I, Lafayette

Lafayette in Continental uniform by Charles Willson Peale. By permission of the National Park
Service, US Dept. of the Interior.

I, Lafayette

CAROL ANNE DOBSON

Appledrane

APPLEDRANE, LLC

Published by Appledrane, LLC, Danbury, Connecticut

Library of Congress Cataloging-in-Publication Data:
Dobson, Carol Anne
        I, Lafayette/Carol Anne Dobson
                p.cm.
        Includes bibliographical references and index.
    ISBN   9798990343009   (pbk.)

    1.Lafayette. 2. American War of Independence. 3. French Revolution.
                Library of Congress Control Number: 2024935138

Printed in the United States of America

To my grandchildren
Xavier and Alicia

CONTENTS

PART TWO: TRIALS OF DESTINY

ILLUSTRATIONS

ACKNOWLEDGMENTS

Acknowledgments are due to Cornell University for allowing the reprinting of part of their five-volume collection, *Lafayette in the Age of the American Revolution, selected letters and papers, 1776-1790,* edited by Stanley J. Idzerda. Acknowledgments are due to the American Philosophical Society for allowing the reprinting of part of the letters in their collection of *The Letters of Lafayette to Washington,* edited by Louis Gottschalk. Acknowledgments are due to the Stuart Jackson Collection of the Marquis de Lafayette manuscripts, General Collection, Beinecke Rare Books and Manuscripts Library at Yale University. Acknowledgments are due to the Fondation Josée et René de Chambrun for the use of part of the letters of Lafayette in their collection which have been published by André Maurois.

INTRODUCTION

Lafayette's own words and those of his contemporaries create this narrative non-fiction in the form of an autobiography. Lafayette's conversations and thoughts are all referenced from original French and English sources. The reader sees what Lafayette sees and knows only what Lafayette knows. It is in the present tense and is chronological. It is history but it is happening now.

A French aristocrat, he was one of the most important European figures of the eighteenth and early nineteenth century. He fought in the American War of Independence; he was a general in the Continental Army; he led a small force in pursuit of Cornwallis over Virginia and trapped him at Yorktown, the resulting victory by American and French armies a key factor in ending the war. He regarded the United States as his adopted country and Washington as his adopted father, his final resting place covered by soil from Bunker Hill, so combining in death his two homelands. He came to America a raw youth, albeit a youth so rich he was able to buy a ship to transport himself and his fellow Frenchmen across the Atlantic, a youth who had married into the powerful Noailles family, a marquis who knew the king.

He remained true to the ideal of liberty for the whole of his life. He was a leader of the liberal nobility who wanted political reform,[1] and on July 11, 1789, was the first person to read a Declaration of the Rights of Man to the Assembly in France. Following the fall of the Bastille he became commander of the National Guard of Paris and attempted to keep order and curb violence in the febrile revolutionary atmosphere. A republican, he nevertheless advocated a constitutional monarchy as the best policy for France in 1789 and tried unsuccessfully to stop the Jacobins from gaining control. On August 19, 1792, he was forced to abandon his army and flee his homeland to escape the guillotine, but subsequent imprisonment by the Austrians and Prussians for five years failed to change him. 'I was imprisoned for wanting to make the people revolt against despotism and aristocracy and I passed my solitude thinking about it and left prison without changing my views at all," he said in Philadelphia, 1824.[2] Napoléon's treaty at Campo Formio liberated him, but he remained at his château, a gentleman-farmer, and increasingly came to revile the man who said he had found the king's crown in the gutter, had picked it up with his sword and the people had put it on his head.

He knew the heights of acclaim but also plumbed the depths of hatred. Initially said to be riding into history on his white horse, his popularity later plummeted. Not enough of a republican for some, not enough of a constitutional monarchist for others, regarded as a traitor by many. He never became the French Washington. He never became the president of a French republic, but he did become the symbol of freedom for oppressed people everywhere. He espoused the liberal causes of the Enlightenment. He fought against slavery. He fought against religious intolerance. He supported revolutionary movements throughout the world. He never submitted to any regime. He remained steadfast to his ideals and was prepared to die for them. 'It is an extraordinary phenomenon that a character like Monsieur de Lafayette should have developed amongst the highest ranks of the French nobility,' wrote Madame de Staël.[3]

Historians and biographers have sometimes treated Lafayette harshly. He has been called weak, naïve, too easily swayed by flattery and craving popularity. This work attempts to reveal his personality and his actions, untainted by an author's own prejudices as has so often been the case. His words have not been cherry-picked to reveal him at his best. His flaws are sometimes only too obvious. His strengths shine from the page, not clouded by the passage of time. This work shows how he matures in his views, escaping from such beliefs of his class that slaves were property and becoming an eminent supporter of the abolition of slavery. It reveals why a republican by 'inclination and education' advocated a constitutional monarchy. 'So long as a constitution consecrates the bases of liberty defined in my Declaration of Rights of July 11, 1789, and so long as it represents the general will of the people, then I will not only submit to it, but sacrifice myself,' he wrote.[4]

It provides an insight into how he experienced warfare, revolution, prison and a multitude of other dramatic events. It reveals the world in which he lived-the world of Washington, of Louis XVI, of Napoléon, and of the Restoration. It reveals a man with a generosity of spirit, who lived his life bravely, who was often, as he said himself, an advocate of initially unpopular views which later became taken up by many; it reveals a man who consistently followed the path of liberty.

I, Lafayette

Part 1

Military Destiny

Chapter 1

Chavaniac

The still depths of the pool mirror my red hair, long face, gray-blue eyes[1] and aquiline nose. I resume my hunt for the enemy who scurries in front of me along the hillside path, flitting like a shadow between the trees, disappearing into the gloom of tangled foliage. I stab the bushes with my sword and pierce the red coated body. I know no mercy. He dies, like my father at Minden, in Prussia, when a British cannon ball struck him. A wild boar suddenly crashes through the undergrowth; I skulk away to keep myself safe for the glorious military future and life of honor I am determined will be mine.

Roman legionnaires once tramped this countryside; the clash of weapons, the shouts and screams of battle echoed across blood-drenched soil; now they frequent the lonely forests as unwisely as the British and are slaughtered as efficiently.

I am a son of the Auvergne, a land buckled by subterranean forces spewing out lava. Eroded cones of extinct volcanoes graze the sky, mountains rising beyond mountain,[2] seamed by valleys where streams tumble down hillsides of oak, beech and pine, soared over by kites and eagles. The Arverni of ancient Gaul lived here. Their chief, Vercingetorix, led fifteen tribes against the Romans, defeating them at Gergovia near present-day Clermont. In 52 B.C. he surrendered to Caesar at the siege of Alesia and was taken to Rome to be dragged behind a chariot through the streets.

"I took up arms for the liberty of all," he declared, his words vaulting two thousand years, making me long to emulate him.

Am I a Gaul or a Frank? I hope I am a Gaul. I prefer Vercingetorix defending our mountains to the brigand Clovis and his abominable successors.[3] I belong to an ancient, noble family. Our name was Motier, which became Motier de La Fayette[4] when we possessed the seigneurie at La Fayette in the mountains of Ambert,[5] called Villa Faya in the Cartulaire de Sauxillanges of 1000 AD when a donation of land was made to the abbey. In 1240, Pons Motier, seigneur de La Fayette, married Alix Brun de Champetières. They had two sons; the elder was Gilbert Motier de La Fayette; the younger was Roch Motier de Champetières, from whom I descend. In 1692, the La Fayette branch had no male inheritor because one son of comte François de La Fayette entered the clergy, and the other, René-Armand, had a daughter, Marie-Madeleine, who later married the duc de La Trémoïlle. René-Armand therefore bequeathed his estates on his deathbed[6] to my great grandfather, Charles du Motier de Champetières, baron de Vissac and de Saint Romain, who took the name La Fayette, and whose eldest son was my grandfather, Édouard du Motier de La Fayette. In 1717, after the death of her husband, Madame de La Trémoïlle deeded the marquisat of La Fayette to Édouard's first son, Jacques Roch, her cousin, and my uncle.

My ancestors have always been warriors; my side of the family only left Auvergne to go to war. We are renowned for bravery on the battlefield and were so often killed that our fates even became a sort of proverb in our province.[7] Fortunately, we also fathered children before we went to fight or I would not be here.

Gilbert 11 took part in the First Crusade in 1095.[8] Pons du Motier de La Fayette was a Crusader at Saint Jean d'Acre in 1250. Jean du Motier was killed at the battle of Poitiers in 1356.[9] In 1421, maréchal Gilbert du Motier de La Fayette, whose motto was *Cur Non?* led the French to victory with the Scots against the English at Beaugé and killed the Duke of Clarence, the heir to the English throne, with his own hand. Seven years later, he fought alongside Jeanne d'Arc at Orléans. In 1557, François Motier de La Fayette was killed at Saint Quentin; Pierre de La Fayette died at Montcontour in 1569;[10] in 1561, Jean du Motier de La Fayette was killed at Cognac. Claude du Motier, chevalier de Vissac, was a soldier for thirty-eight years, participated in sixty-five sieges and five battles and died at Troyes in 1692. My grandfather, Édouard Motier de La Fayette, took part in the sieges of Philipsburg, Mons and Girone, and in the battles of Marseille and Spire, and received so many injuries he abandoned warfare. In 1734, Jacques Roch du Motier de La Fayette, my twenty-three-year-old uncle, died at the siege of Milan. A captain of dragoons, he charged an Austrian detachment at the head of his company; he captured the enemy commander, chivalrously placing the man with his pistols behind him on the horse. His prisoner shot him in the back when they encountered an Austrian detachment.[11]

Finally, on August 1, 1759, my father, Michel Louis Christophe Roch Gilbert du Motier de La Fayette, colonel of grenadiers, was killed in the Seven Years' War, his battalion exposed on the ridge of a hill by lieutenant-général de Saint Pern for no military advantage[12] and decimated by artillery commanded by an officer whose name was Phillips. [13]

I look at his portrait on the wall. His armor gleams. His long face resembles mine. He does not yet know his fate. I hunt in the forests where he hunted. I wander the fields he wandered. I was born in the same tower room he also first took breath.[14] I want to be a soldier like him and like my ancestors and cannot remember a time when I was not enthused by tales of military valor and by schemes to travel the world in search of glory.[15]

Our dark-hued château of Chavaniac, built from volcanic pouzzalana,[16] squats large on the summit of a wooded foothill in the Fix Mountains, at the south-eastern end of the plain of Charlièrgues in the Basse Auvergne, not far from the chateaux of Vissac and Saint Romain. It is said to derive its name, which was Cavaniac[17] in the tenth century, from the local word for the cawing of crows.[18] In the fourteenth century it was a *maison forte.*[19] At the end of the seventeenth century its roof was ravaged by fire and was rebuilt and enlarged in 1701. The principal façade faces north, flanked by two distinctive, campanile towers, inspired, some say, by women's headdresses on fête days at Vélay.[20] On the hillside below, and along the stream at its foot, cluster about forty, dry-stone, red-tile-roofed houses around the small church of Saint Roch. It is in the parish of the *collecte* of Saint-Georges d'Aurat, in the *élection* of Brioude, eight leagues away,[21] and in the *généralité* and *province* of Auvergne.[22]

Our domain is twelve leagues wide and twenty-six leagues long and I can see a great distance from two sides of our château. To the north is Paulhaguet and the undulating Charlièrgues;[23] far away are the high summits of the Monts Dôme, the Luguet, the Plomb du Cantal and the higher summit of the Sancy. About three leagues west is Langeac and the Allier River, dominated by the bare hills of the Margerides;[24] to the east are wooded hills. Châteaux and farmhouses at the foot of small volcanic cones dot a country verdantly green in summer, punctuated with fields of ripening wheat, oats and rye and pine-covered hillsides, encircled by blue, brown, or mauve-tinted mountains. In winter I look out through frost-patterned glass onto a land often shrouded in deep snow, the softened outlines of hills, trees and houses enveloped in a uniform gleaming whiteness under the vast Auvergne sky.

Winds howl from the hills on stormy nights, rattling the windows, spitting rain or snow down the chimneys, hissing against the blazing logs in the hearth. My grandmother, Marie-Catherine de Chavaniac de La Fayette, relates the battles and glory of a family closely tied to memories and sorrows associated with war.[25] Shadows dance over the candle-lit room, pride and sadness are in her voice; she talks about my father.

"He was twenty-seven when he died.[26] You were only two, but you became a marquis even although you were not long out of your cradle."[27]

I was born on September 6, 1757, and baptized next day as the very high and mighty seigneur, Monseigneur Marie Joseph Paul Yves Roch Gilbert du Motier de La Fayette, the legitimate son of the very high and mighty seigneur Monseigneur Michel Louis Christophe Roch Gilbert Du Motier, marquis de La Fayette, baron of Vissac, seigneur of Saint-Romain and other places, and of the very high and mighty lady Madame Marie Louise Julie de La Rivière.[28]

Perhaps all those saints' names will ward off the La Fayette battlefield curse? I do not know, but as my family call me Gilbert, I will put my faith only in Saint Gilbert.

I live with my grandmother La Fayette, my two aunts and my cousin. Marguerite-Madeleine du Motier was my father's elder sister who never wanted to marry as she could not bear to leave her family;[29] she is, in every respect, a person of extraordinary merit who assumes responsibility for my education.[30] My other aunt, Louise-Charlotte, came back to Chavaniac with her five-year-old daughter, Marie-Louise, when I was four, after the death of her husband, Monsieur Guérin de Chavaniac, baron de Montoléoux. Marie-Louise is like a sister to me and never have brother and sister loved each other more.[31]

Our life follows the seasons, like that of the peasants. I help in the harvests. We celebrate the fêtes. Sometimes we visit Vissac or our house at Brioude. Occasionally we make social calls on our neighbors or go to see my two great-aunts, Marie and Gabrielle du Motier de Champetières who live in the convent at Chazes.[32] We are aristocrats, but we are comparatively poor. The soil here is often thin, the climate cold, our revenues meagre from the seigneuries.[33]

My initial attempt to advance my heroic ambitions comes when I am eight in the shape of the Beast of Gévaudan. By all accounts, and there are many, it is a monster. Some suggest it is a hyena, others that it is a wolf or even a werewolf. A few believe it is the Devil. Its flanks are red; it has a black streak along its back and a bushy tail; its head is enormous with ferocious teeth.

The first victim is Jeanne Boulet, a girl of fourteen, murdered near the hamlet of Les Hubacs in the parish of Saint Étienne de Lugdarès at the end of June 1764. After that, attacks happen frequently to people alone in isolated areas of Gévaudan. Fear haunts our region. The bishop of Mende, Monseigneur Gabriel-Florent de Choiseul Beaupré, says public prayers; crucifixes sprout like mushrooms, nailed to doors, draped onto carts or hung round necks when peasants tend fields or milk cows.

"A wolf or a hyena would not cut off the head cleanly like that and tear the body to shreds. It must be a supernatural being," people remark.

"A wild animal does not have long claws. It is possible it is a man dressed in fur. A man who enjoys slaughtering innocents," say others.

Rumors abound that it has killed hundreds although no one knows the exact number. I search for it along the frozen tracks of winter; I search for it by summer fields of oats and rye and along rocky woodland paths, but it constantly eludes me.

Louis XV orders Captain Duhamel and fifty-seven dragoons to Clermont; the Beast eludes them also. François Antoine, the best marksman in France and lieutenant of the royal hunts, comes next and on September 20, 1765, he kills a large wolf in the woods owned by the Abbaye de Chazes, the home of my two great-aunts.[34] It is stuffed with straw and taken to Paris where it entertains the courtiers, but by the spring of 1767 the Beast again rampages through Gévaudan, eating women and children. My hoped-for prey once more occupies my walks when suddenly I read in the local newspaper: 'A Monsieur La Fayette encountered the Beast and ran away in fear.'

The blood rushes to my head. "How dare someone write that! A La Fayette would never be a coward!"

I seize quill and ink and write a furious letter; I give it to a servant to deliver, but my family find out. "The journal and its readers will have to remain in ignorance of your denunciation," they tell me.

A few weeks later, we hear the young marquis d'Apcher is going to search for it in the forest of La Ténazeyre in Nozeyrolles with the hunter, Jean Chastel, and others.

"I will kill it first," I mutter.

Next day I take my father's ancient musket from the wall. I run out of the château; young peasant boys follow; we escape into the countryside; we advance deeper into woods and fields. The day passes. Evening begins to darken the sky; we trudge homewards; I enter the château to recount my exploits.

"And what were your intentions, Gilbert?" says my grandmother, her expression as somber as her mourning dress. "Were you trying to kill the village boys as well as yourself?"

"I wanted to find the Beast and defend the peasants. I am their seigneur. It is my duty to protect them."[35]

The candlelight flickers and smokes. Outside the window the sun sinks below the hills, the blackness of night robbing the land of color. The Beast still prowls.

My grandmother was Marie-Catherine Suat de Chavaniac before her marriage in 1708, at the age of twelve, to my grandfather, Édouard du Motier de La Fayette, baron de Vissac and de Saint Romain. Chavaniac belonged to her family, and she has lived here, apart from her time in Paris, since 1701. My grandfather died in 1740 after an accident at Versailles when he was accompanying the king's carriage and fell from his horse, gravely injuring his head. He lived for four years with no hope of recovery; when he died my grandmother returned to the Auvergne with her children.

My mother, Marie-Louise-Julie de la Rivière, is descended from Breton nobles who trace their descent from Saint Louis, King of France. Her father is the marquis de La Rivière; her grandfather is comte Charles Yves de La Rivière.

When she married my father, she left Paris and came to live at Chavaniac.[36] After his death she gave birth to my sister, Marie-Louise-Jacqueline,[37] who died, only three months old, on April 5, 1760. In 1762, when I was five, she went back to Paris whilst I stayed here. She loves me devotedly, but it would never have occurred to her to take me away from my La Fayette grandmother for whom she had a deep reverence.[38] She was presented at court that year[39] and sometimes participates in court society to help advance me when I am older. In summer, when the road is less treacherous and the season is over, she comes to stay at Chavaniac and spends much of her time in prayer although before the death of my father she had been very lively and liked frivolous activities.

When I was five, my grandmother bought the extinction of the fiefdom of Chavaniac on April 7, 1762, from Yves-Marie Desmarets, the comte de Maillebois.[40] My only allegiance is therefore to the king. She also bought legal rights in the region, including that of the *droit de justice*, for the parish of Aurac and the villages of Soulages, Anglard and Vernède. She is a lady of the highest merit,[41] is greatly respected in the province and people often travel up to twenty leagues to consult her.

She obtained a pension for me from October 6, 1759, of seven hundred and eighty livres from Louis XV after the death of my father. He had not made a will, so a large part of my mother's dowry reverted to her family, the de Rivières, and he had also spent much money on his four campaigns in the Seven Years' War, as was the custom. He went to Paris to live at eleven,[42] and I will soon follow the same path, my heart breaking at the thought of leaving my home, my grandmother, my aunts and Marie-Louise.

The marquis de Bouillé, my cousin, who lives nearby at Le Cluzel, visits Chavaniac for several days. He believes I am much grown and well educated for my age. Abbé Fayon, my tutor, asks what he thinks of my character.

"He is astonishingly advanced in reason and extraordinary for his thinking, his knowledge, his sang-froid and discernment. I believe him to have a trait of self-love and even of ambition. He has the qualities of mind which are proper to great men, namely the power to think and judge, and that if a vigorous character is added to these, he will one day do very great things," is his opinion.[43]

December 1767 [44]

I say farewell to my beloved family; the misery of abandoning all I love filling me with great sadness.[45] The carriage trundles down the winding track towards Saint-Georges d'Aurac; not long after, we take the turning; I glimpse the château and the dark pine trees for the last time.

We jolt along wild roads mended with lava, pozzualana and basalt, past houses and walls of the same materials. We career up and down, splashing through streams laced with ice, an uninterrupted chain of mountains bounding the horizon under a winter sky. We reach the main highway; the wheels roll more quickly, past frozen fields and leafless, skeletal trees; to my astonishment people no longer take off their hats to me as they had done to the little seigneur in the village.[46] I have been torn from my loved ones and from the world I know and have absolutely no curiosity to see the capital.[47] The snow-bound mountains slowly fade into the distance, the Auvergne now a memory, but its hot lava in my blood, its solid granite in my bones.[48]

Chapter 2

Wealth and Marriage

Paris straddles the vast, distant plain, five leagues in circumference, huddling beneath a cloud of smoke. After two weeks travelling one hundred and twenty leagues north, we approach the capital city of France, the tall gothic towers of the cathedral of Notre Dame and the glistening dome of the Hôtel Royal des Invalides slowly becoming visible. Once past the gate we finally come to a halt at the Palais du Luxembourg, a three-storied building of pale stone built for Henri IV's queen, Marie de Médici, where my mother lives with her father and grandfather in an apartment granted to my uncle, the comte de Lusignem, by the king.

My grandfather, the marquis de La Rivière, is an educated, elderly gentleman who lives mainly at his ancient château of Kéroflais in Bretagne and interests himself in the affairs of that region. He had not followed a military career because he had conspired with other Breton nobles against the duc d'Orléans, regent during the minority of Louis XV, and had fled to Spain where he had been wrongly accused of being someone else and had been arrested for a short time. He appears very hard, is very rich and is said to be a miser.[1] He is the son-in-law, not the son, of Charles Yves Thibault, the comte de La Rivière et de Ploeuck, my great-grandfather, although they have the same name as my mother's parents were cousins.

My great grandfather was *lieutenant général* of the *armées du roi* in 1745 and then *capitaine lieutenant* of the second company of musketeers, the Black Musketeers, in 1754. He received the *grand croix de l'ordre de Saint-Louis* in 1756 and is governor of Saint Brieuc. He is charming and a man of society.[2]

My uncle, the comte de Lusignem, is a similar age to the marquis de La Rivière. He married the daughter of the comte de La Rivière but she died and he remarried. He is therefore both the cousin by marriage and the brother-in-law of my grandfather.[3]

Not long after my arrival, I enter the tall, stone arch of the Collège du Plessis in the rue Saint-Jacques, where I will board, just a few streets from the Palais du Luxembourg. The day is chill. Bells ring incessantly from the hundreds of churches, chapels, convents and abbeys already starting to announce the hour, which never seems to be at the same time for any of them. Dressed in the navy uniform trimmed with azur,[4] I bear little resemblance to the boy who had roamed Auvergne forests and hunted the Beast.

Most of my fellow pupils are from the *noblesse de la robe* and will be magistrates who administer justice and government, whereas I am proud to be from the *noblesse de l'épee* who fight for France and the king.

I learn Latin, but unfortunately not Greek. I study Tacitus, Virgil and Cicero and win college prizes, but not those of the university, partly because other students have redoubled their classes two or three times and partly because I do not copy exactly what I write, and a mark is deducted for each word of a sentence I have left out.[5]

For two years I am intensely religious. I have no idea why my faith is so strong, although my mother, who was raised in a convent, is also very devout. Whatever the reason, I put the same effort into it as I do into everything and even my confessor says he is envious of my fervor. Then I cease to be religious, which also remains a mystery to me.[6]

Monsieur René Binet, the teacher of rhetoric, sets a composition on the perfect horse which obeys at the sight of the whip.

'The perfect horse is one which when he sees the whip has the sense to throw his rider to the ground before he can be whipped,' I write. Monsieur Binet laughs and does not chastise me.[7]

I am well-liked by the other pupils who even consider me a leader. When I go to the courtyard, my young friends, most of them larger than I, surround me, eager to appear to be my followers, and, if need be, would fiercely come to my defense. However, one day I try to rouse the other pupils to prevent a friend's unjust punishment, to my disappointment they do not support me as I wish. I am never punished; I have decided to never merit it, but I will defend myself with my sword, if need be, a sword which we all wear when we go to dine in town, along with our embroidered clothes, our curled, powdered and pomaded hair in a bag.[8] Nothing displeases me here except not having my independence.[9]

This enormous city of 700,000 inhabitants is the center of culture and philosophy in Europe. Montesquieu, as long ago as 1748, wrote *L'Esprit des Lois* in which he argued that the power of the executive, the legislature and the courts should be separated. Diderot and d'Alembert have published seventeen volumes of *L'Encyclopédie*, which is intended to be a compendium of all knowledge. The philosopher, Voltaire, talks about the rights of man.

The Louvre, where the Académie de Sciences is based, is divided into different areas for subjects such as botany, chemistry, astronomy and geometry. Scientists like Lavoisier are making exciting discoveries and people flock here from Europe and America to discuss the latest ideas. Even the celebrated American, Dr. Benjamin Franklin, with his new theories on electricity, came in September   1766.

Wide boulevards, created in the seventeenth century by the demolition of the walls and fortifications, surround the city. Some parts are leafy and spacious, with tree-lined squares and convent gardens, such as the area near to the Palais du Luxembourg. Other parts are foul-smelling and dirty.   Streets are often narrow,[10] tall houses obscuring the light.   There are no foot pavements;[11] the mud is filthy, black with grit and metal fragments which have come off vehicles, waste from the houses empties into it, giving off a sulfurous smell with a tang of nitric acid. [12] People swarm everywhere, the poor on foot, the wealthy in carriages or on horseback, as well as a variety of animals, including dogs, pigs and even occasionally a herd of cattle. There are many magnificent buildings, particularly the Palais du Luxembourg and the cathedral of Notre Dame with its enormous, stained-glass windows. An impressive equestrian statue of Louis XV stands in a square which is being built, and the Pont Neuf, recently constructed in 1763, is a broad and elegant bridge across the Seine, whilst other bridges linking the Île de la Cité with the right and left banks still have houses on each side as they have for centuries.

April 3, 1770;[13] spring sunshine brings warmth and light to the Luxembourg gardens but inside the palace my heart breaks as my thirty-three-year-old mother lies dead after an illness of a few weeks during which she was bled thirteen times.

Next day, her funeral takes place at the nearby church of Saint Sulpice, where I sit by my uncle, the only other family mourner, the Latin words echoing into the high, vaulted, baroque ceiling.

Just a few weeks later, my grandfather dies. [14]

"The loss of his beloved daughter has been too great for him to bear," declares my uncle.

I inherit large estates in Touraine and Bretagne. I already own land in the Auvergne and my annual income will now increase from twenty-five thousand to one hundred and twenty thousand *livres* a year. I was born comparatively poor, but I have become one of the richest nobles in France.[15] My new wealth however means little to me, although abbé Fayon is more aware of it. I have never needed money. My only thought is sorrow at my mother's death. I continue at the Collège du Plessis. I am generous, which is appreciated by my fellow students, and buy horses which I let them ride.

I am thirteen so my relations start to look for a bride whose family will advance me at court and in my military career. I burn with desire to be in uniform;[16] on April 9, 1771, I become a second lieutenant in the company of the Black Musketeers that my great grandfather had commanded. I proudly wear the scarlet and gold uniform, its blue cloak embroidered with a silver cross encircled by flames and ride a black horse. I have the honor to participate in a review before the king at Versailles and ride there in ceremonial uniform.

"I do not have any orders," the king tells me. I ride back to my commander and repeat the words which he hears three hundred and sixty-five times a year.[17]

It is proposed that I marry Mademoiselle d'Ayen, the second daughter of the marechal d, marshal of the king's armies, first captain of the king's *garde du corps*[18] and a member of the extremely wealthy Noailles family, one of the foremost of France; his father, the duc de Noailles, is governor of the province of Roussillon.[19] I am fourteen; she is twelve. The oldest daughter, Mademoiselle de Noailles, will marry the vicomtc de Noailles, her cousin.

Not long afterwards I discover the duchesse d'Ayen has refused me. She thinks I am too young, that I have no parents to guide me and that I already have a large fortune at a very young age, which she regards as a dangerous gift.[20] The duc d'Ayen has left his home, the hôtel de Noailles in Paris, and has gone to live at his father's mansion in Versailles because of the dispute.

Kites wheel over hills and valleys blurred by summer heat; rye and wheat are ripening; red cows graze in flower-filled meadows; to my joy I am home in the Auvergne. On my birthday in September we receive a letter to say my marriage has been arranged with Mademoiselle d'Ayen.[21]

The duc and duchesse d'Ayen have agreed a compromise. A marriage contract has been drawn up between the duc and my uncle. It will be signed but will be kept secret for two years and the engagement can be cancelled at any time. The marriage will not take place for two years and then my wife and I will live in the d'Ayen family home. I will finish my education by attending the Académie de Versailles and will live at the Noailles mansion there. I will pay a rent of eight thousand livres a year, bring my own servants and pay for my food and fuel. The duc d'Ayen will give a dowry of 400,000 livres. My future wife, however, will not be told about the contract for the next one and a half years. I will visit the hôtel de Noailles and we will gradually become acquainted with each other, but she will not know that I will be her husband.

In October, a preliminary contract is drawn up, directed on my behalf by the abbé de Murat and Monsieur Jean Gérard, the lawyer. I am content. I do not know what my future wife looks like, but the abbé de Murat has been told she is very pretty.

The meetings take place at the Lusignems' apartment and never at the hôtel de Noailles in the rue Saint-Honoré, Saint Germaine-en-Laye. I am sometimes present but say nothing.

The duc d'Ayen, Jean François de Noailles is a well-built man, whose reputation as a scientist and a soldier is as substantial as his person. He is a member of the Académie de Sciences. At fifteen he became a colonel of the Noailles regiment. He fought in the Seven Years' War and was promoted to lieutenant general. He wears a long, full-bottomed wig which frames a heavily jowled face whose eyes look at me sharply. The duchesse d'Ayen, Henriette Anne Louise d'Aguesseau, the granddaughter of the celebrated Chancellor d'Aguesseau, also regards me seriously, but in a kindly fashion. I know she had not wanted me as a son-in-law and that the contract can be annulled at any time, and I do my best not to appear socially gauche. She has pock marks on her face which cosmetic powder has not managed to conceal; she was stricken with smallpox in 1768, just before she gave birth to a son. She recovered, but the baby died, and as her first son had died at the age of twelve months, the duc d'Ayen has no male heir. He has five daughters and evidently wants them to marry tall young men with a military training to provide him with strong grandsons.

On February 15, 1773, the witnessing of the contract finally takes place, at the home of Monsieur d'Aguesseau, the father of the duchesse d'Ayen. The king will sign in September and has given special permission for everyone to sign before him. I am represented by the comte de La Rivière, Madame de Lusignem and Monsieur Gérard, as well as the abbé de Murat who signs for my aunt, Mademoiselle du Motier. My wife-to-be is represented by the duc d'Ayen, the duchesse d'Ayen and Monsieur and Madame d'Aguesseau. I will receive four hundred thousand *livres*.

The abbé de Murat tries to persuade the duchesse d'Ayen to tell her daughter. "This marriage has become so public that even the boot blacks are talking about it."[22]

She refuses.

"If Monsieur de La Fayette is getting a good bargain, Messieurs de Noailles are getting a better one for their girl," is his opinion.[23]

"My housekeeper, who has been with me for six years, will go to Versailles to take care of you," he tells me. "Every other week, on Sunday and Monday, you will return to stay with the Lusignems."[24]

Next Monday I go to my new home. I become a student at the Académie de Versailles; a tutor, Antoine Fourreton de Margelay, a former *maréchal des logis* in the *compagnie écossaise* of the bodyguard commanded by the duc d'Ayen is employed to instruct me in military matters.

I meet my future wife, Marie-Adrienne-Françoise de Noailles, Mademoiselle d'Ayen, at the hôtel de Noailles. She is a slender young girl with large, intelligent eyes who has no idea she will marry me; her sister, Mademoiselle de Noailles, also has no idea she will marry the vicomte de Noailles; she has three younger sisters, Mademoiselle d'Epernon, Mademoiselle de Maintenon and Mademoiselle de Montcler, who is five.

The mansion is palatial, the salons resplendent with exquisite furniture, classical statues and porcelain ornaments. Paintings hang everywhere, signed by artists called Rembrandt, van Dyck, Watteau and Fragonard whose names mean little to me. Beautiful gardens extend to the grounds of the Tuileries Palace.

I learn behavior and etiquette at the Académie militaire de Versailles where the teachers attempt to make me into a refined member of the nobility. Horse riding, fencing, dancing, and the studying of military texts, such as Le Blond's treatise on artillery, replace my classical education at the Collège du Plessis. Every morning we practice riding at the Manège, reputed to be the best riding school in Europe. I enjoy the army training, but I am often laughed at for my awkwardness by the other students who are mostly from the highest echelons of French society and include the comte d'Artois, the brother of the dauphin, the future king of France, and so do not share my pride in my aristocratic lineage.

I court Mademoiselle d'Ayen at the mansion in Versailles, or sometimes at the hôtel de Noailles in Paris or in its gardens. Louis, vicomte de Noailles, often accompanies me, and there is always a chaperone. I tower over my future bride, my tall, long-limbed, broad-shouldered frame remaining solidly incapable of the flourishes and dainty gestures demanded by society. I do not say much; I lack the refinement considered appropriate for a noble. However, inexperienced and clumsy though I am in matters of social etiquette and of the heart, I sense she likes me. She is not beautiful, but I like her face and character. I am very pleased she will be my wife.[25]

The duchesse d'Ayen is a devoutly religious woman who was raised in a convent, like my mother, and whose principal aim in life is to fulfill the will of God and accomplish his work. She adores her children. She supervises their education and spends much time with her flock of doves as she calls them. I quickly love her like a son, and I feel she loves me.

In April, the duc d'Ayen has me transferred to the Noailles regiment with the rank of second lieutenant.[26] I am becoming part of the Noailles family.

On September 19, 1773, Mademoiselle de Noailles marries the vicomte de Noailles. The younger sisters cry bitterly, and tears are shed by those who receive as well as by those who are losing so precious a charge.[27] In the winter, the duc d'Ayen comes to reside with his family at the Noailles mansion in Versailles, where I live, in order to command the royal bodyguard once a year for four months. The duchesse d'Ayen now informs Adrienne of her marriage to me, nearly a year since we were introduced. Far from being horrified, the vicomte de Noailles tells me his wife, Louise, said her sister had almost fainted in delight when her mother told her.

The early months of 1774 bring reports of a strange event which took place in December on the other side of the Atlantic. More than one hundred men, armed with tomahawks and pistols, their faces blackened with soot, some dressed like Native Americans, gathered on Griffin's Wharf at Boston Harbor. They boarded three ships moored there and forced each captain to give them the keys to the hatches and twelve candles. They opened the hatches and took the cargo of tea chests. They used the tomahawks to split the wood, then threw them overboard and fled back to Boston. The following morning, tea was floating on the sea, and people went out in small boats and beat the leaves with oars and paddles to soak and destroy it.

The colonists had wanted to show their anger at having to pay taxes to Britain without their views being represented in Parliament. They are bitter they can be taxed without their agreement and feel they are being exploited to help pay the large debts incurred by Britain in the Seven Years' War.

The might of Britain is so great, its army so well-trained and formidable, that interesting and diverting although it is to hear of the destruction of the East India Company's tea, it seems only like a flea bite on the flank of a bear, an irritant perhaps, but not likely to affect it in any way. My wooing of my wife-to-be and my struggles to invest myself with the trappings of a noble are uppermost in my mind, not whatever is taking place in Britain's distant colony. On March 26 I take an important step in my future life when the duc and duchesse d'Ayen accompany me to the Château at Versailles to present me to the king.

At ten o'clock in the morning, I wait in the Oeil de Boeuf, the royal antechamber, so-called because it has a large window in the shape of a bull's eye. Hundreds of people are crammed into the salon, each lady taking up an immense amount of space both outwards and upwards because of extravagantly wide panniers beneath her satin gown and immensely tall columns of hair, held in place by tow, wool, pads and wire. Scarlet circles of rouge paint cheeks, like red poppies on white masks; jewels sparkle on necks, wrists and fingers and wreathe through bizarre hair creations; diamond buttons sparkle on coats and waistcoats; the whole glittering spectacle reflected in huge mirrors on the walls.

The Château is magnificent. Its marble floors and pillars adorned with chandeliers, statues, paintings and lustrous, often silver, furniture; the splendor tainted by an ever-present, unpleasant aroma. There is excrement in the corridors. Courtiers and non-courtiers relieve themselves wherever they can, as does a menagerie of dogs and cats; the heady scent of feces and urine overlaid by the perfume of rose, violet and lavender from wigs and clothes, is a strange and powerful mixture.

I am escorted into the chamber of His Majesty, Louis XV, the King of France and Navarre, who is seated at a table between a bishop and a woman I believe is Madame du Barry.[28] People say he is the most handsome man in the kingdom. His eyes and eyebrows are extremely black, his nose is very definitely Roman. Gossip says he has no teeth, and eats, or rather, drinks, his food with a straw.

The maréchal whispers my name; I bow as graciously as I can. I am presented at court; I am advancing along the path I hope will lead to honor and glory. Some days later, the king and his three grandsons sign my marriage contract.

On April 11, 1774, a month after my presentation, I marry Mademoiselle d'Ayen in the flower-bedecked chapel of the hôtel de Noailles. Only forty relations are present. My cousin, abbé Paul de Murat, *vicaire général* of the archdiocese of Paris, officiates; my witnesses are the comte de Lusignem, and the marquis de Bouillé. The duchesse de Mouchy, Adrienne's great aunt who is Marie Antoinette's first lady-in-waiting, named Madame l'Etiquette by her because of her strict ideas of courtly manners, and the comte de Tessé, her uncle, are her witnesses. I sign 'du Motier de La Fayette' in my small and not very elegant handwriting. I am sixteen; she is fourteen.

In the evening, a lavish reception takes place at the hôtel de Noailles, attended by the royal family and aristocrats from France and Europe. We dine from more than one hundred hors d'oeuvres, twelve soups, eight stews, twenty-four pies, thirty salads, thirty dishes of roasted meats, a half-side of veal and beef, and forty-six desserts. I am now a member of the Noailles family.

Chapter 3

Heart enlisted in freedom's cause

Wooded hills alternate with fertile valleys. Streams flow down steep hillsides, flooding over valley floors and meadows. Low, square houses straggle along broad streets, plum orchards at their back, wagons and steaming manure heaps at their front. I travel through Lorraine in the northeast of France to join the *Noailles-cavalerie* in the annual army exercises;[1] the marquise de La Fayette, my dear heart, remains in Paris.

Metz is the headquarters of the Army of the East commanded by the maréchal de Broglie. The town can garrison ten thousand men and bristles with formidable defenses, including a bastioned wall, preceded by fascines and entrenchments extending to the left bank of the Moselle, and a citadel. I am a lieutenant, but the duc d'Ayen intends me to take the place of the prince de Poix, who commands our company, when he becomes a colonel. The petit Poix,[2] as he is called, is so small he needs to sit on a raised chair at the dinner table and is the maréchal de Mouchy's eldest son, the brother of my brother-in-law, the vicomte de Noailles.

I train hard in the equestrian ring; I read books on tactics and strategies; I drill and exercise with the troops on the banks of the Moselle and Seille and on the nearby plain. I participate in Lorraine society with Ségur and Noailles, who is a favorite with the local ladies; I write to Adrienne and tell her whom I meet, with whom I dine and what they say.

A few weeks after my arrival a messenger rides in from Paris: 'The king is dead. He has died of smallpox.'

Within the hour, the whole army knows the ghastly details. Pustules covered most of his body. The stench from his skin was so atrocious it extinguished the palace candles and as his corpse could not be embalmed it was sprinkled with slaked lime and put in a double-lead coffin. It was not possible to drive the funeral carriage through Paris and so it drove from Versailles to Saint Denis to be placed in the cathedral vault. Only two carriages accompanied it. The chaplain and priest of Versailles were in one; the ducs d'Aumont and d'Ayen in the other, followed by servants carrying flaming torches, with cloths protecting their faces, then fifty soldiers. Louis XVI is now king. "*Vive le roi!*" we huzza.

In the evening, we hear more. People had jeeringly shouted "Tally Ho!" when the funeral procession careered past, as though the corpse was hunting. On March 4 the king had sent away his mistress, Madame du Barry, to the château at Ruel, so that he could confess his sins and receive absolution. However, he improved slightly and asked for her, but she had already left. He then lingered between life and death for several days, finally succumbing on May 10, at three o'clock in the afternoon. The courtiers had been waiting in the Oeil du Boeuf, and when they knew he had died they had immediately stampeded with a thunderous noise to the grande galerie, to the new king and queen, who fell on their knees and prayed to God to guide and protect them as they said they were too young to reign, before quickly leaving Versailles for Choisy, as they feared catching smallpox.

The first person to greet them was the duchesse de Mouchy, who four years ago had been the first to welcome Marie Antoinette to France, on the Île d'Epis, in the middle of the Rhine between Strasbourg and Kehl. She is the duc d'Ayen's aunt.

We drink. We celebrate into the early hours of the morning. *"Vive le roi!"* resounds throughout the town.

Louis XVI is nineteen. A plump, but strong man, he is square-shouldered, with very poor posture, and looks like a peasant shambling along behind his plough.[3] He waddles when he walks.[4] He cannot recognize anyone at more than three paces and peers short-sightedly at people as he believes glasses to be undignified.[5] He loves to hunt; he loves to eat. Our new queen, the graceful, fair Marie- Antoinette is eighteen. It is sudden and somewhat unexpected although strangely I was at Versailles with the king when he was first taken ill a few weeks ago. My usual practice is to remain quiet, so I did not mention it to anyone, which my relations now find very strange.

The duc d'Ayen quickly asks the new monarch for my commission as captain in the Noailles-cavalerie; it is agreed I will have it on my eighteenth birthday, but I am listed as having it from May 19, 1774.

In autumn, the wheat harvest is very poor. On September 13, Anne Robert Jacques Turgot, baron de l'Aulne, the *contrôleur-général* of the king's finances, issues an edict to liberalize the commerce of grain to stop its price being set too low, decided until now by the royal administration.

Louis XV's death is influencing people to undergo inoculation against smallpox; I decide to have the procedure done even although I know there is a risk. The duchesse d'Ayen agrees; I return to Paris and we rent a small house at Chaillot.

A physician makes an incision in my skin; he inserts pus taken from a pustule of an infected person into the wound. A few days later I am unwell, but not seriously. My mother-in-law devotes herself to me, helped by Adrienne; I am very content, enjoying the closeness of loving and being loved.

When I recover, I set off to Chavaniac with abbé Fayon; Adrienne stays in Paris as she is pregnant.

We spend much time talking as we drive south. "You are not prudent and lack principles," is his opinion and we discuss this point of view at length. "You are a ne'er do well but at least you have a good heart," he finally declares.[6]

The volcanic uplands of the Auvergne welcome me home. Winter is approaching. It is cold; fires blaze in the hearths of the château; with great emotion I embrace my aunts who are in raptures of joy to see me.[7]

I travel back to Paris and the hôtel de Noailles; I plunge once more into society. I race. I drink. I play cards and drink some more with friends known as the court set. We applaud the republican scenes in the theatres and the philosophical discussions of learned men.[8] Liberty is on our lips. We are nobles; we spend our time amusing ourselves, but we enjoy a plebian philosophy and laugh at the old courtiers and clergy. We have all been enthused by stories of ancient chivalry in our youth[9] and we attempt to bring back the clothes, customs and games of the court of François 1, Henri 111 and Henri IV. We wear silk cloaks, ribbons and plumes, and even the king's brothers, the comte d'Artois and the comte de Provence, join in, as well as Marie Antoinette. "Only men wearing this costume can come to my balls," she decrees.

This fad does not last long; we quickly forget playing at knights and paladins and turn our attention to other pastimes. I often go to the tavern, the *Épée de Bois*, just beyond Paris, at the foot of Montmartre near the hamlet of Les Porcherons, with Noailles, Ségur, Coigny, the Dillons, the Guémenées and others. We call ourselves the *Société de l'Épée de Bois*. We perform a play which ridicules the dignitaries of the Paris Parlement and I have the role of the procureur général. It is a sensitive subject politically. The parlements had been exiled and the king has just re-established them with great support from popular opinion. We, however, are privileged young aristocrats and believe we can mock. A great uproar ensues. Maurepas, the premier ministre, wants to exile us from the court. Ségur talks to the king who finds it amusing and we are not sent away in disgrace.

"I am as guilty as they are, as I laughed when I heard about it," he says. [10]

I dance in the apartment of Marie Antoinette, where the quadrille, an Austrian queen of France, the honor of being her partner,[11] and my two left feet, do not fare well together. She is graceful in her satin shoes and wide-panniered dress; I dance, but somewhat less gracefully. She laughs in disdain at me, her wide-apart blue-gray eyes bright with laughter, her prominent Habsburg lower lip pursing in merriment. I retreat in shame, the courtiers laughing.

During the winter session of the duc d'Ayen as captain of the king's bodyguard at Versailles, the duchesse d'Ayen accompanies Adrienne and I to the queen's weekly balls. Afterwards she invites our friends to supper at the Noailles' mansion, and our closest friends to dinner.[12] She believes that God will bless her efforts to keep her daughters in the path of religion and protect them from the dangers of a worldly life. She therefore allows herself to attend such events, so as not to offend her husband, and to make our home pleasant for Louis de Noailles and myself,[13] and behaves with such a natural and sincere manner she charms everyone.[14]

I find much of our activity trivial. Discussions on topics such as the differences between wigs, or types of snuff, leave me coldly aloof, in despair at this frivolous vacuity. Our social life resembles an orrery, a moving model of the sun and the planets. Marie Antoinette is our sun and the courtiers all circle round, at various degrees from her, whilst I am at the very edge, a stolid body which is both part of the system, yet distant. I am often silent. I only talk when I think there is something of merit to say or hear and this disguised self-love and critical demeanor is not softened by the gaucheness of my manners which invariably creates an unfavorable impression and does not suit the required graces of the court or the demands made upon them by the occasion of a supper in town.[15] My tall, gangly body does not possess the necessary delicacy and I drink heavily to participate more fully. I want to impress Louis de Noailles, who is only slightly older, but far more sophisticated, and drinks, gambles, is a good horseman and has mistresses.

"Tell Noailles how much I drank," I keep telling my friends as they carry me into a carriage one evening, unable to stand upright after drinking large quantities of champagne.

I also want to impress the duc and duchesse d'Ayen. However, I know my social skills to be sadly lacking and unlikely to be remedied; in any case, I have no intention of becoming just a courtier for the rest of my life. My plans are far more ambitious and involve armies, battles and *gloire*. I will be a soldier, like my father, and like my ancestors. My new Noailles family unfortunately does not seem to recognize my overwhelming desire and the maréchal de Noailles endeavors to enlist me in the service of the comte de Provence, a brother of the king.

My whole being rebels at this plan. La Fayettes are soldiers, not courtiers. Republican ideas charm me.[16] I do not hesitate to displease my family in order to save my independence. I bide my time to find an opportunity to make the comte refuse me or for my family to decide on a different path. My lucky star gives me just such a chance at a masked ball.[17] I recognize Provence who is boasting and showing off his good memory.

"It is unnecessary to take so much trouble to prove that memory is the wit of fools," I say to him.

A few days later, we meet at court. "Did you know the masked person on whom you were so severe?" he asks.

"Yes. He who wore that mask now wears a green coat," I reply.

He immediately turns his green-coated back on me; I know I will no longer be considered for his service.

The duc d'Ayen is very annoyed. I am considered to have brought shame onto the family. However, I have achieved what I wanted. I can maintain my independence.[18] The Noailles family no longer talk of my being a courtier.

Louis XVI is also having problems, although of a more intimate nature. People are laughing about his sexual prowess, or rather, lack of it. He and Marie Antoinette were married at a proxy wedding in April 1770, but his obvious difficulties in the marital domain are a constant source of conversation among his subjects. He does not share Marie Antoinette's love of social engagements. He prefers to make locks in his metal-working room or to read historical books, his favorite being Hume's *History of England*. He is passionate about hunting and writes his hunting journal in detail, whereas it is rumored his first meeting with Marie Antoinette only received the short line: 'Met the dauphine today.'

I am very aware affairs are an integral part of aristocratic society. Marriages are arranged and husband or wife are often ill-suited. Louis de Noailles, my brother-in-law, has mistresses, as does the duc d'Ayen. I attempt to conform, but my moth-like attempts to fly dangerously close to the flame of social acceptability threaten to burn me when I decide to have a mistress despite my happiness with my wife. The beautiful Aglaë de Barbentane,[19] comtesse d'Hunolstein, is married to comte Philippe-Antoine d'Hunolstein, colonel of the regiment of the duc de Chartres. I pay court to her, but she pays me little attention. I suspect my friend, the comte de Ségur, is a rival. Jealousy consumes me.

"Fight a duel!" I order him one night at his house.

"I haven't the least intention of claiming her heart," he replies.

We drink; wine befuddles and angers me. I taunt him. "I insist we duel! You are a coward!"

In the early hours of the morning both of us can hardly stand. "I accept your denial," I say.

"Let me escort you to your carriage," he replies. "Let us part friends."[20]

My first romance, scarcely begun, breaks against the obstacles of jealousy with which I collide head-on. My second, I pursue, despite long interruptions, on every possible occasion and goes from esteem all the way to the contrary sentiment and was finally terminated by a catastrophe unconnected with me.[21]

Adrienne has religious doubts about her first communion, which she resolves, and takes the sacrament on the eve of our wedding anniversary. She also, to our sorrow, has a miscarriage.

The price of grain escalates, partly because of the poor harvest last autumn and partly because of Turgot's reform attempting to institute free trade of grain. People say they cannot buy bread. In April, there is a riot in Dijon; riots and unrest spread from one town to another. On May 2 and 3 crowds even gather in front of Versailles; they pillage bakeries in Paris and pamphlets blame the entourage of the king. The army intervenes. There are many arrests and two young men are hanged in the place de Grève in Paris.

Metz is far from this. I go to bed early, spend half the day in the saddle, running after all the troops[22] and longing for letters from my wife. On May 7, five deliveries pass; there is nothing for me at the post, so I leave Lépine and a man on horse-back there to bring me letters immediately.

Two letters finally arrive. To my joy, Adrienne tells me she is pregnant. I write back:

I could never have believed that any news from you would move me so deeply...I am in the first flush of joy...Let us then rejoice and turn our thoughts to the Coronation. It has been decided that you will make the journey. I would go to hell to embrace you...I love you madly...We live in a state of confusion and desolation here. The whole garrison is going into mourning for Monsieur le maréchal has made a clean sweep of women. They are driven away or shut up...Only legitimate passions are allowed. Legitimate or not, my dear heart, it would, I assure you, be a difficult matter to uproot what I have pledged to you for life.[23]

On June 11 I am present with my regiment at Reims where the coronation of Louis XVI takes place at the cathedral.[24] It costs 760,000 *livres*. Turgot tried to spend less. He said there was a deficit of twenty-two million livres in the government's finances and a further seventy-eight million needed to be taken into consideration. He failed.

Louis XVI enters Reims in a carriage modelled on that of Apollo. His head is much larger than that of Louis XV, so a new crown had to be made for six thousand *livres*, even its velvet-lined case costing one hundred and fifty livres. He now rules by divine right, anointed by the holy oil of Clovis; he touches two thousand four hundred victims of scrofula to heal them, and many cures are recorded. Eight hundred small birds are set free. Marie Antoinette is so moved by the ceremony she cries.

The streets of Metz are quiet in the summer heat but on the other side of the Atlantic there are stirrings of rebellion in Britain's colonies. Tea was destroyed at Boston harbor, five months before the death of Louis XV; more recently, there was fighting in April, at Lexington and Concord, near Boston, but detailed reports have not yet reached us.

The Duke of Gloucester, brother to King George 111, is visiting the local fortifications. He and his entourage are travelling in Europe, partly for his health, partly, according to gossip, because the king has disapproved of his choice of wife, the illegitimate daughter of Horace Walpole; partly because he and his brother do not agree about the American colonies, so he has been ordered to Italy to avoid problems in England. I and other officers are invited to a banquet on August 8 in his honor, given by the comte de Broglie, the brother of the maréchal, at his palace.

The evening is hot. I sit in my blue and silver uniform, at the second seat from the bottom of the dining table. No expense has been spared on our feast; we dine on the best cuisine the region of Lorraine can offer to our former enemy who defeated us in the Seven Years' War. The tall, portly duke has just received some letters from England and speaks about the American colonies.

"Why should they pay taxes when they don't have any representation in government? They are a people fighting for liberty. The Bostonians are fighting for the same freedom that the English already have. The battles of Concord and Lexington must make us realize that Americans are truly committed to their insurgency. They have the taste of blood now, and they also have a new Continental Army, commanded by George Washington. They will want to take on our troops again soon. The colonies are a sleeping giant it is better not to wake and there is a large minority in the House of Lords which supports them." He speaks French very well; I begin to listen with interest.

"It was meant to be a secret that our forces were coming to Lexington to arrest Samuel Adams and John Hancock and search for ammunition and weapons and if it had been kept then fighting would probably not have occurred. Two men from Boston, Paul Revere and William Dawes, rode from Boston to alert the colonists, and a system of bells, guns, bonfires, drums and a trumpet also quickly spread the warning. People twenty-five miles away already knew of our coming when our soldiers were still unloading boats at Cambridge. When about seven hundred of our regulars arrived at Lexington, the Minuteman Company was already lined up on the green. There were not many of them though, about eighty. It is thought they were intending to let us pass but shots were fired. It is not really known who fired first. A gunshot went off, the British attacked, and the Americans fled. The regulars then carried on to Concord and one man was said to have been scalped. The Americans had fled some way from the other side of North Bridge at Concord but their numbers steadily increased as news quickly spread through the countryside. They marched back down to the bridge and our soldiers were given the desperate order by Major Buttrick: "Fire, fellow soldiers, for God's sake, fire!" Two Americans were killed. Two British were subsequently killed, and the regulars marched back to Boston, followed by the colonists, and were heavily outnumbered towards the end as men were arriving from farms and hamlets and swelling the ranks of the militia. The colonists also fought from behind walls and trees, instead of being drawn up in battle formation. They would attack, then run away through the woods, and attack again from the side. The regulars were exhausted, their ammunition was nearly gone, and they broke into a disorderly rout to try and escape, but our officers stood in front of them with drawn bayonets and shouted that they would kill anyone who continued to flee. A drummer was also found to summon them to assemble; and they were formed up properly and marched on. Sir Hugh Percy's troops from Boston finally arrived, somewhat late in the day, to save them. The wounded were carried on the cannons and had to keep jumping off so that they could be fired. It is thought that forty-nine Americans and seventy-three British were killed, and many were wounded. Altogether, it is not a large number, but the engagements at Lexington and Concord are important, because they have showed the Americans for the first time that they can attack and perhaps beat us. Strong measures are being adopted by the ministry to crush the rebellion." [25]

I listen with burning curiosity. I abandon my usual taciturnity. I ask questions. By the end of the meal, my heart is enlisted. I am fired with enthusiasm for the cause of liberty.[26] I will endeavor to cross the Atlantic and fight for a cause that is noble and just.

Autumnal Paris has lost the heat of summer; leaves are fading, but society life blooms with all its artificial brightness and gaiety. The glittering honeypot of Versailles attracts like a flower to bees. I visit the salons of Adrienne's aunt, Madame de Tessé, and of the princesse de Poix. I dress in my finery for masquerade balls at the Opéra. I drink with my *Épée de Bois* friends, and all the time I dream of America. I dream of its rebellion. I dream of fighting for its freedom. I tell my pregnant wife about the colonists; she becomes as passionate a supporter as I am. Ségur, Noailles and I discuss it endlessly. We will go together.

I change the motto on my coat of arms from *vissat contra fatum* to *cur non?* that of the maréchal de La Fayette, my ancestor at the battles of Baugé and Orléans. Why not? seems more fitting for what I am intending. It serves to encourage and tell me what to do.[27]

On December 15, in the cold of winter, our daughter is born. We call her Adrienne Henriette Catherine Charlotte. Henriette is the name of her grandmother and the name we will use. Adrienne survives the birth, but our baby is not strong, her baptism taking place next day as is the custom.

Ten days later I join the masonic lodge of Saint-Jean de la Candeur, frequented by aristocrats, where the elderly, studious, abbé Raynal, a former Jesuit, often speaks.

"There should be liberty for the people. There should be religious tolerance. There should be free trade between nations." He talks eloquently in a sharp, clear voice. I listen. I agree. I enthusiastically embrace this wonderful new fraternity which expresses what I believe.

On June 11, 1776, I and many others are placed on the reserve list as a result of the reforms of the comte de Saint-Germain, appointed the new minister of war last year on October 27. He has risen through the ranks and resents inexperienced young noblemen, like me, buying their commands. He considers it has weakened the French army and was partly to blame for our defeat in the Seven Years' War. He abolishes the Black Musketeers.[28] I am now free to go to America.

Chapter 4

A military contract and a ship

The comte de Broglie regards me grimly, his eyes dark, like those of a woman who has enhanced them with belladonna, his face and body plump, but his bearing military.

"No!" he says peremptorily. "Your plan to go to fight in America is so chimerical and fraught with so many hazards, without any advantage to yourself, that I cannot regard it favorably, nor encourage you with any advice except to abandon the idea immediately."

"I am determined to go to America. At least do not betray me," I reply.

"I saw your uncle die in the wars in Italy. I witnessed your father's death at the battle of Minden. I do not wish to be an accessory to the ruin of the last surviving branch of your family."[1]

I stand my ground. "I will go. Whatever you say, I am determined to fight for the freedom of America."

"You are very young. You have a wife and a child. Stay in Europe and attend to your family. You are wealthy and a nobleman. You do not need to risk your life in the British colonies," he says.

I have no intention of abandoning my plan to fight against the British and nor has Noailles and Ségur. Every day we hear of nobles going to see the American merchant, Silas Deane, who arrived here in July, and of their being given high-ranking positions in the American army. How much is true and how much is false, we neither know nor care. We agree to offer our services.

We decide we must keep our intentions secret. The men who have been accepted do not have our social rank and it is possible for the government to say it does not know what they are doing. We are courtiers, however. Our actions make France no longer appear neutral and so the government might decide to directly oppose us. We believe most of the ministers agree privately with our views, but in public they will have to act in a way that does not offend Britain, with whom we are not at war. We also need the consent of our parents and guardians as we are minors. We will continue very carefully.

"We need influence to obtain a post," says Noailles. "I will write to Monsieur Maurepas, the premier ministre, and I will also ask the duc d'Ayen. If he agrees on my behalf, he will also help both of you."

"No!" says our father-in-law, not just once but several times. We start to become desperate, but we are just a few amongst many who want to serve. At every social gathering we hear of Beaumarchais outfitting ships with military supplies and sending men across the Atlantic. How many officers do they need? There will be more Frenchmen than Americans over there soon. There is a rumor the Americans declared their independence on July 4. It is said Vergennes expects to receive a request for recognition and alliance from the Congress. It is also said the British have evacuated Boston and colonial forces have attacked a Spanish post in South America.

Noailles again asks the duc d'Ayen. "I do not have a private fortune, unlike La Fayette. The prince de Poix is the oldest in my family, not me. I need to advance myself militarily."

Our father-in-law looks at his son-in-law, a Noailles like himself; he hesitates.

"I also want to fight in America," I declare.

He turns to me with scorn. "I will make no such request for you," he shouts contemptuously.[2] "Your brother-in-law is strong, energetic and determined. What on earth would you do over there?"

I stride out of the room, humiliated and angry. I immediately go to see de Broglie. I tell him what has happened. I ask again to be considered.

"Good! Get even! Be the first to go to America!" he declares, without any argument.[3] "Say nothing to your father-in-law. I will arrange a meeting with baron de Kalb. He has already agreed a contract to become a major general with Silas Deane who is secretly sending military supplies for twenty-five thousand men, and several engineers, to the insurgents. Lieutenant colonel baron de Kalb will accompany you. He will assist and interpret as he speaks English."

At the beginning of November, Noailles and I meet with de Kalb at his house in Chaillot.[4] Ségur is not with us. He has decided against our venture as his family is vehemently opposed and he thinks the ministry will not give us consent.

I find de Kalb to be a large, well-built Bavarian. He has been an officer in the French army for many years and had been sent by the duc de Choiseul to the American colonies in 1767[5] to report on what was happening but was then never personally questioned by him so little did that minister really think of the Revolution.[6]

"Monsieur the duc d'Ayen has agreed that we can both offer our services to the Americans, through Mr. Deane, if we are made general officers. We congratulate you on your arrangement with Mr. Deane and would take great pleasure in serving in the same army with you. Would you present us to Monsieur Deane?"

"I will do so when you wish," he replies.[7]

Noailles decides he cannot go against the wishes of our father-in-law and writes to de Kalb a few days later to say he has given up the idea of going to America. I visit de Kalb several times alone, very aware the Noailles family will certainly not help me and that they would prevent my going.[8]

De Kalb takes me to meet Silas Deane at his apartment in the hôtel d'Hambourg on the rue de Jacob.

The plump, brown-haired man is the first American I have seen. He is not wearing a wig; his hair is not powdered and is tied back in a queue. His clothes are simple, almost rustic; he wears a black stock at his neck, his coat is plain. His manner is as straightforward as his appearance.

"I wish to fight for the insurgents' cause in America," I declare. I speak more of my ardor than of my experience but dwell much upon the effect my departure would excite in France as I am a noble who is close to both the king and the queen.[9] De Kalb translates for me.

"Monsieur the duc d'Ayen wishes and consents to the going to America of Monsieur de La Fayette," he says.[10]

Deane is formal, speaks very little French, and our conversation has not been copious;[11] however, I leave the rue de Jacob, having advanced somewhat on my plan to fight in America. I go most days to see de Kalb at Chaillot and sometimes he comes to the hôtel de Noailles. I tell only my friends what I intend.

On November 7 Deane receives official notification that a Declaration of Independence was made in America on July 4 and immediately sends it to the ministry. Ségur, Noailles and I celebrate, ecstatic with joy.

By late November, three ships in Le Havre, equipped by Beaumarchais' firm Roderigue Hortalez and Company and secretly financed by both French and Spanish governments, are nearly ready to sail. The adjutant general, colonel du Coudray, has gone to arsenals throughout France and chosen two hundred four-pound field pieces, a hundred thousand balls, thirty thousand stands of small arms, ammunition and four thousand tents for the American insurgents. The government claims these arms and the accompanying officers are sailing to Le Cap and not America. However, everyone seems to know about it and the duc d'Ayen asks Maurepas if Noailles can go. To our not very great surprise, Maurepas refuses.

"His decision is exactly what it should be when a matter meant only to be talked of is committed to writing," is the view of Duboismartin, de Broglie's secretary.

My disappointment is immense. If Noailles had been accepted, it would have opened the way for the duc d'Ayen to agree to my departure. I must now proceed without the support of my family. I continue to keep quiet about what I am doing and family, friends, ministers, French spies, English spies, are all blind to what I am doing.[12] De Kalb will soon travel to Le Havre to sail with the officers already agreed by Deane, and another group, under du Coudray, is expected to set sail at the same time. Time is pressing.

At the end of November I finally achieve what I want. I agree a contract with Deane which de Kalb composed:

> The desire which the marquis de La Fayette shows of serving among the troops of the United States of North America, and the interest which he takes in the justice of their cause, make him wish to distinguish himself in this war, and to render himself as useful as he possibly can; but not thinking that he can obtain leave of his family to pass the sea and serve in a foreign country, till he can go as a general officer, I have thought I could not better serve my country, and those who have entrusted me, than by granting to him, in the name of the very honorable Congress, the rank of Major-General, which I beg the States to confirm to him, to ratify, and deliver to him the commission to hold and take rank, to count from this day, with the general officers of the same degree. His high birth, his alliances, the great dignities which his family hold at this Court, his considerable estates in this realm, his personal merit, his reputation, his disinterestedness, and, above all, his zeal for the liberty of our provinces, are such as have only been able to engage me to promise him the rank of major-general in the name of the United States. In witness of which I have signed the present this 7th of December 1776.
>
> Silas Deane,
> Agent for the United States of America.

> I write:

> On the conditions here explained I offer myself and promise to depart when and how Mr. Deane shall judge proper, to serve the United States with all possible zeal, without any pension or particular allowance, reserving myself the liberty of returning to Europe when my family or my king shall recall me.
>
> Done at Paris, this 7 of December 1776.
> THE MARQUIS DE LA FAYETTE.[13]

December 8. I know de Kalb is going to Le Havre tomorrow to set sail for America. I am not included in the group and my disappointment is immense. I go to see him.

"I cannot help you," he tells me.

"Farewell. Till we meet again in America," I reply.[14]

I call on Duboismartin. "I can do nothing," he says sympathetically.

I visit the home of de Broglie, but he has left for Ruffec, his country residence. I write a letter to him asking for advice and instructions. I am determined to go to America. I hear that Benjamin Franklin has arrived in Nantes and is shortly setting out for Paris.

The *Amphitrite* sets sail with Tronçon du Coudray and his group. The *Seine*, de Kalb's ship, sails on December 14 but returns after a few days because there are problems with the vessel and the cargo. The *Seine* and the third ship are both being detained in port and the authorities at Le Havre have been ordered to stop any vessel leaving.

The reason for the government's sudden change is the arrival of the devastating news that Washington's army was defeated by thirty-three thousand British and Germans at Long Island, New York, White Plains, Fort Washington and the Jerseys. The American army was thought to have been decimated to three thousand men who were being pursued by General Howe.[15] Lord Stormont, the British ambassador in Paris, has been angrily protesting about French officers departing for America and the ministers believe they must attempt to appear to be neutral as we are not at war with Britain and do not wish to be at the current time. They, therefore, withdraw financial support; Vergennes orders Lenoir, the lieutenant général of police, to publicly and severely arrest any officers who say the government has ordered them to America, and a prohibition has been issued against discussing the war in cafés.[16] Even the American envoys admit their discouragement and try to turn me aside from my project.

On December 28, Franklin, Deane and Lee meet with Vergennes. He treats them with politeness and civility but makes it clear that France does not want to offend Britain by openly receiving them or formally negotiating with them as ministers of Congress. They are, however, told that America can use French ports and can import and export. It is known to many that two hundred field pieces and thirty thousand weapons have been removed from the royal magazines to send to America, but Vergennes claims to be ignorant of this.

At the beginning of 1777, French relations with the insurgents improves. In January, France grants a loan of two million livres to America, to be made in four quarterly instalments. The first half million is paid on January 17. In February, Silas Deane is again proposing to send a ship to America and de Kalb will once more be included. I am determined that this time I will go. I am not prepared to wait.

"Perhaps you could buy a ship to transport us," says Duboismartin. "My younger brother, François Augustin, who was a sailor for eleven years, has suggested it."

The proposition excites me. At eight o'clock in the evening, I go with him to the hôtel d'Enghien to see his brother who had recently been to Bordeaux to buy uniforms and arms for his regiment in Port-au-Prince and had intended to sail from Le Havre with the volunteers in order to rejoin his regiment.[17] He tells me of his plan; I quickly agree. I give le petit Dubois, as de Broglie calls him, a box of silver to go to Bordeaux and buy a ship. He sets off in the evening.[18]

I return to Silas Deane. "Thank you for your frankness. Until now, you have only seen my ardor in your cause, and that may not prove at present wholly useless. I shall purchase a ship to carry out your officers; we must feel confidence in the future, and I am buying a ship to transport your officers. It is necessary to show confidence and it is especially in the hour of danger that I wish to share your fortune."[19]

He is delighted. Now I need to obtain money to secretly buy and arm a vessel.

Maurepas sends the prince de Montbarey, a high official in the ministry of war, to talk to me.

"It is suspected that you intend to try and go to America," he says.

I do my best to convince him I will not. "I renounce any idea of fighting in America," I declare repeatedly.[20]

To my great relief, he departs. I am not sure he believes me;[21] I am also not sure if the duc d'Ayen has an idea of what I am doing and has been telling Maurepas. I say nothing to Adrienne. I am not able to tell my beloved I am about to leave her and our daughter for a dangerous voyage to a country at war with Britain as I cannot risk her father discovering my plans. She shares my passion for America, but she is only sixteen; she is pregnant again and I know she will be very distressed.

I agree to visit Britain with the prince de Poix, to stay with the French ambassador, the marquis de Noailles, the duc d'Ayen's brother. It has already been arranged and it would be difficult to decline the invitation without compromising my secret. At the same time, it seems a useful way of concealing my plans. Silas Deane agrees, as do the two other commissioners, Arthur Lee and Dr. Benjamin Franklin.

"It is a good idea to go to London," is the opinion of Dr. Franklin, whom I have not yet met as I fear being seen if I visit his home;[22] I correspond with him and Silas Deane through William Carmichael, an American who is less known, whom I meet in my carriage or at midnight at my home. I learn much from him about the Revolution and its ideals; he becomes a friend.

The frivolous activity of the court keeps me busy in the week before my trip to England. On Tuesday afternoon, February 11, I receive word that Duboismartin has bought a ship, *La Bonne Mère*, from Messieurs Reculès de Basmareins, Raimbaux et Compagnie. The ship and cargo cost 112,000 livres, a quarter of which I pay in cash and the remainder fifteen months from the date of delivery. It is a merchant ship of two hundred and twenty tons, with an experienced captain, a crew of thirty and two cannon. I sign a note to cover the deposit; I rename it, rather more fittingly, *La Victoire*. Then I go to the queen's Mardi Gras Ball. I dance and dine, my head filled with the excitement of my impending escape and my new military career helping the insurgents fight Britain.

February 20. Spires rise from the flat plain; we are approaching Calais. I keep a close watch on my tongue and hope the prince de Poix conducts himself well in London.

"You are always afraid I will say something stupid," he claims.[23]

We drive through the town of bleak, poor, two-story houses and halt at an inn by the harbor, formed by a long quay jutting into the sea. Numerous ships and boats ply backwards and forwards; to the north is the invisible coast of England, the land of my enemy, on which I shall soon set foot.

I write to Adrienne:

We have arrived at Calais without accident, my dear heart, ready to embark tomorrow and see the famous city of London. It will be painful for me to leave the shore; I leave behind all the people I love. I leave you, my dear heart, and in truth, without knowing why. But the die is cast, and I must go. We have proceeded quite slowly, we have broken down because that is always what happens to me, and we arrived with the agreeable hope of staying five or six days, however, tomorrow we shall be able to cross quite easily and we shall only be sick for four or five hours. Please give my news to my aunts, my heart. I shall write to you from London when I arrive, and I hope to soon receive a letter from you…Farewell, dear heart, I will always love you very tenderly in whatever country I go to. I wish you could know how sincere that assurance is and how important your love is to my happiness.[24]

She will think I am writing just a few words before I cross the strait, but when she knows I am sailing across the Atlantic to join the rebels, I believe she will understand.

Next day the packet ship takes five hours to make the crossing. We slowly approach the coast, the white cliffs looming larger and larger; we drop anchor in the harbor.

The small village of Dover has narrow, long and dirty streets; red brick houses replace French pale stone. We leave the valley, dominated by its chalk cliffs, defended by a grim castle on its eastern heights; we travel across a wintry Kent countryside of rolling hills, conical oast-houses and copses of bare trees. Our carriage clatters through the towns of Chatham, Rochester, Dartford, Greenwich and Woolwich, the unpainted houses again of red brick with tile roofs,[25] the streets wide with stone pavements, chimney smoke from coal fires tainting the air. Several times, in the distance, we glimpse the blue-gray ribbon of the Thames, dotted with vessels, until finally we see the dome of Saint Paul's Cathedral arching against the sky, taller than the other buildings, followed by gilded spires, chimneys smoking furiously, and a forest of masts on the Thames.

I enjoy myself in London. On the twenty-eighth, I write to Adrienne: 'For once, my dear heart, I am just like these gentlemen. London is a charming city. I am overwhelmed by kindness, and I only have time to enjoy myself. All the men are sincere and pleasant. To us, all the women are pretty and of an agreeable society.'[26]

I like the ball because my dancing is more on the level of everyone else's.[27] I am happy, after my initial distaste, to leave the dinner table at seven-thirty, have supper between two and three in the morning, and go to bed at dawn. I meet Doctor Edward Bancroft,[28] an American who supports the rebels. I dance at the home of Lord George Germain, the minister for the colonies, as well as at that of Lord Rawdon, who has recently arrived from New York; I revel in the knowledge I will soon be fighting against British oppression. At the opera I encounter Sir Henry Clinton, a short man with a hooked nose, large jaw and intelligent, expressive eyes.[29] I am even offered a tour of British ports, including Portsmouth, to see the ships being fitted out for America, but honor makes me refuse. I am not a spy. I do not, however, remain silent about my support for the insurgents and my esteem for their agents in Paris.

"Trenton was a wonderful victory for Washington," I say,[30] my kinship with the opposition earning me a lunch at the residence of Lord Shelburne who backs the rebels and is a friend of Beaumarchais.

The marquis de Noailles takes me to the court of Saint James and introduces me to His Britannic Majesty, George 111, an older version of the Duke of Gloucester. I bow with dignity, proud at being French.

"You are enjoying our city, I hope," he remarks, looking at me with very pale blue eyes set in his large, Hanoverian face.

My uncle replies as I speak hardly any English. I bow again, inwardly delighted to mock the king I will soon be fighting.[31]

I like the English people I meet, particularly General FitzPatrick, a Whig member of Parliament who supports the insurgents, but I never forget what I am about to do and never reveal my secret. I write frequently to Adrienne. She writes to me, but not as often as I would wish. I tease her: 'I was quite distressed, my dear heart, not to receive any news from you for two posts. Fortunately, I know that you are not sick, but only lazy, because we have had letters from the vicomtesse and our other friends who don't speak of you at all.'[32]

March 9. I write a letter to the duc d'Ayen which I will send when I have departed to America:

You will be astonished, my dear papa, by what I am about to tell you; it has cost me more than I can say not to have consulted you. My respect, my love, my confidence in you must assure you of that; but I had given my word and you would not have respected me if I had failed to keep it; whereas what I am doing, will, I hope, give you a good opinion, at least of my good intentions. I have found a unique opportunity to distinguish myself, and to learn my profession: I am a general officer in the army of the United States of America. My zeal for their cause and my sincerity have won their confidence. On my side, I have done everything I could for them, and their interests will always be dearer to me than mine. Finally, my dear papa, I am in London, waiting for news from my friends. When I receive it I shall leave here and without stopping in Paris, will embark on a ship that I have equipped and which belongs to me. My travelling companions are Monsieur the baron de Kalb, an officer of the highest distinction, a brigadier in the king's army, and, like myself, a major general in the service of the United States; and some excellent officers who want to share my adventures. I am delighted to have found such an excellent opportunity to do something and to learn. I know very well that I am making enormous sacrifices and that it will be painful for me more than anyone to leave my family, my friends, you, my dear papa, because I love them more dearly than anyone who has ever loved. But this journey is not very long, people take longer ones every day just for pleasure, and besides, I hope to return more worthy of everyone who has the goodness to miss me. Adieu, my dear papa. I hope to see you again soon. Keep your affection for me because I want very much to merit it, and I already deserve it because of what I feel for you, and the respect I will feel for you for the rest of my life. Your loving son.
    LA FAYETTE.

Three weeks after our arrival, a note arrives from de Kalb: '*La Victoire* is ready and anchored at Bordeaux.'
    "I would like to take you to the court again," says my uncle.
    "I am sorry, but I wish to go back to Paris concerning a matter of some urgency" I reply.
    "Why?" he enquires in surprise. "Have you a problem there?"
    "No. There is no bad news of any kind. I will return here later."
    "I will say you are ill," he replies.
    It is not what I would have said but I do not object. I take my leave of him and the prince de Poix. I travel again across the county of Kent, fervently hoping not to see it next time as a prisoner of war. I embark once more by the white cliffs, nausea quickly holding me in its dismal grip.
    "It is only a short trip," people say to console me.
    A calm sea meets the packet near Calais. My stomach settles. On shore I quickly forget the ghastly experience.

I meet de Kalb. "Preparations are not yet quite complete," he says.
    I dare not go home to the hôtel de Noailles in case the duc d'Ayen discovers my plans. I therefore rent a room on the first floor at the house of Monsieur Marie, the gardener of the Orangerie, at Chaillot, and anyone who calls must ask for the gentleman who lodges on the first floor.[33] I spend three days closeted there, making my last preparations. I am desperate to be gone. My beloved wife and daughter are not far away; I know it will be a long time before I see them again and that I am about to cause them great unhappiness.
    Basmarein visits and we conclude the purchase of my ship. I cannot consult the duc d'Ayen about raising the money and so I borrow from friends.
    Carmichael comes. He brings the names of the men who are to sail with me, one of whom will be an American, his friend, Edmund Brice. There are thirteen names under the headings of name, rank and commencement of pay:

Mrs. le Marquis de Lafayette; Major General from December 7, 1776: Baron de Kalb; Major General, November 7; Delesser; Colonel, December 1; de Valfort, December 7, De Fayols, Lieut. Colonel, November 20; de Franval, Lieut.Colonel, December 1; de Bois Martin, Major, November 7; de Gimat, Major December 1; De Vrigny; Captain of a French company, December 1; de Bedaulx; Capitaine; Captain, December 1; de La Colombe, lieutenant, December 1; Candon, lieutenant, November 7, 1776.

The mentioned ranks and the pay, which the very honorable Congress shall affix to them, to commence at the period marked in the present list, have been agreed by the undersigned, Silas Deane, Esquire, as Deputy of the American States-General, on the one part, the Marquis de La Fayette and the Baron de Kalb, on the other part. Two copies; Paris, this 7 December, 1776.[34]

It is antedated to December 7, 1776, which makes it look as though it precedes the arrival of Dr. Franklin. De Kalb, Silas Deane and I sign. Carmichael gives us letters of introduction to various members of Congress, and a letter for me to Robert Morris, a banker, for my financial needs.

"Are you not returning to your family?" asks de Kalb.

"No, I fear the anguish and distress of parting from Madame de La Fayette.[35] It would be too much to bear," I say.

March 16. It is the day of our departure. I rise before dawn, not able to resist visiting Noailles and Ségur. At seven in the morning, I rush into Ségur's bedchamber, close the door and sit down near his bed.

"I am going to America to fight. No one knows about it. But I love you too much to leave without telling you."

"How are you going to sail there?" he asks in astonishment.

"I have bought a ship, *La Victoire*. I have fitted it out with a good crew, weapons, ammunition, and many officers who want to fight, including Monsieur de Ternan and Monsieur de Valfort, both of whom are brave and experienced."

"I wish I could come with you," he says, with great regret.

"I would also like you to come with me. Hopefully war will soon break out between England and France and then nothing will stop us joining each other. Do not tell anyone yet. I do not want the duc d'Ayen to know until I am out of reach." I embrace him. "Goodbye, my friend."[36]

Next, I visit Louis de Noailles. I also greatly surprise him. We again sadly say farewell.

I write to Adrienne:

I am too guilty to vindicate myself; I have been too cruelly punished not to deserve a pardon. If I had expected to feel my sacrifices in such an awful manner, I would not be at present the unhappiest of men. But I have given my word, and I woud die rather than go back on it. M. le duc d'Ayen will explain my foolish acts to you. Do not be angry with me. Believe that I am cruelly distressed. I had never realized how much I loved you- but I shall return soon, when I have fulfilled my obligations. Adieu, adieu, write to me often, every day. Embrace our dear Henriette. And, moreover, you are pregnant, all adds to my torment. If you knew how terrible this is for me, you would surely pity me. To add to my misery, the people I love are going to believe that I am happy to leave. Besides, it is a journey no longer than that of your father to Italy. It will be short. Adieu. I have saved this letter for the last; my final farewell is for you. They are going to take me far away. It is terribly hard for me to tear myself away from here, and I do not have the courage to speak to you any longer of a man who loves you with all his heart, and who cruelly reproaches himself for the time he will spend without seeing you. L. [37]

At noon, de Kalb and I leave his house at Chaillot in a carriage I had sent two days earlier to his stables. We travel through Paris; I stop the carriage near the hôtel de Noailles and add a postscript to my letter to the duc d'Ayen: 'I come to Paris for a moment, my dear Papa, but take only the time to say goodbye to you. I wanted to write to my uncle and aunt de Lusignem, but I am in such a great hurry that I must ask you to present my respects to them.'[38]

"Take my letters to the hôtel de Noailles," I tell a servant.

We set off again. We travel as fast as we can, changing horses frequently and stay one night at an inn. I say nothing to de Kalb about the duc d'Ayen's ignorance, until now, of what I am doing. On March 19 we arrive at Bordeaux.

Chapter 5

Flight from king and France

We drive by the brown, fast-flowing waters of the Garonne, the river which cuts a crescent swathe through the town and gives Bordeaux its other name, the Port de la Lune. My thoughts are on my letters which it probably would have been wiser to have dispatched when I left France. It is now too late. I am aware my father-in-law will not appreciate my spending my fortune in this way; what I do not know is the extent of his anger, and what action he might take. He and his family are immensely powerful at court. Will he try to prevent me from going? Will he attempt to bring me back to Paris? Several times in the last few days, cooped up in the carriage with de Kalb, I have nearly blurted out the truth but have so far held back.

The long waterfront is busy; small boats and barges come and go from the sloping, muddy shore, carrying people and goods out to ships moored in the river as there is no quay.[1]

I meet Captain Le Boursier. "I hope to leave soon," I tell him.

"She will be ready to sail in a week. In any case, the rest of your party is not yet here," he replies.

"I would prefer to set sail as soon as the others arrive," I say.

"The wind is contrary. We must wait," he replies.

I finally confess to de Kalb. "My family do not know that I am sailing from France to fight in America."[2]

Astonishment disturbs his calm face. "I know we have had to maintain the utmost secrecy, but I had not realized you had not been given consent and that your family did not know. Madame la marquise was sometimes with you when I visited."[3]

"I will send a messenger to Paris to discover the effect produced by the letters I left my family telling them what I am about to do," I say.[4]

I immediately write a message to my friend, Monsieur de Coigny, who is very close to the court: 'Find out what my family and the ministers think and, if possible, prevent an interdict from being issued.'

"Ride post-haste and return with the reply as quickly as possible," I order the courier.

I go to stay at the palatial residence of the maréchal de Mouchy, lieutenant governor of Basse-Guyenne, Adrienne's great uncle; de Kalb goes to *La Victoire*, saying he is a ship owner.

"I am visiting Bordeaux. I hope to see the vineyards," is my excuse for being here. To my guilt, I am warmly welcomed; I realize the embarrassment I will shortly cause not only to the maréchal, but also to the marquis de Noailles in London, who has just presented me to the king of England.

De Kalb registers with the port's embarkation officers on March 21, as do Duboismartin, La Colombe, Bedaulx, Candon, Franval, Gimat and Brice shortly after they arrive. Huguenots are not allowed to leave France so those who are Protestant register as Catholic. Edmund Brice, who is American, describes himself as twenty-two, born in Sauveterre, and Catholic. Bedaulx writes that he comes from Neufchâtel in Switzerland.

On the twenty-second, I go to register with the other officers who have arrived; De Vrigny, Rousseau de Fayols, Valfort and Redon, as well as my and de Kalb's servants, Camus, Moteau and Argé. I describe myself as Gilbert du Mottié, chevalier de Chavaillac, an ancient form of Chavaniac, which will not be so easily recognized as the usual spelling. I say I am aged twenty, tall, and fair.[5] It is true I am tall and pale, but I am still nineteen. Like the others I declare I am travelling to the Cape in the Antilles for business. Next day, Capitaine, Dubuysson and Lepas register.

No one has arrived to arrest me and I have not received a reply from de Coigny. *La Victoire* has been loaded with barrels of salt pork, biscuits and water and other necessities and has been moved to an anchorage out in the roadstead of Pauillac. She is ready to sail.

In the morning of the twenty-fifth, we all start to board the launch. A horse gallops towards us; it is my courier.[6] He thrusts a bundle of letters into my hand. I clamber down into the boat; the seamen row away from the shore; I tear open the packet and hastily read. The reaction to what I have done is terrible. My family is extremely distressed, particularly my beloved wife. The duc d'Ayen is in a fury. He rushed to see Maurepas at Versailles, and he, the court and the king are incensed because my close connections to the French court suggest their acquiescence and encouragement to fight against Britain. The king is particularly furious that a noble with my high rank and position will be fighting with rebels. There is talk of a *lettre de cachet* by which I could be imprisoned indefinitely, without any reason given, and soldiers and a ship are said to be pursuing me. In great agitation I tell de Kalb what has happened.

"Abandon your plan," he says gravely. "Return immediately to Paris. Leave your ship in the care of the outfitters at a sacrifice of perhaps twenty to twenty-five thousand francs.[7]

"No," I reply. "We only have de Coigny's knowledge of the situation. We are already on our way. We will at least leave France and have the ship anchored out of reach while I await confirmation of the royal orders which my friends say have been issued."[8]

"It is best then to sail to Spain, to Los Pasajes near San Sebastien," he suggests.

"We will sail there while the wind is favorable. Then I will consider what to do. I will send another courier to Paris to try and discover more," I say.

In the night I start to feel seasick.[9] *La Victoire* swings heavily at anchor, the tide making her bulk quiver as though she is trying to escape seawards. During several hours I queasily contemplate the unfortunate turn of events and my foolish sending of the letter to the duc d'Ayen before I had left France. I had not expected such an angry response. My whole life until this venture has been of unhesitating obedience to my family and my monarch. I know I must take the ship and the officers to Spain to escape the clutches of the king and his ministers. However, I believe I am doing what the government wants and what it has already been doing far from the eyes of Lord Stormont.

Morning finally dawns. A few hours later we set sail. Our square-rigged, two-masted ship begins to ponderously sail down the Gironde estuary, the Port de la Lune retreating into the distance. We pass farms, copses, churches, country houses and villages necklaced on the bank by white-sand beaches; at midday on the twenty-sixth we sail past the Lighthouse of the Kings, midway between each bank, and enter the Gulf of Gascony. The Atlantic rushes to meet us; *La Victoire* bucks and kicks like a horse being broken; we turn south towards Spain, following a low, sandy coast, my seasickness worsening. Two days later, we see the dark mountains of the Pyrenees. We cross the border into Spanish waters.

March 28. *La Victoire* anchors at the narrow, rocky harbor of Los Pasajes.

"I wish the ship to stay here until my courier returns from Paris with more definite news of what is happening," I tell the captain and my fellow officers.

De Kalb is impatient at the delay. He wants to sail quickly. He worries he will miss the campaign in America. However, it is my ship and so he must comply.[10]

On the thirty-first, a courier arrives from the comte de Fumel, the commander of the port of Bordeaux, carrying the orders of the court. To my despair I discover that I must go to Toulon and wait there for my father-in-law and his sister, the comtesse de Tessé, to join them for a six-month excursion to Italy.[11] I eat dinner with de Kalb in San Sebastien; we discuss what I should do.

"I find it difficult to believe that it is not in the interests of France for me to go to America. I am sure Maurepas and Vergennes agree but cannot say so publicly because of annoying Lord Stormont and the British. I realize the ministers and the king do not want to appear to be secretly supporting a war against Britain, but many Frenchmen have now gone to America to fight, so I am certainly not the first, although I am certainly the most prominent."

"It is best to do what His Majesty and your family want," he advises. "You have acted with honor in all this. Do not be disheartened. If you do have to sell the ship, try to get the owners to release you from your contract by allowing them to keep twenty thousand, or twenty-five thousand livres, from the forty thousand you have paid them. In the meantime, it is best to keep *La Victoire* at Puerto de Pasajes."

"I do not wish you to set sail until you have heard from me as I will make every possible effort to obtain permission to depart."

"I agree," he says reluctantly. "The ship belongs to you."

My greatest fear is to involve Deane in some disagreeable dilemma and to harm our American friends' interest at the court. If I discover that the orders are serious, I decide to sacrifice myself to the resentment of others, to make sure no one else shares my misfortune and that Silas Deane's security and that of his cause will not be threatened. I will return to Bordeaux to try and change the royal orders.

I set off back towards France; I cross the small river at the frontier; I stop at Saint Jean de Luz where the innkeeper's daughter takes my mind off my dilemma for a short time. Then I continue north through a wretched countryside of barren, watery marshland where stagnant pools are covered in vegetation to entrap the unwary. A few sheep graze on denuded patches of earth, the only crop the hardy rye. Dunes sometimes extend inland from the coast; at least one hamlet has its houses almost completely submerged by sand. Local inhabitants move across their benighted terrain on tall stilts to escape the water; men and women suddenly appear; gangly, elongated figures striding along on high, slender wooden sticks. Green pine forests by the coast and rivers occasionally alleviate the drab swamps, but near to Bordeaux the land metamorphoses into fertile fields and vineyards bordered by the mud-brown river.

I arrive on April 3. I present myself to Monsieur de Fumel. "I am responsible for what has happened and I am ready to suffer the consequences. I want to return to Paris for two weeks to see Madame de La Fayette, at Saint Germain, or wherever they wish. I hope to be able to change the orders and go to America."

"No, the orders from the king are that you must go to Marseille, to accompany the duc d'Ayen and the comtesse de Tessé for a trip to Italy, as you already know," he replies sternly. "I cannot change the order of the king. You must go to Marseille."

He does not, however, arrest me. There have been no soldiers sent from the king. There is no mention of any lettre de cachet. I breathe more easily. I write a letter to Maurepas and plead for a revocation of the order. I send another courier to find out more from Paris.[12]

I write to Carmichael:

I am kept here by order of the king, my dear friend, and I am sending a messenger to obtain a cancellation of it. In the meantime, I have put the ship and the other officers out of danger. I am distressed that my goodwill for you should have been so unsuccessful. I am so hurried that I do not have the time to write more. Express my regrets to Mr. Deane. Adieu. Force can stop me from rendering you the service I should like, but as it has no effects on hearts it will not prevent me from remaining all my life your brother and your friend. [13]

April 5. I write to de Kalb that I have been refused permission to proceed and fear I will be compelled to go to Toulon, that I am waiting for the answer of my courier and will inform him at once when I know more.[14]

Several days pass. There is no word from the government. I obtain a passport from Monsieur de Fumel to travel to the Mediterranean; on the twelfth, I write again to de Kalb. I tell him that I am on the point of leaving for Marseille, where the royal order commands me to report on the fifteenth; the court is devoting great attention to my affair, but I still hope to win over the duc d'Ayen so that I will be free to join him. I tell him not to sail before he receives another letter from me from Toulon or some other place, that the ship is still held in my name and for him to look after my interests and see that my investment is realized as soon as possible.[15]

I set off. Six leagues from Bordeaux I wait for my courier who might bring new entreaties of my family or the opinion of the public. He arrives, along with the vicomte de Mauroy.[16]

"I have been sent by Mr. Carmichael," says de Mauroy.[17] The government and the king have only acted as they have because of the anger of the duc d'Ayen. If you continue the voyage there will be no serious consequences. Everyone in Paris has been cheering you and your expedition. I have been entrusted with a letter from the comte de Broglie to Washington, and a letter from Mr. Deane to the president of Congress. Return to your ship and sail to America."

My spirits soar. My optimism returns. I dash off a second letter to Maurepas: 'As I have not heard from you, I believe I have your approval to carry on with the expedition.'

De Mauroy and I get into a postchaise. We make a detour to avoid Bordeaux[18] and go south to Spain. When we stop at a posthouse to change horses, I disguise myself as an outrider and gallop in front so as not to arouse suspicion. At Saint Jean de Luz de Mauroy goes to do some errands and I sit on a bale of straw in the stables. The innkeeper's daughter unfortunately goes past and recognizes me. I make a sign to her to be silent.

"I will throw your pursuers off your track," she says.[19]

April 16. At nine o'clock in the morning, we reach Puerto de Pasajes and *La Victoire*. I waste no time. I immediately send the first officer to Bayonne to buy one hundred muskets. I decide to have the ship armed with six cannon instead of the pitiful two and order four more to be found.

"I received assurances from everyone in Paris that only the duc d'Ayen had procured the royal order and that everyone is in favor of my enterprise and very dissatisfied with my father-in-law for obstructing me, and that the ministers would have said nothing except for the complaints of the duc d'Ayen. The ministers granted and issued orders to stop my sailing out of mere compliance with the requests of the duc d'Ayen," I tell de Kalb.[20]

On April 19, I write to Adrienne:

My dear heart, they thought that fear would have more effect upon me than love. They do not know me well, and since they snatch me away from you, since they force me not to see you for a year, and since they wish only to humble my pride, without affecting my love; at least this cruel absence will be employed in a manner worthy of me. The only idea that could hold me back was the sweet consolation of embracing you, of being restored to you, and to all the people I love. For these reasons, I asked for fifteen days, only fifteen days, to be with you, at Saint Germain, or wherever was wanted. I was refused. I refuse also, and, having to choose between the slavery that everyone believes he has the right to impose on me, and liberty, which called me to glory, I left.

My voyage will be no longer, perhaps less, and you will have news of me even more often. A thousand ships will bring it to you constantly. I shall not expose myself; I shall take care of myself, I shall think that you love me, you can be very tranquil. It is more as a philosopher than as a soldier that I shall see that country....I was received here with very flattering transports of joy, I am liked here beyond my hopes, but I am far from happy. My heart is broken. Tomorrow is the cruel moment of departure. I am writing to you the day before to be more sure that my letter will be rational. If you do not send word to me that you still love me, that you forgive me, that you will take good care of your health, I shall be in despair. I swear to you by the most sacred honor, by my love for you, that my greatest regret in departing is to leave you, that my greatest anxiety is for you. Make me less unhappy by writing to me quickly. Farewell, I may return sooner than M. le duc d'Ayen. Love me always, even at this moment when I deserve it only because of my pain at leaving you and because of my ardent love.

Embrace our Henriette. Take good care of our other child. I hope to be reunited soon with my whole family. Write to me at once. My address is Major. Gal...You must go with Mde. d'Ayen to Mr. Deane's house, to have your letter forwarded to me. He is a man of the greatest merit, the most honorable man in the world, and my friend. He will take care of your first letter. For the others, the marquis de Coigny will give you the address.

Adieu, once again, do not doubt the love that I feel more than ever at this cruel moment. Nothing, not even adversity, compares with the anguish of leaving you. L.[21]

April 20. Sunday. Flaming torches illuminate the night, revealing the wretched dwellings clinging to the rocky ground. A wind billows out the sails; my ship emerges from the narrow inlet. Lanterns gleam on the focsle, star constellations shine brightly in the black heavens. *La Victoire* sets her prow towards America.

Chapter 6

The sea is so sad, and I am sad with it

La Victoire pitches and rolls, one minute gaining the crest of a wave, the next, lurching sickeningly down into the trough. The sea appears to boil in a storm-whipped frenzy; white foam spewing on to the deck hangs in streamers from the rigging. The masts creak, the timbers shudder as though our floating wooden box is tearing itself apart; I think sadly of Adrienne and my friends. I have left behind everyone I love most in the world. I can find no more excuses for myself and to add to my misery I am seasick, as are many of the others; I lie down or lurch unsteadily as we sail across a watery hell.

"I wish to sail directly for America," I tell the captain a few days after we leave Spain.

"No, it is not possible. Our papers are for the Leeward Islands. If the English capture us making for an American port, we will all be sent as prisoners to Halifax and kept there indefinitely. We also need to replenish our supplies."

"The ship belongs to me. Everyone on board runs an equal risk. I want to sail to America by the quickest route and if you are not willing to follow my orders, I will remove you from your command and give it to the next officer."

I do not mention there might be a lettre de cachet waiting for me at the Islands and I would be arrested. His face is sullen with anger and I mistrust him.

"Alright, I will do as you say," he agrees reluctantly.

I suspect he has other motives besides personal anxiety; I make enquiries among the crew.

"He has goods worth eight thousand dollars in the hold," the second mate tells me.

I speak again to the captain. "I give you a pledge of security that if we are captured and your cargo is lost, I will pay you the eight thousand dollars."[1]

"We will set course for America," he says.

"*La Victoire* is heavy and could not escape even the smallest privateer. She has only two cannons and some guns. If we are captured, I want her sunk."[2]

"No," he shouts.

"I have already said I will reimburse you for the loss of your cargo," I reply.

"I'm not sinking my ship," he retorts.

I go to ask the brave Dutchman, Bedaulx, instead. His fate would surely be the gallows if he is captured.[3] I have faith in his strength.[4]

I am the first to recover. I feel almost the same as if I am on land and am sure that when I arrive in America I will have acquired perfect health for a long time.[5] In the meantime, the tedium of each day is followed by the tedium of the next. There is always the sky, there is always the water and then the next day it is the same again. The sea is so sad, and I am sad with it.[6] Sometimes there are long periods of calm; sometimes the winds blow strongly against us. I do not keep a journal of my voyage. I have not noticed anything which is worth writing about or which has not already been written about by other people,[7] but the miserable plain I am on is somewhat improved by keeping busy. I divide my time between military and English books, between de

Kalb who teaches me warfare and Brice who teaches me English. I discuss America with de Mauroy.

"Don't you believe that the people are united by the love of virtue and liberty? Don't you believe that they are simple, good, hospitable people, who prefer beneficence to all our vain pleasures, and death to slavery?" I ask.

"If the savages of the new continent had united to live together; if some man of genius, virtue, talent and constancy, a new Timoléon, had given North America its laws, such a people could present to us the beautiful picture you have just described, but it was people already civilized who brought to this wild land the views and prejudices of their respective homelands," he replies. "Fanaticism, the insatiable desire to get rich, and misery, are unfortunately the three sources from which flow that stream of immigrants, who, sword in hand, go to cut down under a sky new to them, forests as ancient as the earth, watering a still virgin land with the blood of its savage inhabitants, and fertilizing with thousands of scattered corpses the fields they conquered through crime. In this tableau, which is only too accurate, do you see any less horror than you see in the picture you are able to make of the continent we are leaving? I see you are about to mention the Quakers, and the happiness that at least Pennsylvania must offer us, but beside the fact that such a point of view works to the disadvantage of the other colonies, it is a fact that these supposedly good people yield with regret to the projects of all their neighbors. They piously desire only peace and abundance, and that finally all powers are the same to them because under their monkish constitution, no power can bind them. That is the basis upon which I admit to you quite frankly that I expect to find in America only people like those of our own continent. I think that because of their prejudices, we French must be detested by them, when, as people who come to offer knowledge superior to theirs, we hurt their pride in general and arouse their envy in particular. Don't worry, though, it will be politic to welcome you. I do not know what resources Monsieur de Kalb has, and since I have none, I would be a complete fool if I did not at least reap from such a voyage the fruit which is always within reach of he who looks at it calmly."[8]

I continually refute the darkness of his vision; I maintain my hopes for the American people and their revolution. He is unable to sway me. My idealism remains strong; I long to fight for their cause which represents virtue and liberty.

May 30. I write to Adrienne:

It is from very far away that I am writing to you, my dear heart, and to this very cruel separation is added the even more terrible uncertainty of when I shall hear your news. I hope, however, that it will be soon; among so many reasons which make me long to arrive, nothing else makes me so impatient. How many fears, how many troubles have I to add to the pain which is already so cruel of leaving all that is most dear to me! How did you take my second departure? Did you love me less? Have you forgiven me? Have you thought that, in any case, I would have been separated from you. I would have been wandering in Italy, trailing in a life without glory, with people who are most opposed to my projects and to my way of thinking? However, all these thoughts did not prevent me from feeling great distress in the terrible moments when we left the shore. Your distress, that of my friends, (your pregnancy), Henriette, broke my heart. I could no longer find an excuse. If you knew how I have suffered, the sad days I have spent fleeing from everything I love in the world. Must I join to this misfortune that of learning that you do not pardon me? If that is the case then my heart, I should be truly pitied ...Do not think, my dear heart, that I shall run great dangers in what I will be doing. The post of general officer has always been looked on as a warrant for long life. It is very different from what I should have done in France, for example as colonel...Ask any of the French generals, of whom there are so many, because once having reached that rank they run no further risk, and therefore do not make way for others as they would do in other ranks. In order to show you I am not trying to deceive you, I will admit that we run some danger at the present time because we risk being attacked by English ships and my ship is not strong enough to defend itself. But as soon as I land I shall be perfectly safe. You see that I tell you everything, my dear heart, so be confident and don't worry without reason...But now let us talk about more important things. Let us talk about you, about dear Henriette, about her brother or sister...Henriette is so lovable that she makes me wish for a girl; but whatever our new child shall be, I will welcome it with great joy. Do not lose a moment in hastening my happiness by telling me of its birth...Write, send a reliable man.'[9] On June 7 I add more to my letter until it becomes so dark I can no longer write, as I have forbidden lights on the ship for the last few days: 'I am still on this sad plain, my dear heart...To console myself a little, I think of you and of my friends and of seeing you again....What a wonderful moment when I arrive, when I come in unexpectedly and embrace you. You will perhaps be with our children....You must admit, my heart, that the occupation and the life I am going to have will be very different from that intended for me in that useless trip. Defender of that liberty which I adore, more free than anyone by coming as a friend to offer my services to this very interesting republic I am only bringing with me my own free heart and my goodwill. No ambition, and no particular interest. In working for my glory, I work for the republic's happiness. I hope that for my sake you will become a good American...The happiness of America is intimately linked with the happiness of all humanity; it will become the respectable and safe sanctuary of virtue, of honesty, of tolerance, of equality, and of a peaceful liberty...Adieu...I love you and will love you the whole of my life.[10]

The drinking water is green; there is very little salt pork and biscuit, but I remain cheerful and optimistic. Various birds appear which means we are not far from America. We have sometimes been becalmed or winds have blown strongly against us,[11] but my star has watched over us and we have not encountered British ships.

June 12. At nine in the morning suddenly comes a shout from the crow's nest. "Land ahoy!"

We stampede onto the deck and stare towards an almost invisible coast which slowly becomes more distinct. About forty leagues distant a small ship rapidly approaches. The captain's face goes white, but the officers like me and prepare to resist. She comes nearer; we see with relief she is an American man o' war.

"The British are blockading Charleston. Sail further north," her captain tells us.

Not long after, we have another fright. Two British frigates appear in the distance, but my star continues to shine. The wind gusts strongly in our favor; we speed north for twenty-five leagues and the frigates are blown south.

June 13. Friday. At two o'clock in the afternoon the anchor rattles into the depths. We are by North Island off South Carolina, near the entrance to Georgetown Bay. It is fifty-four days since we left Los Pasajes.

Chapter 7

I swear I will conquer or die for America's cause

La Victoire is alone at the very edge of the Atlantic Ocean, the American continent in the distance.

"We need a pilot to guide us into Georgetown before the British find us," says the captain. "Lower the yawl."

I clamber down into it with de Kalb,[1] accompanied by the ship's lieutenant. Seven sailors row us towards a coast of gently sloping beaches with occasional high dunes, interspersed with swamps glittering in the fierce sun, and dark green thickets where enormous oak-like trees droop low canopies of leaves almost to the ground. The men sweat profusely as they pull on the oars; every so often one rests whilst the others carry on. There are no signs of habitation, no houses, no cultivated fields and no people.

Hours pass. We approach the northernmost point of the island. The sun sinks below the horizon; the thick shroud of night descends. A myriad stars twinkle. A huge moon glows white. The air resembles a blacksmith's forge and the sailors slump at their oars in exhaustion.

Suddenly we glimpse men in a flat-bottomed pirogue. They are black. They are naked. They stare at us, terror on their faces, their bare skin glistening in the moonlight, shells heaped next to them gleaming ghost white.

"Slaves," mutters a sailor.

"Where are we?" calls de Kalb. "Can you take us to your master?"

They reply, but their words are unintelligible. One points to the shore. "Danger!"

"We need a pilot," calls de Kalb.

"Come. Massa Ugee's house," he says, indicating the mouth of a creek.

They paddle their craft; we follow. We proceed upstream past marshland, the night air noisy with croaking frogs and the chirping of cicadas. A short time later an ebbing tide traps our yawl in the mud; the men help us into the pirogue.

"Stay here. We will return when we can," I tell the sailors.

We continue past a low bank and see the flickering of a distant, faint, yellow gleam.

"Massa Ugee's house," says one of the slaves.

The pirogue grates onto the bank. I stumble on to American soil.

"I swear I will conquer or die for America's cause," I declare solemnly, emotion welling up in me.[2]

We set off towards the glimmering light, our sea-legs struggling to walk across soft, water-logged ground. At midnight, we emerge from a copse in front of a large house where a candle burns in an upstairs window. Dogs howl.

"Who goes there? Stop where you are, or I will fire!" A man shouts.

"We are French officers. We have just come ashore to serve in the Continental Army. Our ship is at the mouth of the inlet and we seek a pilot to guide her. We seek shelter for ourselves and somewhere to spend the night," calls out de Kalb.[3]

Candles are immediately lit in every window. The bars grate on the front door. It swings open and the dark bulk of a man steps on to the porch, people with candles standing behind him. We walk forward slowly so that he can see us and our uniforms. We stop near to him.

"May I introduce the seigneur Gilbert du Motier, marquis de La Fayette. I am the baron de Kalb. I am a brigadier in the army of France and aide to the comte de Broglie."

"I am Major Benjamin Huger, of the South Carolina militia, a patriot to the American cause, and I welcome you, sirs, to my house," he replies.

A young child tugs at my sleeve to pull me into the hall. We step gratefully inside.

"Georgetown is not deep enough for *La Victoire* so I will instruct a pilot to take her into Charleston. I don't believe the British are still blockading it as the winds are thought to have driven them north. It is safer for you to ride overland with your party and for the others to stay on the ship. However, it is a difficult road and I can't provide all of you with horses. There are many runaway slaves marauding through the countryside as well as a few Hessians, so it is best to be well armed. High tide is in the early morning, shortly after three, so your yawl will soon be refloated," says Major Huger.

I retire to bed in great happiness. I have at last reached the haven of my wishes, beyond the reach of my pursuers. I have arrived safely in America.[4]

In the morning I wake in paradise. Sunlight streams yellow gold into my room; mosquito curtains draping my bed quiver in a current of air from an open sash window.[5] Outside are bushes and trees with vivid green foliage, heavy with blossom, the air resonating with bird song and the chirping of cicadas.

A black woman enters, followed by two black servants. One speaks in English, but I cannot understand. I jump from my bed. I dress and go to eat breakfast where I sit with the blue-eyed, pink-cheeked, four-year-old Francis Huger on my knee.

Major Huger, a rice plantation owner of French Huguenot descent, is correct. The tide frees our yawl. The sailors row again and at noon we reach *La Victoire*.[6]

On board the officers crowd round me excitedly. "You can either choose to sail with the ship to Charleston and run the gauntlet of the British ships or come with me overland by difficult roads and without horses for everyone," I tell them.

One group decides to remain on board with de Mauroy. The other group consisting of Dubuysson, de Kalb, several officers and two servants, will come with me.

Next day we return to Major Huger's house.

"A ship in Georgetown Bay is sailing soon for France. If you wish to write letters home, I will arrange for them to be given to the captain," he says.

De Kalb hastily goes to write to his wife; I add lines to Adrienne's letter:

I have arrived, my dear heart, in very good health, at the house of an American officer, and by the greatest good fortune in the world, a French ship is about to sail...I have only the time to finish my letter. This evening I shall go to Charlestown and I shall write to you from there. There is no interesting news. The campaign has begun, but there is no fighting, or at least, very little. The manners of people here are simple, honest, and in worthy in every way of this country where everything resounds with the beautiful name of liberty. I was intending to write to Mde. d'Ayen, but it is impossible...Adieu, adieu, my dear heart. From Charleston I will go overland to Philadelphia and to the army. Is it not true, my heart, that you will always love me?[7]

In the evening we say farewell to the Huger family and little Francis. We go by ferry to the mainland; we set off in high spirits, but the humid heat quickly starts to overwhelm us; our weapons are heavy and we only have three horses.

We splash through tidal swamps, evil expanses of unknown danger where an astonishing number and variety of snakes wriggle across the surface and, less helpfully, below it. Trees often grow out of the water, their trunks broad at the base, their roots hiding ghastly and strange creatures; on muddy creek banks bask long-snouted, huge, scaly alligators.

We make our way south in the worst terrain I have ever encountered, contending not just with swamps and their assorted, slithering, wildlife, but also with dense woods where we slash a path through the vegetation. Dubuysson and others are impeded by their boots. They throw them away; the scorching sand burns their bare feet; they find it increasingly difficult to walk in the woods.[8] They fall ill, but the fifty-six-year-old de Kalb remains strong.

It takes us three days to travel seventy-five miles. Exhausted, dirty, our clothes in rags, we finally reach Charleston, situated on a peninsula between the Cooper and Ashley Rivers. We pass through a beautiful entrance where tall magnolias, studded with cream-velvet blooms, pierce through clusters of very green young trees. We enter wide streets laid out from north to south and east to west which intersect at right angles; the houses are attractive, some of wood, others of brick, but all roofed with wood; on paths and in gardens are magnolias and other brightly flowering bushes whilst Spanish moss trails from branches of enormous living oaks. Sandflies swarm around us and we have the appearance of beggars and brigands.[9] People stare with surprise and scorn.

"Which swamp are you from?" someone shouts.

Many others call out mockingly, but my English is not good enough to understand everything they are saying. French voices join in the abuse. I realize there are many of my countrymen here who also wish to join the American army; I am angry and hurt that Frenchmen can behave like this to other Frenchmen.

We find lodgings; Dubuysson and the others limp away to bed; de Kalb and I go to enquire about *La Victoire.*

"She has not arrived. The two British frigates blockading the town will have captured her," town officials inform us.

"We would like pilots and sloops sent to warn the captain and to tell him to transfer some of the cargo or beach the ship near to the shore and the forts, perhaps even burn her, if she is going to be taken," de Kalb says, translating for me.

Next day, a storm blows violently. The frigates disappear. At noon, *La Victoire* sails into the harbor without meeting friend or enemy. I make my way to the waterfront; people crowd round, congratulating me on the success of our voyage. The same Frenchmen who sneered at us now try to join my party.

Captain Foligné, commander of *Le Marquis de Chalotais*, which has just escorted two American munition ships to Charleston, visits me at my lodgings to pay his respects.

"Would you take my letters to my wife in Paris on your arrival and tell her I am in good health and about to go to Philadelphia?"

He agrees; he returns to his ship which then fires a fifteen-gun salute, moving me greatly.

I go to the inn, the meeting place of Freemasons; they welcome me like a brother. Two days after our arrival, a five-hour dinner is given in my honor where I am introduced to Generals Robert Howe and William Moultrie who invite me to inspect the local fortifications.

"To Liberty and to America!" I toast in faltering English.

Very late that evening, at my lodgings, the heat is still suffocating. Swarms of mosquitos compete for my blood, and I write by candlelight to my beloved:

> The country and its inhabitants are as agreeable as my enthusiasm had imagined them. Simplicity of manners, the desire to please, love of their country and liberty, a sweet equality reigns here for everyone. The richest and the poorest man are on the same level; and although some people have immense fortunes, I defy anyone to find the least difference between their manners towards each other...I started off at Major Huger's house in the countryside, now I am in town. Everything resembles the English fashion, except that there is more simplicity, cordiality and kindness towards each other than in England...Charleston is one of the most attractive, best constructed and agreeably peopled town that I have ever seen. American women are very pretty, very unaffected, and of a charming neatness...It enchants me that all the citizens are brothers. In America, there are no poor, nor even peasants. Each person has the same rights as the most powerful landowner....I have received the most agreeable reception possible from everyone. It suffices to have come with me to be welcomed in a most satisfying way....I feel as much at ease in their society as if I had known them for twenty years, the resemblance between their way of thinking and my own, my love for glory and liberty, would make you think that that I am very happy but I miss you, my dear heart. My friends are not here and there is no happiness for me far from you and from them. Do you still love me? I often ask myself that and my heart always answers yes. I hope it does not deceive me. I wait for news from you with an inexpressible impatience. I hope to find letters at Philadelphia...Write long letters often. You cannot know with what joy I will receive them. Embrace Henriette; can I say, my dear heart, embrace our children? Those poor children have a father who roams, but he is, at heart, a good, honorable man, a good father who loves his family very much, and a good husband as well, for he loves his wife with all his heart...Adieu then my dear heart, I must stop for lack of paper and time; and if I do not repeat ten thousand times that I love you, it is not from want of love, but from hoping that I have already convinced you of it. It is very late at night. The heat is intense and I am devored by little flies which cover you with large blisters; the best countries have, as you can see, their inconveniences. Adieu, my heart, adieu. [10]

I also write to my friends, the prince de Poix, Noailles, Coigny and Ségur, as well as to the duchesse d'Ayen. Then I put down my quill, snuff out the candle and go contentedly to bed. I have only been a short time in America. I am far from home, far from my loved ones, but my dreams are being realized. This wonderful new country entrances me and I look forward to serving in the American army and fighting Britain.

On Friday I visit John Rutledge, President of the South Carolina General Assembly, who welcomes me warmly. On Saturday, I visit the fortifications with Moultrie, Howe and Colonel Gadsden. Batteries are being built along the river to defend both the port and the entrance to the town, whilst Fort Johnson is situated on James Island, overlooking the outer harbor. It is decaying and dilapidated but has two batteries one on top of the other, with about twenty guns. [11] There is a treacherous sand bar which can be crossed at five places, but the water is so shallow large ships cannot possibly pass over it. We go to Fort Moultrie across the water from Fort Johnson, on Sullivan's Island. The party is magnificent; people shower me with honors. Colonel Moultrie speaks about the battle on June 28, 1776.

"The British fleet bombarded us all day, but, as you can see, we built the walls of palmetto trunks, packed with sand and marsh clay. The soft, fibrous wood absorbed everything thrown at it. We had twenty-six guns and three tons of powder whilst the British used nearly seven thousand shells. The redcoats were waiting on Long Island," he points to a flat area of land not far from us. "They were going to cross from the marshes at low tide but found that some of the water was about seven feet deep. It was impossible for them to wade across and they did not have enough small boats. It then became a fight between the artillery and their ships were savagely attacked for nine hours and forty minutes. The flagship of Admiral Parker was badly damaged; the frigate *HMS Actaeon* grounded on a sand bank and was burned by its crew so that it was not captured. Clinton stayed for a few days and then he took his men and ships back to New York with his tail between his legs. We had thirty-seven men killed and wounded. The British had two hundred and five killed and wounded."[12]

At the corner of the fort flies a blue flag on which is a crescent and the word liberty. "I designed it," he says proudly. "The blue represents the color of our uniforms, and the moon is the gorget, the emblem on the men's caps. The flag staff was shot down during the battle and it fell outside the fort wall. Sergeant Jasper retrieved it under fire and set it up again. It is a symbol of the Revolution here in the south and we call it the *Liberty Flag*."

"I will give you money to equip one hundred soldiers," I tell him, in appreciation of his clearly very good defense, although it must be admitted that the British appear to have chosen the only plan of attack certain to fail.[13]

I am forced to concern myself with financial matters. I inherited great wealth at a young age which has always been managed for me. I have never visited my lands in Touraine or Bretagne and know nothing of my tenants there. I am used to spending lavishly, much to the disapproval of de Kalb who advises me to exercise economy.[14]

Now, however, I need money to finance our expedition. I write a letter drawing on five thousand five hundred dollars from Paris. I intend to sell the cargo on *La Victoire* to raise more and I advertise it for sale. To my surprise the captain brings me a note for forty thousand livres to be paid to Reculès de Basmarein et Raimbaux, the previous owners, when the new cargo and ship return to Bordeaux.[15] They will also deduct an additional amount of thirty-five percent, twenty-five per cent for insurance and ten percent for a commission. To my chagrin I had not read the contract thoroughly.

I sell the cargo on *La Victoire*. My friends and I manage to borrow thirty-six thousand livres, although at very high interest, de Kalb endorsing letters of exchange for twenty-eight thousand livres drawn on my agent at Paris as I am a minor and would otherwise not be able to obtain it. I begin to appreciate the value of money.

La Victoire sets sail for France and becomes wrecked on the sand bar at the harbor entrance. I will receive insurance both on the ship and the new cargo of rice. My star is shining again.

Vrigny, Candon and La Colombe decide to go by sea. The rest of us divide into two groups and will travel separately. De Mauroy, de Fayolle, Capitaine, Franval and Duboismartin buy two wagons and eight horses for seven thousand livres. My party of de Kalb, Valfort, Delesser, Dubuysson, Gimat, Bedaulx and Brice buy four wagons and carriages for five thousand seven hundred livres.

"I will be your guide even although I do not know this region of America," says Brice.

Chapter 8

An initial shock at Philadelphia

June 26. It is early morning; we set off across the plain near Charleston, the sun already hot. De Kalb and I are in a shay, an open carriage which is a sort of sofa, supported by four springs. In front rides a servant dressed in the gold-braided uniform of a hussar;[1] another servant rides next to us on horseback; the second carriage, with two wheels, has the two colonels; the third has the aides-de-camp, the fourth has our baggage and at the back of our cavalcade is a black servant on horseback.[2]

We pass rice fields where green shoots cover watery ground traversed by canals, dikes and gates to flood or drain the land at high and low tides. On drier ground are fields of tall, blue-flowering indigo, a very valuable crop which is helping to finance the war and whose dye was recently brought in thirty-five barrels to France by Dr. Franklin. Black men and women labor in the heat.

Sometimes there are wide, grassy plains like natural lawns. Elsewhere there are huge cypress and gum trees, forests of tall, large pines, or swamps seething with clouds of hostile insects. My shay and our other vehicles ominously creak over the rough road. Their axles splinter and break four days after setting off, which is not a great surprise. We abandon them for horses. They quickly become lame or die; I buy more. We are forced to leave behind some of our luggage and part of it is also stolen.

The road winds slowly north; we often share it with many others beneath a suffocating sun. Wagons carrying agricultural produce lumber along rutted tracks which are either deep with dried mud or thick with dust; we are occasionally caught up in enormous herds of cattle, pigs, or other animals being taken to market by drovers, the stink of excrement from so many beasts making the air unpleasant and the ground slippery for our horses.

The countryside delights me. Nature adorns the land with youth and majesty. Immense woods and fast-flowing rivers, crossed by ferries, alternate with cultivated land and neatly built homesteads; wild animals roam everywhere. De Kalb is not captivated by our surroundings as I am, but he is always practical and capable. He does not suffer from the hardships of the trek, unlike the others, many of whom are again laid low by fever and dysentery and who are very far from sharing my enjoyment. We often sleep on the ground in the woods at night; we are often almost dead from hunger and exhausted by the heat, but my enthusiasm remains boundless. We constantly think of arriving at Philadelphia and the reception we will have, and slowly we travel seven hundred miles, by way of the Carolinas, then Virginia, Maryland and Delaware, each colony seeming very different. Virginia, two hundred leagues wide and almost three hundred leagues long, appears the wealthiest and the most fertile. Maryland is very beautiful, whilst Pennsylvania is the oldest and the most cultivated but is not richer than Virginia.[3]

July 17. We reach Petersburg and I take the opportunity to write again to Adrienne:

I am very happy, my dear heart, if the word happiness is appropriate for me while I am far from everyone I love. There is a ship here ready to sail for France and I may tell you, before I arrive at

Philadelphia, that I love you, my dear heart, and that you can be content about my health. I did not notice the fatigue of the trip; it was very long and boring by land, although it was even worse when I was on my sad vessel. I am now eight days from Philadelphia and in the beautiful country of Virginia. All the hardships have gone and I greatly fear that those of the war will be very light, if it is true that General Howe has left New York, to go I know not where. But all the news is so uncertain that I will wait until I arrive to have an opinion and will write you a long letter from there. You should have received four from me, if they have not fallen into the hands of the English. I have not yet received your letters and my impatience to reach Philadelphia and receive them is beyond comparison. You may imagine the state of my mind, after this immense time without receiving two lines from any of my friends. I hope this will soon be remedied because I cannot live in such uncertainty. I have undertaken a task that is truly too much for my heart which was not born to suffer so.

You will have heard of the beginning of my journey; you know that I started out brilliantly in a carriage; well now I must tell you we are now on horseback after having broken the wagons in my usual praiseworthy fashion, and I expect to write to you in a few days that we are arriving on foot. It has been somewhat tiring but although several of my companions have suffered greatly, I have hardly noticed it...I hardly dare think of your impending confinement, my dear heart, and yet, I think of it every minute of the day. I cannot think about it without trembling and having a terrible fear. In truth, I am very wretched to be so far from you. Even if you did not love me, you ought to pity me; but you do love me and we shall always love each other and we shall always make each other happy...The farther I go towards the north, the more I love this country and its inhabitants. There are no politenesses or kind attentions that I do not receive, although several hardly know who I am. But I shall write more of that to you from Philadelphia. I have only the time here to entreat you, my dear heart, not to forget a wretch who has paid most dearly for the wrong of leaving you, and who has never so well felt how much he loves you. [4]

Fort Ticonderoga, in northern New York, was taken by the enemy on July 6. General Arthur St. Clair marched two thousand soldiers from it across the bridge to Mount Independence and sent his sick soldiers and supplies off in boats before setting off through the countryside. People are angry, but he has managed to save his corps. The colonies have been divided in half and if the British capture New York and Philadelphia they will be cut into three parts. We hope the insurgency will not be too harmed by this.

Wind and rain whip the countryside. De Kalb and Dubuysson decide to travel on; the rest of us wait for the storm to finish. Seven days later, we reach Annapolis, the home of Brice, and meet up again with de Kalb.

"Dubuysson is ill. He has a fever and is in bed," he says.

"Gimat also has a fever. We had to leave him behind in Petersburg," I tell him.

I write to Adrienne:

I manage to always find, my dear heart, ships which are about to set off, and this time, I only have a half of a quarter of an hour. The ship is already under sail and I can only tell you that I have happily arrived at Annapolis, forty leagues from Philadelphia. I cannot describe the town because as soon as I dismounted, I armed myself with a little quill dipped in invisible ink. You must have received five letters from me unless King George has received some of them. I sent the last one three days ago I told you about my good health which is still the same and of my impatience to reach Philadelphia. I have just learned bad news. Ticonderoga, the strongest post in America, has been taken by the enemy, which is very annoying and which we must act on. We must try to make up for that. In retaliation our troops have taken an English general near Niew York. I am every day more miserable for having left you, my dear heart.....Farewell, my heart, I am so hurried that I do not know what I am writing you, but I do know, dear heart, that I love you more tenderly than ever, that it took the pain of this separation to convince me how very dear you are to me, and that I would give half of my blood to obtain the pleasure of embracing you just once more, and of telling you just how much I love you....My dear heart, if you knew how much I miss you, how much I suffer from being far from you, in truth, you would find me somewhat worthy of your love. There is only space now for Henriette, or may I say, for my dear children. Embrace them, my dear heart, embrace them a hundred thousand times. I shall always share those embraces. [5]

We sail from Annapolis along the wide Delaware. In the morning of July 27, I see the spires and steeples of Philadelphia for the first time, thirty-two days after leaving Charleston. Our clothes are even more dirty and ragged than when we arrived there and much of our luggage has been lost or stolen. We again resemble vagabonds. We have travelled nine hundred miles on horseback.

We enter the city which is as clean as we are dirty. The roads are parallel and straight like those at Charleston and intersect at right angles, forming squares. The roofs are of shingle wood, but the houses are constructed mainly of red brick which also paves the roads. It is hot. Behind the houses are tree-lined alleys where people stroll and it is cooler, but on the streets the red buildings and red ground absorb the heat and throw it back at us, baking our already over-heated bodies.

We find a boarding house. We quickly attempt to make ourselves look somewhat more presentable and meet with Dubuysson and those of his companions who have arrived. It is Sunday; Congress is not in session so the thirteen of us go to the house of John Hancock, the President of the Second Continental Congress.

He is a thin man, who limps towards us, as though his feet are painful. His face is handsome, his eyes very dark, and he is bewigged and dressed more finely than most Americans I have yet seen. He does not greet us courteously; his manners appear to lack the refinement of his clothes.

We give him our contracts signed by Silas Deane, as well as a letter of recommendation from Deane for myself and de Kalb, whilst I also have a letter of introduction to Robert Morris asking him to be my banker in America.

"Go to Robert Morris. He's a representative of Pennsylvania in Congress and a member of the Committee of Congress for secret correspondence which is the body which sent Silas Deane to Paris," Hancock says bluntly.

We stare at him in complete astonishment at his brusqueness. We are speechless. However, we go again through the hot streets to the house of Robert Morris, who turns out to be as plump as Hancock is thin, and not as well dressed.

"I am busy today. Would you please come back tomorrow and meet me at the door of Carpenter's Hall, the seat of Congress," he says rudely.

We regard him with annoyance and bewilderment. We return to our lodgings, not knowing what to think. What has happened is completely unexpected. We have our contracts. We have travelled so far at great danger and at great cost. I am a very high-ranking noble of the French court; de Kalb and de Mauroy are experienced soldiers in the French army.

Carpenters' Hall is a two-story building in the ubiquitous red brick, dominated by a steeple.

"Please wait outside," we are told.

We wait and we wait. At last Morris appears, accompanied by another man.

"This is Mr. James Lovell, the congressman for Massachusetts and chairman of the committee of foreign affairs,"[6] he declares, without any preliminary politeness. "He speaks French very well and is in charge of all dealings with people of your nation. Therefore, it is with him you will deal in future."[7] With that he turns and goes into Carpenters' Hall, leaving us in the street with Lovell.

"We have letters of recommendation and commissions from Mr. Silas Deane," says de Kalb.

"We no longer have any need of French officers. Return to France, gentlemen. America is filled with French officers wanting rank and money sent by Mr. Deane. You are all adventurers. You are wasting our time and yours. Have you seen Mr Deane's commission? We asked him to send four French engineers. Instead, he sent Monsieur Ducoudray with four men who claim to be engineers but are not, and some artillery men who have never served. We asked Mr. Franklin to send us four engineers and they have arrived. French officers are very forward to come and serve us without being asked. Last year we needed officers but this year we have many and they are all very experienced," he shouts.[8] "Even His Royal Highness, the prince de Condé, would solicit in vain a division of the American army and such a thing would be a direct affront to our constitution."[9]

Passers-by stare. We also stare. Words fail us. Lovell turns his back on us, like Morris, and goes into Carpenters' Hall. We stand in complete amazement.

"It is incredible that they should so scandalously abuse officers with their recommendations tolerated, if not openly avowed by the French government. De Kalb particularly is well known in America and even in Congress," exclaims Dubuysson.

"Yes," agrees de Mauroy. "We have all been recommended and we represent the French king and his government. It is an open secret that France is aiding the colonies in their struggle."

"I don't think that our papers have even been read by Congress.[10] I don't know why these men have acted like this, but I refuse to accept what they say. It is best to wait and see why we have been treated so contemptuously before we complain," is my opinion.

We return in subdued spirits to our boarding house and discuss what has happened. Lovell has, in fact, somewhat clarified the situation and although his rudeness is completely unacceptable, we begin to have some understanding of the problem. Many French officers have been sent by Deane with promises of high rank but have not been useful to the American fight.

We discover that Frenchmen who have joined the American army have not always behaved correctly. Some are adventurers and have nothing in common with America's fight for liberty. Monsieur de Fermoy was incompetent at Ticonderoga. Monsieur de Borre is spoken of with contempt. The marquis de la Rouërie is sometimes reckless. Monsieur Conway, a Frenchman of Irish descent, is disliked by the officers of his brigade and envied by the generals because he makes his soldiers work in camp and drills and instructs them himself. Du Coudray appears to have been the worst and has managed to disgust the whole Congress by being extremely arrogant and very demanding of high rank.[11]

"We must not be confused with any of these people. We must write an appeal directly to Congress," we decide.

De Kalb and de Mauroy describe their military qualifications; they demand that Congress either confirm the rank Deane has offered them or pay their expenses to and from America. The others demand the same.

My determination to serve in the American army remains undiminished and I have advantages which the others do not. I am connected to the French king and court, a link it is very much in America's political interest to further. I am extremely wealthy. I have no need of a wage and am a Freemason. I write: 'I would like to serve in the American army on two conditions, first, that I should receive no pay, secondly that I should serve at first as volunteer.'[12]

We send the letters to Congress. We wait. Next day Lovell visits, accompanied by a slightly built man, with a long, narrow face.

"May I introduce William Duer, the congressman for New York, who also speaks French," he says politely. "Congress has read and discussed your proposals."

"We apologize for the reception which was given to you," declares Duer to me. "May I speak to you in private?"[13]

We go to a different room. "What are your intentions?" he asks.

"My chief motive in coming to America is to serve under Washington and to create a sensation in France for the benefit of the insurgents," I reply. "I intend to soon return home."[14]

He and Lovell depart. A short time later he returns and again speaks to me alone.

"Would you agree to break your contract with Deane and accept an appointment as a major general dating from today? Would you also serve without pay and without the command of a division?"[15]

I am now in a quandary. I do not wish to accept unless the claims of everyone are granted and as Duer is speaking only to me, I suspect, to my amazement, that de Kalb and de Mauroy are being offered nothing.

"Our cause is not yours," advises de Mauroy. "As all obstacles have been removed for you, you must only think about your own success. The rest of us do not enjoy in France so great an importance that our fate would cause a sensation there. It is very different for you. I follow what you are doing with the greatest interest and provided that you succeed I willingly resign myself to all the troubles that I have yet to endure here. My career is too far advanced for me to hope for great military rank, but you begin yours under the best possible auspices and I have an opinion of you that redoubles my wishes for your success and which you will undoubtedly justify."[16]

Money does not concern me. I am rich. I want the rank of major general in the American army and I intend to command a division whatever might be said at the present time. For the moment it seems better to accept what is being offered. I cannot return home. I would be laughed at and ridiculed. My honor would be blemished.

"I accept," I tell Duer.

"Would you write this in a letter to Congress?" he asks.

"Yes," I reply.

I immediately start to write. I keep my words succinct. My command of English is still poor and I do not wish to show my ignorance or to confuse the situation: 'I give up any contract with Deane as I do not wish to cause you embarrassment.'[17]

Duer returns to Congress with my letter. Two hours later I discover they have passed a resolution accepting me. I receive the sash of a major general and a letter which declares:

Seeing that the Marquis de Lafayette, on account of his great zeal in the cause of liberty in which the United States are engaged, has quitted his family and country, and has come to offer his services to the United States, without demanding either pay or private indemnity, and that he desires to expose his life in our cause,- resolved, that his service be accepted, and that on account of his zeal, illustrious family and connexions, he shall have the rank and commission of major-general in the army of the United States. [18]

It is an honorary position and it is for George Washington to decide what I should command. It rescinds the earlier date of commission given by Silas Deane and is dated July 31. I appear to be the only one offered anything. I am the youngest. I have practically no military experience. I have been chosen for diplomatic reasons for my closeness to the French court. I am surprised but also relieved.

De Kalb and the others are furious at their rejection by Congress but my usual optimism and my intention to help my companions makes me hope that they will also be taken on. I ask the chevalier Jean-Joseph Sourbader de Gimat and chevalier Morel de La Colombe, both twenty-two, to be my aides-de-camp. They are delighted.

De Kalb writes a letter to Congress to say that if his engagement as major general by Mr. Deane will not be ratified he is ready to return to Europe, but thinks he is entitled to be reimbursed financially, that although he ardently desires to serve America he did not mean to do so by spending part of his and his children's fortune, that what is deemed generosity in my case would be downright madness in him. He says he is very pleased for me as I am a worthy young man, and no one will outdo me in enthusiasm for the American cause. He refers to his military experience of thirty-four years and that he should be placed in a senior position to me. He threatens legal action against Mr. Deane if Congress do not give him full satisfaction concerning returning home. He believes that neither his name, nor his services, nor his person, are proper objects to be trifled with or laughed at; he feels the injury Congress has done to him very deeply; that it seems ridiculous to make people leave their homes, families, and affairs to cross the sea to face one thousand different dangers, to be received and looked at with contempt by those from whom he had expected warm thanks.[19]

Chapter 9

I instantly know Washington from the majesty of his face and body

Late in the evening of July 31,[1] I see George Washington for the first time, at a dinner given in his honor at the City Tavern, a building in the usual red brick on Second Street above Walnut Street, not far from Carpenters' Hall. The British fleet of two hundred and twenty-eight warships and transports which sailed from Sandy Hook on July 23, was sighted at the Capes of Delaware in the forenoon on the thirtieth,[2] so it is now presumed it will sail up the river and attack Philadelphia. Washington has ordered his troops at Coryell's and Howell's Ferry to cross the Delaware and march to Philadelphia and has ridden on in advance with his staff.

He is standing, surrounded by a crowd of officers, congressmen and townspeople, but I instantly know who he is from the majesty of his face and body, the noble affability of his manners,[3] and the dignity with which he addresses those about him. He is a head taller than anyone else and is a large man in every respect, from his feet and hands to his massive thighs.[4] Muscular and broad-shouldered, wearing his uniform of a blue coat with two epaulettes,[5] over buff-colored clothes, he carries himself with an erect, military bearing which, at the same time, seems lithe and powerful.

I sit at the table in the plainly furnished, wood-floored room and watch only one figure hold court. The conversation buzzes animatedly, although fear is apparent in men's voices and eyes as they drink copious amounts of porter from thick tankards, wine, or madeira, and eat turkey pot pie, roast venison, clam chowder and an ice cream, which is evidently Washington's favorite. He holds everyone's gaze. On his shoulders rests their future, their salvation from the eighteen thousand British regulars on ships south of their city.

At the end of the evening, I am introduced to him. He looks very directly at me with widely set blue-gray eyes.[6] There is a fine symmetry in his features, his nose is straight[7] and scarred from smallpox, his powdered hair is pulled back from his forehead and tied in a queue.[8]

"I compliment you on the noble spirit you have shown and the sacrifices you have made for the American cause," he says, revealing darkly stained teeth and speaking in a surprisingly soft voice for a man with such a powerful physique.

"I would be pleased if you would make my quarters your home. Establish yourself there whenever you think proper and consider yourself at all times as one of my family. I cannot promise you the luxuries of a court or even the conveniences which your former habits might have rendered essential to your comfort, but as you have become an American soldier you will doubtless have to accommodate yourself to what you have chosen and submit with a good grace to the customs, manners and privations of a republican army."[9] He regards me with an unwavering gaze which bears the hint of a smile. "I am inspecting the Delaware fortifications tomorrow. Would you care to accompany me?"

I look at him and see, not just a general, but a brother freemason and a friend. War took my father from me, before I was even a boy, and standing next to this large, confident, forty-five-year-old soldier, I feel an instant bond, strengthened by our wish to fight for the same cause of liberty.

Next day, I tour the fortifications. I speak little. I follow in his wake under a hot sun. Fort Mifflin on Mud Island, built by the British engineer John Montresor, has formidable, thick, high stone walls on the east and south side constructed in the form of a tenailled trace, a saw-toothed design, facing the river, but at its rear and on the north it is very weak; there are only ditches and palisades with four wood blockhouses and a battery of ten eighteen-pounder guns.[10] A small, square redoubt is in the center of the main enclosure[11] and it appears insufficiently garrisoned with about three hundred men. North of it is Province Island, a bank of mud mostly under water at high tide but having two small areas of dry land which could be used by the enemy to place guns. On the Jersey shore opposite it at Red Bank is Fort Mercer, a much smaller pentagonal earthwork construction.[12] Nine hundred yards downstream from Fort Mercer to Fort Mifflin are two lines of *chevaux de frise*[13] which consist of wooden crates as large as a two-story house, filled with stone ballast and chained together in a row, a heavy log with a barbed iron point sticking out of each one.[14] A second line of chevaux de frise extends further down the river from Billingsport Island to the New Jersey shore[15] and only ten trusted river pilots know how to negotiate the barrier. Two piers have also been constructed nearer to Fort Mifflin and are linked by a boom.[16]

Washington is an excellent and bold horseman, his posture straight and erect. He rides quickly without standing upon his stirrups, bearing on the bridle or letting the horse run wild.[17] His manner is polite and grave towards me, as well as to the officers accompanying him. I feel very honored to be included in his staff.

"Make common cause with us," demand my companions when I return to my lodgings. [18]

"Should I send back the scarf and not accept the commission?" I ask.

"It is best to join the army without delay as after the sensation produced by your departure from France you need to distinguish yourself in America," is the opinion of de Kalb.[19]

I follow his advice. I buy horses, a carriage, uniforms and weapons and wait for my appointment to be officially reported to the commander-in-chief. A few days later a carriage and four arrives and I receive an invitation to come to headquarters. On August 8, Gimat and I reach the encampment five miles northwest of Philadelphia. The enemy fleet sailed away from the Capes on an eastern course the same day I toured the Delaware fortifications with Washington[20] and the army is remaining here until Howe's intentions are known.[21]

Washington is on horseback reviewing his troops; I stare with amazement at the sight in front of me. My two summers at Metz on exercises with the French Army, in all its colorful glory, have ill prepared me for the Continental Army. About eleven thousand men are badly armed and even more badly clothed. They wear an odd assortment of garments. Many are almost naked.[22] They lack shoes and even the best dressed wear only gray linen hunting shirts as used in the Carolinas.[23] Their drilling tactics leave much to be desired. A regiment drawn up in battle order needing to move forward on the right without breaking rank, is doing so by the left making a continued countermarch, and they are always arranged in two lines, the shortest men in the front.[24] I try to disguise my surprise and disappointment but Washington glances sharply at me.

"We must feel embarrassed to exhibit ourselves to an officer who has just quitted French troops."

"I have come here to learn, not to teach!" I reply.[25]

His austere features soften; he seems pleased at my reply.

Despite their clothes, the soldiers appear fine men, their officers zealous. I meet the generals. Henry Knox is tall and fat, with shrewd blue eyes in a large, pale face. He appears lively and amiable.[26] He owned a bookshop before the war but has succeeded in building up a good corps of artillery. He performed the almost impossible feat of retrieving almost sixty heavy mortars and cannon with ammunition left behind by the British after the capture of Fort Ticonderoga. Teams of oxen dragged the heavy weapons on forty-two giant sleds three hundred miles across mountains, frozen rivers and wild countryside for three months and finally arrived at the American lines outside Boston to the immense surprise of everyone.[27]

Nathanael Greene has a long, straight nose and very blue eyes. He is also tall like Knox, but well-built, rather than plump. He limps and so was rejected by the British as an officer; his talents are only yet known to his immediate friends.[28] He is a fighting Quaker and has been expelled from his church. Lord Stirling is regarded as more brave than judicious, and General Stephen is fond of the bottle.[29]

I go north with the army; it makes camp on the broad meadows near Neshaminy Creek in Bucks County whilst everyone waits to see where Howe and his fleet will go. Since the British attack on Long Island and Manhattan, Washington has been conducting a war of attrition, like the famed Roman General Quintus Fabius Maximus, rather than fighting a pitched battle. Now he needs to know where the enemy will land, in order to decide whether to continue with his Fabian tactics and preserve a good army, furnished with proper necessaries, which takes advantage of favorable opportunities to defeat the enemy piecemeal, or whether to stand and fight. Burgoyne has captured Ticonderoga and possesses all the country between there and Fort George; if Howe now co-operates with him, our army needs to march north to unite with the northern army which is nearly equal in numbers to that of the enemy and is between Fort Edward and Saratoga, as it would take our utmost efforts to counteract them. If, however, Howe goes south, all or most of Burgoyne's success would be lost and he would have to just remain in possession of Ticonderoga and the dependent fortresses and wage a partisan war because if he advanced into the countryside he could precipitate himself into certain ruin. It is thought to be inconceivable from any principle of common sense or military propriety that Howe can be running away from Burgoyne to the south instead of co-operating with him, and so when Washington discovered Howe had embarked his troops, he had marched the army from Middlebrook to Morristown, then from there to the Clove, about eighteen miles from the North River, and had moved two divisions over the river. Then it appeared Howe was sailing south from the Hook, so the army hastily countermarched to about thirty-three miles from Philadelphia to defend it.[30] [31] Now everyone is in a state of suspense, some imagine the enemy has gone south, whilst the majority, with which Washington agrees, believe they have gone east.[32]

Congress asks General Schuyler and General St. Clair to come to Philadelphia to give an account of what has happened in the north and General Gates goes to take command of the army there.

Washington decides to recross the Delaware as he believes the enemy has gone east, but on the tenth an express arrives from Philadelphia to say that they had been seen on the eighth,[33] off Sinepuxent Inlet, about sixteen leagues south of the Capes of Delaware, so the army is again waiting for further intelligence.[34]

I write a letter to Congress:

To the Honorable Mr Hancok, President of Congress, Philadelphia.
the 13 august 1777.

I beg that you will receive yourself and present to Congress my thanks for the Commission of Major General in the Army of the United States of America which I have been honor'd with in their name the feelings of my hart long before it became my duty, engaged me in the love of the American cause. I not only consider'd it as the cause of Honor, Virtue and universal Happinness, but felt myself empressed with the warmest affection for a Nation who exhibited by their resistance so fine an example of Justice and Courage to the Universe.

I schall neglect nothing on my part to justify the confidence which the Congress of the United States has been pleased to repose in me as my highest ambition has ever been to do everything only for the best of the cause in which I am engaged. I wish to serve near the person of General Washington till such time as he may think proper to entrust me with a division of the Army.

It is now as an american most at an annum that I'l mention every day to congress the officers who came over with me, whose interests are for me as my own, and the consideration which they deserve by their merits their ranks, their state and reputation in France.

I am sir with the sentiments which every good american owe to you,

Your most obedient servant the mqis de lafayette. [35]

I badger Washington for a command. "I know I am young and inexperienced, but I am ready whenever you wish to command a division, and in the meantime would accept a smaller position. I would also like commissions for my aides-de-camp as Mr. Hancock has directed."

He looks at me, his expression not revealing his thoughts.

"I will write to Mr. Hancock," he says.[36]

I receive two letters from Dubuysson which he wants me to sign and send to Washington and Congress. He writes that as he had come with me, that I am his relation, served in the same regiment and was recommended by the same people, in order to justify his return to France he would have to say I do not even have enough influence here to obtain a position for the only officer in the camp in whom I have a personal interest.[37]

I return to Philadelphia where de Kalb is lying in bed with a bruised right knee which has given him a fever.[38]

"I will do what I can to help. I will pay for anyone who wants, to return to France," I tell everyone.

"If you remain, I will try to obtain a post for you as major of a cavalry regiment," I tell Dubuysson.

"That is all I ask. I consent to stay here," he replies.[39]

"Thank you for not abandoning me. I will do my best for you," I reply. I say farewell and go back to camp at Neshaminy.

Washington takes me aside. "It is not possible to have a command at the present time. It does not seem to be what Congress intends. However, you must always treat me as a friend and as a father."[40]

'I am his adopted son,' the thought races through my mind.

"I have received letters from Dr. Franklin in France. He does not wish you to hazard yourself too much in battle. It is important to our cause that you have come to help us, and we are very grateful. He also says that your beautiful young wife is big with child."

"Yes, she is," I reply with emotion.

Count Casimir Pulaski, well known for his bravery in the unsuccessful Polish war of independence, arrives at camp from France wanting to fight for the American cause. Washington introduces him to me.

"I have letters for you from your family and from the marquise de La Fayette," says Pulaski, who wears an ornate uniform, has pomaded hair and a curled black moustache and appears very different from the Americans with their clean-shaven faces, their hair tied in a queue and their plain clothing.

"How is she?" I ask.

"Your child was not yet born when I saw her, but the marquise was well and gave me letters for you." To my great delight he gives me a packet.

"I will only fight under you or Washington," he says and writes accordingly to Congress.[41]

Washington now believes the enemy is going to Charleston although he cannot see why Howe has decided to go there. "Is he expecting to drag this army after him by appearing at different places and thereby leave the country open for General Clinton to march out and join with Burgoyne? I am at a loss to determine."[42]

August 21. In the morning, a council of officers is called to discuss the situation. Will Lee, a sturdily built man with skin the color of coffee, Washington's personal slave who is always by his side, places a map on the table in the headquarters' tent; the generals and brigadier generals gather round to see the route taken by Howe's fleet.

"There is the strongest reason to suppose Howe has gone far either east or south. The danger of the sea, the troops so long confined on board and the loss of time so late in the campaign, scarcely admits the supposition that he is merely making a feint,"[43] says Washington.

"I expect he is sailing south to Charleston," replies Knox, stabbing at the map with a hand bandaged by a handkerchief, which is slipping off, revealing two missing fingers.

"The army is exhausted with all this marching about to try and find them," remarks Major General Stephen.

"Congress is as baffled as we are," mutters Lord Stirling. "I heard Laurens say that Howe has gone to the moon."

"Hopefully they are at the bottom of the sea," declares Washington. "They seem to be a long time sailing wherever it is they are going. There have been some bad storms since they set off."

Nathanael Greene's opinion is that the Continental Army's situation is a little awkward. It is buried in the country out of hearing of the enemy and that although Washington is exceedingly impatient and it is said that if Philadelphia is lost, all is ruined, it should be considered a great object, to be sure, but not of that great magnitude which is often claimed. He thinks that we shall not remain idle long. In the spring we had the enemy about our ears every hour; the Northern army could neither see nor hear of an enemy. Now they have got the enemy about their heads and we have lost ours compelled to wander about the countryside like the Arabs in search of them.[44]

The council agrees unanimously: 'The enemy has probably sailed to Charleston. It is not expedient for the army to march south as it would not arrive in time to provide help, and lastly that the army should march immediately towards North River.[45]

"I concur with everything you have said, gentlemen," declares Washington. "Howe is probably sailing to Charleston and so our Continentals can march north, either to halt Burgoyne's invasion from Canada, or even to attack New York."[46]

I hold my tongue in the discussion, although I agree. My English is too poor to contribute, and, in any case, my knowledge of the situation is limited, and I do not want to make a fool of myself. However, I sign the minutes as The Mquis de Lafayette, M.G., below the name of Washington, and after the signatures of Major Generals Greene, Stirling and Stephen, but before those of Brigadier Generals Knox, Wayne, Muhlenberg, Weedon, Woodford, Scott and Conway.[47]

Alexander Hamilton is sent to Congress to inform them of the council's decision; in the evening he returns with their approval of the plan to march the army towards the North River and that General Washington was to act as circumstances may require.[48]

Next day the order is given for the troops to set off north. At one-thirty in the afternoon an express arrives with a letter from President Hancock: 'This moment an express arrived from Maryland with an account of near two hundred sail of General Howe's fleet being at anchor in the Chesapeake Bay. In consequence of this advice Congress has ordered the immediate removal of the stores and prisoners from Lancaster and York in this State to places of greater safety, and the calling out of the militia.[49]

"Our army will march tomorrow to go through Philadelphia and onwards to be closer to where the enemy disembark, to show our colors to Congress, to strengthen the resolve of our soldiers and the townspeople," says Washington.

He orders Sullivan to join the army with all convenient speed, Nash to hasten with his brigade and Proctor's artillery, to Chester. He gives the troops the news of Stark's victory against an enemy detachment under Colonel Baume at Bennington in the Hampshire Grants on August 16.[50] Stark has reported thirty men killed and forty wounded and claims there were two hundred and seven Germans killed, many wounded and seven hundred prisoners.[51] 'It is a signal victory...our troops behaved in a very brave and heroic manner,' he says in General Orders.[52]

Early next morning the army marches down the Old York Road. By nightfall it camps near Germantown, a few miles north of the city. I stay with Washington and his staff at the fine old house of Stenton.[53]

August 24. Sunday. Just after dawn it is dry, but rain starts to fall which luckily stops by seven.[54] Washington leads the army in one column into Philadelphia, down Front Street and up Chestnut where members of Congress come out from Carpenters' Hall to watch; then the men march west to the Common. The townspeople line the streets. They crowd the windows and are even on roofs, waving handkerchiefs and cheering wildly. Washington is an impressive figure at the head of the parade on his great white horse and I ride proudly next to him,[55]John Laurens and Alexander Hamilton close behind. Eleven thousand men follow, twelve abreast, in the four divisions of Greene, Stephen, Wayne and Stirling, field artillery placed between each one, each general at the head of his men. The drums and fifes in the center of each brigade play a slow quickstep, enabling the soldiers to march in time in a lively manner but without dancing along.[56] Each man wears a sprig of green,[57] an emblem of hope, in his hat, which gives a more uniform air to the gray hunting shirts and ragged and motley clothing; every weapon gleams and most have a bayonet. If anyone leaves the ranks to join the crowd they will be brought back and at the next halt receive thirty-nine lashes.[58]

We cross the Schuylkill on the floating bridge. Washington and his staff go along King's Road towards Chester and Wilmington, accompanied by those on horse. The infantry march first to the heights of Derby and then to Naaman's Creek.

August 25. The day dawns hot and close. Intelligence arrives: 'The British have landed about six miles below Head of Elk opposite Cecil Court House.'

"Send scouts to observe their movements and see what they intend," commands Washington from his headquarters at a house on Quaker Hill. "Move the army to the hills beyond Wilmington."

He directs Armstrong to send every man of the militia under his command at Chester and Marcus Hook that is properly armed as quickly as possible; Baylor to bring such men as he has ready; Greene and Stephen's divisions to come; Sullivan's division to come but not to press his men too hard in their march as they have just undertaken an unsuccessful attack on Staten Island. General Smallwood and Colonel Mordecai Gist have been ordered by Congress to command the militia of Maryland and have already left Sullivan's division.[59] Washington orders their militia to patrol near the head of the bay to attempt to attack foraging parties and to threaten and harass the enemy's rear when they start to march towards Philadelphia.[60]

I accompany him on a reconnaissance mission with General Greene and a strong troop of cavalry. We ride down the King's Road to Newport under a threateningly black sky. Our horses scramble up through dense woods on the two-hundred-feet-high Iron Hill, gouged by streams which have exposed striking blood-red soil. We halt at the summit and survey the terrain below; to the east is the broad valley of the Christiana River, busy with many ships; north is Newark, whilst further away are the White Clay, Red Clay and Brandywine Rivers.

Billy Lee gives Washington his small spyglass.

"It is important to know how many have landed and how soon they will push forward," he complains, after looking for some time. "We will cross the border into Maryland and see if we can discover more."

The woods again close round us. We climb to the summit of Gray's Hill; Washington scrutinizes the plain with his spyglass.

"Just a few tents with the British flag," he says in frustration. "We will go back to camp now."

The skies are black with storm clouds as we near Head of Elk and night is drawing in. Torrential rain suddenly pours down, drenching us. Just ahead, a small hamlet is visible and Washington spurs on his horse. "We will take shelter there."

"There are many loyalists round here. It is best to continue," Greene protests.

"We are very near to the British army. You could easily be taken," I say vehemently.

"No, we are more at risk in the dark and with this weather. We might encounter enemy patrols," he replies.

We stop at a stone farmhouse. Billy Lee knocks loudly on the door. A man opens it, an expression of surprise crossing his face as he sees our party and the distinctive figure of our general, a surprise perhaps harboring hostility.

"We would like to stay the night," says Washington. "What is your name?"

"Robert Alexander," the man mutters, stepping back inside.

Washington sleeps peacefully in the main bedchamber. The rest of us spend a very restless, sleepless night, mounting guard at intervals, our weapons at the ready. In the morning we hurriedly depart at dawn, very grateful our commander-in-chief has not been caught by the British.

"You were right," he admits to Greene as we ride out of the hamlet towards the road to Newport. "A single traitor could have betrayed me."[61]

Chapter 10

Blooded at Brandywine

It is hot. Sometimes it rains. Informants report that Howe has about eighteen thousand men[1] in two divisions. Lieutenant General Cornwallis commands one, which moves to Elkton; the other, under Lieutenant General Knyphausen, has crossed the Elk and is camped at Cecil Court House.

Washington orders the grain fields at the head of the Chesapeake to be burned. "Be constantly near the enemy and give them every possible annoyance," he orders Brigadier General William Maxwell's corps of seven hundred and twenty light infantry,[2] formed earlier at the Neshaminy camp to replace Colonel Daniel Morgan and his riflemen sent north to reinforce the Northern Army facing Burgoyne. On September 2 he tells Maxwell to go to Iron Hill near the Maryland line and post men in the night on an advantageous part of the road[3] as the enemy is intending to march tomorrow. "Be prepared to give them as much trouble as you can."[4]

Next morning these troops skirmish with an advance force of Jägers,[5] commanded by Lieutenant Colonel von Wurmb, near to Christiana Bridge. They fight well, although forty are killed or wounded before retreating over White Clay Creek.[6] The new flag of the United States with thirteen alternate red and white stripes and thirteen stars in a circle, white on blue, representing a new constellation, is proudly flown for the first time.[7]

The two divisions of the enemy join at Pencader and encamp there with their right, their left extending across the Christiana towards Newark, leaving General Grant at Head of Elk with six battalions to guard the baggage and communicate with the ships.[8]

Washington continues to deliberate. "Should the army fight a pitched battle? Should it just continue to snipe and attack from the woods?"

He decides he must protect the capital.[9] We will fight. Our troops now number about eleven thousand men fit to soldier, including militia.[10] On September 5, he issues a General Order: 'One bold stroke will free the land from the rapine, devastations and burnings and female innocence from brutal lust and violence We have already endured two years of war…If we behave like men, this third Campaign will be our last. Ours is the main army: to us Our Country looks for protection.'[11]

On September 6, my twentieth birthday, it is ordered that deserters will be instantly shot down as a just punishment to themselves and for an example to others.[12]

The army, with the exception of the light infantry, which remains on the line, moves to a position behind Red Clay Creek where earthworks begin to be thrown up; its left is at Newport on the Christiana, a tidal river where huge flocks of wild fowl often rise in great numbers into the sky, and on the road which leads from Howe's camp to Philadelphia; its right extending along the creek to Hockesson.[13]

The British march towards Brandywine River. Howe advances in our direction, as though to attack, but stops two miles away. Washington is very suspicious and holds a council of war during the night; it is decided to march the army to the high ground on the east bank of the Brandywine near to Chads' Ford.[14]

'Upon reconnoitering their situation, it appears probable that they only meant to amuse us in front while their real intention was to march by our right and by suddenly passing the Brandywine and gaining the heights upon the north side of the river, get between us and Philadelphia and cut us off from that city. To prevent this, it is judged expedient to change our position immediately,' Washington writes to President Hancock.[15]

At two o'clock in the morning of September 9, he orders the army north into Chester County. Near evening we cross the Brandywine River at Chads' Ford.

"It is the last natural defense before Philadelphia. If we fail here, the city will be taken," he says.

Local people flee in a state of great distress. They abandon their houses, take their furniture and drive their cattle. Women and children travel on foot, everywhere resounding with their cries. We hear that the British are plundering amazingly.[16]

Intelligence arrives: 'Knyphausen's division yesterday entered Chester County and is encamped at New Garden and Kennett Square, about seven miles west of the creek, and Cornwallis is a short distance below Hockessin Meeting House.'

"We will deploy along the east bank of the Brandywine and center the troops on Chads' Ford. We will make entrenchments on the hilly ground there and station troops north and south along the river. There are eight possible fords," declares Washington.

"That means we have to station men over five miles," says General Maxwell. "It is a great distance."

"We have no choice," Washington replies.

"Is there strong support for the British in the area?" asks General Knox.

"They have been rustling cattle and stealing horses, as usual, but there are many Quakers living here and I believe their loyalties lie mainly with the British," Washington says.

"That is correct," agrees Greene, a Quaker.

September 10. Information arrives: 'Knyphausen and Cornwallis joined forces at Kennett Square, their parties have advanced on the roads leading to Lancaster, to Chads' Ford and to Wilmington.'[17]

The alarm guns fire. The army is placed under arms. All the wagons are sent to the rear, but the men keep their blankets,[18] Washington ordering and supervising every detail. In the late afternoon four deputies from Congress arrive to see the deployment of the army.

"We agree with your strategy. May God go with you," they declare as they mount their horses to return to Philadelphia. "Make a staunch defense or the city will fall."

In the evening, I ride with Washington and his officers as he makes a tour of the army. The men cheer him. They stand to attention, their clothes often ragged, their muskets often ancient. Some have the young, fresh faces of farm boys, others are old men, but their determination to die in defense of their country is very apparent and they know Washington is also prepared to die for the same cause.

At a wooded bend of the river, the Reverend Joab Trout preaches a sermon: "We have met this evening perhaps for the last time. We have shared the toil of the march, the peril of the fight, and the dismay of the retreat alike…They that take the sword shall perish by the sword…And have they not taken the sword?…Let the desolated plain, the blood-sodden valley, the burned farmhouse, blackening in the sun, the sacked village, and the ravaged town, answer! Brethren, think me not unworthy of belief when I tell you the doom of the British is near…And in the hour of battle when all around the darkness is lit by the lurid cannon glare and the piercing musket flash, when the wounded strew the ground and the dead litter your path, then remember soldiers that God is with you! You have taken the sword, but not in the spirit of wrong and ravage. You have taken the sword for your homes, for your wives, for your little ones. Amen."[19]

His words resound across the men grimly awaiting tomorrow's battle. They settle down to sit or sleep on the red-brown earth scored by the paraphernalia of war. There is a silence, a hush of expectation.

The terrain is dusty and sunbaked. Sometimes there are large, plowed fields, or meadows, which would suit the British who prefer to fight on open ground. Often, however, there are many small fields of barley, oats or corn, with a multitude of split-rail fences and stone walls, as well as farm buildings, peach and apple orchards, woodlands with thick underbrush, and narrow lanes, all of which would be more suitable for the American style of fighting and would hinder the British moving rapidly in formation.

The Brandywine River flows from northwest to southeast into the Delaware. It runs parallel to the Schuylkill and is about fifteen to twenty miles from it.[20] It is fast-flowing, but comparatively shallow and meanders along a valley which is often rocky with trees to the water's edge. Washington's description of it as the last natural defense before Philadelphia is true, but unfortunately the hot summer has shrunk it and although in most places it would not prove a substantial obstruction to the enemy, it is of sufficient depth that fords, of which there are many, have to be used to cross it.[21] Dried creek beds splay out from the river and would pose problems for troops moving in formation and dragging artillery.

Roads dissect the land. The main road goes from east to west and crosses the Brandywine at Chads' Ford. Northwards, one to two miles distant, following the same direction, is the Street Road. At right angles to these roads west of the Brandywine is the Great Valley Road, whilst on the east of the river is another road which leads across the Street Road to the Birmingham Meeting House.

In the late evening, General Sullivan comes to our headquarters at Benjamin Ring's house about three quarters of a mile east of Chads' Ford.

"Guard Brenton's Ford and send off a party to the ford a mile and a half above it, another to Jones's Ford and another to Buffenton's Ford a mile and a half above Jones's," Washington tells him.

"Are there any fords higher up?" Sullivan asks.

"There are no fords within twelve miles, to cross at which the enemy must make a long circuit through a very bad road," is the opinion of a local man.

"All the light horse has been sent to the right to watch the enemy's movements in that quarter," says Washington.[22]

Chads' Ford is about one hundred and fifty feet wide with hills on either side. Brigadier General Anthony Wayne's brigade of Pennsylvania Continentals with Proctor's artillery is stationed about two hundred yards above the ford on the brow of a hill near Chads' House; earthworks and a redoubt have been constructed as a front line. Greene is in command of the center and his division and Brigadier General Francis Nash's North Carolina Brigade are on Wayne's left; Muhlenburg's and Weedon's brigades of Virginia Continentals are immediately east of the ford. Washington himself will be at Chads.' On the west bank opposite, on high ground on either side of the road, is Brigadier General William Maxwell's eight hundred light infantry. Major General Armstrong with one thousand Pennsylvania militia guards Pyle's and Gibson's Fords about half a mile south in rough terrain of steep wooded hills which is not likely to be attacked. General Sullivan commands six brigades and is one mile above Chads' at Brinton's

Ford. He guards all the fords north; Stirling's division is a short distance east of the river, to the right of Wayne; to his right is Stephen's division, and beyond that is Hall's Delaware Regiment at Painter's Ford; one battalion of Colonel Hazen's 2nd Canadian Regiment at Jones' Ford[23] and a second at Buffington's Ford, whilst Colonel Bland's 1st Dragoons are stationed nearly opposite Painter's Ford. Major James Spear with a corps of Pennsylvania militia patrols above the Forks near Buffington's. Count Pulaski commands the cavalry.

I stay the night at headquarters instead of at my lodgings in Gideon Gilpin's small house, a quarter of a mile away.

September 11. A mist cloaks the pre-dawn gloom. Today I will fight against the British, a battle I have spent my life waiting for. A report arrives: The entire British army is marching on the road to Chads' Ford.

Maxwell's force, which also includes three detachments from the Virginia Line, goes towards Kennett Square to impede the approach of the enemy. At six o'clock the mist starts to lift. A second report arrives: 'The Americans are attacking and ambushing Hessian and Loyalist forces from the woods at Welch's Tavern on the other side of the river.' At seven, an alarm gun sounds. I ride with Washington and the other officers to the heights by Proctor's artillery behind an earthwork overlooking Chads' Ford. We can hear firing. From eight, the battery guns fire in support of Maxwell's soldiers, the noise thundering above us, obliterating all other sounds, the mist thickened by the artillery smoke and obscuring what is happening. At nine, the mist has gone, the sun is shining brightly. Washington walks along the two lines of troops. They cheer him wildly and seem to promise success.[24]

Green-uniformed loyalist soldiers appear opposite,[25] but the woods are so close to the bank it is not possible to estimate the size of their force.[26] Blue-coated Hessian soldiers and red-coated British come into sight.

Porterfield's and Waggoner's Virginians cross the river to reinforce Maxwell. Enemy artillery fires repeatedly; Maxwell's men retreat from the woods; they recross the creek. Porterfield's and Waggoner's men also retreat across the river.[27] It is not yet eleven.

"We killed or wounded three hundred enemy soldiers and our casualties do not exceed fifty," Maxwell reports.[28]

Weedon's artillery continues to fire; the enemy withdraws several times.[29] Shot is falling about us; it beheads an artilleryman near to Washington. He does not flinch; he anxiously watches the enemy through his spyglass. "The enemy seems slow to attack," he says.

We return to the Ring House where Washington paces continually, desperate for information as to whether the British are about to mount an attack on Chads' Ford with the Hessians, or are perhaps somewhere else, attempting to outflank us.

I stand at his side. I hear the booming of cannon and smell the powder in the air. I have crossed the ocean for this. I have left my family and my country. I long to join the battle.

At eleven, Colonel Moses Hazen at Jones' Ford, about two and a half miles above Chads,' sends word of an enemy column marching to the forks of the Brandywine.[30] Just after eleven, Washington sends a message to Colonel Bland who is with the light horse on the right: 'I earnestly entreat a continuance of your vigilant attention to the movements of the enemy, and the earliest report not only of their movements, but of their numbers and the course they are pursuing. In a particular manner I wish to gain satisfactory information of a body confidently reported to have gone up to a ford seven or eight miles above this. It is said the fact is certain. You will send up an intelligent sensible officer immediately with a party to find out the truth, what numbers it consists of, and the road they are now on. Be particular in these matters.'[31]

He orders Stirling and Stephen to march their divisions to Birmingham Meeting House about three and a half miles from Chads' Ford which commands the road most likely to be used by a force advancing from the upper streams of the Brandywine. Sometime after eleven o'clock a hastily scribbled note, dated eleven a.m. at the Great Valley Road on the right bank of the river, comes from Lieutenant Colonel James Ross of the Eighth Pennsylvania:

> A large body of the enemy, from every account five thousand, with sixteen or eighteen field-pieces marched along this road just now. This road leads to Taylor's Ferry and Jeffrey's Ferry, on the Brandywine, and to the Great Valley, at the Sign of the Ship, on the Lancaster Road to Philadelphia. There is also a road from the Brandywine to Chester by Dilworth Town. We are close in their rear with about seventy men; Captain Simpson lay in ambush with twenty men, and gave them three rounds within a small distance, in which two of his men were wounded, one mortally. I believe General Howe is with this party, as Joseph Galloway is here known by the inhabitants, with whom he spoke and told them that General Howe was with him. [32]

"It seems a terrible blunder on Howe's part to divide his force and weaken those at Chads'," says Washington, to the agreement of the other generals. "The very magnitude of the blunder is puzzling."[33]

"Tell Stirling and Stephen to proceed to Birmingham Meeting House as ordered and tell Maxwell, Sullivan, Greene and Lincoln to prepare to cross the Brandywine. I will go with General Greene's division to attack Knyphausen in front and General Armstrong's militia will attack Knyphausen's right. Move the troops forward," Washington orders at about eleven-thirty.[34]

Greene's advance guard cross the river to the opposite bank. The rest of the troops prepare to follow.

A note arrives from Sullivan:

> Since I sent you the message by Major Moore,[35] I saw Major Spear of the militia who came this morning from a tavern called Martin's, at the fork of the Brandywine. He came from thence to Welch's Tavern and heard nothing of the enemy about the fork of the Brandywine and is confident that they are not in that quarter; so that Colonel Hazen's Information must be wrong. I have sent to that quarter to know whether there is any foundation for the Report and shall give your Excellency the earliest information. [36]

Major Spear arrives from Sullivan and confirms the information. Some light horse sent to reconnoiter the road also say there appear to be no enemy there.[37] Washington is now very undecided about what course of action to take. Are the British marching down the Brandywine towards our army? Or is it just a feint and they are marching down the south side to reinforce Knyphausen?

"Recall the troops from the east bank and pull back Stirling's and Stephen's brigades to Birmingham Meeting House to support Sullivan. Give the order not to attack. Move the troops back to the high ground so that they are not exposed to the artillery fire," he orders.

"Cross the Brandywine and continue to skirmish with the enemy, he tells Maxwell.[38]

At about two o'clock, a dark, thick-set man gallops in on a horse lathered with sweat and is hurriedly brought to Washington.

"I'm Squire Thomas Cheyney. I've just come seven miles from Sconneltown. The British have crossed the Brandywine and are marching towards Sconneltown and Birmingham Meeting House."

"No, surely not," cries Washington skeptically as one of the officers laughs derisively. "You must be wrong. We were told this earlier and then it was contradicted."

"No, I'm not," he declares. "They fired at me."

"Draw a map of it on the ground," says Washington.

Cheyney bends down and makes a diagram of the roads in the dirt.

"No, I think you must be wrong," cries Washington again.

"My life for it, you're mistaken, General. By hell it's so!" says Cheyney. "Ask Anthony Wayne or Persie Fraser if I'm a man to be believed. I have this day's work as much at heart as e'er a blood of you! Put me under guard till you find my story is true."[39]

A short time later, a message comes from Sullivan:

2 o'clock pm. DEAR GENERAL,- Colonel Bland has this moment Sent me word, that the enemy are in the Rear of my Right, about two miles Coming Down, there is, he says about two Brigades of them. 2 of Clock PM he also says he Saw a Dust Rise back in the Country for above an hour.
He encloses Bland's note:

I have discovered a party of the enemy on the heights, just on the right of the two Widow Davis's who live close together on the road called the Fork Road, about half a mile to the right of the Meeting House. There is a higher hill in front. [40]

Cheyney is right. The enemy is probably outflanking us.

"Tell General Sullivan to march his division to meet the approaching enemy," orders Washington. "Tell Generals Stephen and Stirling to march their men at the quickest step to the Birmingham Meeting House.[41] I will stay here at Chads' Ford with Greene's Division and Wayne's and Maxwell's brigades to keep my hand on all the troops as it is not clear if there are only two enemy brigades to our rear." "Can I join General Sullivan," I ask as it now seems clear that fighting is about to take place along the right flank, whereas the left remains relatively quiet.

"Yes," says Washington.

I throw myself onto my horse, followed by Gimat and La Colombe. I gallop off to fight in battle for the first time in my life, excitement coursing through me. We race near the river for about three miles towards the sound of firing; we arrive at Sullivan's division just as they have formed a line in front of a small wood[42] on the brow of a hill near Birmingham Meeting House. I place myself in the center division under Stirling, where Conway's brigade is stationed; the men cheer my arrival amongst them in my major general's uniform. The music of the drums and fifes of the Grenadier Guards is loud in the air, black bearskin hats and red coats are advancing across the plain in perfect formation.[43] The Hessians fire from split-rail fences to protect the British who clamber over some and move others. The British reform their lines. They march in finest order across the ground, the first line firing muskets and artillery. The infernal fire of the weaponry and the booming of the cannons deafeningly accompany the fifes and drums; bullets whistle like angry bees, plowing up the ground, making trees crackle, branches break, and leaves fall as in autumn. Small arms roar like a drum roll. The fighting is at close quarters, almost muzzle to muzzle. Cannon balls fly thick and many.[44] Men are being cut down; they scream and groan in agony, splattered with blood. Bodies are thick on the ground. Our troops start to run. The right flank is giving way; there is so much firing on the left flank it also starts to give way; it falls back to the land behind the Birmingham Meeting House and along the road leading to Dilworth town.[45] I dismount. "Take my horse to the rear," I order, to encourage my comrades and to show them I have no better chance of flight than they.[46] I throw myself, sword in hand, into the fighting in the center with Conway and about eight hundred men where the enemy is concentrating its fire. The

British aim their muskets and charge. Our force wavers. The British light infantry overrun our artillery battery. Bullets scream. We retreat to a hill near Sandy Hollow, southeast of Birmingham Hill. My fellow officers and I try to organize a bayonet counterattack. I grab the musket of the man next to me; I show him how to fix the bayonet. I do the same with the muskets of other soldiers; I push some in the back to make them fight, but they are inexperienced and lack the confidence to use them. We slowly retreat, but at each fence or ridge we manage to reform. Five times the enemy drives us from the hill; five times we regain it, the summit often disputed muzzle to muzzle. The enemy concentrates their fire on the center; there is extreme confusion amongst our troops; they start to abandon the fight. The British continue to advance. Men flee in panic. I try to stop them. I rear up my horse and gallop right and left to prevent them running away. I jump to the ground and grab at shoulders and arms. "Stand and fight!" I shout.

The soldiers halt. They begin to fight again. Behind us, Stirling and his brigade on a small slope fire over our heads at the enemy. The British advance. Men fall dead or injured about me. Shrieks, groans, the beat of drums, musket and cannon fire, all blend in one hellish cacophony, black smoke wreathing funereally in the air.

"Fall back!" I order the survivors.

We retreat to Stirling's and Sullivan's men. We fight together until the British come up to about twenty yards from us. We retreat into woods.

"You have been injured!" Gimat shouts.

I look down. Blood is seeping out of the boot of my left leg. I have been shot.

The news of my injury is taken to Washington, unfortunately much exaggerated. He evidently expresses his grief that one so young, and a volunteer in the holy cause of freedom, should have fallen so early. Then he is told I will not die; he sends me his love and congratulation that matters are no worse.[47]

Dr Cochran, Washington's personal physician, hurriedly places a light bandage on my wound, but the shot is falling so thickly that if we remain, in a very little time we would both be past all surgery.[48] I try to continue fighting but am too weak. Gimat lifts me on to my horse[49] just as Washington arrives some way off with more troops, followed by Greene and Weedon's brigade. I want to ride to them, but blood is pouring from my boot and I am so light-headed I can hardly stay on my horse.

Men, cannons and wagons are fleeing past. I join the stampede towards Chester to avoid being captured. Dusk is falling. Behind us heavy artillery firing from Greene's men is providing covering fire to impede the enemy advance and enable the rest of our army to escape. Soldiers, cannons and baggage crowd the road. Wagons crush the dead and the dying who lie everywhere.[50] Night conceals our agony and our rout. I cling onto the reins and the saddle, weak and in pain, the chaos sweeping me along. In the darkness and ghastly confusion, it is impossible to recognize anyone.[51] At Chester, about twelve miles from the battlefield, before a stone bridge which it is necessary to pass over,[52] I turn my horse sideways in the panic-stricken mêlée to block the way.

"Halt! Form a column!" I command weakly. "Place guards along the road to the bridge to stop the men fleeing. Join your regiments."

Most obey me; I re-establish a semblance of an army. Washington arrives with the other generals.[53] I finally agree to have my injury dressed and am on the point of fainting. I am taken to Chester, a small town at the junction of Chester Creek with the Delaware; I am carried into a house and placed on a table. Surgeon William Magaw of the First Pennsylvania Regiment examines the wound.

"The ball has passed through the flesh and hasn't touched the nerves or the bone," he says.

Not long after, the general officers arrive.

"You appear to be very hungry. Don't eat me up as I am the only dish upon the table in the house," I tell them.[54]

Washington, his face drawn and tired, looks pleased to find me in such good spirits. In the darkness the exhausted troops, some wounded, have been ordered to assemble behind Chester for the night. Greene's division had reached the fighting a little before darkness fell, having run four miles in forty-two minutes. They had opened their ranks to let the fleeing men through, then had closed them and fought bravely to halt the enemy. In the confusion some of our troops had mistaken Weedon's 3rd Virginia Regiment for the enemy and had fired on it, killing many.[55]

The intelligence Washington had received of the enemy's main body crossing the Brandywine about six or eight miles above on our right had been uncertain and contradictory and it had been late before a disposition was made to receive them on that quarter.[56] The force had not then been adequate to oppose the enemy and had retreated before reinforcements arrived.[57] As soon as Cornwallis's gunfire had been heard by the enemy at Chads' Ford, they had begun a furious cannonade, warmly returned by our forces. They had then crossed the Brandywine and driven Wayne's division to retreat.[58] Howe holds the battlefield, but our loss of men is believed to be less than his.[59] We have lost eleven cannon. Many had to be abandoned on Meeting House Hill because so many horses were killed.

I am placed on a litter and carried to a boat to be conveyed along the Delaware to Philadelphia, twenty-six miles away.[60] I see Washington on the bank.

"Treat him as if he were my son," I hear him say to the surgeon.[61]

The night seems never-ending. My leg pains me greatly, but I have survived my first battle. I am alive. La Colombe and Gimat are with me, as well as James Monroe, Lord Stirling's aide who speaks French. He greatly admires Thomas Jefferson and tries to entertain me with conversation about the house Jefferson is building at Monticello, and about the Declaration of Independence.

The steeple of Christ Church soars gracefully above the threatened city. On shore, people surround me, taking an interest in my youth and my situation.[62]

"Would you like a drink of wine?" asks an old woman.

"Thank you," I say gratefully.

Townsfolk scurry in all directions. Whole families are fleeing, wagons and carts piled high with possessions hastily racketing along the streets. Women are running, children crying, horses galloping, fear and terror on their faces.[63] I am taken to the Indian Queen Tavern, a small, low building with a warren of rooms. Outside, Philadelphia awaits its fate. Every roar of the cannon was heard here, men, women and children filled the streets as though it was market day. loyalist supporters and rebels silent in separate groups in all the public squares and places, until, finally, in the stillness of the bright moonlit morning, one last courier came and announced our defeat. Friends of liberty are escaping to the hills. The Whigs fear they will be killed by the Tories for supporting the rebels. An effigy of Washington has been hanged and people are being tarred and feathered, as had once happened to loyalists and tax gatherers.

My friends visit.

"I am surprised how quickly the Americans were routed," I say to de Mauroy.[64]

"Come back to France with us," says Duboismartin. "Your entire fortune would not buy you the advantages you would now derive from your wound."[65]

"You don't need to fight any more. You will be famous," declares Dubuysson.

"No. I am staying. I want to fight for the American cause and I admire Washington.[66] Can you take letters to my family? They will be worried if they hear false reports about my wound. I need to reassure them."

63

I hastily write to Adrienne:

I send you a few lines, my dear heart, by some French officers, my friends, who came with me but who have not received commissions and are returning to France. I will start by telling you that I am well, because I must finish by telling you that yesterday we were soundly beaten in battle. Our Americans, having held firmly for quite a long time, finished by being routed; while I was trying to rally them the English gentlemen honored me with a musket ball which wounded my leg slightly, but it is nothing, my beloved; the ball touched neither bone nor nerve, and I will now have to lie on my back for some time, which puts me in an ill temper. I hope, my dear heart, that you won't be worried; on the contrary, it is a reason to be less so as I shall be out of combat for some time and intend to take good care of myself. This defeat, I fear, will have unfortunate consequences for America. It is necessary to try to make reparations if we can. You should have received letters from me unless the English have harmed my epistles as well as my legs. I have had only one letter from you and I long for news. Adieu. I am forbidden to write any longer. I have not slept for several days. Last night was spent retreating and my voyage here where I am being very well taken care of. Tell my friends I am well; a thousand tender respects to Mde. d'Ayen; a thousand compliments to the vicomtesse and my sisters. These officers will leave soon. How wonderful for them to see you. Goodnight, my dear heart, I love you more than ever.[67]

John Hancock had received the dispatch of the battle from Washington at four in the morning. At ten, Congress had met and had immediately sent a message to Putnam at Peekskill to march down one thousand five hundred Continentals, and to Dickinson in New Jersey and to Smallwood and Gist in Maryland to send their militia, as well as asking Pennsylvania militia to join Washington.[68] It ordered the commissary general of purchases to buy thirty hogsheads of rum to give to the soldiers in compliment for their gallant behavior. [69] It also ordered at five o'clock that the Continental Navy Board without delay provide a proper boat or vessel to convey me, my attendants and baggage to the Jersey as well as a boat for du Coudray.[70]

There were too many wounded for the British doctors to treat and Washington has been asked for surgeons to go under a flag of truce. Dr. Benjamin Rush, one of the men who signed the Declaration of Independence, is being sent, as well as four other doctors, a hospital mate, and several attendants. Several Congressmen visit me, all booted and spurred and on the wing for a place of greater safety to hold their sessions.[71] They hurriedly depart.[72]

Loyalists call this year of 1777, the Year of the Hangman, as the three sevens resemble a row of gallows from which they intend to hang the rebels,[73] and many now fear the charge of treason. Thomas Paine, the English author of *Common Sense*, published in 1776, which has greatly influenced republican ideas and the Declaration of Independence,[74] writes an essay on the battle to encourage people and gives four thousand copies away free:

Those who expect to reap the blessings of freedom must, like men, undergo the fatigues of supporting it. The event of yesterday was one of those kind of alarms which is just sufficient to rouse us to duty, without being of consequence enough to depress our fortitude. It is not a field of a few acres of ground, but a cause that we are defending and whether we defeat the enemy in one battle, or by degrees, the consequences will be the same.[75]

I wait in pain at the Indian Queen Tavern whilst Congress will probably move to a town such as Reading, Lancaster, York or Easton;[76] on the fourteenth it agrees to pay the expenses of my fellow Frenchmen, submitted to them by de Kalb, so that they can return home.[77]

Our army encamps on the edge of Germantown. The British are at Chester about fifteen miles away.[78] It is no longer hot. There is a strong north-west wind. On the fifteenth, torrential rain pours down, drenching our army and that of the British as they prepare to do battle. Our ammunition is ruined. No flint will flash. No charge would ignite. The ground is a quagmire.[79]

It now seems inevitable the British will take Philadelphia. More townsfolk are fleeing, a third of the population has gone. Congress has sent six wagons of the principal Quakers under guard to Virginia to try to halt their aid to the enemy, and the bells are being removed from Christ Church to prevent the British melting them down for weapons. On the fifteenth, Congress awards de Kalb the rank of major general. Unfortunately, he has already left Philadelphia with Delesser, Valfort and Dubuysson[80] and an envoy is sent after him.

On the sixteenth, du Coudray rides a high-spirited horse on to the Schuylkill ferry. It becomes frightened and plunges into the river, drowning him. Congress resolves that his body will be buried with honors of war at the expense of the United States.[81]

Chapter 11

Moravian succor

September 18. To my relief, there is at last a boat; I will not become a prisoner.[1] I travel along the Delaware to Bristol where I stay at the house of Simon Betz whose niece helps to care for me. Early next day the last few congressmen who had remained in Philadelphia arrive here en route to Lancaster. Henry Laurens, a congressman from South Carolina, a slightly built man with a swarthy complexion, a descendent of French Huguenot refugees, like Major Huger, offers to take me in his coach, a rare sight here, and I happily accept. He had waited in Philadelphia, believing that fear had already driven some great men to inglorious retreat and thinking Washington would be victorious in another battle on the eighteenth or the nineteenth, but had been disappointed.[2]

We set off to Bethlehem in the vanguard of about seven hundred wagons and carts, some of the wounded shrieking in agony as we jolt and bump over rutted, uneven roads. Civilians flood along beside us, walking in the fields on either side, as well as between the vehicles. Army officers ride past, sometimes of high rank, such as Henry Lee. It is a harrowing cavalcade of sadness and suffering, but people do not seem as fearful as at Philadelphia. They appear exhausted. My leg hurts and Henry Laurens kindly allows frequent stops.

Towards evening on Sunday, September 21,[3] we emerge from woods onto an extensive plain, under a brilliant golden-red sky. In the distance, on the right, is the wide, eastern branch of the Delaware, dotted with wooded islands;[4] about a mile ahead is Bethlehem, the town of the Moravian community, its large stone buildings on a majestic, gradually rising hill surrounded by forest, glowing in the rays of the sunset.

We pass the Lehigh River, its rope ferry resembling that opposite the hospital of the invalids at Paris, and slowly approach solid, buttressed, hip-roofed houses and a large three-storied limestone building, the Single Brethren House, which has been commandeered as a hospital. At the entrance to the town is the Sun Inn.[5] We halt; I am carried inside the spacious tavern;[6] a surgeon examines my wound, cleans and bandages it again. Dusk is now night; I lie painfully in bed, a witness in the days since the battle to the convulsions of civil war.[7]

Next day, General Woodford, who has been wounded in the hand, visits. There are now so many sick and injured that their numbers are too great for the hospital and tents have been erected in the garden at the back. So many people are also arriving at the Sun Inn that my room is needed,[8] so the following day I am taken to a nearby house, occupied by the assistants to the farmer,[9] where Mrs. Barbara Boeckel, the wife of George Boeckel, the overseer of the Bethlehem farms, comes to look after me.

"I cannot give you proper attention unless you live at my house," she says after twenty-four hours. I am therefore moved yet again, this time to her own house on the main street just below the inn. Several rooms on the second floor have already been prepared and her daughter, Liesel, will help her.

The Boeckel household is a sanctuary of calm and quiet, guided by their religious beliefs. The handsome, lively Liesel[10] does not live with her parents, but in the Choir, the house for single women, and there are different houses for men and children. She and her mother dress exactly as all the other women in gowns of a plain color which reach to their ankles, fastened down the front with straight pins. On their heads they wear a haulbe, a close-fitting, rather beak-like white cap, tied with a ribbon to denote their status. Mrs. Boeckel's is blue because she is married whilst Liesel's is red as she is single.

George Boeckel attempts to turn me away from military ideas and gives me Cranz's *History of Greenland and the Moravian Missions in that country*, written in English, which I read.

The Moravians lead a gentle and peaceful life,[11] but their community now overflows with injured soldiers and prisoners. There are nine hundred wagons in the fields behind the tavern and the Moravians complain bitterly that one of their workshops is being used to make cartridges. The prisoners even fight among themselves and the British and the Hessians hate each other. There are two hundred and eighteen Highlanders in the Waterworks building who have to be guarded by one hundred soldiers, and the Moravians are hoping they will soon be taken to Lancaster and then to West Virginia.

The archives and money of Congress arrive, escorted by fifty troopers and fifty infantry from Trenton and there is talk of Congress holding its sessions here. About sixteen Congressmen are already in Bethlehem, including John Hancock, Samuel Adams and John Adams. And, of course, Henry Laurens. The army baggage train of about seven hundred wagons camped last night on the south side of the Lehigh River, with an escort of two hundred soldiers. They have ruined the fences and the buckwheat crop which has infuriated the Moravians. The Independence Bell has also been brought from Philadelphia but the wagon carrying it broke down as it descended the hill by the hospital, so it had to be unloaded there.

I lie in bed, hating my inactivity even more than my wound. I long to be able to walk again; I long to fight. We hear of the Paoli Massacre as people are calling it. General Wayne and a division of one thousand five hundred men were sent to observe the British and attack its baggage train or rear. They were encamped south of the Schuylkill, on the edge of thick woods, two miles south-west of Paoli's Tavern, and ambushed in the night of September 20 to 21 as they slept in their tents.[12] The enemy troops, led by General Grey, bayonetted them. At least, two hundred were killed, many wounded, and seventy-one prisoners taken.[13]

I write to Henry Laurens on the twenty-fifth. I ask for a commission of lieutenant for La Colombe whom 'General Canaouay is desirous of having in his brigade...My leg is about in the same state and without your kindness would be in a very bad one.' [14] I send La Colombe to him with the letter.

Gimat arrives, to my delight.

"De Kalb was here before you came. He was staying at the Sun Inn," he says. "He has accepted the rank of major general, dated July 31."[15]

On September 26 Howe crossed the Schuylkill River at Swedes' Ford; Lord Cornwallis entered Philadelphia.[16] The townspeople, now mainly women and children, watched in silence; the only noise that of military boots on the cobbles, the clatter of the horses' hooves, and the tunes of the bands. When the victory parade finished, the soldiers rampaged through the city, looting shops and houses. They said they wanted salt and good bread, but some stole far more than that. Many of the Philadelphians are of German ancestry and are furious at the Hessian and Anspacher troops destroying their homes. About eight thousand British troops have been sent to Germantown five miles before their lines and Congress has moved to York.

On October 1 I write to Adrienne:

Wise reflections have made me rest several weeks in bed away from danger, but I must admit to you that I have been invited there by a slight wound to the leg I received, I do not know how, as, in truth, I did not expose myself. It was the first battle I was in, so you can see how rare they are. It is the last of the campaign, or at least probably the last large battle, and if there was another, you can see I would not be there. Therefore, my dear heart, you need not worry. I am very pleased to reassure you and in telling you not to fear for me tell myself that you love me, and this little conversation with my heart pleases it greatly, for it loves you more tenderly than ever.

I wrote to you immediately on the day following the battle. I told you my injury was nothing and I was right. I only fear that you have not received my letter, that Howe might have exaggerated his exploits to his king and that if he said I had been wounded he might have also said that I had been killed…Let me speak of my wound. The ball passed through the flesh and did not touch the bone or the nerves. The surgeons are astonished with the speed at which it is healing. They are in ecstasy every time they treat me and suggest it is the most beautiful thing in the world. Personally, I find it is dirty, annoying and quite painful, so that depends on your taste, but if a man gave himself a wound for enjoyment, he would regard it in the same light I do. There, my dear heart, that is the story of what I pompously call my wound in order to give myself airs and make myself seem interesting.

As you are the wife of an American general officer, I must tell you what to reply when someone says that we were beaten. You will reply that it is true but between two armies equal in number and on a plain, experienced soldiers always have the advantage over new ones. Besides, we had the pleasure of killing many more of the enemy than we lost. Then if someone remarks 'That might be so, but Philadelphia, the capital of America, the boulevard of liberty, has been captured,' you will politely reply 'You are imbeciles. Philadelphia is a sad town, open on all sides, whose port was already shut, that the residence of Congress there made it famous. (It is full of a wretched sort of people, the Quakers, who are fit only to gather in a hall with large hats on their heads whatever the weather and wait in silence for the Holy Spirit, until one of them, wearied from not seeing it appear, gets up and utters a great deal of tearful stupidities).[17] This is what this famous town is, which we will make them return to us sooner or later. If people continue to question you, send them away with words the vicomte de Noailles will tell you, as I do not want to lose time here talking of politics. I have kept your letter for the last in the hope I would receive your news…but if I do not immediately send it twenty-five leagues away where Congress is, the captain will have left…That is why my writing is more scribbled than usual…I have only received news of you once, by Count Pulaski. I have a bad wound which is making me very wretched. Think how terrible it is to be far from all I love, in such a despairing state of uncertainty, There is no way to support it and yet I feel I do not merit being pitied, why was I so determined to come here? I have been really punished for it. I am too sensitive, my beloved, to do this. I hope you feel sorry for me when you know all that I suffer, especially now when news from you would be so welcome. I tremble at the thought of receiving word from you…Do not worry about my wound. I have a friend who told the doctors I should be well cared for. That friend is General Washington. A respectable man whose talents, whose virtues, I admire, whom I venerate more and more as I get to know him, has wanted to be my intimate friend. His tender interest for me soon won my heart. I live in his family; we are like two brothers, united in an intimacy and a reciprocal confidence…When he sent his chief surgeon to me, he told him to care for me as though I were his son as he loved me the same. Having learned that I wanted to rejoin the army too early, he has written a letter full of tenderness and told me to let my wound heal first…Embrace Henriette a thousand times for me; talk to her of me…my punishment will be not to be recognized by her when I return…Has she a sister or a brother? It does not matter to me, my heart, so long as I have the pleasure of being a father for a second time and I hear about it soon…Adieu, adieu, my dear heart, love me always, I love you so tenderly. [18]

October 4. We hear heavy cannon fire in the far distance. There is a rumor Washington is attacking the British at Germantown and we wait in great anxiety. Many different reports of the battle arrive which all agree our army did well at the beginning. Then wagons come, rumbling heavily over the ground, injured men shouting and screaming, the hospital quickly becoming awash with blood.

I send to headquarters to learn what happened and lie with great impatience in bed. I finally find out that Washington had discovered three thousand enemy troops had been sent to Head of Elk to escort supplies as the chevaux de frise and the forts are preventing them using the Delaware. Part of the army was in Philadelphia under Cornwallis, the other consisted of about nine thousand soldiers at Germantown. Washington decided to attack Germantown. He planned a pincer attack at five in the morning by four columns which would approach on different roads, each man wearing a piece of white paper in his hat so that he could be identified by his fellow-soldiers as it would be before dawn. However, the roads were rough and unfamiliar, and the soldiers with their tattered shoes, or just with bare feet, tired from the marching of the last few months, marched slower than expected. Only Sullivan's column, accompanied by Washington, reached its correct position at the appointed time. Sullivan attacked and the British fell back, their tents and baggage were overrun, one hundred and ten taken prisoner and they were routed.[19] The early morning mist became a fog and the British set fire to fields of buckwheat, creating clouds of smoke and making it impossible to distinguish our men from theirs at a greater distance than sixty yards. The air was also very still and so the fog and smoke hung low and did not disperse.[20] The battle swung against us. Greene arrived thirty minutes late. General Stephen ordered his Virginians in the wrong direction; the Maryland and New Jersey militia never found Germantown and the Pennsylvania militia reached the village but became trapped by a small force of Hessians. About one hundred and twenty redcoats, led by Lieutenant Colonel Musgrave, occupied the large, two-story, stone house of Mr. Chew, the Chief Justice of Pennsylvania. They closed the shutters, barricaded the doors and stationed themselves at the second-story windows.[21] Many officers argued that the house should be ignored but Washington followed Knox's advice that in hostile country one never left a fortified castle in the rear. Lieutenant Colonel William Smith was sent under a white flag to demand they surrender. The redcoats immediately shot him, breaking his leg.[22] Washington then ordered three regiments to take the building. Knox pounded it with four cannon, but the walls resisted stoutly. An hour was spent in an unsuccessful endeavor during which many of our soldiers were killed and the enemy had time to rally before Washington ordered the army to move on, leaving behind a small detachment. Other mistakes were made including the forces of Stephen and Wayne firing at each other in the fog. After three hours the fighting halted. Washington and the officers tried to make the men continue but they refused. The Americans collected the wounded and the field pieces and retreated before British reinforcements arrived. We ran away from the arms of victory ready to receive us.[23] Washington had lost but had so nearly been victorious. About one hundred and fifty-two Americans were killed,[24] five hundred and twenty-one wounded and four hundred taken prisoner, whilst the British had five hundred and thirty-seven killed and wounded and fourteen captured.'[25]

Washington believes the attack nearly succeeded. The troops also think that they nearly won and appear to be in high spirits and keen to fight the enemy again. Washington has now fought two consecutive battles against the British regulars in quick succession and has shown audacity and confidence.

My wound slowly heals; staying in bed is more difficult for my active nature than suffering the pain and I spend much of my time writing letters to anyone I can think of who might be useful to aid the rebellion, despite the good Moravian brethren mourning my war-like folly. I listen to their sermons and plan to set Europe and Asia ablaze.[26] Washington cited me in his report of the battle of Brandywine, so my name has been mentioned in newspapers, which is very useful for my campaign to help the American cause.

I contemplate an attack on the British Indies under the American flag. I write to my cousin, the marquis de Bouillé, who is governor of Martinique.[27] I also write to Maurepas and to de Broglie about leading an attack on Mauritius and from there to coordinate attacks on British trading posts by individuals.[28]

In October we hear there was a wonderful victory at Saratoga by General Gates. On September 19 a first battle was fought at Freeman's farm, resulting in very heavy losses for the enemy, who, however, bivouacked on the field. Next came a battle at Bemis Heights on October 7, and again the British suffered heavy losses with about six hundred killed, wounded or captured as well as the capture of their ten cannon, the Americans had about one hundred and fifty casualties. The British retreated. On the ninth, they reached the heights of Saratoga. The Americans encircled them, ceaselessly bombarding them by artillery or firing at them. The ground was covered by dead horses. The camp was a scene of constant fighting; the soldier could not lay down his arms day or night.[29] Burgoyne had hoped General Clinton would sail up the North River to come to his aid, but Clinton left New York with three thousand men, took two forts, then returned to Manhattan.

"We have yarded Burgoyne," said the New Englanders.

The enemy were trapped. Capitulation came. On the sixteenth, Burgoyne and his magnificently uniformed staff rode to the American camp and met Gates dressed in a plain blue frock coat.

"General, the caprices of war have made me your prisoner," said Burgoyne.

"I shall ever be ready to testify that it has not been through any fault of Your Excellency," replied Gates.[30] Then they enjoyed a meal of ham, beef, goose and mutton, accompanied by cider and rum.

Our victory has been immense. Five thousand eight hundred and ninety-five British and Hessian troops have been captured, including two lieutenant generals, two major generals and three brigadiers, as well as twenty-seven cannon, ammunition and equipment.[31] The defeated troops are marching down through rebel territory to take up winter quarters near to Boston.[32]

October 14. I write to General Gates:

I Can't let go your express without doing myself the pleasure of congratulating you About your happy and glorious succès. The fine opportunity of your victory and the circumstances (the taking Fort Montgommery) which it meet with is to add some thing yet and to your glory and to the gratefulness of everyone who loves the cause we fight for. I find myself very happy to have had the pleasure of your acwuaintance before your going to take the command of the northern army. I am very desirous, sir, to convince you how I wish to cultivate your friendschip. [33]

On the same day I also write to Washington:

My dear general...I do not do myself the honor of wraiting to you as many times as I would chuse, because I fear to disturbe your important occupations but I indulge now that pleasure to me on the occasion of the two nominations of Congress. General Connay is a so brave, intelligent and active officer that he schall justify more and more the esteem of the army and Your approbation. For the Baron de Kalb who is unknown to your excellency I ca'nt tell any particularity of his arrangements since his niew convention with Congress, because I am not well acquainted with them...I don't take the liberty of asking the sentiments of your excellency about those promotions because I do not think that Congress could be able of doing such things in the army without your petition and approbation.

I can'r express to you, dear General, with what pleasure I heard General Gates's advantages upon the queen's light dragoons's colonel-without speaking of my very sincere love for our cause, without speaking of Congress (which (between us) I am not so fond of as I was in France) everything important to your own succès, agreement, and glory procures me the greatest happinness.

Give me leave, dear general, to speack to you about my own business with all the confidence of a son, of a friend, as you favored me with these two so precious titles. My respect, my affection for you, answer to my own heart that I deserve them on that side as well as possible. Since our last great conversation I would not tell anything to your excellency, for my taking a division of the army- you were in too important occupations to be disturbed-for the Congress he was in a great hurry, and in such a time I take my only right of fighting; I forget the others. Now that the horable Congress is settled quiete, and making promotions, that some changements are ready to happen in the divisions, and that I endeavoured myself the 11 september to be acquainted with a part of the army and Known by them, advise me, dear general, for what I am to do. It is not in my character to examine if they have had, if they can have never some obligations to me, I am not usued to tell what I am. I won't make no more any petition to Congress because I can now refuse, but not ask from them, therefore, dear general, I'l conduct myself by your advices. Consider if you please that Europe and particularly France is looking upon me- that I want to do some thing by myself and justify that love of glory which I left be known to the world in making those sacrifices which have appeared so surprising, some say so foolish. Do not you think that this want is right? In the beginning I refused a division because I was diffident of my being able to conduct it without Knowing the character of the men who would be under me. Now that I am better acquainted with no difficulty comes from me.Therefore I am ready to do all what your excellency will think proper...Be certain that I schall be very happy if you judge that I can stay in America without any particular employment when strangers come to take divisions of the army and when myself by the only right of my birth should get in my country without any difficulty, a body of troops as numerous as a division. We have there different ways of advancement as the different ranks of men....I do not tell all that to my general, but to my father and friend. For Congress I'l tell never nothing to them because tho' I like some as Mr Lee, Mr Lawrence etc. some others did not behave with me with that frankness which is the proof of an honest mind....I desire only to know your opinion....If I was to be at the head of a division....I can not help to tell you that a division as they are, principally with General Woodfort would be the most agreeable for me.

I hope that I'll be in camp in three or four days where I'l be able to speack to your excellency about all my businesses. I beg your Pardon for being so tedious- it is for You a very disagreeable and troublesome proof of my confidence- but that confidence is equal to the affection and respect which I have the honor to be with your Excellency's the most obediant servant. [34]

My wound is still not fully closed over, but I abandon my bed.[35] I limp and cannot wear my boot, but I will go back to the army as Washington might soon attack New York. I buy a horse. I say farewell to the Brethren and ask to visit the Sisters' House. They agree.[36]

On the eighteenth, I write to Henry Laurens:

Receive, Sir, as a good american, my very sincere compliments about the heroic bravery, and most finest action in Germain town which illustrated one of your countrymen, who by the same time is so happy as to be a son of your's.....I heared with pleasure the promotions of Congress....Cannway deserves such a distinction for his fighting so well this Campaign, his coming here without particular arrangements, and his leaving a corps where he was actively employed and considered in as a man of great talents....Don't forget Sir to mention to Congress that an immense quantity of clothes are arrived from France I don't know where since last winter and that our poor soldiers the respectable instruments of our glory and liberty are indecently nacked for the next one....I hope, Sir, that a second pacquet of letters is arrived for me because they have been seen by several officers....I fear that some unknown spy should have done a little present of it to his excellency General Howe. Therefore, I'l have perhaps some knowledge of them in the English papers of the next months, and my only consolation would be to let the bearer be hang'd. [37]

I go with Gimat to the Sisters' House where Liesel lives and find it spacious and divided into several rooms where the girls spin cotton, make hemp or wool, embroider and fashion ruffles, pocketbooks or pin cushions like our French nuns. On the first floor is a large, vaulted chamber with a bed for each woman, a bed which has plenty of feathers, as is common in America. In the evening the women pray in the chapel which has several instruments hanging on the walls and an organ.

"It is an admirable institution," I tell them.

I say farewell to Liesel. Gimat, Woodford and I ride away from Bethlehem, through wooded hills now fiercely bright with autumnal red, orange and yellow.

Chapter 12

Under fire again

October 19. We reach headquarters at the house of Peter Wentz in Worcester Township near Methacton Hill.[1]

I am with my general again, exhausted but content. A *feu de joie* took place yesterday just before sunset by the army drawn up in two lines to celebrate our victory at Saratoga; General Gates has not yet sent a detailed report and the text of the agreed convention,[2] although an express arrived yesterday from George Clinton to say that on the fourteenth, at eight o'clock, the capitulation whereby General Burgoyne and the whole army surrendered themselves prisoners of war, was signed, and that on the fifteenth they will march out to the river above Fisher's Creek with the honors of war, and ground their arms.[3]

On October 6 the British had captured Forts Montgomery and Clinton on the west bank of the North River[4] whose loss Washington had always thought could prove fatal to the American campaign in the eastern states and New York, but then the news had come of Burgoyne's defeat, transforming the situation. On the night of the eighteenth to the nineteenth, the British withdrew from Germantown; during the day headquarters moves to the house of James Morris in Whitpain Township, Montgomery County. I have a room on the ground floor, beneath that of Washington.[5]

Twenty-five miles away, the British have constructed a chain of wooden palisades and fourteen redoubts stretching from the Upper Ferry on the Schuylkill to the shore of the Delaware above the city,[6] but we control the Delaware itself with Fort Mercer at Red Bank on the Jersey shore and Fort Mifflin on Mud Island, as well as chevaux de frise, fire ships and fire rafts, a frigate, a brig, a schooner and galleys. Howe is finding it difficult to feed his army as he cannot bring in supplies by river and if the forts can hold out just a few more weeks until the winter cold and ice, then he might have to retreat to his ships or fight across the Jerseys to reach New York.[7] On October 2 we abandoned Billingsport on the Jersey shore of the Delaware, twelve miles below Cooper's Ferry;[8] on the ninth, it was occupied by the British who moved siege artillery on the tenth to Province Island at the mouth of the Schuylkill, and have started to fire at the rear of Fort Mifflin where its defenses are weakest.

Mauduit du Plessis, one of the four French engineers sent by Deane, has strengthened the fortifications. He has reduced the size of Fort Mercer and made it into a large, nearly pentagonal redoubt with a strong earth rampart ten feet high and a deep ditch protected by an abattis in front.[9] On October 22, about one thousand two hundred Hessians commanded by Colonel Carl von Donop attack Fort Mercer which is defended by four hundred Rhode Islanders under Colonel Christopher Greene. The outer part had been deliberately left undefended and the Hessians quickly rushed in, believing they were victorious. They approached the inner section, were fired on for forty minutes and completely defeated. They threw their cannon into a creek so they could carry off their wounded officers. They left their provisions and fled. The garrison had fourteen killed and twenty-three wounded, whilst three hundred and seventy-one Hessians are thought to have been killed, wounded or captured.[10] The prisoners included several officers and

Colonel Donop, who was fatally wounded. The same day, the enemy attacked Fort Mifflin both from land batteries and from six men-of-war which had managed to pass the chevaux de frise as two had been removed.[11] The Americans fired on the frigates *Augusta, Roebuck, Liverpool* and *Pearl*, and the sloop, *Merlin*, which all ran aground. The *Augusta* caught fire and the *Merlin* was burned because it could not be refloated.[12]

I try and do what I can for all my compatriots in America. I write many letters concerning both them and the plans I had started to formulate at Bethlehem. An attack on the British West Indies and India, led by myself, is still very much in my thoughts. I discuss my ideas with General Conway, whose troops I joined at Brandywine and whom I saw fight very bravely. He had served in the French army since the age of fourteen and was a colonel in the Anjou Regiment. He was originally from County Kerry but calls himself comte Thomas de Conway. He had arrived in America in May 1777, shortly before me, and had been given the rank of brigadier general before Congress had become annoyed with all the French officers flocking to their cause. I have seen him at councils of war where he rarely speaks, although afterwards is quick to criticize. He is a lively, genial man who agrees with my schemes for attacks on Britain throughout the world and I considerably enjoy his company.

"I think an invasion of India is not only an excellent idea but also very feasible," he declares.

We discuss plans of campaign at great length; he calls himself La Fayette's soldier which I find very flattering.

October 23. I write a letter to Duboismartin which will be taken by the same mail boat of Congress on which I am trying to obtain a berth for Valfort. I enclose in it a letter describing my ideas for my expedition to the Indies, to be forwarded to Maurepas, or whoever is currently the premier ministre. I say to Duboismartin I would also like Monsieur de Bouillé:

To close his eyes to an expedition based on his island which would not even take two months of this winter; one would have to furnish some ships with congressional commissions, take some men from the estates of my cousin the governor, and fall on some small English islands where the negroes would cover the cost of the enterprise...I shall be content with repeating to you that several members of Congress had made many misjudgments. Du Coudray made them lose their heads, but there are some men of virtue and merit in Congress. As for the rest, among all the accusations and injustices, I hope that we always except General Washington, my friend, my intimate friend, and since I like to choose my friends, I dare say that to give him that title is to praise him. [13]

I tell Maurepas:

I ask only the honor of serving my country under another flag, and I love to see her interests united to those of the republicans for whom I fight, even though I wish I might soon be permitted to serve actively under the French colors. Then I would rather be a grenadier in the king's army than hold the highest rank in a foreign army...It is impossible to leave America when things are going so well and at such a decisive moment...The outbreak of war would cause me to leave immediately, even if I had to swim back...If there is to be an invasion of England, for God's sake do not forget me!
14

On October 29, I write to Adrienne that Monsieur de Valfort will tell her my news but that in my letter I want to say how much I love her:

I have too much pleasure feeling this sentiment not to have also pleasure in repeating it to you a thousand times if I could. I have no other resources, my dear heart, than to write, and write again, without hope that my letters might reach you and search to console myself for the pleasure of conversing with you, for the disappointment and anguish at not receiving any word from France. It is impossible to tell you how much my heart is troubled, and often devastated, by this silence. Even if I could, I would not try, so as not to mix sadness with the sweet moments of my exile when I can speak to you of my love. But do you at least pity me? Do you realize how much I suffer? If only I knew where you are, what you are doing. I will know this later but then I would not be separated from you as if by death. I await your letters with an impatience that nothing can distract...Repeat to me that you love me; the less I merit your affection, the more I need your assurance of it...You must have received so many accounts of my wound that to talk more about it would be useless, moreover if you had believed it to be grave, Monsieur de Valfort will tell you it is not. Soon I will not limp at all...From now on I shall not need to show or expose myself, and I assure you I shall be careful. Moreover, the war is being carried on by small detachments that will not involve me...There has been some difficulty with my finances; M.de Valfort will explain it to you. I think there is a remedy, however. I spend as little as I can, and yet I spend a great deal; the abominable expense of even the smallest articles and the depreciation of paper currency are the causes...What happiness it would be for me to learn that I am a father a second time, that you are well, that my two children and their mother are preparing to make me happy for the rest of my life...It is terrible to be reduced to writing when one loves as much as I love you, and shall love you until my dying breath. [15]

I again write to the comte de Broglie proposing my plans of invasion and ask for it to be sent to Maurepas if he considers my words suitable.

I constantly worry Washington does not trust me and that is the reason I have not yet received a division. The idea makes me very uneasy. It becomes almost an obsession. I brood about it. I am unhappy.[16]

Washington has very strangely still not heard from Gates about his victory, although he had received news of it on October 17 from General Putnam and on the eighteenth from George Clinton. On October 30 he tells Hamilton to ride the three hundred miles north and to order Gates: 'The absolute necessity that there is for his detaching a very considerable part of the army at present under his command to the reinforcement of this.'[17] He instructs Hamilton to get two of the three regiments there to march south to join our army.

November 2. The army, which has at least one thousand men barefoot, marches to Whitemarsh about thirteen miles from Philadelphia and encamps in a wooded range looking south across Whitemarsh valley. It is covered by two commanding hills, is secured by a strong advanced post, [18] its position holding the key to the Bethlehem and Skippack roads.[19] I move with Washington's staff to George Emlyn's mansion.

It is becoming cold. Winter is near. Roads are harder and will perhaps soon be icy. The lack of shoes, or their poor state, means the men cannot easily march. About four thousand men also lack blankets, two thousand of whom have never had one even although they have been in the army for twelve months.[20] The army needs to be fed and clothed. It is not in a fit state to fight, as the council of war on the twenty-seventh had concluded.[21]

Washington's opinion is that:

Our situation is distressing from a variety of irremediable causes, but more especially from the impracticability of answering the expectations of the world without running hazards which no military principles can justify, and which, in case of failure, might prove the ruin of our cause;

patience and a steady perseverance in such measures as appear warranted by sound reason and policy must support us under the censure of the one, and dictate a proper line of conduct for the attainment of the other; that is the great object in view.[22]

November 6. I write another long letter to Adrienne:

A single letter from you; a single letter, my dear heart, has come to me. The others are lost, captured, at the bottom of the sea evidently…surely you do not neglect to write to me by all the ports, by all the packet ships of Dr. Franklin and of M. Deane. However, ships have arrived. I have sent expresses to all the corners of the continent, and all my hopes have been in vain. Apparently, you have not been properly instructed. I beg you, my darling, find out how to send me some letters. To be deprived of them is so cruel. I am so wretched to be separated from all that I love…Do not worry about me; all the large battles are finished. There will only be skirmishes which will not affect me; I am as safe in camp as in the middle of Paris…Do I have two children? Is a second object of my love joined to that I have for my dear Henriette? Embrace my dear little girl a thousand times for me. Embrace them both very tenderly my dear heart. Take care of your health…Will you always love me? I love you more than I have ever loved and will do so for the whole of my life. [23]

On November 10 the British again attack Fort Mifflin which is defended by about five hundred men from the Fourth and Eighth Connecticut Regiments and an artillery company.[24] On November 15 it is attacked at dawn from just below the chevaux de frise by the ship of the line, *Somerset*, the *Isis*, the *Roebuck*, the *Pearl* and the *Liverpool*, whilst the *Vigilant* with sixteen guns and a hulk with three reinforced the floating battery,[25] all within pistol range of the fort on the western side. By midday all our guns in the fort fell silent and our men were being cut up like cornstalks by the British fire.[26] Several American galleys and floating batteries with a frigate attacked the British with their long guns which helped to relieve the enemy cannonade. When darkness fell the fort was abandoned; the men and the stores they could carry were evacuated to the Jersey shore. About seventy men remained who set fire to everything that would burn. Then they were taken in three boats to the shore, one of which was sunk by the British who plainly saw them in the light of the burning fort, but they were hauled onto the other two boats.[27]

I join the military Freemasonic lodge of American Union where Washington is the master mason. From this moment I never again doubt he has complete confidence in me. I enjoy an even greater link with my adoptive father and friend. I am supremely happy.[28]

Conway complains bitterly that a letter he sent to Gates in confidence has been given to Washington. He tells me Washington wrote very briefly to him on the ninth: 'Sir. A Letter which I received last night contained the following paragraph. In a letter from Genl. Conway to Genl. Gates, he says 'Heaven has been determined to save your Country; or a weak General and bad Councellors would have ruined it.'[29] Conway had immediately replied.

I go to speak to Washington who looks at me gravely. "Colonel Wilkinson disclosed information to Major McWilliams which Lord Stirling sent to me with the words 'such wicked duplicity of conduct I feel it my duty to report.' I wish to conceal every matter which could in its consequences give the smallest interruption to the tranquility of this army or afford a gleam of hope to the enemy by dissent within it. I therefore ask you to read this with the greatest injunction of secrecy. My staff already know about this, but you are the only other person to whom I show it."[30]

I agree to keep the secret; I read the letter.

"Conway has written back to say there was nothing improper in his conduct and admitted he had written to Gates congratulating him on the victory at Saratoga. He also admitted that criticism he had previously made of our military methods may have been in the letter, but he denied the words 'weak General' and said that he defied the most keen and penetrating detractor to make it appear that he leveled at my bravery, honesty, patriotism or judgement, of which he had the highest sense. He also said he was willing for me to see the original letter.[31] A faction is plotting for Gates to be exalted on the ruin of my reputation and influence. Conway is my enemy. I loathe the man and there are also certain unnamed concealed enemies who are secret traitors. I have not sought this position. If I displease the people, I will depart but until then I will resist any intrigue."[32]

"The army and Congress need to stand behind you without dissent. This country is very new and still weak. America will be lost if your leadership is not followed," I say.

I make enquiries about Conway. I discover he is an ambitious and dangerous man. It is clear to me he has done all in his power by cunning maneuvers to destroy my affection and confidence in Washington and that he has been attempting to make me leave America.[33]

On November 14 Conway sends his resignation to Congress, complaining he had been criticized for asking to be promoted and blaming de Kalb's commission as major general for his resignation: 'If I patiently bore such wrongs it must be concluded in France that I misbehaved and, indeed, the congress, instead of looking on me as an officer who enjoyed some esteem and reputation in the French infantry, must take me for a vagabond who fled here to get bread.'[34] He also writes to Washington asking for leave to collect his scattered belongings. Washington replies that evening through Colonel Harrison and says he shall not object to his departure as it is his inclination and he wishes him well for a return to his family if Congress allows him to resign.[35]

November 18. I write to Henry Laurens who became President of Congress on November 1, and ask for some favors for fellow Frenchmen. I praise the gallant defense of our forts, particularly pleasing of which was the conduct of Major Fleury and Captain du Plessis. 'I can assure you that everyone who in the defence of our noble cause will show himself worthy of his country shall be mentioned in the most high terms to the king, ministry, and my friends of France when I'l be back in my natal air.' I suggest that as Conway is returning home, he might be useful there to procure equipment for us, particularly that of clothes and ammunition. I tell him that although 'I am near a very hot fire, however as my eyes fall in this moment upon three quite nacked fellows, it congeals my blood and obliges me to tell you again how happy I would be if our army was drest in a comfortable manner. That army is not a very strong one-great many losses, and fiew recruits- indeed, Sir, I wish heartily that some changements in raising militia could help our inlisting continental soldiers- if the sixht part of that American militia was under our command and discipline.'[36]

The same day, Cornwallis enters New Jersey,[37] his frigates now having sailed up from the lower part of the river.

"General Greene will go to discover the size of his army. He will cross the Delaware near Bristol and march down the eastern side to Red Bank Fort. His division will be reinforced by General Varnum's troops from the North," Washington orders.

"I wish to volunteer to accompany General Greene," I say.

"You can," he replies.

November 20. We leave. I cannot wear a boot as my wound is not yet completely healed, but my enthusiasm is unbounded. In the evening I lodge with Greene in a fine country house; next day we cross the Delaware in advance of the troops and go to Burlington in New Jersey. At five in the afternoon an express arrives from Varnum: 'Fort Mercer was evacuated last evening.'

Commodore Hazlewood informs us that that the greater part, if not all, of the fleet, except the thirteen galleys, was burnt that morning and Varnum has now retreated to Mount Holly. Our expedition had already therefore become futile on the same day we started out.

"I do not know where Glover's brigade is. I cannot attack Cornwallis without it. However, if we can strike at the enemy, we will," says Greene.

We go to Mount Holly. "Can I reconnoiter Lord Cornwallis?" I ask.

"Yes," he agrees. "Make an attack if circumstances warrant it." [38]

I ride to Haddonfield on the twenty-fourth in order to be acquainted with all the grounds and roads near the enemy[39] whose main body is between Great and Little Timber Creek and is believed to number nearly five thousand from information given to us by prisoners.

Next day I set off in high spirits, accompanied by my second-in-command, Colonel Armand, the marquis de la Rouërie, who left France because of an affair of the heart and does not use his title. I have about three hundred men; ten light horse under Mr. Lindsay, about one hundred and fifty riflemen under Colonel Butler, two militia pickets under Colonels Hite and Ellis, as well as Colonel Laumoy and the chevaliers Duplessis and Gimat.[40] Colonel Morgan's riflemen, in hunting shirts, leather leggings and moccasins, armed with rifles, knives and tomahawks, run all day next to my horse.[41] One hundred and fifty of his men have come on the expedition, the rest did not have stout enough shoes to do so.

November 25. Scouts locate the enemy on the peninsula of Gloucester, opposite Philadelphia, with ships drawn up to cover the troops.[42] We stealthily creep through the woods, the frontiersmen occasionally climbing trees to gain a better view. I post pickets on each side of the trail to prevent our being surprised; we quickly come up near to the enemy encamped under the protection of the guns of their men-at-war.

I go forward with just a few guides to Sandy Point, a spit of land which extends into the river at the mouth of the New Town Creek. There is only one road; on each side are swamps and thick undergrowth.[43]

"We are in range of their guns," my guides say. "We must turn back."

I ignore them. I continue until I can clearly observe the British troops lined up in great numbers on the bank of the Delaware. It is not obvious if any troops have yet crossed the river, but boats are constantly going backwards and forwards. They appear to be transporting stock and there are as many men on the returning boats as are going over. Many ships are sailing up the river which suggests the chevaux de frise have already been removed.

I am in the sight of the sentries, but I continue, determined to gain information about the enemy. They do not shoot. Instead, a detachment of dragoons thunders out towards me. My guide is fearful but directs me along a back path through the undergrowth.[44] Those who could have killed me counted too much on those who ought to have.[45] My lucky star shines once more.

I return to my men; I send a message to Greene: 'The enemy are very busy crossing the Delaware.'[46]

We continue to scout the wooded countryside, Daniel Morgan's frontiersmen running near my horse without stopping to eat or rest. Late in the afternoon we come to the Gloucester Road between the two creeks; Duplessis and a small group go to discover how near to Gloucester are the first pickets. We hear firing. I rush with my men to help and find that they have come across an outpost of about three hundred and fifty Hessians with field pieces, about two miles from the British at Gloucester.

I lead my troops forward, bullets singing about us, smoke blurring the bushes and trees. Armand's horse is killed under him. He gets to his feet and continues fighting. Men with faces blackened by powder shout and roar savagely in that primeval state of killing or being killed. The dying and the dead lie in our path. We ride in pursuit; I slash and stab at the enemy. Brice's horse falls, shrieking in agony, but Brice scrambles up unscathed. Shortly after, the same happens to Duplessis, but he also is uninjured.

We chase the Hessians for more than half a mile. British reinforcements come up twice, but they fall back. Darkness is making it difficult to fight and we withdraw slowly to Haddonfield. The British advance again, perhaps realizing from the beat of our drums that we are not very near, but Major Morris and some of his riflemen quickly push them back.[47]

We return with fourteen prisoners who say about twenty-five to thirty of their fellow soldiers have been wounded and at least the same number killed, including an officer. We have a militia lieutenant dead and five wounded.[48]

Greene arrives during the night. "You have done wonderfully. I will send a report to Washington and would you also write one."

I proudly do so:

I never saw men so merry, so spirited, so desirous to go on to the enemy, whatever forces they could have as that little party was in the fight. I found the riflemen above even theyr reputation and the militia above all expectations I could have...I wish that this little succès of ours may please you, tho' a trifling one...It will be a great pleasure to find myself again with you. With the most tender affection and highest respect...[49]

Greene writes to Washington that his march has proved fruitless: 'The enemy has drawn itself down upon the peninsula of Gloucester; the ships are drawn up to cover the troops; there is but one road that leads down to the point...all the general officers were against making an attack.' He tells him that it is uncertain whether any of the enemy have crossed the river as the boats appear to be transporting stock and that prisoners say the enemy is going into winter quarters as soon as they get up the river. He says he will leave General Varnum's brigade and the rifle corps here for a few days and that his division, Huntington's and Glover's brigades, will return with all dispatch to join him.[50]

I ride on ahead and arrive at the heights of Whitemarsh a day before Greene who stays with his slow-marching troops. To my delight I finally receive letters from home which Henry Laurens has sent on to me. With joy I discover I am again a father. The maréchal de Noailles writes that my daughter, Anastasie Louise Pauline, was born on July 1, and that it is not the happiest event in the world. To my disappointment there is no letter from Adrienne but there are letters from my friends who say I am famous in France. I am called the American enthusiast and even the duc d'Ayen has spoken of me proudly.

"I have written to Congress, on hearing of your gallantry, to ask for a division for you, as there are some vacant positions now that Stephen has been dismissed. I am waiting for their response," Washington says.

My heart leaps. I will have a division.

Washington receives Congressional orders concerning the appointment of Major General Gates as president of the Board of War, as well as the appointment of three additional members and an order of the twenty-eighth appointing a committee of three members of Congress 'to repair to the army, and in a private and confidential consultation with General Washington, to consider of the best and most practicable means for carrying on a winter's campaign with vigour and success, an object which Congress have much at heart, and on such consultation, with the concurrence of General Washington, to direct every measure which circumstances may require for promoting public service.' [51] The three members of Congress have also been instructed to confer with Washington 'for enquiries into the cause of losses and failures.' [52] It surprises me to see resolves from Congress about military operations. [53]

November 30. Washington holds a council of the general officers to discuss three locations for winter quarters.

"The first is to find a site in Tredyffrin township of Chester County, in the chain from the Schuylkill to Bethlehem, the second is to find a site from Reading to Lancaster and the third is that of building huts near to Wilmington. If we do not attack Philadelphia, Congress wants us to spend the winter at Valley Forge, about twenty-two miles by wagon road from there. It is not my choice, as you all know. I would prefer to have several small camps from Reading to Lancaster."

"I would choose Wilmington as I have said many times before," declares Greene. Cadwallader and a few others agree, whilst most favor a line from Lancaster to Reading.[54]

"One great objection to huts is that they are exceedingly unhealthy and are at best but a miserable shelter from the inclemency of the weather. The mortality among the Hessians at Brunswick last spring as well as common observation will justify this assertion," says General Sullivan.[55]

The council does not come to a decision and Washington asks each of us to make a written reply.

I give my response on December 1:

I am deprived of points of knowledge by my being stranger in this country, and my being stranger in the army, if I can speak so, for I have no officers, no soldiers under my particular direction whom I could consult, and know theyr temper, theyr inclinations, and all what is possible to expect from them…However, (and in making excuses to your excellency for such an indecision and referring myself to your knowledge about the suppositions I will make) if it was not distressing neither for officers neither for soldiers, if going to Lancaster etc. will disaffect and make a bad impression as far as to prevent our recruiting, if we can keep better our officers when we schall be in a kind of encampement near the enemy, if principally you think that we should be fit for some winter march's we should be able to support some disadvantages then I am fully and with a great chearfulness of opinion that we must go to Wilmington. My reasons would be then:

1.This position enable us to do in the course of the winter what we shall think proper to annoy, to deprive of resources of every kind, to attack if possible the ennemy.

2.This position has something shining and military like which will make the best effect and upon the continent and even in Europe.

3.The doctors, and american ones, who know the manners and physik constitution of our soldiers say that nothing is so confortable as wellmade huts.

Prudence orders me to choose Lancaster but if the inconveniences I fear (without being able to know them) if those inconveniences I explain to your excellency are not as strong as they can be, if principally our present civil situation ask from us some thing shining and perhaps bold then I give all my wishes and all my choice to Wilmington. [56]

The same day Congress passes a resolution giving me command of a division.
"You can choose which one you want," Washington says.
"I would like the Virginians," I reply, as they are his countrymen.

We learn the British will quarter their troops at Germantown and Philadelphia for the winter.

"The possession of our towns while we have an army in the field, will avail them little," Washington remarks. "However, Congress has made a formal request for us to attack Philadelphia."

"Howe has built fourteen redoubts on the north and west of the city," says Greene. "There are also reinforcements thought to be arriving from New York. It would be madness to do so."

"A third of our army is confined to tents for lack of shoes, stockings and other clothing," declares General Sullivan. "A winter campaign will only increase the great dissatisfaction among the officers. I am fully convinced and fear that more than half your officers will leave you in a month unless some remedy is found to quiet their minds and relieve their distress. There are more than one hundred deserters from the Delaware regiment and the same number from many of the other regiments. They will have to be brought back to the army before the beginning of a spring campaign."[57]

"The commissary is finding it difficult to provide the army's daily provisions," says General Varnum.[58]

"My first concern is to keep the army together," says Washington. "I cannot attack Philadelphia, and I cannot provide protection for every individual and every patch of ground in the United States. Congress will finish by destroying us with all its demands."

December 3. He asks for our opinions in writing on the practicability of an attempt upon Philadelphia with the aid of a considerable body of militia.[59]

I write that:

Europe has a great idea of our being able to raise when we please an immense army of militia and it is looked upon as our last but certain resource. If we fall this phantom will fall also and you know that the American interest has always been since the beginning of the war to let the world believe that we are stronger than we can ever expect to be. If we destroy the English army, our generous effort will be admired everywhere, if we are repulsed it will be called a rash and laughable expedition. Therefore, we must not let a shining appearance and the pleasing charms of a bold fine enterprise deceive us upon the inconveniences and dangers of a gigantesque and in the same time decisive expedition. [60]

December 4. General Orders to the army announce my new command. During the night, Captain Allen McLane, scouting between the lines, discovers Howe is advancing from Philadelphia with most of his army.

"Go with one hundred horsemen to observe the enemy," Washington tells McLane. "Prepare the army to receive an attack," he orders.

The alarm guns fire at four in the morning. The whole army musters. Battle lines form.[61] The enemy advance in two columns on the Manatawny and Skippack roads. At Three Mile Run on the Skippack road McLane and his cavalry attack so successfully that the front division changes its line of march.[62] At three in the morning the enemy encamps on Chestnut Hill about three miles from our right.[63] We hourly expect an attack and keep constantly on the alert.[64] Washington has the tents taken down and sends the heavy baggage to the rear. Our position is very well defended. Both flanks have strong abattis, the approaches to the center are covered by several batteries and we have fifty-two heavy guns.[65] Washington is determined not to advance but to wait for the main attack on the ground he has chosen.[66] He will not sacrifice the advantages of our situation. If the British are defeated, they can return to Philadelphia. If we are defeated, we risk the loss of the whole army and the downfall of our cause.[67]

At eleven o'clock he orders Brigadier General James Irvine with six hundred Pennsylvania militia to advance towards the enemy. There is heavy fire from both sides; Irvine is wounded and taken prisoner.[68] His men retreat.

One very remarkable night the northern lights paint the heavens crimson velvet; we gaze in awe.

"A bloody battle is about to be fought!" cry the soldiers.

The enemy maneuver in the front and on the flanks of our lines until the following Monday then suddenly retreat during the night to Philadelphia.[69]

On December 10, the committee appointed by Congress send a report to Washington which says they believe: 'a winter offensive is ineligible and that the Army should take up winter quarters where it would be most likely to overawe the enemy, to protect the country and to find provisions and shelter.'[70]

"The army will go into winter quarters at Valley Forge," Washington says.

Next day, at four o'clock, the whole army is ordered to strike tents and parade in order to march. At six 'clock the march commences. At nine the army starts to cross the Schuylkill; two divisions of Sullivan's division and part of Wayne's pass over the pontoon bridge at Matson's Ford.

Intelligence arrives that the enemy is advancing on this side of the river. Sullivan is commanding as he is major general of the day; he orders the troops to recross the river and take down the bridge. He abandons the militia and dispatches a message to Washington who arrives to find the enemy clearly visible on the nearby heights. [71]

"I believe they are foragers, that the meeting is accidental. However, they might make use of this unexpected discovery and might draw as much advantage from it as if the encounter had been premeditated," he says.[72]

Night begins to darken the sky; the army marches about five miles up the river to Swede's Ford, where it encamps.[73] We learn that the enemy only consisted of about two thousand men who have hastily retreated.[74]

In the morning, the men cannot march as there is a lack of provisions,[75] but will hopefully do so later today.

Chapter 13

One half a gill of rice and a tablespoon of vinegar to celebrate Thanksgiving

I meet with Washington and the other officers in the downstairs room of a small stone house on the path opposite Gulph Mill. Outside our soldiers are in a snowstorm. They are without tents or blankets and are trying to shelter under the rocks and trees of the high ground on both sides of the Gulph, a chasm in the hill. Thirty-six wagons with fence rails instead of boards between each[1] were used to bridge Swede's Ford, and at six in the cold sleeting evening the men started to cross in single file, some here, some at the raft bridge below, and some by two fords.[2] Next day the army marched three miles from the west bank of the Schuylkill and reached the Gulph.[3]

It is now three in the morning. The storm continues, snowflakes swirling savagely through the darkness, entombing ragged groups of hardly recognizable human beings. They are in a pitiful state. Some have worn-out shoes; many have just bare feet. Legs are naked or nearly naked, and tattered shirts are the only garment for at least a quarter. Faces are gaunt, hair hangs in dirty strands.

At sunrise, the army stirs. The snow ceases. Frozen, stiffened bodies turn towards the pale light in the east. Bloody footprints mark the virgin white as men straggle to collect wood and make fires.[4] The snow returns. The army resumes a huddled, crouching, immobile state. The fires die, the flames spluttering and hissing.

Provisions do not arrive. There are not enough wagons; it is necessary to ration the few supplies there are.

December 14. I write to Gates: 'The idea of obtaining your friendship is highly pleasant to me- be certain, sir, that you can depend on my attachment forever.'[5]

The same day I also write a long letter to Laurens. I tell him I chose the Virginians because of my tender and warm attachment for our respectable and great general which made me wish to be at the head of his countrymen. I tell him I have heard that clothes and blankets will soon arrive in camp: 'Don't you think that as the Northern provinces have been well provided for sice the beginning of the war (and indeed I saw yet yesterday large parcels of goods distributed amongst them) some more attention should be payed to our poor nacked Virginians who have always fought without any resource, always in the opened field and under General Washington.' I also mention my plan to attack the British in the East Indies, that I have written to Maurepas and Bouillé and that I will explain everything to him when we meet.[6]

On the fifteenth I ride towards the Schuylkill with a small escort to reconnoiter near the ford. We approach the swollen, ice-encrusted river and see redcoats foraging on the opposite bank, as bright as poppies in a summer field. My men level their muskets and shoot. The British immediately halt. They return our gifts with enthusiasm, a bullet singing past my ear. We fire again. They fire back, then withdraw.

"We can't pursue them. We will be easy targets if we try to cross the river," I say.

We go back to the Gulph, my spirits high. I have again been under fire. My lucky star has shone once more. I have survived. [7]

December 16. Wagons and carts trundle into camp laden with tents and baggage sent to Trappe when the enemy threatened to attack. The men quickly erect them; a drab array of canvas matching the sleet-gray day. In the night, snow turns to rain; before dawn, it freezes. [8] The roads are now hard with ice; the barefoot men cannot march. The downpour continues, falling steadily from the sky, transforming the winter landscape into slush and mud.

The rain is unrelenting. It penetrates our clothing. It streams from hats and hair down necks and faces into shirts, streaking dirt-grimed skin. Our army is a mass of sodden men, morosely shivering below trees, underneath wagons, or below improvised awnings of rags, branches and leaves, the unlucky ones huddling together in the open, completely drenched. Powder is wet, or damp at best. We would not be able to fight even if we wished to. My Virginians are undermanned even in proportion to the weakness of the whole army and almost entirely naked, but I hope I will soon get cloth to make clothing as well as obtain some recruits. [9]

"On December 18 we will celebrate the first Thanksgiving of our new country," says Washington. "Congress decreed that date in November to give thanks to God for blessing the nation and the troops in our battle for independence and peace."

The officers are somber. We are only too aware of the dire position of the army and the Revolution. Congress has abandoned Philadelphia. We were defeated at Brandywine and Germantown. Our currency is daily depreciating. Our army is hungry as winter tightens its grip.

The same day, I proudly write my first letter from America to the duc d'Ayen, which John Adams, whom I have not yet met, will carry. I say that the maréchal de Noailles told me about the confinement of Madame de Lafayette:

> He did not speak of it as the happiest event in the world, but my anxiety was too great to worry about distinctions of sex. His kindness in writing to me, in letting me know all the news, has given me a hundred times more pleasure than he could have imagined in telling me I have only a daughter. So now the rue Saint-Honoré is discredited forever, whilst the other hôtel de Noailles has acquired a new luster by the birth of Adrien.

I tell him of military events which have happened since my arrival here; of the British plan to cut America along a line from the Chesapeake Bay to Ticonderoga. I write about Brandywine, Germantown and Saratoga and that the loss of Philadelphia is very far from having the importance given it by Europe. I write of:

> The prodigious superiority of merit of General Washington over General Gates. Our General is a man truly made for this revolution which could not be accomplished without him. I see him more closely than any other man and I see him worthy of the adoration of his country. His tender friendship and his confidence in me for all military and political matters, large and small, which concern him, enable me to judge everything he has to do, to conciliate, and to vanquish. Every day I admire more the beauty of his character and of his spirit. Some foreigners are piqued because they did not receive commissions, although such things were nothing to do with him, others whose ambitious projects he did not wish to serve, are jealous intriguers who would like to tarnish his reputation but his name will be revered throughout the centuries by all lovers of liberty and humanity...America waits impatiently for France to declare for her and one day I hope that France will decide to humiliate proud England...Since I returned from Jersey, Washington asked me to choose from several brigades the division which would suit me best. I have chosen one which is completely composed of Virginians. It is weak, at the moment, even by comparison with the

weakness of the army...I read, I study, I examine, I listen, I think, and from all that I try to form an opinion into which I place as much common sense as I can. I do not talk very much for fear of saying something stupid...When the heart tells me that an opportunity is favorable, I do not refuse to take the risk, but I do not think that the glory of success permits us to hazard the well-being of an army or of a part of it, which is not prepared nor intended for an attack. [10]

Gentle rain falls on December 18, the third day the soldiers are without flour or bread.[11] They file quietly to receive their Thanksgiving ration of one half a gill of rice and a tablespoon of vinegar.[12] They listen in their corps and brigades to the sermons of the chaplains. They stand half-naked, in ragged clothes; they pray, their voices echoing across the high, uncultivated hill.

"All we have to be thankful for is that we are alive and not in the grave with many of our friends," is Dearborn's opinion.[13]

At the commissary's quarters the only food in one of the stores is a barrel two-thirds full of beef hocks.[14]

"We are in a land of plenty. The army is serving our country and yet it is left to starve," is the opinion of my fellow officers.

Washington is displeased that his advice about winter quarters was not taken but pleased that at least the army will not be fighting this winter. A small force will remain as an outpost at Gulph Mills, under the command of Lord Stirling, to give warning if the British advance from Philadelphia.

Chapter 14

The tattered, hungry army at the forested wilderness of Valley Forge

December 19. Friday.[1] At ten in the morning the soldiers start to march from the Gulph. They pass by Hanging Rock which projects so far across the road that men and wagons must skirt round it which causes a delay, the troops cursing in the biting cold as they wait.

The tattered, hungry army tramps slowly north for six miles, bare feet leaving bloody streaks on the ground. By midday, the first soldiers are arriving at the forested wilderness of Valley Forge where Valley Creek flows north into the Schuylkill whose course here runs from west to east.[2] During the night, snow falls, thinly covering the ground; some of the men are in tents; some sleep by the fires. They lack food and many even lack water, not realizing Valley Creek is just a half mile away.[3]

In the third week of September the British burned the sawmill, iron works and grist mill at Valley Creek as they were being used to help our army.[4] They also took twenty-five barrels of horseshoes, several thousand tomahawks and three thousand eight hundred barrels of flour[5] from the magazine. Now there are only twenty-five barrels of flour left. The men make flour cakes by mixing flour with water and cooking it on a stone over the fire.

Washington issues a proclamation on December 20: 'All the farmers within ten miles of Valley Forge must thrash out one-half of their grain by February 1, and the other half by March 1, under penalty of having all that shall remain in sheaves seized by the Commissaries and Quartermasters of the army and paid for as straw.'[6]

Some brigades are given salt pork on the twenty-first,[7] but for most there is no meat, soap, or vinegar.

"No meat!" "No meat!" "Caw!" "Caw!" shout the starving troops. "Tu-Whit!" "Tu-Whoo!" The raucous cawing of human crows joins the screech of owls, the distant vales echoing the melancholy sound of the soldiers suggesting they will fly away.[8]

"We are eating glue! Our guts are turned to pasteboard! No bread! No soldier!" they cry.[9]

Officers run up and down with drawn swords. The shouting slowly fades. The hunger does not. Even the horses lack fodder.

In the afternoon of the twenty-second, Major John Clark Jr. reports: 'a large body of the enemy are on their march to Derby.'

They are presumably foraging, and Washington orders the army to prepare to march against them. Then he receives the terrible news that even if enough men could be found with suitable clothes and shoes, there is no food, so instead he sends a few light parties drafted from each brigade[10] to watch and harass;[11] and orders a search of the countryside and any provisions found to be taken.[12]

I write to Adrienne, a shorter letter than I had intended because the man who will take it to John Adams has just told me he is leaving almost immediately: 'I was filled with the most wonderful joy to hear of your delivery. I have never been so happy in my life as when the news arrived…You can imagine with what impatience I await your letters which I gather are in five or six ports.' I repeat my love for her and for my daughters and ask her to welcome Mr. Adams who will be the bearer of my letter.[13]

Washington writes to President Laurens of Congress that the men had been unable to stir the previous day against a possible threat from the enemy due to the lack of provisions, and that a dangerous mutiny begun the night before which was suppressed with difficulty by the spirited exertions of some officers, was still to be greatly feared because they lack food. He declares that unless there is a great change in the supply of provisions the army must inevitably be reduced to either starve, dissolve or disperse. He says that there are now 2,898 men unfit for duty in camp because they are bare-footed and otherwise naked and that there are no more than 8,200 fit for duty in camp. Many have to sit up all night by fires because they have no blankets. He replies to the criticism of the choice of Valley Forge by the Legislature of Pennsylvania who had said that a great part of this state, particularly that on the east side, together with the state of Jersey would be left to the ravages of the enemy:

> We find gentlemen without knowing whether the army was really going into Winter Quarters or not…reprobating the measure as if they thought Men were made of Stocks or Stones and equally insensible of frost and Snow and moreover, as if they conceived it practicable for an inferior Army under the disadvantages I have describ'd to be wch. is by no means exaggerated to confine a superior one (in all respects well appointed and provided for a Winter's Campaign) within the city of Philadelphia, and cover from depredation and waste the States of Penn., Jersey, aca. but what makes this matter still more extraordinary in my eye, is that these very Gentn. Who were well apprized of the nakedness of the Troops, from ocular demonstration thought their own Soldiers worse clad than others, and advised me, near a Month ago, to postpone the execution of a Plan, I was about to adopt (in consequence of a resolve of Congress) for seizing Cloaths, under strong assurances that an ample supply would be collected in ten days agreeably to a decree of the State, not one article of wch., by the bye, is yet come to hand, should think a Winters Campaign, and the covering these states from the Invasion of an enemy. I can assure those Gentlemen that it is a much easier and less distressing thing to draw remonstrances in a comfortable room by a good fire side than to occupy a cold bleak hill and sleep under frost and Snow without Cloaths or Blankets, however, although they seem to have little feeling for the naked, and distressed Soldier, I feel superabundantly for them, and from my Soul pity those miseries wch. it is neither in my power to relieve or prevent. [14]

Washington moves into a two-story, stone house, near the mouth of Valley Creek, which he rents for one hundred pounds in Pennsylvania state currency from a widow, Deborah Hewes, who rents it from her brother-in-law, Isaac Potts, a Quaker, one of the original owners of the forge which had given the valley its name.[15] Eleven thousand and ninety-eight soldiers shiver in the winter cold on a plateau about two miles long and a mile and a quarter wide, dominated by the steep, forested Mount Joy and opposite Mount Misery on the other side of Valley Creek, so named because William Penn had lost his way on it; the northern end overlooks the Schuylkill River where a wide ford would allow a quick retreat. To the east the British are encamped near to Philadelphia, eighteen miles away, and about ten miles west is our former camp at Whitemarsh. It is strategically and tactically a good situation for our winter camp but unfortunately although there are a few fields without crops and several small houses on the far side of the creek, there is no village, no plain and hardly any valley.[16] There is plenty of water although it has to be carried in buckets for considerable distances; the land is well-drained, and the dense forests, where many ancient oaks have trunks five feet in circumference, provide an abundant source of wood for constructing huts and making fires.

Each brigade has been given a plot of land picked out by Washington himself and the noise of axes felling and cutting the trees resounds from dawn to dusk, the soldiers yoking themselves to wagons to drag the wood as there are not enough horses. Groups of twelve are building the huts whose dimensions had been given in General Orders on the eighteenth, and twelve dollars will be given to the group in each sector which finishes its hut in the quickest and most workmanlike manner.[17] Thomas Paine visits.[18] He describes the men as like a family of beavers. "Everyone is busy, some carrying logs, others mud and the rest fastening it together and a curious collection of buildings in the true rustic order is appearing."[19] He does not join the army. "I tried it and it is not for me. I prefer to fight with words."

I stand at the door of my hut near Valley Creek, a flurry of snow delicately dusting churned earth and sloping roofs. Not far away, men are crammed into small barracks, no gayer than dungeons[20] with either twelve soldiers, or two, four or six officers, in a room sixteen by fourteen feet. The roof and doors are of oak planks, the sides are six and a half feet high of wood sealed with clay, as is also the one- or two-foot-high chimney. To the north-east of my quarters, along the ridge, are about two thousand huts in parallel streets, along with five earth redoubts and extensive trenches which form the outer defensive line.[21] The western edge of the plateau has similar entrenchments and an abbattis as well as redoubts; the steep side overlooking the creek does not need defenses and the north side has the Schuylkill as a defense. The huts are arranged in a grid pattern according to the topography of the land; there are streets as though in a village, each regiment allotted its own area, and a bridge has been constructed across the Schuylkill. I try to be more simple, more frugal and more austere than anyone else. I was brought up in comfort but now I adapt to privation and fatigue[22] and as most of the other general officers live in houses some distance from the camp, I am often major general for the day.

A fire burns in the hearth at the back of the room, the flames flickering in the uneven draw from the chimney. In the woods, unfortunate men wielding dull axes are stripping branches and attempting to hew out logs from newly felled trees. They lack coats, hats, shirts and shoes, their few clothes are in rags, their naked legs and feet are blackening in the cold and amputation is often the result.[23]

So far, I have been spared the itch, which afflicts many. Scabs cover men's bodies and the physicians have been cooking up a concoction of sulfur and pig's fat to smear on the affected skin.[24] The smell is atrocious. It hangs over the camp, combining with the low smoke from the chimneys, the odor of human excrement and the stench of corpses. Washington ordered one lash to be given to anyone who does not use the latrines and since then the smell has diminished. Men who steal food are flogged. There is a ban on cards, dice and other sorts of gambling.

We have a lack of everything. We have hardly any kettles and so cannot make soap, which would help in combatting not just the itch, but other illnesses. Typhus and fevers ravage the men and there are five thousand in the hospital, many of whom are not expected to survive.

The army is living on the very edge of existence here at Valley Forge, beset by hunger and disease, and, like Washington, I fear for its future unless a substantial improvement occurs. Men desert daily. It is easy to wander off through the woods. It is a capital offence, but that does not seem to deter.

The situation has never seemed more critical, even although Saratoga in the north has been a wonderful victory. The British garrison at New York lives sumptuously whilst hundreds of badly clothed, badly fed men, roam the shores of the Hudson.[25] Howe's army quartered at Philadelphia has about eighteen thousand men; we have about eleven thousand here at Valley Forge. Some days there is literally nothing for the men to eat and the patient endurance of both soldiers and officers is a miracle.[26] The paper money has no solid foundation, is often counterfeited by the enemy and discredited by the partisans. Farmers in this part of Pennsylvania are not necessarily unanimous or zealous in support of the war.[27] They often prefer to sell their produce to the enemy for a prompt payment of gold and silver rather than receive a certificate whose value often depreciates before they are given Continental paper money. There are about seventy-five thousand farmers within a fifty-mile radius of Valley Forge, but both our army and the British have already scoured east Pennsylvania and the enemy has not only destroyed the magazine here, but also at Danbury and along the North River. The roads are awash with water in the frequent rain; there are few wagons, horses and teamsters. The quartermaster, Thomas Mifflin, resigned on October 10, without telling Washington, who had to write to Congress asking if rumors about his resignation were true,[28] and no one has yet been appointed. Joseph Trumbull, the commissary general, has been ill for months in New England.[29] Both departments are in complete disarray. While the army is suffering want of shoes and other items, hogsheads of shoes, stockings and clothing are lying at different places on the roads and in the woods, lying and perishing for want of teams and proper management.[30]

Washington not only writes to Congress and to the different states, he also personally writes to suppliers and finds out in detail about every aspect of what is needed; I am with him when he writes to Boston to try and obtain boots and saddles.

"I think the idea of wintering in this desert can only have been put into the head of the commanding general by an interested speculator, or a disaffected man," is de Kalb's opinion.[31] He also believes General Stephen was made the scapegoat for the defeat at Germantown. "He was court martialed and accused of being drunk and retreating when he should not have done. I'm not defending him, but I think he was made to bear the whole of the blame, some of which should be put on the shoulders of others."

A fellow Auvergnat, comte Charles Albert de Moré de Pontgibaud, is now one of my aides-de-camp, after reaching here in rags. He had been imprisoned in the château of Pierre-en-Cize after his family obtained a *lettre de cachet* from the king, a fate which had perhaps nearly been mine. He had managed to escape and had sailed across the Atlantic to join the rebels in America. On his arrival in the Chesapeake his ship had been fired on by the enemy; he had been shipwrecked but had saved himself. Everything he possessed had been stolen; he had walked all the way here to Valley Forge to be with me and I have given him horses and clothes. He says that when people offered Franklin sympathy for the taking of Philadelphia he remarked: "You are mistaken. The English army has not captured Philadelphia. It is Philadelphia which has captured the English army."[32]

Thousands are without blankets and warm themselves by fires all night. Some have so little clothing they cannot leave their huts.[33] It is often difficult to find men fit enough to do camp duties. Those who are naked borrow clothes from those who have them. The officers, and even the generals, also lack clothing; many are wearing coarse woolen blankets like invalids do in French hospitals.[34] Hunger increases. The commissary department still fails to supply food. Many farmers have not obeyed Washington's proclamation. They are Tories and wish to sell their crops to the British for their gold.

December 25. It snows.[35] Washington invites me to be guest of honor at Christmas dinner; we dine on a little mutton, some potatoes, cabbage, crusts of bread; our drink is water.[36]

December 29. Conway rides into headquarters. He informs Washington that Congress has appointed him inspector general of the new Board of War and that he has been given the rank of major general. Washington already knew Gates had been appointed head of the Board of War. Now Conway will be in Valley Forge advising him on the army.

Washington is icily polite, a manner of behaving with ceremonious civility, tantamount to incivility,[37] which people generally find very distressing. Conway professes to be very hurt by how he has been received: "Such a reception as I never met with before from any general during thirty years in a very respectable army."[38]

Washington sees Conway twice; then he sends Lieutenant Colonel John Fitzgerald to ask him what methods he means to use in his new office. Conway replies with a detailed account of his plans and the intention to begin verbal instruction of officers from each regiment: "If my appointment is productive of any inconvenience or anyways disagreeable to Your Excellency, as I neither applied nor solicited for this plan, I am very ready to return to France where I have pressing business, and this I will do with the more satisfaction that I expect even there to be useful to the cause."[39]

Anger erupts among the brigadiers as Conway, the most junior of them, has been promoted over all the others.

"There is almost universal disgust. His military knowledge and experience may fit him for the office of inspector general, but the right of seniority violated, without any remarkable services done to justify it, has given a deep wound to the line of brigadiers," is Laurens' opinion.[40]

Washington replies in writing to Conway, using similar cold words as he employed in speaking to him:

> By consulting your own feelings upon the appointment of Baron de Kalb you may judge what must be the sensations of those Brigadiers who by your promotion are superseded. I am told they are determined to remonstrate against it; for my own part, I have nothing to do in the appointment of general officers and shall always afford every countenance and due respect to those appointed by Congress....nor have I any other wish on that head but that good attentive officers may be chosen, and no extraordinary promotion take place but where the merit of the officer is so generally acknowledged as to obviate every reasonable cause of dissatisfaction thereat. [41]

In the morning I go to speak to Washington, but he cannot see me. I therefore write him a letter:

> My dear General, I went yesterday morning to Head Quarters with an intention of Speaking to Your Excellency But you were too Buzy and I shall lay down in this letter what I wished to say.
> I don't Need telling you How I am Sorry for all what Happens Since some time. It is a necessary dependence of my most tender and Respectful friendship for you, Which affection is as true and Candid as the other Sentiments of my Heart, and Much Stronger than a So new an acquaintance Seems to admit. But an other Reason to Be concerned in the present circumstances is my ardent and perhaps enthusiastic Wishes for the Happiness and Liberty of this Country. I See plainly that America Can defend Herself if proper measures are taken and now I Begin to fear that She could Be lost By Herself and Her own Sons.
> When I was in Europe I thought that Here almost every man was a lover of liberty, and would Rather die free than live slave. You Can Conceive my astonishment when I saw that Toryism was as oppenly professed as Wighism itself. However, at that time I Believed that all good Americans were United together; that the Confidence of Congress in you was Unbounded. Then I Entertained the Certitude that America Would Be independent in case she should not loose You. Take a way for an instant that modest diffidence of yourself (which, pardon my freedom, my dear general, is Sometimes too Great, and I wish you could know, as well as myself, what difference there is Between you and any other man Upon the continent), You Shall See very plainly that if you were

lost for America, there is no body who could keep the army and the Revolution for six months. There are oppen dissentions in Congress, parties who Hate one another as much as the Common Ennemy, stupid men who without knowing a single word about war, undertake to judge you, to make Ridiculous Comparisons; they are infatuated with Gates, without thinking of the different Circumstances, and Believe that attacking is the only thing necessary to Conquer. Those ideas are Entertained in their minds by some Jealous men, and perhaps secret friends to the British Government, who want to push you in a moment of ill Humour to some Rash enterprise upon the lines, or against a much stronger army.

I have been surprised at first, to see the niew establishement of this board of war, to see the difference made between northen and southern department, to see resolved from Congress about military operations - but the promotion of Canway is beyond all my expectations. I should be glad to have niew major generals after me, because as I know that you take some interest to my happiness and reputation; it is perhaps an occasion for your excellency to give me more agreable commands in some interesting instances. On the other hand, Gal. Connway says he is entirely a man to be disposed of by me, he calls himself my soldier, and the reason of such behavior for me is that he wishs to be well spoken of at the french court, and his protector the Mquis. de Castries is an intimate acquaintance of mine - but Since the letter of Lord Stirligg I inquired in his caracter. I found that he was an ambitious and a dangerous man. He has done all in his power by cunning maneuvres to take off my confidence and affection for you. His desire was to engage me to leave this country. Now I see all the general officers of the army revolted aginst Congress. Such disputes if known by the enemy, can be attended with horrid consequences. I am very sorry when ever I perceive troubles raise amongs the defensers of the same cause, but my concern is much greater when I find officers coming from France, officers of some character in my country to whom any fault of that kind may be imputed. The reason of my fondness for Connway was is being by all means a very brave and very good officer. However that part of maneuvres etc. which seems so extraordinary to Congress is not so very difficult for any man of common sense who applies himself to it...I have the warmest Love for my country and for every good Frenchmen. Theyr succès feels my heart with joy. But, sir, besides, Connway is an Irishman, I want countrymen who deserve in every part to do honor to theyr country. That gentleman had engaged me by entertaining my head with ideas of glory and shining projects, and I must confess for my shame, that it is a too certain way of deceiving me.

I wish'd to join to the fiew theories about war I can have, and the fiew dispositions nature gave perhaps to me, the experience of thirty campaigns, in hope that I should be able to be more useful in the present circumstance. My desire of deserving your satisfaction is stronger than ever, and every where you'l employ me you can be certain of my trying every exertion in my power to succeed. I am now fixed to your fate, and I shall follow it and sustain it as well by my sword as by all means in my power. (I beg you will keep the letter secret). You will pardon my importunity in favor of the sentiment which dictate it. Youth and frienship make myself perhaps too warm but I feel the greatest concern of all what happens since some time. With the most tenderest and profound respect I have the honor to be, dear general, Your most obedient humble Servant.

(The Mquis. De) Lafayette. [42]

December 31. I receive a letter from Washington which considerably cheers me:

Your favour of Yesterday conveyed to me fresh proof of that friendship and attachment which I have happily experienced since the first of our acquaintance, and for which I entertain sentiments of the purest affection.' He praises me and denigrates Conway, whom he calls his inveterate enemy, who has practised every art to do him an injury. 'We must not, in so great a contest, expect to meet with nothing but Sunshine. I have no doubt but that everything happens so for the best; that we shall triumph over all our misfortunes, and shall in the end be ultimately happy; when my Dear

Marquis, if you will give me your Company in Virginia, we will laugh at our past difficulties and the follies of others.

G. Washington. [43]

Conway writes brazenly to Washington. He defends his promotion; with clear insincerity he links Washington's name with that of Frederick in Europe; he suggests he has not been properly received by Washington and that he could expect no support in his duties because the commander in chief disliked him personally.[44]

On January 2, Washington sends his correspondence with Conway to Congress and writes:

If General Conway means, by cool receptions…that I did not receive him in the language of a warm and cordial friend, I readily confess the charge. I did not, nor shall I ever, till I am capable of the arts of dissimulation. These I despise, and my feelings will not permit to make professions of friendship to a man I deem my enemy, and whose system of conduct forbids it. At the same time, Truth authorizes me to say that he was received and treated with proper respect to his official character, and that he has had no cause to justify the assertion that he could not expect any support for fulfilling the duties of his appointment. [45]

The brigadiers continue to be angry about the promotion of Conway. They consider that his military knowledge and experience may fit him for the position of inspector general, but the right of seniority has been violated, without any remarkable services done to justify it.[46] Nine brigadiers of the main army sign a letter of complaint to Congress: 'We have commanded with him in the field and are totally unacquainted with any superior act of mind which could entitle him to rise above us.'[47] Nathanael Greene wrote additional words saying that if regular promotion was denied: 'a sense of injury would mean a lessening of military service.'[48]

I now barely speak to Conway; my compatriots behave similarly; we all despise him.[49] I completely support Washington. To the suggestions that an attack should be made on Philadelphia, I say to Robert Morris: "We have at our head a great judge, a man whom America and principally the army is to have a confidence as extended as the love he derives from them, and when he will think it proper to fight, then I shall believe always that we have good reason for it."[50]

It is very evident that there is favoritism between the northern and southern departments which really surprises me; I write again to President Laurens to try and obtain clothes for my men:

I am undone, my dear Sir, our cloathes, the fair object of my Most charming hopes, they are, I am told, detained in York town and confined in a dark jail. Consider, if you please, that they are innocent strangers, traveling tho' this state, and very desirous of meeting the virginian regiments they belong to. If they are detained only for exerting the most respectable rights of hospitality receive here my thanks in the name of Virginia. But if it is possible, I do not want they should be entertained longer, and I wish very heartily they schould appear soon upon the nacked backs of our honest virginians soldiers for whom they have been destinated. [51]

Discipline is very necessary in our critical situation. One night, after heavy snow, I make my rounds; I come across officers who are negligent; I am forced to have them reduced to the ranks.[52] I write to Washington to complain of the use of court martials as men are judged by their inferiors; at the same time, I criticize the disproportionate nature of some of the sentences.[53]

Mrs. Greene joins her husband in early January; I spend much time socializing at their home and write to Adrienne: 'Several general officers are sending for their wives, and I envy them not their wives but the happiness of being able to see them.'[54]

Most of the soldiers have good huts although not the North Carolinians who are the most backward in their buildings.[55] The encampment is finally completed on January 15,[56] but there is often no straw to lay on the earth floor of the huts. Thousands still do not have blankets. The weather, however, is not as cold as it could be. The snow which fell in the early days was only about four inches deep and it is now mainly rain which plagues us. Food is still lacking. At the beginning of January, the commissary again had nothing, but then some flour and cattle arrived.[57]

Conway has gone to Yorktown; Thomas Mullens, his aide-de-camp, a man who is not a wit, tells me that Conway has received two letters from Gates and Mifflin concerning a plan to send him to Canada. I am extremely displeased. I write to Washington:

> They will laugh in France when they'l hear that he is choosen upon sooch a commission out of the same army where I am, and when the project should be to show to the Frenchmen of that country a man of theyr nation who by his rank in France could inspire them with some confidence. [58]

I receive a letter from Henry Laurens who writes that the 'eruption into Canada is an attempt to do honor to the Marquis and benefit to the public.' I am overjoyed. Then I learn from de Kalb that Conway will be my second-in-command. I immediately write to Laurens. I express my gratitude for the honor. I say that I am young and inexperienced but 'every mean in my power, every knowledge in the military way can have got since the first days of my life, everything nature could have granted to me, all my exertions and the last drop of my blood, schall be employed in showing my acknowledgement for such a favor and how I wish to deserve it.' I protest about the choice of Conway: 'How can I support the society of a man who has spoken of my friend in the most insolent and abusive terms, who has done, and does every day all his power to ruin him?'[59] I ask that General McDougall be appointed instead; I go to talk to Gouverneur Morris, a man of quick intelligence, a member of the Congressional committee who is here in camp.

"I am even willing to serve under General McDougall if he would accept the command," I tell him.[60]

Conway writes to me. He talks of the points of view he knows to be most agreeable to me; the utility of this invasion both to American liberty and to my own glory. He assures me he would be very happy to serve under my orders and that he feels a greater pleasure to be under me than if he was commander-in-chief, very happy if he can by every exertion in his power contribute in something to my reputation. I will wait at least two days before replying to this honest gentleman.[61]

Chapter 15

Proposed expedition into Canada

Washington hands me two letters from the Board of War which have come in his mail; I open one.

"It is the official confirmation by Congress of my appointment by the Board of War to command an expedition to Canada," I tell him.

He says nothing. I open the second letter. "It is from Gates. I must go immediately to Albany to meet General Conway who will give me instructions to explain the principles on which the expedition is formed and the opinion of the Board with respect to the best way of executing it...The Board deem it needless to recommend to me as much secrecy in this matter as the nature of the thing will possibly admit of."[1]

Again, he makes no comment;[2] I can only guess at his reaction. I go to see the Congressional commissioners in the camp.

"I am surprised to receive the news of my appointment and the instructions of my commission by any other hand than that of my general. It makes me think that I am not perhaps considered as a detachment of His Excellency's army under his immediate command. The title of being his aide-de-camp appears to me preferable to any other which might be offered to me," I say bluntly. "I believe I should go to Yorktown to consult Congress in order to know in what light I should consider the expedition proposed against Montreal."[3]

They agree with me. I ride back to headquarters. I find Washington in the same room writing a letter and this time I see clearly from his severe expression, that he is displeased.

"I wish to go to York to speak to Congress," I say.

"You have permission to leave tomorrow," he replies.

The Board of War has asked him for his approval on the scheme. He answers: 'In the present instance, as I neither know the extent of the Objects in view, nor the means to be employed to effect them, it is not in my power to pass any judgment upon the subject. I can only sincerely wish, that success may attend it, both as it may be advancive of the public good and on account of the personal Honor of the Marquis de la Fayette, for whom I have a very particular esteem and regard.'[4]

In the morning of January 28, I set off at dawn, the sun filtering through low mist shrouding the trees. Two days later, in warm, unseasonal weather, the bluebirds singing in the trees,[5] I ride into the quiet, rural town of York where Congress has taken over the courthouse. I quickly discover, to my horror, that Conway left for Albany yesterday.

I spend most of the day talking with Henry Laurens, who thinks highly of Conway. John Laurens and I attempt to convince him otherwise. Finally, he begins to address me as 'Your Excellency,' a term used for Washington, so I know he now agrees with me.[6]

Congress gives me written instructions that the troops will consist of two thousand five hundred men, that the commissary of clothing at Albany will provide all the woollens and every comfort his stores can provide and that tents will be unnecessary and cumbersome as the men will be in the woods at night and very used to the mode of covering themselves there. If I find a general disinclination of the inhabitants in Canada to join the American Standard, then I will destroy all the works and vessels at St. Johns, Chamblee and the Isle aux Noix and then retire to the settlements, then Saratoga. If, however, the Canadians want to join our cause 'they must determine to receive the Resolves of Congress and the currency of America. The Grand Object, however, of the expedition is to destroy or possess the enemy's vessels and stores of every kind upon Lake Champlain and in the City of Montreal, and all stores of every kind in the possession of private Persons, which may be necessary for the Service of the States, or Serviceable to the Enemy.'[7] To my disappointment this is very different from the expedition to free New France which I had envisaged; it is more of a ravage or incursion.[8]

I write to Congress to express my warmest thanks for the mark of confidence they have honored me with in appointing me to the command of a northern army. I say I have been surprised to receive the news of my appointment and my instructions from any hand than that of my general. 'It engaged me to make this very stranger to my mind and very strange in itself reflexion...However I hope that idea was groundless, and I find even it was a ridiculous one.' I enclose a list of Frenchmen I wish to accompany me and say that I had wanted to have General McDougal but if his health does not allow him to venture to the cold north, I suggest the baron de Kalb instead.[9]

In the evening, I meet the Board of War at the quarters of Gates, a short, stout man, just four years older than Washington, with whom he had fought in the French and Indian War. Richard Peters, the secretary of the Board of War, and two congressmen, Francis Lightfoot Lee and Wiliam Duer who has the reputation of being a tory, and whom I regard as a rascal,[10] also attend. I voice my opinions frankly.

"If you don't give me McDougall or de Kalb and the French officers appointed according to my ideas, I decline the appointment and will go to France with most all the French officers in the army."

Mr. Lee is, I believe, for me, Duer quite against, the secretary charmed with the dispute, and the old fellow scratching his wig.[11]

We drink toasts. When everyone is about to rise, I speak.

"There is one health, gentlemen, which we have not yet drunk and which I will propose. The commander in chief of the American armies."

My hosts receive it coldly. Duer and Lee flush but everyone drinks.[12]

"I will travel with you to Albany," says Duer. "I will meet you at Ringo's Tavern near Coryell's Ferry on the Delaware. Colonel Robert Trump will precede us and make our path easier."

On February 2, Congress resolves that Major General McDougal should come on the expedition if his health permits it, if not, then the baron de Kalb will have the commission if General Washington deems it proper.[13] Commissions will be granted to Gimat, de Vrigny, Pontgibaud, de Sigonie, de Lomagne, and du Frey, as lieutenant colonel, lieutenant colonel and major, and the last three as captain.[14]

On Tuesday, I celebrate by breakfasting with Henry Laurens, his landlady and Miss Catherine Alexander Ketty, the young daughter of Lord Stirling. I very much enjoy the excellent tea poured out by the charming Miss Ketty and tell her so.

Several congressmen have suggested it would be helpful to tell people in France about the proposed expedition. I therefore return to my lodgings and write to Adrienne:

> What an enchanting pleasure it will be for me to embrace you all; what a consolation to be able to
> weep with my other friends for the dear friend I have lost!...Canada is oppressed by the English...I

am to go there with the title of General of the Northern Army, at the head of three thousand men, to see if evil can be done to the English in that country. The idea of rendering the whole of New France free and of delivering her from a heavy yoke, is too splendid for me to allow myself to dwell upon it...I am undertaking a most difficult task, above all taking into account the few resources I possess. As to those my own merit offers , they are very trifling in comparison to the importance of the place; nor can a man of twenty be fit to command an army...Be so kind to tell the prince that his youthful captain, although now a general-in-chief has not acquired more knowledge than he possessed at the field for military maneuvers, and that he knows not how, unless chance or his good angel should direct him, to justify the confidence which has been placed in him... Adieu, my dear heart. Embrace our dear children. I embrace their charming mother a million times. When shall I find myself again in her arms? [15]

I set off back to Valley Forge with my usual enthusiasm, hoping that when my letter reaches France many people will know of it. I have achieved what I wanted from Congress, and I believe I have been instrumental in destroying the cabal trying to discredit Washington. Conway is now the inspector general of the army without inspection, and second commander of the incursion without any particular command.[16] In the afternoon, beneath a darkly lowering winter sky, I cross the Susquehanna, a somewhat perilous undertaking, the ferry trying to avoid large blocks of ice.

I finally reach headquarters. I tell Washington about events at York. He listens intently, his misgivings about the venture obvious although I am sure he wishes me well and does not want harm to come to me. I leave him to go and speak with Lord Stirling about the best road to take to Albany.

Chapter 16

I am reduced to wish to have never put the foot in America[1]

February 7. Before dawn I write to Gates by candlelight, the rain pitter-pattering on the roof: 'I should be in a terrible concern about my means of succeeding, and the immensity of things which I must be provided for, had I not the greatest confidence in your friendship, and your good care of my reputation, as well as in the public interest. This project is yours, Sir, therefore you must make it succeed. If I had not depended so much on you, I would not have undertaken the operation.'[2]

I also write to Henry Laurens. I tell him I will soon be leaving and that I am enclosing two lines for General Gates. I ask him to give my respectful compliments to his fine landlady and the most charming Miss Ketty.[3]

Just after five o'clock we set off, rain stinging our faces. We ride our horses as hard as we can, the dark slowly transforming into the grayness of a winter's day. The Susquehanna again has treacherous floating ice, but we manage to cross. Next day, we reach Coryell's Ferry, the meeting place with Duer. He is not there which does not surprise me. I dare say he is hurrying everything for the alert and expeditious incursion and calculating very kindly every accident which can break the neck of a gentleman travelling from headquarters to Albany. There is also no sign of Colonel Troup who must fly over like a bird for nobody has seen him along that road where he was to get everything ready for me.[4]

We do not bother to wait. We hurry to cross the wide, icy Delaware. We reach the far bank; the rain turns to snow, shrouding our cloaks, hats and horses so thickly we soon resemble white wraiths on phantom steeds.

Three days later, we reach Flemington. I receive a letter from Laurens who writes that Miss Ketty has spoken of me in a flattering way. I write back: 'If sche had taken any Notice of what my eyes could have signified, she would have read there the greatest admiration for all her accomplished person.'[5]

I write to Washington:

I go on very slowly sometimes pierced by rain, sometimes covered with snow, and not thinking many handsome thoughts about the projected incursion into Canada. If Succès were to be had it would surprise me in a more agreeable manner, by that very reason that I don't expect very shining ones. Lake Champlain is very cold for producing the least bit of laurels, and if I am neither drawned neither starv'd I'l be as proud as if I had gained two battles...I fancy Mr Duer will be with Mr. Cannway sooner than he had told me. They'l perhaps conquer Canada before my arrival, and I expect to meet them at the governor's house in Quebec...Could I believe one single instant that this pompous command of a northern army will let your excellency forget a little an absent friend, then I would send the project to the place it comes from. But I dare hope that you will remember me sometimes...It is a very melancholy idea for me that I ca'nt follow your fortune as near your person as I could wish-but my heart will take very sincerely his part of everything which can happen to you. [6]

My companions feel the biting cold on the four hundred miles north; they wrap themselves in woolen blankets to try and keep warm. We travel slowly, sometimes drenched by rain, sometimes blanketed by snow. The wild, wintry landscape and meeting Americans both enthrall me. I talk to them; I observe; I even take notes despite our hurried trek, so that I can write more later. Their manners and way of life impress me. Their spirit seems wholly republican. Their freedom is exciting. I am particularly interested that they have no arranged marriages; they marry for love and not at such a young age, as is our custom.

Congress has instructed me to visit the government of New York State, so I meet Governor George Clinton at Poughkeepsie. He looks at my orders, but like Washington, makes no comment.

"I will ensure you are helped by army officers in Albany," he says.

We stop briefly at Livingston Manor to see James Duane, a New York congressman, then hasten in sleighs along the bank of the North River.[7]

February 17. We reach the old Dutch and German township of Albany, called Willemstadt until its name was changed to commemorate James, Duke of York and Albany, snowdrifts rearing high along the sides of crooked, winding streets and against wooden, Dutch-style buildings, long icicles festooning windowsills and gables.

I find that Conway only arrived three days ago; he appears active and looks as though he has good intentions, although I am not convinced.

"The expedition is quite impossible. I ordered the regiment commanders to provide the numbers of men fit for marching and they fall far short of what the Board of War expected. The men are destitute of every article necessary for a long and severe march. Colonel Hazen has procured some clothing from Boston, but it is not sufficient. There is a general claim and a dissatisfaction here for want of money. The men have not been paid for five months," he tells me.[8]

I do not believe him. I investigate. After two days I discover he is telling the truth and that this is an ill-devised operation. The Board of War promised two thousand five hundred soldiers at a low estimate, but I cannot find twelve hundred fit for duty and most of these would be too naked even for a summer campaign. Colonel Hazen has managed to ensure some clothes from Boston, but it is nowhere near enough. There also appears to be almost eight hundred thousand dollars due to the Continental troops, some militia, the quartermaster's department and others. I have been promised four hundred thousand dollars to undertake the expedition but so far only two hundred thousand have arrived. A deserter describes the enemy as being much stronger than I thought and there appears to be no straw upon the vessels to burn them.[9]

Gates had told me General Stark will have burnt the fleet before my arrival. The first letter I receive here is from General Stark: 'What number of men, from whence, for what rendezvous, I desire him to raise?'[10]

'I would have done something if I had received money,' writes Colonel Biveld, who was also to join our force.[11]

I beg at every door I can think of.[12] We have not an hour to lose and even if we had everything ready it is now rather too late.

General Arnold, General Lincoln and General Schuyler have all written before my arrival to Conway and they all say that in our present circumstances there is now no possibility to begin an enterprise into Canada.[13] General Arnold, who, like Lincoln, is recovering from his injuries, calls Gates the greatest poltroon in the world.[14]

I visit General Schuyler in his imposing two-story, red-brick mansion in a horse chestnut grove on a steep bluff overlooking the river about a mile from the town. A tall, thin man with an aquiline nose and an aristocratic manner, he moves somewhat stiffly, as though from rheumatism. I dine with him and his wife, Catherine; afterwards, as we drink a glass of Madeira, I show him my orders.

He reads them, his dark eyes alive with interest. "It is a similar plan of attack to that which I recommended to General Washington last November. Someone else at Congress now wishes to claim the honor, I presume," he comments sharply.

It is evident there will be no invasion into Canada. I have been misled. I have been duped.

I write to Laurens:

I intend to wrait to you as the president of Congress but now I will explain my heart to my friend, and let him know which hell of blunders, madness and deception I am involved in...You will find by my letter to Congress how much I had been deceived, and neither words of honor, neither wraiting assurances, my travel to York, my conversations etc. have been able to prevent what I was much affraid of, it is my being sent with a great noise, a schining apparat. For what? For nothing at all. You will condemn, I am sure, Gal. Stark's conduct, but you will be more surprised that Gal. Gates seems not so well acquainted with the northern department as myself who am here since two days...What is your opinion, Sir, about my present situation? Do you think I now have no doubt it is a very pleasant one? How schall I do to get off from a precipice where I embarked myself out of my love for your country, my desire of distinguishing myself in doing good to America, and that so false opinion that there was in all the board of war some feeble light of virtue or common sense? My situation is such that I am reduced to wish to have never put the foot in America or thought of an American war. All the continent knows where I am, what I am sent for, I have wrote it though the whole France and Europe (as I had been expressly desired)...Men will have a right to laugh at me, and I'l be almost ashamed to appear before some...I'l publish my instructions with notes through the world and I'l loose rather the honor of twenty Gatess and twenty boards of war, than to let my own reputation be hurted in the least thing.

I was very glad and quiete with my division, but now, sir, as by the impulsion of many in and about Congress I have vrote to my friends that I had the command of an army, an army must be given to me at the head of which I could do some thing to throw a schade upon this very desagreable part of my military life- unless leave should be granted to me to go and laugh in France of the niew military american ministry of war...I can not give up all ideas of penetrating into Canada, but I give up this of Going there this winter upon the ice...You know that the whole expedition has been put on foot to satisfy one single Man's ambition...There is a project which could make honor to myself good to the country...it is if I was directed to go with a part of the northern forces which I could then command to defend the north River or attak Niew York... [15]

The same day I also write to Washington:

Why am I so far from you and what business had that board of war to hurry me through the ice and snow without knowing what I should do, neither what they were doing themselves?' I tell him what has happened and that I am very distressed by this disappointment. I say that I am afraid it will reflect on my reputation and I shall be laughed at. 'My fears upon that subject are so strong that I would choose to become again only a volunteer, unless Congress offers the means of mending this ugly business by some glorious operation. General Arnold seems very fond of a diversion upon New York and he is too sick to take the field before four or five months. I should be happy if something was proposed to me in that way, but I will never ask, nor even seem desirous, of anything directly from Congress. [16]

February 20. I write to President Laurens of Congress and enclose a report of Conway on the situation indicating that the general officers near to Albany all believe that an invasion into Canada would not only be very hazardous but also extremely imprudent.[17] I also enclose other papers including a letter from the Committee of Albany and various letters to Conway concerning the expedition:

> You will see very plainly that if proper orders, proper money had been sent some time ago we could have been able to carry the expedition, but the time is now too schort...What my perhaps too quick and too warm heart must feel after being so deceived, every sensible man must have some idea of. What can be done for me in this occasion I leave to the own feeling of the honorable Congress. It is in expecting theyr niew instructions for what I am to do and to be that I have the honor to be...[18]

I also write a short letter to Gates. I refer him to my letter to Congress: 'I am sorry that a so displeasant affair came through your hands, but I am not in any doubt that you were fully convinced of everything you induced me to build my hopes upon.'[19]

I am busy paying debts. Every department is after me for money.[20] I have only received $200,000, which I thought was intended for the expedition, although it was later said to be for the department, but it is spent almost immediately on the debts I consider most pressing. I give leave to everyone in the public departments to borrow on my private credit to pay the debts.[21] I send six months' provisions to Fort Schuyler. I hurry the sending for the cannon at Ticonderoga which will be mended as fast as possible and will be needed for the defense of the North River. [22] I divide the army into twenty troops of sixty men with one officer to train and drill each one. I make frequent reviews, buy uniforms and equipment.

Congress has decided that a new oath of allegiance should be taken by civil and military officers and so I have forms printed in Poughkeepsie with the words: 'An acknowledgment of the independence, liberty and sovereignty of the United States; an eternal renunciation of George 111, his successors and heirs and every King of England; a promise to defend the said states against the said George 111.'[23]

On February 25, de Kalb arrives.[24] He is now the second-in-command.

"He is my subordinate in the French army. It is not right that he should be given a superior rank to mine. There is a cabal being conducted against me," says Conway angrily.[25]

I nearly laugh at his words, enjoying seeing the Irishman, as now I always think of him, suffer a taste of the medicine he had been trying to give our commander-in-chief.

General Gates still has the title and authority of commander-in-chief of the northern department. I suspect he wants me to be gone and for Conway to be put immediately under him. However, Conway seems more polite with me than with most. He is gay and very certain of himself and I believe he hopes I will return to France after this disappointment and then he will be master of the field.[26]

General Schuyler visits. "I am one of the commissioners appointed by Congress to work with the New York tribes. There will be a convention of the Six Nations soon, at Johnson Town, to discuss a new treaty. The Senecas, Cayugas, Oneidas, Onondagas, Mohawks and Tuscaroras will all, hopefully, be there. They have always held French people in high esteem, and I think it would be helpful if you and other Frenchmen could attend."

"If I can return in five days I would be delighted to come," I tell him.

Shortly after his visit we receive an anonymous letter at the end of February. The writer says he has been enlisted to help burn the town and vessels of Albany, that many townsfolk are to be killed by their negroes. Several names are mentioned. Next morning, I have them all arrested but nothing is discovered, and the committee tells me to dismiss them.[27] Another plot is alleged by a British deserter serving in the American army. I travel to Schenectady where he is being held. I meet with Conway, and we spend nearly a part of a night interviewing our informant, a very short man with a pock-marked face, whose clothes smell strongly of the local beer.

"Major Carleton, the nephew of Sir Guy Carleton, the commander of the British forces in Canada, is rumored to be making preparations for the insurrection," he says. "He is in disguise here at Schenectady and is preparing for an uprising to burn, destroy and murder."

I dispatch soldiers to the houses where he thinks provisions and munitions are being stored.[28] Nothing is again discovered. I order a court martial of the man.[29]

I decide that these allegations mean it is clearly very important to meet with the Six Nations; I leave de Kalb in command and hurriedly set off from Schenectady with Conway and other French officers to attend the pow-wow in Johnson Town.

February 28. We speed in sleighs along the banks of the Mohawk River, the ice cracking and creaking beneath the horses' hooves and the runners of the sleigh, our breath making clouds of moisture in the air. The hilly countryside is wild and uninhabited; we keep vigilant for any attack.

The evening sky is darkening. On our west are wooded hills; directly ahead is the small cluster of houses of Johnson Town. Our sleigh draws near to hundreds of Native Americans, their bodies peacock-like against the white snow. Despite the cold, many are almost naked. The men are large and muscular, their brown skin decorated with paint and feathers, their hair cut close with a lock in the center,[30] their ears pierced, their noses bejeweled. The women have long black hair, sometimes braided, and several are wearing beaded headdresses.

We stop in front of an elegant, two-story house flanked by two masonry blockhouses.[31] We disembark from our sleighs; the Native Americans surround us, touching our clothes and hair. We are quickly taken into Johnson Hall, a house made completely of wood but fashioned to resemble stone, and greet the three commissioners, Schuyler, Duane and Douw.

The Senecas are not here. There are a few Mohawks and Cayugas, but most are Oneidas, Tuscaroras, and about one hundred Onondagas. There are only about four hundred Mohawks now in existence and they live in the east of the tribal lands, surrounded by forty thousand New Yorkers in Albany and Tryon Counties. They therefore greatly fear their expansion into their territory and support the British who they think will treat them better. They are led by Joseph Brant, whose tribal name is Thayendaneagea and who is the brother of Molly Brant, also known as Konwatsiatsiaienni, who was the wife of William Johnson, the former commissioner for the Crown. He built Johnson Hall where we are staying, which is at the junction of six Native American trails, and which was later owned by John Johnson who fled to Canada when General Schuyler came to arrest him. Joseph Brant used to live here and has even visited King George. His volunteers, composed of Mohawks and Loyalists, have been causing mayhem in the countryside by taking cattle, horses and supplies and making people declare for Britain or leave the area. The Mohawks and the British are therefore very closely linked, and this is the first time in hundreds of years that the Six Nations, the Iroquois, have been divided.

Several days pass. I write to Peter Gansevoort, the commanding officer at Fort Schuyler and ask him to try every exertion in his power to apprehend Carleton who evidently dresses in native clothes, has painted his face, wears a ring in his nose and has had his body decorated. I beg

Gansevoort to prevent his escape by any means. 'You may promise in my name fifty guineas hard money besides every money etc. they can find about Carleton, to any party of soldiers or Indians who will bring him alive.'[32]

On March 9 we assemble in Johnson Hall for the pow-wow. The warriors and their chiefs, the sachem, all very colorfully painted and dressed, with feathers, jewels, shells and bones adorning ears, noses and various parts of their body, sit at one side on benches by the door. We sit opposite, rather more drably dressed, whilst in the middle is the missionary, Samuel Kirkland.

Schuyler rises to his feet to give the speech agreed in December by Congress. "Brothers, sachems and warriors of the Six Nations. The great council of the United States call now for your attention…far from desiring you to hazard your lives in our quarrel, we advised you to sit still in ease and peace…Why have you listened to the voice of our enemies? Is this a suitable return for our love and kindness? Or did you suspect that we were too weak or too cowardly to defend our country; and join our enemies that you might come in for a share of the plunder? What has been gained by this unprovoked treachery? What but shame and disgrace…Brothers, Cayugas, Senecas, Tuscaroras, Mohawks!… We do not desire to destroy you…it is still our wish to bury the hatchet and and wipe away the blood which some of you have so unjustly shed.

Brothers, Oneidas and Onondagas. It rejoices our hearts that we have no reason to reproach you in common with the rest of the Six Nations… You have kept fast hold of the ancient covenant- chain…while the sun and the moon continue to give light to the world, we shall love and respect you. As our trusty friends, we shall protect you and shall at all times consider your welfare as our own

Brothers, of the Six Nations…Remember that our cause is just…Let us, who are born on the same great continent, love one another. Our interest is the same and we ought to be one people, always ready to assist and serve each other…"[33] Schuyler talks slowly, an interpreter translating into the different languages. He finishes his speech. He looks at me. "The great French father across the waters has seen the righteousness of our cause and has sent his young men armed with the weapons of war. A soldier of the French father, the marquis de Lafayette, desires to speak to his Iroquois brothers."

I stand up proudly and confidently. I represent France and the French king.

"I am a soldier for the father of the Canadas. He wants me to tell you he remembers his Iroquois children. He gives you gifts for your young and old and your warriors. The British make many promises but do not keep them. The French father has always loved his Iroquois children and has never broken his promises. The British promise that you may live at peace but then bring armies and death to your valleys.

Now is the time for the Iroquois Confederacy to stand up. By these belts of wampum the French father asks you to join him in this fight. Let us stand together against the redcoat and let us clear the path between your hearths and mine. This I say in the name of my father in France." The interpreter translates my words.

The Onondaga chief speaks for the guilty tribes and blames the headstrong warriors. On the second day of the pow-wow, the Oneida chief, Odatshedeh,[34] also known as Grasshopper, stands up. He speaks slowly with dignity, his words calm. He regrets the actions of the other Iroquois in supporting the British and believes they will destroy themselves. "I, Odatshedeh, Chief of the Oneida, do take this young man and give him the name Kayewla, and adopt him into our nation. By these strings the Oneidas and the Tuscaroras will stand with you at every hazard. We honor our French father by holding fast the Covenant Chain with the United States. With our American brothers we will enjoy the same fruits of victory and peace or be buried in the same grave."

He says he wants a fort built and a small garrison provided. He also criticizes the younger Oneida warriors. "Formerly the sachems were instantly obeyed by the warriors but now they have thrown off all regard to their council…Brother Warriors reflect for a moment that at a future day your locks will be silvered by age and then…will you deplore the neglect which your Elders now experience from you."[35]

I give a medallion to him. I distribute gifts of woolen blankets, small mirrors, écus of six francs that they want because they have the image of the king of France, whom they call their grandfather, colors to paint their skin, ball and powder, and rum.[36] Everyone becomes very excited, particularly with the fire water and the coins and the conversation becomes very lively under a thick haze of blue smoke from the peace pipes.

Grasshopper speaks gravely to me. "The French have always been our allies. My people, the Oneida, fought at Oriskany and Saratoga. We will fight for you, Kayewla, like a bear fights for cubs. We are fearless. We move like strong winds from trees, and hills and swamps, with our tomahawks, arrows and long carabines. We show no mercy, like crazy buffalo stampede."

I would like to embrace him, but restrain myself, not wishing to offend. "You will help us win and drive the British from the land."

The old men, whilst smoking, talk politics extremely well. Their objective seems to be to promote a balance of power, if the intoxication of rum, like that of ambition in Europe, had not often turned them aside from it.[37] An elderly man tries to talk to me in French.[38] His name is Lafleur and he is a former French soldier from the army of the marquis de Montcalm, but he has lived so long with the tribes he has almost forgotten how to speak his language. He proudly shows off his plumes and body paint to me. "I have never had my ears cut though, which is the sign of a warrior."[39]

A treaty is finally agreed. Drums resembling a keg covered with skin beat heavily and rhythmically.[40] The warriors whoop and scream. Someone curses softly, probably Pontgibaud.

When the tribes have departed, we drink toasts. Duane's opinion is that we can expect nothing but revenge from the Senecas, Cayugas and most of the Mohawks for their lost friends and tarnished glory.[41] It is possible that all these tribes will soon be on the warpath against us again. The Mohawks and Cayugas have already declared for the British.[42]

I learn the garrison at Johnson Town has not been paid for a long time and I decide to pay them out of my own pocket. Then I and my fellow Frenchmen speed in sleighs again along the Mohawk's snow-bound banks.

"Europe's beggars seem less disgusting than America's savages," is Pontgibaud's opinion.[43]

At Albany I rush round in my usual fashion, as busy as a bee in a barrel of tar, as the Americans say. Major Brice gives me dispatches he has brought from Congress and the Board of War. I read with pleasure that Congress gives me its approbation for my conduct here. They believe the Canadian enterprise is not possible and should be abandoned. Congress resolves they entertain a high sense of my prudence, activity and zeal and 'that they are fully persuaded nothing has or would have been wanting on his part, or on the part of his officers who accompanied him, to give the expedition the utmost possible effect.[44] Gates tells me that a new arrangement will be made for the general officers in this part of the continent, which I understand to mean that de Kalb and I will leave Conway the chief command of the troops.[45]

Conway enters my room; I angrily show him the letter. I watch him as he reads it.

"I am innocent of this," he protests.[46]

I am even more convinced of his guilt and write to President Laurens of Congress:

In my country we hold a particular military command as an honourable mark of confidence- that if I am recalled to leave this command in the hands of a gentleman who comes from Europe as well as myself, who is not above me neither by birth, neither by his relations or influence in the world, who has not had any more particular occasion of distinguishing himself than I have had, who has not the advantages I can glory myself in, of being born a Frenchman, I will look upon myself as not only ill used but very near being affronted,- and such will be the sentiment of all those of my nation and Europe, whose opinion is dear to me. I am very far from making complaints-but as I hope Congress returns me some of the warm attachement I have schowed for theyr country, they will permit and approuve my going to France immediately. I am sorry that this going away will take off from the army many French officers more useful than myself, but I should be very ungrateful for General de Kalb, Gal. Portail and the engineers, the Mqs. De La Rouerie and almost all the French officers now in the Continental army, was I to refuse theyr instances for following me in my going over to France. I suggest that if General Putnam is leaving the service, I would find Fishkill to be a very agreeable command which would be nearer to Washington to receive his orders. [47]

I also write a personal letter to Laurens; I mention again that the post at Fishkill would make me very happy. I express my hope that 'those noises of truce and peace are groundless. Schall I see the name of Laurens at the end of such a convention when this of Henkock was at the end of the declaration of independency?'[48]

I arrange that Lieutenant Colonel de Gouvion, accompanied by Captain Tousard and Captain Céleron, all engineers, will supervise the building by militia from Tryon County of a small fort at Kanonwalohale for the Oneidas. Washington has said he would like Oneida warriors to come to Valley Forge to help resist British raids and act as scouts; I hope to persuade them by using 'love of French blood mixed with the love of French louis d'or.'[49]

'I will bring down to your excellency some scalping gentlemen for dressing the fine hair of the Howe,' I tell Washington.[50] Gouvion will accompany them to headquarters. They will carry provisions of corn and a woman, Polly Cooper, will be with them to show our soldiers how to prepare it.

I supervise an exchange of the English sick and wounded. I also write to Washington: 'Do'nt your excellency think that I could recruit a little in General Greene's division, now that he is quarter master general?'[51]

A southerly wind replaces the freezing north easterly, melting the thick snow quilting the ground so quickly that torrents of water flood the countryside and roads.

A skirmish takes place between twenty American scouts and forty-five British and Native Americans near Bennington, in Vermont. We kill five men, take six prisoners and fourteen stands of arms. I long to have been there but have to be content with writing to Washington about it.

March 31. I set off to Valley Forge, the sun shining weakly, filtering down through forests where birds sing and animals liberated from hibernation run through the undergrowth. Albany was the defeat of my plan to lead an invasion of Canada, but I believe I have extricated myself without the ruin of my honor; I have also been useful to the army in the region. I have won over some of the tribes. I have attempted to stop uprisings. I have defended and supported Washington in the conspiracy against him and neither he nor I have been destroyed by Gates, Conway and their cronies.

I hurry south. I call on Governor Clinton, then on General McDougal. In less than a week I arrive at Bethlehem; I meet de Kalb at the Sun Tavern.

"I wish to go back to France. I want my patron to recall me. I intend to go to Lancaster and York to ask Congress to release me," he says.

I visit the Boeckel family house by the farmland, no longer limping and unable to wear a boot. I talk of the tribes and the pow-wow and spend several days enjoying the quiet tranquility of their religious life and the kindness of their welcome.

I say farewell. I ride away to return to my general and my military destiny. On April 8 I reach Valley Forge.

Chapter 17

Treaty of alliance with France

Spring sunshine warms the trees and huts, dispersing the stench which gathers in the evening. I learn that conditions had worsened here after my departure for Albany. Food had become even more scarce, inoculations against smallpox had killed many and there had been more amputations of men's limbs and more deaths. Now, however, the situation has greatly improved as General Greene is quartermaster although he was not pleased to be given the post as he said there has never been a famous quartermaster in the history of warfare. General Wayne has obtained cattle and farmers are selling vegetables in the camp. General Lee has also been released from British captivity and exchanged for Major General Prescott, to the delight of Washington who ordered the greatest preparations made for his reception. He rode four miles on the road to Philadelphia with his principal officers to meet him and welcomed him as a brother. The army was assembled at Valley Forge with a band playing; in the evening there was an elegant dinner with music. Next morning, Washington very unusually even delayed his breakfast to wait for Lee, who had been with a woman he had brought from Philadelphia and who came downstairs late, looking as dirty as if he had been in the street all night.[1] He stayed two days. Then he left and is returning in May.

At the center of the camp, on the large parade ground, a voice is loudly shouting commands in German and French. The new Prussian inspector general, Baron von Steuben, a very stout man, with a military bearing, mounted on a horse with magnificent trappings and two enormous pistol holsters on either side of the saddle, drills a group of men as a small greyhound wanders backwards and forwards.

He has achieved an incredible transformation of the army since his arrival in late February. He has trained the soldiers to march and turn in formation and how to change from line to column and then back to line. He is compiling his Blue Book, a manual for infantry drilling and marching, which Hamilton is translating from French. He has also brought about reforms such as having latrines dug at least three hundred feet from the huts and filled in after four days.[2]

Washington has given me responsibility for foreign matters, and I constantly write to France to persuade people of influence to support the American cause. I am doing everything I can think of to draw our two countries together. I continue to beg Congress for commissions for French officers and endeavor to aid Pulaski and Armand in organizing cavalry corps of Frenchmen and Hessian deserters. I would prefer, however, to be more active. I also long for home. It seems a long time since I received a letter from my family. It grieves me, but I do not worry. My anxiety focuses mainly on the recent arrival in New York of a draft of the Conciliatory Bills of the British Prime Minister, Lord North, in which he proposed to Parliament a reconciliation of the dispute between Britain and the American states.[3] The terms he suggests would perhaps have been accepted at the beginning of the war but now I am hopeful it would be unthinkable for most people to revert to a colony. Governor Tryon in New York has had copies widely distributed in the country. They were even dispatched to Washington who sent them to Congress with the words:

Nothing short of independence, it appears to me, can possibly do. A peace on other terms would if I may be allowed the expression be a peace of war. The injuries we have received from the British have been so unprovoked and have been so great and so many, that they can never be forgotten. Besides the feuds, the jalousies, the animosities, that would ever attend a union with them; besides the importance, the advantages which we should derive from an unrestricted commerce; our fidelity as a people, our gratitude, our character as men, are opposed to a coalition with them as subjects, but in case of the last extremity. Were we easily to accede to terms of dependence, no nation, upon future occasions, let the oppressions of Britain be ever so flagrant and unjust, would either pose for our relief; or at most they would do it with a cautious reluctance, and upon conditions most probably that would be hard, if not dishonorable to us. [4]

I know that British commissioners are sailing across the Atlantic to try and agree a reconciliation with Congress. I write to Laurens to alert him to the danger posed by Lord North's proposals:

He can't fight us out but hopes to negotiate us out of our rights, he wants to make friends to the government by foolish hopes...If he sincerely wants peace upon such terms as anyone can accept without without ruin and personal as well as national dishonor let him withdraw his troops and treat afterwards. [5]

On April 20, Washington writes to all the general officers on duty at Valley Forge: 'There seem to be but three general plans of operation which may be premeditated for the next campaign; one, the attempting to recover Philadelphia and destroy the enemy's army there; another, the endeavoring to transfer the war to the northward by an enterprise against New York; and a third, remaining quietly in a secure, fortified camp, disciplining and arranging the army till the enemy begin their operations – and then to govern ourselves accordingly. Which of these three plans shall we adopt?'[6]

On April 22, Congress decides unanimously that the terms offered by the North bills are completely inadequate and that no advances by the British government for peace would be met unless they first either withdraw their armies and fleets or acknowledge unequivocally the independence of the United States.

We all reply in writing to Washington's proposals. Maxwell, Wayne and Paterson want an attempt made on Philadelphia. Varnum, Poor, Muhlenberg and Knox agree with the second suggestion and want to advance across New Jersey and attack New York. Stirling wishes to try both these plans. Von Steuben and Duportail do not want to attack the enemy at this time but to continue to arm, equip and train the army so that success is more certain. Nathanael Greene has a different opinion. He wants four thousand men to march rapidly to New York, to join there with the New England militia. Washington would lead this division whilst Lee remains in command of the main army at Valley Forge.[7] I write that I consider the taking of Philadelphia the best scheme if it can be carried with success.[8]

Washington deliberates on our answers. He decides to remain at Valley Forge for the moment and see what the British do.

I receive permission to accompany American commissioners to Germantown who will meet with British commissioners to arrange an exchange of prisoners. I know that Captain Fitzpatrick, whom I met in England, will be there and I want to see him.

We greet each other with delight. We are both unarmed, a new experience.

"How did it happen that you left France and have chosen such bad company in America?" he asks.

"I do not know how I can ever return to France and join my frivolous countrymen and leave General Washington," I reply. "I do not know how I could bear the loss."[9]

He agrees to take a short letter to Adrienne for me which he will send from England. I quickly write and give it to my kind friend. Then we part.

May 1. I am summoned to headquarters and join the officers already waiting there. Washington enters. "I have received a letter of great importance from Mr. Simeon Deane." He proceeds to read it. "We have now the great satisfaction of acquainting you and the Congress that the treaties with France are at length completed and signed. The first is a treaty of amity and commerce...the other is a treaty of alliance, in which it is stipulated that in case England declares war against France...we should then make common cause of it and join our forces and councils etc. The great aim of this treaty is declared to be 'to establish liberty, sovereignty, and independency, absolute and unlimited, of the United States, as well in matters of government as commerce;' and this is guaranteed to us by France. The preparations for war are carried on with immense activity and it is soon expected. This treaty was signed on February 6 with His Majesty Louis XVl."[10] He looks at us. "This news affords me the most sensible pleasure," he says gravely.

A hubbub breaks out. Everyone cheers and shouts. Tears pour down my cheeks. I am ecstatic with happiness. I rush to Washington. I abandon military protocol. I throw my arms round him and kiss him on both cheeks.[11] For a moment he appears surprised but looks as though he is nearly crying for joy.

Shortly after, I write to President Laurens to present my sincere felicitations to Congress.[12] I also write a personal letter to him: 'Houza, my good friend, now the affair is over, and a very good treaty will assure our noble independence.'[13]

In the distance are shouts and cheers as men learn of the hope France has given them. I wrap my white Bourbon scarf round me and join the festivities where a hastily constructed huge bonfire is flaming and smoking into the blackening sky. I lead a march of French officers and the soldiers cheer.

Simeon Deane arrives in camp. A plump, dark-haired man, he resembles his brother. I ask about my wife.

"When the treaty was announced, my brother, Dr. Franklin and Mr. Adams, were presented to the king and the royal family. Then they went immediately to the marquise de Lafayette who was at Versailles that day and thanked her for the help you have given our cause."

He gives me letters from Europe.[14] I happily open a letter from Adrienne expecting news about the treaty and Versailles. Instead, I read the words in disbelief. My heart freezes to ice. My beloved Henriette died seven months ago. I tell no one. I make my way in misery back to my hut.

May 6. Today there will be a celebration in honor of the treaty with France which was ratified by Congress on May 4, and the army's survival from its winter hell. De Kalb and I visit Washington at his house in the early morning.

"Your Excellency," says de Kalb. "We are here to plead for the life of the Frenchman sentenced to death by court martial."

"We ask for mercy. I know you rarely intervene in the decisions of a court martial, but, in this case, now that France will support the United States in its struggle for independence and French blood will be spilled in your cause, I beg you to overturn the sentence for the young man," I ask.

He reflects for a few moments. "This day is dedicated to our gratitude to the king of France. I can refuse French officers nothing. I agree to your request. I pardon him and he can return to the ranks. I will also set free all the men in the camp's prison," he replies.[15]

We thank him; we hurriedly go to tell the soldier.

At nine o'clock a cannon roars. The brigades muster in the bright sunshine under a cloudless blue sky. The chaplains read out the announcement of the alliance contained in the postscript to the *Pennsylvania Gazette* of the second. Then come prayers and a Thanksgiving sermon, the American *Te Deum*, to each brigade.[16] My Virginians stand in reverential silence, as does the whole army.

At ten-thirty the cannon again boom across the valley. Washington, on his gray horse, rides to a low knoll and waits there with Greene and other officers not on duty for the review to begin. Brigade inspectors inspect the uniforms and arms of each brigade. The battalions form. Brigadiers and commandants appoint field officers to command them.

"Load and ground your arms!"

At eleven-thirty another cannon fires, the signal for the march. In sunshine, under a cloudless sky. The brigades wheel to the right by platoons and proceed by the nearest way to the left of their ground in the new position which the brigade inspectors point out. Ten thousand soldiers march and parade in well-drilled precision under the gaze of von Steuben, his hair powdered, the Star of the Order of Fidelity on his chest. I command on the left flank, wearing my white Bourbon scarf, surrounded by all the Frenchmen; de Kalb commands the second line; Stirling, the right. We advance in five columns towards Washington.

A third cannon fires, followed by thirteen cannon firing in succession, one for each of the states. Then each man in a long line in each company fires a single musket shot in succession from right to left, then left to right, a feu de joie beginning at Woodford's division. A rolling, thunderous noise echoes across Valley Forge, its smoke drifting across the valley.

Another cannon roars out. "Long live the king of France!" the men huzza.

The cannons again fire thirteen times. Once more the feu de joie erupts.

"Long live the friendly Powers of Europe," the men huzza.

The feu de joie fires again.[17]

"Huzza! Prosperity to the American states!" the men shout, as Washington looks on with an expression of the utmost delight.

The army return to their brigade parades and are dismissed. They go back to their huts and celebrate with an allowance of brandy. The officers march arm-in-arm, thirteen abreast, and they, their wives and visitors, go to dine on tables under canopies of tent cloth stretched on poles in the open air. In the center, in marquees, are the guests, the higher-ranking officers, and the ladies who have been here at Valley Forge during the harsh winter months, Mrs. Washington, Mrs. Greene, Lady Stirling and her daughter, Lady Kitty. Fifteen hundred people toast France and its king, and America and its revolution. The band plays patriotic and martial tunes. We eat and drink a profusion of fat meats, strong wines and other liquors.[18] We sing.

Washington rises to depart, and everyone rises as well, clapping, shouting loud huzzas and throwing hats into the air while he rides about one quarter of a mile. Then he and his suite turn around.

"Huzza!" they shout several times.

We continue our festivities until the sky is black, although Washington is cautious, as always. He orders patrols to be increased around the camp, in case of attack, as he had himself done on Christmas night, 1776.

A British spy was seized during the celebrations.

"What shall we do with him?" asks the officer on duty.

"Let him go back and tell his employers what he has seen. Twill pain them far more than to hear of his detection and death," is the reply.[19]

Chapter 18

Thwarts Howe's dinner hopes at Barren Hill

On May 7 the British attack ships and houses at Bordentown, New Jersey. Six hundred men in two galleys and several flat boats burn or sink two frigates, nine large ships, three privateers, brigantines and some sloops and schooners. They burn a store house and several residences.

The same day Washington orders General Maxwell to leave the main army and march with his New Jersey brigade to Bristol and Dunk's Ferry and then cross the Delaware to Burlington to meet up with Colonel Shrew's Regiment at Mount Holly. Maxwell must harass the British if they decide to go to New York through New Jersey. At noon it is raining heavily; the order is given for the troops to set off tomorrow. The rest of the army is placed under marching orders.

Reports arrive: 'Two hundred transport vessels are sailing.'

"It is possible the British are intending to evacuate Rhode Island and move the troops from there to New York and then perhaps to operate along the North River or reinforce Philadelphia, in which case the army at Valley Forge needs to be strengthened," says Washington.[1]

On May 8 Washington convenes a council of war.[2] I attend, as well as Generals Gates, Greene, Stirling, Mifflin, de Kalb, Armstrong and Steuben, and Brigadier Generals Knox and du Portail.

"The British are thought to have more than sixteen thousand men. About ten thousand of these are in Philadelphia, about two thousand in Rhode Island and four thousand in New York. Our Continental troops number about eleven thousand eight hundred, including those who are ill. With the detachments at Wilmington and on the North River and reinforcements we might reasonably count on having about twenty thousand. Therefore, I request the council to decide what measures it is best to take."

Everyone expresses their views; the final decision of the council is unanimous.

Washington declares: "The line of conduct most consistent with sound policy and best suited to promote the interests and safety of the United States is to remain on the defensive and wait events and not attempt any offensive operation against the enemy till circumstances should afford a fairer opportunity of striking a successful blow. As the enemy are strongly fortified by nature and by artificial works in all their positions it would require a greatly superior force to attack them with any hope of a favorable outcome. To take Philadelphia by force is impracticable and thirty thousand men would be needed for a blockade. The Continentals would not be so much increased by the militia. There are strong objections existing against offensive movements. It is best to wait at Valley Forge for the moment and see the development of the enemy's plans."[3]

On May 12, at eleven o'clock, at headquarters, the officers swear the new oath of allegiance demanded by Congress on February 3. Lee is not present, as he is at York. I have already supervised the oath-taking at Albany; now I officiate again in my division for over a week. It is a surprise to me that a twenty-year old Frenchman should be doing this, but I very much appreciate it.

Twenty-six officers in Woodford's brigade take the oath but complain that their patriotism is being questioned and that as each officer's rank is inscribed on the certificate it might fix their ranks for the future.

I write to Washington: 'I have taken the oath of the gentlemen officers in General Woodford's brigade...and want only to let their beloved general know which were the reasons of their being rather reluctant...to an oath, the meaning and spirit of which was, I believe, misunderstood by them.'[4]

He replies: 'Thank you much for the cautious delicacy used in communicating the matter to me...The oath is perfectly consistent with the professions, actions, and implied engagements of every officer...the objection founded on the supposed unsettled rank of the officers is of no validity...I have a regard for them all and cannot but regret that that they were ever engaged in the measure.' [5] His response ends their objections.

"Take two thousand four hundred men across the Schuylkill towards Philadelphia. Try to find out where the British are doing. Attack their rear if they retreat," Washington orders me, to my intense satisfaction and delight.

He talks to me at some length about my expedition and writes detailed instructions:

The detachment under your command, with which you will immediately march towards the enemy's lines, is designed to answer the following purposes; namely, to be a security to this camp, and a cover to the country between the Delaware and the Schuylkill, to interrupt the communication with Philadelphia, to obstruct the incursions of the enemy's parties, and to obtain intelligence of their motions and designs...You will endeavour to procure trusty and intelligent spies who will advise you faithfully of whatever may be passing in the city...A variety of concurring accounts make it probable that the enemy are preparing to evacuate Philadelphia; this is a point of the utmost importance to ascertain and if possible, the place of their future destination...Should you be able to gain certain intelligence of the time of their intended embarkation so that you may be able to take advantage of it and fall upon the rear of the enemy in the act of withdrawing it will be a very desirable event; but this will be a matter of no small difficulty and will require the greatest caution and prudence....You will remember that your detachment is a very valuable one, and that any accident happening to it would be a severe blow to this army. You will, therefore, use every precaution for its security and to guard against a surprise....in general, I would advise that a stationary post is unadvisable, as it gives the enemy an opportunity of knowing your situation and concerting plans successfully against you. In case of any offensive movement against this army, you will keep yourself in such a state as to have an easy communication with it and at the same time harass the enemy's advance. [6]

May 18. Near midnight, in darkness, I lead my little army out of camp, my force including a troop[7] of light horse under Captain Alan McClane, six hundred Pennsylvania militiamen commanded by General Potter, forty-seven of my Oneidas who arrived here recently, and five cannon. We cross the Schuylkill in silence at Swede's Ford. We march for about twelve miles along its eastern bank following the Ridge Road and reach the small hamlet at Barren Hill, about eleven miles from both armies. It is a very good defensive position, and we can reconnoiter in different directions. The hill is part of the ridge which separates the Schuylkill River from the country to the east which drains into the Delaware. It is a good height; we can see for miles. On the right is a steep, rocky ridge and the Schuylkill. In front of us is another ridge and, on our left, a small wood with several excellent stone houses at its edge. Down at the river there are three nearby fords, Swede's, Levening's and Matson's. There are also several roads on the hill. The Ridge Road goes to Philadelphia; to the east a road goes to White Marsh and Chestnut Hill;

another goes in a south-east direction to Germantown whilst on the west there is a road to Matson's Ford.

"Place the cannon at the front. General Porter take your six hundred militia to Whitemarsh to guard the junction of the two roads there so that the British cannot reach the crossroads and cut us off from Swede's and Matson's fords. Captain McLane take the Iroquois and the cavalry to guard the Ridge Road on the right flank. We can retreat across the river by any of the three fords and all the roads are guarded. We will wait the night here and try to find spies to go to Philadelphia to discover what is happening. My headquarters will be at the church and cemetery."

We stay here three days. In the early morning of May 20, I talk with a young lady, who on pretense of visiting her relations, has agreed to go to Philadelphia and spy for us. Suddenly Pontgibaud rushes in with a man.

"This is one of our surgeons. He met a militia captain who saw red coated dragoons passing his house at Whitemarsh today. He jumped out of a back window and ran as quickly as he could to us and says we should retreat across Matson's Ford."

"Return to your post," I tell the surgeon.

"I expect it is Potter's dragoons. Some of them are in red. It is best to see what is happening though. Ride there quickly," I say to Pontgibaud.[8]

He gallops out of camp and returns a short time later. "The surgeon is right. I saw the head of a column and came back immediately."

"Change the front. Move the troops back to the houses, church and cemetery," I order.

A scout arrives. "The British are on the road towards Swede's Ford."

"How can that be? Where is Potter's militia? It should be at Whitemarsh. If the British are there we can also be cut off from Matson's Ford."

Captain McLane arrives at a gallop. "The British dragoons are on Ridge Road. The Iroquois have climbed tall oaks and have seen a very large army with thousands of red coats, some purple and gold, as well as dragoons on horses. They captured two enemy soldiers who say their army is behind us."

"We are surrounded," the soldiers cry, milling round in panic, fear on their faces.

I rapidly climb the church tower; I see thousands of red coated grenadiers and dragoons who completely encircle our position for about two miles. I scramble down.

"Take your brigade down the road by the river past Spring Mill to get to Matson's Ford about three miles away. It is the only road not held by the British. Hurry because Grant is nearer to it than we are. Gimat will accompany you," I order General Poor.

"Go into the woods close to the British," I order the Oneida warriors and some of our troops. "Harass them as they approach. Make it look as though you are the heads of columns of our main force."

They run into the trees; not long after we hear firing and eerie war-whoops and yells. Three cannon fire in succession from Valley Forge, eleven miles away.

"Washington is warning us," says John Laurens. "He is observing what is happening through his spyglass."

"Set off to Matson's Ford," I order the rest of the men. They hurriedly rush down the wooded path; I follow; on the heights above we can see redcoated soldiers making their way towards the summit and the church. We reach the ford; most of the men are already on the opposite bank; others are crossing, chest or shoulder-high in the fast-flowing water, clinging on to each other to stop from being swept away, resembling corks bobbing on a fishing skein. Immediately the troops cross they form and prepare for action.[9] In the distance, the firing stops.

"Tell the last men to retreat from the church, the cemetery and woods," I order.

Not long after, they come rushing along the path; at Barren Hill there is shouting and musket fire from two directions. The British are shooting at each other.

Light cavalry suddenly appear riding along the path opposite. We fire at them, wounding or killing several, as well as their horses. The few soldiers left on the bank hastily throw themselves into the water; on our side the troops have already formed up. The cavalry wheel around and retreat.

During the afternoon the Oneida arrive in groups of three or four, whooping and hallooing like wild animals.[10] I march my force to Gulph Mills; we halt there until late evening and then spend the night in a wood.[11]

"The British have withdrawn to Chestnut Hill," my scouts inform me.

Next day we cross the Schuylkill again. We return to Barren Hill and stay the night. At dawn we go back to Swede's Ford and then to Valley Forge.

Washington appears very pleased to see both myself and my force. I recount the encounter; he listens intently, smiling when I describe the ruse of my soldiers in the woods pretending to be the heads of columns.

"Nine of our men were killed, including six of the Oneida, who fought very bravely. I cannot commend the men and officers highly enough."

Washington's opinion is that by my own dexterity or the enemy's want of it, my retreat had been soldier-like, orderly and well-conducted, that I had come off handsomely, whilst poor Grant has been loaded with obliquy.[12]

We hear that Admiral Lord Howe joined the army as a volunteer and that the English generals felt so certain of my capture that they sent several invitations to a fête at Philadelphia at which they said I would be present.[13] Fortunately, I managed to maneuver rather better than they did; I saved my whole corps and am not now a prisoner on a ship sailing to England.

"A large French fleet bringing four thousand troops will arrive in Delaware Bay by early July," announces Washington. My joy is immense.

It seems almost certain that the enemy intend to evacuate Philadelphia. Their baggage and stores are nearly, if not all, embarked on transports and most have been sent below the chevaux de frise.[14] We believe all their forces will meet at New York, but do not know whether they will depart from America or go up the North River. Greene's opinion is that many circumstances indicate they will leave America.[15] Washington thinks that appearances and a thousand circumstances suggest they will pass through the Jerseys to New York and that they will either march to Amboy or embark below the chevaux de frise.[16]

I receive a reply from the letter I wrote months earlier to the marquis de Bouillé. He approves of my plan and has written to Maurepas. I write to Congress and ask Laurens to give serious consideration to this proposal and suggest it as his own idea.[17] Congress, however, appreciates my zeal and goodwill for their cause, but does not pursue my scheme.

I also receive a letter from Conway who wants my help in obtaining a certificate of honorable service from Congress. I accordingly write to Laurens: 'You know my sentiments for some part of his life, which remain fixed in my mind But General Connway is an officer in the French service, a gentleman of bravery and talents and I ca'nt refuse to my own feelings to beg you would mention to Congress that I have wrote to you in his behalf. I do not believe they will deny some lines to him.'[18]

At the beginning of June, the three British commissioners, Carlisle, Eden and Johnstone who have sailed to the United States to promote North's peace proposals, arrive in Philadelphia, which might explain why the British have not yet evacuated the city. More than probably it will detain them there for a few days.[19]

Washington warns Congress that protection needs to be offered to the people of Philadelphia or hundreds, or even thousands of people, among whom are valuable artisans, with large quantities of goods, will be forced from the city, who would otherwise willingly remain. We hear that their reluctance and distress are scarcely to be paralleled.

June 9. The officers who had not renewed their oath of allegiance on May 12, do so. Lee is among them, as he had arrived in camp with his dogs from York on May 20. He is swearing the oath when he removes his hand from the Bible.

"Why have you done that?" asks Washington.

"As to King George, I am ready enough to absolve myself from all allegiance to him, but I have some scruples about the Prince of Wales," he replies.[20]

We all laugh. Even Washington smiles. As soon as there is silence, Lee again takes the oath of allegiance, this time with his hand on the Bible; no one remarks on what has happened. He has a sharp wit and can be very entertaining, but his turn of mind is caustic, and he is a strange man. His features are plain, his nose enormous, his whole appearance singular and unprepossessing;[21] a pack of dogs which he greatly cares about always accompany him.

June 10. The soldiers go into tents a mile in front of the hut encampment, leaving behind the unhealthy exhalations from mounds of carcasses and filth which have accumulated over six months.[22]

Sir Henry Clinton, whom I met at the opera in London, has replaced Howe. I write my opinion of him to Henry Laurens: 'He is a military pedant, somewhat blunderer and nothing more.'[23]

We believe the British are about to leave Philadelphia. Many of their troops are now in Jersey where they have thrown over a number of their horses and wagons.[24] On June 15 we learn from an informant whose mother is a laundress for the Carlisle commission, that the commissioners have asked for all their laundry to be returned to them immediately, clean or not. The same informant says that the troops still in the city are the Third Brigade composed of the Highlanders and two British regiments, some Hessians, the grenadiers and light infantry and the cavalry. Several houses have been burnt, as well as all the vessels on the stocks; the artillery park has only five field pieces and two howitzers; the horse tenders are at the wharves with slings and the *Vigilant* and some row galleys are at the upper end of the town to cover the passage of the troops. Orders have been given to the Third Brigade to be ready to march that morning at two o'clock. On the sixteenth, three deserters, one from the corps of grenadiers, confirm much of the intelligence we have received.[25]

Washington has sent Major General Dickinson to the Jerseys to assemble the militia there. He has recommended him to be in the most perfect readiness for the British as their march will be rapid when it commences. He has also suggested to him that the militia annoy, distress and really injure the enemy on their march, after having obstructed the roads as much as possible, that it is best they should act in very small groups as the enemy's guards in the front, flanks and rear must be exposed and therefore may be greatly injured by the concealed and well directed fire of men in ambush.[26]

General Gates had asked for reinforcements to guard the highlands on the North, but Washington had decided to keep the army together partly because the enemy had declared that before they left Pennsylvania they would attack Valley Forge and a weakening in our numbers might induce them to do so. He has also ordered magazines to be laid up to support the army if it marches either to Fishkill or to the lower parts of the North.[27]

Captain McLane, who is scouting near the city, sends a letter dated noon. He says that all the enemy's park of artillery has crossed the river; that the Highlanders were then crossing; that he had marched towards the enemy's redoubts, caused several to be manned, and exchanged a few shot with a party in front of them. He believes that Philadelphia will be completely evacuated tomorrow. [28]

I write to Adrienne:

Chance gives me, my beloved, an opportunity, although rather an uncertain one of writing to you…Several ships have sailed which have carried my letters. They will have renewed your pain by the addition of mine. How terrible it is to be so far from you. I have never so cruelly felt how horrible is this situation. My heart is afflicted with my own suffering and that of yours which I cannot share. The immense time that it took me to learn of what happened adds to the sorrow…The loss of our poor child is always in my thoughts…I learned at the same time of the loss of our little Adrien, whom I have always looked on as my own. I receive your news from M. de Cambrai and M. Carmichael…whom I wait for impatiently. I will have great pleasure in chatting with him and in talking about you…If the sadness that I received had arrived immediately I would have left to join you, but the news on May 1 of the treaty kept me here. The campaign which will commence does not let me leave, my heart has always been convinced that by serving the cause of humanity and of America, I am fighting for the cause of France. Embrace a million times our little Anastasie. Alas, she is all we now possess. My whole love is now focused on her. Adieu. I do not know when my letter will arrive, and I fear that it will not reach you. [29]

Chapter 19

British retreat through the Jerseys

June 17. The prevailing opinion is that one division of the enemy will march by way of Trenton and another by a lower road.[1] Washington calls a council of general officers at headquarters to discuss the situation and the likely march of the enemy through the Jerseys.

"I am against attacking the enemy," declares General Lee; most of the officers agree.

"The country must be protected; and if in doing so an engagement should become unavoidable, it would be necessary to fight," Greene declares.[2]

"I ask the following questions," says Washington: "Whether any enterprise ought to be taken against the enemy in their present circumstances? Whether the army should remain in the position it now holds, till the final occupation of the city, or move immediately towards the Delaware? Whether any detachment of it shall be sent to reinforce the brigade in the Jerseys or advanced towards the enemy to act as occasion shall require, and endeavor to take advantage of their retreat? If the enemy march through Jersey, will it be prudent to attack them on the way, or more eligible to proceed to the North River in the most direct and convenient manner, to secure the important communication between the eastern and southern States? In case such measures should be adopted, as will enable this army to overtake the enemy in their march, will it be prudent, with the aid which may reasonably be expected from the Jersey militia, to make an attack upon them, and ought it to be a partial or a general one?"[3]

The officers have many different opinions and so Washington asks each of us to write our views. I write that although an attack against Philadelphia, if successful, would be very glorious for us, the chance of making it without being discovered until the moment of the attack is not likely and so I do not advocate it. I suggest the army should move a short distance from here towards the Delaware. This might make them hurry what they are doing, or alter their plans, or give us some indication of what they intend- all great advantages in war. I do not want to send any large detachments from the line unless it should be a force such as the light infantry which could be joined to the Jersey militia. It is not worth the risk to hazard a large detachment. I do not know the country and the obstacles already put in the enemy's way, but I think nothing should be neglected to make the enemy's route as difficult as possible. If an attack presents itself, apart from small skirmishes, then I believe it should be a general attack. If we can hurry their going through the Jerseys, as was considered yesterday to be their likely route, and prevent them pillaging or stopping, we would gain an advantage. Most people believe we should stay here until the enemy clearly reveal their plans. If we do that we give up deriving a material advantage from their retreat, and I would do that therefore with reluctance. However, every day, every hour brings new intelligence which may give us greater light. When this happens, we should act immediately without the long apparat of a council of war, whereas in almost all councils since men began to make war, nothing will be decided but to remain in the same place where the council has been met.[4]

June 18. At nine o'clock in the morning Washington reads our answers.

Lee stands up. "I am strongly opposed to action. I do not agree with either a partial or a general engagement. The regulars are too strong for our army. It would be very foolish for us to do anything. We need them to reach New York. Now that we have an alliance with the French, we don't want to risk everything. I have the experience of being a former British army officer. I know their strengths."

"We do not want to take any chances. It would be extremely foolish," agrees Lord Stirling.

"It would be almost criminal to hazard a general engagement with such a brilliant and well-appointed army," says von Steuben.

"I agree," says Duportail.

"We should just try to stop the British from ravaging the country," says Lee.

"I am in favor of making as bold a demonstration as possible on the enemy and punishing them in every way and at every point," declares Wayne.

"I agree," says Cadwallader.

I am also inclined to agree with General Wayne," I say.[5]

"I believe that the army should remain at Valley Forge until there is some definite indication of enemy intentions," declares Washington. The council of war agrees.

At eleven-thirty, George Roberts from the militia, gallops up to Potts' House with a small group of light horse which had been scouting near to Philadelphia for the last few days.

"The British evacuated Philadelphia early this morning!" he informs Washington. "I was at the Middle Ferry on this side and received news of it from people gathered on the opposite shore. I could not cross as the bridge has been destroyed. About three thousand troops have embarked on transports."[6]

A short time later, an express rider brings a letter from Captain McLane. He says he is in Philadelphia and confirms that the evacuation has indeed taken place.[7]

The situation has now changed. The only question is whether to attack the enemy as it marches along the poor sandy roads of the Jerseys.

"It is an excellent opportunity to attack. The country and Congress are hungry for a victory. The British are very vulnerable with their army spread out over such a long march escorting so many wagons. We might never have such a good chance again. The country must be protected and if in doing so an engagement becomes unavoidable it would be necessary to fight," says Nathanel Greene.

"Their soldiers are so well-drilled they can quickly wheel round in formation to confront us," Lee replies sharply.

"We must attack. We must Burgoyne Clinton," Wayne vehemently declares, his strong, muscular body aggressively turning towards Lee.

"Yes, we should attack," asserts Cadwallader, a quick-tempered man like Wayne.

"I will postpone the decision for forty-eight hours, and in the meantime, we will harass their army and see what possibilities exist for an assault. By marching at the heels of the British it looks as though we are pursuing them, and they are running from us. Their evacuation is not the sign of a victorious army and it is politically useful to show we are chasing them. It will give the population courage to join the militia," says Washington.

Lee looks as though he has bitten a lemon and leaves the room.

In Philadelphia, McClane and some militia entered the city by way of Bush Hill between the ninth and tenth redoubts. At Second Street they met the last enemy patrol. They fired and captured a captain, a provost marshal, a guide, and thirty privates without losing a single man,[8] whilst in the Jerseys two columns of about seven thousand men are starting to march, one commanded by Clinton, the other by Knyphausen. Their baggage train is extensive and consists of about one thousand five hundred wagons stretching over twelve miles,[9] which will have to traverse the poor roads there. [10]

The British commissioners have sailed on the *Trident*; Howe's flagship is the *Eagle*. Here at Valley Forge, excitement sweeps through the camp. Our enemy is retreating; we are ready to pursue and to fight.

Washington orders General Maxwell who is at Hopewell with five thousand three hundred troops, to cross the Delaware and join Major General Dickinson and his eight hundred men. He orders Major General Benedict Arnold to take control of Philadelphia with about four hundred Continentals from Colonel Jackson's regiment. General Arnold has managed to travel south even although he is still suffering greatly from his injury at Saratoga. His right thigh had been shattered but he had refused to have the leg amputated and now walks with the aid of a cane, one leg shorter than the other. He cannot ride a horse and a soldier helps him get around. A stocky man, with black hair, a dark complexion and strangely pale gray eyes, he is renowned for his bravery at the capture of Ticonderoga, his expedition to Quebec, his participation in a naval engagement on Lake Champlain and a skirmish at Danbury, as well as, of course, his courage at Saratoga. Washington thinks very highly of him, but obviously the state of his wound does not permit his services in a more active line.[11]

At three in the afternoon, Lee sets off with the vanguard of our army, comprising the brigades of Huntington, Poor and Varnum, with orders to halt at the first strong ground after crossing the Delaware at Coryell's Ferry unless he receives authentic intelligence that the enemy has gone by the direct road to South Amboy, or still lower, in which case he is to march to North River.[12] Lee is followed by Wayne with Mifflin's division comprising Conway's brigade and the First and Second Pennsylvania brigades, whose orders are to go by the direct route to Coryell's Ferry. At six in the evening, General Arnold sets out to Philadelphia.

On June 19, at five o'clock in the morning, in heavy rain, I lead out from camp my division consisting of Woodford's and Scott's Virginians and a brigade of North Carolinians. De Kalb follows with Glover's, Patterson's and Learned's brigades; then come the artillery park and spare ammunition. Next is Stirling with the brigades of Weedon, Muhlenburg and the First and Second Maryland. We march along the York Road to Doylestown; that night the three different parts of the army set up camp on the ridge near the Presbyterian church, on the road to Coryell's Ferry and on the west of Main Street in the village. On Saturday, June 20, Washington issues orders for a gill of spirits to be given to each man 'if the commissaries are provided.'[13] That night I stay at the home of Mrs. Thomas Jones, west of Doyleston.

"How did you sleep?" she asks me next day.

"Very well, madam," I reply. "But your bed was a little too short."[14]

We cross the Delaware; on Monday we spend all day in camp near the river and I am now nearer my red friends.[15] We do not know if Clinton is going north or whether he is marching south along the Delaware. Will he retreat to New York or will he fight? Is it possible he intends to occupy the passes in the Highlands along the North River? His slow march perhaps suggests he wants to fight, although as his soldiers have wool uniforms, are carrying sixty-pound backpacks, are being shot at by the militia who have felled trees, filled in wells and destroyed every bridge on the often narrow road of deep sand, causing new bridges or causeways to be built over Cooper's Creek, Moor's Creek, Ballybridge Creek, Ancocus Creek and Bird Creek, as well as having a lumbering baggage train and artillery extending for twelve miles, it is not perhaps surprising.[16]

Washington orders each brigade to provide an active-spirited officer and twenty-five of its best marksmen to join Colonel Morgan's corps early tomorrow morning and continue under his command until the enemy pass through the Jerseys, in order to reinforce Dickinson on the enemy's east flank. He also orders all tents and heavy baggage to be left behind and all weapons to be well-cleaned and afterwards carefully inspected, together with their ammunition, by their respective officers.[17]

The heat is intense. My clothes are wet with perspiration and cling to me as I ride. In the afternoons, thunderstorms erupt. I welcome the rain; unfortunately, the roads become slimy pits of mud, the streams transform into torrents and the soldiers struggle to march in the treacherous conditions.

Congress has rejected the proposals of the commissioners. I, therefore, no longer fear a peace settlement between Britain and the United States. I and my fellow Frenchmen celebrate late into the evening, as do the local mosquitos which bite me so severely my face swells up like a pumpkin. I write to Laurens that: 'the answer of Congress to the commissioners is a fine piece.'[18] 'I beg leave to join here my voice to this of all lovers of liberty, all good Americans, all true French men, in expressing my admiration and my pleasure at the noble, spirited, and ever to be prais'd answer of Congress, to the deceitfull and somewhat impertinent address of the British commissioners. That afforded me a double satisfaction as I felt it in a double capacity.'[19]

June 23. We are at Hopewell, in Hunterdon, on the eastern side of the river, about eight miles from Princeton, about fourteen miles from Trenton. The enemy has reached Black Horse, directly south of Bordentown and is probably moving or preparing to advance on both the Crosswicks Road and the Bordentown Road. Cannon fire had been heard from the direction of Crosswicks Creek and Clinton had evidently been having problems in rebuilding the bridge over the creek which is about four miles from Trenton. It is possible the British are going to Trenton although Moylan has sent a message to say he believes the van has already reached Allentown.[20] Clinton could march north-east from there through Trenton and Princeton, cross the Raritan at Brunswick, then march to Amboy and ferry his troops to Staten Island. Or he could go northeast to Raritan Bay and ferry the troops from different locations between South Amboy and Sandy Hook.

I stay with Washington at Joseph Stout Junior's large, imposing house on a hill above the Hopewell valley. Here, at nine in the morning, on June 24, he convenes a council of war: "Our army, exclusive of General Maxwell's troops, has ten thousand six hundred and eighty-four soldiers fit to fight. The British army is believed to number rather less than ten thousand. Our intelligence says that they are in two columns, one on the Allentown Road, the other on that of Bordentown.[21] Will it be advisable for us, of choice, to hazard a general action? If it is, should we do it by immediately making a general attack upon the enemy, by attempting a partial one, or by taking such a position, if it can be done, as may oblige them to attack us? If it is not, what measures can be taken, with safety to this army, to annoy the enemy in their march? In fine, what precise line of conduct will it be advisable for us to pursue?"[22]

Weak sunshine streaming into the south-east-facing room begins to fade; the wood-paneling loses its luster.[23] Birds singing outside the window fall silent. Darkness envelopes us. Morning becomes night. It is an eclipse of the sun. We say nothing. No one suggests what it might augur for our confrontation with the enemy. The phenomenon passes. Sunshine returns.[24] The council resumes.

"A small detachment, if any, should be sent to help General Dickinson and General Maxwell who are attacking the enemy on its flanks, and the main army should march towards the North River. It would be better to build a bridge of gold for the British to use than to attack or to hinder their passage across the country in any way of a force so well-disciplined. If the armies are about the same size in numbers, then risking an engagement with them would appear to me to be very criminal. The late alliance with France would be a more effective step towards independence than any act of the army, however bold it might be in conception and so it would be better not to hazard any engagement at the present. If a partial attack is made it will soon become a general one with an enemy so well prepared for battle. To risk an action would be to the last degree criminal. The army should proceed to White Plains," Lee declares,[25] his opinion the same as on June 18.

Stirling again agrees with him, as do the brigadier-generals.[26]

"It would be the most criminal madness to hazard a general action at this time," says Knox.

"I am not for hazarding a general action unnecessarily, but I am clearly of opinion for making a serious impression with the light troops and for having the army in supporting distance. There should be two brigades to support them. The attack should be made on the English flank and rear. If we suffer the enemy to pass through the Jerseys without attacking, I think we shall ever regret it. I cannot help thinking we magnify our deficiencies beyond realities. We are now in the most awkward situation in the world and have come to our grief repeatedly-marching until we get near the enemy and then our courage fails and we halt without attempting to do the enemy the least injury. I think we can make a partial attack without suffering them to bring us to a general action," says Greene, hesitating to speak too strongly because he is on staff duty.[27]

I listen to everyone. Late in the meeting, I give my opinion. "It would be disgraceful and humiliating to let the British cross the Jerseys in tranquility. Perhaps a rearguard action could be made or an attack without causing a general action to occur. The long baggage train is particularly vulnerable."[28] I believe we should use a larger force although not to fight unless circumstances should make success certain. I appeal to American honor, patriotism and gallantry not to allow an opportunity such as this to pass unimproved. It would be a shame to the leaders of the army and a humiliation to the soldiers if the British could traverse the whole of New Jersey unmolested. They ought to be pursued, in any event, and if nothing more were done, their rear ought to be attacked. The army should maneuver in such a manner as to take advantage of position and watch for a possible separation of forces to cut off detachments and if any opportunity presents itself to strike."[29]

"I agree," declares Duportail.[30]

"I agree about the larger force. Fight, Sir," declares Wayne angrily.

"If we get near to the enemy but do not attempt to do the least injury the public will conclude that our courage has failed us," says Greene.

The council finally concludes that a general action is not advisable but 'a detachment of fifteen hundred men be immediately sent to act, as occasion may serve, on the enemy's left flank and rear, in conjunction with the other Continental troops and militia, who are already hanging about them, and that the main body preserve a relative position, so as to be able to act as circumstances may require.'[31]

I reluctantly sign when I see the officers sign who share my opinion; so does Greene. Wayne refuses.

We discuss the number of men to be sent against the enemy. Lee, Stirling, Woodford, Scott, Knox and Poor want fifteen hundred. Steuben, Duportail, Wayne, Paterson, Greene and I want twenty-five hundred, or at least, two thousand. There are six officers for more than fifteen hundred and only six for fifteen hundred. [32] Some believe the detachment should attack the enemy, although not to engage in battle. Others believe that we should only skirmish and harass as circumstances permit.[33] It is finally decided: 'One thousand five hundred men should be immediately sent to act, as occasion may serve, on the enemy's left flank and rear, in conjunction with the other Continental troops and militia who are already hanging about them, and that the main body preserve a relative position in order to be able to act as circumstances may require.'[34]

After the meeting, Hamilton is scathing. "I always disapprove of councils of war. This decision would do honor to the society of midwives and to them only." [35]

Generals von Steuben and Duportail come to see me.

"Our English was too poor to speak at the council, but we are very distressed to see the American army about to lose an occasion which may perhaps be the finest ever offered."[36]

"I agree. I will write to Washington on your behalf, as well as my own," I reply.

My letter is blunt. I say I think Morgan should be sent towards the rear of the right flank and the militia to act as it has been already ordered. I believe that a detachment of two thousand five hundred selected men ought to be sent towards the enemy's left flank to attack the enemy as occasion presents. I want the column of the main army to be at a proper distance along the enemy's left flank. If the corps should put such confusion among the enemy that a general attack might be advantageous, then I would not think that with ten thousand men it is not proper to attack ten thousand English.[37] 'I do'nt doubt but a detachment of 2,000 or 2,500 selected men will find an occasion of attacking some part of the ennemy with advantage-of even beating those tremendous grenadiers if they fight with them. In a word I would lay my fortune, all of what I possess in the world, that if such a detachment is sent in proper time, some good effect, and no harm schall arise of it...But I forget that I write to the general, and I was ready to speack freely to my friend.'[38]

Wayne and Greene write similar letters. Greene repeats his words at the council of war. He says that people expect something from us and our strength demands it. He says he is by no means for rash measures but that we must preserve our reputations. He thinks we can make a very serious impression without any great risk and if it should amount to a general action the chance would be greatly in our favour. He thinks we can make a partial attack without suffering the enemy to bring us to a general action.[39]

Washington sends six hundred riflemen under Daniel Morgan to Maxwell's brigade on the right flank. Later in the day he sends a detachment of one thousand four hundred and forty selected men under Brigadier General Scott to reinforce the Jersey militia who are already harassing the enemy on the left and rear. Von Steuben reports that the enemy have taken the direct road from Allentown to Monmouth Court House.[40]

June 25. Washington orders the whole army to leave their tents and go to Rocky Hill, Somerset County, and Kingston, Middlesex County, about seven miles distant.[41] He agrees to the decision of the council and decides to strengthen the advanced forces. "I will give a small force of one thousand five hundred to General Lee."

To my great surprise, Lee does not accept the post. "The proposed task could be discharged more properly by a young, volunteering general, than by the second-in-command of the entire army."[42]

"I appoint you instead," Washington says and gives me the written order:

You are immediately to proceed with the detachment commanded by Gen. Poor, and form a junction (as expeditiously as possible) with that under the command of Genl. Scott. You are to use the most effectual means for gaining the enemy's left flank and rear, and giving them every degree of annoyance. All Continental parties, that are already on the lines, will be under your command, and you will take such measures, in concert with Genl. Dickinson, as will cause the enemy the greatest impediment and loss in their march. For these purposes you will attack them as occasion may require by detachment, and, if a proper opening should be given, by operating against them with the whole force of your command. You will naturally take such precautions, as will secure you against surprise, and maintain your communication with this army. Given at Kingston, this 25th day of June,1778. [43]

I am delighted. I now command the advance Continental and militia regiments. I make preparations. Seven letters pass between us.

"You must not push on with too much rapidity. You may be, in case of action, at too great a distance to receive succor and therefore exposed to great hazard," Washington tells me.

To my chagrin, Lee changes his mind. He writes to Washington that he now finds the command is viewed in a different manner:

They say that a corps consisting of six thousand men, the greater part chosen, is undoubtedly the most honorable command next to the Commander-in-Chief; that my ceding it would, of course, have an odd appearance. I must entreat therefore, after making a thousand apologies for the trouble my rash assent has occasioned you, that if this detachment does march, I may have the command of it. So far personally; but, to speak as an officer, I do not think this detachment should march at all, until at least the head of the enemy's right column has passed Cranberry; then if it is necessary to march the whole army, I cannot see any impropriety in the Marquis's commanding this detachment, or a greater, as an advanced guard of the army; but if this detachment, with Maxwell's corps, Scott's, Morgan's, and Jackson's, is to be considered as a separate, chosen, active corps, and put under the Marquis's command until the enemy leaves the Jerseys, both myself and Lord Stirling will be disgraced. [44]

Lee visits me, accompanied by a small spaniel.

"Would you give up the command?" he asks.

"I could not without great reluctance give it up. It has been given to me freely and I am particularly keen to keep it," I reply.

"I put my career and honor in your hands and appeal to your generosity and magnanimity. You are too generous to ruin either one," he says.[45]

"If I do not meet with the enemy within twenty-four hours, I will give you the command," I say reluctantly.[46]

I go to speak to Washington. "If you believe it is necessary or useful to the good of the service and the honor of General Lee to send him down with a couple of thousand men or any force more, I will cheerfully obey and serve him not only out of duty but out of what I owe to that gentleman's character.[47] I ask only that if this happens Lee would join me with a force similar in size to mine so that the two contingents would appear to unite rather than appear to replace me."[48]

I do not wait for provisions, even although we have much need of them;[49] I set off with the largest detachment I have led, riding next to General Poor. The humid heat is again intense; one hundred degrees in the sun. At nine o'clock in the evening we are at Cranberry, having only marched about ten miles. We camp at the creek; the men splash themselves with the brackish water and gulp it recklessly.

"Stop drinking! Your intestines could burst and kill you! At the least, it will make you sick," the officers order repeatedly.

The men are so desperate with thirst they ignore the command; even if the whole British army suddenly appeared, I do not think they would take any notice. Mosquitos hover in dense clouds over the banks and surface of the slow-flowing stream; bites soon add to our discomfort and the men settle down for an uncomfortable night.

Hamilton is already here; he has been gathering intelligence about the enemy position and that of our forces. He tells me the enemy have all filed off from Allen Town on the Monmouth Road; their rear is said to be a mile west of Lawrence Taylor's Tavern, six miles from Allen Town. I write to Washington, enclosing Hamilton's report; I ask for him to order that provisions should be sent to us as speedily as possible and that I would particularly like to be well furnished with spirits as we expect to make a long and quick march early tomorrow morning.

Next morning, nothing has arrived. The sun has only just risen but the heat is already almost unbearable. There is no rum to help the men make a quick march, but we set off south towards Highstown.

At seven-fifteen we meet there with the New Jersey militia of Dickinson. Hamilton has been riding all night but has not discovered any more about the enemy. A scouting party arrives: "The enemy is in motion; their rear is now about one mile from where it had been last night, about seven or eight miles from here."

I order Maxwell's and Wayne's brigades to march; I will fall lower down with Scott's and Jackson's regiments and some militia. Hopefully, we can attack the enemy before they halt. If we can not overtake them, we can halt at some distance and perhaps attack tomorrow if they do not escape in the night.[50] At noon we reach Robin's Tavern on the road towards Monmouth Court House. Wayne's detachment, however, is almost starving and appears unwilling or unable to march any more until they receive food. I ask the opinions of the general officers of the detachment; their reply is that I should march in the night near them, to attack the rear guard when on the march. We also speak of a night attack, but that seems dangerous. Wayne, Hamilton and other officers go to reconnoiter.

I write to Washington to tell him the situation: 'My motions depend much upon what your army will do for countenancing them. I beg you would be very particular upon what you think proper to be done and what your excellency will do.'[51]

He is now at Cranberry with the army and sends me a letter:

I have given the most pointed and positive orders for provisions for your Detachment and am sorry that they have not arrived...I wish you would send up an active officer to the Commissary who might never leave him till he obtained the necessary supplies...Tho' giving the Enemy a stroke is a very desireable event, yet I would not want you to be too precipitate in the measure or to distress your men by an over hasty march. The Weather is extremely warm and by a too great exertion in pushing the Troops many of 'em will fall sick and be rendered entirely unfit for service...Do not push on with too much rapidity. You may be, in case of Action, at too great a distance to receive succour and exposed from thence to great Hazard. [52]

Another letter arrives from him telling me to march to Englishtown so that the army can support my detachment in case of attack or to cover my retreat if need be. However, as the main army is at Cranberry and my force is at Robin's Tavern, we are unfortunately on two different roads which do not link. He is surprised provisions have not arrived but when the detachments meet, he says it will be easier to be provided for.[53]

A later letter arrives to say he will give Lee a part of the army to reinforce, or at least cover the several detachments at present under my command. He feels for Lee's distress of mind but at the same time has an eye to the delicacy of my situation. He says he has obtained a promise from him that when he gives me notice of his approach and command, he will request me to prosecute any plan I may have already concerted for the purpose of attacking or otherwise annoying the enemy. It is the only expedient he could think of to answer the views of both of us. He concludes: 'General Lee seems satisfied with the measure and I wish it may prove agreeable to you.'[54]

"Can we attack now?" I ask the brigadiers.

"No, the troops are too hungry and tired," they say, to my bitter disappointment.

I write to Washington:

Your orders have reach'd me so late and found me in such a situation that it will be impossible to follow them as soon as I could wish. It is not on account of any other motive than the impossibility of moving the troops and making such a march immediately for in receiving your letter I have given up the project of attaking the enemy, and I only wish to join General Lee....I do not believe Gal. Lee is to make any attak tomorrow for then I would have been directed to fall immediately upon them without making 11 miles entirely out of the way. [55]

At two in the morning, my detachment starts tramping down the road in the darkness. A few hours later we reach the main army at Englishtown; I unhappily cede my command to Lee.

There have now been at least five hundred enemy deserters,[56] as well as some captured soldiers, and they report much fear and suffering. Morgan's Riflemen and Cadwallader's Pennsylvanians are killing many. All the bridges on their route have had to be repaired or new ones built, frequently under fire. The narrow roads are often of deep sand which has bogged down the wagons, and the torrential rainfall in the afternoons has made the sandy mud hold fast the wagons and carriages. Men have dropped dead from the heat as they marched, unfortunately from our ranks as well as the enemy.[57] When Howe marched through the Jerseys in 1776, hundreds of people had wished to sign loyalty oaths. Now the British have devastated the land. They have killed cattle and left them in the fields and pastures, some with just a small piece of flesh cut off from their hind quarters. Houses have been burned, furniture has been hacked and broken, mechanics' and farmers' tools destroyed, wells filled in, and fruiting cherry trees have been chopped down.[58] Local people are furious, and many are joining the militia.

Deserters reach us almost hourly[59] even although the penalty for anyone caught is hanging and a deserter's body has been strung up in chains by the roadside to deter others. The Germans complain bitterly about the British: "Many of us have wives or sweethearts in Philadelphia and so part of the Hessian cavalry and two Anspach regiments were sent on the transport ships as it was feared they would desert. A lot of Germans live in Philadelphia. They are not our enemy. We did not want to come to America. We were conscripted. We hate the British. They are always flogging men for slight offences. Their soldiers are not called the bloody backs for nothing. Our German troops are suffering the most on the march. We are not allowed to ride on the wagons and so our officers are letting the most exhausted ride on their horses. Men are dying from the heat. There is no water and the wells have been filled with sand. The land is mainly brushwood without roads."

June 27. The enemy is encamped in a strong position at Monmouth Court House. Their right extends about a mile and half beyond the Court House to the parting of the roads going to Shrewsbury and Middletown; their left along the road from Allentown to Monmouth, about three miles on this side of the Court House. Their right flank is on the skirt of a small wood; their left is secured by a very thick one, a morass running towards their rear, and their whole front covered by a wood, and for a considerable extent towards the left, with a morass.[60] Our main army is eight miles west of them, the advance troops five miles away. Morgan, with his corps and some bodies of militia are on their flanks. We do not know where the enemy intend to embark. Some think they will go to Sandy Hook; others think they intend to go to Shoal Harbour.[61] If they reach the heights around Middletown, about ten or twelve miles further on, it would be impossible to attack them.

Just after noon I am summoned to headquarters at Penelopen, south of Englishtown. Washington gives Lee his orders; Wayne, Scott, Maxwell and I listen.

"When the British march tomorrow attack their rear with your division.[62] I will bring up the main army to promptly support you. I wish all officers to waive their respective dates of rank and fight wherever General Lee thinks it is desirable. I also wish you to arrange a meeting this afternoon with the general officers of your division and detail your plans to them."[63]

"I do not have intelligence on the strength of the enemy, nor where they are exactly. I do not know the terrain. I cannot devise a strategy, as anything agreed on now might quickly become useless," says Lee.

"Attack," declares Washington. "Your tactics will depend on what happens. General Maxwell is the oldest in commission and should therefore be given preference in the attack if he wishes, although as many of his troops are recruits and there is a scarcity of cartouche boxes in the brigade, perhaps a different brigade needs to be in the advance. I think that an attack, if begun by a picked corps, would probably give a happy impression."[64]

He does not give Lee written instructions, an unusual step for him. He appears to have confidence in him to act appropriately according to the circumstances.

"I advise again that you need to have a meeting to form a plan of attack," he says to Lee.

"Five o'clock at my quarters," Lee tells us; then we all depart to prepare for the next day.

At five, Maxwell, Wayne and I ride to Lee's tent. He comes out to meet us in his usual rough clothing, a spaniel at his heels.

"I do not know the numbers and exact situation of the enemy. The countryside has not been carefully reconnoitered and if we make a precise plan for tomorrow it might throw us into disarray and be useless if anything unexpected happens. It is best to move cautiously and rely on the vigilance of the officers and the prompt obedience of the men when circumstances require us to move. In the meantime, each of must have his troops ready to march at a moment's notice," he repeats what he said at the earlier meeting with Washington.[65]

"I would like to be with you tomorrow," I ask.

"I am pleased you wish to do so and you have my permission for that," he is replying as Lieutenant Colonel John Fitzgerald arrives with the message: "His Excellency commands you to draw up your troops with their arms on the ground on which you are posted, so that you are ready to repel any attack during the night. He does not think it very probable, but it is not impossible. He also says he wishes you to send word to Colonel Morgan and General Dickenson to say how you wish them to cooperate with your division tomorrow. He hopes that you and your generals have been in conference and have agreed plans for a successful attack tomorrow."

"From my knowledge of the senior officers in the British army I think it highly probable they will turn about and strike, and if I had not been personally acquainted with them, I would expect this of them as officers," Lee comments. [66]

Fitzgerald rides away; Lee continues his instructions. "Do not dispute rank as General Washington requested. It might happen that the oldest officer in rank might be ordered on the left and his junior on the right, and I expect to be obeyed. If you have any complaints, make them later."[67] With that, he turns his back on us and goes into his tent, followed by the spaniel. Maxwell, Wayne and I look at each other in surprise.

"Where is Scott?" I ask.

"I saw him an hour ago at the brook,"[68] says Maxwell. "He is probably just late in coming to the meeting. He would not expect it to be finished so soon."

Wayne mounts his horse and canters off. I leave Maxwell and go to my quarters to sleep for a few hours. I presume Lee will take steps to have the terrain and the enemy position reconnoitered and am surprised he has not already done so. Our unfortunate ignorance of the higher ford at Brandywine, which enabled Howe to outflank us, is not easily forgotten. His lack of a plan though, does not weigh heavily on my mind; I look forward eagerly to the coming battle.

June 28. A thunderclap wakes me; a white-brilliant fork of lightning flashes; rain is thudding down. I dress hastily, without any need of a candle as lightning repeatedly illuminates the night. At four in the morning, I send an aide to Lee to obtain my orders.[69]

He returns with instructions for me to join selected troops of Wayne's and Scott's detachments. They will be part of the vanguard, I happily discover. Two hundred men will march first, commanded by Colonel Butler, then Colonel Jackson with two hundred; followed by Scott's brigade, with a part of Woodford's, comprising six hundred men, with two pieces of artillery; next comes General Varnum's brigade of about six hundred, with two pieces of artillery; then General Wayne's detachment of thousand, with two pieces of artillery, then General Scott's detachment of fourteen hundred with four pieces of artillery, and finally, General Maxwell's one thousand men, with two pieces of artillery.[70] The enemy's front has begun to march; our army is marching. Washington has desired General Lee to bring on an engagement or attack the enemy as soon as possible unless some very powerful circumstance forbids it, and that he will soon be up to his aid. [71]

I hurriedly eat breakfast at the house of Joseph Story, two miles from Englishtown. Then I ride in haste along the road to join Scott's detachment, very hopeful I will make the acquaintance of a few grenadiers before the day is finished.

Chapter 20

Disappointment at battle of Monmouth Court House

At seven in the morning the heat is suffocating. A soldier collapses before we have even gone half a mile. We leave him, more dead than alive, in the shade of an oak whose withered leaves droop thirstily. The sandy road is so hot it scorches men's feet, some of which are bare, others only slightly protected by thin soles on their shoes.

We continue along the road towards the Meeting House, past a terrain of fields, orchards and woods with thick brambles. Muddy streams crisscross the rolling farmland; in the distance are rounded hills.

Orders come from Lee to halt.[1] We wait an hour; the men remove most of their remaining clothes, although they are already half naked. They attempt to find shade under trees or by bushes and I order water to be brought for my sweating horse which appears distressed. I fear it will not last the next ten minutes, let alone the day. The sun rises higher in the furnace of the sky; I finally lose patience and go to speak to Lee.

"What is wrong? Why have we stopped?"

"Local people and the militia are giving me different intelligence. Some say the British have marched from the Court House whilst others say they are still there and are reinforcing their rear. I am not sure the enemy is marching." [2]

"We must attack the detachment of British which has just moved towards my right flank. I believe we can cut it off," I declare.

"No, we have to be cautious," he replies. "You don't know British soldiers. We cannot stand against them. We shall certainly be driven back at first. We must be cautious."

"That might be so, but British soldiers had been beaten and therefore it must be presumed they will be beaten again. At any rate I am disposed to make the trial," I retort.[3]

An aide of Washington arrives for intelligence. "Tell the general that his presence at the scene of action is extremely important," I say to him when he starts to return.[4]

Lee orders the men to march once more. He tells Wayne to move forward with part of his detachment to join the advanced troops.

"Show General Wayne how to get in front by the shortest road," I ask General Forman of the New Jersey militia.[5]

The troops march on. A thickly wooded deep ravine shelters us for a short time from the sun, but I hurry the men through it. It is a potential ambush; if we are forced to retreat along its narrow bottom, we could all be massacred. We emerge safely into a field of Indian corn surrounded on all sides by tall trees. The sun shines strongly onto the ploughed, sandy soil, the air only slightly less hot than the mouth of a heated oven.[6] We continue along the road. Shortly afterwards, the main force halts again for half an hour. I wait with annoyance. One of Lee's aides canters up. "Two British battalions are in the nearby woods."

I ride into the trees to reconnoiter. I urge my horse slowly forward; I glance keenly around. Shafts of sunlight break through the leaves, illuminating only plants and bushes, not red coats. There is no enemy in our immediate vicinity, but towards Monmouth Courthouse I can see light cavalry. I ride back. I inform Lee; I return to my troops who are in a hollow, badly exposed; I send an aide to tell Lee, but then we fortunately move again.[7]

Another of Lee's aides arrives. "The enemy's rear is close to us and will certainly be captured."

I hurriedly ride again to Lee. "The rear guard of the enemy is ours," one of his aides tells me.

"My dear marquis," Lee exclaims in what appears to be a state of euphoria. "I think those people are ours. Conceal your men in the woods on the south side of the road."[8]

I go back; I lead one of my regiments into the trees; the shade gives them some relief; they gasp gratefully for breath. The cannon are, however, too large to follow into the undergrowth.

"Send them along the road and then along a fence to the right," Lee orders.[9]

Colonel Oswald and his men cross a morass at our front; they start to fire their two cannon towards the British advance. Hamilton arrives with orders for me from Lee to take three regiments to the right to prevent the British flanking us on the left.

I go to Lee to verify the order. I return. I send the order to Stewart's and Wesson's regiments: 'Support me on the right.'[10] I lead Livingston's regiment forward across a ravine. We come out of a copse and cross a field and I look for the two other regiments, but they are nowhere to be seen. Our position is now very exposed on open ground, north-west of Monmouth Court House, about six hundred yards from the British. Bullets whistle around us. Several soldiers fall dead. A shot from a British twelve-pounder hits Colonel James Wesson of the Ninth Massachusetts Regiment in the back and shoulders. He slumps heavily onto the ground, moaning in agony, his body a broken mass of blood and bone. I leave a soldier to care for him and bring up my men to the right of Oswald whose two cannon are still the only section of the army firing.

"As soon as the other regiments come up, we will attack the British artillery," I say to Livingston.[11]

Oswald's cannonade stops; a few minutes later a message arrives: 'We have no more ammunition.'

My frustration and impatience mounts. We have been scurrying backwards and forwards like ants, marching and countermarching, and being fired on, without making an attack ourselves. The air is thick with sandy dust scuffed up by so many men's feet which merges with the heat haze making it difficult to see. I worry the British might suddenly appear in front of us without warning.

Lieutenant Colonel Laurens arrives with an order from Lee: 'Withdraw to the nearby houses.'

I glance in that direction and see our troops. I rush my regiment across a morass, cannon balls thudding into the soft ground, bullets buzzing like angry bees through our ranks. Men are collapsing everywhere, as much from exhaustion as from enemy fire. We are very dangerously exposed; I quickly need to find a more suitable position. I hastily write another message to Washington: 'We are retreating.'

Wayne gallops up as my men fall back. "What are you doing?" he shouts.

"I've been ordered to recross the morass and form near the village," I say.

"I don't see any reason to retreat," he replies. "I will send my aide to Lee to ask for support."[12]

I continue with my regiment towards the houses. Oswald, on my left, refuses to move his artillery until Lee orders him to do so. I ride to him. "General Lee has ordered your artillery to the rise in the rear."[13] I leave a member of my staff to guide him. He soon reaches it.

Lee orders me: 'Take command of the right flank at the village.'

I quickly ride to the buildings which are of wood and not suitable as a defensive position. Reports reach us: 'The British are on the right.' I inform Lee; he sends an order: 'Retreat to the woods about a mile back to the left and rear.'[14]

My men struggle bravely to comply. Many fall senseless to the ground. The thermometer shows a temperature of over one hundred degrees, ninety-six in the shade.

On our right, cannons roar. British dragoons charge. On our left rear, British infantry advances, firing on us, causing spirals of dust to rise. We fall back again; we join a general retreat of all the brigades, everyone crowding so closely together that if the British send grapeshot into us, the casualties will be terrible. At the best, it is a disorderly retreat; at times it comes near to being a rout. Horses trot with the field pieces down the yellow-sand road; men scramble in panic across the fields. Some units remain disciplined and march in columns, by battalion or brigade, others, particularly at the rear near to the British, are running frantically. We are giving way without firing a single musket.[15]

I ride with Colonel Walter Stewart of the Thirteenth Pennsylvania Regiment. We come over the morass near the causeway bridge and suddenly the distinctive figure of Washington appears, galloping furiously on his white horse. He rides up to us, his face hard with rage.

"We kept changing positions and then a retreat was ordered. The British are now advancing down the road towards us in two columns with their cavalry and artillery between them," I tell him.

"I have just spoken with Lee," he says, his voice harsh with anger. "Damned poltroon! I demanded to know the reason for this unaccountable retreat. He declared the men had fled from a bayonet charge and that all this was against his advice! I have taken command now."

Colonel Nathaniel Ramsay of the Third Maryland Regiment joins us; Washington takes him by the hand. "I shall depend on your immediate exertions to check the progress of the enemy with your two regiments until I can form the main army."

"We shall check them!" Colonel Ramsay immediately replies.[16]

"Take your regiments to the wood on the left of the road and fire to defend the retreating troops," Washington orders Ramsay and Stewart.

The British advance steadily forward through a cornfield towards our small force attempting to halt them. Washington orders two more guns to take position on the right of Stewart's and Ramsay's men. The British artillery sends shot into the woods but our guns keep responding, the men firing them in an extreme state of exhaustion and about to be overrun by the enemy who are now in the woods; I send aides to Oswald to order him to retreat; he and his men move back about a quarter of a mile; four guns joining him, so he has ten.

Shot falls everywhere, pounding the earth and tearing the vegetation. Washington rides backwards and forwards, guiding the men in a disciplined retreat towards the Perrine Ridge behind us. I help collect the remnants of men from the Connecticut and Rhode Island forces[17] and station them and several cannon behind a sturdy split-rail fence with bushes and trees growing in it. Lee is also, strangely, trying to give orders, until an aide reminds him that the commander-in-chief is on the field.

"Supervise these men. Get them over the bridge," Washington shouts to him as he rides by.

"I will be the last to cross," says Lee.

Olney is placed in charge of the men defending the hedgerow; two three-pounder guns are rapidly pulled into place; over at the edge of woods on our right, Wayne is commanding Ramsay's and Stewart's troops. British infantry attack and launch a bayonet charge; Wayne's men retreat towards our Continentals at the hedgerow; the British continue to come forward into a hail of bullets and cannon shot from Olney's troops.

The air is thick with smoke and dust; the drums beat; men shout and scream. The grenadiers follow the dragoons and frenziedly attack the hedgerow fence. Our men in hunting shirts, some nearly naked, make a spirited defense. The fighting is furious, hand-to-hand and bloody; further back, Washington is organizing both the arriving and retreating men and artillery on top of the Perrine Ridge. He gallops among the soldiers. He stops their flight, gathering them into fighting units and summoning reinforcements. He is an imposing presence, unafraid and resolute, the soldiers cheering him as he rides amongst them. He succeeds in organizing a new line of defense behind the West Ravine, very suitable terrain to hold off the enemy, suggested to him by Lieutenant Colonel Rhea of the militia, whose family own part of this land.

The British charge through the hedgerow fence. "Retreat!" comes the order to the soldiers there.

"No, we want to fight!" they shout, wanting to be revenged on the invaders of their country.[18]

"Retreat!" comes the order again.

They reluctantly abandon the fence and fall back over the bridge of the Spotswood Middle Brook towards the Perrine Ridge. They haul two guns over the morass; Olney's men follow. General Lee is the last man to cross, as he had earlier sworn.

"Go to the rear of the army and round up the stragglers," Washington orders him. The British pursue with bayonets. Our artillery on the Perrine Ridge fires; the British guns fire back about six hundred yards away. Our cannons prevent them from advancing for about two hours and Greene moves his division with four large guns onto Coomb's Hill, overlooking the British left flank. The British are now caught in a crossfire from Coomb's Hill and the Perrine Ridge and flounder with difficulty over the streams and morass.

Washington rides continually up and down, the smoke of battle often obscuring him, before suddenly emerging again from the haze, his calm courage inspiring the men who fight with spirit and enthusiasm. His white horse, a present from Livingston, the governor of New Jersey, is killed under him and Billy Lee quickly comes forward to give him his chestnut blood mare.[19]

Clinton is as courageous a commander of the British as Washington is to our men. He leads his troops himself towards the hedgerow and can be heard shouting "Charge, grenadiers, never heed forming!"

The heat is felling more soldiers than the artillery fire. They collapse at their posts, slumping forward unconscious, or dead. Some of our army is luckily partly hidden in woodland and behind hedgerows and has the benefit of slight shade whilst the British make three assaults in the open, each of which we repel, at one point from a distance of only forty yards. The grenadiers wear bearskin hats and what sort of furnace that produces on their heads can hardly be guessed at.

I am placed in charge of the second line,[20] the troops in reserve in the rear of Greene and Stirling,[21] on the left behind a hill; we are there for most of the afternoon. We move into woodland when it seems likely the British will make a flanking movement. They are beaten back; we return to our previous position. I long to fight. I ache to be part of the battle and not restricted to its periphery. I can smell the powder; I can hear the shouting and the firing, but I am not able to play a part.

We stand ready to withstand an attack; it does not come. The British are not able to do it. The heat has savaged them as much as our artillery. Some even remain in the woods in reach of our shot, instead of retreating to a safe position out in the sunlight. They are being killed because they cannot bear to leave the very minimal shade they have found.

Finally, they abandon their assaults. For two hours, until six o'clock, the battle is fought by the artillery. Gimat had been sent to Englishtown to ask for reinforcements to come up under von Steuben; they now arrive. Woodford brings his brigade down from Comb's Hill; Poor leads his regiments and Clark's North Carolina Brigade onto the other flank; and they start to pursue the enemy who retreat into orchards and fields. Our troops are courageous but too exhausted.

They stagger and fall on their weapons after a few yards. Washington gives the order to stop fighting.

Night falls. Dark hides the blood-stained battlefield and its grim human harvest. Shrieks and moans shred the stifling blackness stinking of artillery smoke and death. A slender new moon casts a faint gleam onto our hungry and exhausted army sleeping where it fought amidst the bodies of the dead.[22] Two Connecticut regiments are sent near to the British lines to watch for any sign of movement. We will fight again at dawn.

I rest by an oak tree; Washington joins me. He spreads out his cloak on the hot earth; we lie down together, his officers nearby, and we talk about the conduct of Lee,[23] who is British, not American, and was held by the British in captivity for some time where he perhaps agreed an arrangement with them to try and stop our attacking as they evacuated their army from Philadelphia. He should not have insisted on leading an assault, which, from the outset, he made it clear he did not want. Dr. Griffith, a chaplain and surgeon in the Virginia line, had visited Washington this morning in the early hours and told him that trusted friends had warned of the probable conduct of Lee and that he should be on guard against the bad conduct of those on whose military skill he has to depend on to carry out his orders. In the woods, near the beginning, he thought he would capture many British. If he had, he would probably have become a hero to America and could have helped to agree a reconciliation with Britain so making the treaty with France useless.

We both sleep. We will fight tomorrow.

At six in the morning, we enter the village.[24] To our surprise and great disappointment we discover the British stealthily escaped in the night. They left campfires burning to make our Connecticut soldiers think they were still there and departed at midnight abandoning the most seriously wounded for lack of wagons[25] and leaving surgeons to care for them. Weapons, knapsacks, utensils and clothes litter the ground, revealing their haste to be gone, and fifteen Americans have been released, to their joy, as well as Colonel Ramsay because of his bravery.

The wounded are taken to the English Church, the Court House, a barn and various houses. We bury the British Colonel Moncton with military honor. He fell so close to our troops at the hedgerow that both his body and the colors of his battalion had been captured and he had been heard to shout, "Forward to the charge, my brave grenadiers," as he fearlessly led the attack.

Shortly after the ceremony Nathanael Greene brings a woman covered in dirt and blood and lacking part of her skirt to Washington.[26]

"This is Molly Hayes, Your Excellency. The men call her Molly Pitcher. You saw her yesterday taking over the ramrod after her husband and other men at the cannon had been killed. You wanted to reward her."

"Here is a piece of gold for you," says Washington. "I also confer on you the rank of sergeant. Our success here is partly due to you and to the many women who brought water from the spring in the woods to give to the men and to cool the barrels of the cannon. The British were not so fortunate. They only had their canteens."

Sergeant Molly clutches the coin and I give her a piece of silver; she passes by the other French officers; they cheer and fill her hat with more money.

There is unfortunately nothing to eat as the supply wagons have broken down. "A gill of rum to each man," orders Washington.[27]

Turkey vultures circle in the sky. They mass in pulsating funereal flocks on dead horses, their beaks on their bald red heads ripping open the carcasses. They glide with huge black wings above the carts carrying the corpses, sometimes covering the bodies like macabre shrouds until driven off. They cloak the men lying in the streams where they had tried to find sanctuary from the heat.[28] Many are Hessians whose thick uniforms proved more fatal than our artillery fire; their tongues became so swollen from thirst, they had been choked and not able to breathe, their bloated bodies often with almost black faces. The stench arising from the dead men and horses in the woods is intolerable.[29]

We claim it as a victory.[30] We occupy the terrain. We bury two hundred and forty-five of their soldiers and fifty-nine of our own, including Major Dickinson, on the battle ground, in the Tennent Churchyard, or in a pit to the southeast of Freehold. We have one hundred and thirty-seven wounded. We have made approximately one hundred prisoners.[31] At least six hundred men deserted to our side, of whom four hundred and forty are Germans. It was the longest artillery battle of the war and the largest in the number of combatants. We held our own in open countryside against the British after the initial debacle.

In the afternoon, Clinton sends a message under a flag of truce to Washington: 'I commend the wounded we have had to leave behind to your tender mercies and I thank you for the honors which I gather you have paid to Colonel Monckton.'

We do not pursue the enemy. They have a night's march ahead of us. They have only ten miles to go to a strong post and will soon be under the protection of the guns of Howe's fleet.[32] Our men are extremely fatigued and Washington decides we will march towards the North River in case the British have designs on our posts there.[33] Maxwell's brigade, Morgan's corps and light parties will remain near the rear of the enemy to prevent their making depredations and to encourage desertions.[34]

I am very saddened and unhappy by my lack of distinction in the fight.[35] I had unintentionally participated in a retreat, initiated by Lee, while I had been looking for a better position from which to fight and this had perhaps not helped the situation. I had been unafraid under fire, but I had not commanded a successful attack against the British. My disappointment is also shared by Morgan. He and his riflemen had not even been present.

Lee writes to Washington on June 30. He complains bitterly of such 'very singular expressions' he had used. He claims Washington, or anyone else absent from the scene, would not have been able to judge the merits or demerits of his maneuvers 'to which the success of the day was entirely owing.' He says Washington had 'been guilty of an act of cruel injustice towards a man who certainly has some pretensions to the regard of every servant of this country.' He demands 'some reparation for the injury committed' and unless he could obtain it, he would retire 'when this campaign is closed,' which he believes will end the war, 'from a service, at the head of which is placed a man capable of offering such injuries.' He believed the offence was 'not a motion of Washington's own breast but was instigated by some of those dirty earwigs who will ever insinuate themselves near persons of high office; for I really am convinced that when General Washington acts for himself, no man in his Army can have reason to complain of injustice or indecorum.'[36]

The dirty earwigs we take to mean Hamilton, Laurens and myself.

"He lost his senses on the battlefield and behaved with a certain indecision and hurry of spirits," is Hamilton's opinion.[37]

Washington replies to Lee that he was not conscious he had made use of any very singular expression when he met him; what he recollected to have said was dictated by duty and warranted by the occasion and as soon as circumstances permit he will have an opportunity either of justifying himself to the army, to Congress, to America and to the world in general; or of convincing them that he was guilty of a breach of orders and of misbehavior before the enemy on the twenty-eighth in not attacking them as he had been directed, and in making an unnecessary, disorderly and shameful defeat.'[38]

Lee astonishingly writes another letter in which he says he is pleased: 'he has the opportunity of showing to America the sufficiency of her respective servants and that he trusts the temporary power of office, and the tinsel dignity attending it, will not be able, by all the mists they can raise, to offiscate the bright rays of truth' and concludes: 'Your Excellency can have no objection to my retiring from the Army.'[39]

He later writes another letter the same day saying that reflection convinces him a court of inquiry should be immediately ordered but that he wishes it might be a court martial, for if the affair is drawn into length, it may be difficult to collect the necessary evidences, and perhaps might bring on a paper war between the adherents to both parties, which may occasion some disagreeable feuds on the continent 'for all are not my friends, nor all your admirers.'[40]

Washington orders Adjutant General Scammell to come to headquarters with his sword and sash.

"Give General Lee this document which places him under arrest and give him a copy of the charges on which he will be tried," Washington tells him when he arrives.[41]

We will go in 'easy marches' towards the North River. Tents will be taken down at three in the morning; the men will march ten miles, then set up camp at one or two in the afternoon. They will rest every third day.[42]

It is about twenty miles to Brunswick. I command the second line on the right. On Wednesday, July 1, we are at Spots Wood, and I am major general for the day. The sun continues to blaze down. The column of soldiers struggles through the deep sand; the only water is at South River and the troops and horses become more and more distressed.[43] The wagons carry many men as they are in such a state of exhaustion from the heat.[44]

The enemy marches towards Sandy Hook. General Forman and others who are well acquainted with the area say it would be impossible to annoy them in their embarkation as the neck of land where they are now has a narrow passage which just a few soldiers could defend. [45]

Chapter 21

The French arrive

July 4. It is the second anniversary of the Declaration of Independence. We celebrate at Brunswick as at Valley Forge. Every hat has a sprig of green, reminiscent of the parade at Philadelphia when I had just joined the army; thirteen cannon roar; the whole infantry line fires a feu de joie.

"The perpetual and undisturbed independence of the United States!" shout the men. A double allowance of rum is given.

Lee's court martial begins, Lord Stirling presiding over four brigadier generals and eight colonels. The charges are:

First: For disobedience of orders, in not attacking the enemy on the 28 of June, agreeable to repeated instructions. Secondly: For misbehavior before the enemy on the same day, by making an unnecessary, disorderly and shameful retreat. Thirdly: For disrespect to the commander-in-chief in two letters dated July 1 and June 28. Lee's incorrect dates are given, although they were received by Washington on June 30. [1]

In the evening, I drink, dance and enjoy myself with my friends at a ball at headquarters. We hear that Conway challenged Cadwallader to a duel because of an alleged slur; Conway has been shot through the mouth and will perhaps die.

July 5. To my great unhappiness, I am called as the first witness at the trial. Adjutant General Scammell and Lee, who is conducting his own defense, cross-examine me about every movement I made at the battle and about my conversations.

"What authority had you to suppose that the aide-de-camp, who you were told brought orders from me to move back your corps as you were advancing towards the enemy, was sent by me?" asks Lee.

"I was told so, but I cannot say by whom and as I had only one battalion in the field, and the others had retreated to Freehold, where you were, I thought that such an order was coming of course. I cannot answer so well of the motion of the troops, as there was a great confusion and contrariety in the orders, and a complaint among the troops on account of it," I reply.

"Did you think that the number of the enemy's troops that followed was equal to the number of ours that retreated?" he asks.

"The number of the enemy did not appear to be equal to ours, but I thought that intelligence had been received that all the British army were coming upon us," I reply.[2]

Two days later I can leave, having kept quiet that I suspect he might be 'guilty of something very ugly and that he is very much prejudiced in favor of his English nation.' [3]

The army marches slowly towards New York, after a week at Brunswick; I again ride at the head of the second line, forming the right column. We receive word from New York that the French have reached American shores, but do not know more. [4]

July 13. The French have arrived![5] I am in an ecstasy of joy. A letter from President Laurens confirms it. The news spreads like wildfire through the camp at Paramus. Twelve ships of the line, fourteen frigates and a force of one thousand soldiers, under the command of Vice Admiral Charles Henri Théodat, comte d'Estaing du Saillans, have taken three months to sail from Toulon. They reached the mouth of the Delaware, unfortunately ten days too late to attack the British whose fleet left on June 28. Conrad Alexandre Gérard de Rayneval, the first French minister to the United States, and Silas Deane, who has been recalled by Congress, disembarked and travelled to Philadelphia. The French fleet sailed to New York and is now at Sandy Hook,[6] from where they can clearly see the British flags flying from the masts of their ships at anchor in the safe water within the Hook but owing to the large draught of some of their ships have not so far been able to sail across the sand bar.[7]

Washington writes on the fourteenth to d'Estaing, congratulating him on his arrival and informing him he is planning to cross the North River five miles above New York and then 'move down before the enemy's lines with a view of giving them every jealousy in his power and facilitate such enterprises as d'Estaing may form.'[8]

I also write to d'Estaing, a fellow Auvergnat and a distant relation by marriage. I express very great pleasure both at his arrival and in knowing that he is in command:

> I rejoice to think that you are about to deal the first blow to an insolent nation because I know that you will rightly value the pleasure of humiliating it and because you are sufficiently acquainted with it to hate it. I have the honor of being united with you in this sentiment as well as by the ties of kindred and by our common origin as Auvergnats…I leave it to the general of the army to inform you of his plans; I shall merely say that we intend to cross the North River and threaten New York in order to prevent them from stripping themselves of their vessels. As soon as the French flag is seen near Canada, half of the inhabitants and savages will declare themselves for us…However, I should tell you how awkward is my position here; for however agreeable it is to me to be in America….I should rather be a soldier serving under the French flag than to be a general officer anywhere else. My purpose is, to leave at once for the Antilles, for Europe, even for the East Indies, if in any one of these three parts of the world we are going to wage war….but all I want to know is, whether war has been declared in Europe…If I can be of service to you, Monsieur le comte, command me….May you defeat them; may you send them to the bottom, may you lay them as low now as they have been insolent before.

"Include information about yourself so Count d'Estaing will know the letters we are sending with Lieutenant Colonel Laurens are authentic and that he is not a spy," Washington tells me. Accordingly, I write a postscript:

> I have this moment arrived at headquarters, Monsieur le comte, and I learn with extreme pleasure you are now in a position to seriously embarrass the plans of General Clinton and Lord Howe. I trust that this will end in a brilliant manner…I do not believe you know my handwriting, but when I speak of our estates in Auvergne, of my château of Chavaniac, of the fine land of Pont-du-Château and the excellent salmon fishing of Monsieur de Montboissier; when I mention Mde. de Chavaniac and Mlle. du Motier….These little family details will enable you to recognize me as a true Auvergnat…Allow me to present to you Colonel Laurens, a trusted aide-de-camp of General Washington and the son of the president of Congress…I trust that Colonel Laurens will bring us back the news of some successful movement or the proposition of some plan that gives promise of brilliant results and in connection with which I may be happy enough at last to shed my blood for my country and to be acknowledged by her. I sign my name in full for the first time in America: 'Gilbert du Motier, Mis de Lafayette. [9]

I write to Elias Boudinot, a congressman from New Jersey, as well as to Mr. Caldwell, the quartermaster at Springfield, to arrange for spies to be sent to New York, and to offer a hundred guineas to anyone who provides information to help the French fleet.[10]

Washington orders the commissary department to send, if possible, fifty of their best bullocks, two hundred sheep and a quantity of poultry, to the comte d'Estaing, Admiral of the French Fleet now laying off Sandy Hook.[11]

July 17. In the morning, the emissary of d'Estaing, Major de Choin, a relation of Sartine, the secretary of state of the navy, arrives here in camp from Philadelphia. It had taken him two days and nights to reach the city and two days to see the president of Congress to whom he had given a letter from d'Estaing, as well as a copy of the letter d'Estaing has written to Washington.[12] The French fleet badly needs water and second ovens, otherwise their flour will be spoiled, as well as pilots to guide it over the shallows of Sandy Hook in order to attack the British[13] who are in Amboy Bay behind it.[14] Unfortunately, Congress could not help. The nearby countryside no longer produces anything as it has been stripped bare by the war; the city has neither goods nor craftsmen. De Choin could not even buy himself two pistols however much money he offered and has asked for some to be sent to him from the fleet.[15]

Washington welcomes him warmly. He orders pilots and mariners to be recruited. He also completes the movement of the army to east of the North River.

Congress suggests an attack on Rhode Island[16] where there are approximately three thousand enemy troops, commanded by Major General Sir Robert Pigot,[17] Washington agrees. He sends Hamilton, accompanied by Lieutenant Colonel Fleury, a Frenchman, to d'Estaing, with four ship's captains who have a good knowledge of the coast and two pilots to explain the proposal and to tell him the new location of the Continental Army.[18]

Unfortunately, the pilot with the best reputation, who guided all the English into harbor there during the war, now says he is too ill to help the French. I manage to persuade the precious invalid, as de Choin calls him, and send him to the sea by carriage.[19] The same day I write to d'Estaing from King's Ferry to say Hamilton will be coming and give the letter to Nevill.

Next night, Laurens returns. "I met with Count d'Estaing on his flagship.[20] He had set out in row boats from his ships in very stormy seas and managed to reach the mouth of Shrewsbury River, although an officer and four sailors died, and several rowboats sank.[21] Many of his men are ill with scurvy, and he greatly needs water and provisions. He offered fifty thousand French écus for a pilot to take his ships across the bar to New York harbor to attack Howe's fleet at Raritan within Sandy Hook, but every pilot refused because the largest French ships draw twenty-seven feet against the twenty-two feet of the British, who, in any case, always remove some of their guns to cross the bar, which d'Estaing obviously cannot do. He believes his sixty-four-gun-ships could clear the bar, but the seventy-fours probably could not, and his flagship of ninety guns certainly could not. Each English vessel has a spring line from her stern to the second anchor, so that if the French ships manage to sail over the sand bar with an easterly wind and a flood tide, the English could haul their ships round to be broadside on to face the bows of the French ships which would be unable to use their guns and which would also need to sail across the bar one at a time.[22] He is considering the possibility of attacking the British at Rhode Island instead."[23]

General Sullivan has been stationed at Providence with about one thousand Continentals since March[24] and Washington orders him to apply 'in the most urgent manner to the states of Rhode Island, Massachusetts and Connecticut to raise a body of five thousand men inclusive of what you already have, and to collect boats, engage pilots and in general get ready for a descent on Newport in conjunction with the French fleet and troops.'[25]

The army is now east of the North River and will hopefully deter the enemy in New York from sending reinforcements northwards. At the same time, we know that a fleet commanded by Admiral Byron has set sail from England. D'Estaing, therefore, reluctantly decides he must abandon an attack at New York even although his ships are so near to the enemy. He agrees to an assault at Rhode Island, which he had, in fact, already decided on, and intends to sail from Sandy Hook on July 23.

July 21. General Varnum departs with four regiments to Providence. Next day, to my joy, Washington gives me the order:

> SIR,- You are to have the immediate command of that detachment from this Army, which consists of Glovers and Varnums brigades, and the detachment under the command of Col. Henry Jackson. You are to march them, with all convenient expedition, and by the best Routs, to Providence in the State of Rhode Island. When there, you are to subject yourself to the orders of Major Genl. Sullivan, who will have the command of the expedition against Newport and the British and other troops in their pay on that and the Islands adjacent. If on your march you should receive certain intelligence of the evacuation of Rhode Island by the enemy, you are immediately to countermarch for this place, giving me the earliest advice thereof. Having the most perfect reliance on your activity and Zeal, and wishing you all the success, honor and glory, that your heart can wish, I am, with the most perfect Regard, Yrs. [26]

Major Neville returns with a letter from d'Estaing in which he suggests I may act with his infantry. I am again in raptures of delight. I write back immediately and give Laurens the letter to bring to him:

> I am leaving my detachment at White Plains with very sincere pleasure to command the detachment of which you will hear. You have filled me with joy, Monsieur le comte, by holding out to me the flattering hope that I shall go into action with the infantry that you have on board. I have never heard any news since I came into the world that gave me greater pleasure....I have never before realized the charm of our profession, Monsieur le comte, as I do now that I am to be allowed to practice it in company with Frenchmen. I have never wished so much for the ability I have not, or for the experience I will obtain in the next twenty years, if God spares my life and allows us to have war. No doubt it is amusing to you to see me presented as a general officer; I confess that I am forced myself to smile sometimes at the idea, even in this country, where people do not smile so readily as we do at home....I beg you, in the name of your own love of glory, do not begin the operations before we arrive. I shall hasten the march of my troops as much as possible...I declare that if I were to arrive too late, I should want to go home and hang myself. [27]

The same day I also write to Sullivan that 'nothing can give me greater pleasure than to go under your orders...The comte d'Estaing, a relation and friend of mine, has offered to me the french troops he has on board so that, in addition to your forces we schall add a pretty good Reinforcement....For God's sake, my dear friend, do'nt begin any thing before we arrive.'[28]

I wait two days for Hamilton but no word comes from him and I fear he might have met with a mishap. I cannot delay any longer. I ride from camp at White Plains, accompanied by Gouvion, Gimat, Pontgibaud and Nevill towards my troops who have already set off on the two-hundred and forty-mile march and are now thirty miles away. My star is shining.

At noon, I write once more to d'Estaing:

The item that I mention to you in my first ciphers is very dear to my heart...I offered to join General Sullivan if he is in a great hurry with the quickest troops from the various regiments....the more I think about what you have written me, monsieur le comte, the happier I am. I communicated to M. de Choin an idea that he thinks should conform to those he knows you have, and I am exultant about it. [29]

My hope is that I will command French and American forces fighting together; I must tread carefully to realize my plans.

The many rivers along our route impede our progress and it is often slow and difficult to ferry the men across. General Varnum and his officers suggest that as there is also a lack of flour, it would be better for them to take the upper road. I agree. On July 26, at Lyme, I order Varnum to take his brigade and Jackson's detachment, and go by Hartford, whilst I accompany Glover's brigade through Old Guilford and East Guilford along the coast to Saybrook.

I hurry my men through charming fishing villages and along winding coastal roads. On July 28, from Saybrook, I write to Sullivan:

I hope a pretty decent crop of laurels may be collected upon that island and we will terminate the whole by joining english country dances to french cotillons in compagny with the fine and Reputed ladies of the charming place. How happy I will be to introduce the land, and naval commanders of the expedition one to the other, I wish you will conceive as well as I already do by anticipating that pleasure. [30]

We cross the mouth of the Connecticut River and I send Major Brice with the letter to Providence.

The men march slowly north; I become more and more impatient even although I know that a council of war at Providence will wait for me before beginning action. On July 30 I allow a day of rest at Norwich where the brigade can pray and wash their clothes before they march the remaining forty miles. I write again to Sullivan:

It is a terrible affair for one who is in hurry to march a body of infantry through a long and in some parts difficult journey. That teaches patience extremely well...The honor I have to command troops who may be call'd old ones Glover's and Varnum's brigades engage me to hope that if there is some warm work it will be for us. I fancy the Count d'Estaing will also give me his two battalions, which will afford me great pleasure-but all those things lay in your bosom, and whatever you will think proper to intrust to my care, I will very cheerfully perform. [31]

I also write again to d'Estaing who is probably now near to Newport, as I know his fleet passed the tip of Long Island yesterday. I tell him Sullivan will have militia, state troops and the few Continental troops Washington has given me. I say that if my Continentals are inspired by the example of that type of soldier one finds only among those who have French blood in their veins, then I expect they will behave in a manner which will surpass that of the rest of their countrymen, but where there was something to be done quickly, I prefer, for many reasons, to see French troops go first. I mention, yet again, my hope and pleasure that I might fight alongside my fellow Frenchmen. [32]

August 2. Sunday. The troops halt and pitch their tents at Angel's Tavern, twelve miles from Providence, [33] and I gallop off ahead through the woods. In the evening, I ride into the small riverside town. [34] The narrow, unpaved streets seethe with townsfolk enthusiastically mingling with half-naked, badly dressed soldiers; I thread my way through the crowds, carts and wagons loaded with army equipment and provisions, to the two–story gabled house of Jabez Bowen, the deputy governor, a dark-complexioned, handsome man, who greets me warmly.[35]

I learn that the French fleet arrived on July 29 [36] and is anchored off Point Judith, near Brenton's Ledge, about five miles below Newport. On July 30, two French ships, one of sixty-four guns, the other of fifty, entered the Western Channel to attempt to capture two frigates. The frigates escaped to Newport but the French ships fired on the battery nearby whose magazine exploded.[37] Two frigates, the *Aimable* and the *Alcmène,* with the captured tender, *Stanley,* entered the Eastern Channel whereupon the British set fire under their battery to the *Kingfisher,* carrying eighteen nine-pounders and two three-pounders, the *Lamb,* carrying two eighteens, two nines and two sixes, and the galley *Spitfire,* carrying two eighteens, two twelves and six sixes.[38] One thousand five hundred Hessians were on Conanicut Island, but on the evening of the thirty-first a French reconnaissance party discovered they had abandoned it. [39]

I cannot contain my excitement. I rush to the shore and find a boat to take me to the *Sagittaire.* I climb on board, emotion welling up in me to see the fleur-de-lys and to be on a ship of my beloved country. I embrace my fellow Frenchmen who just as enthusiastically embrace me.

" *Vive le roi*!" " *Vive la France*!" we cry.

I am not arrested for sailing from France against the orders of the king. We drink many toasts and it is long after sunset when I return to Jabez Bowen, his family, and his delightful sister, Mary.

Greene arrived on July 31, having taken only three days to ride from camp.[40] He has brought a letter for me from Washington:

> This will be delivered to you by Major General Greene whose thorough knowledge of Rhode Island, of which he is a native, and the influence he will have with the people, put it in his power to be particularly useful to the expedition against that place; as well in providing necessaries for carrying it on, as in assisting to form and execute a plan of operations proper for the occasion. The honor and the interest of the common cause are so deeply of the greatest importance that it appears to me of the greatest importance to omit no step, which may conduce to it; and General Greene on several accounts will be able to render very essential services in the affair.
>
> These considerations have determined me to send him on the expedition, in which as he could not with propriety act, nor be equally useful merely in his official capacity of Quarter Master General, I have concluded to give him a command in the troops to be employed in the descent. I have therefore directed General Sullivan to throw all the American troops, both Continental, State and Militia, into two divisions, making an equal distribution of each, to be under the immediate command of General Greene and yourself. The Continental troops being divided in this manner to the Militia, will serve to give them confidence, and probably make them act better than they would alone. Though this arrangement will diminish the number of Continental troops under you, yet this diminution will be more than compensated by the addition of militia; and I persuade myself your command will not be less agreeable, or less honorable from this change in the disposition. I am, with great esteem and affection, dear Marquis, Your most Obed. Servant. [41]

I must accept the order of my general. I give one of my divisions to the brave and enterprising Greene whom I like very much.

Rhode Island is about fifteen miles long and three miles wide. The town of Newport is at the south-west and has an enemy garrison of about five thousand men, commanded by Major General Robert Pigot who had fought at Bunker Hill.[42] Four British and one Hessian regiment are entrenched at the north of the island on Butts Hill and Quaker Hill to prevent our troops landing there from the mainland. North of the town are two lines of outworks made of packed earth with a ditch and abattis of sharpened tree trunks or branches in front; the first line has five redoubts in front within musket-shot of each other[43] and extends from Easton Pond, an inaccessible pond covering more than half of it,[44] near to Tonomy Hall, a very strong hill fortification on a high cliff, commanding the nearby countryside,[45] reaching the sea on the north side of Windmill Hill. The second line is over a quarter mile from the first line, extending from the sea to the north side of the island where there is a battery. A redoubt commands the pass in the south, at the entrance by Easton's Beach, and another redoubt is about twenty rods to the north. These lines are surrounded by a wooden palisade whose two ends are on the shore and are supported by a ravine.[46] We believe the enemy to have about six thousand men here.[47]

To the east of Rhode Island is the Sakonnet, or Eastern Channel; between Rhode Island and Conanicut Island is the Middle, or Main, Channel and to the west of Conanicut is the Narragansett, or Western, Channel.

D'Estaing wants to attack immediately. Unfortunately, our Americans are not ready. Even although my troops have marched two hundred and forty miles no preparations have been made.[48] We have only about three thousand Continentals and, at the most, about one thousand eight hundred militia, although men are coming every day.

"All the tailors and apothecaries have answered the call; you can recognize them by their round wigs, nearly all miserably mounted, wearing game-belts as shoulder bags. The infantry appeared dressed by the same person. These warriors are not coming to see the enemy too close, but to help eat our food," comments the sharp-tongued Pontgibaud.[49]

On the twenty-fifth Sullivan had written to d'Estaing that he still needed men although many militiamen were arriving, and he outlined a plan of attack. D'Estaing arrived on the twenty-eighth, but fog made the fleet only visible to the shore the following day. Laurens then went with pilots to his flag ship, the ninety-gun *Languedoc*, to give him Sullivan's plan of operations and Washington's dispatches. Sullivan wanted d'Estaing to send ships up the Eastern and Western channels and seize the enemy's ships there; to block the main channel with the rest of his fleet to cut off the retreat of the enemy ships and stop reinforcements from arriving; The French vessels in the Eastern and Western channels would then cover the passage of the American troops from Tiverton and Bristol. The Americans would not attack the enemy fortifications at the north end of the island but would just leave a detachment as a guard and would proceed to the fortifications by Newport. When they made their attack the French ships would force an entry into the harbor, silence the batteries, cannonade the town and disembark their marines and land forces at the best place to aid the Americans.[50] On the thirtieth, Sullivan visited the *Languedoc*. He again told d'Estaing he still needed more men, but that militia were arriving in great numbers from the states of Rhode Island, Massachusetts, Connecticut and New Hampshire. He asked for three frigates at Bristol Ferry and Tiverton.[51] D'Estaing wanted to act immediately; to attack the Hessians on Conanicut; to destroy the enemy ships at Newport. He repeated that every moment passed in inaction by his ships was one less problem for the English and would increase the numbers of sick in his fleet, and of the suffering caused by the lack of water and fresh food. [52]

D'Estaing has already carried out part of this plan which, to my great disappointment, is very different from the plan I have been envisaging for the last few days in which I command French and American forces.

Sullivan, a major general, later wrote in more detail, telling d'Estaing, a French lieutenant general and vice admiral, who has been a soldier for thirty years, what to do, and I fear the possibility that he has taken serious offence. D'Estaing, however, replied courteously that in war one must be prepared for any event and that whether the enemy is reinforced by troops from Europe, or whether such reinforcements fail to arrive, he will try to be as useful as possible to the common cause, although he makes the point that each moment of his inactivity is an added advantage to the English and that when ships have been at sea for a certain length of time, then cases of scurvy increase to such a degree that a long rest becomes indispensable.[53] He later writes a second letter in which he says that he is shortly expecting Sullivan's final instructions which will be brought to him by Fleury and perhaps Laurens. He says that Sullivan left a plan when he visited and that he has had the presumption to keep it 'because anything made by yourself is too precious a keepsake to be allowed to slip through one's fingers.' He has, instead, made a copy of it to be returned to Sullivan.[54]

"Visit d'Estaing to help complete the plan of attack," Sullivan tells me.

August 4. There is a mist; the wind blows from the south-west.[55] I carry two letters from Sullivan and embark in a skiff with French and American officers, including John Brown, a large, well-built man, a wealthy, local ship owner. He is a Quaker, like Greene, and in 1772 was the leader of a group disguised as Native Americans, who attacked and burned the *Gaspée*, an armed British schooner which had run aground on Namcut Point in Providence River, and who shot its captain.[56]

At nine in the morning, we reach the black-hulled Languedoc, anchored off Brenton's Ledge. We board. *"Vive le roi!"* the crew shout; the officers welcome us enthusiastically.

The comte d'Estaing, a man of over fifty,[57] with a formidable reputation as a soldier and a former close friend of Louis XV, greets me diplomatically. "I welcome you with personal satisfaction, mixed with political anxiety."

"I have come to fight the English in order to learn better how to serve our master," I reply.[58]

He smiles. I have said what he both wishes and needs to hear. I introduce my companions to him, including Mr. Brown who is offering to give maritime advice to Monsieur Pléville le Pelley. Then we go to his quarters, drink toasts and discuss Sullivan's plan.

We agree it would be better if feints were made at other parts of Rhode Island in order to divert attention from two principal attacks. We think it would be best if part of the American army attack at the same place and at the same time as the French which would make it more certain that all would act at the same instant. We also agree that if I was given the command of these Americans then if d'Estaing was called away because the enemy was attacking by sea, I would also be given command of the French troops which would assure the unity of the movement.[59]

"What is your opinion?" d'Estaing asks his officers.

"I agree," replies each politely, but with not much warmth towards him.

"We shall soon be without water as the springs are exhausted, and our biscuit is nearly finished. We do not yet have the six thousand bricks I have requested to make ovens,"[60] says d'Estaing.

"When I return to shore, I will attempt to procure what you want," I tell him.

We leave the *Languedoc* at five in the afternoon, *" Vive le roi!"* ringing out three times. A boat takes me to the frigate, *Provence,* stationed forward of the main fleet, which will land me somewhere near to Providence; I carry a letter from d'Estaing to Sullivan, as well as his orders for Admiral Suffren to attack two frigates the following day in the Sakonnet Passage.

Thick fog rolls in; the frigate glides slowly along the Western Channel like a phantom and is forced to anchor again almost immediately.[61] Late in the evening, I finally reach the governor's house. I am in raptures. My star shines. I hope to command a detachment of French marines and soldiers as well as my Continentals and militia.

"I prefer to attack at a single point, with a union of the American troops, especially of the Continentals, in a rectangular movement to enclose the British, when we have enough militia to commence an assault," declares Sullivan next day, after having read the letter of d'Estaing.

"I agree," says Greene.

"It is the opinion of the comte d'Estaing that the enemy would be far less fearsome if divided by several false attacks and two real ones. It would be difficult for the enemy to ascertain the time needed for marching and fighting and we should not wait every time we make a landing for almost everyone to be ashore before disembarking the best troops," I say.[62] "If a wing of the army is too much to deploy, the comte d'Estaing would be pleased with a detachment. General Sullivan would have the greatest part of the Continental troops and just a small part of them would be joined to some militia, the whole comprising two or three thousand men who would be joined with French troops which would give them an always reliable support and example. This disembarkation would take place under the fire of the ships and would allow us to reach the Americans and for the Americans to reach us, following the diagram which I have given to you. You will also note that if you do not accept the plan to attack the redoubts at two points, you do not lose the advantage of the rectangle but give it an even more regular form by lengthening your side."

"We should not divide our force to send some to d'Estaing," declares Sullivan. "Our army contains a very small proportion of regular troops. It is necessary that a main body capable of resisting the enemy should exist, as a contrary conduct would expose either division to total defeat or a vigorous attack from the enemy."[63]

"The French fleet is destined to take an important part in this action," I say vehemently. "Its landing party should be counted on for a great deal. If they come ashore in total security, it would be no problem to change the arrangement. However, if there is any danger the French troops should have the right to profit from it, and this is the only mark of gratitude they claim. In either case, the landing was to be made at the same time and so arranged that each party might be in a position to take advantage of any opportunity to distinguish itself that fortune might offer. We not only owe to the fleet this whole expedition because without it nothing would have been undertaken but it is the support from the fleet which will assure our success at the moment of attack. It is not acceptable that the French troops should come ashore after the initial descent has mainly taken place. The sound and the effect of their thundering guns, the division of the places where they are feared, a corps of troops of considerable, though as yet unknown, strength, which lands under the protection of those guns, their first steps telling the enemy that there are Frenchmen among them, is the disturbing spectacle we can offer the British.[64] I would like to command the detachment you intend for the French, whether it is great or small and the pleasure of fighting in view of my own countrymen could not be made up to me by being given any conceivable wing, and I should resume command of the number of troops to which I am entitled after I rejoin you."[65]

The American officers do not agree with me. John Laurens believes my private views withdraw my attention wholly from the general interest and accuses me of ambition and national pride.[66]

"I have no objection after the landing party is no longer under the immediate orders of the vice admiral to allow it to be commanded by you," comments Sullivan.

At five that morning, Admiral Suffren's two frigates sailed south from the north of Conanicut Island. The British frigate, the *Cerberus,* attempted to make for Newport harbor but the French started to come up, so her captain ran her aground and she was set on fire. At about eight, she blew up. The same happened to the *Juno*, the *Orpheus*, the *Pigot* galley and the *Lark*, whose gunpowder exploded, sending burning fragments of smoldering debris cascading over the west of the island. The thirty-two-gun *Flora*, the eighteen-gun *Falcon* and several transports were scuttled to stop the French entering the harbor at Newport.[67]

I write to d'Estaing and say that field pieces will be sent to him, as well as boats and horses. A man will show a better place to obtain water and orders have been given for baking biscuits. I relate what I said to Sullivan and Greene of the plan we had devised and that I have not greatly succeeded in that respect:

> If Sullivan sends you a reinforcement it will be so small that it would not enter his head that I would prefer it to the command of his flank of six thousand men as it would give me the happiness of being under your orders, and the companion in glory of my dear compatriots, the French. Besides, he thinks you will keep control of the detachment and believes therefore that with this famous left wing I will be of some use to him in a way that I myself am not aware…Now I ask your permission to add what my slight acquaintance with this country makes me hope for. Your plan seems to me very far from being lost. In your answer to General Sullivan speak of it again as seeming necessary for the success of the expedition and consonant with your desires as well as with the wishes of those who are under your orders. If while adding your military reflections you stress them firmly, these gentlemen will find it easier to agree to them than to answer them and thus will enlarge the detachment that will be given to you. Its number is not established in General Sullivan's letter; you seem to be assured at least two thousand men, of whom one half or one third will be Continentals. If you should add to this the kindness of asking that I shall command them, or at least that it should be proposed to me, I assure you my decision will come from the heart and my dearest wishes will be fulfilled….We plan to attack on Sunday if we are ready. You see that we have time to send you some reinforcements if you answer at once. [68]

I send Gouvion with the letter to d'Estaing. "Describe to him the part of Rhode Island you have seen and reconnoiter another part of the island."

D'Estaing writes back suggesting I acquiesce to Sullivan's plans in the interest of both sides.[69] He writes to Sullivan and says he is willing to do what Sullivan wishes and that he is punishing Monsieur de Lafayette a little too much for a mistake that is his. [70]

I write to Washington. I tell him I am very pleased with the arrival of Greene:

> Who not only on account of his merit, and the justness of his views, but also by his knowledge of the country and his popularity in this state, may be very serviceable to to the expedition. I willingly part with the half of my detachment, although I had a great dependence on them, as you find it convenient to the good of the service. Anything, my dear General, you will order, or even wish, shall always be infinitely agreeable to me, and I will always feel happy in doing anything which may please you, or forward the public good. I am of the same opinion as your Excellency that dividing our Continental troops among the militia, will have a better effect than if we were to keep them in one wing…the admiral wants me to join the French troops to those I command as soon as possible. I confess I feel very happy to think of cooperating with them, and had I contrived in my mind an agreeable dream, I could not have wished a more pleasing event than my joining my countrymen with my brothers of America, under my command, and of the same standards. When I left Europe, I was very far from hoping such an agreeable turn of our business in the American glorious revolution. [71]

D'Estaing writes to Sullivan again the next day and says that the *Languedoc* will enter the Middle Channel on Saturday if the wind is favorable, and that he hopes to position eight ships across the harbor, whilst the *Engageante* and the *Provence* will sail up the Eastern Channel to the place appointed for the descent of the American troops. He says he hopes 'Your Excellency and the General Officers who serve with you, will put it in my power to give an account to the King and to the Congress of the number and goodness of the troops that you shall have joined to the French-This detachment the number of which I will not undertake to point out because on all occasions we endeavor when it is necessary to be sufficient to ourselves- is the first occasion on which the Generals of the United States have it in their power to give an authentic proof of the value which they set upon the alliance of His Majesty and the satisfaction with which they join their troops to his.' He says that he has been a lieutenant general in the Kings Armies for the last ten years and that he will only tell the officer commanding the detachment movements and positions that those of the enemy and the ground require. He also says it will be impossible for him to delay his disembarkation until the American descent has been made. [72]

Sullivan changes his mind on reading d'Estaing's words. "You can have the command of Jackson's regiment, and as many good militia as would amount in total to one thousand men, as a detachment to join the French," he now tells me.[73]

This is disproportionate to the command I should have had, but I decide to accept it for many reasons. D'Estaing's letter has already made a sufficient impression and if I refuse would add to it too much and I would appear to be disrupting the general plan by my fantasies.

"My attachment for America and my even more tender love for my fellow countrymen make my situation very delicate," I reply.[74]

I write to d'Estaing and say I hope he approves, that our army will not be as large as had been expected, and that I will be commanding some strangely dressed figures whom I will blush for, not because of their clothing, but only if they do not fight as well as might be expected of new troops.[75]

On the night of the ninth to the tenth, Greene will lead a detachment across from Tiverton to the north-east of Rhode Island. Early next morning, four French battalions, each of five hundred sailors and marines, some armed with muskets whose bayonets are made of cutlass blades, the hilts removed then inserted into the barrel ends and tied with tarred rope, as well as the ships' infantry[76] which will form two battalions, as well as the troops I have been given, will cross from Conanicut to the west side of the island. The enemy will be attacked on Monday if everything is ready.[77]

On August 8, at three in the morning, the *Languedoc* leads eight ships of the line into the channel between Conanicut island and Newport harbor. The French ships sail past the batteries on Rhode Island which fire heavily on them, and anchor at the bottom of the Middle Channel.[78] The American army goes to Howlands Ferry.

On the ninth, the wind is from the south and so the French remain at their anchorage. During the night, it shifts to the north; about eleven o'clock d'Estaing sets sail. On Sunday morning, at seven o'clock, two thousand French troops and artillery start to disembark at Conanicut Island using flat boats we have sent as well as their own. Once ashore, they march and drill to become accustomed to land after nearly four months at sea; I prepare my troops to join them tomorrow.

To my great surprise and that of the other French officers, we discover that about two to three thousand American troops, using about fifteen flat boats, are crossing onto the north point of Rhode Island a day before they were intended to.[79] Deserters and local people informed Sullivan that on the eighth, the British, frightened by the French ships coming up the river, evacuated their troops to Newport from the redoubts and batteries on Butts Hill and Quaker Hill, in the north part of the island.[80] Sullivan, however, had written to d'Estaing just an hour before, giving a new, written assurance of what had already been agreed.[81] I and the other French officers are angry. It is an insult to France that the Americans are landing first.

We also discover there are unfortunately no cannon left in the forts which we are meant to defend;[82] Sullivan sends Colonel Fleury to inform d'Estaing what he has done and to ask for help to transport over artillery and munitions.[83]

Our anger at what Sullivan has done annoys my fellow American officers.

"You conceive your troops injured by our landing first and now talk like women disputing precedence in a country dance, instead of men engaged in pursuing the common interest of two great nations," is the view of Laurens.[84]

We believe the French will think Sullivan is jealous of French prestige and so had acted without informing them, wanting to gain the glory for himself, making it appear an American victory with the French acting a secondary part. To my relief, a message arrives from d'Estaing: 'The troops already on Conanicut will be transferred to Rhode Island to join you; the *Fantasque* and the *Sagittaire* will protect their passage.'[85]

In the afternoon, an aide-de-camp brings another message: 'A large British fleet is visible near to our previous anchorage near Newport. I will put out to sea to attack it. I am embarking the men from Conanicut and will leave you three frigates and the *Stanley* in the East Channel, and the galley *Dauphin* in the West Channel. I am sending back the flat boats to you; I will return to help finish the siege of Newport.'[86]

At eleven o'clock that morning, the French ships had been preparing to aid the Americans when the fog which had enveloped the island for two days had started to lift and the lookouts on top of the masts had seen more than thirty ships of Howe's fleet approaching the entrance to the harbour at Newport. D'Estaing's first duty was now to his fleet. His situation was perilous. His ships could not remain blocked, shut in and divided in the Channels for the enemy to come and attack. Sullivan's response was to suggest to him that he was imagining the scene although he knew that the British had been expected.[87] The enemy fleet anchored before the sun went down, a little nearer the shore than the previous anchorage of the French, the only movement a small boat, presumably carrying information to Newport. Their forces were unknown. There was little wind[88] but if it became more favorable it would be better to set sail and go out to attack the enemy, in however disadvantaged a position, than to wait.

August 10. Monday. At eight-thirty in the morning, in a slight west-north-west wind, the French fleet cut their cables [89] and quickly set sail. In single file, they pass the enemy batteries and forts which fire much more strongly than when they passed them before.[90] Each ship fires a broadside of thirty-six to twenty-four-pound balls; each battery returns the fire with much smaller balls of ten to twenty pounds. It is a magnificent sight. I have never been so proud and so happy.[91]

By ten-thirty, the ships pass the last battery, the *Languedoc* fifth in the line,[92] watched by both British and American armies, the ships crowding all the sail they can, even to studding sails and royals.[93] When the fourth ship passes the point, the British ships cut their cables.[94] They flee hastily with full sail, leaving behind many of their ships and boats.

I watch until the two fleets disappear. The British have twenty ships to our sixteen, and nine hundred and fourteen guns to our eight hundred and thirty-four but I have complete faith in the superiority of my nation. A great victory will be ours.

In the evening Sullivan decides to march towards Newport as the number of troops who have arrived are now sufficient to advance towards the enemy without waiting for the return of the French fleet.[95] In any case, he expects the French will come back to join us by the time we post before Newport.[96]

The army parades in the afternoon of the eleventh, to prepare to march at six o'clock the following day.[97] The wind gusts strongly; it is raining; but the men are full of spirit. On the twelfth, the weather worsens. General Nature intervenes. The sky blackens. The wind howls from the north-west;[98] a deluge of rain falls from the heavens. What must it be like out in the Atlantic?

Our encampment floods. We wallow in a sea of mud into which the horses sink and die. We see, for the first time, that men are hardier than horses. Powder and cartridges are ruined. Tents blow away. Soldiers huddle next to the stone walls which take the place of fences here, but many cannot find any shelter. Some die.[99] The communication between us and the mainland is cut off; the wind is so violent it would scarcely permit even a whale boat to pass.[100]

"If the enemy attacks us we must depend on the superiority of our numbers and the point of the bayonet," declares Sullivan.[101]

To add to our misfortune, it is reported that Admiral Byron is near the coast and will probably appear before the French return.[102]

Towards dawn of the fourteenth, the wind veers to the south; the storm subsides. Devastation is everywhere. Roofs have been blown off buildings, trees and bushes uprooted, and windows encrusted with salt from sea spray. Some of the militia start to return home, anxious about their harvest; soldiers attempt to dry their clothes and inspect weapons and cartridges.

I constantly wonder what has become of the French fleet. What havoc has this terrible tempest caused at sea?

"I expect the storm will have driven their ships very far away. I have no hope of assistance from them," believes Sullivan.[103]

At six in the morning of the fifteenth, the signal gun fires. The army parades and forms in columns. At nine, under a black, threatening sky, we march towards Newport. The drums beat. I lead half the army, the left wing, with horses and heavy guns, down East Road. Greene leads the other half, with horses and guns, down West Road. The sun shines, brightening the green coats of the New Hampshire volunteers, the white uniforms and blue-feathered plumes of Greene's men, the different-colored hunting shirts of mine.

We halt about two miles from the redoubts before Newport, near Honeyman's Hill, east of Easton's Pond.[104] We set up camp. In the night, we start to build parallels on the east of the town, not far from the two lines of British redoubts and batteries which, at one place, traverse a ravine.

"The French will dig parallels on the west when they return," says Sullivan. "We will try to take the town by regular approaches."

Militia are deserting in shoals. On the sixteenth, Sullivan issues a proclamation:

The Genl having been Informed that many of the Troops, particularly the Militia under his Command, are so base as to Desert the Army, tho engaged in the most glorious Cause, and in the Fairest prospects of Victory; therefore takes this Method to Call on the good people of the surrounding Towns, to apprehend, secure and return to his Camp, all persons who may come within their notice from this Island not having a proper Pass signed by the Commander in Chief, A Major Genl of the Army or one of their aids des camp.[105]

Fog luckily swirls round us, helping to conceal what we are doing. Cannonading commences at dawn. Cannon balls scream down; we fire back. In the dark cloak of night our soldiers resume digging.

I talk with the Reverend Manassah Cutler who is visiting our fortifications. A cannon ball thuds into the earth next to us; I ignore it and carry on speaking.

"I am glad you are so firm about the arrival of a cannon ball. For myself it must be said I am less firm," he says, scurrying away, his coat flapping behind him as I laugh.[106]

I am major-general of the day almost every forty-eight hours and keep very busy, my thoughts always with the French ships. On the eighteenth, we hear cannon fire from the sea. The French fleet is perhaps just off the harbor, but the fog does not allow them to come in. Our batteries within half musket shot of the enemy lines are nearly ready to open; batteries at musket shot distance are ready.[107] So far, we have not lost a man.

"We will accost the enemy today in accents of thunder," Sullivan declares.

In the morning, a battery of four eighteen-pounders silences an enemy redoubt to our delight. On the twentieth, another four-gun battery opens;[108] a lookout sees a sail on the horizon approaching Newport; we wait anxiously for an hour until a spyglass finally reveals the flags. They show the fleur-de-lys. My anxiety is very great.

At midday, the comte de Cambis comes ashore in a small boat from the *Senegal,* a British frigate captured on the fifteenth, and is met at Point Judith by a group of officers sent to the coast.[109] He writes a letter to Sullivan:

Monsieur le comte d'Estaing has sent me to inform you that the French fleet had returned to Rhode Island following the promise he had made, but that the total dismasting of two of his principal ships by a storm during his pursuit of the English has compelled M. le comte d'Estaing to seek a port in order to make repairs and to put himself in a condition to continue the operations against the common enemy; that the French fleet would consequently go to Boston and not approach nearer to Rhode Island because M. le comte d'Estaing feared that with the damaged state of his ships it would not be possible with the usual south-west winds to pass the Banks of Nantucket;that monsieur le comte d'Estaing begged His Excellency, General Sullivan, to tell his three frigates and his corvette in the Eastern Channel of his departure for Boston, with the request that they should join him there promptly by passing the Nantucket Bank with a good pilot. [110]

He then returns to his ship to sail back to the French fleet which is at Brenton's Ledge.

The whole of Monday and that night the French fleet had chased the British. On Tuesday, the weather gage favored them, and they came up to the enemy about four in the morning. Battle started, but then the storm arrived. Both fleets were scattered. By dawn the *Languedoc* had lost her masts and rudder. The *Renown* arrived and tacked backwards and forwards across her stern, firing a full broadside the length of her decks and smashing cannon balls into her for about two hours. D'Estaing was worried the ship would be boarded and started to throw his confidential papers into the sea. Other French ships came up, night fell, and the *Renown* sailed away. The *Marseillaise* was also dismasted. The *Preston* fired on the *Tonnant* which had only one mast and the seventy-four-gun *César,* commanded by Monsieur de Raimondis, has not been seen since. The *Languedoc* now has two small sails jury-rigged and has been towed back here by one of the other ships.

I am bitterly disappointed, but very relieved the French fleet is not destroyed. The American officers are, however, furious that d'Estaing intends to go to Boston. I remain quiet, everyone around me shouting in anger and distress. Sullivan is beside himself with fury. His face reddens with rage. He stamps up and down like a maddened bull.

"Ten thousand men are in danger!" he shouts. "If the French help us, we can defeat the enemy at Newport. Fresh water and provisions will be found for their ships. Masts and other damage will be repaired."

"Sail out to the flagship to try and gain time and persuade d'Estaing either to make an immediate attack on Newport or to station vessels in the Providence river," he orders Greene and me.[111]

August 21. We gallop from headquarters to the coast; we set sail in a skiff. I know that without French assistance we have little chance of success and fervently hope my countrymen and the Americans can be reunited.

"If we fail in our negotiation," remarks Greene, his face pale, as we lurch up and down in the choppy sea, "We shall, at least, get a good dinner."[112]

However, he appears to be an even worse sailor than I am, and I feel it is somewhat doubtful about his prospects in eating at all.

John Brown captains our small craft. He stands next to Greene, talking angrily and rudely and appears to be goading him. He even pulls at his sleeve. Greene says nothing, his skin a sickly white.

I sit by John Langdon, a New Hampshire Continental ship agent, a militia colonel, whose expression suggests a cold hostility. I ignore him, too preoccupied with keeping my food in my stomach and desperate to see the condition of the ships and to talk with d'Estaing.

We slowly approach the *Languedoc*, its black hull jaggedly pitted by a broadside of cannon balls revealing pale wood, its decks covered by broken masts, spars and debris, only small jury sails now governing it. We clamber on board. I embrace d'Estaing, then Greene and I go to his quarters for a council of war. He tells me of the heroic conduct of the sailors during the battle, filling me with the deepest grief and making tears come to my eyes. [113]

"We now have ten thousand troops near Newport, and we believe we are facing six thousand British in an entrenched position. If it is possible, I beg you to agree to General Sullivan's request, or at least to send reinforcements," I say.

"Perhaps," he replies. "If the garrison can be defeated within two days."

"It is impossible to assure you of that," I say.

"Then I am not willing to delay sailing to Boston," he replies.

"We need French help to achieve a victory which is almost certain," says Greene, which I translate for him.

We talk for hours, Greene and I trying to persuade my compatriots to stay and help us.

"It is difficult to think that three thousand soldiers with a fort behind them and trenches in front would be taken in twenty-four hours or even two days," declares d'Estaing. "Our intelligence reports that the British fleet recently sent from England has been sighted off Long Island. I do not want to be trapped in Narragansett Bay facing a far superior force. Many of my men died as we crossed the Atlantic. Twenty were killed as we ran the gauntlet of the battery. We have lost the *César*. I do not want more killed on a mission unlikely to succeed when our ships are so incapacitated. However, I will give you a chance to write out an appeal to persuade my captains as well as myself."

Greene accordingly begins drafting a petition, watched over by Brown. The *Languedoc* swings violently at its anchor; he becomes steadily more seasick as the afternoon wears on. He struggles to bend over the paper and write but still manages to express our views succinctly: 'The expedition was only conceived as a plan for the French fleet to act in conjunction with the American army. It has been difficult to assemble so many militiamen because of the harvest but now large numbers have come and there will be much unhappiness if the French depart. Newport is an important prize which can be taken and for which it is worth taking a risk.' He does not mention that the storm has caused thousands to abandon us.

I continue to do my best to persuade d'Estaing who is honest in his reply to me. "I speak to you, not so much as to the envoy from General Sullivan, but as to my friend. I am in very unhappy circumstances. I am bound by express orders from the king to go to Boston in case of an accident or a superior fleet. All my officers and even some of the American pilots[114] believe I will ruin my squadron by delaying going to Boston. I called a second council of war and everyone was of the same opinion. I do not think I can justify staying here any longer. I am deeply sorry I am not able to assist America for some days."

Outside on the deck, John Langdon paces backwards and forwards and Brown mutters angrily. We eat dinner which I enjoy despite the situation. Poor Greene, however, is too ill to eat.

"We need to go to Boston," d'Estaing finally declares. "I do not consider Providence suitable as a place to repair the ships. However, I will let my captains decide."

"I do not think we should go to Boston," says Monsieur de Brugnon, the second-in-command. Five minutes later, he changes his mind. All the other officers then agree, as well as the American pilots on board.[115]

Greene queasily protests. "I am sure the repairs can be done here."

"We do not request the stay of your fleet and troops for more than forty-eight hours," I say.[116]

"No," replies d'Estaing firmly. "After many months of suffering my crew will rest some days. Then I will man the ships and if I am assisted in obtaining masts and repairs, in three weeks we will come out again and fight for the glory of the French name and the interests of America. In the meantime, we will help transport the troops back to the mainland."

"That is not what we want," says Greene.

"I will leave you my two battalions," d'Estaing tells me, his pleasure in being able to give me a rank in the French army very apparent.

"No, these troops are useful on board," I reply. "I will not expose them to danger for my own private interest."[117]

D'Estaing gives me a letter for Sullivan:

Sir: Our cables were cut, and the fire of the batteries which we were going to cross in order to attack the enemy's squadron had commenced, when they delivered to me the letter which Your Excellency has done me the honor to write me the 9th instant. It has been impossible for me to reply to it other than in pursuing the English fleet and in hindering it from lending assistance. The Count de Cambis was instructed to tell you my actual position and the necessity in which I find myself of going to Boston. I have not been able to fulfill this sad duty, because with a vessel entirely dismantled, its helm broken and unhinged, one is uncertain as to his personal movements. However, I have had the consolation of being still sufficiently master of them to keep the promise I gave to Your Excellency, assuring that I would return dead or alive. This promise and the service which our presence, although temporary, may be to you, has forced me to shut my eyes to all remonstrances: perhaps, even, I have ceased to be prudent and my zeal has blinded me. I have believed that one could not dare too much in the name of the King, to prove how much His Majesty is attached to his allies, but I should become guilty towards America herself if I did not think of preserving for her a squadron designed to defend her. I expressed regret to Lieutenant Colonel Fleury that you landed a day sooner than we had agreed upon. I should have been distressed to know that you were in danger. They told me that you had only two thousand men with you. I do not presume to weigh your motives. I have refrained from criticism and the twelve thousand men actually under your command will probably justify this step by a success which I desire both as a citizen and as one of the admirers of your courage and talents.

PS. I reopen my letter to assure Your Excellency of the grief with which I have just read your dispatch of the twentieth, but I cannot change my plans....The exact orders that I have from the King command me, in case of superior force, to retire to Boston, and if the appearance of the fleet, together with the 12,000 men which according to Colonel ------, were yesterday under your orders, had, fortunately, for us, given Rhode Island into your hands, I should go away to Boston....I pride myself on esteeming and cherishing the Marquis de Lafayette, but when one is a public man one sees only the public weal. Were I to follow the dictates of my own heart you would only need yourself and the interest that I have for your success. [118]

We say farewell, our mood grim. Sullivan and the officers will be very displeased.

"The garrison would be all our own in a few days if the fleet would but only cooperate with us. They have got a little shattered in the storm and are worried Byron and Howe's fleets may prove their ruin. They are obviously determined to leave us immediately. Our expedition is now at an end. To evacuate the island is death. To stay may be ruin," is Greene's opinion.[119]

We deliver d'Estaing's letter to Sullivan at his headquarters. He does not receive it well and nor does anyone else.

"The French fleet can refit here. Our expedition will be a disaster. It will end in disgrace," officers shout in indignation and anger. "We are now in a very difficult position. So much time has been wasted, our hopes have been dashed, and we are facing the enemy alone without naval support."

"I believe there is jealousy between the admiral and the officers," remarks Greene. "I think that if it was solely his decision he would stay here and fight."

"He said that after so many months of suffering his men will rest some days; that he will man his ships and if he is assisted in getting masts etc., three weeks after his arrival he will go out again and then we shall fight for the glory of the French name and the interests of America," I say.[120]

"It is perhaps possible he might still be persuaded to stay," declares Sullivan. "Perhaps he fears to have full responsibility to remain because if there is a defeat he would be blamed."

I write a letter to d'Estaing to tell him the response and that he will receive letters from Sullivan and Hancock about their fears and their frustrated hopes:

I have never seen these gentlemen so positive of the facilities you will find and the hopes for our success... They take responsibility for this with an assurance that I confess, seems persuasive...today I receive the most positive assurances from the persons who are writing you on all the points on which I was unsure. I confess that if I believe Mr. Hancock about it, I am at a loss for your resources in Boston...Pardon me, Monsieur le comte, if I give you either useless regrets or repetitions that are no less useless, but you will excuse me because of the necessity of my doing so and my duty. I strongly feel what you yourself feel on this occasion and I think myself deserving of sharing your affections because of the sincerity of my own. Farewell, Monsieur le comte, my tender affection for you links itself with the limitless love I have for my country and with my wishes for the success of her arms. I shall be at ease only when I may leave to go conquer or die under your orders and with you. [121]

I read the letter to Sullivan, leaving out the last words.

"I approve of the assurances you give on my behalf," he says. [122]

Next day I am summoned to a council meeting. People complain furiously about the action of my compatriots. They deeply offend me, and I retort with impatience and anger. "My country is dearer to me than America. Whatever France does is always right. Monsieur d'Estaing is my friend and I will support my sentiments with a sword that will never have been better employed. Since you have lacked delicacy in summoning me, I will not be delicate in my expressions!"

Apologies come from everyone. "We do not require your opinion." I remain in a fury. From now on, I might need to avenge every word that is said.[123]

Sullivan drafts a letter from himself and his general officers declaring that 'ruinous consequences would result to this army' if d'Estaing abandoned the harbor of Newport and went to Boston with his fleet, and requesting him:

To lay the following many weighty reasons to induce him to remain at his post before his officers. First. Because the expedition against Rhode Island was undertaken by agreement with the Count d'Estaing. An army has been collected, and immense stores brought together, for the reduction of the garrison; all of which will be liable to be lost should he depart with his fleet, leave open the harbor open for the enemy to receive reinforcements from New York, and ships of war to cut off communication with the main and totally prevent the retreat of the army. Secondly. the ships can be repaired sooner here than at Boston. Thirdly: it is very hazardous to sail the damaged ships around Nantucket Shoals and will probably result in the total loss of two of them. Fourthly: Dismasted ships usually have the masts brought to them. Fifthly: The honor of the French nation must be injured by their fleet abandoning their allies on an island in the middle of an expedition agreed to by the Count himself and will create jalousies between Americans and their hitherto esteemed allies. Sixthly: The account of Byron being near the coast is not well-founded. Seventhly: Even if a superior fleet should arrive, the French fleet would be in no greater safety at Boston as at Newport. Eighthly: The order said to be given by the King of France for his fleet to retire to Boston in case of misfortune, cannot be supposed to extend to the removal of his whole fleet in the middle of an expedition after damage having occurred to only two or three ships. Ninthly: Even if it was necessary for the fleet to go to Boston there can be no reason for the Count d'Estaing's taking with him the land forces on his ships which might be of great advantage in the expedition. It concludes: We, therefore, for the reasons above assigned, do in the most solemn manner protest against the measure, as derogatory to the honor of France, contrary to the intentions of His Most Christian Majesty and the interest of his nation, and destructive in the highest degree to the welfare of the United States of America and highly injurious to alliance formed between the two nations. [124]

The general officers sign. I am furious. I refuse.[125]

"How can you expect me to be a party to such an insult to my compatriots? My country is dearer to me than America. Whatever France does is always right. The comte d'Estaing is my friend and I will support my convictions with my sword which could never be better employed. As you have lacked little delicacy in summoning me, then I will not be delicate in my expressions."[126]

Everyone apologizes. "We are very far from requiring you to give your vote."

I write a short letter to d'Estaing to accompany the long protest letter:

From now on I will be fearful that I may have to resent every word I hear spoken. The predicament I am in, the different feelings that stir me, and the emotions of impatience that I just expressed leave me powerless even to speak and write to you with composure...I admit that the general consternation was more extensive than I would ever have believed. It was impossible to foresee the effect this departure has on dispositions here. Excuse me, monsieur le comte, but this is not the first time I sin by too much frankness. I told you the other day all that I knew; today I tell you what I see, and more than I expected. My heart will always be open to a man whom I love as much as you.

Adieu, M. le comte. They describe the monstrous dangers you will meet on your way to Boston, and I am told alarming stories about the risks you run in going to Boston, and I am frightened by them. I shall have no peace until you arrive there. If I leave the Island, I shall go to that city immediately. I hope that nothing will remain after I leave Rhode Island and that no one will have to complain of any loss unless I share in the danger of it. The last boat will be for me; and, at all events, I beg you to receive the homage of my admiration for your virtues, for your patriotism, and for all that can make you respected and loved. [127]

Laurens goes to deliver our letters. [128] He returns, still with the letters. The French fleet had sailed for Boston the night before last even although the wind was not fair. [129]

People erupt with fury. They shout and wish my countrymen all the evils in the world. They malign their allies as a generous one would be ashamed to treat the most inveterate enemies. I am in horror. I am more upon on a warlike footing in the American lines than when I come near the British lines at Newport. [130] I decide to stay only with the French gentlemen who are here. I believe that the leaders of the expedition are so incensed because they are ashamed to return home having spoken of success at Rhode Island, others are annoyed that they have spent a small amount of money and time at a camp just a few miles from home.

"If anything is said against my nation, I will take it as the most particular affront," I declare. [131]

Sullivan sends Laurens with the letter and declaration of protest in a fast sailing privateer to try and catch d'Estaing.

"Once d'Estaing is in Boston, he could send his troops and even those of the navy. Perhaps you could go and ask for them?" people suggest.

"I am under all circumstances prepared to go for the good of America," I reply.

Discussion continues for some time. "I want to go and join the comte d'Estaing in order to try to be of service to him," I tell Sullivan.

"We need you here in case we are attacked," he replies.

I can now only leave if they send me, but I believe they will do so in a few days. [132]

He asks for a written response from the general officers and the commandants of brigades on the situation; should we attack, retreat or continue the siege? The same day he hears from Washington that perhaps one hundred to one hundred and fifty transport boats are off Throg's Point at the southwestern end of Long Island Sound. Washington believes they are either there to reinforce Rhode Island or to evacuate New York. [133]

In my reply to Sullivan I say that I do not approve of continuing the siege and that it would be best to retreat to the north of the island if troops and other means of Congress are expected. If they are not, then I think there should be a complete retreat:

I give you, sir, a public assurance upon my honor that I schall be happy to go any where and to do any thing which will be deem'd useful to my native country and this country for whom I may venture to say I have given proofs of zeal. Do'nt take it as a miss if I avoid occasions of finding myself in numerous compagnies where by taking a false idea of the liberality of the American citizens by the manners of some, I would be expos'd to lessen the Regard I have for them. No body speacks before me, and they are prudent for it, but this will be my friend who willlet me know the authors of some very strange discourses against a country to whom America is good deal indebted. I beg you would let me know if my presence is agreeable to the freedom of your Meetings as I would be very sorry to trouble the board of officers, whose the greatest part I am unacquainted with, and among whom I do not see my best and worthy friend and General. [134]

In the evening I attend a council of war. It is decided to retreat to the north of the island. [135]

I have sent a letter to Monsieur de Pleville for General Heath, a man of much repute at Boston, who commands the Continental forces in New England and have asked him to expedite the refitting of the ships. [136]

"I wish to be useful to the French fleet," Hancock tells me. "I will return to Boston. Would you give me a letter of introduction to the Count d'Estaing?"

I write a very praising letter which is not my view of him at all as I consider he has only the wit necessary to get him out of difficulty wherever he goes and that his vanity equals the reputation he has so readily been given in Europe. I also consider his wanting to return home stems from a lack of eagerness for English bullets.[137] However, he is very powerful in Boston and he can be of great help to d'Estaing. I therefore describe him as a 'Brutus in the flesh whose role in the revolution should make him as interesting to people now as he will be to posterity...he wishes to see the King's fleet soon in a condition to assist the American troops, and that reason wrests him from the Field of Mars to go and offer you his services in Boston.'[138]

I write a second letter to d'Estaing. I inform him we are still at the same place deliberating what to do and that I had not expected the effect his departure had on everyone. I say that offending Sullivan and the people of New England need not mean falling out with General Washington and Congress. I suggest he writes to Washington and to Congress as I am doing and that if he returns here and cooperates with an American army, I should prefer that Washington himself should command it. I say that I would like Congress to send two thousand men to join with d'Estaing's men and then expeditions could be made to Halifax, or perhaps Newport again, or to the conquest of St. Augustine and the whole state of Georgia, as well as to cause the destruction of the British West Indies. 'I think Congress would agree to a request from you if you say that a corps of six or ten thousand Frenchmen would be sent to Canada next year. Washington could advance across Lake Champlain at the same time your troops are disembarking on riverbanks. I think that Congress would give me the command of their auxiliary troops if that proposal seems to please you.'[139] I send him the letter by the marquis de Vienne.

August 25. In the morning, I discover that Sullivan had issued a General Order for the previous day which criticizes d'Estaing, and therefore, my French nation: 'The General cannot help lamenting the sudden and unexpected departure of the French Fleet, as he finds it has a tendency to discourage some who placed great dependence on the assistance of it...He yet hopes that the event will prove America is able to procure with her own arms what her allies refuse to assist in obtaining.'[140]

The whole camp is talking of d'Estaing's desertion. People are again vilifying the French fleet. I go straight to Sullivan in anger. "You do not know what my king's orders were to his fleet," I exclaim, my hand on my sword. "I demand you take back your words!"

I storm out of his quarters and write a long letter to Washington, enclosing the General Orders and saying that 'my reason for not writing the same day the French fleet went to Boston, was that I did not choose to trouble your friendship with the sentiments of an afflicted, injur'd heart, and injur'd by that very people I came from so far to love and support.' I tell him what has happened, and that the generosity of his honest mind would be offended at the shocking sight I see here and that I might soon be forced to go to Boston, which I will do reluctantly as our position on the island is not without danger. I ask him to recommend to chief people in Boston to help the French fleet. 'Farewell my dear general. Whenever I quit you I meet with some disappointement and misfortune. I did not want it to desire seeing you as much as possible, With the most tender affection and high regard...'[141]

Greene writes to me. He is reasonable as he always is, unlike those I complain of. I therefore add to my letter to Washington that I have received a letter from General Greene and that I am very happy when I am in the situation of doing justice to anybody. I send Pontgibaud to Washington with the letter.[142]

I write a long letter to Hamilton, who speaks French, is from the Leeward Islands, and so, like me, is not American:

It is with pain that I will say even to you that I have seen a number of our adopted compatriots united together, and that I have seen them for the most part unjust, ungrateful, selfish, lacking not only in regard to politeness, but in all the impulses of the most common decency...Would you believe that I, I who have the honor of belonging to the first nation of the world, to a nation which may be envied but which is admired and respected by all of Europe, I have been exposed to hearing almost in my very presence the name of France pronounced without respect, perhaps with contempt, by a herd of New England Yankees...I love America. I love especially her savior and protector. It is not against America that I am in anger, it is against those who dishonor her by sentiments which are appropriate only to Tories.' I suggest he uses his influence to ensure that Congress approves and thanks d'Estaing and that Washington should come to Rhode Island. 'If you give me two thousand men to support the attack...I will answer for its success upon my head.... Monsieur d'Estaing appears to me to have an infinity of plans- Newport, Halifax, St. Augustine, etc., etc., and for the coming year, Canada...As for this year, let me know what you think would be most worthwhile to undertake, without forgetting the British Isles. [143]

I try and promote my ideas as best I can, representing my projects as coming from d'Estaing. I roam freely over the world attempting to find ways to attack the British and in which I can be perhaps one of the chief participants.

Sullivan visits me. His opinion remains that he thinks it unnecessary for ten sail of the line and three frigates to lay in the harbor at Boston to watch two ships repairing.[144] We talk angrily; I prepare again to defend my country with a duel. He calms.

"My dear Marquis, I was too severe. It is true I do not know what His Majesty's orders were. I will issue another statement tomorrow," he admits.[145]

On the twenty-sixth, he issues General Orders which somewhat mollify me:

The General having secured his heavy stores and provided a safe and easy for his Army in Case of Misfortune thinks proper to inform the Army that he has the strongest reason to expect (before any reinforcement arrives to oblige us to quit our present position) that the French Fleet will return to cooperate with us in the Reduction of the Island. It having been supposed by some Persons that by the Orders of the 24th Inst. the commander-in-chief meant to insinuate that the departure of the French Fleet was owing to a fixed determination not to assist in the present enterprise- as the General would not wish to give the least colour for ungenerous and illiberal minds to make such unfair interpretations, he thinks it necessary to say that as he could not possibly be acquainted with the orders of the Admiral, he could not determine whether the Removal of the Fleet was absolutely necessary or not, and therefore did not mean to censure an act which the Admirals orders might render absolutely necessary- He however hopes that the Speedy return of the Fleet will show their attention and regard to the Alliance formed between us and add to the obligations the Americans are already under to the French nation. However mortifying the Departure of the Fleet was to us at such a time of expectations we ought not too suddenly to Censure the movement; or for an act of any kind to to forget the aid and Protection which had been offered by the French since the Commencement of the present Contest. [146]

The same day we have a council of war. It is decided to retreat to Butt's Hill at the north end of Rhode Island; to fortify the position and remain there until the return of the French fleet.[147] The board of general officers and Sullivan now want me to go to Boston to hasten d'Estaing's return and to attempt to get the French troops to join the land forces here.[148]

"I will go but I fear I will miss the attack," I reply.[149]

I have no choice. I will go and come back as quickly as I can. I am glad to find a new occasion to cheerfully undertake anything, even if it has only a small chance of success, which might be thought useful to the common cause by one or any number of men. [150] A bad star is influencing

French actions and hopefully it will soon disappear.[151] On the twenty-seventh I leave camp in the evening; I ride my horse hard towards Boston in the dark of night.[152] Seventy miles and seven hours later, I ride over the Neck into the town.

I quickly discover the French fleet, joined by the three frigates and the *Stanley* from the Eastern Channel,[153] had arrived yesterday evening;[154] Laurens had delivered Sullivan's letter to d'Estaing when he was about to sail into the harbor.[155]

D'Estaing has already met Heath and Hancock and he and his officers are at this moment entering Boston. He does not want to speak to me privately; we will meet at a banquet the Massachusetts council is giving. We dine lavishly and then attend a conference of the council. Every word that is spoken is submitted to me first; d'Estaing remarks on this but does not appear hurt.[156]

"The fleet needs to be repaired and provisions obtained. It is impossible to do anything before this and it is militarily impossible to send the sailors as an auxiliary force to Newport. However, I am immediately ready to serve under Sullivan, as a soldier, at the head of the infantry detachments of Hainaut and of Foix," he offers,[157] showing that France had not been offended by the letter he had received [158] and not because it could strengthen the army or to prove what is already well-known, that Frenchmen know how to die, but to show that his countrymen could not be offended at a sudden expression of feeling, and that he, who has the honor of commanding them in America, is, and will be, at all times, one of the most devoted and zealous servants of the United States.[159]

No decision is taken. Next day, the twenty-ninth, I am still at Hancock's three-story granite house near the summit of Beacon Hill.[160] What is happening on Rhode Island? Has fighting started without me? Hancock gives a dinner in honor of d'Estaing and his officers. When d'Estaing arrives he sees the picture of Washington hanging in the hall, a picture which I had asked Hancock for a copy and have been promised one at another time as his copy is destined for d'Estaing who receives it with such joy that I think I have never seen anyone so happy to have his sweetheart's picture as he is to receive Washington's.[161] For myself, I would have been even happier for him if I also had received one.

"I will give it a royal salute as it is brought on board," he says.

"No, that might cause some speculative politicians to remark on the danger of characters becoming too important," Hancock replies.[162]

"It will have a place of honor on the *Languedoc* and will be entwined with laurel,"[163] says d'Estaing.

I cannot ride back in the night as I have to wait for d'Estaing's letter to Sullivan. In the morning, I learn to my immense disappointment that Sullivan had withdrawn from before Newport, that the British had pursued our troops and fighting had taken place at the north end of the island.[164] My star has not shone.

I set off in great speed back to Rhode Island with d'Estaing's letter in which he says that he would have had the honor of answering Sullivan's first letter if the order which the same person presented to him half an hour later had not imposed on the commandant of the king's fleet the grievous but necessary rule of absolute silence. He says that if the plan he has proposed to the council and to the committee of Boston is accepted, Sullivan will find in the detachment that he will lead to him an absolute devotion to the common cause and to the service of his army, as well as the unquestioning obedience military discipline exacts. He says he will give proof of it; the greatest, most inviolable attachment for the United States will be maintained without difficulty; it is graven in their hearts; the king's will has made it their duty and his wisdom has also graciously foreseen that it would be their inclination. French honor demands that the commander should give evidence by his conduct and by his sentiments towards Sullivan and by a declaration that the French delicacy cannot have been wounded by an impulsive moment followed by mutual regrets.[165]

I gallop frantically towards Rhode Island. Less than eight hours later,[166] my horse is more dead than alive; I meet soldiers straggling along the dark road. At eleven o'clock I reach Howland's Ferry, the quay crowded with men and artillery evacuated from the island. Lanterns shine on boats crammed with men reaching the shore; I see Glover's Marbleheads, the Twenty-First Massachusetts Regiment of sailors, helping to save our army as they did in 1776 after the battle of Long Island when they rowed the troops in the night from Brooklyn to Manhattan and who also ferried Washington's troops across the icy Delaware on Christmas night of the same year to attack the enemy at Trenton. Sullivan is on horseback by the water's edge; we talk hurriedly. The British attacked just after dawn. The fighting was fierce, but we maintained our position and they fell back. There are reports of Howe's fleet heading for Newport to reinforce them. The main army is now on the mainland with the stores and baggage[167] but one thousand men are still on the island.

"Go over to command the rest of the withdrawal," Sullivan tells me.

I jump into a boat which quickly ferries me away from the lights at Howland's Ferry to the opposite shore where I find large groups of men waiting quietly in the dark, the silence broken only by whispers, the occasional swear word and the shuffling of feet. I take command of the evacuation.

Our pickets are so close to enemy pickets they almost touch; I do not know how they fail to notice our leaving.[168] By two in the morning, the rear guard and all the posts that had been recalled have been taken on board; not a man has been left behind nor the smallest article lost [169] and the British do not know we have gone. They do not attack, even at the very last, and I am in no way compensated for what I missed yesterday.[170] I am the last to leave. I am pleased we have escaped the enemy but bitterly disappointed I have not fought.

Daylight is breaking. Sullivan returns to Providence with about one thousand men. Greene and I share the rest which we will use along the two coasts in order to defend a whole region, although we would not be able to defend a single place successfully. [171] Our escape has been timely. The morning after the retreat one hundred British ships arrive in the harbor at Newport.[172]

"We got off the island in very good season," is Greene's opinion.

I hear from 'sensible and candid French gentlemen' that the action did great honor to Sullivan. They say he 'retreated in good order, he oppos'd very properly every effort of the enemy, he never sent troops but well supported and displayed a great coolness during the whole day.'[173]

Thirty of our men have been killed, one hundred and thirty-seven wounded and forty-four missing.[174]

Chapter 22

Death threatens unexpectedly

On August 12, when I was on Rhode Island, Lee was found guilty at the court-martial for disobedience of orders, in not attacking the enemy on the twenty-eighth of June, agreeable to repeated instructions; for misbehavior before the enemy on the twenty-eighth of June, by making an unnecessary, and, in some few instances, a disorderly retreat; for disrespect to the commander-in-chief in two letters dated July 1 and June 28. He was sentenced to be suspended from any command in the armies of the United States of North America, for the term of twelve months.[1]

My orders are to defend the east. I command the troops stationed nearest Rhode Island, from Sakonnet Point to Bristol. Sullivan is at Providence; d'Estaing is at Providence repairing and provisioning his ships; Washington is at White Plains with three brigades. The British are entrenched at Newport and spies and deserters say General Grey is marching five thousand men along the coast intending to burn the towns and ransom the small islands.[2] The French hospital has now arrived at Boston after various difficulties which I have managed to diminish a good deal by sending a part of my family with them, with orders to some people, and supplications to others to give them all the assistance in their power.[3]

I go to Tiverton and stay at the house of Mrs. Reynolds. She serves a delicious meal when I arrive but to my surprise looks indignant as I eat. Later, I discover she thought it was presumptuous of me to eat the dinner she had carefully prepared for the marquis de Lafayette, not realizing that the person enjoying her food was, in fact, me.

I write to d'Estaing. I describe the retreat and my present situation. I mention I would now like to return to France and that I would be appreciative of his help in doing so:

> I shall send word to M. le prince de Montbarey that I am here and that I believe I can and even must remain here as long as you are acting in concert with the American army. This formula appears to me to be all the more necessary since in coming here I could take advantage of only a tacit consent, so very tacit as to be presented to me, without any underhand dealing, in the form of an absolute prohibition.[4]

I write to Washington:

> MY DEAR GENERAL,- That there has been an action fought where I could have been, and where I was not, is a thing which will seem as extraordinary to you as it seems so to myself...From what I have heard from sensible and candid French gentlemen, the action does great honor to Gal. Sullivan: he retreated in good order; he never sent troops but well supported, and displayed a great coolness during the whole day. The evacuation I have seen extremely well performed, and my private opinion is, that if both events are satisfactory to us, they are very schamefull for the British generals and troops. They had, indeed so fine chances as to cut us to pieces, but they are very good people...I beg you will pardon me once more, my dear general, for having troubled and afflicted you with the account of what I had seen after the departure of the French fleet. My confidence in you is such that I could not feel so warmly upon this point without communicating it to your

excellency. I have now the pleasure to inform you that the discontent does not appear to be so great...Now everything will be right provided the Count d'Estaing is soon enabl'd to sail....By your letters to Gal. Sullivan I apprehend there is some general movement in the British army and that your excellency is going to send us reinforcements...I long, my dear general, to be again with you, and the pleasure of cooperating with the French fleet under your immediate orders will be the greatest I may feel. [5]

I go to Bristol where most of my troops are encamped and take up quarters at the house of Joseph Reynolds at the north end of the town.[6] I need more men if we want to oppose the enemy and I feel uneasy that we are so scattered along the coast. If the enemy decides to take some of our batteries we would not be able to prevent them and I am here upon a little advance of land where if there is an attack a long stay might be dangerous. I write to Washington and tell him of this but say that we will do for the best.[7]

Pontgibaud returns on the fourth, bringing me a letter from Washington, in reply to my letter of August 25:

I feel everything that hurts the sensibility of a Gentleman; and, consequently upon the present occasion, feel for you and for our good and great Allys the French. I feel myself hurt also at every illiberal, and unthinking reflection which may have been cast upon Count D'estaing, or the conduct of the Fleet under his command. And lastly, I feel for my Country. Let me entreat you therefore my dear Marquis to take no exception at unmeaning expressions, uttered perhaps without Consideration, and in the first transports of disappointed hope. Everybody, Sir, who reasons, will acknowledge the advantages which we have derived from the French Fleet, and the Zeal of the Commander of it, but in a free, and republican Government, you cannot resrain the voice of the multitude. Every man will speak as he thinks, or more properly without thinking- consequently will judge of Effects without attending to the Causes...Let me beseech you therefore my good Sir to afford a healing hand to the wound that unintentionally has been made. America esteems your virtues and yr. services and admires the principles on which you act. Your Countrymen, in our Army, look up to you as their Patron. The Count and his Officers consider you as a man high in Rank, and high in estimation, here and in France, and I, your friend, have no doubt but that you will use your utmost endeavours to restore harmony, that the honour, glory and mutual Interest of the two Nation's may be promoted and cemented in the firmest manner. [8]

His words very much please me and I write to d'Estaing that he shows all the sensibility and delicacy that one could desire.[9]

My information is that the British will evacuate New York and so I expect troops to be sent to Halifax, to the West Indies and to Canada, where I have always wanted to fight. I therefore write to Washington and suggest I will not return to France as I had been planning but would like to fight there with him. 'I much desire to see Your Excellency in Quebec next summer.'[10]

On September 11 I write a long letter to the duc d'Ayen. I tell him I received with heartfelt gratitude the advice he gave me to remain here during this campaign; it was inspired by true friendship and a thorough knowledge of my interest and is the sort of advice we give to those we really love. I relate in detail what has happened to the French fleet, our campaign on Rhode Island and my present situation as well as the injury to Monsieur Touzard. I tell him how impossible it is for me to know when I can return to him:

My great object in wishing to return was the idea of an invasion of England. I should consider myself almost as much dishonored if I were not present at such a moment, I should feel so much regret and shame, that I should be tempted to drown or hang myself as the English do. My greatest happiness would be to drive them from this country, and then to go to England, serving under your command. I would be happiest to first chase them from here, and then go to England and serve under you. [11]

In order to lessen his anxiety about my profligacy with my wealth I tell him that I have become very reasonable with what I spend, that now I have my own establishment I shall spend still less and that in any case, I am very prudent considering the exorbitant price of everything, particularly with paper money.

September 13. I write a long letter to Adrienne from Bristol:

If anything could disturb my pleasure in writing to you, my dear heart, it would be the cruel idea that I am still writing to you from a corner of America and that all I love is two thousand leagues from me. But also, I can hope that it will not be long before we meet again. War which generally separates, must bring us together; it even will bring about my return by sending ships here, and the fear of being captured will soon completely vanish...How wonderful it would be for me to have heard from you; but I am very far from being granted that delight. Your last letter arrived at the same time as the fleet. Since that immense time, two months ago, I have waited but nothing has come....O when shall I be with you my dear heart; when shall I embrace you a hundred times? I thought that the declaration of war would lead me immediately back to France, independently of all the links of the heart which pull me towards the people I love, my love of my country and the wish to serve it, were powerful motives...I will tell you why I am still here and I dare to think you will approve my conduct...I was in the middle of a campaign and it was not the moment to leave the army...Here I was flattered to be able to be able to act in concert with M. d'Estaing. I wrote to you after our success at Monmouth, and I scribbled my letter almost on the field of battle, still surrounded with the wounded. Since then the only events that have taken place are the arrival and operations of the French fleet, joined to our enterprise on Rhode Island. I have sent a detailed account of it to your father. Half the Americans say that I passionately love my country, and the other half say that since the arrival of the French ships, I have become mad, and that I only eat, drink, or sleep according to the wind it makes....Imagine my beloved what joy I had in seeing the whole of the English feet fleeing at full sail from ours in the presence of the English and American armies assembled on Rhode Island. I admire very much the talents, spirit and all the great qualities of M. le comte d'Estaing...We exchanged cannon fire for several days with the enemy which did not harm us and when General Clinton brought reinforcements we retreated from the island... an officer who has been with me since winter, M. Touzard of the La Fère Regiment, tried to seize a British cannon and with great valor threw himself among the enemy....He was badly injured and his right arm has had to be amputated. In France he would receive the Croix de Saint-Louis and a pension. I would be delighted if you and my friends could help to obtain some compensation for him...Cover Anastasie with kisses for me; teach her to love me through loving you. We are too close for someone to love one of us and not the other. This poor little child must now be everything for me. She has two places to occupy in my heart; and it is a heavy burden that our misfortune has imposed on her....I love her madly and the misfortune of worrying for her does not stop me from abandoning myself to the most devoted love. Adieu, my dear heart, when will I be allowed to see you again and never leave you, to make you happy like you make me happy, to demand pardon at your knees? Adieu, adieu, we will not be separated for long.[12]

In Boston the repair of our ships is proceeding at less than a snail's pace. In all honesty it is not proceeding at all. People appear to be furious about the French fleet sailing from Rhode Island. They are strongly Protestant; some see France as a symbol of the Catholic Church and have even sometimes burnt effigies of the Pope and the devil together as they consider them the same. A dislike of France still exists because of the Seven Years' War. They do not seem to realize how useful the French fleet has already been in helping speed the evacuation of Philadelphia, in destroying enemy ships, and that there is still the possibility of it participating in a future battle. We hear of several riots between French sailors and local people in one of which a French lieutenant, chevalier Grégoire de Saint Sauveur, was killed by a mob. He had been attempting to stop the destruction of a French bakery set up to provision the fleet and was beaten to death by fifty men. A fellow officer, a one-legged man, Lieutenant le Pelley, the brother-in-law of d'Estaing's second-in-command, the comte de Brugnon, was left for dead but he has survived.

This atrocious event has several fortunate outcomes. John Hancock now patrols the streets with militia and he has persuaded the ship builders to repair the fleet. The newspapers had previously blamed d'Estaing for abandoning the American troops and preventing our victory; now the editors have been persuaded to stop writing these hostile articles and attribute the riots to bread shortages. The rioters are not discovered. It is not known if they are American, or even perhaps British, however the Massachusetts council promises to erect a monument to Saint-Sauveur.

Reports arrive of a French naval victory at Ouessant where Admiral Keppel was killed, but I know few details. I write to d'Estaing to ask for more information and say that I have also heard of a Spanish fleet: 'Where are they going? If there was an attack somewhere without me, I would hang myself...I would rather be a soldier than a general anywhere else, and the cap of a grenadier would be the full limit of my ambition, provided I had the pleasure of seeing a glorious fire in London.'[13]

The same day I write to Washington and tell him the news of the French naval victory. I also mention I am now behind Warren, ten miles from Providence, a safer place than Bristol, thanks to his letter to Sullivan following my remarks to him. I say I want to see d'Estaing who has written to me about many ideas and does not yet seem fixed on any scheme but burns with the desire of striking a blow and that if he gives me leave, I will ask General Sullivan and will do what I think best for both countries. I tell him I have not yet found out if the queen of France has sent a present to Mrs. Washington which the British have seized and sold at auction, as he had asked me, but will make further enquiries.[14]

I receive a letter from President Laurens in which he encloses the resolutions of Congress which say that the retreat of Major General Sullivan with the troops under his command from Rhode Island was prudent, timely and well conducted and that Major General Sullivan and his officers and troops are thanked for their fortitude and bravery in the action on August 29. Congress also requests Laurens to inform me that it has a due sense of the sacrifice I made of my personal feelings in going to Boston to promote the interests of the states when an occasion was daily expected of my acquiring glory on the battle field, and that my gallantry in going to Rhode Island after the retreat of most of the army and my good conduct in bringing off the pickets and out sentries deserves their particular approbation.[15]

I am very moved. I write back:

Be so good, Sir, as to present to Congress my plain and hearty thanks, with the frank assurances of a candid attachement, the only ones worth being offered to the representatives of a free people. The Moment I heard of America, I lov'd her. The Moment I knew she was fighting for freedom, I burnt with the desire of bleeding for her- and the moment I schall be able of Serving her in any time, or any part of the world, will be among the happiest ones in my life.[16]

A Newport journal prints the address to Congress of the British commissioners: 'France is a preposterous connection. The Americans have a blind deference towards a country which has always revealed itself as an enemy to all civil and religious liberty, and whose offers are only intended to halt our reconciliation and to prolong the war.' It is signed by all the commissioners including Lord Carlisle.[17] It is extremely offensive to France and to my king.

"I cannot stand aside. I am the highest-ranking officer in the American army. I am not unknown to the English and if somebody must take notice of such expressions then it should be me," I exclaim furiously.

I ask the opinion of d'Estaing. I also write to Washington saying that I intend to write to Lord Carlisle concerning his expressions conveyed in an unfriendly manner. I tell him I want very much to see him and that if he approves of my writing to Carlisle then it would be a reason for coming near to him for a short time in case Carlisle is displeased.[18]

"Can I go to speak with d'Estaing at Boston," I ask Sullivan, but then I receive information that about sixty sails have entered Newport Harbor.[19] I must delay my visit. Not long after, news comes that there is no fleet, just small vessels belonging to the port, which have been mistaken in the fog.[20] As everything is now quiet Sullivan says I can safely go to Boston.

I meet d'Estaing at a dinner at General Heath's house; we discuss my plans for world-wide attacks on the British. I write to Sullivan asking for leave to go to headquarters. Greene left two weeks ago; I am now the only major general here and so I anticipate Sullivan might not be pleased. I write to Washington to say that if Sullivan does not object, I will set off immediately but that if he makes difficulties then would he please send me that permission and I will ride as an express in changing horses on the road so that I have enough time.[21]

I visit Boston and nearby places with d'Estaing. We go to the ramshackle barracks near Cambridge where Burgoyne's army is imprisoned, guarded only by two militiamen, one on each flank.[22] We talk much about military schemes. We agree that I will go to Philadelphia and attempt to obtain the permission of Congress for a joint French and American invasion in the spring of an English possession in the western hemisphere.

"I will wait at Boston for you. And if you return by the middle of October with the consent of Congress, I will take you on board my ship to the French West Indies. I will only do this, however, if you are representing Congress, as you are still not in the favor of the king," he says.[23]

I also mention my plans to Hancock and other prominent people. Hancock agrees with me and believes that Congress would offer a force to invade the British Indies or somewhere else.

By October 1 I have not received any reply from Sullivan. I consider myself, like the comte d'Estaing, an 'unfortunate victim of the irascible Mr. Sullivan' and decide to translate his silence as consent, 'as though he had written me four pages of approbation,'[24] it not being the first time in my life I take the liberty to do that.

I have trouble obtaining good horses on the road but on October 6 I arrive at Fishkill and hurry to headquarters.

Washington appears surprised when he sees me. "I thought you were still by Rhode Island. I have just dispatched a letter to give you leave of absence."

"I did not receive it. I must have left before its arrival," I reply.

What is your opinion of my duel with Carlisle?" I ask.

"I give you friendly commands to retract your challenge. Dueling is a European custom and has no place here in America."[25]

"The comte d'Estaing and the other French officers expect it of me. I cannot withdraw now," I say, disappointed at his lack of enthusiasm.

I also talk to him about my plan for an attack on the British in Canada with French troops. "It would be useful to the United States and so I hope that Congress would solicit me to do so. Canada cannot be conquered by American forces alone. Only a Frenchman of birth and distinction at the head of four thousand French soldiers, in the name of the king, would be capable of producing a revolution there." [26]

"I am skeptical about any Canadian invasion," he replies. "It would need a very large French army which Americans would be resentful and perhaps fearful of on our soil. It is a good idea to return to France to see your fair lady. When the war is ended, perhaps she would like to leave the French court for a few months and visit my humble cottage at Mount Vernon."

"Although I would like to return to France I wish to still be considered as an officer of the United States. I don't want to resign. I just wish to have leave of absence. I do not intend my purpose in returning home to be misunderstood either by Congress or the people."

"I will write to Congress saying you should be allowed to keep your rank in the American army when you return to France," he replies.

I send Gimat to New York with a challenge for Lord Carlisle. I write in French: 'I disdain to refute what you have said, but I wish to punish it. As you are the head of the commission, I summon you to make a reparation as public as was the offence.'[27]

"What would you say to my scheme for Canada if you were a member of Congress?" I ask John Laurens.

"I do not think Congress could solicit, or even accept it, because there does not appear to be a sufficient reciprocity in the benefits to be derived from such an expedition. On the one side there will be an immense expense of transporting troops, loss of valuable officers and soldiers etc. There would be all the disadvantages, and on the other, all the gain. You do well to say that the project can only take place by indirect means, for a minister would not in his cool moments deprive his country of so many troops, with no other view than that of killing so many Englishmen and conquering an extensive province for us. France, though powerful in men, has an extensive frontier to guard and in a European war would not have to do with England alone."[28]

I only remain a day at Fishkill. I set off for Philadelphia; on October 13, I ride again through its red-brick streets. I send a letter to President Henry Laurens asking for leave from the army:

> As long as I thought I could dispose of myself, I made it my pride and pleasure to fight under American colours, in defence of a cause, which I dare more particularly to call ours because I had the good fortune to bleed for it. Now sir, that France is involved in a war, I am urged by a sense of duty, as well as by patriotic love, to present myself before the King, to know in what manner he may judge proper to employ my services...Now that I see a very peaceful and undisturbed moment I take this opportunity of waiting on congress...Inclosed you will find a letter from his excellency General Washington where he expresses his assent to my getting leave of absence. [29]

"I can only stay three days," I say.[30] Congress appoints a committee composed of Gouverneur Morris, Richard Lee, Witherspoon, Samuel Adams and William Drayton to examine the scheme of an expedition into Canada.

"Do you think it is His Majesty's intention to make America the principal scene of the war?" they ask. "Could you return with troops to Canada and how could this proposal be brought to his attention?"

"I can see no advantage for France in fighting the war here in America and not in Europe, but I am convinced the king would help America with all his might."[31] France is already aiding the United States with all its power and any joint expedition against Canada would depend on events and circumstances, is my answer, in line with the policy expressed by Gérard, the French minister to the United States.[32]

163

This tiresome prison of Philadelphia keeps me trapped here. I would have escaped long ago if I was only concerned with my own affair of leaving, but I must wait for Congress to prepare instructions to be taken to Franklin as well as take dispatches from Gérard.[33]

I receive an answer from Carlisle: 'I have received Your Letter transmitted to me from from Mons. de Gimat and I confess I find it difficult to return a serious Answer to its Contents...The Injury alluded to in the Correspondance of the King's Commissioners to the Congress I must remind You is not of a private Nature and I conceive all national Disputes will be best decided by the Meeting of Admiral Byron and the Count d'Estaign.'[34]

'Carlisle conceals himself behind his dignity and by a prudent foresight he objects to entering into any explanation in any change of situation,' I write to Washington.[35] However, d'Estaing is relieved as he believes Carlisle has chosen a professional duelist to be his substitute.[36]

I ask Henry Laurens to accompany me to a play as the theater is open. He politely declines but I persist.

"Congress has just passed a resolution recommending to the several states to enact laws for the suppression of theatrical amusements and so I cannot do myself the honor of waiting upon you to the play," he says.

"Has Congress passed such a resolution?" I reply. "Then I will not go to the play."[37]

Many fellow Frenchmen wish to return to France with me and I ask Congress for ranks in the American army for them. They appoint Capitaine a major, Touzard a lieutenant colonel and Failly, a brevet colonel. I had already asked for promotions for Brice and Neville, and they become brevet lieutenant colonels. Congress also decides to recompense La Colombe and Pontgibaud for their expenses in America.

Conway is here in Philadelphia and has recovered well from the severe wound he received during the duel with Cadwallader. He had written to Washington from what he thought was his death bed expressing sincere grief for having done, written or said anything disagreeable to him.[38]

"I want to go home with an honorable mention from Congress. Will you put forward my letter?" he asks me.

I reluctantly agree; Congress, however, does not accede to his wish.

John Laurens is given the rank of lieutenant colonel. "I have gratitude for the unexpected honor, but I feel I cannot accept it without injuring the rights of the officers of the line of the army and doing an evident injustice to to my colleagues in the family of the commander-in-chief,' is his reply.[39] Congress, however, insists, praising his disinterested and patriotic principles.

On October 24, I receive permission from Congress for an undetermined length of leave to return to France. They try to help me with my king and write a letter to him: 'His devotion to his sovereign hath led him in all things to demean himself as an American, acquiring thereby the confidence of these United States, your good and faithful friends and allies, and the affection of their citizens.' Congress has also ordered an elegant sword to be presented to me by Franklin, the American minister at the court of Versailles.[40]

I will be carrying dispatches to Franklin which will mention the plan to invade Canada and will request four to five thousand troops to sail from Brest in May in four ships of the line and four frigates. Congress asks Washington to find out information about Nova Scotia and Canada; then the final plans will be submitted to him. I write to Washington: 'There is a plan going on which I think you will approve. The idea was not suggested by me, and I acted in the affair a passive part.'[41] I cannot bear to depart for home under a cloud in my relationship with the man I love and admire most in the world.

Gérard will also write to Vergennes that he cannot help saying that the conduct of Monsieur de Lafayette, equally prudent, courageous and aimable, has made him the idol of Congress, the army and the American people.[42]

October 26. I write to President Laurens and thank Congress for the leave they have granted me and that my services have met with their approbation: 'The glorious testimonial of confidence and satisfaction repeatedly bestowed on me by the representatives of America, though superior to my merit, cannot exceed the grateful sentiments they have excited. I consider the noble present offered to me in the name of the United States as the most flattering honor; it is my fervent desire soon to employ that sword in their service against the common enemy of my country, and of their faithful and beloved allies.'[43]

Congress resolves that I will sail in the *Alliance,* a newly built frigate with thirty-six guns, originally called the *Hancock,* but renamed to honor France.

October 28. The rain falling heavily, I set off on the four-hundred-mile journey to Boston and will stop at Washington's headquarters to give him the resolve of Congress asking him to comment on the 'plan for reducing the province of Canada,' as well as a letter from Gouverneur Morris.[44] I have been very active at Philadelphia; I have drunk a great deal and spent several nights without sleep and now feel exhausted. I am hot with fever. My clothes are sodden from the rain, but I continue. People everywhere fête me and I try and strengthen myself with rum, tea and wine. On November 1 I reach Fishkill.[45] Illness racks my body; I have severe inflammation of the intestines.[46] I am taken to bed at the Brinckerhof mansion, a Continental hospital one mile east of the town;[47] Washington is twenty-four miles away at Fredericksburg.

I will perhaps die. My head throbs with pain, I ache and shiver. Dr. John Cochran, director of the hospitals, leaves his other occupations and only cares for me. Washington comes every day to ask how I am, but fearing to agitate me only speaks with my physician.

I worsen. "You must pray for death," I am told. Sadness overwhelms me. I will never see my loved ones and my homeland again. If only I could be given three months more to live; to see my family and friends and witness the happy termination of the American war, then I would agree to my death.[48] "Tell me when I am about to die," I say, my head mercifully remaining clear.

Dr. Cochran and his medical expertise help me, as does Nature; blood hemorrhages from my nose for four hours. Everyone thinks I am dying. The weeks pass and I feel much better. D'Estaing has left without me for Martinique, despite the attempts of twenty-one British ships to prevent him. I start to make plans again. Washington is now at Fishkill and comes to visit. We talk of Canada.

"There would be great difficulty in obtaining sufficient provisions, especially if the enemy continues to hold New York and Rhode Island," he says.

He is clearly against the project. I write to Congress to present counter arguments to the ones I know he will propose. I suggest that perhaps some ships could attack New York and Rhode Island. I say that France will want to know how many troops the Americans will send and where they will be deployed and then the French ministry might increase the numbers of ships, provisions and troops if they think it necessary: 'I feel sanguine for such an expedition because if the bad luck of America makes a peace without joining these provinces to the United States I schall ever be fearful for theyr Safety and liberty.' I also mention I would like to serve with these troops.[49]

Washington and I speak together for hours. We talk of what we have done. We talk of the present situation and our future projects. I embrace him tenderly, grief-stricken to part from him.

Other people visit, including Dr. Thacher.[50] I sit in my chair of convalescence, my strength slowly returning.

On November 29 I am still very weak but set off again for Boston with Dr. Bones as I call Dr. Cochran. Before I leave, I write to Henry Laurens: 'A very severe fitt of illness did put me near making a greater voyage than this.'[51]

We halt frequently and ten days later, on Friday, December 18, we reach Boston. [52] The *Alliance* is not yet in the harbor. I must wait. I visit Hancock and Gates and speak about my scheme for Canada,[53] and socialize at assemblies with my doctor who sings and dances charmingly,[54] Madeira wine happily completing my cure.

I write a manifesto:

The Marquis de Lafayette with the Troops of the United States of America, to my Children the Savages of Canada. You will have learned that your father the King has made a treaty of alliance with the Americans...You also know that your fathers want to take the thirteen states with one hand and Canada with the other in order to join them together against our enemies and that the King has sent a declaration to the Canadians in order to promise them his help...There has been a great battle on the other side of the big lake where the French ships have defeated all that remained of the English ships, and their fleet no longer dares show itself so that the big lake along the coasts of England is covered with ships under the French flag...I proclaim to you that all those who leave the side of the English, and become their enemies will be the friends of your father the King of France. [55]

I write much more in this vein and order necklaces to be sent with my words. I also attempt to find out about fortifications and places occupied by redoubts or batteries in Canada.[56]

The *Alliance* sails into Boston harbor. She is magnificent. There are five other frigates moored nearby, but she is the most resplendent, her thirty-six guns rather more impressive than the six of *La Victoire*. I go on board to meet Captain Pierre Landais, who comes from Saint Malo. His small, sharp face[57] has somewhat delicate features commonly found in women, but his manner suggests a more aggressive demeanor. I already know of his fine reputation as a sailor and that, together with the beauty of the ship, seems an omen of a safe voyage.

"I do not have a full complement of men. I need a crew of one hundred and thirty-five," he says.[58] "Privateers have taken most of the sailors round here, as they give a share of the prize money. That is why there are so many ships waiting in the bay. They all lack men and each day the situation worsens as there are more desertions. The Eastern Navy Board has suggested a press gang for the *Alliance*."

"I do not agree with that method," I reply.

"In that case I will offer a bounty of ten crowns and a share of any prize money, and we will see if that is effective," he says.

Monsieur de Valnais, the French vice-consul, manages to find thirty sailors left behind from d'Estaing's fleet and a few days later we reach the required number by taking seventy British sailors from captured privateers who have to swear an oath of loyalty.[59]

"They are a mixture of Scots, English and Irish," says Landais. "I hope they don't cause us trouble."

It is bitterly cold, the most severe, people say, for many years, and three French sailors from the *Alliance* unfortunately freeze to death at Roxbury.[60] On January 11, however, the wind is fair. I am on board, disappointed I still have not received a letter from Congress about Canada. Brice and Neville wrote to me this morning from Boston to say that the North River is passable so I know there is no hope of one now. We will shortly depart, and I add a few last lines to my letter to Washington:

> The sails are just going to be hoisted, my dear general, and I have but the time of taking my last leave from you. I may now be certain that Congress did not intend to send anything more by me. The Navy Board and Mr. Nevill wrote me this very morning from Boston that the North River is passable, that a gentleman from camp says he di'nt hear of anything like an express for me-all agree to be certain that Congress think I am gone- and that the sooner I'll go will be the better.
>
> Farewell, my dear general; I hope your french friend will ever be dear to you, I hope I schall soon see you again, and tell you myself with what emotion I now leave the coast you inhabit, and with what affection and respect I'll for ever be, my dear general. Your respectfull and sincere friend, Lafayette. [61]

I send it to shore. The *Alliance* sets sail, furrowing through the ice of the port,[62] the snow-white hills of Dorchester, the many steeples of Boston, slowly fading from view.

Chapter 23

Perils at sea

We go through the narrow entrance to the roadstead. The wooden timbers shudder; the ship pitches and rolls. We pass rocks streaming with foam and spray and meet the force of the ocean. It is winter, not perhaps the best season to cross the Atlantic. Nausea seizes me; I lie shivering in the cold, salt-tanged air. I eat little. I sip wine. The wind is blowing so violently only the mainsail is hoisted, but even so we career northwards to the Newfoundland Banks at the rate of four leagues an hour.[1]

After three days a blackening sky heralds the approach of a storm, above my head the wind screams across the deck. Night falls. The hours become interminable. The ship resembles a child's top, spinning and diving from crest to trough of mountainous waves which break over our frail vessel. Water pours in, trickling down the cabin walls, flooding into the passages and the hold.

A monstrous crash suddenly sounds from the deck. The *Alliance* shrieks like a living creature being torn apart and Pontgibaud stumbles into the cabin. "The top yards, sails and pinnace have been blown away," he shouts above the din.

"Captain de Raimondis is an experienced sailor. Go and ask him about the storm," I say.

He shortly returns, covered in bruises from continually losing his balance. "He says he has never been in such an atrocious tempest in any of his campaigns. But don't forget he lost his arm when he was captaining the *César* in the recent battle and is suffering great pain."

"*Diable!* I am just twenty. With my name, rank and fortune and married to Mademoiselle de Noailles. I have left all that to come here to be a meal for codfish!" I cry. [2]

"An officer is loading his pistols as he is determined not to die by drowning," says Pontgibaud.

By a miracle we survive the night, but the storm continues for three long days. Finally, it ceases. We drift on a choppy sea in a freezing cold. I warm myself with rum and the sailors make repairs. We resume our course east, the wind now a friendly force rushing us towards France.

"I am still worried about a mutiny," says Captain Landais. "I don't trust many of the crew. Too many of them are British. Mutineers are paid the value of any rebel ship which is brought into an English port. It was a mistake to recruit all those enemy prisoners. A press gang would have been better."

"It is immoral of His British Majesty to have issued such a proclamation as it means that the officers and anyone who opposes the mutiny will be killed.[3] Have you questioned everyone?" I ask.

"Yes, I have found nothing," he replies.

Two hundred leagues from France we are dining at three o'clock when a man from the crew asks to speak to me.[4] I take him aside.

"The English sailors plan to kill you, take over the ship, and sail it to England. They were intending to do it at four this morning but changed that to four this afternoon. The other mutineers, including the leaders, will be armed and in their hammocks. They don't realize I am American as I have lived for a long time in Ireland and have an Irish accent. They want me to command the ship and I pretended to join them in order to save you. They will shout 'sail' and when the passengers and officers come out of their cabins two cannon loaded with canister shot, prepared by the gunner's mate, will fire, and when we reach the deck two more cannon will await us on the forecastle.[5] A sergeant has also managed to obtain loaded weapons."[6]

Duplessis Mauduit, pistol in hand, guards our informant. We hurriedly arm ourselves. Fourteen officers group together; some go to the bravest and most reliable sailors who run to us with weapons. I lead everyone onto the deck, our swords in our hands, and thirty descend below decks to arrest those there.[7] The suspects are brought up individually and each one, hoping not to be put in irons, allows his fellow mutineers to be locked up.[8]

"We only possess enough irons to lock up thirty-three men," Landais tells me.[9]

We agree to trust the rest but will only rely on the French and Americans. At first the mutineers deny everything. Then we interrogate them separately; the fear of being hanged within the hour makes them decide to confess.[10] One of the ringleaders, William Murray, sergeant of marines, says that he and Savage, the master-at-arms, with seventy others, were going to divide themselves into four groups. The first group would take the magazine; the other three would take the cabin, wardroom and quarterdeck, then the chest of weapons, and if there was any opposition they would turn the nine-pounder forecastle guns aft and fire them. The gunner, carpenter and boatswain were to be killed; Captain Landais was to be placed in irons and sent in the cutter, without food or drink; the lieutenants had to walk the plank unless they agreed to take the ship to England; the marine officers and the doctor were to be hanged, quartered and thrown into the sea; the sailing master was to be tied to the mizzen mast, cut all over, then thrown overboard. I was to be put in irons and taken to England.[11]

After this none of us have much sleep. We keep watch over the men tied up below decks, the main cabin filled with charged weapons and drawn swords.

Several days later, at dawn, two Swedish merchant vessels appear nearby. They are carrying cargoes from England and Captain Landais sends crews to take over the ships and orders the captains to come on board. One does not speak French and goes white with fear when he sees our fierce array of weapons in the cabin, four men guarding the hatch with halberds and the rest of us with drawn swords and pistols in our hands. We try to reassure him with signs, but for two days he refuses to eat or drink. Hunger and thirst finally make him agree to join our dining table and he appears to find our dinner good, our wine excellent.

We are tired; we are fearful of meeting an enemy ship and know that if we do, our prisoners will help them. We have also lost our main masts.

An English corsaire with sixteen cannons chases us, presumably believing the *Alliance* is a merchant ship from the East India Company as our starboard portholes are completely sealed. Part of its crew line the sides shouting hurrah; a cannon shot is fired to know our colors. We immediately raise the American flag and salute the corsaire with half a dozen cannon balls. They recognize their error and despair at having met us. We make them throw their cannon into the sea and take all their Madeira wine. They sail away in a pitiful state.[12]

"The coast is visible, but the captain is sailing towards Saint Malo, his home port," Pontgibaud tells me.

"We want to go to Brest," I order Landais; he changes direction.[13]

On February 6, the *Alliance* passes by the Raz passage and Berthaume, having crossed the Atlantic in only twenty-three days. We sail into the harbor of Brest, at the extreme west of Bretagne, the guns on the ramparts roaring a welcome at the sight of the American flag on the frigate. I recall my situation when I left.[14] I had no idea what lay ahead. I was a fugitive, a rebel.[15]

I had no idea whether I would even reach America or whether I would end in a stinking British prison, laughed at and humiliated. Perhaps even executed. I was a raw youth, untested by battle, compelled to act by my desire for glory, by my wish to help the Americans win liberty from British oppression. I now wear the uniform of an American major general. I have been wounded. I have led men through the trials of war. My name is famous in the United States and France, and George Washington, the hero of America, is my adopted father and adored friend.

The mutineers are taken to the prison.[16] I have not received any news of my family and friends for eight months and I think only of seeing them again.[17] We spend two days at Brest and regain our land legs. Then we set off to travel the one hundred and forty-one leagues to Paris.

Chapter 24

War preparations

February 12. It is two in the morning; thousands of candles light the prince de Poix's mansion at Versailles. I enter the ballroom, dressed in my American uniform, to the strains of music and the chatter of conversation.[1] Bejeweled guests turn to look. No one recognizes me. They stare. A few minutes later, they regard me with disbelief.

"It's the marquis de Lafayette," many say.

The glittering assembly stand like statues; the musicians stop playing. Applause breaks out; there is cheering; people rush to embrace and kiss me.

"Is the marquise de Lafayette here?" I ask.

"No, she rarely goes into society," says the prince de Poix. "She is at the hôtel de Noailles."

"I must see the king to ask his forgiveness before I go home to my family. That is why I have come here first. The lettre de cachet needs to be rescinded or I will perhaps be arrested."

"You are a hero in France. You are talked about everywhere. Your fame is immense. I am sure Maurepas and Vergennes will intercede on your behalf. Stay here tonight; in the morning I will accompany you to the Château and introduce you to Maurepas."

Next day I dispatch an aide to Dr. Franklin with the letters from Congress as I do not know my fate and wish to be sure they arrive quickly. I go to the Château with the prince de Poix, my usual optimism expecting the outcome to be favorable. I am not the youth of two years ago. I am a major general in the American army and have fought in battle. I am a close friend of General Washington. I am well known to Congress and have come to France bearing their letters. I am also a noble who is a member of the Noailles family.

I proudly walk the marble corridors in my uniform. People already know I am coming and look at me with excitement and interest. I am escorted to the premier ministre, the comte de Maurepas, an old man who moves stiffly. He greets me politely and courteously, his pale blue eyes peering rheumily, his fresh, rosy face[2] framed by a long, full-bottomed wig. Two hours pass; he questions me on the situation in America and says nothing about my sudden departure from France against the wishes of the king.

Vergennes, a stocky man, much younger than Maurepas, with a broad face and a genial expression, briefly comes to talk. I give him the dispatches I am carrying.

"The British only seem to want to keep New York, Rhode Island and Halifax. Byron sailed from Newport on Rhode Island for the Islands on September 13, with eleven ships and several frigates. It is quiet there at the present time," I tell him.[3]

Other ministers also ask me about America; I feel greatly honored by my reception and, what was far better, being embraced by all the ladies.[4]

"His Majesty will not receive you," says Maurepas. "I will send him a message."

I am disappointed but wait patiently. Messages go backwards and forwards all day from the royal apartment. Aides whisper to each other. Evening approaches. Servants are lighting candles. Finally, the decree of my king arrives.

"You are to be punished and exiled for your disregard of His Majesty's wishes," says Maurepas. "Several of his advisors want you imprisoned in the Bastille, but His Most Gracious Majesty has chosen the hôtel de Noailles as your prison and you are only allowed to see your relations."

"Thank you for your aid," I reply in delight. "Your tact and diplomacy have helped to smooth a very difficult situation. I am extremely grateful."

"There is also another matter," he adds. "Her Majesty the Queen wishes to see you. She cannot do so officially, and she wants you to walk across the courtyard as she drives by in her carriage."

I go outside. A carriage halts. The queen extends her hand which I kiss. She withdraws it and I catch a glimpse of her blue eyes, her pronounced Hapsburg lip, her fine-complexioned face crowned by an immense pillar of hair. Then the carriage speeds away.

I quickly go to my own carriage, desperate to see my loved ones after two long years. In the winter evening gloom, we drive rapidly along the broad highway from Versailles to Paris. We enter the city and clatter through the streets to the hotel de Noailles in the rue Saint-Honoré.

Everyone is waiting for me. I greet the duc and duchesse d'Ayen, then I embrace my beloved, who is faint with emotion. For the first time I see my beautiful Anastasie, her face a pale oval, her eyes large and dark like her mother's. Joy overwhelms me, bitter-sweet because little Henriette is no longer here, and my adored cousin, Marie Louise, has died in childbirth. I talk until I am hoarse. I describe Washington, the battles, American people, their houses, their food. My father-in-law listens, as do all my relations; he treats me with the respect I have always wanted. In the street, crowds gather. At the front door, servants turn away nobles who leave their calling cards. In the evening we dine. We celebrate. I am home in the bosom of my family.

I have no intention of keeping to the orders of the king. I will go out on what I consider essential business.[5] On February 14 I ask Vergennes for permission to see Dr. Benjamin Franklin.[6] He agrees.

Next day, the elderly Franklin visits, dressed in a plain cloth coat, his hair receding wispily from his forehead and hanging lankly onto his shoulders. He peers through large spectacles, but his eyes sparkle with the vivacity of a much younger man. The dispatches that I carried from Congress have told him that he is now the sole American plenipotentiary. I embrace him with delight. We talk about Washington and the difficult situation of the Continental Army.

February 19. I write to the king with the help of the maréchal, my jailor, and the duc d'Ayen. I put aside my republican ideas and compose a suitable apology for my wayward behavior:

The misfortune of having displeased Your Majesty produces such a deep sense of sorrow that I am encouraged not to try to excuse an action of which you disapprove but to present the real motives that inspired it. Love of my country, the desire to witness the humiliation of her enemies, a political instinct that the last treaty would seem to justify: these, Sire, are the reasons that governed the part I took in the American cause. When I received Your Majesty's orders, I attributed them more to the solicitations and tender concern of my family than to the prescribed posture we were maintaining towards England. The feelings of my heart overcame my reason. I believed I saw that no one would disapprove of my departure as certainly as I saw the impossibility of it being permitted. If, in my disobedience, I used means that rendered me even more guilty, I risked, Sire, what every Frenchman ought to risk- his fortune, his hopes, and even public opinion-rather than harm the interests of his country by compromising the government through his conduct. Persuaded that I was blameless I fought for my country with a calm heart...The first rumor of a war with England was recalling me to France at the very time that the arrival of Your Majesty's fleet and the ever patriotic and enlightened opinion of the general who commanded it convinced me that my remaining in America would be more useful...I would not think, Sire, of daring to justify before Your Majesty an act of disobedience of which you disapprove and for which I should repent...But it is important to my peace of mind that Your Majesty attribute to its proper motives a conduct that has put me in your disgrace. The nature of my offences gives me reason to hope that I can efface them. It is through Your Majesty's indulgence that that I shall have the happiness of absolving myself by the means that you will condescend to give me of serving you, in whatever country and in whatever way may be possible. I am with the deepest respect, Sire, your Majesty's very humble and very obedient servant and faithful subject. [7]

Two days later, on Sunday, instructions arrive from Versailles: I must be at the king's *levée* this morning before seeing anyone from the royal family. I believe the *levée* is at eleven o'clock and as I had hoped to see Dr. Franklin today, I write to him: 'In our kingly countries we have a foolish law call'd Etiquette that any one tho' a Sensible man, must absolutely follow. I will See the Ministers, and tomorrow morning I'll have the pleasure to tell you what is the Matter at Versailles.' [8]

Louis XVI is in his dressing gown, looking slightly plumper than when I last saw him. He asks about America, about Americans, and about Washington. He asks about the war.

"I congratulate you on your success and on the good name you have won by your exploits.[9] I reprimand you for your disobedience to my command, but I pardon you. Avoid public places, however, where you might be lauded for your defiance."[10]

He gives me only a gentle reprimand. He even invites to hunt with him. My 'imprisonment' is ended. I am free. I can participate in society. I take my leave and visit Vergennes and Maurepas.

"America desperately needs aid and I also believe it would be useful to invade Canada," I say.

"I am against any plan for an invasion of Canada. It is not of a great advantage to either France or Spain, whom we hope will soon be our ally. I fear any enlargement of the United States. In any case, before adding a fourteenth state it is necessary to deliver the thirteen others from the yoke of England," is the opinion of Maurepas.

The evening is cold and frosty; the horses slow their pace as they reach the summit of the steep hill in Passy, the Seine River visible in the valley far below.

The hôtel de Valentinois, where Franklin lives, is luxuriously decorated and there are many servants, but he is dressed in his usual frugal manner. John Adams is also here; we toast America and Washington. Then we discuss the needs of the army.

"The soldiers often have not clothes or shoes or even ammunition. They are starving although the land is fertile," I say.

We talk about the loan the United States requires; we discuss the sending of a French fleet with perhaps five or six thousand troops to cooperate with d'Estaing and the American army in an expedition directed against New York, Rhode Island and Halifax.

I come home pleased with the conversation and will approach the ministers again. John Adams sends me a letter detailing his proposals and what he believes is necessary to help me. [11]

I am popular everywhere I go. Even Aglaë de Hunolstein seems delighted to see me. "I consider myself lucky to have some place in his esteem," a friend tells me she has remarked. I am sometimes in the party of the queen; I ride with her; she helps me to obtain the post of *mestre de camp* of the regiment of the *dragons du roi* from the marquis de Créquy, for which I pay eighty thousand livres. I am aware there is resentment among some who have been in the army far longer than I, but on March 3 the king approves my new rank.

News arrives of a British victory in Georgia and South Carolina. However, the duc de Lauzun with a small French detachment, retakes Senegal from the British in late January. I write to Maurepas and say that the little state of Georgia is unhealthy and very unpleasant for any troops stationed there. I also suggest a plan for a corps of one thousand five hundred men to harass and raid the English coasts by the Irish Sea.[12] I believe cities or towns such as Liverpool, White Haven, Lancaster or Cork could be taken, then ransomed and the money given to the United States.

On March 20 I spend the day hunting with the king at Versailles; when I return home I write to Franklin: 'I Remember I heard complaints among the Southern Gentlemen of America about the Senegal being in the ennemy's hands and preventing the Nigro trade for that part of the United States- so that I Believe our Conquest will be pleasing to them and I wish to know your opinion Concerning that affair.'[13] On the twenty-second I visit him at Passy. I talk at great length about my plan to attack and ransom the cities of Bristol, Bath, Liverpool, Lancaster and Whitehaven on the west coast of England, the prospect exciting and pleasing him.

"I can offer the services of the fifty-gun ship, the *duc de Duras*, some of her sailors and Captain John Paul Jones," he says. "I have very little success though with the requests I make to the ministers."

"I think you have more reason to hope for this," I reply.

"I will speak to Monsieur de Vergennes at the dinner tomorrow," he says. [14]

I write to Maurepas in more detail. I suggest that the terror we would cause at Bristol, and at Bath in particular, where the best of London society comes at this time of year, would be felt very intensely, and that Bath would provide some well-qualified hostages.[15]

Vergennes appears interested. He asks me to write about my proposal in more detail and on the twenty-sixth I do so. Maurepas has already told me that the prince de Montbarey would cause no difficulties over the number of men he would give, and I say that I sincerely hope there would be no problem about their quality.[16] I send for Captain John Paul Jones to come to Paris and wait impatiently. I also write to the ministry asking them to buy some frigates. Monsieur Leray de Chaumont, a merchant and friend of Franklin, is arranging the preparation of the ships and tells me that the *Bonhomme Richard*, previously the *duc de Duras*, but now named after Franklin's *Poor Richard's Almanac*, will be ready within three weeks, as well as other ships if required. I discover there had previously been a plan for Jones to attack parts of the English coast, but this has now been changed in favor of mine. I ask Sartine for two letters, one telling Jones that his destination has been changed and that the king will entrust him with the transport of troops which I will command and that he will take us wherever I consider to be appropriate, and that he should go immediately to Lorient to be ready as soon as possible, the other letter asking for the service of the frigate, without which he is not prepared to lend it. [17]

On the seventeenth, I go to see the *Comédie Française* perform '*L'Amour Français*,' a one-act play in verse by Rochon de Chabannes. To my delight, there are several lines about me in it, the first time a living person is praised on the stage. The audience applauds wildly; afterwards I thank Chabannes. I later hear that the duc de Chartres, whose name is often romantically linked to that of Aglaë de Humolstein, is furiously denouncing the play.

I talk with the Swedish ambassador. "Could your king lend four ships of the line with half of their crew, which the United States would agree to return in a year under certain conditions with France taking responsibility for the price of hire?" He appears agreeable. I therefore write to Vergennes and tell him of my proposal. I say that the ships could be here in two and a half months and could then sail to Rhode Island, or anywhere else in America, in October, when the weather is still good. I ask him what he thinks.[18]

I send Gimat and Pontgibaud to Lorient to see the preparations but keep secret about what is happening.

"What are your plans, Monsieur de Lafayette?" the queen asks.

"Monsieur de Maurepas has asked me to say nothing," I reply.

A look of anger crosses her face, but I remain silent.[19]

Adrienne is pregnant and I want to leave my affairs in good order when I depart so I go to see Jacques Grattepain and Jacques-Philippe Grattepain-Morizot, the stewards of my estate, appointed by the court after the death of my notaire, Monsieur Gérard, when I was in America.[20]

"I would like to reconfirm your appointment as I am on the point of going to a foreign country," I say, without revealing more.

I am also busy with a book Franklin and I are compiling, relating the atrocities committed by the British in the American war. Number eighteen shows prisoners being killed and cooked for a festival where the Lenape are eating American flesh and where Colonel Butler and his officers are dining. Number twenty-one depicts a prison ship where the American prisoners never see the light of day and are insulted by the British. I send Franklin some of my ideas: 'I Could indeed make out an immense Book upon so rich a matter- but my dear doctor, tho' I hate the British Nation, I however am oblig'd to Confess that those ministers and theyr executors are unhappily of the Same nature (whatever corrupted it may be) as the rest of Mankind.' I also suggest that as there seems to be unrest in Ireland does he think that: 'a corps of two thousand men with four thousand spare arms might not Crowd awround them Many lovers of Liberty and many ennemies to the English tyrannical government? '[21]

I try and find someone to go to Ireland to observe and perhaps encourage the prospects of revolt. Franklin obtains the services of Dr. Edward Bancroft, whom I had met when I visited London, who seems very suitable for the mission.

My hopes to attack the English and Irish coast suddenly suffer a severe blow. I receive the disappointing order to go to my post as commander of the *dragons du roi* at Saintes. My plan to attack the English and Irish coast has been annulled. I am not sure who is responsible. Is it Montbarey, for financial reasons, as well as timidity? I do not know what will happen to Captain Jones's squadron, but I gather the ministers will speak with Franklin about it.

"Couldn't the government spare at least a small force of six hundred men and perhaps two ships?" I ask Vergennes.

"You must talk to Maurepas," he replies.[22]

"No, such an insignificant number of men is beneath your dignity," says Maurepas. "It is unwise to risk the certainty of commanding your own regiment for the uncertainty of this expedition."

"Public opinion has been so kind to me that even setting out with six hundred men would be attributed to its real motive and pardoned," I exclaim hotly.

"Come back in two days," he replies.[23]

I immediately write to Vergennes: 'What would suit me is an advance guard of grenadiers and chasseurs and a detachment of from the dragons du roi, in all one thousand five hundred to two thousand men, which would put me out of the line of rank and in a position to exert myself.'[24]

I return to see Maurepas, but he is still opposed to my original plan of six hundred men, so I do not mention my more grandiose scheme.

I learn that a loan for England arranged in Holland has been cancelled because an extra one per cent interest had been asked. I suggest it might be procured for America, but fear Monsieur

Necker will not be in favor. A second disappointment follows that of the cancellation of my expedition. I receive a letter from the president of Congress saying they have changed their mind about a joint Canadian expedition.

I leave Vergennes to direct Bancroft concerning the mission to Ireland, as my obligation to joining the dragons du roi prevent me from following up this negotiation.[25]

June 1. I arrive in Saintonge. Almost immediately, my commander, the marquis de Voyer, sends me to St Jean d'Angély, near Rochefort harbor, where the dragons du roi are now based, and which is a smaller and even more parochial town than Saintes. I immediately write to Vergennes to make sure he knows where to send any important messages to me. I tell him that any orders made at Versailles must be issued nearly a fortnight before I can arrive back there and that I would like a separate corps or an advance guard.[26] I live in fear I will miss out on the military expedition being planned. Everyone appears to be talking about it, but I know nothing. I want to fight, not to be stuck in the depths of the French countryside, charming though it is.

I inspect my regiment and find it in a poor state. I do not expect to be here long, but I will spend my time reorganizing all the departments so as to leave things in better order and to return the regiment to its proper condition after a certain time.[27] The marquis de Voyer receives orders to return to Paris. I am now, therefore, also in charge of the infantry at St Jean d'Angély.

I write to Vergennes:

I passionately love the profession of war, that I feel myself especially made to play at that game, that I have been spoiled by the last two years by the habit of having large commands and of enjoying great confidence; remember that I am anxious to justify the benefits that my native country has heaped upon me; remember that I adore that native country, that the thought of seeing England crushed and humiliated make me tremble with delight...judge if I ought not to be impatient to know whether I am destined to be the first man to step upon that shore and to plant the first French flag in the midst of that insolent nation. [28]

The chevalier de La Luzerne is sailing to America to replace Conrad-Alexandre Gérard who is ill, and so will be able to take my letters. I send Dr. Bones a watch engraved with a picture of Washington: 'I remember you had to borrow mine to take my pulse,'[29] I tell him. I write a letter to the president of Congress and declare that: 'the affairs of America I shall ever look upon as my first Business while I am in Europe.'[30]

I also write a long letter to Washington:

I had taken such an habit of being inseparable from you, that I can't now get the use of absence and I am more and more afflicted of that distance which keeps me so far from my dearest friend... The chevalier de la Luzerne intends going to Congress through headquarters...I have requir'd him to let you know any piece of news he has been intrusted with...There are two partys in France. Mms Adams and Lee on one part, doctor Franklin and his friends on the other. So great is the concern which these divisions give me, that I can't wait on these gentlemen as much as I could wish for fear of occasioning disputes...my return to Paris is I believe very near. From there I'll get employ'd in what ever will be done against the common enemy...what would make me the happiest of men, is to join again American colours, or to put under your orders a division of four or five thousand countrymen of mine. In case any such cooperation or private expedition is wished for, I think, (if peace is not settl'd this winter) that an early demand might be complie'd with for next campaign...Don't forget me, my dear general; be ever as affectionate for me as you have been - those sentiments I deserve by the ardent ones which fill my heart. With the highest respect, with the most sincere and tender friendship that ever human heart has felt I have the honor to be your excellency's most obedient, humble servant.[31]

It greatly saddens me that I have not received any letters from him since my return, but I am sure this is because of winds, accidents or lack of occasions as I think he would not want to make me unhappy.

June 13. Wonderful news arrives. We will invade England. The comte de Vaux is forming an army at le Havre, Saint Malo and other places, and I will be an aide to the *maréchal général des logis*. I set off immediately to Paris.

I am with my family again to Adrienne's delight; I learn that our main army will be formed of thirty thousand men and that smaller forces will come from Flanders and Brest. Spain declares war on England on the sixteenth; a joint Spanish/French fleet will attack British ships in the Channel before transporting troops across the strait to invade England. I will be in the vanguard with the grenadiers; my dragons du roi will wait at Brest and join me after the first troops have landed.

I visit Vergennes at Versailles. "What are your views on a French expeditionary force to America?" he asks.

I give him copies of the maps of Rhode Island drawn by Capitaine. 'I think there are various ways to attack the island which offer a good possibility of success,' I later write.[32]

I prepare to leave Paris to go to Le Havre; I see Bancroft for just two minutes when he returns from Ireland; to my disappointment he tells me the fruit is not yet ripe.[33] I will lend my new picture of Washington holding the Declaration of Independence and the French treaty, the edicts and proclamations of His Britannic Majesty under his feet, to Franklin for the banquet and ball he is giving on July 5 to celebrate Independence Day. I will not be there, but Adrienne will go instead.

July 1. I am in Le Havre; from my window overlooking the port I can see the ships which will take us to England and wait impatiently for the south wind which will bring Monsieur d'Orvilliers and his fleet. I write to Vergennes: 'Monsieur de Jaucourt is a most agreeable leader to have…He seems not to have lost the habit of discipline. I am delighted by this, since I, who was also a general in my youth, have always found that it was very difficult to lead a large number of troops without discipline.' I also tell him: 'I can be at peace only on the English coast, and we are not there yet.'[34]

On the third, the wind blows from the south and so will hopefully speed d'Orvilliers on his way. By chance, I find an Irish monk who seems willing to act as a spy in England or Ireland.

Vergennes has asked me for some ideas concerning an expedition to America and on July 18 I compile a long and detailed memorandum. I suggest a force of four thousand three hundred men whose squadron should set sail before September 10, to arrive off the Jersey coast in early November. I suggest attacking Rhode Island, but that Georgia and Carolina also need our assistance and December and January could be spent in the south. My mind ranges freely over the continent. Perhaps we could attack Halifax? The idea of a revolution in Canada is very pleasing to all good Frenchmen and we could leave part of the American troops accompanying us in Nova Scotia. I suggest that the Americans are difficult to deal with but that if I were given the command of our troops, or if the person chosen by the king acts with good judgement then all difficulties would be avoided.[35]

D'Orvilliers and the fleet do not appear. There are rumors that he has sailed to the Azores to intercept the fleet from the West Indies or has even sailed to the United States. Should I buy a ship and sail across the Atlantic? A letter from America says that Fort Lafayette has been captured, that the enemy has had successes in Georgia and have been planning to take over West Point and the navigation of the North River. I suggest to Vergennes that a squadron of three thousand men could be sent to Boston to be joined in the spring by warships and a ground reinforcement.[36]

On August 13, the French fleet, comprising sixty-six ships of the line and frigates, finally arrives in the English Channel, delighting me that the French flag now flies in English roadsteads. The comte de Vaux has gone to Saint Malo, but some people are saying that only a part of the army will be employed, not our force at le Havre. I am desperate to be part of the invasion and write to Vergennes: 'You know that ambition does not torment me, but if being useful to my country is my greatest happiness, if leading troops in war by myself is a game I passionately love, then the pleasure of at least seeing others do it is absolutely necessary to my peace of mind.' [37]

It occurs to me that all this preparation for war might result in the British agreeing a truce with the United States. I therefore write again to Vergennes and offer to take such a treaty to the United States. I would go in my capacity as an American general officer so that my appointment would not create any difficulties in relation to that of the chevalier de La Luzerne and I would not wish any payment. If, however, there is an invasion of England, then I offer my services after that event. I also take the opportunity to remind Vergennes again of my wish to actively participate in the expected campaign here in France.[38] We hear reports that d'Orvilliers blockaded Plymouth and has now gone out to sea to meet the British fleet.

Franklin's grandson, William, arrives from Paris with the sword ordered for me by Congress. It is very ornate and depicts the Battle of Gloucester, the retreat from Barren Hill, the Battle of Monmouth and the retreat from Rhode Island. The pommel is of gold; my coat of arms and motto, *Cur Non?* is on one side, on the other is a partly wooded, partly cultivated scene over which is a rising moon, depicting the United States, with the words: *Crescam ut prosim.* The inscription says: *From the American Congress to the Marquis de Lafayette, 1779.* My spirits soar. It is a noble present and has an immense effect on the army here.

Franklin writes: 'By the help of the exquisite artists France affords I find it easy to express everything but the Sense we have of your Worth and of our Obligations to you. For this, Figures and even Words, are found insufficient.'[39]

"Can I be your aide-de-camp in the forthcoming invasion?" requests William Franklin.

I agree and write to his grandfather asking if he can do so, at the same time thanking him for the sword: 'The Sight of these actions where I was a Witness of American Bravery and patriotic Spirit, I will ever enjoy with that pleasure which Becomes a heart glowing with love for the Nation, and the Most ardent zeal for theyr Glory and happiness.' William Franklin returns to Paris with my letter.[40]

We do not know the positions of our fleet and that of the enemy, but it appears the British are trying to postpone any action and are retreating up the Channel. News comes that d'Orvilliers is sailing to Brest. It seems increasingly unlikely there will be an invasion this autumn, but as I had been one of the first to hope for it, I hope to be the last to give up my belief in it. However, there is better news from the Antilles; we have taken Saint Vincent and Grenada. My brother-in-law, Louis de Noailles, commanded one of the four corps which took Grenada. I write to Vergennes: 'A success was becoming very necessary for us; my brother-in-law's conduct delighted me, and I was pleased to see the public come round to my opinion of a man whose very bravery was disputed and in whose favor I was almost the only one who dared to speak up.'[41]

D'Orvilliers and the fleet are unfortunately now in Brest where they arrived on the fourteenth. They have been decimated by illness and it has been decided they can no longer be useful to the proposed plan.[42] There will be no invasion. I will suffer in silence.[43] I decide to visit a place in the countryside near here where Adrienne will join me.

I receive a letter from Vergennes in which he says that our 'concern for America's welfare means that troops should be sent, but that alone would not be doing enough.'[44] His words suddenly give me hope.

We hear that on September 23, John Paul Jones, in the *Bonhomme Richard*, aided by one American and two French ships, attacked the forty-four-gun *Serapis*, which had been escorting a convoy of merchant ships from the Baltic, off the east coast of England. The *Serapis* surrendered; the *Bonhomme Richard* was about to sink, so the two hundred and thirty-seven crew, half of whom were injured, transferred to the *Serapis*. The *Pallas* captured the other ship, the *Countess of Scarborough*. I write, congratulating him. I also congratulate Franklin on the success of 'the little squadron in which you know I have been greatly concerned.'[45]

In November, however, I still look out at the gray sea from my office opposite the harbour. Only now there is no longer the prospect of any glory, my ill-fated passion for the last year.

'Prepare the army to march,' unexpectedly comes the order. None of us have any idea why, but nothing happens.

I return to Paris. Terrible news arrives: d'Estaing and the American forces of General Benjamin Lincoln abandoned an attack at Savannah on October 9. D'Estaing has been injured, about six hundred of his troops and about one hundred and seventy Continentals have been killed, as well as Count Pulaski who had been leading two hundred cavalrymen.[46] More cheering, however, is the report that the British left Newport on October 25.

Adrienne will soon give birth and is at Passy with her mother. I remain busy at Versailles and Paris on behalf of America.

December 24. At two o'clock in the morning, my servant, Desplaces, brings a letter. To my immense joy, we have had a boy:

> Accept my compliments, Monsieur le marquis, they are very sincere and very real. America will celebrate with illuminations and I think Paris should do the same. The number of persons who resemble you is so small that it is public good fortune to see it increase...For once we have set a good example and M. le maréchal will no longer say we give him only girls...Thank you for your letters. You must have many matters to attend to. The occupations of paternity are so sweet. Give in to them; they can only be good.[47]

Despite the hour, I immediately send a message to Franklin: 'The Boy shall be called George, and you will easily gess that he bears that Name as a tribute of Respect and love for my dear friend Gal. Washington.'[48]

I quickly travel to Passy to see my new-born son. Next day, I attend the baptism, my son blessed with the names George Louis Gilbert Washington Motier de La Fayette. I remain at Passy for several days basking in the delights of parenthood with Adrienne. Then I return to Paris to continue my efforts to obtain men and arms for the United States.

Last October Franklin had said he would have to propose the matter of introducing foreign troops into America to Congress: 'I know nothing of their sentiments on the subject...and therefore I could give no expectation of whether the plan would be adopted.'[49]

"I have been directed to ask for subsidies but have no instructions to ask for troops and so dare to go no further," he continues to say.[50] However, he does ask for arms and ammunition and also wonders about the possibility of some ships.

I am only too aware I have been directed not to request French auxiliary troops for the United States because the popular sentiment of jealousy against foreigners, particularly Frenchmen, not only made Congress averse to this plan, but also made them believe it would cause general anxiety and discontent,[51] However, I visit Versailles frequently and continue to press the ministers for what I consider necessary to help the United States win the war. The failure of our proposed invasion makes it more likely that I will succeed, and my spirits, which do not, in any case, need much strengthening, have been boosted by a long letter I finally received from Washington, written on September 30:

> Your forward Zeal in the name of liberty- Your singular attachment to this infant world- your Ardent and persevering efforts not only in America, but since your return to France to serve the United States- your polite attention to Americans- and your strict and uniform friendship for me, has ripened the first impressions of esteem and attachment, which I imbibed for you, into perfect love and gratitude that neither time nor absence can impair which will warrant my assuring you, that whether in the character of an officer at the head of a Corps of gallant French (if circumstances should require this) or whether as a Major-Gen.l commanding a division of the American army- or whether, after our swords and spears have given place to the plough-share and pruning-hook, I see you as a private Gentleman- a friend and companion- I shall welcome you in all of the warmth of friendship to Columbia's shore. [52]

I talk with Maurepas about the letters I have received from Washington and Hamilton which I say insinuate that the Americans are waiting for our troops.[53] Maurepas clearly shows an interest. I go again twice to see him but there are so many interruptions I feel it is better to write, which I do at some length. I include Washington's words about whether I come to America as a commanding officer of a corps of gallant Frenchmen or whether I am coming to take command as an American major general; I say that Hamilton, his premier aide-de-camp, also echoes his views. I say that my belief in a new campaign in America has not changed because 'I know that country too well to change my opinion…The failure of our great preparations in Europe, the defeat at Savannah, the reconciliation with Ireland, perhaps the taking of Charleston: these are the events that will affect the credibility of the cause and on the state of American finances. The total ruin of commerce, the devastation of coastal cities by small English corps, the very dangerous extension of British power in the southern states, offensive operations undertaken from New York; these can be prevented only by obliging the enemy to confine itself to its posts and these considerations, combined with so many others, make our aid almost indispensable.' I suggest six ships of sixty-four and fifty guns and that eight thousand tons of transport ships can be assembled within a month. I also suggest four full strength second battalions, to which their grenadiers would be attached, commanded by lieutenant colonels. I reply to any objections which might be made and spend many lines explaining why I think I should command the force sent, although I also mention I would serve as a volunteer: 'The crossing might take two months; we must be ready at the end of February; we ought to write to America in two weeks and in four days I would like to see the preparations for which we do not need a response from Madrid.'[54]

To my great joy, I am successful. It is decided to send a force to the United States. Vergennes asks me to write the measures I believe should be taken for the expedition before I talk with him. Accordingly, on February 2, I write what needs to be done if, firstly, I am the commander of the expedition and, secondly, if I am not. Again, I make it clear I think I should command the force which I regard as not only a military and political commission, but also social. If I am not chosen, then I say that: 'it would be necessary to act beforehand to counteract the unfavorable effect which would be produced in America by the arrival of another commander. The idea that I could not lead this detachment is the last one that would be thought of there. But in that event, I will say that I preferred an American division.' I also suggest I should take with me one battalion of six hundred grenadiers, three hundred dragoons and one hundred hussars, and that any plan kept secret from me would seem very suspicious in Philadelphia.[55]

The reply is not to my liking. "It is best for you to go back to America to resume your command in the Continental Army and act as a liaison with our forces. An older soldier will be chosen to lead our troops."

I learn it will be fifty-five-year-old Jean-Baptiste-Donatien de Vimeur, the comte de Rochambeau, whom I know. He does not speak English but is a very experienced soldier. He fought in the Seven Years' War and has been a major general for nineteen years; he will be accompanied by Admiral Charles-Henri d'Arsac, the chevalier de Ternay.

I write a list of the matters relevant to the navy for an expedition to North America, such as provisions, the honors to be paid to the Americans, presents for the Native Americans and a printshop on board ship.[56]

I prepare for my departure. I confirm the legal right of the Morizots to act on my behalf with the agreement of Adrienne and my uncle, the comte de Lusignem; Adrienne will make any necessary decisions for me as she is intelligent, practical and shares my beliefs. I trust her implicitly.

Rochambeau is promoted to the rank of *lieutenant général* and will be second only to Washington. I am being sent in advance to tell Washington that ships and men are on their way. Washington's army will therefore nearly double in size and for the first time he will be able to act independently and not have to continually consult Congress. He also does not have to answer to the king's ambassador in America. It is a personal victory for him and one in which I am proud to say I have played no small part. It also pleases me that my brother-in-law, Louis de Noailles, will be part of the force. He is a colonel, a rank below mine.

"You have an old debt of one hundred thousand livres and now you want a new one of one hundred and twenty thousand. You are buying your glory at the expense of your fortune," says Morizot.

"I do not intend to change course. Glory and honor are beyond price," I reply.[57]

On the morning of February 29, I go to Versailles in my American uniform to take formal leave of the king and queen. The court stands in silence.

"I am sure you will be able to advance our common cause," says Marie Antoinette.

Pride fills me. I am sadly not the commander of the French army being sent to fight, but thanks to my efforts the United States will be greatly aided in the war. I am also returning to my general and will be the first to announce the news of our force. I am returning to a battle which I am sure will be won.

In the afternoon I attend a gathering at the home of the duc de Choiseul. I meet Thomas Walpole, the great-nephew of the former British prime minister.

"The splendor of your uniform surprises me, sir," he remarks. "The American army is, I believe, nearly naked."

"The Americans have various uniforms," I reply in a cool tone. "Some are in blue, some are in green or brown, and many have hunting shirts from the Carolinas. It is true not many are dressed as well as I am, but it is also true that those who captured Burgoyne's army were almost naked."

Everyone laughs. Walpole does not. Nor do I. The subject is too serious.

I spend the next few days seeing Americans, including John Adams who has just returned to Paris, and Philip Mazzei who is here as the special emissary of Virginia. I talk with Rochambeau.

"The Americans have a great need of many items, as I have already listed," I tell him.

I return to Versailles where I insist that I and the other Frenchmen in the American army should be regarded only as American officers. I arrange for the leave of my aides, Capitaine and Gimat, from the French army and learn that the frigate, *Hermione*, will take me to the United States.

March 5. Vergennes gives me my orders, which are in two parts. The first instructs me to tell Washington that the king, wishing to give the United States a new testimony of his affection and his concern for their security, has resolved to send to their aid six ships of the line and six thousand regular infantry troops at the onset of spring. The convoy is ordered to land at Rhode Island if there is no obstacle in order to be better able to assist the American army and to join it if General Washington considers it necessary. But since it is possible that after having voluntarily evacuated Rhode Island, the British may have returned there, I am ordered to obtain authorization from General Washington to send a few of the French officers attached to me to Rhode Island to prevent the French squadron being taken by surprise and to say that the squadron can moor at Boston, if necessary. If the winds drive the fleet south there should be an officer stationed at Cape Henry to give information about disembarking at Rhode Island...The corps of French troops will be purely auxiliary and, in this capacity, will act only under General Washington's orders. The French land general will take orders from the American commanding general for everything that does not relate to the internal regulation of his corps.'[58] The second part of my orders is confidential.[59] It suggests that the auxiliary force should be employed in states which are near to Florida to challenge the British there, and also to attack New York so that the British would bring back troops from the south. The last paragraph states that the known humanity of General Washington and the high esteem with which he is held in Europe, as well as in America, do not let us doubt that he will not needlessly endanger the lives of a corps of brave men sent more than one thousand leagues to the help of his country. The same orders given to me will also be taken by Captain John Paul Jones, sailing shortly afterwards, to be delivered to Washington if I am captured.

On the way home I visit Franklin at Passy to take his letters in which he has written to Washington that my zeal for the honor of the United States, my activity on behalf of American affairs, the inviolable attachment that I show for their cause and for Washington, have inspired in him the same esteem that Washington has for me.[60] We say farewell.

March 6. Monday. The day of my departure. Adrienne is distraught, fearing she will never see me again. I embrace my family; I embrace her. Then I set off for Rochefort with my entourage. I write to Adrienne the same day, as well as on the seventh and the eighth. On the ninth, at eight in the evening, I reach Rochefort. On the morning of the tenth, Captain La Touche-Tréville welcomes me, Gimat and Capitaine, my six servants and my secretary, Poirey, on board the *Hermione*; we set sail towards the roadstead by the Île d'Aix.[61]

On March 12 I write to the prince de Poix, enclosing a letter for him to give to the queen. I ask him to buy some different pieces of excellent quality blue cloth so that I can show Americans a sample of our manufactured goods. I also ask him to purchase a tea service for me like that of Madame de Bouffler, except that the china should be very fine white Sèvres and the spoons should be of gold plate, as I would like to give this as a gift to Mrs. Washington. [62] On the thirteenth, we are joined by Commissary de Corny and Rousseau de Fayolle.

"The wind is favorable, and we will put the ship under sail during the night," says La Touche-Tréville.[63]

At nine in the evening, I write to Adrienne:

This, my beloved, is a truly cruel moment, as I write to you. This is the moment of getting under way and addressing you my last farewells. I confess that the emotions in my heart hardly persuade me to write rationally. I know that I am going to lose sight of this land that holds all that is most dear to me, that tomorrow it will disappear from my view. My heart, you must believe that it costs me cruelly to leave you. You should not be concerned by my crossing; our frigate flies; she is commanded by the most likeable man in the world; I am as well-quartered as is possible; and my arrival is assured. I will write you, my dear heart, on arriving in Boston. Think, my dear heart, that my absence will be like an ordinary campaign; in a few months I will come back to spend the winter with you. Take care of your health, my heart take care of it if you love me. Write me often...Look often at my portrait for it will tell you a part of what I feel. My heart is very troubled at this moment, but I do not want to add to your affliction by describing my own. Farewell, farewell, my dear heart. Give a thousand kisses to our dear Anastasie thousands upon thousands of times; kiss our other child. How fortunate they are to be able to see you. Why do I, dear heart, who am made so happy by you, always return unhappiness by leaving you? Forgive me! The sorrow I suffer punishes me for it. Farewell, farewell again. I would never have believed that it would cost so much to leave. My dear heart, I feel at this moment that I love you still more than I ever thought. Farewell, farewell. [64]

My letter is taken to shore. The sailors lift the anchor; the wind catches the sails; the ship moves forward in the darkness, leaving behind the roadstead of La Rochelle.

The *Hermione* rises and falls, waves buffeting her. Nausea holds me in its ghastly embrace. I lie as still as I can; I eat nothing, Gimat, Capitaine and Rousseau de Fayolles attempting to cheer me. A day after our departure, storm winds howl through the rigging, ferocious waves wash over the ship which groans and creaks. Suddenly there comes the ominous noise of breaking wood.

"The main mast is broken. It is not as serious as on the *Alliance* though. We are returning to the Île d'Aix for it to be repaired," reports Gimat.

A short time later, de Fayolle appears. "Three cutters are chasing us. We are preparing to fire on them. Come on deck and watch."

Gimat goes with him, but I am too ill. The cannons roar; I have to wait to hear others tell me about it. The cannons fall silent; the cutters are either sunk or have sailed away. Fog envelops us, the Hermione continuing slowly towards the Île d'Aix.

March 18. I write again to Adrienne to tell her of our return yesterday. To my disappointment a packet of letters sent to me has been taken back to Paris, as we had been more than forty-eight hours out of port. On the twentieth, we set sail once more, fast and skilfully, the main yard repaired. I quickly recover from seasickness. Occasionally there is no wind, the *Hermione* lingering on the calm sea, her sails drooping. Occasionally the winds are contrary; one man dies from fever, but there is no enemy attack.

Chapter 25

Washington enraptured

April 26. We reach the port of Marblehead in Massachusetts.[1] I spend the night on land, then reboard next day along with pilots to guide us into Boston.[2] At the entrance to its harbor, I write to Washington:

> Here I am, My dear General, and in the Mist of the joy I feel in finding Myself again one of Your loving Soldiers. I take But the time of telling you that I Came from France on Board of a fregatt which the king gave me for my passage. I have affairs of the utmost importance that I should at first Communicate to You alone. In case my letter finds you any where this Side of Philadelphia, I Beg you will wait for me, and do Assure you a great public good May derive from it. To Morrow we go up to the town, and the day after I'll set off in My usual way to join My Belov'd and Respected friend and general. Adieu, my dear general, you will Easely know the hand of your young Soldier. [3]

The *Hermione* enters the harbor at noon. She fires a thirteen-gun salute and the cannon at the fort fire in reply. Church bells are pealing; people are rushing towards Hancock's Wharf; a band is playing.

I recognize many members of both houses of the Massachusetts Assembly. I step ashore, the crowd cheering wildly. People help me into a carriage; we set off through the streets to the house in State Street the Assembly has prepared for me, the band marching ahead, people huzzaing wildly. Not long after, I present myself to the two chambers of the town. I struggle to remember my English, but it is not important. People appear delighted to see me. I am a sign France is perhaps coming to help them.

In the evening, the whole of Boston appears to be assembling in front of the house. They build an enormous bonfire. They cheer and shout; fireworks explode colorfully into the sky. I go onto the balcony and make a speech in the best English I can muster. Tiredness tricks my tongue, but people do not care what I am saying. They cheer just at my standing there. They cheer because my arrival gives them hope that France will help to win the war.

"Frenchmen seem more welcome today than they were two years ago," comments Rousseau de Fayolle.[4]

"I must set out to see General Washington at Morristown. I cannot stop for the banquets and festivities which are planned but I thank the Massachusetts Assembly for the kindnesses they are showing me," I say.

On May 2, I write to Adrienne to tell her of my safe arrival. I also write to Vergennes and mention that the value of paper money has fallen considerably, but that Congress is taking wise measures to re-establish the public finances, that General Lincoln's army appears to be growing daily and that although General Washington's army is very small, several states are contributing men. I also say that I am extremely pleased with public opinion in all the respects which may interest him. [5] My usual optimism gives me hope for the future. I am sure we will win. I write a short message to the Massachusetts Assembly thanking them for the flattering reception I have received. Then Gimat, our three servants and I, set off to headquarters in Morristown in the Jerseys, three hundred miles away, about one hundred and twenty French leagues. Huge crowds again gather in front of the house; many people accompany us for some way on horseback, waving and cheering and firing guns. There is the same enthusiasm in every town we come to which moves me greatly.

'In short, my love, my reception here is greater than anything I could describe to you,' I write to Adrienne.[6]

We ride as quickly as possible along poor dirt roads from morning to night. It is often difficult to obtain horses and we go more slowly to spare our animals. I keep quiet about French plans. At Fishkill I even publicly deny a report of the British that the French fleet is coming. I remain constantly vigilant. Some of the region between New York and New Jersey is known for its Tory sympathies and General Knyphausen is believed to be nearby. I hurry everyone through the Clove, a ravine in the highlands on the west side of the North River, and a very suitable site for an ambush.[7] We travel two hundred and fifty miles to Compton and finally see the wonderful sight of Major Caleb Gibbs and Washington's bodyguard.

"We did not know which road you were taking, so I was not able to ride further to meet you," he says.

He gives me a letter from Washington which I quickly read with great pleasure: 'Your welcome favor of the 27 of April came to my hands yesterday. I received it with all the joy that the sincerest friendship could dictate- and with that impatience which an ardent desire to see you could not fail to inspire.'[8]

On May 10 Gibbs escorts us to a three-story mansion with shutters and dormer windows in Morristown. We reach the porch; I leap from my horse just as my general comes out, closely followed by the much smaller figure of his wife. I embrace him, in tears; I kiss him from ear to ear and he also has tears in his eyes, proof of his paternal love for me. With emotion, I kiss the hand of Mrs. Washington. I embrace all the officers. We celebrate together noisily and happily, my joy overflowing to be back with my military family.

Washington and I go to a different room; I finally tell him the message I bring.

"Six ships of the line and six thousand troops were to leave France in early April and hope to arrive at Rhode Island early in June. They will be commanded by the comte de Rochambeau and are intended to join in a campaign to capture New York or to be used in the south."

He beams with delight, his usually impassive face with an expression of almost euphoria.

"We have so much need of it," he declares.

"Perhaps we can attack Halifax?" I suggest.[9]

"We must try and conceal what we are doing. The English will know that our force is coming," he says.

"Their spy system is always excellent. We need to confuse them," I reply. "Perhaps there can be a proclamation to the Canadians to suggest that the French will attack there, and another to the Native Americans to suggest it will be New York."[10]

"We also need to raise a larger Continental Army. However, for that, I need to have the consent of Congress. It is never quick to decide anything, so it would be best if a small committee is formed to enable a decision to be made. La Luzerne might be able to direct Congress to do that. It would be useful if you go to Philadelphia to ask him."

"Yes, I will do that," I reply.

"It will then be possible to mount an attack on New York," he declares.

I discover it has been, and still is, terrible here. It was thought the army might not survive. The winter was the worst old people can remember. In January there was such a blizzard men could not be in it for even a short time without fearing for their lives and there was six feet of snow in the camp. There is often no food, some men were reduced to eating tree bark or boiling their shoes and many illnesses such as typhus have erupted. It resembles the situation at Valley Forge, the army is starving and yet is in fertile farmland. The people want an army, but they are not prepared to support it, and even worse, some are making a profit from it. There is discontent amongst the soldiers who have sometimes demanded food from people in the countryside at the point of a bayonet. The army has been wonderfully patient and heroic, as usual, and has so far survived, although there are constant fears of mutiny. The men have not been paid for five months. Professional soldiers are needed, not men on short enlist. The currency is becoming worthless. In the south General Clinton is besieging Charleston with about ten thousand troops.

I am feverish with a cold caught from the inclement weather during my ride from Boston, but a few large helpings of rum considerably help to chase it away. I visit the encampment where hundreds of log cabins stand in rows, smoke rising from their chimneys. The men come out to cheer and wave. They resemble wraiths. They are emaciated. Their clothes are in rags; many are half-naked and without shoes.

Hamilton and I draw up a report of everything that needs to be done for the French force. Then I set off on horseback to Philadelphia.

I arrive on May 15. I talk with La Luzerne who has received the dispatches I sent him from Morristown.

"There is a lack of detail in the documents from the ministers of war and the navy," he says.[11]

"I will write more fully for you," I tell him. "I expect Monsieur de Corny, the commissary of war, will be at Morristown when I return, and he will then come here. You will need to assist him financially because he has only fifty thousand francs and due to a misunderstanding has not any letters of exchange. You will need to sign all his agreements and obtain the necessary provisions."

I write to Congress to say I have put an end to my furlough from the American army and 'that I have been able again to join my colors, for I may hope for opportunities of indulging the ardent zeal, the unbounded gratitude, the warm, and I might say, the patriotic love By Which I am forever Bound to America.'[12] I also give them a letter from Washington about me.

La Luzerne writes on the sixteenth to Congress and tells them of the coming French force. He suggests a special committee should be formed to help with preparations and to obtain provisions as Washington has wished. On the nineteenth and twentieth, Congress passes resolutions to ask the states to give ten million dollars to the Continental Treasury and to send their troop quotas to the army. It also instructs the committee which is at headquarters to help obtain supplies for the Continental Army. It requests me to make suggestions to Washington and for him to do what is needed to promote the cooperation and success of allied operations.[13]

I visit the delegates of states such as Massachusetts and am hopeful we might soon have an army of fifteen thousand men, and some militia, not counting the southern army.[14]

On Sunday, May 21, I ride away from Philadelphia towards Morristown, my excitement at the prospect of French and American troops fighting together to defeat the British lending wings to my feet and punishing my horses.

Chapter 26

Treachery of the blackest hue

While I was at Philadelphia men at Morristown had mutinied on account of the scarcity of provisions. On May 27 a small amount of meat reaches our camp. Next day there is again nothing. I write to Joseph Reed: 'An army that is Reduc'd to Nothing, that wants provisions, that has not one of the Necessary means to Make war, such is the Situation where in I have found our troops, and however prepar'd I Could have been to this unhappy sight By our past distresses, I confess I had no idea of such an extremity.'[1] I feel I can no longer write a detailed account of what is happening here to the French court and the French generals. Pride is stopping me until 'our army is put in a Better, a more decent situation.'[2]

The night of the thirtieth, we receive a copy of Rivington's paper sent by Colonel Elias Dayton of the Third New Jersey who says he hopes the report of the surrender of Charleston's garrison and all its arms and equipment to the British on May 12 is a lie.[3] I am skeptical, as are others.[4]

"I think it is true," says Washington, who believes that unless Congress speaks in a more decisive tone, unless they are vested with powers by the several states competent to the great purposes of war or assume them as matter of right, and they, and the states respectively, act with more energy than they hitherto have done, that our cause is lost.[5]

La Luzerne writes that he has helped de Corny obtain nearly 600,000 livres and that with the amount he has brought it should be sufficient to fulfill his orders in as far as circumstances and the nature of the country allow.[6] He later writes that he has divided what is needed into what is wanted now and what can wait, and that the final decision shall rest with Washington and myself.[7]

"I do not think the number of wagons and artillery horses that Monsieur de Rochambeau wanted should be reduced, but there does not seem to be an urgent need for the horses of Lauzun's Legion. Fifty or sixty horses to carry messages and to escort general officers seem adequate. If we have more money then enough horses could be bought to form a company according to French regulations," says Washington.

I talk with Greene about provisions; I write to him and ask for one hundred wagons to be ready either on the North River or on the Connecticut River before June 20, and to appoint a man responsible for feeding the horses of the army and the cattle and sheep which will follow. I also institute a system of express riders from Cape Henry to Philadelphia, then to Morristown and north to Providence, which I hope will be ready by the sixth, to tell us when the French fleet is sighted.[8]

Dr. James Craik, assistant general director of hospitals, has gone to Rhode Island to prepare a hospital for the French until Monsieur d'Annemours, the French consul at Baltimore, arrives. Washington instructs General Heath to stop at Providence and make suitable preparations for the reception of the French army and fleet.

The proclamation I have written for the inhabitants of Canada to mislead the enemy into believing it is the objective of the French, has been sent to Benedict Arnold in Philadelphia to be passed on to New York.[9] Five hundred copies will be printed. When the French troops arrive it will be thrown away; I have been able to say what I want in a work never destined to appear.

June 6. Washington calls a council of war. "New York would be a suitable allied target."

We agree unanimously. In the night a report arrives from Colonel Elias Day at Elizabeth Town: 'The enemy has landed in force at De Hart's Point and is advancing.'

Our heavy cannon is parked here and there are also stores of supplies. Washington, therefore, orders our hungry and weak army to march towards Springfield, hoping to maneuver without fighting. I command the Connecticut division on the left wing. Greene commands on the right. On the seventh, we are at Chatham; we hear that Dayton's regiment of Maxwell's Brigade, with militia, had attacked the enemy causing them to retreat to high ground north-west of the Connecticut Farms where they have thrown up earthworks. On the eighth we are near Springfield and establish headquarters on the hills near the town. During the night there is thunder, lightning and heavy rain; in the morning, we find that the enemy retreated to De Hart's Point in the storm. The commander is now known to be Knyphausen, and it is learned a pontoon bridge has been built to the mainland.

"Our situation is embarrassing," says Washington. "When they unite their force, it will be infinitely more so." [10]

I write to General Heath at Providence waiting for the fleet: 'We are not in a settled position and I am writing as fast as I can with bad pens and bad ink upon the corner of a bad table.' I enclose a letter of introduction for him to Rochambeau and de Ternay and tell him about French military customs. I say that clothing will be coming from France for our soldiers and that I hope the states will provide some for their officers: 'In the fighting way they shall see that we are equal to anything-But for what concerns dress, appearance, etc., we must cheat a little.' [11]

News arrives: six men of war and at least sixty other ships have sailed into New York, presumably bringing troops from the Carolinas. Will they attack West Point?

Six enemy ships sail to Verplanck's Point on the North River. Then they sail back, making Washington undecided what to do. Our army is far from West Point but unless an attack there is definite it is not wise to be away from the Jerseys. On the twenty-second he therefore leaves Greene and a small force to see what the enemy are intending and orders the main army to Pompton, sixteen miles from Springfield.

In the early morning, we hear the rumble of cannon from the direction of Elizabeth Town. A message comes from Greene: 'The enemy are out on their march towards this place in full force, having received a complete reinforcement last night.'[12]

Washington orders the army to march back to support him and to move the stores from Morristown, but the men only manage to march about six miles. In the dark of evening a message comes from Greene who has skirmished with the enemy that the British have burned the village and are now withdrawing towards Elizabeth Town. Fourteen of his men have been killed, forty-nine wounded and nine are missing.

I am bitterly disappointed I have not fought. Next morning, June 24, information arrives: 'The enemy have gone across to Staten Island on the pontoon bridge and have removed it.' It is difficult to understand their objective. Is it West Point?

Washington orders the army to march towards the North River. A small enemy force lands at Phillipsburg on the twenty-fifth and he waits to see their intention. After a few days he begins to believe they are just foraging; on July 1 he orders the main army to Preakness. Meanwhile ladies in Philadelphia are raising money to buy clothing for the soldiers and I send them one hundred guineas in Adrienne's name.

July 4. Preakness. My headquarters are near the Singac Brook, next to those of Washington,[13] my thoughts all the time with the French force out in the Atlantic. I have been greatly saddened by the death of Rousseau de Fayolle on June 8, who was boarding the *Hermione* from a boat in Newport harbor, knocked his head and fell backwards, dying instantly, my dispatches promptly saved by La Touche from falling into the water. I have received a reply from General Heath who says that although he will endeavor to: 'pay every attention and civility to those who come to our aid but that in the infancy of the army of his country….it is not to be expected that her officers can vie in dress with the nobility of one of the most affluent nations in the world.' He thanks me for my letter of introduction and for the epaulettes I have sent him.[14]

Our army remains in terrible straits. Sometimes there is no meat, sometimes there is no bread, sometimes there is neither. Many men are nearly naked and at least a fourth are without blankets.[15] I write to Washington about the clothing which I hope will be coming with the French.[16]

I send two officers of the Second Canadian Regiment to spy on British troops and fortifications and try to discover what the population thinks at Quebec and Montreal concerning my usual scheme for Canada, even although I am very aware Washington does not share my enthusiasm.

There is unfortunately now no doubt about the capitulation in Charleston. May 12 was indeed the fateful day, as Rivington's had said. Two thousand five hundred and seventy-one Continental soldiers, three hundred and forty-three pieces of artillery and nearly six thousand muskets were surrendered to the British. Our soldiers were not allowed the traditional honors of defeat. They had to march out from the town without their colors flying. They had to stack their weaponry in silence and were given the choice of either being prisoners of war or to return home after vowing an oath never to fight again, and to become once more loyal subjects of the British crown.

"This defeat will give spirit to our enemies," says Washington. "The British will now use Charleston as a base to launch attacks into the Carolinas and Virginia. It is possible, however, that they are stretching themselves too thinly."

General Clinton and Admiral Arbuthnot have returned to New York from Charleston; a corps of one thousand five hundred men has been sent to St. Augustine and another corps has been left in Carolina under Lord Cornwallis.

Washington instructs me to write to Rochambeau and de Ternay saying what we know of the British position and detailing the preparations being made to receive the French fleet and troops, as well as asking for the clothing, arms and ammunition they are bringing for us to be sent to New London.[17]

On the eleventh I add my name to a memorial sent from the general officers to Congress concerning the suffering of the army, which has become intolerable due mainly to the depreciation of the money. They talk of the deplorable situation of widows and fatherless children of those who have died for our cause. They say that the distress of the army is so great and the claims of an immediate redress so urgent that they will send this representation by a general officer who will be able to give any explanation needed to Congress. All the general officers sign it and I add: 'Tho' from my particular situation the above mention'd demands cannot be applicable to me, I am so sensible off and so sincerely feel for the wants of the Army, that I very cheerfully join with my Brother officers in Representing most respectfully to Congress the Necessary of some provision Being made for theyr troops.'[18]

We receive the terrible news that a second defeat took place in the south on May 29. Banastre Tarleton's Legion killed nearly three quarters of the Virginian Division, in the region of the Waxhaws. Gates is given command of the Southern Department, where there are one thousand four hundred Delaware and Maryland Continentals under de Kalb and some North Carolina and Virginia militiamen who had reached North Carolina when they found out that Charleston had fallen.

I spend four days and nearly four nights questioning pilots and examining maps of New York harbor to try and see if the French fleet could gain control of it, while at the same time our army would destroy the fortifications at Brooklyn.

"I would expect that by August we could have fourteen thousand Continentals and about six thousand militia. These together with the French force would outnumber Clinton, who has about fifteen thousand, at best," says Washington. "I am still, therefore, strongly of a mind to attack New York. Would you please write to Rochambeau and de Ternay to give details of this proposal."

I do so. I send one copy to Rhode Island, another to Black Point, which is by New York, and a third copy to Cape Henry, as we are not sure where they will land.

On July 13 Admiral Graves is reported to have arrived at Sandy Hook with six ships of the line to join Admiral Arbuthnot already there with, we believe, seven large ships, three frigates and a sloop. On July 14, express riders gallop into camp with a dispatch from Heath of July 11: 'Yesterday afternoon the long-expected fleet of our illustrious ally appeared off Newport…the signals were all made and the fleet standing into the harbor.'[19]

I draft a new letter to Rochambeau. I inform him Admiral Graves has reached New York and that although it presents another obstacle it gives us the opportunity to win greater glory and to inflict greater harm on the British nation, and that de Ternay's fleet should sail as soon as possible to Sandy Hook.[20] I say that if the French fleet is superior it can anchor outside Sandy Hook where it can remain at the entrance to block the port until September 20. 'Thus, Monsieur le comte, General Washington does not think that this misfortune should change our earlier land arrangements.'[21]

Hamilton shows Washington the draft; I learn he disagrees as it is not clear that de Ternay's force is sufficient to give the allies decisive maritime superiority which is a fundamental principle and the basis on which every hope of success must ultimately depend. Another letter must be drafted in which the arrival of Graves' fleet must be declared and then de Ternay and Rochambeau must decide whether to proceed. If de Ternay's fleet is superior to that of the British in New York, there could be a joint attack by American and French forces in August.

My disappointment is immense that Washington has proposed a less daring move; I immediately ride a mile from my quarters at Samuel van Saun's house to that of Colonel Theunis Dey where he is staying.

"I believe you are pushing the fear of danger to an extreme," I bluntly declare.

"The king's confidence requires a redoubling of delicacy and prudence," he replies. "However, write down your plans and I will look at them."[22]

Next day I do so. A few hours later he replies:

You have totally misconceived my meaning if you think I have or shall relinquish the idea of enterprizeing against New York till it appears obviously impracticable from the want of force or means to operate. I have not as yet relaxed in any preparation tending to this end, nor shall I till I am convinced of the futility of the measure…What I had in view by discouraging the first draft of yr. letter to the French Genl. and Adml. was 1st. under our ignorance of their strength I thought we ought not to give them more than information of Graves's arrival, and 2dly not to hold up strong ideas of success which probably would not be warranted by the Issue, because I never wish to promise more than I have a moral certainty of performing. [23]

The same day, General Orders announce that a light division will be formed; Washington will perhaps offer it to General Arnold. He decides he cannot go to see Rochambeau and de Ternay.

"It would be best to speak to them in person, but I cannot leave the army. I need to be here to collaborate with the Congressional committee to obtain soldiers, ammunition and weapons. You can go in my place," he tells me.

July 19. I set off to Rhode Island. At Peekskill I hear of an express going through the Continental village and send for him. He is carrying a letter from General Heath to Washington as well as two letters from Rochambeau and de Ternay. I open all of them and find that Rochambeau says he would like to meet with Washington as 'in an hour's conversation we shall reach an agreement on more things than with volumes of writing.'[24] I also learn with great disappointment that the clothing and ammunition I had managed to obtain from the French ministry has not come with the fleet. I therefore decide to try and get powder and weapons from the states I will be riding through.

I write to Washington: 'In case, (what however I don't believe) they would wish to speak to yourself. I shall immediately send an express to inform you of it. But I daresay they will be satisfied with my coming.'[25]

At Danbury I write again and tell him the Connecticut recruits will be at West Point by August 1[26] but they will not have the weapons I had expected. At Lebanon I meet Governor Trumbull who declares that Connecticut will provide at least fifty tons of powder for the present; fifteen more tons will be made up during August by the three Connecticut mills; and lastly, in case of absolute necessity, twenty tons will be found by this state, which will make eighty-five tons. Trumbull will try to increase this to ninety, as well as provide balls and shells, and hopes to find weapons for perhaps half the recruits.[27]

On the twenty-fourth I reach camp at Newport after only four days of riding. Noailles and I embrace with great emotion; he introduces me to the comte de Charlus, the son of the marquis de Castries. Next day I tour the camp with Rochambeau and see the network of coastal batteries they are building which complement the defense formed by the ships of the line. Unfortunately, only three thousand six hundred men are fit for duty and the fleet has a great proportion of sick, so the ships are very poorly crewed at present.

"Is your army in a position to make a diversion or for a part of it to march immediately to our relief?" asks Rochambeau.

"If Washington could do one or the other, he would not lose a minute. However, I cannot tell you anything certain, although I think he will advance the army nearer to New York than he was at Preakness," I reply.[28]

I assist General Heath in his arrangements for the recruits. Everyone here believes Clinton will come although I do not think so. Governor Trumbull is, therefore, not dismissing the extra militia and the French are hurrying to complete their defensive preparations. However, so many detailed accounts of the enemy flood in that I am forced to change my mind. I make myself acquainted with everything that has happened since I left France. I write to Washington about the disagreeable disappointment concerning the clothing and that I have sent what the fleet has brought on a vessel to Providence which will be taken to headquarters when Olney arrives. I tell him there has been a great mismanagement concerning the transporting of men which has prevented the whole fleet arriving here at the same time but that the second division should be here in three to four weeks and even if it is delayed should arrive in the autumn, and the French generals want to hear from it first before acting.[29]

On the thirtieth I have a formal meeting with de Ternay and Rochambeau.

"Firstly, I would like to speak in my own name, before I talk as General Washington's representative. When I arrived, I found the country exhausted, but it has made immense efforts given the state of our finances and the lack of all resources. By November 1 we will no longer have militia. By January 1, half of our Continental Army will be disbanded. I believe it politically necessary to act during this campaign and am still convinced of this after asking people I have met along my route here. I believe that we have slightly overestimated the number of enemy troops in New York as 14,000 and need to subtract the sailors used by Admiral Arbuthnot. The American troops are taking responsibility for New York. The Brooklyn fort, where you could act with a division of our army, is a simple earthwork with four bastions, a ditch and an abbattis, and contains between one thousand and one thousand five hundred men. Nothing stands in the way of regular approaches to Brooklyn and this post is the key to New York."

I outline how Washington plans to take the city. "With our combined forces and artillery, we will soon achieve our objectives in Brooklyn and then in New York. We should start before we have naval superiority and should take possession of the harbor of New York as soon as possible. We need to begin at the latest around early September. General Washington is filled with the umost confidence in you and desires only to have your opinion of this plan. He wishes to undertake only what appears advantageous to you."

"The assistance sent to the United States is not provisional. The second division left shortly after us and we expect it at any moment. We hope to be able to act before the end of the campaign but will provide you with very superior forces for this winter and the next campaign. We are pleased with the plan to attack Brooklyn but feel we need to have a force upon the island at least equal to that the enemy might present. We doubt whether it is possible to keep the enemy in check by the Morrissania Channel," Rochambeau replies.

"We consider naval superiority necessary. It would be difficult to seize New York harbor, but we would hope to achieve the same objective by a cruising position. I do not believe my 74-gun ships could enter," says de Ternay.

"I believe it is important to occupy the harbor," I reply.

"I will study it again," he says.

"Assure General Washington that when I receive an order from him, I will move immediately to the place he considers suitable," says Rochambeau. "We would like to be able to talk with him."

It is decided that they will write to the French government to speed the second division and to make it larger than originally planned. They will also ask Guichen to send five ships of the line. They say that if the French fleet is superior to that of the enemy it will fight at once for superiority, and that as soon as arms, clothing and munitions for the United States arrives, it will be immediately conveyed to wherever General Washington wants. In the meantime, they will lend us all the powder they can spare, which will not be more than 30,000 pounds.[30]

Washington writes that there is no doubt Clinton intends to attack the French. He wishes Rochambeau had taken a position on the mainland and that this might still be the best option. He also does not think his men could make a rapid march to assist the French. He says he is straining every nerve to attack New York and that I can either remain with General Heath or return to the army; it is for me to choose.[31]

I, of course, choose headquarters. I am desperate to be at the battle for New York and very afraid that I will miss it. On August 3 I send a message to General Heath at Howland's Ferry to say that Rochambeau will come to Butt's Hill in the afternoon to make an inspection. I add: 'I Beg, my dear sir, you will Send me immediately my leave of Setting out without I Can't Stir as you are my Superior officer. I am impatiently waiting.'[32]

Several hours later, I am still waiting on de Ternay's flagship for an answer. I decide not to stay any longer and write to him: 'I take it upon myself to set out because I know from your friendship that you will have no objection to it, and because if I was to arrive too late I would for ever lament the time I lost since this morning.'[33] I set off, determined to ride day and night to make up the hours I have lost.

On my return I tell Washington what was said at the conference; he requests a written account. I write the details of our discussion which I also send to Rochambeau and de Ternay. I tell them that shortly after I left Rhode Island General Clinton withdrew to New York as a result of the movement of our army, which is now near Dobb's Ferry, our advance guard about three miles in front. I also take it upon myself to tell them what I think:

> From an intimate knowledge of our situation, I assure you gentlemen, as an individual and speaking for myself, that it is important to act during this campaign. All of the troops that you may expect from France next year, as well as all of the plans for which you may hope, will not make up for the fatal harm of our inaction. Without American resources, no amount of foreign aid can accomplish anything in this country. Although in any case you may count on us entirely, I think it is very important to take advantage of the times when you find an opportunity for cooperation here. Without it you can do nothing in America for the common cause.[34]

Washington gives me command of two Light Infantry brigades of one thousand eight hundred and fifty men. I had been worried Benedict Arnold would desire the post, but he is still suffering from his wound and wanted to be commander of West Point, to Washington's surprise. Major General St. Clair has temporarily been in command of the two brigades while I have been away and he has now been given the Pennsylvania division. General Enoch Poor commands one brigade, General Edward Hand, the other. We have four cannon, one hundred riflemen and three hundred men in the light horse corps, only half of whom have horses.

I receive a letter from Rochambeau.[35] He criticizes many of the points I have made and says he has written to Washington asking to have a meeting. He also expects that the second division is on its way. I am hurt and surprised by his words. Have I expressed myself badly?

I write two letters, the first to Rochambeau and de Ternay. I say that everything I had said about Rhode Island and New York had been on the orders of Washington and that the only part I could reproach myself with had been my urging to act immediately. I say that I will avoid political opinions in the future as they ought to come from Monsieur de La Luzerne, but that as your compatriot, although it was more considerate of me to give them on my own responsibility, they resemble those of Washington.[36]

I write a second letter just to Rochambeau:

> I have an affectionate fondness for you which I have felt and have tried to show since I was very young. If I have offended or displeased you in my letter, I give you my word of honor that I thought I was doing something very simple... I ask your pardon for two reasons, first, because I am earnestly attached to you, and secondly, because my purpose here is to do all that may please you.'
> I do not, however, retract my remarks about the campaign: 'I am convinced that if you had not come, American affairs would have gone badly in this campaign. But at the point where we are, this is not enough, and it is important to have some successes. Please believe that when I sent you this opinion in my name, it was not mine alone. My error was in writing officially with passion...But I acted in such good faith that your letter surprised me as much as it grieved me, and that is saying a good deal. [37]

I do not feel I am in the wrong. I send my letters to Noailles and Charlus to see if they consider my words offensive. They do not and dispatch the letters to Rochambeau.

He replies a few days later: 'Permit an old father, my dear marquis, to reply to you as he would to an affectionate son, whom he loves and greatly esteems.' He proceeds to tell me of my numerous errors: I had wanted him to act in a way that is militarily inadvisable; I had felt humiliated as a Frenchman because an English squadron with a marked superiority of ships and frigates has blockaded the squadron of the marquis de Ternay at Newport:

> But console yourself, my dear marquis, the port of Brest has been blockaded for two months by an English fleet which has prevented the Second Division from setting sail…If you had fought the last two wars, you would have heard of nothing but these blockades. I hope that Monsieur de Guichen, on the one hand, and Monsieur de Gaston, on the other, will avenge us for these momentary chagrins. He criticizes my belief that the French could not be beaten: I am going to tell you a secret from my forty years experience. There are no troops more easily beaten than when they have once lost confidence in their leaders; and they lose it immediately when they have been compromised through private and personal ambition. If I have been quite fortunate to retain their confidence until now, I owe it to the most scrupulous examination of my conscience; that of the fifteen thousand or so men who have been killed or wounded following my orders, in different ranks and in the most deadly engagements, I do not have to reproach myself with having caused the death of a single man on my own personal account.

He says I have said to the chevalier de Chastellux that the interview he has asked for with Washington has embarrassed him because it is during the arrival of the second division and that this would then be the time to act. He says I have forgotten that he has never stopped demanding what is essential so that if one of three opportunities presents itself to act against the enemy, the execution will be rapid and prompt.[38]

It is best to remain quiet, I decide.

My Light Infantry is always three or four miles ahead of the main army and near to the enemy. It is an élite corps of soldiers selected from the New Hampshire, New York, Connecticut, Massachusetts and Pennsylvania Lines. Each man has a black and red plume, and each officer has a sword, as well as a cockade, epaulettes, and a few other adornments. I should prefer that the corps be distinguished by a uniform, or a good pair of shoes, but unfortunately our skin is exposed, and we are sometimes barefoot, not to mention that the inside is no better provided for than the outside but in that case we send them to bed.[39] The ladies of Philadelphia are going to provide some shirts.

I long to fight, perhaps in the south, or perhaps in Canada. I reconnoiter Fort Washington and believe it would be easy to recapture. Our army is now completely without meat. I blame the intendant of the French army who is making unrestricted purchases and paying in gold. It is decided to forage near to Bergen, which at the same time might bring out the enemy to attack us.

On August 24 the main army marches south to near the Liberty Pole Tavern in Teaneck. My Light Division is about four miles away, near Fort Lee, a little below Fort Washington; Major Lee goes north with his Light Horse; in the afternoon, I go to Bergen, whilst Greene advances with part of the right wing to support me. I lead a part of the vanguard as far as the causeway at Paulus Hook. As I had expected, the enemy does not attack but we manage to find some oxen and forage.[40]

On the twenty-fifth Washington receives a dispatch from Rochambeau which says, to my great joy, that the *Alliance* reached Boston on the sixteenth. Food, however, is becoming even more scarce.

"Do I send home the militiamen because I cannot feed them?" declares Washington. "Or do I accept new recruits and let them starve?"

Four thousand five hundred Pennsylvania militia who are moving forward to reinforce the army cannot be fed. Washington orders them to either be dismissed or sent to encamp at places where there are greater provisions but says that recruiting for the Continental Army must continue. He orders the army to march to near Hackensack and tells Arnold to assemble his troops at West Point in case there is an attack on the Highlands.[41]

Even at Washington's table, food is scarce, although we are entertained one day by a branch with thirteen apples on it sent by Major Leavenworth. Washington gives it to me to look at. Two apples fall off.

"You have ruined two of our states," he says.

The branch is handed round the table and when it reaches Greene, there are only four apples left.

"All gone, except for the four New England States," he remarks. "This one, smaller than the others, is Rhode Island."

"And this one which has withered before it has grown is Vermont," I say.[42]

I still have not received my letters sent on the *Alliance*. Pontgibaud is bringing them to me and so far has spent eighteen days on the road from Boston. I curse at him and do not know what more I can say. The only way I can explain his lack of speed is that my secretary, Poirey, whom I left behind at La Rochelle because he was so seasick, appears to be with him, which I only know from reading it in the gazette, and I believe Poirey is stopping at every wonder that he sees.[43]

On the fourth, terrible news arrives that our army in the south was beaten at Camden on August 16. Gates had more men, a three to two majority, but the British had more regulars, more artillery and many more cavalry. He unfortunately positioned his troops so that the Continentals faced the Loyalists, whilst the militia faced the British and German regulars, commanded by Colonel Webster. The British and Germans advanced, and the militia panicked. Some managed to fire a few shots, then they all ran away. Only the one thousand four hundred Maryland and Delaware regulars under de Kalb, and a North Carolina militia regiment, fought. At least six hundred Americans were killed. To my intense sadness, de Kalb was killed. He was my much-loved friend and one of the strongest and most courageous men I have ever met. He was slashed eleven times and propped against a wagon by British soldiers who tore off his coat, prodding and taunting him. An officer ordered him taken to a house where he died three days later; his last words were: 'Tell the lads they did their best.'

Gates fled. Washington says nothing about his cowardice, but the rest of his military family are not so quiet.

"Was there ever an instance of a general running away, as Gates has done, from his whole army," says Hamilton. "One hundred and eighty miles in three days and a half. It does admirable credit to the activity of a man at his time of life. But it disgraces the general and his soldiers."[44]

"Our army in the south is now in a terrible position. Cornwallis can invade Virginia," says Washington.

General Poor dies of a fever and there is an unfortunate rumor he has been killed in a duel with a French officer. People ridicule our army; A piece from a New York newspaper makes me rage:

REWARD
Strayed, deserted, or stolen from the subscriber…a whole army…with all their baggage, artillery, wagons and camp equipage. The subscriber has very strong suspicions from information received

from his aide de camp, that a certain CHARLES, EARL CORNWALLIS, was principally concerned in carrying off the said ARMY...Any person or persons, civil or military, who will give information, whether to the subscriber, or to...the Continental Congress, where the said ARMY is so that they may be rallied again, shall be entitled to demand from the Treasury of the United States, the sum of THREE MILLION of PAPER DOLLARS as soon as they can be spared from public funds.

Signed, HORATIO GATES.

September 6. Washington holds a council of war. He states the condition of the army and says that the British fleet had disappeared from near Newport on August 29, and it is not known where they are. He asks each general officer to write what they consider should be the plan of operations. The decision is unanimous that no attack should be conducted against New York until the second division arrives and we have naval superiority, and that more reinforcements to the south should wait to see what is happening.[45] My opinion is that the general officer who has conducted the retreat of Gates's army should form as respectable body of troops as he can and keep the enemy in check without risking a general action.[46]

September 9. La Colombe finally arrives from the *Alliance*, but without Poirey or Pontgibaud, and with no official dispatches for me, for La Luzerne, or for the French generals.

"Monsieur de Vauban had all the ministerial letters, even including an order from Monsieur de Sartine, but Captain Landais refused to have anything to do with him and left him behind. The *Alliance* has not brought any uniforms and only two thousand guns and some powder. Some uniforms will be brought by the second division.[47] Captain Landais went mad and had to be arrested on board the ship." He also says that Brest, where we have fourteen ships, is still blockaded by twenty-eight English ships; we have thirty-three ships at Calais and the second division escorted by three of five ships was ready. The rest of the supplies will have to be brought by the second division or by Captain Jones. However, as all Paris is running after John Paul Jones[48] I do not think he will be setting sail very quickly.

Some people say Washington should be made dictator. I do not know whether, as his friend, I should desire it for him, but I know that I must never speak of it nor ever appear to wish it, although I think it seems very important. My republican and even entirely democratic principles would make me oppose such a measure; I would not approve of it if I did not know the man and if I did not believe his dictatorship necessary to the public welfare.[49] I am sure, in any case, Washington would never agree, his principles are too strong, his moral stature too great.

Our situation is dire. Washington writes to Guichen to try and persuade him to sail north:'The Government without finances; its paper credit sunk, and no expedients it can adopt capable of retrieving it; the resources of the country much diminished by a five years' war, in which it has made efforts beyond its ability; Clinton...in possession of one of our capital towns and a large part of the state to which it belongs, the savages desolating the other frontiers...Lord Cornwallis...in complete possession of two states, Georgia and South Carolina; a third, North Carolina, by recent misfortunes at his mercy.'[50]

Washington decides to finally meet with Rochambeau and de Ternay. I am aware Rochambeau has been somewhat surprised a meeting has not already taken place, but I know the reasons all too well. Our army is weak, hungry and half naked; Washington's presence is necessary to hold it together and it is also, moreover, an army he feels it difficult to show to the well-equipped, well-dressed French.

On the fourteenth, General Forman writes: 'I am this minute informed that Admiral Rodney with twelve sail of the line and four frigates has arrived off Sandy Hook from the West Indies.'[51]

"Hopefully, it is that of Arbuthnot returning to New York," says Washington.

However, if it is Rodney then the British naval strength is as great as it has ever been. At the same time, we are not sure if Guichen is sailing north from the Indies to reinforce the French fleet. On the seventeenth I spend a restless night worrying about the British fleet. However, in the morning, news comes that the ships have now entered the Hook and it is Arbuthnot, not Rodney; I become somewhat calmer although Rodney still worries me.

We set off for Hartford to meet with Rochambeau and de Ternay, our group comprising Washington, Knox, Gouvion, Hamilton as Washington's aide, Dr. James McHenry as mine, Major Samuel Shaw as that of Knox, three other aides, and an escort of twenty-two dragoons. We travel by carriage and on horseback along the rough roads winding through thick woods. We halt at Joshua Hett Smith's house, midway between Stony Point and Haverstraw. Major General Benedict Arnold, commander at West Point, meets us at dinner, still limping and one leg much shorter than the other, but not appearing as handicapped by his injury from Saratoga as he was at Valley Forge. I have known him since Albany. I regard him highly, as does Washington, and like everyone else, I have affection for his lovely wife, Peggy, who is nineteen, and half his age. However, a few weeks ago, he asked me for the names of my spies in New York. I refused as I felt it would be dishonorable to reveal them, even to a friend such as he and since then there has been a slight cooling in our relationship.[52]

Arnold shows Washington a letter from his former friend, Colonel Beverley Robinson, a British sympathizer who has rejected the oath of allegiance and whose house is now Arnold's headquarters. "He is on the British ship, the *Vulture*, in the North River, and wishes a meeting for a private matter," he says.

"Refuse him," declares Washington.[53]

On Monday morning, September 18, we cross the river at Verplanck's Point in Arnold's barge;[54] I sit next to him.

"Since you have communication with the enemy you must ascertain as soon as possible what has become of Guichen," I say.

"What do you mean?" he cries in a startled tone, which I find strange.[55] At that point, we reach the bank; we clamber out; I think no more of it. We continue to Peekskill where we spend the night.

On the twenty-first, we reach Hartford, a small, respectable and wealthy village[56] of about three hundred houses with just one very long street by the side of the Connecticut River. The Governor's Guards and an artillery company meet us; a thirteen-gun salute roars out; local people cheer; we go to the house of Colonel Jeremiah Wadsworth. A short time later, Count Axel de Fersen, one of Rochambeau's aides, rides into the village.

"There have been accidents to their carriage and they will arrive shortly," he says.

Not long after, we hear the firing of guns and cheering; my compatriots have crossed the ferry. We go outside and see Rochambeau and de Ternay, accompanied by Desandrouin, the vicomte de Rochambeau and Damas who have travelled through friendly territory and so have not needed a greater escort. I proudly introduce Washington to Rochambeau and de Ternay. Our two generals ceremonially clasp hands in front of everyone, then Rochambeau, de Ternay, Washington, Knox and I[57] adjourn to a room in Wadsworth's house where I will translate and act as secretary.

"Rodney has definitely sailed into New York," Rochambeau informs us.

I know how disappointed Washington must be at this news, but his face remains calm, although I cannot say the same for mine.

"If Guichen arrives by the beginning of October and wins a naval victory then he could enter New York harbor and we could make an attack" says Washington. "If we have not naval superiority until later, then a combined force of French and American troops should be sent to the southern states. A second proposal is that the French fleet should go to Boston where it would not need the support of your infantry which could then cooperate with my army near the North River to stop the British from sending more troops towards the south. My final proposal is that there could perhaps be a winter campaign in Canada."

"Our orders are for the fleet and infantry to remain together," replies Rochambeau as de Ternay remains silent.[58]

"There might be political objections to an attack on Canada," is the opinion of both Rochambeau and de Ternay.[59]

"New York is the most important enemy stronghold and can only be attacked if the French control the harbor," says Washington.

The conference lasts two days.[60] Finally, it is agreed a request should be made to the French government to reinforce their fleet and army forces in America with ships, men and money. It is decided that John Laurens should go to Paris to assist these demands. I write the documents in French in two columns, one of which represents the French view, the other column that of Washington. Rochambeau, de Ternay and Washington all sign.

"I am very content with the outcome of our discussion," says Washington.

"So are we," replies Rochambeau.

We say farewell. The French generals leave Hartford whilst we go to lodge nearby for the night. The local population comes out to welcome Washington, children carrying flaming torches to light the night, pressing round him, calling him father, so much we cannot proceed.

Washington, moved, takes the hand of Dumas who is accompanying him to Providence. "We may be beaten by the English, it is the chance of war, but here is an army they will never conquer."[61]

Next morning, we start our journey to West Point. Two days later in the afternoon of September 24, we are riding down the river from Fishkill when we meet La Luzerne and an escort.

"I am going to Rhode Island to speak with General Rochambeau and Admiral de Ternay," he says.[62]

We all adjourn to a tavern and tell him of the meeting at Hartford and discuss the situation. Next day, in a cool light mist just after dawn we assemble rather hungrily and say farewell.

"Go ahead with the baggage to the Robinson house. Tell the Arnolds we will breakfast with them," Washington tells McHenry and Shaw.[63]

We ride off and a short time later turn into a lane which leads to the North River.

"We are going in the wrong direction," I call out. "We will be late for breakfast."

"I want to visit the redoubts between Fishkill and West Point. Major McHenry and Captain Shaw can ride on and say we will arrive later. However, I know you young men are all in love with Mrs. Arnold and wish to get where she is as soon as possible. If you want, you can go ahead," Washington says, smiling.[64]

We decline his offer and follow him towards the river. He carefully inspects each redoubt then we ride on through the dark forests to a two-story, low-studded house, about two miles southeast of West Point, where Arnold lives, and which was previously the home of Colonel Beverley Robinson before being used as American headquarters. It is an isolated place with no other house in view, surrounded on two sides by mountains and trees.[65]

Major David Franks, his aide-de-camp, welcomes us. "General Arnold has gone to West Point and will return in an hour. Mrs. Arnold is indisposed and is in her bedroom and Lieutenant Colonel Varick is ill with a fever but will greet you shortly."[66]

"We will see General Arnold at West Point," says Washington.[67]

It is ten-thirty. We enter the house; we eat breakfast but without quite the company we had expected. Then we ride to Robinson's Landing on the North River, having left Hamilton at the house to receive any messages.

"Ferry us to West Point," Washington orders the oarsmen of the elegant, awning-covered barge.

We travel along the river for about two miles. We approach West Point, basalt cliffs rearing up almost perpendicularly in smooth columns, rocks which look like trees, Weehawken, as the Lenape call them.

"I am glad that Arnold has gone ahead to prepare for our visit as we will now have a gun salute and you will be able to hear the fine roaring that the cannons make among the Palisade," Washington tells me.[68]

We reach the bank. We disembark, but there is no salute. In fact, it is so quiet the only sound is birdsong. There is no welcome guard. The sentries recognize Washington and regard us with what appears to be complete surprise.

"Where is General Arnold?" he asks.

"We have not seen him. We don't know where he is," is the reply.

Washington appears disconcerted for a moment. "I expect he is at one of the further parts of the fortifications and we will see him later. I will take you on a tour myself. West Point is the key which locks the communication between the eastern and southern states. It is the most important post in America."[69]

I look in admiration at the strategic nature of the site. At this point the river flows very slowly and has a double right-angle bend which means that square-rigged ships have to change course under Fort Arnold's guns which are trained onto a giant chain of iron bars whose links are twelve inches wide and eighteen feet long, floating on sixteen-foot logs, extending from Constitution Island, in the middle of the river just below the bend, and on which there is a battery, to the west bank. It is at the northernmost limit of the tide; below it the river widens. The rocky ridges rise one above another; the high summit bristles with redoubts and batteries; its six fortifications, in the shape of an amphitheater, are out of range of naval guns.

We climb to the top of Crown Hill, which is protected by a precipice, overlooks the extensive plain, and has a view of about thirty miles in all directions. Far below, the North River appears like a vast canal cut through huge mountains.[70] Fort Putnam stands here, named after Israel Putnam, who played a prominent part in its construction. It protects the square bastion of Fort Clinton and the plain, as well as overlooking Forts Wyllys and Meigs, but its stone and mortar is crumbling, its east wall and some smaller parts have collapsed, and it resembles the decaying nature of the rest of the fortifications, which are in clear need of being strengthened and repaired. Nearby, but slightly higher than Crown Hill, is Rock Hill, on which is a redoubt to prevent a bombardment of Fort Putnam. Fort Arnold is earthen with four two-hundred-and-forty-foot-long walls and a twenty-foot ditch. Part is unfortunately built of fascines and wood and needs stonework to prevent it burning easily.[71]

The general state of disrepair surprises me, as I can see it does Washington, whose expression usually reveals little.

"Where is Arnold?" he asks the officer-in-charge, Colonel John Lamb.

"So far as I know he has not set foot here this morning,"[72] he replies with difficulty as he lacks part of his face and an eye from the battle at Quebec.

Washington appears even more disconcerted and looks again at the decrepitude of the fort.

"Why are there so few men?"

"Many have been sent to Fishkill and others to different points along the river," replies Colonel Lamb.

"This is very strange," Washington mutters. "Arnold's conduct is peculiar. Where is he?"

By late afternoon he is still nowhere to be found. At three, we finish our inspection.[73] The oarsmen row us back along the river and at about four we reach the landing. We return to Robinson's house.

"There has been no word from Arnold," says Hamilton.

Mrs. Arnold does not come to greet us, and Washington goes into the room set aside for him; an aide brings some newly arrived papers and he and Hamilton prepare to read them. I go to my room and start to dress for a late dinner.

Suddenly, McHenry rushes in. "Where are my pistols," he shouts. He grabs them and without saying more, dashes away. I quickly pull on my coat and run downstairs.

"What has happened?" I ask Washington, as Knox joins us.

"A spy has been arrested who was carrying letters which reveal an account of our council of war on September 6, as well as the state of the garrison and works, observations on various means of attack and defense, the number of troops at West Point and in the locality, the strength of the army, the artillery at West Point and its deployment in the event of an attack, and a summary of the weaknesses of West Point's defenses, all in Arnold's handwriting. I also have a letter by the man arrested who declares he is not John Anderson, but Major André, adjutant general in the British Army. He said he had left the British armed frigate, the *Vulture,* to meet a person who was to give him intelligence, on land not within posts of either army. Against previous stipulations André says he had been conveyed within one of our posts and refused transit back to the ship. He had been forced to put on civilian clothes and set off for New York by land. Near Tarrytown he had been captured by some volunteers and said he had the honor to relate he was betrayed into the vile condition of an enemy in disguise within our posts. He asks for decency of conduct towards himself and the privilege of sending an open letter to General Sir Henry Clinton and another to a friend for clothing. [74] McHenry and Hamilton are pursuing Arnold down the North River to try and stop him reaching the *Vulture.* He has betrayed us. Whom can we trust now?" he asks in a tone of bewilderment and anger.[75]

I stand speechless, as does Knox, his usually jovial expression one of horror.

"We will eat dinner. Mrs. Arnold is sick and General Arnold is away. We will take our meal without them," Washington says a short time later.

At four, I, Knox, Gouvion, Villefranche, Lamb, and our aides sit quietly with Washington at the table, Colonel Varick at its head, even although ill with a fever. The food is plentiful, but our appetites are dull.[76] Washington remains polite and affable; he says nothing about what has happened, although it has been ordered that no one can enter or leave the house.

"Would you take your hat and walk in the garden with me," he asks Varick after dinner.

He tells him of Arnold's treason. He says he does not suspect him or Major Franks, but his duty as an officer means he must place them under arrest. Varick politely acquiesces. He tells Washington the little he knows. He says that he and Franks had begun to suspect Arnold that morning when they saw the hysterics of Mrs. Arnold and her conviction that her husband was not coming back. He and Franks also speak about John Anderson and their mistrust of Smith.

"Where is Mrs. Arnold?" asks Washington.

"She is still in her bedroom," replies Varick. "I heard her shriek this morning about an hour after Your Excellency had gone to West Point. I went upstairs where she seized my hand and asked if I had ordered her child to be killed. She fell to her knees and begged me to spare her babe. I could not raise her from the floor. Major Franks and Dr. Eustis soon arrived, and we carried her to her bed raving mad. She said that General Arnold would never return; that he was gone for ever, that the spirits had carried him up and had put hot irons in his head. She says there is a hot iron on her head, and she wants to see General Washington as only he can take it off."[77]

Hamilton returns. He has not caught Arnold who unfortunately had six hours' start.

"We went near to Verplanck's Point but his boat had already passed it under a flag and he was already on board the *Vulture,* a few miles below.[78] No one from any of the posts had attempted to stop his flight as they had no idea of his traitorous activities. I have written to General Greene to tell him of the blackest treason which has just unfolded here, that Arnold has fled to the enemy, that André, the British adjutant-general, is in our possession as a spy, that West Point was to have been the sacrifice, that all the dispositions have been made for the purpose and it is possible, though not probable, tonight may see the execution, that I came in pursuit of Arnold but was too late and that I advised him to put the army under marching orders and to immediately detach a brigade this way."[79]

He brings a letter which Arnold has sent from the *Vulture* under a flag of truce, as well as a letter from Colonel Robinson which insolently demands the release of the adjutant general on the grounds that he had gone up with a flag at the request of General Arnold and had his permit to return by land to New York.[80]

Arnold writes:

The heart which is conscious of its own rectitude cannot attempt to palliate a step which the world may censure as wrong. I have ever acted from a principle of love to my country since the commencement of the present unhappy contest between Great Britain and the colonies. The same principle of love to my country actuates my present conduct, however it may appear inconsistent to the world, who very seldom judge right of any man's actions. I have too often experienced the ingratitude of my country to attempt it. But, from the known humanity of Your Excellency, I am induced to ask your protection for Mrs. Arnold from every insult and injury that a mistaken vengeance of my country may expose her to. It ought to fall only on me; she is as good and innocent as an angel and is incapable of doing wrong. I beg she may be permitted to return to her friends in Philadelphia, or come to me, as she may choose...I have to request that the enclosed letter may be delivered to Mrs. Arnold and she be permitted to write to me.' A postscript adds: 'Varick, Franks, as well as Joshua Smth. Esq. (who I know is suspected) are totally ignorant of any transactions of mine that they had reason to believe were injurious to the public. [81]

Hamilton, Varick and I go upstairs with Washington to Mrs. Arnold's bedchamber. She is lying in bed, in a lace gown, very revealing of her bosom, to which she is cradling her child.

"The hot iron!" she screams as she sees us. "The hot iron! You are trying to kill my child! Murderer! The hot iron!"

"It is General Washington," exclaims Varick.

"No," she screams. "That is the man who is going to help Colonel Varick kill my child."

"Do you know where your husband is?" asks Washington.

"General Arnold will never return," she cries. "He is gone forever, there, there." She points in a theatrical manner towards the ceiling. "The spirits have brought him there! They have put hot irons on his head!" She sobs. She raves. "Poor child!" she moans, pressing the infant to her bosom. She falls into a convulsion; Washington says nothing and leaves the room.[82]

Hamilton and I stare in some confusion at the beautiful young woman, her hair loose and disheveled, sprawled semi-naked on the bed in front of us. We do everything we can to quiet her, but she sees us as the murderers of her husband. It is impossible to restore her to her senses. The horror of her husband's actions is making her the most unhappy of women.[83] We ask a servant to care for her and go downstairs.

"There is every reason to believe she is innocent of Arnold's plan. Her first knowledge of it was when Arnold went to tell her he must banish himself from hs country and from her forever. She instantly fell into a convulsion when he told her and he left her like that," says Hamilton.

I agree.[84] I am astonished by Arnold's treachery. He is not so highly esteemed here as is supposed in Europe but has nevertheless given proof of talent, of patriotism, and, especially, of that most brilliant courage, and that he should at once destroy his very existence and should sell his country to the tyrants whom he has fought against with glory, confounds and distresses me. It pains me to call him a scoundrel and I would give anything in the world if he had not shared our labors with us and if he had not shed his blood for the American cause. I know of his personal courage and would expect that he will blow his brains out. In any case, he will probably do so when he reaches New York.[85]

Washington sends an aide-de-camp to Mrs. Arnold with the letter he has received for her from her husband and whose seal he has not broken.

"Tell Mrs. Arnold I have done what I could to seize her husband, but not having been able to do so, I have pleasure in informing her that her husband is now safe."[86]

McHenry adds his account to that of Varick and Franks. "When I was having breakfast with Arnold and his wife, he received two letters concerning the arrest of a spy. He became pale and seemed agitated at what he had read. He ordered a horse to be saddled and went to speak to his wife in her bedroom. Then he told his aide-de-camp he was going to West Point and would return in an hour."[87]

At seven, he orders Jameson to bring André immediately to Robinson's House. "I wish every precaution and attention to be paid to prevent Major André from making his escape. He will without doubt effect it if possible. He had better be conducted here by some upper road, rather than by the route of Crompond. I would not wish Mr. André to be treated with insult, but he does not appear to stand upon the footing of a common prisoner of war and therefore he is not entitled to the usual indulgencies which they receive and is to be most closely and narrowly watched. He must not escape."[88]

At seven-thirty, he writes to Greene:

I request that you will put the division on the left in motion as soon as possible, with orders to proceed to King's Ferry, where or before they will be met with further orders. The division will come on light, leaving their heavy baggage to follow. You will also hold all the troops in readiness to move on the shortest notice. Transactions of a most interesting nature, and such as will astonish you, have been just discovered.[89]

He sends Gouvion to Fishkill to arrest Smith. He continues to issue orders to prepare for an attack; all troops of the main army must be ready to march; the militia and wood-cutting parties are recalled to the east bank of the North River; the North and Middle redoubts opposite West Point are to be reinforced; officers known to be true are to be put on duty.[90]

Everyone here remains in a state of shock at this vile conspiracy, and we are amazed at the miraculous way in which it has come to our knowledge. It is the first case of treason in our army, remarkable in such a revolution, but it grieves us as much as it it disgusts us.[91]

By morning, the wind which had been blowing very strongly upriver, now gusts downstream, and we have less fear of a naval attack. Washington writes to Greene at the Tappan camp to tell the troops what has happened:

> Treason of the blackest dye was yesterday discovered. General Arnold who commanded at West Point, lost to every sentiment of honor, of private and public obligation, was about to deliver up that important post into the hands of the enemy. Such an event must have given the American cause a dangerous, if not a fatal wound; happily the treason has been timely discovered to prevent the fatal misfortune. The providential train of circumstances which led to it, affords the most convincing proof that the liberties of America are the object of Divine protection. At the same time that the treason is to be regretted, the General cannot help congratulating the army on the happy discovery. Our enemies despairing of carrying their point by force, are practicing every base art to effect by bribery and corruption what they cannot accomplish in a manly way. Great honor is due to the American army, that this is the first instance of treason of the kind, where many were to be expected from the nature of our dispute; the brightest ornament in the character of the American soldier is their having been proof against all the arts and seductions of an insidious enemy. Arnold has made his escape to the *Vulture*, but Major André, the adjutant-general in the British army, who came out as a spy to negotiate the business, is our prisoner. [92]

He orders Colonel Lamb to take charge at Verplanck's and Stony Point, and Colonel Livingston to come to headquarters.

September 26. Washington is standing outside on the piazza in the early morning[93] when Smith arrives under arrest, having had to walk all the way from Fishkill. He summons Knox, Hamilton and I to his room. We interrogate him.

"I am a very loyal American," he protests. "I should not have been arrested." He says he had taken a letter to the *Vulture* addressed to Robinson, whom he thought he had to bring ashore for important reasons for the United States. Instead of Robinson he had to bring back John Anderson. Anderson then spoke with Arnold, and he was subsequently asked to escort Anderson to White Plains. "I am innocent," he keeps exclaiming very loudly.

"Why was it decided to send Arnold's visitor back to New York by land instead of rowing him back to the *Vulture?*"

"I had such a bad fever I was unable to make the arrangements for the boat."

"If you were so ill how did you manage to accompany Anderson to White Plains?"

He does not reply.

He tells us where Anderson's regimental coat is to be found in his house and he admits he provided civilian clothes for him. However, we do not discover if he knew John Anderson was a British spy. He seemed to have chatted to many people on the journey and he and Anderson even had a drink with officers in a tavern at Stony Point. He also visited Livingston at Verplancks and stayed the night at Crompond. He said he had left Anderson with about fifteen miles still to travel as he had been fearful he might meet Loyalist patrols, whilst Anderson had a pass from Arnold. The guards take him away.

Hamilton and I receive a request from Mrs. Arnold to see her. We go to her bedchamber. This time her beautiful face and expressive eyes are more composed, although she is clearly still in distress. Her fair hair hangs onto her shoulders, but she is not in such a state of undress as before.

"I would like to travel back to my family in Philadelphia. I am very fearful that the resentment of the country will fall upon me because of the guilt of my husband."[94]

"I am sure General Washington will let you do that," I reply, my anger rising as I consider the despicable behavior of her husband to her as well as to her country.

Washington drafts an order guaranteeing her safe conduct back to Philadelphia. Major Franks will accompany her. I write to La Luzerne and implore him to use his influence in her favor:

> I am upon very good terms with her...General Washington and everyone else here sympathise warmly with this estimable woman, whose face and whose youthfulness make her so interesting...It would be exceedingly painful to General Washington if she were not treated with the greatest kindness....Your influence and your opinion, emphatically expressed, may prevent her from being visited with a vengeance which she does not deserve....As for myself, you know that I have always been fond of her, and at this moment she interests me intensely. We are certain she knew nothing of the plot. [95]

André arrives, a slight, dark-haired man wearing a round beaver hat and blue surtout over a shabby reddish coat. He has ridden through the night, escorted by Colonel Tallmadge, three officers and one hundred dragoon and is drenched by the heavy rain which has been falling.

"I do not wish to see him," says Washington, "But I want to know the exact details of his capture and of the disagreement between Jameson and Tallmadge as to how it should be reported. Then send him to Orangetown and imprison him at Mabie's Tavern. Take Smith there as well but do not allow them to communicate with each other."

I take part in his interrogation. He freely admits what he has already written to Washington. I hope he and Smith are hanged, particularly André as he is a man of influence in the English Army and his very distinguished social rank will act as a warning to spies of less degree.[96]

September 28. André and Smith are taken to West Point, conveyed down the North River to Stony Point, and then to Tappan. They are not allowed to communicate. We set off to Tappan, Washington having ordered Gouvion to West Point to undertake the reinforcement of the fortifications.

On Friday, the twenty-ninth, in the old Dutch church at Tappan, Nathanael Greene is president of the Board of Inquiry, asked by Washington to report as speedily as possible a precise state of André's case, together with its opinion of the light in which he ought to be considered and the punishment that ought to be inflicted. [97] I am a member, as well as Lord Stirling, von Steuben, St Clair, Robert Howe, Clinton, Glover, Hand, Stark, Parsons, Knox and Huntington.

André, escorted by Colonel Tallmadge, walks into the room with dignity. He regards us with a direct and confident gaze as Washington's letter authorizing the inquiry is read.

"Read the names of the members and let the prisoner say if he has anything to object to any of them," says Greene.

"I do not object to any of them," he replies.

"You will be asked various questions, but we wish you to feel perfectly at liberty to answer them or not as you choose. Take your own time for recollection and weigh well what you say," says Greene.[98]

"As well as my letter, which I acknowledge to have written, I would like to say that I came on shore from the *Vulture* just before midnight on the twenty-first somewhere under the Haverstraw Mountain. The boat which carried me had no flag and I had a surtout coat over my regimentals. I met General Arnold in the woods. I had been meant to return that night to the boat, but it was not possible. I was therefore concealed in a place of safety until Friday night. At dawn, the Vulture was bombarded from Teller's Point and went downriver and so I could not return that way. The first notice I had of being within your posts was when I was challenged by a sentry the first night I was on shore. Arnold told me to put the papers between my stockings and my feet. He wrote out a pass, either for a boat trip to Dobb's Ferry, which is the route I followed, or to enable me to get through the guards at White Plains. I was told the overland route would be the one used. I was surprised but had no choice."

His account agrees with what we already know from Smith; I have no doubt he is speaking the truth.

"I set off at dawn on the twenty-third and Smith left me when we reached Pine's Bridge on the Croton River. At Pleasantville, a man alerted me to rebel patrols up ahead, so I went to Tarrytown. About nine or ten in the morning, I met the three gentlemen whom I mistakenly thought were Loyalists because one of them was wearing a Hessian overcoat, and I only gave them my pass when I realized my error. I was taken to North Castle where Lieutenant Colonel Tallmadge questioned me and looked at the pass I was carrying, and I think you know the rest, gentlemen. I would finally like to say that I wish to make it clear that I came ashore in uniform. I met Arnold on neutral land and was lured into American territory. When returning to the *Vulture* I had no choice but to discard my uniform and use a false name. I wish to clear myself from an imputation of having assumed a mean character for treacherous purposes or self-interest."

He is shown the papers given to him by Arnold. "They were found on me when I was taken. They were concealed in my boot, except the pass."

He is shown his letter of the seventh, as of John Anderson to Sheldon, saying he would meet Gustavus at Dobb's Ferry. "I wrote it," he says.

He presents a written statement and calls no witnesses on his behalf.

"Did you consider yourself under the protection of a flag?" asks the judge advocate.

"It was impossible for me to suppose I came on shore under that sanction. If I came ashore under a flag, I would certainly have returned under it," he replies.[99]

"You say that you went to Smith's house?" asks Greene.

"I said a house, but not whose house," he replies.

"True," says Greene. "Nor have we any right to ask this of you after the terms we have allowed. Have you any remarks to make upon the statements you have presented?"

"None. I leave them to operate with the Board," he replies.[100]

A guard takes him from the court; he walks out, still dignified and courageous.

Letters from Robinson, Arnold and Clinton are read out to us. They all declare that André had come ashore under a flag and had acted under Arnold's orders within the American lines. He is therefore not a spy with the usual sentence.

"You have heard the prisoner's statements and the documents that have been laid before you by order of the commander-in-chief. What is your opinion?" asks Greene.

"He is to be considered a spy and according to the laws and usages of nations ought to suffer death," we solemnly answer in turn.

I suffer greatly in condemning him[101] but what he has done makes it inevitable. The opinion of the Board is drawn up:

First, that he came on shore from the Vulture sloop of war, in the night of the twenty-first of September instant, on an interview with General Arnold in a private and secret manner. Secondly, that he changed his dress within our lines, and under a feigned name, and in a disguised habit, passed our works at Stoney and Verplanck's Points, the evening of the twenty-second of September instant and was taken the morning of the twenty-third of September instant, at Tarry Town, in a disguised habit, being then on his way to New-York, and when taken, he had in his possession several papers, which contained intelligence for the enemy.

The Board having maturely considered these facts, do also report to His Excellency General Washington, That Major André, Adjutant General to the British Army, ought to be considered as a Spy from the enemy, and that agreeable to the law and usage of nations, it is their opinion, he ought to suffer death. [102]

Greene signs the document.

I have the utmost admiration for his character and feel an enormous sadness at the tragedy which has befallen him. Hamilton feels the same and speaks of it to Washington.

October 1. Washington writes: 'The Commander-in-Chief approves of the opinion of the board of General Officers respecting Major André, and orders that the execution of Major André take place tomorrow at five o'clock P.M.'[103]

At one o'clock he receives a letter from Clinton asking for a delay until Major General Robertson and two other officers could arrive to provide a true statement of the facts and to declare his sentiments and resolutions.

"I am sure there is no more to say on the matter," he says. "However, I will postpone the execution until twelve o'clock tomorrow."

He orders Greene to go to Dobb's Ferry and meet the British. There, Greene agrees only to allow Lieutenant General Robertson onshore from the Greyhound flying the white flag and not the two civilians, Andrew Elliot, lieutenant governor, and William Smith, chief justice of the province of New York, so that there is no question of transferring the matter to a civil case. Robertson attempts to prove that André came ashore under a flag and acted completely by the directions of Arnold.

"These questions have already been examined by the Board. We believe André rather than Arnold," says Greene.

"The question should be proposed to Rochambeau and Knyphausen, as disinterested men, accustomed to European custom," proposes Robertson.

"No," replies Greene.

Robertson produces an open letter from Arnold to Washington. Greene reads it, then throws it contemptuously at his feet.

"I will wait until tomorrow in the expectation of taking either André himself, or at least an assurance of his safety back to New York," says Robertson.

Next day, Greene sends him a written message: 'Agreeably to your request I communicated to General Washington the substance of your conversation in all the particulars, so far as my memory served me. It made no alteration in his opinion and determination. I need say no more after what you have already been informed.'[104]

Washington receives a request from André that he should be shot by firing squad as an officer and not hanged as a common criminal. He asks his officers for their opinion. Six are for and six against.

"If he is punished at all he must be punished as spies are punished by the laws of war. Any other would in the actual state of our relations with England throw a doubt on our conviction of his conduct," Greene says and casts the final vote.[105] Washington makes no reply to André.

"General Robertson wants André released as a personal favor to Clinton. He has also rejected the idea of exchanging Arnold for André," Hamilton tells me.

I remain with him the night before his execution. He is cheerful and polite to me and to everyone else in the room. He draws a sketch of himself.

"My mother and two sisters are in England. I love them dearly," he says. He writes a letter to Clinton asking him to help them.

October 2. "Your execution will be at noon," he is told in the morning. We all fall silent in gloom, but he remains calm and composed. His servant brings in his breakfast which has come every day from Washington's table. He is crying.

"Leave me until you can show yourself more manly," André tells him.

He eats his breakfast, then shaves and dresses in his regimental uniform of scarlet coat with green facings, buff breeches and waistcoat but not his gorget, sash, spurs or sword. He puts his hat on the table. "I am ready at any moment, gentlemen, to wait on you," he says cheerfully to the guards.

He leaves the house and walks in silence, arm in arm with Captain John Hughes and Lieutenant Burrowes, to the beat of a drum, a wagon carrying a black coffin in front of them, a group of officers on horseback leading the way along the road, all the principal officers of the army having been told to attend by Washington. When they reach the turning up the hill, he suddenly sees the gallows of two forked poles and a crosspiece. He stops and stares.

"Must I die in this manner?" he asks.

"It is unavoidable," he is told.

"I am reconciled to my fate but not to the mode," he replies.

He continues to walk; he reaches the lines of the guards and some of the officers he had met at the Inquiry. He bows with a smile.

At the square of execution, he halts for a moment. He looks up several times at the gibbet and, lost in thought, rolls a pebble under one of his shoes and swallows hard. The wagon rolls forward under the gibbet. André climbs quickly into the wagon. He stands on his coffin. He flinches, but then mutters to himself "It will be but a momentary pang."

He opens his collar and unties his stock. The executioner, his face blackened by grease, attempts to place the rope around his neck but he pushes him away, puts the queue of his hair outside it, the second handkerchief around his eyes and the noose around his neck.

Colonel Scammell reads the death warrant. "You can speak now if you wish."

André raises the handkerchief. "I request you will witness to the world that I die like a brave man."

His hands are tied with another handkerchief. The wagon moves away. Death appears to be almost immediate. Tears pour down my face, like many others.[106]

He swings on the gallows for half an hour. Then he is cut down; his body is placed in a plain wooden coffin and buried at the foot of the gallows.[107]

Washington does not attend the execution. I understand why he did not grant André a more honorable death as it might have suggested the conviction was unjust. It was not appropriate in the light of what he had done and what might have been the terrible outcome for the revolution. Washington put his country before his personal feelings as he always does. It would have been very satisfying to have hanged Arnold, but as we lacked him, the unfortunate André was the sacrifice which had to be given. He behaved with so much frankness, courage and delicacy that I cannot help but lament his unhappy fate.[108]

His death contrasts with that of Captain Nathan Hale, a young man from Connecticut, captured in similar circumstances on Long Island. He was also, like André, distinguished, educated, and beloved by his friends and family. He was not given a trial by the British. The letters he wrote to his widowed mother and relations were torn up. He was hanged, his eyes blindfolded in the execution wagon before he even arrived at the gallows, and he was not allowed a Bible or the words of a clergyman at his last moments.

"This is a fine death for a soldier," British officers surrounding the wagon had shouted and jeered.

"Sirs, there is no death which would not be rendered noble in such a glorious cause," he had replied, and died with courage. [109]

Summer is now behind us. There is a chill in the air; the leaves are changing color. We are all greatly shocked by this vile conspiracy and amazed at the miraculous way in which it came to our knowledge. It is the first case of treason in our army, a remarkable thing in such a revolution, but the event grieves us as much as it disgusts.[110] An almost unbelievable combination of chance events has saved us.[111] We will continue to fight.

Chapter 27

Mutiny

I am with my Light Division, at Harrington, on the right side of the North River, three miles below the main army at Tappan. Rochambeau's son, the vicomte de Rochambeau, and John Laurens, will soon be travelling to France and will carry letters from Rochambeau and Washington which the vicomte will memorize in case he is captured. I start to write letters for them to take.

October 4. I write to Vergennes who has already been sent the copy of my account of the meeting at Hartford by La Luzerne:

> Without maritime superiority there will be no certain operation in America.... General Washington has no doubt on the advantage of attacking New York...if we have naval superiority by this autumn we can act against Charles-Town and reconquer the southern states, but if the English stay masters of the sea we will await blows it will be difficult to ward off...the second division gives us much anxiety...each year of delay increases the number of ships, men and money that it will be necessary to send...Congress has no money and little power....By January 1, this army will not have more than six thousand men....You will have learned of the defeat of Gates and the progress of Lord Cornwallis in the south...The French division has saved us from a very dangerous offensive that General Clinton was obliged to abandon and has provided us with a pretext to awaken the states and obtain troops...but that is not enough, and in the present position of America, it is essential to the interest, as well as to the honor of France, that our flag should reign on these seas, that the campaign should be decisive and that it should begin next spring. [1]

I write to Madame de Tessé to tell her of the situation here; the arrival of the French army and the blockading of its ships in Newport harbor; of Gates; of Arnold; of the American army which cannot attack without ships; and the difficult position of our having no money, no pay and no food. I tell her that we Republicans ask our sovereign master, the people, to make extra efforts.[2]

We march towards Totowa.

October 7. Near Fort Lee on the North River, I write to Adrienne, firstly of my love for her and then of my latest news, of my visit to Hartford with Washington to meet the French generals but that Damas was the only one of our friends whom I saw, the unfortunate vicomte de Noailles being shut up on Rhode Island. I tell her I am in excellent health and that she may also rest assured of the health of our friends in America so long as our maritime inferiority continues. I mention my excess of plain speaking with the French generals and that as I did not persuade them, and as it is useful to the public, we should be good friends; I admitted I was in the wrong and asked for pardon.

Next day, on the bank of the Hackensack, I continue my letter and describe the infamous conduct of Arnold. On the ninth, I write to Franklin:

You will fully hear of Arnold's treachery, of another execution. What miraculous escape we made here.' I ask for help. 'We are nack'd. Schokingly nack'd and worse off in that Respect than we have ever been. For God's sake, my dear friend, let us have any how fifteen or twenty-thousand compleat suits (exclusive of what is expected) and let it be done in such a way as will insure theyr timely departure from France. Cloathing for officers is absolutely necessary. No cloth to be got. No money to purchase. I tell him of the pressing need for weapons and powder.[3]

At Totowa Bridge, on the tenth, I continue my letter to Adrienne. I want her to tell my sweet little Anastasie that I love her madly and to embrace George for me. I say that Washington asked to give her his respects and is very appreciative of George being named after him. 'We often talk of you and of our little family.'

"I hope you are not writing so much that you will miss the express who has been waiting since yesterday. Finish your letters quickly," Washington comes to tell me.[4]

I want to attack the enemy, not remain inactive. Accordingly, I write to Washington to propose an attack on Staten Island, which I believe would not be expected and according to my spies is badly defended. If we have enough boats and take other precautions, we should be able to make good our escape: 'Unless we hunt for enterprises, they will no more come in our way this Campaign.'[5]

October 13. News that Gates has been recalled by Congress reaches headquarters at the Falls of Passaic. A resolution was passed on the fifth, and the next day the president of Congress wrote to Washington that a court of inquiry has been ordered into the behaviour of Gates as commander of the southern army and that he should appoint an officer to take his place. Washington has already decided on Greene and this choice is also that of the delegates of the three southern states. Greene will therefore go south. General Heath, if not already at West Point, is on his way from Rhode Island and will command Greene's post.[6] To my delight, Gates is now no longer a threat to Washington.

I write to Noailles on the twenty-third, bemoaning the fatal star which is keeping us apart even although we are both in North America. I tell him Clinton has remained in New York and mention the news of the convoy which was intercepted by our combined Spanish/French fleet. I also treat him to my thoughts on mistresses, whom I hope:

Will never be so demanding as to prevent us from having supper with other girls or we so stupid as to break up a party out of obedience. If I had a mistress, my feelings would be partly based on the delicacy or pride she would display in not showing jealousy and on the freedom I would have to do anything I wanted. That mistress then would bind me forever, at least so I believe, if not by a violent passion, at least by the most tender attachment. I don't like girls because silliness is boring and impudence disgusting, but so long as they have my amiable friends for lovers, their good taste will reconcile me to them.[7]

The same day the Light Division is ordered to move closer to Cranestown for the more effectual security of our right. Washington has agreed to the raid on Staten Island, and we await a suitable coordination of moon, tide and the probability of fog; Pickering, the new quartermaster general, has been asked for boats to be at a certain place at a certain time.

October 26. A review of troops takes place for La Luzerne who is visiting. Tonight we will attempt our raid and the review serves to prepare my men who do not know what we are going to attempt. The trial at Tappan of Joseph Hett Smith finds him not guilty which displeases me greatly.

In the evening I give a dinner for Washington and La Luzerne; just before we eat I tell my commanders of my plan.

We set off towards Elizabethtown in darkness, the men marching as silently as they can. However, the boats arrive too late; Pickering has let us down. The dawn will expose us; there will be no surprise of the enemy and so I abandon the raid. The soldiers march back to our camp in shame. On the way we pass the accursed boats on the wagons; my men shout insults at the carters, the drivers and everyone else around the boats. We are all furious.

October 27. General Orders tells of the success of militia at King's Mountain in North Carolina against mainly Loyalists commanded by Colonel Ferguson on October 7: 'This advantage will in all probability have a very happy influence upon the successive operations in that quarter.'[8]

I write to Washington that far from lessening my wish to finish the campaign by a brilliant stroke, the disappointment of the proposal for Staten Island has made me more determined to try another project. I suggest an assault on Fort Washington.[9]

His reply is disappointing:

> It is impossible, my Dear Marquis, to desire more ardently than I do to terminate the campaign by some happy stroke; but we must consult our means rather than our wishes and not endeavour to better our affairs by attempting things, which for want of success may make them worse. We are to lament that there has been a misapprehension of our circumstances in Europe; but to endeavour to recover our reputation, we should take care that we do not injure it more….I have had an eye to the point you mention, determined if a favourable opening should offer to embrace it…it would be imprudent to throw an army of ten thousand men upon an Island against Nine thousand, exclusive of seamen and militia. All we can do at present is to endeavour to gain a more certain knowledge of the situation and act accordingly… I shall thank you for any aids you can afford. Arnold's flight seems to have all my intelligencers out of their senses.[10]

October 31. Washington holds a council of war to decide what action to take to help the southern army and where and when to go into winter quarters. We all submit written statements, my opinion being that we should stay in the field until December 1, whilst the other officers want to go into winter quarters immediately. I suggest a combined force using the duc de Lauzun's Legion and men from the light infantry; that a corps of one thousand men could be at Hillsborough in North Carolina by January 1 and could serve during the following four months.[11]

Noailles, the marquis de Laval Montmorency, the comte de Charlus, the duc de Lauzun and the chevalier de Chastellux, who is both a general and a learned member of the French Academy, will be visiting me as Rochambeau has agreed leave for them to travel. I write to General Heath to give instructions to the commanding officers at Fishkills, West Point and King's Ferry to direct them how to come by the best road to my quarters. I write to Washington: 'These five gentlemen may By theyr existence at home be Considered as the first people in the French army.'[12]

Washington decides to order an assault against the upper outposts. He sends Heath and his men to stop ships on the North River and attack Fort St. George on Long Island.

Noailles, Damas and Mauduit Duplessis ride into my camp and I greet them with immense delight. Chastellux has taken a longer route but will soon arrive. The following day, we ride seven miles to headquarters as we expect Chastellux to go there first. It is the day of the assault, and I am standing talking to Washington when he rides in, accompanied by McHenry who has brought him from my camp. I introduce him to Washington, but we say nothing about the attack. Washington takes him into the house and presents him to Knox, Wayne, Howe and then to his military family of Hamilton, Tilghman, his aides-de-camp and adjutants. We have already eaten, but fresh food is prepared; claret and madeira are produced.

Next day, Chastellux watches Washington review the main army but there is no salute given to him by the cannon. Washington apologizes and says that his troops on the other side of the river are in motion and that as he had said he might march along the right bank he did not want to give the alarm and deceive the detachments which are out.[13]

They both ride to my quarters near the Ryerson homestead. The rain is falling very heavily but a fire burns warmly in the hearth and there is the usual bowl of grog on my table for officers. The rain ceases and they both come to watch me review my six battalions and one piquet of dragoons all drawn up in battle order on the heights to the left. I ride proudly at their head.

Chastellux is very admiring. 'Fortunate your country if she knows how to avail herself of your talents; more fortunate still if she should not have the need to use them,' is his opinion. [14]

The rain starts to pour down in torrents; I halt the review. Washington and Chastellux gallop back to headquarters but Noailles, Damas and Mauduit return with me and my delight in giving them hospitality in a foreign land partly lessens my worries about the assault.

Next day I learn to my disappointment that Heath's men had killed several enemy and burned some stores at Fort St George but two days of heavy rain and the sudden appearance of British ships on the North River means the main attack is cancelled.[15]

My Light Division is disbanded and will rejoin the main army which will march on the twenty-seventh to winter quarters from West Point to Morristown. I am heartbroken. My corps has not been able to show its mettle.[16]

I ride to Wayne's quarters and wait for Chastellux. Then I take him to meet the other general officers of the line. Knox accompanies us and we visit not only army officers but also a young Dutch man whose head is monstrously swollen. We pay our compliments to Mrs Knox who lives on a little farm nearby with her two children. Then we return to headquarters.

We have known since August the British are assembling troops under Arnold, but we do not know its destination. Spies report that the traitor commands one thousand six hundred men who have sailed from New York. Washington has already written to Jefferson to warn of a possible attack on Virginia at the end of the year. In October Jefferson had summoned six thousand militiamen when Leslie had arrived, but the British had left before most of the militiamen had even reached there. 'I will only call them up again if the target is definitely Virginia,' he has written to Washington.

On November 3, Congress resolves that it has a high sense of the virtuous and patriotic conduct of John Paulding, David Williams, and Isaac Vanwert, and awards them an annual pension of two hundred dollars and that a silver medal should be made for them, with the inscription *fidelity* on one side, and *vincit amor patriae* on the other.[17]

"You should only go to the south if it seems you might be more useful there than in the north, as naval superiority is now not likely until the spring," says Washington.

I find the thought of joining Greene in the south very agreeable. "I am sure that there will be no reinforcements before spring. I will go to Philadelphia and decide there."

On November twenty-seventh, I ride with Noailles, Damas and Mauduit, escorted by twenty dragoons, to see York Island, all of us wishing the enemy might favor us with a few shots. Chastellux has ridden ahead, and we will meet him in Philadelphia. Mrs. Washington is travelling to Virginia to be with her husband for the winter and I am hoping our paths will cross on the road.

Noailles, Damas, Mauduit and I ride towards Philadelphia, my bad fate making me miss Mrs. Washington by my taking another road at the only point when I could have encountered her. We approach the city, the traces of the war still very apparent. Ruins of houses, destroyed or burnt, stand desolate, near prosperous buildings left untouched. We pass through former enemy lines and see their barracks, as well as a large hospital recently constructed by the Quakers. We enter the wide, straight streets of the capital.[18] It is the second day of December; it is very cold, the streets hard with ice.

I stay at the residence of La Luzerne. However, there are vacant apartments where Chastellux, Noailles and Damas are lodging at the house of the Spanish minister, following his death a year ago when his secretary, Señor Francisco Rendon, became the representative of His Most Catholic Majesty; I move there.

"The Spanish are considering an attack on Saint Augustine, in Florida," La Luzerne tells me in great confidence.

I write to Washington and say I am writing to the Spanish generals to try and engage them to either send twelve ships of the line to transport the American army to Charleston or to render their action as useful to General Greene as possible. I tell him I do not have La Luzerne's permission to mention it and so it is entirely confidential.[19]

December 6. In the morning, Noailles, Damas, Mauduit, Gimat, Presley Neville, Montesquieu, Lynch, Chastellux and I set off to ride thirty miles to the battlefield at Brandywine. We cross the Schuylkill at the same ferry where du Coudray was drowned in 1777; we see again parts of enemy entrenchments; we turn to the left and ride fourteen miles to the little town of Chester, whose forty or fifty handsome houses of stone or brick stand at the junction of a creek with the Delaware. We take the road to Brandywine and come to the bridge where I tried to rally the fleeing troops behind the creek. The grim horror of that night is now a tranquil scene but the sky is darkening and we divide into two groups for the night. Chastellux and his two aides-de-camp, Gimat and Mauduit, stay at an inn, and I and the others go to the house of Benjamin Ring, with whom I lodged before the battle; we delight in seeing each other again.

Early next morning, Chastellux and the others arrive. We set off at nine and with the help of a plan executed under the direction of General Howe and engraved in England, as well as with the advice of an American major whose house is on the battlefield, who fought that day, and whom I have arranged to meet, we explore the ground, examining in great detail what happened, the somber tones of winter now settling over the fields and woods.[20]

We send our servants to Chester to prepare a meal and apartments and soon follow them. I ride with Chastellux and Noailles and we pass an agreeable time no longer talking of the battle, but of Paris and society. We arrive again at Chester and almost immediately see state barges coming down the river which have been sent to take us back along the Delaware. We decide to travel tomorrow and ride to Mrs. Witby's Inn, where we spend the evening eating an excellent dinner, followed by an excellent tea, joined by the officer who had brought the barges, as well as the major who had shown us the battlefield. We laugh and sing and dance with great gaiety to the amazement of the people of the house who cannot conceive how it is possible to be so merry without being drunk and appear to look on us as people descended from the moon.[21]

At six in the morning, we assemble by candlelight in the dining room. We breakfast, then go to the Delaware and embark. A little higher up we cross the river and land at Billingsport. The battery fires a welcome although the fortifications are in a state of neglect. We next continue upriver to Fort Miflin. The island on which it is built and that called Mud Island support the right of a second chain of chevaux de frise whose left is defended by Red Bank Fort, but it only blocks the main channel of the river. The fortifications of Miflin Island are being extended to enclose the fort on every side and the Delaware will surround it instead of a ditch. Near the right bank is Hog Island. We see the place where the *Augusta* caught fire and exploded; we see the carcass of the *Merlin* which the British themselves burnt.

We cross the Delaware to visit Red Bank Fort, or rather its ruin, as it is destroyed. Mauduit becomes very impatient for us to see it as he was both the fort's engineer and the artillery officer who defended it, under the command of Colonel Greene.

"The morning is too far spent. The tide is about to turn. We need to forget Red Bank and return to Philadelphia," we amuse ourselves in telling him.

"We will go to the house of a Quaker who lives nearby," he says. "He is a bit of a Tory. I was obliged to knock down his barn and fell his fruit trees, but he will be glad to see Monsieur de Lafayette and will receive us well."

We find the Quaker sitting in the chimney corner, cleaning herbs. He refuses to speak to us.[22] We go to the fort and see a stone with the inscription: 'Here lies buried Colonel Donop.'

"He was a brave man and died in my arms three days after the attack," Mauduit says regretfully. "You cannot tread anywhere here without stepping on some Hessians. Nearly three hundred are buried in the front of the ditch."

We return to Philadelphia. We learn from French ships recently arrived that Henry Laurens is imprisoned in the Tower of London under suspicion of High Treason. Congress seems determined to retaliate. I also learn, to my delight, that the marquis de Castries has been made minister of the navy, replacing Monsieur de Sartine.

I still cannot decide what I should do. Everyone here advises against my going south as there is always the possibility of an expedition in the north where Washington might need me. I feel it keenly that the people in whom he confides the most are mainly far from him. I also hate the idea of leaving the man I love most in the world to seek for uncertainties at a time when he might want me. At the same time, the southern members here want me to go. I might perhaps be useful, and my love of glory spurs me on. I write to Washington to ask his advice.[23]

My friends and I continue our visits to society and to battlegrounds. Noailles, Damas, Chastellux and I visit Germantown and see the Chew House in which Colonel Musgrove's men had barricaded themselves, and the window on the ground floor Mauduit had climbed, with Laurens just behind him, hoping to burn out the enemy with hay and straw but where he had been shot at, the ball missing him, but killing a British officer in the room.

We ride on to Whitemarsh, occupied by our army after the unsuccessful attempt of October 7. We descend from the heights of Germantown, through dense woods. We emerge from the trees and see Chestnut Hill, at the bottom of which is a little stream; behind it are more dense woods and two hills where our army was encamped. Each summit had a redoubt; the slopes defended by an abbattis.

"The advantages of this position are extremely great," says Chastellux.

"Yes, the camp is a very good one. We were so well entrenched it was impossible to attack," I reply.

"The more respectable this position is, the more honor it does to General Washington," we all agree, and it is true that it seems as though he had divined, rather than discovered, the site, that he must have had an eagle-eye's view and hovered above the trees in order to see the ground hidden by the foliage.[24]

We ride back to Philadelphia after eight hours in the saddle covering thirty-six miles. We dine at the residence of La Luzerne and then go to drink tea with Miss Shippen. Miss Rutledge plays the harpsichord; Miss Shippen sings. Noailles takes down a violin; he plays and the young ladies dance, their mothers and other, more serious people talking in another room.

On December 12 I take my friends to visit Barren Hill. I show them the church and the road along which we hastily retreated to the ford, which we passed without losing a man and with all our artillery. We return to dine again at La Luzerne's and find that the comte de Custine and Monsieur de Laval have arrived. In the evening, we go first with them to see the president of Congress, who is not at home, and then to the house of Mr. Peters, the secretary to the Board of War, and his beautiful wife. [25]

In the morning of the fourteenth, John Laurens, Chastellux and I visit Tom Paine. We find his room in a state of disorder, the table covered with books and manuscripts, the furniture thick with dust. His usual untidy appearance complements his surroundings, but his mind is sharp and we spend an agreeable few hours together.

Chastellux is making notes about the American Revolution which he hopes to publish; he is the author of *De la félicité publique*. He is proposed as a foreign member of the Academy of Philadelphia and much to my surprise, so am I. Chastellux is elected unanimously. I am also elected, although there is one black ball against, which is thought to have been an accident. I also meet with James Wilson, author of the pamphlet *To the inhabitants of the United States*.

De Ternay dies of the putrid fever on December 15. I suspect he died of shame because the French fleet is blockaded at Newport by the enemy. He could be obstinate and rough, but he was always firm and had spirit, and everything considered, his death is very much a loss to us.[26] Admiral Destouches is given command for the moment.

I finally decide for various reasons not to go south to join Greene.[27] It is thought that ships and troops are being made ready at Brest and we are also waiting for news from the new minister of the navy, de Castries, as well as learning more about the possibility of a Spanish officer agreeing to cooperate with our army. My presence would therefore be useful to Washington. I think it very likely there will be fighting in the north, and I am also very reluctant to part from Washington and the army here. If new intelligence arrives then I might change my mind, but for the moment, I intend to remain close to my general.

The Board of the Admiralty wrote to me on the thirteenth, asking about the clothing which was meant to be coming from France. I answer as well as I can on the sixteenth. I say that three million livres were lent to Mr. Franklin, but that he had become timid by the frequent drafts of Congress and 700,000 livres were ultimately intended for the purchase of the most necessary articles; this sum was first divided between clothing and military stores, but after I undertook to obtain fifteen thousand stands of arms and one hundred thousand of powder, it was decided that the money should be used to buy ten thousand complete suits. I refer to the taking of the *Alliance* from Captain Jones by Captain Landais, and then his refusal to take the military stores offered in the name of the French court, as well as denying passage to the comte de Vauban who, it is said, was carrying important dispatches. I say that it is my secretary and two other French gentlemen on board who have told me this and that Mr. Arthur Lee, who was also on board, must also know what happened. I declare that Doctor Franklin from time to time mentioned to me his orders to the American agents, which I thought were very proper. 'How far these Gentlemen have forwarded or neglected the business I am not able to ascertain to Congress.'[28]

New Year dawns. I am preparing to travel to headquarters at New Windsor with Laurens, who has finally accepted the wishes of Congress that he should go to France, and who will meet Washington, Rochambeau and Destouches before sailing. I have received a letter from Greene who does not yet know I have decided against joining him and writes: 'It is now within a few days of the time you mention of being with me. Was you to arrive, you would find a few ragged, half starved troops, in the wilderness, destitute of everything necessary for either the comfort or convenience of soldiers; altogether without discipline, and so addicted to plundering that the utmost exertions of their officers cannot restrain them.'[29]

Disturbing news arrives. The Pennsylvania Line at Mount Kemble near Morristown mutinied on New Year's Day. They have taken six pieces of artillery, killed several officers and men and wounded others.[30] They are marching towards Philadelphia, still accompanied by Brigadier General Wayne, Colonel Butler and Colonel Stewart, to present their complaints to Congress and the government of Pennsylvania. Many are drunk on rum, but their grievances are real. "We are not Arnolds," they are shouting. "We want food, clothes and pay. We enlisted for three years, not for the duration of the war."

The aggravated calamities and distresses that have resulted from the total want of pay for nearly twelve months, the want of clothing at a severe season, and the not infrequent want of provisions are beyond description.[31] Is this the end? Will other troops mutiny? Will they desert to the British?

Congress sets up a committee to investigate and sends President Reed to talk to the men. The committee ask General St. Clair to go as he is already here in Philadelphia. They also ask me as my popularity with the men is well-known. We therefore do not wait for Laurens. We set out early in the morning of January 3; later in the day we reach Trenton; the mutineers are at Princeton, still with Wayne, Butler and Stewart.

We are at Trenton on the fourth and will shortly leave for Maidenhead.[32] Commissary Stewart has talked with the sergeants' committee set up by the troops and has given us a copy of the proposals the men have made and of Wayne's replies, and we will send them to Congress. The men want their proposals settled within six days. They evidently said I was the only one for whom they had a depth of friendship, but that they find me too severe concerning discipline. Stewart and Stirling say they will kill St. Clair but that, except for this mudslinging, he does not believe they will touch me, except to take me prisoner. I do not hear anything said about the general and the officers are all in their rear. The militia has been dismissed. I intend to preach peace and unless I was sure I could kill all of them if I wanted, I would not fire a single shot.[33]

January 5. We learn the insurgents intend to march here tomorrow. We will meet them on the way.[34]

Next day, we go to the camp to talk with the mutineers and expect a bad reception. Just outside the town we find several noncommissioned officers and soldiers.

"What is the reason for all this trouble?" we ask.

They appear embarrassed and ashamed, which seems a good omen. We advance to the guard, who stop us. We identify ourselves. We manage to get past, and I give an order to the noncommissioned officer of the guard who says he will not fail to do it. Soldiers take us to the committee of sergeants; they are very respectful.

"Here are the letters between us and General Wayne," they say. "You can see him."

We meet with him and with several more of their leaders, whom I immediately believe to be guided by British emissaries or by sergeants clinging to their new power.

"You cannot meet with the men," they declare and appear to be organized like a small army with their generals, their colonels etc. We had hoped to separate Colonel Stewart's regiment and to enlist the others in returning to Trenton, but this idea clearly does not please the sergeants and finally it just seems best to keep them away from the enemy. Affairs appear to be progressing well enough when suddenly we receive word from the committee of sergeants that the Line is complaining about seeing so many officers. They fear we are plotting something.

"Make a prompt retreat or there will be evil consequences."

"You have just an hour and a half," comes a second message.

"It is impossible to speak to the soldiers," we decide. "It is impossible to negotiate except in the way General Wayne is doing."

We leave Princeton and as we ride away, we meet many soldiers on the road. "Turn back," I tell them.

"We will follow you anywhere if you need us against the enemy or for your personal safety. We will die to the last man under your orders, but you do not know all that we have suffered. We will see to it that our country does us justice. We will see a deputation from the assembly. We will conclude our agreement with General Wayne and then we will come back to Morristown," they reply.

I find their demands extravagant, however, and I think it is difficult to consent to a general pardon. I harangue a group of about thirty. Some mutineers argue against me but finally consent to return to their huts and I hope that rum or the words of the mob's leaders do not change their minds.

We try to muster the few men remaining in the huts and send them a few miles. The rest of the cannon and part of the munitions will be taken to Chatham, where there is a detachment from New Jersey. The munitions will be sent elsewhere. There appears to be discontent in the New Jersey detachment, just ahead, which I believe was caused by some English and Irish soldiers but quelled by the others, and we believe a brigade from Connecticut is marching here. Therefore, we have Princeton behind us, about two hundred Pennsylvanians on our right, three hundred militiamen and three hundred Continentals from New Jersey in front of us, as well as the enemy who has not yet made a move, and so our position is precarious. What alarms me is that the militia do not appear to want to attack the mutineers so long as they do not try to cross over to the enemy, and we also have one of the leaders who has come for the rest of the men and munitions and whom we can neither let go nor keep.[35]

I decide that I can do nothing more as General St. Clair is here. I believe Washington is coming and I will wait for his orders. I write to him: 'Your going there would be extremely imprudent, and the probability of success is not by far such as to justify yourself to any danger of the kind- the less so as the possessing of your person would be an inducement to theyr joining the enemy...we have been advis'd by theyr Committee to make a short retreat.'[36] Then we ride on to New Windsor.

I arrive at headquarters with Laurens on the twelfth. I tell Washington what has happened. That night, news arrives that the emissaries sent by the British are still with the mutineers and have not been handed over to Wayne.

"They seem to say that if you do not grant our terms, we can obtain them elsewhere," says Washington.

We wait with anxiety. I feel there are many disadvantages in drawing our swords against these mutineers and the certainty of crushing them is not great enough to encourage an attack. I believe it is frightening to spend one's winter killing each other without the enemy suffering any loss, and when I think that the majority of the soldiers are being led astray by a few leaders, that these brave people have suffered with us for four years, have been wounded with us, have shared our triumphs and misfortunes, that they can complain not only of their long misery but even of verified deception in their enlistments, then the necessity of fighting them seems very unfortunate.[37] Then we hear that the emissaries have now been given to the American authorities and were condemned to be executed on the eleventh. On the fifteenth, a letter comes from Wayne to say that the terms offered to the Pennsylvanians have been accepted.[38]

Half will be discharged; half will be put on leave until April. They will receive certificates as compensation for the depreciated currency and will be given more clothes. Washington believes the Pennsylvanian authorities have perhaps made the best agreement that they could, but that it would not only subvent the Pennsylvania Line but would perniciously affect the whole army.[39]

The comte de Deux Ponts is already here and to my delight comte Mathieu Dumas rides in, sent by Rochambeau to ask Washington to visit him at Newport; then Damas and Charlus arrive. I write to the prince de Poix about my French friends in North America: 'The vicomte is delightful...You would be quite satisfied with Damas...Charlus is still the same person we love, and in Rhode Island, as everywhere else, the society is distinguished in the grand manner. Without wanting to boast, I cannot help admitting that this society is the most agreeable that has ever been formed.'[40]

We knew at the beginning of the month that the enemy embarkation which took place on December 20, from New York, and which was thought to be going south, was commanded by Arnold. He has sixteen hundred men, chiefly composed of detachments from the British, German and Provincial corps and the only entire corps is said to be that of the Queen's Rangers. However, news of the traitor is offset by a glorious account that Lieutenant Colonel Washington attacked a party of two hundred and fifty Tories on December 28, killing one hundred and fifty, without losing a single man himself.

It is a bleak and grim time for our army but my lively French friends at dinner often make Washington smile. Unfortunately, on January 21, news arrives that soldiers of the New Jersey Line have mutinied at Pompton. They had been allowed some of the concessions given to the Pennsylvanians, but about two hundred men have marched towards Trenton, followed by Colonel Israel Shreve, their commanding officer, who says many are drunk.

Washington determines that there will be no intervention this time by civil authorities. He will march with his best soldiers and subdue the mutiny. He orders Shreve at Pompton to collect all the men of his regiment who have had the virtue to resist the pernicious example of their associates. If Shreve then has enough men he must make the mutineers return to duty.[41] He orders Heath at West Point to select five or six hundred of the most robust and best clothed men from the garrison and place them under proper officers.

"I will inspect them at West Point tomorrow during our inspection there," he declares. He orders the Jersey militia to assemble and tells Sullivan to tactfully oppose any intervention by Congress this time.

Next day we ride with him along difficult paths to the majestically beautiful, strategically important, West Point. I see again the angle of the river; the chain; the batteries guarding it; the six forts ascending like an amphitheater in front of us; Fort Putnam at the summit, still the only one faced with stone, the chain of mountains beyond, an impenetrable barrier, and down near the river the renamed Fort Clinton, with the artillery park behind; the remaining four fortifications whose fires all cross.

Washington inspects the troops. We view the fortifications. It is a long day; my old wound makes me very weary. I try to disguise my fatigue, but Washington notices. "We will not return by horse. We will go back by boat. The tide will help us to go against the current."[42]

We clamber on board, the wind howling about our ears. We move off into the river, the craft pitching and rolling against blocks of ice, the steep cliffs almost invisible through a twilight thick with falling snow. The boat weaves through the ice; it starts to flood. The banks are too rocky to land. The captain appears terrified.

"Courage, my children. I will lead you; it is my duty to take the tiller," says Washington.[43]

The boat lurches along, awash with water, darkness now enveloping us. An eternity passes; we find a place to land; we walk for about a league and several hours later finally arrive back at the house.[44]

Next day, Washington orders General Howe, whom he has placed in charge of the detachment, to march his men towards the mutineers: 'The object is to compel the mutineers to unconditional submission, and I am to desire you will grant no terms while they are with arms in their hands in a state of resistance. The manner of executing this I leave to your discretion according to circumstances. If you succeed in compelling the revolted troops to surrender, you will instantly execute a few of the most active and incendiary leaders.'[45]

He believes it is difficult to know what the troops sent to quell the mutiny might do, but he believes it imperative to bring the matter to a head. He believes that, otherwise, mutinous behavior will spread.

At the same time, the food shortage is desperate. Supplies are very low. Flour is only available from day to day. There has been very little cattle for some time and salted meat, which should be held in reserve, is nearly exhausted. Washington writes a circular letter to the states of New Hampshire, Massachusetts, Connecticut, Rhode Island and New York, informing them of the mutiny and detailing the risks to the army from the lack of supplies. [46]

Snow falls heavily on the twenty-third. We cannot travel and it is also difficult to obtain horses for the artillery and their forage. We hear nothing for two days and then we learn Howe's five hundred men have already started marching from West Point even although the snow was about two feet deep and there was no track. Washington, Charlus, Dillon and I set off in a sleigh pulled by horses which have not eaten for three days.

On the twenty-sixth we reach Ringwood; Washington talks with Howe whose men have been joined by more troops as well as three guns from the Highlands. About midnight Howe sets off with his detachment to Pompton where the mutineers have returned from Chatham, eight miles away.

Before dawn, on the twenty-seventh, his troops surround their encampment and position the three guns in front of the huts where the men are asleep.

"Tell them to assemble without arms," he orders, not knowing if they would comply and if his own troops would support him against the mutineers.

After some time, they do so. Howe asks the officers the names of the chief offenders. They name Grant, Gilmore and Tuttle as the leaders from each regiment, the mutineers standing in line on the snow. They are found guilty and sentenced to be shot. Twelve of their fellow mutineers are selected to execute them which distressed them greatly. Gilmore and Tuttle are shot. Grant is reprieved.[47]

Howe reports what happened to Washington, who determines to prevent any concessions to the soldiers by New Jersey, which would negate his martial handling of the affair. I agree with the summary justice although I understand and sympathize with the soldiers. An army must have discipline or it becomes a rabble.

The English have not made an attack from New York so there is nothing for me to do here; I accompany Washington back to New Windsor, whilst Charlus and Dillon travel to Philadelphia. He writes a circular on the twenty-ninth, to the New England states: 'I hope this will completely extinguish the spirit of mutiny, if effectual measures are taken to prevent its revival by rendering the situation of the soldiery more tolerable than it has heretofore been. It is not to be expected that an Army can be permanently held together by those ties on which we have too long depended.'[48]

Jefferson has written to Washington telling him about Arnold's incursion into his state of Virginia. Richmond has been partly razed. Plantations have been devastated; slaves have escaped; houses have been plundered; two tobacco warehouses, a shipyard and foundry have been destroyed. It is thought Arnold is going towards Portsmouth and von Steuben is following him down the river.

At the end of the first week in February, Rochambeau informs Washington that a storm on January 22 to 23 had blown Vice Admiral Arbuthnot's ships away from their anchorage at Gardiner's Bay off eastern Long Island from where they keep the French fleet penned up in Newport. A seventy-two has been wrecked; another, or perhaps two, has been dismasted. A ninety has disappeared. There is a slight element of doubt in Rochambeau's information, but the Continental prize agent in Connecticut has also reported the same. We are euphoric. We now have naval superiority. We need to act quickly. Washington diplomatically suggests to Rochambeau 'that the confirmation of the reported British disaster will have enabled Mr. Destouches to take advantage of the event, in a manner as advancive of his own glory as of the good of the service.'[49] He suggests Destouches' fleet and one thousand soldiers should attack Arnold in the south. The French agree. Destouches dispatches a sixty-four-gun ship and two frigates on February 9, under Captain Arnaud le Gardeur de Tilly, to the Chesapeake Bay, to transport muskets, as well as, perhaps, to prevent Arnold at Portsmouth from receiving supplies, and to destroy his transport boats. Temporary French naval superiority means they will be able to control the Chesapeake and will be an opportunity for American forces to capture Arnold.

"A naval force might not be enough," Washington tells me. "I will send an army of one thousand two hundred men to Virginia to give the enterprise all possible chance of success. It will leave me with barely enough men to defend West Point, but it is necessary. I will go to Newport to try and obtain the help of French soldiers and more of their fleet."

We learn of a wonderful victory on January 17 by Daniel Morgan with eight hundred Americans at Cowpens in Carolina, against Lieutenant Colonel Tarleton with one thousand one hundred men. The enemy was completely routed and pursued nearly twenty miles. One hundred and ten of them were killed; two hundred wounded; five hundred and twenty-nine were taken prisoner. Morgan had not more than twelve killed and sixty wounded.[50] He stayed out of the reach of Tarleton's men who had been chasing him for twelve days and who became tired. The militia fought bravely this time, as well as the Continentals, and our soldiers successfully used fixed bayonets.

Hamilton does not enjoy the same relationship with Washington as I do. He often finds him difficult and can be critical of him. He is also desperate to resume a fighting role in the army and not continue as Washington's secretary. On February 16 he resigns from his post and is no longer a member of Washington's military family. Washington had asked him to come to speak to him and Hamilton had said he would come immediately. He had then gone downstairs and given a letter to Tench Tilghman. I had come along and delayed him a short time on a matter of business. He had been impatient to leave me and quickly returned upstairs where he found Washington waiting for him. "Colonel Hamilton, you have kept me waiting at the head of the stairs these ten minutes, I must tell you Sir you treat me with disrespect," he said angrily.

"I am not conscious of it, Sir, but since you have thought it necessary to tell me so, we part," Hamilton had replied.

"Very well, Sir, if it be your choice," Washington had said.

An hour later Tench Tilghman had come to see Hamilton on Washington's behalf, assuring him of his great confidence in his abilities and offering to speak candidly together to heal a difference which could not have happened except in a moment of passion. Hamilton had replied that he had taken his resolution in a manner not to be revoked and would prefer to decline a conversation. He had also said that he would not leave him until some gentlemen had returned and that in the meantime it depended on Washington to let their behavior to each other be the same as before.[51]

Chapter 28

Virginia

The detachment Washington has decided to send into Virginia will be a joint operation with French ships and will be composed of three regiments, each of four hundred men, under Colonels Vose, Gimat and Barber; Gouvion will be the engineer. To my great joy he chooses me to lead it as I am his senior French officer. I write to La Luzerne:

> I will command the corps and will have overall command in Virginia of the American troops…our destination is a secret, and everyone thinks it is Staten Island or Bergen Neck… We do not have a sou, a horse, a cart or a wisp of hay…I will be preceded by a troop of agents accompanied by soldiers on horses obtained first in order to go to take other horses…We shall live by our wits and march at the expense of our neighbors until Head of Elk. The general must be very convinced of the importance of our expedition to reduce himself so much here. [1]

February 20. I receive my orders:

> SIR,- I have ordered a detachment to be made at this post, to rendezvous at Peeks Kill on the 19th instant, which, together with another to be formed at Morris Town from the Jersey troops, will amount to about twelve hundred Rank and file.
>
> The destination of this detachment is to act against the corps of the enemy now in Virginia, in conjunction with the Militia, and some ships from The fleet of the Chevalier DesTouches, which he informs me sailed the 7th instant from Newport.
>
> You will take command of this detachment, which you will in the first instance, march by battalions to Pompton, there to rendezvous and afterwards to proceed with all possible dispatch to the Head of Elk.
>
> You will make your arrangements with the Qr. Master General concerning the route you are to take, concerning transportation, tents, intrenching tools and other articles in his department, of which you may stand in need, with the Commissary General concerning provisions; with the Clothier concerning Clothing, shoes etc And with General Knox concerning the artillery and stores you will want for the expedition.
>
> The result of these several arrangements you will report at Head Quarters.
>
> When you arrive at Trenton, if the Delaware is practicable and boats are readily to be had, you will save time by going from thence by water to Christeen Bridge, Marcus Hook, or Chester but if you cannot avail yourself of this mode, you must proceed by land, by the route which the Qr. Mr and Commissary may designate as most convenient for covering and supplies.
>
> You are not to suffer the detachment to be delayed for want of either provision, or waggons on the route; where the ordinary means will not suffice with certainty, you will have recourse to military impress.
>
> You will take your measures with the Qr. Mr. General in such a manner, that vessels may be ready by your arrival at the Head of Elk to convey you down the bay to Hampton Road, or to the point of operations and you will open a previous communication with the officer Commanding the ships of His Christian Majesty, to concert your cooperation, and to engage him to send,(if it can

be spard), a frigate up the bay to cover your passage, without which, or some other armed vessels might be insecure.

When you arrive at your destination, you must act as your own judgement and the circumstances shall direct.

You will open a correspondence with Baron De Steuben, who now commands in Virginia, informing him of your approach and requesting him to have a sufficient body of Militia ready to act in conjunction with your detachment. It will be adviseable for him to procure persons in whom he can confide well acquainted with the Country at Portsmouth and in the vicinity, some, who are capable of giving you a military idea of it and others to serve as guides.

You should give the earliest attention to acquiring a knowledge of the different rivers but particularly James River, that you may know what harbors can best afford shelter and security to the cooperating squadron, in case of blockade by a superior force.

You are to do no act whatever with Arnold that directly or by implication may skreen him from the punishment due to his treason and desertion which if he should fall into your hands, you will execute in the most summary way.

Having recommended it to the Count de Rochambeau to detach a land with the naval force that might be destined for the Chesapeake Bay (though, from the disposition which has already taken place, it is not probable that a land force will be sent yet), if the recommendation should be complied with, you will govern yourself in cooperating with the Officer commanding the French troops agreeable to the intentions and instructions of His Most Christian Majesty, of which you were the bearer and which, being still in your possession, it is unnecessary for me to recite.

You will keep me regularly advised of your movements and progress; and when the object of your detachment is fulfilled (or unfortunately disappointed), you will return to this post with it by the same Rout, if circumstances admit of it, and with as much expedition as possible to this Post.

I wish you a successful issue to the enterprise and all the glory which I am persuaded you will deserve.

Given at Head Quarters, New Windsor, Feb 20, 81. [2]

He writes on February 21 to Thomas Jefferson, the governor of Virginia, informing him of de Tilly's sailing and my departure. I also write a few lines: 'I shall from time to time inform your Excellency of the Movements of the Continental detachement that Has Marched from this place-they will be precipitated as Much as I can, and I'll have the Honor of writing to your Excellency from philadephia where I intend to preceed the troops.'[3]

My one thousand two hundred soldiers are the flower of the army, selected mainly from the Massachusetts, Connecticut, New Hampshire and Rhode Island Lines, many of whom are from my old Light Infantry. They are lean, hardy men in ragged clothes who have marched down cheerfully and in good order from Peekskill along bad roads in pouring rain. On the twenty-third I meet them at Pompton[4] where provisions and wagons are being collected. I give out standards to each regiment.

"Are we only going for a few days?" some men mutter. I do not reply.

I send Lieutenant Colonel Ebenezer Stevens to Philadelphia to obtain artillery. Next day, in the coldness of dawn, rain falling heavily, I ride to Morristown in advance of my troops.[5] On the twenty-fifth, they arrive at the huts.

In the morning, I set off to Philadelphia;[6] my men tramp again along bad roads in the rain. They march five miles, then are joined by five companies from the New Jersey Line so I now have three regiments. The first is formed of the eight first companies of the Massachusetts Line, commanded by Colonel Vose; the second of the two remaining companies from the Massachusetts Line, five from Connecticut and one from Rhode Island, and is commanded by Lieutenant Colonel Gimat. The third is formed of the Jersey companies, two from New

Hampshire, one from General Hazen's regiment, and is commanded by Lieutenant Colonel Barber.[7] In the last rays of the setting sun they reach Somerset.[8] Woken in the night, they march at dawn on the twenty-seventh to Princeton where they are quartered in several houses and in the four-story-high stone college damaged by the occupations of the two armies and now without students. Rioting breaks out between the Massachusetts and New Jersey troops, but the officers manage to subdue the outburst. Dawn sees them once more marching rapidly on the rain-drenched, mud-mired roads. At one in the afternoon, they reach Trenton; I arrange boats to transport them further.

February 26. I reach Philadelphia where I learn that de Tilly has spoken with the Virginians but upon seeing that nothing can be done immediately, he has not yet decided whether to stay or return to Rhode Island.[9] La Luzerne is fearful that our letters might go astray and wishes me to send Gouvion first to the French squadron and then on to von Steuben's camp so that he can give details of our force, our intentions and the likely date of our arrival. I follow his wishes and Gouvion sets off to travel either by land or water, depending on the state of the Bay.[10]

"In case of necessity you can use French provisions of flour and salt meat that are near to the Chesapeake, he says." [11]

Washington writes that clothing has been dispatched which exceeds what I had asked for, but it is too late to send a further supply of shoes and I must try to obtain them in Philadelphia. He says he has received a letter from Rochambeau reporting d'Estaing's success over the fleet of Admiral Howe. He also, unfortunately, says that Admiral Arbuthnot again has naval superiority and so Destouches can no longer help us further. He orders that it is essential to have fast vessels sailing from the Head of Elk to Hampton Roads to correspond with the French commodore or to warn me of danger which may arise from a change of circumstance as the detachment from Destouches' squadron might be followed by a superior one from the enemy in Gardiner's Bay.[12]

Lieutenant Colonel Stevens has obtained artillery; one 24, six 18, two brass, one 8-inch howitzer and two 18-inch mortars. In total, we will have twelve heavy pieces, four six-pounders, two small howitzers and ammunition, all of which will arrive at Head of Elk, either on the second or the third. I manage to obtain one thousand five hundred pairs of shoes, as well as medicines and instruments. Congress agrees to give the troops the advance of a month's pay which will be distributed at Head of Elk and vessels will be ready for us there with thirty days provisions on board. General Wayne is hopeful he will soon collect one thousand men to join me. I am not so sanguine in my expectations but try to prepare affairs for this number.

March 1. At half past two, a schooner and other boats carrying my detachment from Trenton anchor off the city. They stay about half an hour, then proceed downriver in a favorable wind. Next day, I write to Washington to tell him of my preparations and that we will have enough boats to land the detachment, as well as two heavy scows for the artillery. I say that I will, however, confine myself literally to my instructions, and if Colonel Gouvion writes with certainty that de Tilly has gone and it is certain he will not return, I will march back the detachment, but for the present I am going on: 'because upon the increasing of the ennemy's force at Gardner's Bay, you recommend dispatch to me.' I say that as General Duportail has not yet left, then I hope that if we do not go, I may return in time for the journey to Rhode Island. 'I most instantly beg, my dear general, you will favor me with an immediate answer.'[13]

I visit the Board of the Navy. I propose sending the frigates but discover the *Trumbull* does not have a full complement of crew and there has been a mutiny at sea on the Ariel. Later in the day I set off from Philadelphia to Head of Elk. I arrive in the evening and find a dispatch waiting for me from Washington who says the French squadron has returned to Newport, but that Destouches has fitted out a newly captured vessel, the *Romulus*, which will perhaps be sent there with some frigates. 'Embark your troops immediately on transport boats if they are ready, that not a moment's time be lost, after you receive certain advice that our friends are below. But until that matter is ascertained beyond a doubt you will on no account leave the Elk River.' [14]

I write back: 'My exertions shall be such that I hope we may be embarked before we hear of the arrival of our friends.'[15]

I write the same day to the commanding officer in Virginia[16] as I believe von Steuben has gone to join Greene. I also write to Thomas Jefferson, the governor. I say that the departure of de Tilly must have relaxed the preparations against Portsmouth but that I can tell him with great satisfaction the captured, fifty-gun British ship, the *Romulus*, will be sent there with some frigates, which is, of course, a matter of the greatest secrecy. I say that my detachment has marched with the greatest rapidity and will sail when we hear of the arrival of French ships in the Bay. I ask for militia to be collected to join with my men, for a large corps to guard the passes and cut off all possibility of Arnold escaping, some heavy pieces and ammunition to add to our train of artillery, boats to land our troops as near to the enemy as possible, and scows for the cannon. I also want the fort at York to be put into the best state of defense as the safety of the French squadron depends on it, and I would also like good and accurate maps.[17]

My troops arrive in the afternoon, having marched that day from Christiana. They put up tents; they light fires; there are again mutterings of discontent. There are not enough boats to transport men, horses, guns and equipment so I write to Governor Lee asking him to send all the vessels at Annapolis and Baltimore; I also make the same request to Brigadier General Mordecai Gist, commander of the Maryland militia, and send McHenry to Baltimore to ask the merchants for more supplies.

Next day, rain and wind batter men and tents; out in the Elk River boats appear. "More will follow," I am told. I write again to the governments of Maryland and Virginia.

McHenry is successful. Ammunition, bread, clothes, horses, wagons, medicines, stoves and other provisions start to arrive at our camp or at the wharves. However, it continues to rain, the winds are contrary and we still do not have enough vessels so we cannot leave Head of Elk.

A letter arrives from Washington with wonderful news. Letters from Rochambeau and Destouches have informed him of their intention to operate in the Chesapeake Bay with their whole fleet and a detachment of eleven hundred French troops, grenadiers and chasseurs which will be commanded by baron de Vioménil, Rochambeau's second in command. Destouches wishes to sail on the fifth, and Washington intended to go to Rhode Island on the second, to help smooth out any difficulties. He has also received a letter from Greene who says Cornwallis is penetrating the country with great rapidity; he is retreating before him and hopes to pass the Roanoke. Washington is fearful Arnold will escape before the French fleet arrives in the Bay and therefore says he is giving me 'greater latitude than in my original instructions and that I am free to agree a plan with the French general for a descent into North Carolina to cut off the detachment of the enemy which had ascended Cape Fear River, to intercept Cornwallis if possible, and to relieve General Greene and the southern states. He says, however, 'this should only be a secondary consideration in case of Arnold's retreat to New York.' [18]

March 7. We now have thirty boats and believe more are coming. Von Steuben has written that he has three to four thousand men, but whatever may be his views on the ease of taking Portsmouth by the sword, I will not hazard anything until I have seen the situation with my own eyes. I believe Arnold plays a very deep game; he has had much time to prepare; the position is very respectable and many of his men are experienced in action. I do not flatter myself to succeed as easily as may be thought.[19]

The winds will not allow a frigate to come up the Bay and I decide to transport my men tomorrow to Annapolis as it is important for the honor of the American army that it is present in the enterprise with the French ships and troops. I am sure my men will put up with the inconvenience of being crammed into a few vessels and we will also have armed craft, although the largest has only twelve guns. I might then proceed in a small boat to Hampton where I could perhaps obtain a frigate and where I can try to cool the impetuosity, or correct the political mistakes, of both baron von Steuben and baron de Vioménil. I write to Washington: 'Whatever determination I take, Great deal Must Be personally risked. But I Hope to Manage things so as to Commit no imprudence with the excellent detachement whose glory is as dear and whose Safety is much dearer to me than My own.' [20]

March 8. "Embark the men," I order.

My troops march down the river to Plum's Point, seven miles below Head of Elk. Barber's and Gimat's regiments embark onto ships; Vose's regiment marches another five miles and stays at Cecil's Ferry.[21]

Next day, they embark in various boats in a slight wind. They will be defended by twelve guns on the *Nesbitt*, some field pieces on the vessel that carries Colonel Stevens, and one eight-gun and one six-gun vessel which will meet us from Baltimore. I have requested Commodore James Nicholson to take the general command of our fleet and if there is the least danger to continue further down. Our boats are very crowded, but I hope to unload the vessels as we proceed and to commandeer every boat we come across. Captain Martin, of the *Nesbitt*, says he will answer for the safe arrival of my fleet at Annapolis.

Thirty soldiers escort me on the *Dolphin*, a small sloop armed only with swivels, and I also take on board, Charlus, the only son of the minister of the navy, which will help to add weight to my application if necessary when I request a frigate from the French.[22] Malicious people are wrong to say that Rochambeau pays my youth the honor of envying it[23] and I pay no heed to the resentment I am aware of towards me from some of the French officers.

Commander Nicholson joins us sooner than expected, off Turkey Point.[24] On March 10, I am in Annapolis. I speak to members of the Maryland Council to persuade them to aid our expedition.[25] Out in the Bay, the wind is not fair; my fleet sails about four or five leagues to Pools Island. The wind freshens and most of the craft run into Wostan Creek for safety.[26] On the twelfth, the wind is fair; my fleet arrives here as evening darkens.

I set off, leaving my men safe in the harbor and in a good position to move further down the Bay. I have no doubt the French are already in the Chesapeake; I hope to agree our plans with them and obtain an immediate convoy for my detachment.[27] I also hope to gain local knowledge and to try to improve everything that might help the American side of the alliance.

Rain drenches our small, open barge buffeted by the wind. We struggle as far as Herring Bay. There is no *Dolphin*. Has it returned to Annapolis for fear of an attack? We continue down the coast; further out we see British ships and so keep close to the shore. I send a warning to Commodore Nicholson that there is an enemy frigate and a brig off St. Jerome's.[28]

March 14. In the afternoon, we reach York, a small cluster of houses on a high bluff with wharves and commercial buildings by the shore of the south bank of the York River, about fifteen miles from its entrance into the Chesapeake.

"No French fleet has been sighted," I am told to my great surprise. However, I suspect this is probably due to the delays and chances so frequent in naval affairs.[29] I immediately send an express to von Steuben who has been waiting two days at York and Williamsburg for me: 'Here I am, my dear Baron, in consequence of a new arrangement which I will explain to you. I wait impatiently the pleasure of seeing you, and I shall tell you the very important reason which has caused me to precede the detachment.'[30]

My first aim here will be to request nothing is taken for my expedition that could be intended for, or useful to, the southern army whose welfare appears more interesting to me than our success. My second is to see what has been prepared and to gather and forward every requisite for a vigorous cooperation.[31]

I meet von Steuben who has been very active in making preparations but has not yet reconnoitered at Portsmouth where the enemy has been fortifying.

"We will soon have five thousand militia ready to fight," he says.

"When my detachment arrives, we will have enough men to proceed and might very well do without land troops from Newport. [32] I will reconnoiter as soon as possible. I will also not take command until either my troops or the French arrive," I tell him.

"I think you should," he says.

However, I think it more polite not to do so until the detachment arrives, or operations begin.[33]

I ride backwards and forwards from the shore to my boat out in the river. Suddenly, my horse stumbles; I fall into deep water, flailing desperately. Soldiers on the boat jump in and haul me to safety to my great good fortune.

I expect the French fleet hourly[34] and when it comes, I will send a frigate to Annapolis. There is still no *Dolphin*, but I learn that my men are safe in Annapolis. I do not think we will need Wayne's troops; I write to him to say that Arnold will either escape before the French reach here or will be attacked immediately on their arrival and that of my detachment. I would be very happy to have him, but I do not feel he can arrive in time, and I do not wish to delay his joining with the southern army.[35]

March 16. I go to Williamsburg, the capital of Virginia, a town of about two hundred and fifty houses, situated on flat land between two small rivers, one of which flows into the York, the other into the James. It has a wide main street one mile long; the handsome state house, the Capitol, at one end; at the other, the college which, like Princeton, has no students because of the war. A large church is in the center; nearby is the palace where the state governor usually lives.[36]

I reply to Thomas Jefferson's letters of the tenth, twelfth, and fourteenth, which I received yesterday. He 'trusts that my future acquaintance with the Executive of the State will evince to me that among their faults is not to be counted a want of disposition to second the views of the commander against our common enemy.' However, he says 'that mild laws, a people not used to prompt obedience, a want of provisions of war and means of procuring them renders our orders often ineffectual, oblige us to temporize and when we cannot accomplish an object in one way to attempt it in another.'[37] He fears it is not possible to obtain the number of boats I need to land my men.[38] He says Virginia has already provided six thousand pounds of cannon powder, is ordering four thousand pounds more and ten pilots have also been provided. Maps will be given to me when I arrive, as well as supplies requested by the quartermaster's and engineers' departments which will go mainly in wagons to General Muhlenburg's headquarters and will be rather late.[39] These include about one thousand five hundred gallons of rum, flour and twenty seasoned oak planks. Four smiths will accompany the wagons. Four boats suitable for our use will be ready at the public shipyard on the Chickahominy next Friday; one galley will be there, and another is being prepared, but they need men; others will meet at Hoods.[40]

I thank him for that part of his letters which is personal. I write that since the time when I had 'the Honor of Being Admitted to the American Union, when without Means, without foreign aid,

But with a determination either to Conquer or die, our Noble Contest was Carried through so Many Dangers and Difficulties. Long since Have I Been used to those Inconveniences that are so far Compensated by the Numberless Blessings of A popular Governement.' I tell him I shall adopt every measure that he thinks more suitable to the temper of the people, or to the state of our circumstances, and that to the efforts they have already made, I know new ones will be added to ensure the success of our expedition. I say my detachment is still at Annapolis and cannot come unless a superior naval force is sent to protect it, and that as I have just arrived, I will need to obtain more knowledge about the situation before I can either take command of the troops here or ask for more aid.[41]

I talk with the quartermaster to find out what we need. Next day, I write again to Jefferson. I request the impressment of saddle horses, wagons and two hundred oxen instead of the draft horses: 'I am very Unhappy, Sir, to think that My Arrival in this State is Accompanied with a Necessity to Distress its inhabitants. But your Excellency will Judge that a Siege operation Cannot be Carried with-out Great Expenses and Great Means of Transportation- it is with the Greatest Reluctance that I sign any impressing warrant, But I Hope my delicacy in this Matter Will Be such as to Render me Worthy of the Approbation of the State.'[42]

Jefferson replies that expresses have been set up from Richmond to Hampton, and from Richmond to the army before Portsmouth, which are ordered to ride day and night. He says there is no fear of complaint about my impressment powers and only asks that documentation of what is taken must be made.[43]

March 19. I cross the James by boat; I go to General Muhlenburg's militia camp near Sleepy Hole. To my great surprise, no ammunition has arrived there, although it is expected hourly. Most men do not have enough, and some have none.

Muhlenburg moves his men nearer to Portsmouth; we take riflemen and militia who have a few cartridges to reconnoiter the enemy fortifications.[44] We meet Jaegers; we exchange fire. A private is killed, an officer and a private are wounded; I think the enemy lost about twenty, four of whom were taken. We have no more ammunition and decide to postpone our reconnaissance but are pleased at our small success.[45]

I write to Jefferson about our skirmish and the lack of ammunition. I say I believe the supplies from Hoods will not be sufficient even for temporary purposes. I request that immediate measures must be taken to collect flour, live cattle, hard bread and salt meat.[46]

I am still near to Portsmouth when I receive a letter from Major McPherson, written from Hampton on the twentieth, which says that a fleet has anchored within the Capes.[47] Great joy! We all believe it to be Destouches. We frantically start to prepare. Arnold appears to be in much confusion; his vessels seem to fear to venture downriver. Then to our extreme dismay and surprise we discover the ships belong to the enemy and are said to number twelve, including frigates. Some people think they have sailed from Europe, but I believe it is the fleet from Gardner's Bay.[48] I send spies; I will stay here a little longer in the hope that the French fleet will come. Muhlenburg goes back to Suffolk; I request von Steuben to put several articles which have been made ready, out of the enemy's reach.

March 22. I leave camp for Williamsburg.[49] I know the French sailed on the eighth with a favorable wind so either they are still on their way here, or have been defeated by the enemy, or have gone somewhere else.

We receive news that Greene's troops fought with those of Cornwallis on the fifteenth at Guilford Court House, that the honor of keeping the field was not on our side but that the enemy lost more men than we did.

Reports arrive that on the sixteenth, Destouches' eight ships of the line fought with Arbuthnot's eight ships of the line off the Virginia Capes. Since the British fleet has returned and evidently think they are safe in the Bay, there must be very little hope of seeing the French flag in Hampton Road.[50] Our disappointment is immense. The British again control the Chesapeake and it is obvious our cooperation with the French fleet has failed.

March 24. The enemy ships go out to sea at about eleven o'clock. Later we hear a furious cannonading lasting three hours. Next day, to our great disappointment, they appear with transport ships, and I believe what sounded like cannon was really thunder.[51] I must go back to Annapolis. There is now no chance of success against Arnold although never has an operation been more ready on our part nor conquest more certain.[52]

"Contain Arnold within his works on both sides of the Dismal Swamp," I order. [53]

My detachment is composed of the flower of each regiment which Washington has ordered me to march back as soon as we lose naval superiority. I therefore send an order to my officers at Annapolis to move, either at the first notice I will send, or upon a letter from Washington, which my aide-de-camp has been instructed to open.

A request arrives from Greene for me to move south with my troops, following his defeat at Guilford Court House. The Virginia Council has, however, unfortunately decided that their militiamen and their arms ought to remain in their own state. I leave von Steuben to inform Greene's aide, Colonel Morris, and on Wednesday, March 28, start back to Maryland.[54]

I deviate from my route. On the twenty-ninth, I go to Fredericksburg and stop at Mrs. Mary Washington's house at the corner of Lewis and Charles Streets. An elderly lady, whose eyes and bearing remind me very much of her son, I am transported by joy to see her. For her part, she seems somewhat bemused at my visit; we drink tea together and she entertains me delightfully. Next day, I set off towards Mount Vernon, the home of my general.

On the thirty-first I ride up the drive, in delight at seeing the handsome, two-story building, the Potomac just beyond. There are a few trees, but they are not large, and the grounds do not appear fertile. I stop at the house, which has a slight air of decay and neglect; welcome refreshments are given to me, but I can only stay a short time, in great disappointment that my duty and my anxiety to execute my orders mean I am not able to visit Mr. Custis. In the evening I ride several hours through the dark Virginian countryside to make up for my detour.[55]

April 2. I reach Annapolis. I write to Jefferson: 'On the point of setting out for the Grand Army, I will at least do my best for the Relief of the Troops destined to the defence of the Southern States- I hear that General Greene is in Want of ammunition and will send on four field pieces to Him, with twelve hundred Rounds and Near Hundred thousand Cartridges.- Governor Lee Has promised to Have them forwarded to Fredericksburg, where I hope they will meet Horses and Waggons provided By Your Excellency's orders.'[56]

I find there are not enough wagons and horses to carry our supplies, and no boats to cross over the ferries so I and my troops will have to go by sea, a somewhat difficult situation as two small English vessels, the *Hope* with twenty guns and the *General Monk* with eighteen, are blockading the harbor and townspeople want us to remain here.

Lieutenant Colonel Stevens proposes that two merchant sloops should be armed, one with two eighteen-pound cannon, the other with more cannon and crewed by volunteers. They would then advance towards the enemy ships. I accept his proposal.

April 5.[57] Commodore Nicholson takes out the two vessels and challenges the *General Monk* and the *Hope*. They both retreat, whether from the sound of the eighteen-pounders or from the fear of being boarded, I do not know. My troops embark onto about ninety boats in the dark of night. I go in the rear with the sloop and other craft, and we set off in a favorable wind and tide towards the Elk River.

As we come up the Bay two men come on board my vessel[58]. I suspect they are spies and we therefore pretend to be British. They appear cautious, but McPherson, who used to be a lieutenant and adjutant in the British army, describes some army acquaintances of theirs and they believe us to be the enemy. They say they went to the *Hope* and have supplied the enemy with provisions; they offer to pilot us to a sloop loaded with flour. McPherson and six soldiers go with one man to secure the sloop. As soon as they leave, I clap the other into irons. When the second returns, I will have them tried and hanged as spies.[59]

We reach Head of Elk about eleven in the morning of the seventh.[60] McPherson was meant to land in Gun Powder Creek, but I am uneasy as there is no news from him. Many letters are waiting for me from France, as well as two from Washington. In the first letter he laments the miscarriage of an enterprise which had promised so well for success but that we must console ourselves with the thought we have done everything practicable to accomplish it. However, in the second, written a day later, on the sixth, he orders me to go south with my men:

> To reinforce General Greene as speedily as possible, more especially as there can be little doubt but that the detachment under General Phillips, if not part of that now under the command of Arnold, will ultimately join, or in some degree, cooperate with Lord Cornwallis…Your being already three hundred miles advanced, which is nearly halfway, is the reason which operates against any which can be offered in favour of marching that detachment back. You will therefore, immediately, at the receipt of this, turn the detachment to the southward. Inform General Greene that you are upon your march to join him…It will be well to advise Governor Jefferson of your intended march through the state of Virginia. [61]

His orders surprise me. My heart sinks. It would have been far better if I had remained in Annapolis. We have travelled northwards for nothing, and I greatly fear I will miss out on the likely battle of New York.

"We need clothes. In the north it would be easier to obtain them. The air in the south is unhealthy. We are afraid of the ague and the fever. You haven't much hair and you don't wear a wig. The sun could kill you," say my officers.

I write to Washington that our preparations to depart from Annapolis will not be rapid, that there is an immense difficulty in obtaining wagons and horses, no boats to cross over the ferries and that the state wishes us to remain as long as possible as they fear the enemy ships. I tell him that if I had been still at Annapolis, or upon the road by land, his commands would have been immediately obeyed, but now I will need to stay here several days to prepare, and so will be able to receive another letter from him telling me what to do. 'The troops I have with me being taken from every northern regiment have often (tho' without mentionning it) been very uneasy at the idea of joining the Southern Army. They want clothes, shoes particularly, they expect to receive cloathes and money from their States. This would be a great disappointment for both officers and men. Both thought at first they were sent out for a few days and provided themselves accordingly; both came chearfully to this expedition but both have had already their fears at the idea of going to the southward. They will certainly obey, but they will be unhappy, and some will desert.'

I suggest that if the Jersey Line were to join the detachment of their troops at this place it would hardly make any difference as we have been but five days coming from Morristown to Head of Elk. I say my considerations are not influenced by personal motives: 'I should most certainly prefer to be in a situation to attak Newyork, nor should I like, in an operation against New York to see you deprived of the New England Light Infantry, but I think with you, that these motives are not to influence our determination if this is the best way to help General Greene. From the letters I have received from my friends Marquis de Castries and Count de Vergennes I am assured that we shall soon get an answer to our propositions against Newyork and am strongly led to hope that having a naval superiority the army under your immediate command will not remain inactive...I will use my best endeavours to be ready to move either way as soon as possible.'[62]

I wait to see what Washington will reply. Has he given up the idea of attacking New York, which he has considered the main objective to attack for three years? It is very possible French ships and money will soon arrive, in which case New York is where the battle will most likely be. I am desperate to command part of the advance guard there; I do not wish to confine myself to a small group of light infantry which might only have a few skirmishes.

Reports from Greene suggest that although Cornwallis was victorious at Guilford Court House, it was a very costly victory for him. He is now retreating, and Greene is following.

April 9. I dine on board the *Hermione*.[63]

"We will probably arrive at Rhode Island the day after tomorrow," says Captain de La Touche. "When we return, I believe my uncle, Monsieur de La Touche Treville, who I think will command the squadron of the second division, and over whom I can tell you in confidence I have a great influence, will certainly wish to take possession of the harbor at New York and send a force up the North River."

"There are great difficulties transporting our troops," I tell him.

"After I arrive tomorrow at Rhode Island I believe the *Eveillé* and four frigates will be offered to you to transport twelve hundred men to any part of the continent General Washington wishes, unless unforeseen obstacles occur," he says.

I say farewell and leave the *Hermione* already under sail. I write to Washington and report what was said.[64] I suggest that as our march will take forty days and that desertion and sickness, as well as the heat of the sun, will much reduce our numbers, it might be a good idea to convey the men by the ships mentioned by de La Touche, as well as by the two frigates at Philadelphia.

To my great disappointment, the French fleet does not appear. If the project has not been abandoned, they must be expected any minute. I unburden myself to Hamilton, who has perhaps already left Washington and headquarters although I and others have tried to persuade him against doing so:

Had the french fleet come in Arnold was ours. The More Certain it was, the Greater My Disappointment Has Been...After a March of forty days, we will arrive at a time when the Heat of the Season will put an end to operations. This detachement is So circumstanced as to make it very inconvenient for officers and men to proceed. Before we arrive we Will perhaps Be Reduced to five or six hundred men. There will Be no Light Infantry formed no attak Against New York None of those things which Had Flattered My Mind. If a Corps is Sent to the Southward By land it ought to have been the Jersay Line. But if we weaken ourselves Newyork will Be out of the question.' I suggest to him that the Eveillé and the frigates might carry one thousand five hundred men to wherever Washington wishes. I finish unhappily, 'If this matter was So Managed we Can't be so far gone But that we Might Return. Adieu, write me often and long letters. It is probable I will be in the southern wilderness until the end of the War. [65]

All I can hope for is that Washington has met Rochambeau and they have agreed to fight in the south. However, I must obey the commands of my general. On the tenth, I write to La Luzerne:

I expect you know I am going to the south; our soldiers and officers are not pleased; we have no money, no clothes, no shoes, no shirts, and in a few days we shall be making our meals on green peaches; our feet are cut for lack of shoes and our hands have scabies for lack of linen; When I say 'we' I mean it for I think my baggage has been stolen. However, all this will not stop us marching. [66]

Spies tell me the British are dressed in rags and do not have food, but they are probably not as raggedly dressed as my men. I order one officer per battalion, and one from the Jersey Line, to go back to the army to obtain clothes for themselves and the rest of the corps. I send Colonel Barber to Philadelphia with a letter to the Board of War saying what we lack and requesting tents, overalls, shirts, shoes and other articles.[67] We do not have enough wagons and teams and I issue orders to impress. In the night seven men desert.[68]

I receive many letters which report burnings and acts of cruelty by the enemy in the Bay. The governor of the Council of Maryland writes that enemy ships are sailing back up the Potomac and intend to burn Alexandria; he fears for Baltimore and Annapolis. Tomorrow we will march hard in that direction, but I know that defending these rivers is about as easy as defending the rivers on the moon. The governor says that wagons and horses will be collected at Baltimore; fine cattle and flour will be provided; the stores that were left at the Indian landing are now ten miles from Alexandria and on our route and the lieutenant of Harford County has been ordered to Gun Powder Creek to ask about Major McPherson.[69]

Men are deserting; eight from the Massachusetts regiment alone deserted in the night [70] which was very stormy, torrential rain falling in sheets. In the morning, the roads are impassable. I delay our marching.

Chapter 29

The Susquehanna is my Rubicon

April 12. At nine o'clock,[1] we set off, a day later than I had promised Washington.[2] The roads are again mired in mud but as many men do not possess shoes and stockings, they are not greatly impeded by becoming wet. They halt a short time at Charleston, then march a further six miles and encamp in a wood one mile north of the Susquehanna River, not far from the ferry.[3] They do not want to march. "The climate in the south is unwholesome. The climate in Carolina is mortal to us," they say.

The Susquehanna is my Rubicon.[4] Once I am on the far bank my hopes of fighting in the north have gone and I constantly wonder why Washington has decided not to attack New York.

The wind is gusting strongly, so I order the men across the river first, to Harmer's Town. It seems impossible to be able to take over the wagons; I will have to impress on the other side.

A letter arrives from Washington; he says that whether General Phillips remains in Virginia or goes further south, he must be opposed by a force more substantial than militia alone and that I must therefore open a communication with General Greene. I must tell him of the numbers, situation and probable views of the enemy in Virginia and take his directions as to whether I should march forward to join him, or whether I should remain there to keep a watch on General Phillips if he has formed a junction with Arnold at Portsmouth.[5]

I also receive a letter from Greene. He says that fatal consequences will ensue if I go north with my detachment. The situation is critical in the southern states, and he wishes me to march my force south by Alexandria and Fredericksburg to Richmond from where I can cooperate either with him or with the militia in the lower country. He is determined to carry the war into South Carolina to prevent Cornwallis forming a junction with Arnold. If I follow him in support, we might perhaps do harm to Arnold, particularly if Wayne brings the Pennsylvanians.[6]

April 13. McPherson is now back, he and the six soldiers having spent two days and one night pretending to be the enemy. He discovered that a trade of flour has been carried on from the west shore of Maryland and has saved eight hundred barrels of flour from being sold to the British. A court martial is held at ten in the morning to try three men, two of whom are the Tories trying to sell provisions to the enemy.[7] Eight men desert from the Massachusetts battalion.

It is reported that the second division has arrived off the Delaware Capes with nine ships of the line. I write to Washington that if the news is correct, then he will have a brilliant campaign in the north.[8]

On the fourteenth, I write again to Washington, my thoughts still very much on this subject: 'My Heart and every faculty of My Mind Have Been these last Years so much Concerned in the plan of an Expedition against New York'. I am in the middle of my letter when I learn that nine men deserted last night from the Rhode Island battalion. They were their best men, who had made many campaigns and who were never suspected.[9] I feel that dissatisfaction and desertion are greater evils than any other we have to fear. I resume my letter and say that the idea of remaining in the southern states appear intolerable to the men who are amazingly averse to the climate and the people, and who declare they would prefer to have a hundred lashes than to go south. 'I shall do my best, but if this disposition lasts, I am Afraid we will be reduced lower than I dare express.' [10]

I write to La Luzerne that I am going to pursue General Phillips but dare not hope to catch him.[11] I hang Walter Picket, a spy; I also hang a captured deserter and dismiss a second who is a good soldier. It has been a difficult and dangerous crossing of the river for the men, so they are now not so likely to return. I attempt to further halt desertions by announcing in General Orders that our detachment is intended to fight an enemy far superior in number, under difficulties of every sort. I say that the general is determined to do this but that he will not force any soldier who might abandon him to join this expedition, that it is not necessary for the soldier to commit the crime of desertion, he can just apply for a pass to join his regiment in the north in winter quarters.[12]

I have gambled on the men's reaction and am rewarded. Desertions cease. No one asks for a pass and one man with an injured leg even goes so far as to hire a cart to carry him, so he is not left behind.[13]

I have recently learned of a letter from Washington which has been making a great noise at Philadelphia, criticizing the French for Arnold not having been captured; I write to him to say I am also greatly pained by it and that I could have been helpful with my position with both sides of the alliance. I say that La Luzerne has told me the French army has offered to go to North River, that the second division might act against New York, and that I was right in telling him that the court truly wanted their troops to be active. I say I would have sent him La Luzerne's letter if it had not been that it was too expressive of his grief for my departure owing to his friendship for me and the idea the court may have of my services in a cooperation between the French and Americans. I also mention for the first time that I know about his falling out with Hamilton and 'from that moment exerted every means in my power to prevent a separation which I knew was not agreable to Your Excellency.'[14]

I write to Hamilton:

You are So Sensible a fellow that You Can Certainly explain to me What is the Matter that Newyork is Given up-that our letters to France Go for Nothing. This last Matter Gives Great Uneasiness to the Minister of France. All this is not Comprehensible for me who Having Been Long from Head Quarters Have lost the Course of Intelligences.

Have You left the family, My dear Sir? I Suppose So, but from Love to the General for whom you know My affection Ardently wish it was not the Case. Many Many Reasons Conspire to this desire of Mine- But if You do Leave it, and if I go to Exile, Come and Partake it with me. [15]

I try and forget my disappointment. I have crossed my Rubicon. I must now give all my energy to fight the enemy in Maryland and Virginia and will attempt to obtain shoes and clothes at Baltimore. Desertions are lessening. I ride on ahead. Later in the day I reach Baltimore.[16] My men march to Bush Town and encamp in a wood west of the town.

On the sixteenth, my men march again and encamp in woods five miles north of the city. McHenry is president of the Baltimore Board of War and has influence with the merchants. He helps me to obtain credit for two thousand pounds which I will repay in two years' when French law allows me to better dispose of my estate or before then if the French court adds this sum to any loan Congress has obtained from it. The money will procure some shirts, linen overalls, shoes, a few hats and some blankets.[17] I attend a ball in my honor; the ladies agree to make shirts, which will be sent after me, whilst the tailors of the detachment will make overalls.

Von Steuben writes that General William Phillips has either one thousand five hundred, or two thousand men at Portsmouth, which with Arnold's force makes about two thousand five hundred men. Reducing it to two thousand men which Phillips might have, it is essential that my detachment should advance as fast as possible. I therefore intend to leave our tents, the sick, two howitzers and the artillery, which has not yet moved more than a few miles, and they will all follow as fast as possible.[18] I write to Greene that my troops only envisage going as far as Virginia and any further march south would have real and imaginary consequences. I tell him that, however, I am far from throwing the least objection to our marching southerly if a junction of our forces appears to him to be useful. I say that General Phillips' battery at Minden having killed my father, 'I would have no objection to contract the latitude of his plans.' [19] My star appears to be shining again. Unfortunately, nine men drown while crossing the ferry.

The men encamp one mile west of the landing.[20] I write to Jefferson that I will advance by rapid, forced marches to come to the aid of his state and that I will therefore need to impress a great number of wagons and horses, a measure I have reluctantly adopted, but that uncommon dangers require uncommon remedies. I also ask for any intelligence of Cornwallis and Phillips.[21]

I write to Washington on the eighteenth: 'Every one of my letters has been written upon such a lamentable tone but I am now happy to give you a pleasanter prospect.' I tell him about my address to the men, which has resulted in less desertions, and that today I am hanging one deserter and dismissing another because he is an excellent soldier. I tell him of my success in obtaining a loan and therefore able to buy some necessary items and that I will make a quick, forced march with wagons and horses to Fredericksburg and Richmond in order to disturb the calculations of the enemy.[22]

On the nineteenth, I rejoin my men encamped at Elk Ridge.[23] It is again raining heavily, evidently usual at this time of year, and it is not possible to set off. I send an aide-de-camp ahead to Alexandria to apply to the civil authority for wagons when we reach there.

April 20. At eight in the morning, the men begin to march, leaving the tents and heavy baggage on the ground. Colonel Barber's battalion and half of Gimat's ride in the wagons, the other half on foot. We travel sixteen miles; we halt about an hour for the troops to refresh themselves. Then the other half of Gimat's battalion and half of Vose's ride in the wagons, the men delighted with this novel way of proceeding. We travel about twelve miles and arrive at seven o'clock at Bladensburg where the troops are quartered in houses.[24]

Next day, at seven o'clock the men march again. We halt for a short time at Georgetown before crossing the Potomac into Virginia. We march again and just as the sun is setting reach Alexandria, quartering the men again in houses. I find I cannot obtain a single wagon although I had already dispatched my aide on ahead to ask for help. I therefore have no choice; I send my aide, a Virginian, with non-commissioned officers to impress.

I write to Jefferson:

In our Absolute want of Shoes and Cloathes of Every kind it is Impossible for the Men to Make Such rapid Marches Unless we Have An Extraordinary Help of Horses and Wagons. This Method I knew to Be Bigg with Difficulties-But Every letter Urging the Necessity of our Going to the South ward, representing the Vast and Immediate Danger which threatens this State, I Have flattered Myself that Her Inhabitants Could not Deny us the Means of Advancing to their Defense. And Have Been Encouraged by this Idea that in the whole Detachement there is not one Soldier But who Sacrifices more in this Expedition than Would Be the very Loss of the Articles which we Borrow for two or three days...May I Beg Leave to Request Your Excellency that orders be given for the getting of Provisions at Richmond. Backed Bread, fresh and Salt Meat, with a Quantity of Rum will Be Necessary. We are So Entirely Destitute of Shoes that Unless a Large Number of them is Collected the feet of our Men will Be So sore as To Make it Impossible for them to Advance...I Request Your Excellency to Be Convinced that My Respect for the Rights and Convenience of the Citizens Cannot be Equalled But By My Zeal to forward Every Means of Securing their Freedom and that My Happiness will Be Compleat if our Services may be Useful to the State of Virginia...[25]

I also write to George Augustine Washington at Fredericksburg and ask him to take measures to collect cattle, rum and baked bread in order to provide provisions for fifteen hundred men and officers for four or five days. Shoes would also be very welcome. I tell him I will need to impress about thirty wagons and three hundred riding horses, and it would be helpful if he could have some idea of where I could obtain them, although I wish him to keep quiet about my intention.[26] I send Colonel Barber to Philadelphia to ask for more supplies; I write again to request supplies from Congress.

Reports arrive; Phillips is advancing towards Richmond. Other reports say British ships have sailed up the Potomac and have burned and looted plantations. I need to move quickly. On April 12 a raiding party from the *Savage* landed at Mount Vernon, and Lund Washington, Washington's nephew and manager, agreed to give the enemy provisions to stop the estate from being destroyed and the house burnt. I am horrified at this. Horrified and ashamed. I know what Washington's reaction will be.

I receive a letter from Washington sent on the fourteenth. He repeats that there are things he would like to tell me but dare not confide to paper; he also says that following his conversations with Mr. de ------ the enterprise against ------ is unlikely, and would, in any case, be a long time off.[27] A letter from Hamilton writes the same.

'What the devil can he have told them? I would like you to explain this enigma to me,' I write to La Luzerne.[28]

April 23. The men march at six o'clock in the rain. They halt at Colchester.[29] I write confidentially to Washington to say what happened at Mount Vernon: 'When the Ennemy Came to your House Many Negroes deserted to them. This piece of news did not affect me much as I little Value property,[30] But You Cannot Conceive How Unhappy I Have Been to Hear that Mr. Lund Washington Went On Board the Ennemy's vessels and Consented to give them provisions.'

Next day, the men begin to march at six o'clock along roads oozing with mud from the rain. Twelve miles later, they halt at a small town called Dumfries and quarter in houses. They set off at dawn, unfortunately without wagons and in rapidly increasing heat. We find that local people send away their wagons and horses to prevent our taking them. Twenty-six miles of marching on hot, dusty roads brings us to the Rappahannock. We cross. By four in the afternoon, we reach Fredericksburg,[31] the men now very fatigued. The lack of wagons means we will not have our ammunition until tomorrow.

I receive a letter from von Steuben who informs me that the preparations of the enemy at Portsmouth indicate an intention of operating offensively and as the number of militiamen there are too small to offer the least resistance, he has therefore removed public stores some distance into the countryside. Fourteen ships arrived at Jamestown on the twentieth, but he does not know how many troops are on board or judge their intentions with any certainty. Many people have already left Richmond and Petersburg and the government is preparing to leave Richmond.[32]

I receive a letter from Jefferson. He had already written on the twenty-third that he believes the war in Virginia to be of secondary consequence to that happening in North and South Carolina and therefore intends to send their new militia levies to aid General Greene.[33] This time he writes that the British landed near Petersburg and are advancing there.[34] I reply to him that we would have advanced more rapidly if people had given us aid, but that 'the difficulties we Meet with on the Road do not Surprise me as in our Circumstances they Must Be Expected. When we Are not able to do what we wish, we Must do what we Can.' I say that artillery, baggage, and spare ammunition will follow but in the present emergency I cannot think of waiting for them, that however unprovided for is my detachment I believe its arrival at Richmond will be of great service and that as soon as I have arranged everything for the detachment to march, I will come quickly towards Richmond to discover more about the situation. I suggest it is better not to risk the militia in a general engagement until we arrive, but that they can harass the enemy. I say I hope tomorrow evening to be at Bowling Green or Hanover Court House, that I would like some horsemen to be there, if possible, to escort us, and that my journey needs to be kept secret.[35] I also reply to von Steuben. I say I hope to hear from him at Richmond and request his opinion on the practicality of our forming a junction and my crossing James River if circumstances require it.[36]

April 26. The men rest. They wash their clothes and clean their arms. Next morning it is again raining heavily, the roads stream with mud, but they make a forced march of twenty-three miles to Bowling Green. In the evening, at the tavern, I meet Captain William North, von Steuben's aide.

"The enemy landed at City Point, on the south side of the James, with about three thousand men and are by now at Petersburg. Baron von Steuben skirmished with them, and Innis and his militia are on this side of the James River, lower down than Richmond. The enemy are probably intending to go to Richmond"[37]

I write to Weedon and ask that the artillery being brought by Major Galvan should be hurried towards us. I request thirty horsemen from Fredericksburg as I need fifty men to escort me to Richmond in advance of my troops as I believe there are no armed militia there and Jefferson and I will be dangerously exposed.[38] I also write to Jefferson and ask that every boat in the river should be collected above the falls in order to secure a means of communication, and whether it would be possible to fix some heavy cannon on small craft in order to make floating batteries. I say I hope to be with him either this evening or tomorrow morning and would he please write to me on the road to inform me of what is happening.[39]

April 28. Saturday. The men march at sunrise. I set off ahead and ride twenty-four miles to Hanover Court House, about twenty miles from Richmond, which I hope to reach tomorrow. I expect my men in a few hours. They will camp in the woods; their weapons will be inspected, and new cartridges given out.

On Sunday morning I ride into the large town of Richmond, situated on the left bank near the falls of the James, half of it on a high hill, the rest on the slope and at its bottom. The enemy is not yet here. It is quiet, guarded only by General Nelson with a corps of militia.[40]

I meet Thomas Jefferson, the author of the Declaration of Independence, a man of slender build, somewhat taller than I am, with hazel eyes, a pale complexion and red hair, like mine. He speaks quietly, his manner reserved. He is not a military man.

To my intense happiness, my men march into the town in the rapidly darkening evening. They have arrived before the British. I post them on Shockoe Hill at the east end of the town, quartering them in the ropeworks.

In the morning, we can see the enemy troops across the river at Rockett's Landing in Manchester. If we had reached Richmond a day later, it would have been captured as orders to attack it had already been given. About six hundred enemy soldiers cross in boats. Several of Major Nelson's militia dragoons attack them; they rush back into the boats and hurriedly recross the river. Flames and smoke begin to rise from buildings over there; the air is pungent with the strong smell of tobacco, as though large quantities are burning. I collect our force to receive the enemy; I send an urgent message to von Steuben to come here. I wait impatiently. In the night the British retreat to Osborne's.[41]

I receive three letters from Phillips, the last two from Osborne's. I send the first to von Steuben as it is more relevant to him. The other two I find strange. Phillips complains that Americans have fired on his soldiers from a flag of truce vessel. He wants me to give him the men who fired from the vessel and to publicly disavow what they have done. His second letter accuses Americans of imprisoning and mistreating people because they had accepted protection from the British, and he says that he would send to Petersburg and chastise the illiberal persecutors of innocent people. He also threatens to make the shores of the James River an example of terror to the rest of Virginia if anyone is executed because they are considered a spy or a friend to the British government. He believes me to be a gentleman of liberal principles and hopes I 'will not countenance, still less permit, to be carried into execution the barbarous spirit, which seems to prevail in the Councils of the present civil power of this colony.'[42]

I know Phillips was captured at Saratoga and only exchanged in October 1780, so I write back: 'From the beginning of this war which you observe is an unfortunate one to Great Britain, the proceedings of the British Troops have been hitherto so far from evincing benevolence of dispositions, that your long absence from the Scene of action is the only way I have to account for your penegeries.' I tell him that the charge against a flag of truce vessel will be strictly inquired into, and if the report made to him is better grounded than the contrary one I have received, he will receive every redress. This is, however, the only part of his letters which I consider deserves an answer. 'Such articles as the requiring that the Persons of Spies be heald sacred can not certainly be serious…The stile of your letters, Sir, obliges me, to tell you, that should your future favors be wanting in that regard due to the Civil and military authority in the United States, which can not but be construed into a want of respect to the american Nation, I shall not think it consistent with the dignity of an american officer to continue the Correspondence.'[43]

The British retreat down the Hundreds, the neck of land formed by the James and the Appomatox and burn several houses at Warwick. I learn that my swift arrival at Richmond took Phillips by surprise. He expressed his astonishment to an officer on a flag, and Mr. Osborne, who was with him when he reconnoitered the position before making an attack, said he fell into a violent passion and swore vengeance against me and my detachment.[44]

May 1. We hear the enemy has gone from Warwick to Petersburg. Von Steuben and his militia arrive. Between five and six o'clock, the sun still blazing down, they parade with my eight hundred Continentals on a large plain northwest of the town, watched by many local people.

Next day, the men swelter in the heat. "Cut your coats to make it easier to march," I order.

I send Colonel Good and three hundred men to protect a battery and redoubt being constructed at a bend in the river at Hood's between Jamestown and City Point. I send militiamen to harass the enemy's boats and another corps of militiamen under Colonel Innis to march towards Williamsburg. I send an officer to Point Comfort and set up a chain of expresses to find out if the enemy appear to turn towards the Potomac, as I fear that having missed Richmond, Hunter's Iron Works at Fredericksburg, the only support of our operations in the south, will be their next place of attack. [45] I am surprised to have received no order from Greene, but I intend to try and keep Phillips from Cornwallis as far as I can, without the support of ships. If I can with one thousand men oppose three thousand in this state, I think I will be useful to him. He has previously informed me that he wishes to divide the enemy and so I must continue to carry out his intention. I would also prefer him to ask for the Pennsylvanians, whom I do not want here as they would fight with the Jersey and New England troops.[46]

May 3. At dawn, the rest of our troops march about sixteen miles to approximately a mile north of Bottom's Bridge,[47] forty-two miles from Williamsburg, sixty from Fredericksburg. The men encamp in thick pine woods, no one now deserting. In case the enemy appears at the mouth of the Potomac and looks likely to attack Hunter's Iron Works, I tell Weedon to collect about four or five hundred good riflemen, some mounted militia, and any troops which can be armed, although I do not want the men taken from the fields if their labor is necessary there. I say that I can be with him and his men in four days and that he needs to reconnoiter the land and see where the enemy could be best fought. I wish him to impart this information only to Mr. Hunter and Colonel Washington and to have the public stores ready to be moved and everything not immediately needed to be sent to this side of the river.[48]

I write to Washington on the fourth; I tell him what has been happening and how incredibly happy I would be to see him here. He has given me the choice as to whether to return or not, so I reply:

> If you Cooperate with the French against the place you know, I wish to Be at Head Quarters. If some thing is cooperated in Virginia, I will find myself very happily situated. For the present, in case my detachement remains in this State I wish not to leave it as I have a separate and active command tho' it does not promise great glory...It is not only on account of my own situation that I wish the French Fleet may come into the Bay. Should they come even without troops it is ten to one that they will block up Phillips in some rivers and then I answer he is ruined- Had I but ships my situation would be the most agreable in the world...[49]

The sun beats down, the men sweltering in the heat; ticks, mosquitos and midges biting mercilessly. I allow them to rest. Where are the British? We have no idea. Shoes and linen for overalls arrive on the fifth from Baltimore for the non-commissioned officers and soldiers of the light infantry.[50] On the sixth, Major Galvan and his detachment finally reach here with the tents and baggage we left at Elk Ridge, but unfortunately he was not able to obtain horses for the artillery and ammunition wagons. The men erect the tents under the trees. On the seventh, letters arrive which inform me that Phillips landed at Brandon on the south side of James River this morning and is marching with six days' provisions; that Cornwallis, whom I had been assured had sailed for Charlestown, is advancing towards Halifax, on the banks of the Roanoke. I order the troops to march at dawn, without a halt, towards Richmond, the Continentals first, the militia following.

They reach the town at ten o'clock in the morning and quarter again in the rope walks.[51] I write to General Jethro Sumner of the North Carolina militia that it is very important to try and delay the junction of the enemy. I propose to him to annoy the enemy as much as possible, to take down every bridge and seize boats between here and Roanoke and to give me intelligence both of his movements and, if possible, those of Cornwallis. I will send ammunition to him, and some arms, although the last is not very likely.[52]

I write hastily to Wayne: 'Hasten to our relief, my dear sir, and let me hear of you that I may regulate my movements accordingly.' [53] However, unless I am in dire necessity, I shall ask him to carry on south.

"Send the tents and part of the baggage back into the country," I order on the eighth.

At eight in the morning, my Continentals and some militia march from the rope walks; they cross the river to Manchester and set off towards Petersburg, whilst von Steuben remains here to try to obtain more recruits and other requisites. I have, however, forbidden every department to give me anything which may be useful to Greene.

I write to Washington:

> There is no fighting Here Unless you Have a Naval Superiority or an Army Mounted upon Race Horses... now it Appears I will Have Business to transact With two Armies and this is Rather too much....The Bridge at Peters Burg is destroïed, and Unless He Acts with an Uncommon degree of folly He will Be at Halifax Before me. Each of these armies is More than the double Superior to me. We have no Boats, few Militia and less arms. I will try to do for the Best, and Hope to deserve your approbation. Nothing Can attract My Sight from the Supplies and Reinforcements destined to General Greene's army...[54]

My troops quarter at the small village of Osborne, in the enemy's former camp. To my left is Phillips with his army and absolute command of the river, to my right Cornwallis and his army are advancing to swallow me up.[55] Very unfortunately, Major Mitchell and Captain Muir, who went to Petersburg to prepare quarters for my men, have been captured.

I write to La Luzerne:

> I am here in the former camp of my enemies, possessor of the area and of General Phillips's bed but too polite not to give it back to him as soon as he needs it...Everyone says that General Clinton is coming to join the festivity. I am therefore proscribed by that triumvirate, but, not being so elegant as Cicero, it is not my tongue that these gentlemen will cut off....Although my situation is not marvellous, I cannot help smiling at the ridiculous figure we shall cut before the joined forces of these two gentlemen and at how our militia dragoons will look without pistol, sword, saddle, bridle, or boots against the Simcoes and the Tarletons...For the love of God send us Lauzun's hussars.[56]

I want to distract the British from our sending cartridges to North Carolina, so on the tenth I order four guns from Gimat's battalion to bombard the enemy in Petersburg from the north side of the Appomatox, and then to march south to Wilton, a large plantation on the north side of the James. The rest of my detachment marches from Osborne's at one o'clock. They cross the river at Kingsland Ferry, march four miles towards Richmond and halt at Wilton, eight miles below Richmond, where they spend the night in the woods without tents.[57] We need boats desperately. I write to von Steuben and ask for anything that can cross a river; boats, canoes, scows.[58]

Next day, tents arrive; the men pitch them under the trees.[59] On the twelfth, Barber's battalion crosses the river. On the thirteenth, Sunday, at four in the morning, more troops start to cross. First, the cavalry, then two regiments of militia, followed by Gimat's battalion, then a detachment of artillery with two field pieces. At eight o'clock I cross with my staff family. At nine, Vose's battalion with a company of artillery and two field pieces arrive, having covered the retreat of the troops. When it is dark, we recross the river.

I am waiting to hear from Jefferson. Some days ago, I sent Captain Langborne, one of my aides, to him, to ask for four impress warrants for horses, as well as details of the number of militiamen called up, the number of mounted men, and when they might arrive, as well as how many arms are needed.[60] I am not impressed by democracy in action. It works too slowly in such a desperate situation as this. I am also hoping Wayne will arrive with the Pennsylvanians to enable me to perhaps act offensively.

I believe Cornwallis to have two battalions of light infantry and guards, two battalions of Hessians, the Twenty-Third, Thirty-Third, Seventy-First, Forty-Second, Sixty-Fourth and Eighty- Second, Hamilton's and Martin's Corps, and Tarleton's legion.[61] He appears to be marching with extreme rapidity towards Phillips who has about two thousand four hundred men. I have nine hundred Continentals and militia whose numbers vary greatly, more of whom seem to be going off than are coming in, who come without arms and are not used to war.[62]

Jefferson writes on the fourteenth. He encloses the four impress warrants I need and tells me the situation of the militia being called up by each county. He also says Captain Maxwell is building some boats at the shipyard at Chickahominy, some of which will be so light as to be able to be moved on wheels. The General Assembly will meet at Charlottesville and although he was intending to go there this evening, he has now decided to come and see me tomorrow instead. I am grateful for the impress warrants but at the same time having to impress pains me intensely.

I write to Wayne:

Should You arrive before Cornwallis I Hope we May Beat this Army. Should Both armies Be united Your assistance is Indispensable to receive their first Stroke. By Running a Race with Phillips I Reached Richmond Before him. By Coming Here the Same way, You May Baffle Lord Cornwallis's projects of Conquest. I Beg Leave to Recommend that the Baggage Be Left Behind as it will impede Your Movements and a forced march is Necessary for our Relief. [63]

Why do the British not attack? We have no idea.

"General Phillips is gravely ill with a fever and is likely to die," a spy tells me, so this is probably the reason for the enemy's lack of action.

An officer arrives with a passport and letters from General Arnold; I ask him to come to my quarters.

"Is Phillips dead yet?" I enquire.

"No," he replies.

"Then I will not receive a letter dated headquarters, addressed to the commanding officer of the American troops from General Arnold. It ought to come from the British general chief-in-command. However, if any other officer should write to me then I would have been happy to receive their letters."

The troops move back half a mile from the ferry into woods. At three in the afternoon, they march to Wilton.

The officer returns with the same passport and letter on the sixteenth.

"I am at liberty to say that General Phillips is dead and General Arnold is now commander-in-chief of the British Army in Virginia," he says.

I write a formal letter in which I refuse to correspond with Arnold. In the evening, a man under a flag, sent by General Nelson from the advanced corps, returns from Petersburg with a note from Arnold in which he says he will send our officers and men to the West Indies.[64]

Every department seems in confusion; I busily set about their organization. I appoint Captain Langborne as field quartermaster and Colonel Elliot as field commissary general. I send for Dr. Goodwin Wilson, director of the Continental medical department in Virginia, to help establish a hospital.

I receive a letter from Greene on the seventeenth. He has fought an engagement at Camden against Lord Rawdon who was victorious but had many men killed. He directs that I am to remain in Virginia and take command of the troops, so therefore I have done by necessity what he is now ordering. He wants me to keep the new Virginia and Carolina levies to oppose

Cornwallis. I believe he needs to be reinforced so I write to von Steuben that when he has collected such a number that he wants to march, he must forward them to South Carolina and take new levies under General Sumner, who has not received positive orders to remain in North Carolina. I will, however, keep the dragoon new levies here to be added to Colonel White's detachment, as otherwise our cavalry is so inferior to that of Simcoe and Tarleton that they will overrun the country.[65]

I am not sure that Cornwallis will come with his whole force. He might establish a post at Halifax, one at Petersburg, and then another nearer here. I believe it is Greene whose success and offensive operations will relieve the southern states. I write to Greene; I tell him von Steuben will march immediately and any men left behind will be brought along by an officer. 'The Late Engagement at Camden is like Every action You Risk- No ill consequences in a defeat, the Ennemy's Ruin if victorious. I wish I Had abilities, and I wish I Had Circumstances that Could admit of Such opportunities- But with an Expectation of Support Both Continental and Militia, I dare not attak a Superior Ennemy on its own grounds. To Speak truth I Become timid in the Same proportion as I Become Independent. Had a Superior officer Been Here, I Could Have proposed Half a dozen of Schemes. I tell him the size of my force- nearly nine hundred Continentals; thirty-four artillerymen; four six-pounders and two howitzers; two militia brigades under Generals Muhlenburg and Nelson, comprising one thousand two hundred to one thousand five hundred; the Horse and fifty infantry under Major McPherson and some militia under Major Call.[66] However, the British cavalry force is more than ten times our number and led by experienced officers such as Tarleton, whilst our militia is badly armed and constantly coming and going so that I do not know how many there are.[67]

Von Steuben arrives and will leave on the nineteenth to march south to join Greene. On the twentieth, to my disappointment, Cornwallis reaches Petersburg, his army joining with that of Arnold, Cornwallis now commanding the whole army. I believe General Leslie and General O'Hara are with him and about four thousand negro men and women trail behind. There is no doubt Cornwallis will begin offensive operations and I decide to move my men to Richmond.

At two o'clock they enact a sham fight with Colonel Vose on the right wing, Major Galvan, on the left. At five o'clock, they take down the tents, then set off to march rapidly to Richmond, now a ghost town as the inhabitants have fled fearing the approach of the British.

Where are Wayne and the Pennsylvanians? Where is the battalion of Maryland recruits? I had thought Daniel Morgan had gone to the help of Greene but discover he has not. I write to him to request his assistance 'with the freedom of an old, affectionate friend.' I tell him the enemy have complete control of the water, that we have not one hundred Riflemen, and greatly need arms.[68] I write to Governor Lee of Maryland for militia.[69] I write again to La Luzerne:

> For the love of God let me know what has become of the Pennsylvanians. They should have crossed the Potomac ahead of me and if we had taken as long as they have, the British would be in possession of all of Virginia. Their junction with us would make our little army a little more respectable. We would be beaten but at least we would be beaten decently...Lauzun's Legion would be of immense use to us...Use your influence to get them for us and if the Pennsylvanians have not yet left, advise them to start. [70]

To my not very great surprise, I hear the Virginians are complaining about my lack of action.
"Why has he stayed north of the river while the enemy is on the south bank? People here do not like people they cannot understand as well as they used to. Deserters, British, cringing Dutchmen and busy little Frenchmen swarm about Headquarters."[71]

Von Steuben is extremely unpopular, partly from his disputes with the Virginia field officers about his arrangements for the Virginia Line in Virginia, and I am not displeased he is leaving.[72] The hatred of Virginians towards him is truly hurtful to the cause.[73]

I write to Noailles and tell him about my activities here. I say that until new orders arrive, I am destined to command in this state, and cannot understand what has become of the Pennsylvania detachment: 'On their arrival we shall be in a position to be beaten more decently but now we can only run. When the enemy marches here I shall try, however, to fire a few shots, but without engaging to the point of making the retreat too murderous, considering that with militiamen a retreat would soon become a rout, and loss of arms is irreparable in Virginia.' If he writes to France I ask him to say that 'your poor brother is devilishly busy getting thrashed.' I ask him to give Rochambeau my news as I very much want him to approve my conduct. I also mention nastiness being made to someone I love and if he writes to Paris can he let me know if it is spoken of as a joke or if it is a case of serious malice.[74]

A letter arrives from Weedon. 'General Wayne had not marched from Little York the fourteenth but was to set out in two days.'[75] Finally, on the twenty-fourth, I hear from Wayne [76] who wrote on the nineteenth from Yorktown that his troops will set off in four days and march as quickly as possible. He does not give any reasons for the delay and gives no mention of how many men. I hear that there had been some difficulty for their coming which was overcome by an order from Washington. We will therefore need to take to our heels.[77]

"Move all public stores and private property up to Point of Fork," I order. I will not risk the troops for a few houses, most of which are empty. We will only skirmish with the enemy.

I learn that at nine o'clock this morning, the British army marched from Petersburg to City Point and destroyed the bridge they had built over the Appomattox.

I write to Washington:

Had I followed the first Impulsion of My temper, I would Have Risked Some thing More- But I Have Been Guarding Against My Own Warmth, and this Consideration that a General defeat which with Such a proportion of Militia Must Be Expected would involve this State and our affairs into Ruin, Has Rendered me Extremely Cautious in My Movement..Was I to fight a Battle I'll Be Cut to pieces, the Militia dispersed, and the Arms lost. Was I to decline fighting the Country would think Herself given up. I am therefore determined to Skarmish, But not to engage too far, and particularly to take Care against their Immense and excellent Body of Horse whom the Militia fear like they would So Many wild Beasts...Was I any ways equal to the Ennemy, I would be extremely Happy in My present Command- But I am not Strong enough even to get Beaten. Governement in this state has no Energy, and Laws Have no force. But I Hope this assembly will put Matters upon a Better footing.[78]

We hear the British are ravaging the country; the advance guard of Tarleton, mounted on race horses, like birds of prey seizing all they meet with.[79] About thirty or forty militiamen are captured in Chesterfield County.[80] Reinforcements of two thousand men have arrived from New York so their troops now number about seven thousand; I have about three thousand, comprising nine hundred Continentals, the rest, militia, and only forty horses. [81]

I keep the men under arms most of the night on the twenty-fifth. A messenger arrives: "The British have crossed the James."

"Abandon Richmond," I order next day. In the late afternoon, the troops march ten miles along the upper road towards Fredericksburg; they halt in woods near Cooper's Creek. The tents are sent back into the country.[82]

The men stay in the woods the whole of the twenty-seventh, the sun blazing down, the trees providing some shade. Cornwallis is still at Westover.[83] I write to Wayne: 'Hasten to our aid, my dear Sir...Preparations are being made on the road to Fredericksburg; that, at all events will be your best way. From Fredericksburg your march will be regulated by our position...let me know the time when you expect to arrive, and the number of men you have got with you.'[84]

The men march next day from two in the morning; at eight they halt near Ground Squirrel Meeting House until four, the weather being extremely hot. I write to Jefferson from Gold Mine Creek and say we will be moving this evening towards Anderson's Bridge and that we are keeping parallel to the enemy, in the upper part of the country. I ask for a warrant to impress over fifty miles, instead of twenty, as we cannot get a single horse and the British have been commandeering all the fine horses and other cavalry accoutrements as the public refuse to remove them. I tell him we have no arms, no riflemen, no cavalry and very few militiamen coming, and I would like him to order more riflemen to join us. I say that Camden has been evacuated.[85] I also write to Weedon and give him the same information on our whereabouts, then ask if he could collect saddles, swords, and other cavalry accoutrements belonging to the public and that if any former Continental dragoon is willing to join us, he will be given a horse and accoutrements.[86] I write again to Wayne:

Lord Cornwallis moved up in the night to Richmond and obliged our advanced parties to retire. We are falling back...am going to take a position 25 miles from Richmond and will move up there as soon as my Lord takes possession of the town. We are too strong for their light army and will be too remote for a sudden attack from their main body. The position is between the James and Anna Rivers, above Allen's Creek Church. It covers our stores and has a short road to Fredericksburg. The place called Allen's Creek Church, or a place four or five miles above, is probably the point where we are to make our junction...from Alexandria to Fredericksburg is out of your way...I think the shortest route will be the best, and as our point of junction, if it changes, cannot but be still higher up, you ought not to come too low down. [87]

The men march again; the sun is setting as they arrive near Ground Squirrel Bridge.[88]

May 29. The enemy repaired Bottom's Bridge and crossed it last night. This morning their dragoons came as far as Hanover Court House. From Gold Mine Creek on the South Anna River I write to Wayne that I think the enemy will go to Fredericksburg, that my position is nearer to that town than they are, and I hope to arrive there before their main body. I tell him we will be marching this evening by Ground Squirrel Bridge to Anderson's Bridge on the north side of the Pamunkey, that we will be parallel to the enemy but will keep to the upper part of the country. I request my dear friend to leave the baggage behind and make forced marches and I shall not lose a moment in advancing my troops towards his.[89]

I write to Weedon:

The Enemy seem to have abandoned their projects against this Army and to have given up the destruction of our Stores. The third point is Fredericksburg...Call out every Militia Man that can be collected and armed...Prevail upon the Gentlemen to mount and equip themselves as volunteer dragoons...I have ordered all the Militia that might be on the road to return to you. The Post, dispatches, Public Waggons etc. are to be directed to proceed towards Anderson's Bridge and meet me on the road. I wish I may be met by some Dragoons, as we have only forty, to do Duty with the Army. The inclosed is to be sent by an Officer with the greatest speed; and this gentleman is to ride untill he has found Genl. Wayne. All public stores ought of course to be taken out of the way; such Articles as can be transported from Mr. Hunter's Works must be immediately sent off; and every Boat and Bridge below the Falls to be immediately destroyed. Horses, Cattle and Waggons upon Mattaponi and Potowmack to be removed as soon as possible...I request you will in my Name acquaint the Generals Mother with this Intelligence and also Mrs. Washington, Mrs. Lewis and others who mean to move.[90]

The only problem I no longer have whilst I try to keep my small army from being attacked by Cornwallis as we march through the tidewater region of Virginia, crossing and recrossing its many streams and rivers, and attempting to join with Wayne and his men, is that the traitor, Arnold, has gout and is on a ship sailing back to New York.

At four o'clock in the afternoon, the men take up their march in a north-westerly direction, the sun still exceedingly hot. Just after sunset, it starts to rain. A severe storm erupts. About nine o'clock, loud thunderclaps boom, one very close. Some of the horses take fright; the militia who are marching at the front think the enemy is nearby. They throw down their arms and run into thick woods on either side of the road, causing chaos in the rest of the column. About an hour and a half later, order is restored. The men march again, the heavy rain drenching them. [91]

The troops march to Seach Town on the thirtieth; they halt until seven o'clock, then march again until one o'clock in the morning to Anderson's Bridge on the North Anna River where they stay the night in a large field.

The men march at two o'clock next morning and halt in a field by a wood. At three o'clock they march again for about three miles and reach Pamonkey River about sunset. Rain pours down heavily all night.

June 1. At seven in the morning, they wade across the river the river at Davenport's Ford;[92] they march to Mattaponi in the rain and arrive about four in the afternoon where they shelter in some houses and barns.[93]

I believe the intention of the enemy is to turn our right flank and to prevent our joining with the Pennsylvanians.[94] I will, therefore, move up towards Orange Court House.

Next day the roads are very muddy; the men march slowly. They reach their tents at five o'clock and pitch them in a field. Weedon is completing the removal of stores from Fredericksburg and hopes he has not displeased me by not moving to join with my force.[95] I send Colonel Fleming with a letter to Wayne: 'The apprehension of Being turned and the Conviction that without you no material opposition Can Be made will perhaps oblige me to Retire Higher up than I am.'[96]

On the third, Colonel Tupper arrives from West Point accompanied by a gentleman from Massachusetts who has brought money for the non-commissioned officers and soldiers of the Line. I write two letters to Greene, the first informing him of the situation here, the second congratulating him on his success at Camden. 'I enjoy your glory because I heartily love you,' I tell him.[97]

The men march at four; at sunset they halt near Wilderness Bridge.

On the fourth, the men march about five miles; they cross the Rapidan, make a march of about twelve miles and halt near a church in Culpeper County, about eight in the evening.[98] Wayne is now not far away; I send my aide, Major Richard Anderson, to him with messages.

Tarleton attacks Charlottesville, where there are only a few militiamen, a move I had already feared.[99] On his way there he had burnt or destroyed twelve wagons of clothing and arms intended for Greene. In the town he destroys valuable stores, including one thousand muskets, four hundred barrels of gunpowder and clothing with which the Virginia Assembly had intended to fight. He captures seven members of the Assembly and the rest escape to Staunton on the west side of the Blue Ridge.[100]

Rain pours down all day of the fifth. My troops remain in camp. Wayne writes that he has divested himself of all the heavy baggage and is advancing rapidly towards Orange Court House.[101] The enemy appear to be retreating towards the James River.[102]

My force march from ten in the morning for about four miles. Heavy rain has swollen the river, but the men manage to cross at Raccoon Ford. They march just one mile and encamp on a hill.[103]

Von Steuben and his militia are at Point of Fork, a spit of land between the Rivanna and the Fluvanna, which join to form the James. Lieutenant Colonel Simcoe approaches on the opposite bank of the Fluvanna and positions his detachment on the north bank, the redcoats in the front, to make it appear they are the advance guard of the whole army of Cornwallis. Von Steuben is deceived; he retreats thirty miles in the night,[104] leaving two thousand five hundred stands of arms, a large quantity of gunpowder, case shot, several casks of salt peter, sulfur and brimstone, nearly six hundred hogsheads of rum and brandy, sail cloth and wagons, a thirteen-inch mortar, five eight-inch howitzers and four nine-pounders to be taken by the enemy.[105]

The men rest on the seventh. They wash their clothes and clean their weapons. Wayne wrote to me yesterday and asked if I could meet with him this afternoon.[106] I write back and suggest that as the weather has improved, if his detachment advances some distance this side of Norman's Ford, and he rides eight or ten miles, there is a house four miles from here where I would be happy to meet him in the evening and where he could stay the night as his men would pass it tomorrow early in the morning.[107]

Wayne writes that because of the deluge of rain, Norman's Ford is impassable, but that as the water level is falling fast, he is sure his detachment will be able to cross today.[108]

My men march on the eighth and camp in woods near Brock's Bridge. Next day, they march at four in the afternoon, leaving behind the tents. After five miles, they halt in the woods.[109] On the tenth, they march from sunrise for about twelve miles and stay in the woods in Louisa County. One thousand two hundred shirts arrive from Baltimore for the non-commissioned officers and soldiers. I write to Washington from Brock's Bridge about Colonel Vose's decision to remain with our army as an action is now expected, which means that Colonel Tupper can no longer have his command. I suggest that if more troops are sent then Colonel Tupper can command them.[110]

To our great joy, Wayne and his Pennsylvanians, consisting of three regiments commanded by Colonel Butler, Colonel Stewart and Colonel Humpton, arrive with six field pieces.[111] They encamp on our left. I now have about eight hundred light infantry, seven hundred Pennsylvanians, fifty dragoons, and about two thousand militiamen, shortly to be less as harvest time will reduce their number, as well as four hundred new levies; I have also received a message that nine hundred of Daniel Morgan's riflemen will soon arrive.

My army is still inferior, although not much smaller, to that of Cornwallis who appears to be going to Albemarle Old Court House, high up the south side of the Fluvanna, to attack our magazines there. [112] Now that Wayne and the Pennsylvanians are here, I can think of making a defense.

June 11. We cross the North Anna at Brock's Bridge and make a forced march south to the South Anna River.[113] The men cross, march a further mile, and encamp around Boswell's Tavern. Cornwallis is encamped some miles below the Point of Fork, so we quickly need to position ourselves between his army and our magazines.[114]

"There is an old, disused road to Mechunk Creek you can use," say Virginia militiamen.

It is overgrown and very narrow, but soldiers manage to slash a way between the thick woods and pines in the night. Early next morning, the troops hurry along the path with great difficulty, the artillery brought along with even greater difficulty. The sun beats down, there is almost no water, the woods are very inhospitable.[115] We reach Three Chopt Road on the west of Mechunk Creek.

I write to Morgan: 'It appears Lord Cornwallis expected us where We did not intend to go and part of His Army moved up to a place called Byrd's Ordinary 13 miles Below this. Our Stores are again Behind us, what fell in their Hands is very trifling, and our junction with the Pennsylvanians Enables us to Some Resistance-But we are Still Much inferior to His lordship.'[116] Thanks to our rapidity, we now enjoy a very suitable position along the creek, near the road going south to Elk Hill and Point of Fork, near the tavern on high ground west of the small wooden bridge. 'To Morrow or the day after, will decide which way He decides to move'.[117]

I write to von Steuben on the thirteenth. I tell him we have joined with the Pennsylvanians and we are again between the enemy and our stores. I tell him not to go to Greene, unless, of course, he has received different orders from him, but to immediately return with his Continentals and militia to join with us.[118] It is difficult to know what Cornwallis is doing, but we believe him to be going towards Richmond; Tarleton's cavalry is on Three Chopt Road, covering Cornwallis's left flank.

June 14. I march my troops down Three Chopt Road east to Byrd's Ordinary through very poor countryside which has hardly any water. We give the appearance of pursuing Cornwallis; I order the riflemen to yell and howl in the woods, their faces smeared with charcoal. I have made them an army of devils and have given them plenary absolution.[119] The men encamp in the woods.

We hear there might be peace before Christmas. I write to La Luzerne on the sixteenth: 'I give my full powers for peace, Monsieur le Chevalier, but on condition that the thirteen states will be independent...It seems to me that the enemy wants to make us think that the southern states belong to them.'[120]

My regular troops are very good but few in number. My first line is composed of Pennsylvanian and light infantry and is commanded by General Wayne. The second line is composed of militia and led by Nelson who has been newly elected governor of Virginia and will return shortly. The riflemen and light troops are under General Muhlenburg. General Weedon is at Fredericksburg to assemble the militia from the region near the Potomac in case there is an alarm. Von Steuben, General Lawson and General Stevens are on their way, although I am not sure where I am going to put von Steuben as he is so unpopular.[121]

I write to Weedon and request he hurries on militia which does not belong to the counties north of the Rappahannock. I also ask for cartridges, lead and shoes as well as vinegar and rum, as the water here is very unhealthy to northern soldiers. [122] We still lack horses and equipment, but there have recently been more supplies as a result of Nelson's efforts although I have to allow it was Jefferson who initiated it.

The troops march at daylight on the seventeenth and halt at two o'clock near Ground Squirrel Creek. I stay at Colonel Dandridge's house near Allen's Creek, about twenty-two miles north-west of Richmond.[123]

Tarleton's legion moves on the eighteenth, towards an advance corps commanded by General Muhlenburg which had gone towards Meadow Bridge. At sunset, I order the light infantry and Pennsylvanians forward; some rascals inform Tarleton; he retreats into the town, but Lieutenant Colonel Mercer captures one of his patrols, the first to be taken since Cornwallis arrived in Virginia.[124]

I write to von Steuben and tell him the enemy is in Richmond and its vicinity. 'We are upon ground in this neighbourhood, where we shall remain for your junction, which I request may be made tomorrow as early as possible.'[125] I also write to Washington and complain of von Steuben leaving the stores at Fork Point to be taken by the enemy, but say I am writing to my friend and so speak more confidentially than I would to my commander-in-chief: 'His conduct is, to me, unintelligible. Every man, woman and child in Virginia is roused against him. They dispute even on his courage, but I cannot believe their assertions. I must, however, confess that he had 500 and odd new levies and some militia, that he was on the other side of a river which the freshet rendered very difficult to be crossed.'[126] I do not know where I am going to put him without offending people as General Lawson and every officer and soldier in the regulars and militia are so exasperated with him. I tell Washington my forces will soon consist of 800 light infantry, 700 Pennsylvanians, 50 dragoons, 900 riflemen, 2000 militia and 400 new levies, the remainder of whom have deserted, and that harvest time will soon deprive us of the greatest part of the militia.[127]

I receive a letter from Commodore Barron, dated the seventeenth, from Warwick. He says that at five o'clock that afternoon, thirty-five enemy ships anchored in the road from the sea, which he takes to be the fleet which sailed from there thirteen days ago. Only four appear to have troops on board.[128]

June 19. Von Steuben and his force march into camp;[129] I disguise my annoyance at his behavior.

Wayne and I want to attack. However, my aide, McHenry, who has recently arrived, argues strongly against it.

"A partial victory would bring small advantage; a partial defeat would be disastrous, whilst a general defeat would undo everything so far gained." [130]

Cornwallis's behavior is puzzling me. Does he fear our growing army? Does he intend to embark some troops for New York? I will continue waiting.

June 21. At Dandridge's we hear that Cornwallis left Richmond this morning and was, by the last accounts, near to Bottom's Bridge. I immediately write to Wayne and order him to pursue them by whatever route they take and say that this would be a good time for a night attack, or, indeed, for any attack circumstances offer.[131] It seems probable Cornwallis is going to Williamsburg. Perhaps we will know tomorrow. This retreat will not read well for him in the newspapers. I write to Greene that: 'I follow and one Would think I pursue Him. But as the fate of the Southern States depends on the preservation of this Army, if My lord chooses to Retreat I Had Rather Loose Some Share of glory than to Risk a defeat By which Virginia would Be Lost. I also mention that I think New York, if not reinforced, will be the object, but the enemy cannot defend it and conquer the southern states. If the enemy prefer the southern states to New York, then the Grand Army will come here. In a few days we will know if the enemy will just have a post in Virginia or 'if the whole force is Bent to the Conquest of the Southern States.' [132]

June 22. My troops advance through Richmond where there appears much distress; smallpox is in the town and a large amount of tobacco had been thrown in the streets and burned.[133]

I make my headquarters at the plantation and water mill of Thomas Prosser in Henrico County on North Run, not far from Brook's Bridge. Wayne will be four miles east of Richmond tonight; Muhlenburg was eight miles above Bottom's Bridge this morning and marched at seven in the morning. I write to von Steuben and tell him to advance his troops seven or eight miles this evening, to march in the morning by Savage's, continuing along the Williamsburg Road until he joins with the others. 'You will perceive the necessity of expedition,' I say.[134] I write to Wayne and tell him to approach the enemy as close as possible and to send Butler with two hundred well-chosen men to join Muhlenburg.[135]

Next day, our army march twenty-two miles to Mr. Savage's house on this side of Bottom's Bridge. Our advance troops are near the rear of the enemy; Cornwallis's troops are fresh; I wonder if he will attempt an action.[136] The troops halt on Sunday to wash themselves and clean their weapons. The enemy march from Kent Court House to Byrd's Ordinary.

June 25. The enemy marched at two o'clock this morning from Byrd's Ordinary. This morning the advance light corps move after them, followed by the Pennsylvania Line. Wayne sends me a letter he wrote at three o'clock in which he says Colonel Butler will advance to the fork of the road leading to James Town and Williamsburg and will try to fall in with Simcoe's men who have been foraging, and bring up the rear and right flank; the Cattle Drove, he calls them.[137] I reply from Beacon's Ordinary; I say I much approve of his plan to relieve Simcoe of his burden; that I think the light infantry had best remain at the Court House; that I will send a post of mounted riflemen on the road on their right flank and another on their left and that I will ride towards the Court House where I expect to hear from him.[138] The light infantry make a rapid march during the night but not all manage to arrive in time for the action; Major McPherson mounts fifty light infantry behind fifty dragoons and attacks Simcoe's force at Spencer's Ordinary, about six miles from Williamsburg. Riflemen under Major Call and Major Willis arrive to support them. The whole British army come out to save Simcoe and retire next morning. 'Our wounded are two Captains, two lieutenants and ten privates; two lieutenants, one Sergeant, six privates killed; one Lieutenant, twelve privates whose fate is not known, and one Sergeant taken. The enemy had about sixty killed, among whom are several officers, and about one hundred wounded. It was a hot action and I gather Lord Cornwallis was heard to express himself vehemently upon the disproportion between his and our killed, which must be attributed to the great skill of our Riflemen.' [139] We continue to press their rear with our light parties.

I think Cornwallis believes our force to be greater than it is, perhaps eight thousand men. He retreats instead of attacking and is now about one hundred miles from where he first started to march his men to Williamsburg. I am careful to try and conceal our true numbers. I do not let the men encamp in a line and as the militiamen are always coming and going it is difficult to estimate how many there are. The enemy has four thousand regulars, eight hundred of whom are mounted; we have no more than one thousand regulars. The old arms at the Point of Fork have been retrieved from the water, as well as the cannon, which are undamaged. [140]

June 27. I am at Mr. Tyree's Plantation, twenty miles north-west of Williamsburg and review the troops in an old field.[141] It is hot and raining but their ardor has been greatly increased since our success. Next day finds me still at Tyree's; I have put all the riflemen under Campbell. Tomorrow, I intend to reconnoiter a position below Byrd's Ordinary.[142] On the twenty-ninth my men make maneuvers near here.

I write to Captain Ewell on the thirtieth to tell him he is appointed commissary of prisoners and must go within the British lines to settle and arrange matters with Cornwallis's commissary of prisoners. Greene and Cornwallis have agreed that the first contingent of American prisoners should embark at Charlestown on or before June 15, and sail for Jamestown, and that the first contingent of British prisoners shall embark on or before the first week of July and sail to the nearest British port. Ewell must attend to this immediately.

I write to Wayne and tell him that the position by Mrs. Gordon's is the nearest one to Williamsburg I would choose and that whatever baggage is not completely necessary must be sent back as we need to travel as light as possible, with comfort. I have also received information that the enemy are receiving new clothes, an event which seldom precedes an embarkation, and I would like intelligence from Williamsburg.[143] He replies that he thinks near Gordon's is not suitable for an encampment and recommends a temporary encampment near the Red House, before taking a post near Byrd's Tavern and sending the riflemen to the church and meeting house near the Chickahominy at the junction of the roads leading to Williamsburg[144].

July 1. Sunday. It is exceedingly hot at Tyree's. Many men are deserting, but it is almost impossible to stop them fleeing through the woods. They say they were only engaged for six weeks and harvest calls them home. The times of many are expiring and you might as well stop the flood tide as to stop militia whose times are out. The riflemen also want to return home for the harvest so I will soon only be left with the Continentals. I have been forced to make three brigades into two, commanded by Generals Stevens and Lawson.

Perhaps it would be best to fight Cornwallis? But if we do and are defeated, to be followed by the loss of Virginia, then there will be new obstacles in the way of the independence of America. However, we have been lucky that we have managed to avoid smallpox by always taking care to avoid infected grounds.

I write to Nelson and ask for an immediate call of new militia and say that I have already asked for a third of the militia of some adjacent counties. I suggest raising a corps of black pioneers, as well as a corps of one hundred black waggoners, as they could be easily obtained and would provide a great service. In addition, I ask if it would be possible to raise two corps of volunteer dragoons, each of one hundred and twenty. I would also like wagons, as well as shoes for the light infantry, and rum.[145]

The troops march. They halt on a large plain near the York River and build huts of leafy branches to give shade from the sun. In the afternoon, they bathe in the water and, sadly, Dr. Downey and two soldiers drown. At eight, they march again; they halt at midnight near the ground they left this morning.[146]

July 4 is the fifth anniversary of the Declaration of Independence. It stops raining by ten o'clock and the whole army fires a feu de joie from right to left, then Major Reed parades them on a plain in front of my quarters. I thank them.[147]

I receive intelligence that Cornwallis evacuated Williamsburg yesterday and has gone to Jamestown Island. It is reported that the light infantry and 76th Regiment will be going to New York with him and that the rest will stay at Portsmouth, but I suspect this is not correct and many must be intended to go south. I will tell General Sumner to hurry to Greene and will also send the Pennsylvanians, Virginia Continentals and, if possible, some militia.[148]

On the fifth, the enemy encamp at Green Spring Plantation, northwest of the town. We advance to Byrd's Tavern, part of our army taking post at Norrell's Mill, about nine miles from the British.[149] We cross the Chickahominy; spies tell me most of the British crossed the James during the night to the island of Jamestown, that the army is posted in an open field fortified by ships, and that the baggage has been sent under a proper escort. Only a narrow causeway about three quarters of a mile wide by two miles long, between Jamestown Island in the south-east and Green Spring Plantation in the north-west, with a creek in the east, flat, tidal marshes in the west, link his position from our advance.

July 6. In the early afternoon, I send Wayne forward with about eight hundred men and three field pieces[150] towards the remaining enemy troops who have not yet crossed the river. Many of the light infantry have not eaten for twenty-four hours and they move back three miles to cook food. I arrive with my men at about five o'clock with the intention of following Wayne to come up to the British rear which has not yet crossed the river. I become suspicious;[151] the riflemen firing from the woods have killed three of the commanders of the post in front of them. Each time the commander is killed he has been replaced. Why is Cornwallis being unusually obstinate? I leave my detachment and gallop to a neck of land in the river to see what is happening.[152] I notice the British baggage has already been taken to the opposite bank and that the men who crossed the river appear more numerous than they really are. I suddenly fear a trap. Is the main army directly in front of us? I return with all haste. I hurriedly send a message to Wayne.

I am too late. He has been caught in an ambush in sparse woodland at the far side of the causeway. He has bravely decided to fight rather than run and be slaughtered. With horror I see his two flanks have given way; there is confusion and panic amongst the soldiers who are fighting at close quarters with the light infantry brigade of guards and two regiments from the British first line, the rest of their army forming the second. Their cavalry is drawn up but do not charge. Our men are in danger of being surrounded; I gallop forward; I go from one group to another, uncaring about my exposed position.

"Retreat to Colonel Vose's and Barber's light infantry," I order.

My horse my groom is riding is killed next to me.[153] We abandon two field pieces because their horses have been killed, as have been the horses of most of the field officers. The Pennsylvania Line retreat in great disorder,[154] but the light infantry of Colonel Vose and Colonel Barber come forward and form a battle line in a field near Green Springs. We retreat, very grateful for the increasing darkness, until we come to a brick house near Green Springs about half a mile away. I let the men rest. After a few hours they resume their march and at about midnight we arrive back at Chickahominy Church, which we had left that morning.

We have saved ourselves. Four sergeants and twenty-four men of Wayne's detachment have been killed, one hundred and eleven wounded or missing.[155] I do not know the militia numbers. We have lost two pieces of cannon as their horses were killed. Cornwallis had about two hundred and fifty killed and wounded.[156]

Next day Cornwallis crosses the river with the rest of his men; I believe he is going to Carolina. I shall either follow him in case he proceeds with his full army, or join with Greene, as circumstances direct.[157] We take possession of the island; I make my headquarters at Ambler's House. Cornwallis has left stores at Williamsburg, as well as wounded American prisoners and some horses. He has now no post whatever on this side of the James.

'There were serious blunders on both sides but since the enemy chose to retreat in the end, it will look well in a gazette,' I later write to Gimat.[158]

I write to Greene and Washington on the eighth and tell them of our engagement with the British. I say to Washington that as he ordered:

I have avoided a general action and when Lord Cornwallis's movements indicated it was against his interest to fight, I have ventured partial engagements. His Lordship seems to have given up the conquest of Virginia. It has been a great secret that our Army was not superior and was most generally inferior to the enemy's numbers, our returns were swelled up as generally militia returns are but we had very few under arms particularly lately and to conceal the lesning of our numbers I was obliged to push on as one who had heartily wish'd a general engagement...[159]

July 9. My troops occupy Williamsburg. I visit the wounded in the hospitals near here and at Jamestown. I write to Noailles: 'This devil Cornwallis is much wiser than the other generals with whom I have dealt. He inspires me with a sincere fear, and his name has greatly troubled my sleep. This campaign is a good school for me. God grant that the public does not pay for my lessons.'[160] I also write to La Luzerne: 'I am mobilizing to follow him. If he passes the boundary of Virginia my task is accomplished and after having reinforced General Greene I will come to greet you in Philadelphia.' I say that I have neglected him of late: 'because when one is twenty-three, has an army to command and Lord Cornwallis to oppose, the time that is left is none too long for sleep.'[161]

July 10. I tell Brigadier General Allen Jones of the North Carolina militia that Cornwallis is now advancing to Carolina, to harass him by destroying bridges and boats and obstructing fords and to do everything possible to prevent or delay his joining with the army fighting Greene.[162]

Next day, Cornwallis is marching towards Petersburg, but I still think part of his army will go to Carolina and another part to New York. If this is the case, the Pennsylvanians and Virginia new levies with some of the cavalry should go to reinforce Greene who has now raised the siege of Ninety-Six. The militia disappear daily and do not exceed one thousand five hundred, even including riflemen. Our situation is critical if Cornwallis finds out and continues to move up. I therefore ask Nelson to move stores, particularly those at Albemarle.[163] North of the James there is no more burning and taking of property and there is praise for me in Virginia. 'A kind of sorcery and magic,' is McHenry's opinion.[164]

The action of the sixth has greatly reduced the number of the Pennsylvania troops; I make the three regiments into two and send officers to recruit.

At sunrise on the thirteenth, the two Pennsylvania regiments and the Virginia new levy regiment under Wayne march for Bottom's Bridge to go to the aid of Greene. They number only eight hundred, which is inadequate. At eight o'clock, the light infantry and militia march. They proceed seven miles, halt and encamp in a field near Long's Bridge on the Chickahominy. [165] I write to Wayne and order him to Four Mile Creek.[166]

I write from Long Bridge to ask Nelson to assemble at least one thousand militia at or near Taylor's Ferry on Roanoke to also march with Wayne. They are not only very necessary to Greene but also to Wayne if the enemy decides to attack him. I tell him our intelligence reports that the enemy is preparing for an embarkation, but they have not yet left Virginia, and if they come our way, we might also need them here.[167]

The light infantry and the militia still with me set off at five in the morning of the fourteenth; the rain falling. They arrive near Bottom's Bridge at nine in the evening.[168]

I am in Richmond on the fifteenth. My men rest at Bottom's Bridge, the heat intense. Intelligence reports that enemy cavalry is high up in the country, either perhaps to destroy stores or to go to South Carolina. I therefore write to Wayne:

> It becomes important that some troops be advanced further south, which may maneuver them lower down, or should the cavalry reinforce Lord Rawdon, form a junction with General Greene. General Morgan with the riflemen, and what horse we can collect, will march tomorrow towards Good's Bridge from Westham, where he will cross the river. I request, you will tomorrow proceed to Chesterfield Court House, and the day following to Good's Bridge. General Morgan will be able to tell you of the enemy's movements. Should a stroke at Col. Tarleton be found practicable, you have my permission to make it in conjunction with General Morgan. But, in case the enemy are going to the Southward, you will be so far on your way to Gen. Greene.[169]

On the sixteenth, two battalions of light infantry and some militia march to Malvern Hill, halfway between Richmond and Williamsburg, where I have chosen a camp site which is the most airy and healthy place this side of the mountains.[170] It also has good water and is near to stores at Albemarle Old Court House and Amelia.

I write to General Morgan and tell him I have attached to his command the corps of Nelson and the Maryland volunteer dragoons. When they are no longer needed, or when Tarleton is out of reach of being attacked, then he must return them to headquarters so that I can dismiss them.[171]

Intelligence reports on the seventeenth that Tarleton has not gone towards Roanoke but was last night thirty-two miles south of Petersburg. I suggest to Morgan that if it is possible for Wayne to attack Tarleton, then to do so. I suggest Morgan and his men fall back to the woods near Chesterfield Court House so that if Wayne is attacked, he can retreat to him.[172]

On the nineteenth I am with my men at Malvern, my headquarters the house of William Randolph. I have a post at Sandy Point to observe the movements of the enemy. Colonel Parker has some militia on the south side of the James River, and I shall have some militia near to Williamsburg, the Gloucester County militia in their own county. Our few boats are at Four Mile Creek.[173] The Executive have promised they will shortly give me five thousand militia-it needs to be four thousand and light infantry, and then if two thousand troops go to New York, and six hundred are at Portsmouth, although we cannot perhaps prevent their plundering, we can perhaps prevent their forming any sort of establishment in Virginia, provided we can form a body of cavalry, a very difficult task unless the slaves cooperate with us, as they have been finding suitable horses for them.

Intelligence reports on the twentieth that Cornwallis often asks when I am returning to the main army, which he declares must soon be the case, so supporting my belief the enemy think Washington intends to attack New York. I am almost in despair. I will miss the battle.

I write to Washington, to my most intimate and confidential friend I say, and not to the commander-in-chief. I mention my original objections to coming south but that when I realized the detachment had to come, I knew no one else would have been able to lead them here against their inclination. I recount what I have achieved:

> My entering this State was happily marked by a service to the Capital...I had the honor to command an army and oppose Lord Cornwallis when incomparably inferior to him, fortune was pleased to preserve us...Cornwallis had the disgrace of a retreat, and this State being recovered, governement properly reestablished, the ennemy are under protection of their works at Portsmouth. It appears an embarkation is taking place, probably destined to Newyork...A prudent officer would do our business here, and the Baron is prudent to the utmost...The command of this army has been a great matter for me. You may end this campaign of mine in the most brilliant manner by the command I may, with *some arrangements*, get in the combined army. The services I may render with respect to the *cooperation* may be a very good reason, and my coming unexpectedly unless I have many senior officers in the way may entitle me to a great command...If I may be of the least good to you, it will make me happy to serve as a volunteer aid de camp to you.[174]

I have been blunt in saying what I want but think it wise to end the letter on a less demanding note.

A young man from Tarleton's Legion, who has been captured, is brought to my quarters and talks to my aides.

"Lord Cornwallis and Colonel Tarleton are going to New York. The light infantry and a regiment of horse are certainly embarking to sail there, and preference is being given to the troops who are most fatigued by the marches through Virginia. The Guards will remain here, but I do not know which other troops."

I write more in my letter to Washington and include these details, as well as saying I will be able to receive a reply from him near to Fredericksburg if we do not need to move towards Portsmouth.

I write a second letter, this time to my commander-in-chief, not to my friend. I tell him I am 'home sick and if I can't go to Head Quarters wish at least to hear from you.' I ask for his opinion concerning the Virginia campaign and detail the present position here. I repeat that it is said the enemy is about to embark a part of the army here for New York and enclose some plans relating to the islands there. I also mention that George has been very sick but has now recovered and is with me.[175]

July 21. At dawn there is a report the enemy is coming up the river. The patrol guard go to find out what is happening.[176]

I write to Wayne and ask to know how he is at Good's Bridge, a place which seems very suitable for the moment as it protects that side of the Appomatox River; I do not wish his men to return here as if they have to march south it would cause them extra fatigue, and if the enemy advance towards him he can easily cross the river at Tukoae.[177]

The patrol guard cannot find out anything about the enemy, so at about nine in the evening, the battalions of Barber and Gimat, with one field piece, march from the encampment. They go about six miles downriver but see nothing.

I write to Nelson on the twenty-second and complain again about our lack of horses. [178] I write to Greene on the twenty-third:

> I am very desirous of Giving You Immediate Support and Have no Notion of waiting for a demand from You. But the Moment I Can do it without too great an Impropriety, I shall divide with you My Continental force. I am only waiting for Intelligences from Below, and in Case the Spoken of Embarkation amounts to Such a Number as will Render the Remainder Manageable, the Moment it passes the Capes General Waine will preceed to Boid's Ferry....You will Be Sensible, my Dear General that Having no order from you, I should Be Blamed to Send a way Half of my Continental force-Untill the Ennemy's intentions are better explained..Should anything be possible Against Portsmouth I would detain the troops unless otherwise ordered- But there are thousand to one against that Supposition. [179]

I write to Nelson and suggest that Richmond or its neighborhood, if smallpox stops, would be a good place of rendezvous for the exchanged prisoners.[180] I write to Wayne to say that my opinion entirely coincides with his, in 'consequence of which I Requested You would remain some time at Goodes Bridge..Should the Ennemy remain in this State we must not Give them the Credit of having out Maneuvred us By a feint Embarkation.'[181]

I write again to Wayne on the twenty-fifth and tell him that for the moment we do not know the enemy's intentions, that I only wish to act upon certainties and so it might be best that our forces move together towards Portsmouth. I say that intercepted letters from Lord George Germain reveal that the conquest of Virginia was the main object of the enemy campaign. I ask him to find out 'who Tarleton Has Been fighting with Below Petersburg- for fighting He Has Been!- and My flag dragoon Saw His wounded. He Adds that on Hearing we Had Crossed the River Tarleton Burnt His Waggons.'[182]

At six o'clock in the evening a soldier from Gimat's battalion is hanged. [183]

I write to Washington on the twenty-sixth that: 'my conjectures had proved true and 49 sails fallen down in Hampton Road, the departure of which I expect to hear every minute.' [184] I have sent men to inform me of the fleet's movement. I also believe there is some cavalry on board and think it very likely the ships with about two thousand five hundred men on board are bound for New York. I write to Congress telling them the same.[185]

July 27. The British are still in Hampton Roads. They have pilots on board for the rivers and Bay, but I cannot be sure they are sailing to New York. If they move up the Potomac I will move there as rapidly as I can and am keeping my forces ready to defend as many parts of Virginia as possible. I write to Weedon to ask him to make sure he has people he can confide in at the mouths of rivers to give him the earliest information.[186]

Next day, the thirty transport ships remain in Hampton Roads although the winds are excellent. It is believed the Light Infantry, the Queen's Rangers, two British regiments and perhaps two German regiments are there, as well as cavalry on eight or ten brigs.[187] The escort is the *Charon* and at least seven frigates. They also have the pilots for the Potomac and the Bay, which might be a feint. My last reports say that the pilots on board know the upper part of the

Chesapeake and that they are destined for Baltimore.[188] I have many people in Portsmouth to watch Cornwallis, but none has been able to slip out.[189]

Wayne is at Good's Bridge on the Appomatox with the Pennsylvanians and Virginia Continentals. Muhlenburg has a battalion of light infantry, some riflemen and horse, and occupies a position between me and Suffolk where there is a party of militia under Colonel Parker, General Morgan and five hundred riflemen, as well as some dragoons. Weedon is at Fredericksburg and if a fleet arrives, he will call out the militia. Gregory is on the other side of the Dismal Swamp. I have sent him orders to call out the militia, mount some cannon at the passes and remove every boat which might help the enemy to go to North Carolina. When the embarkation sails, Morgan will return, and the others go to Carolina. If only a French fleet should come to Hampton Road, the British army would, I think, be ours.[190]

I write to Nelson on the twenty-ninth and tell him we need to know the enemy's intentions before the two thousand militiamen rendezvous at Boyd's Ferry. If General Greene's need for men is less urgent than that of our's then we shall have them here in readiness to join our army. I suggest he collects the heavy cannon of Virginia and military equipment which would be needed for a siege of Portsmouth.[191]

I receive a letter from Washington on the thirtieth, written on the thirteenth from Dobb's Ferry. He tells me that Rochambeau's men have joined his for the attack on New York. He says he will shortly have occasion to communicate matters of very great importance to me. He tells me to gather as large a Continental force as I can and increase my cavalry. He tells me to keep him informed as quickly and accurately as I can of Cornwallis's movements.[192]

What does he mean? When will I find out? I feel he is trying to tell me something which he dares not reveal in case the letter is intercepted. Does he mean a siege of Cornwallis? If he does, we will need more naval superiority. That means either Barras will sail from Newport to the Chesapeake or de Grasse will come from the West Indies.

I write back: 'Your letter of the 13ᵗʰ is just Come to Hand. The Moment a perfect Intelligence Can Be Got, Major McPherson will be Dispatched. But Some Expressions in your last favor will, if possible, Augment My Vigilance in keeping You well Apprised of the Ennemy's Movements.' I inform him again of the British troop ships and that they have not sailed. I tell him the present position of my forces. I say that with a very small amount of transport the enemy could go by water from Portsmouth to Wilmington and that the only way to stop that is to have an army before Portsmouth and possess the head of these rivers-a movement which unless I was certain of naval superiority might prove a disaster.[193]

I think I understand he wants me to keep Cornwallis where a superior naval and military force could attack him. I need to keep him closely informed of any move. I therefore order reports to be brought to me very frequently from our positions near the enemy. I continue to remain surprised that Cornwallis has not yet sailed, but it is possible he has heard of de Grasse's success in the West Indies and therefore does not want to sail to New York in case he is nearby.

July 31. I receive a letter written on the twenty-sixth by one of my spies, a black servant of Cornwallis, who says that Cornwallis, Simcoe and Tarleton are still in Portsmouth but expect to move, that most of the army is embarked and that there are also many very valuable negroes but without the ships to take them.[194] I write again to Washington to tell him this latest information and say that if only a French fleet were to come here, I think the British army would be ours.[195]

The British have sailed. Commodore Barron wrote two letters today from Hampton to say that forty ships and several large barges full of troops weighed this morning at sunrise from Cape Henry, certainly bound for Baltimore. They stood up the Bay for about fifteen miles; the wind and tide being ahead, they anchored off Cherrystones. He believes the fleet has on board nearly three thousand men and about two hundred horses. Two men o' war, eight ships and other craft remain in the roadstead and a man from Portsmouth informed him last night that Cornwallis is still at Portsmouth with part of his troops. [196] I immediately write to Wayne to inform him and order him to march to Manakin Town where his troops can cross and where he will hear more fully from me.[197]

August 1. The army marches at dawn. [198] I send copies of Barron's letters to Congress, Washington, and Thomas Sim Lee [199] and write to Parker for intelligence of the enemy. [200] I will go to Fredericksburg where my forces will unite.

My men march at dawn on the second; after fourteen miles, they halt two miles south of Richmond, the heat intense.[201] The following day it is again extremely hot; I allow the men to rest, then at six in the evening, they march to Richmond.

I learn that Cornwallis has halted at Yorktown; I write to von Steuben:

> The enemy's embarkation having at last sailed, I supposed it would go to New York; but, to my great surprise, they stood up the Bay and the general opinion was they were going to Baltimore. This movement, I confess, appeared to me very different from what their present interest seems to be. It has, however, been explained by their entering York River and landing at York and Gloucester. One would think they mean to take post there, and perhaps intelligences of our successes in the West Indies have rendered it imprudent for them to venture out of the Capes. Thinking the enemy should go to New York and might send a reinforcement to South Carolina, I had determined to send the cavalry to General Greene; but as they are determined to remain with us, I request, my dear Baron, you will push on every Dragoon that can be equipped to this camp. [202]

I write to Wayne. I order him to cross the river by the nearest route to join with me at Johnstone's Mill, not far from Newcastle on the Pamunkey. I ask him to send his cavalry ahead to join with my army. 'It would look as if they intended something permanent in this quarter; but, be this as it may, we must take a position nearer to Fredericksburg and Potomack. The strongest assurances of their dividing their force between the Southward and New York might not justify our leaving these parts without cover. We must act as if they were in earnest; because, if we do not, they may be in earnest.'[203]

My men march about ten miles from Richmond and halt at ten in the evening on the north side of Brook Bridge.

I am at Newcastle on the fourth. I write again to Wayne. I say that I had been certain the enemy was going to New York and that part of the army would go to Carolina, and that even when their fleet was sailing up the Bay, I still thought it would tack about and go to New York. Their landing at York, although establishing a position there is the next possibility, still appears to me to perhaps be a feint to draw me north. I say that as the enemy do not appear at the present to intend to go up the Potomac, at least in their vessels, we may take positions that are not so much out of the way as the road to Fredericksburg. The light infantry and militia are near this river, so the Pennsylvanians, Virginians and General Campbell's men can take a position between Bottom's Bridge and Westover. I suggest he goes to White Oak Bridge between Long and Bottom's Bridges. I conclude: 'When a General Has Nothing But Horse and foot to Calculate upon, He May Avoid useless Movements. But when He is to Guess at Every Possible Whim of an Army that flies with the Wind and is not within the Reach of Spies or Reconnoitrers He Must forcibly Walk in the dark.' [204]

The men march at dawn; about eleven o'clock they halt at Hanover Meeting House.[205] The heat is still intense. On the fifth, the army encamps in an old field at Newcastle, and I allow them to rest. Wayne replies from Westham that he is closer to me there and would avoid the fatigue of a march to Bottom's Bridge. [206]

I write to Washington on the sixth from the Pamunkey. I say that instead of continuing to Baltimore, Cornwallis has entered York River and landed at York and Gloucester with two battalions of light infantry, two large Anspach regiments, the 43rd, the Queen's Rangers and some horse; that General O'Hara is in Portsmouth with the rest of the troops; that it is said Leslie has sailed to Charlestown; and that I would still not be surprised if the light infantry and Anspachers were not detached to New York:

> We were in time to take our course down Pamunkey River and will Move to Some position where the Several parts of the Army will unite...York is Surrounded By the River and a Morass. The Entrance is But Narrow. There is However a Commanding Hill, at least I am So informed which if occupied By them would Much Extend their works. Glocester is a Neck of land projected into the River and opposite to York. Their vessels the biggest of whom is a 44 Are between the two towns. Should a Fleet Come in at this Moment our Affairs would take a very Happy turn...General Gregory and Clel. Parker Have Been directed to Collect forces and Press near Portsmouth. I Have written to North Carolina to Be Guarded Against Any Movement By land. I Have written to Maryland for their New levies...Had not Your attention Been turned to Newyork Something with a fleet Might Be Done in this Quarter. But I See Newyork is the object and Consequently I attend to Your Instructions By Captain Olney. [207]

I dispatch letters from Governor Nelson, Colonel Davis and Mr. Ross to Wayne in which they complain he has seized shoes and linen from Virginia's stores which were intended for their own troops in the field who greatly need them, and that other excesses are said to have been committed on the property of individuals by the troops of the Pennsylvania Line. I ask him to explain the matter to Nelson. I order him to move to Bottom's Bridge.[208]

On the seventh, I send McHenry to Nelson and the Virginia Executive to ask for supplies, to have all the cannon and mortars in the state collected and repaired, a proper quantity of fixed ammunition, shells, carcasses and ball provided, the necessity of having boats on carriages, wagons, as well as clothing for the new Virginia levies who are almost naked.[209] Next day, the troops remain in camp to rest, wash and clean their arms.[210] Wayne writes on the ninth from Bottom's Bridge that it was presumed the shoes and linen were the property of the United States. If, however, they were the property of Virginia, then they will be delivered to that state, and one hundred and seventy-three soldiers will not be fit for service, and it will therefore be his duty to send them to a safe place until shoes and overalls arrive from Pennsylvania. He says that the insinuations made against his officers hurt their honor and feelings and does not believe Nelson has read the account he sent of a court martial following which a brave old soldier was executed for committing a small depredation. He tells me to have the goodness to put His Excellency right upon this occasion.[211] On the tenth I write to Governor Lee that the enemy are fortifying York as if it is their intention to make it a place of arms.[212]

At nine o'clock in the morning of the eleventh the troops arrive here at New Kent Mountain and encamp in a field on the left of the road where the British were encamped a few days before.[213] I write to Wayne that the feelings of the officers are very proper and I hope Nelson is far from giving offence to them, that the boots and part of the linen must remain with the Virginia Dragoons, that the shoes must be distributed to the soldiers as they are essential for marching, and to keep the Osnaburg linen until I write to Nelson, whom I am sure will want it returned as there is a great quantity of it. If he could write to me how many shoes and overalls the Pennsylvania Line needs, I will then request Governor Nelson to let us have some linen.[214]

I receive two letters from Washington dated July 30. He says that if I return to the main army, he cannot give me the command I want as there are many more general officers in proportion to the numbers of troops and that the Jersey and York troops are reserved for General McDougal. He suggests that I will not regret staying in Virginia 'until matters are reduced to a greater degree of certainty than they are at present' and also that 'from the change of circumstances with which the removal of part of the enemy's force from Virginia to New York will be attended, it is more than probable that we shall also intirely change our plan of operations.' He talks of expelling the enemy from the southern states, if we cannot lay siege to New York. He wants me to inform General Greene of his words, particularly his expectation of being able to transport part of his army south if the operation against New York is declined. He would like to send someone to explain to me what he has hinted at but is at a loss to know of one whose discretion he could depend on.[215]

I write back:

> Be sure, my dear general, that the pleasure of being with you would make me happy in any command you think proper to give me; but for the present I am of opinion, with you, I had better remain in Virginia, the more so, as Lord Cornwallis does not choose to leave us, and circumstances may happen that will furnish me agreeable opportunities in the command of the Virginian army. I have pretty well understood you, my dear general, but would be happy in a more minute detail which I am sensible, cannot be entrusted to letters. Would not Gouvion be a proper ambassador...Count Damas might come, under pretence to serve with me...Cornwallis is entrenching at York and at Gloucester. The sooner we disturb him, the better; but unless our maritime friends give us help, we cannot much venture below. [216]

The men march seven miles to Ruffin's Ferry on the twelfth. At sunrise they start to cross the Pamunkey River; they encamp on a plain on the eastern side.[217] The heat is again intense.

Complaints have been made about the money I have taken to pay for the exchanged officers landed at Jamestown from Charlestown. I write to Nelson and readily confess the sums have been extravagant, but the Executive had said they would give to the officers from Charlestown whatever money was needed, not realizing it would be such a large sum. I also did not conceive it would be so much, my knowledge of finances not being very extensive and my knowledge of value of the paper or commodities in Virginia being less well known to me than to the Executive. I refer to the proposition concerning negroes and horses taken from the enemy, that it might be best to return the negroes to their owners provided they pay half of their value in cash, that some premium might be given to encourage the taking of negroes going into the British lines and that I also need to know what is to be done with horses we have forced the enemy to abandon. I say I intend the army to take a position between the two rivers so that due protection can be given to the north side of York but that the south side should not be entirely neglected.[218]

I write to Greene that we have been marching slowly along the road to York as the prospects of acting against Cornwallis are not good and that I intend to occupy Montock Hill, four miles from Westpoint. General Wayne was formerly on our right but now is between the Chickahominy and James Rivers, some way above us. I tell him I have no cavalry but three times a day take up the matter with anyone I can think of. I also say the Virginia Executive decided, on receiving a letter from him, that he does not want militia, and that my opinion does not agree with his. I can therefore only reinforce him with regulars. I mention I still think the enemy will send a reinforcement to New York and that Clinton and Cornwallis do not agree. [219]

The men march at sunrise on the thirteenth; they march four miles down the river and encamp on an attractive plantation where there are many fruit trees, particularly peaches.[220]   I write a postscript to Greene's letter. I give him the intelligence I have of the British fortifications, adding 'there is an Uncertainty in their Movements for which I am at a loss to Account.'[221]

Greene wants me to increase my cavalry; Washington orders the same. I write to von Steuben and ask for his help to do so. I say I am still surprised that the enemy at Yorktown and Gloucester have sent no troops to New York. To my embarrassment I also ask him to buy another spyglass, whatever the cost, as I have unfortunately broken his. [222]

August 14. Montock Hill is a good, strategic position. Cornwallis is on either side of the York River at York and Gloucester, and we are at the York River's fork, about thirty miles from Yorktown by water, and about thirty-five by land. From here, we can even see ships arriving. 'God willing we may see some with white flags,' I write to La Luzerne.[223]   The light infantry is four miles from Westpoint, the militia eight miles. Wayne is at Bottom's Bridge where he reports there is plenty of forage. We have a few horses and boats patrol the river. Matthews, with some militia, is between here and Williamsburg; militia and volunteer horse are foraging in Gloucester County.[224] The enemy is fortifying, but not so rigorously as one might expect. Perhaps there is some disagreement in the family? If so, it would be pointless for us to try to divine their plans. I write to La Luzerne: 'Why don't we have Lauzun's Legion? If the French army could suddenly arrive in Virginia and be supported by a squadron, we could do some very good things...I still think it probable the enemy will send some troops to New York but I am not certain about this.'[225]

Cornwallis is fortifying at Gloucester, but not at York. If he expects a French fleet then he will confine his defenses to Gloucester. However, if he means to take the offensive, then the Gloucester fortifications are intended to protect his ships, magazines and hospitals, and if events go badly for him, the position can ensure his retreat. 'This latter seems the Most probable. I Soon Expect to be Hard pushed, and Never was worse provided,' I write to Morgan on the fifteenth, who is at the springs in Bath to restore his health. [226]

We are in desperate need of men, weapons, ammunition and horse accoutrements. We have no heavy artillery in order. The army is marching with bare feet. We have hardly any clothing. There is no flour, not even for the officers. There are no candles or soap and the meat is hardly edible. We also need money. Major Jones from the quartermaster's department sends an assistant to Richmond to ask Nelson and the quartermaster general for help,[227] and Colonel Innes is foraging on the Gloucester side and driving off stock. On the eighteenth, clothing arrives for the non-commissioned officers and privates of the light infantry.[228] I write to Henry Knox and say I need an artillery officer.

To my immense joy, on the twenty-first I receive a letter from Washington at Dobb's Ferry, dated August 15, which says the comte de Grasse is coming to the Chesapeake. He tells me to take a position which stops Cornwallis retreating to North Carolina once he knows of the imminent arrival of the French fleet. If Wayne has not yet left for Carolina and the enemy has made no detachment to the south, he and his troops are to remain here and to inform Greene. If, however, he has already left and has gone a considerable distance, to let him continue. Washington says:

> You shall hear further from me as soon as I have concerted plans and formed dispositions for sending a reinforcement from hence. In the meantime I have only to recommend a continuation of that prudence and good conduct which you have manifested thro' the whole of your Campaign. You will be particularly careful to conceal the expected arrival of the Count, because if the enemy are not apprised of it, they (may be) on board their transports in the Bay, which will be the luckiest Circumstance in the World. You will take measures for opening a communication with Count de

Grasse the moment he arrives and will concert measures with him for making the best uses of your joint forces until you receive aid from this quarter.[229]

I immediately write to Nelson and ask him to call out six hundred militiamen to meet at Black River under General Lawson.[230] I send McHenry to Richmond to discuss the provision of supplies with the Executive Council and the Governor. I request Wayne to begin to march tomorrow morning and move quite rapidly to Westover.[231] Boats will be there, but I tell him not to cross until he hears from me. I am expecting five hundred Maryland new levies and already have four hundred Virginians, six hundred Pennsylvanians, eight hundred and fifty light infantry and one hundred and twenty dragoons. I will have, therefore, two thousand five hundred Continentals, and three thousand, or if wanted, four thousand militiamen. I have two hundred more dragoons and horses ready and am waiting for accoutrements. [232] I believe Cornwallis's force to be about five thousand.

I reply to Washington. I tell him most of the enemy force is at York which is not yet being fortified but that they are busy fortifying at Gloucester Neck where there is a large corps under Colonel Dundas. At York they have a forty-four-gun ship; further down the river are frigates and vessels and there is a small garrison at Portsmouth. From their caution and partial movement, I believe their intelligence is not very good and they are not sure of my intentions and prospects. I report that so far we have occupied the forks of York, so have looked both ways. Some militia have prevented the enemy from being at or near Williamsburg, and Innis and his militia have kept them in Gloucester. I give the estimate of my strength; I report the orders I have given Nelson, Gregory, Washington and Wayne, and that I will shortly assemble my little army near to the Chickahominy. The plan I propose is that of 'taking whatever is in the Rivers, taking possession of the rivers themselves, while the Main Body defends the Bay- forming a junction of land forces at a Convenient and Safe point-Checking the Ennemy But Giving nothing to Chance Untill properly Reinforced.' I say what I have done to recruit more men; the difficulty of obtaining provisions without money; that we have no clothing, no heavy artillery in order, that some arms are lacking, as well as some horse accoutrements and a great deal of ammunition, and that only his own entreaties will result in a sufficient quantity of those articles transported to the head of the bay. 'In the present State of affairs, My dear General, I Hope You will Come Yourself to Virginia, and that if the french Army Moves this way, I will Have at least the Satisfaction of Beholding You Myself at the Head of the Combined Armies...Adieu, My Dear General, I Heartly thank You for Having ordered me to Remain in Virginia and to Your goodness to me I am owing the Most Beautifull prospect that I May Ever Behold.'[233]

On the twenty-third we learn the enemy evacuated Portsmouth on the eighteenth. Colonel Parker entered it at five o'clock on the nineteenth and wrote to me the same day, saying that General O'Hara was on a vessel in the Elizabeth River with the Guards, the 17th regiment, Colonel de Bose's Hessian battalion, and many runaway slaves, all prevented from sailing by a contrary wind. In the town were dead and dying slaves, ill with smallpox, and many worn-out horses. Cannon have been thrown in the river; cannon left in the town have been spiked. He says that Portsmouth is a mere heap of rubbish and Norfolk is little better.[234]

I order the fortifications to be demolished. I send Gimat and Camus to Portsmouth under the pretense of viewing the fortifications, but they are really going to Cape Henry to give my dispatches and information to the French commanders.

I write to Washington on the twenty-fourth, my letter to be carried to headquarters by Colonel Morris, Greene's aide, who has arrived from North Carolina, en route to headquarters, and who will convey Greene's ideas on the best ways to improve the assistance of de Grasse. I again list my troops: 850 Light Infantry, about 600 Pennsylvanians, 400 new levies and Virginia exchanged soldiers; 400 Marylanders,120 dragoons and a chance to have perhaps 60 more; if we had accoutrements we could have 200 more, and 3000 militiamen in a few days. I describe the situation at York- 60 ships in the York River, 10 of which are armed, the largest of which is a 50-gun vessel; and say what I have done so far, that Wayne is filing off towards Westover but that when de Grasse arrives, I will collect our forces at Soan's Bridge and wait for intelligences from him. I believe Cornwallis to have more than 5000 men if sailors are included. [235]

I write to Adrienne with my usual sense of humor, proud to be able to tell her just a little of what I have done: The self-respect with which you honor me has perhaps been gratified by the (grand) role I have been forced to play. You must have hoped it was not possible to be equally gauche on every theater stage, but I would accuse you (my dear heart) of a terrible excess of vanity for since we share everything it would be useless to overestimate me if you had not trembled for the dangers that I risk. I am not talking about cannon shots but about the much more dangerous military skill that Lord Cornwallis makes me fear.' I cannot tell her what is about to happen, but I mention Greene's success in Carolina and that 'this campaign has everywhere taken a much better turn than we should have hoped. Perhaps it will end very agreeably.' I speak about our servants here; about Poirey's exploits on July 6, 'a portfolio on the front of his saddle, a portfolio behind, a large writing desk hanging on his left side, holding a saber that once belonged to General Arnold, and smiling at the large quantity of bullets and balls whistling by.' I say I have decided to return to France this winter, despite all my attachment to America.[236]

I also write a short letter to Maurepas and a much longer one to Poix: 'Your affection for me must make you tremble, my friend, to see me installed at the head of a command four hundred miles from any other army and consequently in sole charge of events.' I mention Clinton whom we saw at the opera and say that he remains in New York. I talk about our friends and relations here, that the rank of my brother-in-law distresses me because it is far below his abilities but that he is 'serving with a very good grace as if the rank of lieutenant colonel had been the height of his ambition...Place at the queen's feet my tender respects...But if to be deserving were a question only of loving her, my dear prince, never has a sovereign a more deserving subject.'[237]

I write again to Washington on the twenty-fifth. I recount my latest intelligence; that the enemy have evacuated their forts at Ivy, Kemp's Landing, Great Bridge and Portsmouth; that they are beginning to fortify at York and will make a fort and battery by a windmill in order to defend the river, and I have no doubt they will do something on the land side; they have finished the works at Gloucester, which consist of some redoubts and a battery of eighteen pieces; there are sixty ships in the river-the largest, a fifty-gun ship, two frigates, seven other armed vessels and the rest, transports. I tell him that my light infantry and main body of militia are here at Ruffin's; General Wayne is on the road to Westover and I hope to join our forces in one day; the militia from Maryland are meant to have set off last Monday but I do not know if they have done so; I have parties on the enemy's lines. I reiterate that I have an immense need of clothing, arms, ammunition, hospital stores and horse accoutrements and estimate again the size of the enemy's army to be at least 4,500 rank and file.[238]

I write to Wayne to finally reveal my secret, a secret which I say is for him alone to know. I tell him there is great hope that we will be immediately aided from the sea, that Washington has directed me to keep him here until further orders and that his position at Westover makes Cornwallis think he is going to the south.[239]

August 26. I complain to Nelson about the lack of provisions, that it has been eleven days since the men had one drop of spirits and that consequently the Continentals are falling sick. There has also been no flour seen in camp for a long time. I complain about the behavior of the county lieutenants, that as they think they will not be punished, they are indifferent to the sufferings of the army:

Unless vigorous measures are adopted, we will be involved deeper and deeper in ruin. Few men in the field, not a sixth part of what is called for - a great number without arms- the greatest part of whom live from day to day upon food that is injurious to their health-without six cartridges per man-and the poor Continentals that will soon be our only dependence, falling off for want of spirits and flour. Should it be known to Lord Cornwallis, he may ruin us at one stroke and defeat every project that may have been made for the protection of this state.[240]

I appeal again to the governors of Maryland and Virginia for men, arms and ammunition. I also order more militia to be called up on my own authority so bypassing the civic authorities. I order Colonel White's cavalry to come with whatever arms they can obtain; I order Wayne's men, many of whom are without shoes, to march to Cabin Point, on the south bank of the James, to impede any crossing by the enemy; I also send some militia and dragoons there. The militia march to Ruffin's Ferry on the twenty-eighth; they cross as quickly as they can.[241] Next day, artillery and stores cross.

Duportail arrives. He has Washington's definitive orders and information on what is happening. De Grasse is coming from the West Indies but will only stay three weeks as his ships and troops are necessary to protect Saint Domingo and the other West India colonies; de Barras is sailing from Rhode Island with siege equipment and provisions; Rochambeau's and Washington's armies are marching down to Virginia and will shortly arrive. There will soon be 36 ships of the line here and 20,000 men who will need provisions.

We discuss the situation. Cornwallis has 5,000 men and if he arms the slaves he may have 6,000. 1,500 of his men, at least, are mounted. My regular force is 1,500, exclusive of the new levies, of whom 200 do not have arms. We do not have 1,000 militiamen able to fight. We have no ammunition; we lack provisions and therefore cannot follow the enemy if they leave York. We need 6,000 militia which are effective rank and file we decide.

I write again to Nelson and tell him I have ordered several counties to collect men, although people who refuse to obey the laws of the Assembly and the Executive are even less likely to take notice of me. I entreat him to send any militia south of the James River who can be armed immediately to Long Bridge upon Black Water under General Lawson. Militia of the Northern Neck and bordering on Gloucester should immediately go to the Gloucester camp. I entreat him to immediately collect enough cattle. 'I cannot help repeating to Your Excellency my unhappy situation. It is probable Lord Cornwallis will for a time retire through North Carolina, which may end in the disgrace and destruction of the American troops in this state; and have the most decisive effects against American independence.' [242]

Every minute I expect to hear that our prey is escaping. Lord Cornwallis could land at Westpoint and cross the James River. If only I had some ships above York.[243] My anxiety is immense. I and my troops will fight; our honor will be saved but we will have failed.

August 31. We learn of the arrival of a large fleet. I believe it to be that of de Grasse and write of it to Wayne who has now crossed the river. I am sending forty dragoons, three hundred riflemen and three hundred militiamen to join him at Cabin's Point, and the light infantry here at Holt's Forge and General Stevens at the ferry, is ready to support his force. I request him to move this way when the enemy cannot escape by water, and then we will join with the French troops.[244]

I write to Taylor and tell him to send for Meredith's son near Whiting's Mill, along with any other good pilots, to the fleet, as soon as the fleet is known to be French. If it turns out to be

British, then he must consider this letter as being completely confidential. I also request that all stock animals should be removed from the enemy's reach, that the mills should be made useless, and all meal, corn and flour taken away. [245]

September 1. To my delight, I am correct. It is the French fleet with twenty-eight ships of the line and four frigates.[246] I receive a letter from de Grasse replying to my letter brought to him by Camus and Gimat detailing my position, that of the enemy, and my plans. He agrees he will today send three small frigates into the James River to prevent Cornwallis from going to Carolina, and these ships will also protect the transport boats for the three thousand two hundred and fifty men under the orders of the marquis de Saint-Simon-Montbléru, who will join with mine at Jamestown on September 5. He will send three or four vessels up York River to force Cornwallis to decide whether to hold the right or left side of the river. He wants our combined force to go into action immediately, as divided and stripped of boats, he would be too weak if the combined British naval forces came to the aid of Cornwallis; he says that he has little time to stay here and that if the enemy is forewarned of our attacks, they will put obstacles in our way. He also offers to land one thousand eight hundred men from the ships' garrisons, and, if necessary, to form companies of sailors. He encloses letters to be sent to Rochambeau, La Luzerne and de Barras.[247]

I also receive a letter from the marquis de Saint-Simon who writes how pleased he is to serve with me, to be able to cultivate my friendship and contribute to the glory and success of the American arms. He encloses a report on the strength and composition of the division under his command so that I can organize provisions and the means to transport their artillery and camp effects.[248]

Nelson is with me. I write a list of everything we need for the fleet and for the combined army. We can depend on having cattle, but flour needs to come from Maryland and Pennsylvania. Nelson sends men to immediately obtain horses for the officers and vegetables for the men, then rides off to the Executive Council.[249]

De Grasse has agreed to much that I have suggested, but I would also like him to force the passage at York and then Cornwallis cannot escape. I intend to suggest the taking of a safe position about ten or twelve miles from York which would be difficult to take without a much greater loss than we could suffer and unless matters are very different from what I believe they are. I believe we should disturb the foraging of the enemy and tire them with the activities of our militia without committing the regulars. I intend to be cautious. I think that having so sure a game to play, it would be madness by the risk of an attack to give anything to chance. I write to Washington. I inform him what is happening and what I propose. I also say I cannot provide wagons and horses and that his best chance is to obtain them in Maryland. I finish: 'Adieu, My dear General, the agreable Situation I am in is owing to your friendship and is for that Reason the dearer to your Respectful Servant and friend.'[250]

To my delight, I learn that Lord Rawdon, who had been commander of the British army in the south after Cornwallis left, was captured sailing to England and is a prisoner on board a French ship.

September 2. A sergeant on horseback rides in with a letter from Wayne who informs me that he had sent Butler and Stewart to reconnoiter five frigates anchored opposite Mulberry Island. They discovered that the marquis de Saint-Simon had disembarked three thousand men from five frigates at Burrell's Ferry. Two frigates will be left there whilst the three other frigates and flat-bottomed boats will transport the soldiers to James Island this morning. Four ships of the line have gone up the York River and the rest of the fleet are with de Grasse at the mouth of the Capes. He says he will be at Cobham with his troops by eight o'clock and wants to know where we will join forces. Will it be at Wiiliamsburg, or near the burnt Ordinary or shall we wait until Washington arrives? He suggests I come down by water to meet him at Jamestown by one o'clock to decide.[251]

The troops set off at dawn; they march about eight miles; they pitch the tents in a field near Diascund Creek, rest until three, then march again for seven or eight miles and halt near Chickahominy Church.[252] Wayne comes to see me in the evening gloom. He does not say the password; a sentry fires on him, wounding his thigh with buckshot.[253] Wayne is in a fury. He wants the soldier court martialed. I agree very reluctantly; the soldier was only doing his duty.

My troops set off at dawn on the third. They march about eight miles and halt near Green Springs. They halt three hours, wash and put on clean clothes. They set off again, proceeding six miles towards Williamsburg. They halt briefly, then march back three miles in heavy rain.[254] Wayne's troops rapidly cross the James in the French boats.

I write to Nelson on the fourth, from near Norrell's Mill, to entreat him to send by boat all the flour he has as the French troops at Jamestown are without provisions, particularly flour, and I have not seen and cannot find, a commissary. I ask if he knows the road Washington will take.[255] Wayne's troops set off towards Williamsburg at about seven. At eight the light infantry march. They pass through the town, halt in a field about three miles below it until sunset, then march back to Williamsburg.[256]

My army rests on the fifth. I continue to try and obtain provisions for the French and fortunately they have not yet been one day without flour, meat and salt. I write again to Nelson on the sixth that the French army needs food. My army is in the same situation and as we also completely lack horses and wagons, the two armies are unable to march. I entreat him to help. However, I know Nelson is doing all he can. 'The wheels of his Government are so very rusty that no Governor whatever will be able to set them fiercely agoing. Time will prove that Jefferson has been too severely charged.'[257] I also say to Nelson that the wants of the hospital and the demands of the surgeons are of so pressing a nature as to induce me to trouble him for their relief.[258]

The light infantry march to Williamsburg; they pass through the town and halt at a plain west of the College.[259] On the seventh the officers give their horses and wagons; we leave our baggage. By the evening we take up a strong position near the town. Ravines are at our front; the right flank is covered by a mill pond on the road to Jamestown, the left by Queen's Creek where there are rivulets and small streams. The militia are still in front of our right and left; there is a good look out on the river. Williamsburg and its strong buildings are at our front. General Muhlenburg has an advance force guarding the roads and passes from York to Williamsburg[260] of one thousand men, four hundred men upon the lines, some of whom are Virginia regulars, and one hundred dragoons, and if I borrow White's unequipped horses, one hundred hussars can be added. There is a line of armed ships along the James River and a small reserve of militia which may increase every day. In Gloucester County there are eight hundred militia driving off stock. French armed vessels are at Westpoint.[261]

Saint-Simon insists on being, without any restriction at all, under my command, a command I would never have hoped for. I have three thousand two hundred men from the Auvergne, Béarn and Touraine regiments, the latter being the regiment commanded by my father when he died at Minden. I also have one hundred hussars I shall mount, two thousand five hundred American regulars, as well as militiamen who are arriving daily.[262]

The French are well-dressed in white uniforms faced with blue, with white underclothes. I do not wish to lower their expectations of my Americans by letting them see the tattered clothing and semi-nakedness of my brave men, so I will attempt to keep the two armies away from each other. I find it embarrassing I cannot provide provisions for the French which must seem very strange to them, but I give them as much flour as I can, whilst my own troops eat cornmeal. My men do not complain, even although they are sleeping in the open and the French have tents. They are grateful and overjoyed that they are here.

Fever grips me; I take to my bed on the eighth in the house of militia colonel, St. George Tucker. I sweat; I shake continually; my head throbs with pain. The suffocating heat and the high temperature of my illness are almost roasting me alive. I cannot write but dictate a letter to Washington to tell him of the quick landing of the French troops and the present position of the two armies just outside Williamsburg. I say I think it would be madness to attack the British now and that the marquis de Saint-Simon, the comte de Grasse and Duportail agree; if Cornwallis should come out against such a position as we currently occupy, then he would repent of it and even if he beat us, he would soon have to prepare for another battle. I describe what is happening at York where provisions are being gathered and most of the sailors landed from the ships. 'I am told he has ordered the Inhabitants in the vicinity of the Town to come in and should think they may do Him as much harm as good.' I end by saying that although there is much we need, 'I have good reason for believing that there will be found a sufficiency of supplies in this State and Mayriland for our Armies. With respect to a proper place for the debarkation of your troops it is the opinion of the Marquis de St. Simon, and myne, that it must be in James River, but we have not had an opportunity yet of fixing on the best spot.'[263]

I also dictate a letter to La Luzerne: 'I beg your pardon, Monsieur le Chevalier, for not writing to you myself, but by acting as quartermaster and commissary, stealing salt, impressing cattle and clamoring for flour, I have ended up, very stupidly, giving myself a fever and migraine, which will go away the moment I allow myself a few hours sleep. I do not know if I am withering of old age, but for the past two days my twenty-four years have been well tolled.' [264]

We receive news of an engagement off the Capes on the fifth, between de Grasse and the British fleet commanded by Admiral Graves. We do not know what de Grasse has ordered for the protection of the Bay, the ships in York River have now gone down. James River is still guarded but there has been no letter from de Grasse about his present whereabouts, although it is likely he will soon return. I tell Washington this and say that he will perhaps want to keep his troops at Head of Elk until de Grasse returns. I also say that following his approbation of what I have done, although I know General Lincoln will be in command of the American army, I am emboldened to ask if I can command the division which is composed of the troops I have led here in Virginia as this would be the greatest reward for me of the services I may have rendered, as I confess I have the strongest attachment to them.[265]

I am still very unwell but in the late afternoon I go outside, mount my horse and ride off to review the army at five o'clock with Saint-Simon.[266]

A small skirmish occurred at dawn of the eleventh on the line between some of our cavalry and the enemy. I write to Nelson once more to say there is no flour, neither for the American or French army, and I am distressed in the extreme by this lack. I suggest vessels in the Rappahannock should be loaded with flour seized from that area by his issuing an order.[267]

Wayne writes: 'I have not been pleased with Madam Fortune for some time and she has added to that Displeasure in attacking you at this Crisis with a Caitiff fever. Try my Dear Marquis, to shake it off, and I will endeavour to get clear of my Complaint the soonest possible.' He asks if any orders have been sent to Head of Elk for flour, salt, spirits and entrenching tools and if the militia could start making fascines and gabions. 'What acct. from the Gallant De Grasse?'[268]

In the afternoon, to my delight, Gouvion arrives to help Duportail with preparations for the siege.

"Where is His Excellency?" I ask.

"I left him at Philadelphia with a large army on the march for here," he replies.[269]

He gives me a letter from Washington, written on the tenth, from Mount Vernon. He expects to be with me on the fourteenth and asks that if there is any danger as he approaches, a party of horse should be sent towards New Kent Court House to meet him. He hopes I will keep Lord Cornwallis safe, without provisions or forage, until he arrives.[270]

September 14. At about three o'clock an express arrives: "General Washington and Count de Rochambeau are riding into Williamsburg."[271]

Chapter 30

Yorktown siege

I immediately mount a horse. I gallop frantically along the sun-seared, dusty road towards the town, Nelson at my side, Saint-Simon just behind. We ride through the camp of the Virginia militia; we come near to the French camp, west of the college. Suddenly I see the familiar, beloved figure of my general standing with Rochambeau, General Hand and a group of officers. I gallop to him, throw myself off my horse, take him in my arms and kiss him ardently.[1]

I present Saint-Simon; he invites Washington to visit his troops who are already lining up on either side of the road. Washington does so, then he rides through the Continental lines, the drums beating. The guns from the artillery park and from every brigade roar twenty-one times. Men, women and children eagerly flock round, in great joy to see him. The army parades. Afterwards we gather in Saint-Simon's tent, the French officers making Washington's acquaintance. We eat supper; we laugh and talk, a military band playing the quartet from Grétry's *Lucille*, celebrating the joy of a family with their father. My fever persists; I am forced to leave early.

September 15. In the morning, I discover that letters from de Grasse arrived after my departure. He is back in Chesapeake Bay with two captured frigates, following a four-hour battle on September 6 with the British fleet which resulted in about two hundred French sailors killed or wounded. De Barras managed to enter the Bay on September 10 whilst the enemy was fighting de Grasse. The siege artillery and salted provisions from Newport are, therefore, now here, and the combined French fleet comprises thirty-seven ships of the line, as well as frigates and other armed vessels.

In the afternoon I give a dinner for Washington. I am unwell and it is raining, but it does not quench my delight. Later, officers of the Pennsylvania Line and the light infantry are presented to him; Hand and Wayne give the names of the men he does not know; he stands at the door and shakes each one's hand. Then he reviews the tough, hardy, almost naked Virginia Line. Immediately afterwards he writes to the state Board of War asking for clothes.

Washington and Rochambeau set off to the flagship, the *Ville de Paris*, to talk with de Grasse, on the seventeenth, but I am too ill to accompany them. Next day, Baron Ludwig von Closen, a short, lively, fair-haired Bavarian who speaks excellent French and is an aide to Rochambeau, comes to see me on his arrival in Williamsburg. The six hundred men transported here by de Barras, disembark and camp by the James near to Williamsburg.[2] On the nineteenth, to my great joy, John Laurens rides in. He recently arrived from France, bearing promises from the court of help in finishing the war.[3] He tells me of my family and of my wife and it is an exquisite pleasure to hear my dear friend talk of my loved ones and my home, especially at such a moment in our war.

"Everything is preparing for our grand enterprise, and as far as we have gone, Fortune seems to have seconded all our endeavors," is von Steuben's view.[4]

Washington and Rochambeau return at noon on the twenty-second. They saw de Grasse for six hours then spent four and a half days beset by problems with boats and contrary winds.

However, they are both content with their discussion as de Grasse has said that he will stay for the whole of October even although his orders are to leave by October 15, that Saint-Simon's troops will stay as long as the fleet, that about one thousand eight hundred men are available for a major action and he will provide some cannon and powder.[5] We therefore have forty days in which to defeat Cornwallis. Our star is shining brightly.

Suddenly it dims. Dispatches had arrived from Congress and La Luzerne during Washington's absence to say that Rear Admiral Robert Digby is expected shortly in New York with three ships of the line, as well as a convoy.[6] We fear a new attempt to aid Cornwallis. A council of war takes place at Washington's headquarters; it is decided von Closen should go tomorrow to inform de Grasse. During the night the enemy send five ships prepared with pitch and sulfur to set fire to the four French warships blocking the mouth of the York. Fortunately, the sky is bright and star-lit; the French see the fireships approach; they cut their anchor ropes and escape.

Next day Lauzun's infantry disembark at College Landing on the James. On the twenty-fifth, von Closen returns to headquarters with dispatches from de Grasse, who has now moved his anchorage from Lynnhaven Bay where the tides are very strong, to beyond the shoals of Middle Ground and Horse-Shoe, off Old Point Comfort. At eight in the morning, he speaks at a council of general officers. "I heard many whispers and saw much anxiety on the *Ville de Paris* because of the naval reinforcements which have arrived in New York and which they think have already joined Hood's fleet, so making it far superior to our own."[7]

The dispatches from de Grasse present a similar view. He says he is much distressed by the intelligence brought to him by von Closen. He fears Digby's arrival makes the enemy nearly equal to him in strength and his position is still not favorable for battle nor safe in a gale. He proposes sailing out to sea towards New York as soon as the wind is favorable, so that he would be in a better position to attack the enemy, and to leave only the frigates blockading the James River and two ships at the entrance to the York River, as well as the troops from the ships and those of Saint-Simon. If there is a battle and he is forced to leeward, he might not be able to return. [8]

His words dismay us. This is a catastrophe. We need to be able to command the rivers to stop any retreat of Cornwallis.

It is decided I will go out with letters from Washington and Rochambeau and talk to de Grasse. Washington writes that de Grasse's proposals cause him great anxiety and asks him to follow the agreed plan. He believes Digby's strength is exaggerated, and even if it is true, is not sufficient to give him hope of success. If de Grasse withdraws, Yorktown might be relieved or evacuated, and the Allied Army could not obtain supplies from a distance. If de Grasse feels he must withdraw, he should continue to sail within sight of the Capes, to maintain the blockade. [9]

"Do not go beyond the Capes. If he has already gone out to sea write to ask him to return and give it to Baron von Closen to take to him," Washington tells me.

Rochambeau writes of the vague nature of the reports concerning the British fleets and says that 'the plan to go to New York, of which you ask our counsel, seems to us a matter of the greatest hazard, because in the absence of your fleet from the Bay, the British who will not have lost a minute to come to the succor of Lord Cornwallis...would be able in the night to pass without your seeing them, or they you.'[10]

"Will you accompany me?" I ask von Closen. A short time later, we set off, although he is exhausted having just spent two nights in open boats going out to the *Ville de Paris*.

The sky is darkening at College Landing on a fine beach on the James, where earlier the French first brigade had landed and where the second brigade will disembark tomorrow. Oarsmen row us out to the *Richmond*, a recently captured British frigate; we eat supper with the commander, Monsieur de Mortemart. At ten o'clock, we clamber into a small, open boat, the wind gusting sharply, the water very rough. Water from the oars drenches me and my stomach is pleased my illness has forced me to eat little.

September 26. At nine in the morning, we board the captured frigate, *Iris*, at Hampton. We sleep for three hours in the bunks, then dine well. At two-thirty, we set sail. At seven in the evening, to my relief, we finally reach the *Ville de Paris*, one of the largest ships in the world, carrying one hundred and ten guns and one thousand three hundred men.[11]

The resplendently uniformed comte de Grasse, a large man in his fifties, taller even than Washington, stands on the deck with his officers and welcomes me warmly. He comes from an old noble family and is the chief French naval officer in America, but his manner is plain and straightforward; I instantly like him. I send von Closen to go on board the *Auguste* and the *Duc de Bourgoyne* to tell their commanders I regret that Monsieur de Grasse does not want me to visit de Bougainville and de Barras, and to request them to attend a conference on board the *Ville de Paris*. At ten o'clock he returns with them, and we discuss the situation in de Grasse's quarters.

"I convened a general council of my officers, and it was agreed that instead of my earlier proposal the fleet will anchor at Cape Henry to cover both the James and the York. We will leave the small gun boats in the James for General Washington to use. We will arm three vessels and two large frigates to block the York. Once the right flank of the army has been secured on the York it would be possible to construct two lines of breakwaters to stop fire ships. Then if the British squadron approaches, we can fight in the way best suited to control the Bay. I also request General Washington, when he is in position at York, to provide a hospital at Hampton for our sick who number one thousand five hundred to one thousand eight hundred. We would like some American sailors to serve on the ships which will not leave the Bay. Even if only one hundred French sailors are sent back, they would be essential to us. We would also like to get rid of some of the prisoners aboard our ships and we need spies or trustworthy people to tell us quickly if the enemy lands in the south of the Chesapeake. I have already written to General Washington."[12]

"I will ask for all your demands. Would you also like to consider an attack on Wilmington or Charleston after York has been taken?" I reply, knowing Washington has already unsuccessfully proposed this.

"No, my ships are not suitable for either and I will not remain here beyond the end of October," he says.

Despite this, both de Grasse and his response delight me. We dine, then I sleep that night in a hammock. In the morning, von Closen and I drink chocolate before leaving the *Ville de Paris* at five o'clock.

"I am very well satisfied with the success of our mission. Monsieur de Grasse has agreed to all the proposals of our generals, and he will leave the Bay only after the operation is finished," I tell him.[13]

At seven o'clock in the evening we reach the *Diligente* and curiosity makes us go on board to see the captured Lord Rawdon. We ask Monsieur de Clovard, the commander, for supper, and dine with both Rawdon, whom I had met in England, and Lieutenant Colonel Doyle and his wife. We talk about the campaign in the Carolinas and Rawdon laments the fate which threatens Cornwallis. He complains bitterly about being a prisoner and is even less happy when I suggest he might be given to the Americans.

At ten o'clock we set off from the *Diligente* in extreme darkness. Our oarsmen do not seem very acquainted with the river; to my annoyance our launch runs aground several times into oyster beds.

At eight in the morning, on the twenty-eighth, we finally reach College Landing. I am feeling fit again, but poor von Closen appears even more exhausted than at the start of our mission.

"Lincoln's and Vioménil's troops arrived on the twenty-sixth[14] and joined with the troops already here," are the first words we hear. "The armies left at five o'clock to start the siege at Yorktown."[15]

We immediately mount the horses we had left. We gallop to Williamsburg where I receive a letter from General Jones in North Carolina which says General Greene has had a very lively engagement with Colonel Stewart, that the beginning did not go well but the outcome was quite favorable. [16]

We quickly put our affairs in order. We remount and ride rapidly for six miles along the dusty road under a scorching sun to the rear of the army comprising four thousand American Continentals and seven French regiments marching towards York. The French have taken a direct road to the left, by the Brick House. The Americans have taken the road to the right,[17] to Munford's Bridge, the light artillery placed at intervals in the huge, single column, rather than at the rear, in case the enemy attacks.

The men are suffering terribly in the heat. They are marching very slowly, the hot, sandy soil burning their mostly naked feet. The officers do not even have horses; they are walking with the infantry and complaining bitterly. Several bodies lie by the roadside; flies and insects buzz constantly.

The countryside, once obviously beautiful and fertile, has the devastated appearance of a nation at war.[18] The fields are fallow; houses are deserted, windows and doors broken and wide-open. Grass in the road often reaches to the soldiers' jackets. There are no people. Washington has ordered that if the enemy is encountered, only one round should be exchanged and then the bayonet must be used.[19] Fortunately, however, there is no sign of them.

By nightfall, the French army of seven thousand men has filed off to the left to begin the investment of the enemy; it is encamped on a plain, a large morass in front,[20] its line stretching through woods and creeks from the top of the York River to marshland near the house of Colonel Nelson. Vioménil commands the vanguard of grenadiers and dragoons, and the three French brigades bivouac out of cannon range of the enemy. Not a single man has been killed.[21]

The Americans proceed further towards the river and halt before the marshland at Beaver Dam Creek as the bridges have been destroyed. They camp in woodland and fields, facing the north-east, the right supported by a creek, the left by a marsh, the heat only slightly diminished. I find Washington under the canopy of the heavens, near to his officers, beneath the small, spreading branches of a tree.[22] I give him the note from de Grasse and recount the conversation,[23] pleased I have been instrumental in persuading him to stay.

"I will consider his requests. Now the fleet is back in the Bay, our plans can continue," he says.

Our men lie on their arms; some rebuild the bridges and will continue through the night.[24] Platoons of Tarleton's legion appear in the evening, but duty pickets are ordered forward; there is some grape-shot fire; they soon make a half-turn to the right.[25] At Gloucester, Lauzun's three hundred infantry and cavalry have reinforced the one thousand five hundred militiamen under the command of Brigadier General Weedon.

On the twenty-seventh, while I was away, Washington organized the Continentals into three divisions, each of two brigades. My Light Division now consists of Brigadier General Muhlenburg's brigade, comprising battalions commanded by Colonels Vose, Gimat and Barber, and Brigadier General Hazen's Brigade, comprising the battalions of Hamilton, Huntington,

Laurens and Antill. General Lincoln is second-in-command to Washington of the American Army.

September 29. In the morning, the army crosses Beaver Dam Creek,[26] the enemy firing a few shot from their advance redoubts. About nine or ten o'clock, the riflemen and jagers fire several shots at each other from a small work by Moore's Mill Pond at the dam and a battery on the left of Pigeon Quarter.[27] We establish a position at the bottom of the York River on a plain about half a mile from the forward posts of the enemy, the jagers and riflemen continuing to fire all day, wounding five or six men, one fatally.[28] The encirclement of Yorktown has been made as tightly as it has so far been possible, although enemy boats are still troublesome in the water above the town.[29]

We reconnoiter with Rochambeau and the senior officers to assess the situation of the enemy and find it is difficult to see their defenses clearly. A wide, deep ravine where a swampy stream flows for about eight hundred yards, extends from the river in front of us; an abattis of sharpened tree trunks and branches spike the ground as far as the stream. We can glimpse earthworks surrounding the town, except by the river, and more earthworks about one thousand yards south. Two redoubts are on the British right and guard the river road to Williamsburg. Three are next to the town and three more defend the left. Beyond the earthworks on the British left are three redoubts. One is several hundred yards west of Yorktown; the other two, which are palisaded and protected by abattis, are about one quarter of a mile apart, approximately five hundred yards east of the earthworks and are on somewhat hilly land with pine trees. There are several small camps between the redoubts and the batteries and the whole of this flat, sandy ground has been cleared of vegetation. York, a town of about sixty houses, is on the south bank of the river, where the long peninsula between the James and the York is only eight miles wide.[30] It is on the summit and slopes of a small plateau, traversed by ravines, which go to the shore. The plateau has on the west a marshy ravine beyond which is a large, star redoubt, fraised and fortified, with a double row of abattis. On the left of the town, the plateau finishes at the river. Its main street is on a bluff above the river, a church steeple and two large houses the most prominent landmarks. On the opposite shore is Gloucester Point which extends into the river, narrowing it to about half a mile. It has four redoubts, three batteries, and entrenchments and a detachment of about seven to eight hundred men, commanded by Lieutenant Colonel Tarleton.[31]

In the river there are only two frigates, the *Charon* and the *Guadeloupe* which have about eighty-eight guns and there are about one hundred other small craft. From the mouth of Queen's Creek, up the river, woods conceal everything in Yorktown except the church steeple. In the opposite direction, the French ships can be distantly seen. [32] There are estimated to be from sixty to seventy cannon at York and about nine thousand men. Nearly all the boats from Head of Elk have anchored off College Creek. Our allied armies have now more than nineteen thousand men, most of them regulars, and we also have more cannon.

It is decided to expedite the moving of the artillery from the James, to form large working parties to provide cover as soon as we can begin the advance, and to assume that the enemy will not surrender until they can no longer escape nor fight.[33] Everyone is in high hopes of a successful siege. "The Allies have the most glorious certainty of victory," exclaims Wayne, and I must say I think the same.

"Cornwallis must now tremble for his fate. We have holed him and nothing remains but to dig him out. We have got him in a pudding bag," say others.[34]

The Americans take their station in the front of the enemy's works and extend from the left of Pigeon Quarter to Moore's Mill on Wormeley's Creek near the river.[35] My brigades are on the end of the right, next to Wormeley's Creek. On our left is Steuben's division, comprising Wayne's brigade and Gist's brigade. On their left is Lincoln's division, comprising Clinton's brigade and Dayton's brigade. The Continentals are in the front line, the militia in the second. We also have Knox's artillery brigade and cavalry of sixty men under Moyland and forty from Lauzun's Legion.

The French form the left wing, south-west of the town, and extend to the river above Yorktown.[36] They have four regiments from Newport, with nine hundred men in each; the Bourbonnais, the Royal Deux-Ponts, the Soissonais and the Saintonge. They also have the three regiments each of one thousand men, brought by de Grasse; the Agenais, the Gâtinais and the Touraine which my father was commanding when he was killed at Minden.[37] Rochambeau has four *maréchaux de camp*, Saint-Simon, baron de Vioménil, comte de Vioménil and Chastellux.

Two headquarters, one for Rochambeau, and one for Washington, are about two hundred and fifty yards apart on the land between the two armies. Washington's tents are on the west of Jones's Run, on flat ground, at the side of an old field, near a spring down the hill to the west, Rochambeau's tents on the east of Jones's Run.

September 30. Sunday. Early in the morning, baron d'Esebeck reports to Rochambeau, to his surprise, that the enemy have evacuated the three outposts between the ravine at York Creek and the marshy land above Wormeley's Pond and Moores Mill, which cover the approach from the south-west. Two are on the Goosely Road on Penny's Hill, or Pigeon Quarter; the third is to the north, covering a road across the top of Yorktown Creek. They have now retreated to their interior defences near the town.[38] It is possible they feared their position was too extended, and they could have been outflanked and captured from the rear.[39]

At dawn, Colonel Alexander Scammell went to reconnoiter the ground abandoned by the enemy. He and his men were captured by dragoons from Tarleton's regiment and after he surrendered he was shot in the back before being carried into York. I had initially thought his absence was due to his being officer of the day but now I know what happened.[40] We are furious at the despicable and unsoldierly behavior of the enemy. Sometime later, a letter is sent under a flag for Lieutenant Colonel Huntington of Colonel Scammell's regiment, informing him of his capture and asking him to send his servant and clothes to Williamsburg where he will be conveyed on parole as soon as his wound is dressed.

Between seven and eight o'clock, the French take possession of Pigeon Quarter and hill and the enemy's redoubts, our position now very advantageous, as we command their line of fortifications from nearby. The vicomte de Vioménil orders his men to attack the pickets stationed before his redoubt on the right. The enemy retreat towards their redoubt; cannons fire; there is a small fusillade; nine men are wounded, one is killed. The French brigade on the right which had been positioned behind the marsh, joins the two others whose lines extend to the York River.[41] We are more fortunate, however. On our side of the line, the enemy scarcely fires scarcely a gun today.[42]

I write to Washington that I consider it possible, although not probable, that the enemy might try to retreat by West Point, rather than elsewhere, as we do not have ships above York. I say that Scammell has been captured and suggest it would be best for officers under the rank of generals or field officers not to reconnoiter so close to the enemy's lines. I write a second, confidential, letter to him and ask if he could send Lincoln over to Gloucester and give me his command:

> You was pleased to tell me, My dear General, that you took Gal. Lincoln with You Because you Could not Help it...Since I Returned from France I never Had Anybody Between You and Me. But Now from Being the Commander of the Army against Cornwallis I became one of Gal.

Lincoln's officers who as of Course the General leads the troops Has Nothing almost to Say Even in the light division. Don't Think, My Dear General, that I am in any way disastified. I will chearfully Serve Any How where ever I am in General Washington's Army. But as the Command of the Right Wing in this Siege is of the Highest importance to me- as it Cannot Have Any Similar effect upon Gal. Lincoln's Reputation and Military prospects in Europe and the future Course of His life, I am Sure You Will Be So very kind to me as to adopt any plan Consistent with propriety that May Bring on an Event So Highly interesting to me that it Can Bear no Comparaison. [43]

Washington unfortunately does not agree.

At night, the battery on the Hampton Road is closed at the gorge and a redoubt begun between that battery and those of Pigeon Hill situated near the beginning of one of the branches of the large ravine on the right of the besieged.[44]

October 1. Monsieur de Choisy with eight hundred men from the garrison troops of de Grasse joins the duc de Lauzun near Gloucester.[45] At Trebell's Landing, seven miles away on the James River, boats arrived last night with the siege equipment, so Rochambeau goes there to begin its unloading and commence its transport to the battlefield. Quartermaster Pickering has been endeavoring to obtain horses and oxen to haul the heavy cannon, but it will be four days before some will arrive here because of the long detour necessary to cross the rivers in the narrower places.[46] Here by Yorktown, the enemy abandon many horses in such a wretched state they can hardly walk.

Washington writes to de Grasse acknowledging the note I brought to him and asking if he could station two or three ships above the enemy's posts on York River so that the investment of their works can be completed. Without this action the British remain masters of the navigation of the river for twenty-five miles and not only can they intercept supplies, but they could also in great security land above Queen's Creek and ultimately try to escape by this route.[47]

At three in the afternoon, Washington, Duportail, and several engineers cross at the mill dam to observe the enemy's works and to determine the position of the parallel. Captain Smith and a guard of fifty men march in front and stop at a hill whilst Washington, Duportail and three of the guard advance within three hundred yards of the enemy's main works.[48] A shot rings out, but Washington is looking through his glass at the time and pays no attention.

One thousand two hundred Pennsylvania and Maryland militiamen collect wicker in the woods to make six hundred gabions for the fortifications on this flat, sandy soil. Six thousand stakes will be cut, two thousand bundles of sticks will be bound together to make fascines, and six hundred long pipes, called saucissons, will be filled with gunpowder. Platforms will be made for the batteries.

The enemy release more of their wretched horses which can hardly walk.[49] They continue to fire throughout the night, at fifteen to twenty minutes between each shot, killing or wounding several of our men.[50]

October 2. From dawn, the firing becomes more frequent at our work parties at only five-minute and sometimes at only one-or-two-minute intervals. About ten in the morning the enemy bring up two eighteen-pounders in addition to what they used yesterday. The incessant firing continues all day.[51] One Maryland soldier's hand is shot off and one militiaman is killed.[52]

St. George Tucker goes to Moore's House and sees with his glass between seventy and one hundred dead horses on the York shore or floating in the river, which suggests the enemy has a lack of forage and do not intend to try to march out. He also sees several square-rigged vessels sunk close to the bank. [53]

By sunset about three hundred and fifty-one shot has been fired at us since dawn.[54] At about ten o'clock, the ships in the river start to fire heavily; the enemy batteries continue the onslaught all night.

October 3. About four hundred horse carcasses, stinking in the heat, are in the river and on the bank. There is very little firing today.[55] The sites for the trench depots are chosen; that in the centre in a large ravine, and that on the right on the slope of a branch of the same ravine.[56] In the evening we happily learn that Monsieur de Choisy's corps composed of Lauzun's legion, the infantry from the ships, and one thousand two hundred militia moved forward in the morning to tighten the line around Gloucester. He encountered Tarleton and his dragoons protecting a foraging party; Lauzun's Legion attacked and Tarleton's horse was brought down. Virginian militia formed a line to support the rally of the French and Tarleton had to retreat to the protection of the Gloucester batteries, with thirty-five men killed. Two of our officers and eleven hussars were wounded, three were killed.[57] Washington describes it as a brilliant success and conveys his particular thanks to Lauzun. During the night, one cannon ball kills three men and wounds another from Captain Rice's company. [58]

October 4. Two enemy deserters come into our lines and tell us of conditions in the town. "The army is very sickly with about two thousand men in the hospital. The troops have scarcely any ground to live upon, they lie upon their arms every night, the shipping is in a very naked state and the cavalry is very scarce of forage."[59]

Engineers survey the ground to determine where to make the first parallel. There is very little firing.[60] Wayne and Butler reconnoiter on the York River side; they report that the enemy is busily constructing new works. At nine in the evening, two thousand French marines are landed on the south side of Gloucester by de Grasse. During the night there is constant heavy cannon fire.

October 5. In the morning, there is very heavy cannonading as well as musket firing when one of our patrols met an enemy patrol.[61] A soldier is killed. There is an attack on the frigate and small warships anchored in the river. Captain William Pierce arrives with news of Greene's victory on September 8, at Eutaw Springs. The Americans took five hundred prisoners, killed and wounded a much greater number, have driven the enemy almost to the gates of Charleston and taken nearly one thousand stands of arms.[62]

The engineers believe we now have enough heavy cannon, mortars and stores transported from Trebell's Landing, as well as enough fascines and gabions, to commence operations, and so the digging of the trenches will start tomorrow.[63] The entrenchment will start east of the head of Yorktown Creek, traverse the Hampton Road at a right angle, and then curve to the high bluff of the York River about six hundred yards from the British redoubt, also on the bluff.[64] The terrain has determined its position; the right is flanked by the river escarpment; the left by the large ravine. While this is being built, on the far left by the river and west of the mouth by Yorktown Creek, a narrow trench will be built and a support battery set up so that the French can oppose a redoubt across the creek as well as keep the warships anchored nearby at a distance, an activity also designed to distract the enemy and stop them noticing what is going on elsewhere.

Slaves stagger towards our lines, starving and ill. Many have smallpox and have perhaps been sent to infect us. There are large groups of them in the woods. Most are dead but a few are still alive, so feeble they can hardly walk. They clutch pieces of ears of burnt Indian corn which are also in the mouths and hands of the dead.[65]

After sunset, in the darkness of night, the rain pouring down, the French engineers mark out the line of the first parallel, followed by a third of the soldiers from the sappers and miners laying down laths of pine wood on it. Washington pays a surprise visit even although it is very dangerous for him to be there.

"We did not realize at first it was His Excellency," says one soldier. "He was wearing a surtout and we couldn't see his uniform. He wanted to know where the engineers were. He asked what troops we are and we said the miners and sappers."

"He told us that if we are taken prisoner not to tell the enemy that," says another.[66]

"Where is he now?" I ask.

"He went away, then returned with the engineers. We heard the officers calling him Your Excellency and realized it was General Washington. Then he went away again," the soldier replies, pleasing me that he is now not near the shelling.

The rain starts to fall even more heavily. The men have worked hard and mainly finished so they return to their tents.

October 6. I write to Greene to congratulate him: 'Your late Victory Has Made me Compleatly Happy and Besides public Motives, the Heart of a friend Had Many feelings to Experience at the Narrative of Your operations.'

I have talked with Colonel Morris, Greene's aide-de-camp, who will tell Greene more about de Grasse's intentions when he returns south, so I restrict myself to just a few remarks: 'I am very Sorry the Admiral is so much Hurried. I need not telling you that I will do what I can. If some thing is done I will go there, and probably will join Your Army for the winter Unless I Return to France...The taking of Charlestown is the thing we ought to do. If it is impracticable, at least must we occupy the Harbour.'[67]

Colonel Scammell dies at Williamsburg. The ball had gone in between his hip bone and his ribs, and it had not been thought he would survive. We mourn him; we are all outraged at the manner of his death.

Rain showers fall during the day, the wind from the east and south-east; the gabions and fascines are brought from the trench depots as far forward as possible without the enemy seeing. At five o'clock in the afternoon, one regiment from each brigade of our army parades on a plain near Tarleton's former camp.[68] They join a similar number of French troops who will start digging the trenches after the miners and sappers have laid the laths.

A gentle rain falls. The night is extremely dark, the moon just past full, but not visible. Washington ceremonially strikes the first blows into the sandy soil with a pickaxe. Fifteen hundred men carrying fascines and entrenching tools on their shoulders take over, each three yards from the next and all working in complete silence. To the rear come horses pulling cannon and ordnance as well as wagons piled with sandbags to construct breastworks. To our right is a marsh; a detachment is sent to the west side of it to build fires in front of which soldiers often pass, as a diversionary tactic.[69] The ruse is successful; the enemy directs its fire here as well as on the flying trench being built at the end of the parallel to support a battery intended to fire at the advanced redoubt on the enemy's right, as well as keeping the fire of their warships at a distance.[70] The cannonading continues severely all night, particularly against this flying trench, and is thought to be because a deserter from the Touraine informed the British about it. This, however, considerably helps the men digging the main trench as the British remain in ignorance of their activity.

Towards morning it is cold. The wind shifts to the north-west. Heavy rain falls. By dawn the men have entrenched so well they are protected from the severe cannonade of the enemy. They have almost completed the first parallel, 10 feet wide, 4 feet deep, and 3,840 to 4,480 feet long, supported on the flanks and in the center by four quickly constructed redoubts. It is 2,880 feet to

3,200 feet away from the enemy fortifications, except for the left, which is only 1,920 feet distant, as the enemy's advanced works are nearer opposite the right, and so the trench on this side is more distant. The nature of the terrain determined its outline-the right was flanked by the river escarpment and the left by the large ravine.[71] One officer and six or seven grenadiers of the Touraine regiment on the left have been wounded; one officer and one man in the ranks are the only casualties on our side. [72]

Daylight reveals our work. The enemy bring two field pieces outside their trenches; they fire at our men setting up a battery but hit nothing. A large bulldog with them constantly races across the ground following the shot. Some officers want him caught and given a message to take back to Yorktown, but he is so ferocious no one dares approach him.[73] A short time later their guns fall silent.

October 7. At eleven o'clock, in a cold wind from the north-west, the American light infantry march into the trench on our side, as do the Bourbonnais and Soissonnais regiments[74] commanded by baron de Vioménil on the French side. The men hold the colors high; the drummers beat. We set up our standards on the parapet which is formed by fascines covered with earth. Hamilton orders his men to mount the bank, face the enemy and proceeds to go through the process of ordering the presenting of their arms. The enemy had been firing beforehand but luckily stop, perhaps from astonishment at the spectacle.[75]

We can now see clearly into Yorktown, where the English flag flies upon the parapet. At noon, with drums beating, the Agenais and Saintonge regiments, commanded by Chastellux, take over from the Bourbonnais and Soissonnais. They perfect the work already begun and start the construction of the batteries. The enemy continues to cannonade, firing incessantly on our work parties who complete one large battery on our far right by the river. Five men are killed and nine wounded.[76]

October 8. During darkness, the parallel and the battery for the feint on the left are finished. In the morning, the enemy bring out a small field piece a short distance from their works. They fire, wounding several of our men. A group goes out from our advanced picket and drives them back. At eleven o'clock von Steuben's division relieves the men working in the trenches. Our fatigue parties complete one large battery on our extreme right, on the bank of the river, on which three 29-pounders, three 18-pounders, two 10-inch mortars and two 8-inch howitzers are mounted, whilst over on the extreme left, Saint-Simon also has a battery completed of eight 18 and 12-pounders, two 10-inch mortars and two 8-inch howitzers, both which batteries are made ready to open at the same instant. A very fine battery of twelve 32, 24, and 18-pounders, six 10-inch mortars and six 8-inch howitzers is forwarded, with small batteries on the right and left of this grand centre battery. The enemy seem embarrassed, confused and indeterminate, their fire seems feeble to what might be expected; their works, too, are not formed on any regular plan, but thrown up in a hurry occasionally, and although we have not as yet fired one shot from a piece of artillery, they are as cautious as if the heaviest fire was kept up. [77]

General Orders announces: 'Colonel Laurens will command the Third Battalion of Hazen's brigade, previously commanded by Colonel Scammell.'[78]

October 9. The first parallel is nearly completed and batteries have been erected somewhat in advance of it.[79] Our commanding battery is on the near bank of the river and has ten heavy guns; next is a bomb-battery of three large mortars and so on throughout the whole French and American line, consisting of ninety-two cannon, mortars and howitzers.[80]

The French finish their digging on our left, a few hours ahead of us, and are ordered to wait. About noon we hold a ceremony to mark the occasion, the men full of expectation and impatience. In the bright sunshine, the Star-Spangled Banner is raised in the ten-gun battery on the right. At three o'clock, Saint-Simon and his men have the honor of beginning the bombardment from their battery on the left of four twelve-pounders, six mortars and howitzers.

"Huzza for the Americans!" they cheer.

At five o'clock, on the right, Lamb's American battery of six eighteen and twenty-four pounders, two mortars and two howitzers, opens.[81] Washington lights the first gun; the cannonball soars across to the town. A simultaneous firing of all the guns follows, the tumult thundering up into the sky, the balls clearly visible as they hurtle towards the enemy. I invite Governor Nelson to witness the scene from the battery of Captain Thomas Machin.

"What is a good target for our gunners?" I ask.

"Now my uncle's house is nearly destroyed, that is probably the headquarters of Cornwallis. It is mine," he says, pointing to a large, elegant building.

During the night, Washington orders the batteries to keep firing to stop the enemy making repairs. In the darkness our soldiers labor to bring more guns into position.

October 10. In the morning, thanks to the night-time activity, two French batteries open, one of ten eighteen and twenty-four pounders, six mortars and howitzers; the other of four eighteen-pounders, as well as two more American batteries, one of four eighteen-pounders and the other of two mortars. [82] By ten o'clock our fire becomes so heavy, and we are inflicting such damage that the enemy are only returning about six rounds an hour. They withdraw their cannon from their embrasures, place them behind the merlins, and scarcely fire a shot.[83] The sixty houses of Yorktown are disintegrating into smoking piles of rubble; the air is thick with dust. Some shells go past the town and fall into the river. They explode, sending water cascading into the sky, like the spouting of the monsters of the deep.[84]

A flag goes into York to ask for the release of Thomas Nelson, Governor Nelson's white-haired, sixty-five-year-old uncle, who was the King's Secretary for Virginia before the war, who had retired from public life in 1775 and who is suffering badly from gout. Cornwallis allows him to leave and at noon he escapes the besieged town under a flag. He alights at Washington's headquarters and although not able to walk, sits serenely and describes what is happening there.[85]

"My house has been damaged, and the shells have caused much destruction.[86] Many of the British have taken shelter under the cliff and Cornwallis is living underground in a sort of grotto dug at the bottom of my garden.[87] They have had to kill at least one thousand two hundred horses because they could not be fed. Over at Gloucester General Choisy is containing them and they seem a good deal dispirited although they say they do not fear the garrison will fall. A whale boat from New York with two majors on board arrived there this morning but all I could hear was that it was probable Admiral Digby with his squadron will shortly make an attempt at the Count de Grasse, however inferior he may be to him in strength."[88]

"It appears that Cornwallis's army depends on this and so it is a confession they have no other alternative to save them," says Pickering, an opinion we widely share.[89]

We fire three thousand six hundred shells today, the black balls from our side incessantly crossing the path of those of the enemy in the air. At night, they are like fiery meteors with a blazing trail. They ascend majestically from the mortar, then gradually descend, whirling around, burrowing, excavating the earth and bursting, cause enormous havoc, throwing limbs and other body parts into the air.[90]

At nine in the evening, red-hot balls from the French battery on the left, set fire to the *Charon*, a 44-gun ship, anchored in the river, as well as several smaller vessels.[91] Fire blazes through the rigging to the tops of the masts, the ships burning furiously, glowing a brilliant-red in the darkness, thunder and lightning from the cannon and mortars tearing the night. [92] The enemy send only some flying shells during the darkness.[93]

October 11. In the morning, hot shot sets on fire two enemy transport ships. This results in the enemy attempting to remove their ships as far as possible over to the Gloucester shore.[94] Our batteries continue to fire incessantly all day.[95] At dusk, we open the second parallel, 1152 feet from the main fortifications, and commence the construction of the necessary redoubts as well as the outline of its batteries. Several trenches link the two parallels, that on the right going from the beginning of the large ravine in the center, that on the left intersecting the main Hampton Road. There is much firing from the enemy. There is even a short volley between patrols on the right. However, firing from the batteries on the first parallel causes the enemy to diminish theirs considerably, so helping the men digging. Our guns are now only one hundred and fifty yards from the nearest British defenses and some of our balls even land on the beach at Gloucester across the river. Our shot and shell go over our heads in a continual blaze all night. By dawn, our men in the second parallel are almost entirely under cover. Seven men have been killed, twelve wounded on the French side.[96] One man killed and three or four wounded on our side. [97]

October 12. The second parallel could not come any nearer to the right than the left of the American line because the enemy still possess two redoubts about three hundred yards in front of their principal works. We therefore need to capture these redoubts, one of which is opposite my division, on the extreme left of the enemy. The other redoubt is to the right, about two hundred yards from the end of the second parallel. During the day there is very heavy cannonading both from our side and from the enemy.[98] During the night, the men complete the second parallel and begin the construction of the two batteries, many flying shells and small royal bombs exploding onto us.[99]

October 13. Work continues on the trenches and the batteries.[100] During the night there is very heavy cannonading.

October 14. The enemy keep up a continual firing of cannon. They are unfortunately using five-inch shells which cannot be seen and only make a slight noise as they fall.[101] Washington does not wait for the batteries to be finished but orders all the guns to fire on the advanced redoubts within range. Saint-Simon, on the left, fires heavily against the star redoubt.[102] At about two in the afternoon, Washington is informed that the engineers consider the two redoubts on the left of the enemy's line to be so badly damaged that an assault can now be made.[103] He decides to make an assault this evening.

"It is best to use French troops as they have the necessary discipline and experience," says Vioménil.

"We are but young soldiers, and we have but one sort of tactic on such occasions, which is, to discharge our muskets, and push on straight with the bayonets," I retort, a little offended by his remark.[104]

It is decided the American light infantry, which I command, will attack the redoubt on the extreme left, defended by about forty-five soldiers. A detachment of the French grenadiers and chasseurs, commanded by baron de Vioménil, will attack the second redoubt, defended by about one hundred and twenty soldiers.[105]

"Gimat will lead the assault on our redoubt," I order.

"No," exclaims Hamilton angrily. "It is my tour of duty tonight and I am senior to him. I wish to do it."

"The other officers would like the honor to go to someone who has served throughout the Virginia campaign," I reply. "However, you can appeal to His Excellency."

Washington decides Hamilton will lead our Americans and Vioménil chooses the vicomte des Deux Ponts and Monsieur de l'Estrapade, the lieutenant colonel of the Gâtinais, to lead the French.

In the darkening twilight, men from the Gatinais and Royal Deux Ponts regiments prepare for the assault on their redoubt. My men, led by Hamilton, prepare for the assault on the redoubt near the riverbank. The miners and sappers are given axes to go in front and cut through the abattis, which are made of treetops, the small branches cut off at a slant. [106] Washington goes to the French line and talks with Vioménil. Then he rides to our troops and gives a short speech. "Act the part of firm and brave soldiers in storming the redoubt. The success of the attack on both redoubts depends on you."[107]

"Arnold and the British behaved very cruelly towards the New London garrison after their surrender. And they shot Colonel Scammell in the back after he was captured. We won't forget," mutter the men.

"There must not be revenge," I warn.

As night starts to darken the sky, the Touraine regiment makes a diversionary attack on the left; the enemy reply with a strong fusillade lasting seven minutes. Then the Touraine retire. At nearly the same time de Choisy also attacks at Gloucester to attempt to deceive the enemy more.[108]

At eight o'clock exactly, the detachment advances beyond the trenches and lies down on the ground to wait for the signal to attack. All the batteries in our line are silent; Jupiter and Venus glow brilliantly, close to each other in the western hemisphere, the same direction from where the attack signal will come. The watchword is Rochambeau, a great favorite with the soldiers, who pronounce it Row-sham-bow, which when said quickly sounds like 'rush-on-boys.'[109]

Three shells soar into the sky, their fiery trains rising into the night, giving the signal to advance.

"Up! Up!" order the officers.

Gimat's New England battalion leads the vanguard silently forward, followed by Hamilton commanding the whole force, with his battalion of New Yorkers and New Englanders commanded by Major Fish, all with unloaded arms. On the left is a detachment of eighty men commanded by Laurens with orders to take the enemy from the back of the redoubt and to intercept any retreat. In front of the right column are twenty men led by Lieutenant Mansfield and a detachment of sappers and miners with axes commanded by Captain Gilliland.[110]

The vanguard reaches the abattis; the British see them and open fire. "Rush on boys!" the men shout. "The fort's our own!"[111]

They slash at the abattis and palisades, many falling into craters made by shells, but the soldiers behind do not stop. They pull down the abattis with their hands, scrambling over or through them. They rush forward with fixed bayonets under heavy firing. Shots and screams tear the air. They take the redoubt in just seven minutes from the initial signal.

The French advance a short distance silently forward through the communications trench almost opposite the larger redoubt they are to attack. A Hessian sentry notices them.

"*Wer da?*" he shouts.[112]

They do not reply. The enemy fire overhead, the signal for all their garrison to fire a roulade from the left to the right since they believe there will be a general attack. [113] The French wait until the abattis are axed, ordered not to fire until they reach the top of the parapet, although some do.

"Inform baron de Vioménil we have captured our redoubt and are ready to help him with his," I tell Major Barber.

The enemy fire incessantly. Barber returns, injured by shot, his coat and shirt stained with blood, but refusing to have the wound dressed until he has personally reported. "The French are not yet in control of their redoubt, but shortly will be," is the message from Deux Ponts.

My men do not take revenge on the enemy, except for a captain in the New Hampshire infantry who tried to kill the wounded Major Campbell, the British commander, who is saved by Hamilton.[114] They return in high spirits, their clothes torn, dirty and bloodied. We have thirty-one prisoners. The rest escaped, some sliding down the almost precipitous bank to the river.[115]

"There will be no more duty for you tonight," I tell them; they rest on the sandy ground, grape and canister hailing down.[116]

The French take their redoubt. They capture a major, six officers and sixty-eight men, as well as two small howitzers. Deux Ponts is severely wounded in the face from sand thrown by a ball; his hearing and sight are much feared for. Charles de Lameth is badly wounded in two legs.[117] They have about seventy dead or wounded and we have about forty, including several wounded officers. Gimat was wounded in the foot but has no broken bones.[118] The enemy quickly turn their fire on the captured redoubts, but the men hastily throw up a wall of earth at the rear.

October 15. "You have performed very bravely. I am extremely proud of what you achieved last night," I tell my men when they return to camp.

By dawn the men have been so busy that the parallel extends to the river on our right and is nearly completed. Batteries are quickly being set up. We are now only two hundred yards from the enemy's line of works and small shells rain down into our trenches; there is an extremely hot fire of shells and shot for the rest of the day. In the evening, Captain White is buried.[119]

October 16. About midnight a sudden tempest blows up. Rain pounds the trenches and encampments, the wind howling in one of the most severe storms I have ever encountered.

"An evil omen," say the men.

About two in the morning, the wind dies down, the rain ceases.

I am on trench duty today; I arrive at the first parallel with the troops I have assembled from camp and discover that the enemy made a rather ineffectual sortie shortly before sunrise.[120] Three hundred and fifty men had marched silently from the Horn battery in the center of their lines. They passed between two small redoubts not yet completed and enter the trench. They went to a French battery and spiked the guns,[121] killing four or five. Then they entered the covered way between the first and second parallel where Captain Savage was commanding the battery.

"What troops?" they asked.

"French," he replied.

"Push on my brave boys and skin the buggers!" cried the British commander and was heard by Noailles. "Charge with bayonets!" he ordered the grenadiers.

They attacked, shouting "*Vive le roi!*" They killed or wounded four French officers and twelve privates, and fatally injured one American sergeant. Seven or eight British were killed and six captured. They spiked the touch holes of four French pieces and two American, but the spikes were easily extracted.[122] Within hours the guns were firing again.

October 17. At dawn, we see the enemy have closed the embrasures of most of their batteries. Their cannon is almost silent, but they continue to throw small shells. Several new batteries open in the second parallel. The whole of our works now has cannon and mortars, and not less than one hundred pieces of heavy ordnance have been constantly firing for the last twenty-four hours, the ground shaking under the incessant thundering.[123] Washington orders again that spectators should leave the ground.

We discover the enemy had tried to escape to Gloucester during the stormy night. Tarleton sent sixteen boats and part of their army was ferried to Gloucester Point, but other boats, some with troops on board, were driven down the river. The tempest had defeated them; they had returned to Yorktown, but even if they had succeeded in transferring their army to the opposite shore, I do not believe they would have broken through our lines.

The sky rapidly brightens. We can see their parapets and palisades disintegrating under our onslaught. We will soon be able to attack on foot. We are so near we can see the dreadful destruction of their works. We can even see men in their lines being torn to pieces by the bursting of our shells.[124]

About nine o'clock, a white flag suddenly appears above the British earthworks. A drummer stands on the parapet of the horn work, but the noise of our cannon is so great we cannot hear what he is beating. We stare, almost unable to believe what is happening. Our guns begin to stop firing. Finally, the last batteries to know about the flag and the drumming, cease. There is complete silence.

A British officer in a red coat and very white trousers walks slowly towards our lines carrying a white flag, accompanied by a drummer boy, also in a red coat and with similarly white trousers, who is beating *en chamade*, which means they wish to talk. We gaze in awe.

I send an officer to greet them. They speak together for a few minutes; the drummer goes back to the town. The British officer is blindfolded and brought into our lines; the letter he bears from Cornwallis is taken by an officer on horseback to Washington's headquarters.

The letter is succinct. Cornwallis writes: 'Sir, I propose a cessation of hostilities for twenty-four hours, and that two officers be appointed by each side, to meet at Mr. Moore's house to settle terms for the surrender of the posts at York and Gloucester. I have the honor to be, etc. Cornwallis.'[125]

Washington writes back:

My Lord: I have had the honor of receiving your Lordship's letter of this date. An ardent desire to spare the further effusion of blood will readily incline me to such terms for the surrender of your posts and garrisons of York and Gloucester as are admissible. I wish previously to the meeting of commissioners that your Lordship's proposals in writing may be sent to the American lines, for which purpose a suspension of hostilities during two hours from the delivery of this letter will be granted. I have the honor etc. [126]

Cornwallis sends an officer under another flag to ask for longer than just two hours. Washington agrees; hostilities cease from five o'clock.[127]

During the night it is eerily silent for the first time in many nights. The sky is cloudless; stars shine brilliantly, meteors flash across the heavens. Today is the anniversary of Burgoyne's surrender at Saratoga.

October 18. At dawn we hear the wail of bagpipes; the band of the Deux Ponts regiment replies. The sun rises; soldiers crowd onto the Point of Rock battery; our lines are completely manned. Two hundred yards away, enemy officers climb onto their parapets and stare at our men. In the light of day, we can see the complete devastation of the town. Secretary Nelson's house lacks a corner, has large holes in the roof and walls and appears near to collapse; the other houses are similar. Hundreds of people are busily moving on the beach, and near to the shore ships are sunk as far as the water's edge, whilst further out, only masts, yards and topgallants can be seen, without any sign of the rest of the ship. Over at Gloucester Point the *Guadeloupe* is sunk at the water's edge; enemy fortifications and encampment are visible, whilst in the distance are the French war ships, two of which are under sail.[128]

Trumbull has composed a draft of proposals to make to Cornwallis which Washington finds acceptable, and it is sent off to the British under a flag. Cornwallis replies, no longer asking for his army to be allowed to return home and asking for terms of special honor for the garrison at Gloucester, permission to dispatch a small ship to New York with private property and immunity for the loyalists at the two sites: 'If you choose to proceed to negotiations on these grounds, I shall appoint two field officers to meet American representatives at a time and place Washington can designate to 'digest the articles of capitulation.'[129]

Washington chooses Laurens as the American commissioner; Rochambeau chooses Noailles, my brother-in-law, as the French commissioner, and Monsieur de Grandchain, for the French fleet. They meet the British commissioners, Lieutenant Colonel Thomas Dundas and Major Alexander Ross at Moore's House. By a strange chance of fate, Laurens's father is imprisoned in the Tower of London, whose Constable is Lord Cornwallis. John Laurens is therefore arranging the surrender of the Constable who is now our prisoner, whilst his father remains a prisoner in the Tower to the captured Constable.

Washington and Rochambeau had been inclined to allow the British to march out with full honors, but Laurens and I had vehemently disagreed.

"Don't forget Lincoln's surrender at Charleston," had exclaimed Laurens.

"The same terms should apply to the British now," I had said.

The discussion of the commissioners continues until midnight. Laurens and Noailles return with a rough draft which is to be considered until tomorrow morning and so the truce is being extended until nine o'clock.

October 19. Washington writes his comments on the draft and sends it to Cornwallis.

"Tell Cornwallis I expect to have the papers signed at eleven o'clock and the garrison to march out at two o'clock," he says to Laurens.[130]

Before midday, the document comes back, signed by Lord Cornwallis, lieutenant general of the forces of His British Majesty, and Captain Symonds, commander of the naval forces of His British Majesty in the York River. The British army will surrender to the Americans, the navy to the French. Officers will be able to keep their sidearms and private property. The sloop *Bonetta* will be allowed to carry dispatches and soldiers, but no public property. The soldiers will be kept in Virginia, Maryland or Pennsylvania. Cornwallis and some other officers will be permitted to return to England or New York.[131]

A short time later, in the shade of the captured redoubt near to the river, Washington and Rochambeau sign the fourteen articles of capitulation on which the words have been added: 'Done in the trenches before York in Virginia, October 19, 1781.' G. Washington, le Comte de Rochambeau, Le Comte de Barras En mon nom et celui du Comte de Grasse'.

Washington sends Cornwallis an invitation to dine with him after the surrender. Our troops immediately enter the town and the fortifications, over which hangs a stench of death from decomposing bodies on the battlefield, many of which are black. Steuben's men hoist their flag. The houses are greatly damaged, most in ruins. They lack roofs, windows and often walls. Rich furniture and books are scattered on the ground; horse carcasses and parts of bodies, some black, some white, lie against walls and in corners; blood-stained rags of clothing are everywhere. The force of exploding shells have created huge mounds of earth.[132] It is filthy. However, the magazines still have many stores and our men start to take them to our lines. The few people there seem to fear we will pillage the town.

The trenches which cross the road going to the town are filled in and made flat. After breakfast, our troops start to line the right, the French the left, of the road extending from our front parallel to the forks of the road at Hudson Allen's. A large contingent of spectators from the surrounding countryside gather, perhaps as many as the number of the soldiers, bringing an almost festive air to the proceedings. At about twelve o'clock the allied army is finally assembled. At the same time, a detachment of American light infantry and the Bourbonnais company of grenadiers take possession of the two redoubts of the fortifications, as provided in Article Three.[133]

At about two o'clock the defeated army marches from the town, led by General Charles O'Hara as Cornwallis has pleaded indisposition. Dumas goes forward to direct the troops and rides on O'Hara's left, General Lincoln on his right.[134] The enemy drums covered with black handkerchiefs and fifes with black ribbons play a British march,[135] stipulated by Washington to be either English or German, following the restrictions made to the Americans at Charleston. The troops march slowly between the mile-long lines of Americans and French, the generals and staff officers in front of each regiment, the French magnificent in white uniforms and white gaiters, with different colored collars, buttons and lapels, according to their regiment. The Soissonais have light blue collars, yellow buttons, rose lapels and a rose feather in their grenadier caps; the Bourbonnais have pink collars, white buttons and crimson lapels. Lauzun's cavalry is particularly striking; they have blue jackets with white braid, yellow trousers, scarlet and yellow striped sashes, black boots and black fezzes on their heads. The Deux Ponts, also known as the ZwieBrucken, have blue coats. On the right of each regiment is a white silk flag embroidered with three silver fleur-de-lys. Behind the flag are drummers and fifers, and in front are hautboists, all playing music.[136]

The Americans stand in three ranks. First the regulars, also with musicians, who are decently uniformed, then the militia who have dirty-white, small, ragged coats or hunting shirts. Many are barefoot.[137] Some are just young boys; some are old men. I look at my lean, tough soldiers with immense pride. I know of their bravery and suffering, from famine and from battle. I know of their will to become a free, independent nation, which has led them to continue fighting against an enemy far better equipped and trained.

The Anspach regiments wear immaculate uniforms, better even than the Hessians. They march along smartly, but the same cannot be said of the British, most of whose uniforms look clean and new, although some are soiled and ragged. Many appear sullen. Most are very drunk. They march out of step in broken ranks with shouldered arms and are carrying heavy knapsacks, presumably because they think they will not be returning to their camp. They show great scorn for the Americans,[138] but stare at the French, many with obvious malice in their eyes. I therefore order the band to strike up *Yankee Doodle Dandy* the song which was originally sung by the British to mock the Americans but has been taken up by the Americans who have added patriotic words. Now the British, who appear a small force by comparison with our numbers, for the first time turn their heads towards them.

O'Hara starts to ride to Rochambeau, at the head of the French troops, to surrender his sword. Rochambeau makes a sign to Dumas and points to Washington. Dumas immediately gallops between O'Hara and Rochambeau.

"The French army is auxiliary on this continent. It is the American general who gives the orders," he says. He immediately accompanies him to Washington, at the other side of the road, on his favorite horse, Nelson. O'Hara, already red-faced, flushes slightly more. He removes his hat and turns to Washington.

"I apologize for my mistake," he says, offering his sword.

"Never from such a good hand," Washington declares, refusing to accept it, and indicating that O'Hara should present himself to Lincoln.[139]

Lincoln takes the sword for just a moment. Then he gives it back to O'Hara and tells him where his troops must lay down their weapons.

The soldiers march to the flat heath, which is surrounded by Lauzun's Legion, their sabers drawn, spears held high. Some of the British officers are crying.[140] Others look sullen. Their broad-brimmed hats hide their faces and their shame, but the officers of the foreign regiments appear more manly.[141]

"Present arms. Ground arms. Put down cartridge boxes and sabers!" shout the British and German officers. The soldiers throw down their weapons. Some try to break them.

"Stop that!" orders Lincoln and puts a halt to it.[142] We need their weapons.

Then they turn about. They march back through our lines. A few of our Americans jeer as they pass, but the French are quiet.[143] When the British reach the town, the French encircle them, partly as a guard, and partly to halt plundering by anyone.

At Gloucester, the enemy are surrendering to Monsieur de Choisy. We have eight thousand prisoners, of whom seven thousand are regular troops and eight hundred are sailors. We also have seventy-five brass, and one hundred and sixty-nine iron cannon, seven thousand seven hundred and ninety-four muskets, as well as eighteen German and ten British regimental standards.[144] Sixty-three ships were lost by the British, thirty-two were sunk and thirty-one remain, of which six are armed, and it is thought the *Guadeloupe*, a frigate of twenty-six, can be raised.[145]

The generals and high-ranking officers will be allowed to go to England or New York. The marines and sailors will be prisoners-of-war to the French navy; the soldiers will be prisoners of the army and will be sent in their regiments, with officers, to Virginia, Maryland and Pennsylvania, and will have the same rations as our army.

We dine with the British officers. Cornwallis is not present; O'Hara deputizes for him. He is Irish; his face has the same ruddy complexion as earlier in the day and he talks quickly and in a jovial fashion. I find it difficult to imagine he belongs to the defeated army; he eats and drinks merrily and is very sociable to everyone. Banastre Tarleton is not here. The American officers have refused to allow him to attend because of the excessive cruelty and violence of his troops.

"Why am I not invited?" he asks me.

"It is best to talk with Colonel Laurens," I reply.

"Has this slight occurred by chance?" he asks him.

"No," replies Laurens. "No accident at all, intentional, I can assure you, and meant as a reproof for certain cruelties practiced by the troops under your command in the campaigns in the Carolinas."

"Severities are a part of war," retorts Tarleton angrily.

"A soldier can perform his duty in many ways and when mercy is shown it makes the duty more acceptable to friends and enemies alike," replies Laurens.[146]

The evening passes with the sang-froid and even gaiety of the English officers, to the amazement of some,[147] and I celebrate with everyone.

October 20. Washington issues General Orders: 'I praise the army for the glorious event of yesterday. I thank His Most Christian Majesty and the French fleet and army. The General's thanks to each individual of merit would comprehend the whole army. But he thinks himself bound by affection, duty and gratitude to express his obligations to Major Generals Lincoln, de La Fayette and Steuben for their distinctions in the trenches. He mentions others, but my heart swells with emotion he has mentioned me.[148]

The French had ninety-eight men killed and two hundred and ninety-one wounded.[149] Cornwallis's account of his loss during the siege is one hundred and fifty-six killed, three hundred and twenty-six wounded, and seventy missing, making five hundred and fifty-two.[150] The American army has ten officers killed or wounded, and two hundred and eighty-nine soldiers killed or wounded.[151]

Washington, Rochambeau and I send our aides-de-camp to Cornwallis.

"He hopes you will call on him," Major George Augustine Washington, my aide, informs me when he returns. "He says he has been fighting so long against you in this campaign that he wants to explain to you in detail the circumstances which led to his surrender and that he had abandoned the fight only when he had not been able to continue any longer."[152]

Tench Tilghman will carry news of our victory to Congress in Philadelphia; Lauzun will carry the same news to France, so I write letters for him to take for me.

'The play is over, monsieur le comte; the fifth act has just ended. I was a bit uneasy during the first acts, but my heart keenly enjoyed the last one, and I have no less pleasure in congratulating you on the successful conclusion of our campaign,' I tell Maurepas. [153]

'After this commencing stroke, what English general will ever think of conquering America?' I say to Vergennes.[154]

To the prince de Poix, I mainly talk about our friends and relations, Noailles, Damas, Charlus, and praise Rochambeau 'whose talents have obtained the justice due them in this recent operation' and Washington 'whose genius, his greatness, and the nobility of his manners attach to him the veneration of both armies...Place at the feet of the queen my most tender and respectful homage,' I tell him.[155]

I also write to my beloved. I know how proud she will be and how relieved I am not injured. 'The capture of Cornwallis is a most agreeable reward for me. It has made me forget the disappointments, pains and anxieties with which the superior talents of my enemy only too well surrounded me throughout the campaign.'[156]

I accompany Tilghman and Lauzun to the river where blackened, fire-burnt hulks rear grimly from the water and bloated horse carcasses float half-submerged, as well as putrefying on the shore. A strong wind is dispersing the stench of death; French flags and pennants fly from the captured enemy ships and the American flag representing the thirteen states flies from the water battery.[157]

I embrace Tilghman and Lauzun in turn. "Godspeed. May your journeys go well."

Washington writes to de Grasse to say that the honor of the surrender of York belongs to him and that although de Grasse had not replied favorably concerning Charleston at their previous meeting, the length of the siege at Yorktown had been one of the main reasons he had rejected his proposal, and as it had been concluded unexpectedly promptly, perhaps he would now reconsider. However, if he still believes Charleston is not possible, then perhaps he would consider transporting our troops to Wilmington, as we would then be able to defeat the enemy with very little difficulty and so take away a point of support for the British in North Carolina, which is attended with the most dangerous consequences to us, and at the same liberate another state.[158]

October 21. Sunday. The Reverend Israel Evans, chaplain of the New Hampshire troops, dedicates his sermon to me. He talks of my disinterested services in the cause of America which prove me a friend of mankind and my well-known amiable virtues which render all panegyrics needless. His words bring tears to my eyes.

The prisoners will march today at three o'clock to Williamsburg and then Winchester. General Lawson and Virginia militia will be the escort.[159] The total enemy loss by death and capture is eleven thousand eight hundred, including two thousand sailors, one thousand eight hundred negroes, one thousand five hundred Tories and eighty large and small vessels. Rochambeau has loaned Cornwallis one hundred thousand écus to pay his troops, to be repaid by the English war chest in New York. The Bonetta sets sail without being searched. Tories are certainly on board, as well as deserters, which has pleased Washington, as otherwise he would have had to have hanged them.

I visit Cornwallis. He welcomes me with courtesy and spreads out a map of Virginia on a table. "I intended to maneuver you from a junction with General Wayne," he tells me.[160] He also relates aspects of the siege. "I had wanted to force a passage towards Gloucester, through

Monsieur de Choisy's position, and I gave orders that the Anspach troops should relieve all posts on the night of the sixteenth to the seventeenth so that the rest of the army should cross the river but the storm and not having enough boats to transport them all before dawn had stopped me." [161]

I tell him how we had planned to stop him. He describes his correspondence with Clinton and the reason his army became trapped in Yorktown. His manner is plain and straightforward, and I find him a worthy soldier and foe.

"I know your humanity towards prisoners, and I recommend my poor army to you," he says.

"You know, my Lord, that the Americans have always been humane to imprisoned armies," I reply,[162] very aware of the atrocious conditions of our captured soldiers on board the enemy prison ships and the good treatment of Burgoyne's army. "I also believe your government has made a terrible mistake in imprisoning Henry Laurens in the Tower of London. He is a public minister and not a military man."

"Perhaps I can be exchanged for Laurens," he suggests.

"I will ask His Excellency," I reply.

Many slaves have been reclaimed by their owners, who asked soldiers to find them, offering a guinea a head. Some soldiers refuse to deliver them back to their masters unless they agree not to punish them.[163] Two of Washington's slaves, Lucy and Esther, are returned to him and I know he is intending to find the other fifteen who originally escaped to the *Savage*.

Washington is cautious about our victory, as the British still have two armies, much larger than the one at Yorktown, at New York and Charleston. 'My only apprehension, which I wish may be groundless is lest the late important success, instead of exciting our exertions, as it ought to do, should produce such a relaxation in the prosecution of the war, as will prolong the calamities of it.' [164]

I go with him to speak with de Grasse on the *Ville de Paris*, to try to persuade him to help us against Charleston or Wilmington. Washington does not stay long; he hurries back to the army; I remain on board with McHenry to attempt to persuade de Grasse who wants to return immediately to the Islands.

October 22. I take the opportunity to write more to Adrienne:

This is the last moment, my dear heart, for me to write to you. Monsieur de Lauzun is about to join his frigate and sail for Europe. Various matters with the admiral have given me the pleasure of being able to send you news which is later by two days. Monsieur de Lauzun will bring a detailed description of public events. The end of this campaign has been truly wonderful for the allied forces. There has been a rare unity in our movements, and I should hold myself in contempt if I was not extremely content with the conclusion of my campaign in Virginia...I count among the most beautiful moments of my life that when Monsieur de Saint-Simon's division united with my army, and those when I was by turn commanding the three maréchaux de camp with the troops under their orders. I pity Lord Cornwallis for whom I have the highest regard; he has shown me some esteem and as the capitulation has righted the wrongs of Charleston and I do not wish to carry vengeance any further...If I return as I hope, I will return with the vicomte.[165]

De Grasse asks me to dispatch pilots to him for expert advice on the Carolina coast. I return to land and send Gouvion with experienced pilots. I hope to go with the fleet southward but will have to wait for de Grasse's reply, and whatever that is, I will be in Philadelphia during the winter. If there is no fighting then if Congress thinks I can serve them in Europe, I will cross and recross the Atlantic in a few months, so long as it is of material use to them.[166]

On the twenty-fourth, however, de Grasse writes to me from the *Ville de Paris*, as well as to Washington, to say that if I can sail out with him, he will try to escort me by his frigates to Cape Fear, and from there he will hastily sail to where he ought to be, but that he cannot do more than that. He raises many objections as to why it is impossible to do what has been asked of him and finishes: 'Do not withdraw your friendship from me; on the contrary pity me for not being able to crown your work by giving a second death blow to our enemies. I flatter myself that you will never count me among that number, and, on the contrary, as I become increasingly deserving of your esteem, that you will place me among your friends.' [167]

My disappointment is great. It is now not practicable to besiege Charleston without the help of a superior naval force. I will never forgive the old admiral for so suddenly overthrowing our plan against Wilmington, after which the fleet would have gone to Savannah and joined with Greene.[168] To my even greater disappointment, Washington decides that he must ask Major General St. Clair to command the detachment of Pennsylvania, Maryland and Virginia Continental troops going to Wilmington or other posts in that state to attack the enemy, or if that is not possible then to continue his march to the southern army and put himself under the orders of General Greene.

"If de Grasse is not acting with us there is no need of someone who speaks French, and there are several generals more senior to you who should have the position," he explains.

I have no intention of kicking my heels at Yorktown. I contemplate again the possibility of an expedition to Halifax, Newfoundland or Penobscot. I finally decide I will return to France where I can be useful to the United States by asking my government for money and reinforcements for Rochambeau.

I address my men for the last time. "In the moment the major general leaves this place, he wishes once more to express his gratitude to the brave corps of light infantry, who for nine months past, have been the companions of his fortunes. He will never forget that with them alone of regular troops he had the good fortune to maneuver before an army which after all its reductions is still six times superior to the regular force he had at that time."[169]

I travel north to Baltimore with McHenry, Noailles and others; on November 8 we arrive in Philadelphia. I call on Robert Morris. Two Tories, Lawrence Marr and John Moody, have been arrested after attempting to steal the secret notes of Congress and I am asked to be president of the court-martial; I agree. On the eleventh, we sentence them to death.

A letter from Washington tells me of the unexpected and sad death of his stepson, Mr. Custis, which, along with other business, has delayed his travelling and means he will not arrive at Philadelphia before the last days of November. He is at Mount Vernon and says that if he is deprived of the pleasure of a personal interview with me before my departure then he sends me his ardent vows for a propitious voyage, a gracious reception from my prince, an honorable reward of my services and a happy meeting with my lady and friends. He also says that it 'follows as certain as that night succeeds the day, that without a decisive Naval force we can do nothing definitive-and with it everything honourable and glorious. A constant Naval superiority would terminate the War speedily-without it, I do not know that it will ever be terminated honourably.'[170]

I write directly to Congress on the twenty-second, as Washington is not here, asking for a temporary absence from the army as there is no prospect of active service before the time at which I can return.[171] On the twenty-third, Marr is executed. The same day Congress resolves that I have permission to go to France, to return when it is convenient for me and for a letter about me to be written to His Most Christian Majesty. They commend: 'his zealous attachment to the cause...his judgment, vigilance, gallantry and address in its defence have greatly added to the High Opinion entertained by Congress of his merits and military talents.'[172] They say that the plenipotentiary ministers at the court of Versailles must confer with me and make use of my information, as well as consult with, and employ my assistance, in accelerating the supplies which may be given.

I meet with Livingston, Morris and a representative of the Board of War on the twenty-fifth, to discuss finance and foreign affairs. We agree on the nature of the dispatches I will carry with me to France.

November 26. Washington arrives, accompanied by his wife.[173] In the evening, we confer with Robert Morris about financial matters and decide that I ought to ask for a subsidy or loan of ten million which will probably be sufficient for the next campaign. Washington declares we very much have need of more French land and naval forces.

I have been given the *Alliance* again for my voyage to France with Noailles, Duportail, Gouvion, La Colombe, Poirey and anyone else I wish to take; Morris is responsible for directing the arrangements. He takes leave of us on the twenty-eighth and gives me the orders for Captain Barry.

We set off from Philadelphia; on December 10, we enter Boston, all the church bells pealing a welcome.[174] The *Alliance* is already anchored in the harbor, but, like last time, it is difficult to find enough sailors, as we will be sailing as fast as possible across the Atlantic and therefore there will be no capturing of ships and consequently no prize money. On the twelfth, I enjoy a reception given to me by officers of the Massachusetts Line. On the fourteenth, the town council, headed by Samuel Adams, makes an address to me. I reply.

December 21. I am finally on board the *Alliance* and write to Washington to say I am impatient to be gone, not so much for myself personally but for the next campaign, of which his opinion, when I deliver it, will be of the greatest use to the common cause. As far as foreign affairs are concerned, I shall be happy to justify the confidence of Congress, by giving my view, whenever it is asked for, to the best of my ability, but the question of finances will, I fear, be a difficult point for the American minister, but I will be happy to help him with my utmost exertions:

> Adieu, My dear General, I know your Heart So well that I am Sure no distance Can alter Your attachement to me. With the Same Candor, I assure You that My love, My Respect, My Gratitude for you, are above Expressions, that, on the Moment of leaving You I more than Ever feel the Strength of those friendly ties that for Ever Bind me to you, and that I Anticipate the pleasure, the Most wished for pleasure, to Be again with you, and By my zeal and Services, to gratify the feelings of My Respect and affection. [175]

December 22. I write to George Augustine Washington and ask him 'to get copies of my letters to the General as you know I never kept any, and when I grow old, I will find great satisfaction in reading over our correspondence during the last campaign.' I also ask him to have my orderly books of the light infantry of the last two campaigns copied up by some sergeant, as Washington has done with his, and to be bound as his are.[176]

December 25. The wind is fair. The *Alliance* sets sail in the morning chill under a winter sky.

Chapter 31

Treaty of Peace

1782. January 17. In the dark of night, we pass the citadel's guns at Port Louis, having taken just twenty-three days to traverse the Atlantic. Next morning we cross to Lorient on the opposite coast. I write hastily to Washington:

> From what I pick up on the shore I find that Lord Cornwallis's down fall had a glorious effect and was properly felt in France, England, and indeed throughout Europe. The birth of a Dolphin has given a general satisfaction to the French nation, and from attachement to the Queen I have been made particularly happy by this event. The taking of Statia is a clever affair and I never read of a prettier coup de main. The Dutch will no doubt be greatly pleased with the conduct of the French. Old count de Maurepas is dead. Charlus is Adjutant General of the Gendarmerie of France which his father commands. It appears that the Convoy from Brest to the East and West Indies has met with an accident. 23 Vessels it is said are taken…Adieu, my dear General, we are ready to go and yet when I think you are so many thousand miles off I cannot leave writing to you…[1]

On January 21 our carriage clatters through the faubourg St. Honoré to the hôtel de Noailles. People are already gathering in the street; I step on to the ground and market women clamor round pressing two laurel branches into my hands. I hurry into the mansion.

"Madame de Lafayette is banqueting with the king and queen at the Hôtel de Ville, to celebrate the birth of the dauphin three months ago, and afterwards there will be a firework display," I am told.

To my great disappointment I realize it will be at least five hours before Adrienne and her family return as court etiquette demands she will accompany the queen to the château de la Muette near the Bois de Boulogne. However, my joy overflows to see Anastasie and George, who have grown up so much I find myself a great deal older than I had thought.[2]

Suddenly, there is the noise of carriages. A trumpet sounds. There is shouting. I rush outside; the royal carriage is there, followed by more carriages. The door opens. I see the queen and Adrienne very surprisingly seated beside her, a departure from court protocol. I bow.

"I am pleased for your victories and your safe return. And I have brought your wife to you," she says graciously. Adrienne alights from the carriage, everyone cheering. She sways on her feet. She faints and I catch her in my arms. I carry her inside, the crowd shouting and clapping.[3]

Next day, I go to Versailles where the courtiers flock around me; I present myself to the king.

"I congratulate you on your success. I have much confidence, regard, admiration and affection for Washington," he says.[4]

I cannot visit Franklin quite as quickly as I had intended as he is suffering from gout, however I learn from him that nothing can be expected from the government. Vergennes does not grant me an audience immediately and writes: 'I am not wonderfully pleased with the country you have left; I find it not very active and very demanding.'[5]

I finally see the three ministers, Vergennes, Castries and Maurepas; I spend an hour with each, making all the arguments I can for more money for the next campaign. I visit Franklin to inform him of what was said.

"I still hope to win over the ministers, but the loan is bound to be small, and it would be best to act as though none is to be expected." [6]

I write to Washington:

I am Hitherto Much Satisfied with their zeal and Good Intentions for America. But find it Very Difficult, Next to Impossibility to Get Monney...I Hope, Between us, Some thing May Be obtained, but Would not Have Mr. Moriss to Be Sanguine....But Congress will Be Mistaken if they Build upon Expectations of Monney from this Quarter. However, I will Exert myself for the Best, to Promote that, and Every other Wiew which May Be interesting to America...It is Generally thought in this Quarter that the Exertions of America are not Equal to her Abilities. [7]

Ségur wrote to me on December 5 that the king says he will give me the rank of *maréchal de camp* after the war in America is ended, when I leave the service of the United States to return to his armies, and that I will be considered as having this rank from the date of the surrender of Cornwallis. I therefore sell my existing commission to Noailles for sixty thousand livres, twenty thousand less than I paid for it. I hear rumors of jealousy about my promotion.

"I will decline it," I tell the marquis de Ségur, the minister of war, the father of my friend.

"No, certainly not. I will have to resign if you do," he declares.

"In that case, I will accept," I reply.

The reception I meet with from the king, from my friends, from the nation at large, surpasses my utmost ambition.[8] 'Hero!" people shout in the street as I pass by. I feature in pamphlets and poems. I even receive an invitation from King Gustavus 111 to visit Sweden.

"I am very happy to be counted among his friends," Aglaë de Hünolstein has evidently remarked.

At a production of *Iphigénie en Aulide*, by Gluck, at the Opéra, Mademoiselle Dorlay, who plays the title role, holds out the laurel crown to me, the audience applauding as the choir sings 'Achilles is crowned by the hands of victory.'

The cause of American independence, however, is always my foremost concern. Vergennes asks me for a memoir of all the different points I have made to him and to the other ministers. I write at length and declare that America needs ten or twelve million livres and the desirability of a powerful demonstration against New York or Charleston.[9] On February 25 I am pleased to be able to write to Franklin that following my meeting the night before with Vergennes, he will present the petition for the loan to America this evening to de Castries and will inform Franklin, at Passy, as soon as possible the amount which will be given: 'Mr. Franklin Cannot Render His friend More Happy than in Employing of him for the Service of America, and He feels a particular pleasure in Avoiding for the doctor the trouble of Journeys to Versailles where His Peculiar Situation calls him two or three times a Week.' [10]

We learn the loan will be six million livres given every quarter to the United States, commencing in May 1782.

John Jay writes from Spain that he is not being recognized as America's envoy and so negotiations are not advancing. I write to Vergennes that when Mr. Jay addresses himself to the minister he is always told he is busy or ill and referred to Don Bernardo del Campo who has no instructions and can only promise to talk to the minister about it.[11] I write back to Jay that 'I have Made What Communications I thought to Be Serviceable' and that as 'a french man and of course a zealous lover of the House of Bourbon I earnestly hope the king of Spain Will not leave to Halland the Credit of the Credit of first Entering Into this Measure. Generosity and frankness are the Pillars of the Spanish character.' I ask him to remember me to my friend Carmichael.[12]

At the end of February, Port Mahon in Minorca was taken by siege by French and Spanish forces, which we had not expected quite so quickly; St. Kitts in the West Indies has also been captured. We hear that in London, Lord North is said to be about to resign.

I spend Easter with Adrienne at Antony, the country residence of the marquis de Castries; from there I write to Washington and tell him that since the marquis de Castries has been head of the navy, we have had 'a serie of successes. Had it not been for the storm that Mr. de Guichen met with on his leaving Brest, we should not, independant of the Spaniards, have lost an instant of maritime superiority in the West Indias.'[13] I hear that Lord North has indeed resigned and I write again to Washington to tell him.

Many of my friends, including Ségur and the prince de Poix, are sailing to America, hoping to fight in the final part of the campaign and I write letters of introduction for them to Washington, Knox, La Luzerne and Hamilton; I also write to Washington that:

I Cannot Refrain from A Painfull Sentiment at the Sight of Many French officers Who Are Going to Join their Colours in America. I Shall, thank God, follow them Before Anything Passes that May Have Any Danger or any Importance. I am So far from the Army. So Far from Head Quarters, So far from American Intelligences that However Happy I am Rendered Here, I Cannot Help ten times A day Wishing Myself on the other Side of the Atlantic.[14] My hope is to sail in May.[15]

In London, Henry Laurens, named by Congress last June as one of the five peace commissioners, has been on parole since last December; I arrange for a letter of credit for £500 to be given to him and write: 'The Treatement You met With is So Very Strange that one is at a loss What to Admire the More, its folly or its Insolence. The Law of Nations Being Unrespected, Retaliation was the only Pledge We Had of their Not Blundering You Into the Most Dreadfull Misfortunes.'[16]

Vergennes asks me again for proposals on the French campaign in North America; I write a lengthy memoir detailing my suggestions. I say that the evacuation of both Charleston and New York is beset by problems. We must either take them or take the troops they think should be posted elsewhere. Above all, it is necessary for the allied fleet to be in the Chesapeake during the winter season. It has already been recognized that reinforcements need to be made. I declare that the closer peace comes, the more important it is to gain control of the principal points. I discuss Newfoundland and say that if the expeditions I mention do not take place, then General Washington will move against Canada. If the attacks happen then I think that everything would be ready at the end of winter for a general peace.[17]

I receive a letter from Adams at Amsterdam who believes the British: 'will try the last Efforts of Despair this Summer, but their cause is desperate indeed. Never was an Empire ruined in so short a time, and so masterly a manner. Their Affairs are in such a state, that even Victories would only make their final Ruin the more compleat.'[18]

I do not want to consider partial peace negotiations. I want a general peace which is what the British also appear to want. I write to Adams that both I and Franklin would like him to come here. I tell him that: 'tho the Court Air Has not So Much Altered my republican Principles as to

Make Me Believe the Opinion of a king is Every thing, I Was the other day pleased to Hear the king of France Speack of You to me in terms of the Highest Regard.'[19]

"Perhaps I should be sent to London to aid in the peace negotiations as did the duc de Nivernois during the Treaty of Paris," I say to Franklin. "I am now an American citizen, speak both languages and am well acquainted with our interests. I might be useful, and as peace is likely to take place my return to America is perhaps not so immediately necessary."[20]

"I like the idea," he replies.

I speak with Vergennes. "Grenville, the British agent, has been empowered to only treat with France," he tells me, to my disappointment.

The British had seemed ready to sue for peace on any terms, but they appear to now think that they need not recognize American independence. The situation has probably changed because de Grasse was defeated by Admiral Rodney at the Saints in the Antilles on April 12. He has foolishly allowed maritime superiority to be taken from him, so taking away my hopes that Charleston would follow Jamaica, and then New York,[21] and the defeat has also changed the situation regarding the negotiations. I, therefore, will not set sail until it is certain there will not be a peace.

"When do you expect to go to America?" Grenville asks.

"I have already stayed here longer than I had intended in order to learn whether there will be peace or war, but I see that the expectation of peace is a joke and that you only amuse us without any real intention of making a treaty. I do not expect to stay much longer. I will leave in a few days," I reply.

"It is not a game. We are sincere in our intention of making a treaty and you will be convinced of it in several days' time," he says.[22]

The future tsar of Russia is travelling in France incognito as the comte du Nord and many events are held in his honor. On June 8 there is a grand ball at Versailles, the Hall of Mirrors lit by five thousand candles. The queen, dressed as La Belle Gabrielle, dances with the comte d'Artois to open the ball. Next, she dances a quadrille with me, my dancing skills apparently having taken a turn for the better since our last attempt.

On the twenty-fourth, I am received into the Masonic Lodge of Saint Jean d'Écosse du Contrat Social, my membership already accepted by unanimous acclamation, instead of by ballot. The lodge says this is reserved for heroes and that I am the first. I am now in a lodge which declares there is a social contract between governments to protect the people, who, in turn, must obey,[23] and which also has many notable members such as Chastellux, de Grasse, de Ségur and Roland.

I write to Livingston on the twenty-fifth:

From the Very Beginning, Mr. Adams Has Been Persuaded that the British Ministry Were not Sincere, that the Greater Part of them Were Equally Against America as Any in the old Administration, and that All those Negotiations Were not Much to Be depended upon. His Judgment of this Affair Has Been Confirmed By the Events, tho' at present the Negotiation Has put on a Better out Ward Appearance....I Conclude that the British Ministry are at variance Between themselves.[24]

The same day I write to Washington that I hope to set sail for America by July 20. The possibility of his being in the field torments me:

But from the Moment I Engaged in our Noble Cause I Made it My Sole Point to Sacrifice Every thing to its Better Success...The American Ministers Have Declared they Wanted My presence in this part of the World...I know, in Case of a treaty I May Better Serve our Cause, By the Situation

292

I am in, with Governement, and My knowledge of America, than I Could do in any other Capacity during an inactive Campaign. I tell him Franklin has granted Cornwallis a conditional exchange, with which I had nothing to do, and relate bitterly the defeat of de Grasse which has lost us maritime superiority and the ability to take Charleston, and then perhaps New York harbor and New York. [25]

Grenville tells us the Enabling Act has passed through both Houses of Parliament, but we do not yet know the words. I fear these people are not sincere and envy my friends in the French army who will soon land on the distant shores of America. I write to Washington:

> I am truly Ashamed to let them Be in the field, and to keep at Such a distance from them. They will think I am much altered from what they Have known me to Be, Unless You are pleased, My dear General, to let them know that Your political people Have Kept me Here for Motives of public utility, and that Never Could I Make a Greater Sacrifice to My zeal for America than When I delay so much My Return to the Army where I Heartly Wish I Could Be Immediately transported....Made. Lafayette is well, and I Hope in the Course of Some Months Your God Son will Have a Brother...Adieu, My Dear General, I Hope You Will approuve My Conduct and in very thing I do I first Consider what Your opinion Would Be Had I an opportunity to Consult it. [26]

Negotiations continue slowly. The frigate I was intending to travel on waits three weeks for me and then sets sail. [27]

Adrienne and I decide to help the peasants in the Auvergne by creating a school where they can weave yarn from sheep wool which would enable them to earn more and remain at home during the winter. I submit the scheme to Joly de Fleury, the new *contrôleur-général de finances*, and await his reply, which I gather will not be quick.

I am twenty-five on September 6 and therefore no longer a minor. I now control my wealth which pleases me greatly. I confirm Jacques-Philippe Grattepain-Morizot as my agent and he acts for me in the recent inheritance made between the comte de Lusignem and myself from my great-grandfather. I sell some of my land in Bretagne and hope to buy a house in Paris.

On the seventeenth, Adrienne gives birth to a girl, two months prematurely. I write to Franklin:

> Every child of Mine that comes to light is a Small Addition to the Number of American Citizens...Mme. de Lafayette Has this Morning become Mother of a Daughter Who However Delicate in its Begining, Enjoys a Perfect Health, and I Hope Will Soon Grow Equal to the Heartiest Children. This reminds me of our Noble Revolution, into Which We Were forced Sooner than it ought to Have Been Begun. But our Strength Came on Very Fast, and Upon the whole, I think We did at least as Well as Any other people. [28]

Next afternoon, I attend her baptism. We name her Marie Antoinette Virginie and will call her Virginie, a good saint's name, as well as that of a state of my adopted country. Franklin who is suffering yet again from gout, writes back immediately:

> I think you do well to begin with the most antient state. And as we cannot have too many of so good a Race, I hope you and Mde. De la Fayette will go thro' the Thirteen....While you are proceeding, I hope our States will some of them new-name themselves. Miss Virginia, Miss Carolina and Miss Georgia will sound prettily enough for the Girls; but Massachusetts and Connecticut, are too harsh even for the Boys, unless they were to be Savages. [29]

The British finally recognize the thirteen states as an independent nation, not as thirteen colonies, and peace negotiations can now begin which will perhaps be concluded in five or six months. At the same time, an expedition is being planned to unite French and Spanish armies, commanded by d'Estaing, at Cadiz, to attack the British in the West Indies. He asks for me to serve with him; I decide it will force the British to negotiate over America and is also very much in the interests of France and so I agree. Duportail and Gouvion are returning to the United States and I write a letter to Washington for them to take: 'I am kept in this country by the request of the American Plenipotentiaries and with a view to be serviceable to our cause which with me shall ever be the first object…it is my private opinion that a success is necessary before the general treaty can come to a conclusion.'[30] Gouvion will tell Washington my plan.

The expedition for a joint French/Spanish attack on the British in the West Indies is finally agreed. Seven thousand men and nine warships will sail from Brest to Cadiz, where there are already about thirteen thousand men and forty ships; six thousand Spanish troops will join the French troops at Gibraltar. D'Estaing will command and I will be chief of staff of the French and Spanish armies.[31] I accept as it seems the only way to achieve supremacy in American waters and I now feel able to write to Washington about the expedition, without my previous secrecy:

> My Last Letter Has Informed You that in Case Peace is Not Made, and our Plans do not Immediately take place at this Court, I Would think it Consistent With My zeal for our Cause, and My Obedience to Your Intentions to take a Round About Way to Serve our Military Purposes….I Have Accepted to Go this Winter With Count d'Estaing, But tho' I am to Reenter Into the french line as a Marechal de Camp from the Date of Lord Cornwallis's Surrender, I Will However keep My American Uniform and the out Side as Well as the inside of an American Soldier. I Will Conduct Matters and Take Commands as an officer Borrowed from the United States, as it Were Occasionally, and Will Watch for the Happy Moment When I May join Our Beloved Colours.[32]

We will go first to attack Jamaica with sixty ships of the line and a larger land force than has yet been seen in the Antilles. I obtain from the minister and from d'Estaing the agreement that after having taken Jamaica, d'Estaing will go to New York with a superior fleet, from where he will give me a convoy and six thousand men to fight in Canada, a plan I have long desired.[33]

"I believe we will know in a month if England is willing to make peace," I say at the end of October. "If it is not agreed shortly after Parliament meets then it is certain that another campaign will be necessary."

On November 4, John Adams, who is now in Paris, dines at the hôtel de Noailles; my guests include the prince de Poix, Noailles, Jay, Mr. and Mrs. Price, Mrs. Izard and her two daughters, Dr. Bancroft and William Franklin.

"I intend to go to the West Indies with d'Estaing in about a month," I tell him in confidence.[34] I feel he regards me somewhat unfavorably, but I do not know why.

I visit Vergennes. "Mr. Adams is in Paris and is requesting more financial aid. Do you consider a subsidy of twenty million livres to be possible?"

"The war has already been very expensive for France, but would you ask Mr. Adams to attempt to procure the money from Holland if the king stood guaranty of its return?" he replies. "Go to speak to contrôleur-général de Fleury.

"The war has been very costly for France," Fleury unfortunately also points out. "France has already spent two hundred and fifty million on the American war and cannot give any more money to her. There is a great deal of money in the country, the king's troops have been subsisted and paid there."

"Hardly any of the subsistence or pay of the British has gone into any hands except those of Tories within their lines," I reply. "Mr. Adams has a plan for going to the States-General for a loan or subsidy."

"I do not want the assistance of Mr. Adams to get money in Holland," says Fleury.

"Mr. Adams would be glad of it. He does not want to go but is willing to take the trouble, if necessary," I reply.[35]

To my great sadness, I learn of the death of John Laurens on August 27 when he was attacking the British in a small skirmish in Carolina.[36]

Now I control my wealth I decide to leave the hôtel de Noailles. Jacques-Philippe Grattepain-Morizot finds a house at 183 rue de Bourbon, in the faubourg St. Germain. Adrienne and I visit; we think it is delightful. It is not palatial, but it has two stories with six rooms on each floor, a basement, an attic, and stables which can hold fifteen horses and four carriages.

I pay 200,000 livres, 50,000 livres for the renovations, and 50,000 for the furniture.[37] I sell the hôtel de la Marck to meet the cost. I choose the architect, Adrien Mouton, renowned for his lawsuit against the director of the French Academy in Rome to obtain freedom from religious persecution, to undertake the work needed.

On November 19, I go in my American uniform to Versailles to take leave of the king. I meet Adams.

"I do not think the English as sincere for a speedy peace as I wish," I tell him.[38]

Dispatches arrive from Congress asking for financial help. I write to Vergennes:

The people are war-weary, but right now they love France and hate England. Bestowing help at this moment is an act all the more useful in that it puts the seal on all the previous ones. It restores courage and silences the British emissaries who constantly accuse France of wanting to stir up the fire without extinguishing it...there is very little money in the country.[39]

I go to Passy on the twenty-third and speak about it to Franklin, Jay and Adams. Franklin, particularly, seems displeased. Perhaps he thinks I am trying to get the credit for any loan?[40]

"I have written it because La Luzerne's dispatches have not arrived recently and Vergennes will not act in the affair of money without something French to go upon," I say. "The Count de Aranda has also told me to tell Mr. Jay that as the lands upon the Mississippi have not yet been decided whether they were to belong to England or Spain, he could not yet settle that matter, so that probably the attempt will be to negotiate them into the hands of the Spanish from the English."[41]

I also show them a document I have written which asks their approval for my part in the coming expedition:

Had I not Been Detained By You, Gentlemen, Upon Political Accounts Which You Have Been pleased to Communicate to Congress, I Would Have Long Ago Returned to America. But I Was With You of Opinion That My Presence Here Might Be Useful, and Since it Appears Matters are not Ripe for a treaty, My first Wish is Now To Return to America With Such Force as May Expell the Ennemy from the United States, Serve the Views of Congress, and Assist Your Political Measures...However Certain I Have Been of Your Opinion, I think it A Mark of Respect to Congress not to Depart Until I Have Your Official Approbation of the Measure.[42]

They do not appear pleased, and Adams was, in any case, not here. However, they agree to my request.[43] They send a letter to me on the twenty-eighth: 'The prospect of an inactive campaign in America induced us to adopt the opinion that you might be more useful here than there, especially in case the negotiation for peace on the part of France in England should be committed to your management.' However, now the proposed expedition might put a glorious and speedy termination to the war they approve my going to fight with d'Estaing.[44]

I say farewell to my family and set off to Brest, d'Estaing having already departed at the beginning of November to travel overland via Madrid to Cadiz. I first go to Versailles and visit Vergennes who is doubtful he can obtain any amount above 6,000,000 livres.

Next morning, I write hastily to Franklin: 'The six million, between us, I think we will have.'[45]

I travel with the comte de Roux along roads which are atrocious, the horses bad. After two nights without sleep we reach Lorient, greatly fearing our ship will already have left Brest.

"I will take you there on my ship," says Captain Barry.

December 3. In the morning, we sail into Brest, where, to my relief, the fleet is still at anchor. Roux and I immediately go on board the *Censeur*, commanded by Admiral de Vialis.

"Four infantry battalions, an artillery force and five thousand recruits have already been embarked," I am told.

I write to Washington next day and ask him to refer to the cypher Gouvion has with him:

26 (West Indies) is the first object...We shall have maritime superiority...Please to Prepare Propositions, and Notions about 46 (N Yk), 47 (ChsT), 3 (Penobscot), 2 (New FdLd)...Inclosed, My dear General, I Have the honor to Send you the copy of a Letter to Congress. I Hope You will be able to tell them you are satisfied with my conduct...Peace is much talked of. I think, *betwen* us, much of the difficulty must lie with the Spaniards- and yet I do not think the ennemy are very sincere...[46]

I write to Poix just as we are about to set sail: 'Never was I so unhappy at leaving my friends...Speak of me to the men and women, the charming women, who are our friends.'[47] I also write to Madame de Simiane, the sister of my friend, the comte de Damas, and say that when we said goodbye I did not think that I should be writing to her again but as the winds have been contrary there will perhaps be time for me to receive an answer.

The *Censeur* sets her prow towards the wintry Atlantic. A fierce south-west wind gusts strongly and we cannot make headway; after two days we return to Brest, a very unfortunate delay which will give Lord Howe the opportunity to attack us when we once more set sail.

I receive a letter from Poix who says unpleasant rumors have again linked my name to Aglaë de Hünolstein. I angrily write back: 'Why do they torment my angelic friend? Is that the penalty for her perfection? Or is she to blame if they make trouble for her in order to hurt me in the most painful way? That would show discernment in them for I admit that nothing in the world would distress me more.'[48]

I write to Franklin and suggest I could be useful in London if the final treaty is signed: 'As to my part, if matters were so ripe as to admit of my return, nothing would more highly please me than the happiness, any how, to serve America, and more particularly in the capacity of a man honoured with her confidence.'[49]

Two days later, we are once more under sail; I am seasick, although not as violently as usual. Poor Roux, however, looks less like a composer of letters than a man who is about to carry them into the next world.[50] We sail south, the winter sea happily lacking any sign of enemy ships and my longing for peace even greater, if only for the sake of the unfortunate men entombed in these vile, floating coffers.[51] About fifty miles from Cadiz, I transfer to the frigate, *Richmond*, which is faster than the *Censeur*. It unfortunately becomes becalmed a few miles from the coast, but I am taken to the low, sandy shore and travel the last part on land.

December 23. I go through the clean, paved streets of Cadiz to the house of Richard Harrison, an American who acts as consul and welcomes me with great friendliness. On the thirtieth, d'Estaing appoints me *maréchal-général-des-logis* of both the armies, and of the fleet. French and Spanish forces are still besieging Gibraltar.

Cadiz is a rich, cosmopolitan town of commerce whose merchants have built about one hundred and fifty distinctive watchtowers near the harbor, each with their own flag, to watch for the arrival of their ships. I find it boring, its only merit being that it is less Spanish than the other towns.[52] My friends discover ladies to entertain them, but I remain tranquil in my savagery, although I cannot claim any credit as I do not meet any woman here whose acquaintance is worth having, with the exception of a beauty with black eyes, a baroness and a kind English lady.[53] I visit the camps, which are just outside the town, and keep very busy, in my usual fashion, arranging all the logistics of the army. I am quite satisfied with the soldiers, and the officers all appear to want to serve under me.

A month after my arrival, our armada is ready to sail; d'Estaing goes to Madrid to see Charles 111. On his return he says the king now agrees that I should go to Canada with a French army. However, when he suggested I should be governor of Jamaica after its capture, Charles had said: 'No, never, not that! He would create a republic there!'[54]

We remain in Cadiz, expecting peace shortly and I hope to pay a visit to my friends over the water very soon.

On February 1, an express arrives: 'Great Britain, France and Spain signed a preliminary peace declaration at Paris on January 20.' Both Floridas have been given to Spain. Hopefully, the people there will move into Georgia. Spain will insist on a right to land all along the east bank of the Mississippi, and I believe Lord Shelburne is hoping there will be a dispute between the United States and Spain. The Spanish are also giving up their claim to Gibraltar but will keep Mahon. The Islands of Providence are returned to Britain. Tabago excepted, they give up their conquests in the West Indies and have St. Lucia again.[55]

Carmichael has written to ask my assistance at Madrid so I now feel obliged to go there, instead of to America, and will meet the king, as well as the count de Florida Blanca.

"Can my servant carry the news to the United States in a fast ship?" I ask d'Estaing.

He gives me the *Triomphe*; I write letters to Congress, Greene, Livingston and, of course, to Washington:

Were you But Such a Man as Julius Caesar or the king of Prussia, I Should Almost Be Sorry for You at the End of the Great tragedy Where You are Acting Such a Part. But With My dear General I Rejoice at the Blessings of a Peace where our Noble Ends Have Been Secured.' I tell him that 'at the Prospect of a Peace, I had Prepared to Go to America...Never did Any thing Please me So much as the delightfull Prospect I Had Before me...But on a Sudden I Have Been obliged to differ my Darling Plan and as I Have At Last Been Blessed With a Letter of Yours, I know You Approve of My Lengthening My furlough Upon Political Accounts.' I say I am going to Madrid, from there I will travel to Paris and in June will sail to America. 'Now, my dear General, that You are Going to Enjoy Some Ease and Quiet, Permit me to Propose a plan to You Which Might Become Greatly Beneficial to the Black Part of Mankind. Let us Unite in Purchasing a Small Estate Where We May try the Experiment to free the Negroes and Use them only as tenants. Such an Exemple as Yours Might Render it a General Practice and if We Succeed in America, I will Chearfully Devote a part of My time to Render the Method fascionable in the West Indias. If it Be a Wild Scheme, I had

Rather Be mad that Way than to Be thought Wise on the other tack...Amongst the Many favors I Have Received, I Would take it as a Most flattering Circumstance in My life to Be Sent to England With the Ratification of the American treaty...As to the Army, My dear General, What Will Be its fate?... 'Adieu, my dear General, Had The Spaniards Got Common Sense I Could Have Dispensed With that Cursed trip to Madrid...[56]

I write somewhat differently when I congratulate Vergennes on the successful conclusion: 'My first idea was to go to America, but a sentence in your letter made me think that you advise me to return to France. M. d'Estaing is my witness that this made up my mind, and since you did not think of my making that voyage it is because you think my return is more advisable.'[57]

On February 14, the *Triomphe* leaves Cadiz for the United States. Next day, I set off to Madrid.

Carmichael and I greet each other with delight. "The position remains the same. The Spanish will still not recognize me," he says.

The Spanish slowness and the jealousy of the court towards the emancipation of the American colonies means that the negotiations are still as little advanced as the first day Jay came to Spain.[58] I am only staying a few days here but hope to achieve the inducement of the ministry to give El Campo liberal instructions, see that Carmichael is recognized as the official American chargé d'affaires and suggest they offer a loan of money to the United States.[59]

Proudly wearing my American uniform and my ceremonial sword, I pay my respects to the Bourbon King, Charles 111, at his country residence, the Pardo, on the seventeenth. I find him old, his face long, his complexion swarthy and his nose very large. I see the great Spanish nobles brought low before him, particularly when they are on their knees, a very interesting sight to someone of an independent mind.[60]

He looks at me with intelligent eyes and receives me graciously, despite my uniform and my principles.[61] He asks questions about Yorktown and Cornwallis, as well as America, of which he and the conde de Floridablanca, the minister for foreign affairs, seem to know very little. I reassure him the United States wants only to trade with Spain and that his country would benefit from peace in her American colonies.

During the next few days, I meet many times with the conde de Floridablanca, whose face I find too stiff to be warm, his mind prejudiced and with no knowledge of the whole situation.[62] I suggest France will mediate between Spain and the United States and broach the idea of a treaty between them. I talk about borders and about the navigation of the Mississippi as well as the rights of cod fishing. I speak very proudly of the United States. I act in a private capacity, am both pressing and haughty by turns,[63] and do not commit the United States to anything.[64]

"If Mr. Carmichael is not officially presented next Saturday, the day of the reception of the ambassadors, as the chargé d'affaires of the United States, I will take him away with me and you will not see an American envoy here for a long time."[65]

I am successful. After a week, I go to the Pardo with Carmichael who is received as the chargé d'affaires of the United States. That is as much as I can do. There will now be no Spanish invasion and Spain will have formal boundaries in America.

I leave Madrid and travel towards the Pyrenees. By March, I once more see Bordeaux and stay again at the residence of the maréchal de Mouchy, my situation now very different from that of the youth escaping to America. I learn that Lord Shelburne has resigned, and Lord North has replaced him, but this information is not yet certain.[66] The American flag has already been seen at London.[67]

I continue north; raging floodwaters carry away the bridge across the Seine at Mantes just as I am about to cross. My star luckily still shines.

I reach Paris on March 12, but intend to only stay a short time as I will be going away for three weeks to Chavaniac. To my delight, now that there is peace, I finally receive my rank of maréchal de camp, dating from the capitulation of Cornwallis. I visit Mr. Jay to give him an account of what happened at Madrid and the concessions I obtained from the Spanish court.

Deputies from Bayonne come to see me, very worried about the restrictions of the *Ferme*, the body which controls the production, distribution and sale of goods made or grown in France. They ask for aid in persuading the government to dredge their harbor and hope to obtain more American trade. [68]

Bayonne and Dunkerque have been suggested as free ports. I ask Vergennes for Lorient instead of Port Louis; it is larger, has better facilities and is very agreeable to the Americans. I believe a prompt decision is important to stop the reopening of trade links between Britain and America.[69] I go to see de Fleury, but he is not there; I write instead and say we must try and obtain almost all the American trade and that because of the restrictions we make, we are in imminent danger of losing it. I also mention that while improving Bayonne, opening the port of Marseille, and making Dunkirk as advantageous as possible, I hope he will decide in favor of Lorient, instead of Port Louis. [70]

There is famine in the Basse Auvergne; local people sent a petition while I was away, asking me to present it to the intendant of the province, Charles-Antoine de Chazerat. They say that they had only avoided the horrors of starvation by the extraordinary help their seigneur, Monsieur de Lafayette, had given them. On February 26 Adrienne delivered this petition to him at Versailles.[71]

Aglaë de Hunolstein wants me to end our relationship. She has been trying for more than a year to do so, but now asks me to decide. She is talked of scandalously by society and her family is angry. She is placing her safety, her peace of mind, in my hands.[72]

"Write to me," she says. "You are more master of yourself in a letter than in a conversation."

I look for her mother but am not unhappy when I do not find her. She is correct in her views but so opposed to what my heart wants.

I set off once more from Paris, carrying with me a memorandum from Adrienne for the school, and travel south towards the Auvergne.

The darkening evening sky blurs familiar hills and trees. For the first time in ten years I step across the threshold of my childhood home. Only my aunt Charlotte is here; my grandmother, my dearly loved aunt, Marguerite-Madeleine, and my cousin, Marie Louise, are all dead. Frail and aged, she greets me with tears of anguish. "Gilbert," she cries repeatedly, clinging to me as though she fears I am a ghost. "Gilbert, I can't believe you are here."

She sobs. I embrace her. "I can't believe it is you," she murmurs.

Next day, visitors flock to see me. "Leave your room and come and eat something," I tell my aunt. "Can you help with all these guests?"

More people arrive, some my childhood friends, others from several leagues distant. Many fall to their knees.

"We are starving. I beg you, seigneur, give us food. We need clothes and money. We have not paid our rent and taxes because of the famine and we are being evicted. Help us."

"I will," I reply.

"Have you been ordered to distribute grain to the parishes of Aurat, Jax, Vissac, Auteyrat, Seaugues, Saint Julien and Saint Geneix?" I ask Monsieur Gueyffier, *subdélégué* of Brioude.[73]

The overseer of my granaries shows me they are filled with wheat.

"Now is the best time to sell the grain as prices are high," he says.

"No," I retort. "Now is the best time to give it away. Distribute one thousand eight hundred bushels of wheat and one thousand two hundred bushels of rye to the peasants."[74]

"Why has the famine happened?" I ask officials.

"The crops were poor last autumn and the Ferme has been withholding grain and seeds from sale in order to create shortages and ensure high prices."

I decide to ask the government to allow me to build public granaries which will act as seed banks for grain, and I shall contribute my own grain to it.[75] I visit local towns, " *Vive Lafayette!*" ringing out everywhere; I am now not just a military hero, I am also the adversary of the Ferme.

I decide to do what Aglaë wants. I write to her: 'You know the torments of my heart. You know it is torn between love and duty…I was happy, however, I must admit that you were not, and it is you who risks everything whilst I had nearly all the pleasure…Everything that you are, everything that I owe you, justifies my love, and nothing, not even you, will prevent me adoring you.'[76]

It would be so sweet to be here if my loved ones were still here. There is not a corner in the château, not a tree outside, where I do not feel as if I am about to see my aunt and cousin again. I tell my aunt about Adrienne and my children and America. I give her a portrait of Anastasie; I write to Adrienne to ask to have a portrait made of George and Virginie, as well as a copy of the little portrait she has of me so that when I return to Paris I can send them to her. I tell her my aunt wishes to continue with the legal action against the chevalier de Chavaniac to stop him from obtaining a third of the estate of her husband's family; I would prefer, however, that she gives up all her property so that we can arrange affairs as we wish. I inform her about the weaving school: 'We are hoping for thirty thousand francs for it. You have rendered an immense service to this region. On Monday I will meet a committee of *curés* where we can see what it is best to do.' I tell her to hasten the work in our house and that I plan to leave on Thursday and stay the night in Issoire, that on Friday I will dine in Clermont and on Monday at Saint Germain: 'My loving greetings to maman and to my sisters. I embrace our children. Farewell, my dear heart. Look after yourself; look after your health, love me always and with that be sure of my happiness.'[77]

I stay only five days. I set off back to Paris with my aunt, briefly stopping at Riom to cries of " *Vive Lafayette!*" Local officials make speeches; I drink the wine of honor then resume the long journey north.

May 5. I am recommended for *La Croix de Saint Louis,* and again there are rumors of jealousy. On the twelfth, my sister-in-law, Pauline, Mademoiselle de Maintenon, marries Joachim, marquis de Montagu. A few days later Adrienne and I move to our house on the rue de Bourbon. I hang Washington's portrait on the wall and display the American flag with that of France. We start to give dinners every Monday, at which Noailles is always present; on other evenings I dine at the Tessés, the Neckers and the Boufflers.

I continue my fight to make some ports free for American goods. I write to Vergennes for an official declaration of what constitutes a free port as far as France is concerned. On June 29, I receive a reply that it is a place where all merchandise can be imported and exported freely.

In July I see again the volcanic mountains and rugged countryside of the Auvergne; I once more travel along the rough roads patched with lava, pozzualana and basalt towards the château of Chavaniac, this time accompanied by Adrienne and her sister, the comtesse de Roure.

With pride I show her my home. She makes frequent visits to the church for Mass and occupies herself with our future weaving school at Saint Georges d'Aurac. She seems very content.

I receive a letter from the president of Congress which approves my conduct in Spain and my endeavors for American trade. I write back on the twentieth. Two days later I write to Washington to congratulate him on his decision to return to private life. I tell him how much his action has been acclaimed in Europe: 'Never did one Man live whom the Soldier, States man, Patriot, and Philosopher Could Equally Admire, and Never Was a Revolution Brought about that in Its Motives, its Conduct, and its Consequences Could So Well immortalize its Glorious Chief. I am proud of you, My Dear General. Your Glory Makes me feel as if it Was My own.'[78]

Two weeks pass very happily, then we set off back to Paris. On August 4 we stop at Langeac, an important seigneurie of the Auvergne whose feudal rights are for sale. The townspeople fete me.

"Our town would be flattered to belong to you as it is already yours in its heart," say the nobles.

"Thank you. I will consider whether to buy the seigneurial rights," I reply and accept a goblet of the wine of honor.

September 3. The Treaty of Peace is being signed today at the hôtel de York in Paris, by David Hartlet, in the name of the king of England, and by Benjamin Franklin, John Jay and John Adams, in the name of the United States. A separate treaty is also being signed today by the French and Spanish with the British at the Château of Versailles. I am in Nancy, at the home of my friend, Roger de Damas, who is gravely ill. I write to Adrienne:

Roger's condition is keeping me here, dear heart. It is still very alarming...He has had a recurrent putrid fever, with the addition of worms, inflammation and a particularly disturbing complication. His complete inability to evacuate made us think yesterday that the end was near. Fortunately, however, he managed to do so in the evening and we thought him to be out of danger. But this morning he is as bad as ever....It gives me much concern to know that you are fretting, dear heart, and I share your anxieties to the full. Keep them, I beg, within reason. Excess is injurious to your health and would even make your work less effective should you multiply them. [79]

I asked for my new aide-de-camp, Lewis Littlepage, to take the news of the Peace Treaty to America, but the secretary of Adams has been chosen instead. Littlepage has challenged Jay to a duel, but hopefully this will not happen.

I sense, as I often do, that Adams does not want to make use of my services for American diplomacy. I write to Washington: 'Since I Have Returned from Spain...I Was not Much Consulted Upon Politics by the Commissionners.' I tell him that I hope I will serve the United States concerning trade and that he will approve my conduct. 'I Greave to Be so long from You. My Mind cannot be properly Easy, and Every Mention, Every Remembrance of America Makes me Sigh for the Moment when I May Enjoy the Sight of our free, and Independent shores.[80]

Roger now seems to be out of danger, and I write to Adrienne:

Having seen him near death twice, I am happy to realize he is no more than seriously ill. Madame de Simiane is as well as can be expected. She is deeply touched by your concern for her. My departure will cause a great deal of grieving because they all believe that I am necessary to Roger, and I must confess to you that I feel somewhat embarrassed despite my longing to see you again and to return to my friends and to the dear walls of Paris.[81]

I finally return to Paris, to my new home, to Adrienne and my children. Aglaë goes to live in a convent. She sells her jewels and donates the money to the poor. Her husband gives her a pension of six thousand livres which she mainly gives away. There are rumors I have fathered her child and that a servant has fathered another. Other rumors allege that at night she was with the prostitutes in the Palais Royal and that her mother, the marquise de Brabanton, wrote to the duchesse de Chartres that her daughter's reputation was so terrible she should no longer be one of her ladies-in-waiting and that she should be confined somewhere to prevent any more disgrace on her family.

Adrienne and I give a dinner on October 21, which includes William Pitt the Younger, Edward J. Eliot, William Wilberforce, Franklin, his grandson William, Lewis Littlepage, my brother-in-law, Noailles, and Madame de Boufflers; in all there are a dozen 'rebels', of whom several are ladies.

Mr. Pitt delights me; his intellect, his modesty, his nobility and a character as interesting as the role for which his position destines him.

"As long as London remains a monarchy," he says, "We can hardly hope to see you in London."[82]

However, now that Britain has been defeated, I would very much like to go to England again. I see the English with pleasure, and whether as a Frenchman or as an American soldier, or even as a private individual, I would find myself without embarrassment in the midst of this proud nation. My conversion, however, is not so complete that on occasions when they are enemies of glory or French prosperity I would do them what harm I can.[83]

I ask William Franklin to obtain for me a printed copy of the Declaration of Independence. I intend to have it copied and engraved in gold letters. I will display it prominently in my study, in a double frame, and will say that the empty side is for a Declaration of French Rights.

The new invention of the hot-air balloon interests me greatly. Last June the Montgolfier brothers had made their first flight in such an apparatus. Others follow them; on December 1, the scientist J.-A.-C. Charles takes off from the Tuileries using a balloon made of silk, and hydrogen instead of hot air. The duc de Chartres is his patron and follows his flight on the ground. On the third, I take Charles in my carriage to thank the duc at the Palais-Royal; I write an account of his flight and those of others and send it to the American Philosophical Society.

Major Pierre-Charles L'Enfant arrives in France from the United States on December 8; he brings me two letters from Washington, in one of which I find instructions to buy plated ware proper for a tea table for him.[84] In the second, he tells me of a new society, the Cincinnati, which was created during a meeting at Verplanck's House near Fishkill. It is a society of officers who fought in the war; it will help to preserve their former friendships and will also raise money for widows and orphans. Membership will be hereditary and will pass to the oldest son. There will be a fee. Washington asks me to choose the French officers who are entitled to join and wish to become members; Rochambeau has been asked to choose officers under his command. I am delighted we will be able to remember our common endeavors as well as remembering our beloved general but first I have to ask the approval of the king, as the only award Frenchmen are allowed to receive from a foreign country is that of the Golden Fleece. I also recognize there might be a problem with the hereditary principle, but I find that, generally, people are in favor of it. Educated people are well versed in Roman history and literature and very aware that Lucius

Quintus Cincinnatus left his farm to lead the Roman army to victory against the Aequians and then went back to his land, like Washington. The ribbon is blue and white, blue for the United States and white for Bourbon France; the medal has the emblem of a bald eagle with outstretched wings.

"It looks more like a turkey, which is fortunate. I always consider the bald eagle to be a bird of bad moral character," is Franklin's opinion.[85]

On the eagle's breast is an image of Cincinnatus receiving the sword of office from Roman senators; on the reverse side Fame is crowning Cincinnatus with a wreath. The new society delights me. My happiest days have been spent in the now-disbanded American army; this society will still link me to it and to my many comrades-in-arms, so slightly lessening my sadness. It is sometimes difficult to decide who is entitled to have the honor, particularly in the case of General Thomas Conway, who is stationed in India. I write to Washington:

> A plot was lad to draw me into a snare, and Madame Conway was made a tool of to give me and yourself the air of an implacable revenge against that man who is considered here as having been abandonned and ruined by me in America…and to avoid the odium of having stifled Connway's claims, I have not discouraged a representation being made in his favor- The man is not worth troubling our heads about him- but as he will become a pretence to a sect who have not hitherto found any against me, it may be better either to give him the badge, or if refused, to do it with that secrecy and delicacy which will not subject me to the reproach of having proposed him, in order that he may be humiliated- That whole family is a nest of rogues… [86]

The comte de Mirabeau denounces the society as an example of hereditary principle. Franklin says little, but Jay is critical. John Adams is now minister at The Hague and I learn he speaks very violently against it, calling it a French Blessing. He also remarks that although I have for a long time said I will go to America, I never do it, which he thinks shows a want of zeal to comply with the desire of my American friends. [87]

I write to him and strongly refute his words. I am polite but I speak my mind. I say I had not wanted my conduct to be misrepresented to him and that as far as my democratic principles go, I went to America when the situation there was at its worst and my disobeying the French court might be ruinous to me. I list the reasons why I have not yet sailed to America.[88] I also write to Washington and tell him most of the Americans here are violently against the association and that Jay, Adams and all the others warmly blame the army, a view I have opposed. I ask him to decide for me on the question of the hereditary principle and to vote on my behalf in any debate. I trust his judgement absolutely.[89]

My interest in new science projects continues. I donate money to a watchmaker, whose name no one knows, and whom we call 'D'. He says he has made a pair of elastic shoes with which he can walk across water. I also pay about one hundred louis d'or to Dr. Franz Anton Mesmer who propounds a theory of animal magnetism. Evidently there is a fluid throughout the universe in which light, heat, gravity and electricity flow. It is also the basis of human health and if the fluid is disturbed it causes disease. To cure the patient, the fluid needs to be 'reorientated', an action called mesmerizing, to allow it to flow freely again.

The north and south poles at the head and feet must not be disturbed as this is where the mesmeric fluid from the stars and the earth enter the person. Mesmer and his aides attempt to locate the smaller poles which are situated in the body and if harmony is restored the patient shrieks. I become a disciple and discover some of his secrets. I write to Washington that before I leave France I will get permission from Mesmer to let him into his secret.

A commission appointed by the king and composed of members of the Academy of Sciences and the Faculty of Medicine is set up to investigate evidence for animal magnetism. Franklin is one of the members. I will, however, be in the United States when the commission concludes.

I borrow 1200 livres from my father-in-law for my trip and leave the financial management of my estate in the competent hands of Morizot and my wife as I have done before. Rumors appear to be swirling about that I am going to Ireland to foment revolution and not to America. I believe the situation to be critical there, the lord lieutenant's conduct has been foolish, and some resolutions of the people have been very spirited,[90] however, it is the United States and my revered general who is now living at Mount Vernon whom I will hopefully soon be seeing.

Chapter 32

Washington fears he will never see Lafayette again

June 28. Maurice Riquet de Caraman, my young aide-de-camp, and I try out our hammocks in our small cabins which no longer smell slightly of paint as I ordered them to be varnished.[1] Our ship is the *Courrier de New York*, the first packet ship to regularly cross the Atlantic to America, and Captain Joubert says that as the wind is changing, we will sail tomorrow. I shall fortify myself with magnetism, camphor and treacle tablets to eat on an empty stomach, and ether to drop onto a piece of sugar to ward off seasickness, although, apart from the magnetism, I do not expect they will have any beneficial effects and I will be very ill. I cannot embrace the main mast as Mesmer instructed; it is too large and I had forgotten, and he did not know, that it is coated with tar to a certain height and would therefore tar me from head to foot.[2]

If I had foreseen the long delay at Lorient I would have brought Adrienne with me, but in any case, her sister is about to give birth and she would have been wrong not to have waited for that. However, I have occupied myself talking with Monsieur d'Arlincourt, the farmer general, as well as with the town mayor, who both consider that complete exemption from duties for the town and the port is the best plan which can be adopted.[3] I have also written to John Adams on learning the new regulations of the Cincinnati and have said that I had always been against the hereditary principle.[4]

The *Courrier de New York* sets her prow for America; gulls scream mournfully in our wake, the Breton coast dwindling to a faint dark line until there is only the vast Atlantic and the sky. Seasickness holds me in its nauseous grip, but at least there is no longer the possibility of encountering the enemy.

I recover my sea legs, the voyage taking on its usual tedium, the ocean always the same, occasionally enlivened by dolphins and flying fish.

A cabin boy falls from a rope and lies lifeless on the deck. I rush to him; I apply Mesmer's principles to his body. I find the poles. He twitches; he opens his eyes; sailors and passengers crowd round me in amazement.

"You have brought him back to life," exclaims Josiah Harmar.

"All the praise is due to Mesmer," I reply.

August 4. Wednesday. Thirty-four days after we set sail, we approach the American coast, the smell of the New Jersey pines a wonderful remedy for seasickness.[5]

I enter the port of New York with feelings of great joy, finally arriving in its streets at eleven o'clock, too late to tell anyone I am here. In the morning, I surprise my friends. I travel in an open carriage, escorted by a horse troop with drawn swords. I see the houses of the city for the first time, often four, five or six stories high, covered by wood, their shingle roofs varnished and painted in various colors.[6] Cannon roar out; bells are ringing; bands are playing; flags and bunting flying.

"Marquis! Marquis! Marquis!" shout crowds filling the streets and windows.

In the evening, I attend a banquet at the Masonic Lodge with Saint John de Crèvecoeur, the French consul, and one hundred former veteran soldiers in uniform. Next day, General Gates takes me on a tour of New York's fortifications. We celebrate for two days, then Caraman and I set off for New Jersey and the road to Philadelphia, Baltimore and Mount Vernon, through the now peaceful countryside. Ruined houses I once saw in flames have been rebuilt, fields are being cultivated; the liberty pole is everywhere, set on a firm and, I hope, everlasting foundation.[7]

On the tenth, ten miles from Philadelphia, an escort from former officers, the Pennsylvania militia and the City Troop of Horse is waiting with Robert Morris and many others to take me into town. I enter the city, crowds surrounding my carriage, bells pealing out. I call on President John Dickinson of Pennsylvania who makes a formal speech of welcome. In the evening, I dine at the City Tavern, where I had first met Washington, with the officers of the former Pennsylvania Line who had been with me in Virginia. I delight in seeing my old comrades-in-arms, whilst outside, in the increasing darkness, candles illuminate all the windows.

Wayne, St. Clair and Irvine next day bring me an address me on behalf of the Line: "We very sensibly feel all the warmth of affection arising from the intercourse of the field, and while we look back on the scenes of distress freedom had to encounter, we can never forget that when destitute of foreign friends, you generously stepped forth, the advocate of our rights- the noble experience you gave by early bleeding in our infant cause impress us with an exalted idea of your patriotism..."[8]

"In the wished for meeting with my dear brother officers, in your so kind reception and most obliging address, I am more happily, more deeply affected than words can express...that I early enlisted with you in the cause of liberty shall be the pride and satisfaction of my life. But while on the glorious conclusion, I rejoice with those I had the honor of being a companion in gloomy times..." I reply. [9]

The following afternoon, the Legislature of Pennsylvania sends a committee to welcome me with a flattering speech, finishing with the words: 'May your stay in America be as agreeable to you as it will be to a nation which will never be able to forget the wonderful conduct and the great talents of the marquis de Lafayette."

I reply, much moved.[10]

I visit Barbé de Marbois, who is acting as French chargé d'affaires in the United States. Then I go to the American Philosophical Society where I speak for two hours about Mesmer and animal magnetism and the cure I made on board the ship. The following day I and my party set off to Baltimore, officers escorting me from the city.[11] We arrive late on Saturday evening, the fourteenth. Two days of festivities ensue; on Monday we leave Baltimore for the last stage of the journey to visit my general.

August 17. The trail winds through dense woods and occasional patches of marsh. The horses pull the carriage more briskly, and every so often, in the distance, I catch a glimpse of Mount Vernon. We bowl quickly along a drive parallel to a second drive surrounded by gardens; we arrive.

Mrs. Washington welcomes me. I greet her with tears in my eyes.

"General Washington is at one of the farms. Would you like to wait at the house or to ride there?"

"I will ride," I immediately reply.

A servant on horseback brings me a horse. I mount and follow him through meadows bright with flowers and a profusion of peach, cherry, apple, apricot trees and purple-flowering lilac. Finally, I see Washington. I ride forward and throw myself off my horse. I embrace and kiss him repeatedly. We stand together under the hot Virginian sun and delight in being together.[12]

Later, at the house, he and his wife show me the portrait I have sent of Adrienne, our children and myself which is hanging above the mantelpiece. I meet the little fair-haired Washy and the older Nelly, the grandchildren of Mrs. Washington, who have been adopted by her and her husband following their father's death; to my amusement the children inspect me to see if I resemble my portrait. [13]

I give Washington Adrienne's letter and the letter Anastasie has written in English: 'Dear Washington, I hope that papa whill come back soon here. I am very sorry for the loss of him, but I am very glade for you self. I wich you a werry good health and I am whith great respect, Dear Sir, your most obedient servant, anastasie la Fayette.' [14]

I spend two weeks at Mount Vernon with my general. He has aged, although he is still large and strong. Creases surround his eyes and mouth and, at times, his hands tremble. However, he seems even greater than he was during the Revolution. His simplicity is truly sublime, and he is as completely involved with all the details of his lands and house as if he had always lived here. [15] He rises before the sun and works in his study until it is breakfast. After lunch we talk about the past, the present and a bit of politics about the future. [16] Then he attends to his affairs and gives me documents to read which have been written while I have been absent. [17]

I ride with him over his five farms, which cover about five thousand acres, where slaves work in great numbers. Black women labor in the fields, black men are digging ditches and building walls.

"It has been very neglected here while I have been fighting. The soil is exhausted from the cultivation of tobacco. I intend to stop growing it and am substituting wheat, corn and grass, which I think will be more profitable. I also intend to have a crop rotation of wheat, potatoes, maize, oats and grass in succession in the same field, as well as to use manure for fertilization. I have already written out the scheme for the next few years and I have begun transferring trees from the woods to line the paths by the lawn." [18]

He shows me his greenhouse, built of brick with seven very tall windows along one wall, whose two wings house slaves. Palm, lemon, lime and orange trees are growing, and many exotic plants I have never seen before.

"I will send you some plants from Europe," I promise.

We visit his war horses, now peacefully grazing; the chestnut, Nelson, always steady on the battlefield, Blueskin, the blue-gray. In his study there are at least a thousand books shelved behind glass, including twenty-eight volumes of his wartime correspondence which have all been transcribed by Richard Varick and a team of secretaries and finished in 1783. He believes that if anyone wishes to know anything, they can consult these; he does not give a personal interview. Vanity is not a trait of his character. [19] He intends to use the rest of his life to arrange his papers for history. The Reverend William Gordon from Boston wrote to him during the war and is now writing a four-volume history of it. He believes he has played his part and that now it is for others to act. In his opinion 'there needs to be an enlargement of federal power sufficient to consolidate the energies of an exploding population and the resources of half a continent...The prospect before us is fair, none can deny, but what use we shall make of it is exceedingly problematical, not but that I believe all things will come right at last; but like a young heir come prematurely to a large inheritance...we shall wanton and run riot until we have brought our reputation to the brink of ruin, and then like him, we shall have to labor with the current of opinion, when compelled perhaps to do what prudence and common policy pointed out as plain as any problem in Euclid, in the first instance.' [20]

At three o'clock every day we eat dinner with Mrs. Washington and visitors from the neighborhood and I very much enjoy the old peach brandy and discover Virginia ham to be of a very fine quality.

"I will send some to France for you and the marquise," says Washington.

Servants in smart livery wait at the table, serving the food in silence, very unlike servants in France. We talk about the war or anecdotes we recall.[21] After tea we resume our private conversations and pass the rest of the evening with the family in the shade of the piazza where we watch the deer on the lawns and the blue Potomac dotted with the sails of innumerable vessels.

"Your letter carried by the *Triomphe* was the first to reach our shores, but we did not find out the war was completely over until November 1. I am sure the large Franco-Spanish force assembling at Cadiz helped to decide the British," says Washington.

"What happened to the American prisoners?" I ask.

"The British only surrendered five hundred. A large number had already been freed and great numbers died on the East River prison ships."

I recount my endeavors with American and French trade; we discuss the unity of the thirteen states and the difficulty of American settlement in the west because of the hostility of the Native Americans.

"I think we should buy their land and not treat them harshly," is Washington's opinion. "But there are many who believe we should be more ruthless.[22] I am going to travel to my lands there which I have put off because I was waiting for you. Would you like to accompany me?"

The thought of travelling with him is very enticing but six weeks would delay me too much. "I have already made plans to visit New England," I reply reluctantly.

"In that case, if you do not come with me, you must meet me here again," he says.[23]

"I will return at the beginning of October and we can travel across Virginia together to go to Congress in Trenton in November," I reply.

"I agree," he says. "I visited Fort Schuyler last year on my trip through the north. I believe it would be useful to America if you attend the Six Nation Peace Conference there. The British have been trying to get the tribes to rise against Americans settling in the Ohio lands. I also think that the tribes who lost the war should cede some of their land."

We discuss slavery, sometimes with William Gordon who is here for information for the book he is writing on the war. Mount Vernon now has more than two hundred slaves, but Washington is intending to grow wheat not tobacco and therefore has no need of an enslaved workforce.

"You wish to get rid of all your negroes and the Marquis wisht that an end might be put to the slavery of all of them, doing so would give the finishing stroke and polish to your political characters," says Gordon. [24]

We briefly leave Mount Vernon to go to Alexandria where the local gentlemen entertain us at Lomax's Tavern; Caraman claims the general and I got a little tipsy there.

"That's an abominable slander!" I joke.[25]

"My husband and I are both old," says Mrs. Washington. "You must bring the marquise and your family to come to visit us."

"I promise I will bring madame la marquise here," I solemnly reply.[26]

After ten days my visit comes to an end, rather sooner than I had intended because of Washington's trip to the Ohio. "We will all meet at Mount Vernon in the fall," we agree.

On Saturday, August 28, we say farewell. I travel once more through the dense woods in the summer heat and on the thirty-first reach Baltimore.[27] I attend a banquet at Grant's Tavern where I receive an address from its leading citizens including Tench Tilghman; the Irish in the city also thank me for my defense of an 'injured people.' I reply: 'In the cause of oppressed humanity, all good men sympathize, and happy are they when they can unite their efforts...But in the approbation of the sons of Ireland, every admirer of true honor, liberal patriotism, and national virtue must find a particular delight.'[28]

A ball at City Hall follows, with three hundred guests. Next day, I meet James Madison, previously a member of Congress, and we talk at length about the Mississippi.

"It is to the advantage of France and Spain to have friendly American trade along the Mississippi, but if Spain continues on its present path there is bound to be hostility. It might even be that America will turn to Britain," he says.

"I agree with you," I reply. "I believe Spain wants to exclude America from the Mississippi. I will write to Vergennes and show you the letter at New York before I send it."[29]

Caraman and I leave Baltimore on September 2 with Madison with whom I talk freely of my three hobby horses-the alliance between France and the United States, the union of the States, and the manumission of the slaves.[30] We arrive in Philadelphia on the fourth, where I stay with Barbé de Marbois. Congress is not in session; I express my opinion freely that the ineffectiveness of the central authority would harm America's prestige in Europe. [31]

I visit Madison and find him writing to Jefferson in code. I question him. He says nothing about the subject of his writing, but I infer from his conversation that the Mississippi is most in his thoughts.[32]

September 9. We leave for Philadelphia.[33] On the tenth, we stop at Trenton; on the eleventh, we arrive in New York, people everywhere again overwhelming me with great kindness.[34] On the thirteenth, I enjoy a banquet with Revolutionary officers at Cape's Tavern, presided over by General Alexander McDougall.

On the fourteenth, I attend a reception by the City Councils. I receive the Freedom of the City, an address in a gold box, an English-style compliment which I assure myself beforehand is of no consequence.[35]

I write to Vergennes to tell him of the large exodus of people to the Ohio, the intention to connect the Potomac, Susquehanna and the Ohio more closely by canals, and that as the outlet for this area is the Mississippi, prohibition of trade on it will lead to disputes later than is thought in the United States, but earlier than is thought in Europe. 'The Americans like us, but they very genuinely hate Spain.'[36]

In the afternoon I set off in a barge to travel up the North River to Albany, again accompanied by Madison, who has decided to come with us to the Six Nation Peace Conference, suggested to me by Washington. On the twenty-third, we assemble at Albany where Barbé de Marbois joins us. On the twenty-seventh it is raining. A quiet drizzle which drips steadily from my hat and down my coat. We leave Albany to its Sunday services and ride into the woods, our horses' hooves muffled by the thick autumnal leaf fall. Ahead lies Fort Schuyler and the Peace Conference, but our party of Caraman, Madison, Marbois and our servants, is deviating from the route to visit Niskayuna, the home of the Shakers.

"I have been travelling across America and have an interest in the indigenous peoples. Can I join your expedition to Fort Schuyler?" Barbé de Marbois had asked. "I would also like to visit the Shaker community, which is only eight miles away, I believe."

"I would be very pleased to see the Shakers," I had replied. "I am a student of Mesmer and there seems to be a similarity between their ideas and his. I gather they claim to heal illnesses and broken bones by the laying on of hands."

"I agree to a detour as long as we are not late for the conference," Madison had said.

The track narrows, finally petering out amongst huge bodies of ancient trees. Daylight is obscured and we fight our way through branches and foliage. It becomes impossible to continue by horse; we dismount and go on foot and as we near our destination a slow, melancholic singing of voices in unison drifts eerily through the trees. We follow the mournful melody to its source in a large wooden building and Caraman pushes open the door. We enter the hall just as the chorus stops and see a fire burning at the far end and a congregation of about one hundred and forty men, women and children, dressed alike in gray clothing, who turn to gaze at us. The women are on one side and the men on the other and they shuffle more closely together so that we can stand with them. Their prayer meeting continues and the preacher, an unkempt man in old and dirty clothing, begins to speak.

"Marriage is contrary to the example of the Savior who was never married, and who never had any carnal relationship with a woman."

"If you marry, you do well. If you do not marry, you do even better," a second preacher proclaims.

"I don't think his philosophy would be popular in France," mutters Marbois, "Except among the clergy."

A third preacher, as badly and dirtily dressed as the other two, continues the sermon with a slightly embarrassed air. "Our leader, Ann Lee, was taken from us six weeks ago. A place became vacant in Heaven and she was specially chosen."

Madison whispers. "They believed she would never die and so her death is rather awkward for them. She was often whipped and beaten when she travelled the country in search of converts shortly before her death. She was very fond of the bottle and people used to say that the spirit possessed her."

Two men at the front of the hall start to chant and men, women and children raise their right knees, before dropping onto one foot and lifting the other foot up and down. Everyone moves backwards and forwards three or four steps and whirl around. They shudder with convulsions. The women close their eyes, or raise them upwards, and cry out, as though in ecstasy or pain, their faces as pale as their white caps and all of them resembling a collection of lively ghosts. The men hold their arms towards the sky; their knees give way, and they shake violently before sighing loudly. They are also very pale and both men and women are so thin they resemble twitching sticks.

An elderly, somewhat evil-smelling man, is writhing on the ground near to me; I bend down and feel his body to try and locate the poles of Mesmer.

"Are you acting in the name of a good spirit or of an evil spirit?" another man asks.[37]

"It is certainly in the name of a good spirit," I reply.

My subject appears to be a very simple man. "I fell off a cart and broke my bones and I was cured," he tells me as several of the old men pull at my clothes. "Live with us," they clamor.

It is difficult to concentrate with all the noise and jostling. I do not seem to be succeeding in finding the poles of animal magnetism and I abandon my efforts in great disappointment.

"I am sorry, but we cannot stay any longer," I tell the disciples.

We say farewell and leave the wooden church and its emaciated but very enthusiastic congregation.

Next day we resume our trek towards the Mohawk valley. We follow the banks of the river through a beautiful but desolate land, scarred by the savagery of the war which has left only blackened, charred posts to reveal the previous existence of houses and barns. The houses we do see all have a stockade and sometimes even cannon.

It is bitterly cold. It often rains. My companions shiver and grumble in cloaks and blankets, but the weather does not trouble me. To protect myself from the rain I wear an overcoat of gummed taffeta which has been wrapped in newspapers which have stuck to the gum and which there has been no time to remove, so if anyone wants to read extracts from the *Courier de l'Europe*, or news from various places, they can do so from my back and arms.

The settlers appear poor. Large families with ten or twelve children sleep in the same bed in their log cabins and lack even the most basic of objects. If we ask for a candle holder, a child is pushed forward with a candle in his hand. If we are too hot in front of the fire another child stands in front of it to shield us. We have constructed a wooden spit on which to turn our meat and the children compete noisily for the privilege of doing it.[38]

We knew it would be difficult to obtain food and have brought a sack of cornmeal with us. People bring out pails of milk and we make porridge. We generally have more than enough and are able to give some away.

The roads hardly warrant the name. They are either rocky or swamped with deep mud. Our carriages bounce and lurch and we are in such great danger of overturning and the horses are so exhausted from pulling the vehicles that we unhitch them, use our blankets as saddles and ride.

We begin to meet indigenous people, the women generally carrying heavy burdens, supported by a band around their forehead, the men invariably carrying much lighter loads. They all, however, look at us with the same fierce expression. Luckily, the Iroquois will not want to scalp me as I have not much hair. You do not lose what you have not got, according to the proverb.[39]

Several hours before sunset we ride across the open plain in front of Fort Schuyler. Huts have already been erected; some are solidly built; others are only fragile lodges composed of branches. Men, women and children stand and stare; the women with dark, handsome faces, often in fine clothes, their dress of scarlet, bordered with gold fringe and ornamented with brooches. The men have rings in their noses, their ears are slit, and their heads are plumed with feathers. They are mainly well-built and sinewy, and I know them to be a useful friend and a formidable enemy.

The earthen fort itself, on a man-made hill, is more decrepit than when I last saw it and its four bastions are half-ruined. We enter the compound and the missionary, Kirkland, rushes to greet us.

"Welcome, friends," he says, as we slide from our blanket saddles.

He leads the way into his hut which has a bark roof and no flooring but is happily blessed with a blazing fire.

"I am afraid the other hut is filled with presents for the tribes. There is no room for anyone there. Cabins will be built for you," he says apologetically.

The others warm themselves at the smoking hearth and I step outside with him.

"I am hesitant to speak at the conference. I am French, not American. I do not want to comment when it is not appropriate, although at Albany General Wolcott suggested that I use my influence with the tribes and General Washington also spoke similarly. What is your opinion?" I ask.

"I think you should speak," he replies. "The tribes are very attached both to you and to France. I think your words would be useful to concluding a successful treaty."

"I can only be here for a short time. Perhaps I can have a private meeting with the chiefs?"

"I don't think that would be enough," he replies.

"I will go to Oneida Castle tomorrow and talk to their sachem before the conference."

We sleep on the bare earth that night, the wind whistling through chinks in the log walls. In the morning, not greatly refreshed, we breakfast on our porridge before setting off for Oneida Castle to meet Grasshopper and his Oneida tribe.

The trail is difficult. Streams convert the land to a treacherous swamp; fallen trees block our path; the fords often very fast-flowing and the horses must swim. It is very cold; rain falls constantly, and we become lost. Our guides scout around; they examine trees to see which side is brown and more moss-covered, as that means it is facing north; when they believe they know where we are, we resume our travels, sometimes on foot, sometimes on horseback.

We arrive wet, my companions very tired, at Oneida Castle, a village of huts where Gouvion lived for a long time. A white flag is flying at the council hut; inside the large, single room, Grasshopper greets us, dressed in the Bavarian hunting costume La Luzerne gave him and accompanied by his chiefs and warriors. At either end of the room there are two fires whose smoke goes out of the roof, and my companions immediately make for the nearest. Grasshopper points to beds which are on two sides of the room.

"They are for you," says our interpreter.

I offer the three casks of brandy, which they call milk, which has been carried by three men all the way from Fort Schuyler. Grasshopper and the warriors thank me in their own tongue and present a newly caught large salmon to us, as well as milk, butter, fruit and honey. We cook the salmon over a fire and eat on silverware we have brought. Everyone drinks from wooden goblets, except for me; I am privileged to have a glass mended with resin.

"Can we see your dances?" I ask.

Grasshopper agrees and one of the chiefs goes outside. He blows a horn and young men come running. They rush to the middle of the room and start jumping from one foot to the other, hitting the ground sharply, then sliding their feet to the rhythm of a drum, in the very energetic fashion I remember from before. After two hours we are exhausted, although unfortunately the young braves, who are also by this time very drunk, are not.

"Can we finish now?" pleads Barbé de Marbois.

"No, they want to continue until sunrise," replies the interpreter, to our dismay. At last, one of the dancers who had served under my command takes pity on us. He remonstrates with the others to stop; they abandon the dance and we gratefully go to sleep.

Next morning we depart for the conference; we traverse the same wet, difficult trail. We ride into the fort late in the afternoon and find the three commissioners, General Oliver Wolcott, Arthur Lee and Butler.

"The tribes are here and represent eight nations. The Mohawks, Senecas, Cayugas and Onondagas, who fought against the United States are here, as well as the Oneidas, the Tuscaroras, Wolves, and some from Canada," says Wolcott. "We are giving them all meat, flour and rum, and they are unfortunately eating as much as they want."

"If you would like me to speak at the conference, I will," I say.

They immediately discuss between themselves, and I can see they are not very willing to have a foreigner address the tribes.[40] I find my position somewhat embarrassing, but I raise the issues I have already discussed at Mount Vernon.

"General Washington believes it is necessary to be firm, to treat some of them as conquered enemies, and for them to make substantial land concessions."

The commissioners decide I can speak; I accordingly prepare a speech, show it to them and they agree it is suitable.[41]

Next day, the conference begins outside, even although it is extremely cold. About forty chiefs and warriors sit in a circle around a fire which they use to light their pipes. One warrior is in a bearskin and very much resembles a bear. Another has large ears attached to his head. Many have European uniforms and Grasshopper again wears the uniform given by La Luzerne.

A commissioner speaks first. Then I speak in French which an interpreter translates.

"On meeting my children again, I give thanks to the Great Spirit which led me to this place of peace where you are smoking together the pipe of Peace. If you recognize the voice of Kayewla, do you also remember his advice and the necklaces he often sent you. I come to thank my faithful children, the chiefs of the nations, the warriors, the bearers of my words and if the fatherly memory remembers the bad rather than the good, I would punish those who while opening their ears, have shut their heart, who lifting the hatchet blindly have risked striking their own father.

The American cause is just. I told you then; it is the cause of humanity; it is your cause. Stay neutral at least, and the brave Americans will defend their liberty and yours. Your fathers will take them by the hand; the white birds will cover the shore; the great Ononthio, the Sun, will disperse the clouds around you, and contrary projects will vanish like a fog which disappears. Do not listen to Kayewla, they used to tell you. They also said that an army from the north would enter Boston in triumph, that the army in the south would take Virginia, and that the great war chief, Washington, at the head of your fathers and brothers, would be forced to leave the country. Those who had their hands over your eyes did not forget, however, to keep theirs open. Peace has been made! You know its terms and I shall oblige some among you by not relating them out of pity.

My predictions having been fulfilled, listen to the new advice of your father, and let my voice resound among all the nations.

What have you ever gained, my children, or, rather, what have you not lost in European quarrels? Be wiser than the white men, keep the peace among you, and since the great council of the States wants to negotiate, take advantage of its good dispositions. Do not forget that the Americans are close friends of your fathers the French; this alliance is as enduring as it has been fortunate. The great Ononthio always gives the hand to your brothers who hold out theirs and by this way we will form a strong chain. To assure yourselves of this, trade with the Americans, and with those of your fathers who cross the Great Lake. You know French products. They will become for you the sign of the alliance. When you sell land do not consult a barrel of rum to give them up to the first person who comes but let the American chiefs and yours, united round the same fire, conclude reasonable sales. At the present time, my children, you know that while several are entitled to Congress's gratitude, there are many whose only recourse is in clemency and whose past faults demand reparation.

If you listen well, my children, I have said enough. Repeat my words to each other, while on the other shore of the lake, I will receive your news with pleasure, and until the day when we shall join our pipes, when we shall lie down again under the same bark, I wish you good health, happy hunting, union and abundance, and the success of all the dreams that promise you happiness."[42]

The chiefs and warriors hear me in silence. Then Ocksicanehiou, the chief of the Mohawks, stands up.

"My father. We rejoice that that you have visited your children to give them just and necessary advice...It is true that the Mohawk nation has left the true path. We recognize that we have strayed and become enveloped in a black cloud, but we have returned, and you will find us good and faithful children...We hope that the Great Spirit, which has up to now protected us... will direct our steps to the good path...Children must obey their father and must be punished when they commit faults... but we hope that the great spirit from on high will purify our hearts...We remember what you said seven years ago and we find that that there is nothing which has not been proved true...You have observed, my father, that the alliance between France and America was a chain which could not be broken...You have warned us not to take counsel from strong liquor when we sell our land; we have need of this salutary advice as it is from there that all our misfortunes come...The words which you have spoken today will be told to all the Six Nations, they will renew and reinforce the chain of friendship which we want to see last for always....we welcome here the members of the great council of the United States You say you are leaving tomorrow and if we have more words to add we shall come to see you."[43]

The speeches continue. Smoke from the peace pipes spirals into the cold air; my companions shiver by the fire.

Next morning, Madison's thermometer registers minus three degrees. My little bark hut is not far from the river and there are thin slivers of ice by its banks; the water is even frozen on the top of a wooden basin near the fire which we had made last night and left burning.

Another meeting assembles. Grasshopper, the speaker for the friendly nations, stands up.

"Kayewla, my father, I beg all the nations here to open their ears to the few words I am going to say, and you, great war chief of our father, Ononthio, I beg you to listen to me. Your speech yesterday contained felicitations, reproaches and advice. We received them with as much pleasure as we recalled your words seven years ago. They prevented us from straying from those who were fighting for the cause of America. This necklace was given to us twenty years ago by your fathers." He hands me the necklace Montcalm gave him twenty years before. "Kayewla, my father. All your words have been verified by the events of this great island, we therefore receive with pleasure the new words which you have said to us on this occasion."[44]

I give him back the necklace. "I am very happy you have kept this necklace so well. I am very content my influence might have prevented you from declaring war against the United States. I thank you for your fidelity in following my advice."

"We again admit our error," says one chief. "We were wrong to be on the side of Britain, which has now been defeated."

"Forget all animosity," I declare.

Other chiefs speak. All night and all day, singing and dancing continues round large fires. Grasshopper goes to the huts of the Senecas. They sit with him and his warriors on the grass and all smoke the pipes of peace. Next day, the Senecas go to the Oneida huts and they again smoke the pipes together.

A settlement is beginning to be decided and I am no longer needed. It is agreed that land will be reserved for the tribes, except for two forts in upper New York; the tribes accept that farmers can settle between Lake Erie and the Ohio River.

I speak a few words with Arthur Lee, who has a very disgruntled air and whom I have never liked.

"The tribes have been too occupied with you to pay attention to us," he complains. I ignore his annoyance. They have promised much, and I like to think I have contributed to a treaty that will give us a small commercial outlet and will ensure the tranquility of the Americans. [45]

I go to talk with the chiefs. "Can I take a young Iroquois boy back to France with me, to be educated there?" I request. "It will be very useful for both our nations."

They consult others. Then they return. "We must ask all the relations and some live far away. It will have to be decided later."

My mission is over. I have done what Washington wanted; the commissioners no longer need me. We rent a small boat and five rowers. Eleven of us travel back along the Mohawk to Schenectady, the current in the shallow river and the oars taking us along very rapidly, in fine, but cold weather. At Little Falls the boat has to be pulled overland for about half a mile; then we embark again and continue downriver. On the banks are many burned buildings, the people again appearing poor, but the further south we go, the more cultivated land we see. From Schenectady we travel by land and on October 7 the gabled roofs of the Dutch houses at Albany come into sight.

'Jay is being offered the position of secretary of foreign affairs," Hamilton informs me. "If he does not agree to it the choice will fall on Arthur Lee.'

'I much wish Jay may consent to it. The More So as His probable Successor does not Hit My fancy.' I write to him.[46]

I write to Jay: 'I hope you will accept; I know you must; but in case you are not determined, I had rather change my plans than not to see you before you write to Congress.'[47]

We visit the waterfalls at Cohoes and the battlefield at Saratoga. Then Caraman and I sadly part company from Marbois and Madison and on October 8 set off for Connecticut. Three days later we arrive at Hartford, very content to be back in the world and to have left the wild forests.[48] A gun salute roars; a crowd accompanies me into the town. Next day, there is a banquet in my honor. I make a speech; I talk about the need for Franco-American cooperation and unity.

Maurice Caraman and I talk endlessly of France. We talk about it in the morning; we are still talking about it in the evening. I write to Poix that 'even if the devil offered me all the New World, he would not make me renounce the part of the Old World where I had the good fortune to be born and live. There is nothing in my opinion so charming as to be an Auvergnat, particularly one from the Haute Auvergne it must be said without vanity, and to live in the rue de Bourbon, in a house which might not be the most beautiful but is infinitely pleasing.'[49]

I write to Jefferson who was appointed a trade negotiator for the United States in Europe last December along with Adams and Franklin. He is now in Paris and I say that I am looking forward to the pleasure of seeing him in the French capital and that my house, my family, and anything that is mine, is entirely at his disposal.[50]

October 13. We leave Hartford. Two days later we reach Watertown, immediately west of Boston, kindness continuing to be bestowed on me everywhere. Veteran officers meet me; we eat dinner in an inn to the accompaniment of a band playing military tunes, then they continue as my escort in the afternoon. We go through Cambridge, are ferried across the Charles, and enter Roxbury where members of Roxbury Artillery join us. We cross the Boston Neck; the Boston Artillery salutes us in a roar of guns and the church bells peal out.

Henry Knox greets me, as well as Lecombe, the French consul, and the comte de Grandchain, who had helped to negotiate the capitulation at Yorktown.

"My frigate, the *Nymphe*, is anchored in the harbor," says Grandchain. "It is at your disposal."

We set off, a band marching in front, a military escort bearing the French and American flags. Knox and I ride at the front, along the main streets, Caraman and Grandchain at our flank, Lecombe following with officers and notables of the city in carriages. People hang out of windows, cheering wildly. We reach the Liberty Pole and the cheering increases. At State Street my military escort depart and the crowd escorts me to my lodgings at the Whig Hall Tavern. I make a speech from the balcony; cheers break out again and church bells ring.

Next day, Knox and former officers of the Massachusetts Line call on me. "May patriotic and enlightened historians enumerate the actions of the marquis in the field, and his efforts to promote the happiness of the United States. May he be placed on the same list as Condé, Turenne, and so many other immortal heroes of France."

"I cannot accept praise," I reply. "It must be given to my gallant troops, the French king and the French people."[51] We drink many toasts and become rather merry.

Two days later, Tuesday, October 19, is the third anniversary of the British capitulation at Yorktown; the Legislature invite me to the Senate Chamber. Governor John Hancock makes a speech; I reply: "Massachusetts is the place where the flame of the American Revolution first began to kindle. I will always look after its interests."[52]

At one o'clock the Roxbury and Boston artillery companies march down State Street, then fire a thirteen-gun salute. The cannon of the Castle fire back, as well as those from the Nymphe in the harbor. At two o'clock, I accompany many people to Faneuil Hall, escorted by the artillery. We sit down to a banquet of five hundred guests, given by the Boston merchants, my chair positioned under a fleur-de-lis in an enormous flower arch.

After the dinner Hancock proposes a toast: "To the United States." A thirteen-gun salute follows from the artillery outside in the street and all the guests clap. "To His Majesty King Louis XVI," he proposes, the same gun-salute and clapping following. "To His Excellency General Washington," he proposes. A curtain suddenly opens behind me to reveal his portrait with a wreath of laurel. Surprise overwhelms me, my eyes blur with tears, as do the eyes of many. I rise to my feet.

"Vive Washington!" I declare.

"Vive Washington!" everyone shouts.

Lecombe congratulates me. "It is very helpful to France to celebrate the friendship of our two countries in this way."

That evening, I attend a reception at the house of Mary Hayley, the sister of the British politician John Wilkes.

"This honor pleases me greatly as it comes from an Englishwoman," I tell Major William North.[53]

Fireworks explode into the night sky and lamps illuminate the streets for the first time since the war began nine years ago.

October 21. I go to Harvard University with John Hancock; we dine in College Hall where I am given the rights of a doctor of law. Later I meet again with Henry Knox who is accompanied by James Warren and Samuel Breck. They tell me about the terrible situation of the whaling industry in New England. Many men died in the war and now the British, previously their best customers, are refusing to buy whale oil.

"It would be wonderful if France gives favorable terms to American whale oil."

"I have already mentioned it to the ministers," I reply. "I will do my best to help."

I also speak with James Swan concerning the obstacles to French/American trade and he agrees to write a memorial on it.

Next evening, I attend a children's ball in my honor. Women and girls surround me, all wanting my attention and to dance with me. I am reminded of the words of King Solomon, although God has not given me the great charms of that wise prince[54]

It is so agreeable here I stay longer than I had intended. I write to Washington to tell him of my delay and that I will sail on the first or second of next month on the Nymphe, commanded by Grandchain, who will take me to Yorktown.[55] I also write to Hamilton to say a happy necessity has made me change my plans but that I hope to visit Congress in four weeks' time and after that I hope to be in New York to see my friends. I say I would like him to promote the idea to Congress of my serving the United States and their ministers at home and abroad, an idea which I think has already met with his approval.[56]

I leave Boston on the twenty-second to travel north. Next day, Saturday, I arrive at Providence. A thirteen-gun salute booms out and cheering crowds greet me. On Sunday I sail to Newport to visit Nathanael Greene. I land in the evening; the mayor and local officials meet me and take me to Greene's house. There I embrace my much-loved friend and companion-in-arms, his wife, Katy, still as lively and beautiful as before. We sit down to dine. We reminisce about the war. We talk endlessly. I speak of France. "I am hopeful of the future for my country," I say. We decide that his son might come to France to study, and that my son will attend Harvard.

October 25. At eleven in the morning, I set sail once more to return to Providence. There I enjoy yet another banquet, this time given by the Cincinnati of Rhode Island at Henry Rice's Tavern. Governor William Greene attends, as well as Lieutenant Governor Jabez Bowen, Caraman, Grandchain, Major L'Enfant and James Varnum, who gives a speech of welcome. I reply, congratulating them on the blessings of peace and the firmly established principles of liberty.[57]

The General Assembly of Rhode Island gives me a dinner on the twenty-sixth, again at Rice's Tavern. The governor gives a speech commending my military ardor which 'resulted from a regard to the rights of mankind.' I reply urging that "these rising states unite in every measure."[58] I leave after the dinner and travel to Lynn and Salem, where I dine again, and then attend a ball where unfortunately a stiff knee means I can only walk a minuet. Before sunrise we set off again.

Late in the evening of the thirtieth, we reach Portsmouth. Church bells ring out but there is no artillery salute as we had not been expected. Next day is Sunday and so all is quiet. On Monday, at sunrise, the artillery begins to fire, and flags now decorate the streets. We leave at ten o'clock, people escorting us as far as Greenland.

We continue south. We stop the night at Newburyport; in the morning of November 2, we travel to Marblehead where crowds greet me, many of whom are women.

"They are the widows of men who died during the war. They are the mothers of children for whose liberty you fought. Marblehead lost half of its citizens who were able to fight. They want today to take the place of their husbands, many of whom you knew," says Samuel Breck, who has joined our group.

"Thank you for coming," I tell them. I walk amongst them and talk to everyone.

My welcome parade resumes. We go to Elbridge Gerry's house. He gives a speech and says that the many deaths the war caused here mean that Marblehead cannot fully manifest the principles of hospitality it feels on this joyful occasion.[59] We dine at a genteel house where after the thirteen toasts I propose a fourteenth: "The town of Marblehead and unbounded success for its fisheries."

November 3.[60] We leave, even although Marblehead is going to honour me with a ball; an escort of citizens accompanying us from the town to cheers and the firing of cannon, and later arrive in Boston.

November 5. [61] We set sail on the *Nymphe*, southwards to Virginia. On the fifteenth, I set foot once more at the small town of Yorktown on the bluff above the river, where I trapped Cornwallis and his army. I show Caraman the battlefield, then we go to Williamsburg, accompanied by Grandchain, for a reception. Next day, Thomas Nelson gives a dinner for me at his house. "If my visitors feel too crowded, they must put the blame on the skill of the French artillery, as they destroyed my house in Yorktown" [62]

Amongst the many guests are Philip Mazzei and James Madison, the president of William and Mary College and cousin of my fellow traveler to the Peace Conference. We discuss many topics including animal magnetism, but I cannot stay long as I know Washington arrived last Sunday afternoon at Richmond and is waiting for me.

November 18. We reach Richmond. To my joy, I once more embrace Washington, who has just returned from his tour of the west on horseback, using packhorses for his baggage and tent. We attend a dinner arranged by local merchants at Trower's Tavern; I meet Patrick Henry, who has just been elected governor of the state. Later, the Virginia House of Delegates resolves to present me with their affectionate respects.

Next day I address them. I talk about Franco-American cooperation and the unity of the thirteen states. I praise Virginians for shedding the blood of her sons in defense of her sister states. I say I hope Virginia will continue to give to the world unquestionable proofs of her philanthropy and her regard to the liberties of all mankind.[63] Slavery is a very delicate and difficult subject to mention here and this is the best I feel I can do.

James Armitstead, a slave who had spied for me in the war, comes to see me. "I am trying to obtain my freedom. Can you write a document for me saying that I gave essential services to the war?"

"I am very surprised you are not yet free," I reply and immediately write an affidavit: 'This is to Certify that the Bearer By the Name of James Has Done Essential Service to Me While I Had the Honour to Command in this State. His Intelligence from the Ennemy's Camp were Industriously Collected and Most Faithfully delivered. He Perfectly Acquitted Himself With Some Important Commissions I Gave Him and Appears to me Entitled to Every Reward His Situation Can Admit of.'[64]

"I hope it is beneficial," I tell him.

"If I obtain my freedom, I will change my name to James Armitstead Lafayette," he says.

Banquets and balls occupy the rest of the week, with much firing of cannons. The following Monday, November 22, Washington, Caraman, Grandchain and I set off to Mount Vernon. We arrive on Wednesday and find many of Washington's family here to greet us, including his daughter-in-law, Eleonor Calvert Custis, her new husband, Dr. David Stuart, Harriot, a niece, and Lawrence Augustine and George Steptoe, two nephews. My former aide, George Augustine Washington, who is greatly troubled by a cough, introduces me to an attractive young lady with long curled hair and large eyes.

"May I present my fiancée, Miss Fanny Bassett."

Once again, I am in the home of my beloved general and adopted father. Once again, I see the Potomac with its little bays and creeks, the plain and the hills beyond. We spend much time discussing his recent excursion of six hundred and eighty miles. He went by Braddock's Road through the Alleghenies. He inspected his land on the Monongahela River, then came back by a circuitous route through the wilderness, all the time investigating the possibility of joining the Potomac and the James by internal navigation with the western waters.[65]

"I would like commissions appointed to examine my schemes and the rivers and streams accurately surveyed. It is vital to form close commercial links with these regions. I wish to open the navigation of the Potomac by canals and locks at the Seneca, the Great and the Little Falls. There would be immense advantages from such a measure, in strengthening the union of the States, multiplying the resources of trade, and promoting the prosperity of the country.[66] I don't mind the Spanish closing the Mississippi. I think they might have made a mistake, as if canals connect the Potomac and the James with the Appalachian rivers this would develop renewed interest in east-west relations and resentment against Spain would increase. If Spain reopens the Mississippi it would weaken America and the people living over there would become Spaniards. The western states stand as it were upon a pivot. The touch of a feather would turn them any way. They have looked down the Mississippi, until the Spaniards, very impolitically I think for themselves, threw difficulties in their way," is his opinion.[67]

Just four days later, it is time to leave. The *Nymphe* is already at New York waiting to convey me across the Atlantic before winter sets in too harshly. I say farewell to all the family, to Squire Tub, the plump three-year-old George Washington Parke Custis, and to his delightful sisters, and set off from Mount Vernon with Washington, Caraman and Grandchain. Next day, we reach Annapolis. The governor and the General Assembly welcome us; I make a speech in which I again say the federal union is so necessary to all. I cannot stay long as I need to travel north, to Philadelphia and then to New York to embark on the *Nymphe*.

"Come with me," I beg Washington.

"The season is too much opposed to it," he replies.[68]

December 1. We ride in separate carriages along the same road; we reach the place where it forks, where he will take the road back to Mount Vernon and I will take the other to Baltimore. We sadly part. He looks solemnly out of his window at me as his carriage disappears from view.

I arrive on the seventh at Philadelphia. Congress invites me to Trenton, so I travel there on the tenth. [69] Next day, I meet a committee of twelve members of Congress in the Long Room at the French Arms, every state, except Maryland, having sent a delegate.

"We wish you a happy return to your homeland. We assure you, in the name of the thirteen united states of our esteem, and consideration for you, as well as of our continuing and personal feeling that your talents and zeal for the happiness of America has inspired. The high opinion of you that Congress has so often shown has been again confirmed by your new marks of attention to our political and commercial interests," declares John Jay.[70]

"I embrace with joy this favorable occasion to thank Congress for the confidence with which it has honored me during the whole of this revolution. It started when, young and inexperienced, I was paternally adopted by my illustrious and respectable friend...I recall also my dear companions in arms whose bravery and services have been so useful to their country...After having profoundly felt the importance of the help which our illustrious monarch has sent I rejoice also when I consider this alliance will become reciprocally advantageous through commercial links and and by the happy effects of a mutual affection...I want to see the confederation consolidated, commerce regulated, trade established, frontiers fortified, a uniform militia adopted, and a strong navy. It is only on these principles that the true independence of the United States can be established. May this immense temple we have just raised to liberty, offer for ever a lesson to oppressors, an example to the oppressed, a sanctuary for the rights of man, and to rejoice in future centuries the spirits of its founders. Vive Washington!" I reply.[71]

Everyone stands. "Vive Washington!"

However, when I send a copy of my speech to Jay I add to 'our illustrious monarch' the part France has played in the cause of mankind and tell him 'I have Clapped in a little bit of French sugar plumb, Because I think it fair to Bend a little on that Gentleman's side.' [72]

I am delighted with my reception from Congress and believe Washington is the only other person to have been so honored.[73] The request that I should continue my services to the United States was greeted with the words that no American could harbour any idea that should make it a question and it was agreed both confidentially and affectionately.[74] I am also pleased that my speech is reported in the newspapers, particularly my belief in the French-American alliance and the need to have a strong federation of the states.

December 13. Sunday. We leave Trenton.[75] On the fifteenth, we arrive at New York.

"The *Nymphe* ran aground in the harbor, but she has been little damaged," says Grandchain. "However, just in case, I think we need to sail with the packet ship, which is leaving in a week's time, on the twentieth."

I therefore have more time to meet Hamilton and my other friends, and Nathanael Greene comes to visit from Rhode Island. I talk about trade with merchants and discuss the establishment of an office of commercial information in France with Crèvecoeur. I meet Kayenlaha, a young Native American who has been allowed to accompany me, as well as John Caldwell, whom I am also taking back to France, whose mother was killed by the British, leaving his father, the Reverend James Caldwell, with nine children.

A committee led by Nathanael Greene, including Governor George Clinton of New York, Crèvecoeur, Samuel Webb, John Lamb and Colonel Fisher, escorts me to the Whitehall Stairs on the twenty-first. There is a parade and a reading of the Farewell Ode: 'For sure no bosom greater virtue knew; Or heart more brave, more tender or more true.'[76] Then I embark on the boat to go to the *Nymphe*. We pass the Battery and a thirteen-gun salute roars out. Twelve–year-old Kayenlaha shrieks with fear and John Caldwell comforts him. We arrive on board; the ship's cannons fire back to salute the American flag.

I read the letter from Washington which Clinton has given me:

My Dr. Marqs., The peregrination of the day in which I parted with you, ended at Marlbro': The next day, bad as it was, I got home before dinner. In the moment of our separation upon the road as I travelled and every hour since- I felt all that love, respect and attachment for you, with which length of years, close connexion and your merits, have inspired me. I often asked myself, as our Carriages distended, whether that was the last sight, I ever should have of you? And tho' I wished to say no- my fears answered yes. I called to mind the days of my youth, and found they had long since fled to return no more; that I was now descending the hill I had been 52 years climbing- and that tho' I was blessed with a good constitution, I was of a short lived family- and might soon expect to be entombed in the dreary mansions of my father's. These things darkened the shades and gave a gloom to the picture, consequently to my prospects of seeing you again: but I will not repine. I have had my day…It is unnecessary, I persuade myself to repeat to you my Dear Marqs. the sincerity of my regards and friendship- nor have I words which could express my affection for you, were I to attempt it. My fervent prayers are offered for your safe and pleasant passage- happy meeting with Madame La Fayette and family, and the completion of every wish of your heart- in all which Mrs. Washington joins me; as she does in complimts. to Capt. Grandchean and the Chevr.- of whom little Washington often speaks. With every sentimt. which is propitious and endearing – I am etc. etc. etc.[77]

My whole being rebels at his words; I write back to him:

My dear General, I have received your affectionate letter of the 8th inst, and from the known sentiments of my heart to you, you will easely guess what my feelings have been in perusing the tender expressions of your friendship- No, my beloved General, our late parting was not by any means a last interwiew. My whole soul revolts at the idea- and could I harbour it an instant, indeed my dear General, it would make miserable. I well see you never will go to France- the unexpressible pleasure of embracing you in my own house, of well coming you in a family where your name is adored, I do not much expect to experience-But to you, I shall return, and in the walls of Mount Vernon we shall yet often speack of old times. My firm plan is to visit now and then my friends on this side of the Atlantick, and the most beloved of all friends I ever had, or ever will have any where, is too strong an inducement for me to return to him, not to think that, when ever it is possible, I will renew my so pleasing visits to Mount Vernon…Adieu, adieu, my dear General, it is with unexpressible pain that I feel I am going to be severed from you by the Atlantick- everything that admiration, respect, gratitude, friendship and filial love can inspire, is combined in my affectionate heart to devote me most tenderly to you. In your friendship I find a delight which words cannot express- Adieu, my dear General. It is not without emotion that I write this word- Altho' I know I shall soon visit you again-Be attentive to your health- Let me hear from you every month- Adieu, Adieu. [78]

December 23. It is a cold winter morning. The *Nymphe* sets sail, the American coast slowly disappearing as we head out into the Atlantic. I have travelled more than 1914 miles in four months and twenty-one days. I have been received in triumph in all the cities and towns I visited and have found kindness everywhere. I have promoted as best I can my views on the American/French alliance, the unity of the thirteen states and the manumission of slaves. I have seen again my beloved general and my comrades in the war. I am content and am looking forward greatly to returning home.

The wind gusts strongly; the ship races across the Atlantic. I teach Latin, French and French history to Kayenlaha and John Caldwell during the tedium of the voyage.

"Call me papa," I tell them.

A new year dawns as we traverse the wintry ocean. On January 20, the granite cliffs of Bretagne loom ruggedly before us; thirty days after setting sail the *Nymphe* drops anchor at Brest. Kayenlaha and John Caldwell set foot on French soil for the first time.

We travel east. On Sunday evening we halt at Rennes where the states of Bretagne are in session. I sold some of my Breton land to help pay for my voyages to America, but I still own Ker-Martin, Ker-Garric and Pont-Blanc near to Tréguier, worth 176,000 livres, as well as the smaller properties of Keraufrait, Saint-Michel and La Rivière, which bring me 24,000 livres. Therefore, next day, at eleven o'clock, I go to the meeting.

Applause greets me; I am given a seat at the barons' bench, near to the president of the nobility. The abbé de Boisbilly is in the middle of a speech about the use of canals during peace and war. He stops. "I compliment you on what you have done. It is wonderful to see here today someone who has contributed to obtaining this desirable peace."

"I thank the states for your flattering welcome. I hope to soon become a member of your august company," I reply. "I am a Breton landowner and will always possess a Breton heart."[79]

I intend to arrive on Wednesday evening at Versailles, but it will be too late to visit the court which I will do the following day. I write to Adrienne to ask her to come to Versailles and to bring our children: 'I hope to take you in my arms between eleven and midnight and will write again later to make sure of finding you alone...I love you greatly and am impatient to tell you so.'[80]

Part 2

Trials of Destiny

Lafayette in his Paris National Guard uniform after J.B. Weyler. Courtesy of the Marquis de Lafayette Collection, Lafayette College.

Chapter 33

France

1785. Rue de Bourbon. John Adams watches seven-year-old Anastasie singing in English, a slight smile playing across his homespun features. She finishes and curtsies to her audience, curls framing her pale oval face, her eyes large and serious.

George takes her place and sweetly sings his song. Abigail, John, Nabby and Quincy Adams clap enthusiastically, along with our other guests. Kayenlaha performs next, feathers hardly covering his luridly painted naked body, a plumed headdress completing his ensemble. He dances and whoops in a suitably terrifying fashion, rhythmically moving his tattooed legs and arms and flourishing a tomahawk. John Caldwell is not here, he is at Loiseau and Lemoine's Institution in the rue de Berri where the Benedictine priests want him to abandon his faith and become a Catholic and I keep having to go there to complain.

The oval salon on the ground floor of our house is crowded; four large mirrors reflecting the fine silks and satins of bejeweled French guests and the more somber garments of the Americans. It is Monday evening. We have resumed our soirées; outside in the street crowds excitedly watch the carriages disgorge their occupants.

Thomas Jefferson does not attend. One of the letters I brought back to France sadly told him of the death of his daughter, Lucy Elizabeth, from whooping cough last Fall and I have sent it to him with my condolences. His daughter, Patsy, is at the convent of Panthémont; Adrienne visits her there and has taken her on excursions to her aunt at Chaville and to the fountains at Versailles.

"Catholicism does not seem to be taught to Protestants at the convent, even although it is obviously very much a part of their life," is the opinion of Abigail Adams. "Nabby and I went with Mr. Jefferson to watch a ceremony of the taking of the veil. The poor girls lay on their faces for half an hour and when they stood up it was called rising to the Resurrection, after having been dead to the world. Then they went to the old abbess; she put upon them the nun's habit."[1]

I talk with John Adams, the third time I have seen him since my return. I visited him at his house in Auteuil on my way back from Versailles in the evening of January 30. I had told him about commerce in America and of the increasing union of the states, which had greatly pleased him.

The possibility of war in the Low Countries regarding the Austrian desire to open the Scheldt River for navigation and the refusal of the Dutch to do so, has greatly interested me since my return. The emperor has sent forty thousand men there and France has ordered the formation of an army corps in Flanders and another in Alsace, one of which will probably be commanded by the duc de Broglie, and the other by the prince de Condé.

"Do you receive letters every week and from post to post from there? Do you know if it is the intention of the States-General to place Monsieur de Maillebois at the head of their armies?" I had asked him as he had until recently been posted to Holland.

"I know the comte de Vergennes is a friend of Maillebois and I once heard the comte say that he had wished him to have the command of the American army," he had replied.

"The comte de Broglie had wanted that position," I had said.

"Although I would not serve a foreign prince, I would serve a republic, and although I should hurt myself with the queen and her party to a great degree, if the States-General would invite me, without my soliciting or appearing to desire it, I would accept the command. Maillebois loves money and demands splendid appointments. I do not regard money so much and would be easy about it. You are the first person to whom I have spoken of this. I would like you to think about it and I will call and see you in a few days," I had told him quietly as I left.[2]

A week after my visit to Auteuil, Adrienne and I attended a large reception at Franklin's house in Passy where I gave him Washington's letter. I found him considerably aged, his health much worse.

The framed copy of the Declaration of Independence in my study is a constant reminder of Washington and the republic born on the other side of the Atlantic. The British crown has been defeated; a fledgling union of thirteen states now exists near the eastern seaboard of America, whose vast country of plains and dark-forested hills, cleaved by immense rivers, is held close to my heart, as is also my friend and adoptive father who gives me the inspiration and the principles by which to live my life. I write to him on February 9 to say I had found my wife, children and friends in perfect health, that: 'the politics of Europe are not in a tranquil condition and from their situation a dreadfull war may break out. The prince de Condé and the maréchal de Broglie are spoken of to command the two armies- Where I would serve, I had not yet time to arrange- but it will not be with my dear general and everything is so short of that happiness, that nothing when compared to it, can possibly please me.'[3]

"Our Republican friends, Thomas Jefferson and the Adams family, have accepted the invitation of the marquise to attend a *Te Deum* at Notre Dame Cathedral to celebrate the birth of the king and queen's new son," I tell Gouvion.

"I doubt whether all the ceremony at Notre Dame is acceptable to God Almighty," he declares. "But very few people, I believe, are there for the sake of God."[4]

The prospect of war diminishes. Frederick 11 of Prussia invites me to watch the summer maneuvers of his army; I decide to attend and will travel east to Deux Ponts, then on to Cassel, Berlin, Silesia, Bohemia, Vienna and the German battlefields. I also hope to meet Emperor Joseph 11. Gouvion agrees to accompany me and Adrienne will take the children to Chavaniac for three months while I am away.

I have not forgotten the New England whalers and set about trying to obtain the importation of their product into France. I talk to Monsieur Tourtille Sangrain who has the contract for lighting the Parisian streets; finally, he agrees to buy about a thousand tons of oil in three different qualities at market prices and does not include the spermaceti which is the most valuable part. I also manage to persuade the ministers to exclude this single shipment from duty on the condition that the oil is unloaded at specified ports and French goods are used to pay for it.[5] Negotiations last three days; I have my horses kept ready to rush to Franklin's house with the good news. However, the duc de Choiseul dies at twelve o'clock in the morning of May 8 and I cannot leave Paris. I write to Adams to tell him what I have achieved and that if he thinks the bargain is good, his eighteen-year-old son, John Quincy Adams, who is setting off to America tomorrow[6] to study at Harvard, can take the proposition to our New England friends as well as the samples of oil.[7]

The following Thursday, the Adams family dine at my house. John Adams has been appointed American minister in London and will shortly travel there after first going to Holland, whilst Jefferson will take his place here in Paris. He and his wife are very much looking forward to going to England, but Mrs. Adams believes she will lose the greatest part of American intelligence by leaving France.

"No one is so well informed as you are," is her opinion as I have a correspondence in all the states and newspapers from every quarter.[8]

I think it very wrong that Protestants have no rights in France, and Adrienne, a devout Catholic, agrees.

"Injustice should no longer be committed in the name of religion. I abhor persecutions which alienate the hearts of men, and which are, moreover, so contrary to the spirit of the Gospel." [9]

I talk with Chrétien-Guillaume Lamoignon de Malesherbes, who had been minister in charge of Louis XVI's household. He wishes the Edict of Nantes, which overturned the privileges Henri IV gave to the Protestants, to be revoked.

"The baron de Breteuil, the duc de Castries and others think the same. I will give you books on the legal aspect," he says.

I write to Washington in code in case it is intercepted:

102 (Protestants) in 12 (France) are under intolerable despotism-Altho' oppen persecution does not now exist, yet it depends on the whim of 25 (king), 28 (queen), 29 (parliament) or any of 32 (ministry). Marriages are not legal among them. Their wills have no force by law, their children are to be bastards, their parsons to be hanged. I have put it into my head to be a 1400 (leader) in that affair, and to have their situation changed. With that wiew I am going, under other pretences to visit their chief places of abode with a consent of 42 (Castries) and an other. I will afterwards endeavour to gain 39 (Vergennes) and 29 (parliament) with the Keeper of the Seals who acts as Chancellor. It is a work of time, and of some danger to me, because none of them would give me a scrap of paper, or countenance whatsoever. But I run my chance…when in the course of the fall or winter you will hear of some thing that way, I wanted you to know I had a hand in it. [10]

I entrust the letter, as well as a gift of seven French hounds, to John Quincy Adams. I decide to take my aunt back to Chavaniac and then visit the Protestant communities near Nîmes and Montpellier; I am just getting into the carriage to leave when a letter is given to me. Dr. Bancroft writes that Billy Knox, Henry Knox's brother, is disordered in his head and confined to a house in London.[11] I immediately send a servant to London to bring him to Paris and Adrienne will accompany him to Chavaniac where he can rest.

By June 12, I am in the Auvergne. I travel to Nîmes. "I wish to meet local merchants and encourage trade with the United States," I say to conceal my true intentions. I meet the elderly pastor, Paul Rabaut. "Many people are favorable to the Protestant cause," I tell him.

He listens. Then he repeats the Nunc Dimittis of Siméon when he at last saw the young Jesus. He does not greatly inspire me with confidence, and I speak later to his elder son, the pastor Rabaut de Saint-Etienne. His face has a somewhat vacant expression, but he speaks clearly and confidently, and I have more faith in him than in his father; I talk about the activities of Malesherbes and others.

"Do not even tell your father. Keep it secret. I will help prepare the way at Versailles for you to personally present a plea for toleration to the king."

I travel to Lyon, the second largest city of France, arriving in the morning of the twenty-second. I visit the archbishop to disguise my Protestant activities. I tour local industries and talk about trade with the United States. I eat ices with businessmen at a café, visit the library of a college and climb one of the very steep hills to view the city. We pass the Masonic Lodge, *Le Patriotisme,* who ask me to enter, welcome me with fervor and make me an honorary member.

Next day I watch the manufacture of silk, visit the hospital, tour a gold refinery, see the archbishop again then go to the stock exchange, after which I accompany the local militia to their quarters where I review the changing of the guard.

The commandant of the province gives me a farewell dinner. "The young hero's health!" he toasts, then singers perform a song celebrating the hero of two worlds.

In the morning, I leave the city, which I have visited in my usual energetic fashion, to return to Paris. A month later the Protestant Jacques Poitevin, an astronomer, arrives from Nîmes.

"I will arrange for you to see Malesherbes and you can decide when Rabaut de Saint-Etienne should come here," I tell him.

I visit Franklin to say farewell as he is returning to Philadelphia. He will be accompanied by Houdon whom Jefferson has commissioned to sculpt the bust of Washington for the Capitol in Virginia and the Hôtel de Ville in Paris, and to whom I have already given a letter of introduction to Washington and a set of dinner plates from Adrienne to Mrs. Washington.

"I will write a letter recommending your grandson, William, to Washington," I say. [12]

On July 9, Gouvion and I set off to the east. At Hesse-Cassel are Hessian regiments I fought against in America; at Cassel, the capital, crowds gather in the streets to see me. I meet our friends from America, including 'Old Knyp,' Baron Wilhelm von Knyphausen.

"You were very good soldiers," I tell them.

They reply with compliments and thanks, but I suspect that former enemies meet with a pleasure which is, however, greater for the victor."[13]

At Brunswick, I meet the celebrated Duke of Brunswick, the sovereign prince, but also a general in the army, as well as the grandmaster of Germanic Freemasonry.[14] I immediately dislike him, but do not know what he thinks of me.

"He appears insincere and has no frankness or love of liberty," I say to Gouvion. "I have the impression he wishes me to believe the only purpose of the Prussians in the Netherlands is to maintain the Stadtholder there without increase of power. I am very suspicious of him."

In the last days of July, I am in Berlin. At Potsdam, I am presented to King Frederick 11, who despite what I already know of him, strikes me very forcibly by his face and clothes as resembling an old, broken, dirty corporal, covered with Spanish snuff, his head almost resting on one shoulder, his fingers misshapen by gout. What surprises me most is the fire, and sometimes the gentleness, of the most beautiful eyes I have ever seen, which sometimes give his face a very charming expression, which I later discover can change when he is at the head of his army to be rude and menacing.[15] I also meet his nephew, the Crown Prince, Frederick William.

August 4. I am in Rheinsburg and stay at the château of the king's brother, Prince Henry. I do not know who is the greater general, he or his brother, but I find him to have a perfect literary knowledge as well as an honest heart, philanthropic feelings and rational ideas on the rights of mankind.[16]

We go to Potsdam where Duportail joins Gouvion and I to watch preliminary maneuvers. On the seventeenth, we watch the main maneuvers at Breslau, in Silesia, and I once more see the king. The broken, dirty corporal is now transformed. He sits, tough and imposing, on horseback, at the head of his army, whilst thirty-one battalions, and seventy-five squadrons composed of thirty thousand men, including twenty-two thousand five hundred infantry and seven thousand five hundred of the best cavalry in the world whose horses are very indifferent, but whose boldness and speed is surprising, parade before us on the plain. Twenty thousand men, handsomely dressed, advance in a single line, the soldiers maneuvering better than I have ever seen.

I admire much, but also find much to criticize. The method of recruitment is despotic and the care of veterans almost non-existent. Frederick becomes furious at even the slightest mistake, bellowing that the officers involved should be arrested. I had rather be the last farmer in America than the first general in Berlin.[17]

Several English colonels attend, including England, Abercrombie and Musgrave; I meet Cornwallis again, who has been paroled for Laurens.

"The worst general in England would be laughed at for these maneuvers. The Prussian infantry is slower than the Hessians and nothing could be more ridiculous than two lines coming up within six yards of another and firing in one another's faces till they have no ammunition," he says critically.

We dine for three hours each of the eight days we are here, conversation initially taking place between the king, the Duke of York, who is the second son of George 111, and myself, and then to a few others. I admire the vivacity of the king's wit, his charm and politeness, to the point that I can understand how people can forget how hard, selfish and tyrannical he is. He deliberately seats me between the Duke of York and Cornwallis and asks me about a thousand questions on American affairs, to the obvious annoyance of Cornwallis.

"Is it true General Washington is thinking of taking a house in London?" he says to the Duke of York.[18]

"Does America need a king?" he asks me.

"There will never be either royalty or a nobility there and I have forcibly expressed my own views on this concerning France," I reply.

"Monsieur," he says. "I once knew a young man who, having visited several countries, where liberty and equality ruled, took it into his head to establish the same in his own land. Do you know what happened to him?"

"No, Sire," I reply.

"Monsieur, he was hanged," he says with a smile.[19]

I laugh. I later write to Adrienne: 'As a friend of liberty, I pray God to save us from such a monarch. If I had the honor to be his subject, we would have fallen out long ago.'[20]

On the twenty-fifth, I am in Vienna at the residence of my uncle, the marquis de Noailles, the French ambassador with whom I stayed when he was ambassador in London before my first voyage to America.

"Would you please remain only long enough to recover from the fatigue of the journey," he requests.

His meaning is clear. He does not wish me to visit military garrisons or fortifications, not a very avuncular attitude on his part.[21] However, on September 4, he presents Gouvion and I to Emperor Joseph 11 who talks to us at some length, mainly of America. He asks about the war, Congress, Washington, and American commerce; he talks little of France and nothing of Prussia.

"I believe it would be in the interest of Austria to trade with the United States," I tell him.

In the evening, I meet the Prince de Kaunitz, the Austrian chancellor. The marquis de Noailles has heard that my longer visits to Prussia have been noted with displeasure and has invented the story that I am only here briefly in order to ask for permission to see the whole of the Austrian maneuvers next summer. Accordingly, I take care to say that to Kaunitz, as well as to make mention of trade with the United States.

I meet Generals Laudon and Lacey and watch the infantry and cavalry exercises with interest. I find their system of economy must be more admired than the maneuvers of their troops. Their machine is not simple, our regiments are better than theirs, and I believe that with training we would overtake the advantage they have on us in the line. The Austrian army is much larger than that of the Prussian or French, but costs far less than ours.[22] It is not so well exercised as that of Prussia and is beginning to use the same method of recruiting.[23]

To my uncle's relief, we leave Vienna and travel to Bohemia and Saxony. Near Prague, we see six battalions drilling on the plain, the artillery very impressive. We tour the battlefields of the Seven Years War, then return via Dresden and arrive in Berlin on September 18. We stay two hours, then go to Potsdam.

"It is a great surprise to see you," remarks the Duke of Brunswick. "We had not expected you to return."

"Why is that?" I enquire.

"We thought you would be arrested as a spy or a go-between. Austria and Prussia are in dispute about the exchange of Belgium for Bavaria, and it is not possible to travel from here to there without causing suspicion."

I laugh. I discover people have been betting on me. Frederick's companion, Lucchesini, has made money because he correctly thought I would come back. I would like to have seen Frederick again, but he is gravely ill in Berlin and is thought to be near death. The maneuvers, however, still take place, this time commanded by Crown Prince Frederick William, who is a good officer, an honest man, a man of plain good sense, but does not come up to the abilities of his two uncles.[24]

I greatly admire the Prussian army. Nothing can be compared to the beauty of the troops, the discipline diffused throughout, the simplicity of their motions, the uniformity of their regiments. Were the resources of France, the alertness of her men, the intelligence of her officers, and national ambition and moral delicacy applied to such a constant system, we could be as superior to the Prussians as our army is now inferior to theirs.[25]

Cornwallis thinks differently. "I find the Prussian infantry slower than the Hessians and its maneuvers such as the worst general in England would be laughed at for making."

September 25. I return to Berlin and spend fifteen days with Prince Henry at his country residence. The king remains ill, so I write my adieux to him before we set off back to France on October 7. We stop at Magdebourg; I meet the Duke of Brunswick again, who is commanding maneuvers and mock battles resembling those I saw at Potsdam, and whose instruction and military routine is so good that even a fool could manage his corps in the line almost as well as if he was sensible.[26]

At the end of October, I reach Paris, very pleased with my trip. I have seen battlefields; my military knowledge has increased; I have met ministers, generals, an emperor and a king. To my pleasure Washington's name was everywhere spoken of with respect and enthusiasm, and the spirit and firmness with which the Revolution was carried has excited universal admiration. However, it has been painful for me to hear people who know very little of the advantages of democratic government speak of the want of powers in Congress, of Union between the states and of energy in their government, which will make the Confederation very insignificant. I have attempted to redress many of these ideas but it grieves me to think that the United States will lose the respect of the world if it does not strengthen the Confederation, give Congress powers to regulate trade, pay off their debt or at least its interest, and establish a well-regulated militia.[27] I have perhaps helped to forward the cause of America and I have always spoken of liberty, no matter in whose company.

Chapter 34

Assembly of Notables

I am a friend of Condorcet, the philosopher and mathematician, a member of both the Académie des sciences and the Académie française, and the author of *Réflexions sur l'Esclavage des Nègres* published in 1781 at Neufchâtel under the name pasteur Schwartz. He first knew of my wish to help the cause of the emancipation of slaves when he lived in Basel, from where he wrote on February 24: 'I have just learned that you have honored my reflections on negro slavery with your attentions...No man of our continent has contributed more than you, M. le Marquis, to break those chains Europe gave America. Perhaps the glory of destroying the slavery that we have imposed on the unfortunate Africans will be reclaimed from you. You would be then the liberator of two of the four parts of the world.'[1] I wrote back to Schwartz through the duc de La Rochefoucauld; we met later when he came to Paris and share the same desire to achieve the manumission of slaves as well as other reforms.

"The royal slaves should be freed and given land," I suggest to Castries.

"You must act privately," he replies.

In December I therefore buy *La Belle Gabrielle* and *Saint-Régis* in Cayenne from creditors of the Jesuits for 125,000 livres. I now own a plantation and forty-eight slaves whom I intend ultimately to set free. Adrienne will supervise the project and the manager will be Monsieur Henri de Richeprey, introduced to me by Condorcet.

Adrienne writes to the priests of the Séminaire du Saint-Esprit at Cayenne. She hopes to teach the slaves to know and to love God and to prove to free-thinking people that the success of the scheme will be in great part due to religion, and the priests will help achieve this.[2] The plantation will cultivate spices such as cloves and cinnamon from plants recently imported from the Île-de-France. There will be no corporal punishment. Wages will be paid, and the blacks will be under the same laws as the whites. I do not want a sudden abolition. I feel emancipation must be achieved gradually.

December 3. I renounce my pension from the king of seven hundred and eighty livres which was awarded after my father's death. I ask for it to be given to the widow of a former under-lieutenant of infantry of Chartres and to a man exempted from work on the highways at Langeac. I say that my life has only recently allowed me to reflect on my personal circumstances, but that now my wealth has been so increased since I was first awarded the pension, I wish to only retain the memory of it.

Rabaut de Saint-Etienne arrives in Paris to promote the Protestant cause and bring about an edict of tolerance. He meets La Rochefoucauld and Malesherbes; I have great hopes that the affairs of the Protestants will be put on a better footing, not such by far as it ought to be, but much mended from the absurd and cruel laws of Louis XIV.[3]

In 1786 I pursue my interest in the emancipation of slavery; I write to Washington to tell him I have bought a plantation in Cayenne and that I am going to work to emancipate the slaves, a project which is, as he knows, my favorite dream.[4] I write to Adams that: 'it is to me a matter of great anxiety and concern, to find that this trade is sometimes perpetrated under the flag of liberty, our dear and noble stripes, to which virtue and glory have been constant standard-bearers.'[5]

Houdon returns, but he has not brought the bust of Washington which will come from London. I am very impatient to see it and hope it is a good likeness. I often now see Jefferson who walks from his house on the Champs Elysées to the rue de Bourbon. We discuss the import to France of American products, whose merchandise we think values about twenty-five million livres. We discuss the tobacco monopoly and trade with the New England fisheries, as well as the problem of the Barbary pirates. I find him one of the most amiable, learned, upright and able men who ever existed.[6] His public conduct pleases me greatly. He unites every ability that can recommend him with the ministers and possesses accomplishments of the mind and heart which cannot but give him many friends.[7]

I ask Calonne for a committee to be formed to examine trade between the United States and France. The *comité de commerce* is set up and I am one of its twelve members. I intend to attempt to break the monopoly of the *Ferme*, although I am very aware it will need to be done slowly.[8] On February 9, I propose the abolition of the tobacco monopoly. No one wishes to discuss it and the meeting is adjourned. A week later we meet again. The *fermiers-généraux* on the committee produce statistics which are very favorable to them; Jefferson subsequently works out that they are not including the interest on their original investment.

'The king should, in favor to them, discontinue the bail; and they cannot ask its continuance without acknowledging they have given in a false state of quantities and sums,' he writes ironically.[9]

He and Condorcet instruct me with the facts I need to know for the discussions. However, in March the government renew the contracts with the Ferme and the tobacco monopoly remains in place, the only proviso being that it could be changed if the king decided. For the moment, I do not have to continue my meetings; Jefferson has gone to London, and I turn my attention to other commerce matters including that concerning Greene who has bought a large interest in timber in Georgia and wants to sell it to France. I ask Castries, who agrees to an order for one thousand feet of American oak and cedar. I also suggest to the merchant from whom I buy my furs to obtain them from America. In April, I buy the seigneury of Langeac for 188,000 livres, causing rumors I wish to become a duc.

On May 24 the comité de commerce meets at the château of Calonne. It is decided that the Ferme will annually buy an extra twelve to fifteen thousand hogsheads of American tobacco on the same terms as those of the Morris monopoly, and that when the Morris contract comes to an end, no similar contracts can be made.

'It is very useful. It will at least keep the commerce between the United States and France alive until the Ferme's monopoly can be destroyed, which might happen if Calonne resigns, as is thought,' is Jefferson's opinion.[10]

On May 31 I dine, as I often do, at Saint Ouen with Necker, in the company of his daughter, Madame de Staël, and Madame de Lauzun. Necker had been, essentially, contrôleur-général, but as he is a Swiss Protestant, he had not been able to sit with the other ministers and so had been, therefore, director of finances.[11] Afterwards, I visit the duc de Nivernois to give him a paper on a small project of the reform of the criminal law, written by Condorcet. He is not at home; I leave it for him, more to acquit my conscience than to have any hope of obtaining anything.[12]

I next visit Lamoignan's house to await to hear the court's final judgement in the strange affair of the case of Marie Antoinette's necklace. The cardinal de Rohan had been deceived into buying a diamond necklace for one and a half million livres, in the belief that the queen wanted it but did not have the money to buy it immediately, and that by paying for it himself, he would win her favor. The conspiracy was discovered, and the perpetrators brought to trial, including the cardinal, of whom it was asked: 'Was it reasonable for him to have believed that the queen would act in such a manner? Or was he guilty of treason for having such a low opinion of her?'

The verdict arrives. The cardinal is found not guilty; Madame de Lamotte is to be whipped and branded in public, then imprisoned; Madame Olivia is to be banished from the court; Cagliostro is found not guilty.[13]

Jeanne de Lamotte's trial brief has provided scandalous accounts for the last few months of an imaginary sexual liaison between Marie Antoinette and the cardinal. 'Louis, if you want to see a bastard, cuckold, slut, look in your mirror at the queen and the dauphin,' people mock. The queen's reputation has been greatly tarnished and the verdict is not what she and the king wanted.

She is pregnant and expected to give birth in July. At the beginning of June, she goes to stay at the newly constructed hamlet of Trianon where she can enjoy the delights of the countryside, under the guidance of the farmer and his wife, Monsieur and Madame Valy-Bussard from Touraine. Cows graze; chickens peck at the lawn under a large net; the little lake is stocked with two thousand carp and twenty-seven pike; gardeners cultivate vegetables in small gardens surrounding each house. Marie Antoinette and her friends make butter and cheese and participate in other farming activities, a bucolic idyll not constrained by court etiquette and far from the vile outpourings of the pamphleteers.

I am invited to visit, with the king and his entourage, the new harbor being built at the small Norman town of Cherbourg at the northern end of the Cotentin peninsula. It will be a momentous occasion, only the second time the king has left the Île de France, the first being when he was crowned at Rheims.

June 19. I set off to Normandy with the maréchaux de Castries and de Ségur, the father of my friend and relation by marriage; the king will depart tomorrow. On Wednesday, the twenty-first, we reach Cherbourg. On the twenty-second, I wait at the hôtel de ville with Castries, Ségur, the ducs de Chabot, de Liancourt, de Mortemart, de Volignac, de Polignac and de Guiche for the carriage of His Majesty.

The buildings gleam with lights in the darkness; at eleven o'clock he arrives, in such a hurry to see the new construction that he celebrates Mass at three o'clock in the morning. Shortly after dawn the royal carriage takes him to the waterside.

"*Vive le roi!*" goes up the cry from hundreds of people crowding the street and hanging out of the windows of the tall, stone houses.

"*Vive mon peuple,*"[14] calls out Louis, dressed in a scarlet coat embroidered with gold fleur-de-lys, made for the occasion.

The townsfolk surge forward, exclaiming joyfully. He glances at them, then gazes at the strange spectacle just offshore which he has talked about for weeks. Eight enormous flat-topped cones rear sixty feet above the water, each one hundred and forty-two feet in diameter, made of twenty thousand cubic feet of oak, weighing forty-eight thousand tons and linked by iron chains. The marvelous scheme has been devised by de Cessart, the chief engineer, and there will eventually be ninety cones cemented together to form a harbor, a marvelous enterprise.[15]

"It is just three to four hours to Portsmouth from here if the winds are favorable. The new harbor will be essential to our navy which will be the equal of Britain's. It is our future hope in the world and this port of Cherbourg will help to bring it about," Louis declares.

His plump face looks as excited as at the hunt, one of his three passions, the other two being locksmithing and the sea, which he has never visited before although he is an expert on maritime topics thanks to his former tutor, Nicolas-Marie Ozanne, previously a naval draughtsman.

Charles-Francois Dumouriez, the Cherbourg commander, guides him towards a waiting barge, gilded with gold, flying the royal flag and manned by twenty oarsmen in scarlet and white. He steps eagerly on board, followed by Castries, Ségur and I. The oarsmen row towards the far cone, craft of all shapes and sizes dotting the sea as far as the horizon. Nausea gnaws at me; the barge rises and falls unpleasantly in the swell; I struggle to keep down my breakfast.

In front of us the huge, unwieldly cone nine is being towed into position and will shortly be sunk, which is what we have come to see today. Our royal party is decanted onto cone eight and we watch. Two hours pass, a very long time in the circumstances for some of us. Finally, we see apertures open at the side; workmen start to throw rocks into them.

"Submerge it," orders Louis.

A capstan breaks. A cable tightens too quickly, knocking three men into the sea. They flail desperately. A boat rescues two; a third sinks below the surface.

Louis peers through his telescope, aghast at what is happening. "I will pay a pension of five hundred louis to his widow," he says in distress.

We sit down on the cone to a cold meal underneath an awning. I eat little, knowing we are about to sail around the roadstead on the seventy-four-gun vessel, the *Patriote*. The meal finished, we set off in increasingly choppy water; I retch uncontrollably over the side, much to the delight of the king, who enjoys a very coarse sense of humor.

We spend several days watching naval maneuvers, nausea my frequent companion. The twenty-sixth brings me salvation; in relief I climb into the royal coach with Castries, Ségur, the duc de Liancourt and the king. We pass through Caen, Honfleur, Gaillon and Rouen. Large crowds welcome their monarch, and he smiles happily, the most contented I have ever seen him. We near Paris and people seem far less enthusiastic.

"I see that I am approaching Versailles," he sighs.[16]

In July, Jefferson gives me a detailed estimate of the imports and exports of the United States from Europe and from the West Indies, a document which will aid me in my efforts to promote trade between France and America.[17] We frequently discuss the Barbary pirates and I decide to offer my services as a chief to the antipiratical conspiracy. I will ask for money from Naples, Portugal, Rome, Venice and some German towns, naval stores and seamen from America, a treaty with Malta, a harbor in Sicily, and will have two or three fifties, six large brigs and some smaller vessels filled with marines to board the privateers. [18]

I travel to the Auvergne. On Sunday, August 13, I set off from Chavaniac to receive the homage of the inhabitants of my new seigneurie at Langeac. A small battalion marches in front of me to the banks of the Allier; I cross in a boat; I mount a white horse and receive a welcome from Vealle du Blau, the commandant. We proceed through the nearby streets; the bailli, Vital-Hyacinthe Servant d'Amourette gives a speech comparing me to Alexander, Caesar, Turenne, Villars and Titus; I receive the keys. A grand Mass takes place at the church of Saint Gal, where the singing of the Credo is followed by an American military air; bread and wine are distributed. We parade along the narrow rue de la Boucherie and emerge from the Porte de Farges, one of the town's seven ancient gates. We go to the hospital, then to the Notre Dame convent and finally celebrate with a banquet.

Back in Paris, Jefferson believes that Virginia should give me land, that the day might come when it will be a useful asylum to me. He thinks that the time of life at which I visited America was too well suited to receive good and lasting impressions to permit me ever to accommodate myself to the principles of monarchical government and that it will need all my prudence and that of my friends to make France a safe residence for me.[19]

"I cannot accept any such grant from Virginia," I tell him.

Houdon has finished my bust. Jefferson was going to present it, as well as that of Washington, to Paris, as gifts from Virginia. However, he breaks his wrist and William Short, a former member of the Council of Virginia, now secretary of the American Legation, takes his place at the ceremony on September 28. Military music plays; the crowd cheers; Ethis de Corny, a lawyer and *procureur du roi*, as well as former war commissioner to Rochambeau's army, makes a speech.[20] My laurel and oak crowned bust is placed in the grande salle of the Hôtel de Ville, near to those of French kings and near to that of Washington, so that I will be eternally by the side of, and paying an everlasting homage to the statue of my beloved general.[21] I am greatly honored as the king himself had to give his approval.

Adrienne and I continue our Monday evening soirées at the rue de Bourbon, our house a center for Americans. I also dine frequently at the house of Adrienne's aunt, Madame de Tessé, whose face twitches and grimaces involuntarily, but whose conversation shines with intelligence and wit. People are still talking about the affair of the necklace and the queen remains unpopular with many.

In September the duc d'Ayen is inspecting the troops in the east, so I visit garrison towns there so that I can preserve the habit of seeing troops and their tactics.[22] At Lunéville I learn with immense sadness that Nathanael Greene has died of sunstroke at the age of forty-three.

In October I am often with the court at Fontainebleau. Calonne gives me a letter to Jefferson which details all the concessions the government has made to the United States since 1784. Apart from what has already been agreed concerning free ports and tobacco, it extends the 'most favored' treatment of the Hanseatic cities to American merchants for ten years. It suppresses duties on all kinds of wood for shipbuilding, and on shrubs, trees and bushes, if produced in America and transported in American or French ships. It allows the free import of vessels built in the United States. Books and paper are exempt from duty if carried in American or French ships, and weapons and ammunition will only pay a small duty.

Jefferson is greatly pleased. "I must say, that as far as I am able to see, the friendship of the people of this country towards us is cordial and general, and that it is a kind of security for the friendship of ministers who cannot, in any country, be uninfluenced by the voice of the people."[23]

I write to Washington, enclosing Calonne's letter summarizing the trade agreements given to the United States. I remark on the difference of opinion between Jefferson and Adams on the Algerines-the former wants to attack them, the latter to buy a peace; I also tell him what is happening in Europe, particularly the Dutch quarrels, that there is no present appearance of a war in Germany, and that Russia and Turkey will not fight soon. I mention that the Empress of Russia, Catherine 11, politely hinted that I should go to St. Petersburg, that I had replied I would like to go to the Crimea, to which she has agreed, and I will travel there in February. I write sadly of the death of our great and good friend, General Greene, and that I feel a comfort in condoling with one who knew his value so well and will of course so much have lamented his loss. I mention my hopes that the affairs of the Protestants will soon be put on a better footing as well as my hope that the jackass, with two females, and a few pheasants and red partridges which I have sent to him, have arrived safe. I add a postscript: 'I have received the hams and am much obliged to that kind attention of Mrs. Washington. The first was introduced three days ago at a dinner composed of Americans, where our friend Chattelux had been invited.'[24]

In November, the court is still at Fontainebleau. The king hunts half the day and is drunk the other half, is Jefferson's opinion.[25] His revenue is 130,000,000 livres, more than that of Louis XV, yet he still wants another 120,000,000."[26]

I realize the public debt is great; the American war was very costly but there can be no price put on freedom. I know that the king is concerned about the amount of taxation on the poorest in our society. It is rumored Calonne has been attempting since the summer to persuade him to declare an assembly of the most prominent men of the kingdom, the notables. It last sat one hundred and sixty years ago in the reign of Henri IV, but it would seem essential now. I buy two more plantations in Cayenne.

On December 28 I am a witness at Condorcet's marriage to the beautiful Sophie de Grouchy; afterwards, I open my house to everyone, my daughters merrily talking with the guests in English and French.

Next day, Louis issues a proclamation: 'The Assembly of Notables will meet in January to examine the finances to be adjusted, the means to alleviate the taxes of the people, and of many abuses to be redressed.'[27]

"The king has just resigned," jokes Ségur.

A New Year dawns. The notables are chosen. I am on the initial list of one hundred and forty-four members, but when the list is made public my name is not there.

"I find it difficult to believe the slight originates from the king as he often invites me to Versailles to play cards or hunt," I declare angrily.

"There are only thirty-six nobles, not including the royal princes, you are young in comparison to the others, and they do not want a radical," say my friends.

Before I enquire why I have been excluded, my name is reinstated.[28] The number of notables has already been declared and so the marquis de Noailles is left out. My name is last but one on the list, which includes seven royal princes, fourteen archbishops and bishops, thirty-six nobles, twelve state advisers, thirty-eight magistrates, twelve deputies and twenty-five municipal officers.[29] There will only be twenty-seven people to represent commoners, known as the Third Estate.

"The fact that you were left off the list shows that your character is not considered as an indifferent one and that it excites agitation. However, I hope that the event will pass without crisis," is Jefferson's opinion.[30]

I write to Washington:

> You easily conceive that there is at bottom a desire to make monney some how or other, in order to put the receipt on a level with the expenses, which in this country is become enormous on account of the sums squandered on courtiers and superfluities- But there was no way more patriotic, more candid, more noble to effect those purposes- the King and M. de Calonne, his Minister deserve great credit for that- and I hope a tribute of gratitude and good will shall reward this popular measure- My earnest wish, and fond hope is that our meeting will produce popular assemblées in the provinces, the destruction of many schlakles of the trade, and a change in the fate of the Protestants, events which I will promote by my friends as well as my feeble endeavours with all my heart... [31]

We learn there has been an uprising of taxpayers and debtors in Massachusetts and that Congress has been raising an army there.

"I am against the rebels," I tell Jefferson.

"A little rebellion, now and then, is a good thing, and as necessary in the political world, as storms in the physical," is his opinion.[32]

Calonne falls ill, and then Vergennes, delaying the start of the Assembly. To my great sadness, Vergennes dies on February 13. He has always advised me well. I will miss him, as will both France and the king who sobbed at the news of his death and said he was the only friend he could count on, the one minister who never deceived him. "How happy should I be to repose at your side," he says at his grave.[33]

I am one of twenty people privileged to be given a room at the Château of Versailles. Mine is number seventy-two; the bishop of Blois is next to me at sixty-eight, and other occupants include the comte d'Estaing, Chastellux, the archbishops of Narbonne and Reims, and the maréchal de Mouchy.

February 22. At the first meeting of the Assembly of Notables, I sit with the nobility in the new hall constructed from drab rooms where props for court ballets and balls used to be stored, at the hôtel des menus plaisirs, on the avenue de Paris, at Versailles. The air is redolent of paint and wood; magnificent tapestries of hunting scenes hang on the walls; there are orbs decorated with fleur-de-lys and a throne with a resplendent purple canopy stands on a dais.

I wear, like my fellow nobles, a blue coat and mantle, with a cravat and a plumed hat. The presidents and attorneys of the *parlements* are in black gowns and square hats, the clergy in cassocks, rochets, capes and square hats, the Third Estate are in black.

Trumpets sound. The king enters, the jeweled crown of Saint Louis on his head, dressed in a robe of blue velvet bordered by white ermine, his cape embroidered with gold and white Bourbon fleur-de-lys, complementing the décor of the room. We stand. He walks in his usual awkward fashion, not dissimilar to a waddling duck, across the fleur-de-lys patterned carpet to the throne. He sits down heavily; the ushers and heralds kneel.

At his right, two steps below on the dais, sits Monsieur, his younger brother, the comte de Provence. On his left, also two steps below, is his youngest brother, the comte d'Artois. The other royal princes, the duc d'Orléans, the prince de Condé, the duc de Bourbon, the prince de Conti and the duc de Penthièvre sit on the same step but not on the carpet. I am to his left, at the upper bench of one of the two benches for nobles who are neither princes nor peers and can see Jefferson at the back with the other foreign ambassadors who have been invited.

The king takes off his hat and puts it on again, the sign that he is ready to begin. We remain standing, the ushers and heralds still kneeling. He speaks. His face has an expression of boredom and his voice is barely audible. I can only hear some of the words: "Fairer taxation...A better system needs to be devised...There needs to be less of a burden on the poor... There needs to be greater freedom of internal trade." I think I hear: "Abuses need to be corrected."

After twenty minutes he directs the ushers and heralds to stand. Miromesnil, the *garde des sceaux*, bows deeply. He walks forward a few paces, bows again; he walks to the bottom step of the dais; he bows once more. He kneels. The king speaks to him; he returns to his seat; we now sit.

Calonne bows to the king. He sits down at a table, his papers in front of him. He removes his hat. He replaces it. He addresses us, his voice ringing out in contrast to that of Louis. He mentions an annual deficit in the treasury, which at the end of 1776 reached 37,000,000 livres. He says that one thousand two hundred and fifty million livres have been borrowed since that time, much of it to fight the national war and improve the navy and that while a prosperous nation of around 25,000,000 people could stand such a debt, the deficit shows every prospect of becoming worse before it can be expected to become better. Abuses have occurred and there now needs to be three remedies. There must be fiscal justice. There must be a new land tax on everyone. There must be political consultations from parish, district and provincial level to assess, distribute and administer the tax. There should be freedom of trade in grain. There must be an abolition of internal customs barriers. There must be the reform of the *corvée*, to be replaced by a monetary tax, as well as the introduction of a simple tax to halt the smuggling. He concludes: "His Majesty, King Louis, is a young and virtuous king who has no other desire than to achieve the welfare of his subjects who adore him. He has at last brought about peace within and without his realm and finds it possible to think of reforming the abuses of our constitution. Others may remember the maxim of our monarchy, 'as the king wishes it so be the law.' His Majesty now believes the happiness of the people is the same as that of the king."[34] He sits down.

Miromesnil speaks. "The Assembly of Notables will meet in seven *bureaux*, led by the royal princes. Each will discuss different aspects of the plan and will meet every day except Sunday."

February 23. I am feverish. My nose streams. I cough incessantly. I swallow nearly a bottle of erysimum bought from Jean Maury, the apothecary to the stables of the comte d'Artois. The Assembly convenes again, presided over by Monsieur. Calonne reads out six topics to be examined by the different bureaux: the establishment of provincial assemblies; the tax on land; the reimbursement of debts of the clergy; the *taille*, the land tax collected annually from each person, regarded as unfair and arbitrary and not paid by the clergy or most of the nobility; the grain trade; and the *corvée*.[35]

February 24. We meet in our different *bureau*. Mine is the second, led by the comte d'Artois, and composed of thirty-one people, including the bishop of Toulouse, Loménie de Brienne. I sit on the left side of the table, between my friend, the duc de Laval, and Laurent de Villedeuil. We commence with a discussion on provincial assemblies.

People are calling us the Not Ables and the pamphleteers are savage. Perhaps the most popular picture, particularly with the crowds at the Palais-Royal, the pleasure gardens owned by the duc d'Orléans, shows a monkey speaking to a barnyard of poultry: 'My dear creatures I have assembled you here to decide on the sauce in which you will be served.'

Another favorite depicts animals being told they will be slaughtered: 'You do not have the right of appeal but will have the luxury of deciding how you will be cooked.'

"Enough puns are circulating about the notables to make a larger volume than the *Encyclopédie*," comments Jefferson who is about to travel to the south so will not be here for this important moment in French history.

My cough is worsening. I find it difficult to talk. I mainly listen, fortified by bottle after bottle of erysimum, as well as the delights of syrup of violet, syrup of mallow and purified whey from Maury, but, in any case, I believe that what we are asked to deliberate on is so important that my youth requires me to educate myself by hearing the words of administrators more able than myself.

On March 6, I am one of five members of a committee discussing the grain trade, the corvée and the *taille*.[36] We recommend the taille should be reduced. We suggest the abolition of the corvée. We endorse the king's plan for removing some of the restrictions on the selling of grain. On the seventh, our bureau approves what we suggest. On the twelfth, the bureaux assemble for the third session of the Assembly.

"I congratulate all the bureaux on their observations which agree with the feelings of the king. I now suggest eight different topics to examine; the reform of rights of agreements, the suppression of the rights of *marques*, the manufacture of oils and soaps; anchorage on French ships; the rights to act uniformly on colonial goods; the modifications to make regarding the privileges accorded to certain provinces concerning the tax on tobacco, and on the *gabelle*, the salt tax," says Calonne.[37]

His words are surprising. We are angry. We do not think that what we have agreed corresponds to the observations of the king. Each bureau immediately discusses the subjects given to it but continues to say that Calonne's words do not correspond with what they have decided. My bureau makes a written refutation; on March 14 we ask the king for an exact record of our findings to be noted in the minutes. Other bureaux do the same. On the twentieth, I read out a declaration by the notables of Bretagne, saying that they wish the bureaux to insert into their statements their wish to preserve their rights and liberties, coughing as I do so. I say nothing afterwards. I have become very thin which is greatly worrying Adrienne.

The comte de Simiane, the husband of my beloved friend, Diane Adélaïde de Simiane, has killed himself in Aix. People are saying it was his jealousy towards me which caused him to take his life; that he was unsuccessful as a lover, unsatisfied as a husband, and that life became so unbearable, he blew his brains out.[38]An anonymous open letter vilifies me. It is a new experience to be the butt of insults. It is unpleasant.

On the twenty-eighth, we discuss the gabelle, the salt tax. I am starting to feel much better. I am coughing less. I speak for the first time. "If the idea of a money tax is adopted, it would be humane of the king and the justice to free from the galleys everyone held there for smuggling."[39]

People agree. I read out a proposal from the seventh bureau which wants the suppression of laws on leather.[40]

On the twenty-ninth, the notables assemble for the fourth time. Calonne reads out two memorials on the reorganization of royal lands and forests to increase revenue and to improve conditions for the peasantry. On the thirty-first, we debate this very passionately in my bureau.

"The selling of some domaines has been a loss to the state," says Nicolai, president of the *chambre de comptes.*

"I agree," I reply fervently, as does the bishop of Langres.

April 1. "When such grave allegations are being made, the king has said they should be signed," Artois tells us.

"I claim responsibility for the denunciation," I declare, whilst Nicolai remains quiet. "I wish to read a memorandum signed in my name and I ask Monsieur to take it to His Majesty as coming from me alone." I start to read, but Artois quickly interrupts. "The tone of it is too strong and personal."

"As a gentleman, I have the right to carry my representations to the foot of the throne," I declare.

Castillon, procureur-général to the parlement of Aix, supports me, as do many others. "The king tells us to only mention certain abuses if we sign the statement. What I said last Saturday merits this permission. I will profit by it, Monsieur, with the zeal, the impartiality and the liberty which are in my heart. I have said that it is necessary to attack the monster of speculation, rather than to nourish it. I proposed, and propose, to the bureau, that His Majesty should be asked to order a serious examination by people who are above suspicion, of all the royal possessions, as well as titles of gifts, rents, exchanges or purchases which have been, or will be made, to the *chambre des comptes.* And since this document which is open and signed by me will be given to His Majesty, I repeat with double my confidence the words I have made and given to Monsieur."

I cite two examples, that of the purchase by the Guémenées of the seigneurie of Lorient and that of the exchange of the comté de Sancerre. "The millions that are dissipated are being raised by taxation, and that taxation can only be justified by the true need of the state. The millions abandoned to depredation or to cupidity are the fruit of the sweat, of the tears, and perhaps of the blood of the people, and the calculation of the misery caused by the collection of sums so lightly wasted is truly frightening in comparison with the justice and goodness we know to be His Majesty's natural sentiments." [41]

"I support these words," says the bishop of Langres.[42] "After Easter I will provide proof."

Calonne is now very unpopular; in order to try and defend himself, he publishes a collection of his speeches to the notables, as well as the government's proposals. He also publishes an anonymous tract introducing the proposals, which claim that if they are accepted, the nobility would pay more but the poor would pay less. He gives the tract to priests to read from their pulpits on Sunday; not surprisingly, it causes unrest on the streets.

On April 2, my *bureau* protests. "It misleads the people and serves as a dangerous tocsin," says the duc de Guines.

"The government had never addressed the people in this manner," declares the duc d'Harcourt.

"Even in Boston this appeal would be seen as seditious," I comment.

The king allows our words to be published and the disagreement between the nobles and Calonne is now very evident. My speech becomes well known; it is printed in pamphlets and newspapers; I send a copy to Washington. It greatly angers Calonne. I hear that he asks the king to imprison me in the Bastille.

On the fourth, we adjourn for Easter. I am coughing violently again and am pleased to be able to go home to the rue de Bourbon.

In the morning of April 8, the king dismisses Miromesnil. Later in the day, to my great satisfaction, he dismisses Calonne. The Paris crowds burn an effigy of him on the Pont Neuf; his blue riband of the Order of the Saint Esprit is taken away and he gives up his estate at Hannonville.

He is said to be ill and spitting blood. "Is it his own, or the country's?" people ask.[43]

"I hear that he has asked a monastery near his house to look after one thousand bottles of wine. He is obviously intending to return to power," I remark to Adrienne.

I have won a victory. I am hopeful that the outcome might be to have a similar constitution to that of England and that the amendments proposed by the notables to keep the ancient forms of representation will strengthen the new assemblies and lay a good foundation for what will follow.

On April 10 the elderly Bouvard de Fourqueux becomes the contrôleur-général and submits two topics of taxation to the notables. On the sixteenth, the bureaux meet again. Next day, I speak. "No new taxes should be levied until all economies possible have been made, and that, even then, because of the squandering and luxury of the court, and of the highest classes in society, more taxes would be inhumane. Follow these millions as they are demanded among rural hovels and you will recognize them as the widow's and orphan's mite, the final burden that forces a farmer to abandon his plow, and a family of honest workers to have to beg."[44]

I make a second speech. "I propose cuts in the military and in the royal household and to sell off unused royal property including many of the hunting lodges. I want regular audits for the royal treasury and punishment of those who make undue profits from speculation in government loans and only when all this is accomplished should the notables consider new taxes. The notables can never sanction taxes, as that imprescriptible right belongs to the representatives of the nation alone."

I have learned of the terrible conditions in prison from Adrienne who has recently visited some with friends. "There must be reform of the criminal law and the prisons. The king's heart would disavow these prisons as well as the law of the kingdom that sends prisoners there if he fully understood their uselessness and danger." [45]

A pamphlet denounces my lack of financial knowledge and my personal integrity. There is much criticism of me, even although I was one of the notables most hostile to Calonne. There is also criticism of d'Estaing and du Bouillé; people say we are displaying a blind and servile submission as we are accustomed to military obedience.

April 23. The king presides over the fifth meeting of the assembly. On the twenty-fifth, Loménie de Brienne replaces Fourquet as controleur-général. On the twenty-seventh, my bureau forms four committees to discuss the deficit and ways to stop it becoming worse. On May 2, we talk about the debt owed to France by the United States. Several people criticize America's irregular and often late, repayments.

"If the trade restrictions are lifted, they will be better able to meet their obligations," I say.

Jefferson is still away and so I appeal to William Short, who is acting for him. I write to Washington, Jay and Knox. Gouvion also writes to American friends, describing my defense of their honor, and at the same time asking how they can be so behind with their payments.

May 10. I am in a committee with Chastellux, Le Peletier de Mortefontaine and the mayor of Montpellier, to examine ways of proposing to the king how to prevent an increase in the deficit. I submit a project of budget reform in the belief that now Brienne has replaced Calonne reforms will be proposed by the notables which the king will make law. I feel that the deficit is not so great nor so unremediable that a virtuous and enlightened administration could not meet it, perhaps by small loans or the postponement of some payments.

"The king should name some fixed sum for his private and military establishment, for the support of the royal family, and for gifts. To do away with costly ceremonies no longer valued and only derived from tradition. To give each office a fixed salary. To insist on the keeping of regular accounts; to give pensions and regular gifts only as a recompense for public service; to abolish the custom of anticipating the revenue." [46]

I receive a letter from Jefferson in the south of France: 'From the first olive fields of Pierrelate to the orangeries of Hieres, has been a continual rapture to me. I have often wished for you. I think you have not made this journey. It is a pleasure you have to come, and an improvement to be added to the many you have already made...This is, perhaps, the only moment in your life in which you can acquire that knowledge. And to do it most effectually, you must be absolutely incognito.'[47]

I make a long speech on taxation. "The rights of the nation outweigh the needs of the government. However great the love of the people for the king, it would be dangerous to believe that their resources are inexhaustible...to cite my province, which in truth, suffers particularly from the inequality of taxation and the inattention of the government, which is forcing farmers to abandon their plows, craftsmen their work shops, that its most industrious citizens, stripped of what they earn...no longer have any alternative but to beg or emigrate and that in this part of the kingdom taxes can only be raised by reducing them to the extremities of misery and despair....It seems to me that now is the time when we ought to beg His Majesty to decide the outcome of all the measures and to consolidate forever their happy outcome by the convocation of a National Assembly."[48]

"What, Monsieur! Are you calling for the convocation of an Estates-General!" declares the comte d'Artois.

"Yes, Monseigneur," I reply. "And even more than that."

There is silence in the room. Everyone knows I am asking for a national assembly.

"You want me to write that Monsieur de Lafayette wants the convocation of the Estates-General and take it to the king?" he asks.

"Yes, Monseigneur," I reply, content that my name should be the only one written. There is silence. [49]

"The first time that France sees the Estates-General she will also see a terrible revolution," comments the duc de Pasquier of the Paris Parlement.[50]

May 23. I am named as one of six to undertake a piece of work accomplished by the second bureau. I move two motions. "I propose to ask the king to give civil status to Protestants and to order the reform of the criminal laws." [51]

"These questions have not been put to the bureau and so we are going beyond the remit of the notables," objects the comte d'Artois. "However, I will speak to the king on these issues, if it is the will of the committee."

The members vote almost unanimously that he should do so. Next day, these two subjects are written and submitted to the king. I send a copy of the resolution to Target who is preparing a royal memorandum on toleration.

May 25. The king presides over the final assembly of the notables. I am the fifty-first to sign the minutes; I write only Lafayette, not my titles. Marie Antoinette and her children watch as we file past.

I am pleased with what I have done and said during the last four months. I have taken an active role in the discussion of a more equal distribution of taxes, to include the clergy, until now exempt, and the greater part of the nobility, who were not good at paying; of provincial assemblies based on an elective principle; of savings of at least forty million livres; of the abolition of internal customs dues; of a change in the gabelle and of an annual publication of the financial account and the publishing of all pensions, gifts etc; of better arrangements in some ministerial departments; the habit of thinking about public affairs, etc.; these are the good effects of this assembly, which although it was not national, since it was not representative, conducted itself with much justice and patriotism. [52] 'I feel the spirit of liberty is prevailing in this country at a great rate and that Liberal ideas are cantering about from one end of the kingdom to the other... I can't say I am on a very favorable footing at Court, if by Court you understand the King, Queen, and King's Brothers, but am very friendly with the present administration,' I write to Washington.[53]

In France we have a centralized government which is struggling to gain popular support. In the United States its popular leaders are struggling for more centralized government. I have confidence in the ability of Brienne and find him both great and good. Malesherbes is again a minister and the duc de Nivernais is called to the Council of State; both these men inspire me with confidence.

I am coughing badly so Adrienne furnishes an apartment in the royal château at Saint Germain in order that I can rest without my children. Many of my friends visit, including Madame de Simiane, and I hear from them what is happening. I know that a federal constitutional conference was due to take place in Philadelphia in May. Has it begun?

On June 22, the king issues an edict ordering provincial assemblies to be set up; I am one of the five nobles appointed to that of the Auvergne.

I write to Washington who is in Philadelphia attending the Convention on whose success may well depend the very existence of the United States. I am honest in my words: 'Her dignity is lowering, her credit vanishing, her good intentions questioned by some, her future prosperity doubted.' [54]

Adrienne is already in the Auvergne; she has travelled there before me as she has a cough and we hope the warmer climate will be better for her.

Chapter 35

I have the happiness to please the people and the misfortune to displease the government

Clermont perches on the summit of a rocky hill, a twin-spired gothic cathedral dominating its narrow, winding streets and gray, volcanic-stone buildings, a fine, long avenue of walnut trees and willows linking it to Mont Ferrand. On the morning of August 14, I gather with twenty-five other Auvergnats at the Collège for the first session of our provincial assembly.

The vicomte de Beaune, the father-in-law of Pauline, Adrienne's sister, is the president and was named by the king, which restricts him, so I would not have wanted to be appointed. This first session is only to complete the number of members as the system of deputation will take place in three years' time. The first nomination is made half by the king; we will make the nomination of the other half and we will also name one half of the subordinate assemblies, who will complete themselves by their own choice.[1] I contest this procedure and move the motion that members should be freely elected.

"It is necessary to recall and revive the ancient rights of Auvergne," I declare.[2]

On the sixteenth, the choice of new members begins; the abbé de Murat, my relation and godfather, is chosen for the clergy. On the seventeenth, my friend Chabrol, from Riom, is chosen for the Third Estate. On the eighteenth, I am appointed, along with the comte d'Espinchal, to represent the *élection* of Brioude, in the forthcoming *assemblées d'élection*.

"I cannot attend because of my activities in Paris for American trade," I say.[3]

On the twenty-first, our preliminary assembly ends. 'It has been pleasing for me to remark at the first glance that the Assembly were disposed to act with zeal and good harmony, whereby many abuses may be destroyed, liberal principles be adopted, and a great deal of good be done,' I write to Jefferson.[4]

Here in the Auvergne, it has been quiet. Paris, however, has been very different. On August 6 the king called a *lit de justice*, which he addressed with the words: "Messieurs, it is inappropriate for Parlement to doubt my power…It is always painful for me to resolve to make full use of my authority and depart from custom, but my Parlement compels me to do so today, and the safety of the state makes it my duty."

Lamoignon informed the Parlement he was pleased they had agreed to the principles laid out by the notables regarding the edicts on the grain trade, the corvée and the customs union, and that now the edicts on the tax laws needed to be registered. He announced there would be a stamp tax on every legal agreement and that the proposed land tax would replace the present property tax of the *vingtième*, levied on one-twentieth of nobles' property. "It is the wish of the king," he had declared, who had evidently fallen asleep, following a large lunch, which tends to make him irrational, as well as reducing his conception of where he is. He had, unfortunately, not only fallen asleep, but was also snoring loudly, which made it difficult for Lamoignan to be heard. Next day, Parlement debated its response, led by d'Eprésmesnil and supported by my friend, Adrien Duport, a magistrate of Parlement. Parlement declared the king's registration of the taxes to be illegal: The constitutional principle of the French monarchy is that taxes should be consented to by those who bear them.

On the tenth, Louis suspended Parlement. On the fifteenth, he exiled it to Troyes, by means of lettres de cachet, and on the seventeenth, the Palais de Justice was occupied by Swiss Guards who barred the entrances to prevent anyone entering. The parlement of Bordeaux was exiled to Libourne. Riots ensued, led by law clerks who had lost their employment. People talked of marching on Versailles. Louis, Marie Antoinette and Brienne are being openly vilified in both Paris and the provinces, and effigies of Lamoignon have been burnt. The government has tightened censorship; booksellers have been warned against selling unauthorized publications and some political clubs are banned. Soldiers patrol the streets.

I return briefly to Chavaniac. On August 28 I set off to travel through the mountains of the Auvergne where I find all classes of people receive me with the most affecting marks of love and confidence;[5] on September 4, the Masonic Lodge Sully, at Saint Flour, welcomes me; I attend a banquet where a poem relates 'the illustrious Lafayette who by his noble exploits in the two hemispheres has made all humans his brothers.'[6]

I return to Chavaniac and learn that Ségur, Castries and Villedeuil have all resigned; I write a letter on behalf of American trade to the new contrôleur-général, Monsieur de Cambert. Then I travel north to the court at Fontainebleau. I arrive to find that the Prussian king sent part of his army under the Duke of Brunswick across the Dutch border on September 13. The Dutch are expecting the French to support them, and to my delight, my name has been put forward as general, although I gather the Rhinegrave de Salm is also being considered. I immediately set off to gallop to Paris.

I arrive the same day. A short time later, I set off again. I ride hard through the night and most of the next day towards Holland, but news comes that the Dutch Patriots have chosen the Rhinegrave de Salm, not me, and that the Prussians are pushing back his troops, whilst the French army remains in the same position. My disappointment is great. My journey has been for nothing. I return to Paris, greatly annoyed at the British intrigues, the perfidy of the Berlin government and, above all, at the weakness and bad faith of the French government. The stadthouder is reinstated.

Before the end of September, the parlements are recalled from exile, a compromise agreed. Parlement agrees to prolong the period during which a new vingtième tax might be collected, while the king agrees not to go ahead with Brienne's tax proposals.

I am curious to know what happened at the Convention in Philadelphia and write a long letter to Washington telling him I hoped it had:

> Devised proposals and found in the people a disposition which can assure the happiness, prosperity and dignity of the United States... The affairs of France are still in an unsettled situation. A large deficiency is to be filled up with taxes, and the Nation are tired to pay what they have not voted. The ideas of liberty have been, since the American Revolution, spreading very fast. The combustible materials have been kindled by the Assembly of Notables. After they had got rid of us there were the Parliaments to fight with and altho' they are only courts of Judicature, they have made use of their right of registering, to deny their sanction to any taxes, unconsented by the Nation...and from the proceedings that have taken place these six months past, we shall at least obtain the infusion of this idea into every body's head, wiz- that the King has no right to tax the Nation and nothing in that way can be stipulated but by an Assembly of the Nation. The King in France is all mighty. He has all the means to enforce, to punish and to corrupt. His ministers have the inclination and think it their duty to preserve despotism. There are swarms of low and

effeminate couriers. The influence of women, and love of pleasure have abated the spirits of the Nation, and the inferior classes are ignorant. But on the other hand, the genius of the French is lively, enterprising and inclined to contempt of their rulers....there is a strange contrast between the Turkish power of the King, the regard of the ministry to preserve it untouched, the intrigues and servility of courtiers and the general freedom of thinking, speaking and writing in spite of the spies, the Bastille, and the library laws, the spirit of criticism and patriotism in the first class of the Nation....the frolicking insolence of the mob in the city ever ready to give way to a detachement of the Guards, and the more serious discontents of the country people, all which ingredients mixed together will by little and little, without great convulsions, bring on an independent representation of the people, and, of course, a dimunition of regal authority. But it is an affair of time, and will be the slower on its way, as the cross interests of powerfull people will put bars in the wheels...[7]

I believe the new administration to be composed of good men, among whom are my friends, Malesherbes and the comte de La Luzerne, the new minister of the navy. I meet often with like-minded people at Adrien Duport's house in the rue du Grand Chantier. Condorcet attends, as well as the academician Target, Talleyrand, recently appointed bishop of Autun, La Rochefoucauld, comte César de La Tour Maubourg,[8] who comes from le Puy, not far from Chavaniac, Mirabeau, from Provence, an enormous, ugly man with a large pock-marked face, whom I find decadent and immoral and greatly dislike, and many others. There are generally about sixty of us, although we are sometimes called the Society of Thirty, or the Americans, or even occasionally, the Lafayettistes. Jefferson comes but he is not a member.

November 10. I arrive late at the Collège in Clermont for the second session of the Auvergne Assembly which began on the eighth. Our previous motion requesting the preservation of Auvergne's ancient rights was not presented to the king. We, therefore, reconfirm it.

The king has asked Auvergne to provide 2,038,000 livres. We debate the increase of the vingtième tax; on the twenty-second, I am a member of the committee deputed to examine it. We decide that the continuation of the present system of taxation is both unfair and destructive, but that it is not possible to increase taxes. We make a report to the king in which we protest about the vingtième, and we defy his command to find a way of raising taxes.

On December 3 I give a report in the name of the bureau of agriculture and trade. "The peasant, constant in character, mistrustful from experience, does not like new things. I welcome the new freedoms in the grain trade, but the Auvergne is isolated, forgotten in the distribution of roads. Internal customs dues considerably increase the cost for Auvergne producers and ruin them. We should try and stimulate the local economy. We should create a rope and sailmaking industry, instead of sending raw hemp to the ports, or to Agen, to be manufactured. We should make improvements in sheep farming, by buying rams from Berry and Rouergue, and we need to have a policy concerning forestry, exploited by the navy which has bought huge quantities for the war in America."[9]

On the sixth, I give a second report. "I want life here to be improved so that more children will be born. I want the order of 1666 which exempts from all taxes the fathers of twelve children living or dead in the service of the state to be rigorously followed; I want courses for midwives in the hospitals, as well as for people to travel across the Auvergne giving innoculations against smallpox. I would like to destroy begging which continues to increase, perhaps by establishing workshops. We also have the problem of emigration which has gone on for such a long time."[10]

The eleventh is our last day. "Our assembly has been severely criticized by the government for straying from the function intended by the king. I therefore propose our deep consternation on the unexpected discontent of the king but insist again on the too heavy tax charges weighing on the province and repeat the demand for a fairer tax distribution," I say. My motion is adopted.[11]

Adrienne and I travel north to Paris. At Nemours I receive letters from America which includes a copy of the constitution of the United States sent to me by Washington. He writes just a few lines: 'The document must speak for itself. It is now a child of fortune, to be fostered by some and buffeted by others. What will be the general opinion or the reception of it is not for me to decide, nor shall I say anything for or against it: if it be good, I suppose it will work its way good; if bad, it will recoil on the Framers.'[12]

I send the proposed constitution to Jefferson. 'What do you think of the powers of the president? I am afraid that our friends are gone a little too far on the other side, - But suppose it is the case, and General Washington is the president, I know him too well not to think he will find the danger and take the authority before he goes over.'[13]

While I was in the Auvergne a *séance royale* was held on November 19, when the king introduced an edict to give civil rights to Protestants, and then an edict which proposed to borrow 420 million livres between 1788 and 1792. This time he sat on a dais, not the canopied lit de justice, and spent a day listening to the speeches without falling asleep. However, he refused to allow a vote and ordered the edicts to be registered. Complete silence followed. The duc d'Orléans, his cousin, stood up and said: "Sire, I beg you to allow me to place at your feet and in the heart of this court that I consider this registration illegal."

The king had replied indecisively: "I don't care…it's up to you…yes…it's legal because I wish it."[14]

He and the royal princes left the building where three hours later it was voted that the king's actions had been illegal. Riots followed and Orléans was exiled to his estate at Villers-Cotterets.

In late December the regulations for Franco-American trade are made law. There is no longer a French monopoly of spermaceti candles. A liberal right of entrepôt is granted, which is almost the same as making all French ports free for America, and the privileges given to French trade are now also given to Americans in all French possessions in Asia.

Chapter 36

Will the monarchy fail?

I write to Washington on New Year's Day, 1788:

> It is needless for me to tell you that I read the new proposed constitution with an unspeackable eagerness and attention. I have admired it, and find it is a bold, large, and solid frame for the Confederation….In the name of America, of mankind at large, and your own fame, I beseech you, my dear General, not to deny your acceptance of the office of President for the first years. You only can settle that political machine, and I foresee it will furnish an admirable chapter in your history.
>
> I am returned from the Provincial Assembly of Auvergne wherein I had the happiness to please the people and the misfortune to displease government to a very great degree. The Ministry asked for an encrease of revenue. Our Province was among the few who gave nothing, and she expressed herself in a manner which has been taken very amiss. The internal situation of France is very extraordinary. The dispositions of the people of which I gave you a picture are working themselves into a great degree of fermentation, but not without a mixture of levity and love of ease. The Parliaments are every day passing the boundaries of their Constitution, but are sure to be approuved by the Nation, when among many unrational things, they have the good policy to call for a General Assembly. Governement see that the power of the crown is declining, and now want to retrieve it by an ill timed and dangerous severity. They have monney enough for this year, so at least they think, for my part, I am heartily wishing for a Constitution, and a Bill of Rights, and wish it may be effected with as much tranquillity and mutual satisfaction as it is possible. [1]

On January 4, the *Parlement* of Paris rules all lettres de cachet to be illegal. Louis demands this decree to be rescinded in his presence. It is. Parlement later declares this decision to have also been illegal. In the provinces the parlements are refusing to renew any expiring taxes, or recognize new laws, and are saying that all new affairs should be decided at an *Etats généraux*.[2]

On the twentieth, *Parlement* registers the edict the king made in December, giving civil status to his non-Catholic subjects. Their marriages are to be regarded as valid and therefore their children to be legitimate. The dead can be lawfully buried in specially designated places, and they can own property by certain exemptions made in business or professions.

Jefferson and I are very pleased, although he is also critical: "It is only an acknowledgement that Protestants can beget children and that they can die and be offensive unless buried. It does not give them permission to think, to speak or to worship. The most illiterate peasant is a Solon compared with the authors of this law."[3]

On February 3, I am very pleased to present Rabaut Saint-Etienne at the ministerial table at Versailles,[4] the first Protestant clergyman to be there since the revocation of 1685.

Brissot and Clavière hold the first meeting of the *Société de Amis des Noirs* on the nineteenth. I join, as does Adrienne, Condorcet, La Rochefoucauld, the celebrated scientist, Lavoisier, Mirabeau and many others. I am also a member of the *New York Society for Promoting the Manumission of Slaves*, as well as the *British Society*, and am already a member of the *Gallo-*

American society Brissot and Clavière founded in 1787 which wishes to promote culture and trade between France and America.

I decide to play an active role in the army as the Estates-General will not meet until 1792, although I believe it will probably meet much earlier, perhaps in not much more than a year after this summer. I ask to be sent south, under the command of the duc d'Ayen. From April 1 I am given the command of a brigade of infantry in the division of Languedoc and Roussillon, but for the moment I remain in Paris.

April 11. The *Parlement* of Paris tells the king that his will alone is not enough to make law. On April 29 it refuses to endorse any more collecting of revenues. On May 3 it decrees that some laws are fundamental, that the people should only be taxed by an Estates-General and that there should be no arbitrary arrests. It also swears an oath to resist any attempt at a judicial reorganization. On the sixth, the two leaders in Paris, d'Epresmil and Goislard, are arrested; violent protests erupt in the countryside. Two days later, a lit de justice takes place. Extensive changes are proposed; small provincial courts will, in future, conduct most criminal and civil cases; the parlements will only be concerned with the nobility and cases of more than 20,000 livres; seigneurial courts will be abolished; a *cour plénière*, appointed by the government, will register edicts and will be composed of judges, dukes and courtisans and not a single representative of the nation. I am furious, as are most of my friends, that ministers dare to say that all taxes and borrowing will be registered. Condorcet, however, believes that reforms are necessary.

There is anger throughout France. 'Lamoignan and Brienne are in league with the devil to destroy liberty,' write the pamphleteers.

All courts in France are suspended. *Parlements* announce they want an Estates-General. Lettres de cachet silence many. Orators harangue the people. Hatred towards Marie Antoinette, still tainted by the affair of the necklace, boils over more virulently than ever. "Her extravagance is causing the financial problem!" "Madame Deficit!"

I am ill again. I have a fever. My blood is inflamed, perhaps because of my disappointment that it is the upper classes and the legal professions who are resisting the king and his ministers, not the general populace. The rich love their comfortable life and the poor are subdued by poverty and ignorance. The doctors bleed me to try and cool my blood; I become very weak; I spend weeks in bed and am not able to take up my command in the south.

I write to Washington:

> Governement have employed the force of arms against unarmed magistrates and expelled them....The people, my dear General, have been so dull that it has made me sick....What has the more wounded up my anger, is a Bed of Justice wherein the King has established a Court Pleniere, composed of judges, peers, and courtiers...Discontents breack out every where, and in some provinces are not despicable. The clergy- who happen to have an Assembly, are remonstrating. The lawyers refuse to plead. Governement are embarrassed and begin to apoligise. Their commandants have been in some parts pursued with dirt and stones. And the midst of these troubles and anarchy, the friends of liberty are daily reinforced, shutt up their ears against negociations, and say they must have a National Assembly or nothing. Such is, my dear General, our bettering situation and for my part, I am very easy when I think that I shall before long be in an Assembly of the Representatives of the French Nation, or at Mount Vernon...[5]

I am miserable, a very unusual state for me. I hope for passive resistance rather than armed conflict and bloodshed. I begin to have more hope of a National Assembly as the government is desperate to raise money, and if it does come about then there is hope for a constitution. I no longer talk to Brienne and Lamoignan. I am disillusioned. I hear Brienne has said I am the most dangerous of their opponents because my policy is all action.

Reports reach Paris of a very serious disturbance in Grenoble on June 7. The parlement [6] there had declared the enforcement of the May edicts illegal, as in Paris and elsewhere, and Brienne had ordered the *lieutenant-général* of the Dauphiné, the duc de Clermont-Tonnerre, to exile the Grenoble magistrates. On Saturday, June 7, they were given lettres de cachet. The town was crowded because it was a market day and the law clerks immediately started raising the alarm. They made speeches attacking Brienne and Lamoignon and distributed pamphlets.

At ten in the morning, all the shops and stalls closed; men left their work and rushed to the center of the town to try to prevent the magistrates from leaving. They closed the city gates to stop military reinforcements from entering, but two regiments, the *Austrasie* and the *Marine-La-Royale*, were already there and were quickly sent to the rioting. Many of the townspeople clambered onto house roofs, tore off the tiles, and threw them onto the soldiers below. The Austrasie held firm, but the Marine-La-Royale did not, and fired on the crowd, killing some and wounding others. The tocsin bells rang out from the cathedral and from the churches in the countryside, and more peasants rushed from the countryside to help friends and relations who had come to Grenoble for the market and who, they now feared, were being attacked.

Clermont-Tonnerre fled from his house which the crowds ransacked, stealing and drinking all his wine. A stuffed eagle was taken from one of his natural history cabinets and paraded through Grenoble as a victory symbol.

The magistrates were escorted to the Palais de Justice where a special session was held. Fireworks were let off on the place Saint André and the crowd celebrated. The royal judge, Jean-Joseph Mounier, and the Protestant lawyer, Antoine Barnave, were two of the leaders of the revolt.

The Breton parlement protests against the edicts of Lamoignan and Brienne, particularly the establishing of a *cour plénière*. They say their land is only a possession of the crown by marriage contract and therefore they should continue to have special rights and their own laws administered by their parlement. Royal officials who are sent to Rennes are roughly treated and the king exiles members of their parlement by lettres de cachet.

Three hundred Breton nobles sign a resolution against anyone serving in the new courts and a commission of twelve nobles come to Versailles to present it to the king. He refuses to read it and they visit me. I agree to attend their meeting and to help improve their petition.

July 12. Reports arrive of violent disorder in Bretagne. I meet more than sixty of their nobles in the evening; I sign the petition even although I want a constitution whereas they wish to preserve their rights.

At eight on the following Sunday morning, I am working in my study. The heat of the last few days has abated; the sky is a peaceful blue with small white clouds. My thermometer shows a pleasant eighteen point two degrees Centigrade and my barometer is falling. Suddenly the room darkens as though night is coming. The sky is now an ominous dark gray, tinged with black in the distance. An enormous storm cloud appears, swollen and huge at its base, rapidly moving towards the north-east. Lightning sears the sky, the wind freshens. Then rain falls, cascading against the house and streaming off the roof in huge sheets. Far away there is the faint sound of thunder; the wind soars in octaves of sound, a crescendo shrieking through the trees, whirling debris through the air. Towards the faubourg Saint Antoine the heavens are now as black as the River Styx; hail is hammering the house, carpeting the ground; tiles careering past the window.

Seven minutes later, the black clouds move rapidly away from Paris; thunder booms faintly from the north; it becomes light again and we appear to have only been near the storm's edge.

It is not long before we learn of the catastrophe which has happened. We were spared, but enormous hailstones killed men and animals and ravaged land just before the harvest already harmed by the drought. France's best cornfields are destroyed, a loss estimated at twenty-five million livres.

The twelve Breton deputies who presented the petition to the king are imprisoned in the Bastille. On July 15 I am stripped of my commission in the army of the duc d'Ayen in Roussillon and Languedoc but keep my rank of maréchal de camp. Civil and military posts are taken from three other nobles.

'I am honored more than I merit, for only having done my duty,' I write to César de La Tour Maubourg,[7] whilst Marie Antoinette wonders why an Auvergnat should participate in Bretagne's quarrel.

"I am Breton, in the same way that the queen belongs to the House of Austria," I reply to her displeasure.[8]

Jefferson's opinion is that my disgrace which would previously have had bad consequences for me will now mark me favorably with the nation at present and that although it makes me unpopular with ministers may save me with their successors. He believes that peace or war, they cannot fail now to have an Estates-General, but hopes that the appeal to the sword will be avoided and great modifications in the government obtained without bloodshed."[9]

At the end of July, an immense sorrow strikes us. Adrienne's sister, Clotilde de Thésan, falls ill and dies. The duc d'Ayen is away and Monsieur de Thésan is with his regiment, but Louis de Noailles, Monsieur de Grammont and I are present, and we do all in our power to soothe the grief of Madame d'Ayen and the family.[10]

The summer is long and hot. The drought continues; crops are dying. Rumors fly throughout our stifling city. People suggest the monarchy might fall. They see omens everywhere and even the stone horse of Louis XVl's statue is said to have been sweating blood.[11]

Adélaïde de Simiane is not in Paris, but I often see Madame de Tessé, the Condorcets, Morellet, Mazzei and Marmontel, either at the rue de Bourbon or at their homes. I also see Jefferson who still stops at my house most days on his five-mile walk.

'Peace or war, they cannot fail now to have the *États-généraux* in the course of the following year.[12] I hope that the appeal to the sword will be avoided, and great modifications in the government be obtained without bloodshed,' is his opinion.[13]

I receive a request from Brienne to come to see him. On August 1 I do so for an hour.

"Why have you avoided me for three months?" he asks.

We discuss the political situation; he leads me to believe that the Estates-General will be convened next year. On August 8, I discover it has been decreed that the Estates-General, last convened in 1614, during the Regency of Marie de Médicis, will meet in 1789. On August 11, the date of May 1 is set and the cour plénière suspended. I believe that this will bring calm, that the ministers will regain confidence, that everyone will unite to work with them for the public good.[14]

The government unfortunately suddenly announces it will pay part of its debts in paper money. For payments of more than twelve hundred livres, three fifths would be paid in cash and the rest in paper money; for payments of less than twelve hundred livres, people would receive a slightly higher amount of cash. People rush to withdraw money from the *caisse d'escompte*. It closes and as I have been writing and talking to friends and acquaintances to suggest they should curtail opposition to the government's policies I am nearly as ashamed as if I had done it myself.[15]

The price of bread rises. The streets seethe with agitation and the police are doubled. Textile producers lay off more than 200,000 workers across France. However, there are no riots and the crowd outside the *caisse d'escompte* becomes smaller. [16]

On the eighteenth, the king dismisses Brienne and Lamoignon. People burn their effigies and go wild with joy; bonfires illuminate the night. Ten thousand people throng the pleasure gardens, shops, cafés and arcades of the duc d'Orléans at the Palais Royal, fireworks blazing into the sky. On the twenty-sixth, the king again appoints Necker, whom I consider a clever man of finance, but not a man suitable to prepare for, or to lead, a revolution. The celebrations continue, crowds rampaging through the streets. They stop carriages on the Pont Neuf and force the occupants to descend and bow to the statue of 'good' King Henri IV. They attack guard posts and several houses of government officials.

August 29. Troops fire into the mobs, killing twenty-five, and injuring many, although people are talking of hundreds of deaths.[17] Necker reintroduces controls removed by Calonne on the price of grain, but it is too late; the price of bread still rises; disorder continues.

Washington writes:

I do not like the situation of affairs in France. The bold demands of the parlements and the decisive tone of the King show that but little irritation would be necessary to blow up the spark of discontent into flame that might not easily be quenched. If I were to advise, I would say that great moderation should be used on both sides. Let it not, my dear Marquis, be considered as a derogation from the good opinion I entertain of your prudence when I caution you as an individual desirous of signalizing yourself in the cause of your country and freedom, against running into extremes and prejudicing your cause. Although I believe Louis XVI is really a good-hearted, tho a warm-spirited man, nevertheless if thwarted injudiciously in the execution of prerogatives that belonged to the Crown and in plans which he conceives calculated to promote the national good, he might disclose qualities which he had been little thought to possess. There seems such a spirit awakened in the Kingdom as, if managed with extreme prudence, may produce a gradual and tacit revolution much in favor of the subjects, by abolishing lettres de cachet, and defining more accurately the powers of government. A monarch's own glory and felicity must depend on the prosperity and happiness of his people.[18]

However, even although I believe I often risk imprisonment for treason, I remain very optimistic for the future of my country. I tell my friends in America that not only tranquility, but victory for the liberal cause have come to France. I am very hopeful, as are my fellow-thinkers, that we will have a constitution.

I miss Adélaïde de Simiane. 'My heart counts the days that have passed and the days that remain; they grow longer at the close of separation like shadows at the end of the day,' I write to her.[19]

Peter Otsiquette who has been with me for some years, has returned home, and Joel Barlow arrives from America with Nathanael Greene's son, George Washington Greene. Jefferson, Short, Barlow and I have decided he will attend pension Lemoine, across the street from Jefferson's house on the Champs Elysées. I will pay, just as I had for John Caldwell. 'No affair in my life can be more capital, no task more pleasing than the one I owe to your confidence and that of the good and great man of whose friendship I was proud and happy,' I write to Mrs. Greene.[20]

A cough plagues me again, but to my great pleasure on September 23 it is decreed that the Estates-General will meet in January. On the twenty-fourth, the Paris Parlement reconvenes. The price of bread continues to increase; people again demonstrate violently on the streets. Parlement bans demonstrations and begins a judicial enquiry into the police authorities.

In October, the provincial parlements reconvene and all parlements are asked to register the convocation of the Estates-General whose date is now changed to January 1789, but with no word about how it will be composed or chosen. People are suspicious. Wiil it be without power?

The Paris Parlement declares that the Estates-General should follow the forms of that of 1614 which was organized in three elected chambers of Clergy, Nobility and the Third Estate. However, this presents the problem that each order had voted separately and so the Nobility and Clergy had been of a similar size and able together to outvote the Third Estate.

Necker has stopped the censorship of the press and all writers imprisoned under Brienne have been released. The pamphleteers praise the states of Dauphiné which have already met at Vizille and which, by the end of September, has decided that the Third Estate would be twice the size of the other two groups and that all deputies would be elected.   Necker also lifted the ban on political clubs which are now springing up everywhere and stridently debating the issue. My group meets at Adrien Duport's house several times a week and we oppose the forms of 1614. We wish to double the third estate and vote by head. We produce pamphlets which are distributed throughout France to attempt to persuade municipal authorities to demand this and are hopeful we will have a constitution. Mirabeau wrote in August: 'War on the privileged and privileges is my motto. Privileges are useful against kings, but are contemptible against nations, and ours will never have any public spirit until it is rid of them.' [21]

The king announces the recall of the Assembly of Notables to decide the composition of the Estates-General. On Thursday, November 6, the notables meet at Versailles; I am again in the second bureau, presided over by the comte d'Artois.

A few days later, I catch the illness people are humorously calling Brienne. By the eleventh, which is Saint Martin's Day, it is savagely cold. I cough in every meeting I manage to attend, meetings which greatly displease both me and many others whose vitriolic quills busily criticize. However, my heart remains pure, my spirit free, my character disinterested; my conscience and the public confidence are my two supports; if I lose the second then the former would suffice. [22]

We hear of riots. People are hungry; there is often no work. Snow starts to fall heavily on December 1. At Versailles we discuss the numbers for each order. Should it be equal for each group?

"There should be double the representation for the Third Estate," I argue.

My proposition only receives eight votes against sixteen; my bureau decides the same principles must be followed as for the last four convocations of the Estates-General and on the same forms as those of 1614. [23]

When the final vote takes place in my bureau for the separation of the three orders, I vote for double representation of the Third Estate. One hundred and eleven notables, however, do not want to double the Third Estate, nor to have voting by head, with twenty-three against. On December 12, Louis ends the Assembly in the *salle de gardes* at Versailles. The result is not what he wished nor what people are demanding. On the eighteenth, I and one hundred and eight notables sign a document declaring that Paris must choose its own representatives and not officials of the Hôtel de Ville and a few notables. I go to Adrien Duport's house and find Mirabeau and abbé Sieyès furious for how I voted.

Each day is an icy repetition of the previous day. The Seine freezes from the twenty-sixth. Thousands skate or slide on it, a sight never seen before. Boats are held fast in the ice. People cannot work and large numbers are pouring into Paris. Hunger afflicts many; at Pontamousson in Lorraine public granaries are broken in to and the corn stolen.

Necker and the king spend the week before Christmas in discussion; on December 27, the *Result of the King's Council of State*, is published. It declares that the number of the Third Estate will be doubled, that each order will be able to select its representatives from people who do not belong to it, that the right to grant taxation will be restored to the nation, that there will be an annual budget and that there will be a discussion of lettres de cachet and freedom of the press. However, it says nothing about the method of voting. Necker's New Year Gift to the Nation, people call it.

"I congratulate you on all the king has conceded," says the comte de Bouillé when I encounter him on New Year's Eve.

"We will take him further than that," I reply to an expression of shock on his face.

Later, at a meal of the king, the comte de Provence says, "I hope, Monsieur de Lafayette, that wholly republican as you are, that you do not approve of the murder of Charles 1."

"I do not approve the king's execution," I reply, but I do not deny my republicanism.[24]

The price of bread rises to fourteen sous a loaf. Violence pervades the city. it is not safe to walk the streets in late evening and carriages have been attacked.

Condorcet decides he need not reply to a recent defense of slavery. "It is in the Estates-General that the cause should be pleaded, and it is to you, the hero of American liberty, the wise and zealous advocate of the noble revolution on behalf of negroes, the generous man who has devoted part of his fortune and some of his brilliant youth to the search for ways to break the chains that his eyes ought never to see. It is to you that belongs the defense there of liberty and the rights of man, which are the same for all, no matter what their color or their country might be."[25]

This is the worst winter people can remember for seventy-nine years. Thousands have flocked into Paris and other cities seeking work and food; it is believed there are thirty thousand in the faubourg Saint Antoine alone. Beggars are everywhere. The Seine has frozen from here to Le Havre. Blocks of ice float in the strait between Dover and Calais, endangering ships. Great fires burn at crossroads to help warm the unfortunate wretches who are hungry and homeless. The curé of the parish of Sainte Marguerite, near the Bastille, provides eighteen enormous cooking pots, each making one hundred and twenty-five soups, four times a day, and the same is happening throughout France. The king comes to Paris and distributes money and I hear that Marie Antoinette is giving twelve thousand francs a month, although she remains hated and accused of a love affair with the comte d'Artois. I donate money, like most of the wealthy, and try to negotiate the bringing of American food to France.

On Christmas Day there is a momentary thaw. Stalactites of ice hanging from roofs and branches drip water and crash to the ground, as at Albany. Then the harrowing cold returns. On December 30, my thermometer registers minus twenty-one point eight degrees, whilst the average temperature for the month was minus six point seven degrees. The official price of bread rises again to fourteen and a half sous and market days are often riots. Mobs search for wheat and corn, raiding monasteries and convents, and even breaking into houses.

Chapter 37

Revolution

1789. Snow and ice still paralyze France. Couriers and their horses become lost and die in the snow; communications are nearly cut off and mail becomes increasingly difficult. It is impossible to work watermills or windmills, so the government has arranged for six thousand carriages to bring corn into Paris. Thousands of fields of crops are destroyed. Even in the south the canal du Midi is frozen; in Provence and Languedoc vines and olive trees are decimated, whilst added to the misery is the destruction of the last harvest from hail and drought. People cannot pay their taxes and have either had to sell their land or been evicted. More than half the farmers in Normandy are now without any land and a similar situation exists throughout the country. People are refusing to pay the taxes. They are ignoring the game laws to try and save their few remaining crops; they kill several gamekeepers. It is decided to abandon the cone harbor at Cherbourg which has failed to be constructed. It seems a long time ago that I watched its proud beginnings. It was a high point for the king and events are now taking on a blacker hue for him.

The cold lessens in the middle of January. Snow and ice start to melt, causing flooding. The Loire overflows by Orléans, ruining at least three leagues of land, washing away the great causeway to Blois and sinking many boats.

The rules for the Estates-General are declared on January 24. The recent decision of the king to double the number of the Third Estate is acclaimed by many, even although it is less than the numbers apportioned in the Dauphiné. The two hundred and thirty-four electoral constituencies will be the ancient jurisdictions of *bailliages* in the north and *sénéchaussées* in the south; if they are too small, they will be joined to others, whilst eight large towns will be awarded separate representation. Each constituency will have two nobles, two clerics, and four Third Estate deputies. Lists of grievances, *cahiers de doléances*, will be compiled to help the elected representatives.

I am writing a Declaration of Rights, as are others, and Jefferson has been helping with suggestions and corrections.[1] I hope it will be Europe's first true proclamation matching the American principles. It will not just be a concession or a petition of rights like those of England in the seventeenth century. Once the principles which are indispensable and sufficient for liberty are enunciated and their observance assured, the details of government would be but secondary variations. I think of it as the height of my career, the fruit of my past, the gage of my future life.[2] I write nine points starting with the words: 'I believe Nature has made men equal, and distinctions among them, although required by monarchy, are only acceptable if commensurate with benefit to the general welfare.'[3]

February 3. Gouverneur Morris arrives in Paris, having crossed the Atlantic despite his wooden leg, the result of a carriage accident in 1780. He failed to be elected to the first Congress of the United States and is here to represent American businesses. His French Protestant ancestors had sailed to America from La Rochelle after the restoration of the Edict of Nantes and he speaks French fluently. He comes with Jefferson to the rue de

Bourbon, to my delight bringing me a letter from Washington who writes about the new Congress and my wish for him to become president:

> Your feelings approach those of my other friends more than my own. In truth the differences seem to me to multiply and grow larger as time approaches for me to give a definitive response. In the case when circumstances demand in some way my acceptance, be assured, my dear Sir, I will accept the burden with the most sincere repugnance and a real defiance of myself, which will probably be little believed by the world.[4]

At the end of February, I travel to the Auvergne, the road treacherous with snow and ice, occasional torrents of muddy water making it even more hazardous. I arrive to the blazing hearth fires of Chavaniac and soon begin to feel better than in Paris. I prepare quietly for the hard task ahead. La Colombe has agreed to be my aide and he will also help my friend, La Tour Maubourg, who is standing in Le Puy-en-Vélay where there are many working against him, particularly the bishop and the House of Polignac. 'We will defeat them,' I write to Madame de Simiane. [5]

Slanders are being made against me; I hear they come from the prince de Condé and Marie Antoinette and that more evidence will be sent to blacken my name. It is said I plotted an armed revolt during the crises of 1787 and 1788 and that I wrote 'I am sure of Vélay and Vivarais' and 'It is better to fight than to be slaves,' in a letter which is circulating.

I believe these words to refer to a movement of public opinion, not to an armed rebellion. I have never been criminal enough to want the horrors of a civil war. It is abominable that I, who, on the eve of the convocation of the Estates-General, the person who first demanded it and who has taken no step that did not try to conciliate the *Noblesse* and the Third Estate, should be accused of the intention to rouse the kingdom to flames when we have the means before us of a chance to become free and happy in the most peaceful way possible.

I discover strong support for nobles who agree with several princes who want to maintain the monarchy and keep the ancient constitution and forms. The princes, I call them. I find division and jealousy between the different orders, areas and individuals.

"If you agree to what we want, you will be elected unanimously. If you do not agree you will not be elected," say some nobles.

"I wish to convince, not flatter," I reply.

I preach moderation at the risk of displeasing. It is possible that instead of being nominated I will only bring upon myself many quarrels and esteem, but I will do my duty and will be moderate, although their oppression revolts me and their personalities anger me.[6]

I arrive at Riom on March 11 with my brother-in-law, the marquis Joachim de Montagu de Beaune, and will stay at the home of Guillaume-Michel de Chabrol until my departure for Saint Flour on the twenty-first. On the fourteenth, we go to Mass at the church of the Sainte-Chapelle; we swear the oath 'to proceed in honor and conscience to the writing of the cahiers and to the nomination of the deputies of the Estates-General.' At nine o'clock we all gather in the grande salle of the Palais, then each order goes to its own room. On the fifteenth, I am one of four people nominated to speak with the Third Estate and am also chosen as one of three to write our cahier de doléance. From March 17 to 22, we draw up the cahiers. I persuade them to use passages from my Declaration of Rights and so we begin: 'Nature has made Men equal.' We suggest there can be different ranks in a monarchy, but they must be based on the general welfare. We ask the Estates-General to draft a constitution for a government of three branches. We want legal reform, reform of lettres de cachet, trial by jury and to have equality before the law. We also want nobles to relinquish their tax privileges and for taxes to be proportionate to the ability to pay.

"We must have exemption from taxes for the land known here as the capon's flight, which entails the noble's house, court and garden," argue some nobles.

"The capon's wings need to be clipped close in order to cut its flight short," is my reply.[7]

The nobles agree to the principle of a proportional distribution of tax and an equal tax imposition on the three orders, with the reservation that it should be fixed by the Estates-General; their pecuniary sacrifice, I call it. The Third Estate is delighted by this; the clergy also agrees to the great displeasure of the bishop. I want the adoption of voting by head and not by order, but I am almost alone in this and fail to achieve it. Mirabeau and others at Adrien Duport's house often think I am not radical enough but here people believe I am a dangerous revolutionary. The conservatives propose that if the Estates-General decide to vote by head, the deputies of our nobility wish it to be written in the cahier that their constituents believe that vote by deliberation and vote by order is a constitutional right.

March 23. Langeac, who presides over the nobles and who sold the seigneurie to me, is chosen as deputy on the first ballot, with 382 votes out of 397. Next day, the cahiers are read and approved. Instructions are written for the deputies of the nobility. On the twenty-fifth, I am elected but with only 198 votes out of 393. On the twenty-sixth to the twenty-eighth, the marquis de Laqueuille, the marquis Bégon de la Rouzière and the comte de Mascon are elected.

I sign the instructions given by the *sénéchaussée* of the Auvergne and accept the mandate. I prefer to sacrifice myself and cannot be suspected of self-interest as everyone knows that the Third Estate daily offers me the choice to be nominated by them. I feel it has been difficult to do what I and my friends have attempted and that what we have achieved is very little. Our cahier is a mixture of great principles and trivial details, of popular ideas and feudal ideas. We say that nature has made men equal, yet we forbid workmen to carry arms. We want to tax industry, yet we demand that all tax laws should be abolished which hinder it; we lay down instructions, but we tell our deputies to act according to their consciences. There are two hundred years between one and the other.[8] At the same time, we have been instructed to wait to join the Third Estate until a majority of nobles wish to do so.

March 30. I return to Chavaniac, elected, but not content.[9] On April 1, I write to La Colombe and authorize him, if necessary, to buy a fief of one of La Tour Maubourg's opponents in order to give him an extra vote.[10] On April 4, I am in Brioude; on the fifth, in Clermont; on the sixth, Riom again. At Clermont I receive the news that he was elected at Le Puy on the third. I immediately write to him: 'Join me quickly in Paris where we shall have much to do and say, for men are pretty cowardly and pretty malicious.'[11]

I travel north, the road winding through ruined fields of withered, broken crops and dead chestnut trees, stark reminders of the winter cold. Men, women and children in tattered rags beg pitifully. Occasionally there is violence. Groups carrying pitchforks, knives and axes wander the highway, searching for hoards of wheat and corn, a dispossessed people abandoning their homeland. During the last few weeks there have been grave riots against the clergy and landowners in Provence. The bishop of Sisteron narrowly escaped stoning. The palace of the bishop of Toulon was burnt. Châteaux throughout the region have been attacked. The Hôtel de Ville in Marseilles was ransacked and Mirabeau took command from de Caraman, the local military governor. He stopped a grain ship from sailing and formed a citizens' militia; at Aix, troops fired into the crowd. Mirabeau was elected for the Third Estate at both Aix and Marseilles and has chosen to represent Aix.

April 13. I reach Paris. Desperate men, women and children swarm through the streets, searching for food and begging for help. I learn that the government has moved weapons from the Arsenal to the Bastille and artillery magazines are being well guarded. In the evening, news arrives that the government has announced how Paris will elect its deputies. There will be sixty electoral districts; the electors will be chosen in one day and the qualifications for voters are more restrictive than in the rest of France. A quarter of all men over twenty-five will be discounted, so thousands who had hoped to vote will be deprived. The city is divided into twenty districts for the nobles and sixty for the Third Estate; each district will choose electors who will draw up cahiers and select deputies. I am in the eighteenth district of the nobility.

April 17. In the morning, I tell Morris about my electoral campaign in the Auvergne. We discuss the likelihood of a revolution in Paris. "It can bring about much harm without producing the least good," we agree. "It would therefore be better to direct protest against the way that the elections are being made, whilst continuing to proceed with them."

"The duc de Coigny, said to be a lover of the queen, received the order from his constituents to propose that in the event of an accident she should not be regent. I spoke against this proposal," I tell him.

"The king and the queen detest you equally, but you continue to argue against this proposal," he says.

"I want a republic," I reply.

He, however, thinks differently, basing his opinion on human nature.[12]

April 20. I attend the first meeting of the eighteenth district at the convent of the Théatins. I am nominated as one of four representatives to go to the marquis de Boulainvilliers to protest about the rules.[13] The districts flout the rules and begin to choose their deputies, as well as write a cahier, often using the Society of Thirty's model, which is based on my Declaration of the Rights of Man and Citizen.

Ten thousand troops have now been assembled near to Paris, the French and Swiss Guards are already within the city, augmenting the *maréchaussée* of six thousand men. In the provinces the famine is causing unrest.

On the twenty-second I go to see Jefferson and Morris at four o'clock.

"I think that the Estates-General should distance the Swiss Guard from the king but give their felicitations to the national troops," says Morris.

"It is not important," says Jefferson, but I am convinced by Morris's words.

"Do you think I should take an active part in the debates of the Estates-General?"

"You must only speak on important occasions," they both say. Then we all go to the Palais-Royal to have our profiles drawn.[14]

On the twenty-seventh, Réveillon, a paper manufacturer, and Henriot, a salt petre producer, are falsely accused of wanting to reduce wages. Five or six thousand workers attack Réveillon's house and factory, and he and his family escape over the garden wall. French Guards are sent to halt the rioting. They fire and the mob stones them. A battle ensues, ending at four in the morning, when many have been wounded and twenty-five killed, although claimed to be hundreds.[15] It is reported that there were shouts of 'Long Live the Third Estate!" "Liberty!" and "We will not give way!"[16] There is fury that the government used soldiers to attack the people; it is also evident the government is struggling to control the increasing unrest.

The king changes the opening of the Estates-General from April 27 to May. Unfortunately, eight hundred deputies are arriving at Versailles from all parts of France, not knowing the date has been altered. On the twenty-seventh, they are surprised to learn the king has gone hunting. At the last moment they are told of the new date and are angry at how they have been treated. At the end of April I go to live at the hôtel de Noailles in Versailles; Adrienne will come here on May 2. I hear that even now the comte d'Artois hopes that the Estates-General will not convene. In Paris, two of the rioters at Réveillon's house are executed. On the thirtieth, the deputies of the

Third Estate meet and decide their policies. They want voting by head, fair taxes for everyone and the abolition of privileges.

May 2. The three orders are presented to the king. First, he sees the clergy; early in the afternoon, it is the turn of the nobles, dressed in black silk coats trimmed with gold, waistcoats of silver or gold, white lace cravats and white-plumed, black hats turned up at the front in the style of Henri IV. Last comes the Third Estate who are only announced as a group.

"The king looked at us with as much interest as he would a herd of sheep," a deputy from Clermont complains to me.

On April 30, there was severe disorder at Marseille. A mob took over three forts and killed the chevalier de Beausset, one of the commanders.

May 4. Monday. We attend a service at Notre Dame, the words of the *Veni Creator* soaring into the ceiling. We emerge into the bright afternoon sun, I and my fellow-nobles walking two by two, each holding a long wax taper, the tall white plumes of our hats waving solemnly as we proceed along the streets of Versailles where Gobelin tapestries hang from balconies and windows.

We are part of a spectacle of immense pomp and color. The Swiss Guards are in scarlet and gold. Next are the Royal Falconers, hooded birds of prey on their wrists. In front of us is the third estate in drab black hats, black stockings, short black coats and white muslin neckcloths; behind is the clergy, the bishops and archbishops brightly arrayed in purple or red capes, and square hats, although three quarters are curés dressed in black. The royal carriages follow; the king preceding his two brothers and the younger prince, as the dauphin is gravely ill; then Marie Antoinette, the two princesses, and a gaggle of courtiers and ministers at the rear. We walk very slowly in file to the church of Saint Louis, an immense crowd gazing at us, held back by French and Swiss Guards.

"*Vive le tiers état!*" people shout. "*Vive le roi!*" Trumpets ring out; bands play music. There is silence as the queen passes. A malevolent silence.

We assemble in the church; the Third Estate are at the back and several protest. The archbishop of Paris celebrates a Mass of the Holy Spirit, then Monseigneur de la Fare, the bishop of Nancy, preaches a sermon. He describes the history of the Estates-General. He appeals for reform in the name of Christian ethics; applause erupts from many deputies despite the lack of respect to the church and to the king, who appears to be asleep. I am proud for France. We are standing on the threshold of a momentous time in history.

May 5. We assemble at seven in the morning, in a hall designed by Pierre-Adrien Paris, creator of stage settings for royal performances, at the hôtel des menus plaisirs, on the avenue de Paris, about half a mile from the Château of Versailles. Our body of two hundred and seventy nobles, two hundred and ninety-one clergy and five hundred and seventy-eight deputies of the Third Estate, all wear the same dress as before. The Third Estate enter the hall through a side door, unlike the other two orders, and there are mutterings of discontent. One of them has refused to wear the prescribed black clothes and wears brown. He looks like a French Dr. Franklin and people cheer him at some length. Applause also greets the bishop of Nancy and the duc d'Orléans, the only prince of the blood to be a deputy.

Each deputy is called by name, which takes four hours. A few minutes before the king is expected to arrive, Mirabeau enters alone.[17] He walks to a seat near the middle of the rows of backless benches, placed one behind each other, his large, bear-like body, dressed in the black of the Third Estate, his pock-marked face crowned by a mass of unruly hair powdered and tied in a black silk bag. A subdued, but widespread whistling greets him;[18] the deputies seated in front of him, move one bench forward; those behind shuffle further away. He sits by himself, smiling with contempt, then people move back to fill the empty seats as there is not enough room.[19]

Very strangely, when we had discussed at Duport's house whether the nobles of the popular party should represent the Third Estate, I had argued that we should. Mirabeau had successfully argued that we should not. However, when he tried to stand for the provençal nobility he had been rejected and now represents the Third Estate, whilst I, who had supported the opposite view, have been elected for the Auvergne nobility.

At noon a fanfare of drums, fifes and trumpets sounds; the king and the royal entourage enter. Dressed in the robe with the order of Saint Louis, Louis waddles, in his usual ungainly fashion, to the gold throne on a dais hung by velvet drapes, then sits down abruptly. Monsieur and the comte d'Artois seat themselves below him on his right, as do the other princes of the blood, also dressed in the order of Saint Louis, but their clothes not so embroidered or diamond encrusted as his.[20] The ministers sit under the dais; Madame Élisabeth and Mesdames Victoire and Adélaïde sit on the king's left, behind the queen, who is also below him, and who sits with great dignity, fanning herself with a large fan, as though she is very agitated, her eyes often glancing to the rows of the Third Estate, as though she is looking for a face she knows.[21]

I am seated with the nobles to the left of Louis; the clergy is on his right; the Third Estate at the back. The ladies of the court, resplendent with jewels, sit in two balconies; two thousand members of the public sit in graduated tiers of seats between two columns behind the clergy and nobility.

The king reads a short speech in a clear voice. He talks of the public debt, large when he came to the throne, and which has subsequently much increased. He talks of the American war as being an honorable cause and hopes all three orders will unite with his ideas concerning the general good of the nation: "I have already ordered considerable reductions and I would like your ideas on this. I will place the exact financial situation for you to see and I am sure that you will advance ways of ameliorating it. I deplore the radical ideas which are misleading the public. I wish the happiness and prosperity of my realm."

"*Vive le roi!*" and the clapping of hands constantly interrupt him. The queen is crying, or seems to be crying, but no one acclaims her.[22] Then he sits down on his throne, takes off his hat, as protocol demands, before replacing it. We in the nobility do the same. The Third Estate now also wrongly put on their hats as they do not enjoy our privilege. There is confusion among their ranks. Some take them off and put them on again, whilst others take them off. The queen speaks to the king, as though she wants him to take off his hat.[23] Some of the nobles take off theirs. It is a fiasco.

Barentin, the *garde des sceaux,* speaks next for about twenty-three minutes; he appears tense and unhappy, his voice so soft it is difficult to hear, and muttering comes from the back of the hall.

"His Majesty will consider certain reforms such as freedom of the press, changes in the criminal code, a redistribution of taxes, once the fiscal problems have been dealt with. I urge you to avoid all dangerous changes," is what I think he says. I know he does not want the convocation of the Estates-General, voting by head, or the doubling of the Third Estate, and the words coming out of his mouth do not reflect his true opinions.

Necker speaks next. "There is no danger of bankruptcy. The deficit is only fifty-six million livres. It is necessary to authorize a loan of eighty million livres." He gives financial details, enthusiastic applause every so often interrupting him. After half an hour his voice fails. He gives his speech to his secretary clerk who continues to read it for another two and a half hours.

Disappointment rises in me; there is no mention of voting by head, or by order. He appears to want the three estates to meet separately but is postponing that decision.

"It will be a chance for the clergy and the nobles to renounce their tax advantages of their own accord," reads the secretary.

Necker suggests the Estates-General has been called because the king wants to fulfill his promise and to follow the wishes of his people, He seems to be saying that if we do not do what he wants, the king will end our assembly and take his advice on how to remedy the deficit. He talks about the establishment of an East India Company and of a National Bank to consolidate the national debt. He says that the king pledges to assemble the Estates-General at intervals. At four o'clock, the secretary finishes reading. Louis stands.

"*Vive le roi*!" people cry at some length.

Marie Antoinette stands. "*Vive la reine!*" people shout for the first time in several months. She curtsies gracefully; the cries redouble. She curtsies again, even more gracefully.[24] Then she and Louis walk from the hall.

My disappointment is great. I had been hoping for more. What of a new constitution? Are we only to have a few fiscal reforms and a few improvements in the law code? All three orders should meet as one. As abbé Sieyès says: 'There cannot be one will as long as we permit three orders. At best, the three orders might agree, but they will never constitute one nation, one representation, and one common will.'[25]

May 6. The three estates meet in separate rooms to verify everyone's credentials. My order behaves badly; they all talk at once; they boo; they hiss. It is bedlam. The session is adjourned. On the seventh I propose that credentials should be verified by a commission of all three estates. People oppose me; my motion is lost by forty-six votes against one hundred and eighty-eight. The clergy also vote for separate verification by one hundred and thirty-three votes to one hundred and fourteen. Mirabeau publishes a journal about what is happening and his comments. It is banned; he then publishes the same journal and calls it: *Letters from Monsieur de Mirabeau to his constituents.* By May 11 my order declares it is properly constituted, but the clergy has still has not done so. Our two orders receive an invitation from the Third Estate to join them in verifying credentials, because if there is separate voting we would be agreeing to vote in the different orders. I do not conceal my principles but my four colleagues from the sénéchausseé of Riom constantly remind me of my pledge to conform to the instructions of our cahier. Even so, I consistently maintain there should be voting by head.[26]

Jefferson had written to me on May 6:

As it becomes more and more possible that the Noblesse will go wrong, I become uneasy for you. Your principles are decidedly with the *tiers état*, and your instructions against them. A complaisance to the latter on some occasions, and an adherence to the former on others, may give an appearance of trimming between the two parties. You will, in the end, go over wholly to the tiers état, because it will be impossible for you to live in a constant sacrifice of your own sentiments to the prejudice of the Noblesse. But you would be received by the *tiers état* at any future day, coldly, and without confidence. This appears to me the moment to take at once that honest and manly stand with them, which your own principles dictate. This will win their hearts forever, be approved by the world, which marks and honours the man of the people, and will be an eternal consolation to yourself. The Noblesse, and especially the Noblesse of Auvergne, will always prefer men who do their dirty work for them. You are not made for that. They will, therefore, soon drop you, and the people in that case will perhaps not take you up...If violence should be attempted where will you be? You cannot then take side with the people in opposition to your own vote, that very vote which will have helped to produce the scission. Still less can you array yourself against the people. Your instructions are indeed a difficulty which a single effort surmounts...Forgive me, my dear friend, if my anxiety for you makes me talk of things I know nothing about. [27]

Reinforcements of troops arrive daily to people's fear. Rioting continues in nearby towns. Grain is becoming even more scarce; the government stored large amounts at the beginning of last winter, but it will not be sufficient. Regiments with cannon have been ordered to Provence.

The king orders some game animals in the plain of Saint Denis to be culled because they eat the grain crop. Fifty gamekeepers there have now killed many hares and partridges and there will also be a wall constructed round Monsieur's forest in Brunoy to stop the animals from marauding onto nearby land.

On May 28, my order votes by 197 to 44 that deliberation by order and the right of veto which belongs to each order separately is a principle of the throne and of liberty which constitute the monarchy. On June 3, the deputies from Paris finally take their seats, one of whom is Jean-Sylvain Bailly and another the abbé Sieyès.

"I approve the name *communes* which the Third Estate has adopted," I say to the anger of many of my fellow nobles.

At one in the morning on June 4, at Meudon, the seven-year-old dauphin, much-loved by both his parents, dies from consumption, his body said to be so emaciated his ribs and pelvis protruded oddly. His mother was with him, and his father had visited the previous day. Four-year-old Louis Charles is now dauphin and has been given the order of Saint Louis. Louis goes to his hunting lodge at Marly to mourn.

June 6. Jean-Sylvain Bailly had asked for a deputation from the Third Estate to see the queen to offer condolences on the death of the dauphin. Her grief was too great to enable her to accept their visit but the king, although in the first painful days of mourning, said that he would receive them between eleven and midday. Bailly and twenty deputies go to Marly where the king receives them in his room.

"All the orders of the kingdom have an equal right to my goodwill, and you can count on my protection and my kindness. I ask you, above all, to support promptly, with a spirit of wisdom and peace, the accomplishment of the good that I am impatient to make to my people, and for which they wait with confidence of my sentiments for them." [28]

There will be a simple funeral, like that of princesse Sophie, two years ago, but even so it is reputed it will cost 600,000 livres.

There is much talk of liberty, frightening many clergy and nobles, but the king says nothing. Broadsheets are being continually produced. Today thirteen are made; there were sixteen yesterday and ninety-two last week. Desein's shop is said to be so crowded it is difficult to reach the counter. Provincial presses are also busily working; nearly all want liberty and express violence towards the clergy and nobility. There are hardly any written for the other side, the remarks are often seditious, but the courts do not act. There is a rising sense of hope and expectation.

People debate excitedly in coffee houses and shops at the Palais-Royal; orators stand on chairs or tables as well as go out into the streets; it is said that talk of violence against the government is cheered. The shortage of bread continues. We hear of riots in the provinces and the army struggling to maintain order at markets.

The clergy propose to set up a commission from the three orders to investigate how to lower the price of bread which means that each of the three estates would meet separately. The Third Estate pray. They ask the clergy to join them in the general assembly hall in the name of the God of peace and the national interest, and act in concert to bring about union and concord.[29] When the news of this reaches Paris, even more hatred erupts against the clergy.

On June 10, Sieyès proposes a formal motion in the Third Estate that the deputies from the two other estates should be invited to join them for the common verification of powers and to form themselves into an active assembly capable of starting and fulfilling the object of their mission. They will proceed to the verification, whether the deputies from the privileged classes are there or not. It passes by 493 votes to 41. On the twelfth, my order, and that of the clergy, receive the invitation. We decide to deliberate on it. On the thirteenth, three curés from Poitou join them. On the fourteenth, six curés join. On the fifteenth three more join. On the seventeenth, they pass the resolution of abbé Sieyès to form a National Assembly by 491 votes to 90: 'The Assembly, deliberating after the verification of powers, recognizes that this Assembly is already composed of representatives sent directly by at least ninety-six per cent of the nation.'[30] They say they hope the Assembly will never lose the hope of reuniting in its breast all the deputies absent today. They vote to send a respectful address to the king. On the eighteenth, my order and that of the clergy are in great alarm. Target and Le Chapelier propose that all taxes should be declared illegal but provisionally sanctioned until there is a new system. It is carried unanimously.[31]

The Assembly declares that as soon as it will have fixed the principles of national regeneration, in concert with His Majesty, it will consider the consolidation of the public debt, putting immediately the creditors of the state under the watch of loyalty and honor of the French nation.

The king says nothing for several days. Then it is announced there will be a *séance royale* of all three estates on June 23. On Saturday, June 20, the Third Estate arrived as usual to go into its hall at the hôtel des menus plaisirs. They found it locked, soldiers with drawn bayonets barring their way and placards announcing the *séance royale* on June 23. Bailly had just received a letter from the marquis de Dreux-Brézé saying there will be a meeting on June 23, but not where they should meet in the meantime. Everyone was becoming drenched in heavy rain pouring down and were angry that it looked as though they were being prevented from meeting until the twenty-third. Doctor Guillotin suggested going to the Royal Tennis Court in the rue du Vieux Versailles. The six hundred deputies marched there, accompanied by many others, whose numbers increased as they walked.

They entered the bare, narrow hall, whilst people crammed into the galleries and peered through the windows. A table was borrowed from a tailor next door and used for the desk of Bailly, the president. Sieyès declared they should all go to Paris and finish the charade. Mounier did not agree. He said that, wounded in their rights and their dignities, the members of the Assembly had been warned of attempts to push the king to a disastrous course of action and that instead of a threat of dissolution, they should swear an oath to God and France, never to be separated until they had formed a solid and equitable constitution as their constituents had asked.

Barnave started to write. Then Bailly stood on the table. He placed one hand on his heart; he raised the other and read out what Barnave had written: "As the National Assembly has been called to prepare a constitution, restore public order and uphold the principles of monarchy, nothing will impede the continuation of its deliberations. Regardless of the site it is forced to use and wherever its members assemble, it remains the National Assembly."

Six hundred deputies raised their right arms and swore the new oath, except Martin d'Auch de Castelnaudary, who remained sitting, his arms folded. It was evident to everyone that the king, nobles and clergy had been removed from their position in the legislature of France and Barnave ordered expresses to Nantes in case the Assembly had to take refuge there.

The king is still at Marly; no word comes from him. However, in Paris, crowds pour onto the streets; the Palais Royal erupts. What will happen now? Will the king use his troops? Will the public support the Assembly? In the evening, a committee of council, including Artois and Necker, takes place until midnight.

I have not been present at these momentous events. Should I resign as deputy for the noblesse and go to Riom to ask to stand for the Third Estate? I believe a deputy would give me his seat. The question torments me. I cannot bear to be the man of the sénéchaussée of Auvergne after having contributed to the liberty of another world.[32]

Next day the Assembly votes themselves as the authority in France and now resemble the Long Parliament of Charles 1 of England. The king, nobles and clergy are powerless to legislate any more, unless they act with force. On the twenty-second, the Assembly meets in the church of Saint Louis at Versailles as the comte d'Artois had rented the tennis court. Enormous crowds gather outside; Bailly reads out the king's letter postponing the gathering until tomorrow.

I am writing my Declaration of the Rights of Man and Citizens at home when Jefferson arrives, having looked briefly into the church with Philip Mazzei.

"The first time good use has been made of a church," is his opinion.[33]

On Tuesday, the twenty-third, from about ten o'clock in the morning, French Guards and some Swiss Guards, line the streets of Versailles as well as surrounding the hall at the hôtel des menus plaisirs and posting soldiers in all its passages and at the doors. Only the deputies can enter and the Third Estate is again forced to use a side entrance after the two other estates were seated.

The king arrived, to the cheers of the crowd, accompanied by the princes of the blood, except Orléans, who is a deputy. When he entered the hall, the clergy and some of the nobility cried "Vive le roi" but most people remained silent.[34] He spoke briefly, declaring he was the father of all his subjects. Then a speech was read for him, which suggested thirty-five reforms, hardly any of which were acceptable to his audience. He did not say when the estates should meet, or that feudal rights should be abolished, and did not mention the change in representation of the provincial assemblies. Lettres de cachet would be abolished except for cases of sedition or family delinquency. He then spoke again and said that if the Assembly abandoned him, he would have to proceed alone for the good of his people. He ordered it to leave and go tomorrow morning to the chambers assigned to each order. There was silence. A few clergy and nobles again called out "Vive le roi" but everyone else stayed silent. He left, followed by several clergy and two nobles. The marquis de Dreux-Brézé waited to see if people obeyed the royal command and carpenters came in and started dismantling the dais and platforms. No one moved. "Messieurs, you know the intentions of the king," he said.

There was silence again. Then Mirabeau stood up. "We have heard the intentions of the king and you who do not know how to speak for him in the Estates-General, you who have here neither place, nor voice, nor right to speak, it is not for you to speak his words. However, to avoid all equivocation and delay, I declare to you that if you have been charged to make us leave here, you must ask for orders to use force, as we will only leave by the force of the bayonet!"[35]

Bailly also stood up. "The Assembly cannot adjourn without having met," he told him. "I believe that the Nation when assembled cannot take orders," he declared to his colleagues.[36] Everyone cheered, and they continued to debate. They confirmed all the previous resolutions and passed more, Mirabeau proposing: 'Our persons individually and collectively are sacred and that all who make any attempts against them should be deemed infamous traitors to their country.'[37]

Necker had not come to the meeting and a crowd gathering in the center of Versailles noticed deputies going to see him. About five thousand joined them, shouting, "Vive Necker!" and rushed into the courtyard of the château. Marie Antoinette, in fear, went to see Necker and asked him not to resign. The king also later went to see him, and Necker agreed to stay if he agreed to his original plan to unite the three orders. Necker then went to talk to the deputies and spoke to the crowd.

Nobles go to see the king and are told by the duc of Luxembourg that they are obliged to His Majesty for his declared intention of supporting our rights and the true principles of the constitution.

In the evening, I attend a dinner at the house of Madame de Tessé where I am seated next to Gouverneur Morris.

"You are doing wrong to our cause," I tell him. "Your opinions are continually said as arguments against the true party."

"I am opposed to democracy because I love liberty. I see the nobles running blindly to their ruin and would like to stop them if that is still possible; that their projects concerning the French people are absolutely incompatible with the elements of which they are composed and the worst thing for them would be the realization of their hopes and plans."

"I know that my party has lost all reason and I reproach them for it, but I am none the less determined to follow them to my death. I think that it would be good for them to regain common sense and to live with them. I have decided to resign," I reply.

"I approve of that. The instructions binding you are contrary to your conscience. If the *tiers état* now shows proof of moderation, it will succeed but its downfall is certain if it has recourse to violence," he says.[38]

June 24. Most of the clergy join the National Assembly. In Paris, crowds excitedly throng the streets; it is said ten thousand people are in the Palais-Royal where the king's proposals were read out to them this morning. They cheer the orators and howl down the king's words, particularly that he had said nothing on periodical meetings of the estates, that he had declared all the old feudal rights to be retained as property, as well as the change in the balance of power in the provincial assemblies.[39]

Necker has offered to resign, but people are skeptical; Sieyès, Mounier, Chapellier, Barnave, Target, Tourette and Rabaud beg him to insist on the king accepting his resignation. In the afternoon, Necker walks on foot, although he had not done so in quieter times, across the courtyard to the apartment of the king, in order to court the flattery of an immense crowd shouting out "Father of the People!"

A deputation of nobles goes to the queen, who receives them holding the hand of the dauphin.

"I claim from your honor the protection of my son's rights," she tells them, clearly implying that if the king's position is not supported, the monarchy would be lost. [40]

People gather on the streets of Versailles. The king drives to Marly in his carriage and they watch silently. They shout insults at clergy or nobles who want to keep the separation of the three estates. They hit the bishop of Beauvais on the head with a stone; they hiss and shout abuse at the cardinal de La Rochefoucauld, as well as at the archbishop of Paris when he comes to Versailles, and again when he returns, even although he has an escort of soldiers. They break the windows of his residence and he decides to no longer live there. In the Palais-Royal there are rumors that many of the deputies will be killed, and some houses are even marked with a 'P' for proscribed. Other rumors say the French Guards will not fire on the people and have sworn an oath not to support the king. Is this an end to absolute rule in France?

Next day forty-seven nobles go over to the National Assembly as they believe that the king and his family are in danger and that they must therefore give way. I still cannot accompany them as I am constrained by my instructions, but I decide I will not resign. I wish to be here because several dangers threaten the Assembly which I want to share and because the Assembly will be considering a Declaration of Rights where I hope I can be useful.[41]

June 27. My fellow nobles and I meet again.

"The king has written to us," says our president, the duc de Montmorency-Luxembourg. "He asks us to go to the Third Estate and that deputies whose cahiers do not allow them to vote by head can abstain from voting until they receive new instructions.[42] The comte d'Artois has also written, entreating us to comply with the king's wishes and saying that we are placing him in grave danger if we continue to refuse to join the Third Estate."

Most of the deputies immediately jump up from their seats. "We are ready to give every proof of our zealous affection for His Majesty and tender regard for the safety of his person," cries one.

My group from Riom, as well as others, sign a statement that we have followed the wishes of our constituents but that now we are going to the chamber of the Third Estate because that has been the decision of everyone.[43]

At five o'clock in the afternoon, I walk with forty-six nobles and the duc d'Orléans in silence into the salle des menus plaisirs, accompanied by a parallel column of clergy who had also not yet joined their brethren there.

"We have decided to come here in order to give to the king the token of our respect and to the nation the proof of our patriotism," announces the duc de Montmorency-Luxembourg.

"This day will be celebrated in our history. It makes the family complete. It ends forever the divisions which have mutually afflicted us...The National Assembly will now occupy itself, without distraction, or relaxation, with the regeneration of the realm and the public welfare," replies Jean-Sylvain Bailly, the president.[44]

I do not speak. I cannot until I am released from the orders of my constituents.

Outside, the crowds are celebrating. They gather below the royal windows at the château. "*Vivent le roi et la reine!*"

The king and queen come out onto the balcony of Louis XIV's former bedroom overlooking the cour de marbre, the crowd acclaiming them with joy. Then the queen brings out her two children and people go wild with delight. In the evening, windows in Versailles are bright with lamps and candles; bonfires and torches flaming into the dark sky. People rush to Necker's house.

June 30. A 4000-strong mob frees soldiers who had gone to the Assembly to denounce their commander, the duc du Châtelet, and who had been arrested and sent with about twelve others to the Abbaye prison. They are paraded in triumph to the Palais-Royal, the Liberty Pole as Morris calls it.

July 1. I am finally accredited as a member of the National Assembly. Crowds everywhere are still celebrating and there is sporadic violence. An abbé is heard to criticize Necker and the mob in the Palais-Royal nearly tears him to pieces.

The fourth is the anniversary of the Declaration of Independence; Adrienne and I dine at Jefferson's house, the hôtel de Langeac, with many Americans.

"To the man who sustained so conspicuous a role in the immortal transaction of that day," declares Joel Barlow, honoring me greatly.

Later I talk with Morris about the momentous events taking place at Versailles.

"The triumph of the Third Estate is now considered complete. I am sure all danger of civil commotion is at an end," I say.

"I advise you to keep a certain constitutional authority in the nobility, because it is the only way to assure the liberty of the people. The feeling against the nobility is so violent that I fear its ruin. I fear the most disastrous consequences, even although people are not thinking of it at the moment," he declares.[45]

More and more troops are massing around Paris and Versailles, commanded by the maréchal de Broglie. We hear that regiments are marching towards Paris, that batteries are being thrown up on the hills above Sève and St. Cloud, and that the hills of Montmartre are being made ready for another battery. The government tries to reduce the huge numbers on the streets by employing men on the roads near Paris. Dragoons and hussars patrol even more frequently than during the riots in the faubourg Saint Antoine. The recently arrived Swiss regiment of Diesbach has been sent to St. Cloud to protect the château. Royal Dragoons are at the Champ de Mars with artillery; regiments are at Saint Denis, Besançon and La Fère. The regiments of Provence and Vintimille are stationed in Neuilly, the Royal Cravat regiment and the Royal Polish Regiment are at Sèvres and Meudon. People are hungry and demand bread. A four-pound loaf has increased from eight to fourteen sous, the highest price for twenty years. People are saying that the princes are hoarding grains deliberately to more effectively trip up Necker whom they are so keen to overthrow.[46]

Jefferson's house has been broken into three times and he has asked Montmorin to station a *garde de corps* at the customs house at the nearby grille de Chaillot. He is now not so sure there will be no unrest.

On July 8, Mirabeau addresses the National Assembly: "A great number of troops have already been surrounding us and more are arriving every day. Trains of artillery follow them. Roads, bridges and walks are being changed into military posts; preparations for war are obvious to everyone and fill our hearts with indignation. It was not enough that the sanctuary of liberty should have been soiled by troops, that the Assembly should have been submitted to armed force, it was necessary to deploy all the apparatus of despotism and show to the assembled nation more threatening soldiers than it would have been necessary to have shown the enemy. And why this apparatus? For order, to contain the people? The people have been brought to order, have been contained by an act of clemency and goodness…reason alone suffices to bring them to their duty. The people have never been more calm, more patient than at this moment when their representatives valuing their rights and their complaints, are going to improve their lives…these precautions, instead of calming people, will alarm and agitate them; that the soldiers might become caught up by contact with the capital; that they will become interested in our political discussions; and that anxious citizens, insubordinate soldiers, they will become involved in impetuous actions; sedition will march with head raised high: what will become of the authors of these measures, when a general fire will be lit, when intoxicated people will be precipitated into extreme excesses. Do they know with what horror this good king will look on those who will have lit the flames of sedition, who will have enabled the shedding of the blood of his people, and who will be the premier cause of the violence, the hardships, the tortures of which a crowd of unfortunates will be the victims.[47] Everyone applauds.

"Would you speak in favor of the motion. Your words would carry greater weight than those who have spoken before," people ask me.

I no longer keep silent. I go to the tribune. "I would like to speak before this demand is sent to the bureaux for discussion. There are only two reasons to send a proposition to the bureaux; either that there are still issues to be deliberated or there is still an issue to decide. However, gentlemen, the presence of troops around our Assembly is obvious to all of us. And as to the determination to act in such a case, I will not slight the Assembly by suggesting that any of us would hesitate. I am not therefore, just content to support the motion of Mirabeau, I ask, instead of it being sent to the bureau, that it should immediately be put to a vote."[48]

We vote. The motion passes. Mirabeau writes the admirable address which will be taken to the king tomorrow.[49]

'The ministers wish us never to show our noses,' I tell Jefferson. 'They want to delay action until they resolve their own differences, but it is impossible to go on so.'[50]

July 9. The king told the president yesterday that the troops which have been brought up to Versailles and Paris would never make any attempt against the liberty of the Estates-General, that their presence is just to keep order, and they will only stay long enough to guarantee publlc safety. He said that he will receive the deputation from the Assembly and will again make a response.

Mirabeau's address concerning the need to send away the troops is read and agreed on by the committee overseeing it. The Assembly decides to examine the principles of a constitution; we will debate it three days in the bureaux, followed by three days debating together. We will discuss the rights of man, the principle of the monarchy, the rights of the nation, the rights of the king, the rights of citizens, the organization of the National Assembly, the principles of judicial power, the organization of municipal and provincial assemblies, and the functions and duties of military power.[51] The Assembly will from now be called the National Constituent Assembly.

I intend to present my declaration tomorrow; I write to Jefferson: 'Be pleased to consider it again and make your observations. They are very angry with me for having supported the motion against the coming of troops- If they take me up, you must claim me as an American citizen…I beg you to answer as soon as you get up and wish to hear from you about eight or nine at least. God bless you.'[52]

July 10. I believe that the duc d'Orléans, or at least the people behind him, want to interfere. He has made advances towards me.

"You are both proscribed," says Mirabeau.[53] "There are sinister plans to act against you, as you alone are capable of commanding an army. You must unite with the duc d'Orléans. He can be your captain of the guards and you can be his."

"The duc d'Orléans, in my opinion, is only a man richer than I, whose fate is no more interesting than that of other members of the minority," I reply coldly. "It is useless to form a party if you are with the whole nation. It is necessary to go forward without worrying about the consequences and construct the building or leave the materials behind. In the meantime, I will watch Monsieur the duc d'Orléans, and perhaps I will, at the same time, denounce Monsieur the comte d'Artois as a trouble-making aristocrat and Monsieur the duc d'Orléans as troublemaking by more popular means. All these interfering schemes will be thwarted by the force of circumstances, as certainly as despotic plans."[54]

Mounier later speaks to me. "Mirabeau talked in the same way to me about Orléans. I told him it is treason." [55]

The president addresses us on the eleventh: "The king saw the deputation yesterday evening. He read the address and has replied that everyone knows of the disorders and scandalous scenes which have happened at Paris and Versailles and that it is therefore necessary to use the methods he has in his power to keep and maintain order and even to protect the liberty which allows you to deliberate here. If, however, you wish it, the Estates-General can be transferred to Noyon or to Soissons and the king will himself go to Compiègne in order to maintain the communication which must exist between the Assembly and himself."[56]

"At the same time that this response and these words of kindness give us confidence, the present state of events orders us to be vigilant and there is no other part to take except to insist on the sending away of the troops," Mirabeau replies.

The National Assembly decides to leave the situation as it is, except to demand the sending away of the troops.

Later in the day, I present my Declaration of Rights, the first in Europe. "Although the restraints of my cahier have taken away from me the ability to vote, I believe, however, I can still offer you the tribute of my thoughts. I would like my draft of a Declaration of the Rights of Man and Citizens to be sent to the different bureaux to prompt thought on this matter and induce others to present proposals which might better meet the Assembly's intentions, and which, in that case, I will be pleased to prefer to my own."[57]

Applause breaks out; I start to read: "Nature has made men free and equal. The distinctions necessary for the social order are only founded on a general usefulness. Every man is born with unalienable and imprescriptible rights. These are the liberty of his opinions, the care of his honor and his life, the right of property, the full disposal of his person, of his labor, of all his faculties, the communication of his thoughts by all possible means, the search for his well-being, and resistance to oppression. The only limits of the exercise of the natural rights are those which assure happiness to other members of society. Man can only be governed by laws which have been consented to by himself or by his representatives previously promulgated and legally applied.

The principle of all sovereignty resides in the nation. No body, no individual, can have any authority which does not emanate from it.

All government has its only aim that of the general well-being. This interest demands that the legislative, executive and judiciary powers should be distinct and defined and that their organization assures the free representation of citizens, the responsibility of agents and the impartiality of judges. Laws must be clear, precise, and the same for all citizens.

Subsidies must be freely agreed to and proportionally given out.

And as the introduction of abuse, and the right of generations which succeed it, necessitate the revision of all human establishment, it must be possible to the nation, to have, in certain cases, an extra convocation of deputies, whose sole object is to examine and correct, if it is necessary, the evils of the constitution."[58]

Applause echoes around the hall; I look at the deputies, proud of what I have written. It is my profession of faith, the fruit of my past, the pledge of my future. It is both a manifesto and an ultimatum."[59]

The comte de Lally-Tollendal comes to the tribune to second my proposal. "He speaks of liberty as he has defended it," he says to more applause.[60] "I think this declaration should be the starting point for the constitution, but I am not sure the American experience is the best model for France. I think Lafayette's words should be considered by the bureaux, but that no declaration of rights should be formally adopted until after the rest of the constitution has been adopted."

Mirabeau, Rabaut Saint-Etienne, Sieyès and others are also considering the subject, but I am very content to have written the first Declaration of Rights in Europe. During the night a résumé of my words is printed and distributed throughout Paris and will hopefully form the basis for whatever is decided.

July 12. Sunday. We discover that yesterday, Necker was dismissed and exiled and left Versailles at five in the evening. La Luzerne arrived at Necker's house at midday, bringing a letter from the king, ordering him to leave France. He dined quickly with his wife and then told her to come with him in the carriage. They went to their country house, at Saint Ouen, where it is believed he wrote to his daughter, Madame de Staël, and told her he was leaving for Brussels at midnight. His carriage was last seen heading towards the Belgian border. Montmorin and Saint Priest have also gone.

Many deputies gather in the hall in great consternation. "One can only measure with terror the abyss of misfortune to which yesterday's resolution can drag France. The exile of Necker, so long desired by its enemies, has now happened," says Mirabeau, a personal enemy of Necker and now probably not considering the loss of the minister, but more the disastrous events it might well herald.[61]

We are surrounded by troops who are mainly foreign. There is fear there will be an attack on Paris. There is fear that twelve members will be taken and made an immediate example of. There is fear that the king will dissolve the chambers and go to Compiègne. [62] There are even rumors that barrels of gunpowder have been placed under our meeting place.[63]

We meet on the morning of the thirteenth; we listen in silence to the initial addresses to the decrees.

Mounier speaks. "On recognizing the power of the king to change his ministers, we must say to him that the nation has not withdrawn its confidence from them, and that this confidence will not be given to his successors. The public credit and the wellbeing of the people are in danger. They are in despair; they are being provoked by a menacing display of force; liberty is being attacked; roads are closed; soldiers guard intersections. The king is being told to fear his people; we must enlighten him and show him the dangers threatening his kingdom. I propose to send an address to the king to recall his ministers, and of the danger of these changes and violent measures...It is necessary to declare to the king that the Assembly would never agree to an infamous bankruptcy.[64]

People support his motion. Finally, Monsieur de Guillotin presents the decree taken by the electors of Paris on the eleventh, demanding the authorization of a *garde bourgeois*.

At midday, we learn there have been terrible events in Paris during the night and the morning.[65] News of Necker's dismissal reached the Palais-Royal yesterday afternoon; crowds gathered, demanding that public places should be shut as a sign of mourning. Camille Desmoulins, one of the orators, has been calling for a revolt against the German troops, who, he says, have come to cut the throats of Parisians.[66] Late in the afternoon, unarmed people in the Tuileries were fired on by a detachment of the royal-allemand, led by the prince de Lambesc. People ran to the Palais-Royal crying "*Aux armes!*" An immense crowd went to the Hôtel de Ville demanding weapons and the ringing of the tocsin bells. The doors were broken down, the weapons taken.[67] During the night, the toll gates at the porte de Clichy were burnt as well as the toll houses from the faubourg Saint-Antoine to the faubourg Saint-Honoré and those from the faubourgs Saint-Jacques and Saint-Marcel; parts of the city wall have been destroyed. Brigands, armed with sticks, pikes and other weapons, have been roaming in groups to ransack houses whose owners are regarded as enemies of the public good and citizens have managed to stop them. The city officials have agreed to cooperate with the electors. They have formed a committee to remain in session for the duration of the crisis and have approved a plan for a voluntary citizen's guard of eight hundred men in each of the electoral districts.

A general cry of profound indignation arises from the assembled members. "We must send a deputation to the king to tell him of the dangers which threaten the capital and the kingdom, the need to send away the troops whose presence rouses the despair of the people, and to give the guard of the city to the bourgeois militia."

The archbishop of Vienne, Lefranc de Pompignan, will lead our deputation. If the king agrees, we will send a delegation to Paris to tell them the consoling news, to bring about tranquility.[68]

I expect the new ministers to be dismissed and the previous ones recalled, as well as the withdrawal of troops and the appointment of a National Guard in Paris. If the king appreciates the danger to which he has been exposed and if he lets us act, we shall restore calm, and if there is a faction, we shall destroy it.[69] But if the ministers recover from the fear which they have at this moment, if their outrageousness reasserts itself, great misfortune may befall the state."

The archbishop of Vienne returns from seeing the king who had replied: 'I have already said what my intentions are concerning the measures I need to take for the disorders in Paris. It is for me alone to judge what is needed, and I cannot make any changes. Some towns will look after themselves, but the size of the capital does not allow any guard of this sort. I do not doubt that it is only from the purest motives that you offer your services at this terrible time, but your presence in Paris will do no good. You are needed here to hasten your important work.' [70]

The Assembly is in consternation, fearful at this response.

"If we defy the king, we might expose ourselves to great personal danger," says the archbishop.

"Not to act would seem like surrender," calls out a deputy.

For the second time, I go to the tribune and speak on the earlier motion of Monsieur Biauzat. "Personal safety, even the making of a constitution, is a less important consideration than the danger immediately facing the nation. The king's advisors, perfidious councilors, must be held responsible for the current disorder and for all that might happen. This morning the duc de Clermont-Tonnerre said that the constitution will be, or we shall no longer be. I think that now the constitution will exist, even if we do not."

Confidence returns. We vote unanimously to declare again that there is no intermediary between the king and the Assembly; that the ministers and the civil and military agents of the authority are responsible for any undertaking which is contrary to the rights of the nation and to the decrees of the Assembly, that we hold the present ministers and the king's advisors, of whatever rank and state, personally responsible for the present and future unrest. We express our confidence in Necker. We ask again for the withdrawal of the troops and the establishment of a citizen's guard, and to reassure the state's debtors by repudiating any suggestion of bankruptcy, to reassert the inviolability of deputies, and to reaffirm our oath to separate only after we have finished the constitution. We will send these decrees to the king and we will also publish them.[71]

"We must continue our session throughout the night, so that we cannot be arrested," suggests Bailly.

We agree. The hall in the hôtel des menus plaisirs is probably the safest place, as we are all together, particularly for those like me who are proscribed. Part of the deputies will stay here tonight and in the morning another group will take their place. Our president, the good and old archbishop of Vienne, would be too fatigued to remain in the chair all night and so it is decided we will have a vice-president for the present circumstances. I am appointed by five hundred and eighty-nine votes out of seven hundred and eleven. Applause breaks out. The vice-presidency is for me alone and is only for now.

"Gentlemen, on another occasion I would have reminded you of my inadequacy and the particular situation in which I find myself but the circumstance is such that my first sentiment is to accept with delight the honor which you do me and to exercise with zeal the functions under our venerable president as my first duty is never to separate myself from your efforts to maintain peace and consolidate public liberty."[72]

Everyone applauds again. The archbishop leaves. I take the chair. At eleven-thirty, I suspend the debate. Most people want to remain; homes have been visited to see if they are there. I stretch out to sleep on a bench while some walk round the hall. We believe Paris is quiet and I imagine we will have a deputation from the city in the morning. We are in a very unusual situation; the day will be interesting.

July 14. In the early hours of the morning, I hope we will be able to go to bed because we only have the rumor of Paris as a pretext and it is peaceful now.'[73] At nine, the archbishop takes over the chair. We discuss how to proceed with writing the constitution. People keep looking involuntarily towards the city as we do not know what is happening there. We hear that troops have been stationed on the roads and on the bridge at Sèvres where there is also cannon, and that the prince de Lambesc has been seen riding rapidly into Versailles, surrounded by officers to protect him following the excesses he committed at the Tuileries.

The least noise makes people suspect firing. They put their ears to the ground to hear better. There are continual alarms. It is said the king will flee during the night and will leave us guarded by, and at the mercy of, the foreign and German regiments encamped at the Orangerie.[74] In the afternoon, the duchesse de Polignac and the comte d'Artois walk there and the officers are served refreshments and wine.

At five o'clock, the Assembly reconvenes; people are in a state of consternation but not discouraged.

Suddenly Noailles rushes in from Paris. "The Hôtel des Invalides has been taken. The people have cannons and intend to besiege the Bastille. Noble families have been forced to shut themselves in their houses."[75]

Monsieur Wimpfen, a deputy, then also arrives from Paris with equally alarming news. "I was arrested and taken to the Hôtel de Ville. The armed crowd showed me a decapitated corpse dressed in black, who they said was Monsieur de Launay, the governor of the Bastille, and that they would next execute me. I was set free on the orders of the electors." [76]

We decide to send the deputation again to the king.

"It is the dignity, as well as the duty, of the Assembly not to interrupt its work, and to continue with the calm and the courage that circumstances must not change," I say from the chair. [77]

We propose to establish communication and couriers with Paris so that we can have news from there every two hours, and to remain in sitting until we have made constitutional laws, or at least until after the danger has passed.

Two electors, Bancal-des-Issarts and Ganilh, arrive, sent by the *comité permanent* at the Hôtel de Ville.

"The Bastille has fallen! Men, women, children and priests are working with an equal ardor to defend themselves. They are digging large ditches, setting up barriers, and collecting paving stones which women are taking to the top of the houses to try and stop enemy troops from entering the city. Metal workers are making long pikes, lead makers are making balls and bars. Sentinels are at the top of towers to give the alarm if troops approach."[78]

They read out a declaration from the *comité permanent.* "Paris is in a terrible state. Atrocities happened at the Bastille. It was useless to send deputations from the committee, with a flag and drum, for peace, to de Launay, governor of the Bastille, and demand that the cannon there should not fire on the people; there has been the death of several citizens, killed by firing from the Bastille."

"Let vengeance come down onto the head of the guilty from the Heavens and from men! Vengeance!" shouts Mirabeau and others in indignation.

"The demand made by a multitude of assembled citizens to besiege it; the massacres which can follow; we beg the National Assembly to consider, in its wisdom, as quickly as possible, how it will be possible to avoid the horrors of civil war at Paris. The establishment of a bourgeois militia and the measures taken yesterday, partly by the Assembly of Electors and partly by the committee, have procured for the city a quieter night than could have been hoped for, considering the considerable number of individuals who armed themselves on Sunday and Monday before the formation of the militia, and many of these individuals have been disarmed and brought to order."[79]

"Monsieur le président, at the head of a numerous deputation, has gone to the king to ask him to remove the troops. I invite you, messieurs, to stay with us to hear what he says," I say.[80]

We decide to send a second deputation which is just about to depart when the first deputation returns.

"The king has replied that he is taking all the measures necessary to re-establish peace in Paris and has ordered the prévot des marchands and municipal officials to come here to act in concert with them. He has instructed generals to put themselves at the head of the newly formed garde bourgeoise. He has ordered the troops at the Champ-de Mars to leave Paris and says that the anxiety of the situation affects him greatly."[81]

"Send a second deputation!" people cry.

The archbishop once more departs with another deputation. He returns with the reply: 'Messieurs, you break my heart more and more with the account you give of the misfortunes of Paris. It is not possible to think that the orders given to the troops can be the cause. You know the response I have already given. I have nothing to add."

"Do not allow the king's generals to command the militia," I tell the electors who will return to Paris tomorrow. [82]

The archbishop goes away to rest. I take the chair; we prepare to spend the night again in the hall, many very worried they will be arrested. We discuss until two o'clock. We decide to wait until morning to send another deputation although the duc de La Rochefoucauld-Liancourt had, however, gone earlier to speak to the king believing that if he knows the truth he will behave differently.

"Is this a revolt?" the king evidently asked him.

"No, Sire, it is a revolution," was his reply.[83]

July 15. We decide to send a new deputation to the king, which I will lead, to ask again for the sending away of the troops, the free circulation of provisions for Paris and the authorization of the garde bourgeoise. This can then be taken to Paris where it will help to quell disorder and calm the citizens. We are just about to set off when the duc de La Rochefoucauld Liancourt arrives.[84]

"I have been authorized to say that the king will come to the Assembly," he announces, to the great joy of everyone.

At eleven o'clock, he arrives on foot, without an escort, accompanied by Monsieur and the comte d'Artois. My deputation escorts them into the salle des menus plaisirs where everyone waits in a respectful silence, Mirabeau having already warned that the people's silence is a lesson for kings.[85]

The king does not sit on the chair which has been placed on a raised platform for him. He stands, his head bare, a departure from royal protocol; for the first time he addresses the deputies as the National Assembly. [86]

"The head of the nation comes with confidence into the middle of its representatives, to show them his pain and to invite them to find ways to bring order and calm…I have ordered the troops to leave Paris and Versailles. I authorize and invite you to make my decisions known in the capital," he says.

"*Vive le roi!*" "*Vive la nation!*" deputies cry and applaud.

"Sire, the National Assembly receives with the most respectful feeling the assurances Your Majesty gives regarding the sending away of the troops and supposes that it is not simply their removal to some distance, but their being sent to their barracks and quarters from where they have come," says the archbishop of Vienne. "Would you also re-establish free communication between Paris and Versailles and immediate free communication between them and yourself? We also solicit the approbation of Your Majesty for a deputation to be sent to Paris to help to bring about order there. Finally, we repeat our concerns about your change of ministers which is one of the principal causes of the terrible troubles which afflict us, and which have broken the heart of Your Majesty."

"You know my intentions and desires on a deputation to Paris," replies the king. "I would never refuse to communicate with the National Assembly."[87] However, he says nothing about the ministers.

"*Vive le roi!*" The deputies cheer. They throw their hats in the air; they escort him in triumph, as they had on June 27, twenty deputies forming a chain around him to stop the crowd who are in transports of delight, pressing forward too much.

"*Vive le roi!*" come the shouts all the way to the courtyard of the château where the musicians from the Swiss regiment play the air 'where could one be better than in the heart of one's family.' The queen comes out onto the balcony holding the dauphin and presents him to the people. The sun shines brightly and joy is on everyone's faces.

At eight o'clock in the evening our deputation of eighty-eight deputies sets off in forty carriages from the stables of Monsieur. I am in the first carriage as I am vice-president.

"*Vive la nation!*" crowds shout for the whole of the route. Troops withdraw at our approach. At the   Place de Louis XV, we leave the carriages; I lead our procession on foot across the Tuileries to the Palace where a deputation of four electors meets us in the vestibule.

"Messieurs, we have been deputed by the Assembly of the Electors to receive the angels of peace that the National Assembly sends us," says Monsieur du Veyrier.

We set off together, by the Carrousel, along the roads Saint Niçaise, Saint Honoré, the Arbre Sec and the embankments, towards the Hôtel de Ville. In front ride the night watch, two detachments of French and Swiss Guards, the officers of the prévot of the Hôtel de Ville, and those of the Paris militia. Then walk the electors, followed by the deputies of the National Assembly, several detachments of the French Guards and the Paris militia, who also stand on either side of the route. [88]

"*Vive la nation!" Vive le roi!" "Vivent les députés!*" come the shouts from an immense crowd lining the streets and hanging out of the windows. They press forward; they embrace us; they take our hands. They cry tears of emotion. They give out red, white and blue cockades. The newly born Paris militia keeps order; a huge number of soldier-citizens follow us, like a forest of weapons which has suddenly come out of the ground like the soldiers of Cadmus.[89]

At the Hôtel de Ville the electors wait on the steps. We go into the grande salle which is filled by electors and other people. Tumultuous applause and shouts ring out; Bailly, Sieyès, the comte de Clermont-Tonnerre and the archbishop of Paris take seats beside the desk of the comité permanent, near the mantel on which stands my bust by Houdon.

Moreau de Saint-Méry, the president of the electors, asks me to speak. There is so much noise, I wait. Finally, it abates.

"I congratulate the electors and all the citizens of Paris on the liberty which you have won by your courage…The king was deceived, but he is no longer. He knows our suffering and he will prevent it happening again…By coming here for him to convey words of peace, I hope, messieurs, to also bring back to him the peace which his heart needs." I recount what happened this morning;

then I read the statement of the king, "*Vive le roi!*" *Vive la nation!*" people crying after nearly every sentence.

Lally-Tollendal speaks next, then others. The archbishop of Paris invites everyone to join him at Notre Dame Cathedral to sing the *Te Deum*. We accept. Moreau de Saint Méry asks to pardon the soldiers who were taken while defending the Bastille. We also accept this and are about to leave the room when many voices rise in unison. "Make Monsieur le marquis de Lafayette *commandant-général* of the Paris National Guard."

I am taken by surprise, knowing that La Salle is already the commander. Others join in. "Make Lafayette commandant-général!"

I stand to speak. "I swear to sacrifice my life to the conservation of this precious liberty whose defense is being given to me." Cheering and shouting drown my words. I draw my sword; I raise then lower it to show I am accepting their demand.

People shout for Bailly to be chosen as *prévôt des marchands*. A voice calls out. "Not *prévôt des marchands! Maire de Paris!*"[90]

"*Maire de Paris!*" everyone shouts.

Bailly leans forward, very moved, tears in his eyes. He accepts. "I am not worthy of such a great honor, nor capable of carrying such a burden."[91]

Several deputies will remain in Paris to help the electors; they choose nine, including myself, Bailly, La Tour Maubourg, Clermont-Tonnerre, Target, La Rochefoucauld and Duport. They also choose ten electors to report what has happened to the National Assembly and to agree with them about how to bring calm to the capital.

We set off to the cathedral. I come out of the Hôtel de Ville; hundreds surround me, embracing me, grabbing my hand. "*Vive Lafayette!*" they shout. I thank everyone. I slowly walk through the crowd towards Notre Dame and enter just as the *Te Deum* is finishing. The committee of electors asks me to swear an oath of office.

"I am ready, but I can only accept provisionally as I am a member of the National Assembly and I need its approval," I reply.

They agree.

"I will defend with my life the precious liberty entrusted to my care," I swear. [92]

Then I go with the deputies and a committee of electors next door to the palace of the archbishop, to confirm my appointment.

"I am happy to give my command to hands as pure as those of Lafayette," says La Salle graciously, who will now become second-in-command.

At midnight, most of the deputies return to Versailles; I go with La Salle and La Tour Maubourg to the Hôtel de Ville where Bailly and several electors are discussing the administration of Paris. It is agreed that I will deal with the police as well as with military affairs.

"Search the Bastille as there are believed to be more prisoners still there," I order.

The crowd has arrested and brought from the Bastille a man who says he is the comte de St. Marc and had been sent by his district, St. Gervais, to see if the underground passages of the Bastille contain dangerous communications. He is a victim and not in any way guilty. We make him a prisoner here for the night to save him and I will ensure his freedom tomorrow. [93]

I have hardly slept for three days; I am exhausted. At two o'clock in the morning I feel I can finally go home to my family and sleep. I will return at seven.

Chapter 38

I march my sovereign about the streets as I please

July 16. On my way to the Hôtel de Ville I come across an enormous crowd.

"What is happening?" I ask.

"Only an abbé who is going to be hanged," is the reply.

I force a path through to the middle of the mob. "I am a patriot. I am abbé Cordier," calls out a man in terror.

"No, he is a traitor called Roy," people scream. At that point, my son arrives with a friend; I immediately take the opportunity to distract the crowd from their violence. "Messieurs, I have the honor to present my son to you."

They react with surprise and pleasure and my friends manage to get the abbé to the safety of the Hôtel de Ville.[1]

A *fiacre* appears with another man caught by the armed citizens.

"What is happening?" I demand.

"I am Captain Danton from the Cordelier district," says a tall, large man with an ugly face. "This is the second governor of the Bastille and he is refusing to let people enter the prison. He must be hanged."

"He is Soulès and is an elector. We put him in charge of the Bastille the night of its capture. He is only doing what he has been asked to do," shouts La Salle running towards us.

I walk up to Soulès and shake his hand. "This man is an elector," I tell the crowd. "It is a false accusation. If the authority of the government of Paris is not respected, I will resign."

The captain is forced to free Soulès who walks quickly towards the Hôtel de Ville. On the steps, La Salle gives him his sword. We enter the building; the electors confirm the other man is Cordier. I quickly write him a certificate of good citizenship and send him home with an armed guard.[2]

We hold a meeting of deputies and electors; we discuss how to calm the violent situation here in Paris where people are denouncing anyone thought to be a traitor, and where the new militia, whose only uniform is the red and blue cockade, is meting out summary justice.

A permanent committee is set up, comprising Messieurs Target, Duport, de La Rochefoucauld, Clermont-Tonnerre, de la Coste, La Tour Maubourg and myself. Last night people started to destroy the Bastille so we need to order its demolition to give their action legality, otherwise they might become accustomed to acting in this way.[3] We agree to send two architects there to direct the work under the guard of La Salle.

We decide that the militia of each district will have its own staff but will answer to the Hôtel de Ville, and that the French Guards who have already proved their patriotism can join. All communes in France shall be defended by the new force which I believe should be called the National Guard,[4] with the name of its town or city added. The Assembly decrees this.[5] We also agree measures to try and halt disorder, to open shops and workplaces, and to enable traffic to circulate; copies of these regulations will be sent to all districts to be posted in the streets tomorrow.

Later in the day the electors now believe they do not have the authority to order the demolition of the Bastille. I also do not think I have the authority to order it as it has been agreed that the military authority is subordinate to the civil. In the end, the electors take responsibility, but I will carry it out. I therefore send the city trumpeters to the front of the Hôtel de Ville and to all crossroads in Paris, accompanied by four electors, to proclaim, in my name, that demolition will begin immediately, and I sign an order telling Pierre-François Palloy, a builder, to start work.

Paris needs food. All the city administrators of food have disappeared in fear and there is a risk of famine.[6] A committee on subsistence is set up to supervise the bringing of wheat to the windmills and the distribution of flour to the markets. I ask the committee to authorize me to write to all districts to ask them to each send a representative to the Hôtel de Ville to form a military committee to discuss the organization of the new force.

The deputies are about to set off to Versailles and I go with them to the grande salle.

"We appreciate what you have done to restore order," they say to the electors.

"We also appreciate what you have done," is their reply.

I would like to go to Versailles, but the leaders of the city say the peace of Paris means I cannot leave here for a moment. Eighty thousand people surround the Hôtel de Ville in a state of furious excitement, making a terrible noise. When I appear, they quieten.

"The king must come here!" "The king is not sending away all the troops! We are being misled!" they shout.

If I am absent for more than four hours, we are lost. My situation does not resemble that of anyone else. I reign in Paris over a people in fury pushed by abominable cabals; on the other hand, a thousand injustices have been done to them which they are right to complain about. [7]

People thought to be traitors are denounced and attacked or killed. Two army officers are brought in; I free them after they give their word. Monsieur de la Barthe is dragged before me, accused of offering to pay for the arrest of aristocrats, but then not paying. I regard the promise as worse than the non-payment and make him resign from the citizens' guard.

I receive a letter from Clermont-Tonnerre telling me that Mounier described me in the Assembly as a hero whose name is dear to liberty in the two worlds, and that it has been decided to ask the king to accept me as colonel-in-chief of the Paris National Guard and Bailly as mayor.

A letter arrives from de Broglie which declares, in the name of the king, that all the royal troops now in Paris will today return to their respective garrisons.[8] I immediately report this to the Assembly of Electors. They decide to allow royal soldiers to join the new force and write an oath for the troops to be faithful to the Nation, the King and the Commune of Paris, so that they can swear allegiance to the king, as well as be in the National Guard.

Several deputations of troops, including the Swiss Guards, the *guet à cheval*, the *gendarmerie*, as well as the French Guards, come to the Hôtel de Ville wishing to be in the National Guard. I administer the oath to them in front of the Assembly.

The comte de Montlosier requests a passport as he is setting off today for Riom to ask for new instructions.

"Inform my constituents I also wish to change my instructions," I say. I accompany him to the place de Grève; a disorderly rabble of armed men immediately scramble back to their posts and salute. They give me honors rather than obedience. I may seem to be their chief, but I am far from being their master.

At eleven that night, many electors go home, but there is too much unrest in Paris for me to do so; I remain at the Hôtel de Ville with Moreau de Saint-Méry and members of the permanent committee. At one in the morning, I receive a letter from La Rochefoucauld which says the king is reappointing Necker and that he will come to Paris today.

I immediately write back: 'Events have moved so quickly, with such urgency as to leave no time to bring to His Majesty the explanation of all that I have seen, thought, and considered necessary to risk. I regret that I am unable to come to you in person, but I feel from the duc de La Rochefoucauld's letter that I am ordered not to leave Paris, but to await you here. My situation astonishes me more than anyone else in the world, to which I would owe an inexpressible happiness if Your Majesty deigns to read my heart and find there the sentiments of gratitude and devotion that are eternally engraved thereon.'[9]

July 17. I spend the night busily preparing for the day, my responsibility to keep the king safe weighing heavily on me. There must be no violence. Armed citizens will protect him and the royal garde du corps will wait outside the city. I give posts to the companies under my command; I send aides to each district with their orders and Monsieur le chevalier de Saudray will carry out what I have commanded. [10]

In the morning, I wait in bright sunshine at Point du Jour with nine aides, Gouvion, La Colombe, Jauge, Bouneville, Cadignan Chabot, Curmer, Desmottes and Romeuf,[11] as well as a detachment of mounted guards. I have a sword and wear civilian dress, except for a red and blue cockade in my plumed hat.

At about three in the afternoon, the king's large carriage, drawn by eight black horses, very slowly appears at walking pace, guarded by a large group of armed citizens' militia from Versailles, most in rags, but all wearing red and blue cockades, and carrying pikes, poor weapons, swords, and various agricultural implements. The king has no guards[12] and is accompanied by the duc de Villeroy, the duc de Villequier, the maréchal de Beauvau and the comte d'Estaing, as well as the captain of his bodyguard and two equerries. A second carriage follows with four attendants, then many carriages bringing deputies from the National Assembly, three hundred of whom have already come to Paris.

"*Vive le roi*!" "*Vive la nation*!" crowds shout.

Louis is plainly dressed in a morning coat, his expression anxious and sad.[13] I approach the door of the carriage. I speak with respect to him and attempt to reassure. He is usually received at the place Louis XV, at the Conférence gate,[14] but today it has been decided that Bailly with twenty-five electors, twenty-five members of the municipal authority, the entire company of the *gardes* of Paris with their colonel, and the *echevins*, Messieurs Bufault and Vergue, should go beyond the Conférence, bearing the keys to the city in a red bowl.

"I give to Your Majesty the keys of the good town of Paris. They are the same ones which were given to Henri IV. He had reconquered his people; now the people have reconquered the king," Bailly declares, to applause. "How memorable is today when Your Majesty comes as the father in the middle of this reunited family…Sire, neither your people, nor Your Majesty will ever forget this great day. It is the most beautiful day of the monarchy; it is the time of an eternal alliance between the monarch and the people."[15] Applause rings out again; then Monsieur de la Vigne speaks briefly as president for the electors.

"I receive with pleasure the homage of the town of Paris and of the electors," Louis replies.

We set off in a somber and stately fashion, two long lines of deputies walking on either side of the royal carriage, Bailly walking in front, I on my white horse, Jean Leblanc, sometimes before the carriage, sometimes beside it, with my aides, a detachment of cavalry following.

On either side of the streets are at least one hundred thousand armed men, generally three deep, sometimes four, composed of the new militia, volunteers, and French Guards commanded by their sergeants as I cannot trust the officers. Some possess muskets from the Bastille and the Invalides, the rest have swords, pistols, pikes, pruning hooks, and scythes, and there are even women and monks with a gun on their shoulder. Behind the armed ranks mass women, children and old men, who also fill the windows and crowd the roofs. Discipline is excellent; each armed man stays at his post; the crowd does not try and push through. There is silence.

At the place Louis XV, where I have stationed French Guards with cannon, a shot suddenly comes from near the Palais Bourbon, killing a woman not far from the king's carriage. I brace myself for trouble, but nothing more happens.

"*Vive la nation!*" "*Vive le roi!*" *Vivent Bailly et Lafayette!*" "*Vivent les députés!*" "*Vivent les électeurs!*" people shout. I try and quieten the acclaim. I want the solemnity of silence.

Trumpets sound. A band plays martial music; there is again the occasional crack of artillery as we continue along the rue Saint Honoré, then the rue du Roule, and along the embankments to the place de Grève which I have ordered to be completely empty of people and encircled by many soldiers.[16] The king descends from the carriage; Bailly walks several steps in front. He stands on the bottom step of the Hôtel de Ville above his monarch and presents the cockade to him.

"Sire, I have the honor of offering to you the distinctive mark of Frenchmen."

Louis graciously takes the revolutionary emblem and sets it in his hat.[17]

I escort him up the steps towards the main door above which is a banner with the words: *Louis XVI father of the French, and king of a free people*. The citizens form an arch with swords and pikes, which clash together. People press around him, voices crying out, but the king remains calm.

"Move back!" cries the maréchal de Beauvau.

"Let them alone. They love me well," the king declares.[18]

I remain in the place de Grève with the soldiers to keep order[19] and he goes to the throne prepared for him in the grande salle, which is already filled with people. Not long after, he appears at a window wearing the cockade.

"*Vive le roi!*" the shout goes up, everyone in transports of delight. He returns inside, then shortly afterwards comes to the main door where I meet him to escort him to his carriage.

"Monsieur de Lafayette. I have been looking for you to say that I confirm your nomination to the post of commandant-général of the Paris National Guard."[20]

We leave the Hôtel de Ville. Armed citizens again line the streets, their arms reversed, the symbol of peace; the band of the *gardes françaises* play 'where can you better be than in the bosom of your family' from Grétry's '*Lucile*'.

"*Vive le roi!*" "*Vivent le roi et la nation!*" shout the crowd.

We manage to safely reach the Point du Jour. The king does not want us to accompany him further. I return in exhaustion to the Hôtel de Ville.

In the evening, I meet with a committee to decide on regulations for the Natonal Guard of Paris. Luckily only a few people attend and so I am finally able to make my way home to my anxious wife and family. It has been reported that the comte d'Artois left Paris yesterday evening with the duchesse de Polignac for the north-eastern border. The prince de Conti, the prince de Condé and the abbé Vermond, Marie Antoinette's advisor, are also believed to have fled, as well as one princess and another five princes.

Paris lacks food. Beggars and homeless people gather everywhere. Men armed with whatever implement they can find, are roaming the streets, as well as six thousand soldiers from regiments which have joined the National Guard, including five hundred Swiss Guards and six battalions of French Guards without officers. All the resources of the government have been destroyed, as they are hated and not compatible with liberty; the tribunals, the magistrates, the agents of the former regime are all suspected and regarded with hostility. Agents of the former police are trying to destroy what has happened in order to bring back their despotism. Many aristocrats are attempting to foment trouble; the followers of the duc d'Orléans are working for his cause, and all these people are milling together in the revolutionary cauldron of Paris. There is no military organization, no civil authority. There are no national laws, no legal procedures. Instead, Paris has an armed mass of people in each of the sixty districts, and at the Hôtel de Ville the electors in their patriotism are attempting to control the administration and bring foodstuffs into the city.[21]

Baseless rumors sweep the population. It is said that two new royal regiments are at Saint Denis; that the convoys of flour intended for Paris have been stopped; that twelve hundred hussars from Nassau are here and will attack. Fear is often the cause and even the workers demolishing the Bastille are saying their wine and bread are poisoned. Comperot, an elector, goes there and drinks and eats what they are refusing, to show them it is safe.[22] Bailly and I save many people from being killed, but we are starting to be criticized in the press.

"It was easier when I marched my sovereign about the streets as I pleased," I remark.[23]

July 20. A military committee is set up composed of deputies named by sixty districts to organize the National Guard. I write to the National Assembly to tell them of the measures I have taken to ensure calm in Paris and that it will be possible to open theatres tomorrow.

The prince de Lambesc, hated for ordering troops to charge the people in the Tuileries on July 12, is captured, dressed as his servant, attempting to flee Paris, and brought to the place de Grève. I go out. I shout angrily; I manage to save him.

Berthier de Sauvigny, devoted to the court, the former intendant of the royal army which had threatened Paris, is arrested at Compiègne.[24] He is hated by the people; blamed for the lack of bread and accused of mixing green wheat with ripe to try and suggest the harvest is bad.[25] The electors have decided to protect him, whether innocent or guilty, and I order a detachment of two hundred and forty volunteers commanded by d'Hermigny[26] to escort him, which will be accompanied by two electors, Monsieur de la Rivière and Monsieur de la Prède. The electors decide to institute a tribunal to try people accused by the public and I have the responsibility for the protection of those arrested.

At four in the afternoon, Adrienne and I give a dinner at the rue de Bourbon for friends, who include the duc and duchesse de La Rochefoucauld and Morris. After the meal I give Morris the pass he wants for the Bastille.

"The French Guards should become a city guard, receive special pay and recruit only from superior soldiers," he suggests.

"I agree," I reply.

"It would be best to prepare a plan for the National Guard and to submit it to the committee. Do you know what measures to take to get the king to confer on you the government of the Ile de France?"

"I would prefer to have only that of Paris. I have exercised the most power I could ever have wanted to. have ever wanted to exercise and I am tired of it. I was absolute commander of one hundred thousand men. I walked my sovereign through the streets, prescribed the amount of applause he could receive, and could have taken him prisoner, if I had wanted. All this has made me wish to return to private life as soon as possible," I reply.[27] Morris looks as though he does not believe me.

July 22. At five in the morning, the financier, Joseph-François Foulon, is brought to the Hôtel de Ville, having been arrested at Viry and made to walk to Saint Marcel with a bundle of hay on his back and a necklace of thistles round his neck. He had been the intendant of de Broglie's army in the Seven Years War. He was in the ministry of Breteuil and is now believed to want to be minister of finance and to institute plans of public bankruptcy. It is alleged he remarked when people were starving that they could eat hay, as horses lived on it. Crowds are gathering in the place de Grève, shouting that he has already been tried and has been found guilty. Bailly and I had wanted him taken to the Abbaye Saint-Germain but the electors had wanted him brought here and so I had reluctantly consented.

I arrive and to my surprise find that although the Hôtel de Ville is well guarded and has so far been respected by the people, Monsieur de Rhulièrers has ordered reinforcements of fifty horsemen from the watch, one hundred and twenty-three fusiliers and fifty-three grenadiers, and that many others have also come.

"You cannot increase the troops of Paris at one place without an order," I say to Monsieur Hay, the colonel of the city's guards; I send away a large part of the soldiers.

Foulon is being guarded in the grande salle. A woman enters and starts shouting abuse, calling him an enemy of the people. She leaves, but fearing the consequences, we decide to move him to the room next door. Monsieur Hay stations four guards there and to calm the crowds outside in the square and to show that Foulon is still in the building, asks him to stand at the window. He does and this appears to satisfy them.

I ride from the Hôtel de Ville to visit the districts where disorder might break out. Near the district of the Cordeliers I am invited to a meeting there.[28] I go into a large gathering, part of which consists of French Guards. Applause greets me and I see Danton presiding, the ugly man who had been trying to have Soulès killed.

"To recompense the patriotism of the brave *gardes françaises*, the district has decreed to demand that the regiments should be re-established in their former state and the command should be given to the first prince of the blood, the duc d'Orléans. We have no doubt of the approval of the commandant-général for such a patriotic proposal." Captain Danton's words are accompanied by flattering compliments, to applause from the assembly. I am in a trap and Mirabeau's traitorous words immediately come to my mind.

"That is not a good idea," I reply, very suspicious of any attempt to give power to the duc d'Orléans, whom I fear is trying to usurp the king.

His face darkens with anger for the second time in our very short acquaintance. I dislike and mistrust him. At that point, a messenger arrives from the Hôtel de Ville. "The crowd in the place de Grève is rioting and want to kill the prisoner, Foulon!"

I immediately leave and ride quickly through the streets. I find a mob has forced its way into the building and is now in the room with Foulon who is seated on a small chair in front of the desk of Moreau de Saint Méry, the president, people making a chain around him to distance him from the enraged crowd. I walk unhindered to Moreau de Saint Méry and address the crowd. Complete silence replaces the tumult.

"I am known to you all. You have made me your general and that choice which honors me, imposes upon me the duty of speaking to you with the freedom and frankness which are the basis of my character. You want to kill this man here in front of you without a trial. That is an injustice that dishonors you, that would brand me, that would brand all the efforts I have made in favor of liberty, if I was so weak as to permit it. I will not permit this injustice, but I do not wish to save him if he is guilty. I wish only that the orders of the Assembly should be carried out. I wish the accused to be put in prison until he can be properly tried by a tribunal. I want the law to be respected, the law without which there is no liberty, the law without whose aid I would have contributed nothing to the revolution in the New World and without which I would make no contribution to the revolution now in progress. What I am saying should not be interpreted in favor of Monsieur Foulon. Perhaps even the manner in which I have spoken of him on many occasions would alone forbid me to have the right to judge him. But the more he is judged guilty, the more it is important that the correct procedure should be followed for him, whether to make his punishment more striking, whether to question him legally, and to have from his mouth revelations of his accomplices. Therefore, I order that he should be taken to the prison of the *Abbaye Saint-Germain.*"[29]

The crowd near me falls quiet. "Take him to prison!" some demand who have been guarding him, and two men climb onto a desk. "Take him to prison!" they shout. But at the far end of the large room voices shriek with fury, "Get down!" and I do not think they have heard what I said.

"Let me speak," says Foulon. He starts to talk, but his words are mainly inaudible in the general hubbub. "Respectable Assembly…a just and generous people…I am in the middle of my fellow citizens…I do not fear anything." His words incite the crowd, not calm it. They shriek abuse. There is shouting outside. I see several well-dressed people who appear to be trying to rouse the others and my heart sinks. I suspect a deliberate attempt to cause trouble.

"What need of judgement is there for a man who has been judged for the last thirty years?" bellows a particularly well-dressed man.

I try to speak three times. Each time the crowd subsides and I begin to have hope. Then ghastly, far more terrifying shrieks come from the square.

"The Palais-Royal and the faubourg Saint Antoine are coming to take the prisoner!" people shout from the end of the room. Terrible cries echo from the stairs and all the corridors; a new mob surges into the room, into people already there. Everyone pushes forward to the desk and table where Foulon is seated, knocking over his chair. He falls to the ground.

"Take him to prison!" I bellow to tumultuous applause, running the risk my order will not be carried out.

Foulon applauds as well. A fatal mistake. "Look! They agree!" someone shouts.

Men grab him from the hands of the people surrounding him.[30] I shout in fury, but my voice cannot be heard. I cannot protect him. I am completely impotent. They drag him down the stairs and out into the place de Grève. They hang him from the lamp post opposite the Hôtel de Ville. The rope breaks. He falls onto his knees and begs for pity. People reattach the rope which breaks again. A quarter of an hour later another rope is attached and he is hanged. Once dead, he is decapitated. His head is stuck on a pike, hay put in his mouth. His body is dragged on the ground in triumph towards the Palais-Royal.

In my anger and despair, I know that Berthier, Foulon's son-in-law, is on his way here as a prisoner. The mob will do the same.

"Have more men guard the building and the square," I order. I station French Guards and armed citizens, bayonets at the ready, in the courtyard and on the steps.

Bailly arrives at five and is told the terrible news.

"There will be great danger when Berthier appears," we decide; we send a courier to Monsieur de la Rivière to tell him to take Berthier straight to the abbaye.[31]

Berthier arrives at eight forty-five in the evening. The mob in the place de Grève erupts into fury; they push past the soldiers and enter the Hôtel de Ville. They rampage along the corridors and into the assembly room. Bailly and I hurry to join the electors.

Monsieur de la Rivière has placed Berthier in the next room and tells us what happened en route. "Immense crowds filled the route, shouting, 'Death!' 'Torture!' and Monsieur Berthier replied to them that he had never bought nor sold a single grain of wheat. I received your letter directing me to the abbaye, but the people prevented me, and I had to continue to Paris. In the rue Saint Martin, Foulon's head was thrust at the carriage, but I told Berthier not to look and said it was the head of Monsieur de Launay,"

A strong guard escorts Berthier into the room and Bailly attempts to appear to do what is needed so that Berthier can quickly go to prison and away from the mob.

"Do you have anything to say?" Bailly asks.

"I will answer when I know the accusations against me," Berthier replies calmly.

"What have you done since July 12?" asks Bailly.

Berthier gives a detailed answer. "I have not slept for two days and would like to rest," he concludes. [32]

"Finish it! Finish it! Force the Hôtel de Ville…the faubourg Saint Antoine…the Palais-Royal," people shout from elsewhere in the building.[33] Berthier pales. More people suddenly rush in, pushing him and his escort back to the desk.

"Take him to prison at the abbaye," orders Bailly. "Let the guard look after the prisoner for the nation and for the town of Paris."

The soldiers quickly escort Berthier out of the room. Then a dragoon enters, carrying bleeding flesh in his hands. "Here is Berthier's heart! He has been killed!" [34]

There is complete silence. The faces of some electors go gray. They look away. "Please leave," they ask, almost as one; the dragoon and the mob pour out of the room.

"They are bringing Berthier's head!" shouts a voice.

Moreau de Saint Méry and I immediately send a message: "The Assembly is occupied with its deliberations and the head must not be brought in."

Thankfully, it does not appear. In that, at least, I am obeyed. It is useless to talk. A maddened crowd does not listen. I am angry and distressed. Two men have been killed against my order. My position as commander is now untenable. This is not the revolution I wanted.

"I must resign," I tell Bailly.

"I will do the same," he says.

"No," I tell him. "Our situation is different. The victims were taken from the guards I was commanding. I can no longer be sure my commands will be carried out. You were not present when my commands concerning Monsieur Foulon were ignored and his death was illegally demanded. In the case of Monsieur Berthier, it was more surprising and unexpected. The public interest means that a military commander should always be certain that with enough forces he can always carry out the orders of the civil authority. In any case, I do not believe my resignation will be accepted. I do not seriously intend to resign but it is essential that I should propose it, so that these sad events should provide an example to bring people who have acted wrongly back to order, and also to make people understand that in a time of liberty, if the law is not sovereign and if magistrates are not obeyed, he or other decent people would not agree to command such military forces."[35]

Accordingly, I write to him and to the sixty districts offering my resignation:

Monsieur. Called by the confidence of the citizens to the military command of the capital, I have not ceased to declare that in the present situation it is necessary that this confidence, to be useful, must be entire and universal.

I have not ceased to say to the people, that as much as I am devoted to its interests to the last breath in my body, so I am incapable of buying its favor by an injustice. You know, Monsieur, that two men died yesterday. One was placed under guard, the other was brought here by our troops and they were both intended by the civil power to be tried by a regular process; to satisfy justice, to find out accomplices and to fill the solemn engagements taken by all the citizens towards the National Assembly and the king. The people did not listen to my advice, and the day when I lack the confidence that they promised me, I must, as I have said before, leave a post where I can no longer be useful. [36]

Bailly refuses to accept my resignation. Monsieur de Saint-Méry and the electors come to speak to me at the committee of subsistence where I am with Bailly. "Stay. Do not resign," they implore. "Paris needs you as its general."

"I refuse. The public usefulness itself seems to demand my resignation. The bloody and illegal executions of last night and the importance of my being able to prevent them, convince me that I do not enjoy universal confidence."

"Stay," they plead.

"I will return to the Assembly at six o'clock," I say.

In the afternoon, deputations from the districts come to see me led by the venerable curé of Saint-Étienne-du-Mont. They cry. They swear to obey me. They bring letters refusing to accept my resignation.

What can I do? I suspect atrocious acts are being organized by an invisible hand.[37] I cannot abandon citizens who place all their confidence in me, but if I stay, I am in the terrible situation of seeing evil without being able to remedy it.[38]

I return in the evening. The electors give me more letters refusing my resignation.

"I am very moved by the deputations which have increased my regret at leaving," I say.

"The general will has already acclaimed you. We will give you all the power you need to re-establish respect for the law," they declare.

"I still do not wish to reconsider," I reply.

They crowd round me. Monsieur Osselin, an elector, falls onto his knees; I gently lift him to his feet; I embrace him. I allow myself to be led back to my seat. More deputations arrive from about forty districts, each imploring me to stay. The electors and deputies of the districts who are present write a declaration. They vow complete confidence in my virtues, talents and patriotism. They again proclaim me commandant-général of the National Guard of Paris, and they promise, in their name, as well as in that of our armed brothers in our districts and in other military bodies, the submission and obedience to all my orders, as my zeal, supported by all patriotic citizens, should bring to success the great work of public liberty.[39]

The district representatives take this oath in turn. My tears flow. I fear if I do not accept now there will be serious rioting during the night. I stand and speak.

"I accept. My function is to watch over the safety of the city, guarded by its armed citizens, to execute the decrees of your representatives, to live in order to obey you, and die, if it is necessary, to defend you. These are the only functions, the only rights of the person you have deigned to name commandant-général."

"*Vive la nation!*" *Vive la liberté!*" *Vive Lafayette*!" they shout. They embrace me, many also crying. They all sign the declaration. They applaud and escort me to the meeting of the military committee.

I am pleased with the outcome of a ghastly situation. I have behaved honorably in resigning immediately. I have done what I needed to do, and it is a useful lesson for the crowds. My position is now far stronger, and there will hopefully be a better legal framework for future events.

"I think agitators were responsible," is Bailly's opinion.

July 24. I write to Liancourt that Paris is calm: 'I feel that the infernal cabal which is pursuing me is instigated by foreigners. This idea encourages me because there is nothing so cruel as to be tormented by fellow citizens. You cannot imagine the touching scenes brought about by my resignation. I hope that this will give me the means to be useful.'[40] Next day, Saturday, twenty deputies, nominated by the communes of each of the sixty districts, assemble in the Hôtel de Ville. They proclaim, once again, that Bailly is the mayor and that I command the National Guard.

"I thank you for my nomination. You are the first deputies who truly represent Paris," I say. "It was your devotion which made me decide to continue. I pledge to faithfully fulfill the functions of commandant-général, to keep myself within the limits prescribed by my office and will never forget that the military power is answerable to the civil authority.[41]

They respond by swearing their allegiance to the orders I will give on behalf of the public good.

"There is a third oath to be taken between Monsieur de Lafayette and I, that of always loving each other," says Bailly. We embrace, to the great pleasure of the assembly who know how much the union of its two chiefs can be useful to the public good.[42]

In the evening the Assembly renames itself the Assembly of the Representatives of the Commune of Paris. They approve the principles I have recommended for the organization of the military.

I am at home on Sunday. A messenger arrives. "The Hôtel de Ville is at risk of being invaded by a mob who believe a vast amount of silver is hidden in the building."

I hurriedly rush there. It seems quiet but to avoid any risk I order a large force to come. No mob appears; I have no idea if the threat of force forestalled a problem or if it was just a rumor.

The maréchal de Castries is arrested on the twenty-seventh as he is trying to leave Paris even though I have given him a passport. The electors offer him a special pass if he wants to leave or an escort of electors if he wishes to return. He decides to leave.

I give out passports to anyone who wants them. "It is better that people should leave France than that they should become our enemies," I say. I give a passport to Jefferson, who also obtains one from the royal authorities. "Just in case," he comments.

Deputations arrive from the provinces. They say they have taken weapons and ammunition and want to know what to do. We talk to them as brothers.

July 30. In the morning, we learn that Necker will be coming to Paris today, accompanied by his wife, his daughter, deputies of the National Assembly, Saint-Priest and others. We agree that a deputation will meet him at the gate of La Conférence.

A huge crowd gathers there and Adrienne, with other women, is in the group to welcome him. I wait to meet him on the steps of the Hôtel de Ville, with the members of the committee. He arrives, having been acclaimed by crowds thronging the streets wild with joy, calling him the father of the people and the savior of the nation.

He goes to the Chamber of the Representatives of the Commune where Bailly makes a short speech. Then he addresses the gathering. He says the king has received him with the greatest kindness and has assured him of the return of his most complete confidence. He invites the municipal authority to restore calm in the capital and nearby. He asks for the release of Monsieur Besenval, who has been arrested because he was the commander of the royal troops during the taking of the Bastille and says that accord has always existed between the two of them. He asks for him to be allowed to travel to Switzerland. He also talks of a general amnesty.

All the representatives cry out for grace and grant Besenval his liberty. They immediately sign the order and two members, de Corberon and Montaleau, offer to take it to Versailles. Necker also writes a letter and they set off.

He next goes to the chamber of the electors where he is seated on the dais of the president, Moreau de Saint Méry, who presents him with the national cockade.[43]

"Here are the colors which you undoubtedly like. They are those of liberty."

Necker repeats the speech he has already made to the representatives of the commune.

"*Grace!*" "*Pardon!*" "*Amnistie!*" is the same enthusiastic response. Bailly stays silent. Moreau de Saint Méry presents Adrienne with a cockade.

Necker goes to a window in the Queen's Room overlooking the place de Grève, having been asked to show himself to the crowd. "*Vive la nation!*" "*Vive Monsieur Necker!*" come the cries.

He leaves the Hôtel de Ville to an even greater outpouring of joy, Bailly and I escorting him to his carriage, now decorated with laurel and olive by market women.

Bailly refuses to sign the decree written by Clermont-Tonnerre concerning the amnesty. He regards it as unconstitutional and dangerous for the electors to suggest there should be an amnesty for the enemies of the nation and believes it will cause trouble with the people.

The assembly of electors decides to join that of the representatives; they meet in the room of the electors, the two assemblies now a single body of the commune.

In the evening, crowds sing and dance in the streets and squares; lamps and candles are lit in all the windows, including those of my own house in the rue de Bourbon.

"*Vive le roi!*" *Vive le dauphin!*" *Vive Necker!*" people shout.

July 31. We learn many districts have erupted in anger at what was decided yesterday at the Hôtel de Ville. Many are furious that Necker has dared to reprieve one of their victims and that he is attempting to restore order. They think the electors should not have agreed on an amnesty and that the enemies of the people should not be allowed to return to Paris at this dangerous time. They believe he is sacrificing liberty for his own purposes and that he had promised the queen the release of Besenceval. It is suspected that Mirabeau went last night to the district of the Oratoire to speak against any pardon and that he obtained a decree from them to stop any such act, which they then sent to fifty-nine other districts.

Violence is increasing in the towns and countryside where fear and hunger are causing panic. There are false accounts of invading Austrian forces, the British landing at Saint Malo and Brest, a Swedish regiment at the north-eastern frontier commanded by the comte d'Artois, and thirty thousand Spanish soldiers marching on Bordeaux, all of which are terrifying people.

The rumors often implicate the queen. She is hated. "It is only her desire for revenge which has made her stay," people say. She is accused of intending to mine the National Assembly, poison Louis and replace him with Artois, as well as to have asked her brother, the emperor, for an army of fifty thousand men to invade France.

Brigands are seen everywhere, either paid for by Artois, who is said to have taken a vast amount of gold to pay foreign soldiers,[44] or by the princes or aristocrats. Many are just groups of hungry people searching for food, or local men armed with pitchforks, scythes, or whatever arms they manage to find, trying to defend their areas, who are often then thought to be brigands. Fear and panic create even more fear and panic.

Chateaux are attacked and looted; seigneurial rolls and feudal titles are burnt. Grain stores are seized, bakers' shops looted, the *maréchaussée,* the provincial police, unable to prevent any of it.

"This country now is as near in a state of anarchy as it is possible for a country to be without breaking up," is Morris's opinion.[45]

In the evening, I submit a draft proposal for the National Guard to a meeting of the Commune:

One: Paid, regular soldiers should do most of the work. Volunteers would be used to police the districts and to provide emergency support. They would pay their own expenses. Each of the sixty districts would provide one company of paid troops and four companies of non-paid. All regularly domiciled men aged twenty to fifty, but not including vagrants or servants, would be subject to be called up.

Ten battalions will compose a division and there will be six divisions for the whole city. Two: Staff officers would be chosen by the local authority after being nominated by the general. Three: The uniform will consist of a royal blue coat with white lapels and facings, scarlet collar, white lining, scarlet edging, and yellow buttons, a white vest, white breeches, black leggings in winter and white in summer, and a hat trimmed with black braid. Every soldier and officer to wear a cockade in his hat and the uniforms of officers will have the usual addition of epaulettes, swords and plumes. The cockade will be white, red and blue. [46]

Red and blue, apart from being the colors of Paris, are also the colors of Orléans, whom I detest and suspect of intrigue and treachery, whilst Bourbon white has been the color of France.

"I bring you a cockade which will go around the world, and an institution, civil and military at the same time, which must triumph over the tactics of Europe, and which will reduce arbitrary governments to the alternative of being conquered unless they imitate it and overturned if they dare to imitate it." I tell the committee.[47]

The Commune authorizes me to send my proposals to each district; I include a fourth part, detailing discipline and etiquette, parade and police duties, and other relevant subjects.

Mirabeau, Glezen, Robespierre and Barnave maintain at the National Assembly that the generous principles of civil liberty are not applicable when the people have been right to arrest a man who had put himself at the head of their enemies.[48] Monsieur de Besenval must be judged not by rumors, but on his actions, acquitted if innocent, punished if guilty. No one should be arrested without being accused. Mirabeau and Barnave win. The Assembly overturns the decree of the electors and says that Monsieur de Besenval and the other conspirators must be tried and that a tribunal would be nominated to which people would be sent who had committed treason.

On August 1, deputies from the Commune thank the Assembly for the decree it has passed. They beg it to name a tribunal to judge the enemies of the nation so that this would stop so many excesses happening.[49] Instead, this measure seems to inflame the population even more. Already one hundred and fifty châteaux have been burned in Franche-Comté, the Mâconnais and the Beaujolais. Now flames engulf even more châteaux and atrocities are being committed everywhere. Monsieur de Baras is cut into pieces in front of his pregnant wife. Monsieur de Montesson has his throat slit after seeing his father-in-law killed. Monsieur de Belsunce is killed at Caen, the chevalier d'Ambli is dragged from his bed, his eyebrows and hair pulled out, and is put in the smoke house.[50] More nobles flee.

By the third, the cost and scarcity of bread is increasing the unrest. Monsieur Châtel, the lieutenant to the mayor of Saint Denis, is killed by a furious mob.[51] They dragged his head through the streets and forced the municipal authorities to lower the price of bread to two sous. People then rushed from neighboring areas to buy bread there, quickly depleting the stocks and making famine seem possible. Saint Denis asked Paris for help and the Commune issues a proclamation that the price of bread should be set at thirteen and a half sous for a four-pound loaf, that people must not demand what they cannot be given, and to be peaceful.

August 4. In the morning Bailly and I discuss the situation of two deputies, Garin and Charton, who had been sent to Provins to obtain food. They were badly treated by the townspeople and are now imprisoned in a house and might be killed. We decide we must help them; four hundred men are ordered to go there with a cannon, accompanied by four deputies.[52]

In the afternoon, at the National Assembly in Versailles, it is decided to urgently promulgate a Declaration of Rights.[53] In the evening, Monsieur Target reads out a proclamation to stop arson and the pillaging of châteaux. Louis de Noailles declares that the kingdom is floating between the complete destruction of society and a government which would be admired and followed throughout Europe. He suggests the abolition of serfdom, the abolition of the *corvée* and the redemption of dues. The duc d'Aiguillon, who had been intending to speak first, then speaks of the horrors and violence taking place in France which could be excused by the sufferings of the people and that he supports the motion of my brother-in-law. Other deputies denounce different wrongs, such as private courts or tolls, followed by many nobles and clergy wanting to renounce their privileges. It is a moment of patriotic drunkenness according to Ferrières, and Lally-Tollendal becomes so alarmed he quickly passes a note to Chapelier, the recently appointed president after the resignation of Thouret, who had been criticized by the radicals as being sold to the Polignacs and to the aristocracy: 'They are not in control of themselves. Adjourn the session.'[54]

Bailly and I are not present, although completely in agreement. We applaud the destruction of privileges and here in Paris try also to destroy prejudices such as by making speeches to persuade certain soldiers of the National Guard to have officers from various theaters and a brother of two young men who were executed.[55]

Grain and bread are starting to reach the markets and the price comes down. This dampens the rioting, but unrest remains like a volcano bubbling and exploding at unexpected times and places. The king appoints the archbishop of Bordeaux, Champion de Cicé, as *garde des sceaux*, and La Tour du Pin to the ministry of war.[56]

In the evening of the fifth, we learn from committees that ten thousand pounds of gunpowder from the Arsenal have been loaded onto a boat at Saint Paul. People have become very agitated about this and are saying that La Salle is a traitor as he signed the order. I know nothing about it, which seems very strange, and the electors are starting to worry. Bailly and I order the boat to be arrested, guarded during the night, the powder to be unloaded tomorrow and taken to the arsenal.

Next day, the commandant of the district of Saint Louis de la Culture complains that four of his men have been arrested and must be released. We learn that the arsenal holds four types of powder, only one of which is suitable for military use in Paris and of which they currently have only 240 pounds. The directors of the arsenal therefore decided they would send some of the unwanted powder to Essonne and would then have more space for the powder they want. They asked La Salle for authorization, and he very imprudently signed his name and added 'for Monsieur de Lafayette.' The powder loaded onto the boat is only cheap *poudre de traitre*, used in the slave trade, which has been confused with the word *traitre*, and has caused the problem. I visit the district in the afternoon to explain the misunderstanding. Then I go to Saint Étienne du Mont to see a guardsman who has been injured.

"I will take personal responsibility for your care, and you will have a pension," I say, and send him to the hospital.[57] Then I learn that the scientist, Lavoisier, a director of the arsenal, and his wife, have been arrested and taken to the Hôtel de Ville to be tried.

I rush back. Angry crowds are gathering in the place de Grève, even more furious now at La Salle. Many enter the Hôtel de Ville and surge into the grande salle. I am told that La Salle came in a carriage, but on seeing the mob shouting his name, he hurriedly, and wisely, departed.

I order detachments to occupy the place de Grève and the nearby streets as quickly as possible. "First occupy a small square outside the Hôtel de Ville, and then gradually enlarge it to push back the crowd," I order.

I go into the grande salle and find people flooding in to join those already there.

"What is it you want?" I ask.

"La Salle!" they shout, almost with one voice.

"Why?" I demand.

"Because he has betrayed us and forged your name to an order!"

"La Salle has not forged his name. He acted correctly, as my deputy," I say, in frustration, trying to make myself heard above the belligerent shouting. "He must be taken to prison."

"No, we want him here!" they clamor.

"His safety must be assured," I say.

Most raise their hands in agreement, but a few do not, and the thought again comes to me that this has been deliberately orchestrated to create disorder and panic.

I send fifty soldiers to arrest him in the hope he will not be found. The crowd rampages through the rooms, forcing doors, scattering papers and documents, and even searching the bell tower. A man climbs a lamp post and hangs a rope from it in the place de Gréve.

I play for time. I hope that reinforcements will soon arrive and I see from the window that the troops are beginning to occupy the square and are pushing back the crowd.

At eleven o'clock, the soldiers sent to arrest La Salle return without him; the place de Grève is now completely occupied by my men.

"It is very late. You are tired and so am I. The place de Grève is free of disorder. Let us all go home," I declare.

People go to look out of the windows and realize I am correct. They stampede from the room.

"You must have respect for justice and humanity," I lecture those remaining. Slowly and reluctantly, the last few abandon the grande salle, muttering about me and my troops, but afraid to be violent. "While he was entertaining us with his good speeches and pretending to look for La Salle to justify himself, it looks like the traitor was really hiding between his legs, under the rug at the table," is one of many silly comments I hear.

At three o'clock, we decide we can leave; I go home to my bed to the great relief of Adrienne who worries every time I go out that I will not return.

In the morning, the new powder arrives from Essonne and the agitation does not resume. Bailly proposes a reduction in the price of bread; the Assembly agrees; the four-pound loaf is reduced from fourteen sous to twelve.

August 9. Sunday. The military committee has asked the Commune to order commissioners be appointed concerning the uniform of the National Guard. Today several battalions are having their flags blessed in different parishes[58] and I go to Saint Nicolas des Champs, wearing my uniform for the first time, a coat of royal blue with a red collar, and white breeches, vest and facings, resembling that of my American Light Infantry uniform.[59] In the streets are singers from the Opéra and marching military bands; in the afternoon, in the Palais-Royal, battalions from several districts parade to drums and military bands.

Next day, the National Assembly decrees the structure of the National Guard should follow what I suggested; municipal authorities can ask for them, as well as for police and troops of the line, to keep order. The National Guard, and the troops of the line, officers and soldiers, are to swear an oath to be faithful to the nation, the law and the king; they are subordinate to the civil authority.

Many people with weapons are rushing to the countryside to hunt, following the decree of the National Assembly stopping the exclusive hunting rights of nobles.

"They have not properly understood the decree, or have perhaps not wanted to understand it," says Bailly.

We forbid all patrols, and all citizens, to go to hunt with weapons in the countryside without an express order from myself.[60]

The National Assembly issues a decree on the eleventh concerning the decisions made on the night of August 4, which begins: 'The National Assembly entirely destroys the feudal régime,' but continues to say that most feudal dues were redeemable and should continue to be collected until compensation is paid, although *tithe* is abolished. However, people have already stopped paying both dues and tithes, so this decree vindicates them.[61]

Next day, in the evening, I appoint Gouvion as *major-général*, de la Jard, d'Ermigny and La Colombe, as *aides-majors généraux*, and Poirey as *sécrétaire-général*. My only regret is that Pontgibaud does not wish to join us.

"Monsieur de Gouvion lived in America during the Revolution; he rendered the greatest services to the cause of liberty under the orders of General Washington, whose special friend he is," I say.

"I am not sure I am worthy of the position," he replies. "I will serve without pay for a trial of three months."

August 13. In the morning I confirm their appointments although Bailly does not seem pleased I have acted alone without speaking to him. However, I am delighted to have good men like Gouvion, La Colombe and Poirey with me, whose merit has already been tested in America, and whom I know I can trust and rely on in these difficult, revolutionary times.

My popularity is immense. I am the subject of poems, speeches, paintings and engravings; ladies dressed in white often visit the Hôtel de Ville to honor either Bailly or myself. People also, however, sometimes virulently attack me concerning my military ambitions, the chief of whom is Marat, the former agent of the police, whose journal seems to concern itself only with Bailly or me.

Our house overflows with people and I leave Adrienne to bear the brunt of the entertaining as I am so busy and not often there. The district of the Sorbonne even chooses George as second lieutenant of one of its companies of the National Guard.

"No, he is too young. He can be a fusilier," I tell them, but they continue to want him as second lieutenant.

"Gentlemen, my son is no longer mine. He belongs to you and to our country," I say graciously.

Riots are feared at Montmartre where several thousand work on the terraces. They are in revolt because there is not enough money to pay them, as well as a lack of bread, and they will have to return home. On August 15, I ride there with just a few National Guards. About six thousand thin and anxious men meet me with flowers, not weapons.

"We can pay your wages for a few days but then you must go home. Otherwise, I will have to send soldiers here," I tell them gently, but firmly.[62]

On August 18, the Commune orders the workshops to be closed and that those who do not live in Paris shall be given a passport and twenty sous on the day they leave, as well as three sous per league of their journey. The same day, I present the two division chiefs, Dormesson and Saint-Christian, to the National Guard. On the twentieth, I go back to Montmartre, again with only a few National Guards. Thousands meet me. They listen to what I say. They do not riot but I am not convinced they will leave.

I next visit the faubourg Saint Antoine where trouble is also brewing, even although forty-five thousand livres have been given to the 'heroes of the Bastille'. I quickly discover the distressing state of many. Some injured men have received no medical care; some widows and orphans have not received a sou.

"I will try and get medical help for you, as well as food and clothes," I promise.

In the evening, I describe the situation to the Commune. Physicians immediately offer their services free; a charity school agrees to take two orphans; and the Assembly sets up a new committee to help the sick and poor. The newspapers report my speech and people offer money.

I work to establish a police system for Paris. Ballots are held for company and battalion orders. Each district designs and makes its battalion standard, which is then blessed at the local church in my presence, often accompanied by Adrienne.

The officers so far elected of the National Guard of Paris swear an oath of allegiance in front of the Commune on the steps of the Hôtel de Ville. The officers stand at the front; Bailly officiates, and the officers swear to be faithful to the Nation, the King, the Law and the Commune.

The military committee chooses an ensign for the National Guard of Paris. It approves the uniforms and obtains bids for funds for the uniforms of the paid soldiers.

"We would like the sword to be a model of yours," they tell me.

On the twenty-second, I order all barracks to be ready in two days. I ask for fifty livres per man and 1,2000,000 livres in total to provide the unpaid soldiers with arms and equipment. The Commune agrees.

August 25 will be the day of Saint Louis, the *fête* day of the king, and it has been decided that Bailly and some of the representatives of the Commune will go to Versailles to swear an oath of allegiance to him; I will accompany with part of the National Guard as an escort. I am aware of rumors at court that I will mount a military coup to try to seize power and therefore write to Adélaide de Simiane, who is part of the court circle, as I know she will relay my words and help to allay fears:

> I need to talk with you. We can meet on Tuesday and, in the meantime, I will reply to your propositions. Do not think about my power. I shall make no use of it. Do not reflect on what I have done; I want no compensation. Consider the public welfare, the well-being and the liberty of my country and know that I shall decline no burden, no danger, provided that when calm is restored, I shall again become a private citizen. I am ambitious for only one further step: and that is to arrive at zero.
>
> This is how I will always behave. If the king refuses to have a constitution, I will fight against him. If he accepts it, I will defend him, and the day when he became my prisoner made me more devoted to his service, than if he had promised me half of his kingdom. But we must have a constitution and we are going to work towards it.
>
> My situation is truly extraordinary. I am in a great adventure and I take pleasure in the thought that I shall finish it without having had an ambitious gesture with which to reproach myself, and after having put the world right, I shall withdraw with a quarter of the fortune I had upon entering the world.
>
> We will be arriving with one hundred and thirty men and only about thirty officers and fifteen officials. The ministers will therefore be very content. I shall try to ensure that there will be no armed citizens. It will be extremely difficult.
>
> The food situation is going badly. All Hell conspires against us. Bless us with your angelic prayers.
> I believe that we will bring the kingdom out of this. [63]

The whole National Guard of Paris want to come, an obvious impossibility as the city would be left unguarded and unpoliced. I decide to take men who represent every rank. I will station soldiers double at the city gates and I order that no one in uniform or armed will be allowed out and that cannon loaded with grapeshot will be at the gates to Montmartre. I will station at various necessary places extra soldiers and have patrols.[64]

August 25. At four in the morning, the infantry march from Paris and wait at Versailles for the rest of the procession. The cavalry will escort Bailly and the representatives from the commune from Point du Jour. Aides will be stationed at three different points along the route and a horse will be kept saddled at Versailles so that I can ride quickly back to Paris if there is any sign of trouble.

At Point du Jour I get into Bailly's carriage; we set off, preceded by market women, who usually go to see the king on this day. At Passy, Auteuil, Point du Jour, and Sèvres, the local National Guards and onlookers give honors to the representatives of Paris, particularly to Bailly and I.

At Versailles, our detachment meets us, as well as the National Guard of Versailles, the avenue and the place d'Armes filled with people.[65] We proceed, in beautiful weather, in a column of about one thousand two hundred to the château, through flower-strewn streets lined by innumerable onlookers, who also crowd windows and balconies.

"*Vive Bailly!*" *Vive Lafayette!*" "*Vive la commune de Paris!*" they cry.

At the château, the grandmaster and two aides of ceremonies take us into the royal bedchamber where the king is sitting in the *lit de parade*, accompanied by Monsieur, officers and ministers. Bailly kneels on one knee and swears the oath of loyalty. He gives the king a beautiful bouquet, made by the women of Les Halles, enveloped in gauze on which is written in gold: 'To Louis XVI, the best of kings."[66] He presents me; next I present my officers.

"I count on your zeal for the establishment of order and tranquility in the capital," Louis declares. [67]

We go to the green salon, next to the bed chamber of the queen. She is not in court dress but is wearing many diamonds and other gems; she receives us in state, seated on a large chair, her feet on a stool; several duchesses in court dress on stools seated on either side, whilst behind is the entire household of Ladies and Gentlemen.[68]

"*La Ville de Paris*," the court official announces. Bailly bows deeply, although it is clear the queen had expected him to go down on one knee. She nods her head in a somewhat unfriendly manner and Bailly gives a short speech in which he speaks of devotion, attachment and of the fear of the people concerning the lack of food.

I present my officers. Her face reddens; she appears moved by a strong emotion.[69] She stammers a few words in a shaking voice. Then she nods her head to dismiss us, to the men's displeasure. We also visit the dauphin, Madame Royale, Monsieur and Madame, Mesdames Élisabeth and Adélaïde, the king's aunts, followed by the ministers, Saint Priest, de La Tour du Pin, Necker, Mortmain, de La Luzerne and Lambert. Finally, we dine, Saint Priest our host. During the meal I go with several representatives to visit the dinner the National Guard of Versailles is giving for that of Paris; to my great pleasure, I find it a spectacle of concord and fraternity.

"Would you be commandant-général of our National Guard of Versailles?" they ask.

"It would not be compatible with that of Paris," I tell them.[70]

After the dinner my men want to be presented to the king. He agrees.[71] They stack their weapons and I lead them, accompanied by the representatives, to the cour du marbre, aware that many of the court fear my military ambitions and what I am now doing.

The king stands on a balcony and accepts flowers from the men. "*Vive le roi!*" they shout. At eight o'clock we arrive back in Paris, which to our immense relief, has been quiet.

August 26. After a week of debate, the National Assembly votes for the Declaration of the Rights of Man and the Citizen which it reserves the right to change when the constitution is finally decreed. Its main part is the rule of law, referred to in nine of its seventeen articles, and which is defined as the expression of the general will, made by the direct or indirect participation of all citizens. Sovereignty rests essentially in the nation. In the eyes of the law all citizens are equal; article one states: 'men are born and remain free and equal in rights.' Article thirteen states that taxation will be 'apportioned equally among all citizens according to their capacity and with no other distinction than that of their virtues and talents.'

Although others have contributed to the declaration, including Mounier, Lameth, Talleyrand, Target and Duport to articles 1 to IX, the comte de Castellane to article X; XVI to Duport and XII to XVI to the Sixth Bureau, much of it is based on what I wrote.[72] Articles one to nine mainly derive from my first five paragraphs. The next eight resemble my next three. Only my last paragraph in which I had suggested the amendment of the constitution by a special convention has been completely abandoned.[73] I feel I can claim that the first Declaration of Rights in the American sense proclaimed in Europe is that which I proposed to the Assembly.[74] The king's assent is now needed.

On the twenty-seventh, the battalions of the National Guard parade from each district to Notre Dame. There is a general benediction and abbé Claude Fauchet, a deputy from Caen, preaches a sermon on the holiness of armed freedom.

Adrienne and Anastasie come with me to many of the church ceremonies to bless the flag. They help with the collections, and Adrienne often prays for the souls of patriots. The tricolor is everywhere, not just worn by soldiers; ladies decorate their clothes with it; men attach it to canes, fobs and buckles and sales of dimity cotton are greatly increasing.

Mounier presents a report as spokesman for the National Assembly's Committee on the Constitution. It declares: 'No act of legislation may be considered law unless sanctioned by the monarch.' The deputies debate with great fervor. Should the king have the right of an absolute veto? Should there be a suspensive veto? The people of Paris also angrily discuss the veto. The orators at the Palais-Royal denounce the absolute veto and I fear an attempt to go to Versailles. On the twenty-eighth there are food riots at Les Halles.

I finally find time to write to my beloved Washington to congratulate him on becoming president: 'I am all the more pleased with your election because his paternal friend, with more disinterestedness and moderation than any other, can test in that post what degree of executive power is needed for the maintenance of liberty in a republic.'[75]

Jefferson will soon be returning to the United States. Washington has granted his request for leave and the Senate has confirmed the appointment of William Short as chargé d'affaires in Paris. On the twenty-ninth there are food riots again at Les Halles; National Guards go there to help subdue the crowds. In the evening of the thirtieth, a messenger arrives from the Commune to tell me there is trouble brewing at the Palais-Royal. Orators at the café de Foy and other cafés facing the garden have claimed that some aristocrats and clergy in the National Assembly are conspiring with some of the people. They say that traitors at the National Assembly want the absolute veto which will make France a slave. They want to prevent the National Assembly from granting the veto to the king and to protect the life of Mirabeau,[76] and have asked the marquis de Saint Huruge, recently released from the insane asylum at Charenton[77] where he was imprisoned with de Sade, to convey their demands to Versailles. It is said that he will lead fifteen thousand men there, to invite the nation to dismiss its unfaithful representatives, to name others in their place and to ask the king and the dauphin to come to Paris for their safety. [78] The Commune has sent a message to Saint Priest, the minister of the king's household, to warn him.

"Give the necessary orders to stop the uprising and to arrest its leaders," the Commune tells me.

I send cavalry on the road to Versailles and block the rue Saint Honoré at the place Vendôme with infantry. I order district commanders not to allow any armed groups to pass under any pretext whatsoever. Saint Huruge is arrested and made to return to Paris.[79] At two o'clock in the morning I report to the Commune that the Palais-Royal is quiet. They send another letter to Saint Priest: 'The precautions taken by Monsieur le commandant has been successful: all is quiet.' At three they leave, and I go home to bed.

Next day, Saint Huruge leads patrols in the Palais-Royal; he comes with a delegation of eight citizens from there to present a protest to the Commune. They are not in session, so Bailly and I meet him.

"It is not suitable to cause a disturbance at the Palais-Royal. Your demands are absurd and dangerous. Make people come together in peace," says Bailly.

"I promise," he replies.

"Why don't you join the National Guard to help keep the peace?" I ask.

He agrees; he becomes a sergeant in the district patrols at the Palais-Royal.

"That was very adroit of you," Bailly tells me.[80]

The delegation, however, become angry when they are sent away and dare to put a finger to their necks to suggest the representatives will be hanged. They print a declaration complaining about the profaning of a residence of a cherished prince honored by the nation by atrocious and bloody acts. They charge me to deploy all the forces of the Commune against people disturbing the public peace.

Chapter 39

Specter of famine and counter-revolution

September 2. The Commune at the Hôtel de Ville wish to give me a yearly salary of 120,000 livres, as well as a payment of 100,000 livres for past expenses.

"The amount appears to me to be much too large, not only in itself but also for the obligation it places on future appointments. I ask for a postponement. At a time when so many citizens suffer, when so many expenses are necessary, I do not wish to increase them unnecessarily. My fortune suffices for my present state. I wish that the 100,000 livres, for this year, should be added to the 50,000 livres, and should be given to help those who have suffered the most for the country."[1]

On the third, the Commune decide compensation for the mayor of 50,000 livres, half that I have been offered, which they continue to want me to accept.

"In persisting to refuse, I am not affecting a false generosity...My fortune places me above need. It used to be considerable. It has sufficed for two revolutions and if there should come a third, it will belong to the people in entirety," I reply.[2] After this, there is no longer any question of receiving the money.

Paris continues to ferment with unrest concerning the question of the king's veto. I am busy night and day attempting to keep the city peaceful, as well as directing the National Guard, so I am unable to participate in the heated debates on the constitution at the National Assembly in Versailles. Deputations come to the Hôtel de Ville asking either for a referendum on the issue, as Loustalot is demanding, or for the National Assembly to pass a resolution of neutrality. I fear riots; I order mounted patrols to the Champs Elysées and warn those at the Palais-Royal.

My view is influenced strongly by my experience in America. I would like two elected chambers which are not permanent, but I know that some of my closest friends would vote against me. I do not want the power of an absolute veto to be given to the king, but I would accept a suspensive veto. I would happily see a senate elected for life, if it is a way to unite the patriots, but I do not want a hereditary senate.[3] Mounier, Lally, Mirabeau and Malouet all support an absolute veto and I do not like to see such division between the patriots. I hope all differences can be reconciled. I am prepared to sacrifice my own convictions in order to be united against the enemies of the Revolution. Whatever is finally decided by the Assembly I will attempt to enforce as commandant-général of the National Guard of Paris.

I write to Jefferson to ask him to break every engagement to give a dinner to myself and seven members of the National Assembly whom I wish to agree together on the veto as being the sole means to prevent a total dissolution and civil war. I tell him the only way to unite them is to find some way for a suspensive veto which is so strong and so complicated as to give the king a due influence, and that if they do not agree in a few days we shall have no great majority in favour of any plan and it must end in a war as the discontented party will unite either with the aristocratic or factious people.[4]

September 7. Paris is quiet. I embrace La Salle in the place de Grève when he comes to the Hôtel de Ville to thank the Assembly for his release, which was ordered yesterday.

At four in the afternoon, I meet Duport, Barnave, Lameth, Blacons, Mounier, La Tour Maubourg, and d'Agoult at Jefferson's house, the hôtel de Langeac. The cloth is taken off the dining table; wine is placed on it; we debate. Duport, Lameth and Barnave want a single chamber. Mounier wants an English-style House of Lords or a Senate for life nominated by the king but would be content with an elected Senate if the chamber did not have a majority from among the patriots. [5] We discuss until ten o'clock and finally decide that the king should have a suspensive veto on the laws, that there should only be a single body for the legislature which should be chosen by the people.

Jefferson is silent. He believes we debate well without any gaudy tinsel, rhetoric, or declamation, worthy of being placed in parallel with the finest dialogues of antiquity, such as given to us by Xenophon, Plato and Cicero.[6]

Agitation continues. I post more men at the bridge over the Seine at Sèvres to stop people going to Versailles. I send patrols to the Palais-Royal but cannot use much force.

There is a rumor I have asked the ministers to accept the suspensive veto, but what I wish is to prevent a plan which I believe emanates from those around the duc d'Orléans to manipulate the current unrest and place the National Guard under his control.[7] I am confident my popularity would defeat them, but I do not want any large force in hands other than those of the king, which if they were mine would make me more powerful than he. I want a strong constitutional monarchy. I want two chambers. I want the Upper House to have the exclusive right to initiate legislation and if a bill is passed twice, it should then go to the Senate, which might have a veto of at least one year's duration. I believe the king's veto should only be suspensive; I prefer the royal veto to be binding on two successive legislatives but could be overridden by a two-thirds vote in the chamber of representatives of the third legislature. I would also like many small provincial assemblies, directly responsible to the central authority. I hope this appeals to the court, to Mounier, and to those who wish an English-style constitution, but this has not so far been the case. I am indignant that I am accused of asking ministers to support a suspensive veto. I have asked nothing. I try to be impartial.

I fear France is becoming more divided. We need a plan which would unite the majority and would bring about a constitution. I suspect a conspiracy and am constantly on guard against it. Pamphleteers and journalists virulently attack Mounier and his allies. Camille Desmoulins in *Les Révolutions de France et de Brabant*, denounces the supporters of the veto as aristocrats who wish to preserve the monarchy.

The summer has been hot; rivers and streams are low or even dried up. Watermills frequently cannot work, and the supply of flour is greatly reduced adding to the unrest. Riots are constantly happening, often involving women. There is a rumor that city officials want to starve the people and bakers live in fear they will be hanged from lamp posts.

In the morning of September 8, I address the Commune and report the measures I have taken for the organization of the companies and for the distribution there of the soldiers attached to the Commune. I propose a reform of the criminal procedure, which Bailly has already several times rejected.

"Such a notable change would bring about a serious interruption in the administration of justice, which it would not be sensible to provoke politically now. We are in a time of great unrest, when justice needs to have all its severity and very actively repress disorder," he has always argued.[8]

The Assembly adjourns until the afternoon. I return to try again. Finally, in the evening, my motion is carried.[9] The Commune agrees to petition the National Assembly that an accused should be granted counsel, have a public trial, receive notice of the charges against him, have access to the evidence, and be sentenced to corporal punishment only by a two thirds' vote of the magistrates who tried him. There are rumors the king and the ministers are very displeased with me over what is happening in Paris concerning the veto, although they also blame Duport.

There are also unfortunate rumors that the king intends to leave Versailles with his court and go to Metz. If this happens, Paris will probably rise in revolt.

I write frankly to La Tour du Pin:

There will be trouble if the court is not happy with me. I talked this morning to the Commune about the necessity to punish the troublemakers and have complete submission to the National Assembly...I am accused of wanting to protect my friends, but I demand public trials. I am accused of threatening Versailles, but I am withdrawing my troops. I am accused of trying to influence decisions, but I do not even go to the National Assembly and only use my influence to protect its members and facilitate the liberty of its opinions...I have done what I ought to as a good Frenchman and a friend of peace. I do what I ought to as commandant-général of the only army which dares to show itself.

Anyone other than me would have lost popularity a hundred times...Surely the court lost faith in me when I made my declaration of rights and when I asked for the enlistment of the takers of the Bastille? I was delighted to learn that you are at the head of the councils and armies of the king...You will not be displeased with me. I have calmed the unrest...but I wish that the king would seize all opportunities to please Paris...is it true that M. d'Estaing announces the wish of the king to go to Metz? The government needs to reassure us with openness, with details...I will do what I can for it as much as possible without harming the interests of our dear liberty...P.S. I am too strong today to be joking. [10]

On September 10, the National Assembly decides the national legislature would be permanent, would hold regular annual meetings, with or without the approval of the king, and would consist of one chamber, by four hundred and ninety votes to eighty-nine.[11] The veto is still being very hotly debated. There seems no hope that the patriots can come together. I write to La Tour Maubourg: 'Our society needs to stop voting against Mounier. I prefer an executive power a little too strong, a hundred times more than the plan of federative provinces which will divide France into bits.'[12]

I fear unrest. There are disturbances at the Palais-Royal which the National Guard suppress.

On the fifteenth, the National Assembly votes for the suspensive veto by six hundred and seventy-three votes to three hundred and fifty-two.[13] There are now four groups: Our society; Mounier and his anglophile supporters; the aristocrats; and the faction. On the sixteenth, six thousand rifles and bayonets which had been asked for by the Assembly of Representatives in August, arrive from the Royal Arsenal. There are now four thousand eight hundred men in paid companies. I visit them. I eat with them. I resolve disputes. I demonstrate how a single man, unaided, can load and discharge a cannon.

Gouvion, La Colombe and Poirey live with me at the rue de Bourbon and I pay twenty-five volunteers to be my bodyguard. It has also been expensive to equip myself as commandant-général, even my white horse cost one thousand five hundred louis; Jacques-Philippe Grattepain-Morizot estimates my wealth is now 108,000 livres a year, whereas it was 118,000 livres in 1783. The Revolution will probably cost me a quarter of my fortune.

On the seventeenth, at four-thirty, I go to the hôtel de Langeac for a last dinner with Jefferson before he leaves France. Condorcet, La Rochefoucauld and Morris are already there.

"Some troops of the National Guard are marching to Versailles tomorrow to press for the decisions of the Estates-General," I tell them.

"Will your men obey you?" asks Morris.

"They do not want to stand guard when it rains, but I believe they would follow me into action," I reply.[14]

We spend most of the dinner talking about the threat of famine and the unrest it is producing.

"Perhaps I can come to talk with you about importing food from America?" says Morris.

"Dine at my house," I reply.

I do not stay long; I am too busy. I go to order troops to the bridge at Sèvres to help prevent any advance towards Versailles. I write to Saint Priest to say what I have done. I write to d'Estaing, commander of the National Guard at Versailles, to tell him there have been reports of one thousand eight hundred French Guards and discontented people who wish to come to Versailles which I might not be able to prevent.

September 18. Unrest is increasing because of the lack of bread. Women stop five carts of grain at la place des Trois Mairies and bring them to the Hôtel de Ville; anxious deputations come from the districts to complain and propose solutions. Adrienne insists we only eat dark bread or rye at home.

'Paris is in danger of hourly insurrection for the want of bread...The group of the aristocrats is sowing dissensions in the National Assembly and distrust out of it...the patience of the people is worn thread-bare...civil war is much talked of and expected,' is Jefferson's opinion.[15]

The king replies to the Declaration of the Rights of Man and the Citizen, as well as to the decrees in August. He says he approves, in general, of the spirit in which they have been passed, but has many reservations concerning issues such as the redemption of the tithes, seigneurial dues and hereditary offices.

The Assembly of the Representatives becomes a new body composed of three hundred members, five from each district. People call it the Assembly of Three Hundred.

Since the night of August 4, people have been trying to help France in whatever way they can, and women have been particularly prominent. Earlier in the month, Madame Moitte and other painters' wives, dressed in white, went to the Assembly to offer their jewels to the nation. People have been donating possessions, even silver buckles on shoes, and the king has donated most of the royal silverware to the Mint. Camille Desmoulins' journal *Les Révolutions de France et de Brabant*, publishes lists of donations.

On September 21, the king orders the publication of the decrees but does not agree to them. He also, very unfortunately, says special consideration must be given to the rights of German princes in Alsace. Anger erupts at the Palais-Royal and in the press. Is this a royal coup? Is the king attempting to keep Absolute Rule? Rumors abound and people become even more fearful when Mounier becomes president of the National Assembly and Saint Priest orders the regiment of Flanders to Versailles.

A royal lieutenant, Morel, comes to see me at the Hôtel de Ville. "Four thousand men with one thousand eight hundred horses, some from the prince de Condé, are being gathered, and along with musketeers and gendarmes they will comprise about nine thousand two hundred men. They wish to seize Versailles, dismiss the National Assembly, take the king to a military post, capture the duc d'Orléans and kill Bailly and you. La Montagne, the chief of the voluntary cavalry at the Tuileries is in the plot. If they do not succeed at Versailles they are going to retreat to Montargis and be joined there by the prince de Condé and baron de Vioménil, who will bring troops from Alsace. They hope to summon twenty-five thousand men and start a civil war, funded by the clergy."

"Thank you for your information. You are a good citizen," I tell him. [16]

More rumors of plots spread through Paris; Mirabeau is talked of as mayor. People are in even greater fear of starvation; deputations come to the Hôtel de Ville complaining of spoiled grain being sold in the Halles.

I meet at the Tuileries with military officers. "How can we help the poor and the hungry this winter?" I ask. We decide to create a fund to which members of the National Guard of Paris will contribute and which our wives will manage.

On the twenty-second, Adrienne, George and a cavalry guard of honor go to the church of Saint Etienne du Mont for the blessing of the flag of the local battalion. "You are with your family as the family of the marquis is of all humanity," they tell her.[17] Adrienne sponsors a collection for people in debt in prison. People sing and recite poems.

Morris arrives at my house as arranged, but I cannot stay for dinner. "I am too busy," I tell him. "However, I very much support your plan to import food into Paris." I hurriedly leave to meet officers of the law to try and bring about criminal law reform, a great necessity as the soldiers sometimes refuse to arrest people because sentences are so extreme.

On the twenty-fifth, the Assembly decrees that the nobility, the clergy and others, must pay direct taxation.[18]

September 27. At ten-thirty I come out of the Hôtel de Ville with my staff to join fifty men and all the officers who are waiting in the place de Grève; we march towards Notre Dame for the blessing of the standards of the sixty battalions of the National Guard of Paris. Bands play, the soldiers hold a standard from each battalion, troops line the route, cheering spectators massing behind them. We reach the cathedral square, the officials group around Bailly. I and my officers pass in review before them, so showing our submission to civil authority. The officers go to stand in the nave with their standards, thirty on either side.

Bailly and I enter the cathedral together, in front of the Commune, drums beating, military instruments playing, tapestries on the walls sent by the king from Versailles for the occasion. We sit down to applause, in front of the choir on the right, opposite the orchestra. Adrienne is seated next to Madame Bailly, with other women, the first time the mayor's wife has appeared in public.

Leclerc de Juigné, the archbishop of Paris, says the Mass, then sits between Bailly and I, to applause. The flags are brought to him. He blesses them to cheers and the firing of guns even although we are in a church, and to the obvious anxiety of many. The officers swear an oath. The drums beat again, music plays; it is a very imposing spectacle.

Abbé Fauchet gives a sermon: "Do everything for liberty; do everything for our goodness. Rich people are the enemies of the people and liberty and there is surely more danger than prudence in rousing the people who have nothing against those who have; that saps society by its principal base, propriety."

Finally comes the *Te Deum*. Then I, Bailly, and twelve of the representatives dine with the archbishop.[19]

Next day, Adrienne and I give most of our silverware, valued at forty-eight marcs, to help the national debt. It is one of the largest donations. Jefferson leaves Paris for England, from where he will sail to America.

September 30. Lieutenant Morel comes to see me again. "The queen knows about the conspiracy, as well as Saint Priest, d'Estaing, and several generals and deputies of the National Assembly. They all hope the king will join them and they have obtained weapons."

I give him a written and secret document authorizing him to spy for me. I also pay Coulon de Thévenot, who has invented a technique to write more quickly, to sit in the National Assembly's meetings and give me reports. The press talks about a royal plot.

Montmorin, a friend of the king, and the minister of foreign affairs, whom I have known since I went to Spain, comes to see me.[20] He is fearful of the Orléanist faction.

"Would you consent to not only become *connétable*, but also *lieutenant-général* of France?" he asks.

"This rank would add nothing to my standing in France, nor to my determination to defend the king against the attempts of Monsieur, duc d'Orléans. I believe that if there is an unforeseen plot the king should leave Versailles for Paris, where the National Guard would quickly look after his safety."[21]

He leaves. I talk about his proposition with Adrienne, as well as with friends.

Mounier visits. He also wants me to become *connétable*. I again refuse.[22]

The specter of famine continues. I have ordered that all flour should be taken directly to the flour market, but there is often fighting at the city gates to take flour to the districts. I talk again with Morris about importing American foodstuffs.

I am very fearful of a counter revolution supported by the regiment of Flanders, the *gardes du corps*, some nobles, and even perhaps the National Guard of Versailles. Many share my suspicions and there are increasing demands for citizens to go to Versailles. Soldiers guard routes leading there, but deputies complain as they think the supposition of danger might influence people.

Chapter 40

March to Versailles

October 2. The simmering cauldron of Paris is spitting and boiling with even more anger than usual because people discover that officers from the newly arrived regiment of Flanders were yesterday given a banquet by the officers of the *gardes du corps* in the large theater at the end of the chapel gallery in the Château of Versailles.[1] This is the custom, but there is fear of famine so the spectacle of the royal soldiers feasting is enraging many.

The king returned from hunting at Meudon and he, the queen and the five-year-old dauphin came to sit in the center box during the dinner,[2] whereupon the band played the refrain from *Richard Coeur de Lion*: 'Oh, Richard, oh my King, the world abandons you!' It is said the tricolor was trampled on, white cockades were worn, as well as the black cockades of the queen, there were shouts of 'Long Live the King!' and 'Down with the Assembly', and there is even talk of an orgy.

Les Révolutions de France et de Brabant of Desmoulins, *L'Ami du Peuple* of Marat and Loustalot's words in the *Révolutions de Paris* are adding fuel to the fire. I hear of attacks on people with more royal patriotism than sense flaunting white or black cockades. Violence and demonstrations seem likely; the representatives decree that paid companies should remain under arms and battalion commanders should summon as many citizens as possible.

Morris is one of my guests at dinner; after we dine, I talk with him about American products.

"Go on Monday with Mr. Short before the new committee to give it an air of diplomacy to try and import foodstuffs into France," I tell him.

"Would you write to me what you want as well as to Mr. Short," he requests.

We discuss the unrest here in Paris. "You must immediately discipline your troops to make them obey you," he says. "The nation is accustomed to being governed and it is necessary she should be. If you expect to lead them by affection you will be mistaken."[3]

"I partly agree with you," I reply.

"As the parties are extremely divided, I believe you should attach yourself to that of the king, the only one which can be dominant without danger to the people."[4]

I look at him with amazement.

"I can give you proof," he says.

Mazzei arrives; he joins our conversation and Morris says no more about his aristocratic sympathies.

On Sunday, October 4, I review, as usual, a division of the National Guard on the Champs Elysées. Afterwards, several soldiers bring a defiant-looking man to me.

"He is wearing a black cockade as well as a tricolor," they complain.

"I have the right to wear it!" he protests, and I notice he has somewhat unfortunately placed the black cockade above the tricolor.

"I know of no regulation that says a soldier cannot wear the queen's colors, but as his first loyalty is to the nation, he must, at least, wear the tricolor above the black," I say.

The soldiers go away quietly, but I feel it unlikely their comrade will survive the rest of the day without being attacked, or worse, hung from a lamp post.

I return to the Hôtel de Ville and learn that people are shouting at the Palais-Royal that there is a conspiracy to stop bread reaching the citizens and they must march to Versailles to get bread and stop a counter revolution.

"Send more troops to reinforce those in the place de Grève," I order.

"Some representatives will stay here in the building overnight," Moreau de Saint Méry tells me.

October 5. At nine o'clock in the morning, he unexpectedly arrives at my house, his plump face creased with anxiety.

"Market women with pikes, cudgels and knives are in the place de Grève, demanding to speak to either the mayor or the representatives about bread. The tocsin was rung from the church of Sainte-Marguerite, which brought more people, and soldiers advised me not to risk going to the Hôtel de Ville."

"I will make no concessions to the demonstrators. I will go there immediately," I say.

Jean Le Blanc is quickly saddled; my men scramble to get ready. We set off. Near the Seine a furious human flood, armed with pitchforks, knives, cudgels and a variety of improvised weapons, pours along the streets, entrapping us. Even my huge horse cannot force his way through; for nearly two hours we creep at snail-pace towards the place de Grève.

A strong smell of smoke greets us. An immense crowd, mainly women, is surging against mounted soldiers guarding the Hôtel de Ville, the closely packed ranks rippling and swaying as more people arrive, extending into nearby streets and onto the embankments. "Bread!" they chant. "Versailles!"

I see with relief no one is strung up on a lamp post. I push through the throng which opens to let me reach the soldiers at the front steps. A few minutes later, I am in the calm of the building.

"I ordered reinforcements and stationed cavalry at the entrance, but the demonstrators managed to get in by a back door. They ransacked and set fire to several rooms, but we have chased them out. I think the crisis has passed although they have taken muskets and two cannon," Gouvion says.

I go to the police committee room and preside over a meeting with several representatives.

"I will not go to Versailles. I will order the National Guard not to go there," I declare.

A message arrives: 'Antoine-Joseph Santerre, commander of a battalion, went to Bailly's house with some soldiers from the National Guard and tried to persuade him to go to a small house in the country.'

"I am suspicious," I say.

The others agree; we decide to send an armed escort to fetch him; I give the order.[5]

At about noon, we receive another message: 'An armed mob of women with two cannon set off for Versailles about two hours ago, led by Stanislas Maillard.'

"We must notify the ministers and the National Assembly," I say.

"I will deliver it," cries Claude-Toussaint Fissour, a young representative.

I start dictating. "We know of no reason for this outbreak, other than the ferment caused by people wearing cockades which are not the revolutionary colors, and the fear of a bread shortage. Weapons have been taken from the Hôtel de Ville and an armed mob is thought to be going towards Versailles. Monsieur le commandant-général has restored order in the Hôtel de Ville and is in the process of restoring quiet in Paris."

Reports arrive of rioting in different districts. "This has not just happened spontaneously. It has been planned," I say.

Grenadiers, former French Guards, suddenly burst into the police committee room where abbé Fauchet is presiding, followed by an immense crowd shouting "Lafayette!".

"What is the problem?" I ask.

"My general," replies lieutenant Mercier, a grenadier. "The people do not have bread. The committee of subsistence is misleading you. We do not believe you are a traitor. We believe that the government is betraying you. We cannot fire on women who are asking for bread. We are in a situation which can't last. There is only one way to make it end. Let us go to Versailles. It is said the king is an imbecile. We will depose him. We will have a regency. You will be regent, and everything will go well."

"What! Do you intend to wage war on the king and force him to abandon us?" I reply.

"My general, the king will not leave us. We have Monsieur the dauphin. It is useless to try to convince us. All the grenadiers, all our comrades, think the same. You will not change us."

I immediately again suspect a conspiracy. I think the idea of regent has been suggested to them without a name, and they have naturally thought of their commander.[6]

"General, we must go to Versailles. That is the source of the evil. That is what the people want us to do," they keep saying.

I continue to talk, but they do not change their minds. I go outside with them and try to speak to the crowd.

"Versailles! "Versailles!" people shout, drowning my words. I am completely impotent. At two o'clock I abandon the struggle. I go back inside the Hôtel de Ville and give last instructions to Fissour who sets off.

Reports arrive that more groups of armed people are on their way to Versailles.

"I expect the women will be dealt with by the royal forces," I tell the representatives. "However, the situation appears to be worsening, with greater numbers now going. There are also many National Guards who want to go there, partly because of pride in the national cockade and partly because they want to safeguard the king and bring him to Paris, and they are now being reinforced by the grenadiers. We must alleviate the bread problem. That might calm the crowd as it is one of the main demands."

"Strengthen the guard at the city gates where convoys of grain are expected and send a detachment to Mantes where some of the *basoche* troops are attempting to stop flour being stolen. Try to retrieve as much of it as possible," the representatives order me.

"I should also be authorized to use all the military means in my power to increase the threshing, milling and transporting of breadstuffs," I reply.

"Have your division commanders dispatch troops to rural areas to buy wheat at a fixed price and have it milled and brought to Paris as quickly as possible," they instruct.

"Send ten detachments of twenty men from each of the sixty battalions to search for wheat throughout the nearby countryside," I order.

Bailly's carriage, escorted by soldiers, appears at the far end of the square. He makes a plea to the mob, but they treat him the same as they did me and he retreats into his carriage. A short time later, he manages to enter the Hôtel de Ville and goes to the grande salle to discuss the situation with the representatives.

From the window I see more people with pikes, pitchforks and other makeshift weapons coming into the place de Grève and can hear a steadily increasing din of furious voices. I go outside with some of my officers. I mount my large white horse and ride among the grenadiers.

"I am not going to Versailles! I forbid the National Guard to go! Remember your oath! I know your loyalty! I pledge my own readiness to die in defense of liberty!"[7]

"To Versailles!" "To Versailles!" is the only response. Rain starts to fall but does not dampen the aggressive spirit of the crowd. Some aim guns at me.

"If you do not come with us, we will have our own leaders," a man shouts.

"Take him to the lamp post!" cries another and someone throws a rope over a lamp post.

I am almost a prisoner. I argue and argue. "Hang him!" people shout. Time and again they hang a rope from the lamp post. They push and hit me,[8] my aides constantly running backwards and forwards to the Hôtel de Ville to say my life is in danger.

At four o'clock another report arrives: 'The women have been followed to Versailles by several thousand men and women armed with guns, pikes, and two or three cannon.'[9]

I send an aide to the representatives with the message: 'I can no longer resist the demand to lead troops to Versailles. I will lose control of the National Guard if I do not agree. I also need to try and avert the violence there will obviously be against the king and the royal family, as well as others. I need your authority to do this.'

I am still on horseback when their reply comes back almost immediately: 'We express confidence in the zeal and loyalty of the National Guard of Paris to prevent or to repress disorder. The desire of the people and the representation made by the commandant-général means that it is important to comply with the advice. We therefore pass a resolution to authorize and order the commandant-général to go to Versailles, taking the necessary precautions for the safety of the city he is leaving behind.'

Four commissioners will accompany me to show the civil nature of the military advance and to make certain requests of the king, the most important being that he should come to live in Paris.

"March!" I order.

A large contingent of men carrying pikes, axes, swords, knives and the occasional pitchfork, tramps forward from the west of the Hôtel de Ville. Then come, in correct military formation, four corps of grenadiers and fusiliers commanded by the duc d'Aumont. Next march the National Guards from the place de Grève. Drums beat; standards are raised; the ranks open for me to lead several battalions,[10] accompanied by Gouvion and my staff.

We approach the quai Pelletier, wind buffeting us, rain falling heavily from a funereal sky on to the dark artery of the Seine. Hordes of spectators, oblivious to the weather, stand or rush excitedly along the roads and acclaim the procession. We pass the Pont Neuf; we come to the Tuileries where even elegantly dressed people applaud with delight. The column marches through the place de Louis XV to the gate at La Conférence. Ahead is the road to Versailles. Twenty thousand men march forward. Will the regiment of Flanders attack? Will I have to lead my troops into battle?

I receive word the first mob of women has reached the hall of the National Assembly and that some tried to get into the château but were stopped by the *gardes du corps*. Eight were taken to see the king who has said he will order all bread at Versailles to be collected and given to them. There was a skirmish; a citizen from Paris has been killed and Monsieur de Savonnières, an officer of the bodyguard, had his arm broken. [11]

At Auteuil I send the officers Villars and Desperrières ahead to see if the bridge over the Seine at Sèvres is being defended against our advance.[12]

"Return if it is, but if not, ride to Versailles and tell Mounier and the ministers I am coming on orders from the representatives to maintain order, to respect the king, with no hostile purpose."

They do not return. I assume the bridge is not guarded. We continue. We reach the bridge at Sèvres. I halt the column. The soldiers, but not the officers,[13] of the regiment of Flanders, send a message from Versailles to ask my orders. I tell them to remain in their barracks; I also quickly dispatch a message to Adrienne saying that the regiment of Flanders will not fight. 'Do not worry,' I tell her. 'Inform anyone else who might be interested.'

We cross the Seine, our Rubicon.[14] "Attack everyone who opposes us," I order.

We reach the small village of Montreuil. The rain stops. The moon shines brightly.[15] I again halt the column.

I address the men. "I wish you to swear an oath to the Nation, the Law and the King." [16]

They pledge, their voices reverberating through the evening air.

At Viroflay I receive word from Mounier that the king has unconditionally accepted the decrees.[17] At almost the same time, I receive word from a royal officer: 'His Majesty is glad to know of Lafayette's approach and has accepted the Declaration of Rights.'[18]

Lieutenant colonel Lecointre and the comte de Gouvernet of the National Guard of Versailles ride up.

"We place ourselves and our men at your disposal. We have already offered to do so to the duc d'Aumont with the vanguard of your army which has reached the place d'Armes just outside the Château."

"Tell your men to receive their Paris comrades with distinction," I reply.

The battalions which started late from Paris have now caught up with us as I deliberately made our march slow; the citizens with their makeshift weapons have been persuaded to let the fusiliers and grenadiers precede them. It seems unlikely we will be attacked.

"March at the double!" I order.

Shortly before midnight, we reach Versailles. The soldiers march six abreast down the avenue de Paris, flaming torches and moonlight showing the way. There is silence, the only sounds those of tramping feet and the beat of the drums. Our numbers are so great that although the men are marching quickly it takes an hour to come near to the National Assembly at the hôtel des menus plaisirs. I halt the troops and leave my senior officers in command. I enter the building, accompanied by the representatives, Broussais de la Grey and Louis Lefèvre, to offer my respects to the president.

Men and women from Paris, some drunk, are chaotically and raucously mingling with the Assembly who are debating the code of criminal practice. I walk to President Mounier who is standing with a few deputies.

"It was impossible not to come, but we come in peace. The troops have sworn allegiance to the king. The possibility of famine and anger because of the supposed events at the banquet for the regiment of Flanders have roused many who have followed those intent on causing trouble. I believe much money has been given out to influence people."

"If you have peaceful intentions, what do you want?" he demands.

"I hope that calm can be restored if we go to the Château and the *garde du corps* offers an apology as well as adopt the tricolor cockade. The National Guard can replace the *garde du corps* and it would be helpful if the regiment of Flanders is sent away and if His Majesty displays sympathy with the national cockade."

I speak only very briefly. The representatives and I leave. I ride with my staff to the place d'Armes where d'Aumont has stationed the vanguard. Behind us our army fills the avenue de Paris as far as the hôtel des menus plaisirs. More men are still arriving; I give the order they must swear their oath of loyalty again.

I walk towards the cour des ministres, the courtyard of the Château, which is filled with Swiss Guards.[19] Many grenadiers and my staff follow, worried that I am going into a trap.

The gate to the courtyard is shut and padlocked. "We wish to enter. Your honor and mine require me to give the king proof of my devotion."

"I am surprised you wish to come in," declares their captain.

"Monsieur, I will always find myself with confidence amongst the brave regiment of the Swiss Guards," I say loudly.[20]

"We will not open the gate. We must send to His Majesty for instructions."

We wait. Finally, the reply comes back. "You can be admitted." The comte de Gouvernet and Mathieu Dumas, director general in the ministry of war, arrive to escort me.

The gate partly opens, but the grenadiers do not want to let me go. I am not sure if some do not trust me, but it is certainly evident they do not trust the king and his ministers. I plead with them for nearly half an hour, as do Gouvernet and Dumas. At last I persuade them. I slip through the half-opened gate, but they grab hold of my hands through the grill as it shuts. Gouvernet and Dumas help to pull me free; the two representatives and I walk towards the cour royale, the inner courtyard, Gouvernet and Dumas almost carrying me, I am such a state of exhaustion.[21]

"Do not do anything foolish," I tell the guards.

I cross the guard room and the antechambers; courtiers, ministers and many others, including the duc d'Ayen, watching in grim silence. I am covered with mud from my head to my boots; I am calm. People crowd round me.

"Here comes Cromwell!" Monsieur de Hautefeuille cries out in the salon of the oeil de boeuf.

I stop. I look directly at him. "Cromwell would not be here alone!" I reply with dignity.[22]

I am taken into the king's chamber where Louis is seated, surrounded by d'Estaing, Provence, Necker, Champion de Cicé and others. He appears friendly.

"Sire, I thought it was better to come here to die at the feet of Your Majesty than to perish in vain at the place de Grève," I say respectfully, in such fatigue I can hardly stand.[23] "The representatives and I have come to show our love for your sacred person. We will shed the last drop of our blood for your safety. Twenty thousand men have come to Versailles in obedience to the popular will. I was not able to stop them, but they have sworn an oath to remain under the strictest discipline."

"What do they want?" he asks.

"With the most profound respect we wish that the National Guard of Paris and of Versailles should alone guard his sacred person, that special ministerial decrees promise the citizens of Paris food during the coming winter, that a court system should be provided to improve trials, that the king should cooperate with the Constituent Assembly, and that he should come to live in the Tuileries, the most beautiful palace of Europe, in the middle of the largest city of his empire, and among the greatest number of his subjects." [24]

"I would like you and Monsieur d'Estaing to talk together about the National Guard serving as my bodyguard and I will follow your joint advice. Earlier today I signed the constitutional decrees. I am also ready to accept the reform of court procedure," he replies. "I wish my ministers to discuss the matter of my living in Paris. I will give an answer later."

"I would like to request that my troops should be stationed in the Château," I ask.

"No. The garde du corps will occupy, as usual, the interior; the Swiss Guards will occupy all the posts towards the gardens and the National Guards from Paris can be at the exterior on the side of the town."[25]

I accept this. I leave the king and the ministers.

"What precautions have you taken to secure the château from the gardens?" I ask the comte de Luxembourg, the captain of the garde du corps.

"The garde du corps has been charged with security there," he replies.

I wish to see with my own eyes, so Dumas and I go to the *galerie* from where a large detachment of the guard is visible on the green lawn facing the garden. [26] I leave by the same gate I entered. I shake hands with the officer and soldier on duty there and return to my men. I send an officer down the line to convey the news that His Majesty has given the National Guard the command of the exterior of the Château.

The men are tired and wet after seven hours of marching;[27] churches, the royal stables, the former barracks of the French Guards, and private houses, are requisitioned. I station a battalion near the barracks of the garde du corps and order patrols in the town and around the Château.[28] By two in the morning most of the battalions are lodged and have been given food. Some citizens shelter in stables and coach houses, but most have nowhere and make large fires around which they sing, dance and eat.[29]

At two, I go to the king's apartment, but he has retired to bed. "Please tell His Majesty all is well," I say, knowing my posts are well guarded.

I make my way to the National Assembly where they are still debating the code of criminal practice, citizens singing and shouting around them. Mounier decides not to come to a room to speak to me as that would stop the session, instead he sends Lally-Tollendal and Clermont-Tonnerre.

"The intentions of the National Guard of Paris are good. The posts at the Château are guarded in a way which leaves me no anxiety. I will answer for everything. I am going to rest now," I tell them.

They return to the Assembly and reassure Mounier who adjourns the meeting. I talk to him as he leaves and confirm what I have already said.

"I will reopen the session if there is any cause for alarm," he replies.

"No. Order has been restored, sentries and troops have been posted. I am sure you are as exhausted as I am. I now intend to go to bed. I invite you to follow my example."[30]

I accompany him home with the comte de Virieu; we agree to meet in a few hours' time.[31]

"I believe the evil of today to be the work of a cabal," I say.

"I agree," replies the comte.

I leave Mounier at his home, then I hear of a disturbance at the barracks of the *garde du corps*. I go there with my aide, Jauge, in La Marck's carriage.

A group stops us. "My children, what do you want?" I demand.[32]

"The heads of the *garde du corps*," is the reply. "They have insulted the cockade and must be punished."

"I tell you again," I say. "Stay calm. Trust me, it will be fine."

"Give them three *écus*," I instruct Jauge.

They stop shouting and let our carriage continue, but the incident worries me. I drive back to the château to make sure the soldiers of the garde du corps are not harmed. Near dawn I go with Dumas to see Montmorin. I spend about an hour with him, the comte de Luxembourg joining us, whilst Dumas leaves me to go to my small apartment on the second floor at the hôtel de Noailles, only about a hundred paces from the gate of the chapel.[33]

"Now that the National Guard of Paris is under control, I am worried that they will attack the garde du corps. I have sent a large contingent to the Trianon Palace," says Luxembourg.

He leaves; I talk with Montmorin. I leave. The sky is rapidly brightening; all seems quiet as I make my way towards the hôtel de Noailles. There, I wearily mount the stairs. I speak with Gouvion.

"I have just inspected the posts," he says. "It is perfectly calm. All the entrances to the Château are guarded and the mob of women and brigands has dispersed and is wandering around."

"I have faith in the troops at the exterior of the château and the people have promised me to remain quiet. We need to take urgent measures regarding the policing of Paris," I reply.

"I will ride there shortly," he says and goes to lie down in the doorway so that he can be ready for any alert. I speak with Dumas whilst a servant brings me a bowl of sago and my valet dresses my hair.

We talk about what has happened this terrible day and the measures I propose for the maintenance of order in Versailles. I quickly write the letters to Paris. Dumas leaves. Gouvion is now fast asleep.[34]

The accord between the soldiers has prevented the battle I was fearing. It has gone better than I could have guessed. I had very much feared lawlessness, but I prevented mutiny and the troops have been relatively disciplined. The king received me well and has sanctioned the constitutional provisions. I know I have done my best for him and for the nation. My lucky star has shone many times. I have escaped being hanged or shot. I fling myself down on my bed; I sleep, still in my clothes, exhausted by the last twenty hours.[35]

It seems just a few minutes later a captain is waking me. I notice Gouvion has gone.

"A mob has entered the Château and is attacking the garde du corps and threatening to kill the queen. Two gardes du corps were killed but they stopped the intruders for a short time at the queen's door. She fled to safety and was led to the king by Victor Maubourg."

I leap from my bed; I do not wait for a horse to be saddled. I run towards the Château, followed by my men. "Order the grenadiers at the first post under Cadignan to the Château!"

I jump on the first horse I come across[36]; I gallop frantically, straight into an armed mob parading two heads on pikes and attempting to set fire to about thirty of the gardes du corps. A man with a large beard brandishes an axe dripping with blood.[37]

"I gave my word to the king that there would be no harm done to the gardes du corps. If you make me break my word, I am no longer worthy of being your general. I will abandon you," I shout to my grenadiers.

The rioters surround me belligerently. "Kill him!" one yells.

"Seize him!" I shout in fury. My soldiers drag him towards me, knocking his head on the cobbles.

"Attack!" I order. The grenadiers fall on the would-be assassins and snatch the men. I rush on into the cour de marbre. I must reach the royal family and the fighting. Other units of the National Guard are now arriving. The mob in the courtyard calms.

"Get out of here!" I shout at them.

A few leave by the main gate, but most remain. About eight o'clock I decide the mob has been subdued enough for me to go into the château. There I find the apartments taken over by the National Guard and in the long, inner room of the oeil de boeuf are courtiers, deputies and the three representatives.

"Monsieur, the king accords you the right to enter his cabinet," says a court official.

I enter the chamber. The king, queen, their children, sister, brother and aunts are here. The king appears dazed, the queen is distraught, her eyes wet with tears, her face deathly white. From outside comes the noise of the crowd and occasional shots.

"Sire, would you consent to allow the National Guards who are in your apartments to repeat their oath of loyalty?"

"Yes," says the king.

He and I go to the Oeil de Boeuf and to the other rooms where Gondran's company is in control.

"We swear loyalty to you. We will die for you," the soldiers cry, tears in their eyes, which pleases me greatly as they are men who left his service to join the Revolution.

"My garde du corps is innocent of the insults of which they have been accused," says the king.

It is now ten o'clock. In the cour de marbre, the National Guards stand with fixed bayonets, surrounded by the crowd. "The king on the balcony!" "The king to Paris!" they shout.

"What shall I do?" he asks his advisors. He had already been out on the balcony, before I had arrived, and had been well received.[38]

"We think you should go out again on the balcony, Sire," is their reply.

I stay silent. I do not wish to be seen to be influencing the decision, although it has been my opinion for a long time that the Assembly should be at Paris and that the king would be safer there.

He steps out onto the balcony, accompanied by the queen, their children, Necker, and Champion de Cicé. I stand between the king and the queen.[39]

Applause and cheering greet us. It quietens. "I will go to Paris and entrust myself to the love of my good and faithful subjects," he declares.

The crowd applaud. "*Vive le roi!*" they shout joyfully.

I signal with my hat for quiet. When the noise abates slightly, I address the crowd. "You have been led astray by enemies of the revolution and of liberty!"

The crowd acclaim me. They shout in approval.

The king again speaks to the crowd. "My garde du corps has been maligned. Their loyalty to the nation and to me ought to preserve for them the esteem of my people."

"Can you do something for them?" he asks me.

"Bring one out here," I reply.

A soldier of the garde du corps comes out, three representatives and the king standing next to him. I embrace him; I take off my own cockade and give it to him to wear.

"*Vivent les gardes du corps!*" shout the crowd.

Soldiers of the garde du corps take off their white sashes; they throw away their hats with the white cockades; the National Guards give them their own hats with their cockades.

The crowd does not disperse. "The king to Paris!" "The king to Paris!" they shout; they call threateningly for the queen.

"Madame, what is your personal intention?" I ask.

"I know the fate waiting for me, but my duty is to die at the feet of the king, in the arms of my children," she replies.[40]

"Madame, are you resolved?"

"I am," she says.

"Come out on to the balcony," I tell her, only too aware of the atrocious threats being shouted.

"What! Alone! Have you seen the signs they have made to me?" she exclaims in distress.[41]

"Yes, madame. I will accompany you. Have faith in me."

I go out onto the balcony with her; she carries the dauphin and holds the hand of his sister.

"No children!" shout the crowd.

She takes the children inside. She bravely returns alone. I try to speak but the noise is so great I cannot make myself heard. The crowd is surrounded on three sides of the courtyard by the National Guards who are unable to control the center. They roar. I can even hear shooting.

I bow and kiss her hand, a hazardous, but decisive action. There is complete silence. Shouts erupt. "*Vive le général!*" "*Vive la reine!*"

She retires inside, very proud.

"Go back to Paris now," I tell the crowd, but they continue to shout. "The king to Paris!" "The king to Paris!"

He discusses with his advisors. He decides to go. He and I once more step out on to the balcony.

"His Majesty will carry out his promise and will leave for Paris about noon," I tell the crowd.

"I will," he declares.

More shouts and shots. We go inside once more; Madame Adélaïde, one of the aunts, embraces me.[42]

"Thank you for what you have done for my poor nephew," she says.

"Set off immediately," I order my first division.

The departure of the king will be arranged by his staff. "Some of my *gardes du corps* have been arrested by the people. Can you help them?" Louis asks.

I give an order to release them. I write to Bailly to make sure there is a good reception for the royal family. I sit at a table in the king's cabinet and sign hundreds of passports for people from the château to move to Paris, my signature now valued more highly than that of a royal minister, a very different situation to yesterday.

"I would like to go to Paris rather than to Bellevue with my aunts," says princesse Élisabeth. "Can you please intercede for me?"

I do so. Finally, the king agrees.

I appoint Lecointre as the officer-in-charge of the National Guard of Versailles who will occupy the outer squares and gardens and Captain Gondran from the National Guard of Paris who will replace the gardes du corps in the interior.

The weather is fortunately good. The first division has already gone; at one o'clock I give the order for the rest to set off. I make the people go first, followed by several battalions of the National Guard, which are drawn up along the avenue de Paris. Then comes the king's carriage; d'Estaing and I ride next to it, accompanied by a large enough escort to ensure the safety of the royal family. Then come the carriages of other residents of the Château and some deputies from the Assembly; in the middle is a long line of wagons with flour from the royal household; whilst the National Guard of Paris brings up the rear, thousands of men and women straggling along next to the troops.

"We are bringing the baker, the baker's wife and the baker's boy," some shout in triumph.

"I hope the queen will once more have the affection of Paris," says d'Estaing. "I hope you can give her an opportunity to do so."

"I will try. The factions have made me even more convinced that the king must be defended against those planning to replace him by another. These people have made me a royalist,"[43] I tell him, realizing that the monarch must be defended against those who wish to overthrow him and replace his rule with that of another.[44]

Every so often I halt the procession of about sixty thousand people to allow those on foot to rest. After six hours we near Paris; I send an aide to Bailly to tell him of our approach.

At the gate to Paris, Bailly welcomes the king; he once again presents the keys of the city to him.

"It is always with pleasure and confidence that I find myself among the worthy inhabitants of my good city of Paris," Louis declares.

He and his family wish to go straight to the Palace of the Tuileries, but Bailly and I both think he should go to the Hôtel de Ville. He graciously relents and I ask Moreau de Saint-Méry about the queen.

"It is best if she stays with the king. It is dark and there are many people on the streets. Harm could easily happen to her."

The National Guard march with pride through the streets, lined with a double rank of Guards, people applauding them, lamps and candles in all the windows. *"Vive le roi!"* rings out everywhere, with only a few hostile cries. I send the wounded soldier of the *garde du corps* to my house to be looked after.

At about eight in the evening, we reach the place de Grève, the crowd so immense that the king and queen leave their carriage and go on foot, the deputies and I following them, fearful of what people might do.

Inside the Hôtel de Ville, the king seats himself on the hastily set up throne in the grande salle, his family surrounding him, the representatives very respectful.

Bailly quotes the words the king said earlier. "It is always with pleasure that I find myself amidst the worthy inhabitants of my good city of Paris."

"You have forgotten the word 'confidence,' interjects the queen.

"Messieurs," says Bailly. "By hearing this from the mouth of the queen you are in a happier state than if I had not made a mistake." Everyone cheers. "The National Assembly will soon come to Paris." More cheers sound. [45]

After the speeches the king and queen go onto a balcony overlooking the place de Grève. The crowd roars its delight. Madame Élisabeth clasps my hand. A short time later, I lead the royal cortège escorted by troops from the National Guard to the Palace of the Tuileries. We arrive at nine.

"I owe you more than my life," says Madame Adélaïde. "I owe you that of the king, my poor nephew."

October 7. Gouvion moves out of my house as I have appointed him commander of the forces in the palace of the Tuileries where he will live. I arrange for the injured soldier of the garde du corps Adrienne has been looking after, to be taken to hospital. Then I set off, accompanied by a numerous suite, to the Tuileries for the *levée* of the king. On the way, I encounter the duc de Villeroi, one of the four captains of the garde du corps.

"I took no part in the wrongdoings of my subordinates yesterday," he says.

"So much the worse for you, Monsieur, for they conducted themselves very well indeed," is my reply.[46]

We cross the Seine to the place de Louis XV; we go to the Tuileries. Many people crowd the gardens, shouting, " *Vive le roi!*" " *Vive la reine!*" and calling out for them to show themselves.[47] Soldiers from the National Guard are walking arm in arm with soldiers from the garde du corps, not only in a sign of friendship, but also to protect them.

I enter the dark, drab palace which has not been lived in for many years and seems in complete disorder[48] and am taken to the king. He appears dejected, but I gather his usual good appetite was unaffected by yesterday's events and he dined very well last night.

"Can you give me information on the measures being taken to provision Paris?" he asks Bailly and I.

The queen is sad and tearful. "Thank you, Monsieur Lafayette, for standing by me yesterday in my hour of danger." [49]

I suspect the duc d'Orléans played a part in the revolt and I intend to send him away to prevent him from being able to cause more trouble. I arrange to see him at the home of the marquise de Coigny in the rue de Saint Niçaise. We meet; I speak imperiously. "Your presence in France is causing unrest because ill-intentioned men, abusing your confidence, are using your name to cause trouble. Your departure from Paris would make it easier to keep order."

"I have no intention of leaving," he says.

"It will be dangerous for you to stay in Paris. I will defend the king with my life if necessary. I have contributed more than anyone to upsetting the steps to the throne. The king is now on the last one and I will defend him there against you. You will have to pass over my body and that will not be easy."[50]

Orléans is quiet.

"You can go on the pretext of a diplomatic mission to London. I believe that because of your many English friends you will be capable of serving France well there. The people of the Austrian Netherlands are threatening to revolt against Austria and your appointment will be seen as a sign of confidence in an international crisis."

He is displeased but resigned. He agrees; we part. That evening he changes his mind after speaking to his friends.[51]

Even more people start to pour into the gardens of the Tuileries and the nearby streets, screaming and shouting. We fear a new revolt. The representatives order me to deploy the military force confided to me to prevent dire consequences and ask for the king's help to keep order.[52] I post soldiers and cannon at the main entrances and the gates of the Tuileries, and the king issues a proclamation: 'The commander of the national militia is authorized to preserve peace and invites all good and loyal citizens to give him aid.'

There is a rumor that a mob from the faubourg Saint Antoine is planning to march on Versailles and burn the Château. I send a message to Versailles warning of the danger and station many troops on every road from Paris.

I speak with Mirabeau about the appointment of new ministers.

"I wish to avoid both the aristocrats and the republicans. I particularly dislike Saint-Priest, Duport, de Lameth and Barnave," he says.

"I do not have a preference. I have not yet decided," I tell him.

We both agree it is not yet time, but I realize that when there is a change, he intends to be a minister and will abandon the duc d'Orléans.

I eat dinner at home with my family; at five o'clock I go to the Hôtel de Ville for a meeting of the commune. They stand and cheer me.

"We thank you for the noble, firm and conciliatory line of conduct you have followed during the last few days."

"I thank you for your confidence I would like the representatives to issue an address to the provinces reaffirming the continued respect of Paris for the National Assembly, loyalty to the monarch and fraternal sentiments for the provinces. I wish to show everyone that what has just happened has not divided the king from his subjects."

"We unanimously approve," is the reply.

Market women come into the hall. "We repudiate the unbecoming behavior of the women on October 5. Far from speaking evil of Monsieur Bailly and Monsieur Lafayette we have spoken only good of them and would defend them to the last drop of our blood."

The representatives award them tricolor ribbons and cockades and order their words printed and distributed. Some deputies decide to go back to their regions to attempt to organize opposition to what they perceive as a very worrying situation here in Paris. Mounier returns to the Dauphiné. On the ninth there are threats of riots from many districts and orators are rousing the crowds.

"Put the entire National Guard under arms on special duty," I order.

I send a message to Adélaïde de Simiane that I cannot see her: 'It is hard to exchange supper with you for a revolt, but the black cockades have been followed by an outbreak at the Hôtel de

Ville. It is necessary to arm ourselves and guard it. Someone is trying to starve us, and the situation is black.'[53]

I see the duc d'Orléans again at the home of the marquise de Coigny.

"I insist you leave in twenty-four hours," I tell him bluntly. Again, he agrees; this time I take him to the king, who appears greatly astonished at what I am suggesting.

"I will find out in London who is behind these troubles," says Orléans.

"You are more interested in that than any other as no one is more compromized than you," I reply.[54] "Montmorin will give you your instructions tomorrow morning."

In the evening, many people as usual dine at the rue de Bourbon, including Morris. Afterwards, I talk with him in my study.

"You need a more capable minister than those at the present. I believe the bishop of Autun would be suitable for that of finance," he says.

"He is a bad man and false, "I reply, surprised Morris is suggesting him as I know that he and the bishop of Autun are both lovers of Madame de Flahaut.

"I do not agree," he says. "And if you have the bishop of Autun you are then sure of Mirabeau."

"Surely they are enemies?" I reply.

"You are wrong. According to Autun, the king wants to immediately give you the Blue Ribbon," he says.

"Perhaps you are right," I reply.

"What about Thouret as the *garde des sceaux*?" he asks.

"He has talent, but I doubt the force of his spirit," I reply.

"What about Clermont-Tonnerre?" he asks.

"He is not a man of great value," I reply.

"The coalition I am proposing will remove Necker from the support of the same population which supports him today. He is already frightened and ill."

The duc de La Rochefoucauld arrives; we stop our discussion. [55]

"The National Assembly is coming to Paris," he tells us.

"I will return at nine o'clock tomorrow," says Morris.

On the tenth I receive a letter from the duc d'Orléans to say he has changed his mind again and is not going. I send a message to him to meet me at the ministry of foreign affairs.

During the night the doors of many houses have been chalked red, white or black. It is rumored that red means it is to be burnt, white to be ransacked, and black that the occupants will be killed. The houses of the representatives and the principal officers of the government have been marked.

The king asks me to take command of all the military forces in Paris as well as those within a radius of fifteen leagues in order to provision the capital. He also asks me to deny deserters the right to enlist in the National Guard.

In the Assembly, Talleyrand supports a proposal that church property should be confiscated by the state and that two thirds of it should be used to fund the salaries of the clergy in place of the tithes lost on August 4.[56] Mirabeau believes that the state should have all of it. [57]

On the eleventh I have another conversation with Morris.

"You can't be minister and soldier at the same time, still less minister of each department., and that as to your objections to some because of their morals, it is necessary to consider that it is not possible to regard being minister as a direct route to Heaven. People are driven by ambition and greed, the only way to assure yourself of the help of the most virtuous is to make them interested in acting well," he says.

"I intend to propose Malesherbes as garde des Sceaux" I reply.

"He won't accept," he says.

"He will accept an offer made by Lafayette," I reply.[58] Morris sees I want him to leave, so he departs.

On the twelfth the king agrees to my wish that Mathieu Dumas should be appointed *aide maréchal des logis*. On the thirteenth, I receive word from Orléans, written at daybreak, that he will not leave France. I send him another message asking him to meet me at the office of Montmorin, the minister of foreign affairs. He agrees, somewhat to my surprise.

We meet early next morning. "My enemies can claim that you have evidence against me," he says.

"It is rather my enemies who say so. If I were able to produce evidence against you, I would already have had you arrested. I admit I have looked for it everywhere," I reply sharply.[59]

He gives in for a third time, knowing I have the support of the king and Montmorin.

"I must have a passport. I am a deputy. I will need to ask the National Assembly," he says.

"We would prefer you to ask for it in writing," I tell him, not wanting any public discussion.

He writes a letter to the president of the Assembly to dismiss in advance any attempt at denunciation.

Montmorin also sends a letter there saying it is necessary to have the passport as soon as possible because the prince is about to depart on an important mission for the king. I send an aide with the letter and instruct him to wait for the reply and then bring it back to Paris.

Passports have already been obtained from the Hôtel de Ville for his secretary and the rest of his suite. The police committee signs. I sign and Louis also signs a passport which Montmarin countersigns, all of which greatly pleases me. Orléans finally leaves Paris. I take no notice of the many rumors circulating about what I am doing; I remain steadfast in my effort to rid the country of an enemy to liberty and the king.

I hear that Mirabeau was going to speak on his behalf, but now Orléans has gone he seems to have abandoned him. "They claim that I am in his party. I wouldn't have him for my valet," he is reported to have remarked.[60]

October 15. I meet with Duport, Barnave, de Lameth and Mirabeau at the home of Mirabeau's niece, Madame d'Aragon, at Passy, to discuss the ministries.

"Only the person of the king should be regarded as inviolable," says Mirabeau.

"I will be no party to any hostility against the queen," I retort.

"Very well, general, since you wish it, let her live; a humiliated queen can be useful, but a queen with her throat cut would be good only as a subject for a bad tragedy," he replies, in my opinion deliberately trying to blacken himself.[61]

October 18. I review troops in the rain on the Champs Elysées. The king also attends, leaving the Tuileries for the first time in twelve days. He walks from there wearing a broad hat to avoid being too wet and people appear to take offence at this. However, the five hundred unpaid soldiers of the National Guard I sent to escort him are smart in their uniforms and he is delighted to see them drill.

October 19 is the anniversary of the capitulation of the British at Yorktown. It is also the first day the National Assembly convenes in Paris, at the archbishop's palace. I order all the avenues leading to it to be closed, with barriers, guarded by cannon and many detachments of the National Guard; I station five hundred men on horseback to guard the square before it. There are crowds but they seem to regard the proceedings with a somber or indifferent air.[62] At ten o'clock the National Assembly starts its session.

At about midday, I, Bailly, and a deputation from the Commune, leave the Hôtel de Ville to go to pay our respects to the deputies. We make our way towards the archbishop's palace, escorted by the garde of Paris, as well as soldiers from the National Guard. I wear my uniform of royal blue coat, red collar, white underclothes and epaulettes, as Mirabeau had suggested.

We enter the archbishop's palace; the National Assembly suspends its debate; the deputies and spectators applaud. The president welcomes us. He speaks flatteringly of me: "This hero is a sage, whom only an interest in humanity called to the fields of glory, and who, under the banner of a forever illustrious warrior, seem, like him, to take his lessons from a new Lycurgus."[63]

Mirabeau goes to the tribune. He praises Bailly and I. He declares we had to fear and dare everything. He calls for a vote of thanks to us as an invitation to all good citizens to respect legitimate authority, to facilitate the work of their chiefs, and to inculcate obedience to law and to all the virtues of liberty. Applause erupts. The National Assembly unanimously passes a vote of thanks. Bailly also thanks Mirabeau.

"It belongs more to Monsieur de Lafayette than to me," he says.

I stand and speak, so moved my voice trembles, my eyes fill with tears. "Excuse me, Messieurs, for my emotion. It is a true measure of my profound gratitude."

I pay tribute to Bailly and to the National Guard who have for three months fought the battle for order at my side. I grasp this opportunity to do the National Guard the justice that it has always used its force in a manner befitting the purpose which induced it to take up arms.

During the day three wagons carrying flour are stopped en route to Les Halles; the National Guard   forcibly intervene to defend the chairman of the district committee who wanted their release. The next two days are quiet,[64] but on October 21, the fear of famine again reaps a bitter and gruesome harvest. In the morning an old woman accuses Denis François, a baker, of hoarding a large amount of bread. The National Guard saves him from the fury of the mob and brings him to the Hôtel de Ville. At eight-thirty there are only three police committee members present, but they bravely go into the place de Grève to try and calm the crowd. They do not manage to do so. The mob break into the building. They drag François outside and hang him from a lamp post. Before he is dead, they cut off his head; they stick it on a pike and parade it round the streets.

I am furious that the National Guard at the Hôtel de Ville did not protect him. I summon the district battalions, post cavalry at the Louvre, and order detachments to the archbishop's palace and the Hôtel de Ville.

When Bailly and some of the representatives arrive, they dispatch my aide, La Colombe, and two members of the police committee to the National Assembly to ask for aid to obtain food and the immediate passing of a martial law.

"Without a martial law I cannot answer for the calm of Paris," I declare.[65]

The National Assembly agrees to draft a law concerning riots and to produce a plan for a tribunal to judge cases of treason. It also directs a committee to work with the police committee to discover the reasons for the disturbances.[66]

I tell the Commune the measures I have already taken. They instruct me to find the head of François, which is still being carried around Paris, and to disperse any rioters. I send Lajard, one of my aides to François' bakery. He disperses the crowds, his men using fixed bayonets. Not long after, soldiers from the National Guard arrest the ringleaders of his killers. Reports come of more crowds gathering in the faubourg Saint Antoine, intending to go to Saint Marcel, and attack the monasteries where they believe are weapons and then to come to the Hôtel de Ville to demand that the price of bread should be lowered. The National Guard break up the crowd and arrest the leaders.

The National Assembly passes a martial law which declares that if there is a riot, the authorities should display a red flag; the crowd should be told three times to disperse, and if it does not do so, then force should be used. Duport argues against. He wants the rioters to ask a committee to present their grievances and only if they do not disperse, should force be used. He fails to achieve this; only the elegantly dressed, austere and somber Robespierre opposes the bill,[67] which is passed and sent to the king for his agreement.

I go to the Commune to ask for orders from them if the accused are found guilty and sentenced to death. That night, the man who was mainly responsible for the death of François is arrested. On October 22, he is hanged in the place de Grève. The man who roused the crowds in Saint Antoine is also executed.

There is much criticism of the martial law in the districts; people say it could lead to military excess and there is much heated debate. I order that a military court should investigate what happened. It decides that ten officers and one hundred and eighty men are guilty of disobedience. I cashier all of them. Protests ensue, particularly from the Cordelier district and its president, Georges-Jacques Danton, who want the findings of the military court invalid until most districts had approved the setting up of military committees.[68]

I call a meeting of National Guard officers at my house and ask them to swear loyalty.

"We are the only soldiers of the Revolution; we are the only defenders of the royal family from attack; we are the only ones obliged to preserve the freedom of the representatives of the nation; we are the only guardians of the public treasury."

October 24. The Saint-Roch battalion is the first to take the oath that they would not lay down their arms until I order them to do so or to tell them that the great work of our liberty is completed.[69] The other fifty-nine battalions soon follow.

I hear rumors I am trying to establish a dictatorship. I write to Mounier to ask him to return and not to encourage the Dauphiné to rebel: 'If I perish in my efforts to save my country, at least do not let my last reproaches be for those who, instead of joining together, abandoned us, and whose opposition can make us lose all.'[70]

Chapter 41

Powerful and popular, but enemies circling

November 1. Morris visits at five o'clock and talks about Mirabeau whom he believes would be a dangerous enemy to me if I neglect him, or an even more dangerous friend if I help him in his projects.[1]

"The insult he made recently to a gentleman was so bad that he is ruined by it because he can no longer be in a ministry and the Assembly's view is that he is lost."

"Is there anything more to expect from him," I ask heatedly.

"The bishop of Autun has just expressed the same opinion," he says.

"I don't know the bishop well and would like to know him better," I reply. "Bring him to eat at my house the day after tomorrow." [2]

On November 2 the confiscation of church lands is passed at the National Assembly by 510 votes to 346; they will be placed at the disposal of the nation.[3] On the third, the prince de Poix comes to my house to speak to me favorably of Mirabeau. At nine o'clock, Morris and Talleyrand, the bishop of Autun, arrive. We speak of the riot for bread at the faubourg Saint Antoine and the ways in which food can be provided for Paris.

"I think there should be a committee composed of three ministers, three members of the municipality of Paris and three members of the Estates-General, as there is a man who can provide bread if directed to do so by such a committee," I say.

"I do not think the Assembly would want to be involved," says Talleyrand. "It would not want to run the risk of being responsible for provisions for Paris."

What do you think of a new minister?" I ask.

"Only Monsieur Necker knows how to stop famine and bankruptcy which appears inevitable," he replies.

"Do you think that Mirabeau has a great influence on the Assembly?" I ask.

"His influence is not enormous," he says. "I cannot think of a new minister unless there is a radical change."

"I agree," I reply. "At the present time all the friends of liberty need to unite."[4]

On the fourth, Mirabeau visits me in the evening. I again propose an embassy for him, but he refuses. On the sixth, he moves in the National Assembly that ministers should participate in its discussions. There is much opposition to this and on the seventh the Assembly decrees that deputies are forbidden to enter a ministry, so finishing our various plans concerning ministers and ministries.

Thomas Paine arrives in Paris and frequently visits me. My friend and relation, the comte de Ségur, who has been ambassador to Russia, also arrives.

"I was astonished as soon as I crossed the frontier to see the difference in French people. The changes have been extraordinary. Eight hundred leagues and five years' absence had not prepared me for what I found. Bourgeois, peasants, laborers and even the women, had in their bearing something proud, independent and spirited, which I had never seen before," he says.[5]

"I don't know by what misfortune a party that hides in the dark has come to mix itself with the true people who desire only justice and freedom. Brigands have sprung up from I don't know where, paid by unknown hands, and have committed deplorable crimes by taking advantage of the movements stirred up by the ill-timed resistance of the court and the privileged orders. We tried in vain to drive them away or punish them. They still came back. After the capture of the Bastille they committed dreadful murders. They even threatened to pillage Paris. Only the immediate organization of a National Guard was able to put a check to their disorders. At the same time a small number of them appeared in the provinces and as the false report spread of their near arrival, it aroused such a great dread that the people took up arms. We have made unsuccessful attempts to discover who are the leaders of these brigands. It is a problem which has not been solved. On October 5 these villains participated in the disorders which broke out in Paris owing to what happened at Versailles. While I was trying to re-establish order near the Hôtel de Ville and calm people I was informed that these wretches were on their way to Versailles at the head of a great crowd and threatened the most sinister deeds. When I got to Versailles, they had already besmirched the hall of the Assembly and threatened the Château. The National Guard dispersed them. It all seemed calm. Then, unfortunately, there had been an unwillingness to entrust the National Guard with more than a certain part of the outside posts and towards the end of the night the brigands entered the Château from the garden through a door which was not one of their posts. We happily arrived in time to prevent an atrocious crime. The people had not taken part in that odious conspiracy, but they were very roused and could only be appeased by persuading the king and his family to Paris. I truthfully tell you of these tumultuous scenes which have mixed much sorrow with the lawful hopes of most of the nation for the establishment of a representative government," I tell him.[6]

Ségur visits the king and queen; not long after, the king asks me to write a memorandum on what his council should do to advance the revolution while preserving as much royal authority as is consistent with the national interest. I write that the establishment of a free constitution is the only salvation for the nation and for the king. The king can no longer balance between the parties; on one side is the debris of a powerless aristocracy; on the other is the entire nation the source of his glory, happiness and power. I propose that the court should stop all appearance of constraint and discontent; that it should hold, twice a week, at least, a committee of influential members in the National Assembly to accelerate and regulate what is happening; the work of the Assembly should be the formation of municipalities and provincial assemblies; there should be provisional measures for the re-establishment of calm and provisional support for the finances; there should be the fixation of principles concerning the armed forces; there should be the formation of a judicial system and the creation of a supreme tribunal or of an elective senate; there should be the laying down of the first principles of trade and the basis of a plan for education; the regulation of finances. I say that all the decrees of constitutional power in a general body of constitution will facilitate the change and finish by declaring that the end of the revolution will be marked by my complete abandonment of my political life. [7]

The comte de Moustier, who had been minister of France in the United States, also returns, to my delight bringing me letters from Washington and Hamilton. Washington writes that the revolution in France is 'of such magnitude and of so momentous a nature that we hardly dare yet to form a conjecture about it.'[8] Hamilton says that he rejoices in the efforts which I am making to establish liberty but fears much for the final success of the attempts, for the fate of those he esteems who are engaged in it and for the danger in case of success of innovations greater than will consist with the real felicity of my nation. He dreads disagreements among those who are now united about the nature of our constitution, and the vehement character of our people whom he fears it will be easier to bring on than to keep within proper bounds. He also dreads the interested refractoriness of the nobles who cannot all be gratified, as well as the reveries of our Philosophic politicians. He tells me that he is now head of the finances of the United States and that he will make the debt due to France one of his first tasks. He tells me to be virtuous amidst the seductions of ambitions and then I can hardly in any event be unhappy.[9]

Rumors abound that there will be a counter revolution on November 25. I therefore order the Guards to wear uniform for the next eight days. I double the guard at the Tuileries, call out all my cavalry and order artillery placed near Henri IV's statue on the Pont Neuf to command the Seine and give the alarm. Nothing happens. There is no coup although the rumors continue, and it is said that Bailly and I will be assassinated. On the twenty-ninth, there is a large ceremony on the banks of the Rhône when twelve thousand soldiers of the National Guard from the Dauphiné and Vivarais swear to uphold constitutional freedom. On December 1, Mirabeau writes protesting his fidelity and devotion to me and that he has no other political liaisons. He says that the fatality of my exalted position and personal indecision was blinding me to the impossibility of rendering permanent a state of things that only success can justify. He says that my taste for mediocre men and my weakness for my own views will ruin the most beautiful destiny and, by losing me, will compromise the public good.[10]

I do not reply.

Marat's newspaper, *L'Ami du Peuple*, is very critical of people, policies, and the use of soldiers to arrest debtors. He is arrested and brought to the *comité des recherches* at the Hôtel de Ville. I enter the room as he is being questioned.

"I have been misunderstood," he tells me. "I have never attacked you or your principles. You fought to break the irons of the Americans. Can anyone believe that you wish to put them on your compatriots?"

We talk at some length; he expresses doubt about some members of my staff.

"Who are they?" I ask.

"I will name them later in *L'Ami du Peuple*." [11]

He is released and an escort takes him home.

On December 19 and 21, the National Assembly decrees that a fund will be established, the *Caisse de l'Extraordinaire*, to receive the money from the Patriotic Contribution and from the sale of national lands. Paper currency, assignats, will be issued in 1,000 livre notes, with an interest of five per cent, upon the basis of the anticipated sales to the value of 400 million livres. [12]

I have for a long time been investigating the marquis de Favras who is suspected of counter revolutionary actions. In the evening of the twenty-fourth, I have him arrested and brought to the Hôtel de Ville to be questioned by myself and the *comité des recherches*. Bailly and I discover a letter on him from Monsieur, the duc de Provence, which appears to implicate him in a plot to help the king flee to Picardy, raise troops and kill Necker, Bailly and myself. I immediately go to see Provence at the Palais de Luxembourg and give him back the letter.

"Only Monsieur Bailly and I know anything about this and so therefore you are not compromised, "I tell him, to his delight.

In the morning of the twenty-fifth, Favras is taken to the prison of the abbaye. Early on the twenty-sixth, Monsieur requests to see me and I visit him.

"A note was circulating yesterday evening accusing me of being in a conspiracy," he says in an irritated tone in front of his courtiers.

"I only know one way to discover the authors and that is to offer a reward, which I will do," I immediately say.

In the afternoon, he goes to the Commune. "I have been falsely accused of being at the head of the supposed plot against Monsieur Bailly and Monsieur Lafayette," he declares, his words having been written by Mirabeau.

On the twenty-seventh, I speak privately with Morris and Short in my study and relate the details of what happened.

"Mirabeau is a scoundrel. I now realize the danger of a liaison with him."

"I have already warned you about him," Morris replies. "The comte de Luxembourg asks me to tell you he has sworn to ruin you. Mirabeau has placed advantages in his hands. Monsieur is now at the head of the revolution; he must stay there for if there is a counterrevolution, he preserves the heads of all the others against accidents, and if the revolution is accomplished, the nullity of his character takes away all authority and weight."

"That idea greatly interests me," I reply.[13]

Bailly and I write to the Châtelet to say that one of the two witnesses had denounced the plot, but they decide that the current jurisprudence does not allow this distinction and so the trial can continue.[14]

December 28. A soldier of the National Guard is stabbed while on duty. A stiletto knife is found nearby with a piece of paper with the words: 'Go on ahead and wait for Lafayette.'

Six hundred of the National Guard pledge to avenge any insult to, or any attack, on me.[15]

Favras is indicted. On the twenty-ninth, Malouet visits. He wants to keep the royal power along with constitutional principles in order to avoid anarchy. He wishes me to put myself at the head of the moderates, who want liberty, peace and justice for everyone. I invite La Tour Maubourg and Thouret to join our discussion; Malouet repeats what he has already said. We like what he is saying. We decide we will meet again to discuss further.

Two days later, I go with La Tour Maubourg, Liancourt and Lacoste to La Rochefoucauld's house. Malouet arrives with deputies who usually sit with the right but who appear to wish to reform. It is now clear to us that he represents a formal grouping. I, however, do not want factions. I want agreement between the deputies. We decide however to meet again.

January 1, 1790. I talk with Morris who has arrived before my other dinner guests.

"It is necessary to finish the trial of Besenval because people are starting to take his side and the violence of the torrent can turn against those who pursue him," he says.

"In spite of your criticisms of the Assembly you must recognize the superiority of the new constitution over that of England," I tell him.

"You are really mistaken if you think that is my opinion," he replies.

At dinner we talk of Monsieur and Mirabeau. "They are both closely linked, but one is weak and indolent, the other is an active, clever rascal," I say. [16]

January 2. I lead a deputation of the National Guard to present our respects to the representatives of the Commune, my belief always being to subordinate military power to a civil authority. Next day, I and my friends again meet with Malouet and his associates at the home of La Rochefoucauld. We do not agree. On the fourth, I go to the National Assembly with Bailly. Repeated applause greets us but from one side of the hall only.

My popularity is still immense. There are songs and poems about me, as well as medals, engravings, pictures and acclaim from the patriotic journals. Venom, however, spews out from districts such as the Cordeliers and from the revolutionary press.

The Château and large houses in Versailles have been closed following the king's move to Paris and many have lost their employment. A large crowd gathers in the afternoon of January

7 at the place d'Armes demanding a reduction in the price of bread. The municipality reduces the cost of bread to two sous the pound and the crowd disperses. Next morning, it decides it cannot afford to subsidize it unless the government helps and sends a deputation to Paris. They are advised to raise the price to three sous and the king asks me to send reinforcements to Versailles, which I do. The authorities in Versailles declare martial law and raise the price of bread to two and one-half-sous the pound. The unrest is quelled. On the ninth, the Châtelet sends troops to arrest Marat who flees into the district of the Cordeliers. The same day, the trial starts of the marquis de Favras at the Châtelet. On the eleventh he arrives to testify. Huge crowds gather outside. I order cannon loaded with grapeshot placed there, and cavalry, chasseurs and grenadiers to patrol the streets. There are rumors that explosives have been hidden in my house. I think it unlikely but order a search to be made of it and the neighboring houses. Nothing is found. The rumors continue that Necker, Bailly and I will be killed. The people of the faubourg Saint Antoine want me to move to live in their district as they say I will be safer there than with the aristocrats of the faubourg Saint Germain. At the Tuileries some of the National Guards on duty are treated unpleasantly, as are some deputies of the National Assembly. On the tenth I go to the faubourg Saint Antoine to attend Mass. People surround me grumbling.

"I praise your patriotism; I sympathize with your problems, and I want you to pay less attention to the enemies of the revolution," I say. They quieten. I offer them money.

"We don't want money. Reduce the price of bread," someone shouts.

"I am not in charge of the supply of bread, but I will do everything I can."

"*Vive Lafayette!*" people cry and smother my horse with pats and kisses, all wanting to guard me.[17]

January 11. "Release Favras!" large crowds shout near the Châtelet. There are reports there will be a mutiny of some soldiers of the National Guard because they are against the revolution, they wish to free Favras, and have complaints about their pay. It is said they will assemble on the twelfth, in the Champs Elysées. I arrange for unpaid infantry to assemble in two columns tomorrow in the place Vendôme. I will lead one to the north and west of the Champs Elysées; the duc d'Aumont will lead the other to the east and south; we will be joined by the grenadiers and chasseurs, and I therefore hope to encircle the mutineers. Ruhlières will command the cavalry and intercept any forces from Versailles or Neuilly. I tell the king, but not the Commune as I need to keep it a closely guarded secret.

Information comes next day that men are gathering on the Champs Elysées, and more are arriving. D'Aumont and I set off with our columns, buffeted by a cold winter wind. We reach the mutineers. We surround them.

"You are not worthy to wear your country's uniform," I tell them.

"Mercy!" they cry, falling to their knees.

"Close in," I order. Four men break through and run towards the Seine. One jumps in and drowns.

"Strip them of their uniforms and arms," I order. "Escort them to the military depot at Saint Denis."

I go in the stormy night to the Tuileries to inform the king I have broken the mutiny. Then I go to the Assembly of Representatives. I recount the events of the last few days to applause; they vote me their thanks.

I return home and hastily write a letter to Washington:

I cannot let the packet sail without a line from your filial friend…who wants to express to you those affectionate and respectful sentiments that are never so well felt as in uncommon circumstances-

How often my beloved General have I wanted your wise advices and friendly support. We have come thus far in the Revolution without breaking the vessel of state either on the shoal of aristocraty, or that of faction, and amidst the ever reviving efforts of the mourners and the ambitious, we are stirring towards a tolerable conclusion- Now that everything that was is no more, a new building is erecting , not perfect by far, but sufficient to ensure freedom and prepare the Nation for a Convention in about ten years, where the defects may be mended- I will not enter in all the details I have already related-Common Sense is writing a book for you-There you will see a part of my adventures- I hope they will turn to the advantage of my country and mankind in general- Liberty is sprouting about in the other parts of Europe, and I am encouraging it by all the means in my power...Your most devoted and filial friend, Lafayette. [18]

In the following days people say I acted with much prudence and decision,[19] although some criticize; a poem in the *Actes des Apôtres*, the royalist newspaper, asks 'why the immortal Lafayette thought he had to mobilize ten thousand soldiers just to undress about one hundred and fifty.'[20]

January 21. Bailly orders me to provide men to execute the decree given against Marat who is still   publishing *L'Ami du Peuple*. Next morning, I order Carle, commander of the Battalion of the Barnabites, to help two bailiffs from the Châtelet arrest him. Danton goes to the Assembly with a deputation to protest that it is invalid to do so as the writ antedated the National Assembly's decree to reform criminal procedure. The National Assembly decides otherwise, but Marat had already escaped. Loustalot criticizes me:

Every day you are called the French Washington and the guardian angel of France.... But ask yourself whether you have been more useful to the Revolution than it has been to you. We armed ourselves without you...And took the Bastille... You have moved from inactivity...to absolute power. You have been able to place friends in lucrative posts; the court dare not oppose you, men flatter you, the aristocrats fear you, and patriots applaud you and march under your banner. [21]

Desmoulins talks of Marat's eloquence as being of 'courage, heart and great character.'[22]

January 29. Besenval and Augéard are set free, causing many to erupt in fury because both have escaped their vengeance.[23] The revolutionaries criticise the Châtelet for refusing to give Favras the name of the person who denounced him and to refuse to hear witnesses on his behalf.

February 4. It is believed the king will visit the Assembly today at the manège. A crowd soon fills the galleries; all the deputies are in their seats. At eleven o'clock a note is given to me from the king; I hand it to the president, Bureaux de Pusy.

"His Majesty will come at midday and wishes to be received without any ceremony," he says.

People applaud. Thirty deputies, including myself, are chosen to escort him; we go immediately to the Tuileries. We return with the king, in a black suit, his ministers and two National Guard soldiers.

"*Vive le roi!*" everyone cries.

He stands, his head bare, in front of a chair covered with purple velvet and fleur de lis; and reads out a speech. "I renew the sanction I have given to all the decrees of the Assembly. The Assembly and I are the authors of the new order which will be established, and of the constitution which will be the basis of your happiness. The dauphin will be raised in these principles, and he will learn that one day he will be the guardian and the defender of constitutional laws. Our union is very necessary; peace will help the finishing of the constitution. I invite those who do not believe in the principles of the revolution to reunite and recognize that division can only produce harm and that their efforts against the National Assembly and the king will not change the actual state of things and will not alter the constitution, already founded, already sworn in the hearts of all Frenchmen."

"*Vive le roi!*" people shout and cheer. [24]

"Thank you, sire, for binding yourself to defend the constitution and the laws," says Bureaux de Pusy.

I and the other twenty-nine deputies escort him back to the Tuileries. Marie Antoinette meets us with the dauphin and declares she has the same views as the king. "I promise to educate my son to respect liberty and maintain the law."

We return to the Assembly where we find it has been decided to swear a civic oath. We each stand and pledge in turn: "To be faithful to the Nation, to the Law, to the King."

In the afternoon I return home where I find many people, euphoric with the king's declaration. Jean Maudit de Larive, an actor, who had once played Bayard, gives me a gold chain Bayard was said to have worn and which had been given to him by one of his descendants.

"You are the new Bayard," he says. He recites a poem which has the line: 'Who better than you have the right to the armor of the chevalier without fear and without reproach,' to the applause of everyone.

Morris visits later.

"What do you think of what happened?" I ask.

"If His Majesty's words produce some effect on reasonable people, it will more clearly prove the weakness of his ministers. For three months they have complained about what is happening at the Assembly. Today they seem to give it the full approbation of the king. I find it strange that the Assembly members have sworn to observe a constitution which they are still writing. If His Majesty's words produce some effect on reasonable people, it will be to prove more clearly the weakness of his ministers. For three months they have argued against the Assembly. Today they seem to give their full support to His Majesty. I do not think the king's words can do any good, and that they must then do harm."

His words greatly surprise me. "I can now plead the case of royal authority in the Assembly," I tell him.[25]

In the dark winter evening, I go to the Hôtel de Ville to participate in a ceremony to honor a volunteer of the Bastille who had saved the life of a daughter of an officer there. I ride across the river to the place de Grève; candles light the windows; the people have illuminated the building to celebrate the union of the king and the Revolution.

On February 5, I issue an Order of the Day celebrating the momentous occasion of the previous day when 'the true friends of liberty have rallied more closely than ever around the best of kings and ought to redouble the sentiments of love, loyalty and trust that unite the nation to its chief; sentiments which Louis XVI would find especially in the hearts of the generous soldiers who bear arms for the constitution; the King's promise to defend the constitution ought to become the signal for order and tranquility throughout France.'[26]

I accompany Bailly and a deputation comprising one representative from each district to the Tuileries to express the gratitude of the Commune to the king.

"You will be Louis the Just, Louis the good, Louis the Wise; you will be truly Louis the Great," proclaims Bailly.[27]

Next day, we go again to the Tuileries, this time to see the queen.

"The day of February 4 will be memorable in our history; but the French people will not forget the touching words which Your Majesty addressed to the deputies of the National Assembly…Show yourself to the people with those graces with which you are blessed, and with the goodness you always have," declares Bailly.[28]

On the tenth, I accompany the king, queen and dauphin to Notre Dame for Mass; then the queen takes her son to visit seventy abandoned babies at the *Enfants Trouvés*.

"It will one day be your duty to protect poor orphans such as these," she tells him.

The royal family returns to the palace through crowds lining the streets, shouting, "*Vive le roi, la reine et le dauphin!*"

On the eleventh, eight battalions come to the place de Grève, wishing to take the oath.

"French patriots, citizens, and soldiers, you who unite under these titles have come to promise to defend the law, the nation, the king, and liberty. This is the most beautiful day of our lives. Let us swear then to be faithful forever to our oaths. Let us swear to die in defense of the laws of the Nation," I say.

"We so swear," shout the soldiers. "*Vive la nation, le roi, la liberté, et monsieur le commandant!*"[29]

On the thirteenth, the Assembly decrees all monasteries and convents, except those dedicated to education and charity, to be closed; new religious vows are forbidden. The government now has more land to sell which will help France's finances. Favras is found guilty of counterrevolutionary conspiracy; an immense crowd surrounds the Châtelet, shouting for his death.

"Your death is a necessity for public calm," Quatremère, the judge, tells him.[30]

Next day, Sunday, I ride on my white horse from the *Manège,* leading the deputies to an immense ceremony of oath-taking at Notre Dame; in front are National Guards preceded by the *Dames de La Halle* carrying baskets of flowers and wearing tricolor cockades. The representatives and the mayor march from the Hôtel de Ville, crowds lining the streets. In the cathedral Bailly and I stand at opposite ends of the altar steps.

"I swear to be faithful to the Nation, the Law and the King and to defend the constitution unto death," declares Bailly.

"Unto death!" everyone repeats. "Unto death!" shout the crowds outside.

Bells ring out; drums beat; cannon fire; sun suddenly streams through the stained-glass windows brightening the uniforms and the standards.

Later, in the evening darkness, the windows of the Hôtel de Ville are again bright with lights. Huge transparencies display patriotic sentiments, including the words of the king: 'I shall maintain liberty, and my wishes are in accord with your principles.'[31]

February 15. Alarming riots are taking place in many areas of France, and I spend much time trying to think how to repress them. I talk in the morning with many people, including William Short, of a plan to authorize the officer commanding troops to act alone without the local municipal officers if the need arises in an extraordinary circumstance. Morris arrives later; I tell him of my idea.

"I do not agree," he says. "Bad consequences can result, personal as well as political."

"What can be done if the authorities refuse to use the powers given to them?" I ask.

"There are various punishments which could be used, but they will all be insufficient because the institution of the municipalities is intrinsically bad. They will become the source of infinite confusion and of great weakness. The people have been given such extravagant ideas of liberty that I do not think it is in anyone's power to alter this organization until experience has made everyone wiser. Perhaps commissioners can be sent as administrators to each district?" he says.

"I do not think the Assembly will give the king the power to nominate commissioners," I say.

We finally decide it would be convenient to declare provisionally that certain commissioners nominated for other matters could be given the power in question, until the organization of the municipalities.

"The king must be given some sweets for his speech to the Assembly," I suggest.

He smiles. "There are no sweets to give. Executive power has already been so divided that there is nothing to give the monarch."

"I am thinking of nominating Saint-Priest as minister of war, with Duportail under him," I say.

"I do not know Saint-Priest, but someone who knows him has told me he is false, and I advise you to be sure of him before you make him master," he replies. "I will not say anything about Duportail, but I believe him to be incapable because he is too much a man of the bureau. I know at least that his ideas on the Revolution are very different to yours."

"The finances of the state are on their way to ruin. Anarchy seems to threaten them and even to attack them everywhere. That is why, above all else, you must be sure of the army which promises to be the only institution to survive. If war breaks out, it will be necessary to conduct it according to completely different principles from those of honor up to now; it will be necessary to place strong garrisons in the colonies, then abandon the ocean and completely suspend the commerce which it will not be possible to protect."[32]

On the sixteenth, I review 4,000 men of the Fourth Division on the Champs Elysées. They swear the oath. Then I go to the Assembly, followed by the crowd. I arrive late but in time to participate in a debate on the riots in the provinces. Champion de Cicé had written a letter describing the lynching at Béziers and that the municipality had not assisted the royal soldiers to keep order. The deputies propose various measures to calm the situation. I go to the tribune to speak. There is applause.

"The people above all, want liberty, but they also want justice and peace. They expect them not only as a result of our work but also from our provisional decrees; they expect them from the zeal of civil and municipal officers, who, if they set greater store by their popularity than their duties, thereby become unworthy. The people also expect them from a vigorous executive authority, which must no longer be sought among ruins but where it actually is in the constitution. The executive authority ought to be vested by and for the constitution with sufficient energy to restore public order without which liberty is never either sweet or assured."[33]

February 18. News arrives: a disorder is brewing in the faubourg Saint Antoine. Wagons of military supplies going towards the city's gates have been stopped by people who suspect there is a counterrevolutionary plot or fraud by officials. I go there with mounted troops and find tents and stakes ablaze.

This is needed for soldiers at the frontier," I tell everyone. They immediately put out the fires and allow the wagons to continue. " *Vive Lafayette*!" they shout.

Next day I attend the Assembly in the morning but am impatient there is a debate on a decree on the allowance to be granted to people in monasteries, and not a debate on a law for the disorders. When I leave the meeting, it is proposed to me to have a rapprochement with Mirabeau.

"I do not like him. I do not esteem him, nor do I fear him. I do not see why I should try to come to an understanding with him," I reply.[34]

Favras is hanged in the place de Grève at eight o'clock at night, the crowd screaming insults at him, in delight at the hanging of a marquis. He continues to say he is innocent of conspiracy either against the state or against people. I am not present at the execution. I believe his death to be just as he was guilty. I write to Madame de Simiane: 'I was touched this evening by the courageous death of that man, who was guilty. The public fury hurt me also...Adieu until tomorrow. I need to be softened by your friendship for I am disenchanted with men almost as much as Madame de Tessé.'[35]

On the twentieth, I speak at the Assembly to support the law on local disorders, a law which I consider mediocre, but which will suffice for the establishment of the new order.

"Disorders were necessary for the Revolution; the former order was only servitude, and so, insurrection is the most holy of duties, but for the Constitution it is necessary that the new order strengthens itself, that people must live in security, it is necessary to love the new Constitution, it is necessary that public power should have force and energy." [36]

At the same time there is unrest throughout the provinces, people are also, however, flocking to churches and squares to swear the oath when they hear of the king's words to the National Assembly and the oath-taking of the deputies.

The revolt last October in the Austrian Netherlands has long been on my mind. In November, the town of Ghent fell to the insurgents. Then followed Bruges, Ostende, Mons, Anvers and other towns. Austrian troops were chased from Bruxelles. On December 19 the states of Brabant met for the first time and gave their agreement to the act of joining with the province of Flanders.[37]

My aim is to establish liberty in Belgium with the least excess and misfortune possible, by yielding the wishes of the throne and various aristocrats to the great principle of national sovereignty, to the true liberty of the Belgian people. The French government, the king and his ministers want to avoid a rupture with Austria. I would like to profit from this ministerial fear, from the embarrassment of the Court of Vienna, and of the need that the Belgian aristocracy has with France, to bring all the parties to a national and representative system, but I cannot go against the policy of the French government.[38]

I have sent Sémonville to Bruxelles; he wrote in January that there 'is no doubt that it would be very disadvantageous to France to see ten thousand Hessians here, as well as Brunswickers, the Prussians at Liège, and at the head of all these armies, the two premier military men of Europe.'[39]

I urge Montmorin to assemble troops on the border. I have asked for 25,000 men in Flanders, under Rochambeau, and a second force in Alsace, all of which would already have happened if Necker had been less parsimonious.[40] On February 22, Schlieffen, the commander of the Prussian troops at Liège, writes to me: 'My nation desires the redoubtable Austria to be less powerful in this province, yours must desire the same.'[41]

On the twenty-seventh, I again refuse to accept an indemnity of 100,000 livres from the Commune.

It is distressing my letters have not reached Washington and on March 17, I write again to him:

> Our revolution is getting on as well as it can with a Nation that has swalled up liberty all at once, and is still liable to mistake licentiousness for freedom- the Assembly have more hatred to the ancient system than experience on the proper organization of a new and constitutional government- The ministers are lamenting the loss of power, and afraid to use that which they have- and as every thing has been destroyed and not much new building is yet above ground there is much room for critics and calomnies. To this may be added that we still are pestered by two parties, the Aristocratic that is panting for a counter revolution, and the factions which aims at the division of the Empire, and destruction of all authority and perhaps of the lifes of the reigning branch, both of which parties are fomenting troubles. And after I have confessed all that, my dear General, I will tell you with the same candour that we have made an admirable, and almost incredible destruction of all abuses, prejudices, etc. etc. that everything not directly useful to, or coming from the people has been levelled- that in the topographical, moral, political situation of France we have made more changes in ten month than the most sanguine patriot could have imagined- that our

internal troubles are much exaggerated and that upon the whole this Revolution, in which nothing will be wanting but energy of government just as it was in America, will propagate implant liberty and make it flourish throughout the world., while we must wait for a Convention in a few years to mend some defects which are not now perceived by men just escaped from aristocracy and dispostism.[42]

I send him a picture of the Bastille as it was a few days before I ordered its demolition, and its main key.[43] I entrust it all to Thomas Paine to take to London and dispatch from there.

Near the end of March I accompany the king and queen to a plate glass factory in the faubourg Saint Antoine. A few days later I go with them to the Gobelins tapestry works in the district of Saint Marcel.

Unrest continues. I strengthen the forces at the Hôtel de Ville, drill the National Guard every day and send contingents to help police in nearby towns.

Meetings of National Guards to swear allegiance are starting to be held in different regions of France. On March 20 there is a very large ceremony on the banks of the Loire for National Guards from Bretagne and Anjou; in Strasbourg, fifty thousand National Guards from eastern France do the same.

I am very busy. I write to Madame de Simiane:

My Easter fortnight will be an Orléanist president, the dispute with the Duport party, the priests in the confessional, the parlementarians in the districts, the counter-revolution of M. de Maillebois which is occupying many heads, a plan for the pillage of the caisse d'escompte, the districts and the commune at loggerheads, the rivalry of the civil and military, the army uncertain about its fate, the struggle over judicial reform, thirty thousand hungry workers, M. Necker packing his bags, the vicomte de Mirabeau and company who are sowing aristocratic slanders. [44]

On April 7, I reply to Schleiffen: 'The French nation know too well the price of its liberty to ever try to harm that of other people, or to see with indifference that other powers are trying to intervene in that of their neighbours....His Prussian Majesty will always find in the King of the French, principles of liberty, justice and moderation, as much in conformity with his personal character as with his wish for the nation, and this frank and straightforward conduct which befits a citizen-king, certain to be more than ever supported by a free and vigorous nation.'[45]

April 12. The National Assembly debates the motion that the Catholic religion should be the sole religion authorised in France. Charles de Lameth opposes it and when Mirabeau supports him the right walk out. I double the number of National Guards at the manège and in the streets near the Tuileries so that the deputies of the right are not insulted or attacked. Next day, huge crowds gather wishing to obtain a seat to watch the proceedings. I sit far to the left, wishing to show that I do not agree with the motion. The debate is heated, and La Rochefoucauld suggests that the majesty of religion elevates it beyond debate and that there should be no more discussion. The marquis de Foucault criticizes the number of troops I have employed and says that the Assembly is not free and therefore cannot pass a decree. The Assembly, however, accepts La Rochefoucauld's motion. The right stand and start to profess "In the name of God and the religion" but shouts drown out their words. I go to the tribune. "Messieurs, some persons having told Monsieur the mayor of Paris of their misgivings about the safety of the capital, misgivings that neither he nor I believed to be well founded in any way, he thought nevertheless that it was his duty to order me to provide some reinforcement of the citizen guard with which the National Assembly has seen fit to surround itself. Permit me to take this opportunity to to repeat to the Assembly, in the name of the National Guard, that there is not one of us who would not give the last drop of his blood to assure the execution of its decrees and the liberty of its deliberations and to preserve the inviolability of its members." People applaud loudly with the exception of the very right-wing deputies. I regain my seat and they continue to applaud.[46]

April 14. I write a memorandum for the king. I ask him to reread the memorandum I gave to him last year; my principles, my opinions, my advice will be the same. I write about the Declaration of Rights, the legislative power, the judicial order, the administration, the army and navy, the National Guards and foreign affairs. I list the functions and royal prerogatives.[47]

April 27. I am summoned to speak at the Châtelet which has been investigating the events of October 5 and 6 since last December. I recount what happened from the time of my arrival at Versailles. I say that I spoke from the balcony of the château warning the people against troublemakers; I do not name the duc d'Orléans or Mirabeau.

On the twenty-eighth, Mirabeau writes at length to me about our former relationship, the reasons for our disagreement, the perils threatening the state, and our need to act together. He says he is even ready to now accept the position of ambassador at Constantinople. He says that such confidences are rarely made in writing but that if he ever violates the laws of the political union he is offering me then I can make the letter public but until that time it must remain private.[48] I do not take up his offer.

Dumouriez writes to me on May 2 that it is time to occupy ourselves with the affairs of the Low Countries; he has learned that the king of Prussia has proposed to the king of Hungary to guarantee the Low Countries for him if there is a general pacification, and he has several things to talk about with me concerning this. He repeats that he has never merited any suspicion about his liaisons, that he has never had any with what is called the Orléans faction and that he has a sincere and tender attachment to me.[49]

On May 9 the lands of the king are confiscated, which will provide more money for the state. On the twelfth, Bailly, Mirabeau, Chapelier, Talleyrand, Sieyès and I found the Society of 1789, whose aim is moderation. It is not a party; I must concern myself with the constitution and with order, independently of the intrigues of clubs.[50] The same day, I speak at the Assembly concerning the grave disorders at Marseilles on April 30 and other times, as well as the disorder at Toulon on May 3. I approve the measures taken by the ministry to re-establish order; Mirabeau opposes the motion. On the thirteenth, our new Society of 1789 holds a dinner at the Palais-Royal for 124. We drink the usual thirteen toasts, then make a collection for the poor of nearly 600 livres. The windows are open; people outside hear that I am present.

"We want the hero of the Revolution!" they shout.

I go out onto a balcony, my glass in my hand. Everyone cheers. "To my fellow-citizens," I toast.

"Long live the nation! Long live the king! Long live Lafayette and all the friends of liberty!" they shout.

Bailly also comes onto the balcony; they cheer him. Nearby, a band is playing a new tune. 'Ça ira', which includes the words 'He who exalts himself will be humbled and he who humbles himself will be exalted...Through the prudent Lafayette all our troubles will abate, Ça ira! Ça ira.'

It is decided that a more humane method of execution will be carried out. It is a partly an invention of Doctor Antoine Louis and cuts off a person's head, instead of hanging or the many gruesome and painful executions currently used. Doctor Joseph Guillotin proposed it at the National Assembly and said the criminal will feel nothing but a gentle caress but has not been pleased that it will be called the *guillotine*, and not the *louison*.[51]

May 14. I go with Bailly and National Guard soldiers to stop a crowd wishing to burn the building where a group of the extreme right, the *salon français*, is meeting. We find just a few deputies in the building; I leave the National Guard to control the crowd.

It is reported that Mounier has gone to Switzerland, as well as Lally-Tollendal.[52]

May 25. I am driving in my carriage with Romeuf near to Saint-Germain-l'Auxerrois; we see a man being attacked by a crowd who is accusing him of having stolen a sack of oats. A patrol of cavalry, as well as volunteers, have wanted to take him to the Châtelet, but the crowd is refusing, and several men are beating him with sticks. We immediately force our way into the crowd despite people begging us not to. We get down from the carriage and push further into the crowd. A man lifts his club against Romeuf who snatches the body from him. I stand astride it.

"You are murderers!" I shout. "I don't believe everyone here is guilty. Show me the killers!"

Several soldiers, who have followed me, point to a man. I grab him by the collar. "I am going to show you how everything is honorable when you are executing the law."

I march him as far as the Châtelet by the neck, despite his cries, the National Guard pressing round me.

When I later leave the building, I order the soldiers to move aside. I stand on the parapet, the whole crowd around me again; I harangue them. "You have been fooled by the factions and brigands who want to force the Constituent Assembly and the king to leave Paris and let it burn. The tranquility of the capital is under my jurisdiction. I will destroy anyone who dares to disturb public order. I will be supported, but even if I am alone, I will resist crime and I will have the law respected until my last breath. I do not think there are men brave enough to fight against me."

I suddenly see at the other end of the embankment people hanging the thief whom I had left as I had believed him to be dead. I run there with Romeuf, the National Guard throwing themselves with us into the middle of the crowd. We save the man; he escapes; I continue through the mass of bodies. "Stand aside!" I order. The crowd opens. "*Vive Lafayette!*" they shout. I regain my carriage.[53]

On the twenty-sixth, Bailly speaks in the Assembly of the measures he and I are taking to assure public calm as we have noticed in the last ten days that there has been a great agitation in Paris, that foreign vagabonds have been trying to bring about disorder and have even been giving out money. He mentions my actions yesterday at the Châtelet. "*Bravo! Vive Lafayette!*" people cry.[54] On the thirty-first, Dumouriez writes again, wanting me to immediately persuade Monsieur de Montmorin to let him go to the Low Countries, to place himself under my orders and help the insurrection of the Belgians.[55] However, I do not want a French general to further Belgian independence and wish General Van der Meersch, arrested in April as the leader of the party opposed to that of the states, to be released before any cooperation is given.

Last summer, the Spanish seized American and British ships in Nootka Sound, an excellent anchorage on the west coast of Vancouver Island and are claiming the Pacific North-West for Spain. News of the action reached London in January and has become an international crisis. The National Assembly has spent the whole of May debating whether France should aid the Spanish if there is war, as Pitt is suggesting. Should the family pact of the Bourbons of France and Spain be invoked or has this now been annulled by our Revolution. What are the powers of the king concerning diplomatic matters?

I talk frankly with Lord Robert Fitzgerald, the British chargé d'affaires in Paris. "I believe Britain is exploiting the situation not just to help the Spanish-American colonies free themselves from Spain, but also to harm the French Revolution. However, Britain will never harm the Revolution in France because the spirit of liberty burns in the heart of every French peasant. I thoroughly agree with Britain's intention to help free the Spanish colonies and it might be that in the future France might aid Britain in this respect. We want the same sort of revolution we have here to happen all over the world. I regret that we have to keep a monarchy here in France and I do not despair that one day we will have a better equality between men by an impartial distribution of landed property.[56]

Fitzgerald looks very surprised at my words and does not appear able to answer me.

Mirabeau writes again to me on June 1 and suggests that for the sake of the nation I become like Richelieu at the court, and that instead of the monk, Capucin, he will become my eminence grise. I do not succumb to his proposition. On the third, Bailly and I walk, both holding a candle, behind the king, queen and Monsieur, in a procession of the Holy Sacrament from the church of Saint-Germain-l'Auxerrois to the Louvre. Adrienne is ill and the Assembly of Representatives deputes two members to find out how she is. On the fifth, Bailly comes to the National Assembly leading a deputation from the municipality of Paris to propose a Fête of the Fédération where men who fight for France can swear an oath to liberty and to constitutional equality on July 14, the day of the taking of the Bastille. The duc de La Rochefoucauld supports the motion. On the eighth, Talleyrand reads a decree to organize the means of executing this proposal. On the tenth, I learn that Benjamin Franklin died on April 17, at the age of eighty-four years. Next day, following my request, Mirabeau gives a moving eulogy to the deputies and asks that the Assembly should mourn for three days.[57] I and La Rochefoucauld support the motion, which passes, supported by the left wing of the Assembly. I go to tell the king. On the seventeenth, I go to Notre Dame for a ceremony of the placing of the flags by the deputies of the Basoche. In the evening, the Society of 1789 celebrates the anniversary of the Chamber of Commons in the National Assembly and I dine with Bailly, Mirabeau, Sieyès, Talleyrand and Paoli at a venue in the Palais-Royal; outside the window people cheer and shout.

June 19. I am not yet sure that Adrienne does not have smallpox, so I write to the king instead of going in person, to ask him to wear his review clothes for the review next Sunday and not his ordinary walking clothes. I beg him to believe I would not make such a suggestion if it was not very important to people.[58] In the evening, I go to the National Assembly to support a petition from the clerks of the Basoche. [59] I find Monsieur Lambel speaking: "The day when deputies from all the provinces assemble to swear a constitution which promises liberty and equality to French people must not recall to some of our brothers, thoughts of humiliation and servitude. The figures representing four provinces, whose deputies have always been counted amongst the strongest supporters of the rights of the nation, are chained, like slaves, at the foot of the statue of Louis XVI...Monuments of pride cannot exist under the reign of equality. Let us destroy emblems which degrade the dignity of man. I demand that since we must get rid of all monuments of pride, we must not stop just at statues. Today is the tomb of vanity. We must abolish hereditary nobility. It must be forbidden to everyone to call themselves count, marquis, baron."

I stand at the same time as Lameth and give way to him as he supports Lambel. "The titles Monsieur Lambel invites us to proscribe harm equality, the base of our constitution; hereditary nobility shocks reason and opposes true liberty."

"The motion of Monsieur Lambel is so necessary that I do not think it even has a need to be supported, but if there is a need then I join my whole heart to it," I say. People cheer.

"The title of Monseigneur should only be given to princes of the royal blood," says the elderly Goupil de Préfeln.

"In a free country there are only citizens and public officers," I reply. "There is much truth in the magistrature of the king, but why grant the title of prince to men who are only in my eyes citizens when they no longer have titles?[60]

"Have an adjournment," cry the few nobles present. "Let us discuss this tomorrow. It is such an important matter, but it is being debated without having been stated beforehand. It is also a rule that no constitutional law should be proposed in an evening session."

However, it is very apparent by the applause of the left that Lambel's motion was planned, and that they are determined to pass it.

"You are destroying the distinctions of nobility, but are keeping those of the bankers, the money lenders, the people receiving 100,000 *écus* of income," someone shouts.

"No delay!" calls out my brother-in-law, the vicomte de Noailles. "The only distinctions should be those of virtue. Suppress liveries."

"Let all citizens have their own name and not that of a piece of land," cries President de Saint-Fargeau. "My name is Louis-Michel Le Pelletier."[61]

"Some of you propose to take the symbols of enslavement from the statue of Louis XIV... others are claiming a return to absolute equality. Each of these questions need scrutiny. The nobility in France is constitutional. It is necessary to adjourn the discussion. If there are no more nobles there is no more monarchy. This question is so important it must be discussed in the morning. The wisest decisions are not always taken amidst great enthusiasm" declares abbé Maury.[62]

"It is not a question of a new constitutional article. It is a question of a reglementary decree. We do want to lose the morning sessions in which we are going to discuss the constitution. We only need to decide now a necessary consequence," I say.

There is tumult. Shouting comes from all parts of the chamber. Chapelier reads out a project of the decree. The nobles again call for an adjournment. The debates start again. The adjournment is rejected. The Lameths, who hope to gain much popularity, insist forcefully it must be decided now. I cannot oppose such a motion. Finally we adopt the decree. All titles are abolished. Citizens are only allowed to take their family name. They are forbidden to use livery, coats of arms and incense when it is not being offered to God. I will no longer use the title 'marquis.'

Next morning there is a furore at court. Some members of the Constitution Committee are thinking about revising the decree and request me to ask Montmorin, the keeper of the royal seal, to delay the king's sanction in order to give time for a new proposal. I agree. I believe amendments can be made conforming to the true principles of liberty.[63] People also try to make me act with Mirabeau, who was not present at the debate on the nineteenth, who wishes me to collaborate with the king and queen.

"Monsieur de Mirabeau behaves badly with me. I defeated the king of England in his power; the king of France in his authority; the people in their fury, and I am certainly not going to yield to Monsieur de Mirabeau," I say to Frouchot.[64]

The decree appears to be uniting the nobles, the clergy and the parlements who had previously hated each other before the Revolution. More nobles are emigrating.

On the twenty-fifth, I go to see Necker and Montmorin, then Champion de Cicé. I discover that the king has been advised to pass the bill and Champion de Cicé wants me to write to the king himself. I do so; I say that the three ministers think he should reconsider and therefore I beg him to delay sanctioning it until he talks with Montmorin.[65]

The king writes back. He wants to know why I want to delay the bill. I write again to him. I say that the first fault concerning the bill on the nineteenth lay with the members of the Assembly, starting with myself, who being present at the debate could have demanded a more reasonable wording. I have tried to repair the harm by presenting to His Majesty an occasion less strongly attended when the decree could be changed, according to the observations of the king, to the great satisfaction of the public. [66]

On the twenty-ninth, I go in the evening to the Tuileries as the queen has asked to see me.

"We have complete confidence in you, but you are so absorbed by the demands of your position that you cannot do everything. You need to use a man who has talent and activity and who can do what you, for lack of time, cannot. We believe that Mirabeau with his force, his talent and his ability to manage affairs in the Assembly would be the best suited for this. We, therefore, desire you to act in concert with him concerning matters which interest the wellbeing of the state and that of the king."[67]

Her words surprise me. I have no intention of acting with Mirabeau.

It is decided to celebrate the *Fête de la Fédération* on the Champ de Mars where the flat grass in front of the École militaire will be transformed into an amphitheater. Work begins at the end of June; architects and engineers draw up the plans and mark out a semi-circle. In July, twelve thousand men[68] dig and move the earth to raise the sides by four feet. There is not enough earth and so more is brought from the plain of Grenelle and from the land behind the École Militaire and Les Invalides, where the slightly raised earth is flattened.[69] It is a massive project, and it quickly becomes evident more workers will be needed to finish it by the fourteenth.

It rains heavily. The ground becomes a quagmire making the work even more difficult and so the districts invite good citizens to help in the name of France. People flock to the Champ de Mars, pushing barrows and bringing carriage horses. Rich and poor labor together from daybreak to midnight.[70] Wealthy ladies, Capuchin monks, Knights of Saint Louis, school children and many others come, often carrying spades, and are harnessed to small tip carts, called camions, to transport the earth. Each of the sixty battalions of the National Guard of Paris provides soldiers, and men come from the city workshops, leaving them empty. Many people camp in the nearby streets and free food and barrels of wine are distributed. Signs are everywhere. 'Beware our anger,' write the butchers, whilst the workers of Prudhomme, the printer, have a large banner inscribed on one side: 'Printers of the Revolution of Paris' and on the other: 'For Liberty'.

The paid workers resent the others. There is a fear of riots, so I order a patrol at night. I ride to the Champ de Mars to see what is happening. Soldiers stop work. They salute me; people crowd around.

"*Alors, général, ça ira-t-il?*" shouts a man.

"*Oui, mes enfants,*" I say.

"*Ça ira, ça ira,*" they sing in reply.

I dismount. I take a pickaxe; I shovel earth for two hours and push a wheelbarrow. It is decided that anyone who wants to attend can enter free.

I escort the king to the site to see how the work is progressing. The workmen greet him with a ceremonial arch of pickaxes, and everyone halts what they are doing. "*Vive le roi!*"

He inspects everything, a look of pleasure on his face.

July 3. Dumouriez sets off to Belgium, without my having seen him, although he asks me to place six thousand livres of credit for him in Brussels. However, my view is changing. I think the Belgian revolution is only an intrigue of the aristocracy and the clergy, where the interests of the people have been forgotten and in which I do not see any principle of liberty and the rights of nations.[71]

The same day, the duc d'Orléans dispatched a letter to the National Assembly, to the king, and to me, in which he protests very strongly about Monsieur de Boinville, whom I had sent to persuade him in the name of public calm not to return to Paris and to tell him that I will fight a duel with him if he does.[72] On the sixth, I explain to the deputies, with a certain amount of embarrassment, why I behaved as I did towards the duc d'Orléans.[73] I also express my confidence in the Fête of the Fédération.

July 9. Thousands of *fédérés* start to arrive in Paris. I place detachments of National Guards at the city gates to welcome them and to take them to their lodgings where the owners give them beds, sheets, wood and everything they need to make their stay comfortable.[74] The king opens the royal library, botanical gardens and museums to them and the Opéra gives special performances.

The Jacobins and Cordeliers savage me; they suggest I want to be a dictator. Marat, who spends much time in a bath because of his skin complaint, and truth be told, can be said to be half-mad,[75] makes the same claim in *L'Ami du Peuple*, as does the *Journal du Diable*. However, I know I am still immensely popular, despite my many enemies from the Cordeliers and the Jacobins, as well as the queen, Mirabeau, Orléans, and many aristocrats, and despite the caricatures and slanderous writing about my private life being sold on the streets.

On the tenth, fourteen thousand citizen-soldiers, elected from three million citizen-soldiers from eighty-three *départements* of France, assemble in the place de Grève. They proclaim they are the Assembly of the Fédération and I am the president. On the eleventh, Sunday, three divisions of my National Guard parade on the plaine des Sablons watched by citizens, fédérés, the king, the queen and the dauphin.

"*Vive le roi!*" "*Vive la reine!*" people shout. The king bows and smiles.

I escort him back to the Tuileries; to my surprise I find Orléans. He arrived earlier today and had written to the king to ask if he could pay his respects to him. His unexpected arrival, however, is frightening many. Everyone seems to think he has come to give his name to some new crime. People look at him with horror; ladies turn their backs; men regard him with scorn;[76] a courtier is deliberately insulting and I send two of my aides to protect him. He comes out of the meeting with the king; I am polite; we greet each other in a friendly manner.

On the twelfth, the Assembly approves the Civil Constitution of the Clergy. On the thirteenth I lead a delegation of National Guards to the National Assembly; amidst cheers I stand and speak.

"The National Guards of France come to offer you the homage of their respect and gratitude. The nation, wishing at last to be free, demands a constitution...The rights of man have been declared; the sovereignty of the people has been recognized; powers have been delegated; the bases of public order have been established. Hasten to give all its energy to the state...For us, devoted to the revolution, united in the name of liberty, called from all parts of France...we will bear, without hesitation, to the altar of the country the oath which you dictate to its soldiers. Yes, Messieurs, our hands will rise together, at the same time...Under the protection of the law, the standard of liberty shall never become that of disorder...We swear it on our honor; and free men, Frenchmen, do not promise in vain," I declare.[77] People cheer.

Bonnay, the president, makes a speech; people cheer again. I lead the gardes onto the floor to even greater applause. We go across the gardens of the Tuileries to the palace; I present a deputation to the king who greets us courteously.

"Sire. We wish to revere Your Majesty with the most beautiful of all titles, that of chief of the French, and king of a free people. Enjoy, Sire, the prize of your virtues; that these pure vows never sullied by despotism, should be the glory and reward of a citizen king. You have desired that we should possess a constitution founded on liberty and public order. The National Guard of France swear to Your Majesty an obedience which shall know no other limits than those of the law; a love which will only finish with our death."[78]

Louis appears pleased. He already knew what I was going to say and has prepared a response.[79]

"Tell your fellow-citizens that I would have liked to talk to them as I am to you....I cannot go with you to your homes, but I can be there in my affections and by laws protecting the weak; I can watch out for them; live for them, die, if necessary, for them. Their king is their father, their brother, their friend, that he can only be happy if they are happy."[80]

The soldiers file past him and out into the corridor. "Can we be presented to Her Majesty the Queen?" they ask.

Their request is granted; Marie Antoinette comes into the chamber carrying the dauphin. I present the soldiers, then stand back in the crowd. Several kiss his hand. To their delight, she takes her son round the room so that others can do so. She sees me. She immediately stops the kissing of the hand and confines herself to politenesses.[81]

Chapter 42

Riding into history on a white horse

July 14. Rain pours down from black skies. Fifty thousand National Guards, the Paris electors of 1789, companies of sailors and other corps, soldiers of the line, and veterans and *fédérés* from the eighty-three départements, assemble at the Boulevard du Temple, bearing banners on which is written *constitution*.

At eight o'clock in the morning, I arrive at Porte Saint Martin with my staff, in uniform, a tricolor cockade fastened to my hat. I ride to the head of the cavalry. "March!" I order.

We set off. National Guards of Paris line our route, immense crowds are in the roads, at windows, on the embankments. They cheer; they throw flowers; they give the rain and sweat-soddened men wine, cakes and bread every time they stop. The rain ceases occasionally. Then it resumes. " *Vivent nos frères les Parisians!*" call the *fédérés,* and more wine fruits, ham and other foods are lowered from the windows.[1]

We reach the Manège. I dismount. I go to tell the deputies it is time to join the procession. They immediately set off across the Tuileries in their black coats and holding umbrellas; I ride quickly to the place de Louis XV to rejoin the procession. The battalion of children from the *École militaire* stand at the bridge; the battalion of veterans takes a position nearby; the standard bearers of the sixty Paris battalions form a double line in the center of the square. The deputies arrive. I and the troops salute; the deputies join the procession between the battalion of veterans and the battalion of children; we continue.

" *Vive l'Assemblée nationale!*" the crowd shouts, throwing yet more flowers, the wind and rain lashing furiously. '*Ça ira! Ça ira!*" they sing and clap.

Sweat pours down my face. A man rushes up to me with a bottle of wine and a large glass.

"General, you are hot. Have a drink." He fills the glass and gives it to me.

I take the glass; I look briefly at him then I drink the whole glass to show I have no worry, that I have no anxiety amidst the people. People applaud. I smile and return the glass to him.[2] He immediately refills the glass and drinks it, understanding why I hesitated. People applaud again. I ride on to the bridge over the Seine. "Order the artillery to fire to show that the Assembly is coming."

I lead the procession through the towering Triumphal Arch into the amphitheater and see about four hundred thousand spectators, who started arriving at six this morning, filling the tiered rows, different colors of umbrellas bright in the downpour of rain. Ahead, in the center, are three hundred priests, wearing white cassocks and large tricolor sashes, standing at the four corners of the Altar of the Fatherland, Talleyrand, the bishop of Autun, at their head.

John Paul Jones, Tom Paine at his side, marches in with a small detachment, bearing the flag of the United States, the first time it is displayed in Europe.[3] I stand and salute, my heart overflowing with pride that my two beloved countries are united under the flag of liberty.

The troops assemble. Finally, the grenadiers march in, the last cavalry detachment at the entrance. In front stand the National Guards in a line; in the center around the Altar of the Fatherland stand troops of the line in a multitude of different uniforms.

We wait for the king. The bands play. "*Ça ira, ça ira*," people sing. The National Guards also sing and groups of fédérés start to dance their local dances to *Ça ira*, or to their own provincial songs. People clap to the music and shriek with laughter to see the soldiers dancing in the mud.

"*Vivent nos amis!*" "*Vivent nos frères!*" they cheer.

"*Vivent les parisiens!*" "*Vivent les vainqueurs de la liberté!*" respond the *fédérés*.

"*Vive la nation!*" they all shout.

Artillery fires to announce the arrival of the king. The crowd cheers. He walks, in his glittering robe of the Order of the Holy Ghost, to the throne swathed in purple velvet and decorated with gold fleur-de-lys on a dais in the center of the pavilion covered with a canopy decorated with fleur-de-lys and tricolor bands. He stands briefly beside the throne then sits down. The royal family go to their box, their sparkling finery a contrast with the black-coated deputies in the tiers below; Saint Priest and two other courtiers stand behind him and the queen. I had wanted President Bonnay of the National Assembly to be seated above the king, but Saint Priest had called it a ridiculous idea and has placed him behind and to his right. The officials of Paris and the wives of notables have the remaining seats and Adrienne is there. I know that George is also here, accompanied by Félix Frestel, his tutor.

The guns fire a signal; the fédérés present arms. Incense is lit at the four corners of the altar, but the heavy rain keeps extinguishing it. The priests go past me to the altar. Talleyrand starts to celebrate the Mass, water streaming from his miter down his face, his garments drenched. The noise in the amphitheater diminishes.

"Bless the standards!" I command.

The bearers of the standards of the eighty-three *départements* and of the *oriflamme*,[4] form a line in front of the Altar of the Fatherland. Talleyrand, who appears to be wearing an embroidered coat and a sword under his garments, gives the blessing of the church.[5]

"Sing and weep tears of joy because on this day France has been made anew," he intones.

One thousand eight hundred musicians play;[6] artillery roars from outside the grounds; the spectators clap; the standard-bearers march from the altar, pass in front of the king and return to their ranks.

I ride to the king to receive my orders as I am *major-général* of the *fédération*,[7] the music playing, the fédérés swinging their hats on the points of their swords, everyone shouting and singing. I signal to the band to stop playing. There is a volley of gunfire; everyone quietens. Bonnay and the deputies stand.

"I swear to be faithful to the Nation, to the Law and to the King, and to maintain with all my might the constitution decreed by the National Assembly and accepted by the King," declares Bonnay.

"I so swear," reply the deputies.

Artillery fires again. "*Vive l'assemblée!*" "*Vive la nation!*" shout spectators and fédéré*s*.

I give the signal for another cannonade. Suddenly the rain stops. The sun shines. The king stands and waits for silence. When there is complete quiet, he raises his arm towards the altar.

"I, King of the French, swear to employ the power delegated to me by the constitutional law of the state, to maintain the constitution decreed by the National Assembly and accepted by me," he declares in a loud, strong voice.[8]

An immense cry goes up from everyone, almost drowning the artillery. "*Vive l'Assemblée nationale!*" "*Vive la nation!*"

Marie Antoinette unexpectedly raises the dauphin in his uniform of the National Guard. "Behold my son! He unites with me in the same sentiments."[9]

The cannons roar, the musicians play military tunes. "*Vive le roi!*" "*Vive la reine!*" "*Vive le dauphin!*" everyone shouts.

Some of the fédérés rush towards the royal box. "Go back to your posts," I order.

"What are your commands, Sire?" I ask the king.

"Would you please administer the oath," he requests.

I salute. I turn. I draw my sword and hold it high in front of me. I walk slowly between the *gardes* to the foot of the altar. I mount the steps and place my sword on the altar, to the sound of trumpets. The last note fades away. There is silence. I recite the oath for the fédérés.

"We swear to be always faithful to the Nation, to the Law and to the King, to maintain with all our power the constitution decreed by the National Assembly and accepted by the King; to protect, in accordance with the laws, the safety of people and of property, the circulation of grain and of other supplies within the kingdom, the collection of public taxes in whatever forms they may have; and to remain united with all Frenchmen by the indissoluble bonds of brotherhood."

A man in each of the companies simultaneously repeats the oath for everyone to hear. Swords flash in the air. "I so swear," shout a multitude of voices repeatedly. Salvoes fire from forty cannon; "*Vive l'Assemblée nationale!*" "*Vive le roi!*" people cry.

"In the hero of Liberty as well as in his numerous brothers-in-arms, France will find not only defenders of the constitution, but also friends and brothers whom the same zeal has united for the glory of the nation, for the maintenance of the law and for the splendor of the French throne," I declare, knowing that at the same moment the *fédérations* of other cities of France are proclaiming their oath.

Artillery fires. I descend the steps, but people do not want me to leave the altar. They throw themselves on me. They kiss my face, my hands and my clothes and I can hardly mount my horse. Even when I am in the saddle, they kiss what they can, my boots, the horse's harness, and, finally, the horse itself.[10]

The priests sing the *Te Deum* at the altar. The king stands up; he walks across the amphitheater to the École militaire. "*Vive le roi!*" everyone shouts.

The fédérés gather around me. I lead the procession of soldiers to the Triumphal Arch. We return across the bridge to the place de Louis XV and the Tuileries whilst the king drives in his carriage along other streets to the palace.

I go to the château de la Muette with Bailly, to attend a banquet given by the Commune of Paris for the fédérés. Many of the National Guards are already in the garden and come out to greet me. They crowd round my horse, cheering and trying to touch and embrace me. For a moment, I fear I will be suffocated, but friends and officers come to my rescue.

I do not stay until the end of the dinner. Proud and content, I go home through the brightly lit streets.

Fourteen thousand deputies, chosen by more than three million National Guards, deputations from all land and sea forces, came in the name of armed France to abjure the ancient régime and to pledge allegiance to liberty and constitutional equality.[11] I believe three hundred thousand spectators have attended the *Fédération*. It was a sublime spectacle. There was only harmony, no disorder.

July 17. The Paris Assembly comes to see me. "The deputies of the National Guards of France are leaving with the regret of not being able to nominate you their leader; they respect the constitutional law which prevents at this time the wish of their hearts; and what covers you for ever with glory is that you yourself have proposed this law. But although you cannot be our commander you will always be our friend, our guide, our model."[12]

I am immensely popular. It is said I was riding into history on my white horse. There are pictures of me everywhere, as well as pamphlets, songs and poems. The revolutionary press sneers with rage. Marat calls me General Motié and says I have been bought by the court.[13] They talk of my deification and adulation. The court is also angry; they think I eclipsed the king.

In August, the garrison at Nancy, composed of various regiments, including the *régiment du Roi-Infanterie* and the *régiment Châteauvieux-suisse*, rebels. The soldiers send a deputation to the National Assembly, complaining that their officers have misused funds and have treated them harshly, but it is decided to ask General Malseigne, the local commander, to stop the revolt. He is not successful; the soldiers arrest him, but he manages to escape,[14] and on the sixteenth the National Assembly votes to appoint my cousin, the marquis de Bouillé, a royalist who commands the army in the east, to use whatever force is needed to quell the rebellion.

'This is the moment when we can start the establishment of constitutional order which must replace revolutionary anarchy...The decree concerning Nancy is good; its execution must be entire and vigorous. I am sure that you will serve our constitution and that I have as much need as you of the establishment of public order,' I write to him.[15]

I write to Washington on the twenty-third:

What would have been my feelings, had the news of your illness reached me before I knew my beloved General, my adoptive father was out of danger! I was struck with horror at the idea of the situation you have been in, while I, uninformed, and so distant from you, was anticipating the long waited for pleasure to hear from you....Now we are disturbed with revolts among the regiments- And as I am constantly attaked on both sides by the Aristocratic and the Factious party I don't know to which of the two we owe these insurrections. Our safeguard among them lies with the National Guard...I have lately lost some of my favour with the mob and displeased the frantic lovers of licentiousness, as I am Bent on Establishing a legal subordination. But the Nation at large are very thankful to me for it. It is not out the heads of the Aristocrats to make a counter revolution....But I think their plans will be either abandoned or unsuccessful. I am rather more concerned with a division that rages in the popular party. The Clubs of the Jacobines and 89 it is called, have divided the friends of liberty who accuse each other, Jacobines being taxed with a disorderly extravagance, and 89 with a tincture of ministerialism and ambition....I hope our business will end with the year- at which time this so much blackened Cromwell, this ambitious dictator, your friend, shall most deliciously enjoy the happiness to give up all power, all public cares, and to become a private citizen in a free monarchy, the constitution of which, altho' I could not help it being very defective now, will lay a foundation for the more excellent are to be made in a few years. [16]

On August 24, the king formally promulgates the Civil Constitution of the Clergy. On August 31, the National Assembly discusses the situation at Nancy, a deputation having arrived from there a few days ago to express its views to it. Some want to execute the decree against the rebels.

"We must have an enquiry," demand Robespierre and others.

"Monsieur Bouillé needs a show of support from the Assembly, and we must give it to him," I reply.[17]

Barnave proposes a motion supporting Bouillé in his mission to restore order which the Assembly passes.

On September 2 we learn that Bouillé marched on Nancy, the Swiss regiment of Salis-Samade in the vanguard, which encountered a company of the *régiment du roi* with a cannon at the entrance.[18] A young officer shouted to his men not to fire, but they did so, the grapeshot killing and wounding hundreds, especially officers, who were mainly at the front, as well as the

436

unfortunate young officer, who later died of his wounds. Bouillé then attacked the town and killed at least ninety-four of the rebels. The next day, the *régiment de Châteauxvieux* held trials, a privilege always granted to Swiss regiments. Forty-one were condemned to the galleys for thirty years, twenty-three were hanged, one was broken on the wheel and hundreds condemned to prison. The Jacobin club of Nancy has been closed.

Forty thousand men and women swarm onto the streets near the Tuileries.[19] "The massacres of Nancy!" "Dismiss the ministers!" they shout in fury.

"Disperse them!" I order.

'It is difficult for a patriot to believe he spoke these words,' declares Brissot in *Le Patriot français*, referring to my support of Bouillé in the Assembly. On the third, I write: 'You are the public savior, my dear cousin; I rejoice twice, as a citizen and as a friend.' [20] On the fourth, Necker resigns, but people seem indifferent.

I must stand firm to try and obtain liberty but am becoming increasingly isolated. On September 10, National Guards come to my house, wishing to swear a new oath of loyalty to me. Desmoulins accuses me of idolatry; he says I must reject any oaths except those sworn to the nation, the law and the king. On the fourteenth, the Paris Commune sends a deputation to express their joy at the pitiable nature of those who oppose me.[21]

Marat's *L'Ami du Peuple*, writes of 'the shameful actions of the sieur Motier to engage the Parisian army to cover itself with opprobrium in approving the massacres of the patriots of Nancy.' Two days later, on the fifteenth, Marat savages me again: 'Soul of mud...to the good fortune of being the saviour of France, you have preferred the dishonorable role of a man of small ambition, of avid courtesan, of perfidious meddler, and to surmount it all, as a vile supporter of a despot.'[22] Camille Desmoulins is equally vituperative in *Révolutions de France et de Brabant* and when Elysée Loustalot dies on the nineteenth, Desmoulins even declares I have killed him as Loustalot realized I am just an ambitious officer whose spirit was never great enough to play Washington.[23]

The Paris Commune orders me to seize all the copies of *L'Ami du Peuple,* but they continue to appear. On the twenty-second, I lead a funeral procession for the soldiers who died at Nancy through streets where people stand in silence to the Champ de Mars. The National Altar is covered in black with white crêpe; a band plays a somber tune; sixty priests say Mass.

On the thirtieth, Chabroud makes a report to the criminal procedure taking place at the Châtelet, investigating the events of October 5 and 6 as to whether the duc d'Orléans and Mirabeau instigated what happened. I do not think there are sufficient charges against the duc d'Orléans to impeach him and I am sure there are not against Mirabeau,[24] who asks Ségur to enlist my speaking for him. On October 1 I send a letter I wrote to Saint Priest during that time, to the president of the Assembly. On the second it is decreed that there are no grounds for the accusation, but I do not attend. Mirabeau accuses me bitterly of not doing what he alleges I had agreed. The Orléans party tries to compromise and even to attack me. They fabricate a memoir; they pay people to libel me. However, I do not think anything will come of this, particularly if the king spends more time in Paris to halt intrigues on the absurd suggestion that he will be leaving. [25]

I meet several times with the queen to discuss the present situation and the future government in the hope of saving the monarchy. She endeavors to conceal her feelings but is said to be still angry about the events of October 6. She believes I am one of the principal participants in the ruin of the royal family and detests me. Unfortunately, our meetings give rise to atrocious accusations. *Les Révolutions de France et de Brabant* suggests our meeting for nearly two hours on the twelfth at the château of Saint Cloud is of a sexual nature. Pornographic pamphlets and prints represent us in a variety of sexual encounters, occasionally accompanied by Bailly. At the same time, *L'Ami du Peuple* publishes *Anecdotes on the dictator Motier*. I suspect the duc d'Orléans is partly responsible.

On November 15, Monsieur de Castries, a deputy of the right, wounds Charles de Lameth slightly in the arm. The mob is furious. They rush to the house of his father, the duc de Castries; they vandalize the rooms and throw all the furniture out of the windows. I go there with Bailly and soldiers. I am too late to prevent the destruction, as only the walls are left intact,[26] but I stop it being burnt down.

"The vengeance of the people is just, but it does not mean that the neighboring houses should suffer," I say.[27]

The aristocrats accuse me of deliberately being too slow to give the order to suppress the riot and only arriving after it was over; the National Assembly commend me. We hear that Calonne has joined the comte d'Artois in Turin.

Morris visits on the twenty-sixth. "The time is approaching when all good people should group round the throne; the king is very precious because of his moderation and even if he used to enjoy an excessive power it would be possible to persuade him to agree a suitable constitution. What the Assembly have drafted in the name of a constitution is good for nothing. Your personal situation is delicate. You only command the troops in name, but not in reality. I don't know how you can discipline them, but the best line of conduct would perhaps be to take the opportunity of an act of disobedience and resign. In this way you will be able to keep your reputation in France which would be precious and useful later."

"I only owe my elevation to circumstances and events, so that when the disorders cease, I will fall, and the difficulty is to know how to make them occur again," I reply.

"Events arrive quickly by themselves if you know how to profit by them," he says.

"I would like to re-establish the nobility. I would like to have two chambers, as in America," I reply

"The American constitution would not suit France. France needs a government more authoritarian than England," he says.[28]

On the twenty-seventh Voidel declares to the National Assembly that a league has been formed against the state and against the religion between some bishops and some priests, that religion is the pretext, interest and ambition are the motives. A heated debate ensues for two days, following which it is decreed that the clergy must completely accept the new order and swear an oath to be faithful to the nation, the law and the king; to maintain with all their power the constitution decreed by the National Assembly and accepted by the king, and that those who do not swear would be believed to have renounced their offices and would be replaced.[29] Sunday in eight days time is appointed as the day to swear the oath. Sunday passes. There is hostility from many clergy. On December 6, the king signs the new decree, the deadline for the swearing of the oath now extended to the end of the year.

"Hang priests not taking the oath!" crowds are shouting outside the Assembly at the beginning of 1791. Inside, passions continue to run high. One hundred and nine swear the oath, but only four bishops, the archbishop of Sens, the bishop of Autun, the bishop of Orléans and the bishop of Pamier.[30] Many clergy are still refusing, particularly in the countryside, although some also refuse in the cities.

On the eighteenth, I speak in the Assembly concerning the legal system: "Transplant the same system used in Britain and America. Do not lose it by mixing it with the ruins of the barbarous judicial system you are destroying."[31]

In February, the king's aunts, Adélaïde and Victoire say they want to travel to Rome for Holy Week.

"If you agree it looks as though you are giving the assent to an infraction of the law you have recently signed. And it also looks as though this journey is to rehearse your own flight," Mirabeau says bluntly to the king.

"The aunts should renounce the million livres given to them by the nation if they wish to consume it in Rome," writes Desmoulins.

Tocsin bells call people to district meetings where they all condemn the journey and try to find ways to stop it. The king, however, takes no notice. It is even said he is personally making the arrangements.

Adélaïde and Victoire set off with a small retinue of twenty, accompanied by Berthier, the commander of the National Guard of Versailles. A mob of women rush to the royal château at Belleluron, but the aunts have already gone. The mayor halts them at Arnay-le-Duc; they quickly dispatch a letter to the Assembly asking to be allowed to continue.

There have been rumors that the fortress of Vincennes, where Mirabeau spent four years in prison, will replace the Bastille. On the twenty-eighth, at eleven o'clock in the morning, I receive an order from Bailly: 'A very large crowd, armed with pickaxes and crowbars, is demolishing the keep. Send troops there from your headquarters.'

I had suggested to the king in May last year that he should order its destruction, but it is obvious rioters cannot be allowed to do so. Santerre, who led the storming of the Bastille, is already there to restore order with his battalion of the National Guard from the faubourg Saint Antoine, but he appears to be aiding the demolition.

I send a battalion to the Carrousel to maintain public order. I ride to Vincennes with troops. I angrily harangue the soldiers and they retreat to their lines.

"Attack the rioters!" I order.

They charge towards them. They arrest sixty-four; the others flee. I form a column, the prisoners in the middle, the artillery at the front, and we set off into eastern Paris. People fire at some of my officers, but we continue to the faubourg Saint Antoine where the gates are shut against us.

"Bring up the cannon!" I order.

The gates open. We march through the narrow, dirty streets in the evening darkness. People scream abuse and throw stones, wounding several soldiers, including one of my aides. In the rue Saint-Antoine a grenadier bayonets a man who tries to bring down my horse so that I can be killed. Finally, we reach the Conciergerie, some injured, but with all our prisoners.

"Four to five hundred nobles armed with pistols and daggers have surrounded the king at the Tuileries," are the first words I hear.

"Tell the National Guard to disarm and disperse them," I order.

I quickly ride there; nobles come to meet me, complaining bitterly. "The soldiers treated us roughly. We were protecting the king."

I go to talk to the guards. "In the morning we were given wine at our meal to try and make us drunk. While we were drinking a group of royalists gave entry tickets to the palace to others, some of whom had come from outside Paris. They had swords, sabers, sword sticks, pistols and daggers and went into the apartments separating our room from that of the king's chamber. His Majesty came out of his chamber and the chevalier of Saint Elme went into the room of the guards with a pistol. We were told you had been killed in the faubourg Saint Antoine and rushed in a fury into the room where the king was pleading with the nobles to lay down their arms."

I lecture, at some length, the duc de Villequier, the first gentleman of the bedchamber, whom I consider most guilty. Then I turn my attention to the others.[32]"You have all been foolish. You have shown a lack of confidence in my ability and wish to protect the king."

I return to the guards' room. "Weapons have been put in cupboards of the apartment," they tell me. I go back to the king.

"You must give them up," I say.

He gives an order; a large basket of arms, including daggers, is brought in.

"Destroy them," I tell the guards.

They go to the courtyard where they take great pleasure in breaking them, perhaps rather disrespectfully for the royal palace and for the nobles who have already been brusquely censured.[33]

"The false zeal, or the wild behavior of people who call themselves my friends will finish by killing me," declares Louis.

On the twenty-ninth, I issue an Order of the Day in which I again severely criticize the *chefs de la domesticité,* an expression which greatly annoys the courtiers.[34]

In the evening, at the Assembly, a new law is proposed to control the movement of émigrés in and out of France.

Mirabeau objects strongly. "Restrictions on travelling go against the principles of the Declaration of Rights and the Constitution as I have already argued in the case of the aunts."

"Traitor!" shout the Jacobins.

The aunts are, however, allowed to continue to Rome.

On March 7, I write to Washington:

Whatever expectations I had conceived of a speedy termination to our Revolutionary troubles, I still am tossed about in the ocean of factions and commotions of every kind- For it is my fate to be on each side with equal animosity attacked, both by the Aristocratic, Slavish, Parliamentary, Clerical, in a word, by all ennemies to my free and levelling doctrine, and on the other side by the orleananoise, factious, Anti Royal, licentious and pillaging parties of every kind, so that my personal escape If it is doubtful that I will personally be able to escape so many enemies, the success from amidst so many hostile bands is rather dubious, alth' our great and good Revolution is, thank Heaven, not only insured in France, but on the point of visiting other parts of the world, provided the restoration of public order is soon obtained in this country, where the good people have been better taught how to overthrow despotism than they can understand how to submit to the law. To you, my beloved General, the Patriarch and Generalissimo of Universal Liberty, I shall render exact accounts of the conduct of your deputy and aid in this great cause.[35]

April 2. Saturday. Mirabeau is dead. He has died unexpectedly after a very short illness, at nine-thirty this morning.[36] He was only forty-two. His last words had been to ask for opium to dull the pain, but it is reported that he said: "I take with me the death of a monarchy. The factions will prey upon its remains."[37]

The National Assembly falls silent in sorrow. Several sob. Even those, such as Barnave, who had violently disagreed with him, are sad.

"All members of the Assembly should attend his funeral, not just a deputation," suggests Barère.

Talleyrand stands. "I went yesterday to see Monsieur de Mirabeau. There were many people in the house, and I went with an even greater measure of sadness than that of the public sorrow. The sight of desolation filled one with the picture of death; it was everywhere, save in the spirit of the one in most imminent danger."[38]

'He was killed!' is the rumor flying about the city. His body is cut open for an autopsy, but there is no trace of poison. The whole of France mourns. People cry in the streets. It is proposed he should be the first of the leaders of the Revolution to be placed in the still unfinished church of Sainte Geneviève, which will be a Panthéon where *grands hommes* will be commemorated, men who are not only very important in public life, but also virtuous in private. Everyone knew Mirabeau's vices, but no one speaks against the proposal. Even Robespierre agrees.

On April 4, at six o'clock, I lead the National Guard at the front of the funeral procession. They march slowly to the muffled beat of black crêpe-covered drums, followed by battalions of children and veterans, all the members of the Assembly, officials of the municipality of Paris, and the Jacobins, who are now calling him one of their own, despite their recent denunciations and abuse. There are perhaps three hundred thousand spectators, all respectful and silent. The infantry reverse their rifles.

We halt at the church of Saint Eustache, which has been draped in black. Abbé Cerutti preaches a eulogy; then the procession again wends its way through the night, to the music of Gossec, melancholy notes from wind instruments soaring into the black sky, flaming torches illuminating the cortège. Near the chime of midnight, we reach Sainte Geneviève; shortly afterwards Mirabeau's heart is placed on a catafalque next to the philosopher, Descartes.

Crowds gather angrily in Paris. Many are hungry. There is little work. Thirty thousand men and women are receiving twenty sous a day, but this cannot continue long. The king is ill with fever and bloody coughs and the Assembly enquires about his health to the disgust of Fréron's paper which writes: 'twelve hundred legislators soiling their dignity as men and as representatives of the French nation by going into ecstasies for eight days over the state of the king's urine and his stools to the point of falling on their faces before his toilet as if it were the most resplendent throne.'[39]

On the seventh, in the Assembly, Robespierre proposes: "No deputy should be eligible for public office until four years after the session has ended." The motion passes.

The new constitutional bishop of Paris, Monsieur Gobel, comes to dine at the rue de Bourbon, not as a private person but representing his position. Adrienne dines out as she does not want to receive him as bishop.[40]

"Many rich women have installed chapels in their homes so as not to have to go to their parish churches and hear the praises of the Lord sung by constitutional priests. I refer, in particular, to Madame de Noailles, Madame de Mouchy, and Madame de Poix. Will you give me your support in closing these chapels as well as the religious houses?" he asks.

"You must be aware, Monsieur, that your nomination to the See of Paris is entirely owing to my representations. The appointment is now made and I am not going to say whether I am, or am not, sorry, but I am astonished at being asked to persecute in the name of the constitution, citizens whose opinions are not the same as my own. If you wish to act in this manner, you will therefore always find in your path a general who is firmly opposed to you," I reply in annoyance.[41]

The king wishes to spend Easter in his château at Saint Cloud to hear the service from a non-juring priest. As might be imagined this is not popular with Parisians who consider him duplicitous because he has sanctioned the decree on the clergy, but he himself wishes to attend the prescribed service. They also fear he will try to leave France.[42] They gather near the Tuileries.

April 18. I receive an urgent message: 'The king and his family are in their carriage to go to Saint Cloud, but the crowd is preventing them from leaving.'

I immediately ride there; I arrive at the same time as Bailly and find the royal carriage stationary, an island amidst waves of angry people surging around it, extending along the road as far as place Louis XV, already crammed with citizens. National Guard soldiers stand by the carriage, but they are also blocking its path; the king is leaning out of its window, his face taut with anger.

"It is surprising that I give liberty to the nation but am now denied my own!"

"You are a fat pig whose appetite costs us twenty-five million a year," cries a man.

"What you are doing is against liberty. It is also against the constitution," I shout at the soldiers and the mob, but there is such noise I cannot make myself heard.

"We do not want the king to leave! He will not leave!" people reply.

"The king must be able to leave," I tell them.

"We know we are violating the law, but the safety of France is our first law," they retort. "If he escapes there will be a civil war. Paris will be drowned in the blood of its citizens!"

"Martial law must be declared," I say to Bailly.

"No," he replies.

I approach the carriage and see the queen, in tears, huddled ashen faced against its side.

"If you wish I will force a way through for you. Give me the order," I tell the king.

"It is for you, sir, to attend to what is necessary for the proper fulfillment of your constitution," he replies.

I harangue the mob again, but without success. I go back to the carriage.

"Your departure will be dangerous for you and your family, but give me time to clear the way," I say to the king.

"Form up on the right and on the left to open a path for the carriage," I order the soldiers.

They refuse. I know there is a battalion of the National Guard in the gardens of the Tuileries which has offered to help, but I do not wish them to attack their fellow soldiers, so I go back to the crowd and argue again. Then the king, the queen, the dauphin and princesse Élisabeth descend from the carriage. They walk in humiliation back to the palace after nearly two hours in the vehicle. The crowd has shown itself stronger than the will of the king or the Assembly. My troops have not obeyed me. I have failed as a commander.

On the twenty-first, I write a letter resigning my post: 'As the National Guard no longer obey me, I must cease to retain a command which is merely nominal.'

At nine-thirty in the evening, I go to the Commune. I explain the reasons for my resignation. I collapse.[43]

Next day I return. "I still intend to resign," I declare.

At eleven o'clock that night, in torrential rain, Bailly comes to see me, accompanied by members of the National Guard. Adrienne allows in as many as the house can hold, but some have to remain outside.

"I am very sorry I cannot provide better for all of you. I am very touched by your zeal," she says in distress.

I refuse to reconsider; at midnight Bailly leaves in disappointment.

The following day, the king goes to the Assembly to protest about what happened.

"I pledge an oath again to the constitution of which the civil constitution of the clergy is a part," he declares.

He also tells the foreign ambassadors to inform their monarchs that he is free.

'He is a hypocrite prince who rebels against the people. Parisians, you will be the executioners of three million of your brothers if you are mad enough to let him escape from your walls,' writes Marat in *L'Ami du Peuple*, with similar remarks being made in other revolutionary papers. However, every day for two years these same warnings have been made that the king is on the point of fleeing and the warnings have now become so frequent that people no longer believe them.[44]

On the twenty-fifth, I speak to the Commune: "I very much appreciate the requests made to me by the National Guard, but I shall not resume my command because I have no assurance that the law will be any more respected in the future than in recent days. I do not think that the National Guard has seen with indifference what has caused my discouragement-constitutional authority disregarded, orders despised, the public force opposed to the execution of the law, of which the protection was confided to it. We are citizens, we are free, but without obedience to the law there is only confusion, anarchy, despotism."

Despite my words, however, I suggest a way I might be persuaded to return: "The soldiers must renew their oath of allegiance to me and the companies which rebelled must be disbanded."

The sixty battalions accordingly pass resolutions that every soldier should swear to obey the law and that anyone who refuses should be expelled.

On the twenty-sixth, I agree to resume my command, but I know, as does everyone, that I have been weakened.

"He is an ambitious nobody, the vile tool of a despot," Marat describes me from his bath.

"He lacks the vision of a Washington," declares Desmoulins.

The Jacobins placard Paris. They extol the rebellious soldiers. They call them true patriots. The court treats me with hatred, the queen with dislike and disdain.

May 4. The Pope had sent a letter to the bishops on March 10, criticizing the Civil Constitution. He had sent another letter to them on April 13, asking them not to swear the oath. These two letters are made public and many clergy withdraw their oaths. Angry crowds burn his effigy and prevent non-juring priests from worshipping. Market women cane a convent of nuns in public because they had punished pupils who attended a Mass by a non-juring priest. At the end of May, the Papal Nuncio leaves France. There is now a complete break between Rome and France, to the distress of my wife.

Chapter 43

Royal bid to escape

There continue to be rumors the king is about to escape.

"Is there any truth in what is being said?" I feel compelled to ask him, although ill-at-ease from having to do so.

He looks me steadily in the eyes. "No, there is no truth in any of it. I give you my assurance."

I believe him. I publicly announce: "These suspicions are lies. I will answer on my own head that he is not leaving."[1]

On June 20, I visit Bailly in the evening.

"I have been informed of new accusations from the committee of investigations, that the king is about to flee, but I don't think it is likely," he tells me.[2]

"I am sure there is no cause for alarm. However, I will go to the Tuileries to mention it to Gouvion," I reply.

"I know nothing of any escape," Gouvion says. "Madame de Rochereuil tells me any gossip she hears when she attends the queen and there has been no suggestion anything is planned."

"Assemble the principal officers of the guard and have them patrol the courtyards during the night, just in case," I reply.[3]

I go to attend the *coucher* of the king with many others. He seems the same as always. We all enjoy a lively conversation, nothing suggests he is on the point of escape, and he retires to bed, somewhat later than usual. At midnight I drive around to check the grounds of the Tuileries. There is no moon. The coach lamps cast a pale light in the dark. Candles gleam in the windows of the Palace. It is quiet; my carriage takes me home to the rue de Bourbon.

June 21. In the morning, I am abruptly woken by Monsieur d'André, the deputy for Aix.

"The king and his family have escaped. Lemoine, the valet, found his bed empty at seven o'clock and gave the alert. The queen has also disappeared, as well as Madame Royale, the dauphin and Madame Élisabeth. The Assembly is about to meet. Paris already knows."

I dress hastily as officers from the *garde* arrive with the same terrible news. I rush from the house towards the Tuileries, leaving Adrienne in great fear. We both know I will probably be killed.[4]

I talk in the road outside the palace of the Tuileries with Bailly and Beauharnais, the president of the Assembly.[5] We do not know if the royal escape has been aided by foreign powers and whether there will be an invasion or perhaps a civil war.

"If the king reaches the frontier, he will have the support of the emperor of Austria, as well as the probable assistance of other countries and armies formed by the émigrés," declares Bailly.

"The Assembly has just been convened. Time is being lost while we wait for its orders. Do you think that the arrest of the king and his family is necessary for the public good and can alone guarantee against civil war?" I ask.

"Yes," they both agree.

"Then I will take responsibility for their arrest. We cannot wait for the Assembly. I will say the king has been abducted," I reply.[6]

I write a note declaring that as enemies of France have taken the king and his family, all National Guards and all citizens are therefore ordered to arrest them. I give the same order, which I sign, to all who come to see me, as well as to officers of the National Guard, who immediately set off on every road from Paris.

"Go to Valenciennes," I tell my aide-de-camp, Louis Romeuf, at eight o'clock.[7]

The crowd is growing. They are very fearful, their anger increasingly mounting against the Sixth Division of the National Guard which had been on duty at the Tuileries during the night.[8] I walk calmly through the mass of people towards the Hôtel de Ville. In the place de Grève I suddenly come across a large group tearing the clothes from the duc d'Aumont, the unfortunate commander of the Sixth Division, and dragging him towards the river. "You will drown," they shout.

"Stop!" I command. I extricate him from their hands; he runs to the safety of the Hôtel de Ville. The people surround me, still in a fury against him and against me, but I keep walking.

"Each citizen will gain twenty sous as you will now not be paying for the civil list," I joke, to lessen the mood of terror.[9]

They jostle and push, but I continue to make my way. "You call this a terrible event. I would like to know what name you would give to a counter-revolution which deprives you of liberty?"[10]

"We will have you as king," a few voices call out.

A deputation from the Assembly arrives to escort me to the building as they were worried for my safety, but they find I am still popular with the crowd.

"If you wish I will have an escort out of respect for the deputation, but, for myself, I do not need one as I have never been in such safety since the streets are full of people," I tell them.[11]

I reach the Hôtel de Ville; I walk into the Assembly with Gouvion. Camus immediately leaps to his feet. "No uniform here! We must not have any uniform in the Assembly."

"The Assembly has ordered them to the tribune," says Beauharnais.

"Citizen soldiers are exempt," declares Demeunier.

I go to the tribune. "You have been informed of the attempt by public enemies last night, in the hope of compromising French liberty, to the king and part of his family. Monsieur le maire thinks Monsieur de Gouvion, the commander of the interior guard of the Tuileries, should inform you about what has happened. I say only that I will take upon myself alone the responsibility of an officer whose patriotism and zeal are known to me. Monsieur Duport has told the Assembly what is happening in Paris. Let me add that actions of the National Guard have shown on this occasion the greatest proof of all that the French people are worthy of liberty and that nothing can deprive them of it."[12] I speak briefly, not knowing what has already been said.

"It is impossible that the king left by any of the known places," says Gouvion. "He has been guarded with the greatest exactitude. People near to the royal family told Messieurs de Voidel and de Sillery of the committee of investigation about their worries."

"We knew nothing," protest de Voidel and de Sillery.

"The man charged with bringing this information to them had not found any member but had talked, I believe, with Monsieur de l'Apparent," says Gouvion.

"I have vague ideas of what Monsieur de Gouvion is saying. Monsieur Cochon de l'Apparent came to warn me of rumors concerning a possible escape of the king, and I therefore gave orders to Monsieur le commandant générale," asserts Bailly.[13]

Arnaud de Laporte, the intendant for the civil list, brings a letter to the tribune which the king had left for him.

"How did you receive it?" the deputies ask.

"His Majesty had left it hidden with a note for me," he replies.

"Where is this note?" asks a deputy.

"No, no," others call out. "It is a confidential note. We do not have the right to see it."[14]

We read the king's letter, which I find pitiful. He writes to the French people that the only recompense for all his sacrifices is imprisonment in Paris, violation of property and complete anarchy in all parts of the empire. He denounces the betrayal of the wishes in the cahiers and the lack of power given to the king under the new constitution. He criticizes the power of the Jacobins. He denounces the *Société des Amis de la Constitution*, which he calls an immense corporation, more dangerous than any that existed before. He does not believe it possible to govern a kingdom as large and as important as France by the methods of the National Assembly. He invites the inhabitants of his good city of Paris, and all the French people, to mistrust the suggestions and lies of false friends. He asks them to come back to their king. 'He will always be your father, your best friend; what pleasure he will have in forgetting all his personal injuries and to be in the middle of you again….and when liberty will be placed on a firm and unshakeable base.'

He denounces everything he has said, sanctioned and accepted. He has placed his faithful friend, Monsieur de Montmorin, in great danger, as he had innocently signed the passport for the baronne de Korf, as well as other ministers, and he has also abandoned other loyal friends to their fate, including the duc de Brissac, commandant of the cent-suisses. If the king is not found, I will probably be killed and then there will be slaughter of many others, such as the National Guards on duty that night at the Tuileries.[15]

The deputies remain quiet and dignified. They issue the same instructions I earlier gave for all the roads. The ministers have been told to come to the Assembly and an escort has been sent to protect Monsieur de Montmorin. They arrive; the Assembly tells them to continue their functions under its orders.

There is ferment in the streets of Paris. Crowds are destroying everything which has the name or arms of the king. They are smashing royal statues and shouting abuse at their departed monarch. The National Guard is redoubling its zeal and is managing to restore calm.[16]

To my surprise, Louis Romeuf suddenly enters the room. "I was ordered to go to Valenciennes, but I was caught by the crowd."

The deputies decide he should still go there with a decree to instruct all municipal authorities not to let anyone leave France. At midday he sets off again with two deputies, La Tour Maubourg and Biauzat to ensure his safety, who will go to the gate of Saint-Denis as a large vehicle had been seen going towards Châlons.

They return sometime later. "There is a rumor the king has been arrested at Meaux. We told Romeuf to go there as quickly as possible, instead of to Valenciennes," says La Tour Maubourg.

The Assembly has now taken all possible measures; it attends to the order of the day and debate as though nothing extraordinary has happened.[17]

In the evening, I and other deputies of the popular party, including Barnave, Lameth and Sieyès, go to the *Société des Amis de la Constitution*.[18] I have not been there for a long time and others have never been there, but we have been informed that Danton and Robespierre are planning to announce motions to incite the people and persuade them to riot. We hope to unite the different parts of our group in the face of a very difficult and dangerous situation, as well as to dampen down Robespierre and Danton's extreme measures.

Danton sees us enter the room and immediately goes to the tribune. "Monsieur Lafayette, you promised on your head the king would not flee. Have you paid your debt? Either you have betrayed your country, or you are stupid to have spoken for a person for whom you could not speak. In the most favorable case, you have declared yourself incapable of commanding us. But I want to believe that you can be reproached with more than errors. If it is true that the liberty of the French nation depends on one man, it would only merit slavery and abjection. France can be free without you. Your power weighs on the eighty-three départements. Your reputation has swung from one pole to another. Do you want to be really important? Become a simple citizen again and no longer need the just defiance of a great number of people."[19]

"I have never been so sure of liberty than after having seen the spectacle Paris has shown us today. I come to this society because it is here that all good citizens must meet in these times when we must more than ever fight for liberty. It is known that I was the first to say that when a people want to be free, they will become so."[20] I reply calmly, then leave.

I already know Danton has received one hundred thousand livres from Montmorin to obtain his silence and inaction. I met him at Montmorin's house the same evening that he had made the deal and he even told me he was more monarchist than I am. I believe him to be prepared to sell himself to any party and although he talks in an inflammatory way at the Jacobins, he regularly told the court what was happening. He is therefore counting greatly on my discretion to keep his secret.[21]

The Jacobins scornfully denounce our statement that the king has been kidnapped.

"They have in twenty decrees called the flight of the king a kidnapping. Do you want other proofs that the Assembly betrays the interests of the nation?" demands Robespierre.

"Marat was right when he said the Capet woman wants to escape with the fat Louis with the help of Lafayette and the chevaliers of the dagger," declare many.

"You should be made dictator," others say to me.

Rumors are spreading like flies on a dung heap. The Austrian army is said to be marching on Paris. On the twenty-second all the generals in Paris come to the Assembly to swear an oath of fidelity; on the twenty-third, many soldiers of the National Guard renew their oath of allegiance. I also swear, applause constantly interrupting me.

Rochambeau sets off to take command of the Army of the North, to attack the enemy if it invades France; part of the National Guard from both Paris and the provinces are willing to march under my orders.

However, even now, there is humor. Signs spring up: 'Lost. A king and a queen. A reward to anyone who finds them.' 'To rent,' says a sign at the palace. Life also goes on as usual, much to people's surprise. The streets are calm; workers continue to work; carriages drive along the roads; government functions as the Assembly has invested itself with all the powers it needs. Paris and France learn that the monarch is not necessary to the government which exists in its name.[22]

"One would never have imagined that at this moment there is no longer a king of France," people say.

Wednesday evening is sultry with heat. There are a thousand rumors about the king, but we know nothing. The Assembly adjourns at ten o'clock.

Two couriers arrive, white with dust from the road. They force their way through the clamoring deputies to the table of the secretary; Chabroud seats himself in the president's chair.

"The king has been arrested at Varennes," says one.

Everyone starts shouting at the same time. "Bouillé and his army are at Clermont-en Argonne!" "Shut the gates!" "Announce a state of siege!" The Austrians will invade!"

Chabroud's voice is inaudible. André replaces him, but the din continues, so I meet separately with La Tour Maubourg, Barnave and the other leaders. We decide to send commissioners to bring back the king.

At midnight, the Assembly reconvenes and gives the final decision: "Messieurs La Tour Maubourg, Pétion and Barnave shall go to Varennes as commissioners and Mathieu Dumas will accompany them as adjutant général."

Several deputies and I adjourn to La Tour Maubourg's house in the rue Saint Dominique; we discuss the situation.

"The fat pig is embarrassing!" declares Pétion, his sentiments not far from my own, although I would not have expressed it in quite that way.

At two o'clock, in the morning, the three commissioners and Mathieu Dumas leave in a large berlin coach which clatters away into the hot night air to escort our monarch back to Paris.

June 24. Friday. The heat is torridly unrelenting. I have had little sleep. Romeuf returns. "The royal family are on their way and should arrive tomorrow late in the day. They were recognized at five minutes past eight in the evening at Sainte-Ménéhould, by the postmaster, Drouet, a former dragoon at Versailles. He noticed that the valet sitting in the corner of the coach had a profile which resembled that of the king on the *écus* and the *assignats*. Unsure what to do, he let their two coaches depart. Then our two couriers arrived from Paris with the news of the escape and he realized his suspicions had been correct. He galloped with another former dragoon to Varennes-en-Argonne where he alerted Monsieur Sauce, the procureur, to the probable identity of the travellers about to arrive in his village. Monsieur Sauce and the villagers made the carriage occupants get out and come into his house. A judge who had lived at Versailles was brought and he confirmed it was the king. One hundred and fifty hussars arrived at Varennes, but the peasants defended the road with two cannon. The hussars did not attempt to attack and embraced the National Guard soldiers just as peasants from the countryside, armed with guns, picks and shovels. came rushing into the village. At five, the next morning, the couriers reached Varennes and presented my order to the king. There is no longer a king in France, he evidently replied."

Not long after we hear the news, the Cordeliers Club brings a petition to the Assembly escorted by thirty thousand people, proposing that either the king should be deposed or that there should be a national referendum to decide what to do with him.

June 25. Saturday. I prepare for the arrival of the king and his family. I order cavalry to the woods at Bondy; I send a message to Dumas to go along the external boulevards and enter Paris at the gate of the Étoile, then along the Champs Elysées to the garden of the Tuileries, so avoiding many houses, and not passing through the poor districts which would be the more direct approach.[23] I post the National Guard along this route; placards in the faubourg Saint Antoine order: 'Anyone who cheers the king will be beaten; anyone who insults him will be hanged.'[24]
I ride with my officers to Pantin, the air promising thunder. We wait in the heat. Finally, in the distance, a procession appears, moving at walking pace, throwing dust into the air. The cavalry come first, then a berlin closely surrounded by cavalry,[25] three gardes du corps, dressed as couriers and wearing the yellow livery of the Maison de Condé, are seated on the front with three soldiers of the National Guard, followed by other carriages, a file of National Guards and citizens snaking down the road as far as the eye can see.

I ride up to the berlin which sways to a halt in front of the rotunda of the customs gate. To my surprise I see the king and queen wedged between Barnave. The king also, again to my surprise, appears not very different from his usual self. The queen, haggard and ashen-faced, peers at me with scorn as though I am a ghost, and I know she had expected to find me killed. Opposite them sits Pétion between Madame Élisabeth and Madame de Tourzel with Madame Royale on her lap, and the dauphin; whilst in the second carriage are two ladies of the queen and La Tour Maubourg, whose large body would have even more severely inconvenienced the occupants of the crowded first carriage than was the case.

Dumas rides quickly to me. "I give the command to you."

"You are mistaken," I reply. "Your duty has not yet been fulfilled. The decree concerning the return of the royal family states that your responsibility is to take them to the palace of the Tuileries."

I indicate the route by the new boulevards and the Champs Elysées,[26] then we set off. Lefebvre's grenadiers continue to escort the royal carriage and I ride at the head of the procession. At Monceau the king asks for a drink of wine, probably to prepare himself for what lies ahead in Paris. A glass of wine is brought; he downs it in one gulp.

We travel along the Champs Elysées, the National Guard standing with arms reversed as though for a funeral. An immense crowd looks at the cortège with hostility but remains quiet and orderly; the placards have achieved the desired effect. The carriages enter the Tuileries by the turning bridge at the far end of the gardens; we see large numbers of people.

"Monsieur de Lafayette. Save the gardes du corps," the queen calls out.

The carriage halts. The king descends, calm, his brown coat streaked with dust, his face sweating. Many members of the Assembly are at the foot of the steps, including abbé Grégoire, baron de Menou, le Coulteux and Duport; they come forward to meet the royal party. The queen appears fearful and frail; Louis de Noailles offers her his arm. Next come Madame Royale and the dauphin, to the cheers of the crowd; the baron de Menou takes him in his arms. Then come Madame Élisabeth and Madame de Tourzel. There is silence. No one removes their hats. No one shouts insults. Dumas dismounts and stays close to the vehicle to help protect the gardes du corps. The crowd suddenly explodes as they see the three men in their torn and bloodied livery.[27] "Kill them!" They attack the soldiers and Dumas, tearing his uniform. They wound one of the gardes du corps. I lead the troops forward; I push back the crowd. I take the gardes du corps into the cool of the château. Valets come forward to help the king; he disappears into his rooms.

The king and queen have returned to Paris. I still have my head and Austrian troops, as far as we know, are not advancing into France. I go to the king. I speak with respect and affection. "Sire, you know my personal attachment to you, but you must realize that if you separate your cause from that of the people, my own first loyalty will be to the people."

"It is true that you have followed your principles. It is an affair of party," he replies. "At present, here I am. I will tell you frankly that I had thought to be surrounded by people of your opinion, but that it was not the opinion of France. I see now, with this trip, that I was mistaken, and it is the general opinion."

"In everything that is not contrary to liberty and to my duties towards the nation, I have always wanted you to be content with me," I say. I tell him about the decree of the Assembly. His face remains expressionless.

"Sire, may I have your orders?"

"It seems to me that I am more under your orders, than you are under mine," he says with a laugh.[28]

The queen looks at me with scornful coldness; I behave with my usual calm.[29] She disdainfully offers me the keys of her boxes which are still in the carriage.

"No, thank you, madame," I reply. "No one had thought of, nor will think of, opening them."

She places the keys on my hat which I am holding under my arm.

"Please excuse me for the trouble I cause in asking Your Majesty to take them back for I cannot touch them."

"Very well," she snaps, snatching them away. "I shall find someone less delicate than you."[30]

The king goes into his study to write letters. His valet brings them to me, and I find it very unpleasant that I am accused of wanting to exercise such surveillance.[31]

I learn that it had been the decision of the king and queen to keep the three soldiers of the garde du corps in their livery. Dumas had wanted them to be dressed in the uniform of the National Guard, but the queen had said that the king must return to Paris with his family and servants as he had left it, a decision which could have resulted in the deaths of the three men.[32]

The lawns of the Tuileries are a sea of military tents. The king is forbidden to walk in the gardens or on the terraces. Guards patrol constantly. The doors of the rooms are kept open all the time, even that of the queen. Deputations and deputies continually visit to make sure the royal family is still there, as do I. The king complains bitterly.

Some people consider the Assembly's decree on the twenty-fifth to mean there should be a different guard for each of the royal family and that they should be kept apart.

"When such a serious measure is open to two interpretations, I will always choose the most humane," I reply.[33] I ask for kinder interpretations concerning their treatment and it is proposed that they should be specified by the Assembly. "In that case, I will take the responsibility. It would be unworthy for the representatives of the nation to concern themselves with such painful details. It is best that the blame should fall onto me."[34]

"Pig!" "Coward!" "Fool!" shout crowds at the gate or in the place Louis XV. If they notice the king at a window they shout even more loudly. "We will eat your heart!" "We will cut you into pieces!"

If they see the queen, they are equally venomous. "The Austrian slut must be whipped!" they scream, or other ghastly threats.

The domestic service continues as before, but I give the orders to the soldiers, instead of asking the king. The doors and gates of the gardens are kept closed. "Please give me a list of those you wish admitted," I ask.

I find their list is mainly of people very opposed to the Revolution. I therefore station several officers in a room between the rooms of the guards and those of the king and queen, through which visitors must pass. There is, however, direct access between the chambers of the king and queen which avoids embarrassment to them.

People accuse me of having helped the king to escape. One group says I did so to have a republic, the other that I wanted to help the court. Both are absurd and I continue to try and assure the independence of the debates of the Assembly and obedience to its decrees. The Assembly nominates d'André, Tronchet and Duport as commissioners to question the king. They speak to him with respect and kindness. The queen says she is in the bath, so they question her the following day to enable her to agree her replies with the king.[35]

June 30. A letter is read at the Assembly from Bouillé. He claims the honor of having advised the king's flight. He accuses me of being at the head of a republican party which wants to overturn the constitution. He threatens France with a foreign invasion and Paris of complete destruction if a single hair from the heads of the king and queen is harmed.[36]

July 2. I speak at the Assembly. "Monsieur de Bouillé denounces me as an enemy of the form of government you have established…Messieurs, I will not renew my oath, but I am ready to shed my blood to maintain it."[37]

Adrienne greatly admires the stance I have taken in relinquishing all my republican tendencies to join in the wish of the majority as well as taking every responsibility, bearing all censure in order to assure the safety of the royal family and spare them as much painful detail as I can, despite the difficulties in which my position places me. She goes to the Tuileries to see the queen as soon as she starts to receive. "Politics should not be allowed to rule personal relationships," she says.[38]

I also visit the queen. She looks at me with a cold hostility but is polite. Her face is white; her reddened eyes are unattractively prominent; I know her hair has turned completely gray.

She and the king are openly prisoners. Before, they were watched, but not imprisoned. Now they are not trusted. Nearly every night the officers on duty at the palace are troubled by alarms. I am constantly woken from my bed with false fears of escape. The people and the parties are in a continual state of agitation; the king has either fled or is just about to flee.[39]

Danton, Robespierre and other radical leaders call for a republic and for the king to be put on trial as he had abdicated by fleeing. Jacobin clubs are mushrooming throughout France. On July 10 the Emperor Leopold issues the Padua Circular inviting other monarchs to join a campaign to restore the liberty of the French royal family. The king of Prussia responds favorably.[40]

July 14 is the celebration of the anniversary of the Fédération. Bailly marches with the battalion of the grenadiers; I join them en route. All appears calm. On the fifteenth, the Assembly decrees, nearly unanimously, that the king is inviolable and therefore cannot be included in any action against those responsible for his escape. [41] Robespierre, Pétion and three or four others do not agree. People are furious. I put the National Guard on alert and local authorities authorize committees to maintain revolutionary vigilance. Priests who have not sworn the oath are attacked. In the evening, a club called the Social Circle brings four thousand people to the Jacobin club.[42] A petition is drafted by Laclos and amended by Brissot: 'The king should abdicate and should not be replaced unless a majority of the nation decides it.'

I, the Lameths, and most of the deputies, except for Robespierre and Pétion, decide to leave the Jacobin club. We establish another club in the former convent of the Feuillants.

July 17. The petition is placed on the Altar of the Fatherland at the Champ de Mars for people to sign; fifty thousand soon gather in the heat of the day. They start to sign and then discover two invalids, one of whom is lame, hiding below the altar. Some say the men were trying to see the legs and ankles of the women going up and down the steps of the altar; others that they were going to blow it up.[43] The crowd refuse to believe their pleas of innocence;[44] they drag them to the committee of the Gros-Caillou, but then snatch them away. They hang, then decapitate them, and parade the heads on pikes around Paris.

As soon as I hear what has happened, I ride to the Champ de Mars with a detachment of the National Guard. A barrage of stones rains towards us from the sides of the amphitheater. Someone shoots at me from behind a barricade of wagons. The soldiers jump over the barricade and seize the would-be assassin.

"Let him go free!" I order.

The soldiers tear down the barricade. The crowd at the altar promise two commissioners of the commune and I that they will leave peacefully after signing the petition. I leave a detachment to watch them and ride back to the Hôtel de Ville. Several hours pass; I believe the Champ de Mars is peaceful and leave the building.

I receive a message: 'The Assembly declared martial law at six o'clock to assure its security, as well as that of the Tuileries and Paris.'[45]

Bailly has set off, flying the red flag, with the battalion of grenadiers which is always at the Hôtel de Ville. I ride hastily to join them. At eight o'clock we reach the entrance to the Champ de Mars. The crowd allows the advance guard and the cannons to enter but when the municipal officers appear, they shout insults and throw stones. Someone fires a pistol at Bailly who is trying to read his proclamation; a volunteer dragoon is hit in the leg. The National Guard fire in the air to avoid hurting anyone, but this moderation seems to embolden the attackers who again throw stones from the elevated sides, redoubling their assault on the municipal officers and the soldiers, wounding several, including an aide-de-camp, and killing two volunteer *chasseurs.* The soldiers fire on these people, killing eleven or twelve [46] and wounding ten or eleven. A soldier is knocked off his horse, several are wounded, two dragoons are killed, a cannoneer is stabbed to death. A soldier starts to fire a cannon; I ride my horse in front of it; he luckily holds back.[47] Cavalry attacks the rioters without wounding any and they flee. [48]

I finally arrive home; to my immense relief I find my family are safe even though a howling mob had rushed there, threatening to cut off Adrienne's head and bring it to meet me. She had heard the terrible shouts and had acted calmly to take every precaution against the approaching danger. The guard was doubled and drawn up in front of the house.

"At least they were not on the Champ de Mars trying to kill you. We were fortunate, because just as the brigands were climbing the low wall in the garden which looks onto the place du Palais-Bourbon, a detachment of cavalry rode past and dispersed them."[49]

The Assembly passes a unanimous vote to thank Bailly, myself and the National Guard. Paris remains calm, but there are wild exaggerations of the numbers killed. Marat denounces the 'infernal plot of the atrocious Mottié' and says four hundred unfortunate victims were thrown into the Seine at nightfall.[50]

Fréron writes: 'You should have delayed, Bailly, and you, the traitor La Fayette, using this terrible weapon of martial law. Nothing will ever wash the indelible stain of the blood of your brothers, which spurted over your scarves and uniforms. It has fallen onto your hearts. It is a slow poison which will devour you to the end.'[51] He is arrested, as is Brune, and about two hundred others. Danton goes to his home at Arcis-sur-Aube and then to England. Desmoulins, Marat, Santerre and Legendre are in hiding. The Cordeliers and the Social Circle do not meet and the Club des Feuillants sends a manifesto to provincial authorities declaring that it is the only legitimate *Société des Amis de la Constitution.*[52]

In early August, martial law is lifted. Newspapers can again be published, with the result that there are pamphlets and caricatures of me everywhere, often depicted hanging from a lamp post. The Champ de Mars is called a massacre and Desmoulins, who has reappeared, calls me 'the liberator of the Two Words, flower of the age of janissaries, phoenix of the alguazils-majors, Don Quixote of the Capets and the Two Chambers, constellation of the white horse.'

August 5. I propose a motion to hasten the completion of the constitution. "I will not speak of these painful duties that the nation has had the right to expect from me because all the people of devotion must follow it but which it is permitted to impatiently calculate the length." [53]

The radicals are no longer present at the Assembly to impede it; I am busy maintaining public calm, but I also work with Barnave, Duport and Alexandre Lameth.

It is decided to exclude the Civil Constitution of the Clergy, which has so greatly divided the nation. Swearing an oath to the constitution therefore does not mean an acceptance of the new ecclesiastical order and it also means that the Civil Constitution of the Clergy can be amended without the ten years needed to change the constitution itself.[54] On the twenty-third, a law is passed to restrict the press, only Robespierre speaking against. Any writer who 'deliberately provokes disobedience to the Law or disparagement of the constituted powers and resistance to their acts' might be prosecuted and public officials whose honesty is slandered might sue.[55]

August 27. The 'silver-mark' qualification for a deputy is rejected, but as the elections to the Legislative Assembly have already been held, everyone selected has already passed it.[56] On August 1 the Assembly had already passed a law imposing penalties on émigrés. If they do not return within a month they will be subjected to triple taxation. An official list of émigrés is drawn up.[57] Many of the officers of the army have fled, including Bouillé, who is now in Switzerland, and it is rumored they are planning to invade.

On the thirtieth, I speak against the fixing of a delay of thirty years before the constitution can be modified but am not successful. On the thirty-first, the immediate abolition of procedures relative to the Revolution, of the use of passports and of all restrictions on the freedom to travel within and without France are agreed.

Rumors of invasion intensify as Emperor Leopold had met on the twenty-seventh with the king of Prussia at Pillnitz and had invited other powers to join them in using 'the most effectual means…to put the king of France in a state to strengthen, in the most perfect liberty, the bases of a monarchical government equally becoming to the rights of sovereigns and to the wellbeing of the French nation.' They had declared they are ready to 'act promptly' if the other powers agree.[58] The émigré princes had also been there.

September 3. The constitution is finished and presented to the king. I order the lifting of the surveillance of the palace; there are no more guards within the interior; the royal family now has complete freedom. [59] On the seventh Gouvion is elected a deputy for Paris, Marat calling him the 'damned soul of Mottié, the leader of the country's enemies.' [60] Thomas Paine is elected for the Pas de Calais region even although he does not speak French. On the eighth, a decree suppresses the post of *commandant générale* and its functions are given to six *chefs de légion* who will each perform their duties for a month. On the thirteenth, the king sends a message to the Assembly saying that he accepts the Constitution, that he undertakes to maintain it within France, to defend it against attacks from abroad, and to execute it by all the means given to him.[61]

The left side of the room applauds. "*Vive le roi*!" The deputies on the right are sullenly silent.

The king also writes that he would like a general amnesty. The room erupts again into applause and more cries of "*Vive le roi*".

I therefore propose a decree to stop any pursuit and procedure connected with the Revolution. Applause again breaks out.[62] It is unanimously passed; people will now no longer be investigated and arrested following the riot at the Champ de Mars[63] and there will not be an investigation into the October days and the flight to Varennes. [64] All rioters imprisoned in the three years since the Assembly of Notables will be freed; it will have the advantage that many people who have been victims of obscure injustices or of different parties will now also be freed.[65]

September 14. The king, with all his ministers, comes to the Assembly. He sits at the side of the president and formally swears to accept the constitution. "I come here, messieurs, to solemnly consecrate the constitutional law; I consequently swear to be faithful to the nation and to the law, to use all the power which has been delegated to me to maintain the constitution and to execute its laws. May this great and memorable time be that of the re-establishment of peace, of union, and become the pledge of happiness for the people and for the prosperity of the empire."

Paris erupts in joy, although there are some who doubt his sincerity; caricatures depict him as Janus, facing both ways.[66] I believe that he appears to accept the constitution with good faith, with the intention to observe it and to make it work.[67]

The aristocrats vehemently rail against the constitution, against me, against the Assembly. Morris views it with his customary sarcasm: 'A democracy? Can that last? I think not. I am sure not, unless the whole people are changed.'[68]

On the eighteenth, I ride at the head of the National Guard to a celebration of the adoption of the constitution at the Champ de Mars where a hot-air balloon with tricolor ribbons takes off to fly above Paris. I am very content even although it does not completely fulfill my hopes. I would have preferred two elected Chambers and a Senate elected for life.[69] I deplore that the new power of the judiciary has not been given the independence it needs and whose principal guarantee is in the permanence of judges.[70] I am very critical that the new Assembly weakens too much the power of the executive and the jurisdiction of government.[71] I am also critical that present members of the Assembly could not stand for election so France will not now have the benefit of experienced men. However, even with these flaws, I believe the Revolution is complete and that calm will return to France now there is a proper constitution.

On the thirtieth, the king speaks at the National Assembly for the closure of the last session. "I would have preferred it to have continued its work to add to what has already been done and which only has need of being perfected…You, messieurs, must still fulfill a duty even when dispersed throughout France. You must explain to your fellow citizens the true meaning of the laws which you have made for them.[72]

President Thouret replies: "The Assembly, now having reached the end of its career, is enjoying the first fruit of its work…Sire, you have already nearly done everything; Your Majesty has finished the Revolution by your frank and loyal acceptance of the constitution."[73]

The king leaves. Thouret raises his voice and addresses the large crowd of deputies and spectators.

"The Constituent Assembly declares that its mission is finished and that its sessions cease now."[74]

Outside, people are euphoric. They crown Robespierre and Pétion with oak leaves. They unharness the horses of their carriage and pull them through the streets to shouts of acclaim.

October 1. The seven hundred and forty-five members of the Legislative Assembly meet for the first time. Most are young, half are less than thirty years old. Many lack political experience. There are three groups; the right has two hundred and sixty-five deputies mainly linked to the *Feuillants*; the Jacobin left has approximately one hundred and thirty-five; and there is a center group of about three hundred and forty-five constitutional independents.[75] Three hundred and forty-five of the new deputies join the club of the *Feuillants*.[76] This Assembly which is renewing the social order has had to destroy a vast edifice of oppression and abuse; resistance has made it impossible to reform without demolishing everything. I know the constitution is imperfect, but it has the means of revision and public confidence.[77]

"The Constitutional act is now finished. I will be faithful to my declaration to retire and become a farmer as Washington did in 1783." I say. I resign from the National Guard.

On the eighth, I make my adieux and set out my principles in a proclamation to the National Guard of Paris. "Receive the wishes of the most tender friend for the common prosperity, for the good fortune of each of you, and that his memory, often present in your thoughts, mingles with the sentiment which unites all of us, to live free or die," are my last words.[78] I give up my powers to the municipal authority of Paris and receive the most touching instances of affection and regret. On the eleventh the National Guard vote to present me with a sword forged from the locks of the Bastille;[79] I relinquish my command to Bailly.

"You may be sure that we shall never forget the Hero of Two Worlds who has played so much a part in the Revolution," he declares.[80]

I make my last speech to the Assembly. On the thirteenth, Paris gives me a gold medal and a marble statue of Washington by Houdon.

Chapter 44

Commander of an army on the eastern front

We travel slowly towards Chavaniac as I often stop to walk through towns and villages to receive people's acclaim. Adrienne and I are in one carriage, Virginie and Anastasie in another, our vehicles overflowing with civic crowns and flowers to the excitement of my daughters.[1]

Adrienne has written to her sister, Pauline de Montagu, to ask if we can stay with her at the château of Plauzat, but her reply was unexpected: 'I cannot, without provoking the anger of my father-in-law, offer you the hospitality you wish. However, you will pass through the posting stage of Vaire and we can meet secretly there.'

Pauline therefore waits two days for us at Vaire's posthouse where Adrienne and I embrace her with delight.

"We are emigrating to England. Monsieur de Montagu thinks it is safer to leave France," she says.

"I believe the country and Paris will now be calm," I reply. "I am retiring to Chavaniac with my books, my Swiss cows, my Spanish sheep and a Maltese donkey."

The two sisters say farewell tearfully. "We must write often." [2]

October 18. Ten days after leaving Paris, we arrive at Chavaniac, the anniversary, ten years ago, of the capitulation of Cornwallis's army at Yorktown. I set foot once more in my childhood home, my seventy-two-year-old aunt[3] welcoming me with great joy, only believing I have returned when she sees me standing in front of her.[4]

On the twentieth, I write to Washington. I thank him for his two letters given to me at Brioude and tell him of the warmth of the welcome I received on my journey and of the changes at Chavaniac: 'I rejoice in loving the liberty and equality of this total change which has placed all citizens on the same level, and which only respect legal authorities. I cannot tell you with what pleasure I bow to a village mayor.'[5]

On the twenty-sixth, baron de Frénilly visits and finds me in my study, surrounded by papers and secretaries, dictating letters to be sent throughout Europe.

"I was travelling to Clermont just before your arrival there. The townspeople thought I was you and welcomed me in a state of great excitement. When they discovered I was not you, they stoned me. The mayor later apologized but it was a very unpleasant experience," he says unhappily.

When he leaves, he glances at the main door where I have had the coat of arms erased and painted over by a large red bonnet of liberty.[6] His carriage quickly disappears down the hill.

November 4. Snow already covers the summits of the mountains;[7] My sister-in-law, Louise, and my beloved mother-in-law, the duchesse d'Ayen, come to stay; they grieve to see Adrienne still suffering after so many anxieties and emotions of the last years.[8] The duchesse d'Ayen visited Pauline at Plauzat before coming here, but Pauline did not reveal she will shortly be leaving France, so we also say nothing.

Next day, seven delegates arrive from the National Guard of Paris. I see their uniforms, the color of liberty, and immediately embrace them before knowing why they have come. They read out the address voted for on October 26, which has been sent to eighty-three départements and to sixty battalions of the army, to me, to Adrienne, who is in tears, to my family, and to my friends. They stay two days. I tell them of my esteem, my attachment and gratitude to the citizens of Paris.

"Will we see you again with us?" they ask.

"You see me in my native land. I will only leave it to defend or consolidate our common liberty if it is attacked," I reply.[9]

On the eleventh, a delegation from the département of the Haute Loire visits to say I have been elected a member of the administration.

"No one could be more touched by this mark of esteem and confidence, but I cannot accept, as I intend to live as a simple citizen and occupy myself only with domestic affairs," I reply.[10]

Adrienne no longer fears each day that I will not return to her, that I will be killed by the mob, and is gradually recovering from the ordeal of the last three years. She pursues her religious devotions, as does her sister and her mother who is edified to see the religious devotion she experiences in the village,[11] whilst I pursue my tolerance to all faiths. Priests who have taken the oath are now here, so I have given one of my houses in the village which I keep as a chapel with the inscription *peace and liberty*, to two non-juring priests, and the former curé of Chavaniac lives in the château.[12]

Bailly has resigned as mayor of Paris and my friends asked me to stand in the election on November 16. I decline, but they put forward my name. Pétion wins by 6728 votes to my 3126; I think my defeat has been influenced by what happened at the Champ de Mars, as well as my *Feuillant* beliefs. Pétion also had the support not only of the Jacobins, but also, rather strangely, that of the queen, who is reported to have said: "Monsieur de Lafayette only wishes to become mayor of Paris to soon after become mayor of the palace. Pétion is a Jacobin, but he is an idiot, incapable of becoming the leader of a party. As mayor he will be nothing. Besides, it is possible that the interest he knows we have in his nomination will bring him to the king."[13]

On November 20, the battalions of the Fourth Division of the Army of Paris elect me chief; I again refuse.

I am very active, as always. I am training Félix Pontonnier, the son of the coachman, as my secretary. I employ an Englishman, John Dyson, to teach me how to farm, and I buy English pigs and cows. I commission the architect, Antoine Vaudoyer, to make improvements to the château; I decorate what I call my Tower of Treasure with my mementoes of the American Revolution. I have Aubusson tapestries in my bedchamber, toiles of Jouy depicting American scenes in my dressing room, and I commission paintings from the artist, Houel, depicting scenes of the Revolution. It is all, however, very expensive. My revenues have been reduced to fifty-seven thousand livres and Adrienne intends to try to obtain a loan of two thousand écus.

Flurries of snow dust the trees and hills; December brings winter to Chavaniac. Bitter winds blow under the doors. Log fires blaze in all the hearths. We bid farewell to the duchesse d'Ayen and Louise, Adrienne sad, but not distraught. She is very content with our new life in the countryside and with my being here with her, and, in any case, hopes to see her mother again soon.[14]

On the fourteenth, the king notified the elector of Trèves: 'If the armed groups of French émigrés on your territory have not disbanded by January 15, I will regard you as an enemy.'[15] War now threatens. To Adrienne's great distress, a courier suddenly arrives from Narbonne, the minister of war. I have been appointed commander of the Army of the Center, one of three armies formed on the eastern frontier, the other two commanded by Lückner and Rochambeau.

Our liberties and constitution are seriously threatened. My services can be usefully employed in fighting, and I cannot resist the wishes of my countrymen.[16] Adrienne is beside herself with grief. I will no longer be with her, and, far worse, she fears I will be killed.

I set off almost immediately with Félix Pontonnier and my valet, Chavaniac, the son of the local tailor. We travel day and night and on December 22 we see the lights of Paris gleaming through the evening darkness.

Pillet, one of my aides-de-camp, writes to Adrienne for me to tell her of my arrival:

Madame, Monsieur de Lafayette has arrived here loaded with the blessings and marks of affection of the people who eagerly acclaimed him in all the towns through which he passed. Anxious to arrive on the appointed day, he sacrificed his moments of rest to these complimentary exchanges, but fortunately, although he has been travelling day and night, his health seems not to have suffered at all from the fatigues of the journey, and those friends who saw him leave Paris as a sick man are overjoyed by the renewed vigor and the increase in his weight which he has acquired at Chavaniac. All faces light up here at the mention of Monsieur de Lafayette. He is seen everywhere and is welcomed by all as the liberator of his country and the one man in whom they can place their hopes, and he seems happy to know this. The general opinion is that we shall not have a war, but that in order to put an end to the state of anxiety in which the country has been for some considerable time and especially to rally the friends of order and to make an imposing show of strength. So, as you may see, the future presents no cause for alarm.

Throughout his journey Monsieur de Lafayette seemed deeply affected by the condition in which he left you. He hopes that once the rumors of war have been dissipated, Madame de Lafayette will recover her peace of mind and that her fondness for him will enable her to exercise sufficient self control to prevent any deterioration in her health.[17]

December 23. I visit the king; he receives me with politeness, but not warmth. He had not wanted me as commander, but Narbonne had insisted: "If Your Majesty does not appoint him today, the wishes of the nation will force you to do it tomorrow." On the twenty-fourth, I speak at the bar of the Assembly. "I appreciate your approval for the king's decision."

Narbonne has already gone to the frontier, and I will meet him, Lückner and Rochambeau at Metz. On the twenty-fifth I go to pay my respects to the king; at ten o'clock, I set off to the east, detachments of all the battalions of the National Guard accompanying me through the streets to the cheers of thousands of people. At midday, I reach the gates of Paris; the soldiers on foot halt, but those on horseback continue with me to Gonesse.

Metz. My army is meant to be thirty thousand men but is much smaller and includes many new recruits. A few days after the arrest of the king and the emigration of Bouillé was known, most of the officers of the corps composing the garrison here fled. I impose very strict discipline, to the surprise of Lückner and Rochambeau, and to the annoyance of the Jacobins. I am very popular with the men. I eat with them and visit the hospitals. I form two horse artillery companies similar to those I had seen in Prussia. I place one in Lückner's army under the command of Captain Chanteclair, who served with me in Virginia, and the other in my army, commanded by Captain Barrois. I also substitute eight caliber guns for those of the Prussian three.

I write to Washington that I had to act when our liberty and constitution became threatened:

The most important part of our business is to know what part the Great Powers will act-That everyone of them hates us is obvious but not wistanding they would crush us to pieces, they are afraid to touch us, least their subjects catch what they call the French evil...The Army I command will be of course the first to act. I am to have twenty thousand men to garrison the frontiers from

Montmédy to Bitche and thirty thousand to take the field-I do not hope to come up quite to those numbers, but in case I want reinforcements the National Guards will help me-I will send you an exact return of my Army when it is finally arranged, for I always consider myself, my Dear General, as one of your lieutenants on a detached command.

The regular regiments are short of their complement- The volunteer Bataillons do very well, in general, the soldiers and noncommissioned officers of the Army are patriots but want discipline-A third part of the officers are good – another third gone-the remainder very ill affected and will soon I hope go out-They are tolerably well reimplaced.

M.D'orleans can not recover himself from the muddy swamp into which I have kicked him by the middle of October 1789.[18]

Some of the local aristocrats are rude to me which does not harm my popularity with the citizens of Lorraine.[19] I review the troops every day to the tune of *Ça ira*, delighting both the soldiers and the spectators who beat time with their hands and feet.

By February, war seems very probable and Rochambeau, Lückner and I travel to Paris to see Narbonne. On March 2, the king questions us at a council of state about the armies.

"My army lacks arms and equipment," says Rochambeau. "Discipline is almost completely destroyed and circumstances render its re-establishment impossible. With such troops we must reduce operations to defensive measures."

"I agree that equipment and discipline are far from being perfect, but the troops have plenty of spirit. They will follow me everywhere I want. I wish to attack because it conforms to the French temperament," says Lückner.

"My wish is to attack," I declare, siding with Lückner.[20]

March 3. Narbonne does not attend the committee of ministers. He displeases the court by the frankness of his character, his patriotic conduct and his attachment to me.

"He accuses Bertrand de Molleville of behaving badly in the execution of military laws and of the constitution in general and I would like de Molleville's resignation," I say.

"I refuse," replies de Molleville, his colleagues supporting him.

Lückner, Rochambeau and I do not want to lose Narbonne; we therefore each write a letter saying his services in the ministry of war are indispensable. [21] A few days later he publishes our letters in Le *Moniteur* and the *Journal de Paris* without our agreement.

The intrigues are keeping us here longer than we had intended.[22] I see with deep regret the violent division between the Constitutionals and the Girondins. The Jacobins and their clubs are becoming very popular and control provincial administration. Marat, Robespierre and Danton are very powerful; Pétion, the mayor, is in charge of the National Guard.

Narbonne and de Molleville are dismissed. De Grave becomes the minister of war. Dumouriez is appointed to foreign affairs, Roland to the interior and Lacoste to the navy, all Girondins. I do not, however, reveal my displeasure, and work with Dumouriez. [23]

It is decided that I will go into the Low Countries with 40,000 men, supported by Rochambeau, whilst Lückner maneuvers on the Rhine. It is Rochambeau who has proposed me.

"It is a question of revolution, and Your Majesty knows that Lafayette understands revolution better than anyone," he told the king.[24]

"I will only declare war when our armies are ready to march," promises Dumouriez.

I write to Washington on the fifteenth:

Although the preparations continue for war, it is still doubtful that our neighbours dare approach to extinguish such a communicative flame as that of liberty. The danger for us is in the state of anarchy which comes from the ignorance of the people, of the immense number of non-property owners, of a habitual mistrust against all government measures, which leads to exploitation by ill-intentioned people or disguised aristocrats... Do not believe, my dear General, the exaggerated reports that you might receive, particularly those which come from England. Liberty and Equality will be maintained in France, that is certain, but if they do not, you know that I will not survive...The King has chosen his cabinet from the most violent part of the popular party, that is to say, from the club of the Jacobins....We have still some problems but we have to attain our goal. Disorder, wearing a mask of patriotism is our biggest evil, for it threatens property, tranquility and liberty itself.' I also comment on Morris, as well as the Constitution: Permit me, my dear general, to make an observation on the last choice of ambassador. I am a personal friend of Gouverneur Morris. I have always been very happy with him, but the aristocratic and truly counter revolutionary principles he professes, make him little suitable to represent the only nation whose government resembles ours, since both are founded on the plan of a representative democracy. I tell him I would have preferred to have had an elective senate, a more independent judicial body: You see that I am not enthusiastic about all the articles of our constitution, although I like its principles which are similar to those of the United States, with the exception of the hereditary presidency of the executive power, which I believe is suitable to our circumstances.[25]

March 20. Lückner and I return to the east; Rochambeau remains in Paris as he is ill. My army now consists of 60,000 men and extends on the frontier from Givet to Bitche.[26] We prepare for war.

I receive letters from my friends in Paris informing me what is happening there. On April 15 there will be a *fête* held in honor of the Swiss of Châteauvieux and there seems to be a rumor I have returned to the city with the aim of opposing it. 'What has he come to do?' asks *Le Patriot français*. 'Does he think he will find July 17 again? No, he will only find the men of July 14. He is lost and has no resources.'[27] *Le Pèrc Duchesne* shows Madame Veto, their name for the queen, accusing me 'the faithful Blondinet,' of having organized the massacre at Nancy with Bouillé;[28] Robespierre declares: "The pretended hero of two worlds. Let the sword of the law cut off the heads of the great conspirators."

On April 9, Gouvion protests at the Assembly following an address at the bar from the soldiers of Châteauvieux, freed from prison at Brest on December 31 by the decree of the Assembly, and invited to Paris where they will be given a triumphal fête by the Jacobins. He says that his brother marched in the name of the law with the brave National Guards to Nancy where he was killed.[29] He resigns and comes to join my army.

I write to Adrienne on the eighteenth:

I cannot conceal from you that war is probable. There is still some hope, but I would believe war is more likely. We will be in tents toward May 10. The parties are divided in the following way: Robespierre, Danton, Desmoulins etc. etc. form the Jacobin mire and say that we are beaten without resources and attack Lafayette who, they say, has deceived the people and the court, who has brought M. de Bouillé who is far less guilty, and who is more dangerous than the aristocracy....The other party that people call the high Jacobins and which supports the present ministry, is composed of Bordelais, Sieyès, Condorcet, Roederer etc. They fear and hate Robespierre but do not dare make him less popular; they believe war to be inevitable....and although they hate me personally, they have some confidence in me as a constant friend of liberty, equality and a true defender of the constitution.[30]

Robespierre is demanding that the busts of Bailly and I should be removed from the Hôtel de Ville and that the road bearing my name should be renamed.[31] The Jacobins want my dismissal and Brissot has said 'Those of you who think you see a new Cromwell in Lafayette do not know either Lafayette or your century or the French people. Cromwell had some character and Lafayette has none.'[32]

A courier arrives: 'War was declared against the king of Bohemia and Hungary on April 20.'

I order the troops to remain in their quarters and go to speak to them. "War has been declared against the enemies of our liberty."

"*Vive la nation!*" *Vive le roi!*" *Vive Lafayette*!" they shout.[33]

April 24. Just before five in the evening, the aide-de-camp of Dumouriez arrives with new orders.[34] I am to go from Metz to Givet by the thirtieth, take Namur and cut off communication with Luxembourg. I write back to inform him of the present position of my troops when the new order arrives. I say that it is impossible that ten thousand men and their artillery can march there by the thirtieth, but that I will be at Givet on the twenty-eighth and will be preceded by Monsieur de Gouvion. I ask him on what footing I announce myself at Liège, which is Austrian territory; that if he thinks it useful, I will send some light troops there so that news of them can be known at the Assembly of the States. I also tell him that all the information he gives to me is immediately disclosed by unknown sources and that for the last fifteen days my movements and those of the other generals have been known in Metz societies: 'Your instructions have come to me via several of my friends at the same time as those carried by your aide-de-camp. No one arriving from Paris has known as much as I.'[35]

April 25. Thirty-eight cannons are made ready in twenty-four hours, thanks to the activity of Monsieur de Rissan; horses are obtained by the zeal of the municipal authority and the townspeople; shoes and other necessary objects are also procured.[36]

Next day, at four in the morning, the artillery sets off with three and a half companies of the Auxonne regiment, followed by the rest of the army. The troops nearer to Givet are given the order to march there as quickly as possible. The sun soon beats down ferociously but I order forced marches as I fear that otherwise we will not cover the fifty-six leagues to Givet by the thirtieth, where we are to meet with Rochambeau. The men quickly become very fatigued and lack basic necessities but do not complain. I am the only person who does, knowing what they are having to suffer.

De Grave writes on the twenty-eighth: 'As the Assembly and the king have declared war on the emperor, the French general has the right to pursue the Austrians everywhere which welcomes them.'[37]

On the twenty-ninth our patrols push back those of the enemy. On the thirtieth my advance force overcomes them at Bouvines, half-way to Namur, killing two or three Austrians and capturing four. On May 1, Gouvion takes up position with three thousand men. In the evening, a message arrives from Rochambeau that Dillon and Biron are falling back. A second message arrives later from Biron to say he is returning to Valenciennes. During the night several of my officers go over to the enemy.

A letter arrives from de Grave, written on the thirtieth:

M. de Biron has encountered a corps of six thousand men entranched on the heights of Mons and it is vey uncertain that he will be able to take this town. The unfortunate Thébald Dillon was completely beaten at Bézieux; returning to Lille pursued by the Austrians, the people at Lille cried treason and cut him to pieces.'[38] They killed his aide-de-camp, M. Chaumont, and M. Berthois. Such horrors are a long way from the behavior of people who love liberty. They also killed six Tyrolian chasseurs, prisoners of war....Since the Brabant seems little disposed to revolt, I believe you should only attack if there is a near certainty of success...Perhaps your name will awaken in the heart of these people the love of liberty, but unless there are certain proofs to the wish of the

Belgians to shake off the Austrian yoke, do not hazard anything, as a second defeat would be worse.[39]

May 2. I write to inform de Grave of our movements and that my advance force is still at Bouvines. I say that it is incredible that the artillery and troops under Monsieur de Narbonne should have managed to march fifty-six leagues, along bad roads, in excessive heat, in the short space of five days. I say that the treatment of prisoners of war must be exemplary otherwise our brave soldiers would be too sickened to fight if the fate of their defeated enemies was given over to cowardly acts of cannibalism. I ask for the necessities we lack.[40]

Lückner and I agree I will occupy the camp at Maubeuge. I inspect the troops there; they do not have enough food or munitions.

Next day, I write again to de Grave, denouncing the penury and distress of my army which prevents me from moving forward.[41] It is a very difficult and precarious situation. On the sixth, my army is at Rancennes, the soldiers yet again uncomplaining about the lack of necessary items. I station two forward posts on Austrian territory, one towards Luxembourg, the other at Bouvines; my second division is around Dun; the corps of Riccé is near Longwy.

I write again to de Grave to tell him my position; I add 'I cannot conceive how war has been able to be declared when we are not in any way prepared.'[42]

Rochambeau resigns from ill health and is reported to have declared: "How do you think I can resist Dumouriez and the Jacobins when Lafayette who has so many claims to popularity can hardly defend himself against them?"[43] He is indignant at the change of the plan he had drawn up; he felt insulted and horrified by the tragedy indiscipline has just produced.[44] I want him to stay; I propose to unite my force with his under his orders. I am called to Valenciennes to form a plan of attack on the coast of Flanders. Lückner demands to be in command, and I agree that I will occupy the entrenched camp at Maubeuge.

May 7. My troops are now at Maubeuge. On the ninth there is a light skirmish with the enemy; two or three men are killed and six wounded. On the eleventh, I receive a letter from Rochambeau telling me what measures to take if the enemy attacks.[45] On the nineteenth, his command is given to Lückner. De Grave was replaced by Servan on May 7. On the twenty-third, Gouvion is attacked at Hamptinne, near Florennes, by very superior forces, his troops fighting well before retreating.

June 11. The Austrians under General Clairfait attack our advance force at Glisuelle beyond Maubeuge. They are beaten back but Gouvion, my beloved friend of fifteen years, is killed by a cannonball.

'He is mourned by his soldiers and by the whole army; he will be mourned by the National Guard of Paris and by all who appreciate the value of a pure civism, an unshakable loyalty and the union of courage with talent. I will not speak of my personal affliction. My friends will pity me.' I write to Servan.[46]

On the eleventh, the king used his veto to oppose a law on non-juring priests as well as to oppose the formation of a camp of twenty thousand fédérés on the outskirts of Paris.

I receive complaints about the growing excesses of the Jacobins from administrative and municipal bodies. The Jacobin clubs are taking over all powers, insulting the tribunals and constitutional authorities, dominating the administration, the legislative body and are directing politics and the war.[47] I also receive worrying letters from my friends in the constitutional party. They say that before perishing in the common shipwreck, it is necessary to arm the true friends of liberty against a new and insupportable tyranny. They are plotting to save the nation, to maintain the laws, and to keep the inviolability of the crown.[48] I daily see the violation of the

Declaration of Rights that I was the first to proclaim, and of the constitution to which I had sworn an oath on July 14, 1790, in the name of the armed men of France. [49]

June 16. News arrives at our camp at Maubeuge that on June 12 the king dismissed the Girondins, Roland, Servan and Clavière. On the thirteenth, Dumouriez became minister of war. To my delight I can now make a necessary example to encourage the well-intentioned but very feeble majority of the Legislative Assembly which, however, has some remarkable, strong and patriotic deputies. [50] I therefore write a letter to the president describing the true state of France and denouncing the Jacobins; a copy will be sent to the king:

> I was going to call your attention to grave public interests and refer to, among our dangers, the conduct of a minister whom I have accused for a long time, when I learn that he has succumbed under his own intrigues...Your circumstances are difficult; France is threatened by outside forces as well as disturbed by those within...You must repress them and will only have the power to do so if you are constitutional and just. Can you hide from yourselves that a faction, and, to avoid vague terms, the Jacobite[51] faction, has caused all the disorders? It is this faction I openly accuse. Organized like a separate empire in the capital and in its affiliations, blindly directed by several ambitious chiefs, this sect forms a distinct corporation in the midst of the French people, whose powers it usurps by subjugating its representatives and officers. In the public meetings of that faction, the love of law is called aristocratic and its violation, patriotism....I denounce this sect....It is after having opposed all obstacles, all traps, the courageous and perseverant patriotism of an army, sacrificed, perhaps, to attempts against its leader, that I can today oppose to this faction the correspondance of a minister, worthy product of this club, this correspondence, all of whose calculations are false, the promises vain, the information wrong and frivolous, the advice perfidious or contradictory, when, after having pressed me to advance without precautions, to attack without the means, started to tell me that resistance was going to be impossible, when my indignation pushed back this cowardly assertion...The citizens should rally around the constitution; they should be assured that the rights which it guarantees should be respected with a religious fidelity, which will ensure the despair of either public or hidden enemies.....Let the royal power remain intact for it is guaranteed by the constitution. Let the king be revered because he is invested with the national majesty. Let him choose a minister who does not carry the chains of any faction, and if any conspirators exist, they should be killed. Let the reign of the clubs, destroyed by you, give way to the reign of law, their usurpations give way to the firm and independent control of constituted authorities; their disorganizing maxims to the true principles of liberty; their delirious fury to the calm and constant courage of a nation which knows its rights and defends them. Let their sectarian plots give way to the true interests of the country, which in this moment of danger ought to reunite all those to whom its enthralment and its ruin are not objects of an atrocious rejoicing and of an infamous speculation. [52]

My letter to the Assembly arrives on June 18. According to Mathieu Dumas, it was read out in an almost religious silence. The left side and part of the center of the Assembly applauded; the rest and the tribunes did not dare give the least sign of agreement. Dumas and others wanted to have it printed and sent to the départements; murmurs started, but its printing was voted for. The Girondins, recovered from their astonishment, opposed its sending to the départements. Vergniaud, pretending to believe that my intentions were pure, said that the Assembly could only receive the communications of a general of the army through the minister. Thévenet replied that what I said was true and that it had needed a man such as Lafayette to make them heard at the Assembly. Guadet cast doubt on the authenticity of the letter. Dumas affirmed that the signature was mine. Guadet replied that Monsieur de Lafayette knows that when Cromwell used similar language, liberty was lost in England, but that he would never be persuaded that the emulator of Washington would want to imitate the Protector of Great Britain. Carnot le jeune, of the center, said that the only way to bring calm was to send the letter to a committee. This was decreed.[53] It is the first time the faction has been so strongly attacked and the Jacobins denounce me in newspapers, in clubs and on the streets.

"Strike Lafayette and the nation will be saved. When the decree is given, the entire nation will execute it...The wellbeing of France is attached to the fate of Lafayette. If he is given the time to finish his plotting, liberty is finished, but if he is overturned immediately the cause of the people will triumph, and liberty with them," declares Robespierre at the tribune of the Jacobins on June 18.[54]

"There is no doubt Lafayette is the leader of the nobility which has joined with all the tyrants of Europe, and if it is true that liberty comes from heaven, it will come to help us exterminate our enemies," is Danton's offering.[55]

The Jacobins regard me as their chief enemy to stop them destroying a constitutional monarchy. They are correct. They talk constantly of a republic. Violence and threats of revolution wash the dirty streets of Paris.

June 22. I write to Lajard, a friend who is now the latest minister of war, about the formation of artillery companies of horse and other military matters. Then I continue: 'All this is less interesting than our political situation, on which all the efforts of good citizens should concentrate. There is no one amongst them who would want to see liberty, justice and France sacrificed to the factions. My fight with them is to the death and I want to finish it soon, because if I have to attack them alone, I would do it without considering their force or number.'[56]

I worry about Adrienne. 'Would you like to come here to be with me?" I write to her.

She decides to stay at Chavaniac with our children and my aunt. She fears if she accepts my proposal that in these times of public trouble, I will be accused of wanting to put my family in safety. She also fears to impede my movements which depend on so many uncertain events. [57]

News arrives at our camp at Bavay that thousands of people, many armed, from the faubourg Saint Antoine and the faubourg Saint Marceau, as well as Jacobins, Orléanists, brigands, vagabonds and National Guards, led by Santerre, Legendre, and Saint Huruge, stormed into the palace of the Tuileries on June 20, the third anniversary of the swearing of the tennis court oath, and a day after the king had renewed his veto against the decrees on non-juring priests. They went first to the Assembly, and Santerre, commander of the National Guard of the faubourg Saint Antoine, wrote a letter to say that they only wished to present a petition to the Assembly to be given to the king. A speech was made composed of insolence and threats, complaining of the three ministers' dismissal, that the people would attack traitors, that the hour had arrived, that blood would flow, and much else. Then they were allowed to enter. Enormous tables carried in the Declaration of Rights; women and children danced around the tables carrying olive branches and picks to suggest there would either be peace or war and singing *Ça ira*. Then came men from the markets and workers of all classes armed with poor guns, sabers, and entrenching irons placed at the end of huge sticks, led by Santerre and Saint Huruges carrying naked sabers. Torn *culottes* were waved in the air. "*Vivent les sans-culottes!*" they shouted. The heart of a calf with the inscription, 'The heart of an aristocrat,' was stuck on the end of a pike. Battalions of the National Guard marched behind to keep order; then came more women and armed men and were applauded by the Girondins and people in the galleries. This infernal column then left the Assembly, crossed the garden of the Tuileries, turned the palace by the side of the Carrousel and entered by the royal door which two municipal officers had ordered the Swiss to open. They filled the courtyards and the garden and invaded the building. They besieged the king who was standing on a bench behind a table in the embrasure of a window, surrounded by National Guards and other people trying to protect him. They shouted threats. "No Veto!" "Recall the patriot ministers!" Legendre presented him with a red bonnet which the king placed on his head. He was given a bottle of wine and asked to drink to the health of the nation, which he also did.[58] He remained calm, which does not surprise me, and confronted the mob for hours.

Marie-Antoinette, princesse Élisabeth and the children, were in a different chamber, guarded by a few grenadiers, and huddled in terror behind a barricade of chairs, whilst the crowd hurled insults at the queen, many of a sexual nature. After six hours, Pétion arrived, claiming he had only just heard of the violence. He harangued the mob and persuaded them to leave.

"I must go to Paris. I will defend liberty against tyranny until I die and cannot stay silent at what is happening. Everyone is afraid of these factions, but I am not, and I will speak the truth about them," I declare.

I decide to change the position of my army; I send Pusy to Lückner at Menin to ask him what he is intending to do and if he approves my change of position. I add to my message my proposal to go to Paris unless he believed it was inconvenient for the army:[59] 'I have always lived for the cause of liberty. I will defend it to my last breath against all sorts of tyranny and I cannot submit in silence to what the factions are doing at the Legislative Assembly in making it abandon the constitution to which we have all sworn an oath and to the king by placing him in danger.'[60]

Pusy returns with the message: "He said to coordinate the operation of your troops with his and take the necessary measures if you are not at your post. He also said that if the *sans culottes* get hold of you, they will cut off your head."[61]

June 25. I write to Lajard about the army which I station for safety under the cannons at Maubeuge. Next day, I write an Order of the Day to the troops: "I am going to the National Assembly and to the king to express the feelings of all good Frenchmen and to demand that my army is given what it needs."[62]

I set off with La Colombe, travelling as quickly as possible, halting briefly at Soissons where the officials of the département of the Aisne warn me of the dangers and uselessness of my going to Paris and try to stop me from continuing.[63]

In the pale light of early dawn on the twenty-eighth my postchaise clatters through the Paris streets to 41 rue de Seine.

"I have come to speak to the Assembly," I say to a surprised La Rochefoucauld. I quickly write to the president and ask to address the deputies. He gives his agreement; La Rochefoucauld and I go to the Manège. The Girondins do not want me to enter; Dumas and Jaucourt speak on my behalf, I am allowed to proceed.[64]

It is obvious people know I am coming. The deputies fill the main part of the vaulted hall. The galleries swarm with Jacobin supporters dressed in red bonnets and striped *sans culottes* and more people are still entering. I go to the bar. There is some applause.

"I must first assure you, messieurs, that following the concerted actions of Monsieur le maréchal Lückner and myself, my presence here neither compromises the success of our arms nor the security of the army I command...It has been said that my letter of the sixteenth was not from me.; I have been reproached from having written it from camp. To avow it is mine I must come here alone, having left that honorable rampart which the affection of my troops formed around me. I am here to acknowledge the authenticity of my letter and I am here alone without the protection of my troops.

Another more powerful reason forced me to come, Messieurs. The violence committed on the twentieth at the Tuileries has aroused the indignation and the alarm of all good citizens, particularly those of the army....I have received from different corps messages filled with their love for the constitution, of their respect for the authorities which have been established and of their patriotic hatred for the factions of all the parties....Messieurs, it is as a citizen that I have the honor to speak to you, but the opinion that I express is that of all French citizens who love their country, its liberty ,its calm, the laws which have been given...It is time to guarantee the constitution from attacks being made on it, to assure the liberty of the national assembly that of the king, his independence, his dignity. It is time to thwart the hopes of wicked citizens who are waiting for foreigners to re-establish what they call public tranquility and which would be for free men a shameful and intolerable slavery. Arrest the instigators and the leaders of the violence on June 20 at the Tuileries and punish them for treason. Secondly, destroy a sect which invades the national sovereignty, tyrannizes citizens, and whose public debates leave no doubt about the atrocity of the plans of their leaders. Thirdly, I dare finally beg you, in my name and in the name of all decent people, to take effective measures to ensure the respect of constitutional authorities, particularly that of yours and the king, and give the army the assurance that the constitution will not be attacked from within the country whilst brave Frenchmen are shedding their blood to defend our frontiers."[65]

Most deputies applaud.[66] Others are silent. Guadet is the first to speak. "Has the Austrian army been beaten? No, our enemies are still the same; our external situation has not changed and yet the general of one of our armies is in Paris. What powerful reason calls him here? It is our internal troubles; he fears that the Assembly has not enough power to repress them. Making himself the mouthpiece of his army, the mouthpiece of all the honest people of the kingdom, he comes here to maintain the constitution. I will not examine if he who accuses us of having seen the French people in the brigands who took their name, could not be, in his turn, accused of having seen his army in the staff who surround him, but I will say that Monsieur de Lafayette himself forgets the principles of the constitution which he recommends, when he establishes himself in the legislative body as the spokesman for an army which has not been able to deliberate, the spokesman for all the honest people of the kingdom who have not charged him with the mission. The minister of war must be questioned to see if General Lafayette has been ordered or given leave to come to Paris. From tomorrow the special commission must forbid generals of the army to come to present petitions at the bar of the Assembly." [67]

"Our constitution is still a theory, whose application can still be discussed, according to the circumstances and passions of people, who have many different interests. Recently, an armed multitude came to the Legislative Assembly, and it was argued that there were no laws or prohibitive reasons as to why they should not be here. Today Monsieur Lafayette, who has given as guarantee to the nation his whole fortune, his whole life, a reputation which is worth more than his fortune and his life, comes to the bar, and suspicions and worries abound, passions are let loose. The petition of General Lafayette must be sent to the special commission to deliberate on it and reply as quickly as possible" replies Ramond.[68]

The debate continues in a furious tumult of voices. I remain silent, grave and composed. I have said what I wanted. I hope to reanimate the ardor of the National Guard. It is the only force which can come to our help to save the constitution and the king, but we must act quickly with vigour, disperse the Jacobin club which is already frightened, and push to the end a movement of reaction. I am resolved, as are my friends, to brave all the dangers that this action entails.[69]

I leave before the debate finishes. Outside, a few people cheer, but others shout insults. I walk across to the palace of the Tuileries and ask for an audience with the king.

He receives me with both warmth and reserve,[70] his plump features creasing into a smile. "Thank you for coming."

He is his usual self and appears as unmoved by his recent humiliation as he was when he returned from Varennes.

"Thank you," says Madame Élisabeth. The queen is coldly polite.

"Order must be restored. The Jacobins are strong. They are causing tyranny and anarchy in Paris and the country and need to be disbanded," I say bluntly. "It is necessary to destroy them physically and morally."[71]

"The only way I and my family can be safe is to support the constitution," replies the king. The queen agrees.

"I would be very pleased if the Austrians could be beaten as quickly as possible," he says.[72]

"You are going to review four thousand troops tomorrow. Let me come with you. When you leave, I will appeal to them to do what is necessary for the defense of the constitution and public order," I reply.

He reflects for a few moments. "Yes, you can attend."

"We do not require your help," declares Marie Antoinette dismissively.

I go to the rue de Bourbon, escorted by a steadily growing crowd.[73] At my house, whose entrance has a *mai* adorned with tricolor garlands, there are more people, including many former National Guards whose force has been very changed from how it was and now lacks civic devotion and esprit de corps.[74]

In the evening, I talk with Lally-Tollendal. "I am resolved to declare war on the Jacobins at Paris, to call together all the friends of the kingdom and of true liberty, all the proprietors who are worried, all the oppressed who are many, and to hang in the middle of them, in a public place, a monarchist standard bearing the words, 'no Jacobins, no Coblenz', and to harangue the people, to drag them to follow us to the Tuileries, to arrest their leaders. I swear that when I return to the army, I will work for the means to deliver the king."[75]

The Jacobins denounce me at their clubs. "He has at last taken off his mask, but he has done so too soon," says Brissot. "He is an enemy of France," declares Robespierre. "He is the greatest of criminals," says Couthon. "He is a traitor, an imposter and a scoundrel," says La Source.[76]

I hold a meeting at the rue de Bourbon to attempt to persuade people to attack the Jacobin club. Only one hundred attend, one of the problems being that the National Guard has changed. Working men armed with pikes have now brought disgust and terror into its ranks. The former citizen soldiers come to see me, but the previous patriotic army is no more.[77]

Pétion cancels the review. It is rumored the queen has informed both him and Santerre of my plan, which I am well able to believe.

Madame Élisabeth had said, "It is necessary to forget the past and to throw ourselves with confidence into the arms of the only man who can save the king and his family."

"It is better to die than to be saved by Lafayette and the Constitutionals," the queen had replied.[78]

I meet Morris at the Palace.

"I am leaving Paris tonight," I tell him.

"You need to return soon to your army or go to the duc d'Orléans and decide whether to fight for a good constitution or for the piece of paper which bears its name. In six weeks time it will be too late," he says.

"What do you call a good constitution? Is it an aristocratic constitution?" I ask.

"Yes," he replies. "I believe you have lived long enough under the present régime to see that a popular government is worth nothing in France."

"I would prefer the American constitution with an executive hereditary power," I say.

"In that case the monarchy would be too powerful, and it would need to be controlled by a hereditary senate," he replies.

"I would have some difficulty on agreeing to that," I tell him, and our conversation ends.[79]

I hold another meeting. This time only about thirty come. It seems hopeless. I will try and achieve what I want by other means. I send a letter to the Assembly; I say I am returning to the post where brave soldiers are willing to die for the constitution and I bitterly regret that the Assembly did not decree on my petition. I again denounce the sect which is harming all authorities and threatens their independence and which, after having provoked the war, tries by corrupting our cause to take away from it our defenders. I say that our liberty, our laws, our honour, are in danger.[80]

June 29. At seven in the evening, I abandon Paris, again travelling as quickly as possible. My carriage breaks down twice between Louvres and Senlis and the commandant of the local National Guard lends me his to continue to Maubeuge.

July 2. I issue an Order of the Day saying I had only left my troops because of the imminent danger to the constitution and the king, and that the king had been very grateful for the signs of the army's attachment to him.[81] Next day, Bureaux de Pusy takes a letter from me to Lückner in which I suggest we should unite our armies and attack the Austrians near Mons. I believe that a victory would have political consequences. I tell him I will leave tomorrow for Avesnes and will go to meet him on the fifth at Valenciennes.[82] Lückner replies immediately that my plan is not practical, and he will meet me at Valenciennes.

On the sixth, Lückner and I discuss the situation; we are both in despair at the poor state of the army. We write a letter to the minister to give to the king saying we believe he should make peace, that the means we have been given to defend the kingdom are very disproportionate to those the coalition allies appear to have prepared, that we think, with the king, that we must all die rather than to allow an attack on our national sovereignty and on the sacred cause of our liberty, but that we believe that a prompt and honorable peace would be the most important service the king can give the nation.[83]

I return to my army; the minister writes to me on the ninth, to say that His Majesty, without telling me,[84] and partly to satisfy Lückner who prefers to be in the German parts of France, has changed the départements assigned to each of us. I will now command the Army of the North, from the left of the frontier, from the coast of the Channel to Montmédy; Lückner will command the Army of the Center, from Montmédy to the Rhine; Biron will be under his orders, although still called general of the army, a title wanted for him by the Jacobins. I suspect that this change has been instituted by them to cause trouble for me and to deprive me of reinforcements. [85] At Paris, Torné has described me as wanting to imitate Cromwell without having his ability;[86] the citizens from Croix-Rouge have said that the bar of the Assembly was dirtied by my presence as a rebel leader.[87]

La Rochefoucauld, who is president of the *directoire* of the département of the Seine, had Pétion suspended from his post of mayor of Paris on July 6 for his behavior on June 20, but the Assembly cancels this on the thirteenth.[88]

During all this political intrigue, I am pleased to hear from Adrienne that nine paintings of events of the Revolution by Hoüel have arrived at Chavaniac. I am not, however, pleased to discover that only Lückner is allowed to be at the ceremony of swearing an oath to the constitution at the *Champ de la Fédération* on the anniversary of July 14, as I had hoped it would be a solemn occasion to remind Frenchmen of their civic duties.

Our troops are currently marching to the most exposed part of our territory, the gap between Montmédy and Longwy; two regiments of chasseurs will therefore be at La Capelle, twenty leagues from Compiègne, where the royal château stands at twenty leagues at the most, from Paris, a distance the king is allowed to be from the capital according to the decree of March 28, 1791. This therefore enables a plan to be devised. I propose to accompany him to the Assembly where he can announce he intends to stay at Compiègne for a few days. He will go there with some National Guards of Paris and will be able to count on the National Guard of Compiègne. The loyalty and patriotism of the officers of the two regiments is assured and La Tour Maubourg, maréchal-de-camp and a former member of the Constituent Assembly, will command them. The king will therefore be sheltered from any violence, in a situation of his choice, and can then make a proclamation forbidding his brothers, and the émigrés, to come any closer and declaring himself ready to march, if the Assembly agrees, against foreign enemies, whilst at the same time he can also strongly proclaim his support for the constitution.

My actions will be completely legal; my troops will be there only to protect the king. I do not wish to be accused of a *coup d'état*. It is the only way to save the constitutional monarchy as well as to save France and liberty from the brink of the abyss.[89] I write to La Colombe at Paris to ask the Royalists to suggest my scheme to the king.

The king thanks me but refuses my proposal. Some of his personal friends tried to calm his worries, to inspire confidence in him for the patriot general. They begged him with tears in their eyes, to abandon himself to the only person who can snatch him from his fate and to save so many others who are dependent on such a decision. His most influential advisors are, however, only hoping for the return of an absolute monarchy by an increase in anarchy and a foreign invasion. The life of the king means little to them besides the recovery of their privileges. In the Tuileries they are saying publicly 'We know Monsieur de Lafayette will save the king, but he will not save the royalty.' The queen recalled that Mirabeau, shortly before his death, had said that in case of war 'Lafayette would want to keep the king prisoner in a tent.' She also remarked "It would be very annoying for us to twice owe him our lives."

La Colombe asked the queen from what strange blindness had she and the king taken this decision. She had replied "We are very grateful to your general, but it would be better for us to be shut up in a tower for two months."

"What did she mean?" I ask.

"I have not the slightest idea," he replies. "It is obvious she is still hoping foreign armies will come to their aid."[90]

My proposal to the king becomes known. The *Patriote* and the *Chronique* write furiously about me. Robespierre savages me; Collot-dHerbois attacks me at the bar of the Assembly. I continue my march to Sedan and Montmédy and think only of defending our frontiers.[91]

A report reaches me at Longwy that six Jacobin deputies declared to the Assembly that during a dinner at the episcopal palace given by Gobet, the bishop of Paris, Lückner had said that Bureaux de Pusy had come to him with a proposal from me that we should both march at the head of our armies and attack Paris.

The six deputies signed their declaration; the Assembly now feels obliged to summon Bureaux de Pusy to the bar to give an account of his mission. I write a short letter to the Assembly and finish with the words: 'It is not true.' [92]

I write to Lückner, who is on his way to Strasbourg. He replies: 'The cabal must treat us equally; I have been warned that you and I have been denounced…Paris seems terrible to me!'[93]

Dumouriez writes to me demanding an explanation. I write to Lückner and enclose Dumouriez's letter. I receive his reply on the twenty-fifth: 'You know me enough to recognize an intrigue in the proposals which are as false as they are impossible.'[94]

Bureau de Pusy very bravely goes to the Assembly on July 29. He shows them the letters he carried between Lückner and I and describes the movements of our armies. He narrowly escapes being killed and returns to camp.

D'Abancourt was appointed minister of war on July 23. He writes to me criticizing my movement towards Montmédy, in concert with that of Lückner, when the imperial forces have just occupied Bavay. I reply in detail about our movements. I ask him where my frontier is meant to be-is it from Dunkerque to Givet and Rocroy, is it at Sedan, or does it extend to Montmédy? I tell him what I will do militarily depending on each case.[95]

We hear that the Duke of Brunswick, commander of the allied Prussian and Austrian forces on the frontier, proclaimed at Coblenz on July 25: 'If the Tuileries are invaded, or an assault made on the royal family, Paris will be attacked.'

News comes from Paris that his words have roused people to fury. They want to defend France and great numbers are enlisting in the army. Dumouriez has been made general and is being sent to the front.'

I immediately write to the minister of war: 'I do not believe the news that Dumouriez has been sent to the army I command. I have accused him openly of madness, or of treason to the public good and to me.'

'If Dumouriez comes tell him to go,' I tell Arthur Dillon who commands the left wing. To my immense anger, Dumouriez arrives and takes up his command.

We learn that many fédérés had arrived in Paris for the celebration on the fourteenth. On the thirtieth, the volunteers from Marseille, comprising about 500 men, arrived with three cannon and fought with grenadiers of the Filles-Saint-Thomas, killing one and wounding others. They came to the bar at the Assembly to present a petition for the dismissal of the king. Pétion also demanded his dismissal, and the petition was sent to the *commission extraordinaire*. On August 8, Jean Debry, who reports from the *commission extraordinaire*, accused me of treason and wanted to put me on trial. Brissot spoke to the Assembly and said he is no longer my friend, that if a general had wanted to serve the projects of the enemy, he would not have acted any differently than I had done, that my military movements were just useless walks, designed to fatigue the army and expose the frontiers. He accused me of having abused the power and the forces that the nation had given me, of having compromised the security of the state and violated the constitution, either to harm the deliberation of the legislative body, or to dirty the legislature, or to bring about civil war between all the citizens, or to claim an authority higher than the constituted authorities. I am accused of wanting to play the role of dictator. He said that all these actions are crimes, and the law punishes them by death.[96] Dumolard, Vaublanc, Daverhout, Quatremère and Froudière supported me and were insulted and attacked as they left the Assembly; they took refuge in the *corps de garde* of the courtyard of the Palais-Royal and had to jump out of a window to escape. Mathieu Dumas was attacked and knocked to his feet by those ghastly market women who knit at executions and other grisly events and was rescued by Girardin and two ushers who dragged him away by his legs as he lay on the ground.[97]

The Assembly voted by 406 to 224 to reject the accusation. However, it is evident Paris is spiraling down into greater and greater violence and the Jacobins are becoming more and more powerful. On August 9, nearly the whole Assembly declared that it was no longer free.[98] Tocsins rang throughout that night and citizens armed themselves.

August 12. A tattered and bloodied soldier from the National Guard of Paris arrives at our Sedan camp. "They killed them! The Tuileries! The king!" he raves and shouts.

He is unable to speak coherently, but we begin to fear the worst. Then an officer from the army rides in, his words horrifying us.[99]

"I forced my way with my pistol through the barricades at Saint Denis to escape. All six hundred of the guards at the Tuileries have been massacred, as well as two hundred servants.[100] Santerre and Fournier led troops from Marseilles and mobs from Saint Antoine and Saint Marceau into the Palace. The king told the Swiss Guards not to fire. They obeyed him and were slaughtered at their posts. He and the royal family fled to the Assembly and asked to be protected. The mob followed them, carrying heads on pikes. The king and the queen are imprisoned in the Luxembourg and it is rumored they will be moved to the Temple.

Later we learn more details. One of the two chief authorities is imprisoned, the other is reduced to two hundred and forty members, less than one third of the Legislative Assembly. The Commune elected by the people has been violently replaced by what is being called the Commune of August 10.

I declare to the mayor and to the municipality of Sedan that in the state of captivity and impotence to which the legislative body and king have been reduced, the military power, in order to remain independent, will demand its orders from the département of the Ardennes, as it is a constituted authority which had remained free; that it would also submit to other civil powers nearby. I basically write an extract from the Declaration of Rights and the first constitutional principles. I send copies of my letter to other administrative bodies and to Lückner and the mayor of Strasbourg, who is republican by inclination but faithful to the law.[101]

I write to d'Abancourt:

I learn, monsieur, that there has been much unrest at Paris, and I wait with anxiety for more exact news than that which has reached me. The disorders in the capital are no doubt paid for by foreign powers to help the counter-revolution and this opinion is strengthened by the rapprochement of their activity with that of foreign powers...The news of the disorders at Paris...will spread among the troops and will produce an indignation that the true defenders of France are seeing the country divided by internal factions, whilst everyone should rally around the constitution. [102]

Word reaches me that commissioners have been sent from Paris to inform us of the new government. I write to the council at Sedan: 'Arrest the commissioners when they arrive.'

On the thirteenth, I issue an Order of the Day which I also send to the administrators of the Ardennes département and to the Sedan council: 'I will continue to observe the constitution and I will never bow my head to any despotism, a head which has always been devoted to the cause of liberty and equality and often risked for it in two hemispheres...The king has been suspended. We must rally around the constitution.'[103]

In the afternoon of the fourteenth, the commissioners, Antonelli, Kersaint and Péraldi reach Sedan. There is great indignation towards them in the town and from the troops, not only because they represent a faction which has not consulted the country, but because it is being said that they want to destroy me. The mayor politely interrogates them. He makes them admit that at the time of the vote they are carrying, the Assembly was not free. He talks of the horror of August 10, the duty of all citizens, and above all, of the magistrates, to maintain the constitution, to prevent the deputies of a rebel faction to arouse a patriotic and peaceful commune to violate laws. He takes the unanimous advice of the general council of the commune and arrests them. From their imprisonment in the château the commissioners send a message to me that I will be most powerful in the new government and will have the premier rôle. However, what I want is to see France just and free.[104]

I issue an Order of the Day to calm the agitation in the army which is both surprised and indignant. I say the bare facts as I know them. I recommend the most exact discipline and fidelity to constitutional duties.[105]

On August 15 I review the army on the plain of Sedan by Verdun. "Swear an oath of allegiance to the Nation, the Law and the King," I demand.

Voices of discontent arise from both soldiers and officers. Two battalions refuse.

"Liberty, Fraternity, Equality, these are the only words to which we will swear," says a captain from the volunteers of the Allier.[106]

"Arrest the battalions!" I order.

The other troops refuse. It is a very bitter moment for me. I realize that Jacobin groups have been working to influence the men in each regiment and that their words have borne fruit. I no longer have the loyalty of my soldiers and nor does the king. Liberty is being trampled on. A violent faction is crushing all in its path.

Following my failure, I become the butt of caricatures: *The great fury of the God Lafayette at Verdun*; *So you want to follow the impulse of your heart! Tremble before the conqueror of the Champ de Mars!*

I send Alexandre Romeuf with a letter to Lückner. He gallops to Metz and back in just two days and returns with a written report of the speech Lückner made to his troops, reproducing his strong German accent and making us laugh even at such a grim moment.

Lückner is called before the municipal council at Metz by the Jacobin mayor. He tearfully agreed to their demands and writes to me: 'Keep the commissioners with you. I would not know what to do if they came here.'

Commissioners go to the camps of the other commanders. Montesquiou in the south and Arthur Dillon in Flanders immediately give in. At Strasbourg, Victor de Broglie and Dietrich, the mayor, at first refuse, but the duc de Biron, the commander on the Rhine, forces them to acquiesce to the Jacobins. It is only here in the *département* of the Ardennes, at Mézières and Sedan, that the commissioners are opposed. I appear a rebel, whereas, in fact, I am upholding the legitimate order. I am now completely isolated.

On August 17, the Provisional Executive Council orders me to give the command of the army of the north to Dumouriez and to come immediately to Paris to give an account of my conduct.[107]

I know I will be formally accused and will be executed. I leave Sedan and go to Mairy-sur-Meuse where I discuss the situation with César de La Tour Maubourg.

"Should I refuse to hand over the army to Dumouriez? Should I go to Paris again and argue my case?"

"It is certain death. The troops do not support you. They will probably choose Dumouriez. You will be killed and how does that help our cause?" he says.

"The Jacobins have become too powerful and are supported by the people. My ideas for liberty in France are crumbling into dust. If I thought it would be useful, I would happily go to Paris and face execution. However, I know my sacrifice would be in vain, so that means I will have to leave France."

"It seems the only choice," he replies.

"I will seek asylum in a neutral country and then I will go to America."

"My brothers and I will come with you. We are all at risk of being guillotined," he replies.

"We will invite others who would be in danger if they are abandoned here. We must go as quickly as possible. We will set off tomorrow and must keep our decision secret."

I write to Bureaux de Pusy: 'Come with me tomorrow, my dear Pusy, in the whirligig I have to ride. Leave Sedan for Bouillon where you will have to be before noon. Have a good horse.'[108]

Chapter 45

Flees the Jacobins and France

August 19.[1] A cold dawn; rain drizzling from a leaden sky. I make troop dispositions to help my successor. I try to absolve of blame the mayor and worthy magistrates of Sedan, the administrators of the Ardennes and all the citizens compromised by their defense of the law, by having already antedated a requisition so that all which has been said or done, by whatever civil authority against the insurrection of August 10, was ordered by me, thus enabling them to not bear responsibility.[2]

"I will inspect the front beyond Bouillon," I say as a pretext for the journey. I abandon new military equipment and the greater part of my salary to allay suspicion but take twenty thousand livres. An hour later, I abandon camp with a group which includes the three La Tour Maubourg brothers, La Colombe, the three Romeufs, Victor Gouvion, Langlois, Laumoy, Masson, Pillet, d'Agrain, and our servants.[3] We ride along the meadow road from the Meuse to the Gironne. We cross the river at Gironne and continue north between the Bois du clos le Loup Gironne on the right and the forest of the Ardennes on the left. Towards noon the castle comes into sight on the rocky outcrop above Bouillon. Pusy is waiting at the inn and to my surprise and displeasure I also see Alexandre de Lameth.

"Can I join you?" he asks. "There is an order to arrest me, but I have managed to outride my pursuers."

"Yes," I reply reluctantly.

"Go back to Sedan," I tell my escort. I give them dispatches which order that the advance troops behind the Chiers should entrench their position to withstand a sudden attack and that Lückner, who is not far away, will be in command until the arrival of Dumouriez. I send a letter to the municipal council of Sedan:

> If the last drop of my blood would serve the commune of Sedan I would give it and it would have the right to this sacrifice, but at the moment, for reasons which will not escape you, my presence in a few days would only serve to compromise you; I must prevent misfortunes to Sedan which would be because of me. The best way to serve you is to take away a head which all the enemies of liberty have proscribed, and which will never bow under any despotism, overcome with sadness at not being able at this time to be useful to France.[4]

The hussars canter away; we immediately leave. We cross the bridge over the Semois; we ride north through marshland and hilly terrain before plunging into the thick forest of the Ardennes along steep, rough, narrow paths. Our map, the best we could obtain, is often inaccurate; we struggle to know what direction to take.

Occasionally we notice riders some way off but as they are probably French *émigrés* we keep our distance. We meet a peasant and ask him to guide us. He refuses, even when threatened with a pistol.

"Release him," I order, to the regret of several in our wet, mud-splattered and fatigued party.

We carry on. We know we are in the neutral territory of the bishopric of Liège, but our hope of soon reaching Maastricht in the Dutch republic is fading fast. We have been riding for seven hours. Rain is still falling; the already somber sky is becoming very dark; our horses are exhausted. We suddenly notice the unwelcome red glow of campfires on the crest of the hill near Rochefort. We know the main enemy force is, or, at least, was, not on our route, but we do not have accurate information about Rochefort. We cannot deviate as on our right is a chain of posts by which General Clairfait sends communications from Namur to Luxembourg and on our left are French patrols from Givet or groups of émigrés from the region of Liège.

We halt. It is very difficult to know what to do. Are the fires of Austrians or of émigrés? We are neither émigrés nor do we want to join the enemy. We are in uniform but are non-combatants. We have left the French army and are not a hostile force. We wish only to travel through neutral territory and go to Maastricht. It seems best to talk, so Bureaux de Pusy, who speaks German, sets off towards them.

"They are volunteers from the Duchy of Limburg," he says on his return. "I told the commander, the comte d'Harnoncourt, that we are French citizens who are strongly attached to the constitution, completely opposed to French wearers of white cockades and that we claim the right to have free passage to Dutch territory. He told us to enter the town and stay the night at the *Auberge du Pélican*."[5]

We ride to Rochefort. We enter through the gate at the top of the hill and see soldiers stationed on both sides of a steep street leading to the château.

"It's Lafayette!" someone unfortunately calls out.

I decide it is now better to say the truth. "Go to the comte d'Harnoncourt. Inform him again we merely wish to pass through his post and will leave before morning to go on to Holland," I tell Pusy.

The comte d'Harnoncourt comes to the Auberge du Pélican and offers me hospitality at the château. I politely decline. He leaves. Not long after, soldiers surround the inn; Harnoncourt returns.

"I arrest you," he says.

Fifty soldiers search us and take our weapons. "Monsieur Bureaux de Pusy must go to Namur tomorrow to obtain passports from General von Moitelle," he orders.

"You are violating your word of honor!" we protest.

"You are a scoundrel and deserve a thorough caning which I would be glad to give you!" shouts Maubourg, his hot temper boiling over.[6]

I dictate a declaration:

> The undersigned, French citizens, snatched from extraordinary circumstances from the goodness of serving, as they have always done, the liberty of their country, and not being able to any longer oppose the violations of the Constitution established by the national will, declare that they can not be considered as enemy soldiers as they have renounced their positions in the French army, unlike that section of their compatriots whose views, sentiments and opinions, are absolutely opposed to theirs and who have joined with the powers at war with France. We are foreigners who claim free passage, which the rights of people assure, in order to travel quickly to a territory whose government is not at the present time in a state of war with their country.
>
> At Rochefort, August 19.
>
> Lafayette; La Tour Maubourg; Alexandre Lameth; Laumoy; Du Roure; A. Masson; Sicard; Bureaux-Pusy; Victor La Tour Maubourg; Victor Gouvion; Langlois; Sionville; Alexandre

Romeuf; D'Agrain; Louis Romeuf; Curmer; Pillet; La Colombe; Victor Romeuf; Charles La Tour Maubourg; Soubeyran; D'Arblay; Ch. Cadignan. [7]

August 20. At four o'clock in the morning, Pusy sets out with an Austrian officer to Namur. I write to Adrienne:

Whatever will be the vicissitudes of fortune, my dear heart, you know that my soul is too strong to be brought down; but you also know it too well not to pity my agony in leaving my homeland, to which I have dedicated my efforts, and which would have been free and worthy if personal interests had not acted to corrupt the public spirit, to disorganize the means of resistance abroad, and of liberty and security within. It is I who, proscribed by my own country for having served it with courage, have been forced to traverse a territory held by an enemy of France, to flee my country which it had been so wonderful for me to defend. An Austrian post was on our route; the commander thought he had to arrest us; from here we are going to be taken to Namur, but I cannot believe that they will have the bad faith to restrain any longer foreigners, who by a patriotic and constitutional declaration have taken care to keep separate from French émigrés who hold opinions so opposed to theirs; foreigners who declare they wish to go to a neutral country, Holland or England. Here is a list of those who are here with me…you know better than I, the list of all the patriots who have been massacred, whether by the Marseillais, or whether by the orders of Messieurs Pétion, Santerre and Danton. It seems to me they have attacked men who have served liberty. My own fate was decided a long time ago. I could have enjoyed a life very different from this present one, if I had more ambition than morality; but there will never be anything in common between the behavior of criminals and how I act. I have been the last to maintain the constitution to which I pledged allegiance. You know that my heart would have been republican if my reason had not given me this nuance of royalism, and if my fidelity to my vows and the national good had not made me defender of the constitutional rights of the kIng; the less that people resisted, the more my voice was raised and I became the target of all attacks. The mathematical demonstration of no longer being able to usefully oppose crime and to be the object of one more crime, forced me to bow my head to a struggle where it was evident that I would die for no useful purpose. I do not know how long my journey will be delayed, but I will go to England where I want my whole family to join me, and hopefully my aunt as well. I know that the families of émigrés are being arrested, but they are those of émigrés bearing weapons to fight against their country; whilst, I, Good Heavens! What monster would dare to think I fall into that category. The imperial and jacobite posts will read the few letters that I write; I do not mind, as long as they arrive. I have never hidden a single sentiment.

I make no excuse neither to you nor to my children, for having brought ruin to my family; There is no one among you who would have wished to owe his fortune to conduct contrary to my conscience, but come to join me in England; let us settle in America; we will find there the liberty that no longer exists in France; and my love will try to console you for all the pleasures you have lost. Adieu my dear heart. [8]

Later in the day, we leave Rochefort, escorted by Austrian hussars to the hôtel de Hariscamp at Namur where we find Pusy.

"When Moitelle knew you were here he was carried away by inexpressible transports of joy. He kept repeating your name and sent messages to all the generals and princes he could think of saying you are in custody. However, he has now been ordered to the army and the marquis de Chasteler is in command," he says grimly. [9]

Chasteler bows. I also bow. He addresses me as marquis; I correct him.

"You are a noble defender of liberty. I am flattered to be able to praise Washington's friend," he says.[10]

"Thank you," I reply. "I prefer to be the victim of arbitrary governments rather than of the people.

"Prince Charles of Lorraine is coming from Bruxelles to question you," he says.

"I do not suppose, Monsieur, anyone will permit himself to ask me questions that it does not suit me to answer!" I reply sharply, only too aware that prince Charles is the prince de Lambesc, colonel of the Royal Allemand regiment which charged the crowd in front of the Tuileries on July 12, 1789.[11] I saved him from the mob in the place de Grève and he subsequently fled France.

The prince arrives. He is polite, but I treat him with disdain as I realize he wants me to betray my country.

"Why are you here?" I ask. "Our political opinions are very different."

"We can perhaps come together, as the excess of the last events make it desirable for the whole of Europe and the triumph of the constitution. The court is not unfavorable to you. It will follow international law and give you passports to a neutral country. We would like to be informed about France and its resources and about the army."

"I would never renounce my principles or harm my country!" I retort angrily, which brings the conversation to an end.

Chasteler comes back and tries to calm my annoyance by showing me a letter he has written to the duc de Saxe-Teschen, the uncle of the emperor, and the governor-general of Holland. It appears to be an attempt to minimize my revolutionary principles, which are described as most reasonable.

"Please do not forget my support for the vicomte de Noailles to abolish aristocratic privileges. Please do not omit any such suggestion from your letter," I declare angrily for the second time that day.

The duc de Saxe-Teschen sends an order to transfer us to Nivelles, not far from Bruxelles. On August 23 we clamber into carriages in the courtyard to set off there, a crowd surrounding us to our annoyance, a spectacle for everyone to see.

We arrive in the evening. "Would you please give your word of honor as prisoners of war?" asks Major von Paulus, the commander of our escort.

"I will not cooperate with an injustice by my agreement. You do not have the right to keep us prisoner," I reply.[12]

The others say the same. During the night, guards stand duty at our doors; I am only allowed to walk in the courtyard and not in the little garden at the bottom of my steps.

August 25. I write to Madame de Chavaniac:

I am in good health, my dear aunt, and that is the only consoling news I can give you...For six months I have watched the terrible progress of the disorganization. Fidelity to the constitution appeared the best way to save France. I tried everything possible regarding the Assembly, the king, and good citizens, which without departing from a constitutional position, could unite and strengthen us. My efforts have been in vain...Finally, it was either necessary to die uselessly or to bend under the Jacobin yoke or to distance myself from the infernal machinations which had piled up against me...If I could have hoped for a legal judgement I would have presented myself to the law, even although there is no action of my life which could compromise me in the eyes of true patriots, but since the arbitrary wish of the first group decides on death or life, it was forbidden to a friend of liberty to abase himself by appearing before such tribunals. I was therefore forced to leave the frontier. I took all precautions for the safety of my troops and set off for the neutral region of Liège…We have been arrested and against all justice have been taken to Namur and in this small town we are waiting for the decision of the emperor who is in Vienna. I have said that I would prefer to complain about the injustice of arbitrary governments than of those of the people, and that the imperial persecution appears more natural than that of the people of Paris. However, I must say that we have been treated guilty of with much politeness and they have tried to defend us from the attentions of émigrés with the white cockade. I am sending Monsieur Bureaux de Pusy to Bruxelles to complain to the government of the Pays-Bas about the violation of people's rights, which they are concerning us, and I hope that we will have immediate justice. Then I will go to England to a farm and you can obtain the address from the minister of the United States in London…I am here what I have been all my life. My soul, I admit, is given over to a profound sadness, but my conscience is pure and tranquil and I doubt that the leaders of the different factions who have savaged me can say as much.. Madame de Lafayette and my children are probably no longer at Chavaniac, and I really hope, my dear aunt, that you have agreed to go with them…Adieu, my dear aunt. I love you tenderly. [13]

I also write a long letter to the duc de La Rochefoucauld: 'Where are you, my dear friend? Are you still alive? Is it possible that so many virtues, that such a constant and pure love of liberty should have managed to escape proscription?' I write about the situation since August 10, and that I have stayed faithful to the constitution. I tell him of our flight and what I intend to do if I regain my liberty. I finish by declaring that I will always behave in a way worthy of a free man, that I am incapable of bending under any illegitimate yoke, and that it is at least a consolation that those who are persecuting me here do not profane the name of liberty.[14]

I send a message to William Short at The Hague:

My dear friend, You have been acquainted with the atrocious events which have taken place in Paris, on August 10, when the Jacobite faction overthrew the Constitution, enslaved the Assembly and the King, the one by terror, the other by destitution and imprisonment, and gave the signal for pillage and massacre. I could have had an eminent position in the new order, without even becoming embroiled in the plot; but my principles could not agree to such a scheme. I opposed Jacobin tyranny as far as I could, but you know the weakness of our good people; I was abandoned. The army welcomed the clubs. Nothing was left but for me to leave France. However, we have been arrested on our road and detained by an Austrian detachment, which is absolutely contrary to the rights of people, which you will see in the enclosed declaration which I ask you to publish. You will greatly oblige me, my dear friend, by leaving for Brussels as soon as this letter reaches you and by insisting on seeing me. I am an American citizen, an American officer. I am no longer in the service of France. In claiming this, you will be within your rights, and I have no doubt of your immediate arrival. God bless you.[15]

I write to the princesse d'Hénin, who is in England. I tell her about my refusal to see the commissioners who appeared to be suggesting to La Colombe that I should be the chief man of France. I tell her I was sure my conscience could not agree to their proposals. I could not forget their crimes, nor sacrifice the king and unite with their party. I recount my flight and that I hope to soon be in England. [16]

"Give us the army money chest," demands an officer.

I laugh.

"I advise you to take the matter more seriously," he replies.

"How can I help laughing. For all that I can understand of your demand is that had your prince been in my place he would have robbed the cashbox of the army."[17]

They confiscate personal possessions. They take my gold watch, two medals, gold spurs, and my wallet. They confiscate a toothpick from Alexandre Lameth. "You could use it as a quill."

Later in the day we are divided into three groups. Those who had not served in the National Guard are released and forbidden to stay in the country. Those who have been officers in the French Army, and my aides-de-camp during the Revolution, La Colombe, the three Romeufs, Masson, Charles and Victor La Tour Maubourg, will be taken to the citadel at Antwerp as prisoners of war. César de La Tour Maubourg, Bureaux de Pusy, Lameth and I, who were deputies in the National Assembly, as well as officers in the French Army, will be tried by a tribunal at Luxembourg. I now fear execution.

"I would like to say farewell to my friends," I say.

"No," is the reply.

I manage, however, to embrace Louis Romeuf who bursts into tears, fearing the worst for me. I repeat my beliefs to him and ask him to publish them. "I realized that if I fell into the hands of the arbitrary governments they would take vengeance for all the harm I had done them, but after having defended until the last instant the free national constitution of my country, I abandoned myself to my fate, thinking it was better to die by the hands of tyrants than by the misguided hands of my fellow citizens. It was necessary, above all, to prevent a great example of ingratitude from injuring the cause of the people in the eyes of those who are unaware that there is more pleasure in a single service rendered to that cause than all the pain that personal vicissitudes could give. Besides, they have wasted their efforts; the truths that I have uttered and my labors in the two worlds are not lost; aristocracy and despotism have received a death blow, and my blood, crying for vengeance, will raise up new defenders for liberty."[18]

The guard takes me away, Louis sobbing.

September 3 finds me in a carriage driving along winding roads through wooded hills. Three carriages follow, my friends in each one, guarded by officers, with hussars riding as escort.

I write again to the princesse d'Hénin: 'It is very strange to know that La Rochefoucauld and Barnave are in Jacobin chains whilst I and my companions are in those of Austria....I prefer to suffer in the name of the despotism that I have fought, than in the name of the people whose cause is dear to my heart, and whose name today is profaned by brigands.'[19]

September 4. We reach Luxembourg. People crowd the streets, screaming insults at us, although I occasionally notice a compassionate face. The Austrians give us to the Prussians who take me to the home of the Lontz family, above a shop, a guard outside.

In the morning, I hear the noise of fighting downstairs. Madame Lontz is angrily shrieking. People are shouting and cursing under my window. I have no weapon; I wait. The hubbub subsides. The French émigrés are driven off. At dinner, I learn Madame Lontz used a broomstick to defend me. Major Rochefort d'Ailly, the chief officer of the garrison, bans all Frenchmen from the street and gives strict instructions to the guards not to allow any insults.

I ask to see the Archduchess Marie Christine, the sister of Marie-Antoinette. Prince Heinrich XV zu Reuss and Prince Paul von Eszterhazy, the commander of Austrian troops in Breisgau, come to question me.

"I wish Louis XVI to be a constitutional monarch either by the victories of foreign armies or by a Frenchman who could defend the king militarily," I say, which seems to surprise them.[20] However, nothing results from our meeting.

I receive a reply from the duc de Saxe-Teschen: 'I would have been very honored to have commanded an army against General Lafayette if he had been appointed by the king and the nation; but that since the leader of the French Revolution, forced to leave his country by the same people he had taught to revolt, has fallen into the hands of the allied powers, he will be kept until his sovereign, in his clemency or by his justice, decides his fate.' [21]

I am not allowed at the tribunal of the representatives of Austria and Prussia where our fate is decided in the presence of the former French minister, the baron de Breteuil, representing the king. Schulenburg, the Prussian minister, tells me its verdict. "Monsieur de Lafayette is not just the man of the French Revolution, but that of universal liberty…the existence of Monsieur de Lafayette is incompatible with the safety of the governments of Europe." [22] Maubourg, Lameth, Pusy and I will be held as state prisoners until a restored French king can decide on our fate.

I will not be executed immediately, although it is possible it will happen. However, I face imprisonment for the rest of my life, a very dismal fate.

Marie Christine writes a brief note to me: 'The authorities are keeping you for the scaffold.'[23]

We learn we will be imprisoned at Wesel in Westphalia. My three servants, Chavaniac, Demanges and Pontonnier, will be with us, as well as Maubourg's valet, and an old man, Nicolas Jandel, who has been assigned to Pusy. We will meet them at Coblentz.

We leave Luxembourg. I sit in the first of the four carriages with the commanding officer; three other carriages carry Maubourg, Pusy, Lameth and lower-ranking officers. In front and behind ride an escort of cavalry. At inns we have the joy of being able to speak to each other. At each town people line the streets and look at us with kindness, or with hatred, or just with curiosity, the strong arms of our guards stopping any harm to us.

We halt at Trèves. We are placed in separate cells furnished only with a table and a dirty pallet. A guard holding a pistol constantly watches me, a torture I find almost impossible to endure.

September 15. We arrive at Coblentz. People stare. The émigrés hold their court at the nearby château of Schönbornlust and it feels strange to be here as a prisoner whilst many of my former friends and acquaintances are enjoying a normal life.

Next day I write to the princesse d'Hénin:

The day after tomorrow we will go by boat to Wesel to be imprisoned there in the fortress. Every second of the day and night a non-commissioned Prussian officer, whose language I do not speak, attentively watches me with Prussian exactness. He conscientiously follows his duty but, at the same time as acquitting himself of his master, the king's orders with a scrupulous rigidity, he behaves with all the delicacy which his orders allow. Although I am content with myself, I am far from content with my fate, but am very far from repenting my conduct. I would do the same again. I do not know what will happen to us, but I submit to whatever it is as well as I can. I do not write to my friends in case a letter might compromise them, nor to madame de Lafayette, who is probably on her way to join me. Give news of me to everyone. Also tell the American minister. He will be, like the English, very astonished about what has happened to me, especially when they know the circumstances.…If you have any news of Madame de Maubourg, Madame de Pusy, or of anyone in whom their husbands, Alexandre de Lameth or I would be interested, you will greatly please us by sending it. Address it to Wesel, where I shall say, like the bird in The Sentimental Journey, "I can't get out." I underline the last words. [24]

Chapter 46

Entombed

I suffer the hellish monotony of never-ending days in the dungeon-gloom at Wesel. My guard, a non-commissioned officer, on duty two hours at a time, watches me night and day, like a hawk surveying his prey. It is unbearable.

"I am going to be ill," I complain.

Your king is in a far worse position," he says, turning his back.[1]

An iron stove constantly gives out light. All sorts of vermin and a multitude of rats torment me.[2] I know nothing of my friends. I am not allowed any newspapers or letters. I am suffering with my chest and with my nerves; at night I cannot sleep.

Colonel Friedrich von Tschirschky, the commandant, comes to my cell accompanied by a legal officer. "His Majesty has written to you. If you give us plans against France, to help our common cause, conditions here will improve for you," he says, showing me a letter.

"Your king is very impertinent to connect my name with such an idea. I might be his prisoner, but I will not accept insults from him," I reply angrily.[3]

We are given permission to write to the king's general adjutant of infantry, Major Hermann von Mannstein, to ask that we should be released. Nothing comes of it.

I arrived on September 19; I have now been here nearly three months. What is happening to my wife, my family, my friends, or to France? I know nothing. I am entombed. I am hot with fever; my friends will not even be allowed to visit me on my deathbed.[4]

On December 31 my cell door opens; guards take me outside into the fresh air. I see Maubourg, Lameth and Pusy, my heart swelling with indescribable joy. We clamber into two open carts, furnished with chains and handcuffs, which then slowly trundle east across Westphalia and Brunswick towards Magdebourg. We talk with incredible pleasure, haggard caricatures of our former selves, our breath making clouds of moisture in the bitter winter air. My cough improves. My health slowly returns.[5]

People show a flattering interest in us. Our journey through the Germanic empire can only be called honorable for the defenders of a noble cause.[6]

At the small town of Hamm, we enter the courtyard of an inn. To our amazement, as well as, I think, to theirs, we see the plump Monsieur and his brother, Artois, with their retinues. They stare, they mock our wretched condition as they eat at a neighboring table. I am glacially calm. I prepare myself for violence, but there is none; presumably because they do not want to attack the prisoners of the state which shelters them.

Diane-Adélaïde de Simiane's brother, comte Charles de Damas, comes to speak to me. "I have been given permission to do so. I would like to thank you for your help when I was arrested last year after the king's flight to Varennes."

"How is Madame de Simiane?" I ask.

"She is well. I will tell her I saw you," he replies.

He quickly relates the success of the French army, the injurious management of public affairs, and the king's trial. I am very grateful for the information and pleased to see him. We say farewell. We jolt away in our rustic vehicles leaving him and his richly dressed companions to their carriages and freedom. It is a strange encounter.

We halt at Soest and Lippstadt. My servant, Desmanches, is not well guarded; two people sympathetic to our cause help him escape; he takes with him a message for my friends: 'Rescue us.'

At Minden, guards from Magdebourg replace our guards. We climb into wagons they have brought and set off on the last stage of our trek.

January 4, 1793. It is cold and wintry; we jolt across a flat plain, dread in our hearts, slowly nearing the town of Magdebourg I visited with Gouvion when we travelled to the east. Our destination is the red-brick, star-shaped citadel on an island in the Elbe; we approach its forbidding and grim exterior, heavily fortified with ditches, ramparts and palisades, bristling with many guards, my hopes of escape beginning to fade. Maubourg is unusually quiet. I look at Pusy and Lameth in the other wagon and see their anguish.

Four chained, padlocked and iron-barred doors lead to my cell which is only five and a half feet by three feet wide. It is under the rampart of the citadel and is surrounded by a high, strong palisade. It is dank; the wall nearest the moat is slimy with water and the small, grilled window on the wall opposite lets in daylight, but not the rays of the sun.[7] The whole gloomy tomb is reminiscent of the hold of a prison ship I visited in New York harbor.

Two guards look down into my cell, an intolerable torture; other guards watch them to prevent any communication; beyond are walls, ramparts and ditches and more guards. One guard even stands next to me while I sleep. On a wall are two lines of a verse in French: *The prisoner is to suffer and die*, a distortion of the revolutionary words: *To live free or die.*[8]

In the morning, my servant, Chavaniac, enters my cell. Later I eat dinner in the presence of the guard and of the commandant, Major Sanff von Pilsac, who has been ordered by the king to sleep nearby and who always takes with him my cell keys. I have books, whose blank pages have been torn out. I have no news, no ink, no quills, no paper, no gazettes. Every time the guard changes, an officer reports what I have said; they obviously believe they are holding the devil here in prison.

My health had improved after the journey, now it is deteriorating daily; I wheeze and cough like an old man; I cannot sleep; fever is my constant companion. My physical constitution has nearly as much need of liberty as my moral constitution.[9] Sometimes I glimpse Maubourg when the first two of my four doors are opened for a few hours before dinner to improve the stifling air. His face appears very changed and it distresses me greatly to see him like that.[10] Lameth nearly died at Wesel and is not much better here; Pusy suffers greatly but is less ill.

The poor state of our dungeons, the lack of air and of exercise, and every form of mental agony, is being used as a slow poison. Our imprisonment again resembles a living death. I am buried and am dead to the world in this subterranean rat-hole.

A few weeks after we arrive in January our conditions improve. The United States has sent a thousand florins which will stop my being forced to have bread and water when my money runs out. I can now eat as much roast meat as I wish and can also have a choice of wine. I buy articles through a galley slave, two orderlies and a servant on contract; I also loan large amounts of money to my fellow prisoners with the result that we are all quickly amassing books. I begin to feel more hopeful. I do not know if the United States is trying to obtain my freedom.

"Your king was executed on January 21. It is your fault! You will be tortured and killed!" The guards shout, fury and hatred contorting their faces.

I look at them with as much horror as they look at me, shaken by the trampling underfoot of all the laws of humanity, of justice, and of national agreement.[11]The plump and coarse-mannered Louis, waddling like a duck, mischievously turning on the fountains at Versailles so that people were unexpectedly drenched, who so proudly visited the new harbor at Cherbourg, who loved hunting, has been decapitated. I remember the part I played in bringing him back to Paris after his flight. At least it was not my soldiers who caught him. How did you go to your death? Were you brave at the final moment?

Other terrible news finds its way into the darkness of my cell. There is much killing in Paris. I do not know the details; I pace up and down frenziedly in the tiny space.

"French prisoners of war say they have been told by their commanders that you are dead. There have also been reports of it in journals in Philadelphia and London," an officer tells me.

Will my wife, my family and friends believe this? I constantly worry. I agonize about my family. I know nothing of those I hold most dear.

I hear French armies are winning battles although I gather the prince de Cobourg has been successful against some of Dumouriez's army. It seems strange not to be a part of it. I also learn of the atrocious murder of my virtuous friend, La Rochefoucauld. I grieve for him.

This place might be a latrine of despotism, of servitude, of ignorance and spying, but even under this vile regime, some people are drawn towards liberty.[12] Le Blanc, the chief of the guards, a Protestant émigré, agrees to smuggle letters, as do some others. On March 15 I write secretly to the princesse d'Hénin, on a page I have torn from a book, using a toothpick and soot and vinegar as ink. I describe my cell and daily life. I tell her I long to hear of my family as well as of hers; I ask them to be told we are not dead and of our fate. I finish by saying that I do not know of our plantation in Cayenne, but I hope my wife will have managed that the slaves obtain their freedom.[13]

An officer gives me the February edition of Minerva, a monthly journal published at Berlin. I read an article by Baron Johann Wilhelm von Archenholz who writes that I have shown self-sacrificial devotion to liberty, country, constitution and constitutional king. He says my imprisonment is senseless and illegal and is the greatest cruelty that has occurred in this century. He encourages and praises me and accurately represents my beliefs and my reasons for leaving France.

I write secretly to Archenholz on March 27. I say I do not merit his great praise, but his kind exaggeration is so generous that I thank him for having let me hear the voice of liberty honoring my tomb. I write about the situation in France. I tell him to recall the premeditated aggression of August 10, when soldiers defending the law were killed in the name of the people; when citizens were massacred in the streets, thrown into fires and prisons, to be assassinated in cold blood, the king only saving his life by an illegal suspension; the National Guard disarmed; the oldest and most honorable of friends of liberty thrown to assassins, the duc de La Rochefoucauld killed; the constitution outlawed; the press in chains; opinions punished by death; letters falsified; juries replaced by executioners; the administrative and municipal bodies of Paris broken; the National Assembly forced at knife point to sanction these terrible acts; natural liberty, civil, religious and political smothered in blood. What must I think, I ask him, I who pronounced the first Declaration of Rights and who thought the constitution, despite its faults, as the best point to fight against our enemies. I talk about my reasons for fleeing and about my flight. I finish by expressing my hopes for escape: 'Is it possible to escape from so many barriers, guards and chains? Why not? Already a toothpick, some soot, and a scrap of paper have deceived my jailers. Already, at the risk of his life, someone is bringing you this letter.' I talk about perhaps going to Switzerland, even although America is the homeland of my heart.[14]

The king of Prussia authorizes us to receive and write letters, thanks, I believe, to the efforts of Monsieur Pinckney, the American minister in London. I receive to my inexpressible consolation, a letter from my wife which I am not allowed to keep. I learn that on February 4, she, my aunt and our dear children were at Chavaniac in good health. I write back, the commandant watching while I do so, my words later to be translated into German and dispatched to the council of war in Berlin which will send it on if there is nothing to cause concern to them, in which case it will come back to be corrected.

I say, to conceal the truth, that after eight months of silence I am allowed to know of her, and to tell her that I am still alive. I say that I am tormented by her worries, and those of my aunt and children, and that I am doing all I can to maintain my health, in my narrow cell, where I can not breathe or walk, a situation I can not change any more than I can change my character or my principles, and so I am patient. I tell her I have books and see Chavaniac every day and to give six louis to his father. I say I do not know what has happened to our property and would be more worried about Cayenne if I had not been sure of her zeal and firmness: 'Give news of me to General Washington…Once again adieu. May your situation be softened by thinking of the consolation I find in your tenderness, in the hope of seeing each other again one day, and in what I have been able to do during my life for humanity.' [15]

In June, to my great surprise, General Duke Frederick of Brunswick, whom I last met at Potsdam in 1785, suddenly appears at my door with Hüllesen, the commandant of Magdebourg, Senft von Pilsach, the citadel commandant, the civil president, and an officer. We stand squashed together, half in the hole, half at the door, because I do not want anything confidential to be said between us.

"I have retired from my command in the Pays-Bas and I am on my way to my estate at Sibyllenort. I decided to stop at Magdebourg and visit you," he says in French. "How are you?"

"I am as well as can be expected, but Lameth is gravely ill from these damp conditions," I reply.

"Would you mind if the other prisoners join us?" he asks.

"I would be delighted. We never see each other except on the one occasion we signed the accounts of our expenses at Wesel," I reply.

My friends are brought from their cells, so ill and emaciated it shocks me, only the second time I have seen them since our arrival here when I saw to my surprise the list of letters sent to me, despite my never having been told whether my wife and family were alive.

We ecstatically embrace in the tiny, cramped cell, forcing most of the Prussians to stand in the corridor. We talk about military matters and Dumouriez's betrayal in April when he fled from his army, capturing Beurnonville, the minister of war, Bancal and the two National Convention deputies sent to arrest him and gave them to the coalition forces.

"Dumouriez has sold a list of Dutch patriots who support the Revolution to the prince of Cobourg, but he will not make use of it," says the Duke of Brunswick, to my horror, as I know the implacable princess of Orange.

We also talk about the plots of the foreign powers with the duc d'Orléans and the queen and the recent proclamations of the prince of Cobourg according to which the coalition wants to give France its constitutional king and the constitution.

"It is an irony that I am in the chains of the Allies, whilst their new ally, Monsieur d'Orléans, would never pardon me for having so often prevented the assassination of the king," I remark smiling.

"What is the constitutional position of the coalition?" I question.

"The Allied Powers and the queen and the duc d'Orléans talk of a constitution as they think it is necessary to start somewhere," he says, words which I encourage him to repeat.[16]

Our situation greatly improves following his visit. We are allowed to walk in the fresh air one hour each day. Lameth had been so ill it was thought he would die unless he was able to breathe fresh air and so permission had already been granted to him to do so. Now Maubourg, Pusy and I can also enjoy the privilege; we walk, each at different times of the day, in a little garden at a corner of the south bastion, accompanied by a guard; no favorite of the sultan kept more completely away from any glance of the curious.[17] After more than five months, I feel the outside air on my face; I see the sun again. I can walk more than six paces and it strengthens me for my return to my dank, unhealthy cell. I read newspapers from Leyden, Hamburg and Berlin, as well as the Dutch gazette, *De Leyde* and the *Minerva* of Archenholz. I am allowed to receive visitors. The poet, Klopstock, comes to see me.

"I do not think that your room merits the word dungeon," he says. "You write letters, read, and sometimes Commandant Pilsach visits you for dinner."[18]

On June 22 I write, at length, a secret letter to the princesse d'Hénin in London: 'I will not describe all the precautions with which they surround me. These people must think they are holding the devil.' I mention the visit of the Duke of Brunswick and ask her to tell one of my friends in London to immediately inform Mr. Short, the American minister at The Hague, so that he can warn the two or three Dutch patriots who are most closely linked to me; I write of my extreme sadness at the death of La Rochefoucauld. I say that I constantly think of liberty during my solitary meditations and that whether a miracle extricates me from here, or whether I die on a scaffold, liberty and equality will be my first and my last words. I ask her to inform Mr. Pinckney of my letter and to reassure the families of my three companions that their health is better and to express my love to my family and my friends.[19]

July 4. A letter I was writing to Washington has been seized and I have been forced to destroy others, but despite being imprisoned in this narrow, damp subterranean dungeon, doomed to the moral and physical hardships heaped on me by a revengeful tyranny, I enjoy myself today in cheating the crowned gang and their vile agents by writing secretly to Pinckney to commemorate the seventeenth anniversary of the Declaration of Independence of the United States. I compare the two situations of France and the United States. I talk about the struggle to win liberty for Europe, that soon the chains of France will fall and those of Europe will be shaken, that my contribution to this might only be as a martyr in the depths of a prison or with my blood shed hopefully not uselessly on a scaffold, but I will say Amen to this. I also thank him for his intervention which has meant that after eight months I now know my wife and children are alive. 'Please let them know my health is not too bad. Please give my affectionate respects to my revered general and paternal friend and remember me to my friends in America.'[20]

On the sixteenth, I again write secretly to the princesse d'Hénin, the great advantage of the sound of all the keys grating and turning in the locks being that I can easily hear someone coming. I tell her I think that approaches from the United States might be the most suitable to bring about my freedom but that I fear the slowness and the perfidy of European politics. I do not write to my aunt, my wife or children as my handwriting is too well known to Paris and to the eighty-three départements.[21] On the twenty-third, I write an open letter to the princesse.

Thoughts of escape occupy me. I write to Archenholz on August 23 about the details of a plan we are devising whereby the captain of the guard will withdraw his lieutenant and sentinel for a very short time and we will crawl out of our holes and escape over the ramparts. Horses will be ready to take us five miles from Magdebourg to Helmstead, where I hope that d'Archenholtz will have carriages. 'Each of us should have at least one pistol, as for swords, each should have surely one.'

La Tour Maubourg adds a postscript with his toothpick: 'Le Blanc must make use of the four thousand livres.' He later writes again: 'If M. Münche persists in his refusal, I see no other way but that of the chimney, which can only serve for my neighbour and myself. But to be frank with you, the important point is that he should escape, in the first place, for the public good and also because were he free, we should not long be detained.'[22]

I write to Le Blanc on August 30. I tell him that if our plan is discovered and he is in danger he must not hesitate to place himself in safety; his horse and the four thousand livres will be sufficient to help him initially, then he needs to go to Archenholtz, and from there to my friends in England and await events which might be able to unite us. [23]

In the autumn I learn that a Law of Suspects was passed in France on September 17, allowing committees to arrest people without trial. This terrible news brings back my insomnia and causes me more pain than all the efforts of my prosecutors could bring. I have much more energy to resist my own situation and to defy the vengeance directed at me than to bear the danger threatening those I love whom I want to leave Paris immediately. What is happening to La Rochefoucauld's wife and mother in these terrible times?

The cause of the people is no less sacred to me; I would give my blood drop by drop for it and would reproach each instant of my life that I had not fought for it, but its charm has been destroyed.[24] I hear, to my distress, that Bailly and Malesherbes have been arrested.

October 2. I receive a letter from Adrienne written on August 1. In horror, I read that she was arrested in September a year ago, then released to return to Chavaniac after giving her word of honor. I am intensely proud of her and how she has behaved and am delighted to receive more detailed news than before. I immediately reply to her with an open letter which I send to the princesse d'Hénin as I do not wish to compromise my wife:

The five people so dear to me are therefore reunited at Chavaniac, my dear heart, and in a state of tranquility, I dare to hope, that they merit so well. I was sure that even the desire of obtaining my liberty would not make you say anything which was not worthy of you, but the way in which you talk of it speaks directly to my heart, so that I need to thank you. I had thought that perhaps your fate had been more terrible and sad, but I know that you will find some pleasure in thinking that your tenderness and your esteem are the happiest moments of my life, the consolations of my solitary captivity and if I am ever allowed to rejoin my family will make me happier than ever....I am happy with my health, particularly my chest, despite receiving the opposite to which it needs...I am pulled out of my hole once a day to breathe a bit of fresh air; I have some books and although the unfortunate talent of reading quickly has become somewhat of an inconvenience for me, I have found in English, French and Latin, the means of speaking with the dead, although sequestered from the living...Félix is still kept apart. Adieu, my dear heart...Keep the hope that we will see each other again. It is impossible to think that my star should be completely extinguished since my poor aunt, by a miracle, has had the strength to resist this new shock. I embrace her with all my heart, as well as Anastasie, George, Virginie and Monsieur Frestel who also belongs to our family. Adieu, adieu, I embrace you and love you with all my soul. [25]

October 9. I receive two letters from the princesse d'Hénin, written in May; I realize invisible ink has been used.

"Can I look at the letters again to think about my response?" I ask. I heat the words by the fire; red letters appear. She and Lally Tollendal have asked Bollman, who enabled Narbonne to escape, to go to Berlin to appeal for my release; he will also try to help me escape. I read, then burn it.

"You must have lost the letter," I tell Senft; he fortunately agrees not to send the other compromising letter to the ministers in order to conceal his supposed blunder.

I reply hastily, in secret, to the princesse d'Hénin on the twenty-fourth. I cannot have two plans of escape and I prefer that of Archenholtz and Le Blanc. I therefore ask her to abandon any other plan of escape than mine. It has been extremely complicated to organize what we have so far managed; I cannot talk clearly without compromising many people, but I want everything Monsieur A. wishes to be done immediately without any other project confusing it. I also write to Le Blanc to tell him the problems these two letters have posed for me and ask him to keep to the plan of Archenholtz no matter what happens. I say that delay could be fatal and wish him to return quickly. I detail everything I will need to escape from the fortress. I will say I am English, perhaps American. The best horses must be procured to reach Hanoverian territory where a light carriage will be needed. I tell him that fourteen months in the dungeons of their majesties has not put me in the best of health, but that basically I have a strong constitution, which joined to the memory of my chains, will enable me to make a very quick journey. I believe it will be a long time before my absence is noticed but as it is not impossible that it should become known after two hours we must guard against this accident and hurry to escape pursuit. I will look at the chimney through which I might need to escape if the doors are locked. Maubourg knows how to unlock my padlock; he will come into my cell, he will put my coat in the chimney, take out some bricks, and place a dummy in my bed in case the commandant enters in the evening. In the morning no one will know how I escaped. I mention the problem of the guard who has decided not to help; I will speak to him and offer him a thousand louis in a month if he enables me to leave the fortress. If, however, he refuses the offer and we fear he will betray us, it will be necessary to find another way and I believe that his friend will not run any risk in getting me outside. I tell Le Blanc that after his marriage perhaps he can persuade his wife to leave this cursed country and come to my family who will welcome my liberator. I finally mention the passports which if I do not have Prussian officers with me need to be able to pass careful inspection, and that the Jewish person accompanying me needs to be offered much money as he will be entirely master of my fate. [26]

I await my escape. The dangers of delay are great. There will fortunately be no moon.

There is now a fifth padlock on the doors before my cell. The two doors of the citadel, previously open, have also been padlocked. The daily and nightly inspections of the guards and the commandants have increased; the privations, both small and large, have also increased; the commandant is armed with pistols. However, there is no sign that the escape plan has been discovered. Our cells are not searched. I carry on as before. I believe that the coalition is only intending to tighten our chains more securely. They are enraged by the interest we inspire in people and which some citizens and military men proclaim loudly. They are trying to destroy all communication between the living and us. [27]

I write secretly to the princesse d'Hénin. I say there are only two ways to leave here, that of a well-thought-out escape or that resulting from a declaration of the United States to no longer negotiate with deceitful governments. [28] I learn that on November 12 Bailly was executed.

December 2. There is a rumor that I am going to be transferred. I am sure it is untrue. On the tenth,

I write two secret letters to La Colombe. I say there are four ways in which I can leave my prison: an escape, representations by people, public clamor, and approaches made by the United States. I want him to submit these ideas to my friends. In the second letter I say I would like copies, or relevant extracts, from my letters, to be sent to General Washington and Mr. Jefferson by the ambassadors, and by Mrs. Church to her brother-in-law, Colonel Hamilton. I believe the Irish and English Whigs share a common cause with me and if my correspondance can be conveyed to them, they could render me a great service by aiding the demands of the United States.[29] On the eleventh, I write to Pinckney. I thank him again for what he has done for me- the cessation of the most diabolical torture revenge could invent, that of being told nothing about every person I hold dear; pecuniary support; the allowance of one hour breathing fresh air; and, finally, I say that instead of the lingering method being used to get rid of me, a speedier method has not been taken. I say how pleased I am that he is preparing a formal, public, spirited demand as it appears to me the most likely to succeed and will be, at all events, most agreeable to my feelings.[30]

On the sixteenth, I write secretly to the princesse d'Hénin. I say I am distressed by her news of Madame de Poix and my cousin. I ask her to tell my family I am still alive as I learned from a Prussian officer who had been surrounded by French army prisoners whose leaders had said I was dead, that the Jacobins are still spreading this false rumor.[31] I learn that du Châtelet was executed on December 13.

January 3, 1794, brings distressing news. "You will be transferred tomorrow to a prison on the frontiers of Silesia. Maubourg will go in two days to Glatz in Silesia. Lameth and Pusy will stay here," I am told.

I am not allowed to know my destination but believe I am going to Neise. Maubourg asks to join me in the same fortress, even if we cannot communicate, but has so far not received an answer. I write secretly to the princesse d'Hénin: 'It was evidently thought I was dying too slowly and so to break a soul which was not bending, I am being sent alone one hundred and sixty leagues away....New anxiety about my wife, children and aunt devour me; the fury of the Jacobins make me fearful; taken from this place, from news, from means of communication, snatched from the friend who shares and softens all my pains, I am now going to see the complement of my solitude and the complete closure of my tomb.' [32] I hastily scribble some lines and write a few more in a secret letter to La Colombe to be given to Monsieur Pinckney and others who are trying to obtain my freedom which will now only be achieved by snatching it from the Powers. I say that it will be necessary to establish communication with me and to work on winning over some guards. Perhaps the Jewish people in the region will help me? I want my friends to remember my principles which I have sworn to hold until my last breath.[33] I write to the king of Poland that I will be near to his frontier and offer him my confidence, my affection and respect.[34] I also write to Mazzei and Littlepage, officers of the king, at Warsaw, introducing them to the bearer of the letter.

January 4. My open cart trundles through the cobbled streets. I gasp and cough in the freezing air; the town recedes; we go towards the frontier. The days pass. I begin to feel slightly better. My strength starts to return; I cough less. In the distance I see snow-capped mountains I last saw with Duportail and my beloved Gouvion in August,1785, when I travelled across the region to visit the military maneuvers.

On the sixteenth, my cart reaches Neisse, twelve days after leaving Magdebourg. I enter yet another red-brick, star-shaped fortress which stands on the riverbank opposite the town. Its walls close around me; I am taken down into its bowels to be entombed once more.

My cell receives daylight by small windows iron-barred in a wall eight feet thick. The earth of the rampart which is above my head is separated from it by a vault and a mezzanine, and my ceiling is very low. Three guards stand before it in the day, five at night. The courtyard of the fort is small and often marshy and from it can only be seen black walls and barred windows. My cell is longer than at Magdebourg; it comprises a sort of corridor divided into two parts, which Monsieur le commandant, Major von Hanff, has had covered with very clean planks. I can walk in the small courtyard with officers of the guard, and Chavaniac and Félix are allowed to come to me. I read journals from Hamburg, Leyden and Berlin; I have books. Most wonderful of all, after a month, I am allowed to receive and write letters.

February 16. I write to Madame de Maisonneuve, Maubourg's sister, who has been given permission by the king of Prussia to rejoin him at Glatz:

> If it is true that the Jacobins have declared me dead and buried that I would like to tell my family that at least I am not dead although I do not dare to write to them myself...the recognition of my writing could furnish a pretext for tyranny... My most ardent wish is to know she is not in France. What safety is there in a country where Robespierre is a sage, Danton an honest man and Marat a god?...I think my family would be best in Switzerland.... No consideration of fortune should expose them to personal danger... Assure my aunt, my wife, and my children that I live, that I fare better than at Wesel, that I resist my situation morally and physically...that my heart is constantly occupied with love of them and the good fortune to one day see them again...please spare me the inexpressible anxiety of knowing that they are all in France. Adieu, my beloved. Whatever is my destiny, remember always with gentleness the sentiments of my dear M...L...for his American brother, and the constant and mutual attachment which since that happy time attaches me so tenderly to you.[35]

I receive a letter from the princesse d'Hénin who gives me news from Chavaniac which in the present crisis of France are the least bad I could hope for, although I am in torment to hear of my wife's stay at Brioude. It would be impossible for her to leave without her children, but I would be so happy to know my family was in Switzerland. I think that besides the protection she finds in public affection, she would find in Mr. Jefferson a more imposing safeguard against the Jacobin tyrants. She needs to be taken to the frontier. I write that I am waiting impatiently for a letter from her as I know Madame de Maisonneuve is now at Glatz.

Commandant Hanff, whose wife Caroline is French, adds a postscript to my letter to say that he tries to combine his duties towards his king with an attempt to lighten my imprisonment, and that I am faring well.[36]

To my great delight, Pusy, Maubourg, and their servants, Jules and Jandel, arrive in April from Glatz. They are in cells near mine and Maubourg's sister, Madame de Maisonneuve, comes to live in the town.

He tells me the terrible news that Adrienne was again imprisoned at Brioude on November 13, catapulting me immediately into the blackness of complete despair. My family needs me. I must be with them. Perhaps America will come to my aid as I am an American citizen? So far, I have been bitterly disappointed. The most likely hope seems to be escape.

I hear that our cause is widely supported in different countries. There is even a debate in the House of Commons. Pitt criticizes our imprisonment, as does Cornwallis, Fox and Tarleton. I read in the gazettes of the death of Malesherbes, Madame du Châtelet, Duport's father, and many others who were all executed on April 22. These terrible events, and my fears for my family, torment me.

May 16. I am told that Pusy, Maubourg and I will be transferred from Prussia to Austria. We are being sent to a fortress in Moravia. I write a short letter to the princesse d'Hénin to inform her. I write to my former aides de camp. The king of Prussia has talked of Austrian hatred towards me. Kaunitz, the chancellor, does not like me and Monsieur de Thugut has heard much ill about me.

On the seventeenth, four soldiers and a captain escort I, Maubourg, Pusy and our four servants from Neisse; Commandant von Hanff and his wife follow in their carriage. We cross the frontier and continue to Zuckmantel where Austrian soldiers and officers are waiting.

"Would you write to the princesse d'Hénin to inform her we have arrived at this place and will be going to Olmütz tomorrow," I ask Caroline Hanff. "Here are some letters I would like you to send for me."

"I will do that for you," she replies.

I say farewell to her and her husband. We set off once more down the broad expanse of the imperial highway.

Chapter 47

Olmütz

May 22. Ghostly outlines of fortified walls rear up from the flat plain in the darkness of night. We travel across a long, wooden bridge over the Morava River, then across a drawbridge over a tributary. We enter the town through a narrow, guarded, white stone entrance, behind which looms a cathedral. The wheels clatter on the cobbles; we reach a square where a second House of God is dimly visible at one side. We turn into the inner courtyard of a grim, four-storied building with rows of narrow, arched windows.

Maubourg, Pusy and I glance at each other. The emperor now decides our future, which, in my case, I am not sure will be very long.

Lieutenant General Baron Splényi von Mihaldy, the interim commandant, watches a provost sergeant and a first lieutenant search us and our belongings. Teapots, scissors, forks, knives, pocket watches, knee and collar buckles and razors are all confiscated, as well as thirty double and forty single gold fredericks, and French assignats to the value of five hundred livres.

They examine books and gazettes, any work published after 1789, particularly *L'Esprit* and a French copy of Thomas Paine's *Common Sense*, and even a reprinted medieval religious work by Thomas á Kempis.

"Is common sense considered to be forbidden goods?" I enquire.[1]

Liberty is found in other books, including Rousseau's *Contrat social*, and a *History of Greece*, which not only has the word 'liberty,' but also the word 'republic'. My maps of Belgium also appear to be a danger to the emperor as well as writing materials, mathematical instruments and our letters, which will be stored far away from us in a chest at the commander's quarters in the town.

"We were allowed to have these at Neisse," Pusy complains bitterly.

"The Prussians have no idea how to imprison people properly," is the reply.

My cell is on the ground floor. Two doors are in front of it; one of very thick stout wood, with two enormous padlocks and a lock; the second with just a lock. My cell is large and vaulted and has an adjoining chamber of similar proportions. A tall window, about eight feet tall by four feet wide, is divided into four sections, whose upper parts are padlocked and whose lower part, about four feet square, is covered by a double iron grating. The second room also has a window. The furniture is sparse; a table, two chairs, a wardrobe and a stove, and there is a strong smell of excrement.[2]

"Your future will be only these four walls. You will have news of nothing and no one. Your name will never be said, even by your jailers, and in dispatches to the court you will be known as number two. You will never know anything of your family, nor each of you about the two others, and as this situation will naturally incline you to kill yourself, you have been forbidden to have knives or forks and all means of suicide," says Splényi.

"I am not obliging enough to kill myself," I reply.[3]

May 23. At five o'clock there is banging and rustling from a fire being lit in the stove outside the room. Pale fingers of dawn creep through the iron grills on the outside of the window to reveal the unfamiliar surroundings.

I can see for many leagues as the prison is on a hill at the south end of the town. A building is nearby on the right, another is on the left; between them are two houses whose fenced gardens back onto a terrace just below me, at the bottom of which extends a meadow to a tributary of the river. An incline then extends for about three hundred paces; there are buildings and a causeway, and further away the Morava River flows by fields. A cluster of other buildings and two guardhouses complete the scene and in the far distance is the wispy blur of the Oder Mountains.[4]

At eight o'clock the two doors are unlocked. Lieutenant Jacob and Sergeant Platzer enter; in the corridor soldiers stand guard with drawn sabers; another flourishes a smoking branch, presumably in a hopeless attempt to freshen the foul air. A soldier, a stranger to any sort of cleanliness, carries in coffee or chocolate, bread and water; I sit at the table and eat from dishes of Delft as dirty as the person who brought them. The jailers watch my every mouthful. I finish; they inspect the two rooms and the windows, a task which does not take long as there is not much here.

At eleven-thirty, lunch arrives; the same grimy soldier appears with the same grimy dishes. I have acidic red wine, soup, boiled beef and a *ragout* or vegetables, roast meat, salad, a dessert and black coffee; supper consists of roast meat, salad and half a bottle of wine;[5] I eat with a pewter spoon and my fingers. It is a great improvement on Prussian prison food, and far more plentiful than I had expected, but all of it is unfortunately impregnated with a distinctive flavor of tobacco.

"Is it a novelty to you to eat in this way?" enquires Lieutenant Jacobs.

"No, I have seen it used in America by the Iroquois," I reply coldly.[6]

A few days later, Splényi sends a catalogue of books I can borrow from a library, and another catalogue of books in German from a bookseller. I choose several.

Escape is not far from my thoughts. I watch the arrangement of the guard. Two sergeants command thirty men, and, at any one time, there are fifteen men on duty and one sergeant. Two soldiers stand outside the first locked door and a third stands inside; when the doors are open more guards stand in the corridor with drawn sabers. At mealtimes, or for other reasons, such as a visit of Splényi, the lieutenant and the sergeant watch. Occasionally I am awoken at night for an inspection and even the outside of the windows is examined. Three guards are on duty in the corridor and two are on the terrace. They are forbidden to speak to us and report everything we say or do. The soldiers on the terrace are also ordered to stop communication between any of us from our windows; other guards at the guardhouses watch the guards on the terrace. For the moment, I admit that escape is not likely; my thoughts turn to hopes of a Polish uprising led by my friend, General Tadeuscz Kosciousko.

Maubourg, Pusy and I are not the only French state prisoners held in the Jesuit Barracks. Beurnonville and his servant, Marchand, are also here, and Bancal is in the Clarissa Convent nearby. Beurnonville's room is next to mine and is below that of Félix Pontonnier. The rooms of Maubourg and Pusy are opposite latrines at the end of the corridor, and these latrines, combined with an inadequately covered sewer extending across the terrace and then into the moat, are the source of the continual stench.

Maubourg, Pusy and I remain constantly in our cells. I pace up and down; I read; I eat the meals. I worry constantly about my wife and my family. My cough racks my body and I am feverish. I am becoming very thin.

Dr. Karl Haberlein, the director of the garrison clinic, is a kindly man and speaks to me in French; I discover he is a fervent admirer of Washington. He brings wine with a label he has attached to the bottle as though it is a medicine; he poultices my arm with spurge laurel.

Six weeks pass. Our servants come to our cells. We communicate secretly. Beurnonville's cell is below that of Félix Pontonnier and they can talk through the window. Félix also manages to convey a message by playing pan pipes, whistling French songs and using gestures when he walks on the terrace below the windows. Beurnonville and Bancal are allowed to walk for the benefit of their health; in July, Beurnonville is given permission to take carriage rides.

Near the end of the month, to my surprise, Haberlein gives me a pamphlet and a card.

"This is from a person who has travelled here from London. The friends named on it are well and are thinking of you. We both agree that this knowledge will help your health more than any medication I can give you."

I read the pamphlet and card and see a list of my friends in London, as well as Narbonne, whom Bollman rescued. I also see the name Justus Erick Bollman, Doctor of Medicine, with an address of Steinmetz and Company, his banker in Vienna. Escape suddenly glimmers amidst the darkness.

"I have heard of my supporters in London," I say. "How are my friends?"

Haberlein does not know more; I return the pamphlet and card to him.

In August, Bancal is allowed carriage rides. My imprisonment, and that of my friends, also becomes slightly more lenient. Félix Pontonnier comes each morning when the guards enter with the meal. He serves my breakfast; he bandages my arm with the poultice ordered by Haberlein; Chavaniac comes on Thursdays and Sundays. Sometimes we can order items which Sergeant Platzer buys, such as tooth powder, sugar and lemons.

"Can I walk outside?" I ask, whilst Maubourg and Pusy refrain from making the same request so that I can have more opportunities to escape.

"Beurnonville is at a spa at Slatenitz for the month to improve his health. He has promised not to escape, and it is the emperor himself who has sanctioned it," Haberlein tells me in September. "I have requested for you to have carriage rides for your health."

In October, I learn the emperor has agreed and Haberlein hopes that although the previous commandant, Arco, will soon return, he will not decide differently. Now, every other day, I go out in a carriage from two to four in the afternoon. During the excursion I am also permitted to walk; I can finally breathe fresh air again and the possibility of escape seems more feasible. I wait to hear from Bollmann.

Finally, the silence is broken. Haberlein gives me a novel, *Clarissa*, in which are two sheets of paper on which my friends have written in French, asking to whom to send 20,000 dollars given to me by the United States, as well as writing of other matters. At the end are the words: 'These lines will say more to you than it appears at a first glance if your misfortunes have not too much blunted your understanding and if you are capable of reading it with the same warmth as the letters from the princesse d'Hénin.'[7]

I remain outwardly calm. When I am alone, I heat the back of the page. English words written in lemon juice appear. Bollmann says that he has been sent by my friends to be at my service. He has already tried for several months to let me know he is here and has waited in vain for news of me and has seen me on a drive. He says that I alone can suggest a plan, as I alone know what he does not. He suggests an escape during the night, having bribed the lieutenant or sergeant to bring me out.[8] He says that: 'negotiations are proceeding between the powers engaged in the conflict, with a view to reach a peace which will perhaps be signed next winter. However, I tell you with joy and without worrying about any personal risks I may run, that I will aid no matter what plan of escape.'[9]

I tear the paper with my teeth, then burn it. I write with a toothpick and ink from water and cinders, in French on the margins of two pages of the novel. I thank him for news of my family and friends and ask how they are. I try and give him details of my health, which I say is good, and that I go out for a drive every other day in a frockcoat and round hat with the provost sergeant. I say I have lost faith in diplomacy to obtain my release and so I would like him to follow the method he speaks of. I also mention that I am concerned for Haberlein's safety.' In lemon juice I write:

It is not practicable, my dear friend, now to write about my situation in detail; however, I will do so before I see the timorous doctor again, provided you persuade him to give me your answer, and to smuggle another book to me. I will only say that precautions have been so well taken against all the usual means of escape, that all that remains are the unusual ones. It is true that if the lieutenant or the provost corporal were to fetch me in the evening in the general's name, I think I could escape, but it would be much easier for the lieutenant who has the right to go out in the carriage with me, although he does not use it, or for the corporal who accompanies me- which seems far better- to go on ahead when we have left the town and find another carriage with horses which are ready. The scheme could not fail unless we are betrayed.

To avoid that, I have an equally easy plan, whose success you can count on. The lieutenant is a stupid, servile and stubborn old man; the corporal has more of a weakness for money but is a cowardly rascal. He can be bribed; but his cowardice is such that he may prefer less of a reward and no danger, to a fortune and some risk. It is a thousand times better to go on ahead despite him when we go together in the vehicle.

We are in a phaeton, nobody is with me except the corporal, who, I must mention, has a hernia, and a great, stupid driver, who sometimes, like today, is left at home, and then it is the corporal who drives. We go along different roads, sometimes through byroads, and we do not always return the same way we came, but we always go a half german mile (one league), and sometimes a whole mile (two leagues) from town. If it is half a mile, you can catch us up on horseback, as the vehicle usually goes slowly. Have a trusty man with you, stop the driver. I will frighten our timid corporal with his own sword, so that nothing will stop me from jumping on the horse of your companion who can ride some distance behind me. If the driver is not there, so much the better; if he is, he will only think of saving himself.

Depend upon it, my dear sir, when you choose your time and place where you can have one or two relays of horses on the road, that no-one will have any idea or the audacity to want to stop us; and before the slow German general knows what we are doing or what he must do, we will be safe. My friends Maubourg and Pusy are convinced of it. That is the reason that I have asked to go out in the vehicle, and they have not asked to do it as well, so that I can go out all the permitted days. The more audacious is the scheme, the more it is unexpected, the more likely it is to succeed, and we may say with the poet that 'The presence of spirit and courage in the face of danger, do more than armies to obtain success.'

Take care not to mistake Beurnonville or Bancal for me. They go out on the days when I don't, the first at half past one, the second at four o'clock. I would like you to obtain pocket pistols for me, for when I am on horseback. Until then I have no need of them, and the corporal's own sword will be more than sufficient.[10]

I am going to owe you a thousand times more than life- but do not miss this excellent opportunity....I can also throw a letter from the phaeton, but whatever day you make the attempt, next Tuesday or any day after that, I shall be ready. Adieu.[11]

October 10. Haberlein visits. I wait until he is binding my arm with a poultice and Chavaniac and the sergeant are in the next room, then I slip the novel into his pocket. He takes it out and looks at what I have written. "That seems to be alright," he says. "I will give it to Herr Bollmann."

I wait several days. Haberlein visits; he gives me another book on which is written a note of thanks in ink. When I am alone, I heat the page. 'I need time,' Bollmann has written. I tear it out and burn it.

On my next drive I discover rules have unfortunately been tightened since the return of Arco. A soldier now stands on the back of the carriage and remains with us for the whole of the excursion. I am disappointed, but still optimistic.

November 6. Haberlein gives me another message, written in French, ostensibly from my friends in England: 'John Jay is seeking your release in Vienna. Your family is well.' My hopes rise at this wonderful news.

"Would you write a message for your friends in England," he asks.

When I am alone, I heat the page and see the words: 'I now have everything ready to carry out the plan and to make an attempt on Thursday or Saturday. Huger will help me. We will remove our hats to signal to you and you must wipe your forehead with a handkerchief. Try and take the route to Silésie.'

Huger! The name brings tears to my eyes. I am in a frenzy of excitement but remain outwardly calm. I burn the letter.

November 8. Saturday. Two o'clock in the afternoon. It is market day and the cobbled streets throng with peasants, traders, carts and donkeys. We drive out from Olmütz in the phaeton pulled by two horses. The provost sergeant, Platzer, sits beside me, dressed in an overcoat, white breeches, a hat and boots, and armed with a sword. I am in a blue Prussian army greatcoat; my hair is powdered and I wear a hat. A young soldier with a saber stands on the springs at the back.

The drunken driver manages to negotiate the bridge over the Mittelmarch, then the next over the Morava. We take the right fork and veer onto the imperial highway in a welter of other vehicles and people on foot. We travel north-east towards the villages, across a flat land crisscrossed by ditches, without any hedges or trees except for a small, wooded hill some way off. Peasants work in the fields.

I sit stiffly upright, my handkerchief ready to use, tensed to act. Just south of Chwalkowitz two horsemen ride towards us. They pass on the right. They remove their hats. We salute them back and I catch a glimpse of a stocky man, with fair hair cut very short, and a thinner man, with a pleasing, youthful appearance. I wipe my handkerchief across my forehead; they ride on towards Olmütz. I glance back; they turn and follow slowly as we go through the village to the fields.

"Do you want to walk?" asks Platzer.

"Yes, the weather is pleasant," I reply.

"Go right," he orders the driver.

The phaeton bumps along a track and pulls up near the statue of an angel. I brace myself.

"It is pleasant here and the exercise will give you an appetite and a thirst," says Platzer as he climbs out of the small carriage and helps me down.

"Take the back seat," he orders the soldier. "Wait for us at the tavern at Klien-Wisternitz."

He holds my left arm, and we walk together, the phaeton going slowly towards the village. I ready myself. I listen attentively. At about three o'clock I hear galloping. I can still see the phaeton and there are peasants nearby, but this will be the only opportunity

The riders quickly gallop near to us. "Halt!" they shout.

Platzer turns in surprise.

"Seize his sword!" shouts Bollmann.

I pull it half out of the scabbard.

"What are you doing?" Platzer cries in alarm and tries to push it back.

Bollmann jumps from his horse; he throws the reins to Huger and aims a pistol at the sergeant.

"Give us the man!" he shouts.

Platzer and I struggle for the sword. The horse rears up and canters away. Huger quietens his own animal and dismounts. He puts the reins over his arm and aims a pistol at the sergeant who is holding his sword in his left hand and ferociously pulling at my cravat, choking me with his right. I cannot breathe. Bollmann grabs him, but he continues to grip me tightly.

"He's strangling me," I gasp in French. Huger drags him away from me. "Kill him! Kill him!" I shout in English.

I stumble to my feet. I attempt to mount the horse, but Platzer grabs my coat, forcing me backwards. We both fall onto the ground taking the horse down with us, pain shooting through my arm. The animal tramples Platzer, then staggers upright.

"Help!" Platzer screams. "Help!"

The peasants stand and stare, not sure what is happening as he is not in uniform.

"I will give you money," I say.

"Gag him!" shouts one of my rescuers.

I push a glove into Platzer's mouth, but he bites my finger[12] and spits out the glove, still holding me. Bollmann knees him in the chest and keeps him on the ground. Huger pushes a handkerchief into his mouth and holds a pistol to his head.

"Let the prisoner go!" shouts Bollmann, holding a pistol to his head.

Both men pummel him; one hits him with his riding crop. Platzer lessens his grip; I roll away and Huger kneels on his arm.

"Take care of his sword, sir!" shouts Bollmann. He grabs the sword, drawing blood from Platzer's hand. He throws it some distance, but then the sergeant grabs the pistol and throws it.

"Mount the horse!" Bollmann tells me. "One horse has gone. It's best that you try and save yourself than for all three of us to be taken prisoner."

I shakily mount the chestnut mare. "Can I help?"

"Go off!" Bollmann says. "Follow the main road."

"Get off!" shouts Huger.[13]

I canter slowly away along the road towards Chwalkowitz, blood dripping from my fingers, my hand and my side hurting badly. I am not sure where I am going. I glance back. Platzer is running after me. Bollmann and Huger are on the other horse[14] which will hopefully bear the weight of both.

I dig my heels into the mare's flanks and gallop. Sometime later I am still alone. I hear the warning boom of cannons from Olmütz; I am now being pursued. I come to the small town of Sternberg and quickly ride through it in my bloodied, mud-covered state. I take the road straight ahead, relief flooding through me as I leave it behind. Then almost immediately I feel a shiver of alarm; the road is narrow, twisting and turning up a steep hill, whereas I remember the imperial highway as wide, with trees on each side, and a deep ditch. My route meanders into a myriad of country tracks and I start to despair of finding the road north. The hours lengthen. Where are Bollman and Huger? Have they been caught? Have they taken another road? I will have to cross the border without them and without being recognized. Troops must now be coming closer. It would be senseless to return in the direction of Olmütz. I keep riding in the direction I hope is north, my flagging horse lathered with sweat.

Early evening begins to darken the countryside; in the gloom I see a man walking at the side of the road. He calls to my horse. I stop.

"Good evening. What is the name of the town ahead?" I ask in my heavily accented, poor German.

"Braunseifen," he replies.

"Is this the imperial highway?" I ask.

"No," he replies.

"Where is the nearest posting station?" I ask.

"Lobnig, just east of Braunseifen. Are you a Romanic?" he replies.

"No. I am from England," I say.

"We have a Romanic here who works for a merchant," he replies.

"Are you a merchant?" I ask.

"No," he replies.

"What then? A tanner," I ask.

I do not understand his reply and say nothing, very aware of my dirty, blood-stained clothes and my thoroughbred chestnut mare.

"How far is it to Olmütz, Troppau and Neisse?" I ask.

He tells me.

"Can you show me the way to Neisse? Perhaps you can be my guide?" I ask.

He says something which I do not understand.

"How much do you want?" I ask, in the hope he is willing to lead me to the border.

"One or two ducats," he replies.

"I will give you that," I say,[15] not having any money, but intending to pay later.

He seems to agree, as far as I can tell. He walks in front of me along a footpath; he guides me across a field and into a forest. He does not appear to be armed or aggressive, but I watch him warily as I follow him down winding paths for about an hour in increasing darkness. We splash through a stream, my horse panting and becoming slower and slower. He cuts a branch. I wonder what he is doing. Does he intend to use it as a weapon? However, he hands it to me and indicates I should use it as a switch. I gratefully accept and we continue in the luminous glow of a full moon. Houses become visible. We descend a hillside towards them. I begin to be nervous.

"I need more money," he says.

"Please be quiet," I beg.

I hesitate to go further with him. I stop, but he gestures me to carry on. I do not know what to do. I do not wish to draw attention to myself. My horse is exhausted, so it is not easy to ride away. We reach a barn on the edge of the village.

"You can wait here," he says. "I will be back."

As soon as he has gone, I ride to a nearby field. A short time later, a horse whinnies. My horse whinnies back and my guide appears with another man on a horse. I start to dismount.

"Stay in the saddle," he says, and leads my horse by the bridle. The other man rides in front and we enter the village and onto a road going north. We pass barns and I start to feel anxious but am somewhat reassured by the calm of the rider. He stops and I catch up with the other horse.

"Have a safe journey," he says.

A man steps out from behind a pile of logs, as though he has been waiting. "Where are you going?"

"What right have you to ask" I declare with as much indignation as I can muster but fearing the worst.

A second man steps out from behind the wood pile. Then come several more, holding cudgels. They grab my bridle.

"Dismount!" orders a man. "Who are you? Have you a pass?"

I say nothing and quickly try to think of my reason for being there. Two hold my arms and take me to a house. We go upstairs where a man is eating by the fire.[16]

The leader of the men talks to me in German and in Latin. I stay silent. The man eating speaks to me in Italian and I realize he is the Romanic. I say nothing.

"Are you the mayor?" I ask the leader of the men.

"Yes," he replies.

"I am a customs officer at Neustadt. And I haven't a passport. I left Neustadt without the knowledge of my superiors and therefore I want to get quickly to Olmütz. I have lost my way and as it would be very costly not to be able to return home before nightfall, I hope you will not keep me here any longer and let me go on my way with my guide."

The Italian grabs his sleeve and says a few words to him. "I know this man. It is General Lafayette. He was in the party of prisoners which came to the Lobnig postal station."

I pull the sleeve of the mayor and we go into an adjoining room.

"I am Lafayette," I say. "Have you read about me?"

"Yes, I hold you in esteem," he replies. "Have you been violent towards your guard?" he asks, looking at my bloodied, dirty clothes and hand.

"I have not killed or shot at him," I reply. "If you will let me go, I will give you one thousand ducats."

"No, I cannot. I have to do my duty, and, in any case, my secretary has already recognized you," he relies politely.

"I would like to speak to him," I say.

The mayor goes into the other room; he returns with the Italian, Buricelli.

"Are you married?" I ask.

"No," he replies.

"Would you like to flee with me?" I ask.

"No, I have a house in Milan, under Austrian control."

"How much is it worth?" I ask.

"Three to four thousand florins," he replies.

"That is nothing. I will give you enough money so you can live like a prince for the rest of your life. I will give you twenty-five hundred ducats and pensions to any children you might have."

"No," he replies.

"I will give you two thousand ducats if you just forget this," I tell the mayor.

"It is impossible," he replies. "The tanner, Droxler, has brought you in."

"He does not know who I am. You can say I have a passport and am someone else," I tell him.

"No, I must do my duty," he replies.

"Let Buricelli stay in the room with me as my guard. He can help me climb through the window and escape. No one will blame you as there are no soldiers here and I have managed to escape all the troops in Olmütz."

"No," says the mayor. "But do not worry. Peace is only a few months away. And then you can   return   toParis."

"Not Paris, London," I say.[17] "Do you know about an American envoy in Vienna?"

"No," he replies.

Has an accomplice been found?" I ask.

"I do not know," he replies.

"Could I have a meal?" I ask.

Food, beer and newspapers are brought to me and I eat in the company of a charming lady who is breast-feeding her infant.

"I also have a wife and children," I tell her. "But I do not know what has happened to them."

She tries to comfort me and then leaves me to sleep in the upper bedroom, guarded by three men.

Three more are in adjacent rooms and two night-watchmen stand outside the house. One of the men, Langer, washes the mud from my coat and breeches.

"I beg you to let me get out of the window. I will give you one thousand ducats," I tell the two men who remain.

"No, not even for a roomful of ducats," they reply. "We will be imprisoned for life in Spielberg fortress."

I finally realize there is no hope. I start reading the newspapers and then sleep. At two I am awoken and taken from the bedroom.

"I am Herr Krömer, the senior district magistrate from Eulenberg. You are now my prisoner. Come with me," says a man.

We travel in his calash, my horse following behind, accompanied by five men, two of whom have rifles.

"Do you know about my rescuers?" I ask the magistrate.

"They have been arrested," he replies.

We stop briefly at Eulenberg; Krömer's daughter bandages my finger.

"We tried, but it was all for nothing," I comment.

Back at Olmütz, I am searched in a particularly humiliating way. I am taken back to my rooms which are bare of everything except the furniture and a few clothes. Black despair grips me. I can only think of the two men who tried to save me. Have they been captured? Where are they?

Arco visits the first day. "The two wretches who tried to rescue you are in our hands. We are going to hang them in front of your window, and I will be very happy to be the hangman," he informs me with great satisfaction.[18]

I am not completely convinced he is telling the truth, but his words pierce me.

My side is swollen, my finger red-hot with pain. It is four days before Haberlein comes to examine me.

"It is nothing," he comments, glancing at my injuries and scarcely daring to speak.

I would like to tell him I will say nothing about the messages he has conveyed for Bollmann and I, but the guard is standing next to us.

"Hurry up," orders the officer.[19]

"Would you go into the next room," Jacob requests.

"For what purpose?" I ask suspiciously.

"That your irons may be put on," he replies.

"Your emperor has not given you such an order," I reply firmly. "Beware of doing more than he requires and of displeasing him by exceeding his orders through an ill-timed zeal."

He thinks about my answer for a moment. To my relief, he does not repeat his command.[20]

I often ask about my rescuers. "How do you know that they are here?"is the response. Will they be executed? My fears torture me. What is happening to my friends and family?[21]

December 9. It is bitterly cold and black as the River of Hades. The stove has gone out; I am no longer allowed candles, and no one comes to see me for the fourteen hours of the night. I shake and shiver feverishly, my sweat-soaked shirt clinging to me. I have already stumbled around in the dark and changed into the only other one I possess.[22] I wheeze. I draw the fetid air into my lungs and cough in spasms which rack my body.

In the afternoon, to my surprise, guards take me from my cell and along the dismal corridor. We enter a room where three men are seated and a very welcome fire blazes in the hearth. A tribunal, I immediately guess. My thoughts race. I have been preparing what I need to say since that terrible day and this will probably be my opportunity, perhaps my only opportunity, to find out about Bollmann and Huger and to take all the blame.

"I am Von Okacz, the chief of police at Brunn. We would like to know the details of your attempted escape," says one of the men.

"I agree to cooperate with you for the sake of the two men I call my divine rescuers, my two messiahs. However, no power can be authorized to hold me captive because I am a citizen of the United States of America and not a prisoner of war," I declare.

"We have no authorization to accept your protests," is the reply.

"I was born in France but am now a citizen of the United States of America. I had planned the escape with friends abroad before I came to Olmütz. I seized the saber from Sergeant Platzer and forced the foreigners to help me. It was I who stuffed the glove in the mouth of the sergeant and the two foreigners avoided harming him. It is possible one of them waved a small pistol, but he did not fire it. I must be regarded as the main author of the escape."

"What do you know of Doctor Haberlein?" he asks.

"Who? Do you mean the physician? I did not know his name is Haberlein. I have never spoken to him about Bollmann and he brought me nothing from him."

"Did Haberlein give you three notes from Bollmann?"

"I keep to the previous response, namely nothing."

"These are signed statements," he says, handing me several pieces of paper. I quickly read them and very unhappily discover Bollmann has been captured and he and Haberlein have admitted much.

The three men question me again.

"I refer to my previous responses without pretending to exonerate myself from possible criticism since I have declared I was author of the project."

They continue to question me.

"I must make the same negative response," I say.[23]

December 10. I meet again with the tribunal in front of another blazing fire.

"I am ready to talk. I knew that Mr. Bollmann was extremely generous and sensitive. I abused these two feelings by all arguments that a spirit like his is unable to resist.[24] I agree that he helped me, but I made him abandon his plan and adopt mine, which pleased him less, and which was a lot more dangerous. I did not think, knowing that he was a very courageous man, and ready to sacrifice himself for me, I was flippant in placing him in an impossible situation. He had no other choice but to either refuse, which would have hurt me, or to sacrifice himself. I feel very guilty on his behalf and regret that the state to which I am reduced does not allow me to show him the whole of my gratitude."

"What part did Doctor Haberlein play in your attempted escape?"

"Doctor Haberlein is a well-meaning man who was very reluctant to transgress regulations. He was unable to withstand appeals to his humanity and knew nothing about the escape."[25]

I return a third time to the tribunal but learn nothing about my brave rescuers.

Andreas Axter from Ofen replaces Haberlein in January,1795. He speaks Latin badly, but we manage to communicate. He looks at me solemnly and I see from his eyes and expression he thinks I am near to death. I am inclined to agree with him.

"What is happening to Bollmann and Huger?" I ask the guards.

"What make you think they are here?" is always the reply.[26]

Commandant Arco is particularly cruel in his remarks. The failed escape has humiliated him. It is a blemish on his career, and he plays with me like a cat with a mouse. Sometimes I believe him, sometimes I do not, but I remain in a state of the greatest anxiety for them.

The agony of the trial continues for months, casting me into utter despair, overcome by fears they will be hanged because of me. I fear the vengeance of the Austrian state and its emperor on my would-be saviors. It will be my fault.

I cough and wheeze in my cell, my thoughts torturing me day and night. I have no news of my family. I am at the nadir of my life. I fear I will be publicly executed. Will I be humiliated like Major André and hanged? Will I even survive to be hanged or whatever is the method of execution? Will crowds watch me as I swing on the gallows and choke my last breath?

My friends have been allowed to receive and to write some letters from earlier in the year so long as they do not say where they are imprisoned and only mention family matters. We manage to communicate secretly in early summer by means of Félix's pan pipes and his and Maubourg's servant Jules's whistling and singing, as well as a network of helpers. At the beginning of June, I learn that Bollmann and Huger will soon be released. My spirits soar. Whatever happens to me, my messiahs will be saved. In July,[27] I learn that they were freed on June 24, just before Vienna had sent orders for a new trial which may have resulted in quite a different verdict and in their execution.[28] Very strangely, I catch a glint of pleasure in Arco's eyes but have no idea why.[29]

I also receive a note from Maubourg from friends abroad, which cheers me greatly. I reply, using a toothpick and my blood on a handkerchief.

The heat of summer starts to fade. Storks fly west across the sky; autumn will soon be here. One day I catch the sound of Jules playing his pan pipes; I quickly translate: 'Your family has survived.'

My heart almost stops beating. I am faint. I clutch my rags, tears streaming down my face in joy. They are alive. My Adrienne, my Anastasie, my Virginie, my George. My dear heart, my darling children.

Autumn comes. I have seen the seasons change. I have watched the pale green wheat fields become   yellow, bright with the rays of the sun. Now they are brown. They are newly plowed and await the spring to transform into wheat. Mist swirls up from the river, painting the landscape a pallid gray; even though summer has departed swarms of mosquitos still compete to enter my cell, their fragile bodies insidiously wafting through the smallest gap, seeking out my blood.

Outside in the yard a soldier is being flogged; he shrieks with pain. Yesterday a soldier was forced to run the gauntlet; his cries were hardly human and the men beating him bayed with the bloodlust of dogs at a cornered prey.

I am an emaciated skeleton of a man, with no hair, in ragged clothes, entombed in a stinking room, but now I know my family live. Now my rescuers have regained their freedom.

October 15. The padlocks and locks on the two doors of my cell unexpectedly grate and clang. The doors open. I look in surprise, completely taken aback to see three women I do not recognize. They regard me with anguish and joy. They rush forward and embrace me, tears on their faces, their bodies warm against mine. I tremble in wonderment to realize it is Adrienne, Anastasie and Virginie. I sob and clutch them to my heart.

"We have come to be with you, to share your imprisonment. The emperor has allowed us to do so," says Adrienne.

I can hardly stand. They support me. I touch their faces tenderly; we cling together. The guards demand their purses and confiscate three silver forks as we embrace.[30]

"The room next door is being prepared for your daughters and one further away for your servant," says Major Czernak to Adrienne. "One thousand two hundred and eighteen florins and two kreuzers, a gilt silver fork and spoon, a silver coffeepot, a packet of papers and a silk purse have already been confiscated." [31]

The guards withdraw; they slam shut and lock the two doors.

"George? Where is he?" I ask.

"He has gone to America and has arrived in Boston. I have written to Mr. Washington to say I am entrusting him to his care and am sending him with Monsieur Frestel, who has been our support, our protector, our comfort and his guide.[32] I felt sure this was what you would want."

"Yes, my dear heart. Thank you," I reply.

I do not have the courage to ask what has happened to our family and friends. I know there has been the Terror, but my knowledge of what has happened is slight and I am very afraid of what Adrienne will tell me. She also has not the courage to talk of it and we wait to speak when we are alone.[33] I tremble with fear. Evening comes; the guards take Virginie and Anastasie from my cell, crossing their sabers in the corridor, making my lovely girls walk underneath. Virginie flushes, but Anastasie makes a face, and I am so proud and adoring of them. The door shuts. I hear footsteps, another door opening and shutting and know they are now in what used to be Beurnonville's room.

Adrienne and I look at each other, her face etched with suffering. I now learn part of the ghastly truth, the horror she has experienced.

"My mother, grandmother and Louise were all executed. They were imprisoned at the Luxembourg, but I did not try to send a message to them as I feared it would make their situation more dangerous. Monsieur Carrichon followed the cart containing them to the scaffold. He had given them absolution and he witnessed their execution, on what is now called Thermidor 4, just five days before the end of Robespierre. The duc and duchesse de Mouchy were killed, as well as La Rochefoucauld, Condorcet, Barnave and Bailly and so many others."

"What happened to you, my dear heart?" I ask fearfully.

"I was arrested and taken to Brioude on November 13, 1793."

"I believed you were still at Chavaniac at that time. I received news of you from Madame de Maisonneuve, Maubourg's sister."

"Madame de Chavaniac was arrested in January,1794, but because she was very elderly, she was allowed to stay at the château. At the end of May, now called the 8 Prairial, I was transferred to Paris, but before I went, I made my confession to the curé of Chavaniac. I arrived in Paris on the nineteenth of Prairial, three days before the decree of the twenty-second which organized a terror in the Terror. I was taken to La Petite Force where I heard that about sixty people a day were being executed. When I was there the château at Chavaniac was sold. Aunt bought back her bed, but the picture of your father was taken.

After a fortnight I was transferred to Le Plessis, where I was alone in a small attic on the fifth floor. Every morning I could see about twenty people being taken to the guillotine but the thought of soon being one of the victims made me endure such a sight with more firmness than I would otherwise have had.[34] I many times repeated the first words of the Belief in God, the Father Almighty and made my will.[35] I spent fifty days there, expecting death at every moment, and I think I would have been executed if it had not been for Monsieur Morris, who repeatedly presented my case to the authorities with the result that I lived beyond the 10 Thermidor, which is when the revolution happened. At first, we thought that new massacres would take place in the prisons, but then we heard of Robespierre's death and that the executions of the Revolutionary Tribunal had stopped. At that time, I still believed my mother, grandmother and sister were alive but subsequently discovered their awful fate. We were still not sure whether the executions would continue, but then all the prisoners at Le Plessis were set free, except for me. Monsieur Monroe, the new American ambassador, attempted to obtain my release but was unsuccessful. I was transferred from there to the rue des Amandiers, and from there to the Maison Delmas on rue Notre Dame des Champs. Monsieur Carrichon often visited, pretending to be a carpenter. He prayed with me and very much soothed the anguish of my soul.[36] Monsieur Monroe kept trying to obtain my release and Madame Beauchet went all the time to Colombel, of the Committee, but Legendre refused to sign. Finally, Madame de Duras saw him and obtained his signature, and I was released on the second Pluviose. I went to stay with my aunt de Ségur at Chateney and she awakened in me a great and tender interest in life.[37] After Chateney I spent several days in Paris at the apartment of the princesse de Poix who shares it with Madame de Simiane, and we talked much about you.

I went and thanked Monsieur Monroe for all he had done. I asked him to obtain a passport for myself and my children. I could not leave George in France nor take him to Germany with me, so that was when I decided to send him to America. I sent for him to come to Paris and managed to obtain a passport with the help of Monsieur Boissy d'Anglas who is a friend of my aunt and who is on the new Committee of Public Safety. The name on the passport was Motier, and Monsieur Boissy d'Anglas contrived to obtain the signatures of his colleagues without their realizing who George is. I wrote a letter to General Washington saying that I was sending him my son with Monsieur Frestel who has been our protector, our comfort and George's guide. I said that I wanted him to lead a secluded life in America and that he should resume his studies which have been interrupted by three years of misfortunes, and that far from the land where so many events are taking place which might either dishearten or revolt him, he may become fit to fulfil the duties of a citizen of the United States whose feelings and whose principles will always agree with those of a French citizen.[38] I knew that it would have been your wish for me to send our son there and I found strength in that.[39]

I travelled to Chavaniac and spent a week with your aunt. Then I returned to Paris with Virginie and Anastasie before returning to Paris to obtain my passport. I went to Fontenay-en-Brie and La Grange, my mother's estates, as there has been a decree allowing the heirs of those who had been condemned to death to buy back the property. Boissy d'Anglas helped me greatly again. Finally I received my passport which was not for Germany but for America. We embarked on a small American ship on September 5 and landed at Altona after eight days. Madame de Tessé is living there with my sister, Pauline, and it was wonderful to see them again. She told me that my father, who has settled in Switzerland, has married the comtesse de Golovkine. We went to see the American consul at Hamburg, Monsieur Parish, and he provided me with a passport in the name of Motier, as a citizen of Hartford, Connecticut. I had to keep everything secret, as well as our nationality, as French people are not allowed to enter Austria. We arrived in Vienna and through the kindness of the prince de Rosenberg, the grand chamberlain, I obtained an audience with Emperor François 11, without the knowledge of his ministers.

"What was he like?" I ask.

"He seemed just a small king, neither good nor bad," she replies. "I asked to share your captivity. He agreed but said he could not give you your liberty as his hands were tied. I also asked if I could write to him directly if I have any requests as I had heard of several vexations in Prussian prisons. He again agreed and said that I will find you well fed and well-treated, but that my presence will give you added pleasure and that I will be pleased with the commanding officer. I spent eight more days in Vienna and went to see Monsieur de Thugut, the prime minister. He was polite but clearly hates you and I was very grateful to Monsieur de Rosenberg for having obtained an audience with the emperor for me. While I was in Vienna an exchange took place of the princesse de France, the duchesse d'Angoulême, for the conventionels who were taken prisoner.

"Yes, I know Beurnonville and Bancal have been freed even although they voted for the king's death, whereas Pusy, Maubourg and I tried to keep him safe and have a constitutional monarchy."

"That is true," she replies. "And I feel that unless an unexpected event happens, I do not think you will be freed soon."[40]

After three days Adrienne requests the commandant to let her attend Mass with Anastasie and Virginie. She also requests a servant and for Pusy and Maubourg to spend some time with us. She dismisses her servant, Jean Depuit, and pays him one hundred and forty-seven florins and four kreuzer. Unfortunately, the physician decides he has caught the Venetian disease and needs a month to recover.

"I will have to pay for his care," she says angrily. "He is an idiot."

She is in prison, but she radiates happiness. She deeply feels the privations of the consolations of religion but feels it is God's hand which has led her here. She is convinced it is due to the intercession of her mother, grandmother, and sister that she now owes her present state of joy at being with me, Anastasie and Virginie.[41]

She and I eat breakfast every day at eight. Then she is taken to the cell of our daughters where she stays until dinner. We all spend the rest of the day together until eight o'clock when Virginie and Anastasie are escorted to their cell; we only see the jailers when they bring dinner and supper. Adrienne is starting to write an account of her mother, using a toothpick and a small portion of Indian ink, on the margins of the engravings of a volume of Buffon.

December 14. She has received no reply to her requests, so she writes to Ferraris, the minister of war. She hopes to have a reply by Christmas, but on Christmas Day, my fourth Christmas in prison, she has still not received an answer.

1796. By the new year Adrienne has a fever and is ill. Her arms and legs swell and are blistered. I immediately ask for a physician.

Axter visits our cell. We speak in Latin and I translate Adrienne's words to him.

"I do not know what is causing it. It is perhaps an illness of the blood," he says.

"You must have treatment. You must go to Vienna," I tell her.

She receives a letter from Ferraris written on December 27. He says he is utterly unaware to whom she addressed the request to hear Mass, but he has not the means to comply with her desire, notwithstanding his wish to do so. He says that as she has consented to share her husband's lot, it will not be possible to obtain any change in her situation.[42]

She writes back, repeating her original requests and saying that the emperor had allowed her to write to him by addressing her letters to the prince de Rosenberg. On January 26 Ferraris replies that neither he nor the council of war can grant the requests made by state prisoners and that she must address herself to His Imperial Majesty.[43]

Fortunately, the winter is mild. Anastasie makes me clothes and even a pair of shoes from Adrienne's corset, so I look far more respectable now. She also writes what I dictate to her on the margins of a book. Adrienne teaches the girls and instructs them in religion. I read to them in the evening and tell them about the United States. Anastasie draws a picture of the jailer, Corporal Colomba, whom she and Virginie have named Cataquois, on her thumb nail, and later draws it on paper and gives it to me.

February 6. Adrienne finally agrees to write to the emperor for permission to have treatment in Vienna but she only consents to do so in the hope she might be useful to me and the other prisoners.

Seven weeks' later, her blisters now large, ulcerated sores, the commandant visits her.

"The emperor has said that if you leave this prison, you can never return. He asks for a written answer."

She quickly does so:

> It was my duty towards my family and friends to try and obtain the advice necessary for my health, but they well know that I cannot accept the conditions offered to me. I cannot forget that while we were both on the eve of perishing, I through the tyranny of Robespierre, Monsieur de Lafayette through the physical and moral sufferings of his captivity, I was neither allowed to receive any accounts of him, nor to let him know that his children and I were still alive. I shall not expose myself to the horrors of another separation. Therefore, whatever may be the state of my health, or the hardships of this abode for my daughters, we shall all three take advantage of His Imperial Majesty's goodness in allowing us to share this captivity in all its details. Noailles Lafayette.[44]

The rector of the University of Olmütz, and other German patriots, manage to smuggle letters for us. The rector organizes a secret correspondence for Adrienne's letters to be taken past the Austrian frontier; he also enables us to receive some news. My daughters make use of another method to convey information within the prison. They lower part of their supper in a parcel at the end of a string through the bars of their cell's window to the sentry standing below. He then passes the parcel using the same method to Pusy and Maubourg.[45] Adrienne is also permitted to write in a limited fashion to family as well as to write letters concerning private and financial affairs. She writes to John Parish, the United States' consul in Hamburg.

In spring, the physician, Axter, manages to give Adrienne a note from someone called P. Feldmann, who says he is an old and true friend of our family and will shortly give us letters from many of our dearest friends, who, as well as our son George, are in perfect health. We are in delight at this news.

"Who is P. Feldmann?" we wonder.

Next day, at two o'clock, the hour of our dinner, Axter comes with the jailer. He makes a sign to Adrienne that he will hide something. He looks at the moisture on the walls, then goes to inspect the walls of my daughters' room. He returns to say that their room is not so moist. Adrienne changes color but quickly recovers herself, whilst I and my daughters remain very much in control of our emotions.

Later, Adrienne discovers two packets of letters from our friends under the straw bed, which we devour in great joy. Peter Feldmann, who is really Ducoudray Holstein, is also offering to help me escape. We discuss his proposition.

"I strongly disagree to it," I say. "When Messieurs Bollmann and Huger made the attempt to liberate me, I was alone; of course, no one was exposed on my account, but now my escape must necessarily involve the safety of all of you."

We therefore decide against it; Adrienne writes to thank him for all that he has done and wishes to do but says that I refuse now that my wife and daughters are here.[46]

Our jailers reject a letter she writes to him as they do not want the conditions here known in America. She asks to see the assistant commandant; he visits my room.

"Therefore I am to understand that the government will not permit my letters to be dispatched because of certain details in them," she says.

"This base and cowardly refusal of your government to admit the infamy of its conduct is the last straw, Monsieur," I declare.

"I have too much feeling not to be aware of what is owing to your situation, but there are expressions in this letter which cannot be permitted," he says.

"There is nothing in it which should anger you, Monsieur. The expressions are not aimed at you, nor at your senior officers, who, like you, are merely passive instruments. I have never felt anything but pity for the officers and generals of the Austrian army. I reserve my contempt for their government and therefore it is to the government that I address these words."

Adrienne reads aloud the letter and stops after each passage to ask if what she is saying is true.

"As to the complaint about taking exercise, there is nowhere for you to walk. And even in the officers' quarters there is a smell," he replies.

"That is all the same to me. All I wish to point out is that not one single officer from the major down, and he is about the most stinking creature whom they could have found to fill the position he occupies, not a single officer, I repeat, but holds his nose when he comes in here," I say.

"What then must I write or not write?" asks Adrienne. "I demand to be allowed to write to someone in Vienna asking to be furnished with a model on which I can shape my letters."

"You are right. The emperor or someone else must be asked to let you know how he wishes you to write and what it is that he finds incorrect in your letters," I say.

"As to the emperor, I do not wish to embarrass him, because I cannot help feeling grateful to him for allowing me to enter this place. It may cost me my life but separation from Monsieur de Lafayette would be worse to me than death. I would much rather write to Monsieur von Thugut. He received me as an enemy, though politely, and I am curious to have his reply," declares Adrienne.

"I think perhaps you would be better to write to Monsieur the Baron von Thugut," replies the assistant commandant.

"Excellent. Then let us write to Monsieur von Thugut. He can be the scapegoat!" I say.

The assistant commandant laughs.

"Perhaps they are angry at my being here at all, because the necessity of having my signature before our expenses can be paid forces them to let me write at least a few lines. But since I am here, they are not going to find it easy to tear me away again. No one is going to take me from this place except with Monsieur de Lafayette unless they carry out my dead body; for I believe that this captivity, which has certainly shortened the life of my husband, has done great harm to my health. But of one thing they may be sure, and that is that nobody is going to make me write lies," declares my wife.

"I agree, madame, that no one can ask that of you," he replies.

"It is true, monsieur, that if anyone should flatter himself that he could do so, he would have to be even more idiotic than your court," I say. [47]

Bonaparte's entry into Milan on May 15, followed by the taking of Verona and the investment of Mantua, is known even in our interment in the bowels of the imperial prison system and gives hope we will be freed. With each French victory, and each letter written on our behalf, there is a visible change in the politeness of our jailors. [48]

Masson and Pillet, my former aides-de-camp, work to promote our release. Madame d'Hénin, Lally-Tollendal and John Masclet are in London and are aided by the American consul, Thomas Pinckney. Charles Fox and General Fitzpatrick can be sure that everything that they have said and done has been essentially useful to my friends and I. [49] John Parish, the American consul in Hambourg, the first non-American to represent the United States in the post, is giving money and help, as he did to Adrienne before she arrived here.

I am very concerned, as is Adrienne, that my views on returning to France should be known, as well as affirming that my beliefs have not changed. In June, Adrienne therefore writes my views to my aides-de-camp:

> La Rochefoucauld and Lafayette and a small number of friends were the only republicans in France and although the constitution of 1791 was more republican than anything since, you know, that in general, a hereditary presidency was hardly to their taste....It would be national foolishishness to re-establish a constitutional monarch, as much as it had been cowardly to substitute for it, the Jacobin aristocracy and the arbitrary kingdom of their chiefs. It is a question here of the Declaration of Rights, on which he would never yield, even if he was alone in the universe. He feels honored to be the representative of those who were martyrs for the cause. It is a question not only of a character on whom for the last twenty years the friends of freedom have fixed their eyes, but of a situation which sooner or later, whether by the example of Monsieur de Lafayette, or whether by his personal help, serves the same cause. He was first and foremost the man of liberty for all, rather than the man of a particular country. [50]

Adrienne also writes to Pillet whom we believe to be in France. She asks him to visit Philippe-Nicolas Beauchet, a government official, and the husband of Marie-Josephe, her former maid, to ask for the addresses and names of our friends and relations. She suggests that the deputies Dupont de Nemours, Boissy d'Anglas and Lanjuinais, might be sympathetic to us, as well as Madame de Staël who has constantly spoken well of Monsieur de Lafayette, but that her imprudence and her many liaisons make it necessary to exercise great caution in dealing with her. She also asks him to speak of me to

Madame de Simiane: 'Here is another commission for you which has nothing to do with politics but deeply concerns Monsieur de La Fayette's heart.'[51]

By late summer, it is evident that only France can tear us from the talons of these governments. I am in great delight at the spectacle of my National Guard beating all these famous armies and of Cadignan's grenadiers outwitting all the great tricksters of Europe.

"I ask nothing better than that the prompt arrival of the French in Vienna should be an added pleasure for the emperor," I say. [52]

Vermin bite us. The air stinks and our bed linen desperately needs changing but our spirits are high. We are overjoyed that George is at Mount Vernon with Washington, perhaps standing on the piazza looking at the Potomac, perhaps riding in the hot Virginian sun over the farms, perhaps sleeping in the same bedroom where I slept. We talk endlessly about him which gives us all such sweet pleasure.

In October, Adrienne's condition worsens. She has a fever, probably from the insanitary condition in which we live. She has a violent eruption on her arms which swell so much she cannot use them or lift them up; she cannot move her fingers; her legs erupt in a similar manner; her skin starts to peel; she is in pain and has spasms in her whole nervous system.[53]

She does not even have an armchair in which to sit, although the physician arranges that twice a week she can use the bath which used to be that of Beurnonville. She continues to suffer but she is always serene. Her spirits are not impaired.[54]

Adrienne writes to George on February 12, 1797:

> To be able to exist at all in such bodily discomfort and in the terrible conditions of our captivity is no small achievement...I cannot conceal from you the great deterioration in your father's health...He cherishes the cause of liberty no less in the prisons where he suffers for it than he did when he served it actively...In this living tomb you are the sweetest and most constant preoccupation of all four of us.[55]

We hear that the French army was victorious at Rivoli in mid-January, and that shortly afterwards came the capitulation of Mantua. Major General Henri Clarke, the French plenipotentiary in the peace talks, has evidently asked the Austrians to ease conditions in Olmütz and it is apparent to us that state prisoners Lafayette, Maubourg and Pusy have become useful to the Austrians in negotiations. Klagenfurt falls and Bonaparte arranges an armistice with Archduke Charles. We learn that peace talks began on April 13 in Leoben, and I believe that from the first day of the negotiations Bonaparte spoke of us.[56] The *Directoire* now governing France, composed of Reubell, La Revellière-Lépeaux, Carnot, Barthélemy and Barras, also asked Bonaparte to put as a condition of the treaty that they are demanding the liberty of Lafayette, odiously arrested in neutral territory by a manifest violation of the rights of man.[57]

We know of Thugut's hostility and hatred towards me; in early May he is reported to have said that release will only come with a final peace agreement. Is he perhaps not intending to free us?

I continue to be very thin; Anastasie and Virginie are not unwell but have several problems due to the lack of air and exercise. Adrienne has been very ill with the swelling and blistering of her arms and worrying acute internal pains. They have now gone, but her legs are still extremely swollen and ulcerated.[58]

In July, to our great excitement, we find out that César's brother, Victor, and Florimond, César's son, along with du Coudray Holstein and Christophe von Passy, are here in Olmütz. On the eighteenth, Adrienne writes secretly to Victor: 'to our dear friends, and as we suppose, the travelers with you or near here.' Next day, she writes again: 'I cannot express the joy that your arrival is causing, not only to your brother and Lafayette. You know how dear you are to both, but also to the entire prison of Olmütz, where one is doubly happy to hope for deliverance and the pleasure of having you as liberator.'

We discover they will depart in the second week of August; we smuggle out more messages and suggestions such as to go to Vienna and try to arrange an audience with the emperor.[59]

July 25. At eight o'clock the soldier brings in the usual dirty breakfast, accompanied by Captain MacElligot, the prison supervisor, who gives me a note: 'The marquis de Chasteler will visit you at ten this morning.'

I realize what this means; we are going to be freed. I secretly tell the others when I am alone.

At ten precisely, Chasteler appears, as elegantly dressed and as courteous as the first time we met. I greet him in a friendly manner.

"It is a pleasure for me that His Majesty, the Emperor, has chosen me for such an agreeable commission," he says.

"I will be as obliging as when we last spoke at Namur," I reply.

"His Majesty assumes that allegations of mistreatment are incorrect," he says. "Have you any complaints about people or conditions?"

"The guards have not mistreated me, but conditions could not be worse," I reply heatedly. "No published complaints about them could have been exaggerated."

"Can you elaborate?" he asks.

"The prison is situated between infirmaries; corpses are carried out almost under my windows from the hospital. The constant smell of nearby sewage is disgusting and there is no fresh air in my rooms. I did not have any news about my family for two years while they were under the knives of the Jacobins and I have been kept apart from Maubourg and Pusy."

He looks displeased. I am not saying what he wishes to hear. "The prison is on the highest site in Olmütz. The Jesuits would not have built such a magnificent building in an unhealthy place and where aristocratic canons live next door," he comments.

I continue to speak angrily, and at some length, on the defects of our cells, our living conditions and all our other grievances; he abandons his defense of the prison.

"His Majesty is ready to release you but as you are regarded in Europe as the leader of the new doctrine, and the principles you profess are incompatible with the tranquility of the Austrian monarch, His majesty, the emperor and king must, for reasons of state, only give you freedom if you promise not to return to Austrian territory unless you have the special permission of the emperor," he says.

At first, I am overjoyed, but then I think again.

"I have no wish to set foot either at the emperor's court, or in his country, not only without his permission, but even if I receive a special invitation from him. I owe it to my beliefs and duty not to recognize that the Austrian government has any right over me, and that just as you would do for the man you regard as your sovereign, so I have the same duty to the French people."

"The French government is insisting on your deliverance but is refusing to let you return to France," he says.[60]

"I would like my fellow prisoners to join me," I request.

"The moment has not come for this," is his reply.

"I will write a commitment as fully as I can, as well as a statement on my treatment," I say.

"I will send you a quill, ink and paper to do so. I will return at five o'clock and go now to talk to Madame de Lafayette, Herr Pusy and Herr Maubourg."

Chasteler told Adrienne that there had been criticism of the Olmütz prison in foreign newspapers which had even been heard by the emperor. He also said that she had been given permission to join her husband as his grace and did she therefore have any complaints. Adrienne replied that she had several and listed them, including the lack of an extra bed which meant her daughters had to share, no news of her son, a dirty, clumsy and most sullen soldier served the meals which they had to eat with their fingers and that she had been denied treatment in Vienna unless she abandoned her husband. His answer had been that she had agreed to share her husband's imprisonment under the same conditions, that in a prison it was impossible to find all the attentions in the world that the beautiful sex has a right to expect and that he would put right any deficiencies in medical treatment.[61]

Notwithstanding her conversation with Chasteler, however, she and our daughters are ecstatic with joy, and I am not far from that situation, although I realize I must continue to keep to my principles. I communicate secretly with Maubourg and Pusy; we agree to write a similar response.

In the evening, Chasteler returns. I give him two statements I have written. In the first I refuse to recognize any legitimate right of the Austrian government to my person and what it arrogated to itself concerning disarmed Frenchmen, and strangers to the affairs of the provinces that recognize its domination.[62] I then answer the issues that he had raised. He reads it with an air of embarrassment whilst Anastasie and Virginie attempt not to laugh. We mention more complaints. "They are all as frivolous as the other," he says. "They all conform to your status as a state prisoner."

He reads my other statement in which I say that I undertake not to enter the hereditary provinces of the emperor and king at any time without having obtained his special permission, apart from the rights that my homeland has to my person. [63]

"Since you want to go to America, I only wish to facilitate the means and that the conditions you make to the commitment not to return to the hereditary states make it null and void," replies Chasteler.

"Far be it from me to have feelings of revenge. I would be quite happy to be away from here as soon as possible, but I cannot abase myself," I say. "Let me meet with my fellow prisoners and then we can establish a common position."

"I will think about it and respond later," he replies. "I will send a courier to Vienna with your response tonight."

What time does the courier go?" I ask coldly.[64]

I do not change my position; Chasteler instead decides to send the courier tomorrow at six in the morning and leaves to see Maubourg and Pusy. I start to write another statement. I do not mention the prison conditions but refer Chasteler to Adrienne's letters to Vienna. I do not guarantee to go to America and reiterate that I do not wish to ever set foot in the hereditary provinces of the emperor and king unless I am bound by patriotic duty to do so.[65] Later, to our immense delight, we are told we can meet with Maubourg and Pusy tomorrow.

July 26. Chasteler does not send the letter at six o'clock and says he will send it at midday. He and MacElligot bring Pusy and Maubourg to my cell. It is the first time we have seen each other for thirty-eight months. We embrace; we are ecstatic with happiness; Chasteler has to wait some time before he can continue.

We all criticize the same conditions in the prison.

"Almost everything you describe is consistent with the standards for state incarceration," he replies.

"You refuse to record anything which reflects poorly on Vienna," says Adrienne.

We cannot agree on not returning to Austrian lands.

"His Majesty could refuse any conditions you make," he warns.

"Five years ago, at Namur, I refused political conditions which could have led to my release," I reply. Twenty drafts later he remains in a good humor and agrees to include separate statements from each of us.

"Germans do not need you any more as there are now so many apostles of your doctrine of the Rights of Man," he remarks.

"Can we see our servants," we all ask.

"Yes," he replies.

Soon afterwards, guards bring in Félix, Chavaniac and Jandel, dressed in ragged clothes, their faces pale and haggard. We rush to embrace each other. Chasteler appears embarrassed.

In the evening, we eat together. We talk and talk and talk again. After thirty-eight months it is an exquisite moment of pleasure in our prison existence.

At seven o'clock, Chasteler returns.

"Can we continue to see each other?" we ask.

"No," he replies. "I hope to deliver your statements this weekend and to write to you on Monday that your passports have been sent. You are no longer regarded as dangerous. Your principles are now spoken by the world."

"I am delighted that the world has become so enlightened," I remark.

He smiles and goes away. Later, I am told that I can resume a limited correspondence, but we are, of course, already writing to our friends and supporters. We send notes to Passy, Ducoudray, and Victor and Florimond de La Tour Maubourg. Adrienne says she is very pleased with my declaration to the Austrian government and would willingly pay for it with many months more of captivity.[66]

In August, Louis Romeuf, my former aide-de-camp, now on the staff of General Clarke, writes to me from Vienna where he has been sent from the army of Italy to negotiate our release. He says that Thugut has been annoyed by the way in which I have rejected his demand; he does not go into details of the discussion he had with him but says that the emperor renounces the terms he originally sent. There is no longer any question of any written or verbal word on my part. The new arrangements are that the Austrian government desires that we will be taken to the American consul in Hamburg who will promise before receiving us that we will leave the town before twelve days and that the order to leave all the states of the empire on this side of the Rhine will be given to us on our disembarkation. As it is not a question of any commitment which might compromise our independence, he hopes that I will not disapprove he has communicated this to Monsieur Parish[67] and has spoken both with him and with the minister of the emperor. He has not been allowed to visit me at Olmütz, but Thugut has said he will write to me. Louis Romeuf writes that he will await my reply at Ratisbonne where he will meet Madame de Maubourg and her two oldest daughters, as well as Madame de Pusy and her daughter, with whom he will then travel to Hambourg to meet me.[68]

I receive his letter on the fifteenth. I immediately reply how wonderful it is to receive his excellent letter which expresses so well his ardent friendship, his noble character and all the sentiments for which I have for such a long time cherished him. I say how wonderful it is to owe him so much and that I am very content with the new arrangement. I also say that I would like Generals Clarke and Bonaparte to know how happy I am to be indebted to them and that my deliverance itself is not the only link which attaches me to Bonaparte. I add a few words for my aunt.[69]

Adrienne buys two carriages for five hundred and thirteen florins and eight kreuzer. The days pass. We hear nothing about our release. We start to worry and fear. On September 9 Adrienne writes secretly to Pillet, suggesting that Julienne Bureaux de Pusy should write to Monsieur de Gallo as quickly as possible to try to aid our liberation. We are in poor health. The heat of summer has now passed; my cough and bouts of fever have returned; Adrienne's arms are swollen; the wound on her leg is not healed; Anastasie has been ill with the same malady but is now better. Félix, however, is suffering greatly. [70]

September 18. We will be free tomorrow. The declaration of the Luxembourg military tribunal five years ago is read to me again: 'The existence of Lafayette is incompatible with the security of the governments of Europe.' We sign receipts for the belongings which have been confiscated from us. Adrienne, Maubourg and I cross out our titles before we sign. We give the furniture we have bought to our guards.

Chapter 48

Freedom

September 19. At six o'clock in the morning we emerge from our living tombs. We painfully breathe the fresh air of freedom. Maubourg, Pusy and I climb into the first carriage; Adrienne, accompanied by Anastasie and Virginie, clutching the volume of Buffon on which she has written her mother's life, is helped into the second. Earlier today she was greatly pleased and surprised to be given another Buffon which had been sent while she was travelling here and kept by the prison with the other confiscated possessions.

My friends share my ghostly pallor. Our senses reel at being outside. It is five years and one month since I was arrested and twenty-three months since I was joined by Adrienne and my daughters. For just a moment we glimpse the friend who has taken so many risks to alleviate our sufferings.[1]

We traverse the flat plain, the steeples of Olmütz disappearing into the distance. We are emaciated scarecrows of men, but we have survived.

People sometimes try to approach our carriages but are prevented by our escort commanded by Major Auernhammer who follows in a carriage. We cross the frontiers of the Hereditary States. Madame de Maubourg, her two daughters, two younger sons and Florimond, and Madame de Pusy with her five-year-old daughter, whom Pusy has never seen, meet us at Bautzen. Pusy and Maubourg are ecstatic with joy. Louis Romeuf is also here; I throw my arms around him with great emotion.

We travel to Dresden and go to an inn. A crowd gathers outside, and I address them in my poor German. At Leipsic and Hallë, thousands of students parade in their gowns, shouting "*Lafayette!*" There are torchlight processions; they sing the *Kommerslieder* and the *Marseillaise,* which I hear for the first time. Our journey has become a prolonged triumph.[2]

A gazette falls into our hands; its news shocks us. On the 18 Fructidor, the former September 4, there was violent and unconstitutional aggression in France towards the two chambers of the legislative body. One hundred and eighty-eight representatives of the people and two of the directors were expelled, proscribed, or deported, without being formally accused or found guilty. Forty-nine *départements* have been excluded from the legislature which continues to make the laws which they must follow. Press freedom has been destroyed and arbitrary measures have been taken against journalists.[3] On September 8 a law was passed which has closed forty-two newspapers and has brought about the deportation of editors, newspaper owners and publishers. Freedom of religion has been suppressed and Jacobin clubs have reopened. We now fear for the future of France and Adrienne is in distress at the expulsion of priests.

"This is a crime against the republic. It is a return to Jacobinism," I comment angrily.

Adrienne remains very ill. The journey is too tiring for her, but despite her fatigue she tries to take part in the general joy and to respond to the many marks of respect with which people greet her.[4] Félix is also weak, but the rest of us are recovering our strength.

We reach Harburg on the Elbe River on October 3, Major Auernhammer having gone ahead to Hamburg. Next day, we receive a salute from the *John*, an American merchant ship owned by George Joy, who had been waiting to convey us to Philadelphia. We go out to it in a launch and receive a wonderful welcome on board by many people. George Williams, the United States consul, makes a speech.

I reply. "It is with inexpressible delight that I find myself once more blessed with the sight of American friends and fellow citizens and how could I better feel that I am restored to liberty and life than on beholding again the American flag and amidst the sensations which your hearty welcome could not fail to excite....I am very sensible of the constant and precious interest which the people of the United States have deigned to take on our behalf, of the early and repeated exertions of their government at home and representatives abroad, particularly in this place...let me pay a due and sacred homage to the heroic Huger, who, as well as his worthy companion Bollman deserve universal respect and are entitled to my boundless gratitude."[5]

"I greet you on behalf of the Batavian Republic," says Abbema, the Dutch minister here, a patriot from '87.

We eat a light meal; a short time later, in the afternoon, we again embark in the launch which hoists an immense American flag. We cross the water to the Hanseatic free port of Hamburg, vessels at anchor hoisting their flags, people on board shouting out greetings. At five o'clock we arrive at the landing steps for the Baumhaus, the port gatehouse. We disembark into a crowd; at every step I receive embraces and hand clasps. I notice red, white, and blue cockades on hats. I raise my own into the air, tears in my eyes.

"I bless the soil of liberty on which I stand," I declare.[6]

The carriage sent by Parish waits for us in a sea of people. "What a large crowd!" exclaims a man.

"No matter. I am used to it," I reply.[7]

"*Vive Lafayette!*" the shout thunders round the quay.[8]

I climb into the carriage with Adrienne, my daughters, Maubourg and Pusy. Madame de Maubourg, her daughters, her sister-in-law, Louis Romeuf and René Pillet climb into a second carriage; we set off along narrow alleys filled with crowds.

At Parish's house on the Deichstrasse there are more people. We descend from the carriages; they open a path so that we can reach our friend and I lead the way, followed by Adrienne and my daughters. I rush to embrace him, Adrienne in tears. Anastasie and Virginie cling to him. There is complete silence for a few moments.

"My friend! My dearest friend! My deliverer! See the work of your generosity! My poor, poor wife hardly able to stand!" I exclaim.

He helps Adrienne to a sofa, everyone crying. She sobs and struggles to speak to the man who has helped us so much, who gave her a passport in the name of Motier, and money for her travel to Olmütz. I embrace him again; I am in such a state of euphoria I cannot calm myself for fifteen minutes.[9]

Baron Rudolf von Buol zu Schauenstein, the Austrian representative at Hamburg, arrives, accompanied by Gouverneur Morris. We are introduced; shortly afterwards Parish escorts me, Buol, his secretary, Morris and Auernhammer into another room to speak privately.

"I have great satisfaction to give you over to a friend who loves and respects you so much and I must remind Mr. Parish of his pledge to the emperor to have the marquis taken out of Germany in ten days," declares Buol, in a very dignified manner.

"I agree," replies Parish.

"You are now completely restored to liberty," Buol tells me.

514

Thugut has written to Buol to say that our being freed is due to the United States, not to the demands of France. I politely tell Parish that this was not the case.[10]

Buol and Auernhammer leave to write a report to Vienna. We remain a short time longer. Then, as our first act of liberty, we drive to the house of Reinhardt, the minister of the republic. He is not there so we continue to our lodging at an inn beyond the city gates.

October 5. Reinhardt, a tall, stout man, visits our inn with his wife, Christine, the daughter of the philosopher Hermann Reimarus, whose relations have always been zealous defenders of my cause and whose uncle is Monsieur Hennings whom my friends know well.[11] He greets us in a friendly manner.

"You are the first leader of the Revolution, the author of the Declaration of Rights. What is your opinion on the constitution of the year 111; I need to write to the government." he says, his accent German, even although he has become French.

"I am proud to be the last French man who attempted to defend the constitution of 1791 and I would have had more pleasure to have defended the constitution of the year 111, which is worth much more.[12] We are as inflexible on the violations of the 18 Fructidor as on those of August 10 and our thanks to the victorious winner cannot be separated from our sympathy for the defeated," I reply.[13]

"Please express our thanks to Monsieur de Talleyrand, the foreign minister. Please convey our admiration and gratitude towards General Bonaparte," we say, trying to soften the difficulty.

Reinhardt is a friend of Sieyès, but he remains perfectly pleasant and sincere towards me; he apologizes for what has been done.[14] Our words, however, are not what he wants or needs to hear, but we cannot remain silent.

Frenchmen of all different parties are here in Hamburg and Altona and it is the principal place of commercial speculation and political intrigues.[15] We see my aides-de-camp, my friends, and Klopstock and Archenholtz, all of whom I embrace with great emotion. I go to bed in exhaustion, very soon after finishing dinner.

On October 6, I awake late. I leave my room and find a paper attached to the door on which a royalist has written: 'Monsieur de Lafayette will receive no one today. I will sleep from October 5 to the 6.' It is unpleasantly referring to my short sleep at Versailles on the night of October 5 and 6.

Later in the day I write to Talleyrand to thank him. I also write to Bonaparte:

Citizen General. The prisoners of Olmütz, happy to owe their deliverance to the goodwill of their country and to your irresistible arms had rejoiced in their captivity at the thought that their liberty and their life were attached to the triumphs of the republic and to your personal glory. It is with the utmost satisfaction that that they now pay homage to their liberator. We would have liked, Citizen General, to have offered to you in person, the expression of these feelings, to have witnessed with our own eyes the scenes of so many victories, the army which has won them, and the general who has placed our resurrection amongst the miracles he has accomplished. But you know that the journey to Hambourg has not been left to our choice and it is from this place that we have said our last farewell to our jailors that we address our thanks to their conqueror.

In the solitary retreat on the Danish territory of Holstein where we shall try to recover our health, we shall unite our patriotic wishes for the republic with the most lively interest in the illustrious general to whom we are still more attached on account of the services he has rendered to the cause of liberty and to our country, than for the particular obligation we glorify in owing him, and which the deepest gratitude has forever engraved in our hearts. Maubourg, Pusy and I all sign. [16]

I write to Washington:

You will be sensible of the affectionate and delightful emotions with which I am now writing to you, and I know also it is not without some emotion that after five years of a deathlike silence from me you will read the first lines I am at last enabled to write...Your paternal goodness to my, to our Son, was not unexpected but has been most heartily felt-your constant solicitude in my behalf I have enjoyed as a welcome consolation in captivity...I had the satisfaction to see the United States take a part in this last transaction...Would to God this family might for the first time meet again at Mount Vernon, and be reunited in your friendly and paternal arms. My own health altho' it is impaired, could, I think, tolerably support a voyage. My daughters are not ill. But Mrs. Lafayette's sufferings in this cruel, unhealthy captivity have had such a deplorable effect on her, that in the opinion of every physician, and every man of sense, it would be an act of madness to let her embark in this advanced season of the year...In the present situation of politics, so painful to me, altho' particulars are yet unknown, it might not be quite unserviceable to offer you a safe express to carry whatever instructions you, or some members of the government could perhaps think of sending over... I beg and hope you will read in my heart those sentiments so warmly grateful, so affectionately devoted which I want adequate words to express, but which have so long animated this heart and shall animate it as long as it can vibrate...[17]

I write to General Clarke, who is now disgraced and even perhaps arrested, to General Fitzpatrick in the House of Commons, as well as to Huger. I learn that an English lady, Mrs. Edwards, whom I do not know, but who describes me as virtuous and noble, bequeaths me one thousand pounds in her will, for which I am very grateful. I also discover, with great surprise, that there is a disagreement between the United States and France. I do not yet know the details,[18] but it distresses me, and I hope it will soon be resolved.

Adrienne remains in very poor health. She can hardly walk, but she is very content, and we care for her as best we can. My own strength is gradually returning, and my daughters are no longer so pale.

October 10. Lake Ploën shimmers in the sunshine of a fine autumn day; I cross in a boat with Anastasie, Joachim de Montagu and César de La Tour Maubourg, who steers. Adrienne sits in the stern of another boat, opposite her sister, Pauline, who had hurried across the lake with Monsieur de Mun when she heard the postilion's trumpet announce our arrival at the town; other small boats carry the rest of our party. Adrienne is reciting the hymn of Tobias, some of her words carrying to us on the wind. We reach the far bank; Madame de Tessé rushes to greet us, crying out in excitement and delight.

We stay at her estate of Witmöld, a large, low-lying tract of land with meadows, orchards, ponds and pine trees, which extends on a peninsula into the lake. The government does not concern itself much with this region and although it is despotic, is not actively intrusive or bad. Its tolerance will surely extend to us who will be tranquil in our solitude.[19] We feel relatively safe as Holstein appears to have universal tolerance which even extends to me although I find it inconvenient to live under a government which I had previously declared incompatible with my principles.[20] It is also out of reach of the powers of the coalition and there are many friends of liberty in the towns who wish us well. [21] My health quickly improves; I am now not very different to how I was at the beginning of my imprisonment. My beloved wife, however, remains extremely ill. She cannot walk. She has pain in her teeth, her stomach and in the open sore on her leg. Her arms are not yet better. The doctors say the causes are many and certainly include the foul water we were forced to drink. They think she will always suffer and must be carefully looked after so as not to worsen.

We also worry about Félix. We initially feared for his life, but he has begun to recover, although his lungs and nervous system are still damaged. I have a very deep affection for him, and his death, brought about by his loyalty to me, would have been a worse tragedy than I can describe.[22]

We talk endlessly from morning to night. There is so much to know; so much has happened during our years of captivity. I am greatly indignant at the *Directoire* in France now working against national sovereignty, the constitution, the representation, and against all the principles of liberty, of humanity and justice.[23] It dismays me that the opposition to the *Directoire* consists mainly of royalist and aristocratic supporters who openly want a return to the *ancien régime*. My views have not changed. I do not regret any of my actions or beliefs. My faith still lies in the Declaration of the Rights of Man and the beginning of the Revolution.

I like Madame de Tessé very much; her views and mine agree on every point, as they always have.[24] Pauline, however, avoids talking to me, as far as possible, about anything connected with revolution.[25] Without meaning to, I sometimes cause her offence.

"The origins of the Revolution came from abuses of the *ancien régime*," I say. "The rest was a great misfortune, a tissue of accident, deplorable and a great misfortune but not any more discouraging than stories of shipwrecks to good sailors."[26]

"I wonder that you can find distraction or consolation for so much misery in niggling arguments about the abuses of the *ancien régime*," Pauline cries out and leaves the room.[27]

She and Adrienne spend much time together in religious devotion. They read the *Book of Job*, the sermons of Fénelon and the funeral orations of Bossuet whilst my daughters sew as Pauline believes they will be poor and so will have need of such a skill.

We receive two letters from Adrienne's father. He writes of his happiness at seeing Adrienne's handwriting on a letter addressed from Brunswick. In the second he writes of his marriage, which he had not mentioned in the first even though his wife, the former comtesse de Golovkine, had written several lines. Adrienne replies to her in a postscript to her letter to her father: 'You have well judged the deep and painful impression made upon my heart by your letter and by my father's, an impression which will remain as ineffaceable as my regrets.'[28]

Parish gives us money based on promissory notes; five weeks later we rent a large château at Lemkühlen, between Ploën and Kiel, and one and a half hours from Witmöld. We move there on December 3 with the Maubourgs, including César's younger brother, Charles, as well as our servants and friends; Pusy will arrive shortly with his wife and daughter. We cannot return to France as we are still on the proscribed list.

Alexandre de Lameth writes, wanting to join us. However, although we were friends in the first months of the Revolution, our disagreement, which lasted a long time, now destroys all possibility of an intimate friendship between us. I write back: 'We cannot regard ourselves or be regarded, as friends.'[29]

I start to prepare notes for a work on the Revolution, which I will write with Bureaux de Pusy and which will clearly expound our principles. I intend to write about liberty under a well organised government restrained by democratic laws. I will blame the judgement of Louis XVl, deplore the deaths of Bailly, La Rochefoucauld, Marie Antoinette, Dietrich, Barnave and Condorcet, and will violently attack the Jacobins, Robespierre, Saint-Just and Barère, as well as accuse Danton of corruption.

On December 27 I write again to Washington. I say that Adrienne's health is slowly mending and that with a great deal of care, tranquility, and patience, she will become well again, but any kind of travel and in particular a sea voyage, would harm her. I thank him again for looking after George and imagine he is now closer to the shores of Europe than to the banks of the Potomac, even if he will shortly re-embark for America. I tell him how unhappy the disagreement between France and the United States has made me.[30]

1798. In January I write to Masclet and say that 'although I prefer a republic to a monarchy, I prefer liberty to a republic, and I am very far from believing that liberty exists today in France...the declaration which contains all of my doctrine is that of July 11,1789.' He has complained that I have not written to the *Directoire*, but I tell him that 'the idea of appearing to abandon my friends who are proscribed, and to applaud measures which I disapprove, has shut my eyes to any other consideration.'[31]

I receive a letter from Doctor Clarkson, one of the leaders of the English society of the *Amis des Noirs*, who says that Parliament has authorized the continuation of slave trading. I write back to say that I am angry to find Parliament so backward on the subject, but that I am far from accusing the nation as I know only too well that it is badly represented.[32]

In February, George arrives from America. We embrace and cry with happiness. I hardly recognize him; he has grown so much since I last saw him in the winter of 1791 at Chavaniac. He is nineteen and now a man. He is tall, his face resembling mine, although he is much darker.

"I set off as soon as I heard of your release. I went to see Bonaparte in Paris to thank him for your liberation and to ask him to allow your return to France, but he was reviewing the troops at the Channel ports. I saw Madame Bonaparte and she said she hoped you and her husband should make common cause."

We debate at great length what she meant, her words giving us hope I might be able to return to France.[33]

He brings me a letter from Washington:

Your young son will tell you, better than I can express, the part I took to try to alleviate your suffering, the measures which I adopted, although without success to bring about your deliverance from an injust and cruel captivity, my joy to see the end of it. I hurry to congratulate you and for you to be assured that no one can do it with a deeper and more sincere affection. Each action of your life gives you a right to the enjoyment of this liberty which you have regained....The conduct of your son since he set foot on American soil has been exemplary in every respect and has procured for him the affection and the confidence of all who have the pleasure to know him...Monsieur Frestel has been a true mentor for George; a father could not have cared more for his own cherished son...At no epoch, you can be assured, have you ever played a higher part in the affection of this country....I have once again returned to my home where I will stay wishing the prosperity of the United States, after having worked hard for years to establish its independence, its constitution and its laws....If your memories or circumstances bring you to visit America, accompanied by your wife and daughters, none of its inhabitants would receive you with more cordiality and affection than Mrs. Washington and I; our hearts are full of admiration and affection for you and for them.[34]

My heart overflows as I read his words. George and I talk endlessly about Mount Vernon and about the man we both now consider a father.

I write and thank Bonaparte for his wife's reception of my son and entrust the letter to Louis Romeuf who is staying here at Lemkühlen but is about to return to the army.

Adrienne's health improves; she goes to Hamburg for three days to get our accounts in order and to arrange a power of attorney and will be able to consult an excellent French doctor there.[35]

In mid-February we have the excitement of the arrival of Adélaïde de Simiane and Madame de Maisonneuve, César's sister, who both stay at Witmöld with Madame de Tessé. I greet Adélaide de Simiane with delight. She has survived, as we have, and although she is thinner and looks older, she still retains her beauty.

Charles de La Tour Maubourg requests to see me. He is a tall young man, although not so tall as César, whom he much resembles in looks although he has almost the opposite of his older brother's fiery personality and is always quiet to the point of being taciturn.

"I would like to ask for your consent to marry your daughter, Mademoiselle Anastasie Lafayette. I will have thirty thousand livres a year from my brother when I marry, but that is all. I do not fear poverty although I know what it is." [36]

I do not even consider his lack of money. I am delighted our two families will be united. "I will ask my daughter and if she agrees, then so do I," I reply, and he leaves the room far more happily than he entered.

Our relations and friends at Witmöld react with much dismay. They are horrified, as is my dear aunt at Chavaniac.

"Nothing like this has been seen since Adam and Eve," exclaims Madame de Tessé.

"Only the savages of America behave in this way," declares Monsieur de Mun.[37]

Adrienne's opinion, however, is very different. "The mutual love of these two young people is all that is important. Charles has always known poverty and the simplicity with which he accepts it only serves to make him greater."

'What is here in question is nothing less than marriage, the mutual love of two young people,' she writes to my aunt.[38]

My aunt cannot reply to this and nor can the rest of the family. Anastasie and Charles will enjoy a union of love as happens in America.

"I will provide the trousseau and the wedding can take place here at Witmöld," offers Madame de Tessé.

We cannot continue to pay the rent for the château so return to Witmöld to live. Adrienne's health is again deteriorating. She has an abscess on her arm and her leg is very swollen and ulcerated. However, she refuses to postpone the wedding.

On May 9, we assemble in Witmöld's finest room which has been converted into a chapel. Adrienne cannot walk and George and Charles carry her on a sofa.[39] The elderly abbé de Luchet, given a home by Madame de Tessé despite her irreligious views, conducts the ceremony.

"When I think of the fearful situation my children were in a short time ago, when I see them all three about me, and find myself on the point of adopting a fourth child according to my heart, I feel unable to thank God sufficiently," Adrienne says with joy;[40] my fatherly heart swelling with pride to see my beautiful daughter, so recently sharing my imprisonment at Olmütz, today so radiant and happy.

Pauline gives birth to a baby girl, Stéphanie, on May 19. The abbé baptizes the infant which Madame de Tessé mistakenly sprinkles with eau-de-cologne instead of holy water.

The threat of war looms over us. The imperial forces might invade Holstein, or France might be declared an enemy. Madame de Tessé decides to sell her estate.

I have written several times to Bonaparte, but without success. My friends say I am too unyielding. I write to Washington that I cannot complain personally of the directors, except in as far as they wish for my temporary absence so long as arbitrary measures are considered necessary which I completely oppose, and that the Directory is now afraid of the very Jacobins who had supported the Fructidorian coup de main and that I suspect the Jacobins will be in their turn fructidorited. I do not pretend to know when a system more congenial to the pure and liberal ideas of liberty will prevail in the Commonwealth, but when it does it shall be proper for me to revisit France, which I very much wish.[41]

I say I had hoped to embark for America this year, but Adrienne's health would not enable her to undertake the voyage. However, she is somewhat better than she was, and will travel to France to attempt to restore some of the family estates to herself and her sisters, and to try to obtain permission for me to return. She has never been an émigré. Her name is not on the proscribed list. She has a passport. She is free to travel whilst I must wait in Holstein. I tell him that I also hope to travel to America with George in July unless Adrienne's health deteriorates.[42]

Unfortunately, the deplorable dispute between the United States and France is causing me great anxiety and unhappiness. The French ambassador had campaigned against the election of President Adams, who wanted the United States to be neutral and to trade with Britain. Talleyrand, the foreign minister, is accused of having sent three agents to demand a bribe of fifty thousand livres for him to negotiate, which angered the Americans, and Talleyrand threatened war. I hope my heart will not be rent with the dismal news of a declared war between the two nations.[43] However, despite this situation I intend to travel. I believe it is now reasonable to accept the land I was offered at the end of the war as my situation is very different. [44]

July. Adrienne will go to Paris with Anastasie, Charles and Virginie, where she will stay with her former maid, Marie-Josephe Beauchet, and her husband. We all travel together to the Elbe where we very sadly part. Anastasie is slightly unwell, so she and Charles continue to his family who are living near Utrecht. Bonaparte has sailed to Egypt and Louis Romeuf is on his staff. I know that he has tried to speak to Bonaparte about me but has so far been met only with silence. George and I return to Witmöld and I await anxiously to know how my dear traveler, in her low state of health, has borne the fatigue.[45]

Alexander Hamilton writes: 'In the present state of affairs with France, I cannot press you to come here and until there is a radical change in France, I would be angry to learn that you have returned there. If the prolongation of a bad order of things in your country makes you think of searching for a permanent asylum, you can be assured of a tender and cordial reception. The only thing in which our parties agree is in the affection in which they both hold you equally.'[46]

I write to Washington that I believe the French Directory are earnest in their actual wish to be at peace with the United States and that the British government is now exulting at the prospect of a rupture between two countries who have been allied in the cause of liberty and are trying to precipitate a war. I tell him Adrienne is in Paris trying to establish what property remains to her, and that in her present enfeebled and agitated state George and I cannot come to the United States. I need first to hear from her in Paris about her health and our affairs. [47]

In the salon at Witmöld we discuss what Adrienne needs to do and I write to her with some of these ideas: 'You must get either a discharge for Victor and Charles as *émigrés*, or at least a surveillance, at once. Perhaps you should have let Chavaniac return to the Auvergne instead of leaving him in Holland to help Anastasie.'

To my surprise she writes back critically. I immediately write again: 'I am so sorry, my dear heart, that I have hurt you…You have badly judged the impression I received from what you wrote which has only ever given me satisfaction. You would be unjust in thinking that I have not counted on your exactness in doing what we had agreed. I agree, however, with pleasure and with all my heart, that it was I who was wrong and you who were right. There only remains to me the chagrin of having tormented you with our speculations on the lake of Ploën and thereby to have provoked from that your injustice towards me.'[48]

In my anxiety I may have added to her difficulties, I write another letter eight days later to again reassure her. I say I am unhappy she has decided not to return in December and that we cannot remain in Holstein if there is a general coalition against France in which Denmark joins. I suggest we should go to the United States to live even although they now have a new alliance with England which is a cruel obstacle to my plans, but my hopes are that there will be a reconciliation with France. I finish by telling her: 'The only place I have is in the hearts of my friends and I must not lose any of the place I hold in yours…Adieu, my dear heart, to whom I ask forgiveness for having caused you pain.'[49]

I am not sure, however, if she is still in Paris; I believe she may already be at Chavaniac with my aunt.

When Adrienne returns to Paris, she goes to see the president of the Directory, La Revellière-Lépeaux, with a letter I have written asking for the small number of officers who accompanied me when I left France to be able to return as I was their general and so I alone should be held responsible for our being captured.

He tells Adrienne he regretfully cannot accede to my wish but that she would be allowed to travel freely between France and her husband's home. She believes this means the Directory would permit me to live in Holland and so we could all live near to Anastasie and Charles at Vianen near Utrecht.

In January 1799 I receive a long letter from Washington:

> No one would receive you with more open arms and with more ardent affection than I when harmony is re-established between this country and France. But it would be less than sincere and completely contrary to the friendship I have for you to say that I want you to arrive before then. The scenes you would witness, the role you might be forced to play, would place you in an untenable position. They were guilty of violating treaties, international law and all the rules of justice and decency. But they fooled only themselves…for once the citizens of this country recognized the nature of the quarrel (with France), they rose up as one, they offered their services, their lives, their fortunes, to defend the government they had chosen and they have pledged that if the French should try to invade they would be the first to repel such an attack.
> You say that the Directory is disposed to resolve all our differences. If they are sincere let them prove so with deeds! Words cannot do much at present…The tactic of France and of the opposition has been to assume that those who work for peace are acting from their attachment to Great Britain. You can rest assured that this assertion rests on no foundation and has no other aim but to excite public clamor against men of peace…After my farewell address to the people of the United States you will have been surprised that I have consented to take up my sword.…My belief is very simple. I think that each nation has the right to establish the establish the form of government from which she expects the most wellbeing, provided that she does not infringe any right or be a danger to any other country. [50]

Anastasie will shortly give birth and Adrienne will soon be with her at Vianen. George, Victor de La Tour Maubourg and I set off from Witmöld to join them. We pass rapidly over the frozen lake of Ploën in our carriage, but then floods delay us. We finally arrive in the darkness of evening, seven days after Anastasie's confinement. I joyfully embrace Adrienne and discover I am a grandfather.

"Anastasie had two girls who both appeared at first to be healthy. On Tuesday we took them to the church and although the eldest had a red nose she seemed fine. She gradually fell ill. On Saturday, her feet were swollen. By Sunday evening she could not swallow properly and died on Monday. However, the younger baby is well and has been named Célestine."

I am sad for the little one who died, but very grateful the second is healthy and Anastasie is recovering. Tomorrow, as soon as I can, I will go to the wet nurse, who lives nearby, and see my granddaughter.

It is better here at Vianen than at Witmöld as it is in one of the seven provinces of the Republic of Batavia which are governed by a legislative assembly elected by the people, and I am an old Batavian patriot.

General Van Ryssel, whom I first met when he led the Dutch patriots in 1787, lives in Utrecht and often invites my family and I to his house. Gouvion, a brigade general, the cousin of my beloved friend, is also here. One cold, gray, February day, I suddenly come across French troops and for the first time in many years, I see the tricolor cockade on soldiers. Emotion and pride well up in me.

Their commander is General Brune, the former secretary of the Cordeliers and a friend of Danton and Marat.[51] He is not pleased I am in Holland and wishes me to leave. However, the minister at The Hague and the consul at Amsterdam evidently think differently and I am left in peace.

In March, Pauline and Joachim de Montagu arrive from Witmöld, and Monsieur and Madame de Grammont from France. It is eight years since the three sisters have all been together and their excitement and joy is only tempered by their remembrance of their mother, sister and grandmother. They pray frequently together. Food is a little scarce and *oeufs á la neige* make a regular appearance on the table.

"The only decent meal I have eaten is at the home of General Van Ryssel," remarks Joachim, a large man.

The sisters discuss how to share the estates to be inherited from the duchesse d'Ayen, my great hope being that we will receive land which I can farm, and I constantly plan how to cultivate our future property.

May 5. Adrienne sets off once more for Paris, accompanied by Rosalie de Grammont, as well as George, who needs his passport authorized before going to Chavaniac. I have decided to stay in Vianen. Anastasie, Charles and Célestine are here; I know many patriots of '87; it is nearer to France; it has good institutions, civil and religious liberty; the people governing are well intentioned and the people being governed know their rights and their duties, although I must say that what distresses me is the political oppression of the Batavian republic which I believe to be contrary to the true interests of France as much as to the great principles of national independence.[52] I return home immensely sad to be separated again from Adrienne. I worry about her health; I wait impatiently to hear from her.[53]

At the end of April, Pusy gave me his notes on *les fragments historiques* as he will soon set off for the United States. On May 9 I write to Washington as Pusy can take my letter with him. I tell him that it has become both dangerous and inconvenient for me to live to the east of the Rhine now that war has broken out. I say it is not only that he has convinced me, but out of deference to his opinion that I am delaying my departure until I hear from him. In the improbable case that I should arrive suddenly, he can be sure that my motives would be powerful enough to convince him of the urgency of my determination. [54]

The French plenipotentiaries, Roberjot and Bonnier, were assassinated at Rastadt on April 28, following the leaving of that town by the imperial ministers who had protested about the crossing of the Rhine by the French Army. Generals Van Ryssel and Gouvion give me new details about this atrocity and about the indignation of people. Patriots of all parties are being asked to defend liberty against this detestable House of Austria, and the prisoners of Olmütz must not be strangers to such an invitation.[55] Bonaparte and his army took Jaffa on March 7 after defeating the Mamelukes by the Pyramids in Egypt.

May 14. I go to see Célestine at the home of the wet nurse and meet three tinkers from Cantal. I ask about the Revolution.

"It has already much improved the life of peasants in our region, despite the crimes and violence which blackened it," they say to my great pleasure. They seem men of sense and I find their judgement on my questions far superior to that in the salons.[56]

I am very sad Adrienne is not here and am beginning to feel impatient at the thought of seeing her again. On the sixteenth I write to her: 'We are waiting for your news. I have too much confidence in you to fear that you have forgotten to take care of your health, as you solemnly and tenderly promised....Our garden has new charms every day, but a weasel has eaten my poor female wood pigeon and her eggs...Adieu, my dear Adrienne, my heart follows you, regrets you are not here, speaks to you and loves you tenderly.'[57]

On the twenty-eighth, at Utrecht, I meet Rouget de L'Isle who is on his way to visit me at Vianen; he is the writer of the *Marseillaise* and aide-de-camp to General Daendels. He accompanies me home; we talk about poor Bailly, who was his uncle.

"He heard someone shout out his sentence of execution an hour and a half before it was actually pronounced," he says to my horror.

I receive a letter from George who is still in Paris: 'I have found great changes here and you will realize that my personal affairs are for the moment in abeyance.'[58]

I hear rumors of unrest and violence there and a letter from Adrienne does not soothe my fears as she says 'Do not be alarmed for my safety. I hope to be with you before there is any danger for women or the poor.'[59]

I read Arthur Young's books on agriculture, which Liancourt has lent me; I write to Adrienne about the estate we hope to have at La Grange: 'I would like to know the number of large and small animals there, how much it costs, how many workers are there to look after them.' I also want to know about the park and the woods. I tell her we are worried about the progress of Suvarov, who is nearing Milan, and of the situation of General Macdonald at Naples. 'The future appears threatening. We should be together as soon as possible. Why are you not already here?'[60]

News arrives that on 30 *Prairial*, the former June 18, Treilhard, de Douai and La Reveillère-Lépeaux, three of the five directors, were replaced by Sieyès and Ducos, Rewbell having already gone, and that repressive laws against the press were voted for.

I learn that Bureaux de Pusy has been captured by the English, just four hours after leaving port, and is now being held at Yarmouth. His capture does not encourage me to also risk the voyage. If I was not living here, I would have to go and live with the fish for all avenues are shut to me.[61] Between the ocean where the British are masters, the Empire which is forbidden, and France which I would evidently poison with my royalty and aristocracy, I can only find security in the Batavian retreat. If the aerial squadron makes a successful flight, I would be tempted to make a crossing of the Atlantic by balloon.[62]

August 3. I think sadly and lovingly about Adrienne; to my surprise George, whom I had thought was still travelling, suddenly appears. I embrace him. He tells me about all the subjects dear to my heart. He has been to Chavaniac and has seen my aunt. He gives me the gold hilt of the sword presented to me by America, which he has managed to dig up, the rest of it having rusted away. He has also retrieved the sword given to me by the National Guard.

"Perhaps the hilt can be attached to it?" he suggests.

He tells me Adrienne is very fearful of an invasion of Holland and that my friends in France fear more for me from the hatreds of the coalition than those of the Jacobins.[63] She went to see abbé Sieyès and was very offended by his words. She told him that there is talk in Paris that Holland might be invaded by the coalition armies bringing a counter revolution. If this happens then I would be in danger and would take refuge on French soil. He replied that it would be imprudent to return to France and that I would be safer in the states of the king of Prussia.

"Who kept him prisoner," Adrienne had replied. "He would prefer, if necessary, a prison in France but he has more confidence in his fellow-countrymen."[64]

He assured her of his desire to see the patriots of '89 return, and that he would be very angry if any harm came to me. He repeated how awful it would be if I fell into the hands of the Great Powers. When Adrienne asked him what he wanted me to do at Clèves with the Prussian king he replied that I should continue to wait. [65]

This does not reassure me. I remember Sieyès well. He is timorous, moody, and does not know how to make himself pleasing. He does not speak well nor ride a horse. He is an abbé in the fullest sense of the word; he has much spirit, great faculties for intrigue and excellent intentions at the present. Everyone expected to see him on a pedestal, and everyone is astonished to see how small he is. However, I think that circumstances could make him go higher...His spirit, infinitely superior to that of his colleagues, makes him see the reality of our situation, and the ways to come out of it, he has not done all that he could have done, but since his return to France he has followed a good path.[66]

It seems to me that French people who profited by the Revolution are determined to hold onto their gains, whilst the ultras, the fanatics and the adventurers are all busy scheming and hoping for another monarchy. Between these two groups is the nation which dreads a complete victory for the counter-revolution, would like a limited monarchy, could manage quite happily with a free republic and fears major upheavals more than anything.[67]

"Russia and Turkey are now enemies of France, and Austria and England are on the point of attacking. If the English invade Holland I shall go to the United States," I say to George. "We could perhaps have a farm in the beautiful valley of the Shenandoah in Virginia, not far from the federal city and Mount Vernon? Or the beautiful meadows of New England, near to Boston, of which I am very fond."

However, as I write later to Adrienne, perhaps not the Shenandoah because just as I complain about the situation of the serfs in Holstein as sad to a friend of liberty, I would feel the same about the slaves there. In the northern states equality is for everyone but is only for white people in the south. However, as we do not have even one dollar to buy our farm, we will have to delay it for the moment.

I tell Adrienne that George has arrived:

When are we to see a reunion of the whole family...I shall go to America only when I have lost all hope of serving my country here. When I see the coalition advancing against France, and against the whole of humanity, with the most detestable intentions; when I see my personal enemies at the head of this atrocious league, I feel that there is nothing for me to do but to place myself on the other side and to fight until I am killed. However, this is not possible. The other side shows me almost as much hatred. Nothing tells me that they want to defend liberty.[68]

An Anglo-Russian army lands at three places; the Helder by Texel, Helvoet-Sluis and Groningen on August 27. By the thirty-first the fort of Helder has been evacuated. There is talk of some agitation at Rotterdam, but it has not led to unrest. However, around here it is so tranquil that if it were not for the movement of troops, a stranger would not suppose that a counter revolutionary army has landed in the republic. George, Victor and I want to help the country which is giving us refuge and where liberty is not a useless name. However, I feel it would be difficult to send them to fight under Daendels or Gouvion and we all stay in our garden when the National Guard of Utrecht marches.

The Helder is abandoned and captured; the Dutch withdraw with the loss of a thousand men. It is being said that France is playing the same game as in '87. I do not feel I can go against the wishes of George and Victor; I ask my friend, Van-Ostrum, to take two voluntary grenadiers and not to disclose their names. He agrees to their joining a battalion at Harlem.

I write to Adrienne and say I hope she approves what we have done. 'You see that I have confined myself to the civic duties of a patriot, an inhabitant of an invaded Holland. It would have gone against my convictions to have objected to George and Victor's plan. I do not think they will be exposed to the dangers which they would like to run. That will be a consolation to you, and to me also, for I think that sending someone to war or to wage war oneself are two very different things...The day after tomorrow I shall begin my forty-third year. It is time to choose a proper home.'[69]

We await news from France with extreme anxiety. It is at Paris that liberty can usefully be served. It has always been the center of this grand movement which has agitated Europe. The enemies are still at the Helder where the Duke of York has arrived, but apart from at the dining table, he is a poor reinforcement.[70]

News from the invasion remains much the same by the sixteenth, but if it is true that the Russians have arrived, this will be very important. I am impatiently awaiting the arrival of twelve to fifteen thousand French soldiers. Madame de Tessé has written to me to say that it is thought my retreat is threatened here if France does not withdraw its troops.[71]

September 19. The bells at Vianen are ringing out to celebrate Brune's defeat of the British and Russians at Bergen. I write to Adrienne: 'It is two years ago today, dear Adrienne, that we left the prison where you came to bring me consolation and life. If only, after two years of exile added to five years of captivity, I could give you the assurance of being reunited forever in a peaceful place of retreat...George and Victor are guarding the battery on the right of the army, but I do not feel the enemies will recommence the adventure of the other day. Therefore, we can be tranquil, dear Adrienne, about the danger to our dear volunteers.'[72]

Brune is victorious at Kastricum on October 6. In the newspapers I read that Bonaparte is trying to obtain the independence of Egypt. 'If Egypt is removed from Ottoman rule, if it is closely linked to France, you will see what a considerable advantage this will give us,' I write to Adrienne.[73]

Should I suddenly arrive in Paris so that the rulers of France must either act or kill me? Should I ride with Beurnonville and Lefebvre and proclaim and give assurances of liberty in the capital and then throughout France?[74]

October 18. The Convention of Alkmaar stipulates the departure of the enemy. To my delight George comes home although he is very disappointed he did not fight. A few weeks later I am at General Van Ryssel's house playing chess with him, our children playing Lotto. We learn, to our amazement, that Bonaparte left Egypt, landed at Saint Raphaël on October 6 and marched to Paris.

I am again playing chess with Van Ryssel when a letter arrives from Adrienne. She has seen Bonaparte; he was courteous towards her and said that my life is attached to the conservation of the Republic. She tells me to write to him. I quickly follow her advice; I write a letter which is very short and perhaps a bit terse, but, in any case, no letter is a match for half an hour of conversation. Bonaparte's supporters see me in opposition to him. They are right if he wants to oppress liberty, but if he wants to serve it, I would be with him completely, for I do not believe that he stupidly only wishes to be a despot.[75]

I tell him that as I love liberty and my country, his arrival fills me with joy and hope. I say that I owe him life, that I rejoice in all my obligations towards him, the citizen-general, and have the happy conviction that to cherish his glory and to wish for his success, is a civic act, as much as is an attachment and gratitude to him.[76]

Ten days later, Alexandre de Romeuf, the brother of Louis, arrives in great haste at my house in Vianen, carrying a letter from Adrienne and a passport for me in a false name.

"On the eighteenth *brumaire*,[77] the Council of the Anciens and the Council of the Five Hundred, whose president was Lucien Bonaparte, went to Saint Cloud as they were afraid of a Jacobin plot. The next day, Bonaparte entered the Council of the Anciens who resisted him. Then he entered the Council of the Five Hundred who were very hostile, causing him to faint. He went outside, followed by Lucien, who demanded that the grenadiers should defend his brother. Murat marched the grenadiers into the Orangerie and evicted the Council, many of whom jumped out of the windows. He later brought some of them back to vote for the decree which the Council of the Anciens had passed. The constitution of the year 111 is abolished. France is still a republic but instead of the Directory, Bonaparte will be first consul; Sieyès and Ducos will be second and third consul. There will be a new constitution," he says.

Adrienne tells me that if I want to set off for France, I must not spend many days deciding.[78] I do not hesitate for a second. Two hours later I am on the road to Paris.

Chapter 49

I bid farewell to my beloved and to all my happiness in the world.

I reach Paris; I stay at the home of Adrien de Mun; I immediately write to the provisional consuls, Sieyès and Bonaparte. To Sieyès I talk of our long-standing friendship; the wish he has expressed to establish the republic on the bases of liberty and justice, to reunite around him his companions of '89, and to see me again. I say that when France becomes free, I will not be proscribed, but before going with my family to the mountains of the Haute-Loire, I will hurry to ask when I can talk to him myself of the former sentiments which attach us to each other. [1]

To Bonaparte I write:

> Since the time when the prisoners of Olmütz owe you their liberty, up to now when the liberty of my country imposes on me even greater obligations towards you, I thought that the continuation of my being proscribed does not suit either the government or myself. Today I have arrived in Paris. Before leaving for the distant countryside where I will reunite my family, even before seeing friends, I have not waited a moment to write to you; not because I doubt I should not be anywhere the republic is founded on bases worthy of it, but because my duty and my feelings make me convey to you myself the expression of my gratitude. [2]

General Clarke takes my letter to Bonaparte; I quickly learn he is very angry I have returned.[3] Talleyrand asks to see me. I visit him with Louis Romeuf; Regnault de Saint-Jean d'Angély is already here. We all embrace.

"Bonaparte is in a fury. He says he will take violent measures. We beg you not to expose your friends to such danger. Go back to Holland," they say.

"Do not compromise yourselves. But as Consul Bonaparte has judged it suitable for me to return to France, it is now for him to judge whether it would be proper to leave me alone. You are acquainted enough with me to know that this imperious and threatening tone would only fix me on the path I have already chosen," I reply.

"Leave France," they continue to say.

I do not give way. Midnight strikes. Louis and I start to leave on foot. "It would be very pleasant if I was arrested tonight by the National Guard of Paris and imprisoned in the Temple tomorrow by the restorer of the principles of 1789," I remark.[4]

In the morning, I ask Adrienne to visit Bonaparte and explain what I have said so that I do not compromise anyone. She has not yet gone when Roederer arrives. He prefers Bonaparte to his old friend, Sieyès, and confirms what I had already guessed, that Sieyès is delighted by my return.

"Go back to Holland," he says. He repeats the words of Talleyrand and Regnault de Saint-Jean d'Angély. I reply with the same words I spoke to them.[5]

Bonaparte is again courteous to Adrienne. "You do not understand me, madame, but General de Lafayette will, and since he is no longer at the center of the situation, he will realize I am in a better position to make a correct judgment than he is. I therefore beg him to avoid any outburst. I rely on his patriotism."

"This was always the intention of Monsieur de Lafayette," she replies.

He is very polite and leaves her to go to the council, where he arrived, I am told, in an extremely bad temper.[6] I hear that Sieyès speaks well of my spirit of enterprise and independence. He recommends me not to cause any trouble and talks of me with interest. I do not think it useful to see the third consul, Roger-Ducos, whom Madame de Staël compares to a piece of cloth put between two precious bodies to prevent their shock.

Roederer and Volney visit again.

"I am little disposed to take any notice of Bonaparte's threats, but I feel bound by his advice," I tell them.

It is intolerable to me to stay any longer in Paris, stained as it is with the blood of my relations and friends;[7] I set off for Fontenay-en-Brie, to the dilapidated château of Adrienne's mother where we will live until it is decided what part of her estate we will inherit. I am very content to have seized the moment to come back when liberal declarations make it possible and to have smoothed the principal obstacle to the return of my friends.[8]

Bonaparte leaves me in peace. I write to my aunt to tell her I am now in France, but I am unable to come to Chavaniac to ensure my return remains generally unknown in order not to provoke the attentions of my enemies and avoid their malevolence.[9]

We hope Adrienne's share of her mother's property will be La Grange-Bléreau. It would be slightly less than we had anticipated but would delight us greatly. It is in the countryside, thirteen leagues east of Paris, between Melun and Meaux, and near to Rosay-en-Brie. It is situated on a plateau between two valleys, one occupied by the Yères, the other by a stream of the Ivron and forms a circle of more than eight hundred acres, a medieval château in the center.[10] It once belonged to the Courtenay and La Feuillade families and was owned in the eighteenth century by Louis Dupré, a councilor to the Paris Parlement. His daughter married the son of chancelier d'Aguesseau and their daughter became the duchesse d'Ayen.

The château is impressive although it needs much repair as it has been left derelict for many years and the roof is letting in the rain. A moat is crossed by a wooden drawbridge to an entrance with two doors, the first larger than the second. At the front are two towers with narrow windows and conical roofs. There is a large courtyard, surrounded on three sides by the château, the fourth side being open, which makes it seem spacious and bright. It has a ground floor and two stories and three more conical-roofed towers.[11] A farm is adjacent. I roam the fields, woods and meadows, longing to cultivate it. I would make a good handsome farm here for myself and shall then envy the lot of none.[12]

To my delight, it is decided we will receive La Grange and the Montagus will receive Fontenay-en-Brie where we will continue to live while La Grange is being restored.

Adrienne asks Antoine Vaudoyer, the architect who had worked for us at Chavaniac, to renovate the château, and Hubert Robert to design the park. Robert was the artist standing behind me in 1790, when I said, as I was admiring a painting of the storming of the Bastille, "Fortunate the man who is going to possess that picture!" whereupon he immediately replied: "General, it is yours."[13]

528

We owe two hundred thousand livres, to Morris, Parish and others, a very large amount; I estimate the farm might provide ten thousand livres a year, rising to fifteen thousand if I include the value of the timber. Chavaniac has been bought back by my aunt and will ultimately come to me or my children; my estates in Bretagne and Touraine, although sold as national property, might bring us some sort of payment whilst the Cayenne plantation is already occupied by the state, to which I could perhaps sell it.[14]

In Paris a new constitution is decreed by the legislative commission on December 13. Citizens are asked to vote for or against it in each commune. It is accepted.

1800. My apartment and library are ready at La Grange. They are on the second floor and comprise an antechamber, a bedroom, and a library, circular in form, illuminated by casements, and composed of three bodies whose shelves are held up by elegant white columns which I intend to surmount with cameos in oil consecrated to the memory of men of liberty who were my companions, such as Washington and Franklin, as well as Bailly, Dietrich and others. Its windows look out on the park and a short distance away can be seen the farm buildings.[15]

I go to live there, whilst Adrienne travels constantly to Paris to try and resolve our finances, as well as my status and that of my friends. I appoint Félix Pontonnier as my farm manager; Vaudoyer builds cow sheds and sheep pens. In a few years, I hope to breed two hundred sheep, fifty cows and a hundred and fifty pigs.[16]

Washington is dead. I learn that he died on December 14, just before the end of the century. An immense sadness grips me, my heart breaking. He was right when he said we would not meet again. He has bequeathed me two finely wrought steel pistols taken from the enemy in the Revolutionary War and they will be a shrine to his memory. On February 8 there is a ceremony to commemorate him at Les Invalides. I am not invited, nor is any American. George attends but is not welcomed.

"The eulogy of Louis de Fontanes hardly mentioned Washington. There was nothing said about you, but Napoléon and his exploits were highly praised," he tells me.

Le Moniteur writes: 'Critics have reproached the speaker to have forgotten the hero of the United States for that of Egypt.'[17]

I write to Jefferson to say I have read he is being nominated for the presidency of the United States and that he will almost certainly obtain it. I tell him I am now wholly addicted to farming occupations and preserving in my solitary abode the principles and the sentiments which no vicissitudes in the public or personal times have ever been able to alter.[18]

On March 1 Bonaparte reinstates the civil and political rights of émigrés who had voted for the abolition of privileges on August 4, 1789. This, therefore, applies to me, but not to my friends who accompanied me on August 19. I immediately write to Fouché, the minister of police; he agrees to take their names from the proscribed list.

In May, George is made an under-lieutenant in a regiment of hussars. On the sixth, Bonaparte leaves for Italy. I admire him. He has just obtained a position of supreme power and yet is going over the Alps to fight for France. Our new under-lieutenant also sets off and Adrienne is very brave. She writes to him: 'Those, my dear boy, who love one another make a pact to look at the moon at the same moment. Let us rather look to Heaven. Be with your mother in spirit morning and evening and on Sunday at the hour of the Mass whether or not you attend it.' [19]

She is invited to a reception at her former home, the hôtel de Noailles, by Lebrun, who now lives there. He says he will present me and my companions to Bonaparte when he returns. Perhaps to recompense me for his occupation of it.

On June 14 there is victory at Marengo. If it had been lost, I would have offered my services to Bonaparte to defend the independence of France, and I have written a letter to this effect which a friend will deliver.[20] However, it is not needed, and we all hope there will soon be peace.

Bonaparte and the army return in triumph to Paris. George brings back an engraving of him in the red uniform he wore at Lodi and Adrienne hangs it in her bedroom next to the picture of the prisoners of Olmütz.

In July, I finally meet Bonaparte at the Tuileries; Lebrun presents him to La Tour Maubourg and I. He is a short, thin man, his features delicate, his skin very pale; he is plainly dressed in an olive-green coat, not in a military uniform. I compliment him on his victory at Marengo; he smiles in a charming manner which reminds me of Frederick the Great.

"Thank you. The Austrians perhaps want more. It is Moreau who will make the peace."

"Thank you for helping with our release," I say.

"It was not easy to obtain your freedom. I don't know what the devil you had done to the foreign powers, but they hated to let you go," he says.

"I must also give you thanks from Monsieur Bureaux de Pusy who has gone with Monsieur Dupont de Nemours to the United States."

"He will return to France," he replies. "And his father-in-law, Dupont, as well. People always return to the waters of the Seine." [21]

Cabanis asks me to enter the Senate, but I refuse. I am offered a seat in the general council of the Haute Loire. I again refuse. Talleyrand suggests I could be ambassador to the United States. "I wish to live quietly in retirement," is my response.

We jolt along wild roads, mended with lava, pozzualana and basalt, in the volcanic countryside of my birth. We take the turning from Saint Georges d'Aurac; not long after, the château of Chavaniac, jostled by dark pine trees, comes into sight. We climb the hillside, the mauve-blue necklace of hills and mountains in the distance.

I embrace my aunt. She sobs. She clings to me; I take her into the house. Her head trembles slightly, but otherwise she appears no different to when I left on Christmas Day seven years ago to command the army in the east.[22]

Adrienne and Virginie are in Bretagne attempting to recover rents from my previous tenants, as well as to meet my former agent. Adrienne's health has improved, but even so, it will be very taxing and dangerous for her to travel in public vehicles along the rough Breton roads often frequented by brigands.

News arrives: their diligence has been held up, but she and Virginie are not harmed. I write back: 'My dear Adrienne, you have stolen a march on George so far as seeing the enemy is concerned. I congratulate Virginie on coming under fire before the second lieutenant of hussars.'
[23]

I tell my aunt what has happened as I know she will read it in the gazette, but it does not frighten her.

August 10. Sunday. My aunt goes to church, the sun beating down. She returns, spends some time at the dinner table with guests, then retires with a migraine. She comes back later but goes to bed early. In the morning, she is ill with fever and a headache. To our alarm she becomes increasingly drowsy; we send for Doctor Pissis.[24] A few days later, she recovers.

"What have been the economic and tax consequences of the Revolution?" I question people.

"The suppression of local taxes has increased trade and the price of land in the Limagne has increased," is the reply. I find the peasants not so poor, which greatly pleases me; I write a summary of the present situation.

I visit Le Puy and see the places where Adrienne was imprisoned. I thank everyone who helped her. I am even extremely polite to the elderly royalist ladies, one of whom is more yellow than an old lemon and another who is blacker than a mole.[25] They, in turn, also treat me politely.

I enjoy a superb dinner given by the *préfet*. "To the memory of the martyrs who have perished in the cause of true liberty," I give the toast.

I write to Jean-Antoine Huguet, my former colleague in the National Assembly, who is now *préfet* of the Allier: 'My personal sufferings have been little in comparison with the terrible misfortune of seeing our cause destroyed, our homeland pillaged and stained with blood, the worthiest of people brought down in to the dirt, our most virtuous citizens assassinated by a band of wild animals, not least vile as execrable, to which the nation, heroic abroad, has been within its borders so cowardly laid low. I have lost relations, friends, comrades of liberty and of patriotism whose attachment to me was the reason for their death.'[26]

Adrienne writes to say she has retrieved 16,200 livres from the peasants in Bretagne and will go to stay at Chenonceaux in Touraine to try and recover some La Rivière assets and the payments of former debts.

I reply: 'I would like to meet you somewhere between Orléans and Amboise. I have not accomplished much, but at least I have not done any harm and you can be as completely reassured in this matter of mishandling of which you accuse me, as I am satisfied with all the good you have done since we parted.'[27]

I stop in Brioude on my return home. I embrace everyone then climb into my little gray trap, very glad to say goodbye to the squalid walls of the town. 'You had not told me how arrogant and impertinent the local ladies were when you arrived there,' I write to Adrienne. 'I can only suppose it was because you demanded that women and men should not sleep in the same room; in any case I did not feel it my duty to handle the self-esteem of the inhabitants with kid-gloves.'[28]

In October I go from La Grange to Paris to see my father-in-law who has recently arrived from Switzerland with his wife. I also visit Talleyrand; he comes out of his study accompanied by a man older and plumper than Bonaparte, but with the same pale face, expressive eyes and aquiline nose. Talleyrand introduces me to Joseph Bonaparte, his brother. He invites me to the celebration at Mortefontaine of the treaty of reconciliation signed on September 30 between France and the United States.

There, on October 3, I meet American ministers, former French colleagues, several generals, the first consul and the Bonaparte family. There are fireworks on the river, Rode plays the violin and there is a drama by Marivaux. It all reminds me of the epochs and successes of my youth.[29] Mortefontaine is one of the great pleasures of my life.

"You must find that the French people have gone cold on liberty," Bonaparte remarks to me.

"Yes," I reply, "But they are in the state to receive it."

"They are really disgusted," he says. "Your Parisians, for example. The shop keepers do not want it."

"They are in the state to receive it," I reply. "I do not employ that expression lightly, general. I do not know the effect of the crimes and the madnesses which have profaned the name of liberty, but the French are more than ever in a state to receive it. It is for you to give it. It is from you that it is expected."

He talks to me of military and political interests of France, of royalist intrigues, of the cooperation of the extreme parties. He asks about my campaigns in America.

"The greatest interests of the universe were decided by encounters of patrols," I tell him.

"Several members of the federal convention want to have a presidency for life," I remark and see his eyes light with interest. "With a national representation and suitable barriers, this idea could be good for France." He looks at me attentively.

"The American president does not have pomp and ceremony and is without guards," I say.

"This would not happen in France," he declares.

"People are starting to be removed from the proscribed list. I would like to ask for the removal of Monsieur and Madame de Tessé," I say.

"I promise to do so," he replies.[30]

In December Adrienne stays with Madame de Tessé in the rue d'Anjou in Paris to try to obtain her father's reinstatement. I am not pleased. I want her with me. I write:

> You have married a man whose role it is to live in retirement with his family, and it is unbecoming that his wife should appear to be intriguing in Paris while he plays the philosopher at La Grange…If you could really be of service to your father, I would gladly sacrifice my own feelings to that duty and would do all this trotting round myself…He has in Paris two daughters, two sons-in-law, a brother-in-law and, unfortunately, a wife…What it comes to, dear Adrienne, is this: that my happiness depends too much on having you with me for me to consent to your spending the winter tramping the streets of Paris for no better purpose than that of truckling to vague ambitions which cannot be satisfied by such ill-conceived measures as have so far been decided. Madame de Simiane wanted to leave the day after tomorrow with Virginie but has consented to delay her departure until Monday…She will be at Madame de Tessé's by six and will drop Virginie there without going in herself. I count on her to help you carry out your wish of returning here. [31]

On the twenty-third, a bomb intended to kill Bonaparte explodes in the rue Saint-Niçaise. I congratulate him on his escape.

"The comte de Provence has written to me to say he played no part in what happened. There was nothing wrong with his letter, nor with my answer, but he finished by asking me for something I could not do, which was to put him back on the throne. The Royalists often make proposals to me through my wife. They promise me a statue in which I shall be represented offering the crown to the king, to which I reply that I should be afraid of being shut up in the pedestal. The danger means nothing to me, but if I restore them to power it would be a piece of infamous cowardice on my part. You may disapprove of the government. You may think me a despot but one day they will see whether I have been working for myself or for posterity. I am the master of the movement, I, whom the Revolution, whom you, whom all patriots have put where I am, and if I brought back those people it would be to hand us all over to their vengeance," he says. His eloquence and his patriotism move me greatly; I take his hand.[32]

On December 25, George, who is in the army of General Brune, is wounded by two bullets at the passage of the Nuncio. When I learn of it, I am proud and happy.[33] He has been blooded, like me, at his first battle, and he has survived.

In 1801 Napoléon tells me of his desire to have a concordat with the Vatican. He wants to reinstate Catholicism as the religion of France.

"You will not complain," he says. "I will replace the priests below where you have left them. A bishop will think himself very honored to dine with the préfet."

"Admit that your only object is to anoint your head with the little phial," I say, laughing.

"You don't care about the little phial," he replies. "And nor do I, but it is necessary to make the Pope and all those people there declare against the legitimacy of the Bourbons. Every day I find a stupidity in the negotiations. The dioceses of France are still ruled by the bishops for the benefit of our enemies. You reproach me for an act of tyranny against priests. I agree, it is an act of tyranny, but what other way to contain them while they are not submitted to discipline."[34]

He also talks of the aristocrats and kings of Europe and never fails to remark how much he is struck by their hatred towards me.

"I am really hated," he says. "As are others by these princes and their entourages, but it is nothing compared to their hatred towards you. I would not have believed that human hatred could go so far. How on earth did the republicans have the stupidity to think that their cause was separate from yours?"[35]

I travel once more to Chavaniac, this time with George who is living at La Grange while his wounds heal. Then we go to stay with Madame de Simiane at her country house at Cirey; from there, on June 21, I write to Jefferson, who has become president of the United States:

> While the Rights of Man Have Become in the old World Quite Unfashionable it is to me a Comfort to Hope that when peace May Give time to look at My Young Adoptive Country she will By the perfect Harmony of philanthropy and freedom with Energy and Good Order Once More set her Elders to Rights…Your Speech Has Had Among the friends of Liberty and the pretenders to Be So, the Great Success it deserves- Every eyes are fixed Upon You and from My Rural Retirements the Heart Goes with them.[36]

We return to La Grange. The peace at Lunéville means that France now has the left bank of the Rhine; George will soon go back to his regiment quartered in Milan, which worries Adrienne, although her health is improved.

In September, I travel again to Chavaniac. We are hoping to arrange a marriage for George with Émilie de Tracy, the daughter of comte Destutt de Tracy, a philosopher, a member of the Senate, and my former colleague in the Constituent Assembly; we therefore need to make financial arrangements concerning his future inheritance. My aunt wishes to cede the château and the estate to me and my children.

In February 1802, Adrienne is in Paris trying to resolve payment for the lands in Cayenne, confiscated on August 10, '92. She had written a letter at the time to Brissot about the workers there, but they had been sold as slaves. It is agreed an indemnity will be paid but there is still much negotiation to be done. She travels to Chavaniac to discuss George's inheritance with my aunt and I go to Paris to take over the negotiations concerning the Cayenne lands.

March 15. I ask Berthier, the minister of war, for my retirement. I am forty-four and it is now more than thirty years since I entered the second company of the musketeers in April 1771. On the twenty-seventh, the Peace of Amiens is signed. I visit Cornwallis who has negotiated for the British; I express my opinions in my usual way.

I later see Napoléon. "I should tell you that Lord Cornwallis declares you have not changed," he says laughing.

"Of what?" I say sharply. "Is it of loving liberty? Who will have disgusted me from it? The extravagances and crimes of the terrorist tyranny? It has only made me hate all arbitrary régimes more and to attach myself more and more to my principles."

"Lord Cornwallis says you have talked to him of our affairs, and this is what he has said," he replies.

"I don't recall anything precise," I answer. "No one is further away than I am from looking for an English ambassador to denigrate what happens in my country, but if he asked me if this is liberty, I would have said no, although I would rather have said it to anyone other than him."

"I must tell you, General Lafayette, I unhappily see that by your manner of expressing yourself on the actions of the government, you give to its enemies the weight of your name," he says gravely.

"What can I do better?" I reply. "I live in the countryside. I am retired. I avoid any occasion to speak, but when someone asks me if your régime conforms to my ideas of liberty, I reply, no, for, at the very end, General, I want to be prudent, but I do not want to be a renegade."

"What do you mean by your arbitrary régime?" he asks. "Yours was not so, I admit, but you had against your adversaries the resource of riots. I was only in the foyer whereas you were in the theater, but I watched closely. Yes, in order to put right these actions, you needed to cause riots."

"If you call the national insurrection of July 1789, a riot, I will lay claim to it, but after that time I wanted no more. I have repressed many. Many were made against me, and since you mention my experience, I will tell you that I did not see any injustice in the Revolution, no deviation from liberty which would have destroyed the Revolution itself and, at the end, the authors of those measures."

"But will you not acknowledge that in the state in which I found France I was forced to act in an irregular way?" he asks.

"That is not the question. I speak neither of the time nor of such and such an act. It is the tendency, General. It is the tendency of which I complain, and which afflicts me," I reply.

"I have spoken to you as head of the government and in this position I have cause to complain of you, but as an individual I am content, for in all that I hear of you, despite your severity on the actions of the government, you have always shown personal goodwill towards me," he says.

"A free government, with you at its head, is what I want," I tell him.[37]

The concordat, signed last July 15, at Paris, is submitted in April to the legislative body and adopted by it. I finish negotiating with the council and with General Decrès, the minister of the navy, concerning my estates in Cayenne. My rights are now recognized to the property, but I am not allowed to keep it; instead, I am offered 140,000 francs, half its value.

"As the agreement has been agreed, can you execute it?" I ask Napoléon.

He gives the order, but when I read the contract I see that the negroes are being sold with the land and therefore there are rights of property over those who are found there. I realize, for the first time, that there is a plan to bring back slavery.

"There is nothing to be done," I say, leaving the table.

Our two lawyers, the clerk and the witness, come between us. The sentence is changed. We sign.[38]

April 10. I go to see Tracy at eight o'clock in the morning, after first looking in on Maubourg.

"My aunt has finally agreed to renounce her intention of leaving me a half share in Chavaniac, so assuring George of his half," I tell him.

He falls on my neck and embraces me ten times over with a joy which makes it more and more clear to me that, as we knew already, he had raised these objections simply and solely as a matter of principle.[39]

On the thirteenth, I obtain a pension of six thousand francs for my army service, the maximum for my grade. In May, Bonaparte decrees there will be a plebiscite on becoming consul for life. I vote against. I write to him on the twentieth and say I must follow the principles and actions of my whole life and that in order to vote for him it must be founded on bases worthy of the nation and of him.[40] I hear that when it is said to him that only Jacobins have voted against, he replied that there were also some enthusiasts for liberty such as Lafayette.[41]

I busy myself on my estate and buy rams and sheep at Rambouillet, helped by Tessier, the agriculturalist.

On June 7, George marries Émilie de Tracy. We all travel to Chavaniac to share the new joy of their union with my aunt.[42] Pauline de Montagu comes from Plauzat with comte Louis de Lasteyrie du Saillant, a lieutenant of dragoons, who is staying with her; she presents him to our family and to Virginie. She had met him at Brives in the Limousin and had thought he might be a suitable husband for her. Adrienne agrees as she is content with his religious principles and good character.

We return quickly to La Grange as many English people are in Paris due to the Peace of Amiens, including Charles Fox and General Fitzpatrick, whom I last saw near Valley Forge, who want to see me.

Charles Fox, Mrs. Fox, Mr. John, Mr. Trotter, and General Fitzpatrick, come to stay at La Grange; in Paris I also see Lord Holland, Lord Lauderdale, the new Duke of Bedford, Mr. Adair and Mr. Erskine and find my English friends little encouraging about the Revolution.

"The first years were welcome, but its excesses ruined a good cause," is their view.

"Do not worry too much about a necessary delay," says Fox. "Liberty will be reborn, but not for us; for George at the earliest, and surely for his children."[43] He plants ivy, the symbol of constancy, at the foot of the towers at La Grange.

Adrienne receives a letter from a priest who writes that he has discovered from Mademoiselle de Paris, a lacemaker, the burial place near the place du Trône of the one thousand three hundred and seven victims killed in the last six weeks of the Terror.

Adrienne and Pauline visit Mademoiselle de Paris, whose father and brother had been executed, and learn of the ghastly scenes which happened. They visit the ground where the bodies had been thrown into a grave, now in a long strip of the garden of a house in the rue de Picpus. The small enclosure is owned by the Princess of Hohenzollern, whose brother, the Prince of Salm-Kyrbourg, is buried there. Adrienne and her sister try to persuade the princess to relinquish her ownership and to consecrate it to the common veneration of the bereaved families, but she refuses. However, it will be possible to buy the field surrounding it, and the chapel, and so they appeal to relations of the victims to buy it by subscription. [44]

February 23, 1803. I slip heavily on the ice as I leave the ministry of the navy. In great pain, I am taken to Madame de Tessé's house in the rue d'Anjou.

I have broken the head of my left femur; the surgeons Boyer and Deschamp offer me the choice of a reduction of the fracture which would leave me lame for life, or the use of a machine devised by Boyer, which keeps the fractured limb in a constant state of tension.

"I agree to support the pain caused by the machine as long as you think it necessary for the cure," I tell them.

Eleven days later the inflammation has sufficiently diminished to allow its use. The pain becomes agonizing; the most, I believe, that any human being could endure. Pus oozes from various points. Forty days later, the doctors take off the machine. A part of my hip comes with it, as well as one of the branches of the triceps artery very near to the main artery. Deschamp turns pale, Boyer appears stupefied.[45] The doctors cut it.

"You must remain immobile for another fifteen days," they say.

Finally they remove my foot from it. It emerges crushed, deprived of its small tendons and the inside tibialis muscle which they cut.[46]

I go to convalesce at Aulnay, Madame de Tessé's summer home. Many people visit, including Joseph Bonaparte, with whom I have remained friends, as well as Kosciousko, Moreau, Bernadotte, and Arthur O'Connor.

On April 20, the wedding of Virginie and Louis de Lasteyrie du Saillant takes place in the chamber next to mine. Père Carrichon gives the blessing. Nine days later, I write to my aunt: 'Louis de Lasteyrie is madly in love with Virginie, who reciprocates his passion with all her heart. Everyone thinks her charming in this new role. So, the younger branch is assured.'[47]

I learn from the American ambassadors of a new treaty signed on April 30 with the United States which undertakes to pay fifteen million dollars for Louisiana, which pleases me greatly.

On May 23, to our immense joy, Natalie Renée Émilie, the daughter of George and Émilie, is born at Auteuil.

In August, Adrienne and Pauline's scheme regarding the ground at Picpus where the victims of the Terror were buried, bears fruit. The whole of the convent site is bought for 24,000 francs, although the ground containing the burial graves owned by Princess Hohenzollern remains her property.

By September I am still on crutches; I write to Jefferson saying I hope he has received my previous letters to him and to Madison, respecting the grant of land with which I have been honored and for which I have sent him a blank power of attorney requesting him, Madison and Mr. Gallatin, who has been particularly kind in this affair, to act for me. [48]

1804. "I don't like the sale of land which belonged to France," Moreau tells me when I visit him.

"I agree," I reply. "But it is a happy wrong, useful to both countries, which stops me from having the misfortune to see the countries engaged in hostilities. Besides, my dear General, Louisiana is too far away for us to be too rigorous about it at a time when neither, you, nor I, nor anyone else, can be sure of sleeping at one's own home."[49]

We talk at length about the future. "My views are the same as yours," he tells me.

He appears to dislike Bonaparte and to have little esteem for his character, but without any jealousy towards him, and without any tendency to conspiracy. He gives me his arm to help me to my carriage when I leave. "I will come to hunt near La Grange to see you."

On February 15, several days after our talk my friends rush to warn me that Moreau has been arrested and sent to the Temple and there is a rumor that I am also about to be arrested.

On the twenty-sixth I reply to Jefferson who wrote to me last November. He had said that he sincerely wished I was in America as then I could be given the governership of Louisiana. He also assured me that they are doing their best concerning my land and hoped to have permission from Congress to locate it anywhere they have that is suitable.[50] I thank him.[51]

Pichegru is arrested on the twenty-eighth. The same day the functions of the jury are suspended for two years for crimes against the first consul. Next day, Georges Cadoudal and forty-seven others are arrested and brought before a special tribunal.

Towards the end of March, I learn from *Le Moniteur* that during the night of the fifteenth to the sixteenth, the duc d'Enghien, the son of the duc de Bourbon, was arrested at a château on the right bank of the Rhine by French gendarmes. Five days later he was shot. There is great consternation in Paris. I believe that Bonaparte decided that the death of one of the French princes would suffice to stop their activities for ever. [52]

On April 6, Pichegru dies, strangled, in his prison cell. No one believes it is suicide; Bonaparte is generally thought to be responsible. Prisoners complain to the tribunal of having been tortured.

The senate proclaims Napoléon Bonaparte the hereditary Emperor of the French on May 18. I do not refuse to do what all governments demand of an inhabitant of the country, but I prudently follow a more retired life than ever. Even so, my behavior is not sufficient to allay Bonaparte's need to subjugate everything. He declares several times that I am his enemy, the enemy of his government. Alexandre Lameth says to him one day that he likes to think that his enemies are those of His Majesty. "You are speaking of Lafayette," Bonaparte replies sharply.[53]

General Moreau is being allowed to live in exile in the United States and I write to Jefferson to say that I know too well the citizens of the United States and their government not to be assured that this great and good man will meet there with the reception due to his public and private character.[54]

Adrienne is at Villersexel where her sister, Rosalie de Grammont, is about to give birth. I stay at Cirey in Lorraine with Diane-Adélaïde de Simiane and write and tell Adrienne she is daily missed and wished for by the lady of the house and all those gathered here.[55]

From Cirey I go to Mount Dore in the Auvergne to take the waters with Adrienne and Virginie. I can now walk a little and find the hot springs beneficial; I will perhaps return to complete the cure.

We travel to Chavaniac. My aunt is now eighty-three and as sorrow always overcomes her greatly when we leave, we start to prepare her for our departure some time before. In September Ségur writes that Prince Joseph has given him a message for me.

When I return to Paris, I meet with Ségur. "Prince Joseph likes to attribute your retirement to a feeling of philosophy but sees with sorrow and disquiet that his brother looks upon it as a state of hostility. He regrets that you didn't accept the position of senator and wants you to accept the newly created *Légion d'Honneur*." [56]

"I am touched by Joseph's kindness, but I regard the award as contrary to my principles," I reply.[57]

I am grateful that my friends in the United States, discovering how distant I am from the government in France and fearful of the dangers I am running, have tried to help me to go to live there and create a new fortune for me and my children. I am particularly grateful to President Jefferson in this respect and place him in the forefront of the most noble models of human nature. [58] I write to him on October 8, to express my gratefulness to Congress for their munificence in giving me land in Louisiana and the obligation that I feel towards him personally; the land will be a source of pecuniary independence to myself and future wealth to my family. I say that I do not intend to leave France at the present although it is possible that several of the members in both houses have connected the gift of land in Louisiana with my immediate embarkation. [59] I feel that liberty in America no longer needs me, but I can perhaps be useful in Europe.[60] My friend, Alexander Hamilton, died in a duel with Aaron Burr on July 12 and I finish my letter to Jefferson by saying how afflicted I have been by the tragedy: 'I am sure that whatever have been the differences of Parties, you have ever been sensible of his merits and now feel for his Loss.'[61]

On December 2, Bonaparte is crowned Emperor of the French in Notre Dame. Pope Pius VII gives Charlemagne's crown to him and Bonaparte places it on his own head before swearing on the Gospel to preserve equality, liberty, the rights of property and the integrity of France. I do not witness the spectacle and remain at La Grange.

In 1805 Pauline learns of a religious order, founded by Henriette Aymer de la Chevalerie Sacre-Coeurs, now Mère Henriette, who pray constantly before an altar on which is the Blessed Sacrament. She offers the former convent at Picpus to them; they agree.[62]

Jefferson was elected for a second term on December 5 last year. I write to him praising his admirable speech, saying it is very suited not to the situation but to the wants of this part of the world.[63]

In the summer I go to Chavaniac with Virginie and Anastasie whilst Adrienne visits her father in Switzerland. It is said Bonaparte is planning to invade England. On August 20 I write to Adrienne that my last news of George was dated the 20 *Thermidor*, when General Grouchy and his staff were about to embark in the corvette *Iris*. I try to reassure by saying her that a vessel of that type is unlikely to be exposed either to the dangers of the line of battle or to the discomforts of a transport ship.[64]

On October 20, Ulm is captured; I am in Paris when the guns announce the capitulation. "Please say to Prince Joseph that I would visit him if I had the habit of etiquette," I tell Jaucourt. This is my last contact with the Bonapartes. [65]

George is aide-de-camp to General Grouchy who says he has fought with honor and praises him highly. Bonaparte, however, refuses to allow either him or Louis de Lasteyrie to be promoted. There is hatred towards me. I am bitter and now always call him Bonaparte, not Napoléon.

On October 21, the French and Spanish fleets are defeated at Trafalgar although the nation is told nothing; Bonaparte's plan to invade England is abandoned. On December 2, I rejoice in our victory at Austerlitz against Prussia and Russia. I do not congratulate Bonaparte. No one since Caesar has showed as much prodigious activity of calculation and execution which, after a certain time, assures Bonaparte the advantage over his rivals. But his policy has only ever had one objective, the construction of himself.[66]

In 1806 there is a commemoration service at Picpus. Many people attend, all dressed in black. There will now be constant prayer and veneration for everyone buried there.

On May 16 the British begin a naval blockade of French coasts and ports allied to France. October brings the Fourth Continental Coalition between Prussia, Britain, Russia and Sweden. On October 14, France is victorious at the battle of Jena. On November 21, in response to the British blockade, Bonaparte issues the Berlin Decree, installing the Continental System, implementing an embargo against trade with Britain and even excluding from European ports all neutral vessels which had even stopped briefly at a British port.

On February 7, 1807, George saves the life of General Grouchy at the battle of Eylau. Grouchy recommends he should be made a captain. Yet again, George is not promoted.

Our grandchild, Pauline, is born, and is baptized in the chapel at La Grange. I was hoping for a grandson who would have been named after Thomas Jefferson, but little Tommy becomes a girl, I write to Jefferson.[67]

On June 14 the French are victorious at the battle of Friedland. In July, Bonaparte agrees the Treaty of Tilsit with Tsar Alexander of Russia; France and Russia are now allies and the subsequent peace brings great happiness to Adrienne, freed from her worries about George.

George and Louis de Lasteyrie return home on August 22, having resigned from the army, knowing they will never be promoted due to the hostility of Bonaparte. A few days later, Adrienne suffers violent pains and a strong fever and becomes increasingly weak.[68]

George and I visit Chavaniac. At Brioude, on our return to La Grange, I receive a note from Madame de Tessé which immediately pierces me to the heart; she says that Adrienne is very ill and is at her house. It had never crossed my mind that she might die. In great fear, George and I travel back to Paris as rapidly as we can.[69]

Adrienne is lying in bed in a feverish state, but immediately recognizes me and smiles. I sit by her and hold her hand.

Next day, she improves slightly, probably because George and I have arrived. Then she worsens.

"I was going to have a malignant fever, but I shall be well looked after and shall get the better of it," she tells Diane-Adélaïde de Simiane. However, I am not reassured even though Doctor Lobinhes has asked Corvisart, the physician to the emperor, for advice.

Her mind begins to wander. Her confessor comes to see her. In the evening she tells me. "If I go to another dwelling, you know how much I shall think of you there. Although I shall leave you with reluctance, the sacrifice of my life would be little, if it could ensure your eternal happiness."

She often tells me she will go to heaven. "This life is short and troubled. Let us reunite in God; let us pass Eternity together," she says several times." [70]

She receives the sacrament and wants to see me near her. She becomes delirious in a way which is so touching and so extraordinary. She imagines herself in Egypt and in Syria, in the reign of Athalie in the family of Jacob, which she has been describing recently to Célestine. Her mind wanders, but she is always kind; she always seeks to say something pleasing. She speaks with refinement; she has a loftiness of thought which surprises everyone. She is always tender towards her children, to her sister, to her aunt. She thinks she is with them at Memphis; her mind wanders to different places; it is only where I am concerned that her mind remains fixed. It is as though that impression is too deep to be obliterated, that it is stronger than sickness, stronger than death itself. She presses my hand; it is as though life has already fled and feeling, warmth, existence has taken refuge in it.[71]

She is constantly grateful for the care being given to her. She fears she is tiring people and wants to feel useful. She is, in fact, the same as she always is. The only difference is that she believes herself to be somewhere else. Her thoughts are disordered, but what she says is admirable, charming, and elegantly spoken.

She often begs me to stay longer. "How grateful I am to God that such passionate feelings should have been a duty. How happy I have been. What gratitude I owe to God."

Sometimes she wants me to attend to other matters. "My only concern is to look after you," I reply.

"How good you are. You are too kind. You are spoiling me. I do not deserve so much. I am too happy," she says, weakly but clearly.

"Does your present way of life please you?" she often asks anxiously, while I sit next to her, beside myself with worry as I see her slipping away from me.

"You are looking cheerful, but not too cheerful. I dare say you have been suffering with your chest, haven't you?" she says.

Her delirium increases and she believes I am much beloved in Athalie's time.

"Would it not be strange if being your wife I am obliged to sacrifice myself for a king?" she wonders.

"Am I not mad?" she asks. "Come nearer and tell me if I have lost my mind."

"I should be very sorry to take the kind words you have said to me for absurdities," I reply.

"Have I said anything kind? But I have also said many silly things. Have we not acted the tragedy of Athalie? What! I am married to the most sincere of men and yet I cannot know the truth. It is still your kindness. You want to spare my head. Do speak. I am resigned to the disgrace of being mad."

"Calm, my beloved," I reply. "You are both valued and loved."

"Ah," she answers. "I do not care to be valued as long as I am loved."

She often prays in her bed; my daughters read prayers to her. She recites Tobit's prayers, as she had done on seeing the steeples of Olmütz.

"I have to recite it because I sing badly," she says.

She composes a most beautiful prayer which lasts an hour. Twice she believes I am a fervent Christian. "You are not a Christian," she says.

I do not answer.

"Oh, I know what you are. You are a Fayettiste."

"Do not think me presumptuous," I reply. "But are you not also a bit of a Lafayettiste yourself?"

"Oh yes," she exclaims. "With all my soul. I feel I could die for that sect."

"You are so gentle," I tell her.

"Yes," she says. "God has made me gentle, though my gentleness is not like yours. I have not such high pretensions. You are so strong as well as so gentle; you see things from so high, but I will allow that you are gentle, and you are very good to me."

"It is you who are good," I answer. "And generous above all. Do you remember when I first went to America? Everyone was against me, and you hid your tears at Monsieur de Ségur's wedding. You tried not to appear in grief for fear of bringing down more blame upon me."

"True. It was rather nice for a child. But how kind of you to remember so far back," she says.

"My daughters are happy, and my sons-in-law have good and noble characters, but I have not been able to make them as happy as I am. It would have required all God's power to have brought about that again," she says.

"You will be returning home soon to La Grange," I tell her.

"That would be too wonderful," she replies. "You start there before me."

"Let me stay," I say. "You rest a little."

"I will do my best," she replies, more calmly. "Wait a little. I shall go quietly to sleep."

One night I hear her say to the nurse. "Do not leave me. Tell me when I am to die."

I come up to the bed; she quietens. "You will recover. We will go to La Grange," I tell her.

"Oh no. I am going to die. Have you any cause of concern against me?" she asks.

"For what, my beloved? You have always been so good and so loving."

"Have I then been a gentle companion to you?"

"Yes, certainly."

"Well then give me your blessing."

"We have been so happy. I assure you of my love," I say.

"Promise me to keep that love for ever. Promise me," she replies.

"I promise you," I say.

"Are you satisfied with your children?" she asks.

"They completely satisfy me," I reply.

"They are very good. Support them with all your love for me. How do you think they feel with respect to the house of Jacob?"

"They enter into all your own feelings," I say.

"Ah," she replies. "My feelings are very moderate except those I have for you."

"I am not suffering," she says.

"No doubt she does not suffer," says the nurse. "She is an angel."

On Christmas Eve, the day of George's birth, twenty-eight years ago, she becomes ecstatic with joy at the thought of an anniversary dear to our hearts when she had given him to me.

"Today I shall see my mother," she says calmly. I shudder. "When you see Madame de Simiane, give her my love."

"Perhaps it is best you leave us so that she can pray easily," request Pauline and my daughters rather timidly.

I do not want to go. I am afraid her last moments might be troubled. I even confess that as a husband of thirty-four years I feel for the first time a pang of jealousy. I want to occupy her thoughts completely. However, I give my seat to her sister.

"Have you anything you wish to say?" she asks.

"No," replies Adrienne. "Go to supper." She seems impatient I should return and just a few minutes later, she calls me. I return quickly; I come near to her; she again takes my hand in hers and everyone sits in a semi-circle so she can see without difficulty.

"What a charming sight," she says. She speaks to our daughters in turn. She blesses each of them.

"How happy I have been," she says to me. "What a wonderful fortune to be your wife."

I speak to her of my love. "Is it true? Is it indeed true?" she replies. "How good you are. Repeat it again, it does me so much good to hear you. If you do not find yourself sufficiently loved, lay the fault upon God."[72]

"Have you been happy with me? Are you kind enough to love me? Well then give me your blessing."

"You love me also, you will give me your blessing," I reply.

"I bless you," she says in a solemn and loving manner.

Our children and her sons and daughters-in-law each kiss her hand and her face. She looks at them tenderly.

She makes a sign for me to step back, perhaps fearing a convulsion. I stay near her. She places my hand on her eyes, with a look of loving gratitude so showing me what my last duty to her will be. I try not to speak too much to her so as not to exhaust what remains of her life.

"I love you, my beloved," I tell her.

"Is it then true! You do love me. How happy I am. Kiss me," she murmurs, reviving slightly.

She raises her almost lifeless arms and clasps one round my neck. She draws my head to hers; she strokes my cheeks; she presses me to her heart.

"What joy! How happy I am to belong to you!" She takes my hand. "I am all yours."

She brings my head with her right hand to her heart. "What a blessing! How happy I am to be yours!" She continues to keep bringing my hand to her lips and heart. I clasp her left hand; I feel it move; it is as though it is repeating her words, 'I am all yours.'

Our daughters place hot towels on her arms and hands to endeavor to keep the last remnant of warmth in her body. We hold a spoon of wine to her lips and believe the end has come. "Stand back to give her some air," I say. She begins to breathe again. We kneel; we follow the slow movements of her breathing. She does not appear to be in pain. She smiles, my hand in hers. She dies. It is a quarter to twelve o'clock on Christmas night. We let our tears fall on her body.

Monsieur de Mun and Monsieur de Tracey lead me away. My dear son supports me in his arms. They let me kiss her once again. I bid farewell to her and to all my happiness in the world.[73]

Pauline goes with George to the Picpus cemetery on Christmas Day and designates the place where Adrienne had wanted to be buried. On Monday she is buried there, near to the pit where her grandmother, mother and sister lie with one thousand six hundred victims of the Terror.

Chapter 50

Bonaparte makes fat Louis flee

1808. Fires blaze in the hearths. Winter's cold embraces La Grange. The door of Adrienne's chamber has been walled up; I enter by a secret entrance. My beloved is no more.

I write a long letter about her and her illness to La Tour Maubourg:

> During the thirty-four years of our marriage, her tenderness, her goodness, her dignity, her delicacy and the generosity of her soul charmed, embellished and honored my life. I was so accustomed to all she was for me that I did not distinguish my own existence from hers…I loved her and needed her but it is only in losing her that I can discern what remains for the rest of a life which had appeared given over to so many distractions, and for which now there will no longer be any happiness or pleasure….Although she was attached to me, I must say, by the most passionate feeling, I never noticed in her the slightest hint of demand, of discontent. There was never anything which did not allow me to pursue what I wished to do….It was not only that she came to me at Olmütz, as Charles Fox said, 'on the wings of duty and of love' that I want to praise her here, but it is that she only came after having assured herself, as well as she could, of the well-being of my aunt and the rights of our creditors, and to have had the courage to send George to America-What noble imprudence of heart to remain almost the only woman in France compromised by her name but who never wanted to change it. [1]

I write to Masclet:

> I have neither the power nor the wish to struggle against the calamity which has befallen me or rather to surmount the deep affliction which I will carry with me to my grave. It will be mingled with the sweetest recollections of the thirty-four years during which I was bound by the tenderest ties that perhaps ever existed and with the thought of her last moments in which she heaped upon me such proofs of her incomparable affection. [2]

I wear her portrait in a gold medallion around my neck. 'I am yours' is engraved round the edge; on the back is 'I was then a gentle companion to you! In that case, bless me!' Every morning I ask Bastien to leave the room; I look at her portrait for about a quarter of an hour and kiss it.[3] I buy the books she wanted me to read: *Pensées* by Pascal, *Vérités de la Religion Chrétienne* by Abadie and *Oeuvres de La Berthonie*.

Winter turns to spring. I walk with a cane and drive over the estate in my small hackney carriage. I have become quite a good agriculturist, and lame though I am, I husband my strength where walking is concerned and manage to do and to oversee what is essential.[4]

My financial state is dire; I hope to be able to sell the land I have been given in Louisiana in order to pay my debts. 'I am on the brink of ruin,' I write to Jefferson. 'I would have been, by this time, passed every possibility of redemption, had not the benevolent patience of creditors enabled me, hitherto, to wait the effect of expectations formed several years ago.'[5] My children have agreed to follow the intention of their mother rather than the letter of the civil code, and will take a few landed purchases that complete my fields, as well as the three thousand francs already enjoyed by them, in Bretagne and Auvergne. I have the house for life, the timber, and the part of La Grange which I farm myself.[6]

I write every morning for two hours. Now George is no longer in the army I write about Bonaparte, who could have with less effort and more glory fixed the destinies of the world and place himself at the head of humanity. His secondary ambition has to be pitied in such circumstances, to reign arbitrarily in Europe; but to satisfy his geographically enormous and morally bereft desire, he had to apply all his Machiavellian genius to the degradation of liberal and patriotic ideals, to the soiling of parties, opinions and people, for those who devote themselves to his fate are only the more exposed to this double consequence of his system and his character…I feel he needs to search his heart, to justify himself for his scorn of man, and to the lowness of others to maintain him….He needs to base his existence on continuing success, and by exploiting for his own profit the revolutionary movement, to take from the enemies of France, and give to himself, all the ghastliness of those wars whose only motive is the establishment of his power and of his family.[7]

In July Bonaparte attempts to implicate me, as well as some friends, in a conspiracy connected with General Malet. Fouché, his minister, deflects his attack but I owe my escape from this capital accusation to the imperturbable firmness of Monsieur Jacquemont, whose friendship is as enlightened as it is generous and whose denial of any dealings with me cuts short the serious claims.[8] He is imprisoned and will be exiled.

My agricultural pursuits flourish. I sell my fleeces for an average of nine pounds the piece, every part and age included, fifty-seven sols, which is the highest pitch of weight and value I have heard of in France.[9] Many visitors come to La Grange, including Diane Adélaïde de Simiane who has her own room. I visit Chavaniac with George who has escaped the duties of an an aide-de-camp to the governor of Madrid; [10] then we travel to Switzerland to see my father-in-law.

In February,1809, I write to Jefferson to tell him of my great happiness that England has abolished the slave trade. I always expected France would have that honor, but even so, I welcome it heartily and now expect the total and speedy annihilation of that abominable practice.[11]

My farm continues to thrive; if only my debts could be reduced, little more than its income would be enough for my family and I to live in the frugal way we have adopted. I write again to Jefferson asking to have the titles and documents necessary 'to fix the Opinion Respecting the location and Value of the precious grant for the location and grant of the land.'[12]

By 1810 there are many French armies doing well in the south of Spain. There is an invasion of Holland and there is also a quarrel with the Pope following Bonaparte's marriage with the daughter of Emperor Francis, a marriage which now connects him with the house of Austria and every branch of the house of Bourbon, to the delight of people from the *ancien régime*, whilst at the same time displacing those who acted in the Revolution.[13]

To my great joy, Virginie gives birth to a boy, Adrien Jules de Lasteyrie. In the summer I visit Chavaniac. My debts, however, are still very pressing, and I have not yet received the documents for my tract of land in the United States so that it can be sold. I write in November to Jefferson: 'Above all, My dear friend, Let Me Know as Soon as possible whether I have your Approbation for what I Have thought a Matter of Imperious necessity for me, of justice to a part of My Condition, and the only means to do justice to the other, and avoid, If I can, impending and in a Great Measure Unmerited Ruin.'[14]

On May 6, 1811, Aunt Charlotte sadly dies at Chavaniac at the age of 92.

Bloody wars are now raging in Europe but whatever are their motives or their results, it is a happy prospect to see the whole American continent advancing to independence and freedom, which, I think, must be the end of the actual movements in the former Spanish colonies.[15] I continue to live quietly at La Grange with my fourteen children and grandchildren.

The following year I hear that Bonaparte says in one of his frequent diatribes on liberty: 'Everyone in France has changed; the only person who has not is Lafayette. He has never retreated from his position; you see him peaceful; I tell you that he is all ready to start again.'[16]

"Your existence is truly miraculous; danger to you lies less in the character of the emperor than in the hatred of people of the old régime," Bernadotte tells me.

"I live in retirement with my family on the estate where I have a farm. I have not, however, ever failed to express my opinion on the famous system of the emperor and my ardent desire to see it ended," I reply.[17]

In July, I write to Jefferson: 'At this moment immense Continental forces under Bonaparte are going to attack the Russian Empire, starting with Niemen. Will Alexander fight on the battlefield? Will he negotiate? He runs a risk, in either case, of defeat or caught; but if he stretches out the war for a long time, he could well embarrass his opponent.'[18]

The first battle is at Smolensk, which is taken, but had already been abandoned. On September 7 is the battle of the Moskova, called Borodino by the Russians. The land and the forests are being burnt as our army advances and when it reaches Moscow on September 14 the buildings are set on fire.

Bonaparte delays there. When he finally gives the order to retreat, he has left it too late; by November 6, winter has set in and savages his force. Cossacks attack the rear; snow and blizzards destroy what the Russian army failed to do; by the end of November only about ten thousand men are fit to fight.

Terrible news arrives in December. General Louis Romeuf was killed at the Moskova; Alfred Noailles, my nephew, was killed at the crossing of the Beresina; Victor Destutt de Tracy, Émilie's brother, has been taken prisoner and we fear he might be wounded; Octave Ségur has also been taken prisoner and has had all his toes amputated.

Bonaparte abandons the army and returns to France. I continue to farm as this tragedy happens. I have obtained more than five hundred arpents which I have joined to my existing land, so I now possess seven hundred arpents.

In 1813 Prussia declares war on France. General Moreau dies miserably in a Russian uniform, killed by a French cannonball at the battle of Dresden,[19] which takes place on August 26 and 27 and is a victory for our army. Then comes our defeat at Leipzig on October 16 to 19, before victory at Lutzen. In November Bonaparte rejects Metternich's treaty which would enable him to remain emperor, but France would have to retreat to her natural frontiers and lose control of most of Italy, Germany and the Netherlands.

He retreats across Germany, a shadow of his former self. He finds his military talent again on French soil but has exhausted his resources, extinguished patriotism, and when the legislative body dares for the first time to permit itself some observations, he quickly hurries to adjourn it, on December 31, instead of joining it to the defense of the state. [20]

1814 brings a dire situation. Six hundred thousand Russians, Austrians, Germans and English are invading France from the east and from the southwest. The comte de Lusignem becomes gravely ill and I go to Paris. The comte de Tessé also falls ill and I spend my days between the two. The comte de Tessé dies, assisted to his last hour by Madame de Tessé.

"A habit of fifty-eight years is not one of those one can lose. Death is at my heels," she says to Pauline. Her delicate frame cannot withstand such sorrow. Ten days later, on February 1, she dies.[21] On the same day, Blücher defeats Bonaparte at La Rothière. On the tenth, our army is defeated at Champaubert; on the eleventh, at Montmirail. I am in torment at the storm Bonaparte has brought on France; I am in torment at my powerlessness to combat domestic tyranny and the foreign invasion. I remain in Paris.[22]

George and Louis de la Lasteyrie enroll as grenadiers in the National Guard. My other son-in-law, Charles de La Tour Maubourg, rejoins the army; he is wounded and taken prisoner. George tries to rally some patriotic volunteers. I offer my services to the leaders of the National Guard and agree with Ternau, commander of the Third Legion of the National Guard of Paris, to march at the head of a battalion. I also make offers to the army. I suggest to one of the chief maréchaux that Bonaparte should abdicate, but we part company after our third meeting as he fears being found out by him. My civil efforts do not fare any better. Everyone thinks I am too bold and, right up to the end, too hasty.

Talleyrand, meanwhile, is negotiating with the Bourbons. On the morning of the Allies' attack some senators meet at Lambrecht's house; I await a resolution to which I can rally but they disperse. Next day, March 31, at six in the morning, Tsar Alexander, Frederick William III and several generals enter Paris at the head of their armies. I return home to the rue d'Anjou, shut myself in a room and sob.[23]

Marmont goes over to the Allies and marches his troops to Versailles. Bonaparte attempts to abdicate in favor of his son, but Marmont's actions mean he has no chance of success, and a message is sent to him at Fontainebleau to tell him of the capitulation. The Allies declare they will not negotiate with Bonaparte, nor with any of his family, and that they respect the integrity of the former France. Tsar Alexander stays at the house of Talleyrand, whom he already knew, and who is, in any case, the only dignitary left in Paris. It is there, that after some hesitation, it is decided to bring back the Bourbons.[24] Talleyrand is proclaimed president of the government and he chooses the members. France is humiliated. A week later, Bonaparte signs his abdication and goes to Elbe. France returns to her 1790 frontiers and a new map of Europe will be made by a Congress in Vienna. There is a new Constitutional Charter. It restores the king's divine right and Catholicism as the state religion. France does not pay any indemnity and is even allowed to keep the works of art stolen by Bonaparte.

I am invited to the Tuileries for the first royal audience with King Louis XVIII. I wear my old uniform, and with the greatest reluctance, a white cockade. I find Louis not just large, but positively whale-like, sitting in a chair pushed by servants, his three chins wobbling as he speaks.

He receives me graciously but the courtiers stare with dislike and turn their backs. I will not go again. It is doubtless a disadvantage to replace the conqueror of Europe, the most active, the most commanding of men, and to present to the public and to his troops, an ugly body, although with quite a pleasant face, who reviews troops in his chair and only waves his arms from a balcony, repeating "I am content, very content."[25]

I see the comte d'Artois in the street and feel very moved. I go home and write a letter: 'Monseigneur. There is no period or sentiment in my life that does not conspire to make me happy to see your return become the signal to the pledge of public liberty and happiness. Profoundly joining in that national satisfaction, I feel the need of offering to Monsieur the homage of my personal attachment and of the respect which I am, etc.'

Alexis de Noailles, my nephew, brings me his thanks.

War continues between Britain and America; John Adams, Gallatin and Henry Clay are in London attempting to negotiate peace. Gallatin wishes my help in persuading Tsar Alexander to mediate and I meet him at a soirée at the salon of Madame de Staël.

"I have tried twice to obtain peace between Britain and America. I promise to make a third attempt at mediation," he says.

We talk; I find him polite, aimable, and above all, liberal; his manner is noble and simple. He appears touched by some words of mine on gradual emancipation.

"I know what you are thinking. The leader of a country which has serfdom does not have the right to speak in this way, but many aristocrats are engaged in trying to abolish it and I hardly receive a letter which does not bring me satisfying news in this respect." He complains of the servility of our newspapers. "We will do better in Russia."

"You judge badly our nation by its writings, by its speeches, and the words of courtiers. France wants liberty and will have it," I reply.

He makes a sign for me to follow him to another room. There we find more people, including Talleyrand. He leads me to a corner; he lowers his voice, at the same time putting his ear towards me to hear what I am saying as he is slightly deaf.

"My good intentions have turned out badly, both for your liberty and your glory. I have found neither patriotism nor help in France. The Bourbons only have the prejudices of the ancien régime," he declares.

"But surely their misfortunes must have somewhat changed them," I say.

"They have not changed and are unchangeable. The only one with liberal ideas is the duc d'Orléans, but do not hope for anything from the others," he replies.

"If that is your opinion, why have you brought them here?" I ask.

"It is not my fault. They arrived from everywhere. I at least wanted to stop them so that the nation could impose a constitution on them, but they came like a flood," he replies.[26]

I visit the duc d'Orléans at the Palais-Royal. We talk of America and Washington. I feel he is the only Bourbon compatible with a free constitution and I like him. I remain, as always, an optimist. I write to Jefferson:

> Yet the advantages derived from the first impulse, the philanthropic impulse of the Revolution, not wistanding all what Has Since Happened, are Widely Extended, and deeply Rooted-Most of them Have Resisted the Powerful Hand of Bonaparte-They are More than a Match for the feeble, Uncertain devices of their present adversaries...I am Convinced that those Rights of Mankind which, in 1789, have Been the Blessing of the end of the last Century, shall Before the End of the present one be the Undisputed Creed and insured property Not only of this, But of Every European Nation.[27]

In 1815 the Allied troops are still in Paris. Large numbers of émigrés and Chouans return and I very much fear a counter-revolution. The old guard is reinstated; laws are passed against the freedom of the press, which all shows that the Bourbons have forgotten nothing and have learnt nothing. The new régime is not for me, but I prefer it to that of Bonaparte, even although Louis has not held elections, nor summoned a legislative body. The royalists are behaving as they did before the Revolution; they are spiteful and vicious towards the first constitutionalists. Lettres de cachet start to be used. Pamphlets malign me for my actions towards Louis XVI and Marie Antoinette. The royal press prints one from Monsieur Hue, the premier valet de chambre of Louis XVIII, concerning October 5 and 6. Another pamphlet sanctioned by the duchesse d'Angoulême maintains Bailly and I suggested to the king to flee to Varennes. I write a reply of twenty pages to these falsehoods; I describe the *ancien régime* and name the indispensable conditions to improve the Restoration for the nation, all of which will be published at the beginning of April. To our surprise, news arrives that Bonaparte has landed at Golfe Juan in the south of France. I immediately set out for Paris with George. There I find that the king has just agreed to hasten the meeting of the legislative body.

Bonaparte is welcomed by peasants in the south even before soldiers there join him. People flock to his side; at Mâcon, Tournus, Châlons and Lyon they chase away the royal authorities and seize cannon before his troops arrive. "*Vive l'empereur!*" rings out everywhere. Ney joins him. Bonaparte suggests he has arranged an agreement with Austria and England which facilitates his approach, but it is above all his mix of military ways and of republican forms which make people recall ideas of glory and of liberty, although it is noticeable he first calls them citizens, then Frenchmen mid-route to Paris, until finally at Paris they become subjects.[28] When he reaches Fontainebleau the fat Louis takes fright and flees to Ghent. He abandons the Palace of the Tuileries on March 20 in such great haste he even forgets his money. His bed is still warm when Bonaparte arrives. I stay three days in Paris so as not to appear to be afraid, then I return to La Grange.

Bonaparte had said at Fontainebleau: "It is not the coalition of sovereigns, but liberal ideas which have overturned me." Now he attempts to link himself to those liberal ideas and to conciliate, at least, the French. He says he owes everything to the people. He recognizes liberties, but at the same time, his indomitable character falls back on the opinions and sentiments of tyranny.[29] He is a republican in Provence, half a republican at Lyon and absolute emperor at Paris but finds he must appear to want a constitution.[30]

On April 19, my old friend and comrade, Mathieu Dumas, writes to me by an express that if I believe in the constancy of his opinion and his wishes for the independence of our dear country, to come to Paris tomorrow evening as prince Joseph wishes to see me.[31] I think the only chance of salvation for France lies in the immediate convocation of an assembly of freely elected representatives.[32] I therefore wish to use any means my situation gives me to influence what is happening.

I meet Joseph Bonaparte at ten o'clock in the morning of April 21. We embrace. We speak about the interval of time since we last met during which he occupied two thrones. We talk about the reason for our meeting; he paints a picture, which is only too true, of the dangers facing France.

"I am personally indebted to the emperor, but I have regretted that his character is irreconcilable with public liberty," I say frankly.[33] "I hoped last year that a national insurrection would happen against the foreign invasion and against internal despotism. I even had some hope that the Bourbons would become constitutionalists. However, now after Pilnitz and Coblentz, the invasion of France by the armies of the whole of Europe, the occupation of our territory and our fortresses, the humiliating and ruinous tributes, and even a complete counter-revolution if national opinion does not show our resistance, I do not hesitate to regard the government of the emperor as the least of two misfortunes. I will unite with your efforts to push back the foreign powers and the Bourbons who brought them here, but if the government of the emperor continues to be as I fear, I wish it to last the least time possible."

"I regret that the new constitutional act was decreed yesterday without having shown it to you. There is a Chamber of Peers and you can be sure that your name is first on the list," he says.

"I have always been against hereditary peerages, but I agree that there are sometimes reasons in its favor," I reply. "However, I do not wish to return to public life by means of a peerage, nor by any other favor of the emperor. I am a man of the people. It is only by the choice of the people that I can leave my retirement. If I am elected, I will unite with you, as a representative of the nation, in order to repel the invasion and foreign influence, and by keeping nevertheless my independence." [34]

I receive a letter from Joseph on the twenty-second telling me that the constitutional act will be published today in *Le Moniteur*. It has been mainly written by Benjamin Constant and consists of sixty-seven supplementary articles to the constitution of the empire. There are two legislative assemblies, a chamber of hereditary peers and a chamber of six hundred and twenty-nine representatives elected as agreed on August 3, 1802. Article sixty-seven forbids any proposal to re-establish the Bourbons.

On May 1, I learn that the decree ordering the meeting of the deputies has been published. I am content. The immediate convocation of an Assembly of Representatives appears our only salvation. [35] There is a large ceremony at the Champ de Mars where delegations of deputies of the electoral colleges, of the National Guard and of officers, pledge allegiance to the constitutions and to the imperial dynasty. Bonaparte, in Roman dress, also pledges to support the new constitution and declares peace with the European powers.

I am elected member of the Chamber of Representatives for Seine et Marne on May 8. I am therefore again in political life, after twenty-three years. On June 4, the Chamber of Deputies votes to elect a president. Lanjuinais obtains 277 votes in the second round. I obtain 73. On the fifth, I am elected vice president.

On the seventh I meet Bonaparte for the first time in twelve years, at the imperial *séance*. I am sitting next to George and forget I am part of the deputation to receive him. Someone comes to tell me; I go to the salon and see a plump, aged man, who has lost the agility of his younger years.

"It is twelve years since I had the pleasure of seeing you," he says.

"Yes, it has been twelve years," I reply somewhat coldly. [36]

We go into the chamber where the tedious ceremony of taking the oath takes place. Bonaparte's speech is suitable, but he looks like an old despot irritated by the role his position is forcing him to play. Sometime later, I accompany him to his vehicle.

"I find you rejuvenated," he says. "The country air has done you good."

"It has done more than that for me," I reply, not able to return the compliment as he is so changed, his muscles contracted in an extraordinary fashion. Neither of us want to lower our regard and we each see what the other is thinking. [37]

June 9. It is said that the emperor will leave after tomorrow to fight the European powers. The Assembly and a part of the public do not have a clear idea on the war and forget it is being waged against one man at the expense of a great country. It is very painful to think that without him perhaps war could be avoided, but that as he is here, it is not possible to abstain from giving him help unless we wish to bring about the dismemberment, or at least the subjection, of France, that he, in his turn, will subject to his own design when he can do so. Our position is false and sad but it is the only one we can take with some gleam of hope of saving our country. [38] However, I believe that if the enemies accept the battle, they will probably be beaten. If they retreat before the emperor, his position will become embarrassing.' [39]

June 16. Bonaparte wrote yesterday from Beaumont at three o'clock in the morning that the enemy are marching against him and that he was going to meet them. We will soon have the news of a battle. [40] Everyone talks of a victory. The bells ring out; no one doubts he will be successful.

June 21. We hear that our army was defeated at Waterloo on the eighteenth. Scarcely has this terrible news been confirmed than I am told of the arrival of Bonaparte and of a discussion at the Elysée where he appeared determined to dissolve the chambers, to become dictator, and bring down everything into his ruin. I hurry to see Fouché who confirms this. Regnault de Saint-Jean d'Angély arrives from the Elysée and also confirms it.[41] "The parade vehicles are already being prepared for the ceremony," he says.

I resolve to defend the representation of the country, at least against the immediate danger, by giving ourselves the only remaining chance of suspending the march of the coalition armies and of negotiating with them. We do not have an hour to lose.

I ask to speak at the opening of the Chamber. "When for the first time in long years I raise a voice that the old friends of liberty will still recognize, I feel called upon, messieurs, to speak to you of the dangers confronting the nation, which you alone, at present, have the power to save. Sinister voices are being heard…We must rally round the old tricolor flag, that of 1789, that of liberty, equality and public order. That is the only way in which we can defend ourselves against foreign interference and internal attempts. Permit, messieurs, a veteran of this sacred cause, who was always a stranger to the spirit of faction, to propose five resolutions to you…Article one: The Chamber declares that the independence of France is threatened. Article two: The Chamber must declare itself in permanent session. Any attempt to dissolve it is a crime of high treason….Article three: The army of the line and the National Guards who have fought and are still fighting to defend liberty, independence and the territory of France, have really merited the gratitude of the nation. Article four: The minister of the interior is invited to reunite the chief of staff, the commanders and legion majors of the Parisian National Guard, in order to advise on the means of giving arms and to bring to completion this citizen-army….Article five: The ministers of war, of foreign affairs, of the police and the interior, should be invited to come immediately to the Assembly."

"Vote! Vote!" people shout.

My resolutions are adopted, except the fourth, that of raising the National Guard, which is postponed until the ministers come. It is voted that my words should be printed, put up in Paris and sent to all the départements. However, Bonaparte still has his Guard and a part of the fédérés who are being encouraged to march against us. Our honorable colleague, Benjamin Delessert, runs to the Chamber of Representatives with a part of the legion he commands, to defend us.

Article five very much displeases Bonaparte; we make several requests to ministers before he allows them to come. They arrive, preceded by Lucien Bonaparte, whom his brother has delegated as *commissaire extraordinaire*, as otherwise he would have to remain in the Chamber of Peers.

Lucien speaks eloquently in the defense of his brother but unfortunately maligns France: "The French nation has always been accused of lacking perseverance. It has always been taxed with lightness. If it does not imitate the conduct of Spain, of Russia, of Germany, towards their sovereigns, history will place her below the Spanish, the Germans, the Russians."

I reply angrily. "The remark you have just made at this tribune is a calumny. By what right do you dare to accuse France of being faint-hearted, of having lacked perseverance towards the Emperor Napoléon? She has followed him in the sands of Egypt and in the steppes of Russia, on fifty fields of battle, in his defeats as well as his successes, and it is for having followed him that we have to mourn the blood of three million Frenchmen!"[42]

Lucien says nothing.

"Go back to your brother," cries Jay. Tell him he can save France by abdicating." Manuel, Lacoste and Dupin add their voices to his.

"Our salvation depends on our union. You cannot separate yourselves from the emperor and abandon him to his enemies without losing France, without failing your vows, without bending forever the national honor," says Lucien. [43]

It is decided to hold a council at the Tuileries. Cambacérès will be the president and it will include the four vice presidents of the Chamber of Representatives, five members from the Chamber of Peers and ministers. There is unrest in Paris. There is fear of violence. The National Guard is deployed on the orders of a commission from the Chamber. We debate from eight o'clock in the evening until three o'clock in the morning; we first discuss financial measures, the recruitment of the army and how to resist the enemy. All the propositions made by the ministers pass unanimously.

"I repeat my agreement to all measures of defense," I say at nearly three in the morning. "Are there any other sacrifices to make? Any other measures to take? I consider our first duty is to repel the invasion and foreign influence, but the final question is that of abdication which was raised in the Chamber of Representatives."

"If the friends of Napoléon had believed his abdication necessary for the well-being of France, they would have been the first to have asked him," says a minister.

"You are speaking like a true Frenchman," I reply. "I adopt this idea and change it to a motion. I demand that we all go to the emperor to tell him that, after all that has passed, his abdication has become necessary to save France."[44]

My motion is seconded by Lanjuinais and Flaugergues, but Cambacérès refuses to move it. It is now nearly dawn; we discontinue the meeting.

Bonaparte decides to dissolve the Chamber of Representatives, leaving us with the only choice to either be dissolved or to dethrone him.

In the early morning, the Assembly is impatient to know what happened in the night; the talk is more and more of abdication; there is anger the subject has not been more advanced. State advisors and ministers, namely Benjamin Constant, the duc d'Otrante, Regnault and others, are pressing Bonaparte to resign. Some deputies including Flaugergues, Bedoch and Durbach are doing the same. He continues to refuse. I send a message to him through a ministerial state advisor: 'If the emperor does not send his abdication, I will propose he be dethroned.'

The meeting halts for an hour. A message arrives from Bonaparte. He is abdicating in favor of his son. The Chamber solemnly accepts the abdication of Napoléon Bonaparte in the name of the French people but does not mention his son. A deputation goes to thank him; Bonaparte receives it calmly and with nobility. "There has been a great disaster, but the territory of France is intact. I am making a great sacrifice to the wishes of the Chamber and to the public situation. I have a great love of my son."

"We had not considered him, but we would take note of His Majesty's words," replies the president respectfully.[45]

"Tell the Chamber that I recommend my son to them," he says.

"The liberty and the life of Napoléon must be protected by the French nation," we decide. "We hope the United States will give him asylum."[46] Everyone agrees. I try to arrange a passage for him on a ship.

We discuss what to do. We need a revolutionary government which will inspire enthusiasm and security. There is a fear of the return of the Bourbons. M. Dupin demands that the Assembly should be called Constituent and that there should be an executive commission of five members, three named by the chamber of representatives and two by that of the peers. It is thought that Fouché and Carnot will be named from the peers and I, Lanjuinais and Flaugergues from the deputies. However, I am not chosen. Instead, it is Fouché, Carnot, Grenier, Vicence and Quinette, the intrigues of all the parties uniting against me.

I had also hoped to command the National Guard, but Masséna, who has saved France twice, is appointed. I am nominated, however, to join a deputation to go to talk to the leaders of the Allies to tell them of the intentions of the French people and to ask them to abandon their march towards Paris. I refuse, greatly displeased by my new situation. I want to stay in Paris to help found the new articles of the constitution, to help with the defense and to get the nation's support.[47]

"Your mission is important," says Fouché and many of my friends. I therefore acquiesce as I would have always reproached myself if I could have been useful and had not done so and it is also the best way to determine if there is anything which can be done.[48]

I leave Paris on June 25, with Monsieur Laforest, a veteran of diplomacy, the duc de La Rochefoucauld, General Sébastiani, Monsieur de Pontécoulant, Monsieur d'Argenson and Benjamin Constant who knows almost all the foreign diplomats and has had personal contact with Tsar Alexander.

"*Vive la nation!*" "*Vivent nos députés!*" people call out as we pass.

We would like to go to Metz, which would have saved us a day, but the provisional government, after learning recent information on the march of the emperors towards Bruxelles, wants us to go to Laon where General Morand commands the rear guard of our army.

We reach Laon. We write to Generals Wellington and Blücher to demand a cessation of hostilities and passports. The first aide-de-camp of Blücher, the comte de Nostitz, arrives with two other officers, one of whom is the Prince of Schoënburg.

"The respective state of the armies makes it impossible to suspend our march and to deprive ourselves of the advantages which would result from it," he says. "The Allied powers wish to be ceded the principal places, not only of Flanders, but of the whole frontier, including Metz and Thionville."

"I have a personal message from General Blücher to you," he tells me. "You can count on the German commanders who would be assigned to these places, rather than on Bonaparte's generals."

"That is very obliging of you but knowing my countrymen who at the moment command there, I believe them to be in very good hands," I reply.

"We demand to go to talk to the Allied Powers," we say.

We are desperate to stop the march of our enemies; we write immediately to the government to ask that new commissioners should be sent to Wellington and Blücher. It is very evident to us that the Allies, or at least the British and Prussians, are determined to march to Paris as soon as possible. We talk with the French generals about how to rally our troops, but it seems impossible to do this before several days' time. We decide that, if necessary, we will become prisoners, in order to try our utmost to help France. The passports arrive, however, brought by the Prince of Schoënburg, and we immediately set off towards Mannheim. We travel day and night, encountering many difficulties, and reach Kaiserslautern; General Barclay de Tolly advises us to go to Wissembourg. We take the road to Haguenau to reach there before the sovereigns. We arrive but they are already here. A courier tells us we can only speak to them at Wissembourg, as arranged.

I write to the Tsar; I go to meet him as a private person, but his chief of staff says it is against his duty to announce me. The Tsar sends Monsieur Capo d'Istria with a message: 'My engagements with the Allies do not permit me to see you at Haguenau, but I assure you that the sentiments you knew me to have last year are still the same.'

However, instead of making us travel back ten miles, it is decided that four representatives of the sovereigns will speak to us here. Lord Stewart, the brother of Lord Castlereagh, represents

Britain, General Walmoden represents Austria, Count Capo d'Istria represents Russia, and General Kenesbeck represents Prussia.

We meet. Monsieur Laforest speaks first; each of us say some words. Then General Sébastiani speaks. "The only object of the war no longer exists. Bonaparte has become a private individual under the surveillance of the government and only wants a passport to go either to Britain or to the United States. Monsieur Otto has gone to London to demand this. The Bonaparte brothers are not in th government. The name of the young Napoléon, detained at Vienna, is less disquieting for the Allies. A provisional government has been appointed completely different to an imperial regency and nothing now opposes an immediate suspension of arms and the establishment of conferences for peace. Nothing has been prejudged, neither concerning things nor people, the question remains whole. The plenipotentiaries have great authority and if the Allies would indicate what would suit them, we will immediately refer it to our government." We all voice our agreement with his words.

The emperor of Austria has the consideration to send his staff with food and we have just finished eating when the foreign ministers return, Lord Stewart in front, holding two copies of *Le Moniteur.*

"You say, gentlemen, that no question has been prejudged, and yet here is a proclamation which announces that the king of Rome is at the head of the empire."

"If the *Moniteurs* had provided an obstacle to an armistice, it would have been imprudent to have given them, as we have done, to one of your aide-de-camps." We repeat what we have already said and lift any doubts on any Bonapartist contender for the throne, the foreign ministers appearing to be very satisfied with our explications.

"If you treat with the French, it will be without England, for I declare that I do not have the authority," says Lord Stewart.

"We can only agree jointly," say the others.

Lord Stewart places his chair forward so that the other three ambassadors cannot be seen or heard easily; he proceeds to talk on behalf of all of them and interrupts if they say something with which he disagrees. He is much more polite towards us than he is to his fellow representatives.

More conferences follow. The problem appears to be Bonaparte. What happened three months ago can only be explained by an excessive enthusiasm for Napoléon and a general discontent for the royal government.

"General Lafayette, I must warn you that no peace is possible with the Allied Powers unless you give up Bonaparte," he says to me.

"I am astonished, milord, that to propose such a cowardly act to the French people, you choose to speak to a prisoner of Olmütz," I reply indignantly.

"I would dispute the legitimacy of a chamber convoked by Napoléon," he says.

"I am astonished, milord, that a public man of your country does not recognize that the power of a national assembly derives from who elect it rather than the person who convoked it," I reply.

"England did not make a similar objection to the Parliament of its glorious revolution of 1688," declares Constant.

"Since we are speaking of those times, I ask milord to recall that in the same revolution, which I will also call glorious, the situation of the army and of Charles 11 was a little different to that of the French army relative to Louis XVIII. It had been formed; it had fought with him; it owed him gratitude, which did not prevent all its troops, and particularly the favorite of the king, your great Marlborough, to desert in the night, not to unite with the national flag, but to rejoin an army, a prince and a foreign flag," I say.

Next day, the Prussian, Russian and Austrian representatives arrive without Lord Stewart. The conference can therefore no longer take place as none can negotiate separately and can only make peace or conclude a truce together. The representatives say that the three monarchs regard it as an essential condition of a true state of peace that Bonaparte must be removed from ever troubling again the peace of France and of Europe. This official declaration of the impossibility of making an agreement at Haguenau and the announced resolution to conduct talks nearer Paris means that all we can do is return.[49]

We set off back to Paris, escorted by two enemy officers who place all possible delays in our way.

"*Vive la nation!*" "*Vivent nos députés!*" people call out along the route and I find many signs of willingness to help the French army.

We finally reach Paris on July 5; we find the capitulation was signed a few hours ago. I learn to my profound regret that we are no longer in any state to risk a new battle against the Prussians and the English whose armies have been momentarily separated by the Seine, thereby giving us an advantage if attacking the Prussians.

In the evening, there is a declaration of the Chamber of Representatives, which appears to me to be a manifesto of a national ultimatum, the symbol of which all power must conform in order to become legitimate. We hold a meeting at the Tuileries of the provisional government, the six plenipotentiaries of Haguenau, the general-in-chief and several ministers, to discuss our future negotiations with the Allies.

"It is necessary in our present circumstances to make transactions, but they must be resolved in common, having only as aim the general interest, and made with the knowledge of the Assembly and the people, any transaction made individually being infamous or cowardly," I declare.[50]

On July 6 I go to the Assembly to speak about our trip to Haguenau and to agree on behalf of myself and Messieurs d'Argenson and Sébastiani to the declaration of the representatives. I talk of my opposition to inherited peers, along with my son, Monsieur d'Argenson and several other deputies. Our minority is numerous, but it is not supported.

"The Allies are going to bring back the king without negotiations or pact," announces Fouché.

The provisional government immediately dissolves itself, as do the peers, but the representatives, in the middle of foreign troops, continue their constitutional act. I am still not far from the idea of resistance on the Loire.

July 8. The Chamber of Representatives is closed by Decazes, the new préfet de police, under the order of Louis XVIII; National Guard soldiers stand in front of the gates.

"We have been ordered not to let anyone enter," they say.

"Is this an order from the Prince Regent of England?" I ask. "I am going to my house where I will receive my colleagues with pleasure."

They soon fill my home, so we go to that of President Lanjuinais. We draft a document declaring that the Chamber is not being allowed to meet. We protest in front of the gates. We are impotent. Our only consolation is that we have neglected nothing to try and avoid the catastrophe which has struck France.

Bonaparte is a prisoner; Louis XVIII is king; the white Bourbon flag flies over the Tuileries, defended by the encampments of the Prussians and English with cannon, the wick already lit. There is pillaging around Paris; the Prussians are destroying our monuments; the French army is behind the Loire. I would like to return to La Grange with my children, but it would be insupportable to me to host a German, English or Russian garrison. I therefore stay in my little room and only come out feeling the most painful sentiments.[51]

The émigrés return, filled with hatred and desiring vengeance. They want the generals of the Grande Armée punished. "We are going marshal hunting," remarks the duc de Berri.

In October, I am finally back at La Grange, where I will remain unless any foreigners are quartered here. I write to Jefferson:

> The Imperial destroyer of french Liberty Reassuming a Republican Language, Bowing to National Sovereignty, Allowing a free press, and although Vindictive or Arbitrary, and too often Betray'd old Habits, persuading Many patriots to rejoice at his Conversion-Not So did I- But while I Shunned personal Communication With Him, I declared that if a free Representation was Convened I Would Stand a Candidate- We were, My Son and Myself Elected. At the Same Time a million of foreign invaders Were in Concert with Lewis the 18th, and the elder branch of his family...The defence of National Independence and territory Became, of Course, our principal object...It was My Opinion that Unanimity and Vigour could better be aroused by a popular than By the Imperial Government- The Majority of the Assembly and Army depended more on the Generalship of Napoléon although his Whole troops did little exceed two Hundred thousand. So we all joined on that Line of Resistance. No impediment was thrown, every Assistance was Given. Never did our Heroic Army fight Better than at Waterloo. A stubborn Mistake of Bonaparte Lost the day. He deserted His Soldiers, and Determined to Dissolve our Assembly, Usurp dictatorial powers....that part of the Impending Evil was timely prevented.' I tell him of my hope for the future and of the birth of my eleventh grandchild, George's son, who 'in addition to the family name of Gilbert, Received the friendly Name of Thomas. He is Born to freedom- the cause of French, of European liberty is far from Being Lost. [52]

The second Peace Treaty is signed on November 20, the terms far harsher than those of the first. The frontier of France is changed to that of January 1, 1790, so losing the Saar and Savoie. France will have to pay an indemnity of 700,000,000 francs and endure an army of occupation of 150,000 men for three to five years.

The violence against Bonapartists and Protestants continues, particularly in the south. Men are burned to death and seventeen heads of families are shot at Uzès. People are massacred, their homes destroyed. Many flee France. On December 7, Ney is executed by firing squad.

I write to Jefferson on January 21, 1816:

> Let Me only firmly Assert that the Cause of European Liberty far from Being Lost in France Has Never Been so well understood by the Mass of the people and that the Reactionnary Spirit of the day is Doing More for it than Either the Conventional or the Imperial System, the Medicine is Bitter and to Obnoxious Characters Not Very safe. Yet to the party of privileges and to the party of Rights, the Result Not only in this But in other Countries Cannot fail to prove what for Upwards of forty years You and I have wished it to be.[53]

I keep busy on my estate, my days always much the same. Servants wake me at five and I spend one or two hours in bed reading or writing. I dress; I look at Adrienne's portrait in the gold locket for a quarter of an hour, before writing letters, or occasionally my memoirs, in my study. At ten, I breakfast and read the journals. I call down through a speaking trumpet to my estate manager who shouts back. At midday, until about three o'clock, I go to the farm which has approximately forty cows, about one hundred to one hundred and fifty pigs, and one thousand merino sheep, of which I am particularly proud, some of American origin from Baltimore, as well as five thousand feet of apple and pear trees which produce cider which sells well. I walk to the nearest buildings and parts of the farm as exercise is favorable to my health, but ride to the more distant areas. I write letters until six when the bell rings for dinner which I eat with my family and friends, always at least thirty in number. My children, their husbands and wife, and eleven grandchildren live here, as well as General Carbonel, George's commander in Italy, and Monsieur Frestel. Many people visit, including Lady Morgan, the Tracys, the La Tour Maubourgs, Lasteyries and Ségurs.[54] Madame de Staël dies on July 13; we mourn her. Her daughter and husband come to stay at La Grange for a few weeks as they do not want to be in Paris.

Ary Scheffer paints my portrait. "What pose did he choose?" asks Pauline de Montagu. "Did he paint you holding in your hand your Declaration of the Rights of Man?"

"Well, my dear sister," I reply. "I am standing as though out walking, my cane and my hat in my hand."

"And your other hand?" she asks.

"It is in my pocket, which is better, dear sister, than to have it in the pockets of others," I reply.[55]

Famine rears its head in the winter and spring of 1817. I give up to seven hundred people soup, bread and a sou every day at La Grange.

"In six weeks there will be nothing left here," says my steward.

"Very well. My family will go to Chavaniac. We can therefore leave for others what we would have eaten if we had stayed. That will enable people to eat until the harvest."

We return to La Grange in the autumn and the celebrated Englishman, Jeremy Bentham, visits, as well as Constant and many others.

I am in an opposition group called the *Indépendants*, formed by Laffitte, Casimir Périer and Dupont de l'Eure and including Constant. I stand for election in Paris on September 20 but to my disappointment only receive 2,762 votes out of 7,378. I am finally elected as the representative of the Sarthe in the Chamber of Deputies on October 26, 1818, with 569 votes out of 1,050, despite some shameful intrigues against me. The king is greatly displeased. France and Europe are shaken by my return to the political scene, and I am regarded as a leader of the left.

At the royal *séance* of the Chamber on December 10, the seats are filled with spectators wanting to see me swear the oath. They receive the king quite well, but without enthusiasm. I stand up but refuse to call out ' *Vive le roi!*' along with Manuel, Chateaubriand and others. "[56]

I go to the tribune for the first time on March 22, 1819. I speak against the adoption of a royalist amendment of the election laws. I demand the maintaining of the Charter and the electoral law: "France wants liberty and repose...We must not forget that behind us are abysses in which a single retrograde step could plunge us. The adoption of the resolution of the Chamber of Peers would be, in my opinion, this first retrograde step, and it is with this conviction that I vote to reject it."[57] On May 30 the law is passed to my displeasure.

The royalist newspaper *L'ami de la Royauté*, accuses me of calumnies during the Revolution. The *procureur général*, Bellart, pursues the newspaper; I write to him to say I oppose such action and that I have never asked a journalist to write well of me. When I speak in the chamber the royalists shout insults and abuse.

"You want to have the guillotine again!" a priest accuses me.

"The guillotine is no more the Revolution than the massacre of Saint Bartholomew is the Catholic religion," I reply.

Unrest is growing throughout Europe, particularly in Germany. "It is necessary to put a cordon around France and raise barriers between it and Europe. It is a country which has the plague, says Tsar Alexander."[58]

I am again elected deputy, this time in Seine and Marne on September 14. Abbé Grégoire, a radical republican from 1789, a man who opposed me, is also elected; the royalists denounce him as having killed the king and demand that his election must be cancelled. Everyone is talking of it in Paris.

"If he is excluded, that act alone will re-elect him in twenty départements," I say at the soirée of the duchesse de Broglie.

Grégoire's election is cancelled on December 6; I protest until two in the morning and later visit him.

In 1820, on February 13, Quinquagesima Sunday, the duc de Berri, the king's nephew, is killed by a madman at the Opéra. The duc de Richelieu, supported by the ultraroyalists, replaces Decazes. On March 2, I speak in the Chamber to maintain the Charter. On the eighth, I speak in favor of individual liberty: "On one side was the Revolution with all its moral, political and material advantages; on the other is the counter-revolution with its privileges and its perils. It is for the Chamber; it is for France to choose. Messieurs, it is thirty-three years ago, at the Assembly of Notables in 1787, that I was the first who demanded the abolition of lettres de cachet. Today I vote against their re-establishment."[59] On the twenty-third, I speak concerning the censure of the press; on the twenty-seventh, I speak on the law concerning elections which intends to create a double college and vote for the wealthiest.[60] I declare that such projects of law violate the Charter, which therefore means the dissolution of the mutual guarantees between the nation and the throne.

Monsieur de Serre, ill and dying, accuses me: "When civil war breaks out, the bloodshed is on the heads of those who have provoked it. You know it better than any other. You have more than once learned, death in your soul, and red on the brow, that he who raises the furious ranks is obliged to follow them and almost to lead them."[61] He is referring to October 5 and 6.

I stay silent. People jump to their feet to defend me. I make a sign to them to sit down. The debates rage passionately and angrily.

"Your ideas are abominable!" "He still thinks he is on his white horse!" "Have you been asleep since October 6?" shout the royalists.

"Keep on your guard," my friends tell me, but I take no notice. I remain calm.

Later, at the house of Monsieur Mérilhou, I declare to Voyer d'Argenson and Dunoyer: "This law is a declaration of war to the death against the Revolution. The Royalists want to end the principle of liberty and equality. All we have left against them, and their attacks, is to resist with weapons."[62]

July 4. I enjoy our American dinner and make the toast: "American liberty! May forever be preserved in its original purity the source which must fertilize the two hemispheres!"[63] On the twentieth, I write to President James Monroe: 'The ideas of liberty ferment everywhere...Revolution and counter-revolution are here. Our new generation is enlightened and generous, superior to the ideas of Jacobinism and Bonapartism. It will maintain, I am sure, the rights of a pure liberty. Although we have lost ground this year, our debates have served to advance the public spirit, even if the government and the Chambers are further away from this aim, the nation, I hope, is closer to it than eight months ago.'[64]

In 1821 I enthusiastically support the Charbonnerie, the most important of the various secret societies being formed, whose aim is to overthrow the king and to establish, if not a republic, then a constitutional monarchy. I am a republican by inclination and education but believe that so long as a constitution consecrates the bases of liberty defined in my Declaration of Rights of July 11, 1789, and so long as it represents the general will of the people, then I will not only submit to it, but sacrifice myself.[65] In the present situation in France, I believe I am authorized to appeal to the nation, in conformity with the principles I have followed all my life, to act against the abuse of authority of the king and of the chambers.[66]

I receive a book *Views of Society and Manners in America* by Frances Wright which I read and enjoy. I write and tell her so. She writes back thanking me 'for my kindness and esteem' and hopes to visit me in France to place herself 'in the presence of the generous assertor of the liberties of America, of France and of Mankind.'[67] We meet in Paris in September; she is tall with fair hair and blue eyes which fill with tears when she sees me, and I must admit my own are not dissimilar. We talk until midnight about America and about liberty, and although there are thirty-eight years between us, we have much in common. She was born on my birthday, September 5, in 1795, in Scotland; at twenty-two she sailed to America. I give her tickets to the Chamber and introduce her to my friends.

The Charbonnerie plan to stage revolts at the garrisons of Belfort, Neuf-Brisach, Colmar, Marseille, Toulon, Saumur and La Rochelle. Voyer d'Argenson, Koechlin, Manuel, Dupont de l'Eure, Courcelles and I agree to participate. The first will be at Belfort and we will proclaim a provisional government of Voyer d'Argenson, Koechlin and I. The night of December 29 to 30 will be the uprising; my fellow conspirators will wait until I arrive and give the signal to the garrison.

December 24 is the anniversary of Adrienne's death and I spend the night as always in her room. Next morning, George and I get into the carriage and Bastien climbs onto the box.

"What are you doing, Bastien? We are going to risk our lives. I must warn you that death may wait those who are arrested with us."

"You do not tell me anything new. I know what we are going to do, but I go on my own account, and, in any case, it is also my opinion."[68]

We set off. On January 1, 1822, we are some distance from Lure when Bazard and a son of Courcelles come riding towards us.

"The plot has been found out," they say.

We immediately change direction; we go to the house of Monsieur Martin, the former deputy for the Haute-Saône. We stay for a few days, as though just visiting a friend, then return to La Grange.

General Berton and Lieutenant Colonel Caron are arrested at Saumur; Sergeant Major Borries, Sergeant Major Pommier, Sergeant Goubin and Sergeant Raoulx are arrested at la Rochelle. Mangin, the *procureur général*, declares at Poitiers that Foy, Constant, Manuel, Laffitte and I are suspects. Baudrillet, one of the conspirators, had at first confessed he had gone to Paris, as well as having made two visits to me, before retracting his words.

We protest at a meeting of the Chamber on August 21. We demand an enquiry, but the government has no intention of making the debate public. We attempt to bribe the director at the Conciergerie with more than seventy thousand francs, most of which I contribute. Unfortunately, a priest betrays us, and he is arrested just as the money is being handed over. Other attempts also fail and we continue to be accused. Police spies watch me constantly and Albert Gallatin gives me sanctuary at the American Legation. To my great distress, General Berton, Lieutenant Colonel Caron, and the four sergeants at La Rochelle are found guilty. The four sergeants are guillotined on September 21; Berton and Caron are executed on October 5.

I return to La Grange, watched constantly.

557

"You are a statue looking for a pedestal. It does not matter to you if it is a scaffold," accuses Laffitte.[69]

"I have had a long life. I think I might worthily finish my career on the scaffold, as a sacrifice for liberty," I reply.

In November I am again elected deputy for Meaux with 169 votes to 136.

Fanny and Camilla Wright often stay for long periods at La Grange. They introduce me to their friends, Harriet and Julia Garnett, and Frances Trollope, who also come to stay. In 1823 Fanny starts to write a biography of me. 'I am sure that my beloved Fanny is occupied with me in her study, on her walks, and everywhere,' I write to her when she is not here.[70]

Manuel makes a speech on February 26, about the intervention of the French government in Spain. The right demand he should be expelled; on March 3, I stand by my bench and say loudly: "We agree with everything Monsieur Manuel has said and we make common cause with him."[71]

The Chamber decides on March 3 that Manuel will be excluded from it for the duration of the session. On the fourth, he goes there surrounded by many colleagues.

"I will only leave if made to do so," he says.

Soldiers from the National Guard enter. I stand up.

"What! The National Guard to execute such an order! It would dishonor them!" I exclaim.

"I will not obey the order," Sergeant Mercier who commands them, bravely declares.

The veterans follow; General Foy speaks to the officer commanding them. They appear to hesitate. Then the gendarmes execute the order of the president.

We sign a protest against this new attack on the Charter and on the representation of the country. We do not attend the rest of the sessions which will finish on May 9. Monsieur Quatremère Poissard, colonel of the Fourth Legion, publishes an order of the day in which he disavows the behavior and principles of Mercier and his men. I publish a response to the article in which I relate the first principles of the National Guard.[72] On December 24, the Chamber is dissolved.

I stand for re-election on February 25, 1824. I obtain 152 votes against 184 and so, like most of the other opposition candidates, I am no longer a deputy. I retire to La Grange and again contemplate a visit to America. In January, President James Monroe had written, inviting me to visit the United States.

I decide to go. I choose an American merchant ship, the *Cadmus*, commanded by Captain Allyn, instead of the frigate offered by Congress, as I do not wish to profit by such an offer which would entail considerable costs and inconvenience to my adoptive country. I reread a letter concerning the extreme kindness he and his wife showed Adrienne when she was in prison and with great emotion write to him to say I am not sure which month I will travel but that the summer will not pass before I have the satisfaction of embarking for the United States. [73]

Fanny travels to England. I become ill; I miss her. 'You will be sorry that you have left me without any news of you just when I am so full of anxiety. You promised to write to me before your departure…I have counted on this promise, day before yesterday, yesterday and today…and as they tell me there is no English mail on the first days of the week, my hopes are adjourned indefinitely,' I write. It distresses me to think of having such a long separation from her when I go to America. To my relief, she returns in late May.

"Adopt me as a daughter," she suggests. "It angers me that there is gossip about our relationship. You are the father I have always wanted, and this would help my relationship with your family."

I do not agree with this idea and my family certainly does not.

"Meet her in America," they propose. "And for the sake of propriety she should sail there with her sister Camilla, two weeks after your departure."[74]

Chapter 51

I kiss the tomb of my adoptive father

July 12. George, Auguste Levasseur, Bastien and I arrive at Le Havre. There are many police officers, gendarmes and Swiss soldiers, but no violence. The sun shines, the sea is very calm; at noon on the thirteenth, we embark on the *Cadmus*. The crew parade on the deck; they give three cheers when I pass below the American flag. Three cheers ring out from the crews of the other boats and ships; three cheers resound from the crowds on the waterside despite the police. A breeze catches our sails; the *Cadmus* sets its prow seawards.

Next day, a squall blows. Two of the top-gallant masts break, but Captain Allyn quickly and efficiently organizes the repairs. We continue, the voyage soon taking on its usual tedium. On August 1 we lie becalmed and to our surprise receive a visit from several young English soldiers who row from their transport ship nearby.

A dark smudge of land appears on the fourteenth. My adopted country slowly approaches; a more distinct outline of low coast becomes visible. At dawn the pilot comes on board and guides the Cadmus into the bay towards Staten Island, bright with verdantly green trees and white-washed houses. We see people gathering on the shore, then long narrow boats race towards our ship. They reach us; they shout questions and greetings as cannons boom from Fort Lafayette announcing our arrival. I stand at the rail, tears streaming down my face.

A steamboat comes alongside, the first I have ever seen. Its passengers transfer to our ship; a young man addresses me.

"I am the son of Vice President Tomkins. The city of New York wishes to give you a resplendent reception but today is Sunday and it is not wished to break the Sabbath. Final preparations also need to be made and so they want to postpone it until tomorrow. In the meantime, my father would like to invite you to his house on Staten Island."

A boat takes us to shore. I stand once more on American soil. Vice President Tomkins walks to meet us, wearing an army cap and without a coat, to the obvious surprise of George and Auguste.

"Welcome to America," he announces. I embrace him. He takes us to his house; his wife and daughters receive us in a very kindly fashion whilst out in the bay an increasing number of boats are bringing crowds of people.

On Monday morning, I rise early. I walk on the shore, the sun bright in the east, a beautiful rainbow arching across the sky in the west, an omen of welcome as well as promise.[1] Sometime later, a deputation arrives of several members of the municipal body and the commander of the militia from New York.

"The steamboat, the *Chancellor Livingston*, will take you to the city," they say.

At one o'clock the cannon at Fort Lafayette fire as a signal; we immediately go to the shore where a flotilla of eight steamboats, all resembling floating palaces, are decked out with flags. Bands play, ladies wave white handkerchiefs, men shout a welcome, the steam frigate *Robert Fulton* fires a salute. We embark, two boats taking the *Cadmus* in tow. Deputations welcome me, including generals, officers of the militia, army and navy, a detachment of infantry, and more

560

than two hundred leading citizens comprising many former veterans. My old comrades and I fervently embrace; we set off across the water, the band playing Gretry's ' *Where can you be better than in the bosom of your family?*', boats of every size and shape accompanying us, bedecked with flowers and crammed with people.

"Do you remember when I was an aide to General Scott at the Battle of Monmouth?" asks Colonel Willett.

"Yes, I do," I reply.

The cannons from the forts boom out as well as those from warships. We disembark at the Battery, cheering crowds wave hats and handkerchiefs. I am introduced to people; we enjoy refreshments at Castle Garden. Then I climb into an open barouche, pulled by four white horses, and sit with General Morton. We drive across Bowling Green and along Broadway, bells ringing, bands playing and people cheering in flag-adorned streets, from windows and by triumphal arches, so many flowers cascading down that the horses are trotting through piles of blooms. It is overwhelming. At City Hall I go into a side room for a moment, my tears flowing, in order to compose myself. Then I enter the Hall. The mayor makes a speech; I reply.

We go to the governor's room; people mob me; they shake my hand thousands of times; I kiss babies; I embrace more veterans; my eyes are not dry and nor are those of anyone else. At five, we drive to the City Hotel, magnificently decorated in my honor, a sign over the door inscribed *The Nation's Guest*. It is quiet here; I rest, my heart overflowing with emotion. In the evening, there is a marvelous dinner attended by all civil and military authorities; the following morning I receive the public in City Hall.

On the eighteenth, we cross the East River in a steamboat to Brooklyn where officers at the naval yard and marine arsenal entertain us. I inspect a steam frigate, a truly formidable structure which cannot go in the open sea but is very suitable to defend the coast. We enjoy the view over New York, its harbor and bay, as well as the wharves on East and Hudson Rivers where there is the wonderful sight of a forest of masts flying flags of all nations.

On Friday, the twentieth, I send a servant in the morning for a carriage to take us to Boston. A fine carriage arrives with an officer and an escort.

"How much will it cost?" I ask.

"General Lafayette, you are the Nation's Guest. You can pay nothing while you remain in America. Everything will be abundantly supplied by a grateful people, without money and without price," the officer says.[2]

We set off to Boston, escorted by the Horse Artillery, the Lafayette Guards, the mayor and aldermen in their carriages and many people on horseback. We stop at New Rochelle; I meet more of my former companions in arms.

We take the lower road near the coast and often travel at night, escorted by riders carrying torches, fires burning on hilltops and bells ringing from churches. Every so often, in the day, the sea is visible on our right. We stop briefly at New Haven and visit the College of Yale. At Providence, to my great regret, I cannot visit the sites I knew during the Revolution, but I take some refreshment.

We travel towards the frontier of Massachusetts and reach Dedham at eleven, the village illuminated and people waiting for me.[3] We continue and arrive by torchlight at Roxbury, a village two miles from Boston, where we stay at the house of General Eustis. I embrace him; tears flow; we reminisce into the early hours of the night. Two hours later, at dawn, a military band awakens me; I look out of the window and see infantry drawn up, dressed in the uniform of my former Light Infantry.

"My brave Light Infantry! This was their uniform! What courage! What resignation! How much I loved them!" I exclaim in delight.

A young man is introduced to me, his face sad. He gives me a sword.

"Do you know this sword?" he asks.

"It strongly resembles those I brought from France to arm the under officers of my Light Infantry," I reply.

"It is one of them," he answers. "You gave it to my father who has kept it. It has served gloriously in gaining our independence. He religiously kept it in memory of his general and would have been happy to present it to you himself. He still hoped to do so and this hope softened his last moments on that day he died. He has not bequeathed me wealth but has left me this sword, which will be the most precious of legacies if you sanction his gift."

I look at the sword with interest. "Take it. Guard it carefully in order that it may, in your hands, be used to preserve the rights it has so gloriously contributed to acquire in the hands of your father."[4]

He joyfully takes back the sword and goes out of the room murmuring my name and that of his father.

We set off in an open carriage to Boston, only two miles away, but which takes two hours. Troops on foot and horseback line both sides of the road, in front run sixty boys with two small cannon which they stop to fire every so often.

At noon we reach the city entrance; we halt in the shade of a triumphal arch. The mayor, Mr. Quincy, also in an open carriage, draws up next to our carriage and stands to salute me. I stand and return the gesture.

We travel along the main streets resplendent with triumphal arches, bells ringing, cannons firing, crowds cheering. We reach Beacon Street. "Is Mrs. Hancock still alive?" I ask the mayor.

"Yes, she is not only alive she is in quite good health for a lady of her age," he replies. "You will notice her at her window as we pass."

I look and see her. I stand and wave my hat and hand; I bow. She waves her handkerchief and curtsies; the crowd applauds.

We travel on to State House in front of which lines of boys and girls, each wearing a Lafayette badge, all raise their arms and cry out with joy. A small girl is lifted up to my carriage; she places a wreath of laurel and flowers on my head. "Father," she says, embracing me. I kiss her cheek.

Troops fire. I go inside to the Senate Chamber where the governor, council, judges, revolutionary veterans and many citizens are waiting. Governor Eustis makes a speech; then I start to read the first line of the speech I have already prepared. My emotion, however, is too great. I cannot continue and my words have to be read for me.

Two hours later we are taken to a hotel in Park Street where we find very richly furnished rooms.

"Here you are at home. I hope you will find everything that is necessary. If you find no superfluities remember that you have been received by republicans," we are told.

George and Auguste discover that fine horses and carriages are also provided for us. "What do Boston republicans consider necessary?" they wonder.[5]

In the evening, we dine at the Exchange Coffee House with the governor, his staff, the corporation and other public bodies, French and American flags hanging above the president. Chief Justice Parker gives a toast to Louis XVI. "None of the friends of liberty should be forgotten, even although they might have worn a crown."

August 25. We visit Harvard University. We go into the chapel, the galleries filled with young ladies adorned with flowers and all waving their handkerchiefs. Next day, we return to the university, to a meeting of the Hellenic Society, with an escort of cavalry and a great line of people. On the twenty-seventh, we go to the naval yard at Charlestown, passing over an impressive bridge about a mile long. We inspect the dockyard, then climb Bunker's Hill, the first place the Americans fought the British in a regular battle. We gather at a pyramid commemorating General Warren; I meet veterans.

Doctor Thompson makes a speech. I reply, with great emotion. The crowd acclaims me; artillery roars; battalions of young troops parade.

August 28. We visit the militia training camp at Savin Hill. I am invited to fire at a target floating on the water. I do so; I knock it to pieces prompting much applause from the soldiers and onlookers.

I very much want to see John Adams who lives at the nearby town of Quincy. I do not wish to be surrounded by pomp and so travel in a carriage with two gentlemen from Boston, Auguste and George following in a second carriage.

At two o'clock we arrive at a small and simple house of wood and brick. Inside, the eighty-nine-year-old John Adams is waiting with his family. He is much changed and appears very elderly but smiles to see me and talks in a lively fashion throughout dinner where his family feed him.

On the thirtieth I attend a review of nearly nine thousand troops on Boston Common. In the evening, we go to the theater; to my surprise the curtain rises to reveal a picture of La Grange. I stand, wave my hat and bow my head. I had intended to return to New York, but people are so insistent that I consent to travel at least as far as Portsmouth.

Next day, we leave Boston early. We breakfast at Marblehead, dine at two at Salem, enormous crowds welcoming me, escorted by the militia, bells ringing out and artillery firing. It is late when we arrive at Newbury Port. It is raining and the roads are bad, but the citizens of Salem have ridden next to our carriage for nearly nine miles. Fires burn in the streets, torches flame, bells ring. People shout a welcome and armed troops march to the beat of drums. We stay at Tracey's Inn and to my immense joy I sleep in the same bed where Washington slept, thirty-five years before.

September 1. We reach Portsmouth at noon. Rain is falling, but crowds still gather. One thousand children line the roads, wreaths of flowers covering their heads. Many corps of infantry escort us into town, our procession about two miles long. We stop at Franklin Hall and Governor Morrill makes a speech.

Next day, I promise to return in the spring; at midnight we leave for Boston. We arrive at two o'clock, then set off again to travel through Lexington, Lancaster, Worcester and Tolland. We reach Hartford and enjoy a reception at the State House, the elderly General Wadsworth showing us the epaulettes and scarf I wore at Brandywine, the scarf still stained by my blood. Eight hundred children present me with a gold medal; we proceed to an institute for the deaf and dumb where about sixty wait in silence and when I arrive they place their hands on their hearts. Then I go to review the troops before embarking on the steamboat, the *Oliver Ellsworth*.

We travel down the Connecticut River, bounded by fertile and beautiful banks. We stop at Middletown, only resuming our journey at seven. At dawn, we enter Long Island Sound; at noon, we arrive at New York. I had wanted to enter unnoticed, but our steamboat has so many streamers and flags this is a vain hope. *The Franklin*, a ship of the line, fires a thirteen-gun salute and people come to line the shores and wharves of East River, shouting greetings. We disembark at Fulton Wharf, into an immense crowd, as many as on our first day, and go back to the City Hotel.

September 6. Today is my sixty-seventh birthday and the Cincinnati veterans are holding a dinner in my honor. About four in the afternoon, a military band leads former soldiers along the street to greet me. I am given a decoration of the Order of Cincinnatus which Washington had worn and place it with reverence in my buttonhole. Then we all march together, the crowds quiet and respectful, to Washington Hall, decorated with army trophies and six hundred banners on which are names of heroes of the revolution, and a triumphal arch above my chair. Colonel Varick is the president of the society. We dine; towards the end of the meal a curtain opens to reveal a transparency of Washington and I holding hands before the altar of liberty, receiving a civic wreath from America. General Swarthout reads out the Order of the Day at Yorktown on October 17, 1781, to much applause.

On Tuesday I visit Columbia College; on Wednesday I embark once more on the *Chancellor Livingston* and visit sites in the Bay. We go to the Narrows, where Fort Lafayette is situated, near the point of Long Island. It is unfortunately raining, but I inspect the fort and the troops. Then we dine.

To my intense emotion, Francis Huger, my would-be rescuer when I was in prison, travels from Carolina to see me, now rather stouter than the slight young man I saw at the foot of the statue of the angel. We fall sobbing into each other's arms.

On the ninth, there is a concert of sacred music in Saint Paul's Church. We enter to the sound of the *Marseillaise*, forbidden in France. Later, we watch a marvelous display of the fire department in the Park from a balcony. The ladders of the forty-six companies are stationed in the shape of a pyramid, at the top of which is a tiny house. It is set ablaze; the forty-six engines aim their water hoses at it, quickly extinguishing the fire and producing a spray like silver rain. The sun shines, rainbows appear in glorious colors, to my delight and that of the huge crowd. Also, to my great delight, Fanny and Camilla reach New York safely and I once more hold them in my arms.

September 15. I say farewell to Captain Allyn and the crew and present everyone with gifts. Later that evening, I go to a ball at Castle Garden, a circular fort situated on the mole in front of the Battery. We walk to it over a carpeted bridge, bordered by trees, in whose center is a pyramid about sixty-five feet high, lit with colored lamps and surmounted by a star with my name in the middle. A triumphal arch of flowers is at the entrance with an enormous statue of Washington; the band plays: *See the conquering hero comes*, and there is a large picture of La Grange with the words: *Here is his home*. About six thousand people attend.

At two, we leave and embark on the *James Kent*, accompanied by as many people as the steamboat can carry, most of the gentlemen sleeping on the deck as the ladies have the cabins.

At dawn, I see once more the magnificent banks of the North, the high mountains on either side, sometimes wooded, sometimes bare, bordering the river for almost its whole length. The steamboat chugs against the current at about six miles an hour. We pass Tarrytown. We pass Arnold's house, which stands alone at the foot of the hill.

At West Point I go in a boat to the shore. Cannon roar, echoing across the river and the mountains. Major Thayer greets me, as well as Generals Brown and Scott and their staff. I step into an open carriage with Mrs. Hamilton, and we set off, followed by a long line of ladies who had come with her, as well as many other people. We slowly drive up the road to the military academy, two cannon incessantly firing on a rock far above, the ruins of Fort Putnam visible on a high peak.

I review the cadets on the plain; then they maneuver. At six, we return to the shore and embark again on the *James Kent*. At seven we arrive at Newburgh. I cannot stay long, but I dine and greet many of the citizens in a hall. We set off again in the darkness and by sunrise we are near to Poughkeepsie where the wharves and shores are crowded with people.

We continue along the river and disembark at four at Clermont. We stay the night at the residence of Mr. Robert Livingston, then resume our travel, the beautiful, brown Catskill Mountain soon coming into view, some miles from the river. We stop at Hudson, but despite all the festive preparations I can only spend a short time before re-embarking. At Overslaugh our steamboat draws too much water; we abandon it for a barouche, escorted by dragoons, and reach the village of Greenbush.

We finally arrive at Albany at night. We cross the river on a ferry; a band leads the way; we proceed slowly through the streets, the houses all illuminated and huge wood fires blazing. An Arch of Triumph stands at the entrance to the street leading to the Capitol, an enormous live eagle perching on it which flaps its wings as I pass. We enter the Senate Chamber. The mayor gives a speech.

I reply. "It is not a half century since the town, then ancient, it is true, but still very small, served me for headquarters upon the frontier of a vast wilderness. I received here, as commandant of the northern departments, the renunciation of the royal power and the acknowledgement of the more legitimate sovereignty of the people of the United States. Today I find Albany a rich and powerful city, the central seat of government of the state of New York and the surrounding wilds have changed into fertile and well cultivated plains."

In the evening, there is a celebration ball; at midnight we finally go to bed.

We leave Albany, the huge bonfires flaming again, and embark once more on the *James Kent* to go back down the river. At dawn, on Monday, we arrive at New York. On the twenty-second, we cross the North River to Jersey, the crowds at New York silent and sad at our departure, whilst in Jersey they welcome us with joy and excitement. Mr. Williamson, the governor, makes a speech of welcome and gives a detachment of militia to us as an escort as we travel across the state. Everywhere I am fêted; there are speeches; the firing of artillery; the ringing of bells. The land appears very fertile, there are numerous streams and beautiful farms in this region known as the Garden of the United States. We pass through Bergen, Newark, Elizabeth town, Rahway, New Brunswick, Princeton and Trenton. On the twenty-sixth, I visit Joseph Bonaparte at Bordenton. We dine together and talk about the past.

September 27. Monday. We cross the Delaware into Pennsylvania over a bridge about nine hundred feet long and entirely roofed. There is a sidewalk for people on foot, and two roads, one for carriages coming and the other for going. We go to Morrisville, then to Bristol.

On a plain near Philadelphia, officers and about six thousand militia wait to welcome me. Cannon roar and I review the troops under General Cadwallader. Then I enter the fine streets of the city in a barouche drawn by six horses, preceded by a detachment of cavalry, followed by carriages containing the mayor, the city council and judges, four large open carriages resembling tents, each carrying forty veterans,[6] and a column of infantry at the rear. Spectators acclaim me from stages on each side of the street; we reach the State House and go into the Hall of Independence, where I had waited at the door in 1777. I am taken to the statue of Washington and the mayor gives a speech.

I reply with great emotion to be speaking in the room where independence was declared.[7] For several hours I greet people and children by the hand, my tears often flowing. I stay eight days and find the city much larger than when I last saw it. It now extends from the right bank of the Delaware to the left bank of the Schuylkill, about two miles long by one mile wide. Buildings occupy about two thirds of this area; new houses are being constructed and it is probable that in a few years there will only be buildings between the city and the Schuylkill.[8]

I go to many events including a masonic dinner, a civic ball and a party at the house of General Cadwallader. I tour the arsenal and naval yard and also visit an immense prison which is being constructed, where each prisoner can be kept in solitary confinement and be constantly watched.

I have to speak out. I cannot remain silent. "Solitary confinement is a punishment which needs to be experienced to be appreciated and the virtuous and enlightened Malesherbes who during his administration under the monarchical government of France had ameliorated the conditions of prisoners of state, regarded solitary confinement as leading to madness. During my five years of captivity I passed an entire year in solitary confinement, and another part of the time just seeing someone for only a single hour, but I did not find it reformed me. I was imprisoned for wanting to make the people revolt against despotism and aristocracy and I passed my solitude thinking about it and left prison without changing my views at all." [9]

October 1. I write to Jefferson and say that I hope to join him after the celebration of the anniversary of Yorktown. I tell him that two filial friends, Miss Wright and her sister Camilla, are now at Philadelphia on their way to Washington.

Miss Wright is the author of *A Few Days in Athens*...She is very Happy in your Approbation; for, You and I are the two Men in the World the esteem of whom she values the Most. I wish Much, My dear friend, to present these two adopted daughters of Mine to Mrs. Randolph and to You; they being orphans from their Youth and preferring American principles to British Aristocracy, Having an independent, tho not Very large fortune, Have passed the three last Years in Most Intimate Connection with My Children and Myself and Have Readily Yielded to our joint Entreaties to Make a Second Visit to the U.S. [10]

October 5. We say farewell to Philadelphia; at eight in the evening, we embark on the Delaware to go down to Chester. We arrive at eleven o'clock at night, the whole town illuminated. We go to the very same hall in which my wound from Brandywine was dressed, the speaker mentioning it. An excellent supper follows, before spending the night at the house of Colonel Anderson, my former comrade.

Next morning, we continue. At the border of Delaware, to my immense pleasure, a committee meets us, at the head of which is Captain McLane, now eighty, on horseback, proudly wearing his revolutionary hat and feathers.

We dine at Wilmington; then proceed to Frenchtown where we embark on the steamboat, the *United States*. The night is stormy as we cross the Chesapeake; at nine o'clock in the morning we enter the river Palapsco where Baltimore is situated; the sun comes out, revealing the spires of the city, the forest of masts in the harbor and the bastions of Fort McHenry.[11] Four steamboats bedecked with flags and crammed with people shouting three cheers, come towards us, and follow as we advance shorewards. We transfer into small boats and are quickly rowed to the wharf of Fort McHenry. I enter the fort, whose raised flag is still marked by a British shell, to the roar of cannon and shouts of welcome from huge crowds on the peninsula between the city and the fort.

Magistrates, veterans and infantry stand in a line. They open their ranks; to my astonishment, I see Washington's tent. Emotion overcomes me. George Washington Custis meets us; George and he embrace and sob silently, remembering their two years spent together at Mount Vernon.

Governor Stevens makes a speech; I reply. We go into the tent where Colonel Howard, who fought with me, and who later also fought in the defense of Baltimore against the British in 1814, delivers an address; then my former comrades rush towards me. I recognize everyone; we embrace and talk for a long time.

I leave the fort in an open carriage, followed by militia on foot and on horseback drawn up on the plain. At the entrance to the city is a triumphal arch adorned by twenty-four young ladies dressed in white with myrtle crowns and carrying lances inscribed with the names of the states. They place garlands round me and crown me with laurels.[12] Cannon roar. The crowds shout and I drive along the streets to City Hall where the mayor greets me with a speech in the main hall.

The city is very changed from how it was forty-five years ago when it was only a small collection of badly built houses, although on one side is still the river and in the distance is the same dark forest. Its streets resemble those of Philadelphia, but because it is on more hilly ground it has a more interesting aspect and different parts of it can be seen from various elevated places.[13] We stay five days. I meet deputations; I visit the waterworks and wonder if a similar method might be used at La Grange. I attend a magnificent ball, brilliantly lit by gas, where the band plays *Lafayette's March*.

"If only my granddaughters could be here to enjoy it," I say.

October 17. We leave Baltimore in the evening. The sun soon disappears making it difficult to travel. I wish to enter Washington in day-light and we decide to stay the night somewhere. Unfortunately, the first inn we reach is named *Waterloo* so we continue more miles in the dark to another, my escort now very tired, having been in the saddle all day.

We enter Washington but travel for half an hour without meeting a single inhabitant, the plan of the city being so large it will perhaps be a century before it is finished.[14] Finally, we reach the buildings which are situated between the house of the president and the Capitol. Cannon fire; crowds swarm about us.

I enter the Capitol where the mayor addresses me. We go to the president's mansion, which is only one story tall and built of white stone. A servant opens the door, and we are taken into a large oval room where President James Monroe is seated at the far end on a chair no different from those of anyone else, and grouped round him in a semi-circle are senators and public officers, all dressed, like himself, in blue, without any decorations. Everyone stands; James Monroe comes to meet me. He shakes my hand and that of George and Auguste and presents us to everyone.

We leave Washington. We cross the Potomac by a wooden bridge nearly a mile in length and are met by a corps of troops commanded by General Jones. Cheering and artillery fire greet us and we enter Alexandria. We dine with magistrates and citizens; just as the meal commences, Mr Calhoun, the Secretary of State, announces: "King Louis XVIII has died."

From Alexandria I travel to Mount Vernon in the steamboat, *Petersburg*, with Generals Macoub and Jones, the Secretary of War, Mr. Calhoun, and many officers and citizens. Two hours later, the guns of Fort Washington announce we are approaching our destination. The military band on the steamboat plays a somber melody and we go on deck. Before us is Mount Vernon.[15] We all kneel. Then boats convey us to shore. I step into a carriage whilst the others walk; it takes me to the house, my emotions overflowing.

I stay just a short time, leaving our companions to wait, whilst Mr. Lewis, the family of the judge, and George Washington Custis, take George, Auguste and I down the hill to the river.

Dark cypress trees surround the unremarkable brick vault, its roof covered with earth. The wooden door has no inscription, but wreaths are fastened to it, some withered, some green. The door is opened. I walk alone into the vault. My tears flowing, I kiss the tomb of my adoptive father; I kiss the tomb of his venerable wife. After a few minutes, I go outside in a state of inexpressible emotion, the funeral salvos of artillery echoing through the sacred hills of Mount

Vernon. I take George and Auguste into the vault. I indicate the coffin. We kneel and kiss it. We stand. Sobbing, we embrace each other.

We leave the gloom of the sepulcher and go into the bright light outside where Washington's nephews stand in great solemnity. George Washington Curtis gives me a gold ring containing some of Washington's hair.[16]

"You are the only surviving general of the Army of Independence. At this solemn and touching moment when you come to bow with respect before the remains of Washington, one of the children of Mount Vernon offers you the ring which encloses the hair of he you have loved. The ring has always been the emblem of the union of hearts...In time to come may it recall to your descendants the virtues of their illustrious ancestor, who receive it not in a palace, but at the tomb of Washington."

"The sentiments which oppress my heart deprive me of the means to be able to reply. I can only thank you, my dear Curtis, for your precious gift, and render a silent homage at the tomb of the greatest and best of men."

We return in sadness to the house.

"Everything is exactly the same as when I saw it twenty-eight years ago," says George.

He shows us the key of the Bastille which I had sent Washington.

"Yes, I have not changed anything out of respect," replies Judge Washington.

We only stay a short time, then we go silently down the path to the Potomac River, each carrying a branch of cypress cut from over Washington's tomb. We embark on the steamboat; we remain quiet as Mount Vernon disappears into the distance. The evening darkens; on the deck I talk of my beloved, adoptive father whilst the others listen. We meet the steamboat, *Potomac*, which has on board a volunteer company from Fredericksburg, as well as many passengers, and we continue together down the river.

Next day at noon, we reach the mouth of the York River. We board five small boats and go upriver to Yorktown. I see again the small town where I trapped Cornwallis. Many boats gather near the waterside and crowds of ladies congregate on the upper banks. We disembark; the Yorktown committee greets us, accompanied by the governor of Virginia and council, and by John Marshall, the chief justice of the United States, as well as many army officers.[17]

I make a speech in reply. Then we go to my residence which was where Cornwallis lived. There are still houses in ruins, fire-blackened or scarred by bullets. The ground is covered with parts of weapons, broken shells and abandoned gun carriages. Tents are haphazardly placed and units of soldiers positioned at different locations. Even my lodgings contribute to the illusion of war. I have a simple bed; for other people there are just mattresses, or piles of straw, in ruined houses. During the night sixty officers from a volunteer company guard our headquarters.

October 19. At dawn, cannons fire from the plain, calling the troops to arms. I go with the committee to Washington's tent, which has come with us, and I receive the various corps of officers from the regiments.

Two veterans shake my hand and faint. Colonel Lewis, dressed in the uniform of a Virginian militiaman, addresses me on behalf of Virginia. Applause breaks out. I take his hand. "Please express my gratitude to the Virginia militia, who performed so well during the war."

At eleven o'clock the troops march to the headquarters. They form two columns, then conduct me to a triumphal arch positioned at the exact place of the redoubt taken by my men. I march through a double row of elegantly dressed ladies; the different corps assemble; the crowd falls silent and General Taylor makes a speech. I am decorated with a wreath which I take off and give to Colonel Fish.

"Take it. This wreath also belongs to you. Preserve it as a deposit for which we must account to our comrades,"[18] I say, with great emotion. I turn to General Taylor. "I am happy to receive such honorable evidence of friendship from my former companions in arms, in the place where the American and French armies were so gloriously united in a holy alliance in favor of American independence and the sovereignty of the people. I am also happy to be received on the very place where my dear comrades of the light infantry acquired one of their most honorable rights to the love and esteem of their fellow citizens. I pay a tribute of gratitude to the officers who directed the attack on the redoubt. It is only in their name, in the name of the light infantry, and only together with them, that I accept this wreath."

The troops march past. Then we return to Yorktown and celebrate for the rest of the day. Servants discover candles in the cellar of Cornwallis's former house. They are black after forty-three years but are arranged in a circle and lit. They burn well, the soldiers and ladies dancing until the flames die.

We believe several officers from a French squadron moored in Hampton Roads attend the festivities in civilian clothes, but they do not celebrate with us even although it would be regarded as a family commemoration by both the nations, and we can only assume they are acting on the commands of a higher authority.[19]

October 20. In the morning, we travel to nearby Williamsburg, situated on the plain between the James and York rivers. Two creeks before the town narrow the road and I recall placing an excellent post there which the British unsuccessfully attacked when trying to escape from their position. There are more houses now; about fourteen or fifteen thousand people live here including many of my former friends with whom I celebrate.

Next day, we go to the tiny hamlet of Jamestown where we embark and travel down the river; five hours later, we reach the Hampton Roads, the setting sun shining onto the fort of old Point Comfort, making it appear to float on the sea; further away, the high-sided ships of the French squadron are visible.

We approach Norfolk, which also seems, like the fort, to be floating on the sea until we come close. We disembark on flat marshy ground at the mouth of the Elizabeth River and travel through the town's narrow, winding streets. We see many black slaves owned by French families who have left Saint Domingo and who are hiring them to others. A very sad sight.[20]

Next morning, we cross to the small town of Portsmouth on the opposite bank, which the traitor, Arnold, occupied with his troops. We visit the good naval yard and see a sixty-four-gun ship, the *North Carolina*, which has only been recently launched.

We return to Norfolk to a welcome from the Freemasons who make George, Auguste and I honorary members. Festivities continue; there is a ball at which I yet again do not see any officers from the French squadron, although I suspect some are present in civilian clothes. At eleven o'clock in the evening we board the steamboat in heavy rain to travel up the James to Richmond, where I posted my troops on Shockoe Hill on April 29, 1781, arriving before the British and preventing them entering the town.

Next morning, we land at Osborne. Forty veterans are waiting, some of whom I remember by name, emotion welling up in me. Next day, the rain stops; I go to the State House where Chief Justice Marshall welcomes me. Many celebrations ensue and although I had intended to travel on to Monticello, I accept the invitation of the citizens of Petersburg to go there.

We travel along the sandy road; we near the town and I see again the old wooden church which was my headquarters when I was trying to prevent the forces of Cornwallis joining those of Phillips. I also recognize the place from where my troops fired cannon to attempt to dislodge the British whose march had been too rapid for me to prevent it. Much of Petersburg had caught fire from the cannon balls, but the townspeople seem delighted to see me.

"Look how much better Petersburg is today than it was then. At that time, we had only miserable wooden houses to receive you in and now we have large, well-built brick houses where we can offer you all the comforts of life."

Twenty-four hours later, we return to Richmond; we rest for two days. To my great sadness, I learn from the latest packet boat of the death of my wonderful friend, the princesse d'Hénin, whom I have known for forty-five years.[21] People are celebrating around me and I attempt to carry on, my heart heavy.

Then we set out for Monticello, about eighty miles away, Richmond volunteer cavalry and a deputation accompanying us. We sleep the night at Milton, the local plantation owners fêting us. Next morning, Auguste is ill.

"I will stay here with him whilst you continue," says George.

My carriage travels the winding road up to Monticello, at the summit of a mountain, far above a fertile valley. We approach the house of Thomas Jefferson, my emotion welling up.

We rush to greet each other. He is frail and elderly but still has the same tall, spare, erect frame as thirty-five years ago. We embrace; we sob; we talk; we talk and we talk. So many years to recount, so much to discuss.

Jefferson has designed the house which reflects his cultured and educated mind and is in the shape of an irregular octagon with porticoes at the east and west, peristyles at the north and south and a Doric façade surmounted by balustrades in Ionic, Doric, Corinthian and Attic styles. In the large salon are many paintings, including the *Holy Family* by Raphael, the *Flagellation of Christ* by Rubens and the *Crucifixion* by Guido; in the dining room are busts of Washington, Franklin, Paul Jones and myself; at the entrance is a collection of indigenous weapons, ornaments, clothes and other tribal objects and there is a good library.[22]

His land extends for several thousand acres, mostly wooded, but with about twelve or fourteen thousand acres of tobacco and grain. He has slaves who have a gaiety not generally seen elsewhere. They do not fear being torn from their families and their work is light. They are still, however, slaves.

Auguste and George soon rejoin me, and, to my delight, so do Fanny and Camilla, as Jefferson had written back to me that he and Mrs. Randolph would be delighted to see them. In the afternoons, George and I drive with Jefferson, animatedly discussing.

"Slaves should be free. No man should rightly hold ownership in his brother man. I gave my best services to and spent my money freely on behalf of the Americans becauseI felt they were fighting for a great and noble principle- the freedom of mankind. Now, instead of being free, some are held in bondage," I say.

"The time will come when slaves will be free," replies Jefferson.

"It would be beneficial to both slaves and owners if they were educated," I say.

"I am in favor of teaching them to read print but to teach them to write would mean that they could forge papers and then they could no longer be kept in subjugation," he replies.[23]

Camilla has unfortunately caught a cold, so she and Fanny remain at Monticello when we travel to Montpelier where James Madison lives. He is now seventy-four but still strong and healthy. He appears severe, but speaks in a very lively manner, as does his wife. I meet plantation owners;

I never hesitate to defend the right which all men have to liberty and we discuss slavery very frankly. They condemn it which heartens me.

At Charlotteville we enjoy a public dinner which includes both Madison and Jefferson.

"We held the nail, but it is he who drove it in,"[24] declares Jefferson to the toast. Everyone cries.

November 19. We travel to Fredericksburg and stop at Orange Court House. I walk through two lines of people and am greeted by Colonel Barbour, the governor of Virginia. Many veterans are here; we talk and reminisce; after the dinner I say farewell to Madison. We set off; we reach a triumphal arch where a narrow path leads from the road into thick woods and see young girls strewing flowers along it.[25]

"This is the road where you made a forced march from the banks of the Rapidan to Mechunk Creek surprising Cornwallis," I am told.

"It was here that by using this path I effected a movement which if we had been unsuccessful would have been terrible as the men abandoned their harvests to join my little army. They were separated from their families and endured every kind of fatigue and remained with the army far beyond the time we had any right to ask of them," I reply.

November 20. It is long past sunset as we drive into Fredericksburg which is illuminated with lights. We attend a supper and a ball. Next day, there is a service at the Episcopal Church. On Monday evening we set out for Washington. At the Strafford County line, militia wait and escort us to the Potomac where we embark on a boat.

In Washington, I receive many invitations from all the southern and western states. Their congressmen tell me of the preparations their fellow citizens are making to receive me. I feel it would be difficult, if not impossible, to refuse. I say I will travel again at the end of the winter, part of which I will spend in Washington. I wish to be in Boston on June 17, as I have promised to be at the celebration of the anniversary of Bunker Hill. We will, therefore, travel more than twelve thousand leagues in four months.

"Please have my large carriage," Mrs. Eliza Curtis insists.

"I accept," I reply. We buy good saddlehorses and reduce our baggage as much as possible and on February 23, at nine in the evening, we descend the Potomac and go towards Norfolk.

We visit Lafayetteville on the bank of Cape Fear River, the rain pouring down.

"You are here in your own town, in your own house, surrounded by your children. Dispose of all- everything is yours," says the chairman of the welcoming committee.

We travel through pine forests, across sand plains and some cultivated land of rice and indigo. Twenty-four hours after leaving Lafayetteville, in the middle of a pine forest we meet the deputation of South Carolina. We continue through sands and pines towards Camden, the sun hot even though it is March; we approach the small town and find the trees flowering.

It is here that de Kalb died. I lay the corner stone of a monument to him over his remains. Artillery fire. My hand rests on the stone, following as it slowly descends. The crowd stand in silence; I make a speech extolling the virtues and bravery of my friend-in-arms with whom I first came across the sea from France.

We go to Columbia, the state capital, then travel to Charleston which I last saw in 1776. The pine forests disappear; we enter the beautiful entrance to the town, magnolias rising among clusters of saplings, the air perfumed with scent from orange, peach and almond trees. Colonel Francis Huger joins me in my carriage and I once again welcome my would-be liberator with the same emotion I had felt on seeing him in New York.

We spend three days here in this delightful city, which honors me with the present of a miniature of Colonel Huger, as well as a map of South Carolina in a silver case. On March 17, we leave by sea to travel to Savannah, situated on the right bank of the Savannah River about seventeen miles from its mouth. Here I lay another corner stone, this time to the memory of General Greene, and speak with emotion of my beloved comrade.[26] We go to Chippeway Place where I lay the corner stone of a monument to Pulaski.

We sail to Augusta; from there we travel along bad roads to Milledgeville, then towards the state of Alabama, through many miles of land inhabited by the Creek nation. My carriage jolts and shudders over a very rough road, Auguste and George following on horseback. In the evening we arrive at the Native American Agency in the middle of ancient forests, where the chiefs and the commissioners of the United States last year drew up a treaty which gives a large amount of money to the Native Americans when they go to live on the right bank of the Mississippi. There seems to be considerable anger about this and they are accusing their chiefs of betrayal.

On the banks of the Chatalouche we meet with the first gathering of Native Americans in my honor. They carry my small carriage and insist that I sit in it so as not to tread on wet ground. From Uchee Creek we travel to the village of Big Warrior, about one day distant. We stay one night and continue to Line Creek at the boundary of the Native American lands.

April 3. We arrive at Montgomery; at two in the morning, we embark on the steamboat *Anderson.* A band accompanies us, playing music as we travel past the often high, wooded shores during the next three days.[27] Below Claiborne, the banks of the Alabama are much lower; we pass the mouth of the Tombigee and see low, marshy meadows. On the seventh, we reach Mobile, situated on a plain more than twenty feet above the level of the water. Fort Condé fires an artillery salute; at the wharf, an immense crowd welcomes us. A dinner, ball, and a masonic celebration follow, then we board the Natchez to travel to New Orleans.

Night falls. A storm howls, the craft rocks violently. I am not the only person to fall seasick and we all lie down, the wind screaming, the waves pounding the boat, sweeping into our cabin through the portholes, drenching our beds. At dawn, we reach the Belize River where thousands of tree trunks carried down from the north, pile on the low islands at its mouth; powerful waves crash against those of the sea and there are enormous alligators. On the shore, cypresses are the only vegetation, dark strands hanging from them of the parasitic plant, tillandsia, which local people call Spanish Beard. At midnight we hear the firing of one hundred guns announcing our imminent arrival.

" *Vive la liberté!*" " *Vive l'ami de l'Amérique!*" " *Vive Lafayette!*" awakens us in the morning. We hasten on deck and see men in French uniforms on the shore. Artillery roars. Rain pours down. I disembark onto the levée, the artillery thundering again. We proceed to an immense arch where Mr. Roffignac, the mayor, receives me. We go to the City Hall; I review the troops from a balcony. Grenadiers, chasseurs, Lafayette Guards, and many others, parade; at the rear of the riflemen march a single line of one hundred Choctaws, the allies of the Americans in the Seminole War. I would have liked to visit the battlefield of the 8 January, when General Jackson defeated a British army of fifteen thousand, four times the size of his own force, but it is not possible.

We leave New Orleans; we go to Baton Rouge. We embark again on the *Natchez* and travel to its namesake, about one hundred and thirty-seven miles away. From Natchez, we go up-river to Saint Louis; the banks of the Mississippi are now flat and forested, there are very few houses, and everywhere swarm clouds of mosquitos.

At St. Louis, to my great pleasure, I meet Mr. Hamilton, the son of Alexander Hamilton, as well as Bellisime, a French sergeant from Rochambeau's army. From St. Louis we travel to Nashville; after a ball we go on board the *Artizan* to continue our journey. We rapidly descend the Cumberland and on May 7 again enter the Ohio.[28] On the eighth, we arrive opposite Shawneetown. We dine there, then set off again, still accompanied by deputations from Missouri, Tennessee and Kentucky, most of whom sleep in the great cabin, whilst I share a cabin with George, Auguste and Mr. de Syon.

At twelve o'clock that night the steamboat suddenly jolts and stops. Auguste goes to find out what has happened and Bastien helps me dress.

"What news?" I ask when he returns.

"We shall go to the bottom, General, if we cannot extricate ourselves, and we have not a moment to spare," he replies.[29]

"You go on," I tell George.

"What! Do you think that in such circumstances I shall leave you for a moment," he declares.

The boat is rolling violently; there is a great noise above us. We go to the deck where it is very dark; the boat keels over to starboard; it is difficult to stay on our feet.

"Lafayette! Lafayette!" the captain shouts from a small boat at the side.

"General Lafayette is here," calls Auguste.

Everyone falls silent. A path opens in front of me; they all refuse to move until I am in the boat. I therefore reluctantly agree.

The small boat rocks backwards and forwards. Auguste jumps into it. Two men hold me under my shoulders and heave me over the side. Auguste catches me but our combined weight nearly capsizes the craft. Auguste falls, but Mr. Thibeaudot, the former president of the Louisiana Senate, manages to save us.

The boat rapidly traverses the water to the shore in less than three minutes. We clamber out and look at each other. There are nine of us, the captain, two sailors, Mr. Thibeaudot, Dr. Shelly, a young child, Auguste and I. George is not here.

"George! George!" I call in great fear, my usual calm in the face of danger completely deserting me.

From the darkness of the river come the cries of people still on the boat and the terrible sound of hissing steam from the engine.

George does not reply. I rush up and down the bank. "George!" "George!" I shout frantically.

Auguste goes in the small boat with the captain to rescue the others. They quickly return with many people from the sinking steamboat; others are swimming towards the bank where a fire is now blazing. Suddenly I see George who had made sure everyone had left the steamboat before leaving it himself.

"Mr. George Lafayette must often have been shipwrecked for he has behaved tonight as if he was accustomed to such adventures," says the captain.[30]

More fires are lit for people to dry themselves and I lie down on a mattress which is only partly wet. Heavy rain is falling, then ceases. In the early morning, the captain with Governor Carroll of Tennessee, and a young Virginian, Mr. Crawford, row out many times to the steamboat to retrieve what they can; the shore is strewn with possessions; the fires burn brightly and a salvaged case of claret, keg of whisky, biscuits and a leg of smoked venison considerably cheer people's spirits. The sky looks threatening, and I am persuaded to go to a house nearby with Bastien and Mr. Thibeaudot. We set off but then Auguste and George arrive to tell me that two more steamboats have arrived.

We return; we embark on the *Paragon*, a large and attractive vessel, and set off down the river. We reach Louisville; from there we travel to Lexington and Frankfort. On May 19, at ten in the morning, we arrive on the left bank of the Ohio and see opposite us the beautiful city of Cincinnati, situated in an amphitheater, the river at its foot.[31] On the twenty-second, we set off on board the *Herald*. On the twenty-fourth, we arrive at Wheeling in Virginia, a distance of more than three hundred miles. From here we enter Pennsylvania. At Uniontown, Mr. Gallatin, my old friend, welcomes me and I go to stay with him at New Geneva. Then he takes us back to Uniontown and we set off to Elizabethtown, a small town on the banks of the Monongahela. We travel in a rowing boat to Braddock's Field where the British were defeated in July 1777, by the French and Native Americans. The young Washington was here as an aide-de-camp to Braddock, who unfortunately took no notice of his advice. From there we travel to Pittsburg where I meet veterans from the Revolutionary Army.

"Do you remember the young soldier who offered to carry you in a litter when you were wounded at Brandywine?" asks an elderly man.

I look at him carefully, then throw myself into his arms. "No, I have not forgotten Wilson and it is a great happiness to be able to embrace him today."[32]

In Pittsburg I meet Fanny again. She tells me of her plan to buy a cooperative farm where slaves would learn skills and become free. She will therefore not return to France with me. I pass a night without sleep; her vision of a practical way to pursue the emancipation of slaves is one in which I completely concur and I will help her as much as I can by contacting people who might support her, and by giving copies of her pamphlet *A Plan for the Gradual Abolition of Slavery in the United States without danger or loss to the Citizens of the South*, to important people in political life, but I will lose my beloved Fanny. I will be in France and she will be in the United States.

From Pittsburg we travel by Franklin, Meadville, Waterford and Erie. We reach Lake Erie. Then to Buffalo, from where we go to Manchester, a small village on the right bank of Niagara. We visit the famous Falls which thunder majestically, creating a most sublime spectacle; then to Fort Niagara, followed by various villages, before rejoining the canal at Syracuse. On June 12, we arrive at Albany. We still have one hundred and fifty miles to travel to reach Boston, but the roads will be good. Nevertheless, we only stop for the shortest time possible. On the fifteenth we reach our destination, having travelled nearly five thousand miles in less than four months.

June 17. The sun shines. At ten-thirty, I am part of an enormous procession of about seven thousand people which sets off from the Capitol. Two hundred revolutionary soldiers are at the head; then forty veterans of Bunker's Hill; I am next, in a calash drawn by six white horses, followed by a file of carriages containing people of distinction.[33] Bands play. Bells ring out.

The pyramid has gone; in its place I help the Grand Master of the Grand Lodge of Massachusetts, Mr. Webster and the principal architect, lay the first stone for the monument in the manner prescribed by Masonic ritual. Next, we go to an amphitheater on the north-east side of the hill; speeches are made from a platform and then we dine.

I rise to my feet; I thank the association for erecting the monument and finish by saying "Bunker's Hill and that holy resistance to oppression which has already disenthralled the American hemisphere. The anniversary toast at the jubilee of the next half century will be to Europe freed."[34]

On the twenty-second, we leave Boston; we travel to Portland, Burlington, Whitehall, Troy and Albany. There we board a steamboat to descend the river to New York.

July 4 is the anniversary of the Declaration of Independence. The sun shines radiantly. People throng the streets. I lay the corner stone of a building for a mechanics' library at Brooklyn; after church I review the militia and firemen in the Park before going to the City Hall where the Senate receives me. Later, we dine and then I visit the Park Theater. On the fourteenth, we leave the city watched by silent crowds. We are filled with sadness.

We travel to Philadelphia where we stay a week. On the twenty-sixth, we go to the Brandywine. We arrive at about noon; at Chads' Ford I learn that Gideon Gilpin, in whose house I stayed before the battle, is confined to bed. I visit him and our tears flow. Then I tour the field of battle and recognize many places.

"Long Live Lafayette!" people cry. My emotion is profound. I speak of the courage of Washington and the soldiers on that day.

We stay two days at Baltimore and then travel to Washington. John Quincy Adams is now president, and he invites me to stay at the president's house. I visit my old friend, James Monroe, the former president.

On September 7 I dine with President Adams who makes an eloquent speech. "To February 22 and September 6, the birth dates of Washington and Lafayette," he toasts.

"To July 4, the birth date of liberty in both hemispheres," I reply with great emotion.[35] I throw myself into the arms of Adams, whose tears flow with mine.

Twenty-four guns announce my departure, and we go to board the steamboat *Mount Vernon*, all the militia of Alexandria, Georgetown and Washington drawn up on the plain above the river.[36]

At the entrance to the Potomac, we board the new frigate, the *Brandywine*, named after a stream, not a river, a defeat instead of a victory, solely to recall my first battle and wound. Next day, we enter the Chesapeake. We depart in the middle of a brilliant rainbow, one foot of the arch seeming to rest on the Maryland coast, the other on that of Virginia.[37]

Chapter 52

Revolution again

October 3. The pale cliffs near Le Havre steadily approach after only twenty-four days. Louis XVIII was reigning when I left. Now the comte d'Artois is King Charles X. The *Brandywine* fires a salute. The fort fires back.

"Lower the American flag at the stern," says First Lieutenant Gregory. "Take it, General. We cannot give it to more glorious hands. Let it forever represent your alliance with the American people."

I step again onto French soil to the acclaim of thousands waiting on the quayside. On the fifth I set off by road to Rouen; George goes along the Seine and will meet me there on the seventh.

I dine in the ancient Norman city with Monsieur Cabanon, a former liberal colleague from the Chamber. Crowds begin to gather outside the hôtel, pressing against the windows. I go on to the balcony to speak. Suddenly, detachments of the Royal Guards and the gendarmerie gallop down the street, slashing with sabers at men, women and children, who run, shrieking with fear, blood streaming from their faces and bodies. Many are arrested. Such is my welcome home.

On the ninth, we finally reach La Grange; we drive along the wide, curved avenue, bordered with apple trees; we turn left, pass the farm and go through the copse of chestnut trees towards the tall conifers shading the approach to the stone bridge, guarded by the two towers. The carriage halts. I descend, my family, friends and local people crowding around me. I embrace and kiss everyone and they escort me into the château. In the evening, they take me by the light of illuminations to a triumphal arch they have erected, bearing the inscription *The People's Friend*.

Next day, young girls come with flowers and sing; the company of the National Guard of Court-Palais arrives, as well as a deputation from Rosay.

On Sunday, at five o'clock in the evening, the inhabitants of Rosay and its neighborhood hold a fête for me attended by four thousand people. Young girls sing and present me with flowers. Monsieur Vigné makes a speech; I reply, then am escorted to a tent on the meadow; lanterns illuminate the evening; fireworks cascade in fiery brilliance across the dark sky; everyone dances until dawn. "Long live the people's friend!" echoes until the sun rises.[1]

I know that people were attacked at Rouen but still feel able to write to President Adams: 'France is in a peaceful state, and still less inclined to unrest than she was at the time of my departure, but while the government pursues its anti-revolutionary march, a liberal opinion is gaining ground.'[2]

My friends believe my trip to America will be recognized as one of the great events of our century and they organize a poetry competition to recount it. Béranger writes a song *Immortal glory to the man of two worlds*. I feel very honored. I am also honored by the many presents I have received and order a pavilion built for the canoe given to me by the Whitehallers of New York after their mockfight with a boat from the English frigate, the *Hussar*. [3]

"Can you prepare some medical instruments for Monticello?" I ask Doctor Cloquet. "I am very worried about Jefferson's health."

General Foy dies on November 22. At his funeral an immense procession, hostile to the government, marches to the cemetery of Père Lachaise. I do not attend.

1826. I live at La Grange with my large family and occupy myself with farming, letter-writing and receiving my friends, all the time supporting liberal ideas and movements for independence throughout the world. I miss Fanny. I write to her: 'La Grange is like it used to be-only it is lacking you; and the void is immense. It is even worse in Paris.'[4] On May 16 a law is passed, much hated by most, which gives émigrés compensation for land confiscated during the Revolution. I have never considered myself an émigré, but I nevertheless apply. On August 16 I receive from the préfet of the Haute-Loire, 325,767 francs and 90 centimes for my properties sold there, only the duc d'Orléans receiving more than I do from this scheme. There are other unpopular laws proposed, including a law to make stealing from churches sacrilege which will be punished by cutting off a hand and a head, and the restoration of primogeniture. Heavy taxes are placed on publications, which means their printing will be impossible.

In late summer, I learn, to my immense grief, that Thomas Jefferson and John Adams both died on July 4, fifty years after the signing of the Declaration of Independence. At least I have the consolation we lived long enough to see each other again.

On October 11, I write to the Argentine president, Rivadavia, about the war between his country and Brazil, whose throne I want to see removed. On the nineteenth, I write to the government of Guatemala, congratulating it on the institution of a constitution based on that of the United States. On December 16, I write to Bolivar, saying that nothing can surpass the high price I place on his esteem and his friendship, that my admiration dates from his first efforts for the patriotic cause.

At the funeral of the duc de La Rochefoucauld-Liancourt there is a struggle between the police and the mourners who want to carry his coffin. The coffin falls to the ground and breaks open, the corpse unfortunately rolling out.

On April 27, 1827, Charles holds a review of the National Guard at the Champ de Mars to attempt to raise confidence in his government.

"Down with the ministry!" "Down with the priests!" troops shout as he rides along their lines.

Next day, the National Guard is disbanded. Shop windows in Paris display uniforms and muskets with the sign: *Uniform for sale; the musket will be kept.*

In May, baron de Pinteville, who defeated me in the 1824 elections, dies. The electors of Meaux ask me to stand for his seat; I agree immediately. On June 22, I receive 133 votes against 138 for Nicolas Tronchon in the first round of voting. On the twenty-third I am elected by a narrow margin with 141 votes to 139. Charles, however, dissolves the Chamber; new elections will be held on November 17.

On August 20, my friend, Jacques-Antoine Manuel, dies at the early age of fifty-two. On the twenty-fourth, I attend his funeral at the cemetery of Père Lachaise where there are more than one hundred thousand people.

"It has been said, and all the friends of Manuel will attest to it, that since the day of his retirement until the last day of his life, he wished, hoped, fervently desired, the liberty of his country. As to us, citizens, it is on the tomb of the faithful servants of the people that we must penetrate more and more from our respect, from our devotion for its rights, to make it the principal object of our most virtuous, strongest desires, the most important of our interests and the most holy of our duties," I declare at his open tomb.[5]

Alexis Mignet publishes an account of both the funeral and my speech, which become known throughout France. He is arrested, along with Sautelet, the seller, and Gauthier-Laguionie, the printer. I write to the president of the police tribunal: 'I have the right and the duty to declare that I addressed these words to the immense gathering of citizens at the funeral of Monsieur Manuel; I approved, and even demanded, their publication....It is evident that if blame attaches to these words, the responsibility falls completely onto me and that if there is need of clarification, I should be the person asked."[6] There is no such request; Mignet, Sauthelet and Gauthier-Laguionie are fortunately acquitted.

On November 17 I am re-elected at Meaux by 197 votes to 129.

In January,1828, the eloquent right-wing orator, Martignac, becomes minister of the interior. There is rioting in Paris. Meanwhile I continue with my soirées every Tuesday at the rue d'Anjou, my guests frequently including Odilon Barrot, Matthieu Dumas, James Fenimore Cooper, Christine de Belgiosojo and Constant.

On August 31, while travelling to Alsace, the king stops the night at Meaux. He asks if he is in the electoral district of Lafayette. "I know him well. He has rendered services to our family that I will not forget. We were born in the same year; we learned to ride at the Manège in Versailles, and he was in my bureau at the Assembly of Notables."

On another occasion he asks Royer-Collard about my health. "I will give him justice, that he has not changed any more than I have. In 1787 he was in my bureau, and we had a lively discussion on the *capitaineries*. He wanted to suppress them, and I said that I could not see why one would want to give liberty to poachers who are bad people."

On September 27, I declare my political aims at a banquet in Meaux: "I want the abolition of the double vote, the reorganization of the National Guard and the improvement of the system of education."[7]

Towards the end of the year, I occupy myself with my archives and memoirs. Jared Sparks is compiling the writings of Washington and comes to work at La Grange; I talk to him about the past and show him many documents.

The session finishes in July,1829, and I decide to visit the Auvergne which I have not seen for fourteen years. I will also visit my granddaughter, Nathalie de Lafayette, at Vizille, near Grenoble, who is married to Adolphe Périer and has recently had a child, so making me a great-grandfather.

I travel south with George. We stop at Clermont where I am fêted; I speak about the similarity of our time to that when the Gauls, led by Vercingetorix, had attempted a last resistance against the Romans and when the army of the Loire had established its last defense. In the evening of July 30, I arrive at Brioude, its streets illuminated. Monsieur Grenier, a former member of the Constituent Assembly, gives a speech to welcome me; then there is a banquet, followed by a ball with local dances such as *La Montagnarde* and *La Bourrée*.

Next day, I go to Chavaniac, escorted by people from Paulhaguet, Langeac and Issoire.[8] The villagers greet me. Young pupils of the two schools founded by George form a double line and give me flowers and crowns of leaves, the day concluding with dancing and bonfires.[9] I stay ten days. On August 11, I go to Le Puy where the streets are lit and there is a triumphal arch. A banquet is given in my honor, and I am seated opposite a portrait of Washington and a portrait of myself. I talk about the kindness of the townspeople to Adrienne when she was arrested and the noble resistance of the départemental authority to which I owe the saving of a life more precious than my own.

News arrives: Martignac has been dismissed and prince Jules de Polignac, the son of Marie Antoinette's favorite, has been appointed. He is an ultra, a light, presumptuous man, with little insight; he believes himself to be called by God to raise up the throne and the altar and has religious visions. In 1815 he had refused to swear allegiance to the Charter.

"Be sure that if the Chamber of Deputies sees a plot against public liberty, it will find, as well as the nation itself, the necessary energy to repress it," I declare.[10]

We leave Le Puy; we travel to the borders of the Ardèche and the Isère where the people of Annonay, de la Côte Saint-André, de Rios and other places, are waiting. The following day, forty horsemen escort me to La Tour Maubourg's château near Issingeaud. We embrace each other with joy. We spend several days talking and talking, of Olmütz, and of what is happening today.

I go to Grenoble to visit Augustin Périer, the brother of Casimir, but also the father of Adolphe, my granddaughter's husband. With great emotion I enter the town which gave the first signal of French liberty;[11] I receive a silver crown interlaced with oak leaves from Monsieur Rosset-Bresson, a seventy-four-year-old who had been the first elected mayor.

"I accept it not for me alone but for the dauphinois patriots of '87,'88, and '89, of all the years which showed your ideals, and particularly of that memorable day when the Austrians learned from you what a National Guard, infused with love of liberty and country can do." [12]

I attend a banquet of two hundred guests. I propose a toast: "Here flew the first flag of liberty, the first sign of political liberty. Here there will be an anchor of safety if it is needed."[13]

I leave Grenoble and travel with George and Auguste Perrier to visit Nathalie at the château of Lesdiguières facing the majestic Alps; in the evening, bonfires light up the sky and there is a dance. Then I travel to Lyon; there is an immense crowd and Doctor Prunelle, a liberal deputy, makes a speech.

"I find myself in your midst at a moment which I would call critical, if I had not seen everywhere on my journey, as well as in this powerful city, this calm and even scornful strength of a great people who know their rights, feel their force and will be faithful to their duties," I reply.[14]

Next day, my birthday, I go to the island of Barbe, accompanied by highly decorated boats, people again acclaiming me. On the seventeenth, I attend a banquet, where there are several deputies of the left.

"They threaten us with hostile projects but how will they accomplish them? Will they do it in the Chamber of Deputies? All those of our colleagues who are here at this dinner will attest to you that in a time of danger, our chamber will show itself faithful to patriotism and to honour. Will they dare to exercise an illegal power using laws? The French nation knows its rights," I say.[15]

I return home to La Grange, content I have encouraged the people of the Dauphiné, the Auvergne and Lyon towards liberty. The opposition publishes 100,000 brochures of my trip which are distributed throughout France, and I resume my Tuesday soirées either at the rue d'Anjou or at the home of Destutt de Tracey. George is generally with me and Anastasie or Virginie take it in turn to be my hostess.

The beginning of 1830 is rife with rumors. There is talk of a coup d'état. People are studying history to see how the 1640 revolution happened in England without too much disorder; some are speaking of the duc d'Orléans as a successor to Charles X. My young friend, François Guizot, is elected as deputy at Lisieux on January 23. He had asked for my assistance to become a candidate, so I had written to Dupont de l'Eure for his help: 'Monsieur Guizot is more of a monarchist and less of a democrat, I think, than you or I but he loves liberty.'[16]

Guizot supports the duc d'Orléans, as do many others, including the young journalist, Adolphe Thiers, who has founded the newspaper *Le National.* Lord Palmerston visits Paris and is reported to have said that there will be a change of name in the occupant of the Tuileries and that the duc d'Orléans might be invited to step over the way from the Palais-Royal.

In February, Polignac decides to send an expedition to Algeria. I suggest this could be avoided and that the government is only doing it to win popularity if it is successful. On March 2, an enormous crowd gathers at the opening of the Chambers at the Louvre. The king stumbles as he goes up the steps to the throne, his hat falls from his arm and the duc d'Orléans catches it. He gives it to the king and the deputies cast meaningful glances at each other.

"If guilty maneuvers and perfidious insinuations raise obstacles for my government that I do not wish to anticipate I will find the force to overcome them in my resolution to maintain the public peace in the just confidence of the French and the love they have always shown to their king,"[17] declares Charles, his voice weak, but his words menacing.

We meet afterwards in secret to decide what our response should be.

"We must use vigorous expressions in my opinion," I say.

Royer-Collard, the president of the Chamber, agrees. "We must strike quick and hard. Let us not leave to the folly and incapacity of a few men the time to destroy liberty."[18]

Guizot writes the response to the king with the help of Étienne: 'The Charter consecrated the right of the country to participate in discussions of the public interest and that this participation creates a permanent co-operation of the political views of the government with the wishes of your people. Sire, our loyalty, our devotion forces us to say to you this co-operation does not exist. We demand the dismissal of Polignac and his ministry.'[19]

This is passed by two hundred and twenty-one votes to one hundred and eighty-one and a deputation goes to the Tuileries to tell the king. Royer-Collard's voice falters when he reads the last passage, but he manages to finish it.

Charles X listens, badly hiding his indignation. He produces a paper, rather strangely from beneath his bottom. "Messieurs. I announced my resolution in my speech opening the session; these resolutions are immovable...My ministers will make known my intentions to you."

Next day the Chamber meets again, the galleries packed with people. The minister of the interior prorogues Parliament. There is silence. The president adjourns the Chamber.

"*Vive le roi!*" shout the right.

"*Vive la chartre!*" shout the left.

"*Vive la constitution!*" people shout from the galleries.

"Clear the galleries!" calls a deputy from the right. Royer-Collard leaves the presidential chair. "The Chamber is no more," he says solemnly.

I attend an electoral banquet for the two hundred and twenty-one given by the deputies of the Seine. I make a speech and receive an ovation. "I am deeply touched by the proofs of affection with which the present electors of Paris, sons of my contemporaneous electors of 1789, are kind enough to overwhelm me!" [20]

The counter-revolutionary newspapers attack our words; civic banquets mushroom and I am often a guest. The king announces the dissolution of the Chambers on May 16; new elections are scheduled for June 23 for the *arrondissements*, July 3 for the *départements*. The liberals form a coalition with the republicans of Cavaignac's group; Charles X issues a proclamation against the liberals. Orators fill the streets, haranguing the crowds; disturbances break out.

On July 4, the French fleet captures Algiers. People fear that this military victory will turn the heads of the king and his ministers and bring about new follies. On the eighth I am re-elected in Meaux with 264 votes against 72, the largest vote I have yet received. The 221 are re-elected; the Assembly will be composed of 274 opposition deputies and 145 supporters of the government; the session will commence on August 1.

I talk with Laffitte who wants my support to make the duc d'Orléans king.

"The masses are inert," he declares. "Only a small part of the nation wants to break with the monarchy.

"It is necessary to move them," I reply.

"But where are your republicans?" he asks. "They are only a handful and against them are the new and ancient nobles, the clergy, the religious devotees, the bank, the commerce, the landlords, the rentiers and the bourse. There are several financial and economic dangers to proclaiming a republic. They can only govern by violence inside the country as well as outside A republic will only unleash a grave economic and financial crisis."

"You talk as though my republic will resemble our Convention which alone caused the Terror," I say.

"One is the forced consequence of the other. We need to have the duc d'Orléans," he replies.

"No one knows him. And he is Bourbon which is a bad recommendation," I say.

"He is debourbonized since 1789," he replies.[21]

July 27. Tuesday. An express arrives at La Grange bringing yesterday's *Moniteur* from Charles de Rémusat, my granddaughter's husband. I abandon my meal and read that the king has issued four decrees: 'The freedom of the press is suspended; every publication has to be submitted for approval, which is given for three months and can be revoked at any time; the newly-elected Assembly is dissolved and new elections will take place on September 6 and 13; the electoral law is modified by diminishing the role of the local *collèges* and by increasing the importance of large, rural owners by changing tax calculations according the right to vote.' High positions in government have been given to the ultras, the faithful and very right-wing supporters of the king.[22]

I immediately call Bastien and Carbonel. Within the hour I am in my carriage on the road to Paris, dust flying from beneath the wheels and the horses' hooves. I fear I will be stopped from entering the city, but soldiers let me pass. The streets are dark from the breaking of the new lanterns, making it harder for the royal troops to act in an unknown district in the night;[23] the heat of the day still lingers, infused with the smell of gunpowder and burning wood. At place Louis XV an officer recognizes me but does not arrest me or turn me back.

I reach six rue d'Anjou; I quickly send messages to Charles de Rémusat and my grandson, Jules de Lasteyrie, as well as to my friends, Joubert and Levasseur. They soon arrive and tell me what has been happening. A manifesto was drawn up by Adolphe Thiers, Cauchois-Lemaire and Châtelain at the office of *Le National*.[24] It was placed in the constitutional journals and proclaimed that: 'the legal régime has been abandoned; that of force has commenced. The government has lost its legality which brought it obedience. We will resist it for that which concerns us. It is for France to judge how far its resistance should go.'

Mangin, the préfet de police, ordered the newspapers closed and the presses destroyed. Locksmiths and mechanics refused, so he had to use a man whose only expertise lay in riveting chains for galley slaves, with the result that the equipment has only been partly destroyed.

The first member of the Chamber to protest yesterday was the comte Alexandre de Laborde. He met with journalists and accepted the presidency of the gathering which called for resistance to the decrees and for strong and powerful unanimous action which can alone save our country. He summoned the deputies who were in Paris, but by eight in the evening only a few had come.

For much of yesterday the people were indignant, but calm. However, the widely distributed manifesto has caused anger. The print workers armed themselves, and the students from the École polytechnique led the first stirrings of revolt, assisted by students from the Écoles de droit and de médecine. At midday today, the unpopular Marmont, the duc de Raguse, the betrayer of Bonaparte, was appointed commander-in-chief of the royal troops. At five o'clock, he stationed soldiers at strategic sites in Paris; troops fired on a crowd at the Bourse, killing many, as well as on groups of workers and students in the rue Saint-Honoré, the place Vendôme and the vicinity of the Palais-Royal; guard posts have been attacked and one was burnt.[25] Royal coats of arms, including those of the Orléans family, have been removed or defaced. The king, meanwhile, is at Saint Cloud.

This morning about thirty deputies met first at Laborde's house, then at two o'clock at the house of Casimir Périer, which was tragically preceded by a slaughter. Many young people heard of the meeting; they rushed to the rue Neuve de Luxembourg and were encircled and stabbed with sabers by two detachments of cavalry. They tried to find refuge in neighboring houses and knocked at Périer's house, but the doors were closed against them. Several were seriously injured and were taken to the ministry of foreign affairs. [26]

The deputies appear to be divided into two groups. One group is defending the constitutionality of the dissolution, the need to remain within the law and to only demand the retraction of the decrees. The other group declares that the position of the deputies had not been destroyed by the decree of dissolution, that Charles X, by violating the Charter by the decrees, has removed his right to dissolve the Chamber. They debated for a long time at Périer's house but decided nothing, except to ask Guizot to draft a text protesting at the decrees. They regard themselves as not dissolved, the social pact as being broken, and will not abandon their powers.[27]

"It is difficult to understand the folly of what has happened. All that needed to be done was to stay tranquil under the Charter and to keep within the ameliorations it brought. Use my name to help the revolt!" I declare.

At four in the morning a delegation of cadets arrives from the École polytechnique. "We are going off to fight."[28]

"I give you my blessing," I say.

July 28. Wednesday. In the pale light of dawn, people are fighting in the streets. Trees are being cut down to strengthen barricades erected on many roads where troops might pass;[29] a huge crowd is marching on the Hôtel de Ville. At eight o'clock comes the noise of artillery and the tricolor is said to be flying above Notre Dame. Marmont sends a column against the Hôtel de Ville, another to the faubourg Saint Antoine, and a third to the quays on the Seine. It is again intensely hot; the temperature rises to 98 degrees F. which must be very difficult for the uniformed soldiers.

At midday, the tocsin peals out; I make my way to forty rue de Faubourg Poissonnière, the house of Audry de Puyraveau, to the noise of cannon and the staccato of muskets. Men, many with arms, are gathering in the street. "*Vive Lafayette! Vive la liberté!*" they shout.

I am one of the first to arrive, along with Laffitte; about sixty deputies soon follow. The room is on the ground floor and Audry de Puyraveau throws open all the windows so that people outside can hear. Initially there is silence. Then we discuss how to save the liberty for which citizens have been fighting and dying during the last thirty-six hours.

"Listen to the noise of the cannon and the death rattle of the dying. They are coming to you. These courageous people are fighting a revolution that you must lead. It is no longer possible to hesitate; our place, messieurs, is between the people's battalions and the troops of despotism. Don't lose any time; the royal troops will not; once more, it is a revolution which is calling us!" declares Mauguin.

Several deputies rise to their feet fearfully at the word revolution. "We will leave immediately," they say.

"Don't speak so loudly," plead others.

"I protest against any act which is not legal!" cries Dupin.

"What are you saying about resistance?" says Sébastiani angrily.

"The only question here is to save the legal order. The least imprudence compromises our right, our duty," replies Guizot. "For us it is not, as has been said, to take part, for or against the people, but to make ourselves mediators, to stop the people's movement and to convince the king that his ministers are mistaken."[30]

"I profess I fail to understand the legality which appeared in the *Moniteur* yesterday and the firing which has been going on for two hours," I say, with a smile. "This is truly a revolution. I propose the immediate formation of a provisional government." [31]

"No!" exclaim many of the deputies. "It is premature! It is too extreme!"

Suddenly a man rushes into the room. "The people have taken the Hôtel de Ville after terrible losses, but the battle is continuing. Reinforcements have reached the royal troops. It is feared they will be victorious."

Timid deputies who want to act lawfully seem to revive at this news.[32]

"We must make our protest known, but we must be faithful to the king and only do what is legal." We must write a respectful letter to the king," some say.

"No," declares Guizot, but the proposal is adopted.

"This is insufficient and below the legitimate demands of a people who have already spilled so much of their blood," exclaims Laffitte.[33]

"We need to send a commission to Marmont to ask for a truce during which the deputies can take their complaints to the foot of the crown," proposes Périer.

"No. We need to order Marmont, in the name of the law, and under his personal responsibility, to institute a ceasefire," I reply indignantly.

The meeting, however, nominates Périer, Laffitte, Mauguin, Lobau and Gérard to talk with Marmont to my fury at all these delays while the blood of so many citizens is flowing in the streets.

"My name has already been placed by the confidence of the people, and with its wish, at the head of the insurrection. I ardently desire your agreement of my colleagues, but whatever happens, I consider myself bound by honor to establish my headquarters tomorrow in Paris," I declare.[34]

The meeting finishes at two o'clock, its only result being a weak, timid proclamation which will not be published until tomorrow. We agree to meet at the house of Bérard at four, and the deputation goes to the Tuileries.

In the next two hours the situation changes greatly. The citizens are defeated at various places. The Hôtel de Ville, already taken and retaken twice, is back in the control of the royal troops, although brave patriots are still fighting there. People are beginning to be discouraged. There is no leader. They fear defeat.

At four o'clock, we meet again, but this time only about half of the previous deputies come. The deputation report: "We said that we are unanimous in our resolution to maintain our titles as deputies. We do not regard ourselves as being dissolved. The people who are shedding the blood of citizens are those responsible for what is happening. The only method of bringing about peace is to recall the decrees and to return to our previous situation. Marmont asked us to influence the people to return to their duty, to use what influence we have on the people. We replied that we do not have any influence on the insurrection, but we think that the people are right and that if the king does not change his mind, our influence, such as it is, will be used to maintain the resistance. Marmont replied that he has been charged to bring back order, and so he must deploy the means to do it, but that the king will be told in a quarter of an hour what we have said. He asked if we had any objection to speak to Monsieur de Polignac. We said we had not. He went into another room, then returned to say that the conversation would not be necessary, but that the king would be told, although he did not think we would achieve what we needed. He said that the submission of the people is necessary for there to be any negotiation."

People shout angrily at this; others again appear very fearful. We discuss the proclamation of the earlier meeting which some journalists have printed, having first removed words which were too servile.

"We are not signing this. We are leaving," exclaim Sébastiani, Villemain and Bertin de Vaux and start to walk out of the room.

"No, don't go. Don't abandon France on the edge of this precipice!" deputies shout.

"I am resolved to throw myself body and soul into this revolution. At daybreak tomorrow I will set up my headquarters at the Hôtel de Ville, or whatever other place is occupied by the people," I declare.

News arrives: the citizens have again taken the Hôtel de Ville. The Swiss and the royal troops have retreated and there are many dead and wounded at the place de Grève, the quays and the bridges.

The flagging, timorous spirits of some of the deputies now revive somewhat.

"We will print the proclamation of the deputies and Marmont's reply," says Guizot. "There are only ten deputies here, but I propose that we add at the bottom of it the names of all those absent as well as present, whose liberal opinions are well known."

"I protest!" says Sébastiani, who has come back.

"Let us do it!" exclaims Laffitte, with his usual courage. "If we are defeated, they can say they did not sign, and that in reality there were only eight, but if we are victorious, they will be happy that they have signed."

The proclamation is adopted; the names of sixty-three deputies are added. I sign for George. I hope he will arrive today from the Auvergne, although I fear it will not be until tomorrow or the next day. We adjourn again. The duc d'Orléans appears to be doing nothing, although it is reported he has gone to the king, which I very much doubt.

At eight, we meet again at the house of Audry de Puyraveau and the same signs of weakness and courage seen at the previous meetings quickly become apparent.

"We should stop these shameful actions. The deputies in Paris should wear their uniforms and a tricolor cockade. We should show ourselves boldly at the head of the people," I say.

Laborde, Laffitte, de Puyraveau and Mauguin agree. Sébastiani and Méchin disagree violently. They want a legal order and concessions to mediation obtained from the king.

I stand up angrily. "What is the post that you want to assign to me in the name of our country? I am ready to occupy it at this very instant."

Sébastiani and Mechin leave the meeting; we are now reduced to five. It is midnight. We agree to meet at five tomorrow at Laffitte's house. I go out into the streets, into a beautiful night. People are preparing themselves and the barricades for the fighting tomorrow. There is silence, broken occasionally by the sound of paving stones being dug up, the groans of the injured as friends help them into their houses, and the calls of sentries. One hundred thousand Parisians are working for liberty. I inspect the barricades which have been set up at every point which might be threatened, and which would have made Vauban himself proud.

"Who has taught them how to wage war in just a day, in just a night?" I cry in admiration.

I clamber over the barriers with difficulty, my friends helping me. At two o'clock, we come to a barricade closing off the rue Cadet from Montmartre.

"Halt!" cries the sentry. "Come here, corporal, to inspect these people."

The corporal, a worker, looks us up and down suspiciously. "Go to the sentry post, lame old man and the rest of you and tell us what you are doing out walking so late."

We go into the sentry post where workers stare at the four of us with hostility.

"What are you doing, old man?" demands the captain.

"My captain, I am moved to the bottom of my heart at what I have just seen. Come and embrace me and you will know I am one of your old comrades," I say.

He hesitates. "It is General Lafayette," one of the men whispers, whereupon the soldiers throw themselves into my arms.

"Present arms!" the captain orders; I review them with the greatest solemnity as though I have the very best of a regular army in front of me.

July 29. Thursday. During the night, the Charbonniers set up revolutionary committees in the twelve *arrondissements* of Paris. Fighting starts again at daybreak along the avenues of the place de Grève, the boulevards Saint Denis and Saint Martin, and in houses, churches and theaters, from where the royal forces had been pushed back yesterday. Barricades appear, as if by magic, directly behind soldiers attacking the barricades in front of them. Women throw stones, furniture and hot embers from the windows, scorning the soldiers firing at them. Even children are waving the tricolor, and some are attempting to stab the cavalry horses of the royal troops as they are too short to reach the riders.

There are many acts of compassion. A wounded soldier is no longer the enemy. He is a citizen and is looked after. Many of the churches and the theaters have been transformed into hospitals and the surgeons are treating both sides equally.

After several hours of bitter fighting, victory appears to be favoring the citizens, and several battalions of the line have been detached from the royal army. The Guards and the Swiss are fighting with tenacity, but they are beginning to be dislodged from their positions in the center of Paris and are falling back towards the Louvre and the Tuileries.

Since Wednesday evening the citizens have felt abandoned by the deputies. They have failed many times to awaken their courage and have now announced the formation of a fictitious provisional government composed of myself, Choiseul and Gérard. When citizens go to the Hôtel de Ville, which remains under patriot control, and ask to speak to the government, they are told it is in conference, and this imaginary government is lifting the spirits of the men fighting.

Whole companies of the previous National Guard appear in uniform, armed and with drums beating, which emboldens the people who rush to fight. They form many columns; they march towards the enemy under the command of twenty-year-old students from the École polytechnique. They now believe they will win.

"You have been nominated commandant of the National Guard," I am told to my delight.

I return along the rue de Surène to my house and see my path blocked by a royalist force occupying the Madeleine which is firing at everyone. I escape. A short time later, the soldiers retreat, and I rush as quickly as I can, helped by Jules, de Puyraveau, Carbonel and Poque, to Laffitte's house in the rue Neuve de Luxembourg. The tocsin is still ringing, cannons are roaring and muskets firing in the neighboring streets. People recognize me; they open the shops to prevent my being hindered by the barricades.

"*Vive Lafayette!*" they mutter softly so that the enemy is not alerted to my presence.

Finally, we reach Laffitte's house which has become the center for information about what is happening. Workers, strangers, soldiers, rich and poor fill the rooms resplendent with wealth, the tables covered with silver, but do not take or harm a single item. Bullets from the barracks in the rue Verte have been carried here in wine baskets and are being given to the fighters, as well as bread and other essentials; instructions are being given to patriots from many different départements.

"Promote rebellion and come to the help of Paris if we need you," Laffitte tells them, and the mayor of Rouen immediately departs with Monsieur Carel to rouse his town. Dispatches intercepted by the patriots have also been brought here, as well as demands for safe conduct or passports for foreign ambassadors; I even see prisoners from the royal troops.

Three soldiers report that two hundred royal soldiers were going to be sent, disguised as citizens, to take Laffitte by force to the foot of the Colonne where he would be executed.

Several of my colleagues are here, as well as a deputation of citizens. "Take charge. Lead our forces," they say.

"My friends, if you believe me useful to the cause of liberty, make use of me," I reply.

"*Vive Lafayette!*" "*Vive Lafayette!*" people shout in the salon and in the street.

I turn towards the deputies. "Messieurs, this morning I received the first news of my nomination as commandant of the National Guard. Many citizens wish me to accept it and I will do so, not as a deputy, but as a private individual. An old name of '89 can perhaps be of some use in the grave circumstances in which we find ourselves. Attacked on all sides we must defend ourselves."[35]

An officer runs into the room and interrupts me. "The Louvre and the Tuileries have been taken after stubborn resistance by the Swiss and the Guards. They are retreating!"

Everyone erupts in excitement, then I continue. "I have been invited to organize the defense. Instructions and orders are requested everywhere from me. I learn that similar proposals have been made to my colleague and friend Monsieur de Laborde. It would seem strange that those above all who have given old promises of devotion to the national cause would refuse to respond to the appeal now addressed to them. This refusal would make us responsible for future events. Instructions and orders are being asked from me everywhere. They are waiting for my reply...My conduct at seventy-three will be what it was at thirty-two. It is important, I think, that the Chamber should remain the Chamber, but for me, citizens, my duty is to address myself to the general defense."[36]

"I do not want anything better than to serve under your orders," declares General Gérard. Everyone then agrees that the management of active orders should be given to him.

"I think a civil commission of deputies should be formed," I say.

"Yes," replies Guizot. "It is important that the honorable general follows the wishes of his fellow citizens. The security of Paris depends on his determination. But we also have a duty to fulfill. It is important that we establish, not a provisional government, but a municipal authority which will occupy itself with the re-establishment and maintenance of order."

"I completely agree with this proposition," replies Bertin de Vaux. "It is essential to regularize as quickly as possible what is happening in Paris and even although we do not have the virtuous mayor of Paris in '89, let us congratulate ourselves on having reconquered the illustrious leader of the National Guard."

"Let us vote on the establishment of a municipal authority composed of five members," says Laffitte. This is unanimously agreed.

"Would you like to nominate them?" I am asked.

"No. The municipal authority should be nominated by the Chamber," I reply.[37] Laffitte, Périer, de Schonen, de Puyraveau, Lobau and Mauguin are chosen.

"There is great agitation outside amongst the citizens. The name of General Lafayette is being said everywhere. It is important that the honorable gentleman should show himself to the citizens," declares Bertin de Vaux.[38]

"General Lafayette must accept the command of the National Guard which has just been offered to him by citizens who are united in their pursuit of the defense of the capital," says Laborde.

News arrives: the Tuileries have been taken; the Swiss and the Guards are in retreat everywhere.

I leave the meeting; I go outside into the embrace of an immense crowd, many of whom are armed. They escort me, General Carbonel and Jules along the street towards the Hôtel de Ville which is again in the hands of the insurgents.

"*Vive la nation! Vive Lafayette! Vive la liberté!*" people cry to the sound of fighting from the barricades, the roads and the houses.

Our procession is military and triumphal. Five hundred thousand men, women and children fill the streets and wait at the crossroads. They hang out of windows or stand on the roofs, waving handkerchiefs and acclaiming me. We walk slowly in the middle of this enormous crowd, who for three days have been without a leader, but who now seem filled with joy and hope. A cloud of tricolor ribbons rain down from the windows of the mercers' shops in the rue aux Fers. I pick up the three colors and wear them; others near to me do the same. We march slowly; we take one and a half hours to go from the rue Cerutti to the Hôtel de Ville. At the place de Grève there are many wounded amidst much debris and shell casings. I talk to them. I press them to my heart.

"Now that General Lafayette has taken my hand, I am ready to die," one exclaims.

I walk up the steps into the Hôtel de Ville, into its dark gloom, which reveals a man with a pale face and a long beard, in an odd assortment of military clothes, calling himself General Dubourg. He welcomes me, as does Colonel Zimmer.

"Let me show you the way," someone says.

"No, I think I probably know this building better than you," I reply with a smile.

Crowds drunk with victory fill the gloomy courts and splendid halls, the fleur-de-lys hangings slashed, Louis XVlll's bust overturned, Charles X's bust broken. There are more wounded. Men run in carrying flags captured from royal forces, euphoric about the taking of the Louvre, the Tuileries and the Babylon barracks.

"Fly the tricolor over the Hôtel de Ville," I order.

I establish my headquarters. I dictate an Order of the Day to be put up on walls: 'My dear fellow citizens and brave comrades. The confidence of the people of Paris calls me once more to the command of its public force. I have accepted with devotion and joy the duties confided to me, and just as in 1789 I very strongly appreciate the approbation of my honorable colleagues today reunited in Paris. I will make no profession of faith: my ideas are already known. The conduct of the Parisian people, during these last days of trial, make me more than ever proud to be at their head. Liberty will triumph or we will perish together. *Vive la liberté! Vive la patrie! Lafayette!*'[39]

I write a second Order of the Day concerning the re-establishment of the Parisian National Guard: 'The colonels and officers are invited to immediately reorganize the service of the National Guard; non-commissioned officers and soldiers must be ready to unite at the first beat of a drum; they are provisionally invited to unite with the officers and non-commissioned officers of their former companies; colonels, or in their absence, chiefs of battalions, and asked to come immediately to the Hôtel de Ville to discuss the first measures to take in the interest of the service; it is expressly forbidden to fire weapons except as a necessary defense by the most odious aggression against public liberty.'[40]

Generals Pajol and Gérard organize the defense. The Fifty-Third and Fifth Regiments of the Line stationed at the place Vendôme have rebelled, their only demand being that they should not be asked to fire on their fellow soldiers and have been directed to the Popin and Poissonnière barracks; Marmont is falling back towards Saint Cloud. News comes that Joubert helped to take one of the royal residences and that Auguste Levasseur was gravely wounded at the barricades.

In the evening, d'Argout, Sémonville and Vitrolles arrive at the foot of the stairway of the Hôtel de Ville, sent by Charles X to announce the retraction of the decrees, the dismissal of Polignac and the nomination of a new, liberal ministry with Mortemart as president of the council and minister of foreign affairs. They are brought to the room where the council sits; I come to speak to Sémonville. I listen to him.

"But at least, my old comrade, have you thought about assuring the tricolor cockade for us? For it is necessary that we others, patriots, should not leave here without gaining something." [41]

Sémonville is embarrassed. He does not reply. During the night we constantly fear an attack, but there is no fighting in Paris although it continues in the Bois de Boulogne and on the line of retreat of the royal forces.

July 30. Friday. We are well protected by barricades. The enemy will repent if it advances again into our streets.[42] I take measures to ensure public order and open the gates of Paris so that vehicles can come and go freely. The commission organizes general services.

In the early morning, posters placard the walls of Paris, written by Mignet and Thiers: 'Charles X can no longer enter Paris. He has made the blood of the people flow. A republic will expose us to terrible divisions; it will cause trouble for France with Europe. The duc d'Orléans is a prince devoted to the cause of the revolution. He has never fought against us. He was at Jemappes. He will be a citizen-king. He has worn the colors of the tricolor and he is the only one who can still wear them. We do not wish anyone else.'

"Tear them down," I order, but many have already seen them.

At the Hôtel de Ville, the words 'republic' and 'Napoléon' resonate everywhere.[43] The young and worker insurgents want me to be president of a republic. They do not want another Bourbon king. However, the deputies, the representatives of only 80,000 electors, are still arriving in Paris; they are divided; some want the duc d'Orléans as king, others are suggesting he should be lieutenant-general; some want a republican government and there are even a few who still want Charles X.[44]

Discussions rage endlessly. Deputations keep arriving who wish me to form a popular government.

"If you refuse, you will lose your popularity," they say.

"Popularity is a precious treasure, but like all treasures, it is necessary to know how to use it in the interests of the country," I reply.[45] "Only France and its representatives can form a government."

My first thought in the middle of the revolutionary movement, engaged in measures of combat and public order, is that the national will should be regularly consulted in the forms indicated by the constituent assembly.[46]

"The deputies are trying to impose a king," people tell me. I quickly write to Lafitte, the president, to tell him not to rush. Just as I finish, another deputation comes in, this time from the house of Lointier, in the rue Richelieu, the main assembly point for the various republican assemblies which have sprung up throughout Paris.[47] They demand, in very threatening voices, that the nation must be consulted.

Colin de Sussy arrives, sent by de Mortemart. He had to walk from Saint Cloud and had reached Paris so exhausted he had not been able to continue after first going to the Chamber at the Palais Bourbon. He brings a letter and a document from Charles X cancelling the decrees, but Constant had told him the government is no longer recognized.

He gives me the letter and the document, watched by many people including the Lointier deputation.

"I am here with friends. I have no secrets from them," I say. I open the packet and read out the new decrees.

"There is no longer a king of France," people shout. "Down with the Bourbons!" They threaten de Sussy.

"It is too late," I say.[48]

I am courteous. I ask Lobau to take de Sussy to the commission. There, de Puyraveau and Mauguin violently reject the decrees. I go to the grande salle with him; I tell the crowd what Charles is offering.

"What right does a peer of France dare have to bring to the people of Paris the decrees of a dethroned king?" they shout angrily.

It is difficult to speak above the din. "You see," I say to de Sussy. "You must resign. The Bourbons are finished."[49]

"Meet with Monsieur de Mortemart at the Luxembourg," he replies.

"The people have themselves rejected the decrees," I say. "I am their representative. I have nothing in common with the representative of the fallen monarchy."[50]

Odilon Barrot takes my letter to the meeting of deputies. He demands to be heard; he says he has come from a man to whom glory has been reserved to preside twice over our political regeneration; he says I am fearful that the people of Paris would not be unanimous on what will be decided without the intervention of the Chambers; that I think in order to stop all dissent and give unanimity to the revolution which alone can assure its duration, before taking a decisive part it is necessary to start by stipulating, in a general assembly, the conditions wanted by the people, and to defer the crown until the stipulated guarantees are given.[51]

Charles de Rémusat comes to the Hôtel de Ville. "If there is a monarchy the duc d'Orléans will be king. If there is a republic, you will be president. Do you want the responsibility of a republic? If you do not, you must help put the duc d'Orléans on the throne."[52]

I talk with delegates from the provinces. They give me their devotion and their sympathy, but they do not talk of a republic; they see me as a mediator.

In the evening, thousands of young people come to the Hôtel de Ville to ask me to be president of a provisional republican government which many groups had already decided will be proclaimed on the place de Grève tomorrow at midday, but which has now been delayed because they do not yet have a republican government to reveal to the nation. Some are carried away by emotion, some appear to be in a fury. I am greatly moved. I hesitate about what I should do. I have long wished for a republic in France. I am on the point of accepting.

"Please do not decide until tomorrow morning," pleads Odilon Barrot.

"I agree to do that," I reply.[53]

After midnight, General Heymes arrives from the duc d'Orléans to say he is now at the Palais-Royal and will call on me tomorrow.

July 31. Saturday. Odilon Barrot comes to see me shortly after I wake.

"If you accept to be president of a republic you could plunge us into an abyss," he declares vehemently.

"I promise to refuse," I reply.[54]

William Rives, the American ambassador, visits.

"What will our friends in the United States think if they hear we have proclaimed a republic?" I ask.

"They will think that forty years of experience have been lost on the French," he replies.[55]

I receive a resolution from the deputies in Paris which says that in these urgent circumstances they have nominated the duc d'Orléans as lieutenant-general of the kingdom. I therefore sacrifice my most dearly held wishes.[56] I support his nomination. I send Odilon Barrot again to the Chamber of Deputies to say that the national flag has been reconquered and looked after for three days by the people and that no one has the right to concede it.[57]

I issue a proclamation to the people of Paris:

> It is by this choice that the representatives of the electoral colleges, honored by the agreement of the whole of France, will be able to guarantee liberty, equality and public order, which the sovereign nature of our rights and the firm will of the people claim....It has already been recognized that thanks to the heroic, rapid and popular effort of a just resistance to the counter-revolutionary aggression, the demands of the re-establishment of elective administrations, communal and départemental, the formation of the National Guards of France on the basis of the law of 91, the extension of the application of the jury, the questions relative to the electoral law, the liberty of education, the responsibility of people in power, and the necessary way to achieve this responsibility, must be objects of legislative discussion before all votes of subsidy....Whilst waiting for this, France knows that the lieutenant-general of the kingdom, called upon by the Chamber, was one of the young patriots of 89, one of the first generals who brought triumph to the tricolor flag. Liberty, equality and public order, have always been my motto: I will always be faithful to it.
> [58]

I also address a proclamation to the soldiers of the royal army:

> Brave soldiers! The inhabitants of Paris do not hold you responsible for the orders you have been given; come to us, we will receive you like brothers; come to put yourselves under the orders of General Gérard, one of the brave generals who has shed his blood for the defence of the country so many times. The cause of the army cannot be separated for long from the cause of the nation and liberty...Let us therefore be friends, since we have common rights and interests. General Lafayette declares, in the name of the whole population of Paris, that there is no hatred or hostility towards French soldiers; the people of Paris are ready to fraternize with all those who who come to the cause of our country and liberty. Let citizens and soldiers, reunited under the same flag, finally bring about the happiness and the glorious destiny of our beautiful country. *Vive la France*!
> [59]

Monsieur Durran, chief of staff, who had been sent to the royal troops at Saint Cloud, returns to find out what is happening now that the decrees have been withdrawn.

I write a letter for him to take to the commander: 'I am asked for an explicit response on the situation of the royal family since its last aggression against public liberty and the victory of the Parisian people; I will speak frankly: all reconciliation is impossible; the royal family has ceased to exist.'[60]

The day becomes increasingly hot. An immense crowd, nearly all armed, gathers in the streets. At two o'clock, the duc d'Orléans arrives on a white horse at the place de Grève, wearing the uniform of a general, a tricolor cockade in his hat, a tricolor ribbon in his buttonhole, accompanied by an aide-de–camp. I wait at the bottom of the steps in front of the Hôtel de Ville.

"No more Bourbons!" people shout. He ignores them and appears brave and calm.

About eighty deputies follow him, not in uniform, many in their travelling clothes. Benjamin Constant is carried on a chair as he is half paralyzed; Laffitte is also carried on a chair as he has a sprain. This motley group makes its way very slowly through the immense crowd. There are a few calls of " *Vivent les députés*!" " *Vive le duc d'Orléans*!" but people nearby appear hostile.

He dismounts; I greet him graciously and cordially; I shake his hand.

"Messieurs. I am an old National Guard soldier come to visit his former general," he says.

"*Plus de Bourbons!*" people shout with an increase of fervor. "*Vive Lafayette!*"

We enter the building; we pass rooms filled with people, some of whom appear not to be very favorably disposed towards him, whilst others welcome him with joy.[61]

We reach the grande salle; Monsieur Viennet loudly reads out the declaration of the Chamber adopted today: 'Sovereignty of the people over the head of state and the constitution; abolition of hereditary peerage; reform of the judiciary; municipal and communal elections based on widest possible public participation with no property qualifications; popular election of lower-level judiciary; reform of privileges and monopolies that restrict industry and free commerce; all these points to be accepted provisionally before being put to a referendum to the nation which has the sole power to establish the system of government it prefers.' His words are received coldly.[62]

The duc d'Orléans replies to numerous shouts of acclaim. 'General' Dubourg addresses him in a very severe voice to the astonishment of everyone. "It is said you are an honest man and therefore incapable of acting incorrectly. I want to believe so, but you should be prepared that if you do not, you will be made to do so."

Bérard speaks sharply to him; the crowd opens to let Dubourg step back; they close ranks immediately and he disappears.[63]

I grasp the arm of the duc d'Orléans; I wrap a tricolor flag round him. I take him to one of the windows. I embrace and kiss him. I do what needs to be done.

"*Vive Lafayette!*" "*Vive le duc d'Orléans!*" people shout in the building and outside.[64]

The duc d'Orléans returns to the Palais-Royal, the crowd acclaiming him.

The commission creates provisional ministers, including Dupont as that of justice, Gérard that of war and Rigny that of the navy. The commission and I decree the creation of a mobile National Guard of twenty regiments and give pay of thirty sous a day to each soldier.[65]

A large group of republicans come to the Hôtel de Ville threatening to take up their arms again. "France needs liberty and public order, I say, firmly but affectionately. [66] I share their views; I feel charged with the future fate of our country. I believe I am invested with the authority and the confidence of the people to speak frankly, in their name, with the proposed king.[67]

"Will you give me your word that you will not disturb the present peace in Paris for forty-eight hours? A manifesto of our propositions will be drawn up and I will go to the Palais-Royal to speak with the duc d'Orléans to obtain its guarantee."

They accept. Accordingly, they write the program of the Hôtel de Ville, whose principal articles I agree with, which includes national sovereignty recognized at the head of the constitution as the fundamental belief of the government; no hereditary peers; complete renewal of the magistrature; municipal and communal law according to the largest electoral principle. The abolition of the land tax eligibility; the re-establishment of the National Guard, according to the principles of the constitution of '91; and the suppression of monopolies contrary to the general interest of commerce and industry.[68]

August 1. I go to the Palais-Royal, accompanied by members of the municipal commission wearing tricolor sashes, workers holding out their bare arms to me. The commission gives its powers to the duc d'Orléans, who asks that they should remain provisionally in charge of the security of Paris.

He takes me into a private room. I talk of the program of the Hôtel de Ville; he agrees. I do not make him read or sign it.

"You know I am a republican and that I regard the constitution of the United States as the most perfect which has ever existed," I say.

"I think like you. It is impossible to have passed two years in America and not to be of that opinion, but do you think in the present situation of France, and according to public opinion, that we should adopt it?" he replies.

"No. What the French people need today is a popular throne, surrounded by republican institutions," I say.

That is what I think," he replies.

I believe he is sincere. I believe that although I am helping to make him king, he will have obtained his power from the people and the government will finally be, after fifty years, the one I have always wanted. A constitutional monarchy is best for France at this present time.[69] I think that the choice of the duc d'Orléans, patriot of '89, soldier of the tricolor in '92, known for his citizen ways and his domestic virtues, gives the best chance of liberty and public order that we can have.[70]

I return to the Hôtel de Ville where people crowd round me, wanting to know what was said. I recount our conversation.

"He and his son share all our opinions. What we have proposed is what they also think, and they believe we must quickly give to them the power to ensure the well-being of France." [71]

People are displeased, but they have faith in me; Armand Marrast and other republicans leave to relate our words to their fellow citizens at different places in Paris. I continue to wish to have primary assemblies which would limit the function of the lieutenant-general to his powers at this time until a constitution is written. We need to obtain all we can for liberty as far as circumstances permit.[72]

Odilon Barrot mediates between the Hôtel de Ville, the Palais-Royal and the deputies. We want the sovereignty of the people, all the National Guards of towns and countryside armed and able to nominate their officers, electors aged from twenty-five, eligibility from thirty years, the chamber nominating its president; the electoral colleges naming their own bureau. We try to influence the decisions being made.[73] However, we are also at war, and we must establish relations with all the départements. I need to rally the public spirit round the tricolor flag.

The suffocating heat continues. The four thousand barricades are still standing in Paris; in many places they have stopped streams flowing and unhealthy lagoons of water are spreading out over the streets. Men who were fighting last week are, however, returning to work.[74]

Charles X stayed at Saint Cloud until July 30. He wanted to go to Versailles, but the town refused to open the gates and he went to the Trianon. When he left there, the duc d'Angoulême took a picket of cavalry, which was defending the bridge at Sèvres, and ordered them to fire on a crowd at the far end of the bridge, wounding several women and a child. On Saturday night, the court retreated to Rambouillet, still with many troops. [75]

On August 2, he sends a letter to the duc d'Orléans in which he says he will abdicate in favor of his grandson, the duc de Bordeaux, and that the dauphin also agrees to renounce his rights if the duc d'Orléans, in his capacity as lieutenant-general of the realm, will proclaim the duc de Bordeaux as Henri V. Schonen, Maison and Odilon Barrot are sent as commissioners to see him. The provisional commission and I order Colonel Poque with a small force to follow the movements of the royal troops and to reclaim the diamonds of the crown.

By evening, the citizens of Paris are aware of the demand of Charles X that his abdication is conditional on the making of his grandson, king, and that he does not appear to be leaving. The streets seethe with angry people. Different factions, particularly the republicans, disconcerted by the proclamation of the duc d'Orléans, begin to have hope again that they might succeed in their wishes.[76]

Next day, I am awoken at six o'clock, having only just gone to bed. Charles X refused to see the commissioners. Men are rushing to the Champs Elysées saying they intend to march on Rambouillet and finally put an end to these Bourbons.

I need to regularize this movement of armed men. I order drums to beat. I mobilize six hundred from each of the twelve legions of the National Guard. General Pajol will lead the men, with Colonel Jacqueminot as his chief-of-staff; George will be his aide-de-camp.

By the afternoon, about twenty thousand men have gathered on the Champs Elysées. A few have uniforms of the National Guard, some wear uniforms taken from the royal troops, most wear ordinary clothes. They have armed themselves with whatever they can find, including muskets, pistols, sabers, broomsticks and knives. Vehicles of all sorts and sizes have been requisitioned and about eight hundred are ready to transport them. It is a strange diversity of clothes, arms and vehicles, but animated with the most ardent patriotism.[77]

"*Vive Lafayette!*" they shout.

I review the citizen-army. Then the whole cavalcade slowly starts to trundle down the Champs Elysées with its cannons, the commissioners, Schonen, Barrot and Maison having already set off to talk to the king. I have just received information about the royal troops from a general officer of the army who was present at the king's review of his troops; there are more than twelve thousand men, including three excellent cavalry regiments and forty cannon.

"The men will immediately run away if attacked," says Pajol.

"If they attack get the men from the plain at Rambouillet into the woods and fire from behind the trees," I tell him.

I go to the Chamber by way of the grande cour, the opposite side to the main doors; I hear a threatening tumult of voices; I enter; I see the deputies in an agitated state, preparing to courageously resist a violation of their freedom. I leave the Chamber and walk into the shouting, menacing crowd. I raise my hand. There is a sudden silence.

"My friends. It was my duty to take measures to defend the Chamber of Deputies against all attacks on its independence. I did not do so, and I was wrong. But I had not foreseen, after all that has happened during the revolution, the violence of today. I have no force to oppose you, but if the liberty of the Chamber is violated, the dishonor of it will fall onto me as I am responsible for the maintenance of public order. I place my honor then, in your hands, and I count sufficiently on your kindness to be sure you will go away peacefully."[78]

"We will go away! *Vive Lafayette!*" people immediately shout and start to disperse. The Chamber returns to its discussion.

Late in the evening, a letter is received at the Palais-Royal announcing the success of the commissioners who are now with the king and his family en route to Cherbourg where he will embark for England. The royal troops are being directed to Épernon and tomorrow morning it will be decided which will follow Charles.[79]

Maison had told the king that in another hour the Paris army would be at the château."

"How many?" he had asked.

"About sixty to eighty thousand," Maison had replied.

He had then agreed to go and to give up the crown jewels.

On the fourth, Bérard proposes modifications to the Charter and to make the duc d'Orléans king. He wants to finish with the old dynasty, create a new one, and establish the constitutional conditions to which it will owe its existence.[80] On the fifth, the duc de Broglie is drawing up an agreement between the Charter of 1814 and Bérard's proposal.[81]

I issue an Order of the Day in which I express my gratitude for the promptness and zeal with which the National Guard and the volunteer corps rushed to Rambouillet to put an end to the last resistance of the ex-royal family. I thank the brave men of Rouen, Louviers and Elbeuf who joined our forces, as well as our brave brothers-in-arms of the patriotic town of Le Havre who also marched to help. I speak of the bravery of Colonel Poque who was gravely injured.[82]

On the sixth, Bérard reads to the Chamber the intended modifications to the Charter. In the evening, crowds gather by the Palais Bourbon.[83] During the night of the sixth to the seventh, the duc d'Orléans sends the duc de Broglie and Casimir Périer to me and we discuss the plan to reform the Charter for five hours. We do not manage to agree on the question of hereditary peerage. Next day I learn that attempts are being instigated to interrupt the proceedings of the Chamber today when we debate the new Charter and the making of the duc d'Orléans king. I can see a terrible situation ensuing if this is not stopped. We have not achieved all that we wanted but on the other hand we must think of all the troubles which will come about from an attempt against the liberty of the representatives of eighty thousand electors. We must not spoil this beautiful revolution in the last week. I believe my honor to be at stake in protecting the deliberations of the Chamber. If necessary, I will defend it with my life.[84]

The session starts at eight o'clock, not at ten o'clock which had been expected, but there are not enough deputies to begin the debate. While everyone is waiting, groups of young people surround the hall, shouting in great agitation and frightening some of the deputies. They send a deputation to me, to Salverte, to Tracy and to some other deputies, and finish by promising to welcome what we believe will be agreed.

"If it is not decided by the end of the day, we cannot say what will happen to public calm," they declare. The session begins at ten o'clock. Monsieur de Conny, a defender of Charles X and his régime, speaks first. His words fall on deaf ears. The legitimacy he invokes is dead. The reign of Charles X is finished. Benjamin Constant refutes what he has said.[85]

The deputies discuss the different articles of the proposition originally made by Bérard to make the duc d'Orléans king, not lieutenant general of the kingdom, and to institute a new constitution.[86] Finally, we come to the subject of a hereditary peerage, and I go to the tribune.

"When I express an opinion contested by many friends of liberty, I cannot be suspected of being dragged by a sentiment of effervescence, or of courting a popularity that I would never prefer to that of following my duty. The republican sentiments which I have always evinced have not prevented me from being the defender of a constitutional throne. Therefore, Messieurs, in the present crisis it has appeared suitable to create another national throne, and I must say that my wish for the prince whom you are considering has increased since my knowing him, but I must differ from you on the question of the hereditary peerage. I am a disciple of the American school; I have always thought that the legislative body should be divided in two chambers with differences of organization. However, I have never been able to understand that it is possible to have hereditary judges and legislators. The aristocracy is a bad ingredient in public institutions. I therefore, express as strongly as I can, my wish for the abolition of the hereditary peerage, and, at the same time, I beg my colleagues to not forget that although I have always been the man of liberty, I have never ceased to be the man of public order."[87]

"Bravo!" "Bravo!" people shout.

The new constitution is adopted by 219 votes to 33. Some deputies declare they do not wish to participate in the proclamation of a new royal family; some abstain timidly and secretly. The president proposes not to send a delegation, but for all the deputies to go together to the Palais-Royal, to bring the act by which we have just made him king, to the duc d'Orléans. The deputies agree; everyone immediately sets off. Outside, people are angry, but I manage to bring calm. The

National Guard escorts the deputies through the crowds; just before five o'clock we arrive at the Palais-Royal.

We find the duc seated in a vast salon with his entire family, joy on the faces of everyone around him. Laffitte loudly reads out the new social pact we have just given France.[88]

"We offer you the crown," he says.

The duc makes a short speech, then takes Laffitte's hand and bursts into tears.

"*Vive le roi!*" "*Vive la reine!*" "*Vive la famille royale!*" everyone shouts.

I step out onto the balcony with him; I embrace him again.

"This is the king we need. This is the republicanism we have been able to do," I say.

Those who want to link the new throne to that of the old wish the king to be called Philippe V. I strongly disagree as it a name unworthy of a republican monarch who must have nothing to do with the pretensions of former kings of France.[89] I want him to be called Louis-Philippe I. He agrees and writes to me in English: 'You see you have carried the point.'[90] The Chamber decides that Louis-Philippe I and his male descendants will be kings of the French, and not kings of France.

August 9. Today is the coronation. Paris is both calm and lively. Outside the Palais Bourbon people have been gathering since early morning; before nine o'clock there are already immense crowds waving tricolors and singing the *Parisienne* and the *Marseillaise*, the National Guard keeping order. I arrive shortly after one o'clock, several of the deputies having already taken their seats. I wear town clothes, as do all the other deputies, the peers are in petit costume. The throne is an armchair covered in red velvet; placed near to it are several stools covered with the same red velvet. Two tables, also covered in red velvet, are to the left and right; on one is a writing desk and quills and on the other are the royal insignia, the crown, scepter, sword and the hand of justice. A dais of red velvet, adorned with gold gauze and surmounted with white feathers, is below this modest throne, which enjoys the shade of numerous tricolor flags.[91]

The duchesse d'Orléans, dressed simply, enters with her children and Madame Adélaïde and sits in the royal box. Salvos of artillery announce the arrival of the duc d'Orléans. A deputation of twenty members go to receive him at the door. Musicians play patriotic tunes. The duc d'Orléans enters, his head bare. "*Vive le duc d'Orléans!*" "*Vive le roi!*" people cry. He acknowledges the assembly and sits down with his sons on the stools, the duc de Chartres on his right, the duc de Nemours on his left.

Four marshals of France, Mortier, Oudinot, Macdonald and Molitor take the royal insignia. The ministers Jourdan, Gérard, Dupont de l'Eure, Guizot, Bignon and Louis stand on both sides of the throne; the prince's aides-de-camp Dumas, Rumigny, Heymès and Athalin stand behind. The peers and the deputies also stand, their heads bare.

"Please be seated," says the duc. They sit down.

Casimir Périer, the president of the Chamber, reads out the new Charter.

"I accept without restriction or reserve the clauses and engagements which are in this declaration, and the title of king of the French which it confers on me, and I am ready to swear my allegiance to it," declares the duc. He stands up, his head uncovered, and swears his oath. "In the presence of God, I swear to faithfully observe the constitutional Charter, with the modifications expressed in the declaration, to only govern by the laws, and according to the laws, to render good and exact justice to each according to his right, and to act in all matters in the sole view of the interest, of the happiness and of the glory of the French people."

He signs three original declarations which will be placed in the royal archives, in the Chamber of deputies and in the chamber of peers.

The marshals present the royal insignia to him. Then he sits down on the throne. "*Vive le roi! Vive la reine! Vive la famille royale!*" people shout, waving handkerchiefs and hats.

"I would have preferred not to be given the throne to which the national wish has called me, but France, attacked in her liberty, saw public order in peril, the violation of the Charter....the wise modifications you have made, Messieurs, to the Charter, guarantee the security of the future, and France will, I hope, be happy within her borders, respected beyond them and peace in Europe will be strengthened," says the new king.

He leaves the Chamber giving numerous handshakes to deputies, peers and citizens. The queen immediately follows. She stops and speaks in the conference room to several people.

"It is really to you, General, that we are indebted for this," she says to me.

The deputies and peers go to their respective Chambers to swear fidelity to the king, to the Charter and to the laws of the kingdom. The royal family returns to the Palais-Royal; later, I dine there with many others.

On August 10 Louis-Philippe appoints me commander of the National Guard of France. I issue an Order of the Day: 'I refused in 1790 the wish of three million of my comrades, because the position would have been permanent, and this could, one day, have become dangerous. Today the circumstances are different. I think I must, to serve liberty and France, accept the rank of commandant général of the National Guards. Lafayette.'[92]

I begin the task of forming the National Guard everywhere in France. I decide to meet each week with the colonels and lieutenant colonels of the legions, the artillery and cavalry in order to concert with them not only the means of perfecting the organization of the citizen-army but also on the measures to take to maintain public order and the best way to divide up the service.[93] There have been no executions or massacres. The situation is very different to that in 1789.

August 12. The ex-royal family is embarking today. They have travelled across France without receiving the slightest insult. The people have done everything. Courage, intelligence, clemency towards the vanquished; all has been marvelous. What a difference from the first days of '89. Our republican party, master of the terrain, can make our opinions prevail. We have thought that it is better to unite all the French under the régime of a constitutional throne, but free and popular. The choice of the prince was indicated by diverse circumstances; he would not have had my vote if I had doubted his sincerity and patriotism.[94]

Liberty has made great progress and will make still more. For the rest, I have done what my conscience dictates, and if I have been wrong, then it was in good faith...I think it is useful to provisionally correct the electoral law and finally to have another Chamber. It will be necessary to replace this one as soon as possible by new, larger elections, more in agreement with the principles of the last revolution...with a child's joy I delight in seeing the tricolor flag everywhere.[95]

Demonstrations occur near the Palais-Royal; the National Guard disperse them.

Paris gives a municipal banquet in my honor, on the fifteenth, for three hundred and fifty guests including peers and deputies, ministers, National Guard soldiers and students. I reply with emotion to the toast given by La Borde, préfet of the Seine.

"You are no longer those generations from the *ancien régime*, astonished to learn you have rights and laws; you are the children, the pupils of the Revolution and your conduct in the great days of glory and of liberty has just shown the difference." [96]

On the sixteenth, Louis-Philippe formally names me commander of the National Guard of France, which Guizot had proposed. The same day, the prince de Polignac is unfortunately arrested at Granville just as he is about to embark for Jersey. De Peyronnet, Chanteleuze and Guernon-Ranville are arrested near Tours. I do not want the new régime to begin with executions.

On the seventeenth, I support the motion of Victor de Tracy for the abolition of the death penalty, which I had first proposed forty years before.

"What misfortune, Messieurs, that the abolition of the death penalty was not adopted by the Constituent Assembly! What irreparable suffering we would have been spared! I avow to you messieurs, that since our political storms I feel an invincible horror for the death penalty."[97]

The proposal is sent to a commission. I organize a petition to support its abolition and thousands sign.

In the evening of the eighteenth, I receive an official letter from Guizot, the minister of the interior, saying that Louis-Philippe today signed an order regularizing my position as commandant général of the National Guard. I write to Guizot that I would like permission from the king and his minister to appoint Dumas as major general of the National Guard of France.

I send officers of the National Guard to Tours and Saint-Lô on the twentieth, with as many troops as they think necessary, to oversee the bringing of Polignac and the other ministers to Paris to be judged in conformity with the law. 'I have replied for you; I have replied on my honor of the security of the prisoners; my honor is in your hands,' I write to them.[98]

On the twenty-third, I appoint Mathieu Dumas major general of the National Guard; Carbonel is chief-of-staff and George an aide-de-camp. On the twenty-fifth, there are riots in Paris. I issue an Order of the Day to the people, asking them not only to be calm in the exercise of their public duty but also as a mark of personal friendship.[99] There is fighting in the streets of Brussels. On the twenty-ninth there is a review on the Champ de Mars; about 300,000 people gather on the earthen banks at the edge of the ground; at twelve-thirty, artillery fires; Louis-Philippe arrives, to shouts of acclaim, accompanied by four squadrons of the mounted National Guard, the duc d'Orléans and the duc de Nemours. I welcome him in a tent in front of the École militaire, near to which are two detachments of citizens who had been wounded during the July fighting and who now gather under a flag which commemorates their victory.

"*Vive le roi!*" shout thousands of voices from sixty thousand armed and uniformed men from fifty-two battalions of the National Guard of Paris, four legions of the suburbs, the corps of artillery and the cavalry of the National Guard. Caps and hats are waved on bayonets.

Deputations advance from the battalions, the commanding officers in the center of each. "My comrades. I give you these flags with pleasure, and it is with great satisfaction that I give them again to the man who, forty years ago, was at the head of your fathers in this same place. These colors have marked for us the dawn of liberty," says Louis-Philippe.[100]

He gives me the four flags for each legion. I say the oath.

"*Je le jure*," the commanding officers declare.

The colonels and the deputations return to their men and give them the standards. The men swear the oath, as in 1790. "*Je le jure!*" rises to the heavens. Artillery fire.

"*Vive le roi!*" "*Vive Lafayette!*" everyone shouts.[101]

Louis-Philippe throws himself into my arms. "This is worth more to me than a coronation at Rheims!" he exclaims.[102]

"*Vive le roi!*" "*Vive Lafayette!*" people shout again.

The Revolution, started forty years before, has now bloomed into the sovereignty of the people and of a citizen-king. In the evening, he writes me a letter: 'I must know, my dear general, how you are after this wonderful day, for I fear that you must be very tired…I also want you to tell the National Guard of the admiration it has inspired in me today.'[103]

August 30. I issue an Order of the Day: 'The marvellous review of yesterday, the admirable appearance of the citizen-army, whose rapid formation has been in harmony with the rapidity of the triumph of liberty; the manner in which the National Guard presented itself under arms and

597

paraded before the kIng, excited the enthusiasm of the immense population which surrounded us.'[104]

The Belgians fight for five days. I would like Belgium to be a federal republic in close alliance with France, but it becomes apparent that they would like a republican monarchy. I urge the government not to influence either their choice of prince or their constitution. I believe France should protect the Belgians from interference by foreign powers.[105]

My popularity is immense. I am once more the subject of songs and poems. People say I am the author of liberty. The citizens of Paris bring two cannon to the rue d'Anjou as a gift. Delegations visit me from everywhere in France and Louis-Philippe writes almost nightly to ask about my health.

"There are no patriots in France more enlightened than the king and his son," I say to Duponceau. "I did not know them well before, but they have inspired in me the greatest friendship and trust, and this sentiment is mutual."

September 25. I speak at the session of the Chamber about the treaty concerning black people. I say that after so many sacrifices and misfortunes, France lags behind some other nations in this regard and that to avoid the lengthy nature of special propositions, of their being sent to bureaux, I ask the minister of the navy, who is here today, to tell us what the government determines to do concerning this treaty, and on the state of free men of color in our colonies.[106]

In the morning of the twenty-seventh, I learn from a man just arrived from Belgium that rockets and other incendiary devices have been used against Bruxelles; Prince Frederick has been trying since the twenty-third to occupy the city with a Dutch army corps. I am sent a note by other Belgian arrivals which suggest that one hundred thousand Prussian troops are marching to, or are already at, the border. I find their words somewhat exaggerated but believe their ministers think there are at least sixty thousand. I write to Louis-Philippe and suggest the ostensible reinforcement of our garrisons and the sending of National Guards and troops of the line to our frontier, which could, in my opinion, have a good moral effect.[107]

I support the idea of a monument to be erected to the four sergeants of La Rochelle and collect signatures for it. I propose their remains should be taken to the Panthéon.

Frederick was pushed back after five days of fighting in Bruxelles. On October 4 the provisional Belgian government declared that the Belgian provinces, now separate from Holland, would constitute an independent state, and that a central committee would decide on a constitution to be submitted to a national congress. The Belgians ask me to be either their president or their king.

"It should be at least a civic crown. However, it was already too much for my republicanism to have helped to found a throne and as the maréchal de Saxe remarked when asked to become a member of the Académie Française, that would suit me as much as a ring would a cat."[108] I suggest they should choose a Belgian citizen to be head of their government.

October 2. People condemned for their political views since 1815 ask me the favor of being presented to Louis-Philippe. The surviving electors of the 1789 Assembly of the Hôtel de Ville, as well as those who were *basoches* in '89, also request the honor of offering him their respects. Accordingly, I write to him.[109]

On the eighth most of the members of the commission concerning the abolition of the death penalty propose the adjournment of this question. I therefore speak again in the Chamber. "Without doubt they have not had the misfortune of seeing their family, friends, the best citizens of France perish on the political scaffolds. Messieurs, I support again and without hesitation the proposition of my friend...I particularly support its abolition concerning political crimes and demand its immediate adoption."[110]

On the tenth, the Freemasons of the *Grand-Orient* of France and of the *Rite écossais* give a banquet in my honor at the Hôtel de Ville, presided over by the duc de Choiseul. I am nominated thirty-third of the *Rite écossais* and will soon be a member of the Supreme Council of France. On the eighteenth there is rioting at Vincennes and the Palais-Royal where the king still lives, which continues in the night. People want the heads of Charles X's ministers. The National Guard disperses them. In the morning, I accompany Louis-Philippe and Gérard, the minister of war, to the courtyard of the Palais-Royal. The king assembles the National Guard around him and thanks them for the zeal with which they have maintained public order. Later I issue an Order of the Day also thanking them for the zeal, firmness and devotion which they have showed. 'It is evident that today, as in the first years of the revolution, the enemies of liberty, which is the sovereign justice, would like to see it spoiled by anarchy, sullied by crime.'[111]

I receive a letter from Maria Malibran, the celebrated opera singer. She asks me to help her obtain a divorce from her husband, whom she married in America. We meet; she is as beautiful in person as she is on the operatic stage.

"I will help you," I tell her.

On the thirty-first, eighty thousand National Guards, comprising twelve legions from Paris, four from the suburbs, corps of artillery and cavalry, parade on the Champ de Mars before Louis-Philippe and myself.

November 8. I speak in favor of the liberty of the press. "You cannot impose on human thought."

On the eleventh I attend a banquet given by the Seventh Legion of Paris. Mathieu Dumas makes a speech: "Seventy years ago General Washington, accompanied by General Lafayette, made his first visit to the French army disembarked at Rhode island...He was approaching a village when so many children surrounded him he was forced to stop...Washington said that here was the army our enemies would never be able to conquer....ten years later General Lafayette said the same words when surrounded by a group of young people at the Champ de Mars....his words were prophetic because you were those young people and it is you in the memorable days of July who have caused liberty to triumph, who have affirmed the new government, our representative and popular monarchy."[112]

On the fifteenth, I send to the minister the report of the commission on the Panthéon which I have just received. I say that my colleagues and I are ready to defend it in front of his colleagues; that we regard it as important to include Manuel, General Foy, and the four sergeants of La Rochelle.[113]

I start to prepare for the forthcoming trial of Charles X's ministers. I give orders to the National Guard that a battalion should be ready to march at the first command without the drums beating and frightening the citizens. Two non-commissioned officers must be with the mayor of each arrondissement during every twenty-four hours. The ministers are associated with a sentiment of unconquerable hostility to our liberty. They were the promoters of all the intrigues and the executors of all the acts of violence by which France had been subjected during the restoration. They were the men who conceived and signed the ordinances. They were the men who directed Paris to be attacked for three days and made twenty thousand families mourn the deaths of their loved ones. Their hands are still red with the blood of thousands of patriots. I will, however, bring them to trial unharmed. I will keep public order. I am determined that the honor of the revolution should be safeguarded for history as the ideal of popular omnipotence.[114]

November 16. I feel that the Chamber is resisting popular measures and that the king's council is managing the Chamber and the foreign powers more than I would like.[115] On the eighteenth I lead a delegation from Philadelphia, which has made the voyage to congratulate Parisians on their success, to a banquet at the Hôtel de Ville.

"I hesitated this morning, not knowing on which side I ought to take my place, whether I should stand with those who presented the address or those who received it. This evening I find all the memories as well as all the sentiments of my life fused together here, the grandsons of my companions in America, the sons of my comrades of '89, and my new brothers-in-arms of the Revolution of 1830. It is in this Hôtel de Ville, twice the cradle of European liberty, that have just been presented the resolutions of Philadelphia, that city, where on July 4, 1776, was promulgated the Declaration of Independence, date of a new era of liberty in the Two Worlds; a liberty that, for the first time, was founded on the veritable rights of humanity. Five years ago, at a great anniversary at Boston, in proposing a toast to the emancipation of the American hemispheres wrought during half a century, I added that the toast of the quinquagenary following would be 'Europe freed!' May that prediction be verified! Please raise your glasses." To the memory of Washington!"[116]

General Lallemand gives me a letter from Joseph Bonaparte in New Jersey. He congratulates me, although he would have liked to have seen his nephew, the duke de Reichstadt, on the throne, and hopes he might now be able to return to France. I write back:

> No personal consideration could enter into the deliberation. The first consideration of republicanism is to respect the general wish; I was not able to propose a purely American constitution, the best, in my opinion; it would have been to have disregarded the wish of the majority, risk civil disturbance, bring about foreign war... a popular throne in the name of national sovereignty is what we thought possible; such was the program of the barricades and of the Hôtel de Ville, of which I made myself the interpreter...the Napoleonic system was bright with glory but tainted by despotism, aristocracy and servitude...besides, the son of your immense brother has become an Austrian prince....one of my first actions after the elevation of the duc d'Orléans to the throne was to express the wish that you, your children and their respectable mother, should be able to return, if you wanted, to France. He received this wish very cordially but said that treaties with foreign powers would necessitate some negotiations. Since then the situation has worsened. [117]

On November 29 the Poles rebel against Russia. On December 4 I oppose the extradition of deserters. On the eighth, the king gives me the command of the troops of the line on duty for the duration of the trial of the ministers. I issue an Order of the Day to the National Guard, announcing this, as well as the measures which will be taken. Most of the National Guard want the law of high treason to be invoked against them. They want them executed, but I will do my duty even if it means I will lose my popularity. True popularity is not to be judged of by a complaisance in doing what will please the multitude but by the success with which we persuade the people that they ought not to do that which is wrong, and the firmness with which, when necessary, we prevent them from doing wrong without losing any of their affection.[118] I wish the ministers to be the object of a severe example of national justice. I know that Paris is in great agitation, but I do not wish the people of the barricades, who had shown such generosity towards Charles X, to be vindictive or implacable towards the executors of the counter-revolutionary projects of that despot, and I do not think I am less bound to act correctly from knowing that I, who am now their only safeguard, had been ordered to be arrested and executed by them. Even among my own staff, as among the National Guard, and the students, there is a feeling of indignation that the ministers should go free while the graves are scarcely closed over their victims. Everyone cries for vengeance, and it is only in the expectation that they will obtain it from the law that they refrain from procuring it for themselves. However, I cannot allow a return to the system of the scaffolds.

The court no longer treats me with suspicion, jealousy and low sarcasm. They give me unlimited confidence, respect and an almost filial display of feeling. I pity them; I know they will change when the trial reaches its conclusion.[119]

As well as the troops of the Line and the National Guard, I have been given the command of the police of the Palais-Royal, of the Luxembourg and of the Chamber of Peers. Since July, fifteen thousand soldiers of the National Guard can, at any moment, be assembled at given points, the spaces in between occupied by troops of the line. I divide Paris into four sections; I pay special attention to the safety of the Palais-Royal, the Hôtel de Ville, and the Luxembourg in particular, where Colonel Fisthamel is in charge. My principle for public order remains the same I held in 1789. It is always important to avoid sudden and violent movements. It is always better to prevent rather than to repress. What I most dread is to excite the animosity of the workman's jacket against the uniform of the National Guard.[120]

On the tenth, I order the ministers transferred from Vincennes to the Luxembourg at ten in the morning as it is not possible to take them twice a day from Vincennes to the court.

"Move them during the night," the government tells me.

"No," I reply. "It will be done openly, in daylight."

At noon, the ministers travel through the popular areas of the city, protected by mounted National Guards commanded by Carbonel, *chasseurs* commanded by General Fabvier, and a detachment of artillery, the crowds angry, but silent.

Paris teeters on the brink of a catastrophe. No one knows what will happen. Nobles are in terror. People fear homes and shops will be ransacked and are hiding their possessions. Near the Luxembourg shops put up their shutters. Foreign countries watch closely and most appear to think the new monarchy will not weather the storm.

My headquarters are at the Luxembourg whose garrison consists of both the National Guard and troops of the line. The National Guard patrol the streets, often having to disperse angry crowds whose numbers increase daily and who gather in all parts of Paris.

December 13. Today is Benjamin Constant's funeral. I make a speech at the Père Lachaise cemetery to a sad and respectful crowd: "The love of liberty and the need to serve it always dominated his conduct. It is only fair that this be acknowledged at his tomb by an old friend, the confidant of his most intimate thoughts."

On the nineteenth, I issue an Order of the Day where I lay before my fellow citizens the principles and experience of my life:

> He thought during the barricades that the present government founded on the sovereignty of the people, and having at its head Louis-Philippe, was the best which under the circumstances of France and Europe, we could adopt. He thinks it still and defends the government, not only because he has promised to do so, but also because he has not changed his opinion...A popular throne, surrounded by republican institutions was the motto adopted at the Hôtel de Ville, by a patriot of 1789, now become a citizen-king. Both people and king will prove themselves faithful to this contract....The commander-in-chief, quite sure of being supported by his patriot fellow-citizens and his brothers-in-arms...in his adherence to those principles of liberty and public order, which he will never abandon, even if he stood alone, relies now for their cooperation in the strict and faithful discharge of their duties.[121]

Many dislike my words. They cry for vengeance and death. Paris is in tumult.

From early in the morning of the twentieth, angry mobs gather throughout the capital as the verdict will be given today after five days of the trial. An immense crowd fills the rue de Tournon, the rue de Vaugirard and the front of the Luxembourg Palace. They attack the great gate there and break through the ranks of the battalions defending the advance posts. Shouts come from the tribunal; the mob will soon be inside it and perhaps kill the accused and even their judges.

I do not hesitate. I leave the protection of the National Guard and go on foot into the mob, only allowing George and a few aides-de-camp, to accompany me.

"It is imprudent to do so. These men are not the men of July. Some are criminals and some are instigators of violence," they say.

I take no heed of their words and walk along the rue de Tournon towards the Luxembourg. People open a path for me.

"Death to the ministers!" "Polignac's head!" " *Vive la republique!*" they shout angrily.

"Don't go any further," pleads George.

I continue to walk down the rue de Tournon through the mob. They do not insult me; they quieten.

"Have columns of the National Guard advance at walking pace, taking up the whole of the road towards the Luxembourg."

The crowd retreats. The soldiers clear the avenues; by ten o'clock the crowd has been pushed back in the adjacent streets, but their shouts are still audible, even in the Chamber of Peers.[122]

Darkness falls. The National Guard bivouac in the street, their fires smoking furiously into the sky, the flames lighting the sides of buildings and the ground. I spend the night discussing with Montalivet, Pasquier, Sébastiani and Odilon Barrot, how to protect the prisoners when the sentences are announced.

"I want to return them to Vincennes when the sentence is announced and take them back through Paris the same way they came," I say.

However, the government wants them to be secretly transferred the night before the sentence is given and as the forms of the Court of Peers do not require the presence of the accused as the sentence is read, it is therefore decided, with my agreement, that the ministers should be removed at the end of the trial.

A few hours before the sentence is passed, rumors fly through Paris that the prisoners have been sentenced to death. The crowds celebrate. From nine in the morning an immense crowd fills the whole quarter, from the Panthéon to the faubourg Saint Germain. In the afternoon, after the final pleadings, and before the verdicts are given, I arrange with the president, Pasquier, that the prisoners should be taken back to the part of the Luxembourg which serves as their prison and from where General Febvier will escort them back to Vincennes. The prisoners fear the people will kill them. Polignac appears extremely anxious, Peyronnet is calm, de Chanteleuse is clearly struggling to contain his emotions and de Ranville seems resigned. They all, however, behave with dignity and courage. Lieutenant Colonel Lavocat consigns the prisoners to Colonel Fisthamel; the National Guard on duty inside the Luxembourg are silent and do not attempt to harm them.[123]

At four o'clock, a light calèche takes them away, surrounded by a detachment of cavalry commanded by General Febvier, on horseback, accompanied by Montalivet, the minister of the interior, also on horseback. Posts of soldiers have been stationed the whole length of the route. At six o'clock a gun booms from Vincennes informing us of their safe arrival.

At nine-thirty in the evening, the verdict is given: all four are guilty. Polignac is condemned to be deported by one hundred and twenty-eight votes, only twenty-four votes for the death penalty. Peyronnet, Chanteleuze and Guernon-Ranville are condemned to life imprisonment.

Crowds rage in fury; riots break out; everyone expected a sentence of execution. The battalions of the National Guard at the Luxembourg demand to be relieved. I hurry to speak to them. They listen. They do not oppose me. I am very proud of them; they maintain their lines despite the violence of the crowd. They remain calm. They do not use their weapons. Strong patrols disperse the furious groups in the streets. At eleven o'clock they bivouac again in the boulevards and on the quays, the crowd making angry threats. I issue an Order of the Day thanking the National Guard for their zeal, firmness and devotion.[124]

In the morning of the twenty-second, the unrest continues, this time against the Palais-Royal, where there is great consternation and fear. I remain firm; the National Guard continues to keep order, helped by the students, and again do not use their weapons.[125]

I issue another Order of the Day thanking them and I also make public the letter the king has sent me in which he talks of the National Guard as being more wonderful than it has ever been and assures us of the sacred cause of liberty.[126]

On the twenty-third, there is calm; order is restored. I receive yet another letter from Louis-Philippe who wishes to go riding in Paris past the town halls to once more thank the reserves of the National Guard. He says he does not ask me to accompany him as I would find it too tiring but would like General Carbonel to do so. 'You know my friendship for you,' he writes, signing it with his familiar 'D'.[127]

On Christmas Eve, the anniversary of Adrienne's death, the day of George's birth, I issue another Order of the Day: 'The Revolution has emerged pure from this new trial; it has refuted the falsehoods of its calumniators from all countries; the accused have been protected, the verdict respected....confidence will be re-established, industry will work again; all has been done for public order; our recompense is to hope that all will be done for liberty.'[128]

Chapter 53

Life is like the flame of a lamp; when the oil is out the lamp is extinguished and all is over

People immediately attack me again now they are no longer afraid. The old suggestions that I am greater than the king, published in some English and German newspapers, resurface. Louis-Philippe is once more described as a puppet whom I, as the commander of an armed nation, am using to create a vast republic as well as bringing my beloved American institutions into the whole of Europe. Caricatures are everywhere. I am called milord protector, a new Cromwell, and mayor of the palace.[1]

The courtiers hope to restore the royal etiquette, but I am a constant reminder of the program of July. The old European aristocracies loathe me; I am an opponent of divine right, of privilege, of the abuses they would like to have restored. They see me as the leader of a purely popular revolution, only acknowledging thrones based on institutions which are essentially republican. They hate the system of non-interference in other nations which I have supported. Foreign cabinets suggest to Louis-Philippe that my removal is the price of their friendship, and a refusal would mean he would have to prepare for all the consequences of the displeasure of the Holy Alliance.[2]

I do not attend the debate in the Chamber of Deputies as I am working at my headquarters in the chaussée d'Antin. The news is brought to me that the government and the Chamber have proposed: 'In those communes or cantons where the National Guard may form several legions, the king shall have power to appoint a superior commandant, but he cannot appoint him superior commandant of the National Guard of a whole département, or even of an arrondissement of a sub-prefecture.' The Chamber has therefore pronounced the abolition of the post of commandant-général.[3] I am dismissed!

December 25. In the morning, I write my resignation to the king but do not allow it to be made public.[4]

He replies: 'I have this moment received your letter and am as much grieved as surprised at the resolution you have taken. I have not yet had time to read the accounts of the debates…The council of ministers assembles at one o'clock: after that, I shall be at leisure-that is to say between four and five. I hope to see you there and to prevail on you to retract your decision.'[5]

I meet the king who seems inconsolable at what has happened. "My ministers acted maladroitly and without any ill intention. But the unfortunate article has not yet become law and I know well…"

I interrupt him. "Sire, the distrust of my colleagues, and my dismissal, which they have pronounced as much as it was in their power to do so, make it a point of delicacy with me no longer to retain an authority which is offensive to them, and the principle of which, notwithstanding its transient utility, has been at all times condemned by myself. Besides being bent on promoting to the utmost of my power the abolition of the hereditary peerage, it would not be consistent in me to await, from the Chamber of Peers, a confirmation which would place that assembly in a state of hostility to me; or a favorable amendment, which would place me under a sort of obligation to the Chamber. Indeed, I can assure Your Majesty that I regard all this not only as a duty to be performed, but also as an opportunity."

"Explain yourself," he says.

"Sire, your system of government is not what I approve. I feel that the public confidence has given me a mission. I will not tell you where it is written. It is perhaps in public opinion-perhaps in the air. But, in truth, the French people, and many patriots of all nations, persuade themselves that where I am, there liberty will suffer no injury. I find, however, that liberty is menaced, compromised, and I do not wish to deceive anyone. The policy of your government, both with respect to its internal and external relations, is not such as I think salutary for the interests of liberty, and I should not be acting with sincerity if I longer remained like an opaque body between the people and the government. When I retire from my post everyone will better see on what he has to depend."

"I assure you of my boundless friendship," he assures me repeatedly; he endeavors to overturn what he terms my prejudices. "The article can be retracted."

"Sire, you offer me personally many concessions, but none for the advantage of the public interest. It is the public interest, and not mine, that is the subject of consideration," I reply.[6]

"Wait twenty-four hours so that I can deliberate on it," he says.

I agree in the hope there might be more mature reflection and better views.[7] I wish to set aside all personal consideration. I will consent to every insignificant reparation such as adjourning the execution of the article of the law which concerns me and to yield to all which is required in the hope of obtaining at this difficult time a better system of government.[8] I return to my headquarters. General Carbonel, Major General Tracy and George resign.

Next day Louis-Philippe sends Ségur to try and make me change my mind, evidently fearing the effect of my dismissal on the people.

"No, my dear cousin. I know my position. It is time I retire. I weigh, I know, like a nightmare on the Palais-Royal, not on the king and his family, who love me and are the best people in the world, and whom I love tenderly, but on those who surround them. Have I not heard Viennet say in front of the king when he sees me coming, "Here is the mayor of the palace!" Is it also without any meaning that the king himself reads me newspapers from America where I am depicted showing to Europe my puppet of a republican king to seduce her? We laughed about it, but even so. Without doubt I have been useful in making him a king but if I sacrificed some of my convictions for him, it has only been on the faith of the program of the Hôtel de Ville. I announced at that time a king surrounded by republican institutions, and this declaration that appears to have been forgotten is one which I hold greatly. And this is what the Court cannot forgive. I do not know if they go as far as accusing me of orchestrating the last riot, that which demanded the heads of the ministers of Charles X, and to have enlarged the danger in the eyes of the king. For now, when the danger has passed, they pretend to no longer believe it. Laffitte himself pretends that the king did not feel a moment's anxiety, which is false because I was asked for news a hundred times an hour! I therefore conclude that I have become an embarrassment. I will do my part. I will keep the same friendship for the royal family, but I will only have one word and I cannot change my convictions. As for the National Guard of Paris, as it is wished that I should remain its chief, I understand the motive, but I cannot submit. And what do you think? Suppose that Marshal Soult is offered a position similar to that which they are pretending to offer me, do you think he would reduce himself to remain at the head of one of the divisions of an army from which he has just been stripped of his command."[9]

I talk with Laffitte and Montalivet for two hours; Laffitte, however, does not wait for my reply and says he has guests waiting for him at dinner. Monsieur Guinard, a chief-of-staff of the National Guard, suddenly enters the room. "Reports indicate an insurrection is being planned for tomorrow."

"You must moderate your demands and not become the pretext of this riot," says Montalivet.

"Please convey my conditions to the king," I say. "I will make the concession of waiting for his reply. I will stay tonight at headquarters and will give my resignation tomorrow. For liberty everything, for myself nothing."[10]

Montalivet goes away to convene the colonels of all the legions at the Palais-Royal. Later, de Marmier and de Schonen come to see me. I again refuse to change my mind and they leave with tears in their eyes.

In the evening, I write to Louis-Philippe:

Sire, Your Majesty told me yesterday that the object of our conversation must be finished today. I saw Messieurs Laffitte and Montalivet; they talked of the amendment that the president of the council was intending to propose. But, Sire, you know the objections that I have already taken the liberty to say to you. I told Monsieur de Montalivet that I regarded myself as having already given my resignation. And I think that he will have given orders in consequence of it. Believe me, Sire, that what I am doing is more painful than I can express; today, more than ever, I need to join to the homage of my respect that of my profound and unchanging attachment. [11]

Shortly after midnight comes his reply. He regrets that I cannot accept the amendment which he had waited for with some confidence, but he will now take measures so that there is no interruption in the command of the National Guard. It is not what I had hoped for.

December 27. I say farewell to the National Guard in an Order of the Day: 'He will know to appreciate the new witnessing of their affection and their indissoluble union with him by their devotion to liberty and public order... It is with all his soul and not without sadness that their old and grateful friend dictates these words to them.' [12] Dupont de 'L'Eure resigns as minister of justice.

Later I go to the Chamber which creates a sensation. I stand at the tribune. "Messieurs, it is usual in a neighboring country, for citizens when they leave high office to explain to the Chamber how they stand with their colleagues. Allow me to avail myself of this privilege. I would be deeply hurt if anyone believed, and no one who has known or read about the last fifty-four years of my life, can believe that my conduct has been influenced by the least feeling of personality. I will go further: This opinion of the Chamber has afforded me an opportunity of tendering my resignation. The great power with which I was invested was looked upon, as you, Messieurs, are aware, with jealousy....My power is now broken. I have no longer the honor of being your colleague...I would not have tendered my resignation, which has been received by the king, with all the expressions of his kindness for me, before the crisis we have just passed through. My conscience concerning public order is now perfectly satisfied but I must confess that it is not the same with my conscience of liberty. We all know the program of the Hôtel de Ville; a popular throne surrounded by republican institutions. This has been accepted but we do not all understand it in the same way...However, there are some points on which we shall always be united against internal and foreign enemies. I think that in the course we have taken since the Revolution of July we have acted, not only for the best, but the only way in which we could have done. In leaving my uniform, I do not leave our device of liberty and public order."[13]

1831. January 1. I write a farewell letter to the National Guard of France and to that of Paris, my popularity still immense in Paris and in the country. I also write to Eugène Malibran to try to convince him to divorce his wife, and to a friend to wish him a happy New Year: 'Last year passed well for France; for Europe and for me it snagged a little in its last days. I am neither angry nor depressed, although it was not wonderful. I did all I could to put the world on a good road. I try and remain there myself but I raised much ill feeling among the doctrinaires...The only one who wishes me well is Monsieur de Polignac for not having let him be killed....the essential part was to pass the trial of the ministers without problem- they loved me so much during that time! But afterwards they did not lose a day.'[14]

On the sixth, at the Hôtel de Ville, I present to Odilon Barrot, the préfet de la Seine, an address from the people of Ireland to the French. He replies: "It is with good reason, General, all people address you when they want to congratulate France on the wonderful rôle she has just played in the history of civilization. They would certainly not know how to find a person anywhere else more true to all the principles which for forty years have fought against despotism and the ignorance of all the virtues which make a people worthy of liberty. You have been able to leave the military command which placed you at the head of all the enlightened classes of the nation, but you will never be able to abdicate from your influence, your moral standing, which thanks to fifty years of a life without reproach, you exercise on all spirits, and you will always be the standard around which all the friends of civilization and of the liberty of the people will come to rally.'[15]

On the twenty-third, I congratulate Palmerston on becoming the minister of foreign affairs and ask him what will he do, what can we do, for Poland.[16] On the twenty-eighth, I speak in the Chamber: "Two principles divide Europe; the sovereign right of people, and the divine right of kings; on one hand, liberty, equality; on the other: despotism and privilege..."Every time a country in Europe wants to exercise its sovereignty, any intervention of a foreign government to stop it is a declaration of war against France. If this leads to war, then we will have to submit to it." I talk of Belgium, of Poland and of Portugal.[17]

February 14. A riot erupts following a Mass said at the church of Saint Germain de l'Auxerrois for the assassinated duc de Berri and continues through the night, the next day and night. The rioters ransack the palace of the archbishop of Paris, Monseigneur Hyacinth de Quélon; I offer him residence in my home.

On the twentieth, I speak at length in the Chamber, firstly about recalling to the throne the republican conditions by which it came into existence, it being essential to know where the incompatibility lies between the contract of the Hôtel de Ville and the recently avowed system of the Palace. Then I refer to increasing the number of electors[18] before referring to the riots: 'Some excesses took place which were grievous to the friends of liberty and which, unfortunately, assumed an irreligious character, which might cause it to be believed in France and out of France, that the popular sentiments opposed to the liberty of worship, which is so sacred a principle, that not even a whole nation is not entitled to deprive a single individual of it.'[19]

Russia had invaded Poland on the fifth, sixth and seventh; on the nineteenth they defeat the Poles at Cracow, then take Warsaw. When news of it arrives, mobs again take to the streets.

On the twenty-fourth, I vote in the Chamber for two hundred francs to be the level of eligibility at which a man can vote, although I would prefer it to be lower. [20] On the twenty-fifth, Russia and Poland fight at Olszynka Growchowska and many men are killed on both sides. I consider going to Poland to fight as I realize France will not help the Poles.

There is a rebellion in Italy against the Pope and the Dukes of Parma and Modena which is put down by the Austrians. Riots occur in France; people want work and bread and there is a demonstration at the Palais-Royal. Laffitte is replaced by Casimir Périer; the government has become more conservative.

"Agree that you have been a naïve fool. I am fool number one; you are fool number two and in this way justice is given to everyone!" I say to Laffitte.[21]

On the twenty-ninth, I speak in the Chamber on the law concerning rioting. On May 6, the Chambers are dissolved; new elections will be on July 5. I return to La Grange from where I write a long letter to Casimir Périer concerning Italians who have been proscribed and have sought refuge in France. On the eighteenth, I reproach the minister of foreign affairs for having officially declared that the French government would never consent to the Austrians entering Italian regions in rebellion, but not having done anything to oppose them. On the twenty-eighth, I receive word that César de La Tour Maubourg is dying; I drive hastily to Paris. I sit by his bed. "Hold my hand," he asks.

I can see he does not believe he will survive. "Do not stay long," he says, not wanting to hurt me by watching him suffer. He dies that morning, his death a terrible loss for me. We have been close friends since the age of fifteen and he has given me such wonderful proofs of his friendship.[22]

I write at length on June 13 to my constituents in Meaux of my motives for how I voted in all the great legislative questions discussed in the Chamber and also of my thoughts and hopes during the events of July. I recount the words concerning the program of the Hôtel de Ville I had with the duc d'Orléans when he had just become lieutenant-général, words which had the effect of rallying round us both those who had objected to any monarch and those who desired one in every way contrasted to a Bourbon….this was, prior to the intervention of Louis-Philippe, a republican measure, for the popular overthrow of despotic ordinances, of a granted charter, and a dynasty of divine right, and to substitute for them the patent principle, and the choice of a monarch, an undisguised act of the sovereignty of the French people.[23] The letter is published, printed in nearly all the newspapers and widely distributed; I intend it not just for my constituents in Meaux but also for people throughout France. It evidently greatly angers the king, the minister and the Court.[24]

I am again elected deputy for Meaux by 486 votes to 162, as well as for Strasbourg where I had not actually stood as candidate, but where I received 117 votes to 92. I choose Meaux and am also regional councilor for Seine-et-Marne. On July 25, the new Chamber convenes. On the twenty-eighth, I attend the anniversary of the July revolution and the inauguration of the names in the Panthéon of those who were killed in the fighting. I am seated in the first row of deputies as the king passes by. He ignores me.

"We are in the position of two gentlemen who have given each other the lie; circumstances will not permit us to go to the Bois de Boulogne, but they prevent our exchanging visits," I remark later.[25]

In the new Chamber I advocate the cause of Italy and Poland. On September 6, my birthday, Warsaw falls to the Russians.

"War on Russia!" "Vengeance!" shout crowds in Paris when they find out the news. They break the windows of the ministries. Shops and theatres are closed.

Thiers accuses me of being bellicose. [26]

"If we do not wish war at any price, we do not want peace at any price either." I say in the Chamber on September 20.[27]

The deputies vote for peace. On October 5 the rest of the Polish army surrenders to Prussia, rather than to Russia.

On October 6, I reiterate my view in the Chamber that I have always wanted two chambers and oppose the institution of a hereditary peerage. On the tenth I put down an amendment. I fail, but we manage to halt the hereditary transmission of seats by 324 votes to 94. The same month, I become mayor for Courpalay, the commune where La Grange is situated. On the twenty-ninth, there is a celebration of the insurrection of Poland which I attend wearing a uniform of a grenadier of the Polish National Guard.

In 1832, my grandson, Jules de Lasteyrie, goes to fight with Dom Pedro against Dom Miguel in Portugal for the campaign of Portuguese independence; I write to Dom Pedro to recommend him. Prince Leopold de Saxe-Coburg is elected king of the Belgians; Louis Philippe had refused the title for his son, the duc de Nemours, last February.

Last October, cholera, which had started in India, reached France and has been killing people for five months. In late March, the poor districts of Saint Antoine and Saint Marceau have the first cases of cholera in Paris. It quickly spreads. The streets smell of death; carts take away the dead at night; red lights signal posts to help people. Mourning drapes decorate churches; theaters are shut. We do not understand the illness which strikes at random. People carry bags of herbs; bottles of aromatic liquids and large jars of chloride water are placed in the streets. On April 9 there are eight hundred and sixty-one deaths. Fear terrorizes the people and rumors abound that wells and the buckets of water carriers are contaminated with arsenic and other poisons.

"Down with the doctors!" "Death to the poisoners!" mobs shout and drown two accused people in the Seine at the Pont-Neuf. George goes to La Grange to help the peasants.

Casimir Périer becomes ill; I visit him at his house in the rue Neuve du Luxembourg. His face already has the distinctive bluish tinge and I fear there is no hope. He dies at eight o'clock on the morning of May 16. I mourn him as a friend and a relation, even although I did not share his views; I hope people only attack his memory in order to condemn the government, of which he was, unfortunately, a member.[28]

The press continues to vilify Louis-Philippe, commonly portrayed as a pear, a simpleton in slang. He does not appoint a premier ministre. The deputies flee Paris in terror and the government does what it wants without any discussion.

'The laws which issue from this extraordinary session ought to be classed separately and named the cholera laws. They should only be used provisionally until they can be properly voted on in the next Chamber,' declares a patriotic journal.[29]

On May 28 I attend a banquet where we drink toasts to a republic. Next day at Laffitte's house we draw up a declaration of our beliefs: 'The France of 1830 thought, like that of '89, that hereditary royalty, surrounded by republican institutions is not irreconcilable with the principles of liberty. We are united in our devotion to the great and noble cause France has fought for during forty years. We will not abandon it either in success or failure. We have faith in its triumphs.' One hundred and forty deputies sign. Mauguin signs for General Lamarque, who is dying of cholera. On June 1, he dies; on the fifth is his funeral. Calm prevails throughout Paris; the sun shines brightly. As early as ten o'clock, people of all classes and nationalities, and many uniformed soldiers of the National Guard, stream towards the boulevards next to where Lamarque's body lies in the funeral house. Patriots dispute over who will have the honor of pulling the funeral carriage; shortly after eleven the cortège sets off to cries of " *Vive la liberté! Vive Lafayette!*"

I walk behind it, bareheaded, arm-in-arm with maréchal Clausel, followed by liberal deputies, war veterans, Polish, Spanish, Italian and German refugees and others. Students from the École Polytechnique have been told to stay in barracks, to the great indignation of everyone.

We reach the boulevard de la Madeleine. " *Vive la liberté!*" "*Vive Lafayette!*" people shout. Then there is silence; a silence of respect and mourning, punctuated by the waving of at least twenty different kinds of flags and a muffled beating of drums. We hear that town sergeants have grievously wounded a young man shouting " *Vive la liberté*" and that they, in turn, are saved from the crowd by some of the newly disbanded National Guard. The crowd also erupts into fury when Monsieur de Fitz-James refuses to bare his head as the procession passes underneath his windows, but he quickly disappears from view.

The cortège deviates from its intended route; it goes to the column in the place de Vendôme, maréchal Clausel and I at its head. We walk around its base, former National Guards ecstatically applauding this homage to France's military glory; the outpourings of patriotism and the sharing of our principles which I see and hear, greatly moving me.

Rain starts to fall; the procession sets off again. We reach the place de la Bastille, rain now falling in torrents. Students from the École Polytechnique are here, having ignored their orders. They help the former National Guards to form a protective cordon around the cortège, the stage from where people will speak, and the invalid bearers of the flags. Maréchal Clausel, as the representative of the army, gives a speech from the stage to shouts of applause. Monsieur Mauguin speaks for the deputies, to more applause. Foreign speakers follow: Monsieur Pons de l'Herault, the Polish General Uminski, the Nuncio Lelewill, and the Portuguese General Saldanha, all of whom are applauded loudly.

It had been agreed that I would not speak, but I have to say some words in honor of Lamarque, in memory of '89 and 1830, and as a compliment to the people's flags. I step near to the stage. The crowd roars. I point to the site of the Bastille.

"Look at where the Bastille stood. We must pay tribute to the Revolutions of 1789 and 1830 and to the flags of Poland, Portugal, Spain, Italy and Germany here today to represent their people, not their kings. These flags are the children of our tricolor."

The crowd roars again. "Take the body to the Panthéon!" many shout.

"Disperse peacefully. Do nothing to harm the remembrance of this day. Respect the wishes of General Lamarque and his family to have his body taken to Mont-de-Marsan. Do not spoil this day of patriotism."

The cortège continues to the place d'Austerlitz. Suddenly, to everyone's astonishment, a red flag appears in the crowd, the words, *Liberty or Death,* inscribed on it, the revolutionary slogan which meant *to live free or to die,* corrupted during the reign of Terror into *Liberty or I will kill you*! As the flag approaches the coffin, a red Phrygian bonnet is placed above it. It passes in front of the stage where I am; some foreigners throw crowns of *immortelles,* for whom it is only a symbol of liberty; another is thrown by a man who is perhaps from the police. A crown is placed on my head; I throw it to the ground to show my disagreement and disgust at what is happening.

My three companions by the coffin have left; George and I hurriedly follow. We cannot find my carriage; we scramble into a small carriage which men have unharnessed to pull along. I do not want them to do this, but it is the only way to escape from the crowd. I am helpless. Men surround me, mostly young.

"Go to the Hôtel de Ville!" they shout threateningly. "Order the people to attack. It is by order of the people."

"You are not the French people," I reply. "In any case, the first order for me is that of my conscience and of good sense."

A detachment of dragoons arrives, interrupting the conversation.

"What if we kill General Lafayette and throw his body in the river? The people would think the government had done it. His death would be a good call to arms!" a man calls out.

We pass the post at the Madeleine. Some of the crowd shout to the soldiers to take arms "Would you like an escort?" asks the officer on duty.

"No thank you. I am surrounded by friends," I reply.

He returns to his post, to the satisfaction of the crowd, and the men continue to pull my vehicle towards the rue d'Anjou, not threatening in any way except for a man armed with a saber, evidently from the police, who keeps shouting " *Vive la république!*"

Many hours later we arrive. It is six-thirty. I am exhausted. I shakily step onto the ground, my dignity in tatters, but with my usual calm. I enter the house and go on to the balcony to address the crowd.

"My dear comrades. Please go home," I tell them, my voice weak with emotion. I go inside and they reluctantly begin to disperse.[30]

At the place d'Austerlitz, mounted dragoons had appeared from behind the Grenier d'Abondance and had ridden into the crowd. Citizens and students from the École polytechnique had formed a line to try and form a barrier between the crowd and the dragoons. Other squadrons of dragoons had appeared. I cannot say who had started the fighting, whether it was supporters of Charles X, dragoons, young people, or simply people in anger. I was no longer there.[31]

We can hear the noise of the firing; I become deeply anxious. Between seven and eight o'clock several patriots come to see me to ask what should be done, but I can do nothing. For several months now I have felt that the throne is not open to persuasion. The opposition deputies in Paris decide to meet at Laffitte's house and at ten o'clock about twenty of us are there, as well as some others. Two measures are proposed-an address and a deputation to the king. I agree to neither, but an address is approved. Many want to express their indignation at the sight of the red bonnet, approve the vigorous measures which have secured public order and hope the guilty will be severely punished.

I disagree. "The government has committed errors of the greatest magnitude for which it would not be right to grant a bill of indemnity, and in the present circumstances, more than any other time, it is the duty of the representatives of France to remind the throne of July of the conditions of its existence, the engagements it has violated, the rights of the nation disavowed and trampled upon, and the disasters brought about by its broken faith. We should urge the necessity of abandoning the disastrous system of March 13 which daily widens the abyss that separated all that the revolutionaries of July wished to unite."[32]

It is again proposed to send a deputation to Louis-Philippe. I refuse to take part.

"My last conversation with the king convinced me that his opinions on government are so tenacious that any persuasion, at least from me, would have no effect on the system adopted. My second reason is that my presence will remind the king of having violated or forgotten a solemn engagement. I therefore wish to spare His Majesty, and to spare myself, an interview which bitter recollections would make mutually painful."[33]

We finish the meeting at midnight without deciding anything and agree to meet again at ten o'clock tomorrow.

Partial fighting continues during the night, the forces very unequal between the combatants. Nearly eight hundred workers and young men, nearly all unarmed, face thirty thousand troops of the line, five thousand National Guards, and formidable artillery. Next morning, the sun rises on more bayonets within the walls of Paris, to conquer the republic, than the mists of Austerlitz and Jena had seen march against the Prussians and Russians.[34] Grief and indignation move me. I hate to see French blood spilled by Frenchmen. I condemn the government, but I also condemn the violence of the young men who should leave their grievance to time, the law, the chambers and the press.[35]

We meet again at ten at Laffitte's house, but this time there has been a change in events since last night. The government has won. I repeat the same arguments I had made yesterday.

I leave before there is any agreement on what to do. In my absence, it is decided to send a deputation to the king; Laffitte, Odilon Barrot and Arago are nominated. On their return they say that the king replied he has a legitimate right to defend himself, that he had more than fulfilled the pledges he had made and had given to France as many republican institutions as he had promised, and even more. He declared that the program of the Hôtel de Ville had only existed in the mind of Monsieur de Lafayette, whose incessant appeals were evidently the result of a mistake, that with respect to the system of March 13, it was wrong to give the credit of it to Monsieur Périer, that the system belonged to the king and resulted from his own convictions and that he had only consented to take the crown on the conditions indicated by the development of this system, which was most comfortable to the wishes and wants of France, and from which he would not deviate even if they should mince him in a mortar. He concluded by saying that he would make no change in the system pursued by his government.[36]

While the king is speaking to the deputies, cannon fire on people near the Clôitre Saint-Méry and the rue Saint Transnonian, killing eight hundred. The insurgency ends. The evening is perfectly calm.

In the following days there is an attempt to smear me by suggesting that when the emblem of '93 was raised on the coffin I was eager to place a crown of *immortelles* on it. I write to the *Courier du Gard* to deny the accusation: 'I have always been opposed, with sincerity and with the approval of my countrymen, to the criminal violence of which, in 1792 and 1793, this red cap became in France the bloody symbol.'[37]

There is a deluge of calumnies against me. The old accusations resurface, including that I fell asleep on the night of October 5 and 6, that I said 'this is the best of republics.' I will stay here in Paris to brave this onslaught and show myself before the government.[38]

I believe that if the insurgency in the evening had not happened then the system called the 13 of March would have been reversed. One hundred and thirty thousand citizens of Paris had pronounced in favor of the opposition, if there had been calm the king would next day have been forced to consider talking to the left. Instead, the following day, there was a counter-revolutionary movement which violated the Charter and what distressed me was the lightness with which my compatriots have treated these infractions of their liberty.[39]

I ignore the pleas of my family to remain in Paris because of the cholera; I return to La Grange with Doctor Thierry, as well as with many blankets, linen, food and medication for the peasants. I visit all the sick, whom Virginie and Anastasie have been helping to nurse.[40]

On June 21 I resign as mayor of Courpalay and from the council of Seine-et-Marne, to which I have been nominated; I remain as a deputy and a municipal councilor, to which I have been elected.

The cholera appears to be coming to an end in Paris and will shortly leave us here in our area. Our political situation, however, continues. The anniversary fêtes of the July days pass rather sadly at Paris and at Rozoy we only have the reunion of the battalion.

"The tricolor cockade has just been brought to Portugal on the head of my grandson," I say, which pleases people. [41]

The Chamber will not be sitting until November. I write to Dupont de l'Eure on September 20 and ask that my seat should be marked beside his, on the fourth bench of the left. Ten days later, to my great pleasure I win four prizes at the agricultural competition of Rozoy-en-Brie.

The chill of winter is here. I return early in November to Paris. On the nineteenth, a man fires a shot from the crowd at Louis-Philippe as he rides across the Pont Neuf to the *séance royale* of the Chamber; I suspect the police. He is not injured and gives a speech which is harsh towards republicans and towards the problems arising from the landing in the Vendée of the duchesse de Berry, the mother of the duc de Bordeaux. He wants the government to be granted greater powers. Many deputies rush on foot to the Tuileries to congratulate him on his escape. I do not. I feel that after the lie which has been presented to the whole world, it is more respectful for me not to show my face there.[42] The king and the court complain of my absence.

'They will not suspect me of applauding methods of assassination, even supposing this to be serious, which I gravely doubt,' I write to Dupont de l'Eure.[43]

The session opens rather sadly for the opposition. Several of our colleagues believe that we were too vehement last year. We are not in the majority and have only one nomination for both small and large *bureaux*.

I attend a dinner given by James Fenimore Cooper. He gives me a beautiful jewel in gold from North Carolina which profoundly moves me as it is the latest sign of confidence and of affection which has been shown to me for the last fifty-five years.

December 3. I support an amendment of Monsieur Bignon in favor of the Polish nation. On the seventh, I announce the commencement of the siege of Anvers, being conducted brilliantly by our troops and artillery.

On January 15, 1833, I speak in the Chamber on the law concerning the organization of the départements. I want more power for local assemblies. I say that instead of going backwards we need to go forward in our national system. On the twenty-third we debate a project to give a pension to the conquerors of the Bastille. Gaetan de La Rochefoucauld, one of its opponents, declares "It is not the taking of the Bastille which made the revolution, on the contrary, it is its taking, which by turning it from its natural course, precipitated it into all the excesses of anarchy; it is its taking which gave rise to the example of riots, of massacres etc."

I go to the tribune and fulfil a duty by defending the Revolution of July and the famous July 14 which was the signal for the European revolution. I describe that memorable day and quote the words of Monsieur de La Rochefoucauld's illustrious father to Louis XVI who had said "It's a great riot." "No, Sire," La Rochefoucauld had replied. "It's a great revolution." I finish by saying "In the same way that July 4 was the American era of the liberty of the world, that is to say of a liberty founded on the simple doctrine of natural and social rights; the taking of the Bastille has been recognized throughout time as the signal of European emancipation, set back by many obstacles but which nothing will prevent from achieving."[44]

February 26. I speak on behalf of the political refugees. On March 11, I speak indignantly in the Chamber about the arrest at La Grange of Lelewel, the Polish patriot, who was taken as prisoner to Melun, and then to Tours. On the fifteenth, I write to General Jackson, the President of the United States, to say with what anxiety I had received the news of the wish of South Carolina to cede from the Union and that I am now happy to learn that this collision has been avoided.[45] On June 6 I preside at a banquet in the Bois de Vincennes given by German republicans, to the great annoyance of Metternich. At the same time, a liberal demonstration takes place at the château of Hambach in Bavaria. On the twelfth, I attend a Breton dinner. "To Breton patriotism of 1789 and of 1830. To France and European emancipation!" I toast.[46]

A treaty had been signed on July 4, 1831, by which France had agreed to pay five million dollars in indemnities and to cancel the claims of the heirs of Beaumarchais against the United States. It has not yet been ratified and on the thirteenth, I speak in its favor. My enemies believe I have to choose between my two countries, the United States and France. Instead, I declare: "It will be said that I am a good American. Messieurs, it is a title which I honor; it is a title dear to my heart, but nobody, I believe, will say that I have ever been a bad Frenchman."[47]

I go home to La Grange for the summer; I now drive round the estate in my calash, rather than ride. 'The days are warm, pure and all alive, as beautiful as any you will find at Tours, the paradise of France,' I write to the Princess de Belgiojoso. There have been riots in Lyons and I tell her that: 'it is forbidden at Lyon to sing *La Marseillaise*, which Louis-Philippe used to sing so well, and that would seem to be jealousy between virtuosos.' However, I happily also tell her: 'There is the best news from Oporto; they are expecting an insurrection at Fiqueras.'[48]

On January 3, 1834, I speak in the Chamber. "I thought, and I still think that, under the charm of our national colors, with the help of a dynastic change and the displacement of the aristocracy, that one is walking along a retrograde path, and towards the system of this restoration that the wind of a great week of the people had made disappear." I talk about the abandonment of Poland and Polish refugees, some of whom live at La Grange.[49]

February 1. It is the anniversary of the death, two years ago, of César de La Tour Maubourg. Today is also the funeral of Monsieur Dulong, the son of Dupont de l'Eure, a young liberal deputy, who was killed in a duel with General Bugeaud in the Bois de Boulogne. The bullet penetrated his head, but he did not immediately die. I visited him in his agony and George remained the whole time with him, both of us grief-stricken.

I walk for several hours behind the hearse from the rue de Castiglione to the Cemetery of Père Lachaise. I struggle; it is a long way, but I must continue, both to the memory of Dulong and to patriotism.

In the evening, I am extremely tired; I am not able to urinate; I feel ill and go to bed. Two skillful surgeons are called for during the night and they attempt to help me without success. Next morning Doctor Cloquet returns to Paris. He immediately places me in a hot bath which is somewhat beneficial. Then he operates.

I stay in bed and Doctor Cloquet visits daily, at first prescribing antiphlogistic and derivative treatment and then stimulating frictions and sulfurous douches. My health somewhat improves, although gout attacks my lower limbs, lungs, digestive organs and eyelids. I leave my bed and sit at my desk; I see my family and some of my friends. Princess Christine de Belgiojoso visits when my health permits. She sits by my bedside, entertaining me so well I forget my suffering. I speak often of her to Doctor Cloquet, of her rare merit, her nobleness of character and her kindness towards her compatriots.

My doctors decide that fresh air will benefit my recovery; they recommend my going out in a carriage and so I frequently visit my granddaughter, Nathalie de La Tour Maubourg, now Madame Adolphe Périer, at Beauséjour, a country house by the entrance to the Bois de Boulogne. My appetite improves, my strength increases; I am more cheerful, more like my old self and urination is not such a problem.

I frequently tell anecdotes of my past, particularly of America. "The Americans are aware of my situation. They know that I have need of repose and they will not trouble mine," I say to Cloquet.

Madame Joubert dies. "Poor woman! It was she who made that handsome sketch of La Grange! What a loss to her husband, her children and myself!" I tell Cloquet.[50]

A handful of discontented people erupted into armed violence here in Paris during the evening of April 13. In the morning, I can hear firing from the rue Transnonian where a greater force defeats the rioters. At Lyon there was fighting between workers and troops of the line for four days and it is thought that illiberal laws and measures are being prepared. I write to Fenimore Cooper who is in New York and tell him what is happening here and of my health.[51] I am beginning to feel much better and Doctor. Cloquet believes I might recover almost completely.[52]

On May 1, I write a letter to Murray at Glasgow, the president of the *Society for the Emancipation of Slaves*, thanking him for the Society's mention of my long-standing and constant sympathy for this great cause.[53] On the ninth I make my usual excursion in the morning. It is warm, but at midday thunder rumbles above the trees. The air becomes cold. A wind blows icily from the northwest. Rain suddenly drenches me. I return home, feeling ill, my legs and arms hurting painfully.

Next day I shiver violently and have a painful swelling in my groin. Fever grips me. My symptoms worsen. At times I lapse into a coma. My little white dog acts as a thermometer of my health; when I worsen, she is sad, when I improve, she is happy. My death is announced in a journal.

"The Swiss Gazette has just killed me, and yet you know nothing of the matter!" I say to Doctor Cloquet. "Even more, so that I might die in due form, the celebrated Doctor...whom I hardly know, has been consulted." I give him the journal. "After that believe the public journals if you can!"[54]

"Monsieur Guersent and I would like to consult Professors Fouquier, Marjoin and Andral," he tells me.

"Why? Have I not complete confidence in you both so how can there be any addition made to the care you take of me, and to the interest you feel in my welfare?" I ask.

"We think we have done what is best for you but were there a single remedy which might escape us, it is our duty to see it. We want to restore you as soon as possible to health, for we are responsible for your situation towards your family, your friends, and the French nation, of whom you are the father," replies Monsieur Guersent.

"Yes, their father. On condition that they never follow a syllable of my advice," I reply.[55]

Professors Andral, Marjolin and Fouquier therefore also come. They agree with Doctor Cloquet and his colleagues and try more remedies. I become sad. "I want to talk with you in private," I say to George. Then I recover my spirits and again have hope of recovery.

"Quinine and the fever, my dear doctor, are battling together. Give me plenty of quinine that it may gain the upper hand," I tell Cloquet.

Next morning, I feel myself worsening. "I fear the quinine is in the wrong and I shall be obliged to pay the costs of the suit. Life is like the flame of a lamp; when the oil is out the light is extinguished and all is over," I say.[56]

I am only allowed to see my family.

"You will tell the good Princess de Belgiojoso how grateful I feel for her visits and how much I suffer at being deprived of them," I say to my grandson, Jules.

My body is failing. I am resigned to the passing of my life, although at times I am immensely sad. Messieurs Cloquet and Girou constantly attend me.

May 20. I gasp for breath. I am suffocating. Fever is taking hold. I am prostrate with weakness.[57]

Epilogue

At one o'clock in the morning of Tuesday, May 20, 1834, Lafayette worsened. His breathing became more labored, and it was not apparent that he could see. He fell in and out of a delirious sleep; he became weaker and at three o'clock in the morning his whole family and some of his most intimate friends assembled in his chamber. George noticed him struggling to touch something on his chest and immediately placed his mother's locket into his hand. Lafayette brought it to his lips and kissed it. He opened his eyes and looked with affection at his children surrounding the bed. He pressed the hand of Doctor Cloquet. A contraction appeared in his forehead and eyebrows. He breathed deeply. He sighed. His pulse stopped beating but there was still a murmur by his heart. A stimulating massage was unsuccessfully used. His face was calm.

Sobs and shrieks of the gathering rent the chamber. George, in tears, said a last farewell. The family knelt by Lafayette, kissed his hands, then embraced each other. Bastien stayed at the foot of the bed, tears flowing down his face. Those who had come to visit Lafayette and were present in the house were allowed to see him. Bastien lit the candles of Cornwallis and placed them round the bed. Anastasie knelt and drew a sketch, as did Doctor Cloquet.

People everywhere expressed their grief on hearing of his death, even some who had been opposed to his views.[1] President Dupin announced his death to the Chamber; a delegation of twelve members were designated as representatives at the funeral. American ships at Le Havre lowered their flags.

David d'Angers fashioned a plaster mask from Lafayette's face; Ary Scheffer drew a portrait; Gudin copied the sketch Cloquet had made.

On Thursday, May 22, at nine o'clock in the morning, fifteen Polish refugees from La Grange, led by General Dwernicky, carried the coffin to the bier which was decorated at the four corners with the tricolor. The cortège left the rue d'Anjou preceded by a corps of lancers, a detachment of the National Guard on horseback, two battalions of the National Guard on foot and two battalions of infantry. The ropes of the bier were held by deputies Jacques Laffitte, Eusèbe Salverte and Odilon Barrot, by Eugène Laffitte representing the National Guard, by General Febvier for the army, by Monsieur Baston for the United States, by General Ostrowski for Poland, and by an elector from Meaux. Bastien followed immediately behind, carrying a black velvet cushion on which were Lafayette's sword and epaulettes. Next came the family, the members of the two Chambers, and civil and military officers, surrounded by troops of the line. Armed soldiers lined each side of the street. Marshal Lobau led three thousand of the National Guard in uniform, with black crêpe arm bands but without arms. An immense crowd followed.

When the funeral procession reached the Church of the Assumption former soldiers of the National Guard rushed forward wanting to carry it into the church and to touch it. The interior of the church was simply decorated; the catafalque was surrounded by tricolor flags, at each of its corners was a funeral lamp, flickering with blue flames. After the service the cortège proceeded slowly to Picpus, the crowd even more numerous than before, many in tears. It crossed the place Vendôme; about a hundred young people with a flag unsuccessfully attempted to break through the ranks of soldiers. It continued along the rue de la Paix, along the boulevards to the place de la Bastille, then through the faubourg Saint Antoine to the rue de Picpus.

'I was at the entrance of the rue Grange-Batelière when Monsieur de Lafayette's cortège passed by. At the top of the boulevard it stopped. I saw it gilded with a fugitive ray of sun, shining above the helmets and the weapons. Then the cloud returned,' wrote Chateaubriand.[2]

'Hide yourselves Parisians! To approach the coffin of Lafayette it would have taken a pitched battle. No one tried and indeed the spirit of Lafayette must have been indignant. The true friend of the people of Paris was separated from them by bayonets and sabers,' wrote Armand Carrel in the *National*.[3]

'The death of Lafayette was the occasion of a military parade only; the government had not forgotten the disturbances at the funerals of General Foy and General Lamarque. He was there, but as in the dungeons of Olmütz. The French army kept him imprisoned in a coffin like the Austrian army had kept him imprisoned in a state prison. The funeral carriage marched unnoticed in the middle of a battalion whose bayonets, still covered in French blood, prevented the people from paying homage to their liberator,' wrote Barère.[4]

Lafayette's coffin was carried slowly through an avenue of lime trees in the small, narrow cemetery at Picpus, forever linked to so many deaths in the Revolution; it was placed next to that of Adrienne and covered by earth taken from Bunker Hill in 1825 as he had wished. There were no speeches, only the family were present. At three-thirty, the ceremony finished; there had been no riots nor demonstrations. The Picpus cemetery was now the eternal resting place of a son of the Auvergne, the Hero of Two Worlds, who had steadfastly pursued the course of liberty throughout the whole of his life. [5]

The packet ship, Silas Richard, docked at New York on June 19, bearing the news of Lafayette's death to the country where he had shed his blood for its independence, where he had fought at the side of Washington and where he had trapped Cornwallis and his army at Yorktown.

On June 24 the Senate and the House decreed a resolution expressing the sadness of Congress and requesting the president to send a copy of the resolution and a letter to George Washington Lafayette. There were thirty days of national mourning. The halls of Congress were draped in black. Lafayette was given the same honors as Washington. At dawn, twenty-four guns were fired from every army post and every naval ship and station; flags flew at half–mast; a cannon boomed out every half an hour for a whole day; naval and army officers wore black armbands for six months. Memorial services were held in every city. People wore mourning emblems. The Lafayette Guards marched. Veterans marched. On December 31, the former president, John Quincy Adams, gave a three-hour speech about Lafayette to both Houses, subsequently printed in sixty thousand leaflets. "Pronounce him one of the first men of his age, and you have not yet done him justice....Born and educated in the highest order of feudal Nobility, under the most absolute Monarchy of Europe, in possession of an affluent fortune, and master of himself and of all his capabilities at the moment of attaining manhood, the principle of republican justice and of social equality took possession of his heart and mind, as if by inspiration from above. He devoted himself, his life, his fortune, his hereditary honors, his towering ambition, his splendid hopes, all to the cause of liberty."[6]

The small boy who hunted the Beast became a man whose name was known throughout Europe and America. He was a prominent figure in three revolutions on two continents. He was one of the few original leaders of the 1789 Revolution to survive, escaping the guillotine by fleeing his army and his country. A friend of the oppressed, he knew imprisonment and the threat of death. Hated by many aristocrats, hated by Jacobins, he always pursued the course he believed was best for France and which he hoped would lead to a fair and just society. Guided initially by Freemasonry with its tenets of freedom, virtue and equality, these beliefs were reinforced by his experience in the United States. An immensely wealthy aristocrat who knew the king, he nevertheless absorbed the republican ideals of his adopted country and found a figure to revere and to emulate in George Washington. A republican, he advocated a constitutional monarchy as the best policy for France in '89 and tried unsuccessfully to stop the Jacobins from gaining control. In 1821 and 1822 he participated in failed Carbonari plots to overthrow the government and later played a pivotal role in the 1830 Revolution, making Louis-Philippe a king, once more setting aside his republican views to do what he thought best for France. He felt he lacked the support to do otherwise; the workers fighting at the barricades wanted him as president of a republic, but fellow political colleagues such as Thiers and Laffitte wished the duc d'Orléans to be king, a citizen king, but a king nevertheless. The elderly Lafayette hesitated but after hearing the views of people such as the American ambassador, William Rives, and failing to discover support for himself in the provinces, he acquiesced. As he later wrote: 'The first consideration of republicanism is to respect the general wish; I was not able to propose a purely American constitution, the best, in my opinion; it would have been to have disregarded the wish of the majority, risk civil disturbance, bring about foreign war.'[7] Disillusionment followed. "I was a fool," he said. The republican program to which he had thought Louis-Philippe had agreed was portrayed by the king as a figment of Lafayette's imagination.

He was brave both in battle and in refusing to submit to adversity. He kept to his beliefs. 'Everyone has changed; the only one who has not is Lafayette,' said Napoléon. 'I will give him this justice; he has no more changed than I have,' said Charles X.

'He always acted correctly in the role which the situation assigned to him, that of executing the law,' wrote Adolphe Thiers.[8] He was a military man, like his ancestors. He understood the use of force to ensure peace and stability but obeyed the principle he had learned from the United States, that the military should be subordinate to the civil authorities.

He was a man of his era, but also beyond it. He was not a great philosopher or orator, but he embodied for many, in countries throughout the world, a vision of liberty. His voice has echoed down the years. A voice which resonates with people fighting for freedom. "Lafayette, we are here," said Lieutenant Colonel Stanton for General J. Pershing, commander-in-chief of the American Expeditionary Force, at his tomb in Picpus, on July 4, 1917,[9] followed two years later, on June 7, 1919, by President Wilson who placed a bronze wreath there inscribed: *To the Great Lafayette, from a Fellow Servant of Liberty.*[10]

He had 'an unchanging firmness of character which always tended inflexibly towards the same goal. To work unceasingly to establish, extend and consolidate liberty was the dominating idea which for more than fifty years had guided his conduct, warmed his heart and dictated his words,' wrote the comte de Ségur.[11]

In conclusion, the last words will be those of Lafayette, who spoke truthfully when he said: 'Until my last breath, true and pure liberty will find me always ready.'[12]

Portrait of Old Lafayette by Thomas Sully 1825-1826. By permission of the National Park Service, U.S. Dept. of the Interior.

NOTES

Mémoires, correspondence et manuscrits du général Lafayette are in French and have been translated by the author when quoted. The original French text has also been used from Lafayette in the *Age of the American Revolution, Selected Letters and Papers 1776-1790*, vols. 1-5, edited by Idzerda, and so the translation by the author can sometimes differ from that given in the same volume.

French titles have been written in lower case as they would be in French. French usage has also been followed for street names or squares.

Introduction

[1] Charavay, 598.

[2] Levasseur, 1:54.

[3] *Recherches historiques et politiques sur les États-Unis de l'Amérique septentrionale* (4 vols.: Paris,1788), IV, 117, and n, cited by Gottschalk, *The Letters of Lafayette to Washington*, vii.

[4] *Mémoires*, Sociétés Secrètes, 6:137.

Chapter 1

[1] Cloquet, M., Jules, *Recollections of the private life of General Lafayette* (New York:Leavitt, Lord and Co.,1836) 1:8. Thacher, James, *A Military Journal during the American Revolutionary War, from 1775 to 1783, describing interesting events and transactions of this period, with numerous historical facts and anecdotes from the original manuscript* (Boston; Richardson and Lord,1823) says Lafayette has a fine, animated hazel eye, 186. However, Cloquet knew Lafayette far better and over a much longer time, so is far more likely to be correct in saying his eyes were gray-blue.

[2] Young, *Arthur Young's Travels in France During the Years 1787,1788,1789*, 149.

[3] La Fayette, *Autobiography* (Archives of the La Fayette family); Appendix in Charavay, Étienne, *Le Général La Fayette,1757-1834* (Paris: Société de la Histoire de la Révolution française, 1898) 531.

[4] The spelling La Fayette was changed by Lafayette during the American Revolutionary War to Lafayette as it was quicker to write. In the French Revolution he abandoned the title marquis and the de and retained the simplified spelling.

[5] Mosnier, Henry, *Le Château de Chavaniac-Lafayette* (Le Puy;1883) 12.

[6] La Fayette, *Autobiography* (Archives of the La Fayette family), Appendix in Charavay, 531.

[7] La Fayette, *Autobiography* (Archives of the La Fayette family), Appendix in Charavay, 532.

[8] Mosnier, Henry, *Le Château de Chavaniac-Lafayette,1883*, 12.

[9] Ibid.

[10] Ibid.

[11] La Fayette, *Autobiography* (Archives of the La Fayette family), Appendix in Charavay, 532.

[12] Ibid.

[13] Note: Lafayette says in *Mémoires, Correspondances et Manuscrits* that he died before his birth. He also calls Saint-Pern, Saint-Péru.

[14] Donnet, Hadelin, *Chavaniac Lafayette; Le Manoir des deux mondes*, Paris, le cherche midi éditeur, 1990, 23. According to tradition, Lafayette was born in the room on the first floor of the tower on the right of the north façade.

[15] *Mémoires*, 1:20.

[16] Doniol, Henri, *Histoire de la participation de la France à l'établissement des États-Unis d'Amérique* (Paris; imprimerie nationale, DCCC LXXXV)1:658.

[17] Charavay, 532.

[18] Donnet,14, note 1.

[19] A fortified, or semi-fortified, house.

[20] Donnet, 23.

[21] Mosnier, Henry, 61.

[22] Doniol, 1: 656.

[23] Mosnier, Henry,1.

[24] Ibid.

[25] La Fayette, *Autobiography* (Archives of the La Fayette family), Appendix in Charavay,534.

[26] Maurois, André, *Adrienne The Life of the Marquise de La Fayette*, trans. by Hopkins, Gérard (London : Jonathan Cape, 1961), 36. *Mémoires, correspondence et manuscrits du Général Lafayette* (Bruxelles : société belge de librairie,1837)1 :18. Note says he died before the age of twenty-five. *Life of Madame de Lafayette* by Virginie de Lafayette de Lasteyrie.

[27] *Mémoires* incorrectly says Lafayette's birth followed the death of his father at Minden, 1:18.

[28] Mosnier, Extrait des registres baptismaux de la paroisse de Saint Roch de Chavaniac,15.

[29] Charavay, 533.

[30] La Fayette, *Autobiography*, (Archives of his family), Charavay,533.

[31] Ibid.

[32] Charavay, 3.

[33] Doniol, 1:659. *Mémoires*, 1:2.

[34] Doniol,59.

[35] Castries, 26.

[36] Charavay, 3, 11.

[37] Taillimite, 552.

[38] Maurois, 39, from unpublished letter, Collection Fabius.

[39] Charavay, 11.

[40] Gottschalk, Louis, *Lafayette in America*, (Arveyres, France: L'Esprit de Lafayette Society), 5.

[41] *Autobiography of La Fayette* (Archives of his family), Charavay, 533.

[42] Taillimite, 552, Note 4 says Lafayette is 11 in 1768. *Mémoires*, 1:18 says he is 11. *Memoirs*, 2, says 12.

[43] Maurois, 40, from Ulysse Rouchon, 15-18. *Mémoires du marquis de Bouillé*, cited by Taillimite,14.

[44] Mémoires,1:18. Castries, duc de, *La Fayette* (Paris: Librairie Jules Tallandier,1981), 3. Maurois says 1768.

[45] *Autobiography* of La Fayette, (Archives of his family), Charavay, 534.

[46] Ibid.

[47] *Autobiography* of La Fayette, (Archives of his family), Charavay, 534.

[48] Gaines, James R., *For Liberty and Glory* (London, New York; Norton and Co., 2007), 34, citing Holbrook,5, citing *Mémoires, correspondence et manuscrits du Général Lafayette*, publiés par sa famille.

Chapter 2

[1] Lafayette, *Autobiography*, Charavay, 552.

[2] Ibid., 534.

[3] Gottschalk, Louis, *Lafayette Comes to America* (Univ. of Chicago Press, Chicago,1935), 17.

[4] Bois, Jean-Pierre, *La Fayette*, Paris, 2015, Perrin, 25.

[5] Lafayette, *Autobiography*, Charavay, 535.

[6] Letter of Lafayette from *Collection du Edmond de Lafayette*, cited by Castries, 28.

[7] Lafayette, *Autobiography*, Charavay, 536.

[8] Ibid., 535,536.

[9] Lafayette, letter to M. d'Hennings, Wittmöld, January 15, 1799, *Mémoires*, 3:220.

[10] Adams, Abigail, *Letters of Mrs. Adams, the wife of John Adams*, letter to Miss Lucy Cranch, September 5, 1784, Auteuil, 2:54.

[11] Young, 56.

[12] Popkin, Jeremy D, *Panorama of Paris; Selections from Le Tableau de Paris by Mercier, Louis-Sébastien*, (Pennsylvania; The Pennsylvania State University Press,1999) 41.

[13] Note: Charavay says April 3, the date given by Jal, A., *Dictionnaire critique de biographie et d'histoire* (Paris,1867) according to the death certificate,3. *Mémoires*,1:18. Note says April 12.

[14] *Mémoires*,1:18. Note.

[15] Taillimite,15. *Mémoires*, 1:18.

[16] Lafayette, *Autobiography*, Charavay,535.

[17] Letter of Lafayette from *Collection of Edmond de Lafayette*, cited by Castries, 28.

[18] Bodyguard.

[19] Acte de marriage de La Fayette, April 11, 1774, cited by Charavay, 557.

[20] Lafayette, Marie Adrienne de Noailles, Virginie de Lafayette Lasteyrie du Saillant, Marie Antoinette, *Life of Madame de Lafayette* (Paris; Techner; Barthès and Lowell; M DCCC LXXII) 34,35.

[21] Lafayette, *Autobiography*, Charavay, 536.

[22] Gottschalk, Louis, *Lafayette in America, 1777-1783* (Arveyres; L'Esprit de Lafayette Society,1975)30.

[23] Ibid.

[24] Ibid.

[25] The comte de La Rivière, letter to Mlle. du Motier, November 13, 1772, Paris, cited by Gottschalk, *Lafayette Comes to America*, 28.

[26] Maurois, 43.

[27] Adrienne de Lafayette, *Life of Madame de Lafayette*, 39.

[28] Morgan, Lady, 233. Note: She is a prostitute. Taillimite, 17.

Chapter 3

[1] The Noailles-Cavalerie became the Noailles-Dragons in 1776.

[2] French for pea.

[3] Madame de La Tour du Pin, *Memoirs de Madame de La Tour du Pin*, ed. trans. by Félice Harcourt (London: Century Publishing,1985) 72.

[4] Bernier, Olivier, *Words of Fire, Deeds of Blood; The Mob, the Monarchy and the French Revolution* (Canada: Little, Brown and Company, Inc., 1989) 27.

[5] Madame de La Tour du Pin,71.

[6] Castries, *La Fayette* (Paris: Librairie,) 41.

[7] His grandmother died in 1773.

[8] Gottschalk, *Lafayette comes to America*,43.

[9] Ségur,19.

[10] Castries, 43.

[11] *Correspondances de Mirabeau*, La Marck, cited by Taillimite, 18.

[12] *Mémoires,* 1:7.

[13] Lasteyrie, Virginie de Lafayette ; Lafayette, Marie Adrienne de Noailles, *Life of Madame de Lafayette*,44.

[14] Ibid.,43.

[15] *Mémoires,*1:19.

[16] Ibid.

[17] Ibid., 1:21.

[18] Ibid., 1:8.

[19] Taillimite, 20.

[20] Ségur, comte de, *The memoirs and anecdotes of the Count de Ségur*, trans. by Shelley, Gerard (John Hamilton; London) 53.

[21] *Memoir* of Lafayette of 1779; Idzerda,1:389. Note: As Idzerda points out, this paragraph about the two romances has been left out from the *Mémoires* published by Lafayette's family. 1:13, note 8.

[22] Lafayette, letter to Adrienne, May 8, 1775, Metz, Maurois, 58, cited by Bois, 431.

[23] Maurois, 54, from Fondation Josée et René de Chambrun.

[24] Bois,34.

[25] Sparks, *The Writings of George Washington*, 5: Appendix, no.1, 445. It is not known what the duke actually said, just the general tenor of his words.

[26] *Memoirs*, 1:6,7; Sparks, *The Writings of George Washington*, 5: Appendix, no.1, 445. Note: Gottschalk thinks that the Duke of Gloucester's conversation at dinner in Metz did not make Lafayette decide to come to America, *Lafayette Comes to America*, 50,51.

[27] *Mémoires*, 1:23.

[28] Ibid.

Chapter 4

[1] Sparks, *The Writings of George Washington*, 5 :Appendix, no.1, 446.

[2] Bacourt,1:65-67. Lameth, 106,107, cited by Gottschalk, *Lafayette Comes to America*, 73.

[3] Lameth, 107, cited by Gottschalk, *Lafayette Comes to America*, 74.

[4] *Mémoires,* 1:24.

[5] Tower, Charlemagne, *The Marquis de Lafayette in the American Revolution* (Philadelphia: Lippincott, J.B. Company, 1895) 1:23.

[6] *Memoirs,* 1:8.

[7] De Kalb, letter to Pierre de Saint-Paul, November 7, 1777, with the army of the United States of America; Idzerda, Appendix, French Texts, 1:448-451.

[8] *Mémoires,*1:23.

[9] *Memoirs,*1:8.

[10] De Kalb, letter to Pierre de Saint-Paul, November 7, 1777, with the army of the United States of America; Idzerda, Appendix, French Texts, 1:448-451.

[11] Sparks, *The Writings of George Washington,* 5: Appendix, No.1, 446.

[12] Memoirs written by Lafayette, Idzerda, Appendix, French Texts, 1: 391.

[13] A translation of the original agreement probably prepared for Congress, as Idzerda suggests, following Lafayette's presenting his copy to Congress on July 27, 1777, December 7, 1776, Paris, Idzerda, 1:17.

[14] De Kalb, letter to Pierre de Saint-Paul, November 7, 1777, with the Army of The United States of America, Idzerda, Appendix, French Texts,1:448-451.

[15] *Mémoires,*1:25.

[16] *Mémoires,*1:25.

[17] Gottschalk, Louis, *Lafayette in America; Lafayette comes to America,* Univ. of Chicago; Chicago,1975, 84.

[18] Dubois Martin, François Augustin, exposé, Idzerda, 1:21.

[19] *Memoirs,* 1:9,10. *Mémoires,* 1:25.

[20] Gottschalk, Louis, *Lafayette in America,* 1:86.

[21] Note: *Mémoires de M. le prince de Montbarey,*2:261-263, cited by Gottschalk, *Lafayette in America,* says Montbarey was convinced Lafayette would persist but that he and the ministers thought they had done enough for the moment, 1:87.

[22] Memoirs, 1:10. Note: Idzerda, Stanley J., *Lafayette in the Age of the American Revolution,* says Lafayette did not meet Franklin until 1779, 1:29, note 1.

[23] Lafayette to Adrienne, letter, London, February 25, 1777, courtesy of the comte de Chambrun cited by Idzerda, Cornell Univ., Ithaca,1977, Appendix 1, French Texts, 1:407,408.

[24] Lafayette to Adrienne, letter, Calais, February 20, 1770; Idzerda, Appendix, French Texts, courtesy of the comte de Chambrun, 1:407.

[25] Karamzin, N.M., *Letters of a Russian Traveller,* New York; Columbia Univ. Press, 1957, 261.

[26] Lafayette to Adrienne, letter, London, February 28, 1777, Idzerda, courtesy of the comte de Chambrun, Appendix, French texts, 1:408.

[27] Ibid.

[28] *Mémoires,* 1:26. Note: Idzerda says Bancroft was a British agent but there is no evidence he informed the British of Lafayette's plans, 1:14, note 18.

[29] *Mémoires,*1:26. Chernow, Ron, *Washington, A Life* (New York; Penguin, 2010) 337.

[30] Note: Washington crossed the icy Delaware. 150 Hessians were killed or wounded, 900 were taken prisoner and the Americans lost few men.

[31] *Memoir of 1779,* Idzerda, Appendix, French Texts, 1:391.

[32] Lafayette to Adrienne, letter, London, March,1777, Idzerda, courtesy of the comte de Chambrun, Appendix, French texts, 1:408, 409.

[33] De Kalb to William Carmichael, letter, Paris, March 14, 1777, 18.s of William Carmichael, tray 742, item 93, Idzerda, 1:31,32.

[34] The Agreement of the Infantry Officers and of the lIght troops to serve in the armies of the States General of America, Idzerda, 1:405,406.

[35] De Kalb, letter to Pierre de Saint-Paul, with the army of the United States of America, November 7, 1777, Idzerda, Appendix, French Texts, 1:448-451.

[36] Ségur, 54.

[37] Lafayette, letter to Adrienne, Letter, Paris, March 16, 1777, Idzerda, Appendix, French Texts, 1:.411.

[38] Lafayette, letter to the duc d'Ayen, *Mémoires,* A postscript to his letter of March 9, Paris, March 16, 1777, 1:109.

Chapter 5

[1] *Arthur Young's Travels in France during the Years 1787,1788, 1789,* 43.

[2] De Kalb, letter to Pierre de Saint-Paul, with the army of the United States, November 7,1777, Idzerda,1:147.

[3] De Kalb, letter to Silas Deane, Bordeaux, March 25, 1777, Idzerda, 1:39. De Kalb, letter to Pierre de Saint-Paul, Idzerda, Appendix, French Texts, 1:448-451.

[4]Ibid.,1 :448-451.

[5] *Pièces justicatifs*, Acte d'embarquement de La Fayette sur le vaisseau *La Victoire*, Charavay,561.

De Kalb, letter to Pierre de Saint-Paul, with the army of the United States of America, November 7,1777, Idzerda, Appendix, French Texts, 1:448-451.

[7] De Kalb to his wife, Los Pasajes, April 6, 1777, *The Life of John Kalb*, Friedrich Kapp,104,105.

[8] De Kalb, letter to Pierre de Saint-Paul, November 7,1777, Idzerda, Appendix, French Texts, 1:448-451.

[9] De Kalb, letter to his wife, *La Victoire*, March 26, 1777, Note by Charavay, 10 citing Kapp, 6, and Doniol, 3:206.

[10] De Kalb, letter to his wife, April 6, 1777, Los Pasajes, *The Life of John Kalb*, Friedrich Kapp, 107.

[11] De Kalb, letter to his wife, April 1, 1777, Los Pasajes, The Life of John Kalb, Friedrich Kapp, 104.

[12] De Kalb, letter to his wife, April 6, 1777, Los Pasajes, Kapp, 106.

[13] Lafayette, letter to Carmichael, April 3, 1777, Bordeaux, Idzerda, 1:412.

[14] Tower, Charlemagne, *The Marquis de La Fayette in the American Revolution* (Lippincott; Philadelphia, 1895)1:52.

[15] De Kalb, letter, April 15, 1777, Kapp, 107.

[16] De Mauroy, *Memoir*, December 6, 1776- July 31, 1777, Idzerda, Appendix, French Texts, 1:414-416.

[17] Lafayette, letter to William Carmichael, April 19, 1777, La Victoire, Idzerda, Appendix, French Texts, 1:413,414.

[18] De Mauroy, *Memoir*, Idzerda, Appendix, French Texts, 1:415.

[19] Lafayette's *Memoir of 1779*, Idzerda, Appendix, French Texts, 1:392.

[20] De Kalb, Letter to Deane, April 17, 1777, Los Pasajes, Kapp,108.

[21] Lafayette, letter to Adrienne, April 19, 1777, *La Victoire*, Idzerda, Appendix, French Texts, 1:412, 413.

Chapter 6

[1] Sparks, Jared, *The Writings of George Washington, V:* Appendix, cited by *Mémoires*,1:29.

[2] *Mémoires*,1;29.

[3] *Memoir of 1779*, Idzerda, Appendix, French Texts, 1:392.

[4] *Mémoires*, 1:29.

[5] Lafayette, letter to Adrienne, May 30, 1777, La Victoire, *Mémoires*, 1:112.

[6] Ibid.,1:111

[7] Ibid.,1:112,113.

[8] De Mauroy, *Memoir*, Idzerda, Appendix, French Texts, 1:415,416.

[9] Lafayette, letter to Adrienne, May 30,1777, *La Victoire*, Idzerda, Appendix, French Texts, 1 :416-419.

[10] Lafayette, letter to Adrienne, June 7, 1777, *La Victoire*, Idzerda, Appendix, French Texts, 1 :416-419.

[11] *Memoir* by the Chevalier Dubuysson, Idzerda, Appendix, French Texts, 1:427.

Chapter 7

[1] Du Rousseau de Fayolle, *Journal of a Campaign in America*, Idzerda, Appendix, French Texts, 1: 425. Note: Gottschalk, *Lafayette joins the American Army*, 1, says Edmund Brice was also there, citing Doniol, *La Participation de la France à l'établissement des Etats-Unis de Amérique*, 3:212,213.

[2] *Mémoires*, 1:30.

[3] Sparks, Jared, *The Writings of Washington*, 5:450.

[4] Ibid.

[5] Ibid., 5, Appendix.

[6] Du Rousseau de Fayolle, *Journal of a Campaign in America*; Idzerda, Appendix, French Texts, 1:425.

[7] Lafayette, letter to Adrienne, June 15, 1777, Major Huger's house, Idzerda, Appendix, French Texts, 1:419.

[8] Dubuysson, Memoir; Idzerda, Appendix, French Texts;1:427.

[9] Ibid.,1:427,428.

[10] Lafayette, letter to Adrienne, June 19, 1777, Charleston, Mémoires, 1: 118-124.

[11] Dubuysson, *Memoir,* Idzerda, Appendix, French Texts,1:428.

[12] Chartrand, R, *Forts of the American Revolution*, 1775-83, (New York; Osprey Publishing),2016; 40,41.

[13] Lafayette's Memoir of 1779, Idzerda, Appendix, French Texts, 1:393.

[14] De Kalb, letter to Pierre de Saint-Paul, November 7, 1777, *With the Army of the United States*, Idzerda, Appendix, French Texts, 1:148.

[15] Dubuysson, *Memoir,* Idzerda, Appendix, French Texts, 1:428.

Chapter 8

[1] Dubuysson, *Memoir*, Idzerda, Appendix, French Texts, 1:429.

[2] Dubuysson, *Memoir*, Doniol, 3: 215-222.

[3] Du Rousseau de Fayolle, *Journal of a Campaign in America*, Idzerda, Appendix, French Texts, 1:426.

[4] Lafayette, letter to Adrienne, June 17, 1777, St. Petersburg, *Mémoires*, 1:124-127.

[5] Lafayette, letter to Adrienne, July 23, 1777, Annapolis, *Mémoires*,1:127,128.

[6] Sparks, Jared, *The Writings of George Washington*,1:248.

[7] Dubuysson, *Memoir*, Idzerda, Appendix, French Texts, 1:430.

[8] Ibid.

[9] De Mauroy, *Mémoire*,3:219, Idzerda, 1:85, note 11.

[10] *Memoirs,* 1:17, note.

[11] Dubuysson, *Memoir*, Idzerda, Appendix, French Texts, 1:430.

[12] *Memoirs*, 1:17. Sparks, *The Writings of George Washington*, 1:248.

[13] Dubuysson, *Memoir*, Idzerda, Appendix, French Texts, 1:431.

[14] Harrison, letter to Washington, August 20, 1777, Burnett, 2:458,459, cited by Gottschalk, *Lafayette joins the American Army*, 21.

[15] Dubuysson, *Memoir*, Idzerda, Appendix, French Texts, 1:431.

[16] De Mauroy, *Mémoire*, 3:219, note by Idzerda, 1:86.

[17] Harrison, letter to Washington, August 20, 1777, cited by Gottschalk, *Lafayette joins the American Army*,22.

[18] *Memoirs*, 1:17, note.

[19] De Kalb, letter to Congress, Philadelphia, August 1, 1777, Kapp, 114-116.

Chapter 9

[1] Nolan, *Lafayette in America, Day by Day*, 8. Pickering, *Pickering's Journal*,148, cited by Marshall, George *Washington*, 447.

[2] Washington, letter to Major General Putnam, July 31, 1777, Coryell's Ferry, correspondence in Sparks, The *Writings of George Washington*, 5:8. Archives 111, 1380-81, cited by Ward, Christopher, *The War of the Revolution*, 330. Note: Ward says 260 ships.

[3] *Memoirs,* 1:18.

[4] Pontgibaud, comte de Moré, *Mémoires*,111.

[5] Thacher, James, *A Military Journal during the American Revolutionary War, from 1775 to 1783, describing interesting events and transactions of this period, with numerous historical facts and anecdotes from the original manuscript* (Richardson and Lord; Boston,1823) 182.

[6] Ellis, *His Excellency, George Washington*, 12. Thacher, *A Military Journal during the American Revolutionary War*, says his eyes are inclined to blue, 182.

[7] Thacher, 182.

[8] Ellis, *His Excellency George Washington*; he says his hair is light brown, 12.

[9] Sparks, *The Writings of Washington*, 1:249.

[10] Freeman, Douglas Southall, 4:526.

[11] Bradford, Colonel, letter, *The British view of the Delaware; Defence of the Delaware River*, Ward, Christopher, *The War of the Revolution*, 376.

[12] Chartrand, René, *Forts of the American Revolution*, 27.

[13] Plan of the City and Environs of Philadelphia, 1777, Freeman, 4:527.

[14] US Dept. of the Interior National Park, Freeman, 4: 527.

[15] Ibid.

[16] Anon. Diary recording Howe's military operations in 1777.

[17] Chastellux, marquis de, *Travels in North America in the Years 1780-81-82,* 69.

[18] Dubuysson, *Memoir*, Idzerda, Appendix, French Texts, 1:431.

[19] Doniol, 3: 223.

[20] Washington, letter to Major General Putnam, August 1, 1777, Chester, Correspondance in Sparks, 5:11,12.

[21] *Mémoires*, 1:35.

[22] Note: Idzerda says 'naked' means they wore whatever clothes they had and they were not naked, although sometimes it can be taken to mean so. 1: 101, note 5.

[23] *Mémoires*, 1:35.

[24] Ibid.,1 :36.

[25] Ibid.

[26] Chastellux, Marquis de, *Travels in North America in 1780-81-82,* 70.

[27] Chartrand, 1775-83; 15.

[28] *Memoirs*, 1:19.

[29] Lafayette's *Memoir of 1779,* Idzerda, Appendix, French texts; 1:394.

[30] Hamilton, Alexander, letter to Dr. Knox, July 5,1777, *The Official and Other Papers of the Late Major-General Alexander Hamilton* (Wiley and Putnam: New York and London,1842). Note: the whole of this paragraph is taken from the letter.

[31] Washington, letter to John Augustine Washington, August 5, 1777, Germantown, Correspondance, Sparks, 5:20.

[32] Ibid.

[33] Washington, letter to Major General Gates, August 20, 1777, Head Quarters, Bucks County, Correspondance cited in Sparks, 5:37.

[34] Washington, letter to Major General Putnam, August 11, 1777, Correspondance cited in Sparks, *Writings of Washington,* 5:26,27.

[35] Lafayette, letter to Congress, The Archives of the Dept. of State, Washington, cited by Tower, Charlemagne, *The Marquis de La Fayette in the American Revolution* (Philadelphia: J.B. Lippincott Company, 1895) 1:185.

[36] Washington, letter to Benjamin Harrison, Neshaminy Bridge, August 19, 1777, Correspondance in Sparks, 5:35.

[37] Dubuysson, *Memoir,* Idzerda, Appendix, French Texts, 1:431.

[38] De Kalb, letter to Mme de Kalb, July 19, 1777, Doniol, 3:222- 223.

[39] Dubuysson, Memoir, Idzerda, Appendix, French Texts, 1:432.

[40] Lafayette, letter to Washington, October 14, 1777, Bethlehem, Idzerda; 1:122.

[41] *Journals,* VIII, 673 (August25, 1777), cited by Gottschalk, *Lafayette joins the American Army,* 38.

[42] Washington, letter to Major General Gates, August 20, Head Quarters, Bucks County, Correspondance cited in Sparks, 5:37.

[43] Washington, Letter to the President of Congress, August 21, 1777, Neshaminy Camp, Correspondance cited by Sparks, 5:38.

[44] Greene, letter to Varnum, August 17, 1777, *The Crossroads, The Life of Nathanael Greene, Major-General in the Army of the Revolution,* 1:431.

[45] Sparks, *The Writings of Washington,* 5:41, cited by Greene, *The Life of Nathanael Greene,* 1:432

[46] Ibid.,1:250.

[47] Ford, W.C., *The Defences of Philadelphia in 1777,* Pennsylvania Magazine of History and Biography, XVIII, 1894, 329-30, cited by Gottschalk, *Lafayette in America, Lafayette joins the American Army,* 40.

[48]Journals of Congress, August 21, 1777, cited by Greene, 1:432.

[49] Hancock, letter to Washington, August 22, 1777, Correspondance in Sparks, 5:41.

[50]Ward, Christopher, *The War of the Revolution,* 333.

[51] Urban, K., *Rebels and Redcoats,* 265.

[52] General Orders, G,W.,122-123, cited by Freeman, Douglas Southall, *George Washington,* 4:462, note 138.

[53] Tower, 1:221.

[54] Adams, John, *The Letters of John and Abigail Adams,* letter to Abigail, August 14, 1777, Philadelphia; 300.

[55] *Mémoires,* 1:37.

[56]General Order, Saffell, *Records of the Revolutionary War,* 333-336, cited by Tower, 1:221.

[57] Greene, *The Life of Nathanael Greene,* 1:433.

[58] Freeman, *George Washington,* 4:463, citing General Orders.

[59] Ward, 335, citing Fitzpatrick, IX,128,14. Journals, VIII,667.

[60] Marshall, John, *The Life of George Washington,* 3:139.

[61] *Mémoires,* 1:37.

Chapter 10
[1] Marshall estimates 18000 men, cited by Sparks, *The Writings of George Washington,* 1:253.

[2] Ward, 338, says 72.; *Mémoires* says 1000, 1:38.

[3] Marshall, *The Life of George Washington,* 3:141.

[4] Fitzpatrick, IX,146-147,148, cited by Ward,338.

[5] *Mémoires,* 1:38.

[6] Marshall, 3:142.

[7] Morgan, George, *The True Lafayette,* 100; Note: Congress resolved on June 14, 1777, the design on the flag. This was at Cooch's Bridge.

[8] Marshall, 3:142.

[9] Washington, letter to Heath, September 7, 1777, cited by Sparks, *The Writings of George Washington,* 5:55.

[10] Marshall, 3:141.

[11] General Orders, cited in Moore 1860:493; Bonk, David, *Continental versus Redcoat*, 26.

[12] General Orders, PWR, September 6, 1777, cited by Chernow, *Washington, A Life*, 302.

[13] Marshall, 3:142, Washington, letter to General Heath, September 7, 1777, cited by Sparks, *The Writings of George Washington*, 5:55. *Pickering's Journal*, September 6, Nolan, 14.

[14] *Mémoires*, 1:39.

[15] Washington, Letter to Hancock, September 9, 1777, eight miles from Wilmington, Correspondance cited in Sparks,5:56.

[16] Greene, letter of General Greene to his wife, September 10, 1777, cited by Greene, 1:438.

[17] Marshall, 3:144.

[18] Freeman, 4:472.

[19] *Grace Barclay's Diary*, ed. by Sidney Barclay. 1866.

[20] Freeman, 4:471.

[21] Freeman, 4:471.

[22] Sullivan to Washington, October 24, 1777, cited by Freeman, 4:472. Sparks, 5:458.

[23] Note: The ford later known as Wistar's, was known as Jones' in 1777; Charlton Thomas Lewis, *Lafayette at Brandywine*, 74. Freeman, 4:484. Note:72; after the Revolution the names of some of the fords were changed.

[24] *Mémoires*, 1:22.

[25] Note: The van of Knyphausen's column of 5,000 men comprised loyalist troops; Major Patrick Ferguson's Riflemen and the Queen's Rangers, followed by two British brigades commanded by Grant, three Hessian regiments, half of the 16th dragoons and two brigades of heavy artillery, the rest of the artillery, the provision and baggage train and cattle; a rear battalion of the 71st Regiment of Highlanders, with two flanking regiments, Ward, 342.

[26] *Mémoires*, 1:39.

[27] Ward, 343, citing Irving,111, 194. Fitzpatrick, IX, 451-452. Stephenson,11, 20. Greene, G.W., 1, 444. Hughes, 11, 150.

[28] Freeman, 4:474, citing George Washington, 206.

[29] Weedon, cited by *Rebels and Redcoats; The American Revolution through the eyes of those who fought and lived it*, ed. by Scheer, George F. and Rankin, Hugh F. (The World Publishing Company; New York, 1957), 235.

[30] Freeman, 4:475. Note: Freeman says the note is not thought to be in existence.

[31] Reed, 1847, 309, cited by Bonk,30.

[32] Ross, note to Washington, 11 a.m., 1777, Great Valley Road, Correspondance in Sparks, 5:459.

[33] Muhlenburg, 492, cited by Ward, 346.

[34] Cope, Gilbert, *Historical Address*, 22. Ward, 346.

[35] Freeman says this may refer to Hazan's report.

[36] Sullivan, letter to Washington, September 11, 1777, Brenton's Ford; Sparks, 5:459. Freeman, 4:476.

[37] Marshall, 3:147.

[38] Freeman, 4:477.

[39] Edgar, Gregory T. *The Philadelphia Campaign 1777-1778*, Bowie, MD; Heritage Books, 1998, cited by Gaines, *For Liberty and Glory*, 73. Freeman, 4:478.

[40] Sullivan, letter to Washington, 2 p.m., September 11, 1777, enclosing Bland's note written at 1.15p.m., Sparks, correspondence, 5:460. Ward, 347. Ward's note 18, 467, says that it is impossible to be sure as to when the different messages were sent and received.

[41] Weedon letter, cited by Freeman, 4: 479.

[42] Lafayette, *Memoir of 1779*, Idzerda, Appendix, French Texts, 1:396.

[43] *Mémoires*,1:40.

[44] Ward, citing a captain of the Delawares, 352.

[45] Sullivan,23. Cope, 479. Charlton Thomas Lewis.

[46] Interview with Lafayette, published in Poulson's Advertiser, February 25, 1825, cited by Charlton Thomas Lewis, *Lafayette at Brandywine* (West Chester; The Chester County Historical Society,1896), 88.

[47] Ibid.

[48] Ibid.

[49] *Mémoires*, 1:40.

[50] Knouf, *Soldiers Revolution*,128, cited by Ferling, *Almost a Miracle*, 250.

[51] *Mémoires*, 1:41.

[52] Ibid.

[53] Ibid.

[54] Interview with Lafayette, published in Poulson's Advertiser, February 25, 1825, cited by Charlton Thomas Lewis, *Lafayette at Brandywine*, 88.

[55] Freeman, 4: 482, 483.

[56] Pickering; *Life of Thomas Pickering*, 1:154-156, cited in *The Spirit of Seventy-Six*, 614.

[57] Washington, letter to the president of Congress, Chester, September 11, 1777, *The Spirit of Seventy-Six*, 616.

[58] Pickering,1:154-156, cited in *The Spirit of Seventy-Six*, 614.

[59] Washington, letter to the president of Congress, Chester, September 11,1777, *The Spirit of Seventy-Six*, 616. Note: General Greene estimated that Washington lost 1,200 to 1,300 men. About 400 of these were prisoners. 11 guns were lost. Howe lost 577 killed and wounded and 6 missing, from an estimated 12,500 rank and file. Cited by Boatner, *Encyclopedia of the American Revolution*, 109.

[60] Lafayette, *Memoir of 1779*, Idzerda, Appendix, French Texts, 1:396,397, says: 'taken by water to Philadelphia...the same evening the departure of Congress was decided.' Lafayette says 'the last night was employed in our retreat and in my voyage here', letter to Adrienne, September 12, 1777, Philadelphia, *Mémoires*, 1:130.

[61] Leepson, Marc, *Lafayette; Lessons in Leadership from the Idealist General* (New York: Palgrave Macmillan, 2011) 37, cited by Stockwell, Mary; *Marquis de Lafayette*, W. Smith National Library for the study of George Washington. Lafayette, letter to Adrienne, October 1; 1777, Bethlehem, *Mémoires*, 1:134.

[62] *Mémoires*, 1:42.

[63] Logan Fisher, Sarah, quoted by Robinson, Martha K., *The Encyclopedia of Greater Philadelphia, The British Occupation of Philadelphia*.

[64] De Mauroy, *Mémoire*, 3:219, fol. 5 vols; cited by Idzerda, 1:101,102, note 12.

[65] Statement of Duboismartin, Maryland Historical Society, Baltimore, portfolio 9; cited by Gottschalk, *Lafayette joins the American Army*, 47.

[66] Lafayette, letter to Adrienne, October 1, 1777, Bethlehem; Idzerda, Appendix, French Texts; 1:437.

[67] Lafayette, letter to Adrienne, September 12, 1777, Philadelphia, Idzerda, Appendix, French Texts, 1:433,434.

[68] Ward, 355.

[69] Journals of Congress, September 12, 1777, cited by Greene, 1:446.

[70] Journal of the Continental Congress, 8:738, cited by Nolan, J Bennett, *Lafayette in America, Day by Day*, (Baltimore; The John Hopkins Press, 1934) 16.

[71] Interview with Lafayette, Poulson's Advertiser, February 25, 1825, cited by Charlton Thomas Lewis, 88.

[72] Greene, 1:446.

[73] Fleming, *Washington's Secret War*, 71.

[74] Watson, 109.

[75] Paine, Thomas, *Reflections on the Battle of Brandywine*, The American Crisis, September 12, 1777, Philadelphia.

[76] Adams, John, letter to Abigail, Philadelphia, September 14, 1777, 309.

[77] Kapp, Friedrich, 117.

[78] Adams, John, letter to Abigail, Philadelphia, September 14, 1777, 309.

[79] Marshall,1:188.

[80] Kapp, 117.

[81] Thacher, 140.

Chapter 11

[1] *Mémoires*, 26, cited by Nolan, 17: he left by water 'the same evening that the departure of Congress was decided upon.' Congress decided to leave and go to Lancaster on September 18; *Journals of the Continental Congress*, 8:754.

[2] Laurens, Henry, letter to John Lewis Gervais, September 18, 1777, Philadelphia, LMCC, 2:497,498, cited by Fleming, 71.

[3] September 21, 1777, *Diary at Single Brethren's House*, Moravian Archives, Bethlehem.

[4] Chastellux, Marquis de, *Travels in North America in the years 1780-81-82* (New York, 1828) 348, Note.

[5] Ibid.

[6] Ibid.

[7] *Mémoires*, 1 :43.

[8] Jordan, John W., Historical Society of Pennsylvania, cited by Tower, note1 :1: 237.

[9] Ibid.

[10] Boeckel, G.F., quoted by Myers, Elizabeth, an article in the Easton Express, January 3,1932, cited by Nolan, 18.

[11] Memoir of 1776, Idzerda, 1: 91.

[12] *Mémoires*, 1:42.

[13] André, *Journal*, 49-50, in *The Spirit of Seventy-Six*, 622. Freeman, 4:495, note 37: Numbers of dead and injured varied greatly. Major Samuel Hay who helped the injured reported 300 casualties.

[14] Lafayette, letter to Henry Laurens, September 25, 1777, Bethlehem, cited by South Carolina Historical and Genealogical Magazine,1906, 7:3, cited by Nolan, 18.

[15] Kapp, 119. Note: the date is the same as that given to Lafayette.

[16] *Mémoires*, 1:43.

[17] Lafayette, letter to Adrienne, October 1, 1777, Bethlehem, Idzerda, Appendix, French Texts,1:436,439. Note: These lines have been erased from the letter in *Mémoires,* referenced below.

[18] Lafayette, letter to Adrienne, October 1, 1777, Bethlehem, *Mémoires,* 1:130-137.

[19] Thacher, 141.

[20] Pickering, *Journal of Timothy Pickering,*1:166-170.

[21] Ward; 366.

[22] Pickering, October 3,1:166-170.

[23] A general officer cited by Thacher, 142.

[24]Sparks citing Dr. Cromond on the authority of the Board of War,259.

[25] Boatner, 429.

[26] *Mémoires,* 1:44.

[27] Ibid.

[28] Ibid.

[29] Riediesel,1:174, cited in Ward, 536.

[30] The details of Freeman Farm, Bemis Heights and Saratoga taken from Ward, 521-542.

[31] Ward, 539.

[32] *Mémoires,* 1:48,49.

[33] Lafayette, letter to Gates, October 14, 1777, Bethlehem, Idzerda, 1:121.

[34] Lafayette. Letter to Washington, October 14, 1777, Bethlehem, Idzerda, 1:121-123.

[35] *Mémoires,*1:46.

[36] *A Diary at the Single Brethrens' House*, October 16, 1777.

[37] Lafayette, letter to Henry Laurens, October 18, 1777, Bethlehem for the last time the Saturday, Idzerda, 1:124-126.

Chapter 12

[1] Montgomery County Historical Society, *Historical Sketches*, 2:196, cited by Nolan, 22.

[2]Freeman, 4:525.

[3] Ibid., 4:524.

[4] Ibid., 4:520.

[5] Montgomery County Historical Society, *Historical Sketches*, 2:199, cited by Nolan, 23.

[6] Chartrand, *Forts of the American Revolution, 1775-83*, says ten redoubts, 27. Ward says 14 redoubts, 379.

[7] Greene, 1:475.

[8] Freeman, 4:526.

[9] Chastellux, *Travels in North America in the Years 1781-82*, 124.

[10] Ward, 376, citing Dawson,1:355; Stedman,1:302; Lossing,2:87-88, 208.

[11] Freeman, 4:528.

[12] Ward, 376, citing Stedman, 1:303,304; Trevelyan,3:256-260.

[13]Lafayette, Letter to Duboismartin, October 23, 1777, camp at Whitemarsh, Idzerda, 1:439-441.

[14]Lafayette, letter to Maurepas, October 24, 1777, camp near White Marsh, Idzerda,1:441-443. Idzerda says Lafayette sent Sparks a copy of this letter and said it had been addressed to Vergennes but contemporary references in other letters indicate it was written to Maurepas.

[15] Lafayette, Letter to Adrienne, October 29, 1777, camp near Whitemarsh, *Mémoires*, 1:142-143; Idzerda,1:443-445, note: there are lines included which are not in *Mémoires.*

[16] Lafayette, Freemasonic Lodge, Four of Wilmington, 1824, cited by Castries, *La Fayette,* 81, 82.

[17] Washington, letter to Hamilton, October 30,1777, PWR 12: 60-61, cited by Chernow,316.

[18] Freeman, 4:553, citing Laurens, John,62.

[19] Morgan, 121.

[20] Freeman, 4:530, citing G.W., 42.

[21] Ibid.,4:553, citing Council of October 27,9 G.W., 461ff.

[22] Ibid., 4:553, citing G. W., 106.

[23] Lafayette, letter to Adrienne, November 6, 1777, camp at Whitemarsh, Idzerda, Appendix, French texts,1:446-448.

[24] Plumb Martin, 52.

[25] Ward, 377.

[26] Plumb Martin, 52.

[27] Ibid.,53.

[28] Lafayette's words to the Freemasonic Lodge, Four of Wilmington, 1824, cited by Castries, 81, 82.

[29] Washington, letter to Gates, January 4, 1777, Valley Forge, cited in *The Spirit of Seventy-Six*, 653-655.

[30] Ibid.

[31] Freeman, 4:556.

[32] *Memoirs*, 38.

[33] Lafayette, letter to Washington, December 30, 1777, Valley Forge,137.

[34] Freeman, 4:557, citing *Papers Continental Congress,* 461, LC.

[35] Ibid., 4:558, citing letter of Washington, November 16, 1777, 10 G.W.71-72.

[36] Lafayette, letter to Laurens, November 18, 1777, Headquarters, Idzerda, 1:152-154.

[37] *Memoirs*, Lafayette, letter to the duc d'Ayen, December 16, 1777, Camp Gulph, 1:129.

[38] Sparks, 5:171.

[39] Lafayette, letter to Washington, November 26, 1777, Haddonfield, *Memoirs,* 1:120-123.

[40] Ibid.

[41] Ibid.

[42] Greene, letter to Washington, November 26, 1777, Haddonfield, cited in Greene, 516.

[43] Ibid.

[44] Sparks, 5:171.

[45] *Mémoires*,1:50.

[46] Lafayette, letter to Washington, November 26, 1777, Haddonfield, *Memoirs,* 1:120-123.

[47] Ibid.

[48] Ibid.

[49] Lafayette, letter to Washington, November 26, 1777, Haddonfield, *The Letters of Lafayette to Washington*,6,7.

[50] Greene, letter to Washington, Nov. 26, 1777, Haddonfield, Greene,1:516-518.

[51] JCC, 9:972, cited in Idzerda, 1:165.

[52] Gaines, 84.

[53] Lafayette, letter to Washington, December 30, 1777, Valley Forge, Memoirs, 1: 136.

[54] Greene, 524.

[55] Ford, *Defences of Philadelphia*, 20:229, cited by Idzerda, 1:164, note 2.

[56] Memorandum on Winter Quarters, December 1, 1777, Whitemarsh; Idzerda, 1:162-164.

[57] Ford, Defences of Philadelphia, 20:521, 523,524, 548, cited by Idzerda, 1: 176, Note 1 and 2.

[58] Ibid., 20:521,548.

[59] Washington to the general officers, December 3, 1777, Fitzpatrick, X, 135, cited by Gottschalk, *Lafayette joins the American Army*, 86.

[60] Washington Papers, Ser. F, vol.1, fols. 392,393, cited by Gottschalk, *Lafayette joins the American Army*, 86,87.

[61] Dearborn, *Journals of Henry Dearborn*, 1776-1783, 11.

[62] Ward, 379.

[63] Sparks, 1:261.

[64] Plumb Martin, 56.

[65] Baurmeister, 36, cited by Ward,380.

[66] Sparks, 1:261.

[67] De Kalb, letter to de Broglie, December 12, 1777, Whitemarsh, cited in Kapp, 134.

[68] Dearborn, 11.

[69] Sparks, Washington, 5:182.

[70] Committee's letter of December 10, 1777, to Washington, Freeman, 4:562.

[71] Laurens, 95; De Kalb, postscript to letter to de Broglie, December 14, 1777, Gulph's Mill, cited by Kapp, 136.

[72] Laurens, 96.

[73] Journals of Henry Dearborn, 12.

[74] De Kalb, letter to de Broglie, December 12, 1777, cited by Kapp, 136.

[75] Laurens, 96.

Chapter 13

[1] Waldo, Albigence, Surgeon of the Connecticut Line, Diary, December 12, *The Spirit of Seventy-Six,* ed. by Commager, Henry S, and Morris, Richard B.,639. Laurens, 97.

[2] De Kalb, letter to de Broglie, A postscript written on December 17, 1777, Gulph's Mill, cited by Kapp, 136.

[3] Waldo, letter cited in *The Spirit of Seventy-Six*, 640.

[4] Washington confirmed the authenticity of the bleeding feet when he told the historian, Gordon Ramsay, some years later: "You might have tracked the army from White Marsh to Valley Forge by the blood of their feet," cited by Ward, 543, citing Gordon,3:11-12.

[5] Lafayette, letter to Gates, December 14, 1777, The Gulph, Idzerda, 1:182.

[6] Lafayette, letter to Laurens, The Gulph, December 14, 1777, Idzerda, 1:183-187.

[7] *Mémoires*, 1:52.

[8] Ward, 453.

[9] Lafayette, letter to the duc d'Ayen, December 16, 1777, camp at the Gulph in Pennsylvania, *Mémoires*, 1:155-168.

[10] Ibid.

[11] *Journals of Henry Dearborn*, The Gulph, December 18, 1777,13.

[12] Plumb Martin; 57.

[13] *Journals of Henry Dearborn*, The Gulph, December 18, 1777, 13.

[14] Plumb Martin; 57.

Chapter 14

[1] De Kalb, letter to de Broglie, December 25, 1777, Valley Forge, cited in *The Spirit of Seventy-Six*,646.

[2] Freeman, 4:563, note 106.

[3] Plumb Martin, 59.

[4] Mitchell, Charles, 48.

[5] Montresor*, Journal*, 454-55, cited by Freeman, 4:564.

[6] Proclamation, December 20,1777, Ford,VI:248, cited by Stryker, 6.

[7] Freeman, 4: 566.

[8] Waldo, *Diary*, cited in *The Spirit of Seventy-Six*, 6

[9] Fleming, Thomas, 24,25.

[10] Laurens, 97.

[11] Freeman, 4:568; citing G.W., 184 and 183-184.

[12] Marshall, 3:327.

[13] Lafayette, letter to Adrienne, December 22, 1777, Valley Forge, Idzerda, Appendix, French Texts, 1:547,458.

[14] Washington, letter to President Laurens, December 23, 1777, Valley Forge, cited in *The Spirit of Seventy-Six*, 644-646. Fitzpatrick, ed. Writings of Washington X,192-196.

[15] Fleming, 33.

[16] Freeman, 4:566.

[17] Order of the Day, December 18, Washington, 5:524; cited in Greene, 1:527.

[18] Fleming, 82. Note: Fleming says the visit was in December.

[19] Paine, Thomas, letter to Benjamin Franklin, May 16, 1778, *Writings of Thomas Paine*, 392, Cited by Freeman, 4:571.

[20] Lafayette, letter to Adrienne, January 6, 1778, in camp near to Valley Forge*, Mémoires*, 1:15.

[21] Mitchell, *Travels through American History in the Mid-Atlantic*,52.

[22] *Mémoires*, 1:54.

[23] *Mémoires*, 1:53.

[24] Fleming, 135.

[25] *Mémoires*,1:53.

[26] Ibid.

[27] Marshall, 3:332.

[28] Fleming, 90.

[29] Freeman; 4:573.

[30] Gordon, 111,13-14, cited by Ward, 543, 544.

[31] De Kalb, letter to de Broglie, December 25, 1777, Valley Forge, cited by Kapp, 137.

[32] Pontgibaud, 108. Pontgibaud says he met Lafayette at Valley Forge in November. Idzerda says this is incorrect, 1:212, note 3.

[33] Sparks,1:277.

[34] Pontgibaud, 109.

[35] Orderly Book of George Weedon;165, cited by Nolan, 34. *Journals of Henry Dearborn,1776-1783*; December 25,1777, Valley Forge, 13. Note: He contradicts Weedon. He says it rains but is warmer.

[36] Reed, *Valley Forge*,12, cited by Fleming,33.

[37] Washington, letter to Reed, December 15, 1775, cited by Freeman, 4:588.

[38] Conway, letter to Washington, January 27, 1778; Sparks 5:503, cited by Freeman, 4:588.

[39] 64 Papers of G.W., 10, LC, cited by Freeman, 4:589.

[40] Laurens, letter to Henry Laurens, January 1, 1778, Head Quarters, *The Army Correspondance of Colonel John Laurens*, 100.

[41] Washington, letter to Conway, December 30, 1777, cited by Freeman, 4:598,590.

[42] Lafayette, letter to Washington, December 30, 1777, Valley Forge, Idzerda, 1:204-206.

[43] Washington, letter to Lafayette, December 31, 1777, Headquarters, *Memoirs*, 1:139,140.

[44] Conway, letter to Washington, December 31, 1777, Valley Forge, cited in Freeman, 4:590,591.

[45] Washington, letter to Congress, January 2, 1778, headquarters, cited by Freeman, 4:591,592.

[46] Laurens, letter to Henry Laurens, January 1, 1778, headquarters, *The Army Correspondance of Colonel John Laurens in the years 1777-8*, 100.

[47] 162 papers Cont. Congress., 276, L.C., cited by Freeman, 4:594.

[48] *Greene's Greene*, 1:547,548; cited by Freeman, 4:595.

[49] Greene to Jacob Greene, January 3, 1778, Greene, 1:544, cited by Gottschalk, *Lafayette joins the American Army*, 109.

[50] *Collections of the New York Historical Society*, XI, (1878), 410-412, January 9, 1778, cited by Gottschalk, *Lafayette joins the American Army*, 109.

[51] Lafayette, letter to Laurens, January 2, 1778, Valley Forge, Idzerda, 1:209,210.

[52] *Mémoires*, 1:54.

[53] *Memoirs*, 1: 146-150.

[54] Lafayette, Letter to Adrienne, Mémoires, Camp near to Valley Forge; January 6, 1778, 1:181.

[55] Laurens, John, letter to Henry Laurens, *The Army Correspondance of Colonel John Laurens in the Years 1777-8*, January 1, 1778, Hcadquartcrs, 100.

[56] Stryker, William S.,4.

[57] Freeman, 4:575.

[58] Lafayette, letter to Washington, January 20, 1778, Valley Forge, *Memoirs*, 1:238,239.

[59] Lafayette, letter to Laurens, January 26, 1778, Valley Forge, *Memoirs*, 1:253-256.

[60] Gouverneur Morris to the President of Congress, January 26, 1778, camp at Valley Forge, 1:256,257.

[61] Lafayette, letter to Laurens, January 27, 1778, Valley Forge, Idzerda, 1:258-260.

Chapter 15
[1] Gates, letter to Lafayette, January 24, 1778, Gates MSS, box 19, cited by Gottschalk, *Lafayette joins the American Army*,116.

[2] Gottschalk, *Lafayette joins the American Army*, 116, citing *Mémoires*, 1:73.

[3] Lafayette, letter to Laurens, January 31, 1778, Yorktown, Idzerda, 1:267-271.

[4] Washington, letter to Gates, January 27, 1778, Idzerda, 1:250.

[5] *Diary of Samuel Armstrong*, New England Genealogical Society, cited in Fleming, 129.

[6] Gottschalk, *Lafayette joins the American Army*, 118.

[7] Instructions from Congress for the Marquis de Lafayette Major Genl. in the Army of the United States of America, and commanding an Expedition to Canada, January 31, 1778, York, Idzerda, 1:263-267.

[8] Gates to Congress, January 31, 1778, PCC, no.156, fol.63, cited by Gottschalk, *Lafayette joins the American Army*, 123.

[9] Lafayedtte, letter to the President of congress, January 31, 1778, York, Idzerda, 1:267-271.

[10] Lafayette, letter to Laurens, January 27, 1778, Valley Forge, Idzerda, 1:258-261.

[11] Lafayette, letter to Laurens, January 31, 1778, York, Idzerda, 1:272.

[12] Sparks, VI: 271. Note.

[13] Lafayette, letter to Laurens, February 3, 1778, Anderson Ferry at three o'clock in a great hurry, Idzerda, 1:276, 277.

[14] Resolution of Congress, February 2, 1778, Idzerda, 1:273.

[15] Lafayette, letter to Adrienne, February 3, 1778, York, *Mémoires*, 1:186-188.

[16] Lafayette, letter to Laurens, February 3, 1778, Anderson Ferry, Idzerda, 1:276,277.

Chapter 16
[1] Lafayette to Laurens, February 19, 1778, Albany, Idzerda, 1:295.

[2] Lafayette, letter to Gates, February 7, 1778, Valley Forge camp, Idzerda;1:283,284.

[3] Lafayette, letter to Laurens, February 7, 1778, Valley Forge camp, Idzerda, 1:282,283.

[4] Lafayette, letter to Laurens, February 9, 1778, Flemingtown, Idzerda, 1:285, 286.

[5] Ibid.

[6] Lafayette, letter to Washington, February 9, 1778, Flemingtown, *The Letters of Lafayette to Washington*, 24,25.

[7] Pontgibaud, 119.

[8] Conway, letter to Gates, February 19, 1778, Albany, Idzerda, 1:301, 302.

[9] Lafayette, letter to Washington, February 19, 1788, Albany, *Memoirs*,1:154-158.

[10] Ibid.

[11] Ibid.

[12] Ibid.

[13] Ibid.

[14] Lafayette, letter to Laurens, February 19, 1778, Albany, Idzerda, 1:295-297.

[15] Ibid.

[16] Lafayette, letter to Washington, February 19, 1778, Albany, *Memoirs*, 1:154-158.

[17] Gottschalk, *Lafayette joins the American Army*, 138. Note: he says the letter is not to be found in the original.

[18] Lafayette, letter to the President of Congress, February 20, 1778, Albany, Idzerda,1:305-308.

[19] Lafayette, letter to Gates, February 20, 1778, Albany, Idzerda, 1:311.

[20] Lafayette, letter to Laurens, February 23, 1778, Albany, Idzerda, 1:319.

[21] Lafayette, Letter to Gates, February 23, 1778, Albany, Idzerda, 1:316.

[22] Lafayette, letter to Washington, February 27, 1778, Albany, *The Letters of Lafayette to Washington*, 31-33.

[23] Lafayette, Memoirs of myself, *Memoirs*, 1:44.

[24] Kapp,154.

[25] Conway, letter to Gates, February 25, 1778, Kapp, 154.

[26] Lafayette, letter to Laurens, February 23, 1778, Albany, Idzerda, 1:318-320.

[27] Lafayette, letter to George Clinton, March 3, 1778, Schenectady, Idzerda, 1:327-330.

[28] Ibid.

[29] Lafayette, Letter to Laurens, March 11, 1778, Albany, Idzerda, 1:345.

[30] Thacher, 138.

[31] Chartrand, 22.

[32] Lafayette, letter to Gansevoort, March 5, 1778, Johnson Town, Idzerda, 1:335.

[33] Speech to the Six Nations, *Journals of the Continental Congress*, 1774-1789, Wednesday, December 3, 1777.

[34] He was known as Ojistalale in the late 80s.

[35] Grasshopper's words at the conference, March, 1778, Glathaar and Kirby Martin, *Unfriendly Allies:The Oneida Indians and the American Revolution*.

[36] Pontgibaud, 119.

[37] Memoirs of Myself, *Memoirs*, 1: 43.

[38] Pontgibaud, 120.

[39] Ibid.

[40] Thacher, 139.

[41] Duane, letter to Clinton, March 3, 1778, Livingston Manor.

[42] Gottschalk, *Lafayette joins the American Army*, 144.

[43] Ibid.,120.

[44] *Secret Journal of Congress*, March 2, 1778, cited by Tower,1:290.

[45] Lafayette, letter to President of Congress, March 12, 1778, Albany, Idzerda, 1;349.

[46] Lafayette, Letter to Laurens, March 20, 1778, Albany, Idzerda, 1: 366.

[47] Lafayette, letter to President of Congress, March 12,1778, Albany, Idzerda,1:347-350.

[48] Lafayette, letter to Laurens, March 12, 1778, Albany, 1:350-352.

[49] Lafayette, fragment of a letter to the President of Congress, March 20,1778, Albany, *Memoirs*, 1:164.

[50] Lafayette, letter to Washington, March, 1778, cited by Glathaar and Kirby Martin, 9, ref.39.

[51] Lafayette, letter to Washington, March 25, 1778, Albany, Idzerda, 1:381.

Chapter 17

[1] Elias Boudinot, Journal or Historical Recollections,76-78, cited in *The Spirit of Seventy-Six*, 706,707.

[2] Chernow, 332.

[3] Stryker, 20,21.
[4] Sparks, 1:286,287.
[5] Lafayette, letter to Laurens, April 21, 1778, camp near Valley Forge, Idzerda,1:32.
[6] Sparks, 5:319; *Greene by Greene*, 2:68.
[7] Greene by Greene, 2 :68,69.
[8] Lafayette, letter to Washington, April 25, 1778, Valley Forge Camp, Idzerda, 2:35-39.
[9] Major Carl von Baurmeister, April 30, 1778, *Bicentennial notes on George Washington issued by the Michigan Commission* (Grand Rapids, 1932), 7,7-10, cited by Gottschalk, *Lafayette Joins the American Army*,174,175.
[10] Franklin and Deane to the President of Congress, February 8, 1778, Passy, Wharton 11:490-491, cited by Unger, 71.
[11] May 1,1778, S.C.h. mag.VIII (1907),124-26, cited by Gottschalk, *Lafayette joins the American Army*,175.
[12] Lafayette, letter to President of Congress, May 1, 1778, Camp near Valley Forge, Idzerda, 2:40.
[13] Lafayette, letter to Laurens, May 1, 1778, Camp near Valley Forge, Idzerda, 2:41-43.
[14] Idzerda, 2:43. Note: 2. Simeon Deane reached York on May 2. He brought letters with him from Europe.
[15] De Kalb, letter to Mde. De Kalb, May 12,1778, cited by Kapp, 158,159; cited by Gottschalk, *Lafayette Joins the American Army*, 182.
[16] *Greene by Greene*, 2:72.
[17] Orders issued by Washington, May 5, 1778, Headquarters at Valley Forge, Thacher, 151,152.
[18] De Kalb, letter to de Broglie, May 5-7, 1778, 821 Stevens Facsimile, cited by Freeman,5:2.
[19] De Kalb, 145. Sparks, 5:356, cited by *Greene by Greene*, 2:75.

Chapter 18
[1] Sparks, 5: 359, 360.
[2] *Greene by Greene*, 75.
[3] Sparks, VI: 371.
[4] Lafayette, letter to Washington, May 17, 1789, Valley Forge Camp, Memoirs, 1:170.
[5] Washington, letter to Lafayette, May 19, 1789, Valley Forge Camp, Memoirs, 1:171,172.
[6] Washington, Orders to Lafayette, May 18, 1778, Head Quarters, Idzerda, 2:53,54.
[7] Pontgibaud,125.
[8] Ibid., 127.
[9] Plumb Martin,69.
[10] Ibid.
[11] Ibid.
[12] Washington, letter to Morris, May 29, 1778, Fitzpatrick, XI,484-485, cited by Gottschalk, Lafayette Joins the *American Army*, 193.
[13] *Memoirs*, Fragment D, 1:77,78.
[14] Washington, letter to John Augustine Washington, June 10, 1778, Camp, near Valley Forge, cited by Sparks, 5:398.
[15] *Greene by Greene*, 2:79.
[16] Washington, letter to Major General Dickinson, June 5, 1778, Headquarters, Valley Forge, cited by Sparks,5:395.
[17] Lafayette, letter to Congress, May 25, 1778, PCC, no.156, 21-23, cited by Gottschalk, *Lafayette joins the American Army*, 194.
[18] June 1, 1778, S.C. h. mag., VIII,182, cited by Gottschalk, *Lafayette Joins the American Army*, 196,197.
[19] Washington, letter to John Augustine Washington, June 10, 1778, Camp near Valley Forge, Sparks, 5:398.
[20] Sparks, 1:184-89.
[21] Memoirs until the year 1780, *Memoirs*, 49.
[22] Laurens, letter to Henry Laurens, June 9, 1778, Headquarters, *The Army Correspondance of Colonel John Laurens...,181-183*.
[23] Lafayette, letter to Henry Laurens, June 12, 1778, Valley Forge, Idzerda,2:75.
[24] Washington, letter to General Gates, June 12, 1778, Head Quarters, Valley Forge, cited by Sparks, 5:403.
[25] Laurens, Letter to Henry Laurens, June 16, 1778, Head Quarters, *The Army Correspondance of Colonel John Laurens...,191,192*.
[26] Washington, letter to Major General Dickinson, June 5, 1778, Head Quarters, Valley Forge, Sparks, 5:395,396.
[27] Marshall, 3:456.

[28] Laurens, letter to Henry Laurens, June 16, 1778, Head Quarters, *The Army Correspondance of Colonel John Laurens....,191,192.*

[29] Lafayette, letter to Adrienne, June 16, 1778, Valley Forge, Idzerda, Appendix, French Texts, 2:400-402.

Chapter 19

[1] Laurens, letter to Henry Laurens, June 16, 1778, Head Quarters; *The Army Correspondance of Colonel John Laurens, 191-193,*

[2] *Greene by Greene,* 2:86,87, citing Marshall, 1:249.

[3] Sparks, 5:410, note.

[4] Lafayette's opinion on the military situation to Washington, June 17, 1778, Valley Forge, *The Letters of Lafayette to Washington,* 44-46.

[5] Stryker,57,58.

[6] Washington, letter to the president of Congress, June 18, 1778, Headquarters, Sparks, 5:409.

[7] Ibid., 5:410.

[8] Ward, 571, citing Marshal, 1:292.

[9] Tower, 1:347.

[10] Boatner, 716.

[11] Washington, letter to the president of Congress, June 18, 1778, HeadQuarters, six o'clock, p.m., cited by Sparks, 5:411.

[12] Washington, Instructions to Brigadier General Wayne, June 18, 1778, Head-Quarters, Valley Forge, cited by Sparks,5:411.

[13] Stryker, 69.

[14] Davis, W.W.H., *The Marquis de Lafayette,* A collection of papers read before the Bucks County Historical Society, 1(1908),72,158-159, cited by Gottschalk, *Lafayette joins the American Army,* 207.

[15] Lafayette, letter to Carmichael, June 21, 1778, House of Representatives Collection, cited by Gottschalk, *Lafayette joins the American Army,*207.

[16] Stryker, 56.

[17] Washington's orders, June 22, 1778, Coryell's Ferry, General Hand's Orderly Book, 285, cited in Stryker,70-72.

[18] Lafayette, letter to Laurens, June 23, 1778, camp, Idzerda, 2:84.

[19] Lafayette, letter to Laurens, June 23, 1778, camp; cited by Gottschalk, *Lafayette joins the American Army,* 206.

[20] Dickinson, letter to Washington, June 23, 1778; Reed, June 23, 1778, cited by Freeman, 5:15.

[21] Marshall, 3:462.

[22] Sparks, *Washington's Writings,* Appendix, no. XVIII, 429, 5:552.

[23] Stryker,76.

[24] The United States Naval Observatory has estimated the time of the eclipse and says that totality in the Princeton area was at approximately 10 a.m. Freeman, 34, 5:16, note.

[25] *Memoirs,* 1:50,51.

[26] Tower, 1:350.

[27] Greene, letter to Washington; he says he spoke of this earlier in the day at the council of war, June 24, 1778, cited by Freeman, 5:17, ref. 42.

[28] *Oxford History* citing GW Writing,247.

[29] *Memoirs,* 1:50-52.

[30] Ibid.

[31] Sparks, *Washington's Writings,* Appendix XVIII,429, 5:553.

[32] Lafayette, letter to Washington, June 24, 1778, Hopewell, Idzerda, 2:85.

[33] Sparks, 5:553.

[34] Sparks, Appendix, no. XVIII,429;5:553.

[35] Hamilton, letter to Boudinot, Hamilton, July 5, 1778, 52.

[36] Lafayette, letter to Washington, June 24, 1778, Hopewell, Idzerda, 2:85,86.

[37] Idzerda suggests that Lafayette is quoting Lee in these last words, 2:86, note 2.

[38] Lafayette, letter to Washington, June 24, 1778, Hopewell, Idzerda, 2:85,86.

[39] Greene, letter to Washington, June 24, 1778, 78 Papers of G.W.,35, LC., cited by Freeman, 5:17.

[40] Dispatch from von Steuben of 3 p.m. from Lewis's Tavern, 78 Papers of G.W., 44, LC., cited by Freeman, 5:19.

[41] Stryker,79.

[42] 2 Lee Papers, 417, cited by Freeman, 5:18,19.

[43] Washington's orders to Lafayette, June 25, 1778, Kingston, *Memoirs,*1:178.

[44] Lee, letter to Washington, June 25, 1778, Camp at Kingston, cited in Sparks, Appendix, 5:554.

[45] *Mémoires*,1:52, cited by Gottschalk, *Lafayette joins the American Army*, 211.

[46] Gottschalk, *Lafayette joins the American Army*, 211.

[47] Lafayette, letter to Washington, June 26, 1778, HiceTown (Highstown), *The Letters of Lafayette to Washington*,49,50.

[48] Washington, letter to Lafayette, June 26, 1778, Cranberry, cited by Gottschalk, *Lafayette joins the American Army*, 212.

[49] Lafayette, letter to Washington, June 26, 1778, Cranberry, cited by Tower, 1:355.

[50] Lafayette, letter to Washington, *The Letters of Lafayette to Washington*, June 26, 1778, 7-15 a.m., Highstown,49,50.

[51] Lafayette, letter to Washington, June 26, 1778, half past four, Robin's Tavern, Idzerda, 2:92,93.

[52] Washington, letter to Lafayette, June 26, 1778, Cranberry, Idzerda, 2:91,92.

[53] Ibid., 2:93,94.

[54] Ibid., 2:94,95.

[55] Lafayette, letter to Washington, June 26, 1778, 10.30.p.m., Idzerda, 2:95,96.

[56] Washington, letter to the President of Congress, June 28, 1778, Englishtown, cited in Sparks, 5:420.

[57] Ibid.

[58] Plumb Martin, 70.

[59] Ibid.,71.

[60] Washington, letter to the president of Congress, July 1, 1778, Englishtown, in Sparks,5:422-429.

[61] Washington, letter to the president of Congress, June 28, 1778, Englishtown, in Sparks, 5:420.

[62] Testimony of Scott, Wayne, Fitzgerald, Meade and Hamilton, at the court martial held at Brunswick, July 4, 1778, cited by Gottschalk, *Lafayette joins the American Army*, 218.

[63] Stryker, 107.

[64] Ibid.

[65] Stryker,107.

[66] Fitzgerald in 3 Lee Papers,6, cited by Freeman, 5:23.

[67] Stryker,107.

[68] The stream is now called the Wemrock Brook according to Stryker, 114.

[69] Testimony at Lee's court martial,1-208, cited by Gottschalk, *Lafayette joins the American Army*, 220.

[70] Wayne's testimony at the Court Martial, cited by Tower, 1:369.

[71] Sparks,1:297, Meade's testimony at Lee's court martial, cited by Stryker,121.

Chapter 20

[1] Ward,578.

[2] Testimony of Lafayette at the court martial of Lee, July 5, 1778, *Lee Papers*, New York Historical Society, cited by Tower, Appendix C, 2:482-487.

[3] Sparks,1:297, 482.

[4] Ibid.,1:297.

[5] *Lee Papers, III*,11 (Lafayette) and 147, Brooks, cited by Gottschalk, *Lafayette joins the American Army*, 221.

[6] Plumb Martin, 72.

[7] Gottschalk, Lafayette joins the American Army, 221.

[8] Lafayette's testimony at Lee's court martial; Lee Papers, New York Historical Society, Tower, 2:482-487, Appendix C.

[9] *Lee Papers*, III,11, (Lafayette) and 147, Brooks; cited by Gottschalk, *Lafayette joins the American Army*, 221,222.

[10] *Lee Papers*, III, 12, (Lafayette), cited by Gottschalk, *Lafayette joins the American Army*, 222.

[11] *Ibid.,11,12.*

[12] *Lee Papers*, 20 (Wayne), cited by Gottschalk, *Lafayette joins the American Army,* 224.

[13] Lee Papers, 20 (Oswald), 134,135, cited by Gottschalk, *Lafayette joins the American Army*, 225.

[14] Lee Papers,23,24 (Lafayette), cited by Gottschalk, *Lafayette joins the American Army*,225.

[15] Laurens, cited by Stryker, 165.

[16] McHenry, writing on the margin of Marshall's *Life of George Washington*,111:473, cited by Stryker,183.

[17] Plumb Martin,73.

[18] Ibid.

[19] Stryker,205.

[20] *Memoirs,* 1:53.

[21] Stryker, 206.

[22] Pontgibaud,130,131.

[23] *Memoirs,* 1:54.

[24] Pontgibaud, 130.

[25] Urban,153.

[26] Plumb Martin,75.

[27] Ibid.

[28] Stryker,201.

[29] Lieutenant Colonel Samuel Smith, cited by Lender and Stone, *Fatal Sunday.* Clinton, July 4, 1778, *Documents of the American Revolution*, vol.15, 162.

[30] Gottschalk says the British also claimed it as a victory, *Lafayette joins the American Army*, 229.

[31] Washington, letter to Gates, July 3, 1778, Brunswick, in Sparks, 5:429.

[32]Stryker, 232.

[33] Washington, letter to John Augustine Washington, July 4, 1778, Brunswick, 431-433.

[34] Washington, letter to Gates, July 3, 1778, Brunswick, Sparks, 5:429-431.

[35] McHenry, letter to Cox? July 1, 1778, Thomas H. Montgomery, The battle of Monmouth as described by Dr. James McHenry, cited by Gottschalk, *Lafayette Joins the American Army*, 229,230.

[36] Lee, letter to Washington, June 30,1778, cited by Freeman,5:34.

[37] Ferling, 307.

[38] 12 G.W.132-133, Freeman, 5:35.

[39] *Lee Papers*, 2;437,438, cited by Freeman,5:35,36.

[40] *Lee Papers*, 2;438, cited by Freeman,5:36.

[41] 12 G.W.,133, verbatim, cited by Freeman,5:36.

[42] Plumb Martin,75.

[43] Washington, letter to Gates, July 3, 1778, Brunswick, in Sparks, 5:429-431.

[44] Fitzpatrick, XII,146,147,165,182, cited by Ward, 905.

[45] Ibid.

Chapter 21

[1] *Lee Papers*, 2, cited by Freeman,5:37.

[2] Lafayette's testimony at Lee's court martial, *Lee Papers*, New York Historical Society, cited by Tower, 2:482-487.

[3] Lafayette, letter to Laurens, July 6, 1778, S.C. h.mag.,60, cited by Gottschalk, *Lafayette Joins the American Army*, 231.

[4] Lafayette, letter to d'Estaing, at camp near Paramus, July 14, 1778, Idzerda, Appendix, French Texts, 2:402-404.

[5] 12 G.W., 176, cited by Freeman,5:45.

[6] Doniol, *Histoire de la Participation à l'établissement des États-Unis d'Amérique: Correspondance diplomatique et documents*, 3:323.

[7] Schactman, 153.

[8] Washington, letter to d'Estaing, July 14, 1778, cited by Shactman, 329.

[9] Lafayette, letter to d'Estaing, at camp near Paramus, July 14, 1778, Idzerda, Appendix, French Texts, 2:402-404.

[10] Lafayette, letter to Elias Boudinot, July 15, 1778, camp near Kekeate Meeting House, Idzerda, 2:107,108.

[11] Fitzpatrick, XII,182, cited by Ward,587.

[12] Doniol, 3:322.

[13] Ibid., 3:323.

[14] Morgan, 158.

[15] Doniol,3:323.

[16] Burnett, 3, 324,325, acknowledged in G.W., 209; cited by Freeman, 5:50.

[17] Boatner, 788.

[18] Freeman, 5:50.

[19] Choin, letter to d'Estaing, July 18, 1778, cited by Doniol, 3:329, note 3.

[20] D'Estaing, letter to Congress, Freeman, 5:49.

[21] Report of d'Estaing, November 5, 1778, Freeman, 5:49.

[22] Morgan,158.

[23] Report of d'Estaing, November 5, 1778, Freeman, 5: 51.

[24] Ward, 588.

[25] Fitzpatrick, XII, 184, cited by Ward, 588.

[26] Washington, Order to Lafayette, July 22, 1778, Headquarters, White Plains; Idzerda, 2:110,111, cited from George Washington Papers, Series 43, draft.

[27] Lafayette, letter to d'Estaing, July 22, 1778, Headquarter, *Revue d'Histoire diplomatique, ui supra*,407, cited by Tower, 1:423,424.

[28] Lafayette, letter to Sullivan, July 22, 1778, headquarters, Idzerda, 2:111.

[29] Lafayette, letter to d'Estaing, July 24, 1778, Stamford, Idzerda, Appendix, French Texts, 2:113-115.

[30] Lafayette, letter to Sullivan, July 28, 1778, SayBrook, Idzerda, 2:119,120.

[31] Lafayette, letter to Sullivan, July 30, 1778, Norwich, Idzerda, 2:125-127.

[32] Lafayette, letter to d'Estaing, July 30, 1778, Norwich, Idzerda, Appendix, French Texts, 2:406-408.

[33] Nolan, 73, citing Wild.

[34] Lafayette, letter to Major Neville, August 1, 1778, in Sparks MSS LXX, cited by Gottschalk, *Lafayette joins the American Army*, 243.

[35] Sally Drowne to her sister-in-law, August 3, 1778, Fraunces Tavern, Henry Russell Drowne Collection, cited by Gottschalk, *Lafayette joins the American Army*, 244.

[36] Sullivan, letter to Henry Laurens, August 1, 1778, Continental Congress Paper, no.160, Library of Congress; in *Letters and Papers of Major-General John Sullivan...*,165,16.

[37] Sullivan, letter to Henry Laurens, August 1, 1778, Providence, *Continental Congress Papers*, No. 160, Library of Congress, in Letters and Papers of Major-General John Sullivan...2:165-167.

[38] D'Estaing, letter to Sullivan, July 31, 1778, at sea, Sullivan Papers, New Hampshire Historical Society, cited in *Letters and Papers of Major-General John Sullivan, Continental Army*, v: 2, 1778-1779,154, 155; Cornell, General Ezekiel, letter to Sullivan, July 31, 1778, Fall River, *Sullivan Papers*, New Hampshire Historical Society, in Letters and Papers of Major-General John Sullivan...2:157, 158.

[39] Laurens, letter to Henry Laurens, August 4, 1778, Providence, cited in *The Army Correspondance of Colonel John Laurens...*209-217.

[40] Greene, letter to Sullivan, July 31, 1778, Coventry Iron Works, *Sullivan Papers*, New Hampshire Historical Society, cited in Letters and Papers of Major-General John Sullivan, 2: 158.

[41] Washington, letter to Lafayette, July 27, 1778, Head Quarters, White Plains, Idzerda, 2:118, 119.

[42] Urban,158.

[43] Sullivan, letter to Henry Laurens, August 16, 1778, (Materials for History, Moore, 1861, 121), cited in *Letters and Papers of Major-General John Sullivan...*,2:218-220.

[44] Ibid.

[45] Ibid. Dohla, *A Hessian Diary of the American Revolution*, trans. ed. and introduced by Burgoyne, 84.

[46] Whittemore,97.

[47] Sullivan letter to Henry Laurens, August 16, 1778, (Rhode Island Archives), *Letters and Papers of Major-General John Sullivan...*, 2:218-220.

[48] *Memoirs,* 1:56.

[49] Pontgibaud, 144,145.

[50] Laurens, letter to Henry Laurens, August 4, 1778, Providence; *The Army Correspondance of Colonel John Laurens...*,209-217.

[51] Doniol,3:337.

[52] D'Estaing, letter to Sullivan, July 30, 1778, At sea, *Sullivan Papers*, New Hampshire Historical Society, in *Letters and Papers of Major-General John Sullivan....*2:151-153; Doniol, 3:337,338.

[53] D'Estaing, letter to Sullivan, August 3, 1778, At Sea, *Sullivan Papers*, New Hampshire Historical Society, Letters and Papers of Major-General John Sullivan, 2:169,170.

[54] D'Estaing, letter to Sullivan, August 3, 1778, At Sea, *Sullivan Papers*, New Hampshire Historical Society, *Letters and Papers of Major-General John Sullivan*, 2:170, 171.

[55] Extraits du Journal tenu par le comte de Cambis à bord du *Languedoc*, Doniol, 3:374.

[56] Watson, 21.

[57] Doniol, 3:337.

[58] Doniol,3:460, annexes of chapter VIII.

[59] D'Estaing, letter to Sullivan, August 4, 1778, *Sullivan Papers*, New Hampshire Historical Society, in *Letters and Papers of Major-General John Sullivan...*,2:172-174.

[60] D'Estaing, letter to Sullivan, translation, July 4, 1778, on the Languedoc, *Sullivan papers*, New Hampshire Historical Society, in *Letters and Papers of Major-General John Sullivan.....*,2:172-174.

[61] Extraits du Journal tenu par le comte de Cambis à bord du *Languedoc*, Doniol, 3 :374,375.

[62] Lafayette, letter to d'Estaing, August 5, 1778, Providence, Idzerda, 2:128-131.

[63] John Laurens, letter to Henry Laurens, August 22, 1778, *The Army Correspondance of Colonel John Laurens in the Years 1777-78*, 217-221.

[64] Lafayette, letter to d'Estaing, August 5, 1778, Providence, Idzerda, Appendix, French Texts, 2:408-411.

[65] Ibid.

[66] John Laurens, letter to Henry Laurens, August 22, 1778, Laurens, *Army Correspondance*,218, cited by Whittemore, 93.

[67] Urban, 157. Sullivan, letter to Henry Laurens, August 6, 1778, Head Quarters, Providence, *Materials for History*, Moore, 1861, 116, in *Letters and Papers of Major-General John Sullivan...*2:181,182.

[68] Lafayette, letter to d'Estaing, August 5, 1778, Providence, Idzerda, Appendix, French Texts, 2:408-411.

[69] Gottschalk, *Lafayette joins the American Army*, 247.

[70] *Archives des Affaires Etrangères*, corr. Pol., E-U., Supplement 1, fol. 94 v, cited by Gottschalk, *Lafayette joins the American Army*, 247.

[71] Lafayette, letter to Washington, August 6, 1778, Providence, *Memoirs*, 1:183-185.

[72] D'Estaing, letter to Sullivan, August 7, 1778, *Sullivan Papers*, New Hampshire Historical Society, in *Letters and Papers of Major-General John Sullivan...*2:183,184.

[73] John Laurens, letter to Henry Laurens, August 22, 1778, Laurens, *Army Correspondance*, 218, cited by Tower, 452; Lafayette, letter to D'Estaing, August 8, 1778, At General Sullivan's Quarters, Idzerda, Appendix, French Texts, 2:134, 135.

[74] Lafayette, letter to d'Estaing, August 8, 1778, at General Sullivan's Quarters, Idzerda, Appendix, French Texts, 2:411,412.

[75] Ibid.

[76] Doniol, 3:342.

[77] Lafayette, letter to d'Estaing, August 8,1778, at General Sullivan's quarters, Idzerda, Appendix, French Texts 2:411,412.

[78] Doniol,3:342.

[79] Ibid., 3:343, note 1.

[80] John Laurens, letter to Henry Laurens, August 22, 1778, *The Army Correspondance of Colonel John Laurens*, 220.

[81] Lafayette, letter to Washington, August 25, 1778, Camp before Newport, *The Letters of Lafayette to Washington,* 56-61.

[82] Lafayette, letter to Washington, August 25, 1778, Camp before Newport, *Memoirs,* 1:186-194.

[83] Report of the comte d'Estaing to the Secrétaire de la Marine, November 5, 1778, à bord du *Languedoc,* Doniol,3:451; annexes du chapitre 8.

[84] John Laurens, letter to Henry Laurens, August 22, 1778, 220.

[85] Le comte de Cambis, extraits de son journal, August 9, 1778, à bord du *Languedoc,* Doniol, 3:375, annexe of chapter 7.

[86] Le comte de Cambis, extraits de son journal, August 10, à bord du *Languedoc* 1778, Doniol, 3:377.

[87] Rapport du comte d'Estaing au Sécretaire de la Marine, November 5, 1778, à bord du *Languedoc,* Doniol,3:452, annexes of chapter VIII.

[88] Sullivan, letter to Jeremiah Powell, August 12, 1778, (Massachusetts Archives, vol. 199, 412), Letters and Papers of Major-General John Sullivan, 2:201.

[89] Extraits du Journal tenu par le comte de Cambis à bord du Languedoc, August 10, 1778, à bord du *Languedoc,* Doniol, 3:377, Annexe du chapitre VII.

[90] Ibid.

[91] Lafayette, letter to the duc d'Ayen, September 11, 1778, Bristol, near Rhode Island, *Memoirs,* 1:204-214.

[92] Ibid. The report of the comte d'Estaing to the Secrétaire d'Etat de la Marine, November 5, 1778, on board the *Languedoc,* says the *Languedoc* was fifth in the line of ships, Doniol, 3:452.

[93] Mackenzie,2:345, cited by Ward,590.

[94] *Rapport du comte d'Estaing au secrétaire d'Etat de la Marine,* November 5, 1778, à bord du *Languedoc,* Doniol, 3:452, annexes of chapter VIII.

[95] Sullivan, letter to Washington, August 13, 1778, Headquarters on Rhode Island, *Sullivan Papers,* New Hampshire Historical Society, *Letters and Papers of Major-General John Sullivan,* 2:205, 206.

[96] Sullivan letter to Governor William Green of Rhode Island, August 13, 1778, (Rhode Island Archives),2:202,203.

[97] Sullivan letter to Governor William Greene of Rhode Island, August 12, 1778, Headquarters, (Rhode Island Archives), *Letters and Papers of Major-General John Sullivan,* 2:199,200.

[98] Freeman, 5:64.

[99] Greene, *The Life of Nathanael Greene,* 2:114; citing Cowell, *The Spirit of '76* in Rhode Island, 167.

[100] Sullivan, letter to Washington, August 13, 1778, Headquarters on Rhode Island, *Sullivan Papers,* New Hampshire Historical Society, cited in *Letters and Papers of Major-General John Sullivan,* 2: 206.

[101] Ibid.

[102] Sullivan, letter to William Greene, August 13, 1778, Portsmouth, (Rhode Island Archives), *Letters and Papers of Major-General John Sullivan...*, 2:203.

[103] Sullivan, letter to Washington, August 13, 1778, Headquarters on Rhode Island, *Letters and Papers of Major-General John Sullivan...*, 2: 206.

[104] Whittemore,100.

[105] General Sullivan's Proclamation, August 16, 1778, (Rhode Island Archives), *Letters and Papers of Major-General John Sullivan...*, 2:220,221.

[106] *Life, journals and correspondence of Manasseh Cutler,* (2 vols., Cincinnati,1888), 1:69, cited by Gottschalk, *Lafayette joins the American Army*, 250.

[107] Sullivan, Letter to Governor William Greene, August 19, 1778, (Rhode Island Archives), *Letters and Papers,* 2:232,233.

[108] Whittemore, 101.

[109] Extraits du journal tenu par le comte de Cambis, August 20, 1778, à bord du *Languedoc,* Doniol, 3 :379,380.

[110] Ibid.

[111] Memoirs,1:57.

[112] Greene, citing the words of Lafayette to him, 2:117.

[113] *Memoirs,* 1:57.

[114] Lafayette, letter to Washington, August 25, 1778, Camp before Newport, *Memoirs*,1:186-194.

[115] *Memoirs,* 1:57,58.

[116] Sullivan, letter to Washington, August 23, 1778, Camp before Newport, *Letters and Papers...*,2:264,265.

[117] *Memoirs,* 1:58.

[118] D'Estaing, letter to Sullivan, August 21, 1778, (Washington Papers, Library of Congress), *Letters and Papers of Major-General John Sullivan...*,2:240-242.

[119] Greene, letter to Charles Pettit, August 22, 1778, in *The Life of Nathanael Greene,* 2:119,120.

[120] Lafayette, letter to Washington, August 25, 1778, Camp before Newport, *The Letters of Lafayette to Washington,*56-61.

[121] Lafayette, letter to d'Estaing, August 21, 1778, General Sullivan's Quarters, Idzerda, Appendix, French Texts, 2:413,414.

[122] Ibid.

[123] Lafayette, letter to d'Estaing, August 22, 1778, Sullivan's headquarters, Idzerda, Appendix, French Texts, 2:414.

[124] Sullivan and his Officers to the Count d'Estaing, August 22, 1778, camp before Newport, (Amory's *Life of Sullivan*), Letters and Papers of Major-General John Sullivan..., 2:243-246.

[125] Lafayette, letter to Washington, August 25, 1778, Camp before Newport, *Memoirs,* 1:186-194.

[126] Lafayette, letter to d'Estaing, August 22, 1778, Sullivan's headquarters, Idzerda, Appendix, French Texts, 2:139.

[127] Lafayette, letter to d'Estaing, August 22, 1778, Sullivan's Headquarters; Idzerda, Appendix, French Texts, 2:414.

[128] Laurens, letter to Henry Laurens, August 22, 1778, *The Army Corresondance of Colonel John Laurens,*217-221.

[129] Sullivan, letter to Washington, August 23, 1778, Camp before Newport, *Letters and Papers....*2:264,265.

[130] Lafayette, letter to Washington, August 25, 1778, Camp before Newport, *Memoirs,*1:186-194.

[131] Ibid.

[132] Lafayette, letter to d'Estaing, August 24, 1778, Rhode Island, Idzerda, Appendix, French Texts, 2:415-419.

[133] Washington, letter to Sullivan, August 22, 1778, Headquarters, White Plains, (*Sullivan Papers,* New Hampshire Historical Society); *Letters and Papers of....,* 2:246-248.

[134] Lafayette, letter to Sullivan, August 24, 1778, Rhode Island, Idzerda, 2:147,148.

[135] Lafayette, letter to d'Estaing, August 24, 1778, cited by Gottschalk, *Lafayette joins the American Army,* 262.

[136] Lafayette, letter to Heath, August 23, 1778, Rhode Island, Idzerda, 2:145.

[137] Lafayette, letter to d'Estaing, August 24, 1778, Rhode Island, Idzerda, Appendix, French Texts, 2:415-419.

[138] Ibid.

[139] Ibid.

[140] Sullivan, General Orders, Idzerda, 2:154, note 7.

[141] Lafayette, letter to Washington, August 25, 1778, Camp before Newport; *The Letters of Lafayette to Washington,*56-61.

[142] Ibid.

[143] Lafayette, letter to Hamilton, August 26, 1778, Rhode Island, cited by Gottschalk, *Lafayette joins the American Army*, 261.

[144] Sullivan, letter to Powell, August 26, 1778, Camp before Newport, (Massachusetts Archives, 200: 26); *Letters and Papers...*2:266, 267.

[145] Gottschalk, *Lafayette joins the American Army*, 258.

[146] General Orders of General Sullivan, August 26, 1778, *Glover's Orderly Book MSS*, in the Essex Institute, cited by Freeman, 5:71, note 143.

[147] Sullivan, letter to William Greene, August 29, 1778, Headquarters Rhode Island, (Rhode Island Archives); *Letters and Papers...*2:273.

[148] Greene, letter to Washington, August 28, 1778, *Life of Greene*, 2: 127.

[149] Lafayette, letter to Washington, September 1, 1778, Tiverton, *Memoirs*1:199-202.

[150] Lafayette, letter to Henry Laurens, August 28, 1778, Boston, Idzerda, 2:155.

[151] Lafayette, letter to Washington, September 1, 1778, Tiverton, *Memoirs,* 1:199-202.

[152] Lafayette, letter to Henry Laurens, August 28, 1778, Boston, Idzerda, 2:155.

[153] Report of d'Estaing to the Secrétaire d'Etat de la Marine, annexes of chapter VIII, Doniol, 3:457.

[154] Doniol, 3:359.

[155] D'Estaing, letter to Sullivan, August 30, 1778, Boston, *Letters and Papers of Major-General...*2:277,278.

[156] *Memoirs,* 1:59.

[157] Report of the comte d'Estaing to the secretaire d'état de la marine, annexes of chapter VIII, Doniol, 3:457.

[158] Doniol, 3:360.

[159] D'Estaing, letter to Washington, September 5, 1778, cited in Sparks,6:58,59, cited by Gottschalk, 264.

[160] Boston Independent Ledger, August 31, 1778, cited by Nolan, 78.

[161] Lafayette, letter to Washington, September 1, 1778, Tiverton, *The Letters of Lafayette to Washington,*61-64.

[162] Greene, September 16, 1778, Boston, *The Life of Nathanel Greene*, 2:144.

[163] Pennsylvania Packet, November 10, 1778, cited by Fitzpatrick, XII, 501, n.56, cited by Gottschalk, *Lafayette Joins the American Army*, 264.

[164] Lafayette, Memoir of 1779, Idzerda, Appendix, French Texts, 2:383-392.

[165] D'Estaing, letter to Sullivan, August 30, 1778, Boston, *Letters and Papers of Major-General John Sullivan*, 2:275,276.

[166] Lafayette, *Memoir of 1779*, Idzerda, Appendix, French Texts, 2:383-392.

[167] Sullivan, letter to President of Congress, August 321, 1778, Tiverton, (Continental Congress Papers, No. 160, Library of Congress), *Letters and Papers of Major-General John Sullivan...*2:280-286.

[168] Lafayette, letter to d'Estaing, August 31, 1778, Tiverton, Idzerda, Appendix, French Texts, 2:420-422.

[169] Sullivan, letter to President of Congress, August 31, 1778, Headquarters Tiverton, (Continental Congress Papers, No.160, Library of Congress), *Letters and Papers of Major-General John Sullivan...*2:280-286.

[170] Lafayette, letter to d'Estaing, August 31, 1778, Tiverton, Idzerda, Appendix, French Texts, 2:420-422.

[171] Ibid.

[172] Sullivan, letter to President of Congress, August 31, 1778, Headquarters Tiverton, (Continental Congress Papers, No. 160, Library of Congress), *Letters and Papers of Major-General John Sullivan...*2:280-286.

[173] Lafayette, letter to Washington, September 1, 1778, Tiverton, *The Letters of Lafayette to Washington*, 61-64.

[174] Greene, FV, 154, cited by Ward,592; Note: 38 British were killed, 210 wounded and 12 missing.

Chapter 22

[1] Journals of Congress, December 5, 1778, cited by Tower, 1:393.

[2] *Memoirs,*1:210.

[3] Lafayette, letter to Washington, September 1, 1778, Tiverton, *The Letters of Lafayette to Washington*, 61-67.

[4] Lafayette, letter to d'Estaing, August 31, 1778, Tiverton, Idzerda, Appendix, French Texts, 2:420-422.

[5] Lafayette, letter to Washington, September 1, 1778, Tiverton, *Memoirs,* 1: 199-202.

[6] Preston, *Lafayette's Visits to Rhode Island,*5, Nolan, 79.

[7] Lafayette, letter to Washington, September 3, 1778, camp near Bristol, *The Letters of Lafayette to Washington,* 64.

[8] Washington, letter to Lafayette, September 1, 1778, White-Plains, Idzerda,2:164-166.

[9] Lafayette, letter to d'Estaing, September 5, 1778, Bristol, Idzerda, Appendix, French Texts, 2:423,424.

[10] Lafayette, letter to Washington, September 7, 1778, Camp near Bristol, *Memoirs,* 1:203.

[11] Lafayette, letter to the duc d'Ayen, September 11, 1778, Bristol near Rhode Island, *Memoirs,* 1:204-214.

[12] Lafayette, letter to Adrienne, September 13, 1778, Bristol, near Rhode Island, *Mémoires,* 1:264-270.

[13] Lafayette, letter to d'Estaing, September 21, 1778, Warren, Idzerda, Appendix, French Texts, 2:429,430.

[14] Lafayette, letter to Washington, September 21, 1778, Warren, *The Letters of Lafayette to Washington,* 65-67.

[15] Resolutions of Congress, September 9, 1778, Idzerda, 2:172.

[16] Lafayette, letter to the President of Congress, September 23, 1778, Camp near Warren, Idzerda, 2:180.

[17] Lafayette, letter to Washington, September 24, 1778, Camp near Warren, *The Letters of Lafayette to Washington,* 67,68.

[18] Ibid.

[19] Lafayette, letter to Sullivan, September 23, 1778, camp near Warren, *Letters and Papers of Major-General John Sullivan...,* 2:356.

[20] Sullivan, letter to Henry Laurens, September 25, 1778, headquarters at Providence, *Letters and Papers of Major-General John Sullivan...,* 2:362.

[21] Lafayette, letter to Washington, September 28, 1778, Boston, *The Letters of Lafayette to Washington,* 68,69.

[22] *Memoirs,* 1:60.

[23] Lafayette, letter to d'Estaing, October 1, 1778, Boston, (R.H.D., VI, (1892), 447, Gottschalk, *Lafayette Joins the American Army,* 282.

[24] Lafayette, letter to d'Estaing, October 1, 1778, Boston; (AN: Marine B, 146, fol.188); Idzerda, Appendix, French Texts, 2:185,186, note:2.

[25] Gottschalk, *Lafayette joins the American Army,* 287.

[26] Laurens, letter to Henry Laurens, October 7, 1778, Headquarters, *The Army Correspondance of Colonel John Laurens...,* 230,231.

[27] Lafayette, letter to Carlisle, October 6, 1778, Fishkill, *Mémoires,* 1:282,283, Challenge to Lord Carlisle, October 6, 1778, (Harvard Archives), Nolan,85.

[28] Laurens, letter to Henry Laurens, October 7, 1778, *The Army Correspondance of Colonel John Laurens...,* 230,231.

[29] Lafayette, letter to Henry Laurens, October 13, 1778, Philadelphia, *Memoirs,* 1:233,234.

[30] Lafayette, letter to d'Estaing, October 20, 1778, Philadelphia, Idzerda, Appendix, French Texts, 2:430,431.

[31] Gottschalk, *Lafayette Joins the American Army,* 291,292.

[32] Gérard-Vergennes Correspondance, 339,340, Idzerda, 2:192, note :2.

[33] Lafayette, letter to d'Estaing, October 20, 1778, Philadelphia, Idzerda, Appendix, French Texts, 2:430,431.

[34] Lord Carlisle, letter to Lafayette, October 11, 1778, New York, Idzerda, 2:189.

[35] Lafayette, letter to Washington, October 24, 1778, Philadelphia, *Memoirs,* 1:236,237.

[36] D'Estaing, letter to Washington, October 22, 23, (Washington Papers, Vol. LXXXIX), cited by Gottschalk, *Lafayette Joins the American Army,* 294, note 44.

[37] *Diary of Frank W. Moore,* 2:100. New York Journal, November 2, 1778, Lafayette to the President of Congress, Library of Congress, Nolan, 86.

[38] Sparks, Writings, July 23, 1778, V:517, cited by Gottschalk, *Lafayette joins the American Army,* 294.

[39] Journals, XII,1104-6, (November 5,1778), cited by Gottschalk, *Lafayette joins the American Army,* 297.

[40] The President of Congress, letter to Lafayette, October 24, 1778, Philadelphia, Idzerda, 2:193-195.

[41] Lafayette, letter to Washington, October 24, 1778, Philadelphia, *The Letters of Lafayette to Washington,* 69,70.

[42] Gérard, letter to Vergennes, Correspondance, 346, Idzerda, 2:195, note 1.

[43] Lafayette, letter to Henry Laurens, October 26, 1778, Philadelphia, *Memoirs,* 1:238, 239.

[44] Morris, letter to Washington, October 26, 1778, Sparks, Gouverneur Morris,1:177, cited by Gottschalk, *Lafayette joins the American Army,* 306.

[45] Nolan, 89.

[46] De Kalb, letter to Broglie, November 7, 1778, cited by Gottschalk, *Lafayette joins the American Army,* 304, note 4. *Memoirs,* 1:63, note: Lafayette says eight miles from headquarters.

[47] Nolan, 89.

[48] *Memoirs,* 1:64.

[49] Lafayette, letter to President Laurens, November 29, 1778, Fishkills, Idzerda, 2:205-207.

[50] Thacher, *A Military Journal during the American Revolutionary War, from 1775 to 1783*....186. Note: He describes Lafayette: 'He is nearly six feet high, large, but not corpulent, being not more than twenty one years of age. He is not very elegant in his form, his shoulders being broad and high, nor is there a perfect symmetry in his features, his forehead is remarkably high, his nose large and long, eyebrows prominent, and projecting over a fine animated hazel eye. His countenance is interesting and impressive. He converses in broken English, and displays the manners and address of an accomplished gentleman.' Note: His description of the color of his eyes varies from that of Cloquet, who says they are blue-gray.

[51] Lafayette, letter to Henry Laurens, November 29, 1778, Fishkill, (South Carolina Historical and Genealogical Magazine, IX:110.)

[52] *Le Courrier de l'Europe*, 5 : no. XIII, February 12, 1779, citing an extract from the Trenton Gazette, December 31, 1778, cited by Charavay, 41.

[53] Lafayette, letter to Congress, January 9, 1779, PCC, no.156, fol. 86; cited by Gottschalk, 316, note 41.

[54] Lafayette, letter to Washington, January 5, 1779, Boston, *The Letters of Lafayette to Washington*, 71, 72.

[55] Lafayette, Manifesto to the Canadian Indians, December 18, 1778, Boston; Idzerda, Appendix, French Texts, 2:434-436.

[56] Lafayette, letter to Colonel Vedaloos? December 16, 1778, Boston, A.W.D. Item no. 31628; Nolan, 96, cited by Gottschalk, 315, note 37.

[57] Adams, John; *Diary, Essays, Autobiography*, 3:120.

[58] *Le Courrier de l'Europe*, 5:18, March 2, 1779, 138, cited by Charavay, 41.

[59] Pontgibaud, 151.

[60] Boston Gazette, Nolan, 99.

[61] Lafayette, letter to Washington, January 11, 1779, on board the *Alliance* off Boston, *The Letters of Lafayette to Washington*, 73, 74.

[62] Pontgibaud, 151.

Chapter 23

[1] Pontgibaud, 151.

[2] Ibid., 152.

[3] *Memoirs,* 1:66.

[4] Pontgibaud, 153.

[5] Memoir of 1779, Idzerda, 2:225.

[6] Pontgibaud, 153, 154.

[7] Ibid.

[8] Memoir of 1779, Idzerda, Appendix, French Texts, 2:383.

[9] *Memoirs,* 1:66. The testimony of Franklin to the Marine Committee, June 2, 1779, Smyth, VII, 338, says it is 38 men, cited by Gottschalk, 326, note 26.

[10] Pontgibaud, 155.

[11] N.E. Independent Chronicle, April 29, 1779, cited by Morgan, 171, 172.

[12] Pontgibaud, 156, 157.

[13] Ibid.

[14] *Memoirs,* 1:67.

[15] *Mémoires,* 2:7.

[16] They are exchanged a year later for American prisoners in England.

[17] *Memoirs,* 1:67.

Chapter 24

[1] *Lettres de la Marquise du Deffand,* 111, 496, cited by Gottschalk, *Lafayette and the Close of the American Revolution*, 2, note 3.

[2] Adams, *The Works of John Adams*, Diary, Essays, Autobiography, 3:71.

[3] Vergennes, letter to Montmorin, February 12, 1779, (Arch.des affaires étrangères, espagne, t. 592, no.110), cited by Charavay, 43.

[4] *Memoirs,* 1:67.

[5] Adrienne, letter to Mlle. du Motier and Madame de Chavaniac, February 16, 1779, Paris, Idzerda, Appendix, French Texts, 2:438, 439.

[6] Lafayette, letter to Vergennes, February 14, 1779, Paris, Idzerda, Appendix, French Texts, 2:437, 438.

[7] Lafayette, letter to Louis XVI, February 19, 1779, Paris, Idzerda, Appendix, French Texts, 2 :439, 440.

[8] Lafayette, letter to Franklin, February 21, 1778, Paris, (*Franklin Papers*, 42: no.142), Idzerda, 2:234.

[9] Tower, 2:57.

[10] *Mémoires,* 1:65; cited by Gottschalk, *The Close of the American Revolution*, 8.

[11] Adams, letter to Lafayette, February 21, 1779, Passy; Idzerda, 2:234-236.

[12] Lafayette, letter to Maurepas, March 14, 1779, Paris, Idzerda, Appendix, French Texts,2:440-443.

[13] Lafayette, letter to Franklin, March 20, 1779, Paris, Idzerda, 2:241.

[14] Lafayette, letter to the comte de Maurepas, March 23, 1779, Paris, Idzerda, Appendix, French Texts, 2:443-444.

[15] Ibid.

[16] Lafayette, letter to the comte de Vergennes, March 26, 1779, Paris, Idzerda, Appendix, French Texts, 2:445-447.

[17] Lafayette, letter to Sartine, April 16-20, Paris, Idzerda, Appendix, French Texts, 2:449.

[18] Lafayette, letter to Vergennes, April 26, 1779, Paris, Idzerda, Appendix, French Texts, 2:449,450.

[19] *Correspondance secrete entre Marie Thérèse et le Cte de Mercy-Argenteau* (3 vols.; Paris, 1874), 111, 315, cited by Gottschalk, *Lafayette and the Close of the American Revolution*, 13.

[20] Gottschalk, *Lafayette and the Close of the American Revolution*, 15.

[21] Lafayette, letter to Franklin, May 19, 1779, Paris, Idzerda, 2:265.

[22] Lafayette, letter to Vergennes, May 17, 1779, Paris, cited by Gottschalk, *The Close of the American Revolution, 16.*

[23] Lafayette, letter to Vergennes, Paris; Stevens, Facsimiles, XVII, No. 1613, cited by Gottschalk, *The Close of the American Revolution*, 16.

[24] Lafayette, letter to Vergennes, May 19, 1779, Paris, Stevens, Facsimiles, XVII. No.1613, cited by Gottschalk, *The Close of the American Revolution*, 17, who says that May 19 is the correct date for this letter and not June 1.

[25] Lafayette, letter to Vergennes, May 23, 1779, Paris, Idzerda,2:268,269. Note: Bancroft is, in fact, a double spy; Bemis, S.F., British Secret Service and the French-American Alliance, American Historical Review, XXIX (1924), 474-95, cited by Gottschalk, *Lafayette Comes to America*, 92.

[26] Lafayette, letter to Vergennes, June 1, 1779, St. Jean d'Angely, Idzerda, Appendix, French Texts, 2:452,453.

[27] Lafayette, letter to Vergennes, June 3, 1779, St. Jean d'Angely, Idzerda, 2:377, note 1.

[28] Lafayette, letter to Vergennes, June 10, 1799, St. Jean d'Angely, cited by Tower,2:64, citing Doniol, 4:291.

[29] Lafayette, letter to Dr. Cochran, June 10, 1779, St. Jean d'Angely near Rochefort, June 10, 1779, Idzerda, 2:271,272.

[30] Lafayette, letter to the President of Congress, June 12, 1779, St. Jean d'Angely, near Rochefort; Idzerda, 2:272-275.

[31] Lafayette, letter to Washington, June 12, 1779, St. Jean d'Angely, June 12, 1779, *The Letters of Lafayette to Washington*, 74-78.

[32] Lafayette, letter to Vergennes, June 24, 1779, Paris, Idzerda, Appendix, French Texts, 2:454.

[33] Lafayette, letter to Vergennes, July 1, 1779, Le Havre, Idzerda, Appendix, French Texts, 2:454,455.

[34] Ibid.

[35] Lafayette, letter to Vergennes, July 18, 1779, Le Havre, *Memoirs*, 1:540-551, Appendix 2.

[36] Lafayette, letter to Vergennes, July 30, 1779, Idzerda, Appendix, French Texts, 2:457,458.

[37]Lafayette, letter to Vergennes, August 13, 1779, Le Havre, Idzerda, Appendix, French Texts, 2:459-461.

[38] Lafayette, letter to Vergennes, August 16, 1779, Le Havre, Idzerda, Appendix, French Texts,2:461-463.

[39] Franklin, letter to Lafayette, August 24, 1779, Passy, Idzerda, 2:303,304.

[40] Lafayette, letter to Franklin, August 29, 1779, Le Havre, Idzerda, 2:305,306.

[41] Lafayette, letter to Vergennes, September 11, 1779, Le Havre, Idzerda, Appendix, French Texts, 2:463,464.

[42] Doniol, 4:243.

[43] Lafayette, letter to Vergennes, September 11, 1780, Le Havre, Idzerda, Appendix, French Texts,2:463,464.

[44]Vergennes, letter to Lafayette, September 16, 1779, Versailles, Idzerda, Appendix, French Texts, 2:464,465.

[45] Lafayette, letter to Franklin, October 6,1779, Le Havre; APS, *Franklin Papers*, XVI, no.7, cited by Gottschalk, *The Close of the American Revolution*, 47.

[46] Freeman, 5:138.

[47] Adrienne, letter to Lafayette, December 24, 1779, Passy, Idzerda, Appendix, French Texts, 2:465,466.

[48] Lafayette, letter to Franklin, December 24, 1779, Paris, Idzerda,2:341.

[49] Franklin, letter to Jay, October 4, 1779, Smyth, VII,388, cited by Gottschalk, *The Close of the American Revolution,*59.

[50] Sparks, *Works of Franklin*, viii, 379, cited by Tower, 2:87.

[51] *Memoirs*, 1:248.

[52] Washington, letter to Lafayette, Sepember 30, 1779, West Point, Idzerda, 2:313-319.

[53] Doniol,4:277.

[54] Lafayette, letter to Maurepas, January 25, 1780, Paris, Doniol, 4 :Annexes du chapitre 5:308-312.

[55] Lafayette, letter to Vergennes, February 2, 1780, Doniol, 4: Annexes du chapitre 5:312-314.

[56] Lafayette, Observations on some matters pertaining to the Navy for an expedition to North America, February 21, 1780, Versailles, Idzerda, Appendix, French Texts,2:474-476.

[57] Mazzei to Jefferson, March 2,1780, Howard R. Marraro, (ed.), Philip Mazzei, Virginia's agent in Europe, 31, cited by Gottschalk, *The Close of the American Revolution*, 69.

[58] Instructions from Vergennes, March 5, 1780, Versailles, Doniol, 4:Annexes du chapitre 5,314-318.

[59] Doniol, 4: Annexes du chapitre 5,318-320.

[60] Franklin, letter to Washington, March 5, 1780, Passy, cited by Charavay,54, note 2.

[61] La Touche-Tréville, March 11, 1780, Ile d'Aix, (Arch. de la Marine, B, fol.6), cited by Charavay, 54, note.3.

[62] Lafayette, letter to the prince de Poix, March 12, 1780, on board the *Hermione*, Idzerda, Appendix, French Texts, 2:484,485.

[63] Lafayette, letter to the prince de Poix, March 13, 1780, on board the *Hermione*, cited by Charavay, 54.

[64] Lafayette, letter to Adrienne, March 13, 9 'o clock at night, 1780, cited by Maurois, 102.

Chapter 25

[1] Rousseau de Fayolle, *Journal d'une campagne en Amérique*, 48, cited by Gottschalk, *The Close of the American Revolution*, 77.

[2] Emmanuel de Fontainieu, *The Hermione*, De Monza editions, Commemorative book.

[3] Lafayette, letter to Washington, at the entrance of Boston harbor, April 27, 1780, Idzerda, 3: 3.

[4] Rousseau de Fayolle, *Journal d'une campagne en Amérique*,48, cited by Gottschalk, *The Close of the American Revolution*, 78.

[5] Lafayette, letter to Vergennes, May 2, 1780, Watertown on the road from Boston to camp, Idzerda, Appendix 1, French Texts,3:427,428.

[6] Lafayette, letter to Adrienne, May 6, 1780, Waterbury, Idzerda, 3:8-10.

[7] Note: Knyphausen planned to capture him here but narrowly missed him, cited by Gottschalk, *The Close of the American Revolution*, 82, citing Robertson to Germain, May 18, 1780, Documents relevant to the Colonial History of the State of New York, VIII,792.

[8] Washington, letter to Lafayette, May 8, 1780, Morristown, 10,11, Idzerda, 3:10,11.

[9] Washington, letter to Heath, May 15, 1780, Fitzpatrick, XVIII, 368-88, cited by Gottschalk, *The Close of the American Revolution*, 82.

[10] Washington, letter to Lafayette, May 19, 1780, Fitzpatrick, VVIII, 386-88, cited by Gottschalk, 82.

[11] Lafayette, letter to La Luzerne, May 17, 1780, Philadelphia, Idzerda, Appendix 1, French Texts, 3:433,434.

[12] Lafayette, letter to Congress, May 16, 1780, Philadelphia, cited by Tower, 2:109.

[13] JCC,17:437-39, 442, 443, cited by Idzerda, 3:25, note 1.

[14] Lafayette, letter to Vergennes, May 20, 1780, Philadelphia, Idzerda, Appendix 1, French Texts, 3:435-437.

Chapter 26

[1] Lafayette, letter to Reed, May 31, 1780, Headquarters, Morristown, Idzerda, 3: 43-45.

[2] Ibid.

[3] Freeman, 5:167.

[4] Lafayette, letter to La Luzerne, June 3, 1780, Morristown, Idzerda, Appendix 1, French Texts, 3:445-447.

[5] Washington, letter to Joseph Jones, May 31, 1780, Morristown, cited by Freeman, 5:167.

[6] La Luzerne, letter to Lafayette, May 28, 1780, Philadelphia, Idzerda, Appendix 1, French Texts, 3:443,444.

[7] La Luzerne, letter to Lafayette, May 31, 1780, Philadelphia, Idzerda, Appendix 1, French texts, 3: 444.445.

[8] Lafayette, letter to La Luzerne, June 3, 1780, Morristown, Idzerda, Appendix 1, French Texts, 3:445-447.

[9] Proclamation to the Canadians, May 25, 1780, Morristown, Idzerda, Appendix 1, French Texts, 3:441-443.

[10] Freeman, 5:170, citing Burnett, 19. G.W., 8, 10, 12-13.

[11] Lafayette, letter to Heath, June 11, 1780, On the Heights of Springfield, Idzerda, 3:53-56.

[12] Greene, *The Life of Nathanael Greene*,2:197.

[13] Nolan, 114.

[14] Heath, letter to Lafayette, June 20, 1780, Providence, Idzerda, 3:61.

[15] Washington, letter to Fielding Lewis, July 6, 1780, Preakness, Freeman, 5:177.

[16] Lafayette, letter to Washington, July 4, 1780, camp at Preakness, *The Letters of Lafayette to Washington*,82-84.

[17] Lafayette, letter to Rochambeau and de Ternay, July 9, 1780, Preakness, Idzerda, Appendix 1, French Texts, 3:69-76.

[18] Memorial of Grievances from the General Officers to Congress, July 11, 1780, Camp at Preakness, Idzerda,3:455-461.

[19] Heath Papers, 82; 19 G.W., 167, 171, cited by Freeman, 5:178.

[20] Gottschalk, *The Close of the American Revolution*, 97.

[21] Lafayette, draft to Washington, July 15, 1780; Idzerda, 3:96, note 2.

[22] Lafayette, letter to Vergennes, July 19, 1780, At camp in New Jersey, Idzerda, Appendix 1, French Texts, 3:466-468.

[23] Washington, letter to Lafayette, July 16, 1780, Headquarters, Idzerda, 3:95.

[24] Comte de Rochambeau, letter to Washington, July 16, 1780, Newport, Idzerda, 3:96,97.

[25] Lafayette to Washington, July 20, 1780, Peekskill, *The Letters of Lafayette to Washington*, 88.

[26] Lafayette to Washington, July 21, 1780, Danbury, *The Letters of Lafayette to Washington*, 89.

[27] Lafayette to Washington, July 23, 1780, Lebanon, *The Letters of Lafayette to Washington*, 92.

[28] Lafayette, letter to Washington, July 26, 1780, Newport, *The Letters of Lafayette to Washington*, 93,94.

[29] Lafayette, letter to Washington, July 29, 1780, Newport, *The Letters of Lafayette to Washington*,97-100.

[30] Lafayette, letter to Rochambeau and de Ternay, August 9, 1780, in camp before Dobb's Ferry, Idzerda, 3:131-136.

[31] Washington, letter to Lafayette, July 31, 1780, Robinson's in the Highlands, Idzerda, 3:120,121.

[32] Lafayette, letter to Heath, August 3, 1780, Newport, Idzerda, 3:125,126.

[33] Lafayette, letter to Heath, August 3, 1780, Newport, Heath Papers, 99, Idzerda, 3:126, note 4.

[34] Lafayette, letter to Rochambeau and de Ternay, August 9, 1780, camp before Dobb's Ferry, Idzerda, 3:131-136.

[35] Rochambeau, letter to Lafayette, August 12, 1780, Newport, Idzerda, Appendix 1, French Texts, 3:139,140.

[36] Lafayette, letter to Rochambeau and de Ternay, August 18,1780, Gottschalk, *The Close of the American Revolution*, 115.

[37] Lafayette, letter to Rochambeau, August 18, 1780, in camp, Idzerda, Appendix 1, French Texts, 3:479,480.

[38] Rochambeau, letter to Lafayette, August 27, 1780, Newport, Doniol,4:380, note 4.

[39] Lafayette, letter to Noailles, September 2, 1780, Light Camp near Fort Lee, Idzerda, Appendix 1, French Texts, 3:485-487.

[40] Lafayette, letter to La Luzerne, August 27, 1780, Camp of the Light Division; American Historical Review, 371; cited by Nolan, 124.

[41] Freeman, 5:186.

[42] Woodbridge, Major Thomas, memorandum, August 26,1780, *Magazine of American History*, September,1882, cited by Morgan,185.

[43] Lafayette, letter to Noailles, September 2, 1780, Light Camp near Fort Lee, Idzerda, Appendix 1, French Texts, 3:485-487.

[44] Hamilton, letter to Duane, September 6, 1780, Bergen County, *The Founding Fathers; Alexander Hamilton, A Biography in his own words*, 88.

[45] Freeman, 5:189.

[46] Memorandum to George Washington on Military Operations, September 10, misdated according to Idzerda, 3:171-173.

[47] Lafayette, letter to La Luzerne, September 10, 1780, at the Light Division camp near Hackensack, Idzerda, 3:167-170.

[48] Lafayette, letter to La Luzerne, September 10, 1780, at the Light Division camp near Hackensack, Idzerda, 3:490-492.

[49] Lafayette, letter to La Luzerne, September 10, 1780, at the Light Division camp near Hackensack, Idzerda, Appendix 1, French Texts, 3:490-492.

[50] Washington, letter to Guichen, September 12, 1780; Fitzpatrick, 39-42, cited by Gottschalk, *The Close of the American Revolution*, 129.

[51] Freeman,5:190.

[52] Sparks, MSSXXXII, 97,98, cited by Gottschalk, *The Close of the American Revolution*,131.

[53] *Mémoires,*2:15.

[54] Life of Jonathan Trumbull, Stuart, Boston, 1859; Nolan,128. Arnold, Sparks, 180.

[55] Sparks, MSXXXII, 98,99, cited by Gottschalk, *The Close of the American Revolution*, 131.

[56] Watson, 27. Chastellux,1:40.

[57] Doniol,4:381, cited by Charavay, 64.

[58] Report of de Ternay to Vergennes, October 18, 1780; cited by Freeman,5:193, note 101. De Ternay thought the French fleet should go to Boston as he considered Newport to be a funnel through which the enemy could come. He also thought it was wrong to insist on keeping the French army and navy together in all circumstances.

[59] Gottschalk, *The Close of the American Revolution*, 133.

[60] The minutes of Lafayette and Hamilton, September 22, 1780, Fitzpatrick, XX,76, cited by Gottschalk, *The Close of the American Revolution*, 133, note 47.

[61] Dumas, *Souvenirs du Lieutenant Général Comte Mathieu Dumas*, de 1770 à 1836; 1:44,45.

[62] Gottschalk, *The Close of the American Revolution*, 134.

[63] Lafayette, letter to La Luzerne, September 26, 1780, Robinson's House across from West Point, Idzerda, 3:179,180.

[64] Nolan, 129, citing *Life of André*,327.

[65] Thacher, 131, cited by Van Doren,285.

[66] Varick, letter to his sister, Jane, October 1, 1780, Varick Court of Inquiry, 130; cited by Freeman, 5:197.

[67] Varick, letter to his sister, Jane, 130, Freeman, 5:197.

[68] Note: Sparks says this, Arnold, 244, but Freeman disagrees; he says Washington would not have wanted to waste powder 5: 198, note,11. Sparks is probably correct as when Chastellux visits Heath at West Point he is given a 13-gun salute in the name of the United States, Chastellux, *Travels in North America in the years 1780-81-82*,46.

[69] Thacher, 257.

[70] Ibid., 258.

[71] The description of West Point comes from: Chastellux, 46; Von Closen,60,61; Thacher, 257,258; Chartrand,6; Freeman,5:198.

[72] Lear's Account, Rush, 83, cited by Freeman, 5:198.

[73] Lear's Account, 831, cited by Freeman,5:199.

[74] Letter of September 24, 1780, *André Court Minutes*, 11-13, Freeman, 5:200. *Mémoires*, 2:139.

[75] Sparks, MSSXXXII,123, cited by Gottschalk, *The Close of the American Revolution*, 137.

[76] Varick, Court,192,193, cited by Van Doren, 351.

[77] Van Doren, 347, 348.

[78] Washington, letter to Heath, September 26, 1780, Robinson's House; Sparks, *The Writings of George Washington*, 7:216-218.

[79] Hamilton, letter to Greene, *The Life of Nathanael Greene*, Greene, 2:227.

[80] Lafayette, letter to La Luzerne, September 26, 1780, Robinson's House, Idzerda, 3:179,180. Robinson, letter to Washington, September 25, 1780, *Vulture* off Singsing, Sparks,7:533,534.

[81] Letter from Arnold on the *Vulture*, Sparks, *The Writings of George Washington*, VII, 533.

[82] Hamilton, letter to Elizabeth Schuyler, September 25, 1780, Robinson's House, Highlands, New York, *Alexander Hamilton; a biography in his own words*,89,90. Note: he says he goes to see Mrs. Arnold with Washington after his return from chasing Arnold.

[83] Lafayette, letter to La Luzerne, September 25, 1780, Morgan,183.

[84] Hamilton, letter to Elizabeth Schuyler, September 25, 1780, Robinson's House, Hamilton, 89,90.

[85] Lafayette, letter to La Luzerne, September 25, 1780, Robinson House; Tower,2:164-168, Note: Tower takes this letter partly from Lafayette's *Mémoires, Correspondance et manuscrits*,1:367, dated September 26 and fully given from the *Revue de la Révolution*, 5, Année 1885, in an article by Ernouf.

[86] *Memoirs*,1:255,256.

[87] Lafayette, letter to La Luzerne, September 26, 1780, Robinson House, *Memoirs*, 1: 349-351.

[88] Washington, letter to Jameson, 7.00, September 25, 1780, Robinson's House, Sparks,7:214.

[89] Washington, letter to Greene, 7.30, September 25, 1780, Robinson's House, Sparks, 7:215.

[90] Freeman, 5:202,203.

[91] Lafayette, letter to Rochambeau, September, 26, 1780, Collection of Paul Mellon,Upperville, Virginia; Idzerda,3:180, Note 6.

[92] Greene, *The Life of Nathanael Greene*, 2:229.

[93] Freeman,5:205.

[94] Hamilton, letter to Elizabeth Schuyler, September 25, 1780, *Alexander Hamilton, A Biography in His Own Words*,90.

[95] Lafayette, letter to La Luzerne, September 25, 26, 1780, Robinson House; Tower,2:164-168.

[96] Ibid.

[97] Washington, Writings, (Fitzpatrick), XX,101, cited by Van Doren,355.

[98] Greene, *The Life of Nathanael Greene*, 2:234.

[99] Van Doren,357.

[100] Greene, 2:234,235.

[101] Lafayette, letter to Noailles, October 3, 1780, Light Camp, Harrington,Idzerda, Appendix 1, French Texts, 3:497-500.

[102] *André Court Minutes*,22-23, Freeman, 5:216.

[103] Greene, 2:236.

[104] Ibid., 2:239.

[105] Ibid., 2:240.

[106] Nolan, 131, citing Laune (Lauzun?) from Sargent, *Life of André*, 399.

[107] Description of André's death, Thacher, 272-274. Freeman, citing various sources,5:221.

[108] Lafayette, letter to Adrienne, October 8, 1780, on the Hackensack River, 1:356,357.

[109] *Memoirs*,1:256,257.

[110] Lafayette, letter to Rochambeau, September 26, 1780, Robinson House, cited by Tower, 65, citing *Correspondance du comte de Rochambeau*,1:158.

[111] Lafayette, letter to Vergennes, October 4, 1780, Light Infantry camp near Harrington, Idzerda, Appendix 1, French Texts, 3:500-503.

Chapter 27

[1] Lafayette, letter to Vergennes, October 4, 1780, at the camp of the Light Division at Harrington, Idzerda, Appendix 1, French Texts, 3:500-503.

[2] Lafayette, letter to Madame de Tessé, October 4, 1780, at camp on the right bank of the North River, near the island of New York, *Mémoires,* 2:140-142.

[3] Lafayette, letter to Franklin, October 9, 1780, Light Infantry camp, *Franklin Papers*, 20: no.16, cited by Idzerda,3:192, note7.

[4] Lafayette, letter to Adrienne, October 7, 8, and 10, 1780, near Fort Lee; on the bank of the Hackensack; Totowa Bridge, *Mémoires,* 2: 143-147.

[5] Lafayette, letter to Washington, October 12, 1780, Light Camp near Totowa, *The Letters of Lafayette to Washington*,112,113.

[6] Greene, *The life of Nathanael Greene*, 2:372-374.

[7] Lafayette, letter to Noailles, October 23, 1780, at camp, Wagaraw, Idzerda, Appendix 1, French Texts,3:510,511.

[8] Freeman, 5:227. Note: King's Mountain was in North Carolina at the time this took place.

[9] Lafayette, letter to Washington, October 30, 1780, Light Camp, Idzerda, 3:211-213.

[10] Washington, letter to Lafayette, October 30, 1780, Headquarters, Totowa, Idzerda, 3: 214.

[11] Lafayette, letter to Washington, November 1, 1780, Light Camp, *The Letters of Lafayette to Washington*,120-123.

[12] Lafayette, letter to Washington, November 13, 1780, Light Camp, *The Letters of Lafayette to Washington*,124-126.

[13] Chastellux, 65.

[14] Ibid., 66.

[15] Ibid., 69.

[16] Thacher, 286,287, cited by Gottschalk, *The Close of the American Revolution*, 156,157.

[17] Lafayette, letter to Franklin, November 19, 1780, Light Camp near Totowa on the Passaic, Idzerda, 3:228-230.

[18] Chastellux, 89.

[19] Lafayette, letter to Washington, December 4, 1780, Philadelphia, *The Letters of Lafayette to Washington*, ed. by Gottschalk, 131-133.

[20] Chastellux,115.

[21] Ibid.,121.

[22] Gottschalk, *The Close of the American Revolution*, 162.

[23] Lafayette, letter to Washington, December 9, 1780, Philadelphia, *The Letters of Lafayette to Washington*, 136-138.

[24] Chastellux, 18,19.

[25] Ibid.,141-143.

[26] Lafayette, letter to Adrienne, February 2, 1781, New Windsor, *Mémoires*, 2:179-184.

[27] Lafayette, letter to Washington, December 16, 1780, Philadelphia, *The Letters of Lafayette to Washington*,139,140.

[28] Lafayette, letter to the president of the Board of Admiralty, December 16, 1780, Philadelphia, Idzerda, 3:263-265.

[29] Greene, letter to Lafayette, December29, 1780, camp on the Pedee, Idzerda, 3:274-276.

[30] Washington, letter to Meschech Weare, President of New Hampshire, January 5, 1781, New Windsor, Sparks, 7:352-354.

[31] Ibid.

[32] Lafayette, letter to La Luzerne, Trenton, January 4, 1780; Idzerda, Appendix 1, French Texts, 3:517,518.

[33] Ibid.

[34] American Historical Review, XX:578, cited by Nolan,148.

[35] Lafayette, letter to La Luzerne, January 7, 1780, Morristown, Idzerda, Appendix 1, French Texts, 3:518-520.

[36] Lafayette, letter to Washington, January 7, 1781, Morristown, *The Letters of Lafayette to Washington*, 143.

[37] Lafayette, letter to La Luzerne, January 14, 1781, New Windsor; Idzerda, Appendix 1, French Texts, 3:520,521.

[38] Wayne, letter to Washington, Freeman,5:242,243.

[39] Circular to New England and New York, January 20, 1781, 21, G.W, cited by Freeman,5:243.

[40] Lafayette, letter to the prince de Poix, January 30, 1781, New Windsor, Idzerda,3:528-531. Note: according to Idzerda, he is speaking about the Society of the Wooden Sword.

[41] Washington, Order to Shreve; 21, G.W., 124, Freeman,5:245.

[42] Dumas, 1:55,56.

[43] Ibid.

[44] Ibid.

[45] Washington, Order to Howe, January 22, 1781, HeadQuarters, Sparks,7:380,381.

[46] Washington, letter to President Weare, January 22, 1781, New Windsor; Sparks,7:381-383.

[47] Thacher was present at the execution; Thacher, 302-304.

[48] Circular of January 29 to the New England states, Freeman, 5:250.

[49] Washington, letter to Rochambeau, February 7, 1781, New Windsor, cited by Freeman, 5:256.

[50] Thacher, 305.

[51] Hamilton, letter to Schuyler, February 18, 1781, Headquarters, New Windsor, *Alexander Hamilton; A Biography in his own words*, 94-96.

Chapter 28
[1] Lafayette, letter to La Luzerne, February 19, 1781, New Windsor, Idzerda, Appendix 1, French texts;3:330-333.

[2] Instructions of Washington to Lafayette, Sparks, 7: 417-420.

[3] Lafayette, letter to Jefferson, New Windsor, February 21,1781, *The Letters of Lafayette and Jefferson, with an introduction and notes by Gilbert Chinard* (John Hopkins Univ.), 17.

[4] Wild,56.

[5] Lafayette, letter to Washington, February 23, 1781, Pompton, *The Letters of Lafayette to Washington*,146,147.

[6] Smith, to Washington, February 25, 1781, Morristown, Washington Correspondance, Library of Congress, Nolan,157.

[7] Wild, 56.

[8] Ibid.

[9] Lafayette, letter to Washington, March 2, 1781, Philadelphia, *The Letters of Lafayette to Washington*, 150-153.

[10] Ibid.

[11] Ibid.

[12] Washington, letter to Lafayette, February 25, 1781, New Windsor, cited in Sparks, 7:430-432.

[13] Lafayette, letter to Washington, Philadelphia, March 2, 1781, *The Letters of Lafayette to Washington*, 150-153.

[14] Washington, letter to Lafayette, February 27, 1781, New Windsor, Sparks, 7:439-440.

[15] Lafayette, letter to Washington, March 3, 1781, Head of Elk, *The Letters of Lafayette to Washington*, 153.

[16] Lafayette, letter to the Commanding Officer in Virginia, March 3, 1781, Head of Elk, Idzerda, 3:363,364.

[17] Lafayette, letter to Jefferson, March 3, 1781, Head of Elk, Idzerda, 3:367-369.

[18] Washington, letter to Lafayette, March 1, 1781, Headquarters, Sparks,7:444-446.

[19] Lafayette, letter to Washington, March 7, 1781, Head of Elk, Idzerda,3:376-378.

[20] Lafayette, letter to Washington, March 8, 1781, Elk, *The Letters of Lafayette to Washington*,156,157.

[21] Wild, 57.

[22] Lafayette, letter to Washington, March 9, 1781, On board the *Dolphin, Memoirs,* 1: 391.

[23] Lafayette, letter to La Luzerne, March 8, 1781, Elkton, Idzerda, Appendix 1, French Texts, 3: 384.

[24] Lafayette, Letter to Washington, March 9, 1781, off Turkey Point, *The Letters of Lafayette to Washington,* 158, 159.

[25] Shriver, 58,59, cited by Gottschalk.

[26] Wild, 58.

[27] Lafayette, letter to Washington, March 23, 1781, Williamsburg, *The Letters of Lafayette to Washington,* 161-163.

[28] Maryland State Archives, XLVII (1930),127, cited by Nolan, 160.

[29] Lafayette, letter to Washington, March 23, 1781, Williamsburg, *The Letters of Lafayette to Washington,* 161-163.

[30] Lafayette, letter to von Steuben, March 14, 1781, York, Idzerda, Appendix 1, French Texts, 3:546.

[31] Lafayette, letter to Washington, March 23, 1781, Williamsburg, *The Letters of Lafayette to Washington,* 161-163.

[32] Lafayette, letter to Washington, March 15, 1781, York, *The Letters of Lafayette to Washington,* 159,160.

[33] Lafayette, letter to Washington, March 15, 1781, York, *The Letters of Lafayette to Washington,* 159,160.

[34] Lafayette, letter to Wayne, March 15, 1781, York, Idzerda, 3:399.

[35] Ibid.

[36] Thacher, 333,334.

[37] Jefferson, letter to Lafayette, March 10, 1781, Richmond; *The Letters of Lafayette and Jefferson with an introduction and notes by Gilbert Chinard* (John Hopkins Univ.), 20.

[38] Jefferson, letter to Lafayette, March 12, 1781, Richmond, *The Letters of Lafayette and Jefferson,* 21.

[39] Ibid., 22

[40] Jefferson, letter to Lafayette, March 14, 1781, The Letters of Lafayette and Jefferson, 23.

[41] Lafayette, letter to Jefferson, March 16,1781, Williamsburg, *The Letters of Lafayette and Jefferson,* 24-26.

[42] Lafayette to Jefferson, Williamsburg, March 17,1781, Idzerda, 3:402,403.

[43] Jefferson, letter to Lafayette, March 19, 1781, Richmond, *The Letters of Lafayette and Jefferson,* 27-29.

[44] Lafayette, letter to Weedon, March 20, 1781, Camp at Sleepy Hole, Idzerda, 3:406.

[45] Lafayette to Jefferson, March 20, 1781, Camp near Sleepy Hole, *The Letters of Lafayette and Jefferson,* 30.

[46] Ibid.

[47] Washington Correspondance, Library of Congress, cited by Nolan,162.

[48] Lafayette, letter to Washington, March 23, 1781, Williamsburg, Idzerda, 3:408-410.

[49] Nolan,162.

[50] Lafayette, letter to Washington, March 26, 1781, Williamsburg, *The Letters of Lafayette to Washington,* 167.

[51] Ibid.

[52] Ibid.

[53] Lafayette, letter to Washington, March 25, 1781, Williamsburg, *The Letters of Lafayette to Washington,*164,165.

[54] Nolan,163.

[55] Lafayette, letter to Washington, April 8, 1781, Elk, *The Letters of Lafayette to Washington,* 168-171.

[56] Lafayette, letter to Jefferson, April 4, 1781, Annapolis, *The Letters of Lafayette and Jefferson,* 36.

[57] Wild, 59.

[58] Lafayette, letter to Washington, April 8, 1781, Elk, *The Letters of Lafayette to Washington,* 168-171.

[59] Ibid.

[60] Wild,60.

[61] Washington, letter to Lafayette, April 6, 1781, New Windsor, *Memoirs,* 1: 395,396.

[62] Lafayette, letter to Washington, April 8, 1781, Elk, *Memoirs,* 1:397-401.

[63] Lafayette, letter to Washington, April 10, 1781, Elk, *The Letters of Lafayette to Washington,* 172-174.

[64] Ibid.

[65] Lafayette, letter to Hamilton, April 10, 1781, Elk, Idzerda, 4:16,17.

[66] Lafayette, letter to La Luzerne, April 10, 1781, Elk, Idzerda, Appendix 1, French Texts,4:453,454.

[67] Lafayette, letter to Washington, April 12, 1781, Elk; *The Letters of Lafayette to Washington,* 176,177.

[68] Wild, 60.

[69] The Governor's Council of Maryland, letter to Lafayette, April 12, 1781, in council, Idzerda, 4:27-29.

[70] Wild,60.

Chapter 29
[1] Ibid.
[2] Lafayette to Washington, Elk, April 12, 1781, *The Letters of Lafayette to Washington*, 176.
[3] Wild, 60.
[4] Lafayette, letter to La Luzerne, April 14, 1781, Susquehana ferry, American Historical Review, XX:98, cited by Nolan, 166.
[5] Washington, letter to Lafayette, April 11, 1781, Head quarters New Windsor, Idzerda, 4:24-26.
[6] Greene, letter to Lafayette, April 3, 1781, Head quarters Col. Ramsey's Deep River, Idzerda, 4:3-5.
[7] Wild, 60.
[8] Lafayette, letter to Washington, April 13, 1781, Susquehana Ferry, *The Letters of Lafayette to Washington*,178.
[9] Lafayette, letter to Washington, Susquehanna Ferry, April 14, 1781, *The Letters of Lafayette to Washington*, 180-182.
[10] Ibid.
[11] Lafayette, letter to La Luzerne, April 14, 1781, Susquehana Ferry, American Historical Review,XX,598, cited by Nolan, 166.
[12] *Mémoires historiques de La Fayette*,1:268, cited by Tower, 2: 260.
[13] *Mémoires,* 2:22.
[14] Lafayette, letter to Washington, April 15, 1781, Susquehana Ferry, Idzerda,4:183,184.
[15]Lafayette, letter to Hamilton, April 15, 1781, Susquehana, Idzerda, 4:32.
[16] Baltimore Advertiser, April 17, 1781, cited by Nolan,167.
[17] Lafayette, letter to Washington, April 18, 1781, Baltimore, *The Letters of Lafayette to Washington*, 184-186.
[18] Lafayette, letter to Greene, April 17, 1781, Baltimore, Idzerda, 4:35-41.
[19] Ibid.
[20] Wild, 61.
[21] Lafayette, letter to Jefferson, April 17, 1781, Baltimore, Chinard,37.
[22] Lafayette, letter to Washington, April 18, 1781, Baltimore; *The Letters of Lafayette to Washington*, 184-186.
[23] Shriver; Nolan,168.
[24] Wild, 61.
[25] Lafayette, letter to Jefferson, April 21, 1781, Alexandria, Idzerda, 4:48,49.
[26] Lafayette, letter to George Augustine Washington, April 21, 1781, Alexandria, Idzerda, 4:50.
[27] Washington, letter to Lafayette, April 14, 1781, cited by Gottschalk, *The Close of the American Revolution*, 221.
[28] Lafayette, letter to La Luzerne, April 22, 1781, Alexandria, Idzerda, Appendix 1, French Texts,4:455,456.
[29] Wild, 61.
[30] Idzerda;4: 61, note1: 'Property' changed later to 'concerns.'
[31] Wild, 61.
[32] Von Steuben, letter to Lafayette, April 21, 1781, Chesterfield Co. Ho., Idzerda, 4:51.
[33] Jefferson, letter to Lafayette, April 23, 1781, Richmond, *The Letters of Lafayette and Jefferson*, 38.
[34] This letter from Jefferson has not been found, but Lafayette refers to it in a letter to von Steuben, referenced below.
[35] Lafayette, letter to Jefferson, April 25, 1781, Fredericksburg, Idzerda, 4:62,63.
[36] Lafayette, letter to von Steuben, April 25, 1781, Fredericksburg, Idzerda, 4:63,64.
[37] Lafayette, letter to Weedon, April 27, 1781, Bowling Green, Idzerda, 4:67,68.
[38] Ibid.
[39] Lafayette, letter to Jefferson, April 28, (letter wrongly dated the 27), 1781, Bowling Green, *The Letters of Lafayette and Jefferson*, 39.
[40] Lafayette, letter to Greene, May 3, 1781, Camp on Pamunkey River, Idzerda, 4:80,81.
[41] Ibid.
[42] Phillips, letters to Lafayette, April 28 and 29, 1781, British Camp at Osborn, Idzerda, 4:69-72.
[43] Lafayette, letter to Phillips, April 30,1781, American Camp, Idzerda, 4:73.
[44] Lafayette, letter to Washington, May 4, 1781, Camp near Bottom's Creek, *The Letters of Lafayette to Washington*, 188-190.
[45] Ibid.
[46] Ibid.

[47] Wild,62.

[48] Lafayette, letter to Weedon, May 3, 1781, Richmond, Idzerda,4:77-79.

[49] Lafayette, letter to Washington, May 4, 1781, Camp near Bottom's Creek, May 4, 1781, *The Letters of Lafayette to Washington*, 188-190.

[50] Wild, 62.

[51] Wild, 62.

[52] Lafayette, letter to Sumner, May 7, 1781, Richmond, Idzerda,4:87.

[53] Lafayette, letter to Wayne, May 7, 1781, Richmond, *Wayne Papers*, Historical Society of Pennsylvania, cited by Tower, 2:307.

[54] Lafayette, letter to Washington, May 8, 1781, Richmond, Idzerda, 4:88,89.

[55] Lafayette, letter to La Luzerne, May 9, 1781, Osborne's, Idzerda, Appendix 1, French Texts,4:457,458.

[56] Ibid.

[57] Wild, 63.

[58] Lafayette, letter to von Steuben, May10, 1781, Osborne's, Idzerda,4:91.

[59] Wild, 63.

[60] Idzerda, 4:101.

[61] Lafayette, letter to Wayne, May 15, 1781, Camp Wilton, Idzerda, 4:102,103.

[62] Lafayette, letter to Hamilton, May 23, 1781, Richmond, *Hamilton's Works of Alexander Hamilton*, 1:262; cited by Tower,2:315.

[63] Lafayette, letter to Wayne, May 15, 1781, Camp Wilton, Idzerda,4:102,103.

[64] Lafayette, letter to Washington, May 17, 1781, Camp Wilton on the James River, *The Letters of Lafayette to Washington*, 192,193.

[65] Lafayette, letter to von Steuben, May 17, 1781, Wilton, Idzerda,4:106-108.

[66] Lafayette, letter to Greene, May 18, 1781, Camp Wilton on James River, Idzerda, 4:110-113.

[67] Lafayette, letter to Noailles, May 22, 1781, Richmond; Idzerda, Appendix 1, French Texts,4:460-463.

[68] Lafayette, letter to Morgan, May 21, 1781, Richmond, Idzerda,4:117-119.

[69] Lafayette, letter to Lee, May 21, 1781, Sparks MSS XXIX,528-30, cited by Gottschalk, *The Close of the American Revolution*, 234.

[70] Lafayette, letter to La Luzerne, May 22, 1781, Richmond, Idzerda, Appendix 1, French Texts, 459,460.

[71] Captain Young to Colonel Davies, May 21, 1781, Virginia state papers, 11,111,112, cited by Gottschalk, *The Close of the American Revolution*, 234.

[72] Lafayette, letter to La Luzerne, May 22, 1781, Richmond, Idzerda, Appendix 1, French Texts, 4:459,460.

[73] Lafayette, letter to Hamilton, May 23, 1781, LC, Hamilton Papers, *Works of Hamilton*,1:262-264, cited by Gottschalk, *The Close of the American Revolution*, 235.

[74] Lafayette, letter to Noailles, May 22, 1781, Richmond; Idzerda, Appendix 1, French Texts,4:460-465.

[75] Weedon, letter to Lafayette, May 22, 1781, Fredericksburg, Idzerda,4:125,126.

[76] Lafayette, letter to Washington, May 24, 1781, Richmond, *The Letters of Lafayette to Washington*,196,197.

[77] Lafayette, letter to Greene, May 24, 1781, Richmond, Idzerda,4:128-130. Note: There was a mutiny on May 20 by the Pennsylvanians who wanted to be paid in hard money, not paper. Wayne had twelve of the leaders executed.

[78] Lafayette, letter to Washington, May 24, 1781, Richmond, Idzerda, 4:130,131.

[79] *Memoirs*, extract of Manuscript, No.2;1:418,419.

[80] Gottschalk, *The Close of the American Revolution*, 237.

[81] Jefferson, letter to Washington, May 28, 1781, *Writings of Jefferson*, IV,182,183, cited by Gottschalk, *The Close of the American Revolution*, 237.

[82] Wild,64.

[83] Lafayette, letter to Wayne, May 27, 1781, *Wayne Papers*, Historical Society of Pennsylvania, 2: 21, cited by Tower,2:321,322.

[84] Lafayette, letter to Wayne, May 27, 1781, The Forks of the Chickahominy, *Wayne Papers*, Historical Society of Pennsylvania, cited in Tower, 2:321,322.

[85] Lafayette, letter to Jefferson, May 28, 1781, Gold Mine Creek, Idzerda,4:136,137.

[86] Lafayette, letter to Weedon, May 28, 1781, Hanover County, Idzerda,4:137,138.

[87] Lafayette, letter to Wayne, May 28, 1781, Hanover County, *Wayne Papers*, Historical Society of Pennsylvania; cited in Tower, 2: 323,324.

[88] Wild,64.

[89] Lafayette, letter to Wayne, May 29, 1781, Gold Mine Creek South Anna River, Idzerda,4:141142.

[90] Lafayette, letter to Weedon, May 29, 1781,Gold Mine Creek, Idzerda, 4:142,143.

[91] Wild,64.

[92] Maas, 69.

[93] Wild,65.

[94] Lafayette, letter to Weedon, June 2, 1781, Weedon Correspondence, no.99, Archives of the American Philosophical Society, Philadelphia, cited by Nolan,177.

[95] Weedon, letter to Lafayette, June 1, 1781, Fredericksburg, Idzerda,4:158.

[96] Lafayette, letter to Wayne, June 2, 1781, Corbin's Bridge, Idzerda,4:160.

[97] Lafayette, letter to Greene, June 3, 1781, Idzerda,4:165, note.

[98] Wild, 65.

[99] Lafayette, letter to Greene, June 3, 1781, Camp between Rappahannock and North Anna, Idzerda,4:162-165.

[100] Marshall, *The Life of George Washington*, 4:433.

[101] Wayne, letter to Lafayette, June 4, 1781, Mr. Carter's near the Red House, Idzerda,4:169.

[102] Lafayette, letter to Wayne, June 5, 1781, Wayne Papers, Archives of the Historical Society of Pennsylvania; Nolan,178.

[103] Wild,64.

[104] Marshall,4:434.

[105] *Simcoe's Military Journal*,222,223, cited by Tower, 2:332.

[106] Wayne, letter to Lafayette, June 6, 1781, Elk River Church, Idzerda, 4:171.

[107] Lafayette, letter to Wayne, June 7, 1781, Raccoon Ford, Idzerda, 4:171,172.

[108] Wayne, letter to Lafayette, June 7,1781, Norman's Ford, Idzerda, 4:172.

[109] Wild, 65.

[110] Lafayette, letter to Washington, June 10, 1781, Brock's Bridge, *The Letters of Lafayette to Washington*, 200,201.

[111] Captain John Davis of the First Pennsylvania Regiment says they joined the marquis on June 10, Journal, Pennsylvania Magazine of History and Biography,5: no.3, cited by Tower, 2:328, note 1. Gottschalk, *The Close of the American Revolution*, 244, says June 10. Wild says Wayne and the Pennsylvanians arrived on June 11 and encamped on their left, 66.

[112] Lafayette, letter to Greene, June 18, 1781, Allen's Creek, *Memoirs*,1:522,523.

[113] Nolan, 179.

[114] Lafayette, letter to Greene, June 18, 1781, Allen's Creek, 22 miles from Richmond, Idzerda, 4:191-193.

[115] Wild, 66.

[116] Lafayette, letter to Morgan, June 12, 1781, Mechunk Creek; Idzerda, 4:176.

[117] Ibid.

[118] Lafayette, letter to von Steuben, June 13, 1781, Mechunk Creek, *Steuben Papers*, New York Historical Society, cited in Tower,2:336,337.

[119] Lafayette, letter to La Luzerne, June 16, 1781, Camp near Pamunkey, Idzerda, Appendix 1, French Texts,4:466-469.

[120] Ibid.

[121] Ibid.

[122] Lafayette, letter to Weedon, June 16, 178q1, Deep Creek, Idzerda, 4:189.

[123] Capitaine's map of the Virginia campaign, cited by Gottschalk, *The Close of the American Revolution*, 251.

[124] Mercer to Simms, Tarleton, 308,309, cited by Gottschalk, *The Close of the American Revolution*, 254.

[125] Lafayette, letter to von Steuben, June 18, 1781, Steuben Papers, New York Historical Society, cited by Tower,2:341.

[126] Lafayette, letter to Washington, June 18, 1781, Allen's Creek 22 miles from Richmond, *The Letters of Lafayette to Washington*, 202-203.

[127] Ibid.

[128] Lafayette, letter to Greene, June 18, 1781, Allen's Creek, *Memoirs,*1:522,523.

[129] Lafayette, letter to Greene, June 27, 1781, Tyree's Plantation, Idzerda,4:216,217.

[130] McHenry, letter to Greene, June 20, 1781, catalogue of the American Autograph shop, cited by Gottschalk, *The Close of the American Revolution*, 253.

[131] Lafayette, letter to Wayne, June 21, 1781, Headquarters, Idzerda,4:205.

[132] Lafayette, letter to Greene, June 21, 1781, Dandridge's, Idzerda,4:202-204.

[133] Feltman, 5.

[134] Lafayette, letter to von Steuben, 5 o'clock, June 22, 1781, Proces' House, Idzerda, 4:206.

[135] Lafayette, letter to Wayne, 5 o'clock, June 22, 1781, Proces' House, Idzerda,4:206,207.

[136] Lafayette, letter to Nelson, 6 a.m. June 26, Rawson's Ordinary, Idzerda, 4:214.

[137] Wayne, letter to Lafayette, June 25, 1781, New Kent Court House, Idzerda,4:211.

[138] Lafayette, letter to Wayne, June 25, 1781, Beacon's Ordinary, Idzerda, 4:212.

[139] Lafayette, letter to Nelson, June 28, 1781, Mr. Tyree's Plantation, Idzerda, 4:217,218.

[140] Lafayette, letter to Washington, June 28, 1781, camp, *The Letters of Lafayette to Washington*, 203,204.

[141] Wild, 67.

[142] Lafayette, letter to Nelson, June 28, 1781, Tyree's Plantation, Idzerda,4:217,218.

[143] Lafayette, letter to Wayne, June 30, 1781, Idzerda, 4:222,223.

[144] Idzerda, 4:223, note 1.

[145] Lafayette, letter to Nelson, July 1, 1781, Tyree's Plantation, Idzerda,4:228-231.

[146] Wild,68.

[147] Feltman, 6

[148] Lafayette, letter to Greene, July 4, 1781, Camp twenty miles from Williamsburg, Idzerda, 4:231-235.

[149] Lafayette, letter to Greene, July 8, 1781, Ambler's Plantation opposite James Island, Idzerda,4:236-239.

[150] Lafayette, letter to Greene, July 8, 1781, Ambler's Plantation, Idzerda,4:236-239.

[151] *Mémoires*, 2:28.

[152] Ibid.

[153] Ibid., 2 :29.

[154] Wild, 69.

[155] Idzerda, 4 :238, note 4.

[156] Lafayette, letter to Jones, July 10, 1781, Quarters near Soan's Bridge, Idzerda,4:241,242.

[157] Ibid.

[158] Lafayette, letter to Gimat, July 9, 1781, typescript in the Gardner-Ball Collection, cited by Gottschalk, *The Close of the American Revolution*, 267.

[159] Lafayette, letter to Washington, July 8, 1781, Ambler's Plantation, *The Letters of Lafayette to Washington*, 204.

[160] Lafayette, letter to Noailles, July 9, 1781, Williamsburg, Idzerda, Appendix 1, French Texts, 4:469.

[161] Lafayette, letter to La Luzerne, July 9, 1781, Near Williamsburg, *American Historical Review*. Vol.XX, 604; cited in Nolan, 185, cited in Gottschalk, 269.

[162] Lafayette, letter to Allen Jones, July 10, 1781, Quarters near Soan's Bridge, Idzerda, 4:241,242.

[163] Lafayette, letter to Nelson, July 12, 1781, Holt's Forge, Idzerda,4:243,244.

[164] McHenry to T.S. Lee, July 11, 1781, Kite,24, cited by Gottschalk, *The Close of the American Revolution*, 271.

[165] Wild,69.

[166] Lafayette, letter to Wayne, July 13, 1781, Wayne Papers, Idzerda,4:249, note 2.

[167] Lafayette, letter to Nelson, July 13, 1781, Headquarters Long Bridge, 244,245.

[168] Wild,69.

[169] Lafayette, letter to Wayne, July 15, 1781, Richmond, Idzerda,4:248,249.

[170] Lafayette, letter to Washington, July 20, 1781, Malvern Hill, *The Letters of Lafayette to Washington*, 209.

[171] Lafayette, letter to Morgan, July 16, 1781, Richmond, Idzerda,4:251.

[172] Lafayette, letter to Morgan, July 17, 1781, Richmond, Idzerda, 4:253.

[173] Lafayette, letter to Washington, July 20, 1781, Malvern, *The Letters of Lafayette to Washington*, 205,206.

[174] Ibid.

[175] Lafayette, letter to Washington, July 20, 1781, Malvern, *The Letters of Lafayette to Washington*, 207-210.

[176] Wild, 70.

[177] Lafayette, letter to Wayne, July 21, 1781, Malvern, Idzerda,4:263264.

[178] Lafayette, letter to Nelson, July 22, 1781, Malvern, Idzerda,4:264-266.

[179] Lafayette, letter to Greene, July 23, 1781, Malvern, Idzerda,4:269,270.

[180] Lafayette, letter to Nelson, July 23, 1781, Malvern, Idzerda,4: 271.

[181] Lafayette, letter to Wayne, July 23, 1781, Malvern, Idzerda,4:274.

[182] Lafayette, letter to Wayne, July 25, 1781, Malvern, Idzerda, 4:277,278.

[183] Wild,70.

[184] Lafayette, Letter to Washington, July 26, 1781, Malvern, *The Letters of Lafayette to Washington*, 210,211.

[185] Lafayette, letter to Congress, July 26, 1781, Malvern, PCC, no. 156,fol.204, cited by Gottschalk,276.

[186] Lafayette, letter to Weedon, July 27, 1781, Malvern Hill, Idzerda,4:280,281.

[187] Lafayette to Washington, Malvern Hill, July 30, 1781, *The Letters of Lafayette to Washington*, 211.

[188] Lafayette, letter to Thomas Sim Lee, July 30, 1781, Malvern Hill, Idzerda, 4:285,286.

[189] Lafayette, letter to Washington, July 30, 1781, Malvern Hill, *The Letters of Lafayette to Washington*, 211, 212.

[190] Ibid.

[191] Lafayette, letter to Nelson, July 29, 1781, Malvern, Idzerda,4:283,284.

[192] Washington, letter to Lafayette, July 13, 1781; Fitzpatrick, XXII,367-369, cited in Gottschalk, *The Close of the American Revolution*, 279.

[193] Lafayette, letter to Washington, July 30, 1781, Malvern Hill;Idzerda,4:286-288.

[194] Lafayette, letter to Washington, July 31, 1781, Malvern Hill, *The Letters of Lafayette to Washington*, 213,214.

[195] Ibid.

[196] Barron, letter to Lafayette, July 31, 1781, Hampton, Idzerda,4:292,293.

[197] Lafayette, letter to Wayne, July 31, 1781, Malvern, Idzerda,4: 296, note 1, Wayne Papers, Historical Society of Pennsylvania, cited by Tower, 2:412.

[198] Wild, 71.

[199] Idzerda,4:293, note,1.

[200] Lafayette, letter to Parker, August 1, 1781, courtesy of Mrs. Chalmers, cited by Gottschalk, *The Close of the American Revolution*, 280.

[201] Wild, 71.

[202] Lafayette, letter to von Steuben, August 3, 1781, Richmond, *Steuben Papers*, New York Historical Society; cited by Tower, 2:412.

[203] Lafayette, letter to Wayne, August 3, 1781, Richmond, *Wayne Papers*, The Historical Society of Pennsylvania, cited by Tower, 2:413.

[204] Lafayette, letter to Wayne, August 4, 1781, Newcastle; Idzerda,4:294-296.

[205] Wild,71.

[206] Wayne, letter to Lafayette, August 5, 1781, Westham, Wayne Papers, cited by Idzerda, 4:296, note:1.

[207] Lafayette, letter to Washington, August 6, 1781, Camp on Pamunkey, *The Letters of Lafayette to Washington*,215,216.

[208] Lafayette, letter to Wayne, August 6, 1781, Wayne Papers, Idzerda,4:296, note 1.

[209] McHenry, letter to Nelson, August 8, 1781, Richmond, Idzerda,4:303-307.

[210] Wild, 72.

[211] Wayne, letter to Lafayette, August 9, 1781, Bottoms Bridge, Idzerda,4:307-309.

[212] Lafayette, letter to Governor Lee, August 10, 1781, Pamunkey Camp, Maryland State Archives, vol. XLVII,406, Nolan, 191.

[213] Wild, 72.

[214] Lafayette, letter to Wayne, August 11, 1781, New Kent Mountain, Idzerda,4 :313.

[215] Washington, letter to Lafayette, July 30, 1781, Headquarters near Dobb's Ferry, Idzerda,4:288-290.

[216] Lafayette, letter to Washington, August 11, 1781, New Kent Mountain, Memoirs,1:426,427.

[217] Wild,72.

[218] Lafayette, letter to Nelson, August 12, 1781, Ruffin's Ferry, Idzerda,4:314,315.

[219] Lafayette, letter to Greene, August 12, 1781, Camp between the forks of the Pamunkey;Idzerda,4:315-317.

[220] Wild, 72.

[221] Lafayette, letter to Greene, August 13, 1781, Idzerda,4:317, note.

[222] Lafayette, letter to von Steuben, August 13, 1781, Montock Hill, Idzerda,4:320,321.

[223] Lafayette, letter to La Luzerne, August 14, 1781, Montock's Hill, Idzerda, Appendix 1, French Texts,4:469,470.

[224] Lafayette, letter to Morgan, August 15, 1781, Montock's Hill, Idzerda, 4:323,324.

[225] Lafayette, letter to La Luzerne, August 14, 1781, Montock's Hill, Idzerda, Appendix 1, French Texts, 4:469,470.

[226] Lafayette, letter to Morgan, August 15, 1781, Montock's Hill, Idzerda,4:323,324.

[227] Lafayette, letter to Nelson, August 16, 1781, Camp Forks of York River, Idzerda,4:331,332.

[228] Wild,72.

[229] Washington, letter to Lafayette, August 15, 1781, Dobb's Ferry, Idzerda,4:329-331.

[230] Lafayette, letter to Nelson, August 21, 1781, Camp, Idzerda,4:336,337.

[231] Lafayette writes to Wayne on the twenty second, although he has said to Washington on the twenty first that he had already done so. August 22, 1781, Colonel Braxton's house Westpoint, Idzerda,4:341.

[232] Lafayette, letter to Washington, August 21, 1781, Forks of York River, Idzerda,4:337-339.

[233] Ibid.

[234] Parker, letter to Lafayette, August 19, 1781, Portsmouth, Idzerda,4:334-336.

[235] Lafayette, letter to Washington, August 24, 1781, Mattapony River, *The Letters of Lafayette to Washington*, 221, 222.

[236] Lafayette, letter to Adrienne, August 24, 1781, Camp between the branches of York River, Idzerda, Appendix 1, French Texts, 4:470-473.

[237] Lafayette, letter to the prince de Poix, August 24, 1781, Camp between the banches of York River, Idzerda, Appendix 1, French Texts, 4:473-476.

[238] Lafayette, letter to Washington, August 25, 1781, Mr. Ruffin's, *The Letters of Lafayette to Washington*, 223, 224.

[239] Lafayette, letter to Wayne, August 25, 1781, Mrs Ruffin's, Idzerda, 4:359-361.

[240] Lafayette, letter to Nelson, August 26, 1781, Camp, Idzerda, 4:361.

[241] Wild, 73.

[242] Lafayette, letter to Nelson, August 29, 1781, Ruffin's Ferr, Idzerda, 4:365.

[243] Lafayette, letter to Washington, September 1, 1781, Holt's Forge, Idzerda, 4:380-383.

[244] Lafayette, letter to Wayne, August 31, 1781, Holt's Forge, Idzerda, 4:378.

[245] Lafayette, letter to Taylor, August 31, 1781, Holt's Forge, Idzerda, 4:377.

[246] Feltman, 11.

[247] De Grasse, letter to Lafayette, August 30, 1781, Chesapeake Bay, Idzerda, 4:373-376.

[248] Marquis de Saint-Simon-Montbléru, letter to Lafayette, August 30, 1781, *La Ville de Paris* in the Chesapeake Roadstead, Idzerda, 4:376, 377.

[249] Lafayette, letter to Washington, September 1, 1781, Holt's Forge, *The Letters of Lafayette to Washington*, 225-227.

[250] Ibid.

[251] Wayne, letter to Lafayette, September 2, 1781, Surrey Court House, Idzerda, 4:386, 387.

[252] Wild, 74.

[253] Feltman, 12; Wild, 74.

[254] Wild, 74.

[255] Lafayette, letter to Nelson, September 4, 1781, Near Norrils Mill, Idzerda, 4:387.

[256] Wild, 74.

[257] Lafayette, letter to Washington, September 8, 1781, Williamsburg, *The Letters of Lafayette to Washington*, 228-230.

[258] Lafayette, letter to Nelson, September 6, 1781, Camp near Williamsburg, Chinard, 58; cited by Nolan, 197.

[259] Wild, 74.

[260] St George Tucker, *Journal of the Siege of Yorktown*, 377.

[261] Lafayette, letter to Washington, September 8, 1781, Williamsburg, *The Letters of Lafayette to Washington*, 231, 232.

[262] Lafayette, letter to La Luzerne, September 8, 1781, Williamsburg, Idzerda, Appendix 1, French Texts, 4:478.

[263] Lafayette, letter to Washington, September 8, 1781, Williamsburg, *The Letters of Lafayette to Washington*, 231, 232.

[264] Lafayette, letter to La Luzerne, Sepember 8, 1781, Williamsburg, Idzerda, Appendix 1, French Texts, 4:478.

[265] Lafayette, letter to Washington, September 8, 1781, Camp Williamsburg, *The Letters of Lafayette to Washington*, 231, 232.

[266] Wild, 75; Feltman, 13.

[267] Lafayette, letter to Nelson, September 11, 1781, Williamsburg, Idzerda, 4:398.

[268] Wayne, letter to Lafayette, September 11, 1781, James Town, Idzerda, 4:399.

[269] Wild, 75.

[270] Washington, letter to Lafayette, September 10, 1781, Mount Vernon, Idzerda, 4:397.

[271] Butler, September 14, 1781, cited by Tower, 444,

Chapter 30

[1] Tucker, letter to Mrs. Tucker, September 15, 1781, *The Spirit of Seventy-Six*, 1224.

[2] Von Closen, *The Revolutionary Journal of Baron Ludwig von Closen*, 1780-1783, translated and edited by Acomb, Evelyn, M., Chapel Hill (The University of North Carolina Press, 1958), 132.

[3] Von Steuben, letter to Greene, September 19, 1781, Kapp, 456.

[4] Von Steuben, letter to Greene, September 19, 1781, Kapp, 456, cited by Gottschalk, *The Close of the American Revolution*, 309.

[5] Von Closen, note 1, 132. Fitzpatrick, (ed.), *Writings of Washington*, XXIII 122-25.

[6] Von Closen, 133.

[7] Ibid., 134,135.

[8] Ibid., 134,135, note citing Doniol, V: 544.

[9] Ibid.,135.

[10] Arc. Nat. Marine, B4,184, cited by Freeman,5:341.

[11] Von Closen,134,135, Note citing *an Account of the Campaign of the Naval Armament under the command of comte de Grasse, Magazine of American History*, 7 (1881) 292.

[12] Observations by the Comte de Grasse during his Conference with the Marquis de Lafayette, Idzerda, Appendix 1, French Texts, 4:479,480.

[13] Von Closen,136.

[14] Gottschalk, *The Close of the American Revolution*, 313,314.

[15] Von Closen, 137. St. George Tucker,380.

[16] Jones, letter to Lafayette, cited by Lafayette in letter to La Luzerne, September 30, 1781, Camp before Yorktown,407,408.

[17] Wild, 76.

[18] Von Closen, 139.

[19] Joseph Plumb Martin,129.

[20] Wild, 76.

[21] Von Closen,139. Dumas, *Souvenirs du Lieutenant Général Comte Mathieu Dumas, de 1770 à 1836*, 1:79.

[22] Trumbull, *Journal*, cited in *The Spirit of '76*, 1227.

[23] Washington, letter to de Grasse, October 1, 1781, Before York, Sparks,8:170.

[24] Von Closen, 139.

[25] Ibid.

[26] Freeman says it was often called Beaver Dam Creek in the eighteenth century, but Great Run now, and was much more of a barrier then, 5:346, note 9.

[27] St. George Tucker; 380,381, Washington, letter to the President of Congress, October 1, 1781, Camp, near York, Sparks,8,168,169.

[28] St. George Tucker, 381.

[29] Trumbull, *Journal*, September 28, 1781, *The Spirit of Seventy-Six*, 1227.

[30] Marshall, 4:480,481.

[31] Marshall, 4:481. Von Closen;139.

[32] Freeman, 5:350.

[33] 23 G.W.,152, cited by Freeman, 5:350.

[34] Joseph Plumb Martin,130.

[35] Trumbull, *Journal*, Mass.Hist.Soc. Proc., XIV,334-335, *The Spirit of Seventy-Six*, 1227,1228.

[36] Ibid., 1228.

[37] Boatner, Encyclopedia of the American Revolution, 1240,1241.

[38] Trumbull, *Journal*, *The Spirit of Seventy-Six*, 1228.

[39] Von Closen, 139.

[40] Lafayette, letter to Washington, September 30, 1781, Camp before York, Idzerda,4:409-411.

[41] Von Closen,140.

[42] Trumbull, *Journal*, Mass. Hist. Soc. Proc., XIV, 334-335; *The Spirit of Seventy-Six*, 1228. See Cornwallis for account of works being constructed: 'The enemy constructed on the 30th, and the two following days and nights., two redoubts, which with some works which belonged to our outward positon occupied a gorge between two creeks on each side of the town.' Cornwallis, letter to Clinton, *The Spirit of Seventy-Six*,1236-1238.

[43] Lafayette, letter to Washington, September 30, 1781, Camp before York, Idzerda, 4:411,412.

[44] Von Closen, 141.

[45] Ibid.,142.

[46] Von Closen,142; Rochambeau's Journal; Doniol, 5,576, cited by Freeman,5,347.

[47] Washington, letter to de Grasse, October 1, 1781, Before York; Sparks, 8:170,172.

[48] Feltman,16.

[49] Ibid.

[50] Wild,77.

[51] Butler, *Journal*, *The Spirit of Seventy-Six*, 1228.

[52] Feltman, 16.

[53] St. George Tucker, 382.

[54] Butler, *Journal*, *The Spirit of '76*, 1228.

[55] Feltman, 17.

[56] Von Closen, 142.

[57] Ibid.

[58] Feltman, 17.

[59] Butler, *Journal, The Spirit of Seventy-Six*,1229.

[60] Feltman, 17.

[61] Ibid.

[62] Greene, letter to Lafayette, September 17, 1781, Head Quarters High Hills Santee, Idzerda,4:401,402.

[63] Washington, letter to the President of Congress, October 6, 1781, Camp before York; Idzerda, 4:173.

[64] Tench Tilghman, op.cit. 104, cited by Freeman,5:358.

[65] Thacher, *Military Journal*, 337; Joseph Plumb Martin,136.

[66] Joseph Plumb Martin,130,131.

[67] Lafayette, letter to Greene, October 6, 1781, Camp before York, Idzerda, 4:413,414.

[68] Wild, 78.

[69] Joseph Plumb Martin, 131.

[70] Von Closen, 143.

[71] These lines were taken mainly from the Engineers' Journal, note 22, Von Closen, 143.

[72] *Rochambeau's Journal*, Doniol, 5:577; Tilghman, *Journal*, 104; Washington, letter to the President of Congress; October 12, 1781, HeadQuarters before York, says 'the loss of only one officer of the French artillery wounded, and sixteen privates killed and wounded, the greater part of whom were of the French line.' Sparks,8:177, 178.

[73] Wild,131.

[74] Von Closen, 145.

[75] Duncan, *Diary, The Spirit of Seventy-Six*, 1229.

[76] Von Closen, 145.

[77] Wild, 78; Butler, '*Journal,' Historical Magazine*, VIII, 107,108; cited in *The Spirit of Seventy-Six,*1230.

[78] General Orders, October 8, 1781, Fitzpatrick, XXIII,199; Gottschalk, *The Close of the American Revolution*, 316.

[79] Washington, letter to the President of Congress, October 12, 1781, Headquarters before York; Sparks, 8:177, 178. Washington says the line is now completed.

[80] Joseph Plumb Martin,132.

[81] Washington, letter to the President of Congress, October 12, 1781, Head Quarters before York; Sparks, 8:177,178.

[82] Washington, letter to the President of Congress, October 12, 1781, Head Quarters before York; Sparks,8:177,178.

[83] Ibid.

[84] Thacher, 340.

[85] Chastellux, 221.

[86] Tench Tilghman, 105.

[87] St George Tucker, 387.

[88] Ibid.

[89] Pickering, cited by Freeman,5:363,364.

[90] Thacher, 340,341.

[91] Von Closen, 146.

[92] Thacher, 339, 340.

[93] Von Closen, 147.

[94] Washington, letter to the President of Congress, October 12, 1781, Head-Quarters before York, Sparks, 8:177,178.

[95] St. George Tucker, 386.

[96] Von Closen,147.

[97] Tench Tilghman, 105. Feltman says two men killed and one badly wounded from the French batteries, 19.

[98] Feltman, 20.

[99] Von Closen, 148.

[100] Von Closen, 148.

[101] Feltman,20.

[102] 2 Diaries, 266, cited by Freeman, 5:368.

[103] 23 G.W., 229; Anon. Diary in 7 Mag. Am. His.223, cited by Freeman, 5:368. Washington, letter to the President of Congress, October 16, 1781, Headquarters before York, Sparks, 8:177,178.

[104] *Memoirs,* 270. Le Chevalier de Villebresme, *Souvenirs*, Paris 1897, 93, Idzerda, 4:421,422,note 2.

[105] Washington, letter to the President of Congress, October 16, 1781, Headquarters before York, Sparks, 8:179.

[106] Joseph Plumb Martin, 132.

[107] Olney, *Biog. of Revolutionary Heroes*, in Williams, 276, cited by Freeman, 5:370.

[108] Von Closen, 148.

[109] Joseph Plumb Martin, 133.

[110] Hamilton, account of the attack upon the redoubt on the left of the enemy's lines on October 14 to Lafayette, Idzerda, 4:418-420.

[111] Joseph Plumb Martin, 132.

[112] Deux-Ponts, *My Campaigns in America*, 144-147, cited in *Rebels and Redcoats*, 486.

[113] Von Closen, 149.

[114] Thacher, 341.

[115] St. George Tucker, 389.

[116] Joseph Plumb Martin, 134.

[117] Von Closen, 149. Dumas, 1:85, 86.

[118] Lafayette, letter to La Luzerne, October 16, 1781, Camp before Yorktown, Idzerda, Appendix 1, French Texts, 4:482, 483.

[119] Wild, 79.

[120] Lafayette, letter to La Luzerne, October 16, 1781, Camp before Yorktown, Idzerda, Appendix 1, French Texts, 4:482, 483.

[121] Döhla, Univ. of Oklahoma Press, 1990, 171.

[122] Washington, letter to the President of Congress, October 16, 1781, Headquarters before York, Sparks, 8:178-181.

[123] Thacher, 343.

[124] Ibid.

[125] Tarleton, 343; cited in Freeman, 8:377, St. George Tucker, 391.

[126] G.W., 236, 237; cited in Freeman, 8:378.

[127] St. George Tucker, 391.

[128] Ibid., 391, 392.

[129] Freeman, 8:382.

[130] Laurens, letter, October 18, 1781, Freeman, 8:384.

[131] Johnstone, The Yorktown Campaign, 185-187; *The Spirit of Seventy-Six*, 1240, 1241.

[132] Thacher, 350.

[133] Von Closen, 153.

[134] Joseph Plumb Martin, 136. Dumas, 1:87, 88.

[135] Thacher, 346.

[136] Döhla, 177.

[137] Von Closen, 153.

[138] Ibid.

[139] Dumas, *Memoirs*, 1:52n, 53n, cited by *Rebels and Redcoats*, ed. by Scheer and Rankin, 494.

[140] Moore, Diary, 2:508n, cited in *Rebels and Redcoats*, 494.

[141] Ibid.

[142] Thacher, 347.

[143] Döhla, 178.

[144] Thacher, 351.

[145] Von Closen, 154.

[146] Ketchum, 257.

[147] *Rebels and Redcoats, The American Revolution hrough the eyes of those who fought and lived it*, 495.

[148] General Orders, October 20, 1781, Fitzpatrick, XXIII, 244-247, cited by Gottschalk, *The Close of the American Revolution*, 326.

[149] Von Closen, 154.

[150] Thacher, 351. Von Closen says 556; 154.

[151] Von Closen. 154.

[152] Tower, 2:457.

[153] Lafayette, letter to Maurepas, October 20, 1781, Camp before Yorktown, Idzerda, Appendix 1, French Texts, 4:483.

[154] Lafayette, letter to Vergennes, October 20, 1781, camp near York; *Memoirs*, 1:445.

[155] Lafayette, letter to the prince de Poix, October 20, 1781, camp near Yorktown, Idzerda, Appendix 1, French Texts, 4:484, 485.

[156] Lafayette, letter to Adrienne, October 20, 1781, Camp before York, *Mercure de France,* December 1, 1781,35,35; cited by Gottschalk, *The Close of the American Revolution,* 331.

[157] Döhla, 182.

[158] Washington, letter to de Grasse, October 20, 1781, Head-Quarters; Sparks, 8:185,187.

[159] Döhla, 182.

[160] Lafayette, letter to von Steuben, October 26, 1781, Camp near York, Idzerda, 4:432,433.

[161] Von Closen, 155.

[162] *Memoirs,*1:273.

[163] Joseph Plumb Martin,136.

[164] Washington, letter to Nelson, October 27, 1781; 23 G.W., cited by Freeman, 5:394

[165] Lafayette, letter to Adrienne, October 22, 1781, on board the *Ville de Paris* in the Chesapeake Bay, Idzerda, Appendix 1, French Texts, 4:485.

[166] Lafayette, letter to Samuel Cooper, October 26, 1781, Camp near York, Virginia, Idzerda, 4:429-432.

[167] De Grasse, letter to Lafayette, October 24, 1781, *Ville de Paris,* Idzerda, Appendix 1, French Texts, 4:486,487.

[168] Lafayette, letter to Greene, November 22, 1781, Philadelphia, Idzerda,4:438,439.

[169] Thacher, 536.

[170] Washington, letter to Lafayette, November 15, 1781, Mount Vernon, Idzerda, 4:435-437.

[171] Lafayette, letter to Congress, November 22, 1781, Philadelphia, Idzerda,4:437,438.

[172] Resolution of Congress, November 23, 1781, Idzerda, 4:440,441.

[173] Nolan, 210.

[174] Ibid., 211.

[175] Lafayette, letter to Washington, December 21, 1781, Alliance, off Boston, Idzerda, 4:450.

[176] Hunt, *Fragments of Revolutionary History,* 63-64, cited by Gottschalk, *The Close of the American Revolution,* 345.

Chapter 31

[1] Lafayette, letter to Washington, January 18, 1782, L'Orient, *The Letters of Lafayette to Washington,* 241,242.

[2] Lafayette, letter to Washington, January 30, 1782, Versailles, *The Letters of Lafayette to Washington,* 242 -244.

[3] *La Gazette d'Amsterdam,* February 1, 1782, cited by Charavay, 85.

[4] Lafayette, letter to Washington, January 30, 1782, Versailles, *The Letters of Lafayette to Washington,* 242-244.

[5] Vergennes, letter to Lafayette, January 23, 1782, Versailles, Idzerda and Crout, Appendix 1, French Texts, 5:361.

[6] Franklin, letter to Morris, January 28, 1782; Ferguson, Papers of Robert Morris,4:133, cited by Idzerda, 5:7.

[7] Lafayette, letter to Washington, January 30, 1782, Versailles, Idzerda and Crout, 5:8-10.

[8] Ibid.

[9] Stevens, Facsimiles, XVII, no.1641, cited by Gottschalk, *The Close of the American Revolution,*355.

[10] Lafayette, letter to Franklin, February 25, 1782, Paris, Idzerda and Crout, 5:15.

[11] Lafayette, letter to Vergennes, March 20, 1782, Paris, Idzerda, Appendix 1, French Texts, 5:362.

[12] Lafayette, letter to Jay, March 28, 1782, Paris, Idzerda and Crout, 5:19,20.

[13] Lafayette, letter to Washington, March 30, 1782, Antony, *The Letters of Lafayette to Washington,*244-247.

[14] Lafayette, letter to Washington, April 12, 1782, Paris, Idzerda and Crout, 5:26-28.

[15] Lafayette, letter to Laurens, April 14, 1782, Paris, Idzerda and Crout, 5:28-30.

[16] Ibid.

[17] Proposals for the French Campaign in North America; April 18, 1782, Paris, Idzerda and Crout, Appendix 1, French Texts, 5:364-366.

[18] Adams, letter to Lafayette, April 6, 1782, Amsterdam, Idzerda and Crout, 5:25,26.

[19] Lafayette, letter to Adams, May 7, 1782, Paris, Idzerda and Crout, 5:36,37.

[20] Franklin's Journal, Smyth, VIII, 492,493, cited by Gottschalk, *The Close of the American Revolution,* 362.

[21] Lafayette, letter to Washington, June 25, 1782, St. Germain, *The Letters of Lafayette to Washington,* 250-252.

[22] Franklin's Journal, Correspondance, 2:242, cited by Charavay,90.

[23] Gottschalk, *The Close of the American Revolution,* 369.

[24] Lafayette, letter to Livingston, June 25, 1782, Paris, Idzerda and Crout, 5:43-47.

[25] Lafayette, letter to Washington, June 25, 1782, St. Germain, Idzerda and Crout, 5: 48,49.

[26] Lafayette, letter to Washington, June 29, 1782, Paris, Idzerda and Crout, 5:49-51.

[27] *Mémoires du duc de Lauzun,* 25:210, cited by Gottschalk, *The Close of the American Revolution,* 373.

[28] Lafayette, letter to Franklin, September 17, 1782, Paris, Idzerda and Crout, 5:56,57.

[29] Franklin, letter to Lafayette, September 17, 1782, Passy, Idzerda and Crout, 5:57.

[30] Lafayette, letter to Washington, October 14, 1782, Paris, *The Letters of Lafayette to Washington,* 254,255.

[31] *Mémoires,* 2 :4.

[32] Lafayette, letter to Washington, October 24, 1782, Paris, Idzerda and Crout, 5:64,65.

[33] *Mémoires,*2:4.

[34] *The Works of John Adams,* 3:174.

[35] *Ibid.,* 3:180.

[36] *The Army Correspondance of Colonel J. Laurens in 1777-78,* 37.

[37] Mosnier,57, cited by Charavay,99.

[38] *The Works of John Adams,*3:182.

[39] Lafayette, letter to Vergennes, November 22, 1782, Paris, Idzerda and Crout, Appendix 1, French Texts, 5:368-370.

[40] *The Works of John Adams,*3:187.

[41] *Ibid.,*3:188.

[42] Lafayette, document to the American Peace Commissioners, November 21, 1782, Paris, Idzerda and Crout, 5:68,69.

[43] Adams, J., *Diary and Autobiography,* 3:71.

[44] Franklin, Adams and Jay, letter to Lafayette, November 28, 1782, Warton, VI,89, cited by Gottschalk, *The Close of the American Revolution* 384.

[45] *Mémoires,* 2:4, note 1 from Lafayette.

[46] Lafayette, letter to Washington, December 4, 1782, Brest, *The Letters of Lafayette to Washington,* 257,258.

[47] Lafayette, letter to Poix, December 4, 1782, Brest, a private collection, cited by Gottschalk, *The Close of the American Revolution,* 391.

[48] Lafayette, letter to Poix, December 6,1782, Brest, private collection, cited by Gottschalk, *The Close of the American Revolution,* 392.

[49] Lafayette, letter to Franklin, December 6, 1782, Brest, cited by Gottschalk, *The Close of the American Revolution,* 393.

[50] Lafayette, letter to Poix, December 18, 1782, private collection, cited by Gottschalk, *The Close of the American Revolution,* 394.

[51] Ibid.

[52] Lafayette, letter to one of the ladies he calls his cousin, probably Madame de Tessé, January 1, 1783, Cadiz, *Mémoires,* 2:49-51.

[53] Lafayette, letter to Poix, January 28, 1783, Cadiz, private collection, cited by Gottschalk, *The Close of the American Revolution,* 395.

[54] *Mémoires,* III, 198, cited by Gottschalk, *The Close of the American Revolution,* 398.

[55] Lafayette, letter to Livingston, February 5, 1783, Cadiz, Idzerda,5:86-88.

[56] Lafayette, letter to Washington, February 5, 1783, Cadiz, Idzerda and Crout, 5:90-93.

[57] Lafayette, letter to Vergennes, February 5, 1783, Cadiz, Idzerda and Crout, Appendix 1, French Texts,5:371.

[58] *Mémoires,* 2:5,6.

[59] Lafayette, letter to Jay, February 15, 1783, Madrid, Idzerda and Crout, 5:94-96.

[60] Lafayette, letter to Madame de Tessé, February 17, 1783, Madrid, *Mémoires,* 2:60,61.

[61] Lafayette, letter to d'Estaing, February 18, 1783, Madrid, Idzerda and Crout, 5:371,372.

[62] Ibid.

[63] Lafayette, letter to Washington, March 2, 1783, Bordeaux, *The Letters of Lafayette to Washington,*262,263.

[64] Lafayette, letter to Livingston, March 2, 1783, Bordeaux, *Mémoires,* 2:64-69.

[65] *Mémoires,*2:6.

[66] Lafayette, letter to Washington, Bordeaux, March 2, 1783, *The Letters of Lafayette to Washington,*263.

[67] Lafayette, letter to Livingston, March 2, 1783, Bordeaux, Idzerda and Crout, 5:102-107.

[68] *Mémoires,* 2:4.

[69] Lafayette, letter to Vergennes, March 19, 1783, Paris, *Mémoires,* 2 :69-71.

[70] Lafayette, letter to de Fleury, March 19, 1783, Paris, Idzerda and Crout, Appendix 1, French Texts, 5:375,376.

[71] Charavay, 97.

[72] Lafayette, letter to Aglaë, March 27, 1783, Chavaniac, cited by Gottschalk, *Lady-in-Waiting*, Appendix 111, 128,129.

[73] Gueyffier, to Chavarat, March 27, 1783, Doniol, *Correspondance administrative*, 60-62, cited by Gottschalk, *The Close of the American Revolution*, 418.

[74] Doniol, *Correspondance administrative*,47, cited by Gottschalk, 418.

[75] Lafayette, letter to Adrienne, March 27, 1783, Chavaniac, Idzerda and Crout, Appendix 1, French Texts, 5:377,378.

[76] Lafayette, letter to Aglaë, March 27, 1783, Chavaniac; Gottschalk, *Lady-In-Waiting*, 128-129. The letter is not signed by Lafayette.

[77] Lafayette, letter to Adrienne, March 27, 1783, Chavaniac, Idzerda and Crout, Appendix 1, French Texts, 5:377,378.

[78] Lafayette, letter to Washington, July 22, 1783, Chavaniac in the Province of Auvergne, Idzerda and Crout, 5:145-147.

[79] Lafayette, letter to Adrienne, September 10, 1783, Nancy, cited by Maurois, 133.

[80] Lafayette, letter to Washington, September 8, 1783, Nancy, Idzerda and Crout, 5:151-154.

[81] Lafayette, letter to Adrienne, September 17, 1783, Nancy, cited by Maurois, 133.

[82] Lafayette, letter to someone unknown, possibly Madame de Simiane, October 21, 1783, Idzerda and Crout, Appendix 1, French Texts, 5:382.

[83] Ibid.

[84] Washington, letter to Lafayette, October 30, 1783, Princeton, Idzerda and Crout, 5:159-161.

[85] Franklin, letter to Sarah Bache, January 26, 1784, Passy, from Founders Online, National Archives, The Papers of Benjamin Franklin, vol.41, ed., by Ellen R. Cohn, 503-511.

[86] Lafayette, letter to Washington, March 9, 1784, Paris, *The Letters of Lafayette to Washington*, 278-281.

[87] Lafayette, letter to Adams, March 8, 1784, Paris, Idzerda and Crout, 5:201-203.

[88] Ibid.

[89] Lafayette, letter to Washington, March 9, 1784, Paris, *The Letters of Lafayette to Washington*, 276,277.

[90] Lafayette, letter to Washington, May 14, 1784, Paris, *The Letters of Lafayette to Washington*,283,284.

Chapter 32

[1] Lafayette, letter to Adrienne, June 28, 1784, Aboard the *Courier de New York*, Idzerda and Crout, Appendix, 400, 5: 400. Note: Lafayette wrongly addresses the letter from the *Courrier de l'Europe*, according to Idzerda, 5:232.

[2] Ibid.

[3] Lafayette, letter to Calonne, June 25, 1784, Idzerda and Crout, 252, 253, citing Louis Gottschalk Collection, misdated by Lafayette as February 25, 1784.

[4] Lafayette, letter to Adams, June 25, 1784, Lorient, Idzerda and Crout, 5:227,228.

[5] Lafayette, letter to Adrienne, August 13, 1784, Philadelphia, Idzerda and Crout, Appendix 1, French Texts, 5:401-403.

[6] Döhla, 25.

[7] Lafayette, letter to Samuel Adams, August 7, 1784, NYPL, Bancroft Collection, in Gottschalk, *Lafayette between the American and the French Revolution*,85.

[8] Address of the Committee of Officers of the Late Pennsylvania Line, August 9, 1784, Philadelphia, Idzerda, 5:233,234.

[9] August 10, 1784; Pennsylvania Journal, August 14, 1784, Idzerda and Crout, 5:234.

[10] Saint-John de Crèvecoeur,3:319-321, cited by Charavay,106,107.

[11] Nolan says Lafayette probably slept at Head of Elk that night, 218.

[12] Lafayette, letter to Adrienne, August 20, 1784, Mount Vernon, Idzerda and Crout, 5: 403,404.

[13] Ibid, 5: 237,238.

[14] Unger, *Lafayette*, 194. Anastasie, letter to Washington, June 18, 1784, Paris, Photocopy of the original letter, Idzerda and Crout, 5:239. Note. It is often said that Lafayette gave Washington a masonic apron which Adrienne had embroidered but Lafayette makes no mention of this in his letter to her on April 20.

[15] Lafayette, letter to Adrienne, August 20, 1784, Mount Vernon, Idzerda and Crout, 5: 237,238.

[16] Lafayette, letter to Poix, August 20, 1784, privately communicated, Gottschalk, *Lafayette between Two Revolutions*, 88.

[17] Ibid.

[18] Sparks, The Life of George Washington, 386,387.

[19] Washington, letter to James Craik, March 24, 1784, PWCF 1:234-236, cited by Ellis, His Excellency, George Washington,152.

[20] Washington, letter to Benjamin Harrison, January 18, 1784, Mount Vernon, Founders Online, National Archives, Original Source: *The Papers of George Washington*, Confederation Series I, 1, January 1784- 17 July 1784, ed. W.W. Abbott. Charlottesville: Univ. Press of Virginia, 1992, 56,57.

[21] Lafayette, letter to Adrienne, August 20, 1784, Mount Vernon, Idzerda and Crout, Appendix 1, French Texts, 5: 403-404.

[22] Gottschalk, *Lafayette between Two Revolutions, 89.*

[23] Lafayette, letter to Adrienne, August 20, 1784, Mount Vernon, Idzerda and Crout, Appendix 1, French Texts, 5: 403-404.

[24] Ellis, *His Excellency George Washington*, 166.

[25] Lafayette, letter to Poix, September 15, 1784, privately communicated, cited by Gottschalk, *Lafayette between the American and the French Revolution*, 89.

[26] Lafayette, letter to Adrienne, August 20, 1784, Mount Vernon, Idzerda and Crout, Appendix 1, French Texts, 5:403-404.

[27] Crèvecoeur, 3:326, cited by Nolan, 221, who says that the New York Packet and the Maryland Gazette place it on September 1.

[28] Gottschalk, *Lafayette between the American and the French Revolution*,89.

[29] Madison, letter to Jefferson, September 7, 1784, Philadelphia, Idzerda and Crout, 5:241-243.

[30] Madison, letter to Jefferson, October 17, 1784, Philadelphia, Idzerda and Crout, 5:271-274.

[31] Read, letter to Guerard, September 9, 1784, cited by Gottschalk, *Lafayette between the American and French Revolution*, 91.

[32] Madison, letter to Jefferson, September 7, 1784, Philadelphia; Idzerda and Crout, 5:241-243.

[33] Nolan says the ninth is the probable day of departure for New York, 223.

[34] Lafayette, letter to Vergennes, September 15, 1784, New York, Idzerda and Crout, Appendix 1, French Texts, 5:404,405.

[35] Ibid.

[36] Ibid.

[37] Barbé de Marbois, *Journal of Visit to the Territory of the Six Nations*, September 23, 1784, Idzerda and Crout, Appendix 1, French Texts, 5:405-411. Much of the account of Lafayette's visit comes from the account of Marbois.

[38] Ibid.

[39] Lafayette, letter to Poix, October 12, 1784, Hartford, Idzerda and Crout, Appendix 1, French Texts, 5:419,420.

[40] Madison, letter to Jefferson, October 17, 1784, Philadelphia, Idzerda and Crout, 5:271-274.

[41] Ibid.

[42] Account of Lafayette's Meeting with the Six Nations, October 3,4, 1784, Fort Schuyler, Idzerda and Crout, Appendix 1, French Texts, 5:411-412. *Mémoires*, 2:99-101.

[43] The Chief of the Mohawks' speech, October 3, 1784, Fort Schuyler, Idzerda and Crout, Appendix 1, French Texts, 5:413,414.

[44] The speech of the Chief of the Friendly Nations, October 4, 1784, Fort Schuyler, Idzerda and Crout, Appendix 1, French Texts, 5:414.

[45] Lafayette, letter to Adrienne, October 4, 1784, Fort Schuyler, Idzerda and Crout, Appendix 1, French Texts,5:416.

[46] Lafayette, letter to Hamilton, October 8, 1784, Albany, Idzerda and Crout, 5:263,264.

[47] Lafayette, letter to Jay, October 7, 1784, Albany; Idzerda and Crout, 5:263.

[48] Lafayette, letter to Adrienne, October 10, 1784, Church's Tavern near Hartford, Idzerda and Crout, 5: Appendix 1, French Texts, 416,417.

[49] Lafayette, letter to Poix, October 12, 1784, Hartford, Idzerda and Crout, Appendix 1, French Texts, 5:419,420.

[50] Lafayette, letter to Jefferson, October 11, 1784, Hartford, Idzerda and Crout, 5:266, 267.

[51] Crèvecoeur,3:349-352, cited by Gottschalk, *Lafayette between the American and French Revolution*,114.

[52] Boston Magazine, 1, (October 1784), 540, Gottschalk, *Lafayette between the American and French Revolution*, 114.

[53] North, letter to Steuben, October 19, 1784, Boston, cited by Gottschalk, *Lafayette between the American and the French Revolution*, 115.

[54] Lafayette, letter to Poix, October 22, 1784, privately communicated, cited by Gottschalk, *Lafayette between the American and the French Revolution*, 118.

[55] Lafayette, letter to Washington, October 22, 1784, Boston, *The Letters of Lafayette to Washington*, 287.

[56] Lafayette, letter to Hamilton, October 22, 1784, Boston, Idzerda and Crout, 5:275,276.

[57] Newport Mercury, October 30, 1784, cited by Gottschalk, *Lafayette between the American and French Revolution*, 120.

[58] Bartlett, Records of the State of Rhode Island and Providence Plantation, X (1865), 67,68, cited by Gottschalk, *Lafayette between the American and French Revolution*, 121.

[59] Massachusetts Centinel, November 20, 1784, cited by Gottschalk, *Lafayette between the American and French Revolution*, 123.

[60] Nolan, 232. He cites the *Boston Centinel* and the *Essex Journal* as saying that Lafayette spent the night at Marblehead.

[61] Nolan says this was probably the date, 232.

[62] Mazzei, Recherches,2:201, n.1, cited by Gottschalk, *Lafayette between the American and the French Revolution*, 125.

[63] *Journal of Delegates beginning October 18, 1784*, 30, cited by Gottschalk, *Lafayette between the American and the French Revolution*,126,127.

[64] Lafayette's Recommendation for James Armitstead, November 21, 1784, Richmond, Idzerda and Crout,5:277,278.

[65] Sparks, The Life of George Washington,378.

[66] Ibid, 381.

[67] Ibid, 380.

[68] Washington, letter to Duane, April 10, 1785, Fitzpatrick, XXVIII,125, cited by Gottschalk, *Lafayette between the American and the French Revolution* 131.

[69] New Brunswick Political Intelligencer, January 4, 1785, New York Journal, December 30, 1784, cited by Nolan, 238.

[70] Jay, address to Lafayette, December 11, 1784, Meeting of Congress at Trenton, *Mémoires*, 2:104,105.

[71] Lafayette, address to Congress, December 11, 1784, Trenton, *Mémoires*, 2:105-107.

[72] Lafayette, letter to Jay, December 12,1784, Trenton, *Letters of the Marquis de Lafayette in the Collection of Stuart Wells Jackson*, 16, cited by Gottschalk, 136.

[73] *Mémoires*, 2:8.

[74] Lafayette, letter to James Madison, December 15, 1784, New York, Idzerda and Crout, 5:285-287.

[75] Crèvecoeur, 3:376, cited by Nolan, 238.

[76] New York Journal, December 23, 1784, cited by Nolan, 239.

[77] Washington, letter to Lafayette, Mount Vernon, December 8, 1784, *Mémoires,* 2:109,110, Idzerda and Crout, 5:279,280.

[78] Lafayette, letter to Washington, December 21, 1784, on board the Nymph New York Harbor, *The Letters of Lafayette to Washington*, 288-90.

[79] *Mémoires secrètes*. V. xxviii. February 24.

[80] Lafayette, letter to Adrienne, January 23, 1785, Rennes, Idzerda and Crout, 5:420,421.

Chapter 33

[1] *Journal and Correspondance of Miss Adams*, October 14, 1784, cited by Rice, *Thomas Jefferson's Paris*,67.

[2] Adams, *The Works of John Adams*, 3:223,224.

[3] Lafayette., letter to Washington, *The Letters of Lafayette to Washington*, February 9, 1785, Versailles, 271.

[4] *Journal of Miss Adams*,1,65-69, March 29,30,1785, *Memoirs of John Quincy Adams*, March 28-April 1, cited by Gottschalk, *Lafayette between the American and the French Revolution*,161.

[5] Gottschalk, *Lafayette between the American and the French Revolution*, 165.

[6] Abigail Adams, letter to Mrs. Cranch, May 8, 1785, Auteuil, *Letters of Mrs. Adams, The Wife of John Adams*, 93-95.

[7] Lafayette, letter to Adams, May 8, 1785, Paris; Chinard,89,90.

[8] Abigail Adams, letter to Mrs. Cranch, May 8, 1785, Auteuil;93-95.

[9] Virginie de Lafayette, *Life of Madame de Lafayette*, 183,184.

[10] Lafayette, letter to Washington, May 11, 1785, Paris, *The Letters of Lafayette to Washington*, 296,297.

[11] Gottschalk, *Lafayette between the American and French Revolution*, 174.

[12]Lafayette, letter to Washington, July 14, 1785, Sarreguemines, *Mémoires*, 2:123,124.

[13] Lafayette to Washington, Paris, February 8, 1786, *Mémoires*, 2:130, according to Gottschalk the date is the sixth.

[14] Castries, 13.

[15]Lafayette, letter to Washington, February 8, 1786, Paris, *Mémoires*, 2:130-143.

[16] Ibid.

[17] Lafayette, letter to General Knox, February 11, 1786, Paris, *Letters of the Marquis de Lafayette,* in the collection of Stuart Wells Jackson, 17-19.

[18] Lafayette, letter to Washington, February 6, 1786, Paris; *The Letters of Lafayette to Washington*, 303-310.

[19] *Mémoires*,3:199.

[20] Lafayette, letter to Adrienne, cited by Taillimite,122.

[21] Maurois, *Adrienne The Life of the Marquise de Lafayette*,149.

[22] Lafayette, letter to Washington, February 6, 1786, Paris, *The Letters of Lafayette to Washington*, 303-310.

[23] Lafayette to General Knox, Paris, February 11,1786, Letters of the Marquis de Lafayette in the collection of Stuart Wells Jackson, 18, cited by Gottschalk, *Lafayette between the American and French Revolution*, 187.

[24] Lafayette, letter to Washington, February 6, 1786, Paris, *The Letters of Lafayette to Washington*, 303-310.

[25] Ibid.

[26] Lafayette to General Knox, February 11, 1786, Paris, *Letters of the Marquis de Lafayette,* in the collection of Stuart Wells Jackson, 17,18, cited by Gottschalk, *Lafayette between the American and French Revolution*, 187.

[27] Lafayette, letter to Washington, February 6, 1786, Paris, *The letters of Lafayette to Washington*, 303-310.

Chapter 34

[1] Condorcet, letter to Lafayette, February 24, 1785, Basel, Idzerda, 5:421,422.

[2] Virginie de Lafayette de Lasteyrie, *Life of Madame de Lafayette*, 181,182.

[3] Lafayette, letter to Washington, October 26, 1786, Paris, *The Letters of Lafayette to Washington*, 313-316.

[4]Lafayette, letter to Washington, February 8, 1786, Paris, *Mémoires,* 2:130-142.

[5] Lafayette, letter to Adams, February 22, 1786, Works of Adams, VIII, 376,377, cited by Gottschalk, *Lafayette between the American and French Revolution*, 229.

[6] Lafayette, letter to McHenry, October 26, 1786, Paris, cited by Gottschalk, *Lafayette between the American and French Revolution*, 258.

[7] Lafayette, letter to Washington, February 6, 1786, Paris, *The letters of Lafayette to Washington*, 303-310.

[8]Lafayette, letter to Washington, October 26, 1786, *The Letters of Lafayette to Washington*, 311-313.

[9] Jefferson, letter to Lafayette, February 20, 1786, *The Letters of Lafayette and Jefferson*, 91-92.

[10] Jefferson, letter to Jay, May 27, 1786, Ford, Writings of Jefferson, IV, 234, cited by Gottschalk, *Lafayette between the American and French Revolution*, 237.

[11] Morgan,238.

[12] Lafayette, letter to Washington, May 31, 1786, Paris; *Mémoires,* 2:155,156. (the date of August is incorrect).

[13] Ibid.

[14] Bachaumont, XXXII, July 7, 1786, 167, cited by Gottschalk, *Lafayette between the American and French Revolution*, 240.

[15]*Mémoires,* 2:139.

[16] Maurois, 149.

[17] Jefferson, letter to Lafayette, July 17, 1786, Paris, *The Letters of Lafayette and Jefferson*, 95-98.

[18] Lafayette, letter to Jefferson, not dated, 1786, *The Letters of Lafayette and Jefferson*, 101.

[19] Jefferson, letter to Madison, February 8, 1786, Paris, *The Letters of Lafayette and Jefferson*, 66.

[20] Castries, 128.

[21] Lafayette, letter to Washington, October 26, 1786, Paris, *The Letters of Lafayette to Washington*, 313-316.

[22] Ibid.

[23] Gottschalk, *Lafayette between the American and French Revolution*, 256.

[24] Lafayette, letter to Washington, October 26, 1786, Paris, *The Letters of Lafayette to Washington*, 313-316.

[25] Jefferson, letter to Jay, October, 1787, Paris, cited by Morgan, 240.

[26] Jefferson, letter to Adams, October, 1787, cited by Morgan, 240.

[27] Lafayette, letter to Washington, January 13, 1787, Paris, *The Letters of Lafayette to Washington*, 317-319.

[28] Ibid.

[29] Taillimite,133.

[30] Jefferson, letter to Carrington, January 16, 1787; Lipscomb and Bergh, VI,56, cited by Gottschalk, *Lafayette between the American and French Revolution*,285.

[31] Lafayette, letter to Washington, January 13, 1787, Paris, *The Letters of Lafayette to Washington*, 317-319.

[32] Jefferson, letter to Madison, January 30, 1787, Lipscomb and Bergh, VI,65, cited by Gottschalk, *Lafayette between the American and French Revolution*, 283.

[33] Morgan, 241.

[34] *Procès-verbal de l'Assemblée de Notables tenue à Versailles en l'année MDCCLXXXVII* (Paris,1788), cited by Gottschalk, *Lafayette between the American and French Revolution*, 287,288.

[35] Charavay, 140.

[36] Corvée: forced labor; Taille: tax.

[37] Charavay, 141.

[38] Comte d'Espinchal, *Journal d'émigration*, ed., Ernest d'Hauterive, 276,277; cited by Maurois,156.

[39] Archives nationales, C.2, cited by Charavay,142.

[40] Charavay,142.

[41] *Mémoires*, 2:166.

[42] Lafayette, letter to Washington, May 5, 1787, Paris, *The Letters of Lafayette to Washington*, 322-324.

[43] Letter from Fondation Josée et René de Chambrun, Maurois,155.

[44] *Mémoires*,2:168.

[45] Lafayette, letter to Washington, May 5, 1787, *Mémoires*, 1:225-226, cited by Unger, 222.

[46] Assemblée des notables, *Mémoires*, 2:169.

[47] Jefferson, letter to Lafayette, April 11, 1787, Nice, *The letters of Lafayette and Jefferson*,110-112.

[48] *Mémoires*,2:171-177.

[49] *Mémoires*,2:177.

[50] Morgan, 244.

[51] *Mémoires*, 2:179.

[52] Lafayette, letter to Jay, May,1787, Charavay, 149.

[53] Lafayette, letter to Washington, August 3, 1787, Paris, *The Letters of Lafayette and Washington*, 324-326.

[54] Ibid.

Chapter 35

[1] Lafayette, letter to Washington, October 9, 1787, Paris, *The Letters of Lafayette to Washington*, 326-332.

[2] Comte d'Espinchal, journal inedit, cited by Mège, cited by Charavay,152.

[3] Lafayette, letter to Washington, October 9, 1787, Paris, *The Letters of Lafayette to Washington*, 326-332.

[4] Lafayette, letter to Jefferson, August 27, 1787, *The Letters of Lafayette and Jefferson*, 113,114.

[5] Lafayette, letter to Washington, October 9, 1787, Paris, *The Letters of Lafayette to Washington*, 326-332.

[6] Delmas, *Les loges maçonniques de Saint-Flour au XVIIIe siècl*, Clermont-Ferrand,1897,8:10, cited by Charavay,153.

[7] Lafayette, letter to Washington, October 9, 1787, Paris, *The Letters of Lafayette and Washington*, 326-332.

[8] La Tour Maubourg's name is often spelled in different ways and the form has been chosen in which he himself wrote it on the declaration he signed when captured.

[9] Taillimite,154,155.

[10] Ibid.

[11] *Mémoires*,2:187,188.

[12] Washington, letter to Lafayette, September 18, 1787, Ford, *Writings of George Washington*, XI: 155.

[13] Lafayette, letter to Jefferson, Tuesday, December,1787, Nemours; *The Letters of Lafayette and Jefferson*, 123. Note: Chinard suggests the date as 1788 but Lafayette sent it from Nemours on his way back to Paris in 1787.

[14] Doyle, *The Oxford History of the French Revolution*, 80.

Chapter 36

[1] Lafayette, letter to Washington, January 1, 1788, Paris, *The Letters of Lafayette to Washington*, 334-336.

[2] Estates-General.

[3] Jefferson, letter to William Rutledge, February 2, 1788, Paris, Lipscomb and Bergh, VI, 418, cited by Gottschalk, *Lafayette between the American and French Revolution,* 373.

[4] Lafayette, letter to Washington, February 4, 1787, Paris, *The Letters of Lafayette to Washington*, 338.

[5] Lafayette, letter to Washington, May 25, 1788, Paris, *The Letters of Lafayette to Washington*, 342-345.

[6] The Parlement of Paris is written with a capital 'P', the provincial parlements are written with a lower case.

[7] Lafayette, letter to César de La Tour Maubourg, Charavay, 159.

[8] *Mémoires*, 2:183, note 1.

[9] Jefferson, letter to Jay, August 3, 1788; Lipscomb and Bergh, VII,106, cited by Gottschalk, *Lafayette between the American and French Revolution*, 392.

[10] Adrienne de Noailles, *The Life of the Duchesse d'Ayen*, 83-85.

[11] Schama, *Citizens: A Chronicle of the French Revolution*, 228.

[12] Jefferson, letter to Adams, August 2, 1788, Paris, cited by Gottschalk, *Lafayette between the American and French Revolution*, 392.

[13] Jefferson, letter to Jay, August 3, 1788, Paris, cited by Gottschalk, *Lafayette between the American and French Revolution*, 392.

[14] *Mémoires*, 2:235.

[15] Ibid., 2:235,236.

[16] *Ibid,* 2:236.

[17] Doyle, 87.

[18] Washington, letter to Lafayette, June 19, 1788, Fitzpatrick, XXIX,524, cited by Gottschalk, *Lafayette between the American and French Revolution,*401.

[19] Lafayette, letter to Madame de Simiane, 1788, August 28,1788, Paris, Mémoires,2:237, 238.

[20] Lafayette, letter to Mrs, Greene, September 5, 1788, Paris, Jackson Collection, cited by Gottschalk, *Lafayette between the American and French Revolution*, 405.

[21] Egret, *La Pre-Revolution*, 334, cited by Doyle,90.

[22] Lafayette, letter to unnamed person, November 19, 1788, 2:239,240.

[23] Charavay,160.

[24] *Mémoires,* 3, 198.

[25] Léon Cahen, *La Société des Amis des Noirs et Condorcet, Révolution française*, L (1906), 503, cited by Gottschalk, *Lafayette between the American and French Revolution*, 424.

Chapter 37

[1] *The Letters of Lafayette and Jefferson*, 80.

[2] *Mémoires,*3:227.

[3] *Mémoires,*2:252.

[4] Washington, letter to Lafayette, January 29, 1789, *Mémoires*, 2:241,242.

[5] Lafayette, letter to unnamed person, probably Madame de Simiane, March 8, 1789, Chavaniac, *Mémoires*, 2:240,241.

[6] Lafayette, letter, probably to Madame de Simiane, March 8, 1789, Chavaniac, *Mémoires,* 2: 240,241.

[7] Mosnier, *Les Élections de 1789 dans la Sénéchaussée d'Auvergne*, cited by Bois, 129.

[8] Lafayette, letter to La Tour Maubourg, April 1,1789, Chavaniac; Charavay, 166.

[9] Ibid., 165,166.

[10] Lafayette, letter to La Colombe, April 1, 1789, Chavaniac, Archives nationales; cited by Charavay, 167.

[11] Lafayette, letter to Maubourg, April 5,1789, Clermont; Mortimer-Ternaux,1:429, cited by Gottschalk, *Lafayette in the French Revolution*, 38,39.

[12] Morris, *Journal du Gouverneur Morris, minister plénipotentiaire des États-Unis en France de 1792 à 1794, pendant les années 1789,1790,1791 et 1792*, 15,16.

[13] Charavay, 169.

[14] Morris,19.

[15] Doyle, 98; McPhee, *Liberty or Death; The French Revolution*, says 300 killed, with some estimates of 900, citing Godechot, *Taking of the Bastille*, 133-51.

[16] McPhee,67.

[17] *Memoirs of Madame de la Tour du Pin*, 106.

[18] Morris, 27.

[19] *Memoirs of Madame de la Tour du Pin*,106.

[20] Ibid., 105.

[21] Ibid., 106.

[22] Morris, 28.

[23] Ibid.

[24] Ibid., 29.

[25] Sieyès, Emmanuel, *Que-est-ce que le tiers état?* cited in Dunn, Susan, *Sister Revolutions: French Lightning, American Light* (New York, Farrar, Strauss and Giroux), 1999),61, cited by Unger, 232.

[26] D'Espinal; cited by Charavay, 170.

[27] Jefferson, letter to Lafayette, May 6, 1789, Paris, *The Letters of Lafayette and Jefferson*, 125,126.

[28] Bailly, 1:112,113.

[29] Doyle, 102,103.

[30] Bailly,1:158.

[31] Doyle, 105.

[32] An undated letter, written after June 25, Thursday, Versailles, *Mémoires*, 2:312.

[33] Anecdotal.

[34] *Arthur Young's Travels in France during the Years 1787,1788, 1789*, 82.

[35] Gottschalk says Mirabeau's words are in dispute as his account is the only contemporary source, *The Era of the French Revolution*, 128,129. Arthur Young recounts Mirabeau's words in his *Travels in France during 1787,1788,1789*, 82.

[36] Gottschalk, *The Era of the French Revolution*, 129.

[37] *Arthur Young's Travels in France during 1787,1788,1789;* 82,83.

[38] *Morris*, June 23, 1789, 50.

[39] Young, 83.

[40] Ibid., 84.

[41] Taillimite, 172.

[42] Gottschalk, *Lafayette in the French Revolution*, 69.

[43] Ibid.

[44] Point du Jour, June 28, 66, cited by Gottschalk, *Lafayette in the French Revolution*, 70.

[45] Morris, 52.

[46] Rudé, *The Crowd in the French Revolution*,46; Bonn, *Camille Desmoulins ou la plume de la liberté*, cited by McPhee, 71.

[47] Bailly, Jean Sylvain, *Mémoires de Bailly, Avec une notice sur sa vie, des notes et des éclaircissements historiques*, 1:293,294.

[48] *Mémoires*, 2:250,251.

[49] Ibid., 2: 251.

[50] Lafayette, letter to Jefferson, July 8, 1789, Boyd, XV,254, cited by Gottschalk, *Lafayette in the French Revolution*, 80.

[51] Bailly, 1:305-307.

[52] Lafayette, letter to Jefferson, July 9, 1789, *The Letters of Lafayette and Jefferson*, 134,135.

[53] Gottschalk is probably correct that it was Mirabeau who spoke to him, *Mémoires*, 2:251.

[54] Lafayette, letter to unnamed person, July 11, 1789, Versailles, *Mémoires*, 2:313.

[55] Mounier, Appel,13,14, cited by Gottschalk, *Lafayette in the French Revolution*, 92.

[56] Bailly, 1:310,311.

[57] *Mémoires*, 2:252.

[58] *Ibid.*, 2 :252,253.

[59] Lafayette, letter to Hennings, January 15, 1799, Witmöld, *Mémoires,*3:227.

[60] Bailly, 1:314.

[61] Bailly, 1:332,333.

[62] *Mémoires*, 2:251.

[63] Taillimite, 175.

[64] Bailly, 1:333,334.

[65] *Mémoires,* 2:254.

[66] Bois,138.

[67] Bailly,1:327,328.

[68] Ibid., 1:338,339.

[69] Taillimite, 176.

[70] Bailly,1:339,340.

[71] Ibid., 1:341,342.

[72] *Moniteur*, 1 :156, *Archives parlementaires*, July 13, 1789;230, cited by Bois, 139, Bailly,1 :344.

[73] Lafayette, letter, 6 o'clock in the morning, 1789, Versailles, *Mémoires,* 2 :316.

[74] Bailly, 2:121.

[75] Ibid.,1:363.

[76] Ibid.,2:124.

[77] *Archives parlementaires* cited by Bois, 138; Bailly,1:363.

[78] Ferrières, 1:9.

[79] Bailly, 2:126.

[80] Ibid.,1: 365,366.

[81] Ibid.,1:366.

[82] Ibid.,1:367.

[83] Famous anecdotal words, according to Schama, 353.

[84] Bailly,2:164.

[85] Ibid.,2:166.

[86] *Mémoires*, 2:255.

[87] Bailly, 2:166-169.

[88] Ibid., 2:182,183.

[89] Ibid., 2:184,185.

[90] *Mémoires*, 2:261.

[91] The account of this day comes from Bailly, 2:164-191. He says that from his memory and that of some of the electors he was named before Lafayette despite the account of the procés verbal, 2:192. *Mémoires*, 2: 260, says Bailly is proclaimed mayor after him.

[92] *Journal du Duquesnoy*,1:214; Duveyrier,196, cited by Gottschalk, *Lafayette in the French Revolution*,113.

[93] Bailly,2:198.

Chapter 38

[1] *Mémoires*, 2:264.

[2] Gottschalk, *Lafayette in the French Revolution*, 115,116.

[3] Bailly, 2:216.

[4] Garde nationale.

[5] Extract from the *procès verbal* of the electors, *Mémoires*,2: 263,264.

[6] Bailly, 2:218.

[7] Lafayette, letter to unnamed person, probably Madame de Simiane, July 16, 1789, Paris, *Mémoires*,2:317,318.

[8] Bailly, 2:208.

[9] Soulavie, VI, 385,386, cited by Gottschalk, *Lafayette in the French Revolution*, 125.

[10] *Réimpression de l'ancien Moniteur*, Ray,1:596.

[11] Ibid., 1:596.

[12] *Mémoires*, 2 :265. Other sources say the king has 4 bodyguards.

[13] Ferrières,1:150.

[14] Bailly, 2:230.

[15] Ibid., 2:231,232.

[16] Ibid., 2:234,235.

[17] Ibid., 2:236.

[18] Ibid. 2:236.

[19] Ibid., 2:240.

[20] *Histoire des premiers électeurs de Paris*, par Ch. Duveyrier, secrétaire de leur assemblée, *Mémoires*, 2:266, note 1.

[21] *Mémoires*,2:273.

[22] Ferrières,1:154.

[23] *Morris*, 67.

[24] *Mémoires*, 2:278.

[25] Ferrières, 1:155.

[26] *Mémoires*, 2:278.

[27] Morris, 67.

[28] *Mémoires*, 2:272, clearly suggests this meeting is before this day. Gottschalk, *Lafayette in the French Revolution*, however, suggests it is July 22, 146.

[29] *Mémoires*, 2:275.

[30] *Mémoires*, 2:275-278.

[31] Bailly, 2:295.

[32] Ferrières, 1 :159.

[33] Ibid.

[34] Bailly, 2:303.

[35] Ibid., 2:310-312.

[36] Ibid., 2:310.

[37] Taillimite,180.

[38] Lafayette, letter to duc de Liancourt, July 24,1789, Paris, *Mémoires*, 2:320.

[39] This account taken from *Mémoires*, 2:281-285; Bailly,1:313-318.

[40] Lafayette, letter to duc de Liancourt, July 24, 1789, Paris, *Mémoires,*2:321.

[41] Bailly, 2:329,330.

[42] Ibid., 2:330.

[43] Gottschalk, 166, cites *Courrier de Versailles à Paris* which says it is Lafayette, July 31,50. Ferriéres says it is Saint-Méry, 1:171.

[44] Schama, 369.

[45] Morgan, 275.

[46] *Souvenirs du lieutenant général comte Mathieu Dumas, de 1770 à 1836*; Dumas writes that the red, blue and white cockade was already being sold at the foot of the statue of Henri IV on July 14.

[47] Charavay,183.

[48] Ferrières,1 :176,177.

[49] Ibid.,1 :177.

[50] Ferrières,1:178.

[51] Bailly, 3 :11.

[52] Ibid., 3:13,14.

[53] Ibid., 3:17,18.

[54] Ferrières, 1:186.

[55] *Mémoires,*2:290.

[56] Bailly,3:16.

[57] Hardy, *Patriote français*, August 7,423,429, cited by Gottschalk, *Lafayette in the French Revolution*, 178.

[58] Bailly, 3:50.

[59] Gottschalk, *Lafayette in the French Revolution*, 182.

[60] Bailly, 3: 52,53.

[61] Doyle, 117.

[62] Bailly,3:85.

[63] *Mémoires*, Lafayette, letter to unnamed person, probably Madame de Simiane, 2:321,322.

[64] Bailly, 3:120.

[65] Ibid., 3:121.

[66] Ibid., 3 :122.

[67] Ibid., 3: 122.

[68] *Memoirs of Madame de La Tour du Pin*,122.

[69] Ibid.

[70] Bailly, 3:123.

[71] Ibid., 3:124.

[72] *Mémoires*, 2:303, cited by Gottschalk, *Lafayette in the French Revolution*, 225.

[73] Ibid.

[74] *Mémoires*, 2 :306.

[75] Lafayette, letter to Washington, August 1789, Paris, *Mémoires,* 3:200, cited by Gottschalk, *Lafayette in the French Revolution*, 253.

[76] Bailly, 3 :148.

[77] Schama, 386.

[78] Bailly,3:148,149.

[79] Ibid., 3:152.

[80] Ibid., 3:152.

Chapter 39

[1] *Mémoires,*2:292,293.

[2] Ibid., 2:293,294.

[3] Ibid., 2:298,299.

[4] Lafayette, letter to Jefferson, undated but probably September 6, 1789, Paris, *The Letters of Lafayette and Jefferson,*10.

[5] Mémoires, 2:299.

[6] *The Writings of Thomas Jefferson*,1:104, cited by Charavay,187,188.
[7] Bailly,3:159.
[8] Ibid., 3:184,185.
[9] Ibid., 3:185.
[10] Lafayette, letter written to La Tour du Pin, September, 1789, Paris, *Mémoires*, 2:324-327.
[11] Bailly,3: 188; Doyle,120.
[12] Lafayette, September 10, 1789, Paris, cited by Gottschalk, 255, citing *Mémoires,* 2 :299.
[13] Doyle, 120.
[14] Morris,75,76.
[15] Jefferson, letter to Rutledge, September 18, 1789, Boyd, XV, 452, cited by Gottschalk, *Lafayette in the French Revolution*, 287.
[16] *Mémoires*, 2: 329,330.
[17] *Journal de Paris*, September 23 and October 3,1789, cited by Gottschalk, *Lafayette in the French Revolution*, 298.
[18] McPhee, 93.
[19] Bailly, 3:225.
[20] *Mémoires*. 2:297.
[21] Ibid., 2:297, 298.
[22] Ibid., 2:298.

Chapter 40
[1] *Memoirs of Madame de La Tour du Pin*, 124.
[2] Ibid.
[3] Morris, 84.
[4] Ibid.
[5] *Mémoires*,2:336.
[6] *Mémoires*,2:336. Note: Gottschalk says Lafayette is wrong about wanting him as regent.
[7] Ibid.
[8] Ibid.
[9] Ibid., 2:337.
[10] Ibid.
[11]Ibid.,2:338.
[12] Gottschalk, *Lafayette in the French Revolution*, 342.
[13] *Mémoires*, 2:338.
[14] Ibid.
[15] Gottschalk,343.
[16] *Mémoires*, 2:347.
[17] Taillimite, 194.
[18] *Mémoires*, 2:338.
[19] Ibid.
[20] Ibid., 2:339.
[21] Dumas, 1:454,455.
[22] Ibid., 1:455,456.
[23] *Memoirs of Madame de La Tour du Pin*, 130.
[24] Ibid.
[25] Dumas,1:456.
[26] Ibid., 1:456,457.
[27] *Mémoires*, 2:341.
[28] Ibid., 2:340.
[29] *Memoirs of Madame de La Tour du Pin*,130. Ferrières, 1:319.
[30] Ferrières,1:322.
[31] Gottschalk, *Lafayette in the French Revolution*,362.
[32] *Correspondance entre le comte de Mirabeau et le comte de La Marck*; 1:117, cited by Charavay,189.
[33] Dumas, 1:457.
[34] Ibid., 1:457,458.
[35] *Mémoires*, 2: 348.
[36] Ibid.
[37] Ferrières, 1:325,326.
[38] Gottschalk, *Lafayette in the French Revolution*,373.

[39] Ibid., 375.
[40] *Mémoires*, 2:341.
[41] Ibid.
[42] Ibid.,2:349.
[43] *Mémoires,*3:201.
[44] Ferrières,1:498. Gottschalk, *Lafayette in the French Revolution*, 382.
[45] Ferrières, 2: 343,344.
[46] Ibid., 2:344.
[47] *Dispatches, 1784-90*, 2:265.
[48] *Mémoires*, 2:344.
[49] Taillimite, 202.
[50] Brand Whitlock,1:372.
[51] *Mémoires*, 2:357.
[52] *Dispatches*, 2:265.
[53] *Mémoires,*2:414.
[54] Ibid., 2:358.
[55] Morris, 93. He records the whole of this conversation.
[56] McPhee, 92. Doyle,132.
[57] Doyle, 132.
[58] Morris, 95.
[59] *Mémoires,*2:358.
[60] Bacourt,1:128; cited by Gottschalk, *Lafayette in the French Revolution*, 24.
[61] Mémoires, 2:364.
[62] Ferrières,1:340.
[63] Lacroix,2:360,361; cited by Gottschalk, *Lafayette in the French Revolution*, 42,43.
[64] *Mémoires*, 2 :375.
[65] Ferrières, 1:342.
[66] Gottschalk, *Lafayette in the French Revolution*, 58.
[67] Ferrières, 1:345.
[68] Gottschalk, *Lafayette in the French Revolution*,62.
[69] Ibid.
[70] Lafayette, letter to Mounier, October 23, 1789, Paris, *Mémoires,*2:415-420.

Chapter 41
[1] Morris, 115.
[2] Ibid., 119.
[3] Doyle,133.
[4] Morris, 120-122.
[5] Ségur, 1:273.
[6] Ibid.
[7] Mémoire addressed to the king, *Mémoires,* 2:436-439. Note: the date is not clear although note 1 suggests it was shortly after December 14.
[8] Washington, letter to Lafayette, October 14, 1789, New York, Charavay,200.
[9] Hamilton, Hamilton, *Writings,* letter to Lafayette, October 6, 1789, New York, 521,522.
[10] *Correspondance entre Mirabeau et La Marck*, 1:423-425; cited by Charavay, 206,207.
[11] Gottschalk, *Lafayette in the French Revolution*, 119.
[12] Doyle,133,134.
[13] Morris, 158,159.
[14] *Mémoires,* 2:393.
[15] *Journal général de la cour*, January 6, 1790, 44, cited by Gottschalk, *Lafayette in the French Revolution*, 128.
[16] Morris, 163.
[17] Desmoulins, *Révolutions de France et de Brabant*, No.8, 349,350, cited by Gottschalk, *Lafayette in the French Revolution*, 173.
[18] Lafayette, letter to Washington, *The Letters of Lafayette to Washington*, January 12,1790; 346. Note: Common Sense is Thomas Paine.
[19] Morris, 169.
[20] Gottschalk, *Lafayette in the French Revolution*, 177.
[21] Ibid., 185.

[22] Desmoulins, *Révolutions, No.9,* 426-428;No.10,464-466, cited by Gottschalk, *Lafayette in the French Revolution,* 186.

[23] Ferrières, 2:580.

[24] Bailly,3:282.

[25] Morris, 179,180.

[26] Order of the Day, February 5, 1790, Paris, *Journal of Paris,* February 5-7, 1790, cited by Gottschalk, *Lafayette in the French Revolution,* 213.

[27] Bailly, 3:283-285.

[28] Ibid., 3:285,286.

[29] *Journal général de la cour,* February 12, 1790, 341, cited by Gottschalk, *Lafayette in the French Revolution,* 216.

[30] Lafayette, letter to M. d'Hennings, January 15, 1799, Witmold; *Mémoires,* 3:247.

[31] *Courier national,* February 15, 1790, Paris, cited by Gottschalk, *Lafayette in the French Revolution,* 228.

[32] Morris, February 15, 1790,181-183.

[33] Gottschalk, *Lafayette in the French Revolution,*232,233.

[34] Lafayette, letter to Madame de Simiane, February 19, 1790, Paris, *Mémoires,*2:443,444.

[35] Ibid.

[36] Charavay, 214.

[37] *Mémoires,*3:13,14.

[38] Ibid., 3:16,17.

[39] Sémonville, letter to Lafayette, January 27, 1790, Bruxelles, *Mémoires,*3:22-24.

[40] Lafayette, letter to Sémonville, February 8, 1790, Paris, *Mémoires,*3:28-31.

[41] Schlieffen, letter to Lafayette, February 22,1790, *Mémoires,*3:31.

[42] Lafayette, letter to Washington, March 17, 1790, Paris, Mémoires, 2:446-448.

[43] Lafayette, letter to Washington, March 17,1790, Paris, *Mémoires,* 2: 446-448.

[44] Lafayette, letter probably to Madame de Simiane, not dated but before Easter, 1790, *Mémoires,*2:458,459.

[45] Lafayette, letter to Schlieffen, April 7, 1790, *Mémoires,*3:34-36.

[46] Poncet-Delpech, 277-278, Tuetey, II, 431, cited by Gottschalk, *Lafayette in the French Revolution,* 321,322.

[47] Lafayette's Memoir to the king, April 14, 1790, Paris, *Mémoires,* 2:449-456.

[48] *Correspondance entre Mirabeau et La Marck,* 2:1-6, cited by Charavay,217.

[49] Dumouriez, letter to Lafayette, May 2, 1790, Paris, Mémoires, 3:40.

[50] Lafayette, letter probably to Madame de Simiane, undated, 1790, Mémoires,2:458,459.

[51] Anecdotal, French Ministry of Culture, cited by Unger, Harlow Giles, Lafayette, (New Jersey: John Wiley and sons,2002), 263.

[52] Madame de La Tour du Pin, 138.

[53] Lafayette, letter probably to Madame de Simiane, May 25, 1790, Paris, *Mémoires,* 2:462-464.

[54] Ibid., 2:402.

[55] Dumouriez, letter to Lafayette, May 31, 1790, Paris, *Mémoires,*3:41,42.

[56] Fitzgerald, letter to Leeds, June 4, 1790, Paris; Browning (ed.) 325, Thompson, 80,81, cited by Gottschalk, *Lafayette in the French Revolution,* 466.

[57] Charavay,226.

[58] Lafayette, letter to Louis XVI, June 19, 1790, Paris, *Mémoires,* 2:470,471.

[59] Note: Ferrières, *Mémoires du Marquis de Ferrières,* 2:71, writes very differently of this. He says that Lafayette was furious that the Lameth brothers should alone have the merit of abolishing titles of nobility and rushed there.

[60] Ferrières, 2 :69,70.

[61] Ibid., 2:70.

[62] Ibid., 2:71.

[63] Mémoires, 4:153.

[64]Mirabeau, letter to La Marck, June 26, 1790, cited by Charavay, 228.

[65] Lafayette, letter to Louis XVI, June 25, 1790, Paris, *Mémoires,* 2:471,472.

[66] Lafayette, letter to Louis XVI, June 27, 1790, Paris, *Mémoires,* 2:473,474. Note 1: Lafayette says that he and his friends only wanted, on June 19, to declare there would be no hereditary nobility in France.

[67] Letter written by the king to Lafayette but not sent, June 28, 1790, Paris, cited by Charavay, 229.

[68] Ferrières, 2:90.

[69] Madame de La Tour du Pin,141.

70 Ferrières, 2:90.

71 *Mémoires,* 3: 46, note 1.

72 Ibid., 2: 430.

73 Ferrières,2:84

74 Ibid., 2:90.

75 *Mémoires,* 2:286.

76 Ferrières, 2:89.

77 Lafayette, declaration to the Assembly, July 13, 1790, *Mémoires,* 3 :4.

78 *Mémoires,* 3:6.

79 Ibid.

80 Ibid.

81 Ibid.,3:215.

Chapter 42

1 Ferrières, 2: 92.

2 Ibid., 2: 93.

3 Unger, 266.

4 Note: The Oriflamme is not a religious or military banner. It was later hung in the hall of the National Assembly. On it was written: *conféderation national,*14 juillet,1790 consecrates this now more and more; *Mémoires,*3:7.

5 *Memoirs of Madame de La Tour du Pin,*145.

6 *Mémoires,*3:7.

7 Ibid. Note: Lafayette says the king leads the oath-taking, *Mémoires,* 4:155. Others, such as Ferrières, write differently. Mignet*, History of the French Revolution,* 1:69, cited by Cloquet, 2:133, says Lafayette leads the oath-taking.

8 Ferrières,2:95.

9 Mignet,1:69; cited by Cloquet, 2:133. Ferrières,2:95.

10 Charavay,234.

11 *Mémoires,* 3:3.

12 Address to Lafayette from the Assembly from the *gardes nationales* of France, July 17, 1790, *Mémoires,*3:8,9.

13 Charavay, 238.

14 Madame de La Tour du Pin,151.

15 Lafayette, letter to Bouillé, August 18, 1790, *Mémoires,* 3:133-135.

16 Lafayette, letter to Washington, amended, August 23,1790, *The Letters of Lafayette to Washington,*348-350.

17 *Moniteur,* V,530, cited by Charavay, 244.

18 Madame de La Tour du Pin, 311.

19 *Mémoires,* 4:156.

20 Lafayette, letter to Bouillé, September 3, 1790, Paris, *Mémoires,* 3:143,144.

21 *Procès verbal,* cited by Charavay, 246.

22 *L'Ami du Peuple,* September 15, 1790, no.222,5-8, cited by Charavay, 245.

23 Pellet, *Élysée Loustalot et les Révolutions de Paris,1872,* in12, cited by Charavay, 245.

24 Lafayette, letter to Washington, August 23, 1790, Paris, *The Letters of Lafayette to Washington,* 348-350.

25 Lafayette, letter to Bouillé, October 3, 1790, Paris, *Mémoires,*3:146,147.

26 Madame de La Tour du Pin,157.

27 Moniteur, 3:137; cited by Castries, 199,200.

28 Morris,1:302.

29 Ferrières, 2:185-189.

30 Ibid., 2:209.

31 *Mémoires,* 3:54.

32 Ibid., 3:57.

33 Ibid.

34 Ibid., 3:58.

35 Lafayette, letter to Washington, March 7,1791, *The Letters of Lafayette to Washington,*352.

36 Charavay,263.

37 Schama, 464.

38 Ibid.

[39] Ibid., 468.
[40] Lasteyrie, Virginie de Lafayette, 195.
[41] Journal de la Cour et de la Ville, April 13, 1791, cited by Maurois, 201.
[42] Morris, 227.
[43] Taillimite, 275.
[44] *Mémoires*, 3:74.

Chapter 43
[1] *Mémoires*, 3:76.
[2] Ibid.
[3] Ibid.
[4] Note: Taillimite, 282, says Lafayette first went to see Thomas Paine where he told him the birds have flown. This seems unlikely given the urgency of the situation unless Paine was living in his house which he might have been.
[5] *Mémoires*, 3:78.
[6] Ibid., 3 :79.
[7] Ibid., 3 :82.
[8] Ibid., 3 :79.
[9] Ibid.
[10] Ibid., 3 :80.
[11] Ibid.,3 :81.
[12] Ibid.
[13] Ferrières,2:333.
[14] *Mémoires*,3: 83.
[15] Ibid., 3 :77.
[16] Ibid., 3:83.
[17] Ibid.
[18] Charavay,269.
[19] Aulard, *La Société des Jacobins*,2 :534-36, cited by Charavay, 270.
[20] Ibid., 2 :537, cited by Charavay, 270.
[21] *Mémoires*, 3:85.
[22] Ferrières,2:339,340.
[23] Dumas;1:498. *Mémoires*,3:90.
[24] Ferrières, 2:370.
[25] Dumas;1:502
[26] Ibid.
[27] Ibid.,1:503.
[28] *Mémoires*,3:92.
[29] Dumas,1:505.
[30] *Mémoires*,3:92.
[31] Ibid.
[32] Dumas,1:499.
[33] Ibid., 3:93.
[34] Ibid.
[35] *Mémoires*,3:95.
[36] *Le Moniteur*, cited by Charavay,272. *Mémoires*,3:96.
[37] Ibid. *Mémoires*,3:97.
[38] Lasteyrie, Virginie de Lafayette, *Life of Madame de Lafayette*, 198,199.
[39] *Mémoires*,3:94, note 1 by Lafayette.
[40] Doyle,156.
[41] Morris:247.
[42] *Mémoires*;3:104.
[43] Ibid., 3 :107. Ferrières, 2:457.
[44] Ibid.
[45] Ibid., 3:105.
[46] Doyle, 154. He suggests 50 were killed. A pamphlet supporting Lafayette published next day says ten killed and twenty injured, *Grand récit de ce qui s'est passé hier au Champ de Mars et des assassinats qui y ont été commis avec le nombre des morts et des blessés*, Paris, s.e., 1791, cited by Bois, 198. Lafayette says the number killed was widely exaggerated; *Mémoires*,3 :106.

[47] *Mémoires*,3:109.

[48] Ibid.,3 :106.

[49] Lasteyrie, Virginie de Lafayette, 200, 201.

[50] Marat, *L'Ami du peuple*, no.523, July 19,1791, no.524, July 20, 1791, cited by Bois, 198.

[51] Fréron; cited by Bardoux, 1:342.

[52] *Mémoires*, 3:108.

[53] Bardoux, 1:345.

[54] *Mémoires*,3 :108.

[55] Doyle,155.

[56] Ibid., 174.

[57] Ibid., 155.

[58] Ibid., 156,157.

[59] Bardoux, 1757-1792, 346.

[60] Marat, *L'Ami du peuple*, no.552, September 11, 1791 ; cited by Bois, 200.

[61] Ferrières,2:492.

[62] Ibid., 2:493.

[63] *Mémoires*, 3:117.

[64] Taillimite, 297.

[65] Bardoux, 349.

[66] Taillimite,298.

[67] Ibid.

[68] Morris, letter to Carmichael, July 4, 1789, Paris, in Davenport, 1 :134-138, cited by Unger, 235.

[69] Mémoires; 4:28.

[70] Ibid., 3 :118.

[71] Ibid., 3 :118

[72] Ferrières,2:497,498.

[73] Ibid., 2:499,500.

[74] Ibid. 2:500.

[75] Taillimite, 303.

[76] Doyle, 175.

[77] *Mémoires*, 3:119.

[78] Ibid.,3:120.

[79] Mosnier, *Le Château de Chavaniac-Lafayette*, 64. *Mémoires,*3 :123.

[80] Robiquet,465, cited by Charavay, 276.

Chapter 44

[1] Lafayette, letter to Washington, October 20, 1791 Chavaniac, *Mémoires*,3:188,189.

[2] Callet, A., Anne-Paul-Dominique de Noailles, marquise de Montagu,72,73, letter from Fondation Josée et René de Chambrun, cited by Maurois, 211,212.

[3] Lasteyrie, Virginie de Lafayette, 202.

[4] Lafayette, letter to Washington, October 20, 1791, Chavania, *Mémoires*, 3:188,189.

[5] Lafayette, letter to Washington, October 20, 1791, Chavaniac, *Mémoires,*3 :188,189.

[6] Frénilly, 155,156, cited by Bois,203.

[7] Mosnier,61.

[8] Lafayette, Madame de, *The Life of the Duchesse d'Ayen*, 94,95.e et Ren

[9] Journal de Paris, November 23, 1791, 1329, cited by Charavay, 279. Mosnier,61.

[10] Letter from Fondation Josée et René de Chambrun, Maurois,215.

[11] Lafayette, Madame de, *The Life of the Duchesse d'Ayen*, 95.

[12] Lafayette, letter to Washington, October 20, 1791, Chavaniac, *Mémoires*, 3:188,189.

[13] Bardoux, 354.

[14] Lafayette, Madame de, *The Life of the Duchesse d'Ayen*,96.

[15] Bardoux, 354.

[16] Lafayette, letter to Washington, January 22, 1792, Metz, *The Letters of Lafayette to Washington*, 358-360.

[17] Letter from Fondation Josée et René de Chambrun, in Maurois,215.

[18] Lafayette, letter to Washington, January 22, 1792, Metz, *Mémoires*,3:418-420.

[19] *Journal de Paris*, April 25,1792, no.57, cited by Charavay, 294.

[20] *Le Patriote français*, cited by Charavay, 285. Taillimite,314,315.

[21] Lafayette, letter to Narbonne, March 4, 1792, *Mémoires,*3:421.

[22] Ibid., 3 :304.

[23] Ibid., 3 :306.

[24] Ibid. 3 :303.

[25] Lafayette, letter to Washington, March 15, 1792, Paris, *Mémoires*,3:426.

[26] Ibid., 3 :425.

[27] *Le Patriote français*, April 10, 1792, no.974,404, cited by Charavay,289.

[28] Charavay, 289.

[29] Dumas: 2:127.

[30] Lafayette, letter to Adrienne, April 18, 1792, Metz, *Mémoires*,3:428-430.

[31] Taillimite,318. Aulard, La Société des Jacobins,3 :515, cited by Charavay, 291.

[32] Aulard,3:528; cited by Taillimite, 572.

[33] Charavay, 292.

[34] *Mémoires*, 3:318.

[35] Lafayette, letter to de Grave, April 25, 1792, Metz, *Mémoires*,3:432-434.

[36] Lafayette, letter to de Grave, May 2, 1792, Givet, *Mémoires*, 3:318-320.

[37] *Mémoires*,3: Note 1;434.

[38] Note: It was his own soldiers who cut him into pieces at a farm where he had taken refuge, injured. They threw the pieces into the fire. *Mémoires*, 3:317.

[39] De Grave, letter to Lafayette, April 30, 1792, midnight, *Mémoires*,3:434,435.

[40] Lafayette, letter to de Grave, May 2, 1792, Givet; *Mémoires*,3:318-320.

[41] *Archive historical de la guerre, armée du Centre*, cited by Charavay, 296.

[42] *Archive historical de la guerre, armée du Centre*, cited by Charavay, 296.

[43] Anecdotal.

[44] *Mémoires*,3:317,318.

[45] Copy certified by Rochambeau, *Archive historical de la guerre, armée du centre*, cited by Charavay,298.

[46] Lafayette, letter to Servan, Charavay,302.

[47] *Mémoires*,3:323,324.

[48] Dumas, 2:196,197.

[49] *Mémoires*,3:324.

[50] Roederer saw Lafayette when he received the news and said he had a '*bruyante explosion de joie,*' cited by Taillimite,35.

[51] Note: Lafayette often uses the word 'jacobite' to allude to the plots of the Stewarts and to also suggest that the two parties are similarly contrary to the principles of liberty. *Mémoires*,3: 326, note 2.

[52] Lafayette, letter to the Legislative Assembly, June 16, 1792, camp at Maubeuge, *Mémoires*, 3:325-331.

[53] Dumas, 2:206-208.

[54] Aulard, La Société de Jacobins, IV:11, cited by Charavay.

[55] Charavay, 305.

[56] Lafayette, letter to Lajard, June 22, 1792, Bavay camp, *Mémoires*, 3:440.

[57] Lasteyrie, Virginie de Lafayette, 204,205.

[58] Dumas partly cites *Histoire de la Révolution française* by Thiers and partly describes his own eye-witness account, 2: 211-217.

[59] *Mémoires*, 3:333.

[60] Lafayette, letter to Lückner, June 20, 1792; Copie, Arch.nat.C 358, cited by Charavay,307.

[61] *Mémoires*,3:333.

[62] Taillimite,331.

[63] Charavay,311.

[64] Ferrières,3:130.

[65] *Mémoires*,3:334,335.

[66] Dumas,2:243.

[67] Ibid., 2 :243,244.

[68] Ibid., 2:244,245.

[69] Ibid., 2:247.

[70] Ibid., 2 :247.

[71] Lameth, *Mémoires,* 112, cited by Taillimite, 335.

[72] *Mémoires*,3:336.

[73] Journal de Paris, cited by Charavay,314.

[74] Ibid., 326. Dumas, 2 :248.

[75] Lameth, *Mémoires*, 112, cited by Taillimite, 335.

[76] Aulard, La Société de Jacobins, cited by Charavay, 312.

[77] Dumas,2:248.

[78] Mémoires,3: 336. Note by Lafayette.

[79] Morris,312.

[80] *Mémoires*, 3:339,340.

[81] *Le Moniteur*,13:69, cited by Charavay,315.

[82] Lafayette, letter to Lückner, July 2, 1792, camp at Maubeuge, *Mémoires*,3:363,354; Note: The date is really July 3, according to Charavay,315.

[83] *Archives historiques de la guerre, armée du Nord*, cited by Charavay,315,316.

[84] *Mémoires*,3:341.

[85] Ibid.

[86] Taillimite,338.

[87] Bois,223.

[88] Ibid., 222.

[89] Dumas,2:361.

[90] Ibid.

[91] *Mémoires*,3:349.

[92] Ibid.,3:352.

[93] Lückner, letter to Lafayette, July 19, 1792, en route to Châlons, *Mémoires*, 3:368,369.

[94] Lückner, letter to Lafayette, July 25,1792, Strasbourg, *Mémoires*, 3:369,370.

[95] Lafayette, letter to d'Abancourt, July 29, 1792, Longwy, *Mémoires*,3:445-448.

[96] Dumas,2:447-449.

[97] Ibid., 2 :452.

[98] *Mémoires*,3:375.

[99] *Ibid.*, 3 :388.

[100] Ferrières, 3:198.

[101] *Mémoires*,3:388,389.

[102] Lafayette, letter to d'Abancourt, August 12, 1792, camp near Sédan, *Mémoires*, 3 :460,461,462.

[103] *Le Moniteur*, V : XIII, Chuquet, *La Première Invasion Prussienne*, cited by Charavay,55.

[104] *Mémoires*, 3:387.

[105] Ibid.,3:391.

[106] Cloquet, cited by Charavay, 326.

[107] The decree of the Provisional Executive Council, August 17, 1792, Paris, cited by Charavay.

[108] Original letter reprinted, Chambrun, *Les prisons des Lafayette, dix ans de courage et d'amour*, 89.

Chapter 45

[1] Note: On August 19, the National Assembly debates: 'that General Lafayette has used the most odious maneuvers to sway the army he had been entrusted with…is accused of the crime of rebellion against the law, of conspiracy against liberty and treason towards the nation.' The motion is passed. *Archives parlementaires*, August 19, 1792, Paris, cited by Bois, 228.

[2] *Mémoires*,3:402.

[3] Lafayette, letter to Madame de Lafayette, August 21, 1792, Rochefort, *Mémoires*, 3:466.

[4] Letter of Lafayette to the council at Sedan, *Mémoires*, 3:403.

[5] Lafayette, letter to La Rochefoucauld, August 25, 1792, Nivelles, *Mémoires*, 3:472.

[6] Anecdotal.

[7] Declaration by Lafayette and his compatriots, Rochefort, August 19, 1792; cited by Charavay, 331. Note: Du Roure and five other officers join Lafayette's group at Rochefort, probably after their arrest, according to Spalding, *Lafayette, Prisoner of State*, 243.

[8] Lafayette, letter to Adrienne, August 21, 1792, Rochefort, *Mémoires*, 3:465-467.

[9] *Mémoires, Guerre et Proscription*, 3:410,411.

[10] Chasteler, report to Thugut, July 26,1792, in Büdinger, cited by Spalding,13.

[11] *Mémoires, Guerre et Proscription*, 3:410.

[12] Lafayette, letter to La Rochefoucauld, August 26, 1792, Nivelles, *Mémoires*, 3:473.

[13] Lafayette, letter to Madame de Chavaniac, August 25, 1792, Nivelles, *Mémoires*,3:474-476.

[14] Lafayette, letter to the duc de La Rochefoucauld, NIvelles, August 25, 26, 1792, *Mémoires*,3 :467-473. Note: the duc de La Rochefoucauld never receives the letter. He is killed by a mob at Gisors in front of his wife and mother.

[15] Lafayette, letter to William Short, August 26, 1792, Nivelles, cited by Charavay, Pièces justificatives, 582.

[16] Lafayette, letter to Madame d'Hénin, August 27, 1792, Nivelles, *Mémoires*, 3:477-481.

[17] Cloquet, 1:13.

[18] Chambrun, 96,97.

[19] Lafayette, letter to Madame d'Hénin, September 3, 1792, Arlon, *Mémoires,* 4 :215.

[20] Espinchal, *Journal of the comte d'Espinchal,* 331 (1-11 September 1792 entry, cited by Spalding, 17.

[21] *Mémoires, Guerre et Proscription,* 3:413.

[22] Lafayette, letter to Madame d'Hénin, November 16, 1793, Magdebourg, *Mémoires,* 4:250-252.

[23] Lafayette, letter to Archenholtz, September 21, 1793, *Lafayette Letters,* 38,39, cited by Spalding, 247.

[24] Lafayette, letter to Madame d'Hénin, September 16, 1792, Coblentz, *Mémoires,* 4:216-219.

Chapter 46

[1] *Le Moniteur,* October 4, 1792, XIV:110, cited by Charavay, 341.

[2] Madame de Lafayette, letter to Madame de Tessé, May 10, 1796, Olmütz, *Mémoires,* 4:270-284.

[3] Lafayette, letter to Madame d'Hénin, June 22, 1793, Magdebourg, *Correspondance inédite,* 196-266.nin

[4] Lafayette, words ascribed to Maubourg in a letter to Madame d'Hénin, March 13, 1793, Magdebourg, *Mémoires,*4:219-224.

[5] Madame de Lafayette, letter to Madame de Tessé, May 10, 1796, Olmütz; *Mémoires,* 4:270-284.

[6] Lafayette, secret letter to Madame d'Hénin, March 15, 1793, Magdebourg, *Correspondance inédite,*181-186.

[7] Lafayette, letter to Madame d'Hénin, March 13, 1793, Magdebourg, *Mémoires,* 4:219-224.

[8] Lafayette to Madame d'Hénin, March 13,1793, Magdebourg, *Mémoires,* 4:219-224. *The Letters of Lafayette and Jefferson,* 175. Note: these lines in this letter have been omitted from the same letter in *Mémoires,* cited above.

[9] Lafayette to Madame d'Hénin, March 15, 1793, Magdebourg; *Correspondance inédite,*181-186. *Mémoires,* 4:219-224.

[10] Ibid.

[11] Lafayette, letter to Madame d'Hénin, March 13,1793, Magdebourg; *Mémoires,*4:219-224.

[12] Lafayette, letter to Madame d'Hénin, June 22, 1793, Magdebourg, *Correspondance inédite,* 196-206.

[13] Lafayette, letter to Madame d'Hénin, March 13, 1793, Magdebourg; *Mémoires,*4:219-224. Note: the date is actually March 15, and has been modified and shortened, according to Chinard,112. It was found in Washington's papers in 1828 by Jared Sparks.

[14] Lafayette, letter to Archenholtz, March 27, 1793, Magdeburg; *Mémoires,* 4:224-231.

[15] Lafayette, letter to Adrienne, April 25, 1793, Magdebourg, *Correspondance inédite,* 193-196.

[16] Lafayette, letter to Madame d'Hénin, June 22, 1793, Magdebourg, *Correspondance inédite,*196-206.

[17] Lafayette, letter to Madame d'Hénin, June 22, 1793, Magdebourg; *Mémoires,*4:231-239.

[18] Spalding, 58.

[19] Lafayette, letter to Madame d'Hénin, June 22, 1793, Magdeburg, *Mémoires,*4:231-239; *Correspondance inédite,* 196-206.

[20] Lafayette, letter to Pinckney, July 4, 1793, Magdebourg; *Mémoires,*4:239-243, *Correspondance inédite,* 206-210.

[21] Lafayette, secret letter to Madame d'Hénin, July 16, 1793, Magdebourg;*Correspondance inédite,* 215-221.

[22] Morgan, 362,363. Letter not found elsewhere.

[23] Lafayette, letter to Le Blanc, August 30, 1793, Magdebourg, Chambrun,122. (The original of this letter belongs to the Bostonian Society (Collection Colburn).

[24] Lafayette, letter to Madame d'Hénin, June 22, 1793, Magdebourg, *Correspondance inédite,* 196-206.

[25] Lafayette, open letter to Adrienne, October 2, 1793, Magdebourg, *Mémoires,*4:248,249. *Correspondance inédite,* 225-227.

[26] Lafayette, letter to Le Blanc, October 24, 1793, Magdebourg, Chambrun,126-134.

[27] Lafayette, secret letter to Madame d'Hénin, November 16, 1793, Magdebourg, *Correspondance inédite,* 228-236.

[28] Lafayette, secret letter to Madame d'Hénin, November 16, 1793, Magdebourg, November 16, 1793, *Correspondance inédite,* 228-236.

[29] Lafayette, secret letters to La Colombe, December 10, 1793, Magdebourg, *Correspondance inédite,* 236-242.

[30] Lafayette, secret letter to Pinckney, December 11, 1793, Magdebourg, *Correspondance inédite,*243-246.

[31] Lafayette, secret letter to Madame d'Hénin, December 16, 1793, Magdebourg, *Correspondance inédite,* 250-253.

[32] Lafayette, letter to Madame d'Hénin, January 3, 1794, Magdebourg, *Mémoires,* 4:255, 256. *Correspondance inédite,* 259-261.

[33] Lafayette, letter to La Colombe, January 3, 1794, Magdebourg, *Mémoires,* 4:256,257.

[34] Lafayette, letter to the king of Poland, January 3, 1794, Magdeburg, *Mémoires*, 4:258.

[35] Lafayette, letter to Madame de Maisonneuve, February 16, 1794, Neisse, *Correspondance inédite*, 263-265.

[36] Lafayette, letter to Madame d'Hénin, April 1, 1794, Neisse, *Correspondance inédite*, 270-275.

Chapter 47

[1] Madame de Lafayette, letter to Madame de Tessé, Olmütz, May 10, 1796, *Mémoires*, 4:276.

[2] Part of this description comes from the official report of Chasteler, July 26, 1797, Olmütz, Lasteyrie and Noailles Lafayette, 451-456.

[3] Madame de Lafayette, letter to Madame de Tessé, May 10, 1796, Olmütz, *Mémoires*, 4 :270-284.

[4] Description taken from letter of La Tour Maubourg, Cloquet, 74-86.

[5] Official report of Chasteler, July 26, 1797, Olmûtz, Lasteyrie and Noailles Lafayette, 451-456.

[6] Cloquet,1:56.

[7] Chambrun,156,157.

[8] Spalding, 95.

[9] Chambrun, 156,157.

[10] Lafayette, letter to Bollmann, October,1794, Olmütz, *Mémoires*, 4:269.

[11] Lafayette, secret letter to Bollman, October 19, 1794, according to *Lettres inédites*, 287- 289, but is perhaps wrong.

[12] Madame de Lafayette, letter to Madame de Tessé, September 3, 1792, Arlon, *Mémoires*,4 :277.

[13] Lafayette mistook the words. His rescuers were shouting "Get to Hof." *Mémoires*, 4:269,270; note:1.

[14] *Mémoires*, 4:270, note.

[15] Lafayette's testimony, 9, December 11, 1794; 247v,255r-v, cited by Spalding, 296, note 33.

[16] Lafayette's testimony,9, December 11, 1794,247v,255r, Droxler's testimony, November 28, appendix T,161r-62r, Richter's testimony, November 28, appendix,162v-63v,HKR, cited by Spalding, 115..

[17] Richter to local lawcourt, November 9, 1794,43v/b, cited by Spalding,117.

[18] Madame de Lafayette, letter to Madame de Tessé, May 10, 1796, Olmütz*; Mémoires*, 4:270-284. Moires,

[19] Ibid.

[20] Cloquet,1:56

[21] Madame de Lafayette, Letter to Madame de Tessé, May 10,1796, Olmütz; Mémoires, 4: 270-284.

[22] Ibid., 4 :270-278.

[23] Lafayette's testimony, December 9, 10,1794, 248r-50r, HKR2, cited by Spalding,129.

[24] Lafayette's testimony, December 10, 1794,249v-50r, HKR2, cited by Spalding, 129.

[25] Ibid.

[26] Madame de Lafayette, letter to Madame de Tessé, May 10, 1796, Olmütz, *Mémoires*, 4 :270-284.

[27] Maubourg, letter to Cadignan, July 26, 1795; Washington, *Writings of Washington*, 11:494; cited by Spalding.

[28] Lafayette believed this and informed Huger on his American trip in 1824 but Spalding says there was no basis for it, Spalding,138.

[29] Arco developed an unexpected relationship with Huger according to Spalding, 134.

[30] Adrienne, letter to Madame de Tessé, May 10, 1796, Olmütz, *Mémoires*, 4:270-284.

[31] Lasteyrie, Virginie de Lafayette*, Life of Madame de Lafayette*, 342, Spalding,147.

[32] The words are from Adrienne's letter to Washington, Lasteyrie, Virginie de Lafayette, 317-322.

[33] Lasteyrie, Virginie de Lafayette, 341.

[34] Ibid., 297.

[35] Ibid., 298.

[36] Ibid., 310.

[37] Ibid., 313.

[38] Ibid., 321.

[39] Ibid, 322.

[40] This account is taken from that of Lasteyrie, Virginie de Lafayette,323-336.

[41] Ibid., 353,354.

[42] Ferraris, letter to Adrienne, December 27, 1795, Vienna, Lasteyrie, Virginie de Lafayette, 344,345.

[43] Ferraris, letter to Adrienne, January 26, 1796, Lasteyrie, Virginie de Lafayette, 350,351.

[44] Adrienne, letter to the Emperor, April 4, 1796, Olmütz, Lasteyrie, Virgine de Lafayette, 355,356.

[45] Lasteyrie, Virginie de Lafayette, 361.

[46] Ducoudray Holstein, *Memoirs of Gilbert Motier La Fayette*, 262.

[47] Document drafted by Anastasie de Lafayette, letter from Collection Fabius, cited by Maurois, 305.

⁴⁸ Adrienne, letter to Madame d'Hénin, July 25, 1796, Olmütz, *Mémoires*, 4:290-293.
⁴⁹ Ibid.
⁵⁰ Lafayette, dictated by him to his former aides-de-camp in England, June 24, 1796, Olmütz, *Mémoires*,4:287-290.
⁵¹ Adrienne, letter to Pillet, June 22? 1796, Olmütz, Collection Fabius, cited by Maurois,311.
⁵² Adrienne, letter to Madame d'Hénin, September 15, 1796, Olmütz, letter from Fondation Josée et René de Chambrun, cited by Maurois, 313.
⁵³Adrienne, letter to Parish, dictated by her to Anastasie, December 1796, Olmütz, letter from Fondation Josée et René de Chambrun, cited by Maurois, 315.
⁵⁴ Lasteyrie, Virginie de Lafayette, 359.
⁵⁵ Adrienne, letter to George, February 12, 1797, Olmütz, letter from Collection Fabius, cited by Maurois, 315.
⁵⁶ Spalding,193.
⁵⁷ Ruault, *Gazette*, 294-300, cited by Taillimite, 376.
⁵⁸ Adrienne, letter to Pauline, May 19, 1797, cited by de Chambrun,285.
⁵⁹ Spalding, 295.
⁶⁰ Virginie Lasteyrie de Lafayette, 362.
⁶¹ Spalding, 210.
⁶² Ibid.
⁶³ Ibid., 211.
⁶⁴ Adrienne, on the visit of Chasteler, July 25, 1797, *Mémoires*, 4:294-296.
⁶⁵ Adrienne, letter to nos chers amis in Olmütz, July 25, 1797, Olmütz, cited by Spalding,211.
⁶⁶ Lasteyrie, Virginie de Lafayette, 363.
⁶⁷ Parish was no longer American consul but had agreed to receive Lafayette and the others.
⁶⁸ Louis Romeuf, letter to Lafayette, August 9, 1797, Vienna, *Mémoires*, 4:298-301.
⁶⁹ Lafayette, letter to Louis Romeuf, August 15, 1797, Olmütz, *Correspondance inédite*, 309,310.
⁷⁰ Adrienne, letter to Pillet, September 9, 1797, Olmütz, *Correspondance inédite*, 310-320.

Chapter 48
¹ Lasteyrie, Virginie de Lafayette, 364.
² Lasteyrie, Virginie de Lafayette, 365.
³ Lafayette, letter to Masclet, December 15, 1797, Lemkuhlen, *Mémoires,* 4:388-392.
⁴ Lasteyrie, Virginie de Lafayette, 365.
⁵ Lafayette, his response to George Williams, October 4, 1797, on the merchant ship, the *John*, moored at Harburg, *Correspondance inédite*,324,325.
⁶ Varnhagen von Ense, his childhood account of Lafayette's arrival at Hamburg, cited by Spalding, 225,226.
⁷ Anonymous, 1797b;626-629, cited by Spalding, 226.
⁸ Varnhagen von Ense, his childhood account of Lafayette's arrival, cited by Spalding, 225,226
⁹ Parish, his account, cited by Morgan,389,390.
¹⁰ Lafayette, letter to Masclet, October 11,1797, Witmöld, *Mémoires*, 4:380-386.
¹¹ Ibid.
¹² Ibid.
¹³ Souvenirs, *Mémoires,* 4:368,369.
¹⁴ Lafayette, letter to Masclet, October 11, 1797, Witmöld, *Mémoires*, 4:380-386.
¹⁵ Souvenirs, *Mémoires*, 4:370.
¹⁶ Lafayette, La Tour Maubourg and Bureaux de Pusy, letter to Bonaparte, October 6, 1797, Hamburg, *Mémoires*, 4 :369,370 ; Lasteyrie, Virginie de Lafayette, 366-368.
¹⁷ Lafayette, letter to Washington, October 6, 1797, Hamburg, *The Letters of Lafayette to Washington*, 363-365.
¹⁸ Lafayette, letter to Huger, October 8, 1797, Hamburg, *Mémoires,* 4:375-377.
¹⁹ Lafayette, letter to Masclet, October 11, 1797, Witmöld, *Mémoires*,4:380-386.
²⁰ Mémoires, 5:7.
²¹ Lafayette, letter to Masclet, October 11, 1797, Witmöld, *Mémoires*,4 380-386.
²² Lafayette, letter to Madame d'Hénin, letter from Fondation Josée et René de Chambrun, cited by Maurois, 340,341.
²³ Lafayette, letter to Masclet, October 11, 1797, Witmöld, *Mémoires,* 4:380.
²⁴ Lasteyrie, Virginie de Lafayette, 373.

[25] Pauline, letter to Rosalie de Grammont, letter from Fondation Josée et René de Chambrun, cited by Maurois,337, 338.e

[26] Callet, A., Anne-Paul-Dominique de Noailles, marquise de Montagu,252,253, letter from Fondation Josée et René de Chambrun, cited by Maurois, 337.

[27] Callet, A., Anne-Paule-Dominique de Noailles, marquise de Montagu,252,253, 304,305, cited by Maurois, 337, 338.

[28] Unpublished letter, Collection Fabius, cited by Maurois, 340,341.

[29] Lafayette, letter to Alexandre Lameth, November 30, 1797, Lemkühlen, *Mémoires*,4:386-388.

[30] Lafayette, letter to Washington, December 27, 1797, Lemkühlen, *The Letters of Lafayette to Washington*, 363-365.

[31] Lafayette, letter to Masclet, January 7, 1789, Lemkühlen, *Mémoires*, 4:401,402.

[32] Lafayette, letter to Clarkson, January 27, 1798, Lemkühlen, *Mémoires*, 4:402-404.

[33] Maurois, 350.

[34] Washington, letter to Lafayette, October 8, 1797, Mount Vernon, *Mémoires*, 4 :372-374.

[35] Lafayette, letter to Madame de Chavaniac, March 7,1798, Lemkühlen, letter from Fondation Josée et René de Chambrun, cited by Maurois, 351.

[36] Lasteyrie, Virginie de Lafayette,375.

[37] Callet, A., 312,313, letter from Fondation Josée et René de Chambrun, cited by Maurois, 352.

[38] Adrienne, letter to Madame de Chavaniac, March 22, 1798, Lemkühlen, letter from Collection Fabius, cited by Maurois,353.

[39] Lasteyrie, Virginie de Lafayette, 375.

[40] Ibid., 376.

[41] Lafayette, letter to Washington, May 20, 1798, Witmöld, *The Letters of Lafayette to Washington*,369-372.

[42] Ibid.

[43] Ibid.

[44] Unpublished letter, Collection Fabius, cited by Maurois,352.

[45] Lafayette, letter to Washington, August 20, 1798, Witmöld, *The Letters of Lafayette to Washington*, 373-377.

[46] Hamilton, letter to Lafayette, April 28, 1798, New York, *Mémoires*, 4:410,411.

[47] Lafayette, letter to Washington, August 20, 1798, Witmöld, *The Letters of Lafayette to Washington*, 373-377.

[48] Lafayette, letter to Adrienne, November 1, 1798, Witmöld, *Correspondance inédite*, 356-360.

[49] Lafayette, letter to Adrienne, November 9, 1798, Witmold, *Correspondance inédite*, 361-364.

[50] Washington, letter to Lafayette, December 25, 1798, Mount Vernon; *Mémoires*,4:438-444.

[51] Lafayette, letter to Masclet, March 7, 1799, Vianen, *Mémoires*, 5 : 9.

[52] Ibid., 5 :7-13.

[53] Lafayette, letter to Adrienne, May 16, 1799, Vianen, *Mémoires*, 5:47,48.

[54] Lafayette, letter to Washington, May 9, 1799, Vianen, *Mémoires*, 5:36-41.

[55] Lafayette, letter to Louis Romeuf, May 11, 1799, Vianen, *Mémoires*, 5:41-47.

[56] Lafayette, letter to Adrienne, May 16, 1799, Vianen, *Mémoires*, 5:47,48.

[57] Ibid.

[58] George, Letter to Lafayette, cited by Maurois,373.

[59] Ibid.

[60] Lafayette, letter to Adrienne, May 29, 1799, Vianen, *Mémoires*, 5:48-52.

[61] Lafayette, letter to Adrienne, July 1, 199, Vianen, *Mémoires*, 5 :52-54.

[62] Lafayette, letter to Adrienne, July 4, 1799, Vianen, *Mémoires*, 5:61-63.

[63] Lafayette, letter to La Tour Maubourg, October 17, 1799, Utrecht, *Mémoires*, 5 :99-139.

[64] Lasteyrie, Virginie de Lafayette, 380,381.

[65] Lafayette, letter to La Tour Maubourg, October 17, 1799, Utrecht, *Mémoires*, 5 : 99-139.

[66] Ibid.

[67] Ibid.

[68] Lafayette, letter to Adrienne, August 5, 1799, Vianen, *Mémoires*, 5:70-72.

[69] Lafayette, letter to Adrienne, September 4, 1799, Utrecht, *Mémoires*, 5:77-79.

[70] Lafayette, letter to Adrienne, September 12, 1799, Utrecht, *Mémoires*, 5:79-81.

[71] Lafayette, letter to Adrienne, September 16, 1799, Utrecht, *Mémoires*, 5:82-84.

[72] Lafayette, letter to Adrienne, September 19, 1799, Utrecht, *Mémoires*, 5:84-86.

[73] Lafayette, letter to Adrienne, October 13, 1799, Vianen, *Mémoires*, 5:97-99.

[74] Lafayette, letter to La Tour Maubourg, October 17, 1799, Utrecht, *Mémoires*,5:99-139.

[75] Lafayette, letter to Adrienne, October 30, 1799, Vianen, *Mémoires,* 5:143-146.

[76] Lafayette, letter to Bonaparte, October 30, 1799, Utrecht, *Mémoires,* 5:146,147.

[77] The former November 9.

[78] Lafayette, mes rapports avec le premier consul; *Mémoires,* 5 :153.

Chapter 49

[1] Lafayette, letter to Sieyès, Paris, 1799, *Mémoires,* 5:154.

[2] Lafayette, letter to Bonaparte, Paris, 1799, *Mémoires,* 5:154.

[3] *Mes rapports avec le premier consul, Mémoires,* 5:155

[4] Ibid.

[5] Ibid., 5:155,156.

[6] Ibid., 5:156.

[7] Lafayette, letter to Mademoiselle de Chavaniac, December 1, 1799, Fontenay-en- Brie, letter from Fondation Josée et Renée de Chambrun, cited by Maurois, 395, 396.

[8] *Mes rapports avec le premier consul, Mémoires,* 5:156.

[9] Lafayette, letter to Mademoiselle de Chavaniac, December 1, 1799, Fontenay-en-Brie, letter from Fondation Josée et René de Chambrun, cited by Maurois, 395,396.

[10] Cloquet, 1:165.

[11] Ibid., 1 :169.

[12] Lafayette, letter to Masclet, December 1801, Cloquet, 1:162.

[13] Maurois, 402.

[14] Ibid., 403.

[15] Cloquet, 170. Bois,294,295.

[16] Maurois,408.

[17] *Le Moniteur,* February 12, 1780. *Mes rapports avec le premier consul, Mémoires,* 5:157, note 1.

[18] Lafayette, letter to Jefferson, February 10, 1800, La Grange, *The letters of Lafayette and Jefferson,* 207-210.

[19] Unpublished letter, Collection Fabius, cited by Maurois, 411.

[20] Cloquet,1:107.

[21] *Mes rapports avec le premier consul, Mémoires,* 5:164,165.

[22] Lafayette, letter to Adrienne, August 14, 1800, Chavaniac, Fondation Josée et René de Chambrun, cited by Maurois,415.

[23] Lafayette, letter to Adrienne, August 1, 1800, Chavaniac, Fondation Josée et René de Chambrun, cited by Maurois, 414.

[24] Lafayette, letter to Adrienne, August 14, 1800, Chavaniac, Fondation Josée et René de Chambrun, cited by Maurois, 415.

[25] Maurois, 413.

[26] Lafayette, letter to Jean-Antoine Huguet, August 13, 1800, Chavaniac, *Pièces justificatives,* cited in Charavay,586,587.

[27] Lafayette, letter to Adrienne, 1800, Chavaniac, Fondation Josée et René de Chambrun, cited by Maurois, 417.

[28] Lafayette, letter to Adrienne, Fondation Josée et René de Chambrun, cited by Maurois, 418.

[29] *Mes rapports avec le premier consul, Mémoires,* 5:166.

[30] Ibid., 5:166,167.

[31] Lafayette, letter to Adrienne, December 2, 1800, cited by Maurois, 422,423.

[32] *Mémoires, Mes rapports avec le premier consul,* 5:178.

[33] Lasteyrie, Virginie de Lafayette, cited by Maurois, 421.

[34] *Mes rapports avec le premier consul, Mémoires,* 5:182,183.

[35] Ibid., 5:185,186.

[36] Lafayette, letter to Jefferson, June 21, 1801, Cirey, *The Letters of Lafayette and Jefferson,* 213,214.

[37] *Mes rapports avec le premier consul, Mémoires,* 5:195,196.

[38] Ibid., *Mémoires,* 5:180,181.

[39] Lafayette, letter to Adrienne, April 10, 1802, Fondation Josée et René de Chambrun, cited by Maurois, 433.

[40] Lafayette, letter to Bonaparte, May 20, 1802, La Grange, *Mes rapports avec le premier consul, Mémoires,* 199,200.

[41] *Mes rapports avec le premier consul, Mémoires,* 5:200

[42] Lasteyrie, Virginie de Lafayette, 387.

[43] *Mes rapports avec le premier consul, Mémoires,* 5:203.

⁴⁴ Lasteyrie, Virginie de Lafayette, 398,390,391.

⁴⁵ Cloquet, 1:20.

⁴⁶ *Mes rapports avec le premier consul, Mémoires*, 5:204.

⁴⁷ Lafayette, letter to Madame de Chavaniac, April 29, 1803, Fondation Josée et René de Chambrun, cited by Maurois, 437.

⁴⁸ Lafayette, letter to Jefferson, September 1, 1803, La Grange, *The Letters of Lafayette and Jefferson*, 223,224.

⁴⁹ *Mes rapports avec le premier consul, Mémoires*, 5:208.

⁵⁰ Jefferson, letter to Lafayette, November 4, 1803, Washington, *The Letters of Lafayette and Jefferson*, 225,226.

⁵¹ Lafayette, letter to Jefferson, February 26, 1804, La Grange, *The Letters of Lafayette and Jefferson*, 227-229.

⁵² *Mes rapports avec le premier consul, Mémoires*, 5:210,211.

⁵³ Ibid., 5:217,218.

⁵⁴ Lafayette, letter to Jefferson, July 1,1804, Draveil, *The Letters of Lafayette and Jefferson*, 225.

⁵⁵ Lafayette, letter to Adrienne, July 9, 1804, Cirey, Fondation Josée et René de Chambrun, cited by Maurois, 443.

⁵⁶ *Mémoires, Mes rapports avec le premier consul*, 5: 218. Note: La Légion d'Honneur was instituted on May 19, 1802, for a citizen of merit.

⁵⁷ *Mes rapports avec le premier consul, Mémoires,* 5:219.

⁵⁸ Ibid., 5:221.

⁵⁹ Lafayette, letter to Jefferson, October 8, 1804, La Grange, *The Letters of Lafayette and Jefferson,*230-233.

⁶⁰ *Mes Rapports avec le premier consul, Mémoires*, 5:222.

⁶¹ Lafayette, letter to Jefferson, October 8, 1804, La Grange, *The letters of Lafayette and Jefferson*, 230-233.

⁶² Maurois,456.

⁶³ Lafayette, letter to Jefferson, April 22, 1805, Auteuil, *The Letters of Lafayette and Jefferson*, 236-239.

⁶⁴ Lafayette, letter to Adrienne, August 20, 1805, Chavaniac, Fondation Josée et René de Chambrun, cited by Maurois, 446.

⁶⁵ *Mes rapports avec le premier consul, Mémoires,* 5: 223,224.

⁶⁶ Ibid., 5:232,233.

⁶⁷ Lafayette, letter to Jefferson, February 20, 1807, La Grange, *Mémoires*, 5:265,266.

⁶⁸ Lasteyrie, Virginie de Lafayette, 393.

⁶⁹ Lafayette, letter to La Tour Maubourg, January 1808, Lasteyrie, Virginie de Lafayette, 423-432.

⁷⁰ Ibid.

⁷¹ Ibid.

⁷² Ibid.

⁷³ Lafayette, letter to La Tour Maubourg, January,1808. The account of Adrienne's death is taken from this letter from the Fondation Josée et René de Chambrun, cited for the first time in full by Maurois, 458-473.

Chapter 50

¹ Lafayette, letter to Maubourg, January,1808, *Mémoires*, 5:275-281.

² Lafayette, letter to Masclet, La Grange, 1808, cited by Cloquet,1:33,34.

³ Cloquet,1:33.

⁴ Maurois, 481.

⁵ Lafayette, letter to Jefferson, April 8, 1808, La Grange, *The Letters of Lafayette and Jefferson*, 272-275.

⁶ Ibid.

⁷ *Mes rapports avec le premier consul, Mémoires,*5:237,238.

⁸ *Pièces et souvenirs, Mémoires,*5:298.

⁹ Lafayette, letter to Jefferson, July 28, 1808, La Grange, *The Letters of Lafayette and Jefferson*, 282-284.

¹⁰ Ibid.

¹¹ Lafayette, letter to Jefferson, February 20, 1809, La Grange, *The Letters of Lafayette and Jefferson*, 284,285.

¹² Lafayette, letter to Jefferson, October 26, 1809, Paris, *The Letters of Lafayette and Jefferson*, 291-293.

¹³ Lafayette, letter to Jefferson, February 20, 1810, Paris, *The Letters of Lafayette and Jefferson*, 296-300.

¹⁴ Lafayette, letter to Jefferson, November 16, 1810, Paris; *The Letters of Lafayette and Jefferson,*318-321.

[15] Lafayette, letter to Jefferson, December 26, 1811, La Grange; *The Letters of Lafayette and Jefferson,* 330-332.

[16] *Pièces et souvenirs, Mémoires,*5:302,303.

[17] Ibid., 5:302.

[18] Lafayette, letter to Jefferson, July 4, 1812, La Grange, *The Letters of Lafayette and Jefferson,*336,337.

[19] *Pièces et souvenirs,* 1814-1815; *Mémoires,* 5:300.

[20] Ibid.

[21] Lafayette, letter to Jefferson, August 14, 1814, La Grange, *The Letters of Lafayette and Jefferson,* 340-347.

[22] *Pièces et souvenirs, Mémoires,*5:303.

[23] Ibid., 5:305.

[24] Ibid.

[25] Ibid., 5:349.

[26] Ibid.,5:311,312.

[27] Lafayette, letter to Jefferson, August 14, 1814, La Grange, *The Letters of Lafayette and Jefferson,* 340-347.

[28] *Pièces et souvenirs, Mémoires,* 5: 369,370.

[29] *Mémoires,*5:398.

[30] Lafayette, letter to Madame d'Hénin, May 15, 1815, *Mémoires,*5:497-502.

[31] *Pièces et souvenirs, Mémoires,*5:414.

[32] Ibid., 5:415.

[33] Ibid., 5:415-419.

[34] Ibid.

[35] Ibid., 5: 424.

[36] Lafayette, letter to his family, (probably Emilie de Tracy), June 8, 1815, *Mémoires,*5:505.

[37] Ibid.

[38] Lafayette, letter to his family, June 9, 1815, Paris, *Mémoires,*5:507-510.

[39] Lafayette, letter to his family, June 14, 1815, Paris, *Mémoires,* 5:511,512.

[40] Lafayette, letter to Madame d'Henin, June 16, 1815, Paris, *Mémoires,* 5: 513,514.

[41] *Pièces et souvenirs, Mémoires,*5:451.

[42] Ibid., 5:453,454.

[43] Bardoux, 242,243.

[44] *Pièces et souvenirs, Mémoires,*5:455.

[45] Ibid., 5:456,457.

[46] Ibid., 5:455,456,457.

[47] Ibid., 5:463.

[48] Ibid.

[49] The whole of this account comes from *Pièces et souvenirs, Mémoires,* 5:469-474.

[50] Ibid., 5:474-476.

[51] Lafayette, letter to Madame d'Hénin, July 11, 1815, Paris, *Mémoires,*5:525-527.

[52] Lafayette, letter to Jefferson, October 10, 1815, La Grange, *The Letters of Lafayette and Jefferson,* 375-377.

[53] Lafayette, letter to Jefferson, January 21,1816, La Grange, *The Letters of Lafayette and Jefferson,* 378,379.

[54] Cloquet,2:43-45.

[55] Anecdotal.

[56] Taillimite, 442. Correspondance de M. de Rémusat,5:153, cited by Charavay,414.

[57] *Correspondance et Discours, Mémoires,* 6:34-38.

[58] Duchesse de Broglie, *Journal,* cited by Taillimite,443.

[59] *Correspondance et Discours,* March 8,1820, Séance, *Mémoires,* 6:67-70.

[60] *Correspondance et Discours,* March 27, 1820, Séance, *Mémoires,*6:75-85.

[61] Bardoux, 274.

[62] Bardoux, 275,276.

[63] Lafayette, letter, July 5, 1820, *Correspondance et Discours,* Mémoires, 6:91,92.

[64] Lafayette, letter to Monroe, July 20, 1820, Paris, *Correspondance et Discours, Mémoires,* 6:93.

[65] *Mémoires, Sociétés Secrètes,* 137.

[66] *Mémoires, Sociétés Secrètes,*135, Note 1.

[67] Fanny Wright, letter to Lafayette, July 16, 1821, Chicago, cited by Kramer, 155.

[68] Bardoux, 286,287.

[69] Ibid.,293.

[70] Lafayette, letter to Wright, May-June 1823? Chicago, *Gottschalk et al., Lafayette Guide to Letters*, cited by Kramer,159.

[71] Bardoux, 295.

[72] Lafayette, letter to the editor of the *Constitutionnel*, March 9, 1823, Paris, *Mémoires,*6:155,156.

[73] Lafayette, letter to President Monroe, April, 1824, La Grange, *Mémoires*, 6:163,164.

[74] Kramer,161, says 'that the fullest account of the conflicts, proposals and complex negotiations' which went on before Fanny's visit to the US, is in Fanny Wright to Camilla, June 10, 1824, in Waterman, *Frances Wright*,79-82, copy in Wolfson Papers.

Chapter 51

[1] Parker, Andrew Amos,3.

[2] Ibid., 20.

[3] Ibid., 20.

[4] Levasseur, 1:11.

[5] Ibid., 1 :12.

[6] Ibid., 1 :50.

[7] *Mémoires,*6:174.

[8] Levasseur,1:55.

[9] Ibid., 1 :54.

[10] Lafayette, letter to Jefferson, October 1, 1824, Philadelphia, *The Letters of Lafayette and Jefferson,*421-423.

[11] Levasseur,1:57.

[12] Ibid.,1 :61.

[13] Ibid.,1 :59

[14] Ibid.,1 :61.

[15] *Mémoires,* 6:179.

[16] The American Journal, *Niles Register,* says Curtis gave Lafayette the ring before he entered the sepulchre, *Mémoires,* 6:178,179. Levasseur said it was after he left it, Levasseur;1:63.

[17] Levasseur,1:64.

[18] Ibid.

[19] Ibid., 1 :68.

[20] Ibid.

[21] *Mémoires,* 6:181.

[22] Levasseur,1:77.

[23] Brodie, *Thomas Jefferson, an Intimate History,* 481. An account by Israel Jefferson which first appeared in the *Pike County Republican,* December 25,1873, cited by Diane Windham Shaw, essay in *Symbol in Two Worlds,*40.

[24] *Mémoires,* 6:184.

[25] Levasseur,1:79.

[26] Ibid., 2 :64.

[27] Ibid., 2 :84.

[28] Ibid., 2 :157.

[29] Ibid., 2 :189.

[30] Ibid., 2 :163.

[31] Ibid., 2 :172.

[32] Ibid., 2 :183.

[33] Ibid., 2 :203.

[34] Ibid., 2 :205.

[35] Ibid., 2 :248.

[36] Ibid., 2 :256.

[37] Frances Wright remains in the US in order to attempt social reforms concerning slavery.

Chapter 52

[1] The description of Lafayette's homecoming is from Cloquet, 2:55,56.

[2] Lafayette, letter to Adams, October 27,1825, La Grange, *Mémoires,*6:222.

[3] Cloquet,2:37.

[4] Lafayette, letter to Wright, March 29,1826,Wolfson Papers, cited by Kramer, 168.

[5] Lafayette, speech at the tomb of Manuel, October 24, 1827, Père-Lachaise Cemetery, *Mémoires, Correspondance*,6:249.

[6] Lafayette, letter to the President of the Tribunal of Police, September 17, 1827, La Grange, *Mémoires, Correspondances*,6:248-250.

[7] Taillimite,477.

[8] *Mémoires* 6:325.

[9] *Mémoires*,6:461.

[10] Bardoux, 344.

[11] *Mémoires*, speech at Grenoble, 6:327,328.

[12] Bardoux, 345,346.

[13] Castries, 409.

[14] *Mémoires,* 6:331, cited by Castries, 410.

[15] *Mémoires*, 6:333, cited by Castries, 410.

[16] Taillimite, 481.

[17] Castries, 414.

[18] Brand Whitlock, 2:307.

[19] Ibid.

[20] Ibid.

[21] Laffitte, *Mémoires*,125-133, cited by Taillimite, 485,486.

[22] *Mémoires*, 6 :469.

[23] Bérard, *Souvenirs historiques sur la Révolution de 1830* (Paris,1834), 75.

[24] Bérard, 64.

[25] Lafayette, letter to his family, July 28, 1830, Paris, *Mémoires*,6:382.

[26] Sarrans, *Memoirs of General Lafayette and of the French Revolution of 1830*,1:221.

[27] Lafayette, letter to his family, Wednesday, July 28,1830, Paris, *Mèmoires,* 6:382.

[28] Sarrans,1:228.

[29] Bérard, 77.

[30] Sarrans,1:230.

[31] Ibid.

[32] Ibid.,1:231.

[33] Ibid.

[34] Ibid.,1:232.

[35] *Mémoires, procès verbal* of the meeting, at the house of Laffitte, Thursday, July 29, 6:388.

[36] Bérard,460. Sarrans, 1:221.

[37] *Mémoires*, 6:389.

[38] Ibid., 6 :390,391.

[39] *Le Moniteur*, Order of the Day, July 29,1830, cited in *Mémoires*, 6:391.

[40] Ibid.,6:391,392.

[41] Bardoux, 360,361. Note: Bardoux says Lafayette did not say it is too late, the words frequently ascribed to him.

[42] Lafayette, letter, July 30, 1830, Paris, *Mémoires*, 6:393,394.

[43] Lafayette, letter to the electors of Meaux, June 13, 1831, La Grange, 6:576-591.

[44] Bérard, 110.

[45] Bardoux,362.

[46] Lafayette, letter to the electors of Meaux, June 13, 1831, La Grange, *Mémoires*, 6:576-591.

[47] Bardoux,363; Bérard, 117.

[48] *Mémoires*,6:405, note 1.

[49] Bardoux, 364.

[50] Ibid.

[51] Ibid., 366.

[52] Guizot, *Mémoires*, cited by Charavay,473.

[53] Bérard, 129,130.

[54] Ibid., 130.

[55] Whitlock, 11:333.

[56] Bérard,130.

[57] Mémoires,6 :402.

[58] Proclamation by Lafayette to the Citizens of Paris, July 31, 1830, Paris, *Mémoires*, 6:408,409.

[59] Proclamation to the French Army by Lafayette, July 31, 1830, Hôtel de Ville, *Mémoires*,6:407.

[60] Document from Lafayette, July 31, 1830, Paris, *Mémoires*,6:405.

[61] Unfinished note of Lafayette on July 31 reception, *Mémoires*, 6:410.

[62] *Ibid.*

[63] Bérard, 148.

[64] *Mémoires*, 6 :410

[65] A decree of the Municipal Commission and Lafayette, July 31, 1830, Hôtel de Ville, *Mémoires,* 6:405,406.

[66] *Mémoires,*6:410.

[67] Lafayette, letter to the electors of Meaux, June 13, 1831, La Grange, 576-591.

[68] Programme de l'Hôtel de Ville, ou récit de ce qui s'est passé depuis le 31 juillet jusqu'au 6 août, extrait de la *Tribune politique et littéraire,* article du 7 avril 1831, non démenti par le gouvernement, par Armand Marrast, Paris, Rouanet, 1831, cited by Charavay, 476.

[69] Odilon Barrot says that although he had never heard these words, the phrase 'a constitutional monarchy is the best of republics for France' was the exact thought of Lafayette, Barrot, *Mémoires,*1:126. Lafayette himself always denied the phrase, cited by Charavay,477. In a letter to General Bernard, August 17, 1830, Lafayette says in the new regime a 'very republican monarchy susceptible of improvement,' cited by Taillimite, 493.

[70] *Mémoires,*6 :580.

[71] Marrast, *Mémoires,* 1:7, cited by Charavay, 477,478.

[72] *Mémoires,* 6 :412.

[73] Ibid.

[74] Bérard, 163,164.

[75] Ibid., 157.

[76] Ibid., 171.

[77] *Mémoires,* 6 :413.

[78] Sarrans, 1:299,300.

[79] Schonen, Maison and Odilon Barrot, letter to lieutenant-général, Bérard,174.

[80] Bérard,1:188.

[81] Ibid.,1: 203.

[82] *Mémoires,* 6 :416-418.

[83] Ibid., 6:419.

[84] Lafayette, letter, 5 o'clock in the morning, August 7, 1830, Paris, *Mémoires,* 6:419.

[85] Bérard,1:272,273.

[86] Bérard, 1:345-381.

[87] *Mémoires,* 6 :420,421.

[88] Bérard,1 :383-389.

[89] Sarrans, 1:311.

[90] Bardoux, 381.

[91] The description of the coronation comes from Bérard, 400-411.

[92] Order of the Day, August 10, 1830, Paris, Sarrans, 1:312,313.

[93] Sarrans, 1:314.

[94] *Mémoires,*6:423,424.

[95] Lafayette, letter, August 12, 1830, Paris, *Mémoires,*6:421,422.

[96] Words of Lafayette spoken at the banquet given by the city of Paris for him, August 15, 1830, Paris, *Mémoires,* 6 :424,425.

[97] Lafayette's speech for the abolition of the death penalty, August 17, 1830, *Mémoires,*6:426,427.

[98] Order to the National Guards, August 20, 1830, *Mémoires,*6:431,432.

[99] Taillimite, 496.

[100] Speech of Louis-Philippe on giving the flags to the soldiers at the Champ de Mars, August 29,1830; *Mémoires,* 6:429,430.

[101] Cloquet, 2:141,142.

[102] Sarrans,1:315,316; Lafayette, speech to the 7th legion of Paris, November 11, 1830, Paris, *Mémoires,* 6 :458,459.

[103] Louis-Philippe, letter to Lafayette, August 29, 1830, *Mémoires,*6:430,431.

[104] Order of the Day, August 30, 1830, Mémoires, 6: 228,429.

[105] Sarrans, 2:11.

[106] *Mémoires,* 6:439,440.

[107] Lafayette, letter to Louis Philippe, September 27, 1830, Paris, *Mémoires,* 6:437,438.

[108] Lafayette, letter to the comte de Survilliers, November 26, 1830, Paris, *Mémoires,*6:473-475.

[109] Lafayette, letter to the king, October 2, 1830, *Mémoires,* 6:440,441.

[110] Lafayette speaking to the Chamber, October 5, 1830, *Mémoires,*6:443,444.

[111] Order of the Day, October 19, 1830, *Mémoires*, 6:448,450.

[112] Dumas, speech at the banquet given by the 7th legion of Paris, November 11, 1830, Paris, *Mémoires,* 6:457,458.

[113] Lafayette, letter, November 15, 1830, Paris, *Mémoires,*6:459,460.

[114] Sarrans, 2:51,52.

[115] Taillimite, 498.

[116] Whitlock, 351,352.

[117] Lafayette, letter to Joseph Bonaparte, November 26, 1830, Paris, *Mémoires,*6:468-472.

[118] Sarrans, 2:65.

[119] The above lines are taken from Sarrans, 2:51.

[120] Sarrans, 2:61.

[121] Order of the Day, December 19, 1830, Paris, *Mémoires,*6:489-493.

[122] *Le Moniteur*, cited in *Mémoires*, 6: 489.

[123] Sarrans, 2:78,79.

[124] Order of the Day, December 21, 1830, Paris, *Mémoires,*6:493,494.

[125] *Le Moniteur*, December 22, 1830; Mémoires, 6:493,494, Sarrans, 2:82.

[126] Order of the Day, *Mémoires*, 6:494-496.

[127] Louis-Philippe, letter to Lafayette, December 23, 1830, *Mémoires*, 6:496,497.

[128] Order of the Day, December 24, 1830, Paris, *Mémoires,*6:497,498.

Chapter 53

[1] Sarrans, 2:83.

[2] Ibid., 2:84,85.

[3] Ibid., 2:89.

[4] Bernier believes Lafayette was 'attempting to repeat his old stand-by, the resignation in a huff. In 1789 and 1791 it had worked and he had been called back by a repentant crowd,' 317. It is clear from the words of Sarrans that he was hoping to achieve some sign of a change of system, 2:95.

[5] Sarrans, 2: 92.

[6] Ibid., 2: 93,94.

[7] Ibid., 2:94.

[8] Ibid., 2:95.

[9] Ségur, recounting the conversation of Lafayette, cited by Bardoux,398.

[10] Sarrans, 2:93,94.

[11] Lafayette, letter to Louis-Philippe, December 26, 1830, *Mémoires,*6:501,502.

[12] Order of the Day, December 27, 1830, Paris, *Mémoires,*6:503.

[13] Lafayette's words in the Chamber of Deputies, December 27, 1830, *Mémoires*, 6:504-506.

[14] Lafayette, letter to a friend, January 1, 1831, *Mémoires,*6:518,519.

[15] Speech by Odilon Barrot, February 6, 1831, Paris, *Mémoires,* 6:521.

[16] Lafayette, letter to Palmerston, January 23, 1831, Paris, *Mémoires,* 6:526,527.

[17] Lafayette, speech to the Chamber, January 28, 1831, *Mémoires,*6:527-532.

[18] Sarrans,2:144.

[19] Lafayette, speech in the Chamber, February 20, 1831, *Mémoires,*6:535-539.

[20] Lafayette, speech in the Chamber, February 24, 1831, *Mémoires,* 6: 542,543.

[21] Pinkney, 433, cited by Taillimite, 503.

[22] Lafayette, May 28, 1831, *Mémoires,*6:576.

[23] Lafayette, letter to the electors at Meaux, June 13, 1831, La Grange, *Mémoires,*6:576-591.

[24] Sarrans,2:185; Lafayette, letter, June 22, 1831, La Grange; *Mémoires*, 6:591,592.

[25] Whitlock, 2:380.

[26] Castries,464.

[27] Lafayette, speech in the Chamber, September 20, 1831. *Mémoires,*6:605-614.

[28] *Mémoires*, 6:660.148.

[29] Sarrans,2:256.

[30] The description of Lamarque's funeral comes from Sarrans, 2:272-283. Lafayette, letter to Dupont de 'Eure, June 9, 1832, Paris, *Mémoires,*6:667-671.

[31] Lafayette, letter to Madier de Montjau, June 20, 1832, La Grange, *Mémoires*, 6:675.

[32] Sarrans,2:291.

[33] Ibid., 2:292.

[34] Ibid., 2:286.

[35] Ibid., 2:287.

[36] Ibid., 2:298.

[37] Lafayette, letter to the *Courrier du Gard*, June 13, 1832, La Grange, Sarrans,2:283,284.

[38] Lafayette, letter to Dupont de l'Eure, June 9, 1832, Paris, *Mémoires*,6:666,667.

[39] Lafayette, letter to Madier de Montjau, June 20,1832, La Grange, *Mémoires*,6:673-678.

[40] Whitlock,2:396.

[41] Lafayette, letter to Madier de Montjau, August 1, 1832, La Grange, *Mémoires*,6:690,691.

[42] Lafayette, letter to Dupont de l 'Eure, November 19, 1832, Paris, *Mémoires*, 695,696.

[43] Lafayette, letter to Dupont de l'Eure, November 19, 1832, Paris, *Mémoires*,6:695,696.

[44] Session of the Chamber; January 23,1833, *Mémoires*,6:707710.

[45] Lafayette, letter to General Jackson, March 15, 1833, Paris, *Mémoires*, 6:716,717.

[46] Charavay, 507.

[47] Lafayette, speech to the Chamber, June 13, 1833, Paris, *Mémoires*, 6:738-740.

[48] Whitlock, 2:401,402.

[49] Lafayette, speech in the Chamber, January 3, 1834, Paris, *Mémoires*,6:753-757.

[50] Cloquet, 2:95.

[51] Lafayette, letter to Fenimore Cooper, April 14, 1834, Paris, *Mémoires*,6:759,761.

[52] All the above description comes from Cloquet,2:91-95.

[53] Lafayette, letter to Murray, President of the Society for the Emancipation of Slaves, May 1, 1834, Paris, *Mémoires*, 6:763-767.

[54] Cloquet,2:96.

[55] Ibid., 2:97.

[56] Ibid., 2:98

[57] Ibid., 2:98,99.

Chapter 54

[1] This account taken mainly from Cloquet, 2:98,99.

[2] Chateaubriand, *Mémoires d'Outre Tombe*, II :371, cited by Charavay,515.

[3] Carrel, Armand, the *National,* May 23,1834, cited by Charavay, 516.

[4] Barère*, Souvenirs historiques sur la Révolution de 1830,* 4:272.

[5] This account of the funeral is mainly taken from Cloquet; 2:105-108.

[6] Adams, John Quincy, *Oration on the Life and Character of Gilbert Motier de Lafayette* (Washington:1835)3-88.

[7] Lafayette, letter to Joseph Bonaparte, November 26, 1830, Paris, *Mémoires*, 6 :468-472.

[8] Thiers, Adolphe, *Histoire de la Révolution française*, 123,124, cited by Bois, 422.

[9] Letter from the American Expeditionary Forces, January 4, 1919, France, Morgan,8.

[10] Morgan, 479.

[11] *Mémoires, Souvenirs et Anecdotes par M. le comte de Ségur, de l'Académie française. Correspondance et Pensées de Prince de Ligne, Avec Avant-Propos Et Notes,*199.

[12] Lafayette, letter to Monsieur Prunelle, July 12, 1832, La Grange, *Mémoires*, 6:688.

Bibliography

Adams, John and Abigail, *The Letters of John and Abigail Adams* (New York: Penguin, 2004).

Adams, Abigail, *Letters of Mrs. Adams, the wife of John Adams* (Boston: Little and Brown, M DCCC XL, vol.2).

Adams, John Quincy, *Oration on the life and character of Gilbert Motier de Lafayette, delivered at States, the request of both Houses of Congress of the United States before them, in the House of Representatives at Washington, on the 31st day of December 1834* (Washington:1835).

Adams, William, Howard, *The Paris Years of Thomas Jefferson* (New Haven and London: Yale Univ. Press, 1997).

Angell, Israel, *Diary of Colonel Israel Angel; commanding the Second Rhode Island Continental Regiment during the American Revolution, 1778-1781* (Providence: Preston and Rounds Company, 1899).

Auricchio, Laura, *The Marquis, Lafayette Reconsidered* (New York: Vintage Books, 2015).

Bailly, Jean-Sylvain, *Mémoires d'un Témoin de la Révolution, ou Journal des faits qui se sont passés sous ses yeux, et qui ont preparé et fixé la Constitution française* (Paris: Levrault, Schoellet cie, 3 vols.).

Balch, Thomas, Balch E.S. and Balch, E.W., *The French in America during the War of Independence of the United States. 1777-1783* (Philadelphia: Porter and Coates, 1891, vol.1; 1895, vol.2).

Bardoux, Agénor, *Les Dernières années de La Fayette 1792-1834* (Paris: Ancienne Maison Michel Lévy Frères, 1892).

Bartram, William, *Travels of William Bartram*, ed. by Doren, Mark von (New York: Dover Publications Inc., 1955).

Bédollière, Émile de la, *Vie politique de Marie-Paul-Jean-Roch-Yves-Gilbert Motié: Marquis de Lafayette, né à Chavagnac (Haute-Loire) le 6 septembre 1757...* (Paris:1833).

Bérard, Simon, *Souvenirs historiques sur la Révolution de 1830* (Paris: Perrotin,1834).

Bernier, Olivier, *Words of Fire, Deeds of Blood; The Mob, the Monarchy and the French Revolution* (Canada: Little, Brown and Company, 1989).

Bernier, Olivier, *Pleasure and Privilege; Life in France, Naples and America, 1770-90* (New York: Doubleday and Company, Inc., 1981).

Bicheno, Hugh, *Rebels and Redcoats* (London: HarperCollins, 2003).

Blanchard, Claude, *Journal de campagne de Claude Blanchard sous le commandement du lieutenant général comte de Rochambeau (1780-1785)* (Paris: Bureaux de la Revue militaire française, 1869).

Bloomfield, Joseph, *Citizen Soldier; The Revolutionary War Journal of Joseph Bloomfield*, ed. by Lender, Mark Edward and Martin, James, Kirby (Yardley: Westholme, 2018).

Boatner, Mark M., *Encyclopedia of the American Revolution* (Mechanicsburg, PA: Stackpole Books, 1966).

Bois, Jean-Pierre, La Fayette; *La liberté entre révolutions et modération* (Paris: Perrin, 2015).

Bonk, David, *American Revolutionary War; Continental versus Redcoat* (New York: Osprey Publishing, 2014).

Brancion, Laurence Chatel de, *Lafayette; La traversée d'une vie* (Saint Rémy-en-l'Eau:2017).

Caldwell, Charles, *Memoirs of the life and campaigns of the Hon. Nathaniel Greene, Major General in the Army of the United States, and Commander of the Southern Department, in the war of the Revolution* (Philadelphia: Robert Desilver, 1819).

Carlyle,Thomas, *The French Revolution* (Oxford: Oxford Univ. Press, 2019).

Castries, duc de, *La Fayette* (Paris: Librairie Jules Tallandier, 1981).

Chambrun, René de, *Les Prisons des Lafayette, dix ans de courage et d'amour* (Paris: Librairie Académique Perrin, 1977).

Charavay, Étienne, *Le Général La Fayette, 1757-1834* (Paris: Société de l'Histoire de la Révolution française, 1898).

Chartrand, René, *Forts of the American Revolution, 1775-83*, illus. by Spedaliere, Donato (New York: Osprey Publishing, 2016).

Chastellux, François, Jean de, *Travels in North America, in the years 1780, 1781, and 1782* (London: Robinson, G.G.J. and Robinson, J., 1827,1828, vols 1,2).

Chernow, Ron, *Washington, A Life* (New York: Penguin, 2011).

Chinard, Gilbert, *The Letters of Lafayette and Jefferson, with an introduction and notes by Gilbert Chinard* (John Hopkins Univ.).

Cloquet, M. Jules, *Recollections of the private life of General Lafayette* (New York: Leavitt, Lord and Co., 1836, vols,1,2).

Closen, Ludwig von, *The Revolutionary Journal of Baron Ludwig von Closen, 1780-1783*, trans. and ed., by Acomb, Evelyn, M. (Williamsburg, Virginia: The Univ. of North Carolina Press, 1958).

Commager, Henry, Steele, and Morris, Richard, B.,eds.,*The Spirit of Seventy-Six; The story of the American Revolution as told by its participants* (New York: Castle Books, by permission of Harper Collins, 2002).

Crèvecoeur, J. Hector St. John de, *Letters from an American Farmer and Sketches of Eighteenth-century America* (New York: Penguin,1988; first published 1782).

Dann, John C. ed., *The Revolution Remembered; Eyewitness accounts of the War for Independence* (Chicago: Univ. of Chicago Press, 1980).

Dearborn, Henry, *Journals of Henry Dearborn,1776-1783* (Cambridge: John Wilson and son, 1887).

Great Britain Legation; Sackville, John Frederick, Duke of Dorset; *Despatches from Paris, 1784-1790.* Selected and ed. from the Foreign Office by Browning, Oscar, *Correspondance, 1784-1790* (London: Offices of the Society, 1910).

Deux-Ponts, Guillaume de Forbach, count de, *My campaigns in America: a journal...1780-81*, trans. by Green, S.A. (Boston: Wiggin J.K. and Parsons Lunt, W.M., 1868).

Dohla, Johann, Conrad, *A Hessian Diary of the American Revolution*, trans., ed., by Burgoyne, Bruce, E. (Oklahoma: Univ. of Oklahoma Press, from the 1913 Bayreuth ed., 1990).

Doniol, Henri, *La Fayette dans la Révolution, 1775-1799 (*Paris: Librairie Armand Colin).

Doniol, Henri, Histoire de la participation de la France à l'établissement des États-Unis d'Amérique, complément de tome 5 (Paris: Imprimerie nationale, MDCCC XCIX).

Doniol, Henri, *Histoire de la participation de la France à l'établissement des Etats-Unis d'Amérique* (Paris: Imprimerie nationale, MDCCC LXXXV, vol.1; M DCCC LXXXVI, vol.2; M DCCC LXXXVIII, vol.3; M DCCC XC, vol.4; M DCCC XCII, vol.5).

Doniol, Henri, *La Fayette dans la Révolution: Années d'Amérique, Années de Pouvoir et Années de Geole, La Veille du Consulat,1775-1799* (Paris:Librairie Armand Colin, 1904).

Donnet, Hadelin, *Chavaniac Lafayette le Manoir de deux mondes* (Paris: Le Cherche Midi Éditeur, 1990).

Doren, Carl van, *Secret History of the American Revolution; an account of the conspiracies of Benedict Arnold and numerous others drawn from the Secret Service Papers of the British headquarters in North America, now for the first time examined and made public* (New York: Viking Press, 1951).

Doyle, William, *The Oxford History of the French Revolution* (Oxford: Oxford Univ. Press, 2002).

Dumas, Mathieu, *Souvenirs du lieutenant général comte Mathieu Dumas de 1770 à1836 publiés par son fils* (Paris: Gosselin, M DCCC XXXIX, 3 vols.).

Ellis, Joseph, P., *His Excellency; George Washington* (New York: Borzoi Book; Random House Inc., 2004).

Feltman, William, *The Journal of Lieut. William Feltman, of the First Pennsylvania Regiment, 1781-82* (Philadelphia: Henry Carey Baird for the Historical Society of Pennsylvania, 1853).

Ferling, John, *Almost a Miracle; the American Victory in the War of Independence* (New York: Oxford Univ. Press, 2007).

Ferriéres, Charles-Élie, marquis de, *Mémoires du Marquis de Ferrières* (Paris: Baudouin Frères 1822, vols. 1,2).

Fitz-Henry Smith, *The French at Boston during the Revolution* (Boston: Bostonian Society,1913).

Fleming, Thomas, *Washington's Secret War; The Hidden History of Valley Forge* (New York: Harper Collins,2005).

Fleming, Thomas, *Liberty! The American Revolution* (New York: Viking Penguin, 1997).

Fleming, Thomas, *Beat the Last Drum; The Siege of Yorktown* (New Word City, 2016).

Freeman, Douglas Southall, *George Washington, a biography* (London: Eyre and Spottiswoode, vol. 4 1951).

Freeman, Douglas Southall, *George Washington, a biography* (New York: Charles Scribner's Sons, 1952, vol.5).

Gaines, James R., *For Liberty and Glory; Washington, Lafayette and their Revolutions* (London: Norton, W.W. and Company, 2007).

Gallo, Max, *Révolution française; Le Peuple et le Roi* (XO Editions:2008).

Gallo, Max, *Révolution française; Aux armes, citoyens!* (XO Editions:2009).

Gottschalk, Louis, *Lafayette in America; Book 1; Lafayette in America;Book 2;Lafayette joins the American Army; Book 3; Lafayette and the Close of the American Revolution* (Arveyres, France: L'Ésprit de Lafayette Society, 1975).

Gottschalk, Louis, *Lafayette comes to America* (Chicago: Univ. of Chicago, 1935).

Gottschalk, Louis and Maddox, Margaret, *Lafayette in the French Revolution* (Chicago: Univ.of Chicago Press, 1969).

Gottschalk, Louis; Lach, Donald, *Toward the French Revolution; Europe and America in the Eighteenth-Century World* (New York: Charles Scribner's Sons, 1951).

Gottschalk, Louis, *The Letters of Lafayette to Washington, 1777-1799* (Philadelphia: The American Philosophical Society, 1976).

Gottschalk, Louis, *The Era of the French Revolution* (Cambridge: Houghton Miflin Company,1929).

Gottschalk, Louis, *Lafayette between the American and the French Revolution, 1783-1789* (Illinois: The Univ. of Chicago Press, 1950).

Hamilton, Alexander, *Hamilton, Writings,* ed., by Freeman, Joanne, B. (New York: Penguin Random House Inc., 2001).

Hamilton, Alexander, *The official and other papers of the late Major- General Alexander Hamilton* (New York and London: Wiley and Putnam, 1842, vol.1).

Hamilton, Alexander, *The Founding Fathers; Alexander Hamilton; A Biography in his own words,* ed., by Kline, Mary-Jo (New York: Harper and Row).

Hardman, John, ed., *The French Revolution Source book* (London: Hodder Headline Group, 1999).

Greene, George Washington, *The Life of Nathanael Greene, Major-General in the army of the Revolution* (Boston and New York: Houghton, Mifflin and Company, 1878, vol.2; 1884, vol.3).

Greenman, Jeremiah, *Diary of a common soldier in the American Revolution, 1775-1783, an annotated edition of the military journal of Jeremiah Greenman,* ed. by Bray, Robert and Bushnell, Paul (Illinois: Northern Illinois Univ. Press, 1978).

Hibbert, Christopher, *The French Revolution* (London: Penguin, 1982).

Hitchens, Christopher, *Thomas Jefferson; Author of America* (New York: HarperCollins, 2005).

Holstein, Ducoudray, *Memoirs of Gilbert Motier La Fayette by Gen. H.L. Villaume Ducoudray Holstein, who contributed under the fictitious name of Peter Feldmann, to his liberation from the prisons of Olmutz,* translated from the French Manuscript (New York: Wiley, 1824).

Idzerda, Stanley J., ed., *Lafayette in the Age of the American Revolution, Selected Letters and Papers, 1776-90* (Ithaca and London: Cornell Univ. Press, 1977-83, 5 vols). Vol.5 edited by Stanley J. Idzerda and Robert Rhodes Crout.

Idzerda, Stanley. J. *The Background of the French Revolution* (Washington: Service Center for Teachers of History).

Idzerda, Stanley, J., Lovel and, Anne C., Miller, Marc H., *Lafayette, Hero of Two Worlds, the Art and Pageantry of his Farewell Tour of America, 1824-1825* (New York: The Queen's Museum, 1989).

Idzerda, Stanley, J., *France and the American War for Independence* (Ithaca: Cornell Univ.).

Institut Français, *Washington, Lafayette in Virginia, unpublished letters from the original manuscripts in the Virginia State Library and the Library of Congress* (Baltimore: The Johns Hopkins Press, 1928, vol.2).

Idzerda, Stanley J., ed.; Smith, Roger E., ed. *France and the American War for Independence* (Ithaca: Cornell Univ.,).

Jefferson, Thomas, *A Bundle of Thomas Jefferson's Letters, now first published* (Ithaca: Cornell Univ. Library, 1994).

Jefferson, Thomas; Brandt, Anthony, ed., *Thomas Jefferson; Travels; Selected Writings 1784-1789* (Washington, D.C: National Geographic, 2006).

Jefferson, Thomas, *The Autobiography of Thomas Jefferson* (New York: Dover Publications, Inc., 2017).

Johnston, Henry P., *The Yorktown Campaign and the Surrender of Cornwallis 1781,* (Harper and Brothers, 1881).

Kapp, Friedrich, *The Life of John Kalb, Major-General in the Revolutionary Army* (Leopold Classic Library).

Karamzin, N.M., *Letters of a Russian Traveller, 1789-1790,* trans and abridged by Jonas, Florence (New York: Columbia Univ. Press; London: Oxford Univ. Press, 1957).

Ketchum, Richard M., *Saratoga; Turning Point in America's Revolutionary War* (Henry Holt and Company, 1997).

Ketchum, Richard, M., *Victory at Yorktown* (New York: Henry Holt and Company, 2004).

Kramer, Lloyd, *Lafayette in Two Worlds; public cultures and personal identities in an Age of Revolutions* (Chapel Hill and London: The Univ. of North Carolina Press, 1996).

Lafayette, Gilbert Motier, Mémoires, Correspondance et manuscrits du général Lafayette publiés par sa famille (Bruxelles: société belge de librairie, 1837, 3 vols.).

Lafayette, Marie Joseph Paul Yves Roch Gilbert du Motier, marquis de, *Mémoires, correspondance et manuscrits du général Lafayette publiés par sa famille* (Paris: H. Fournier ainé, éditeur; London, 1838, 6 vols.).

Lafayette, Marie Joseph Paul Yves Roch Gilbert du Motier, marquis de, *Memoirs, Correspondence and Manuscripts of General Lafayette* (New York: Published by his family, MDCCCXXXVII, vol.1).

Lafayette, marquis de: *Mémoires, Correspondances et Manuscrits du Général Lafayette*, (Bruxelles: Société belge de librairie, 1837).

Lafayette, *Letters of the marquis de Lafayette* in the collection of Stuart Wells Jackson (Publications of the American Friends of Lafayette).

Lafayette, Letters from Lafayette to Luzerne, 1780-1782 (London: Forgotten Books).

Lafayette, Marie Antoinette Virginie de; Lafayette, Marie Adrienne de Noailles, *Life of Madame de Lafayette*, trans by Louis de Lasteyrie (Paris: Leon Techener; London: Barthès and Lowell, M DCCC LXXII).

Laurens, John; Simms, William Gilmore, *The army correspondence of Colonel John Laurens in the years 1777-8* (New York: 1867).

Lauzen, duc de, *Mémoires, duc de Lauzun, le temps retrouvé* (Mercure de France, 2017).

Levasseur, Auguste, *Lafayette in America in 1824 and 1825 or Journal of a Voyage to the United States* (Philadelphia: Carey and Lea, vol.2, 1829).

Levasseur, Auguste, *Lafayette in America in 1824 and 1825* (Memphis: General Books, 2012).

Lewis, Charlton, Thomas, *Lafayette at Brandywine, containing the proceedings at the dedication of the Memorial shaft erected to mark the place where Lafayette was wounded in the battle of Brandywine, with supplementary paper on Lafayette and the historians* (West Chester, PA: Chester County Historical Society, 1896).

Linguet, Simon Nicolas Henri, *A tour of two cities; eighteenth century London and Paris compared*.

Lothrop, Samuel Kirkland, *Life of Samuel Kirkland, Missionary to the Indians* (Boston: Little and Brown, MDCCCXLVII).

Maas, John R., *The Road to Yorktown; Jefferson, Lafayette and the British invasion of Virginia* (Charleston: The History Press, 2015).

Madame de la Tour du Pin, *Memoirs of Madame de la Tour du Pin*, ed. and trans by Félice Harcourt (London: Century Publishing, 1985).

Marshall, John, *The life of George Washington, Commander in Chief of the American forces during the war which established the independence of his country and first President of the United States* (Philadelphia: Wayne, C.P., 1804, vols. 2,3,4).

Maurois, André, *A History of France*, (London: Jonathan Cape,1949).

Maurois, André, *Adrienne; The Life of the Marquise de La Fayette*, trans. by Hopkins, Gerard (London: Jonathan Cape, 1961).

McPhee, Peter, *Liberty or Death; The French Revolution* (New Haven and London; Yale Univ. Press, 2017).

Merriman, John. M., ed., *1830 in France* (New York: New Viewpoints, 1975).

Middlekauf, Robert, *The Glorious Cause. The American Revolution, 1763-1789* (Oxford: Oxford Univ. Press, 2005).

Moore, Warren, *Weapons of the American Revolution....and accoutrements* (New York: Promontory Press, 1967).

Morgan, Lady, *Lady Morgan's Memoirs; Autobiography, Diaries and Correspondance* (Leipzig: Bernhard Tauchnitz, vol.1, 1863, vol.1).

Morgan, Lady, *France in 1829-30* (London: Saunders and Otley, vol.2, 1830, vol. 2).

Morgan, Lady, *La France en 1816* (Paris and London:1817, vol.2).

Morgan, Lady, *Lady Morgan in France*, ed. by Suddaby, Elizabeth, and Yarrow, F.J. (Newcastle: Oriel Press, 1871).

Morgan, Lady, *La France* (Paris and London: Treuttel et Wurtz, 1817).

Morris, Gouverneur, *Journal de Gouverneur Morris, minister plénipotentiaire des États-Unis en France de 1792 à 1794, pendant les années 1789, 1790, 1791, et 1792* (Paris: Librairie Plon, 1901).

Morse, Horace H, *The Lafayette Letters in the Boston Society*, (Leopold Classic Library; 1924, vol.4).

Mosnier, Henry, *Le Chateau de Chavaniac-Lafayette* (Le Puy:1883).

Mitchell, Charles W., *Travels through American History in the Mid-Atlantic* (Baltimore: John Hopkins Univ. Press, 2014).

Neimeyer, Charles Patrick, *America goes to War; A social history of the Continental Army* (New York and London: New York Univ. Press, 1996).

Nolan, J. Bennett, *Lafayette in America Day by Day* (Baltimore: John Hopkins Press, 1934).

Parker, James Andrew, *Recollections of General Lafayette on his visit to the United States in 1824 and 1825, with the most remarkable incidents of his life from his birth to the day of his death* (Keene, N.H., 1879).

Plumb Martin, Joseph, *Memoir of a Revolutionary Soldier. A republication of a Narrative of a Revolutionary Soldier: some of the Adventures, Dangers and Sufferings of Joseph Plumb Martin* (Maine: Glazier, Masters and Co.,1830), Dover: 2006.

Popkin, Jeremy D., ed., *Panorama of Paris; selections from Le Tableau de Paris*, Mercier, Louis Sébastien (Pennsylvania: Pennsylvania State Univ. Press, 1999).

Ramsay, David, *The History of the American Revolution* (Indianapolis: Liberty Classics, vol.1).

Rice, Howard C., *Thomas Jefferson's Paris* (New Jersey: Princeton Univ. Press, 1976).

Roberts, Lemuel, *Memoirs of Captain Lemuel Roberts; containing adventures in youth, vicissitudes experienced as a Continental soldier* (Bennington, Vermont:1809).

Rochambeau, Jean Baptiste Donatien de Vimeur, Count, *Mémoires militaires, historiques et politiques de Rochambeau*, (Paris: MDCCC IX).

Rochambeau, Yorktown: *Centénaire de l'indépendance des États-Unis d'Amérique, 1781-1881* (Paris: Champion, 1886).

Rochambeau, *Mémoires militaires, historiques et politiques de Rochambeau, ancien maréchal de France, et grand officier de la Légion d'Honneur*, (Paris:M DCCC IX; vols. 1,2).

Sarrans, Bernard, *Memoirs of General Lafayette and of the French Revolution of 1830* (Boston: Lilly, Wait, Colman and Holden, 1833, 2 vols.).

Savas, Theodore P., Dameron, David J., *A Guide to the Battles of the American Revolution* (New York and California: Savas Beatie, 2006, 2013).

Schactman, Tom, *How the French saved America; soldiers, sailors, diplomats, Louis XVI and the success of a Revolution* (New York: St. Martin's Press, 2017).

Schama, Simon, Citizens, *A Chronicle of the French Revolution* (London: Penguin, 1989).

Scheer, George, F. and Rankin, Hugh, F., ed., *Rebels and Redcoats; The American Revolution through the eyes of those who fought and lived it* (New York: Da Capo, 1957).

Scribner, Kimball, *A Continental Cavalier; The Record of some Incidents pertaining to the Chevalier de Marc, Brevet Major in the army of the colonies, aide-de-camp to General, the Marquis Lafayette* (New York: The Abbey Press, 1899).

Ségur, comte de, *The memoirs and anecdotes of the count de Ségur*, trans. by Shelley, Gerard (London: John Hamilton Ltd.).

Ségur, Louis-Philippe de, *Mémoires, souvenirs et anecdotes par M. le comte de Ségur, de l'académie française, Correspondances et pensées du Prince de Ligne; avec avant-propos et notes* (Paris: Librairie de Firmin Didot frères, fils et cie., 1859).

Shaw, Diane Windham, ed., *Symbol in Two Worlds; Essays on Lafayette* (Easton, Penn.: The American Friends of Lafayette, 2013).

Sichel, Edith Helen, *The household of the Lafayettes* (London: Constable and Company Ltd., 1910).

Slavin, Morris; Smith, Agnes M., ed., *Bourgeois, sans-culottes, and other Frenchmen; Essays on the French Revolution in honor of John Hall Stewart* (Ontario: Wilfred Laurier Univ. Press, 1981).

Smith, John Spear, *Memoir of the Baron de Kalb, read at a meeting of the Maryland Historical Society*, 7 January,1858 (Baltimore: 1858).

Smollett, Tobias, *Travels through France and Italy* (Oxford: Oxford Univ. Press,1979).

Snuff, Mary, Hazel, *A study of army camp life during the American Revolution* (Univ. of Illinois: thesis, 1917).

Spalding, Paul. S., Lafayette, *Prisoner of State* (South Carolina: Univ. of South Carolina: 2010).

Sparks, Jared, *The Writings of George Washington; being his correspondence, addresses, messages, and other papers, official and private* (Boston: American Stationers Company, 1837).

Sparks, Jared, *The Life of Washington* (Boston: Tappan and Dennet, 1843).

Sparks, Jared, *The Life of George Washington* (Cambridge, Mass.: Metcalf and Company, 1839).

Sparks, Jared, Life of Samuel Kirkland, Missionary to the Indians, (Boston, Little and Brown; MDCCCXLVII).

Steiner, Bernard Christian, *The Life and Correspondance of James McHenry, Secretary of War under Washington and Adams* (Cleveland: The Burrows Brothers Company, 1907).

Stryker, William S., Myers, *The Battle of Monmouth*, ed.by Starr Myers, William (Princeton: Princeton Univ. Press, 1927).

Sullivan, John; *Letters and Papers of Major-General John Sullivan, Continental Army, 1778-1779*, ed. by Hammond, Otis G. (New Hampshire: New Hampshire Historical Society, 1931, vol.2).

Taillimite, Étienne, *La Fayette* (Paris: Fayard, 1989).

Tannahill, Reay, ed., *Paris in the Revolution; A Collection of Eye-witness accounts* (London: The Folio Society,1916).

Thacher, James, *A Military Journal during the American Revolutionary War, from 1775 to 1783, describing interesting events and transactions of this period, with numerous historical facts and anecdotes, from the original manuscript* (Boston: Richardson and Lord, 1823).

Thiers, Louis Adolphe, *Histoire de la Révolution Française* (Paris: Furne et Cie.,1865, vol.1).

Thomas Lewis, Charlton, *Lafayette at Brandywine, containing the proceedings at the dedication of the memorial erected to mark the place where Lafayette was wounded in the Battle of Brandywine* (West Chester, PA: The Chester County Historical Society, 1896).

Thomas, Jules, *Correspondance inédite de La Fayette, 1793-1801, lettres de prison, lettres d'exil, précédée d'une étude psychologique* (Paris: Librairie CH Delagrave).

Tilghman,Tench, *Memoir of Lieutenant Colonel Tench Tilghman, Secretary and Aid to Washington, together with an Appendix containing revolutionary journals and letters, hitherto unpublished* (Albany: Munsell, 1876).

Tocqueville, Alexis de, *L'Ancien Régime et la Révolution* (Paris: Michel Lévy Frères, 1866).

Tucker, George and Riley, Edward M., *St. George Tucker's Journal of the Siege of Yorktown,1781* (The William and Mary Quarterly, Third Series, vol. 5, No.3, July, 1948).

Tuckerman, Bayard, *Life of General Philip Schuyler 1733 to 1804* (New York: Dodd, Mead and Company, 1903).

Tower, Charlemagne, *The Marquis de La Fayette in the American Revolution* (Philadelphia: Lippincott, J.B. company,1895, vols. 1,2)

Unger, Harlow Giles, *Lafayette* (Hoboken: Wiley, 2002).

Urban, Mark, Fusiliers; *Eight years with the Redcoats in America* (London: Faber and Faber,2007).

Volo, Dorothy Denneen and Volo, James, *Daily Life during the American Revolution* (Westport, Conn.; London: The Greenwood Press, 2003).

Ward, Christopher, *The War of the Revolution*, ed., by Alden Richard (New York: Skyhorse Publishing, 2011).

Watson, Elkanah, *Men and Times of the Revolution* (New York: Dana and Company, 1856).

West Point Military Academy, *The West Point History of the American Revolution* (New York: Simon and Schuster, 2017).

Whitlock, Brand, *La Fayette*, (New York and London: Appleton, D. and Company, MCMXXIX, vols. 1,2).

Whittemore, Charles, P., *A General of the Revolution; John Sullivan of New Hampshire* (New York and London: Columbia Univ. Press, 1961).

Wiencek, Henry, *An Imperfect God* ((Farrar, Strauss and Giroux: 2003).

Wild, Ebenezer, *The Journal of Ebenezer Wild (1776-1781) who served as corporal, sergeant, ensign and lieutenant in the War of the Revolution*, ed., by Bugbee, James M. (Cambridge: John Wilson and son, 1891).

Wood, W. J., *Battles of the Revolutionary War, 1775-1781* (Cambridge: Da Capo Press, 2003).

Young, Arthur; Betham-Edwards, Matilda, *Arthur Young's Travels during the years 1787, 1788, 1789* (London: W. Richardson, 1792).

Index

Estaing, Charles Henri, comte d', 136, 137, 138, 142, 143, 148, 152, 153, 160, 162, 336, 376
Estates-General, 340, 341, 347, 349, 351, 352, 353, 354, 355, 356, 357, 358, 359, 362, 366, 396, 415
Favras, marquis de, 417, 418, 419, 420, 422, 423
Fayon, abbé, 7, 10, 15
Ferme, 299, 300
Fête de la Fédération, 430
Fishkill, 104, 116, 162, 163, 165, 185, 198, 200, 202, 203, 302
Floridablanca, Franco Antonio, Count, 298
Fort Ticonderoga, 44, 51
Fouché, Joseph, 529, 543, 548, 550, 551, 553
Foulon, Joseph-François, 378
Fox, Charles James, 489, 507, 535, 542
Franklin, Benjamin, 9, 24, 25, 172, 301, 428
Franklin, William, 178, 294, 302
Frederick II, King of Prussia, 325, 327
Frederick William III, King of Prussia, 545
Freemasonry, 327, 618
French Revolution, IV, 427, 479, 480, 629
Frestel, Félix, 434, 486, 502, 503, 518, 555
gabelle, salt tax, 337, 338, 341
Gallatin, Albert, 536, 545, 557, 574
Garnett, Harriet and Julia, 558
Gates, Horatio, 196
George III, King of Great Britain, 18, 26, 100, 328
Germaine, George, Lord, 10
Germantown, 54, 64, 67, 68, 69, 73, 81, 84, 89, 108, 113, 214
Gimat, Jean-Joseph Sourbader de, 28, 30, 42, 44, 47, 50, 61, 62, 63, 67, 72, 78, 95, 113, 131, 138, 163, 164, 175, 182, 183, 185, 213, 222, 223, 226, 235, 240, 251, 254, 260, 263, 270, 278, 279, 280
Girondins, 459, 463, 464, 465
Gloucester, Duke of, 18, 26
Gobel, Jean-Baptiste, 441
Gouvion, Jean-Baptiste, 104, 138, 144, 197, 200, 202, 204, 222, 224, 258, 265, 286, 288, 294, 312, 325, 327, 328, 340, 376, 388, 395, 400, 402, 405, 406, 409, 444, 445, 453, 460, 461, 462, 474, 475, 482, 488, 522, 523, 525
Grasse, François Joseph Paul, comte de, 255, 259, 260, 262, 263, 265, 267, 268, 269, 270, 272, 273, 274, 275, 277, 282, 285, 286, 287, 292, 293
Grasshopper, 102, 103, 311, 312, 314
Grattepain-Morizot, Jacques-Philippe, 175, 293, 295, 395
Great Britain, 201, 238, 297, 463, 521
Greene, George Washington, 350
Greene, Nathanael, 51, 53, 92, 107, 132, 204, 316, 319, 320, 334, 350
Haberlein, 493, 494, 495, 499, 500, 501
Hamilton, Alexander, 54, 520, 537, 572
Hancock, John, 18, 45, 64, 67, 161, 315, 316
Hénin, princesse de, 478, 479, 480, 483, 485, 486, 487, 488, 489, 490, 493, 570
Hessians, 39, 59, 61, 67, 69, 73, 78, 79, 80, 115, 133, 140, 141, 214, 241, 283, 328, 329, 424
Houdon, Jean-Antoine, 327, 331, 334, 372, 455
Howe, Richard, 224
Howe, William, 24, 44, 54, 60, 72, 213, 219
Huger, Benjamin, 39
Huger, Francis, 39, 564, 571
Hunolstein, Élise-Aglaë Barbentane, comtesse de, 17, 173, 299
Indian Queen, 63, 64

Moultrie, William, 40, 41

Mounier, Jean-Joseph, 348, 361, 363, 366, 368, 375, 391, 393, 394, 395, 396, 398, 402, 403, 405, 410, 414, 427

Mount Vernon, 163, 229, 236, 266, 287, 304, 306, 307, 308, 312, 318, 319, 320, 347, 507, 516, 518, 524, 566, 567, 568, 575

Muhlenburg, John Peter Gabriel, 58, 119, 227, 228, 242, 247, 248, 255, 264, 270

Murat, abbé de, 10, 11, 13, 342, 526

National Assembly, 340, 466, 552

Native American, 142, 185

Necker, Jacques, 176, 331, 350, 351, 352, 358, 359, 362, 363, 364, 365, 367, 368, 369, 375, 383, 384, 390, 404, 407, 411, 415, 417, 419, 424, 425, 429, 437

Neisse, 488, 490, 491, 497

New Jersey Line, 225, 230

Newport, 55, 56, 138, 139, 140, 141, 143, 145, 146, 147, 148, 149, 152, 153, 154, 155, 156, 157, 158, 161, 162, 171, 179, 188, 190, 191, 194, 196, 209, 215, 218, 220, 222, 224, 227, 255, 267, 272, 316

Noailles, Emmanuel Marie Louis, marquis de, ambassador of France, 25, 26, 30

Noailles, Louis, vicomte de,10, 11, 12, 14

North River, 51, 53, 54, 70, 73, 89, 98, 100, 111, 114, 117, 119, 120, 133, 134, 136, 137, 138, 166, 167, 177, 185, 187, 188, 197, 198, 199, 200, 202, 204, 209, 211, 212, 231, 234, 309, 565

North, Lord, 106, 107, 291, 298

O'Hara, Charles, 242, 257, 260, 283, 284

Odatshedah. See Grasshopper

Olmütz, 490, 491, 495, 496, 497, 498, 499, 500, 505, 508, 509, 511, 513, 514, 515, 519, 523, 527, 530, 539, 542, 552, 579, 617

Oneida, 100, 101, 102, 103, 104, 112, 113, 114, 312, 314

Orléans, duc d', 8, 336, 337, 345, 350, 357, 364, 366, 378, 379, 394, 396, 398, 409, 410, 411, 426, 431, 437, 438, 467, 484, 485, 546, 577, 579, 580, 581, 584, 588, 589, 590, 591, 592, 593, 594, 595, 597, 600, 608, 618

Paine, Thomas, 64, 88, 415, 425, 453, 491

Palais-Royal, 302, 350, 361

Panthéon, 441, 598, 599, 602, 608, 610

Paoli Massacre, 67

Parish, John, 505, 507

Parlement of Paris, 16, 341, 351, 528

Paul, Tsar of Russia, 292

Périer, Augustin, 579

Périer, Casimir, 580, 608

Phillips, William, 243

Pichegru, Charles, 561

Picpus, 560, 562, 563, 566, 645, 646, 647

Pillet, 478, 495, 497, 530, 534, 537

Pinckney, Thomas, 506, 507, 510, 530

Pitt, William the Younger, 313, 446, 512

Poix, Philippe Louis de Noailles-Mouchy, prince de, 14, 19, 22, 25, 27, 41, 171, 182, 218, 261, 285, 291, 294, 296, 315, 415, 441, 488, 503

Poland, 511, 635, 636, 637, 638, 642, 645

Polignac, Jules, prince de, 345, 369, 385, 394, 605, 606, 610, 614, 624, 629, 630, 635

Pommier,583

Pontonnier, Félix, 477, 478, 501, 514, 515, 553

Protestants, 336, 338, 343, 348, 349, 354, 359, 360, 580

Provence, comte de, 16, 17, 349, 366, 556

Prussia, 3, 308, 337, 341, 445, 471, 473, 479, 501, 506, 511, 512, 547, 562, 563, 569, 577, 637

Pulaski, Casimir, Count, 52, 555, 579, 582

Yorktown, VII, XI, 93, 94, 243, 256, 259, 267, 268, 270, 271, 272, 273, 274, 276, 277, 280, 285, 286, 287, 298, 315, 316, 317, 412, 456, 564, 566, 568, 569, 617

Printed in Great Britain
by Amazon

46999625R00399